Principles and Practice of
Stress Management

SECOND EDITION

Principles and Practice of
Stress Management

SECOND EDITION

Edited by

PAUL M. LEHRER
UMDNJ–Robert Wood Johnson Medical School

ROBERT L. WOOLFOLK
Rutgers–The State University

Foreword by Gary E. Schwartz

THE GUILFORD PRESS
New York   London

*To my parents, Samuel and Ethel Lehrer,
who introduced me to relaxation training
and provided unswerving support to me
throughout my life.—P. M. L.*

To Izzy.—R. L. W.

© 1993 The Guilford Press
A Division of Guilford Publications, Inc.
72 Spring Street, New York, NY 10012

Printed in the United States of America

This book is printed on acid-free paper.

Last digit is print number: 9 8 7 6 5 4 3 2

Library of Congress Cataloging-in-Publication Data

Principles and practice of stress management / edited by Paul M.
    Lehrer and Robert L. Woolfolk; foreword by Gary E. Schwartz. — 2nd
    ed.
        p.   cm.
    Includes bibliographical references and index.
    ISBN 0-89862-766-4 — ISBN 0-89862-162-3 (pbk.)
    1. Stress management. I. Lehrer, Paul M. II. Woolfolk, Robert L.
    [DNLM: 1. Relaxation Techniques. 2. Stress, Psychological—
prevention & control. 3. Stress, Psychological—therapy. WM 172
P957]
RA785.P75 1993
155.9'042—dc20
DNLM/DLC
for Library of Congress   92-49253
                                                              CIP

Contributors

Theodore Xenophon Barber, Ph.D., Research Institute, Ashland, Massachusetts

Aaron T. Beck, M.D., Department of Psychiatry, University of Pennsylvania School of Medicine, Philadelphia, Pennsylvania

Douglas A. Bernstein, Ph.D., Department of Psychology, University of Illinois, Champaign, Illinois

James A. Blumenthal, Ph.D., Department of Psychiatry, Duke University Medical Center, Durham, North Carolina

Thomas H. Budzynski, Ph.D., St. Luke's Hospital, Bellevue, Washington

Charles A. Carlson, Ph.D., Department of Psychology, University of Kentucky, Lexington, Kentucky

Richard Carr, Psy.D., Department of Psychiatry, UMDNJ–Robert Wood Johnson Medical School, Piscataway, New Jersey

Patricia Carrington, Ph.D., Department of Psychiatry, UMDNJ–Robert Wood Johnson Medical School, Piscataway, New Jersey

Steven L. Fahrion, Ph.D., Center for Applied Psychophysiology, The Menninger Clinic, Topeka, Kansas

Roger B. Fillingim, Ph.D., Pain Management Center, Jacksonville, Florida

Robert Fried, Ph.D., Department of Psychology, Hunter College, City University of New York, New York, New York; Institute for Rational–Emotive Therapy, New York, New York

Jack M. Gorman, M.D., Department of Clinical Psychobiology, New York State Psychiatric Institute, College of Physicians and Surgeons, Columbia University, New York, New York; Phobia, Anxiety and Stress Disorders Clinic, Hillside Hospital, Glen Oaks, New York

Paul M. Lehrer, Ph.D., Department of Psychiatry, UMDNJ–Robert Wood Johnson Medical School, Piscataway, New Jersey

Wolfgang Linden, Ph.D., Department of Psychology, University of British Columbia, Vancouver, British Columbia, Canada

Cheryl Dileo Maranto, Ph.D., R.M.T.-B.C., Department of Music Education and Therapy, Esther Boyer College of Music, Temple University, Philadelphia, Pennsylvania

F. J. McGuigan, Ph.D., Institute for Stress Management, U.S. International University, San Diego, California

Donald Meichenbaum, Ph.D., Department of Psychology, University of Waterloo, Waterloo, Ontario, Canada

Patricia A. Norris, Ph.D., Center for Applied Psychophysiology, The Menninger Clinic, Topeka, Kansas

Laszlo A. Papp, M.D., Department of Clinical Psychobiology, New York State Psychiatric Institute, College of Physicians and Surgeons, Columbia University, New York, New York; Phobia, Anxiety and Stress Disorders Clinic, Hillside Hospital, Glen Oaks, New York

Chandra Patel, M.D., F.R.C.G.P., Department of Community Medicine, University College, London, and Middlesex School of Medicine, London, England

Deepa Sargunaraj, Ph.D., Department of Psychiatry, UMDNJ–Robert Wood Johnson Medical School, Piscataway, New Jersey

Johann M. Stoyva, Ph.D., Department of Psychiatry (Psychology), University of Colorado Health Sciences Center, Denver, Colorado

Robert L. Woolfolk, Ph.D., Department of Psychology, Rutgers–The State University, New Brunswick, New Jersey

Foreword: Biofeedback Is Not Relaxation Is Not Hypnosis

A colleague recently told me of an elderly woman she was seeing for stress management. The client was a 100-pound, 5-foot 2-inch, 65-year-old lady who road a Harley–Davidson motorcycle for "relaxation" (and fun). However, save for these times on her "machine," she claimed to have significant difficulty relaxing. Electromyographic (EMG) recordings confirmed that she had high resting muscle tension levels. Being machine oriented, she resonated with biofeedback-assisted relaxation, and made rapid progress in therapy.

It is improbable that this spry pixie of a biker would have accepted meditation as readily as she accepted EMG biofeedback. It is improbable that meditation would have reduced her forehead muscle tension as readily as EMG-targeted biofeedback did. In this specific instance, EMG biofeedback was probably the right choice. What has become clear is that "stress management is not stress management is not stress management." The second edition of *Principles and Practice of Stress Management* provides us with the most comprehensive and cohesive picture of theory, research, and practice of stress management ever painted.

Since ancient times, numerous techniques have been devised to help people cope with life's challenges, to relax, and to find peace of mind. Music, fragrance, yoga, meditation, tai-chi, massage—the list is long and varied. Recent additions to the list include hypnosis, autogenic training, progressive muscle relaxation, biofeedback, and aerobic exercise. Advances in pharmacological and cognitive treatments extend the list that much further. The most essential and seminal of these techniques are contained in this volume.

The field of stress management has progressed substantially since Woolfolk and Lehrer edited the first edition of *Principles and Practice of Stress Management* in 1984. This now classic text was authored by a "who's who" of stress management. The present volume reflects the evolution of the field, and contains an equally authoritative (in many cases, overlapping) set of contributors. Collectively, the chapters express the breadth and depth of the field. They explore the concepts, examine the findings, explicate the techniques, and envision the future. As such, the volume should be required reading for all students in clinical and health psychology, behavioral medicine, and psychosocial nursing. As a reference work, the volume belongs on the shelves of clinicians and researchers involved with stress management.

The chapters by Lehrer, Woolfolk, and colleagues (Chapters 16–19) deserve special study. In a talmudic fashion, they carefully review the literature on similarities and differences among techniques and reach some important conclusions:

- EMG biofeedback produces greater decreases in tension in targeted muscle regions than does progressive muscle relaxation.
- Progressive muscle relaxation (a "whole"-body somatic technique) produces greater decreases in physiological arousal than does EMG biofeedback (a single-muscle technique).
- Thermal biofeedback and autogenic training produce greater autonomic effects than do muscle relaxation treatments, while the latter produce greater muscular relaxation.
- Cognitive therapy is more effective than progressive muscle relaxation for generalized anxiety symptoms.
- Drug therapies, particularly those involving benzodiazepines, are prone to higher relapses rates than are behavior therapies for anxiety-related conditons.
- Combinations of treatments (e.g., stress inoculation) are more effective than individual treatments (e.g., progressive muscle relaxation and behavioral rehearsal alone, which are components of stress inoculation) in the treatment of excessive anger. Cognitive components are particularly effective in reducing self-reported hostility, while biofeedback components are particularly effective in reducing hostility-related physiological responses.
- Persons high in internal locus of control are more likely to engage in internal self-management strategies such as aerobic exercise and multicomponent stress management programs, whereas persons high in external locus of control are more likely to respond to external self-management techniques such as EMG biofeedback.
- Persons low in hypnotic susceptibility respond better to EMG biofeedback and progressive muscle relaxation, whereas persons high in hypnotic susceptibility respond better to hypnosis. Although hypnotic susceptibility is associated with responsiveness to treatment with most relaxation techniques, this is not the case for biofeedback. Indeed, biofeedback and hypnosis may be mutually incompatible as self-management interventions.
- Facial EMG biofeedback is selectively effective for certain kinds of asthma. Skin temperature biofeedback is selectively effective for certain kinds of migraine, hypertension, and Raynaud's disease. Forehead EMG biofeedback is selectively effective for certain kinds of tension headache.

Nine years have passed since the first edition of *Principles and Practice of Stress Management* was published, and in my opinion it served us well. I suspect that the second edition will serve us another 9 years and take us well to the year 2000.

GARY E. SCHWARTZ, Ph.D.
University of Arizona

Preface

Our intent in both this and the first (1984) edition of *Principles and Practice of Stress Management* has been to provide a definitive picture of the stress management field. We include the stress management methods that have received the widest clinical use, and which have been evaluated scientifically in parametric research at multiple sites. Each method covered in this volume has met the dual tests of scientific respectability and clinical acceptance.

As authors of the various chapters, we invited individuals who are closely identified with the origination and/or propagation of each method. Our aim was to invite individuals with unimpeachable credentials to describe and evaluate each approach. We asked each chapter author to write for the interested but critical-thinking clinician as well as for the scholar. Each chapter therefore includes a sophisticated and nuanced description of the method and a case example of its use, as well as a review of the research literature on its applicability. Research on adverse effects and contraindications is covered, as is that devoted to clinical effectiveness.

The first chapter and the final four chapters are our own. We both think of ourselves as scientist-practitioners, with equal investment in each of these professional roles. In Chapter 1 we present our philosophical orientation to research and clinical practice of stress management, influenced by our experience in both areas. Chapters 16–19 review the research literature on comparisons among stress management methods. There we provide answers to questions the clinician and/or researcher may ask about the relative merits and liabilities of the various techniques for treating a variety of disorders among clients with diverse personal needs and personality styles. Although written as scholarly literature reviews, these chapters focus on questions of central interest to stress management clinicians.

The second edition is an update and expansion of the first. Research has mushroomed since publication of the previous edition, as reflected in the replacement of our final review chapter by four chapters in the present volume. The conclusions are similar, but much more definite. We can now say with certainty that the various relaxation and stress management techniques are *not* completely interchangeable. Although their effects do overlap, they each appear to have specific strengths, liabilities, and applications. At times they even may be incompatible with each other. Also we cover several additional methods, which although widely used since time immemorial, we now consider to have been evaluated by a sufficient body of research literature: listening to music, doing controlled breathing, and performing aerobic exercise. We also include chapters on two methods that justifiably could have been included in the first edition as well: stress inoculation training and the "traditional" approach to autogenic training as conceived of by Johannes H. Schultz.

Preparing these two volumes has been very exciting. We have had the honor of working with some of the most creative and eminent contributors to our field. They have been generous with their time and expertise, and they have been impeccably cooperative in holding to our preordained outline and publication schedule and in re-editing their materials to render them parallel and comparable to those provided by other authors. The high acceptance given to our first edition was due primarily to their efforts, and we are greatly indebted to them. We feel this more strongly for the second edition. Our contributors were willing to revise, update, and improve upon chapters that already had been accepted as definitive statements. Doing this required humility and courage on their part, and, we think, some "chutzpah" on ours for even asking this.

We also have felt the thrill of seeing patterns emerge from mountains of research studies and hours of computer searches through *Psychological Abstracts* and *Index Medicus*. Anyone who has engaged in this process is aware of both the difficulty and the rewards of such an enterprise. We hope that our work has been sufficiently thorough and that the results have been fairly presented and properly interpreted. If not, the fault is entirely our own.

The conclusions of this work have already been applied in our own clinical practices. It is our hope that others will find this volume similarly useful, both as a primer for students and as a refresher for experienced professionals.

PAUL M. LEHRER
ROBERT L. WOOLFOLK

Contents

SECTION THREE. INTEGRATION

Principles and Practice of
Stress Management

SECOND EDITION

INTRODUCTION

1

The Context of Stress Management

ROBERT L. WOOLFOLK
PAUL M. LEHRER

Research versus Clinical Practice in Stress Management

In the midst of the hoopla and ballyhoo that have surrounded the burgeoning public concern with stress and its deleterious consequences, meticulous scientists have systematically investigated the efficacy of numerous stress reduction techniques. Their efforts are the basis upon which we warrant and legitimize the methods employed to solve varied and complex human problems. Applications of general knowledge to unique, concrete human situations, however, are always problematic. In the treatment of stress-related disorders, bridging the gap between laboratory and clinic presents numerous challenges to which the research literature is an insufficient guide.

The clinician who attempts to learn therapeutic strategies from reading the empirical literature on stress management techniques inevitably experiences disappointment. The descriptions of treatment methods are cursory and terse; only those already intimately familiar with the interventions studied can understand clearly what procedures were involved. Treatments typically are not adapted to individual cases, but are uniform for all subjects. Frequently the "clinical version" of the treatment undergoes some modification so that a standardized form can be achieved. Moreover, stress reduction techniques often are abbreviated to make them easier to teach, easier to learn, and consistent with control or comparison conditions on such dimensions as length of training or amount of therapist contact.

Due to the presence of experimental controls necessary for the preservation of internal validity, treatment outcome studies do not provide a veridical picture of the clinical practice of stress management. Furthermore, because of the methodological requirements of research designs seeking to isolate causal influences, a given group of subjects often is administered a single stress management technique. Overly recalcitrant or disturbed subjects may be excluded at the outset, or they may become casualties of experimental attrition and be dropped from the final data analysis. The exigencies of research often dictate the random assignment of subjects to treatment conditions, making it impossible to observe the interactions among individual differences and factors related to treatments. Stress problems are intertwined in complicated ways with other pathological life circumstances and personal characteristics; the standard factorial design is not well suited to an examination of these complexities.

In behavioral science experiments, the emphasis on statistical significance as an index of treatment success creates a different emphasis from that in the world of clinical application. It is, of course, necessary to demonstrate that differences between treatment and control conditions are unlikely to have occurred as a result of chance factors. Efficacy versus a control is a necessary but insufficient basis for a technique to be utilized clinically. A technique not only must be better than nothing; it must be clinically powerful enough to justify its use. It must provide sufficient relief of suffering and enhanced ability to cope with life's travails to make it worth the time and effort to invoke it.

Many of the issues having to do with application to the clinic are amenable to systematic study via empirical methods. Interactions can be examined, effect sizes computed, and cost–benefit analyses conducted. Some investigations do exist that shed some light on the practicalities of clinical application; a number of these are reviewed in Chapter 17 of this volume. It is doubtful, however, that any number of such studies can provide answers to all the questions that arise in the course of clinical practice. Applications of scientific knowledge to the clinical arena will inevitably contain elements of art and of pedagogy. A mistake made often by newcomers to this field is to assume that the extensive scientific foundation of self-regulation technology obviates the necessity for clinical sensitivity, perspicacity, and wisdom. Although stress reduction techniques are more standardized and explicit than some other therapeutic methods, their success is no less dependent on the tacit skills and know-how that experienced and effective clinicians develop as they face the intricate and thorny problems clients present to them.

Given the plethora of methods and claims on their behalf circulating through the mental health culture and society at large, clinicians and students interested in the treatment of stress problems need not only to learn techniques but also to evaluate their efficacy. The present volume has been produced to provide the practitioner with a single source through which all those approaches to stress reduction that rest on firm empirical footing can be explored and contrasted. It is designed primarily to serve the clinician rather than the researcher. Although each of our contributors has research credentials, we have asked them to refrain from providing comprehensive and exhaustive surveys of the empirical literature; such reviews are readily available in scientific journals.

Our contributors are the consummate artists of their crafts, each a master of his or her respective area. We have commissioned them to make personal statements based on their clinical experience, and to hold in abeyance some of the circumspection and reserve that might characterize their activities as scientists. Our charge to them has been to wear their clinical hats—to communicate to their fellow clinicians those aspects of clinical acumen, artistry, and sagacity that so often are missing from descriptions of stress management methods. We have asked our contributors to become teachers—not only to convey the readily specifiable, technical aspects of their crafts, but also to explicate those seemingly ineffable therapeutic nuances and intuitive rules of thumb that are the hallmarks of clinical virtuosos. We have asked them also to describe pertinent research findings regarding therapeutic and adverse consequences of their techniques and to show how they utilize research findings to guide their practice.

Overview of the Volume

In Chapters 2 and 3 of this collection, two versions of the progressive relaxation first devised by Edmund Jacobson (1938) are presented. Jacobson originated the method as a treatment for "neuromuscular tension"—a term he used to cover a variety of emotional and somatic difficulties. Most early applications of the method were in the area that more recently has come to be known as "psychosomatic medicine." Jacobson's original method was later modified and drastically abbreviated by Joseph Wolpe (1958) and used in his systematic desensitization procedure as a "reciprocal inhibitor" of fear. Wolpe's modifications of Jacobson's original technique subsequently were refined and codified in manuals authored by Paul (1966) and Bernstein and Borkovec (1973). Progressive relaxation is a widely used method; it is perhaps more familiar to psychotherapists than any other stress management technique. Virtually all behavior therapists are familiar with it, at least in an abbreviated form.

There are some key, rarely appreciated differences between the classical form of progressive relaxation and the modified versions. In contrast to the latter methods, Jacobson's approach emphasizes acquisition of a generalizable muscular skill, and eschews the use of suggestion or other devices that may enhance the experience of relaxation during a therapy session. These are viewed as impediments to the ultimate therapeutic task: teaching the trainee to perceive the most subtle of muscle proprioceptions and to voluntarily eliminate even the most minute traces of skeletal muscle tone (Jacobson, 1970). As outlined in Chapter 2 of this volume by F. J. McGuigan, the patient is taught from the very beginning of training to recognize and to control decreasingly intense levels of muscular tonus. The primary aim is to make the individual able to recognize and eliminate even the most minute levels of tension, to remain as tension-free as possible at all times, and to eliminate unnecessary tension continuously during everyday activities. In abbreviated methods, the emphasis tends to be somewhat less on the awareness of tension and more on the active "production" of relaxation. Whereas the trained Jacobsonian "releases" minute amounts of tension continuously throughout the day, the trainee in a modified method tends to "create" a relaxed state through the use of tension–release cycles or some other activity that has been paired with sensations accompanying tension release.

A number of differences between the two approaches are elucidated by a comparison of McGuigan's chapter with that of Douglas Bernstein and Charles Carlson (Chapter 3). First, training in the classical method can be quite lengthy, because only one muscle group is addressed in any training session. Many months or even years may be necessary before full proficiency is acquired. This is not, however, always the case; therapeutic results have been obtained in as little as one session of training (Jacobson, 1970). Jacobson was also careful to avoid the use of suggestion, because he felt its effects to be transitory and unreliable. In fact, he believed that the suggestion of relaxation by the therapist actually impedes the learning of requisite neuromuscular skills. In his clinical work, Jacobson never told a trainee *where* to expect to feel a muscle sensation after a muscular contraction. He felt it essential that the trainee experience proprioception without any therapist influence. The therapist may leave the room between instructions, while the client works alone on becoming familiar with newly discovered muscular sensations and learning how to control them with newly developed muscular skills and sensitivities. Moreover, Jacobson did not consider it essential that a profound experience of relaxation be achieved in the initial sessions; skill development is all. In this method, deep relaxation occurs as skill in the procedures improves. Each muscle is tensed from the outset only to the degree required for the client to identify the "control sensations," or lowest perceptible level of tonus. Subsequently, with the "method of diminishing tensions," each muscle is tensed progressively less and less until the trainee is able to recognize minute amounts of tension. Indeed, most of each training session involves no muscular contraction at all, but only practice in *eliminating* tension by remaining completely passive.

Bernstein and Carlson (Chapter 3) illustrate some modern variations on Jacobson's therapeutic theme. As distinct from the classical method, all of the major skeletal muscles are addressed in the very first session; the trainee tenses muscles tightly before releasing the tension; and the therapist attempts to produce a deep sense of relaxation in the initial training session. Moreover, in contrast to Jacobson's method, some elements of suggestion are employed. These include telling the trainee the sensations that may be experienced, choosing a relaxing environment, having the therapist use voice modulation during tension–release cycles, avoiding having the trainee converse during the training itself, and using some hypnotic-like relaxation suggestions. These authors view progressive relaxation as only one technique among many possible interventions, and advise the use of other treatment tools in conjunction with relaxation.

In Chapters 4 and 5, we move from the Western disciplines of psychosomatic medicine and behavior therapy to a consideration of methods derived from the Eastern practice of yoga. Yoga has been an integral feature of the Hindu culture for over 2000 years. Elements of that tradition, especially meditation, recently have been appropriated by Western therapists in their efforts to find more effective tools to combat tension and stress. Bolstered by studies indicating the therapeutic potential of Eastern forms of meditation to produce decrements in physiological arousal (Woolfolk, 1975) and improvement in stress-related disturbances (Shapiro & Giber, 1978), clinicians were encouraged to devise Westernized forms of meditation (Benson, 1975; Carrington, 1977; Woolfolk, Carr-Kaffashan, McNulty, & Lehrer, 1976). These methods are technical distillations of the meditation procedures, removed from the complex frameworks of philosophical and religious belief within which they traditionally have been practiced.

In Chapter 4 Chandra Patel describes a stress management program that was originally designed for hypertensive patients, but that has general applicability. Patel's program is multifaceted, incorporating muscle relaxation, breathing exercises, meditation, and creative visualization. Although the techniques of Patel's method can be described and used outside the context of Hindu philosophy, this context is of more than historical interest. Patel provides a rich description of the "spirit" or cognitive underpinnings of stress management techniques used in her approach. What emerges is a vision of existence, a stress-reducing "philosophy of life" and life style that are integral and essential components of Patel's method.

In Chapter 5 Patricia Carrington describes her method of Westernized meditation, "clinically standardized meditation" (CSM). This method derives from the tradition of yoga and its familiar Western instantiation, transcendental meditation (TM). Although devoid of the cultic overtones of TM, CSM continues to emphasize certain ceremonial aspects that Carrington believes to be important aspects of treatment. CSM involves the more permissive and less routinized approach to mantra focus characteristic of TM, as opposed to the more disciplined, Zen-like approach of other approaches (e.g., Benson, 1975; Woolfolk et al., 1976). Carrington also draws upon her thousands of hours of experience in teaching meditation to describe the limitations and side effects of mediation. The result is a rich discussion of the occasional psychic discomfort that clients may encounter during training in any form of relaxation training.

Hypnosis and suggestion are much-misunderstood topics. Theodore Barber (Chapter 6) presents the wide-ranging approach of a consummate clinician for whom hypnosuggestive methods often are the most direct and expedient means of aiding clients in discomfort. His chapter demonstrates how readily the clinician can incorporate uncomplicated techniques from the tradition of hypnosis without becoming a full-fledged hypnotherapist or subscribing to some of the more extravagant claims that frequently are made for hypnosis. Indeed, Barber argues that many other stress management methods contain some elements of suggestion, and he outlines how these elements can be used most effectively in the treatment of stress disorders. Barber's approach has a considerable cognitive emphasis, as he attaches considerable importance to modifying clients' beliefs in a comprehensive treatment program for stress.

Wolfgang Linden (Chapter 7) provides a description of autogenic training, one of the earliest Western systems of physiological self-regulation, developed by the German physician J. H. Schultz out of his experiences with hypnosis. Although used widely by general practice physicians in Europe and in Asia as a method for treating psychosomatic disorders, autogenic training is used infrequently in the United States. It is essentially a collection of autosuggestive exercises whose focus is somatic. The reader unfamiliar with the technique will recognize a family resemblance between autogenic training and a number of other, more familiar approaches. Linden gives a lucid account of what he believes to be the distinctive features of autogenic training. Detailed accounts of training protocols make this chapter a useful introduction to this valuable but neglected technique.

Strictly speaking, biofeedback is a method for representing somatic activity as information available to cognition. It is a measurement–information tool that is used either by itself or in conjunction with other tools for lowering arousal. Biofeedback is a highly specific intervention, targeting only one somatic area at a time. It is usually not sufficient by itself as a stress management treatment, although it often is a core intervention in other applications of self-regulation therapy (e.g., in physical rehabilitation) and in the treatment of some stress-related physical problems (e.g., Raynaud's disease). For stress management, biofeedback is usually combined with other, more global techniques, and often is found to potentiate them.

Patricia Norris and Steven Fahrion (Chapter 8) describe the method of autogenic biofeedback, first developed by Elmer and Alyce Green of the Menninger Foundation. This approach to stress management is a blending of biofeedback and a modified version of autogenic training. The training begins with the use of autogenic-like phrases, imagery exercises, and deep diaphragmatic breathing. These procedures subsequently are integrated with machine-generated skin temperature and electromyographic (EMG) feedback.

In Chapter 9 two biofeedback pioneers, Johann Stoyva and Thomas Budzynski, describe the use of electronic technology in the teaching of relaxation skills. They detail how the patient and therapist can benefit from the objective measurement of physiological events that is integral to every biofeedback device. An important and novel feature of this chapter is the very extensive discussion of the facial musculature and its relation to emotion and stress-related disorders. The authors pay considerable attention to the use of multiple techniques in combination with biofeedback. Their treatment is a sophisticated clinical guide to producing comprehensive, multifaceted stress management interventions with clients.

In Chapter 10 Robert Fried describes a very straightforward method of stress management: control of respiration. Abdominal breathing (also employed by Patel and by Norris and Fahrion) is a technique that dates back centuries to its appearance in yoga as a form of "pranayama" (breath control). Fried's approach to respiration is systematic and fine-grained. A fuller understanding of the role of breathing in arousal and relaxation could enhance the clinical efforts of practitioners of a variety of stress management strategies. He also introduces the clinician to the vocabulary of respiratory physiology and to the useful and increasingly affordable technology involved in monitoring respiratory variables. Evidence is accumulating indicating the central involvement of respiratory variables in the etiology and maintenance of a broad array of emotional and psychosomatic symptoms. It now behooves the stress management clinician to become familiar with this area of psychophysiology, which in previous decades received little attention from mental health practitioners.

In the first of two predominantly cognitive chapters (Chapters 11 and 12), Aaron Beck presents a cognitive model of stress and its associated emotionality and psychopathology. Drawing on both theories of emotion and his own cognitive theory of psychopathology, Beck has fashioned a description of the etiology, operational dynamics, and treatment of stress symptomatology as one of the leading cognitive theorists views it. This perspective is an important corrective to approaches that fail to emphasize the causal role of cognitive appraisal in the genesis of stress. Beck's discussion of cognitive treatments is structured and highly specific.

In Chapter 12 Donald Meichenbaum, one of the pioneers of cognitive-behavior therapy, depicts his adaptation of cognitive methods to the management of stress, stress inoculation training (SIT). SIT is conceptualized within a coping skills model and attempts to develop or enhance clients' capacity to respond to stressors with minimal aversive emotionality and behavioral disruption. The treatment is multifaceted and includes education on the nature of stress and training in identifying circumstances that trigger stress. Extensive use is made of cognitive restructuring. Clients learn to practice relaxation, effective communication, and rational problem solving, and to substitute salutary self-statements for those that are stress-inducing.

Novel features of the treatment are graded exposure to initially low levels of stress and extensive rehearsal of coping skills. This chapter includes one of the most comprehensive reviews of treatment outcome studies in the literature.

Cheryl Maranto (Chapter 13) describes the use of music in stress management. Music may be one of the oldest informal techniques of stress reduction, used by millions of people daily to help them relax. The systematic use of music in clinical stress management treatment is relatively new, however. Although it long has been utilized in this fashion by the music therapy profession (as well by commercial disseminators of "atmosphere" music), a substantial empirical literature exists showing salutary effects, as Maranto documents. She guides us through the complexities of music therapy, educating us to the nuances and distinctions that are fundamental to this discipline. Music is easily integrated with other approaches to stress management, and listening to music is already a response in the repertoires of most patients. Its systematic use, however, requires a broad knowledge of the musical literature, general psychotherapeutic skills, and an understanding of the mechanisms by which music may affect stress reactivity. The ultimate therapeutic potential of this modality is still unknown, but it currently represents a treatment tool that may appeal to many clients.

Roger Fillingim and James Blumenthal (Chapter 14) describe the use of aerobic exercise as a stress management tool. The beneficial psychological effects of exercise have been highly touted in the popular media and among physical fitness proponents for many years. Recently, an increasing number of empirical studies have begun to document the significant effects of exercise on reducing stress reactivity. From a clinical perspective, there are a number of advantages to exercise regimens. In our experience, exercise may appeal to individuals who are loath to learn relaxation methods, and thus may be an acceptable alternative in some cases. In other cases, exercise can be combined with relaxation therapy in a multifaceted program. Exercise approaches require closer links with physicians and exercise physiologists than do other stress reduction techniques. The authors provide protocols that should be followed when prescribing exercise.

Laszlo Papp and Jack Gorman (Chapter 15) provide an overview of the pharmacological treatment of stress and anxiety disorders. The chapter covers such issues as the biochemical action of drugs useful in the adjunctive treatment of stress reactions, their most commonly observed side effects, and potential drawbacks and contraindications. Particularly useful is the discussion of the utility of various medications for various disorders and symptom patterns described in the revised third edition of the *Diagnostic and Statistical Manual of Mental Disorders* (DSM-III-R). In addition to describing current thinking on the older anxiolytics (the benzodiazepines), the authors give extensive treatment to recent developments in the chemotherapy of stress and anxiety.

In Chapter 16 we review comparisons between and among stress management techniques *across* treatment targets, with the aim of addressing broad questions of efficacy. We place particular emphasis on theoretical issues and mechanisms of action, as well as on procedural differences among the techniques that may account for differential effects. We conclude that there is considerable evidence for symptom–treatment specificity, but that this is superimposed on a general "relaxation response."

Until very recently there was little systematic investigation into the procedural complexities of clinical applications of stress management techniques. The inferences of practitioners, based on their own clinical experiences, were our only source of data. In the last decade, however, a substantial body of research has shed light on clinical issues in stress management. In Chapter 17 we examine the empirical literature on factors influencing the efficacy of stress management technology. A review is provided of these issues: variables that influence adherence to treatment regimens; validity issues in the assessment of adherence; the effects of practice; expectancy effects; and individual differences that mediate the effects of treatment.

In Chapters 18 and 19 we, with Richard Carr and Deepa Sargunaraj, review the empirical literature that has made direct comparisons of efficacy among stress management techniques applied to emotional and behavioral disorders and to treatment targets falling within the domain of behavioral medicine, respectively. We report and analyze results of comparative outcome research on stress management techniques *within* particular problem areas (e.g., headache, insomnia). The added effects of treatment–symptom specificity are of clinical importance for some disorders.

All of the contributions to this volume address the basic clinical questions that cut across techniques: assessment, selection of appropriate techniques, the client–therapist relationship, the limitations of stress management technology, potential impediments to therapeutic success, client cooperation, resistance, and adherence to therapeutic regimens. The clinical experience of our contributors represents a unique and invaluable repository of knowledge—the kind of practical knowledge and clinical rules of thumb that can only be acquired through experience.

The Philosophical and Sociocultural Aspects of Stress Management

Despite the impressive array of clinical wisdom and empirical data accumulated to date about modifying stress responses in individuals, it is likely that some issues related to stress management can only be comprehended at the levels of history, society, and culture. The stressors, diets, toxins, and activity patterns of industrialized urban life take their toll on our minds and on our bodies. Diseases such as coronary heart disease, hypertension, and cancer, which are rare among primitive peoples, are our chief causes of death and disability. A major reason for the rise of the degenerative physical diseases, as well as the high levels of psychological distress in contemporary Western societies, may well be the stress of modern life. This stress seems inescapable; no matter what we do, we cannot avoid it entirely.

Why should stress be such a problem in the contemporary world? Were there not terrible happenings and awful circumstances that troubled our ancestors, just as our current frustrations and tribulations beset us? Clearly, premodern life was (and still is, in contemporary developing nations) very difficult. Wars, pestilence, and dangers from the elements have undoubtedly produced emotional arousal throughout human history. Yet there are key differences in the sociocultural environment that can foster a kind of unremitting tension in modern individuals—a level of stress that is chronic, as opposed to the episodic stressors that were (and are) more characteristic of less complicated societies. The modern world is fundamentally and qualitatively different from that of the past. These differences provide some important clues to the capacity of contemporary Western society to create great distress and tension in its citizens.

Among the distinctive features of modernization are the ordering of life by the clock and a large increase in time-pressured work. Caplan, Cobb, French, Harrison, and Pinneau (1975) found that machine-paced assembly workers reported more somatic complaints and anxiety than did assemblers who were not machine-paced. Levi and his colleagues (Levi, 1972) reported that piecework pressure produced increases in noradrenalin levels and in blood pressure. Tax accountants were found to show substantial increases in serum cholesterol when working under the pressure of deadlines (Friedman, Rosenman, & Carroll, 1958).

As Alvin Toffler (1970) and various other observers have pointed out, not only is modern society an ever-changing panorama, but the rate of that change is ever-increasing. Many of the implications of this condition are rather straightforward. An individual is constantly required to make adjustments to a varying sociocultural matrix. We have earlier reported how such social disruptions can elevate levels of stress. In the areas of job skills, interpersonal relationships, management of personal finances, and sex roles, to name just a few, such rapid and fundamental changes have occurred that old assumptions are in continual need of revision.

Three hundred years ago, it was possible for one individual, the German philosopher Gottfried Wilhelm von Leibniz, to assimilate the entire scope of human knowledge. Fifty years ago, an individual could know the entire fledgling field of psychology. But today the knowledge explosion makes it impossible for one person to possess a significant fraction of the pertinent information in even a small domain of that field, or any other. And the pool of knowledge is growing every day. Professionals who are not inclined toward voracious reading within their specialties are soon out of date, their knowledge obsolete. Life is a little like this for all of us: We must keep changing, ceaselessly adapting to a world that transforms itself more rapidly each day. We must move faster and faster just to maintain our places.

One effect of industrialization and modernization is almost universally regarded as beneficial—that of enhancing the freedom and material well-being of individuals. The removal of many of the economic and social barriers to personal growth and self-expression presents the modern individual with a dazzling array of choices, as well as an awesome set of responsibilities. Today we choose our own careers, our circles of friends, our places of residence, and, perhaps most importantly, our own values. We must make decisions on a number of issues that would have been given or fixed in prior eras. We decide everything from whether to alter our appearances through dieting, exercise, or cosmetic surgery to what religion (if any) to follow. We are able to create for ourselves the rules that will govern relations with both intimates and acquaintances. The plasticity of the human being is such that even alteration of gender is now possible. Very little is set, fixed, or taken for granted. In the absence of some generally agreed-upon set of values or beliefs that provides practical wisdom to guide the making of choices, too many options can be difficult to bear. The great French sociologist Emile Durkheim (1897/1958), writing at the turn of the century, called this lack of values and norms "anomie"; he demonstrated that under anomic conditions, suicide rates rise dramatically.

The sociologist Ferdinand Tönnies (1963), describing the changes in society that took place at the time of the Industrial Revolution, described two basic kinds of social organization. Modern American sociologists often continue to call them by the German words *Gemeinschaft* and *Gesellschaft*, or, literally, "community" and "society." The *Gemeinschaft* form of social organization is the preindustrial form. It is characterized by group cohesiveness and coherent social order, but little freedom. In communal cultures, status is ascribed and jobs, wealth, and marriage are determined on the basis of who a person is, rather than what he or she can do. *Gemeinschaft* contains small social units (e.g., the family, the small village), as well as diffuse relationships in which various social roles (e.g., family member, boss, friend, teacher, healer, and church member) are extensively intermixed within the same small group of individuals.

In contrast, the *Gesellschaft* form encourages individual freedom and ambition, but at the price of social isolation and anomie. It is characterized by achieved rather than ascribed statuses. Units of social organization are large, so that even many of the people in a particular congregation or factory work force, let alone in a neighborhood or town, may not be known to each other. This form is also distinguished by role specificity; thus we pray with one group of people, work with another, and socialize with a third. Few, if any, formalized activities take place within the extended family. The extended family all but disappears, and even the nuclear family is weakened. Social isolation and anomie are significant sources of stress in this more modern form of society (Nisbet, 1973).

In the contemporary West, individuals continually are thrown back upon themselves and their own psychic resources. The German sociologist and philosopher Arnold Gehlen (1980) has written that one of the functions of society is to protect the individual from the burden of excessive choice. If this be so, contemporary industrialized societies are less than completely successful in this function. Never before has such a large percentage of the population been without durable and dependable social support.

The loss of community is related to the lack of meaning that is so often described by sociologists and existential philosophers as a concomitant of contemporary life. The premodern world view was communal and spiritual, as contrasted with the individualistic and materialistic consciousness of contemporary times. Premoderns felt themselves to be useful and necessary elements of a cosmological order that had inherent purpose and meaning (Taylor, 1975). But the replacement of religion by science as the ultimate source of epistemic authority; the desacralization of nature; the ascendency of technology and its associated rationality and means–ends perspective; and the relativization of values have disrupted the human security that emanated from a sense of belonging and the confidence that each individual life had some larger purpose and meaning. Existential writers such as Albert Camus have described this shift in human self-perception in compelling terms: "In a universe suddenly divested of illusions and lights, man feels an alien, a stranger. His exile is without remedy since he is deprived of the memory of a lost home or the hope of a promised land" (Camus, 1960, p. 5).

There is much evidence that people who find some purpose in existence, who believe that their activities are meaningful, and who view life as possessing coherence and lawfulness are less likely to manifest stress-related reactions (Antonovsky, 1987; Kobasa, 1979; Shepperd & Kashani, 1991). This evidence brings to mind the writings of the great sociologist Max Weber and his concept of "theodicy." Theodicies are elements of a cultural world view that explain and confer meaning on experiences of suffering and wrongfulness. Berger, Berger, and Kellner (1973) have pointed out that despite the great changes that have accompanied modernization, the "finitude, fragility, and mortality" of the human condition is essentially unchanged; at the same time, those previous definitions of reality that made life easier to bear have been seriously weakened by modernization.

Psychotherapy and stress management (especially the cognitive aspects) may very well be in the business of supplying secular theodicies to people who look to science and scientifically grounded professional to alleviate the discomforts of life. The world views we proffer typically are justified on the basis of some instrumental criterion: They reduce stress, promote health, enhance happiness, or the like. Determining the beliefs that reduce the stress of life is, however, not equivalent to establishing the truth or legitimacy of those beliefs. Any world view that is advanced solely on the basis of its instrumental benefits to health and happiness will be subject to various forms of criticism. One such criticism is the ethical rejoinder suggesting that many beliefs may be worth being stressed for—indeed, worth dying for. A world view whose ultimate claim to authority is pragmatic may be inherently self-limiting and self-defeating if an "inherent" sense of purpose is what provides people with the capacity to withstand the corrosive aspects and vicissitudes of living.

The activities of stress management professionals are orchestrated within the sociocultural matrix and also—along with the ubiquitous mental health and self-improvement industry of which they are part—serve to constitute this matrix. It would seem important for practitioners to have a grasp of the moral and sociohistorical aspects of their role. With respect to existential issues, they may not possess any ultimate answers, but they should at least know what the questions are.

REFERENCES

Antonovsky, A. (1987). The salutogenic perspective: Toward a new view of health and sickness. *Advances, 4,* 47–55.

Benson, H. (1975). *The relaxation response.* New York: Morrow.

Berger, P. L., Berger, B., & Kellner, H. (1973). *The homeless mind.* New York: Random House.

Bernstein, D. A., & Berkovec, T. D. (1973). *Progressive relaxation training.* Champaign, IL: Research Press.

Camus, A. (1960). *The myth of Sisyphus and other essays.* New York: Vintage.

Caplan, R. D., Cobb, S., French, J. R. P., Jr., Harrison, R. V., & Pinneau, S. R. Jr. (1975). *Job demands and worker health* (DHEW Publication No. NIOSH 75–160). Washington, DC: U.S. Government Printing Office.

Carrington, P. (1977). *Freedom in mediation.* Garden City, NY: Doubleday/Anchor.

Durkheim, E. (1958). *Suicide.* Glencoe, IL: Free Press. (Original work published 1897)

Friedman, M., Rosenman, R. H., & Carroll, V. (1958). Changes in serum cholesterol and blood clotting time in men subjected to cyclic variation of occupational stress. *Circulation, 17,* 852–861.

Gehlen, A. (1980). *Man in the age of technology.* New York: Columbia University Press.

Jacobson, E. (1938). *Progressive relaxation.* Chicago: University of Chicago Press.

Jacobson, E. (1970). *Modern treatment of tense patients.* Springfield, IL: Charles C Thomas.

Kobasa, S. (1979). Stressful life events, personality, and health: An inquiry into hardiness. *Journal of Personality and Social Psychology, 37,* 1–11.

Levi, L. (1972). *Stress and distress in response to psychosocial stimuli.* Elmsford, NY: Pergamon Press.

Nisbet, R. (1973). *The social philosophers: Community and conflict in Western thought.* New York: Crowell.

Paul, G. L. (1966). *Insight versus desensitization in psychotherapy: An experiment in anxiety.* Stanford, CA: Stanford University Press.

Shapiro, D. H., & Giber, D. (1978). Meditation and psychotherapeutic effects. *Archives of General Psychiatry, 35,* 294–302.

Shepperd, J. A., & Kashani, J. V. (1991). The rationship of hardiness, gender, and stress to health outcomes in adolescents. *Journal of Personality, 59,* 747–768.

Taylor, C. (1975). *Hegel.* Cambridge, England: Cambridge University Press.

Toffler, A. (1970). *Future shock.* New York: Random House.

Tönnies, F. (1963). *Community and society.* New York: Harper & Row.

Wolpe, J. (1958). *Psychotherapy by reciprocal inhibition.* Standord, CA: Stanford University Press.

Woolfolk, R. L. (1975). Psychophysiological correlates of meditation. *Archives of General Psychiatry, 32,* 1326–1333.

Woolfolk, R. L., Carr-Kaffashan, L., McNulty, T. F., & Lehrer, P. M. (1976). Meditation training as a treatment for insomnia. *Behavior Therapy, 7,* 359–365.

STRESS MANAGEMENT METHODS

2

Progressive Relaxation: Origins, Principles, and Clinical Applications

F. J. McGUIGAN

History[1]

Influences on Jacobson

In 1905 Edmund Jacobson, the originator of Progressive Relaxation (PR), was sent to graduate school at Harvard University by Walter Dill Scott, psychologist and president of Northwestern University, to study with three of the great minds of the day: William James, Josiah Royce, and Hugo Münsterberg. All three had a considerable influence on him: James by exhorting him to study "the whole man"; Royce by nurturing his philosophical paper on truth; and Münsterberg in a negative way that, however, was beneficial for PR. Münsterberg discharged Jacobson as his assistant because, as Jacobson later related, the data he collected were at odds with Münsterberg's theory. Thus freed to work on his own, Jacobson studied the startle reaction to an unexpected loud noise. He found that there was no obvious startle to sudden noise in more relaxed subjects. This was the first systematic study of relaxation, and it marked the birth of PR.

On graduating from Harvard, Jacobson worked with Edward Bradford Titchener at Cornell University. I suspect that he was influenced by Titchener in two very important ways: through Titchener's expertise in introspection, and through his context theory of meaning. Titchener's context theory held that the meanings of words originate in part in bodily attitudes (postures) involving the skeletal muscle system. Related to these two avenues of influence, two contemporary applications of PR for clinical purposes are (1) detailed observation of ("introspection" on) minute kinesthetic sensations and accompanying mental processes; and (2) clinical interpretation of localized bodily tensions as meanings of acts that occur in one's imagination.

---

[1]Portions of this section are adapted by permission from Jacobson (1977).

Objective Measurement of Tension

On leaving Cornell, Jacobson received his M.D. and worked in the Department of Physiology at the University of Chicago from 1926 until 1936; he also conducted a private clinical practice. At Chicago, collaborating with A. J. Carlson, Jacobson discovered an objective measure of tension: They found that the amplitude of knee-jerk reflexes varied directly with the degree of patients' tension. Consequently, as overly tense patients learned to relax, the amplitude of their knee-jerk reflexes decreased. Jacobson's (1938) further research on several reflexes established that chronic tonus (sustained tension) of the skeletal muscles increased the amplitude of reflexes and decreased their latency; conversely, reflexes diminished in amplitude and increased in latency as patients relaxed. In general, general skeletal muscle tone decreased, and this could eliminate the involuntary startle reflex. Charles Sherrington (1909) also made this point when his research established that it was not possible to evoke the patellar tendon reflex in an absolutely toneless muscle. More generally, Sherrington concluded that the appearance of reflexes depended on the presence of tone in the muscles constituting part of the reflex arc. (After about 2 months in my own PR classes, I sometimes drop a large book onto the floor when the students are well into their relaxation period. Seldom is there even a blink of the eye in these well-relaxed students.)

As successful as it was, measuring the knee-jerk reflex was cumbersome. Through arduous efforts with the aid of scientists at Bell Telephone Laboratories, Jacobson eventually was able to measure tension directly. He recorded electrical muscle action potentials as low as a microvolt, a unit unknown to the physiologists of the day. Thus, quantitative electromyography (EMG) was launched. The resultant use of objective measures of degree of relaxation and tension guided Jacobson to develop and validate PR, the most effective method of relaxation that was reasonably possible.

Measuring Mental Events

With this new instrumentation, Jacobson made important discoveries about how the mind and body function. He found that in a relaxed subject, just the *thought* of moving a limb was accompanied by unique covert EMG responses in that limb. For example, if the subject imagined hitting a nail with a hammer three times, there were three unique EMG bursts in the preferred arm. Through extensive research he concluded that all thought is accompanied by skeletal muscle activity, though response amplitude may be extremely low. The eye and speech muscles, he found, were especially important during visual and speech imagery. Conversely, his data indicated that mental processes diminished and even disappeared as the skeletal musculature relaxed toward zero. As Jacobson concluded, "It might be naive to say that we think with our muscles, but it would be inaccurate to say that we think without them" (cited by McGuigan, 1978, p. iii).

Therapeutic Consequences

Jacobson's research showed that to relax the mind and the body, one must relax all of the skeletal musculature. Jacobson applied this basic principle of PR for more than 70 years, with immense therapeutic consequences. His numerous scientific and clinical studies gave the world effective methods for directly controlling the various systems of the body, including those that generate mental processes. I now turn to an exposition of these methods.

Theoretical Underpinnings

PR begins with the ancient and venerable concept of rest. Physicians have long known the value of rest, frequently prescribing it in the form of "bed rest." However, many people who are instructed to rest in bed simply toss and turn. Mere prescription is not sufficient; patients may be told to rest but do not know how. These patients must diligently learn habits of effective rest. Such habits may enable them to prevent the development of a serious tension malady and to use bodily energy with greater efficiency. When relaxation is applied therapeutically, it has often helped restore the body to a normally functioning condition—providing, of course, that the tension malady is reversible. How tension develops in the body is a straightforward physiological event.

How Stressors Evoke Tension

Each stressful situation ("stressor") people meet in everyday life reflexively evokes the primitive startle pattern of rising (covertly or overtly) on the balls of the feet and hunching forward. The entire skeletal musculature reacts immediately. Within a matter of 100 or so milliseconds, people thereby ready themselves for fight or flight, as Walter Cannon (1929) theorized. This startle reaction, followed by complex autonomic and endocrine changes, has had great survival value. However, it is often prolonged beyond the immediate emergency, resulting in a condition of chronic overtension and continued hyperactivity of the systems of the body. In particular, consistent, excessive covert tightening of the skeletal musculature overdrives the central nervous system and increases activity of the autonomic, cardiovascular, endocrine, and other systems, as depicted in Figure 2.1. Prolonged, heightened skeletal muscle tension may then result in any of a variety of pathological conditions, as I soon explain. To reverse the process of overtension, a person needs to learn to relax the skeletal musculature, whereupon there is reduced activity in the other systems of the body.

Principles and Physiology of Progressive Relaxation

In learning PR, one cultivates the ability to make extremely sensitive observations of the world beneath the skin. To acquire such heightened internal sensory observation,

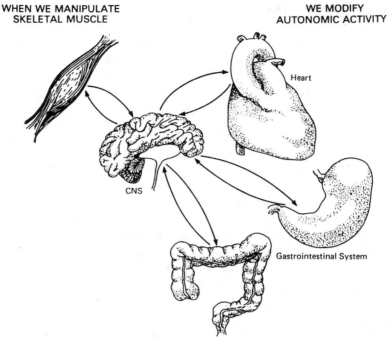

WHEN WE MANIPULATE
SKELETAL MUSCLE

WE MODIFY
AUTONOMIC ACTIVITY

Heart

CNS

Gastrointestinal System

FIGURE 2.1. A model of the functional relationship between the skeletal musculature and other bodily systems. As tension increases, activity of the central nervous system increases. In turn, various autonomic functions, such as those of the cardiovascular and gastrointestinal systems, are heightened. Conversely, relaxation of the skeletal musculature produces a tranquil state throughout the body.

which is a kind of physiological introspection, one first learns to recognize subtle states of tension. When a muscle contracts (tenses), volleys of neural impulses are generated and carried to the brain along afferent neural pathways. This muscle–neural phenomenon—the generation of afferent neural impulses—constitutes the local sign of tension that one learns to observe. This tension sensation is the "muscle sense of Bell," which was reported in the early 19th century by the eminent physiologist Sir Charles Bell.

"Tension" is the contraction of skeletal muscle fibers that generates the tension sensation. "Relaxation" is the elongation (lengthening) of those fibers, which then eliminates the tension sensation. After learning to identify the tension sensation, one learns to relax it away. For this, one learns to allow the muscle fibers that generated the tension to elongate. In the learning process, one contrasts the previous tension sensation with the later elimination of tension. This general procedure of identifying a local state of tension, relaxing it away, and making the contrast between the tension and ensuing relaxation is then applied to all of the major muscle groups. In PR one thus learns to control all of the skeletal musculature, so that any portion thereof may be systematically relaxed or tensed as one chooses. Those familiar with EMG biofeedback may wish to think of PR as a method of "internal biofeedback" in which the learner internally monitors feedback signals from the muscle instead of perceiving their representations on external readout systems.

The Skeletal Muscles Control Other Bodily Systems through Neuromuscular Circuits

In the 19th century, the famous psychologist Alexander Bain (e.g., Bain, 1855) held that the skeletal musculature is the only system over which a person has direct control. Hence, as Bain, Jacobson, and others held, skeletal muscles are "the instrument of the will." They contain the only receptor cells in the body that can be directly shut off, which is accomplished merely be lengthening muscle fibers. A synonym for "skeletal muscles" is "voluntary muscles," precisely because when one wishes to perform an act, one systematically contracts and relaxes the voluntary muscles. For instance, a person who decides to walk, contracts muscles to put one foot in front of the other. This point is so obvious that it does not need elaboration. What is not so obvious is that the internal (covert) functions of the body are similarly controlled by means of the skeletal muscles, as depicted in Figure 2.1. PR is predicated on the principle that covert functions of the body can also be controlled through slight muscle tensions.

Thus, the tension sensation (the muscle sense of Bell) is called "the control signal" because it literally controls the body's activities. Muscles exercise such control as they interact with the brain through "neuromuscular circuits." Jacobson (1964) illustrated this principle in a figure, reprinted here as Figure 2.2. When volleys of neural impulses generated by contracting muscles feed back to the brain, extremely complex events result, following which neural impulses return to the muscles along efferent neural pathways. The muscles then further contract, directing additional neural impulses to and from the brain, and so on. Numerous neuromuscular circuits throughout the body simultaneously reverberate in this way to carry out the body's functions.

By learning internal sensory observation, one can become quite proficient in recognizing control signals wherever they may occur throughout the skeletal musculature. Through practice, those controls may be activated or relaxed. Relaxation of the skeletal muscle controls produces a state of rest throughout the neuromuscular circuits, including reduced activity of the brain itself. The long-range goal of PR is for the body instantaneously to monitor all of its numerous control signals, and automatically to relieve tensions that are not desired. The trained body has an amazing capacity to monitor the many neuromuscular circuits that reverberate in parallel fashion throughout the body. The ultimate goal is to develop "automaticity," wherein one automatically, unconsciously, and effortlessly identifies and relaxes unwanted tensions.

Jacobson (1964) emphasized the control functions of PR when he used "self-operations control" as a synonym for PR. "Self-operations control" was a precedent for contemporary use of such terms as "self-regulation" and "stress management." Its aims are to increase behavioral efficiency by programming oneself to eliminate tensions that interfere with one's primary purposes. A person can thereby control blood pressure, emotional life, digestive processes, mental processes, and the like, as I later illustrate.

The Concept of Neuromuscular Circuits Has a Venerable History

The concept of reverberating neuromuscular circuits driven by muscle controls is ancient. Dating from the period of the early Greeks, its evolution can be impressively

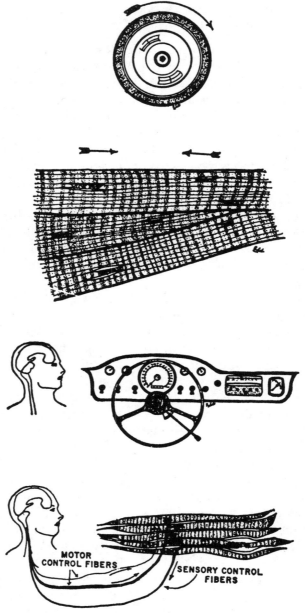

FIGURE 2.2. "You run your car by manipulating the controls on and near the dashboard, whereby you make the wheels move at the rate and in the direction you desire. Likewise, you can run yourself by going on and off with the power in the controls which lie in your muscles, whereupon your muscles contract and relax in the patterns which suit your effort-purposes" (Jacobson, 1964, p. 2). Reprinted by permission from Jacobson (1964).

traced through the writings of philosophers, through the scientific Renaissance, through the research of later physiologists and psychologists, and into the very forefront of contemporary scientific and clinical thinking (see McGuigan, 1978). Some of our the most prominent thinkers have recognized that the human body functions in terms of information generated and transmitted between the muscle systems and the brain. One of the most influential presentations of this concept was provided by Norbert Wiener (1948) in his classic book *Cybernetics*. In greater depth than all others before him, Wiener developed the model that the body functions according to principles of feedback circuits. As he put it,

> The central nervous system no longer appears as a self-contained organ, receiving inputs from the senses and discharging into the muscles. On the contrary, some of its most characteristic activities are explicable only as circular processes, emerging from the nervous system into the muscles, and re-entering the nervous system through the sense organs, whether they be proprioceptors or organs of the special senses. (Wiener, 1948, p. 15)

A similar neuromuscular concept was put forth by Alexander Bain in 1855:

> The organ of mind is not the brain by itself; it is the brain, nerves, muscles, and organs of sense. . . . We must . . . discard forever the notion of the sensorium commune, the cerebral closed, as a central seat of mind, or receptacle of sensation and imagery. (cited by Holt, 1937, pp. 38–39).

Neurophysiology of Relaxation

In various publications, Gellhorn (e.g., Gellhorn, 1958; Gellhorn & Kiely, 1972) sought to specify the neural mechanisms by which the skeletal musculature leads to relaxation of the body. Gellhorn was especially impressed with Jacobson's method, and Jacobson approved of Gellhorn's theorizing as to those neural mechanisms (Jacobson, 1967). Gellhorn started with the basic fact that PR decreases afferent neural impulses from the skeletal musculature. He then noted that the reticular formation receives considerable innervation from those skeletal muscles, so that relaxation reduces activity there. The reticular formation in turn functions in circuits with the posterior hypothalamus and thence with the cortex. Consequently, muscular relaxation reduces proprioceptive input to the hypothalamus, with a resulting lessening of hypothalamic–cortical and autonomic discharges. Gellhorn concluded that lessened emotional reactivity during muscular relaxation is the result of reduced proprioceptive impulses to the hypothalamus, which then decreases excitability of the sympathetic nervous system. Jacobson summarized research by Bernhaut, Gellhorn, and Rasmussen (1953) as follows:

> These findings suggest that a relaxation of the skeletal musculature is accompanied by a diminution in the state of excitability of the sympathetic division of the hypothalamus and, through a reduction in the hypothalamic–cortical discharges, by a similar reduction in the state of excitability of the cerebral cortex. (Jacobson, 1967, p. 155)

In these ways, then, the skeletal muscles can control other systems of the body, including the reduction and elimination of mental (including emotional) events.

Differential Relaxation

"Differential relaxation" (DR) is the optimal contraction of only those muscles required to accomplish a given purpose. Those and only those muscles should contract, and they should contract only to the extent required for accomplishing the purpose at hand. All other (irrelevant) muscles of the body should be relaxed. In the moment-to-moment monitoring of tensions throughout the day, people can often catch themselves wasting energies. Some needlessly clasp their hands together; others tap their fingers and feet, wrap their legs around the legs of a chair, or needlessly rock back and forth. In learning DR, while studying a particular tension signal that is to be controlled, the learner recognizes other tensions elsewhere in the body. For example, when practicing the position in Figure 2.3, the learner may recognize tensions in the leg, trunk, and so forth. These are unwanted tensions that can be relaxed away when the learner later practices there. By learning DR 24 hours a day, one can save considerable energy, so that relevant tensions can be more efficiently directed toward the accomplishment of specific goals. Later I consider some specific applications of the principle of DR.

The Method of Diminishing Tensions

In developing control over one's muscles, it is necessary (eventually) to detect the most subtle control signals. For this purpose, PR starts with relatively obvious control signals generated in the dorsal surface of the forearm by raising the hand at the wrist at a 90° angle (see Figure 2.3). Thus the learner initially perceives a localized sensation of tension in the forearm. With the "method of diminishing tensions," one then studies tensions of ever-decreasing intensity. Thus, after the control signal generated by raising the hand vertically at the wrist is studied, for the next practice the hand is raised only half as much—at a 45° angle from the horizontal. Then the third practice

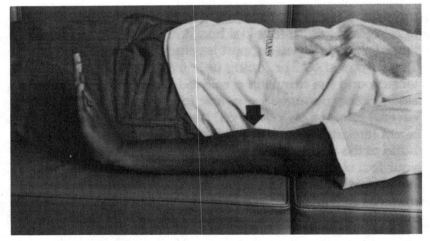

FIGURE 2.3. The first practice position (not "exercise") is to bend the hand back at the wrist to produce tension in the upper (dorsal) surface of the forearm.

position is to raise the hand only half as high as before (at about a 20° angle); on successive practice positions the hand is raised lower and lower until movement is imperceptible. The eventual goal is to identify tension signals of perhaps 1/1000th the intensity of those with which the learner began. Such signals are common in the minute muscles of the tongue and eyes.

Some practitioners give instructions to generate high-intensity tensions (e.g., to clench the fist tightly), which are counterproductive in the study and control of low-intensity tensions. Many covert responses are below 1 μV. To control small tensions, one should study them rather than large tensions.

Avoiding Suggestion

In learning PR, patients are never told that they are doing well, that they are getting better, that they are relaxing, that their hands feel heavy, that they are getting sleepy, or the like. No attempt is made to convince the patients that they will be "cured" in any sense of the word, nor are any such promises made. Instead, the patients are aided by instructions just as in any other learning procedure. Thus a teacher may interrupt a patient's practice with criticism whenever the patient is failing to relax.

Jacobson (1938) listed a number of reasons for avoiding suggestion. As with the placebo effect, any method will accomplish something (though usually only temporarily) if it instills into the patient the belief that he or she will benefit from its application. Jacobson pointed out that relaxation is a fundamental physiological occurrence that consists of learning to elongate muscle fibers systematically. He specified definitive physiological changes in the body that differ from those occurring during suggestion. The patient may be skeptical in regard to the procedure, but still can learn very well when presented with objective evidence of progress. Moreover, the patient learns to be independent of the therapist; in "suggestion" therapies, by contrast, dependence on therapists is engendered. As Lehrer, Woolfolk, and Goldman (1986) added,

> [Jacobson held that] the danger of suggestion . . . is that it may make the individual feel that relaxation is taking place even when it is not. The *perception* of relaxation is not so important as actual physical relaxation, according to Jacobson. Therefore, suggestion may be deleterious because a person may stop devoting the time and concentration necessary to learn relaxation if he or she feels relaxed already. (Lehrer et al., 1986, p. 202; italics in original)

Relaxation Practice Is Not an Exercise

Many suggestions for how to relax use a lay meaning of the term, which is inappropriate in a scientific/clinical context. For instance, advice to exercise is not advice to relax, because exercise is work. Exercise is very advisable on other grounds. For the same reason, terms such as "relaxation exercises" or "relaxation response" are self-contradictory, because "exercise" and "response" are "work words." The essence of relaxing is to allow the muscle fibers to elongate, which is physiologically impossible when one *tries* (through exercising or responding) to accomplish it. One simply cannot make an *effort* to relax, because an effort to relax is a failure to relax.

Is There a Shortcut?

From a naive learner's point of view, the amount of time required to learn PR may seem excessive. Indeed, one needs to learn to control a large mass of muscle comprising almost half the body weight. Recognizing the desire on the part of the learner for brevity, Jacobson spent many years attempting to shorten the method. For example, in the 1950s he developed a method that has since been called "biofeedback" (see Jacobson, 1978, Fig. 25, p. 146-K). However, he abandoned it because patients did not sufficiently generalize from what they learned in the clinic to everyday life, nor was the effect sufficiently permanent. His conclusion was that there simply is no satisfactory brief method for learning to relax a body that has been practicing overtension for decades. Nevertheless, Jacobson (1964) did offer a "briefer course," reducing the time devoted to each muscle group. For instance, instead of practicing for 3 hours on the first position (see Figure 2.3), one practices three positions in 1 hour, starting with the first three in Table 2.2 (see below). Similar abridgements have been made for other muscle groups. The complete course can thus be shortened to one-third of the time it ordinarily takes. However, in this world "you get what you pay for," so that you learn considerably less control from a briefer than from a longer course. An appropriate analogy is learning to play the piano: Certainly you can practice for shorter periods, but your competence is thereby reduced. One exception, though, is with children. Jacobson's research in school systems and in clinical work led him to conclude that children learn PR quite rapidly. His reasoning was that they have not spent so many years acquiring maladaptive tension habits that must be reversed. Teaching PR in elementary school would have amazingly beneficial consequences for society.

With this explanation of the principles of PR, I now turn to the psychologically important topic of clinical control of mental (cognitive) processes. To establish a basis, I first consider the scientific nature of mind and its component mental events.

A Psychophysiological Model of Mind

Mental (cognitive) events are generated by the selective interaction of reverberating neuromuscular circuits. Various functions of the everyday notion of "mind" are indicated by such terms as "ideas," "images," "thoughts," "dreams," "hallucinations," "fears," "depressions," and "anxieties." According to the present model, all such mental (cognitive) events are generated when selective systems of the body interact through highly integrated neuromuscular circuits. Most mental processes are generated when muscles of the eyes and speech regions tense, whereupon specialized circuits to and from the brain are activated. Other pathways are activated also, including those involving the somatic musculature and the autonomic system. A detailed presentation of, and perhaps the most extensive documentation for, this neuromuscular model of the generation of mental events are provided in McGuigan (1978).

    1. Muscular events are present during cognition. The McGuigan (1978) summary of relevant research over an 80-year period provides a firm basis for the conclusion that muscular contraction in selected regions of the body corresponds to the nature of the mental activity present. During visual imagery, the eyes are uniquely active (e.g., when one is imagining the Eiffel Tower, the eyes move upward in imaginal scanning as detected through electro-oculography). During imagining, somatic activity EMG readings detect localized covert responses (e.g., imagining lighting a cigarette produces a distinct covert response in the active arm). Covert muscular responses have been recorded in the speech musculature during a great variety of thinking tasks; for example, there was heightened tongue EMG while subjects were performing a verbal mediation task using Tracy Kendler's paradigm (McGuigan, Culver, & Kendler, 1971; see Figure 2.4). In addition, there is heightened speech muscle activity in both children and adults during silent reading; increased speech muscle activity covertly occurs while individuals are engaged in cursive handwriting; covert responses occur in the fingers of deaf children while they think, which is the locus of their "speech" region; rapid, phasic speech muscle activity occurs during night dreams involving auditory content; heightened speech muscle activity occurs in paranoid schizophrenics during auditory hallucinations; and so on for other mentalistic activities (see especially Ch. 10 of McGuigan, 1978). Conversely, there is no conscious awareness at all when people are well relaxed, as objectively determined by a lack of tension measured through EMG readings (Jacobson, 1938).

The reasoning here is that since specific muscle activity occurs during cognitive activity, and since cognitive activity disappears when this muscle activity is reduced to zero, it may be concluded that muscle activity is a critical component of those cognitive events.

2. *Numerous covert reactions during cognition are related by neuromuscular circuits.* While there are foci of muscular activity in selective regions of the body, depending on the nature of the cognitive activity, there are also other covert responses simultaneously occurring throughout the skeletal musculature. For example, while sub-

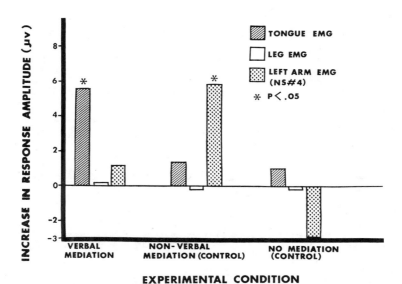

FIGURE 2.4. Tongue EMG increased significantly more for an oral–verbal mediation group than for two control groups. Left-arm activity was greatest for the directional (right-to-left) nonverbal mediation group. From McGuigan, Culver, and Kendler (1971).

jects in one study processed a silent answer to a question, events were simultaneously recorded in the arms, lips, neck, and eyes, as well as in the left temporal lobe and left motor area of the brain (McGuigan & Pavek, 1972; see Figure 2.5). The conclusion is that these unique, simultaneously occurring events throughout the body are not independent. Rather, they are related by means of rapily reverberating neuromuscular circuits between the brain and the extensive skeletal musculature. Since those widespread events occur simultaneously with the silent thought, it is assumed that the neuromuscular circuits generate that thought. I turn now to how such a verbal thought is generated.

3. *There are general linguistic, visual, and somatic components of cognition.* Focusing on linguistic cognition, research has indicated that speech muscles generate a phonetic code, which is presumably transmitted to and from the linguistic regions of the brain (see especially McGuigan & Winstead, 1974; McGuigan & Dollins, 1989). When those speech muscles and linguistic brain regions function in unison, perceptual understanding of linguistic cognitions occurs. No doubt similar processing occurs to generate nonlinguistic cognitive activity. Thus, circuits between the eyes and the brain generate visual imagery, and circuits between the nonspeech skeletal musculature and the brain generate somatic components of thoughts (see McGuigan, 1989, 1991b).

Control of cognitions. From a practical point of view, this model of the mind makes it abundantly clear how people can volitionally control their emotions and other cognitive activities, as well as other bodily functions. That is, if cognitive activities are identical with the energy expended when neuromuscular circuits reverberate, those cognitive events can be eliminated when the neuromuscular circuits cease to be active. They stop reverberating when a person relaxes the skeletal muscle components. I

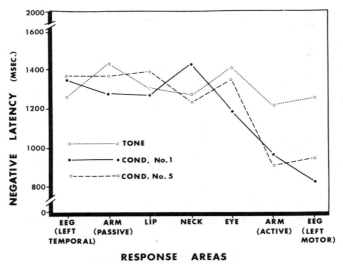

FIGURE 2.5. Mean latencies of covert reactions identified in various bodily regions indicate that the reactions occur simultaneously and are related by means of neuromuscular circuits. The specific conditions are not relevant for this main point. From McGuigan and Pavek (1972).

soon follow up on the clinical significance of this neuromuscular model of mental processes.

The Meaning and Purpose of Tensions

Recalling Titchener's context theory of meaning, a compatible basic principle of PR is that every tension has a purpose—that every tension means something. This point is obvious in many instances. For example, in Figure 2.3, the purpose of the tension in the upper surface of the forearm is simply to raise the hand at the wrist. Similarly, the purpose of tensions in the muscles of the legs while walking is simply to move the body. What is not so obvious is the interpretation of subtle muscular tensions in the application of clinical PR.

Distinguishing between "meaning" and "process." To interpret control signals, one learns that "process" is the way in which meaning is generated—process is the actual tension sensation that one observes within one's body. "Meaning" designates the purpose of the tension, the reason why one tenses. In generating mental events, "process" consists of the muscular contractions within neuromuscular circuits that generate the relevant images, sensations, and so on. "Meaning" is thus the content of those mental processes.[2]

In therapy, a patient is first carefully trained in detecting (proprioceptively introspecting on) subtle tensions throughout the body that constitute process. Then she or he is carefully trained in developing the ability to introspect on and report the content of mental activity in considerable detail. Process usually occurs in unexpected places in the body. The patient first identifies the nature and locality of process. When these are identified, the question to be answered by clinician and patient working together is this: Why do those tensions occur in particular regions and during a given kind of mental activity? Establishing the meaning of the tensions can give the patient better understanding of and control over his or her difficulties. For example, while learning to relax, a man observed subtle tensions throughout his entire right leg. That was process. After some study, the tensions were interpreted as follows: The man was tensing *as if* he were about to fall out of a treehouse and crash into a board with the leg. The mental content generated by the covert tensions in the leg was his remembrance of actually having fallen out of a treehouse when he was a boy. As the muscles in the leg covertly contracted in the present, he relived that experience in his memory as if it were overtly occurring. Rolfers report similar experiences when muscles are stimulated.

Consider a case of a lady whose complaints included anemia, chronic constipation, nervous tension with inability to sit quietly, slight dizzy spells during excitement, and a slight discharge from the nose (Jacobson, 1938). After training, she reported process of sitting stiffly and formally. The meaning of this apparently was that she sought to maintain proper posture in her back because of a fear of developing a habit

---

[2]This theorizing is quite prominent in contemporary psychology, as in Charles Osgood's derivation of meaning from overt responding. In his symbols, R, such as being burned by a lighted match, contributes to the meaning of "fire"; meaning is his r_M. The works of Jerome Bruner and of Hans Werner employ similar principles.

of faulty posture. That is, the purpose served by maintaining a stiff and formal posture was the prevention of an incorrect everyday posture. To control the tension on the meaning level, she came to understand the reasons why she held herself stiffly and was persuaded to change; on the process level, she learned how to relax the relevant controlling muscles.

In clinical work, it may take a long time to identify tensions characteristic of the "nervous" condition of the patient, to interpret those tensions, and to deal with them effectively. But the history of clinical PR is one of considerable success in following this paradigm. For example, anxiety is regarded as a fearful condition represented in the skeletal musculature. Once the clinician can ascertain the meaning of the skeletal muscle representations, it is then possible to relax those critical tensions, whereupon the state of anxiety can be diminished or eliminated. I return to anxiety later in this chapter.

Assessment

Applications of the Method

There are two general purposes of tension control—prophylactic and therapeutic. By learning to relax differentially 24 hours a day, a person can increase the likelihood of preventing a stress/tension disorder. For a person already thus victimized, clinical PR can often ease or eliminate the condition.

Stress/tension disorders fall into two classic categories: cognitive ("psychiatric") and somatoform ("psychosomatic") disorders. Elsewhere (McGuigan, 1991a), I discuss applications within the first category, which includes such neurotic disorders as anxiety state, panic disorder, phobic disorders, neurotic depression, and neurasthenia, as well as lesser fears and worries. The second category includes such disorders as colitis with accompanying diarrhea and constipation, teeth grinding (bruxism), essential hypertension, coronary heart disease, rheumatological pathologies, chronic fatigue, and such pains as those of headaches and backaches.

For over seven decades, Jacobson (e.g., 1938, 1970) collected an abundance of scientific and clinical data that validated the therapeutic application of PR for "psychiatric tension pathologies" (his term). These included nervous hypertension, acute insomnia with nervousness, anxiety neurosis, cardiac neurosis, chronic insomnia, cyclothymic depression, compulsion neurosis, hypochondria, fatigue states, nervous depression, and phobias. Somatoform disorders to which he successfully applied PR included convulsive tic, esophageal spasm, mucous colitis, chronic colitis, arterial hypertension, and tension headaches.

Therapy

Cognitive ("psychiatric") and somatoform ("psychosomatic") disorders, as well as lesser conditions, are characterized by excessive, chronic tension and may be reversed by relaxing the skeletal muscles as represented in Figure 2.1. To summarize, practice in the gradual lengthening of skeletal muscle fibers can result in a generalized state of relaxation, which in turn can produce a state of relative quietude throughout the central nervous system. Consequently, the viscera can also relax, as evidenced by a lowering of blood pressure, a reduction of pulse rate, and a loosening of the gastrointestinal tract. In this way, numerous somatoform disorders can be alleviated or eliminated.

The rationale for treating cognitive aspects of neurotic and related disorders is to interrupt the reverberation of neuromuscular circuits, preventing undesired thoughts from occurring. Some drugs can interrupt neuromuscular circuits, especially by acting on the brain. However, the most natural way to cause these circuits to be tranquil is to relax the tense muscles that are their peripheral components (a "natural tranquilizer"). Verbal components of undesired thoughts, such as those of phobias and worries, can be eliminated by relaxing the speech muscles (tongue, lips, jaws, throat, and cheeks). The eye muscles are the focus for eliminating the visual imagery of thoughts. When the eye muscles are totally relaxed, one does not visually perceive anything; the eyeballs must move in order for visual perception or visual imagery to occur. Thoroughly relaxing all of the muscles of the body can bring all undesired mental processes to zero.

Developing Emotional Control

Jacobson (1938) demonstrated that relaxation and the experience of emotions are incompatible—that it is impossible to experience emotions while simultaneously relaxing. The paradigm for controlling emotions, as for controlling other mental events, is to control the skeletal musculature that generates them when neuromuscular circuits are selectively activated.

The goal is to determine rationally when to experience and when not to experience particular emotions. One can thus be wisely emotional by wisely tensing to allow favorable emotions to flow freely, and inhibiting such wastes as those that occur during temper tantrums. As has been observed clinically in numerous cases, patients who learn to control the skeletal musculature in both its tonic and phasic activity diminish undesired emotions, such as proneness to anger, resentment, disgust, or embarrassment. Conversely, as general tension increases, the proprioceptive impulses thereby generated increase emotionality by exciting the central nervous system, the autonomic system, the endocrine system, and so on, presumably through the pathways specified by Gellhorn (Gellhorn, 1958; Gellhorn & Kiely, 1972).

Both increased and decreased emotionality are objectively evidenced by the amplitude and latency of patients' reflexes, as discussed earlier. Everyday examples of this point are obvious, such as when a saucer is accidentally dropped at a tea party. The excessively tense guest will emit an exaggerated startle reflex with heightened emotionality, while the well-relaxed person may not even blink or interrupt ongoing conversation.

Individuals who are excessively anxious often continually rehearse their griefs, worries, and difficulties with life. If they can acquire control of the skeletal muscle tensions that key this internal speech, they can consequently control their emotions and other negative mental processes. These controls occur principally in the eye muscles for visualizing their difficulties and in the speech muscles for verbalizing their problems, though the remaining mass of skeletal musculature also helps to control mental processes. Thorough training in PR makes it possible to change gradually from a condition of continually attending to difficulties and to develop a habit of turning attention away from those issues. Anxious individuals thus become better able to verbalize relevant contingencies and to react to problems more rationally. That is to say, instead of reacting reflexively to a difficulty, they can stop and reason about the problem (unless, of course, it is something like an onrushing truck). As they become relaxed, then, they attend less frequently to disturbing issues, and can instead focus on other matters and become less emotionally disturbed about problems. A trained person can stop, momentarily relax, and assess a situation—verbalizing, for instance, that "This other person seems to be yelling and screaming at me, and it is to his advantage as well as to mine if I do not yell and scream back."

Specific Applications of Differential Relaxation

The term "tension control" does not mean the same as "tension reduction," because people could not function in life without tensions. The purpose is not to eliminate all tensions, but to control them so that they can be wisely used. In other words, the purpose is to relax differentially, which can be prophylactic as well as therapeutic.

For instance, relaxed eating behavior is as appropriate for healthy people as it is for patients with ulcers. Many people exhibit bizarre, often frantic, eating patterns. Such an individual may be hunched over a plate with elbows on the table, eating tools grasped in the hands, tensed legs, and bent shoulders—all as if the eater is ready to leap in animalistic protection of the food, should an adversary momentarily appear. The eating process is often a continuous shoveling of food from plate to mouth, with no interruption of the chewing process. Conversation, if any, is through half-ground food, with particles exuded in the direction of the listener. Such overtense eating habits most assuredly do not contribute to smooth digestion. People should be differentially relaxed when eating in order to help prevent a variety of gastrointestinal difficulties, as well as to enjoy dining as a pleasant process.

A major industry that dispenses a wide variety of products dedicates itself to helping people alleviate their sleep problems. The complaints of such people include not getting to sleep when they first get in bed, as well as waking up during the night and not getting back to sleep. One patient reported that he had only about 2 hours of actual sleep over a period of four nights in bed. The consequences of night after night of inadequate sleep can be catastrophic, producing chronic fatigue and inefficient work performance. Nonprescription medicines, opaque blinds for the windows, ear plugs, and covers over the eyes are meant to satisfy complaints that the room is "too hot," "too noisy," "too bright," "too cold," and so forth. The effective solution for the insomniac's problems is to learn to practice DR 24 hours a day, which includes sleeping at night! By applying the principles of DR, one can carry the habit of automatic relaxation into the sleeping state.

Several other common applications of DR discussed by McGuigan (1991a) include relaxing while hurrying; conquering the fear of flying by differentially relaxing on an airplane; controlling one's own temper; and learning how to deal with unreasonable people by controlling the tempers of others too. All applications of DR can have both prophylactic and therapeutic benefits.

Support for Various Applications: Problems in the Literature

Jacobson's clinical applications of PR are impressive indeed. However, there apparently are no experimental (vs. clinical) data validating the method, probably because of the extensive methodological difficulties in conducting an éxperiment. That is, a true experimental test would require randomly assigning a sufficient number of patients to two or more groups, and giving the experimental group(s) extensive training over an extended period of time with an hour of practice each day. A procedure approximating that of the clinical case study presented at the end of this chapter would have to be employed with a number of experimental subjects—a demanding requirement indeed. The problem of comparable activity in a control group (or groups) to contrast with such an extensive treatment presents another difficult issue.

Although the literature on various forms of relaxation therapy is impressive, descriptions of the length and nature of training indicate either that the research has not used Jacobson's PR procedure or that this procedure has been confounded with other methods. Several examples should illustrate. Nicassio and Bootzin (1974) gave their subjects four 1-hour individual sessions using something of an approximation to PR; however, in a short training period, "the entire sequence of muscles was covered at each session" (p. 255). Such a compressed learning session must have been overwhelming to the subjects and is contrary to Jacobson's directions. Murphy, Lehrer, and Jurish (1990) taught subjects a combination of PR training and autogenic training, and used a headache diary, a cognitive questionnaire, and an expectancy measure for their dependent variables. Because their subjects learned both methods, however, specific conclusions about PR are precluded. Schaer and Isom (1988) confused PR with hypnosis, stating that "progressive relaxation has some similarities to hypnosis" (p. 513), and used a scale of hypnotic susceptibility to specify subjects "susceptible to progressive relaxation."

Despite the lack of experimental data on this original version of PR, extensive clinical and related data do lend credence to the effectiveness of the method. For example, there is a large body of experimental literature on other methods that involve briefer muscle training (consult Chapters 3, 9, 16–19). Because of the relative intensiveness of Jacobson's original method there is reason to believe that its effects may be considerably more robust than those of the briefer methods.

Limitations and Contraindications

We have seen that PR is appropriately applied for the reduction of everyday tensions, as in DR, and clinically for the elimination of syndromes related to stress and tension.

I have listed a number of cognitive and somatoform disorders, along with other tension maladies that have been shown empirically to benefit from PR. This specification of potentially beneficial applications means that other applications are probabilistically excluded; these would constitute the limitations of the method. One thus could not expect to use relaxation directly to remove a cancer or to cure a viral infection. At the same time, PR can be an adjunctive therapy that can ease discomfort resulting from any malady.

Wolfgang Luthe once asked me about contraindications of PR—a question that had never before presented itself. My answer was that wherever rest is prescribed, PR is appropriate. Later I checked with Jacobson, and he could recall no contraindications from his lengthy experience. There are no reasonable contraindications for rest; so also are there none for relaxation.

PR does not induce anxiety. Some investigators have reported an adverse effect of relaxation therapy, referring to it as "relaxation-induced anxiety" (e.g., Heide & Borkovec, 1984; Lazarus & Mayne, 1990). It is reported that learners become frightened of sensations, fear losing control, fear the experience of anxiety, engage in worrisome cognitive activity, and the like. "Relaxation-induced anxiety" apparently results from the use of methods of relaxation that differ from PR. Lehrer, Batey, Woolfolk, Remde, and Garlick (1988) specified several differences between what they called "post-Jacobsonian progressive relaxation techniques" and Jacobson's PR. "Briefer methods," in which learners engage in large tensions, do not use the method of diminishing tensions, and rely heavily on suggestion, clearly depart from PR. "Relaxation-induced anxiety" apparently results from such other methods of relaxation, but does not occur in PR and is not a contraindication for PR. What sometimes does happen in PR during the early stages of learning to observe and control internal tension signals is that patients say such things as "I think my body is floating." In the initial stages of learning to control anxiety, a learner experiences the world beneath the skin for the first time, and lacks words to describe novel sensations adequately. However, these experiences are minor, causing no undue discomfort. In any event, they are forgotten after the first month or two of training, when such ambiguous statements are replaced with more precise reports of process, such as "Tension in my lower left calf."

Another event that sometimes occurs early in the learning process is the "predormescent start," in which the trunk and limbs may give a convulsive jerk. Apparently it takes place in individuals who have been hypertense during the day's activities or are experiencing a traumatic event.[3] The physiological mechanism may be similar to that of a nervous start, so that it disappears as relaxation progresses, but may appear again after exciting experiences. In any event, the learner some months later never recalls having made the predormescent start.

---

[3]In my own experience, one day after some years of training, Jacobson instructed me to recall the most terrible event in my life. My reaction, similar to the predormescent start, was that my legs involuntarily flew directly into the air. My recollection was of a horrible event involving the use of my legs on the brakes of an automobile. (Later I asked Jacobson whether that was a normal reaction, but apparently I was being used as a guinea pig, because he said he had never given that instruction before.)

The Method

Introducing the Method to the Client

The basic physiology of neuromuscular circuits and the nature of tension and relaxation are explained to the learner. Muscles, the learner is told, contain muscle fibers that are about the diameter of the human hair and are aligned in parallel. Their action is very simple, in that they can do only two things; By sliding alongside each other, they can contract (tense) or lengthen (relax). When muscles contract, they generate the control signal that is used within neuromuscular circuits to control the functions of the body. Relaxation of the body is achieved when a person learns how to allow the muscle fibers to elongate.

The learner is provided with a realistic estimate of how far an overly tense individual has to go. It is explained that there are some 1030 striated muscles in the human body, which comprise almost half of the body weight. A lifetime of injudicious use of such a mass of muscle simply cannot respond to "quick and easy cures" for tension maladies. Just as the learner has spent a lifetime learning how to misuse the muscles, it is reasonable to expect that prolonged practice is required to re-educate them. It simply takes time and practice to learn to reverse long-standing maladaptive muscular habits. Fortunately, this cultivation of a state of bodily rest can be achieved in much less time than it took to learn deleterious muscle habits in the first place.

A frequently asked question is this: "How long will it take me to learn to relax?" A reasonable answer is to counter with the question "How long would it take you to learn to play the piano [or become a good golf, chess, or tennis player]?" The answer, of course, depends on where one starts and on how proficient one wishes to become. An answer more acceptable to the prospective learner is that the basic course specified in Jacobson (1964) and in McGuigan (1991a) is about 13 weeks in length. In my experience, students who take a university course covering those practice positions become quite proficient by the end of a semester. For those who have a neurotic disorder such as a phobic reaction, 6 months or a year of therapy may be required.

A disadvantage of PR is that some people complain that "it takes too much time." Such naive individuals simply do not understand the physiology of excessive tension and the disastrous consequences thereof. To do a proper job, as I have discussed earlier, there is no shortcut. People who complain that they "don't have enough time to practice an hour a day" can only suffer the consequences. If they let their bodies get into the painful condition of being phobic, having intense headaches, having bleeding ulcers, or the like, then they might wish that they had learned preventive PR. Jacobson's clinical experience led him to conclude that learning PR sufficiently early can add 20 years to a person's life. If one totals up all of the hours of practice and compares that with an additional 20 years of life, the practice time would seem well worthwhile. Other suggestions include the one that Jacobson gave Paul Lehrer—to awaken an hour earlier each day for practice; the relaxation would give him the extra rest he needed. Certainly if one is practicing DR 24 hours a day, a considerable amount of energy *is* saved.

These are some of the essential points to get across to the beginning learner. To a large extent, the success or failure of the application depends on the learner's self-discipline—on his or her willingness to practice the method for the prescribed hour each day. Regarding self-discipline, I once asked Jacobson what types of people make the best learners. Without hesitating an instant, he replied, "Catholics and engineers."

The Physical Environment and Equipment

The physical environment for teaching PR can be varied. Groups have been taught in such places as gymnasiums, dance studios, and classrooms. The learners should have something reasonably soft to lie on, such as a thick carpet, gymnasium mats, blankets, or sleeping bags. In clinical treatment, individual rooms in relative quietude with cots, pillows, and blankets are provided. An adept clinician can treat several patients simultaneously, one in each individual room. But whatever the learning situation, no effort is made to eliminate external distractions completely. The goal is to learn to relax in a "normal" environment, which is usually somewhat noisy. The learner should anticipate any possible distraction during the hour of practice (e.g., eliminating), and should cover the body with a blanket at the start to prevent chilling (with successful relaxation, the body temperature may fall noticeably).

Electromyographic confirmation of progress. Ideally, the clinician obtains objective EMG tension profiles as treatment progresses over the weeks. This is done to confirm any therapeutic observations of potential progress, especially reports of diminishing complaints from the patient. For illustration, abbreviated tension profiles for a nervous individual and for a relatively relaxed subject are presented in Table 2.1. This table indicates that the goal for a nervous individual is to achieve a tension profile typical of normotensives. One simplistic way of characterizing this application of PR is that it may turn a "Type A" individual into a "Type B"; the person's excessively tense body regions then become relatively relaxed. Observation of the nervous subject with the naked eye would typically yield such traits as the following: wrinkled forehead, frown, darting eyes, exaggerated breathing, rapid pulse and respiration, and habits of fidgeting. But even the experienced clinical eye may not properly diagnose an excessively tense individual when such obvious symptoms are absent. EMG readings are required for proper diagnosis.

The Therapist—Client Relationship

I have emphasized that the clinical application of PR minimizes suggestive effects so as to produce definitive and permanent, rather than fleeting, physiological changes— changes that differ from those resulting from suggestion and the placebo effect. Thus the hypochondriac who continually seeks reassurance is not suggestively reassured. Instead, if the patient starts to discuss maladies during the instruction period, he or she is merely told to relax the relevant tensions away. The patient should become as independent of the clinician as possible. The teacher emphasizes that it is the learner who successfully eliminates the control signal, thus putting emphasis on the learner rather than the instructor. The clinician as teacher merely guides the learner. PR is a trial-and-error process that has to be learned step by step, with moments of success

TABLE 2.1. Tension Profiles of a "Nervous" versus a Normotensive ("Normal") Subject

Measures	Nervous subject	Normotensive subject
Brow EMG (μV)	8.68	2.95
Left-arm EMG (μV)	2.10	0.58
Tongue EMG (μV)	5.57	2.75
Right-arm EMG (μV)	3.10	0.59
Right-leg EMG (μV)	1.36	0.53
Pulse/minute	70	69
Respirations/minute	17	15
Blood pressure (mm Hg)	117/71	96/70

Note. Adapted from Jacobson (personal communication, 1978). EMG values are based on peak-to-peak measurement.

and failure. Through this process, relaxation, like any other habit, can become permanent.

Description of the Method

Preparation

The psychological set with which the learner starts each practice period is critical. This is the period in which the patient is to do absolutely nothing at all but learn to relax. The session is planned in a quiet room, free from intrusion so that practice may be continuous for an hour, without interruption from telephones, doorbells, or people entering. Any unnecessary movement such as getting up or fidgeting is discouraged, because these added tensions retard progress. An hour-long practice period seems optimal because the individual progressively relaxes, getting to lower- and lower-intensity tensions throughout the body as the hour progresses. Once, perhaps after 2 years into my own training, I asked Jacobson whether I could have a second hour as he was about to terminate my period. The reason was that I was only then discovering very slight tensions in my back "popping loose" that were not previously recognized.

Program Overview

The 1030 or so skeletal muscles in the body are studied in groups. Another meaning of PR is that an individual progressively relaxes regions of the body, progressing from one muscle group to the next in a specific order. The muscle groups progressively studied are first those in the arms, then those in the legs, followed by those in the trunk, neck, and eye region, and finally by those in the speech musculature. There are, for instance, six localized muscle groups in the left arm to be studied. Table 2.2 describes the practice program for the left and right arms.

The First Practice Session

The learner starts by lying on a couch, bed, floor, or mat with arms alongside the body. Only one position is practiced each hour, the control signal being observed

TABLE 2.2. Practice Program for the Arms

Day	Left arm	Day	Right arm
1.	Bend the hand back.	8.	Bend the hand back.
2.	Bend the hand forward.	9.	Bend the hand forward.
3.	Relax only.	10.	Relax only.
4.	Bend the arm at the elbow.	11.	Bend the arm at the elbow.
5.	Press the wrist down on books.	12.	Press the wrist down on books.
6.	Relax only.	13.	Relax only.
7.	Progressive tension and relaxation of the whole arm (general, residual tension).	14.	Progressive tension and relaxation of the whole arm (general, residual tension).

Note. Practice is for one period each day, performing the indicated tension three times at intervals of several minutes. Then go negative for the remainder of each period. Thus, on Day 1, bend the left hand back. On Day 2, bend the left hand forward, and on Day 3 do nothing at all. After 14 days, you are ready to go on to the leg. From McGuigan (1991a, p. 155), as adapted from Jacobson (1964).

three times in each period (as specified in Table 2.2). The eyes are open for several minutes and then gradually allowed to close. (The specific amount of time that elapses is not important, as the learner should not concentrate on timing or anything else. Nor should the individual actively close the eyes, as that would be work; he or she simply allows the muscle fibers around the eyes to lengthen.) When the eyes have remained closed for another several minutes, the learner raises the hand at the wrist steadily as shown in Figure 2.3, without fluctuation; there should be no seesawing or wiggling. While the hand is being bent back, the vague sensation in the upper surface of the left forearm, a "tightness," is the signal of tension—the control signal—that the individual is to learn to recognize. The learner holds the position for a minute or two, studying the tension sensation. Then "power goes off" for a few minutes.

Thus, in each practice hour, the learner studies one major muscle group as follows: (1) identifying the control signal, and thereupon (2) relaxing the control signal away. The learner is not told where the control signal is, but should find it for herself or himself. For example, when the instruction is to raise the hand vertically at the wrist, the learner comes to identify the control signal at the dorsal surface of the forearm (see Figure 2.3). As the learner searches for the control signal, there may be some uncertainty about what is being sought. Some people identify the control signal immediately, while others have great difficulty. It is very subtle, and only a vague guess as to its location may be sufficient, but with repeated practice the control signal can become as obvious as a loud noise. Even the subtle tension sensations in the small muscles of the tongue and eyes can eventually be identified easily.

During this initial learning phase, a number of irrelevant tensions may be identified, whereupon the instructor merely informs the learner that they are incorrect and searching must continue. Often the learner will erroneously report that the control signal is at the base of the wrist; this sensation, which is more prominent than the subtle control signal, is "strain." Strain is the *result* of tension and is generated by receptor cells in the tendons and joints. That is, tension in the muscles pulls on the tendons and joints, so that tension causes strain. One cannot learn to run oneself by means of effects (strain), but only by causes (which are tension signals). Consequently, one must learn to control the body through the tension signals.

An effort to relax is a failure to relax. The process of relaxing is one in which an individual gives up the tension—just lets it go and allows the muscle fibers to elongate. Instructions that are synonymous to "relax the tension away" are to "let the power go off" and "go in the negative direction." It is to be emphasized that no work is required to allow "power off." All the learner needs to do is to discontinue working; no effort is required to follow the instruction "Just don't bother to do anything at all." Untrained people often fail to relax because they work to relax. Typically, at first the learner works the hand down, which is merely adding tension. The key is that one cannot *try* to relax; all one does is to discontinue tensing. Instruction largely consists of preventing the beginner from doing the wrong thing—that is, making an effort to relax. For instance, when the muscle fibers in the dorsal surface of the forearm elongate, the hand simply collapses like a limp dishrag that is released. When successful, all sensations in the relaxed area cease because receptor cells in the muscles "shut off." Although the learner cannot cease activity of the eyes or the ears, only the muscle fibers can be instructed to stop generating signals.

After the learner successfully identifies and relaxes the control signals away, the teacher may leave the room for some minutes, perhaps attending to other patients and later returning to give the next instruction. This sequence is repeated two more times on Day 1. At the end of the session the therapist reviews progress and other matters of interest to the patient, answering any questions raised. A program of practice can then be scheculed for the patient; for example, following Table 2.2, the individual can be instructed to practice for 14 days on the positions specified. At the end of 2 weeks, the patient may then be asked to return to go on to the next practice area. The precise schedule and length of time between visits to the therapist can vary, depending on the requirements of patient and therapist. Sometimes a patient travels long distances, so that the amount of instruction covered can be concentrated if necessary.

After the First Practice Period

On Day 2, the learner bends the left hand forward instead of backward (see Table 2.2), and so on for 14 days. As in Jacobson (1964) and McGuigan (1991a), the entire practice sequence while lying down is as follows: left arm, 7 days; right arm, 7 days; left leg, 10 days; right leg, 10 days; trunk, 10 days; neck, 6 days; eye region, 12 days; visualization, 9 days; speech region and speech imagery, 19 days.

The last region to be studied, the speech musculature, is critically important. As shown in Table 2.3, specific practice positions for the various parts of the speech musculature are presented in the first 8 days. Then the concluding days are practiced in developing speech imagery, so that the individual can learn to control the linguistic components of mental activities. In an analogous way, the individual learns to control the visual components of thoughts through eye control with imaginal practice of visual scenes (the "visualization" practice noted above).

After these positions are practiced lying down, they are practiced again in the same order, but in a sitting position. Repetition is the keynote of PR.

TABLE 2.3. Speech Region Practice

Day

1. Close your jaws somewhat firmly.
2. Open the jaws.
3. Relax only.
4. Show your teeth (as if smiling).
5. Pout.
6. Relax only.
7. Push your tongue forward against your teeth.
8. Pull your tongue backward.
9. Relax only.
10. Count to 10 out loud.
11. Count half as loudly.
12. Relax only.
13. Count very faintly.
14. Count imperceptibly.
15. Relax only.
16. Imagine that you are counting.
17. Imagine that you are saying the alphabet.
18. Relax only.
19. Imagine saying your name three times.
    Imagine saying your address three times.
    Imagine saying the name of the President three times.

Note. For this, as with the other procedures, practice one position each day, performing the indicated tension three times at intervals of several minutes. Then go negative for the remainder of each period. Thus, on Day 1, close jaws somewhat firmly. On Day 2, open jaws, and on Day 3 do nothing at all. From McGuigan (1991a, p. 194), as adapted from Jacobson (1964).

Generalized and Localized Tension

In Table 2.2, Days 7 and 14 call for practice with generalized, residual tensions. In addition to localized tension (that confined to specific muscle groups), the body also generates a more widespread kind of tension that is carried chronically throughout the skeletal musculature. This general tension is a residual tension in which there is fine, continuous contraction of the muscle fibers. Localized relaxation allows the individual to relax a particular group of muscles, but a different technique is required for general tension. An effective procedure for controlling this widespread phenomenon is very slightly, gradually, and uniformly to stiffen (tense) an entire limb for perhaps 30 seconds or a minute. The learner then studies this sensation, which is uncomfortable and insidious. General tension differs from local tension in another respect—namely, that it has no useful purpose (at least none of which I am aware). After the learner studies the general tension for a brief period, it is then gradually relaxed over an extended period of time. If the general tension is built up within the first 15 minutes or so of the period, the remainder of the hour may be spent in reducing the general tension in the limb so that the learner gradually relaxes over an extended period of time. This procedure, with sufficient practice, can allow the individual to relax residual tension down to zero, which can be verified by objective EMG measurements. Needless to say, the untrained person is not directly aware of either localized or generalized tension.

A Learner Can Relax!

Sometimes a learner asserts that he or she *cannot* relax; the point is that the learner *did not* relax. To make the point vividly, the instructor can ask the learner to push down the wall of a room. The learner fails to do so, it can be further explained, because such an act violates the laws of physics. On the other hand, elongating the muscle fibers does not violate the laws of physics. The fact that the person did not relax does not mean that the person cannot relax.

A learner who complains that he or she finds it hard to lie quietly at practice is confused about what is wanted, for there has never been an instruction to hold still (*holding* still is not relaxing). It is never "hard" to relax, for "hard" implies effort. If a learner stiffens when requested to relax, she or he is making a task of it, which is not relaxation but only an unsuccessful attempt. When the learner replaces a statement that "Relaxing makes me nervous" with the statement that "I am beginning to enjoy it," this indicates progress.

If Thoughts Occur

Some learners ask, "What shall I think about when I lie down?" They are instructed not to think, not to bother to *make* the mind blank, not to focus on anything. If they find themselves thinking about something, they should merely "let the power go off" in all the muscle regions on which they have practiced. If the thinking recurs, they should go negative again, no matter how often. But since they do not yet have control of all of their muscles, they should not expect perfection; complete elimination of thoughts can come later if they are diligent.

Also, patients should not think frequently about their symptoms as they continue relaxation training. Signs of progress may appear soon after they start, or there may be a delay, depending upon such matters as how tense they are and what everyday pressures they experience. The essential point is to practice daily; if they do that, they can expect improvement. Furthermore, they should be aware that learning relaxation skills is like learning any other performance skill: two steps forward and one step back, two steps forward and one step back.

An Overview of a Clinical Application

This section concludes with a brief illustration of PR as a method of pain control in treating cardiac patients. In the case of a patient who has angina, with some difficulty in breathing and difficulty in assuming a supine position comfortably for sleep, the following technique may be productively applied.

First, the therapist should start with the patient sitting on the side of the bed, legs off the side. Carefully assisting the patient onto the bed so as to reduce excess exertion, the therapist should help the patient assume a reclining position, with pillows at a 45° angle. Then there should be a progressive let-go ("power off") of the legs for several minutes. Next there should be a slow, progressive let-go of the entire trunk, then of the shoulders and neck, and then of the remaining musculature in order (the forehead, the brow and eyes, the speech musculature). Each instruction is followed by a minute or two of slow, progressive let-go. In this way, the discomfort from the pain and the breathing difficulties can be alleviated with restful sleep.

Resistance, Compliance, and Maintenance of Behavior Change

Perhaps half of those individuals who take the first step in learning PR go on to succeed in developing reasonably adequate control over their bodies, including their mental processes. This estimate covers a wide variety of potential learners, including patients who come to clinics; heterogeneous members of the community in evening classes; college, medical, and graduate students; and even professionals who participate in specialized workshops. To explain this difference in behavior would require a complex research project. Short of that, it can be said that some people have the discipline to see themselves through the program, while others simply do not. Clearly, the difference cannot be explained according to the need to relax, for many with the greatest need have shunned the opportunity immediately after requesting it. I recall the president of a successful company who came for treatment of a peptic ulcer. On our second session, he confessed that he had not practiced a single day since our first instruction period. His explanation was that he had spent his life giving other people ulcers and now he resented having to deal with one for himself. It was agreed that further "treatment" would be a waste of time for all concerned.

Healthy individuals seem to learn more quickly than do patients in distress. Those with neurotic disorders, for instance, are distracted, and their learning is thus prolonged. People who are engaged in cultist activities and fads are especially suggestible and dependent, which makes it more difficult for the teacher to get them to rely on themselves. They have many bizarre ideas that interfere with their learning to relax, and much time can be lost if the teacher chooses to argue with them. Similarly, people who have excessive faith in the clinician also generally fail to observe tensions for themselves and take longer to relax than do average individuals.

Such illustrations of resistance and failure to comply could be enumerated indefinitely, but the problem is not unique to PR. In many spheres of life people behave in a self-destructive fashion, even when they can verbalize the contingencies between their behavioral inadequacies and the consequences thereof. Failure to take prescribed medication for high blood pressure, drug (including alcohol) abuse, and smoking are examples of such self-destructive behaviors. There is often little anyone can do for individuals who engage in denial processes, such as the hospital nurse who asserted that her cigarette smoking was healthy for her. For those individuals who can verbalize the contingencies, perhaps there is some limited hope if they will at least try to discipline themselves in efforts to develop self-operations control—in other words, to enhance their "willpower" (McGuigan, 1991a).

On the other hand, many of those individuals who have dedicated themselves to daily practice and to regular instruction have made amazing progress. A wide variety of symptoms have been alleviated or eliminated with lasting effects, as shown by follow-up testing (Jacobson, 1938, 1970). The following is a classic illustrative case reported by Jacobson (1970).

Case Example: A Case of Anxiety, Exhaustion, and Acrophobia[4]

Summary

In 1929, an attorney, 32 years old, believed that he had overworked to the point of permanent exhaustion; in his words, [he felt] "burned out" for life. He was uneasy, irritable, and often dizzy, and could not appear in court or drive a car for fear of fainting or other discomfort. His fears kept him from high places. "Reasoning" and "fighting" these "ridiculous" symptoms only made them worse. The symptoms appeared first about 4 or 5 years previously. Instruction in progressive relaxation was begun in 1929, omitting all reassurance and other "suggestive therapy." Soon he discontinued treatment and went elsewhere; but after several weeks he returned. Gradually with persistence he developed excellence in observation and report on his tension patterns. Voluntarily he acted as a subject in electrophysiological studies on mental activities. Action-potential measurements indicated increasing skill in maintaining relaxed states, when lying, when sitting quietly, or when reading. He "made it a rule to relax any phobia or disturbing thought-act." In 1931 his symptoms and complaints had diminished; he was able to resume appearances in court and to drive without nervous difficulties. He was discharged in 1931 anxiety-free. Evidently acrophobia was no longer present, for without telling the doctor he moved his law offices to the tower of a high building. Twenty-nine years thereafter he reports that he still practices, although not so regularly as he should. Throughout this period there has been no recurrence of the anxiety, phobias, or other disabilities about which he complained in 1929.

Complaints

In October of 1929 an exceedingly busy attorney, 32 years of age, was referred by his brother, a physician, for an anxiety state which included fears of heights and of dizziness, general uneasiness and irritability, and headache at the vertex and the occiput. He stated that he had been living at high tension all day long and in his opinion was "burned out" for life. Walking down the street or appearing in court, he was suddenly beset by fears of dizziness, making him feel very uncomfortable. At times he felt as if about to faint, and since he had never fainted, he felt that this was "all ridiculous." "Fighting" the above-mentioned symptoms only had made them worse; he had tried to reason matters out and had tried to relax, he had tried to get his mind off of himself, but all had been in vain. He was particularly concerned because when at court examining a witness, he suddenly began to fear becoming dizzy. In consequence, he had been caused to stay out of court, feeling, however, that sometime he would return.

---

[4]This section is reprinted by permission of Charles C Thomas, Publisher, Springfield, Illinois, from *Modern Treatment of Tense Patients* by E. Jacobson (1970, pp. 91–104).

Onset

The onset had been 4 or 5 years previously in the middle of a lawsuit when he was confronted with a difficult opposing attorney. At the time he suffered from pain in the left lower portion of his thorax, both subcardially and laterally. He won the case, however, and finally the symptoms disappeared after the use of belladonna plasters and the administration of a tonic. But he had begun to feel anxious about one set of matters, and the anxiety turned gradually to others. His brother, the doctor, had suggested that if he would pay no attention to his symptoms, they would disappear. Accordingly, he had said to himself, "Get your mind off it. Forget it." This seemed to bring him relief for about 1½ years. Nevertheless, about January 1, 1929, the symptoms insidiously recurred.

Personal History

Among previous diseases had been influenza during the epidemic of 1920. In May of 1929 he suffered from cystitis following cystoscopy, and since then occasional blood cells had appeared in his urine. As a rule he slept well, but there were exceptions of late when he continued to worry. He was married in 1920 and had two children, a boy and a girl, both well. His parents were well, excepting that his mother was rheumatic and worrisome.

General Examination and Clinical Laboratory Tests

General examination disclosed a fairly well-nourished man looking the age stated. His pulse was regular at the rate of 96 in the sitting posture, while his blood pressure was 130/96. His temperature was 98.6°F. He was 5 feet 7¼ inches [tall] and weighed about 157 pounds. General examination revealed a somewhat pendulous abdominal wall but otherwise no significant findings, aside from an extremely lively foot-flexion reflex. Laboratory tests supplied by his brother indicated Wasserman and Kahn reactions negative; basal metabolism, −12; blood nonprotein nitrogen, 27 mg%; urea nitrogen, 15 mg%; blood sugar, 84 mg%; red blood count, 4,310,000; white count, 6500; hemoglobin, 75% with a color index of 0.8. The differential count fell within normal limits. Fluoroscopy of the chest proved negative. Urine analysis was completely negative, aside from a few mucous threads.

Instruction Begun

Instruction in progressive relaxation as outlined in the published text was begun in October 1929. At this time, over a 10-year period, I was attempting to rule out from our procedures all use of any form of suggestive therapy, so far as this might be possible. To this end, I tried to avoid not only reassurance to the patient in any possible form, but also unnecessary conversation. I attempted to confine our relationship to instruction in the forms of progressive relaxation appropriate to the patient's needs in my judgment. Accordingly, when the patient asked questions bearing upon the outcome of the instruction, hoping that it might prove favorable, or when he was in doubt that the instruction really applied to his case, I avoided answers that might possibly be interpreted by him suggestively. However, since from the patient's standpoint he was paying fees for a practical result, some of the individuals treated failed to continue with the instruction. Some never even began, for want of assurance that it would help them. The patient whose history and instruction [are] presented in the present [section] likewise lost confidence after a month or two of instruction, suddenly leaving to go elsewhere for "psychiatric treatment." After 3 weeks of absence with little ado or comment on either side, he returned to complete his course.

I shall omit the early months of instruction, referring the reader to the next mentioned.

November 22, 1929. He has been learning. He states that when emotionally disturbed he localizes the tension patterns and lets them go.

May 3, 9, 1930. Instruction devoted to review of tension patterns in the eyelids and eyeballs. Practice is given in observing tension patterns and going negative upon looking in various directions with eyelids closed and looking from finger to finger with eyelids open.

Visualization Found Impossible during Complete Eye Muscle Relaxation

May 13, 1930. He is requested to imagine that he is seeing the fingers held about 10 feet away from his eyes, but at the same time to remain perfectly relaxed. He reports that he finds this instruction impossible to carry out. He finds it necessary to exert effort tensions of the eyes, that is, to look in specific directions, if he is to imagine objects seen. This request and report are typical of our endeavors to secure objective reports from highly trained patients, without leading them to anticipate the answers. Indeed, these autosensory observations with patients have been carried out under strictly controlled methods characteristic of laboratories of experimental psychology.

Autosensory Observation during Emotion

May 23, 1930. He mentions fear of being in a high building, but fails to give a clear-cut sensory and imaginal report, evidently not yet prepared to describe his experiences, but losing himself in the emotion. He is given further instruction in observing and in reporting matters of visual imagination of indifferent affect.

May 29; June 3, 13, 1930. He continues to be emotionally disturbed from time to time. Training is devoted to the musculature of speech, with particular reference to steady or static tensions.

July 17, 1930. He states that today he has suffered from phobia of high places. Instruction is given in verbal imagination. As yet he fails to recognize tension patterns in the various muscles of speech and to state their locations.

Autosensory Observation during Unemotional Experiences

July 18, 1930. He enters the clinic exultant over his personal discovery that attention to the object of fear diminishes the fear. Instruction today begins in the lying posture with the request, "Think of infinity." He fails to report the imaginal, the tension, and other signal patterns, stating only the meaning of his reflection. However, when requested to engage in simple multiplication, as of 14 by 42, he gives a complete report, not only of the meaning but also of the tension pattern. He is given repeated practice in observation of sensory experiences, distinguishing the report thereof from the interpretation or meaning.

Anger Tension Relaxed

July 22, 29, 1930. He announces that he now relaxes spells of anger [and] has been gaining in weight; and, as noted by his family physician, he no longer fidgets as he did formerly upon receiving a hypodermic injection. Upon being requested to describe an experience of phobia, he still engages in the "stimulus error" but to [a lesser] extent than formerly.

September 3, 5, 1930. Differential relaxation is begun, with training devoted to the right arm. He has been at home with a fever of 101°F at times, due to an infection of the right kidney and of the bladder.

October 14, 17; November 2, 10, 1930. Instruction on the limbs is continued in the sitting posture. At times during the period while sitting, he is on the verge of sleep.

Efficiency

December 5, 1930. He asserts that now he does his legal work effectively and without nervous excitement in a manner which he never accomplished previously in his entire life.

December 12, 1930. He complains of tension in the right side of the scalp.[5] After drill in wrinkling of the forehead, he reports relief.

December 16, 23, 1930. Instruction is devoted to the abdomen and back in the sitting posture.

February 13, 1931. He affirms [that] his nerves are greatly improved. At times a little phobia persists, but he is becoming accustomed to observe tension patterns at such moments and to relax them. His brother, the doctor, recently was amazed at his calmness in trying a lawsuit, in contrast with his extreme excitability in former years. Friends who do not know of the instruction which he has been receiving spontaneously say to him that he is a changed man.

---

[5]He mistakes pull or strain on the scalp for muscular tension.

Phobic Tension Patterns Now Recognized and Relaxed

February 20; March 3, 1931. He states that he has been in very good nervous condition and has been efficient. He makes it a rule to relax any phobia or disturbing thought-act. Instruction concerns brow tensions. He often sleeps during the period.

March 19; April 4, 10, 17, 18, 21, 1931. Repeated practice is given on imagining falling objects of indifferent affect. The purpose here is to teach him [to] observe the pattern of mental processes when any object falls. Thus a first step is taken without him knowing it to lead him to observe what he does in high places when he imagines himself jumping and falling. Thus, without telling him, we proceed in the treatment of acrophobia.

Return of Ability to Try Cases

May 1, 2, 14, 29; June 3, 5, 10, 1931. For the first time in years, he tries cases in court without nervous difficulties. His phobia in the court has disappeared. Instruction is devoted to musculature of speech.

Return of Ability to Drive and to Go on Trips; No Acrophobia

June 13, 1931. He reports that he has taken for the first time in about 7 years a long drive. Previously fearful, but not knowing why, he now finds that he enjoys [driving]. Previous to present instruction, he dreaded and avoided trying cases outside of Chicago. Recently, in contrast, he has gone on three long trips with no difficulty. Nowadays, he tries cases enjoyably, [whereas] previously he met them with dread. The phobia of jumping from high places has been completely absent. Last month was a very difficult time in his business, because large loans for which he was responsible came due at the height of the panic and bank failures of the Great Depression. Nevertheless, he was relaxed and not nervous. He adds that he relaxes concerns about law trials. He no longer argues the legal matters out within himself, but he instead "relaxes the whole thought." Instruction is devoted to tension signals from the tongue and relaxation of tongue muscles.

July 14, 30, 31, 1931. Instruction concerns imagining making various statements. He is still slow to relax to the point where he is ready to observe and report. However, his reports are clear.

September 4, 1931. Instruction is begun on reading while relaxing the left arm so far as possible.

September 8, 18, 22, 25, 29; October 2, 6, 15, 27, 1931. Instruction on reading is continued, while observing tension patterns and learning to relax those not required for the reading in various portions of the anatomy. He fails to report verbal tensions during reading, claiming that there are none, but only visual images and ocular tension patterns. Obviously his training is not yet sufficient, but he is not so informed.

November 6, 1931. His brother-in-law died suddenly. Instruction is devoted to exposing a single printed stimulus word within the instruction to read and get the meaning. At first his reports are confused, for he gives interpretations in place of observations. Finally he begins to report more accurately, as follows: "Ocular tension in seeing the word. Ocular tension in imagining what the word indicates. Tensions in the tongue as in saying the word."

Slight Relapse, yet Patient Not Told What to Look For

November 20, 1931. Yesterday he experienced some nervous distress while in court, pleading a lawsuit. Upon relaxing, the unnecessary emotions disappeared. He has been through various trying ordeals. He even ventured for the first time in 10 years to look at a corpse. For 2 months he has failed to report tensions in the organs of speech while reading. Accordingly he is requested to count while reading, employing the method of diminishing tensions. Finally he succeeds in observing the speech tensions. This occurs with no hint from the instructor that he has been omitting anything.

Relaxes Differentially

December 5, 1931. There have been four deaths in the family which ordinarily would have disturbed him much more, he believes. However, in place of engaging in fears and worries each morning, now he goes to work relaxing and preparing himself to relax during the day. He has found that he does not have to postpone relaxation to the weekend but can relax during the work of each day. Accordingly he is greatly relieved.

Discharged

December 8, 18, 1931. Instruction is given in reading aloud, relaxing so far as possible during this occupation. He is discharged, apparently free from emotional disturbance. Electrical recording has shown excellent technique. He has been a volunteer subject at the University of Chicago, Department of Physiology, for electrical measurement during mental activities.

Freedom from Acrophobia

Following [this patient's] discharge in 1931, the phobia of high places had so evidently disappeared that, without suggestion from the doctor, he moved his office to the tower of a very high office building. In his new office, he felt no fear or phobia. In regarding his nervous condition, he considered himself well. He volunteers to act as an experienced observer with skill at tension reduction in the physiological laboratory of the University of Chicago. He practices differential relaxation every day. On some days he fails to lie down, but as a rule after dinner he practices in a lying posture for

45 to 90 minutes. On about one-half of these occasions he falls asleep. If he awakens at night and finds himself tense, he locates the tension patterns and relaxes accordingly. Uneasiness no longer is experienced and he no longer shows marked irritability. When engages in difficult matters, he relaxes so as to avoid becoming irritated. He has no dizziness, no fears, and no headaches. His technique shows excellent form.

March 3, 1943. Electrical recording is performed with the eyes open. The right thigh averages little over 0.5 μV. The right biceps averages little over 0.075 μV, with low $\bar{V}$. The right jaw muscles average in [the] neighborhood of 0.2 μV. The eye regions [average] about 3.5 μV. The values are fair for a trained subject, except that variability ($\bar{V}$) is a little high.

August 6, 1945. He reports that for the first time in his life, he has completely lost fear of being in high places. He flew in an airplane and at first was fearful when breathing through tubes of oxygen provided for this purpose, but he used his relaxation technique and enjoyed the flying trip from then on. He relaxes differentially to an extent that is readily appreciated by a professional observer.

Persistent Freedom from Anxiety Tension, Although Difficulties Are Met

July 22, 1949. He relates that he was "wonderfully well" for many years following the instruction. In 1939 his daughter married and in 1940 she became very unhappy, which was a "terrific jolt" to him. "During that whole year I suffered from worry, hoping that the situation would straighten out." His daughter was operated on for appendicitis and recovered. She joined him for a few weeks only, after which she returned home, since her husband needed her. "This," continued our patient, "took quite a bit out of me." "Then my son was drafted for the war; usually parents worry about that. In 1940 loose [bowel] movements had occurred once or twice a year and I didn't know what started them. Certain medication overcame any spell promptly. Also I could avert the spells by avoiding raw fruits and vegetables. In 1945 the spells became more intense and frequent. My brother-in-law got me into a business of his own, in which I sunk time and a small fortune. In January 1947 I foolishly let him leave the partnership. Thereafter he enticed the plant manager away, which proved irritating and took my time and interfered with my practice of law. Engineers called in to help the business gave bad counsel with resulting further loss. In December 1947 I sold the business for a pittance."

Irritable Colon

During the summer of 1945, a severe spell of diarrhea was followed by X-ray examination and a diagnosis of duodenal ulcer. The symptoms disappeared after a short period of diet restriction and medication. Since then, there have been only two light spells and one severe spell with burning in the rectum.

Practice Neglected

"It was in the attempt to get rid of nervous disturbance that I sold the plant and returned to more or less regular periods of relaxation, which I had been neglecting, and to which I ascribed alone my lasting improvement. My downfall had been that practice was not regular."

July 25, 1949. A brief refresher course is begun.

July 27, 1949. Roentgenological examination by Dr. James Case indicates negative findings as to duodenal ulcer. The colon, however, is found to be spastic. A similar examination made previously suggested that possibly there had been an early ulcer. At this time, however, he has been relaxing a little more frequently than before and has been able to partake once more of solids.

August 1, 3, 8, 10, 15, 17, 24, 25, 29; September 7, 9, 14, 26; October 10, 1949. Review practice is given on limb tension patterns and relaxation.

1959. His wife writes from her observations in retrospect that through relaxation training he learned "a new way of life."

October 30, 1960. He reports that he has been free from anxiety tension, phobias, fears, and other emotional disturbances these many years. He is able to try lawsuits when and where he desires, [is] able to plead cases at will, and has continued to be generally more relaxed than he had ever been in the decade before he reached the age of 32, when instruction was begun.

Comments and Reflections

The contemporary scene has been flooded with stress management procedures varying from thinking certain colors while breathing into one nostril through repetitiously talking to oneself. There are a variety of muscular relaxation procedures too, which are generally acknowledged as having flowed from PR. In the last analysis, which methods are most effective must be empirically determined. The primary criterion for assessing the effectiveness of a stress management procedure that purports to teach a person to relax is the extent to which the individual is able to selectively allow his or her muscle fibers to elongate on command—that is, to relax differentially in the face of stress. Once the person can thereby exercise self-operations control, he or she can more rationally deal with the stressful situation instead of just reflexively responding to it.

Edmund Jacobson spent over seven decades collecting data documenting the effectiveness of PR clinically and scientifically, including the use of EMG. We should all be indebted to him for giving the world PR, the grandfather of all relaxation methods. I can think of no better way to close this chapter than to quote Jacobson as follows:

> Until I see proof I incline in the direction of skepticism. Progressive relaxation, as developed in our laboratory and clinic, was to me a matter of skepticism at every step. Thirty years ago as I went from room to room trying to get individuals with different maladies to relax, I recall saying to myself, "What kind of nonsense is this that you are practicing?" The careful accumulation of data has vindicated the procedure. (1977, p. 123)

ACKNOWLEDGMENTS

I am deeply indebted to Edmund Jacobson for so many things that it would be impossible to list them all here. First and foremost, though, I would specify the innumerable hours and limitless energy that he spent in personally training me in PR. More specifically for this chapter, I am indebted to him for the ideas, principles, and applications, and in fact often even for the use of his words, which have become part of my own repertoire.

REFERENCES

Bain, A. (1855). *The senses and the intellect*. London: Parker.

Bernhaut, M., Gellhorn, E., & Rasmussen, A. T. (1953). Experimental contributions to the problem of consciousness. *Journal of Neurophysiology, 16*, 21–35.

Cannon, W. B. (1929). *Bodily changes in pain, hunger, fear, and rage*. New York: Appleton-Century.

Gellhorn, E. (1958). The physiological basis of neuromuscular relaxation. *Archives of Internal Medicine, 102*, 392–399.

Gellhorn, E., & Kiely, W. F. (1972). Mystical states of consciousness: Neurophysiological and clinical aspects. *Journal of Nervous and Mental Disease, 154*, 399–405.

Heide, F. J., & Borkovec, T. D. (1984). Relaxation-induced anxiety: Mechanisms and theoretical implications. *Behaviour Research and Therapy, 22*, 1–12.

Holt, E. B. (1937). Materialism and the criterion of the psychic. *Psychological Review, 44*, 33–53.

Jacobson, E. (1938). *Progressive relaxation* (2nd ed.). Chicago: University of Chicago Press.

Jacobson, E. (1964). *Self-operations control: A manual of tension control*. Chicago: National Foundation For Progressive Relaxation.

Jacobson, E. (1967). *Biology of emotions*. Springfield, IL: Charles C Thomas.

Jacobson, E. (1970). *Modern treatment of tense patients*. Springfield, IL: Charles C Thomas.

Jacobson, E. (1977). The origins and development of progressive relaxation. *Journal of Behavior Therapy and Experimental Psychiatry, 8*, 119–123.

Jacobson, E. (1978). *You must relax* (4th ed.). New York: McGraw-Hill.

Lazarus, A. A., & Mayne, T. J. (1990). Relaxation: Some limitations, side effects, and proposed solutions. *Psychotherapy, 27*, 261–266.

Lehrer, P. M., Batey, D. M., Woolfolk, R. L., Remde, A., & Garlick, T. (1988). The effect of repeated tense–release sequences on EMG and self-report of muscle tension: An evaluation of Jacobsonian and post-Jacobsonian assumptions about progressive relaxation. *Psychophysiology, 25*, 562–569.

Lehrer, P. M., Woolfolk, R. L., & Goldman, N. (1986). Progressive relaxation then and now: Does change always mean progress? In R. J. Davidson, G. E. Schwartz, & D. Shapiro (Eds.), *Consciousness and self-regulation* (Vol. 4, pp. 183–216). New York: Plenum.

McGuigan, F. J. (1978). *Cognitive psychophysiology: Priniciples of covert behavior*. Englewood Cliffs. NJ: Prentice-Hall.

McGuigan, F. J. (1989). Managing internal cognitive and external environmental stresses through progressive relaxation. In F. J. McGuigan, W. Sime, & J. M. Wallace (Eds.), *Stress and tension control 3: Stress management* (pp. 3–11). New York: Plenum Press.

McGuigan, F. J. (1993). *Experimental psychology: Methods of research* (6th ed.). Englewood Cliffs, NJ: Prentice-Hall.

McGuigan, F. J. (1991a). *Calm down: A guide for stress and tension control* (rev. ed). Dubuque, IA: Kendall/Hunt.

McGuigan, F. J. (1991b). Control of normal and pathological cognitive functions through neuromuscular circuits: Applications of principles of progressive relaxation. In J. G. Carlson & A. R. Seifert (Eds.), *International perspectives on self-regulation and health* (pp. 121–131). New York: Plenum Press.

McGuigan, F. J., Culver, V. I., & Kendler, T. S. (1971). Covert behavior as a direct electromyographic measure of mediating responses. *Conditional Reflex, 6*, 145–152.

McGuigan, F. J., & Dollins, A. B. (1989). Patterns of covert speech behavior and phonetic coding. *Pavlovian Journal of Biological Science, 24*, 19–26.

McGuigan, F. J., & Pavek, G. V. (1972). On the psychophysiological identification of covert nonoral language processes. *Journal of Experimental Psychology, 92*, 237–245.

McGuigan, F. J., & Winstead, C. L., Jr. (1974). Discriminative relationship between covert oral behavior and the phonemic system in internal information processing. *Journal of Experimental Psychology, 103*, 885–890.

Murphy, A. I., Lehrer, P. M., & Jurish, S. (1990). Cognitive coping skills training and relaxation training as treatments for tension headaches. *Behavior Therapy, 21*, 89–98.

Nicassio, P., & Bootzin, R. (1974). A comparison of progressive relaxation and autogenic training as treatments for insomnia. *Journal of Abnormal Psychology, 83*, 253–260.

Schaer, B., & Isom, S. (1988). Effectiveness of progressive relaxation on test anxiety and visual perception. *Psychological Reports, 63*, 511–518.

Sherrington, C. S. (1909). On plastic tonus and proprioceptive reflexes. *Quarterly Journal of Experimental Physiology, 2*, 109–156.

Wiener, N. (1948). *Cybernetics*. New York: Wiley.

3

Progressive Relaxation: Abbreviated Methods

DOUGLAS A. BERNSTEIN
CHARLES R. CARLSON

In the first edition of this volume, this chapter began with an observation that we live in a world full of tension and anxiety where relaxation is a much-sought-after goal. The same is true in the 1990s—perhaps even more so, as major events such as the Persian Gulf war (which dominated the news during the preparation of this chapter) enfold us. The search for relaxation is important for people in general, but it is especially so for those in whom emotional arousal produces severe subjective distress, overt behavioral problems, and damage to various organ systems. Clinicians and researchers seeking nonpharmacological methods for promoting relaxation and combating anxiety have developed a number of useful procedures, the most popular of which is referred to as "progressive relaxation training." As noted in the introductory chapter, progressive relaxation training is not a single method, but a group of techniques that vary considerably in procedural detail, complexity, and length. Our goal in this chapter is to focus attention upon the form known as "abbreviated progressive relaxation training" (APRT).

History

The history of APRT as we now know it originates in the work of Edmund Jacobson during the early part of this century. The course of its development and use in Jacobson's laboratory and clinic has been reviewed by McGuigan in Chapter 2 of this volume. Jacobson's technique can be lengthy and painstaking. The entire training in all muscle groups may sometimes require 100 or more sessions over a period of several months or even several years.

A considerably condensed version of progressive relaxation training was presented by Joseph Wolpe (1958) in the context of the classic work on counterconditioning methods for fear reduction, which ultimately led to the development of systematic desensitization. Wolpe saw relaxation not as an end in itself, but as one of several responses (including assertiveness and sexual arousal) that are incompatible with, and thus capable of inhibiting, anxiety. Accordingly, he shortened Jacobson's original procedures to make them fit within the framework of systematic desensitization. "The reason why I have not resorted to Jacobson's intensive program is that by the desensitization method . . . I have been able to overcome anxieties . . . on the basis of such relaxation as is attained by my brief method of training" (Wolpe, 1958, p. 136).

In contrast to Jacobson's program, which focused on a single muscle group for several sessions before moving on to the next, Wolpe's brief method taught the client to relax several of 16 major muscle groups in each of about seven sessions. By shortening the procedure in this way, Wolpe was able to get on more quickly to the main component of treatment—namely, desensitization proper. Wolpe's methods also contrasted with Jacobson's in offering instructions and suggestions (such as "Smooth it out" or "Let it go further") about what the client should do following tension release.

The APRT methods described in this chapter represent a further modification of Jacobson's procedures as described by Paul (1966) and formalized by Bernstein and Borkovec (1973). Among these modifications are tension–release cycle times that are considerably shorter than Wolpe's; inclusion of practice with all 16 muscle groups in every training session; introduction of the "pendulum" analogy for explaining the need for tension cycles; and much more elaborate and active verbal input from the therapist (in the form of indirect relaxation suggestions) during training. These changes came about in the late 1960s and early 1970s, and represented not only an effort to streamline progressive relaxation further for use in systematic desensitization, but to supplement and facilitate other methods (such as participant modeling) in the then-burgeoning list of behavioral approaches to anxiety-related problems.

Theoretical Foundation

The theoretical basis of APRT is consistent with the rationale presented in Chapter 2 for Jacobson's progressive relaxation training. Briefly, it is assumed that anxiety and other emotional states involve subjective, behavioral, and physiological components that interact to create the ongoing emotional experience (Lang, 1977, 1979). For example, when physiological activation is perceived and labeled as "fear" or "anxiety," the client reports being afraid or anxious or nervous. Such reports and/or the cognitions preceding or accompanying them may act as additional fear-provoking stimuli that further amplify the autonomic arousal. This can lead to increased subjective discomfort and even more physiological activation, in a continuing spiral that may lead to panic, cognitive flooding, or a variety of other behavioral and physiological consequences.

APRT is believed to intervene in this process by providing a way of reducing autonomic activation. The early laboratory research of Jacobson (1938) and Gellhorn (1958; Gellhorn & Kiely, 1972) suggested that overactivation of the sympathetic branch of the autonomic nervous system is primarily responsible for excessive skeletal muscle activity. When skeletal muscle activity is reduced with progressive relaxation, Gellhorn proposed that there is a corresponding reduction in sympathetic nervous system activity as a result of negative feedback from the skeletal muscle proprioceptors to the ascending reticular activation system and hypothalamus. Resting muscles send little or no feedback information from the skeletal muscle proprioceptors to central brain structures; the lack of feedback information is believed to result in decreased autonomic activation. Direct supportive evidence from human studies of this model has been sparse. However, indirect evidence (e.g., decreased heart rate and blood pressure) from human research supports the efficacy of APRT in reducing autonomic activation (see reviews by Borkovec & Sides, 1979; King, 1980; Lehrer, 1982). Once autonomic activity is reduced, the client should be more capable of (1) providing meaningful assessment information to the clinician, (2) tolerating fear-provoking stimuli, (3) learning more adaptive responses to such stimuli, and (4) learning or using rational cognitions that help to forestall or eliminate subsequent problematic activation.

APRT seeks to reduce the autonomic activation component of anxiety by altering one of its manifestations—namely, skeletal muscle tension. As muscle tension drops, other less directly accessible aspects of autonomic activation, such as heart rate and blood pressure, are also lowered. It is unclear whether alteration of peripheral muscle tension alone is sufficient to explain the effects of progressive relaxation training. For example, it has been argued that central nervous system events—primarily focused attention and pleasant cognitions—may be vital to clinically significant reductions in autonomic activation (Davison, 1966; Benson, 1975; King, 1980). When a client learns how to tense and release muscle groups and to use other relaxation techniques to be described later, he or she is, at the very least, developing a set of voluntary skills that can then be used to reduce maladaptive autonomic activation and to prevent such activation from reaching a troublesome level in the first place.

It is worth noting that the skills the client learns through APRT represent but one way of achieving a state of deep relaxation. There are many other routes to that state (e.g., biofeedback, autogenic training, stretch-based relaxation, and quiet meditation), all of which appear to capitalize on similar or related psychophysiological mechanisms (see Smith, 1985). Thus, the choice of APRT for use in a given clinical situation must be made not because it leads to a relaxed state that is unique, but because it meets the needs of the client and clinician.

Assessment

Clinical Indications

APRT has been successfully used, alone or in combination with other methods, to deal with a wide range of behavior problems in adults and children. Reviews of the progressive relaxation literature (see Borkovec & Sides, 1979; King, 1980; Lehrer, 1982; Lehrer & Woolfolk, 1984; Hyman, Feldman, Harris, Levin, & Malloy, 1989) consistently affirm the clinical efficacy of progressive relaxation training for insomnia, generalized anxiety/stress, specific anxieties and phobias, hypertension, and tension headache. The list sometimes includes asthma in children (Borkovec & Sides, 1979; King, 1980, Lehrer & Woolfolk, 1984), aversion to chemotherapy and spasmodic dysmenorrhea (Lehrer & Woolfolk, 1984), and chronic pain (Hyman et al., 1989). Unfortunately, however, not all of these reviews have distinguished between APRT and other forms of progressive relaxation.

In order to identify the current status of research on the effectiveness of APRT, a computer search of 91 papers concerning progressive relaxation published since 1981 was conducted. The "Methods" sections of 30 of the resulting studies indicated that APRT was employed. Of these 30 studies, 14 specified the treatment population and used multiple controls (a placebo or attention/treatment comparison group, a waiting-list control, and/or a no-treatment control). These 14 studies are summarized in Table 3.1 and generally suggest that APRT can lead to improvement in depression in adolescents and postpartum women, aversion to chemotherapy, muscle contraction headache, stress reactivity, immunocompetence in the elderly, spasmodic dysmenorrhea, hypertension, and low back pain. However, with hypertension there are conflicting reports of success with APRT (see Chesney, Black, Swan, & Ward, 1987; Hoelscher, Lichstein, & Rosenthal, 1986; Hoelscher, Lichstein, Fischer, & Hegarty, 1987). Most notably, there is some question as to whether or not APRT provides any additional therapeutic gain over regular blood pressure monitoring by the individual (Chesney et al., 1987).

In the other 16 studies identified from the literature review, placebo or attention/treatment comparison groups were not used or there was no waiting-list or no-treatment control. Borkovec and colleagues (Borkovec et al., 1987; Borkovec & Mathews, 1988) noted that these experimental conditions were eliminated in his studies for reasons related to the need for having a credible treatment available for research participants; Burish, Carey, Kozely, and Greco (1987) expressed similar reasons for not including waiting-list or placebo conditions.

Summaries of these 16 studies are presented in Table 3.2. On the basis of these studies, generalized anxiety and chronic tinnitus can be added to the list of disorders showing positive outcomes following APRT-based treatments. Given the converging evidence of these outcome studies and the conclusions of earlier reviews, we can place confidence in the clinical utility of APRT for selected disorders.

The use of APRT is governed by the judgment that maladaptive levels of autonomic arousal are at least partly responsible for the development and maintenance of the problems that bring the client to treatment. However, recognition of the fact that APRT can play a beneficial role in dealing with many diverse human problems must not lead to the conclusion that it will always be useful or that it is the treatment of choice for all clients whose complaints match those reported in the clinical literature. It is imperative that clinicians be sensitive to the needs of their clients in determining whether or not APRT may be of benefit.

It is generally safe to say that in the vast majority of cases involving clinical problems similar to those listed above, the use of APRT is probably going to be of some help and is not likely to do harm even if a client is unprepared for the very small possibility of undesirable side effects (to be discussed later in this chapter). Furthermore, the time spent in teaching relaxation skills may provide a positive experience for both therapist and client; such an experience helps establish a good, task-oriented working relationship. Still, it must be recognized that time spent on APRT for, say, general tension cannot be spent in working directly with other problems, which in a given case may require immediate attention.

Thus, as is true for any clinical method, the decision to employ APRT must be based upon careful evaluation of the full range of causal, contributing, maintenance, and complicating factors that may be related to a client's complaints. The information

TABLE 3.1. Clinical Efficacy of APRT: Designs Including Multiple Controls

Study	Treatment target	Design	Major findings
Lyles, Burish, Krozely, & Oldham (1982)	Aversion to chemo-therapy	$n = 50$ Conditions: APRT + guided imagery Therapist support No-treatment control # of sessions: 3 Mode of training: Individual Practice: Once daily Practice tapes: No Compliance: Not determined APRT dropout: None reported	APRT yielded less pretreatment nausea, anxiety; lower heart rate (HR), systolic blood pressure (SBP). APRT also had less posttreatment anxiety, depression, and nausea.
Turner (1982)	Low back pain	$n = 36$ Conditions: APRT Cognitive–behavioral (Cog-Beh) Waiting-list control # of sessions: 5 Mode of training: Group Practice: Once daily Practice tapes: Yes Compliance: Not determined APRT droupout: None reported	APRT = Cog-Beh: improved on pain, depression, disability. Cog-Beh yielded better pain tolerance than APRT. 1-month follow-up: Both groups maintained depression, disability gains. APRT had greater pain report. 1- to 2-year follow-up: Both groups reported decreased use of health care. Cog-Beh reported increased work time.
Halonen & Passman (1985)	Postpartum depression	$n = 48$ Conditions: APRT APRT + stress management (SM) SM Attention control # of sessions: 2 Mode of training: Individual Practice: When upset Practice tapes: No Compliance: Not determined APRT dropout: None reported	APRT, APRT + SM had lower depression scores than SM and attention control.
Kiecolt-Glaser et al. (1985)	Immuno-competence in geriatric population	$n = 45$ Conditions: APRT + guided imagery Social contact No-contact control # of sessions: 12 Mode of training: Individual Practice: No report Practice tapes: No Compliance: Not determined APRT dropout: None reported	APRT had better immunocompetence (as indicated by increased natural killer cell count and herpes antibody) and less distress.
Hoelscher, Lichstein, & Rosenthal (1986)	Hyperten-sion	$n = 50$ Conditions: APRT (individual) APRT (group)	All relaxation conditions showed greater reductions in SBP/ diastolic blood pressure (DBP) than control. Gains were main-

(continued)

TABLE 3.1. Continued

Study	Treatment target	Design	Major findings
		APRT (group) and contingency training Waiting-list control # of sessions: 4 Mode of training: Individual or group Practice: Once daily Practice tapes: Yes Compliance: Self-report of 120 minutes per week; electronic record indicated 100 minutes per week; 32% reported daily practice APRT dropout: 8%	tained at 6-week follow-up.

Reynolds & Coats (1986)	Depression in adolescents	$n = 30$
		Conditions:
		  APRT
		  Cog-Beh
		  Waiting-list control
		# of sessions: 10
		Mode of training: Group
		Practice: home practice; Frequency not reported
		Practice tapes: No
		Compliance: 68%
		APRT dropout: 30%
			APRT and Cog-Beh yielded less depression than control. Gains were maintained at 5-week follow-up.

Carey & Burish (1987)	Aversion to chemotherapy	$n = 45$
		Conditions:
		  APRT + guided imagery delivered by trained professional
		  APRT + guided imagery delivered by trained volunteer
		  APRT + guided imagery delivered by tape
		# of sessions: 3
		Mode of training: Individual
		Practice: Once daily
		Practice tapes: Not reported
		Compliance: Not determined
		APRT dropout: None reported
			Professionally administered APRT training resulted in lower prechemotherapy respiration and nervousness than in other three groups. Professional training also resulted in lower postchemotherapy respiration and HR than in other conditions.

Chesney, Black, Swan, & Ward (1987)	Hypertension	$n = 158$
		Conditions:
		  APRT + diaphragmatic breathing (DB)
		  Blood pressure monitoring
		  APRT/DB + cognitive restructuring
		  APRT/DB + biofeedback
		  APRT/DB + cognitive restructuring + biofeedback
			APRT = blood pressure monitoring for reduction of SBP/DBP. The addition of cognitive restructuring resulted in lower SBP readings. Gains were maintained at 54-week follow-up.

(continued)

TABLE 3.1. Continued

Study	Treatment target	Design	Major findings
		APRT/DB + cognitive restructuring + health education # of sessions: 13 Mode of training: Individual Practice: Twice daily Practice tapes: Yes Compliance: 70% APRT dropout: 19%	
Hoelscher, Lichstein, Fischer, & Hegarty (1987)	Hypertension	$n = 48$ Conditions: APRT APRT + practice tapes Waiting-list control # of sessions: 4 Mode of training: Group Practice: Once daily Practice tapes: Tape condition only Compliance: Both experimental groups reported equal amounts of home practice; subjects in tape condition that had electronic recording of practice reported 150 minutes of practice versus electronic record of 126 minutes APRT dropout: None reported	APRT and APRT + tape had greater decreases in SBP/DBP than control. Results were maintained at 2-month follow-up.
Roth & Holmes (1987)	Physical and psychological health after stress	$n = 55$ Conditions: APRT + mental imagery Aerobic exercise No-treatment control # of sessions: 29 Mode of training: Group Practice: Once daily, if class did not meet for training. Practice tapes: None Compliance: Not determined; subjects did attend an average of 24.8 sessions APRT dropout: 10%	Aerobic exercise had better cardiac fitness and lower depression than other conditions. There was no treatment effect on self-reports of health status.
Holmes & Roth (1988)	Cardiovascular activity during stress	$n = 49$ Conditions: APRT + imagery Aerobic exercise No-treatment control # of sessions: 33 Mode of training: Group Practice: Not specified Practice tapes: No Compliance: Not reported for	Aerobic training resulted in lower HR than APRT, which in turn resulted in lower HR than the no-treatment condition.

(continued)

TABLE 3.1.   Continued

Study	Treatment target	Design	Major findings
		practice; subjects attended 24.8 sessions APRT dropout: 17%	

Sigmon & Nelson (1988)	Spasmodic dysmenor-rhea	$n = 40$
		Conditions:
		  APRT
		  Activity scheduling
		  Waiting-list control
		# of sessions: 6
		Mode of training: Individual
		Practice: Once daily
		Practice tapes: Yes
		Compliance: Average number of practice sessions was 22.4 during the 3-week treatment phase
		APRT dropout: Not determinable from description
			APRT and activity scheduling had reduced symptom severity and discomfort ratings, as well as improved activity level. The results were maintained at 1-month follow-up.

Blanchard et al. (1990)	Tension headache	$n = 66$
		Conditions:
		  APRT + imagery/DB
		  APRT + cognitive therapy
		  Attention-placebo control
		  Control (headache monitor)
		# of sessions: 10
		Mode of training: Individual
		Practice: Once daily
		Practice tapes: Yes
		Compliance: Not determined
		APRT dropout: Not reported
			APRT = APRT + cognitive therapy, which both showed greater reductions in headache index and medication usage than either control condition.

Blanchard et al. (1991)	Tension headache	$n = 33$
		Conditions:
		  APRT (home practice)
		  APRT (clinic practice only)
		  Headache monitoring
		# of sessions: 10
		Mode of training: Individual
		Practice: Once daily
		Practice tapes: Yes
		Compliance: Unclear, but appeared to range from 83% to 100%, according to self-report for those instructed to practice
		APRT dropout: None reported
			APRT had less headache activity than controls. Home practice was marginally beneficial.

gathered in assessment should determine whether APRT is the intervention of choice, alone or in combination with other treatment modalities (e.g., assertiveness training), or whether the client's problems reflect factors (e.g., basic skill deficits) suggesting that other initial interventions would be more appropriate. Relaxation training is most effectively used when it addresses client needs that are recognized and understood by both the therapist and client.

TABLE 3.2. Clinical Efficacy of APRT: Designs Not Including Multiple Controls

Study	Treatment target	Design	Major findings
Burish & Lyles (1981)	Aversion to chemotherapy	$n = 16$ Conditions: 　APRT + guided imagery 　No-treatment control # of sessions: 2, during chemotherapy Mode of training: Individual Practice: Once daily Practice tapes: No Compliance: Not reported APRT dropout: None reported	APRT showed less distress and nausea than no treatment. APRT had lower HR than no treatment.
Blanchard et al. (1982)	Vascular and tension headache	$n = 91$ Conditions: 　APRT with tension headache patients 　APRT with migraine headache patients 　APRT with combined migraine and tension headache patients # of sessions: 10 Mode of training: Individual Practice: Once daily Practice tapes: Yes Compliance: Not determined APRT dropout: Not reported	Subjects with tension headache were 64% improved on headache index; migraine headache patients were 53% improved; subjects with combined headaches were 54% improved.
Southam, Agras, Taylor, & Kraemer (1982)	Hypertension	$n = 42$ Conditions: 　APRT 　No-treatment control # of sessions: 8 Mode of training: Individual Practice: Once daily Practice tapes: Yes Compliance: Not determined APRT dropout: 16%	APRT group had lower SBP/DBP during the working day than did no-treatment control group. Results were maintained at 6-month follow-up.
Teders et al. (1984)	Tension headache	$n = 35$ Conditions: 　APRT (clinic program) 　APRT (home-based program) # of sessions: 10 Mode of training: Individual Practice: Once daily Practice tapes: No Compliance: Not determined APRT dropout: None reported	Both groups showed pre–post reduction in headache index, headache peak, headache-free days, and medication use.
Blanchard et al. (1985)	Tension headache	$n = 53$ Conditions: 　APRT (clinic program) 　APRT (home-based program) # of sessions: 10 Mode of training: Individual	Both treatments decreased headache index and medication use.

(continued)

TABLE 3.2.　Continued

Study	Treatment target	Design	Major findings
		Practice: Once daily Practice tapes: Yes Compliance: Not determined APRT dropout: None reported	
Jakes, Hallam, Rachman, & Hinchcliffe (1986)	Chronic tinnitus	$n = 24$ Conditions: 　APRT + imagery 　APRT + attention switching # of sessions: 5 Mode of training: Individual Practice: Once daily Practice tapes: Yes Compliance: Not determined APRT dropout: None reported	APRT and APRT + attention switching were equally effective in reducing annoyance of tinnitus.
Blanchard et al. (1986); Blanchard, McCoy, et al. (1988)	Hypertension	$n = 87$ Conditions: 　Thermal biofeedback (BF) 　APRT # of sessions: 8 Mode of training: Individual Practice: Once daily Practice tapes: Yes Compliance: Not determined APRT dropout: None reported	BF better than APRT for keeping persons off medications at 2- and 12-month follow-up. BF equal to APRT in decreasing reactivity to laboratory stressors.
Agras, Taylor, Kraemer, Southam, & Schneider (1987)	Hypertension	$n = 137$ Conditions: 　APRT 　Blood pressure monitoring # of sessions: 8 Mode of training: Group Practice: Once daily Practice tapes: Yes Compliance: Not determined APRT dropout: 11%	APRT better than monitoring in reducing SBP/DBP. Results were maintained for 2 years.
Attanasio, Andrasik, & Blanchard (1987)	Headache	$n = 25$ Conditions: 　APRT + cognitive therapy 　　(office) 　APRT + cognitive therapy 　　(home) 　APRT only (home) # of sessions: 11 Mode of training: Individual or 　self-paced alone Practice: Yes; frequency unclear Practice tapes: Yes Compliance: Not determined APRT dropout: 4	At 1 month, all patients reported less headache activity. Self-administered relaxation was as effective as office-based treatment.
Borkovec et al. (1987)	Generalized anxiety disorder	$n = 30$ Conditions: 　APRT + cognitive therapy	APRT + cognitive therapy reduced anxiety more than APRT + nondirective therapy. Results *(continued)*

TABLE 3.2. Continued

Study	Treatment target	Design	Major findings
		APRT + nondirective therapy # of sessions: 12 Mode of training: Individual Practice: Twice daily Practice tapes: No Compliance: 82% APRT dropout: 10%	were maintained at 6- to 12-month follow-up.

Burish, Carey, Krozely, & Greco (1987)	Aversion to chemotherapy	$n = 24$
		Conditions:
		  APRT + guided imagery
		  No-treatment control
		# of sessions: 1–3 during chemotherapy visit
		Mode of training: Individual
		Practice: Once daily
		Practice tapes: Yes
		Compliance: Not determined
		APRT dropout: None reported
			APRT condition had less nausea, vomiting; lower blood pressure, HR, and anxiety.

Blanchard, Appelbaum, et al. (1988)	Long-term follow-up of tension headache	$n = 58$
		Conditions:
		  APRT (clinic-based)
		  APRT (home-based)
		# of sessions: 10
		Mode of training: Individual
		Practice: Once daily
		Practice tapes: Yes
		Compliance: Not determined
		APRT dropout: None reported
			All treatments showed 78% improvement in headache index at 1-year follow-up.

Borkovec & Mathews (1988)	Generalized anxiety disorder	$n = 30$
		Conditions:
		  APRT + cognitive therapy
		  APRT + nondirective therapy
		  APRT + coping desensitization
		# of sessions: 12
		Mode of training: Individual
		Practice: Twice daily
		Practice tapes: No
		Compliance: Not determined
		APRT dropout: None reported
			All treatments were equally effective in reducing self-report and assessor ratings of anxiety.

Long & Haney (1988)	Stress reduction in working women	$n = 61$
		Conditions:
		  APRT
		  Aerobic exercise
		# of sessions: 7
		Mode of training: Group
		Practice: Three times weekly
		Practice tapes: No
		Compliance: Not determined
		APRT dropout: 19%
			APRT was equal to aerobic activity in decreasing anxiety and increasing self-efficacy.

(continued)

TABLE 3.2.   Continued

Study	Treatment target	Design	Major findings

Wisniewski, Genshaft, Mulick, Coury, & Hammer (1988)	Adolescent headache	$n = 10$
		Conditions:
		  APRT
		  Waiting-list control
		# of sessions: 8
		Mode of training: Group
		Practice: Once daily
		Practice tapes: Yes
		Compliance: 90% according to self-report; 53% according to electronic monitoring
		APRT dropout: None reported
			APRT had less headache activity than did control.

The questions outlined below do not comprise an exhaustive list of items to consider in assessment, but they do provide a basic framework for inquiry that can easily be elaborated according to the dictates of each unique situation.

1. *Is there evidence that the client's complaints are related to anxiety, tension, or other aspects of maladaptive emotional arousal?* In some cases, this is a relatively easy question to answer: The client reports being tense and anxious, and there are obvious physiological and behavioral signs that coincide with the subjective experience. In other instances, the emotional arousal may not be the focus of the client's report, nor are there obvious signs that maladaptive arousal is at issue. For example, an adult client may report reduced energy level, lack of motivation, significant absenteeism from work, and mild depression. Though tension or anxiety is not mentioned spontaneously, it may not take much exploration to determine that new job pressures or other events may have threatened, frightened, or stressed the client.

Perhaps the client's initial response to the stress involved some obvious tension or anxiety, but by the time help is sought, an avoidance strategy may have been developed to mask the more fundamental problem. As is well known, anxiety may also play a role in the appearance of other escape or avoidance behaviors, such as alcohol or drug abuse, somatoform disorders, and a wide variety of interpersonal conflicts. Other subtle behavioral signs of anxiety can include insomnia, sexual dysfunction, restlessness, irritability, compulsive or stereotyped response patterns, and changes in appetite.

Physiological indicators of maladaptive arousal may include nausea, backache or headache, unusual or irregular bowel activity (or other gastrointestinal problems), genitourinary system problems, hypertension, and a variety of other psychophysiological disorders. Subjectively, anxiety and its consequences may appear in the form of inability to concentrate, loss of memory, confusion, "flooding," or obsessional thoughts.

2. *Is anxiety or tension the primary focus of treatment?* Anxiety may play a significant role in a client's problems, but before choosing APRT as a component of treatment, the clinician should be satisfied that it is an appropriate initial treatment target. It is in regard to this issue that a distinction between "conditioned" and "reactive" anxiety

must be made (Paul & Bernstein, 1973). If the client's overarousal has developed primarily through a series of unfortunate learning experiences (e.g., fear of driving stemming from having been in several serious auto accidents), new learning experiences (including the use of APRT) may help alleviate the problem, assuming that the client possesses adequate driving skills. However, if the client's fundamental problem primarily involves a reaction to punishment brought about by a lack of driving skills and/or the presence of maladaptive cognitive habits (e.g., "I'll never learn to drive safely"), APRT may be of little more than temporary help. In fact, if treatment does not focus upon the development of new cognitive and overt behavioral skills, the disappointing effects of supplemented relaxation procedures could have a negative influence on the client's motivation to continue working with the therapist.

Recognition of the "conditioned versus reactive" dimension requires the clinician to go beyond the client's self-reports of discomfort to look for indications of skill deficits or for other problems that may be responsible for overarousal. This can be done in a variety of ways, including interviews with family members, *in vivo* behavioral observations, role playing, and informal observation during routine interviews.

In most cases, the clinician is likely to find that anxiety-related problems have both conditioned and reactive components. The point to keep in mind is that unless relaxation training is needed as an immediate rapport-building procedure, it may be postponed or eliminated altogether when assessment reveals anxiety that is primarily reactive. If a significant conditioned residue remains after this aspect of the problem is dealt with, relaxation training may then be brought to bear.

3. *Are there organic components in tension-related problems?* It should go without saying that before progressive relaxation (or any psychologically oriented intervention) is chosen to help deal with physical problems apparently brought on by tension, the client should be examined by appropriate medical personnel in order to rule out organic causal factors. This is especially important when the client complains of such "traditional" psychophysiological disorders as pain in the head, neck, or lower back; cardiac symptoms (such as chest pain, tachycardia, or arrhythmia); asthma; and gastrointestinal difficulties. However, it should also be kept in mind when a complaint could have a less obvious organic base. Examples include disorders of memory, concentration, logic, or other cognitive functions; depression; irritability; and aggressiveness. Furthermore, if the client has an illness or disease for which he or she is taking regular medication (e.g., insulin), a physician who is knowledgeable about relaxation effects should provide medical approval before relaxation treatment is begun.

Adverse Effects

In the general clinical population, significant adverse effects of relaxation training are uncommon. Edinger and Jacobsen (1982) surveyed 116 clinicians—who had conducted relaxation training with an estimated 17,542 clients—and noted that intrusive thoughts were the most frequently encountered problem (15%), followed by fear of losing control (9%), disturbing sensory experiences (4%), muscle cramps/spasms (4%), sexual arousal (2%), and emergence of psychotic symptoms (0.4%). Among clients with generalized anxiety disorder, Heide and Borkovec (1983) found that 30% reported increased tension during APRT. Bernstein and Borkovec (1973) noted from their clinical experience that problems with APRT included client coughing and/or sneezing, excessive movement, muscle cramps/spasms, sleep, anxious thoughts, laughter, and sexual arousal. In general, then, relaxation training does not appear to have significant and frequent adverse effects, but clinicians should be wary of any potential side effects and ready to address them. More is said in later sections about coping with common problems in relaxation training.

Adverse effects of relaxation training have been described as representing either "relaxation-induced anxiety" (RIA) or "relaxation-induced panic" (RIP) (Adler, Craske, & Barlow, 1987). RIA refers to the gradual increase in behavioral, physiological, and psychological components of anxiety during relaxation training. RIP describes the rapid development of severe anxiety during relaxation training. Both of these phenomena might better be understood as "procedurally induced" than as "relaxation-induced," given the general meaning of "relaxation." Nonetheless, the "relaxation-induced" nomenclature is more commonly used in the empirical literature.

Several mechanisms have been proposed to account for the development of RIA and RIP. These include fear of losing control (Bernstein & Borkovec, 1973; Carrington, 1977), fear of relaxation sensations (Borkovec, 1987; Borkovec et al., 1987), and interoceptive conditioning (Adler et al., 1987). Ley (1988) hypothesized that RIA and RIP phenomena are actually minute episodes of hyperventilation in persons who are susceptible to these because of unusually low concentrations of carbon dioxide (CO_2) in the blood. When the concentration of CO_2 is unusually low, very small changes in CO_2 production from metabolism or variations in respiration rate or volume can precipitate the sensations of hyperventilation. Symptoms of hyperventilation include breathlessness, rapid heart rate, muscle contractility, and palpitations. Ley believes that these symptoms of hyperventilation may be triggered during relaxation by slight increases in the volume of inspired air or by reduction in CO_2 production as a result of the lower metabolic activity produced by the abrupt change in physical activity level when a person rests quietly. As of yet, however, there is not a consistent body of evidence to support either the hyperventilation theory or the various other theories developed to account for the adverse effects of relaxation training.

Management of Adverse Effects

Effective management of adverse effects associated with relaxation training begins with a careful evaluation of the client and recognition of the potential for side effects. Clients with a history of generalized anxiety disorder or panic disorder are likely to experience adverse side effects; so, too, are persons with a history of hyperventilation. Extra effort should be made to inform such clients of the potential complications, and steps can be taken to reduce the likelihood of difficulties. For example, teaching clients diaphragmatic breathing skills prior to APRT may pre-empt difficulties, as well as provide skills to control any panic or anxiety that may result from breathing changes occurring during therapy. Providing clients with a thorough description of APRT may also aid in reducing adverse responses; if clients feel as though they have been prepared for the experiences they encounter during relaxation, they will be more likely to manage them effectively. Moreover, a therapist can remind a client that in the unlikely event that difficulties occur, they may actually serve as an important assessment tool; that is, they may clarify more fully the client's presenting complaints.

If adverse effects should occur despite the therapist's best efforts, several courses of action can be pursued, depending on the needs of the client. One strategy is to pause and reassure the client that the symptoms are transitory and will gradually subside with continued relaxation practice (Cohen, Barlow, & Blanchard, 1985; De-Good & Williams, 1982). Another strategy is to switch to an alternative relaxation technique. Several authors (Adler et al., 1987; Heide & Borkovec, 1983) suggest decreasing the focus on somatic experiences if adverse effects should emerge. Lastly, APRT can be discontinued if adverse effects persist or the client is unwilling to carry on. The clinician's calm management of adverse reactions is important to enabling the client to continue working toward alleviation of his or her presenting complaints.

Contraindications

In spite of the generally benign and pleasant nature of APRT, the clinician considering its use should take care to assure that no past or current physical conditions exist that would contraindicate some of the required tension–release cycles. Consultation with the client and his or her physician about this matter is especially important in cases where certain muscles or connective tissues have been damaged or are chronically weak. In some cases, medical advice may suggest that it would be better to focus on strengthening certain muscle groups (e.g., in the lower back) than on learning to relax them. In such instances, APRT may still be feasible, but it would have to be modified to delete or alter procedures for problematic muscle groups (see Bernstein & Borkovec, 1973). The same is true in the case of an individual who, as the result of a neuromuscular disability, is incapable of exercising voluntary control over all muscles in the body (see Cautela & Groden, 1978). Finally, if the client is taking medication regularly (e.g., insulin for diabetes or propanolol for hypertension), medical consultation is necessary prior to beginning APRT, because relaxation training could change the amount of medication needed for management of the dysfunction.

Beyond these considerations, the clinician should also assure that the client is both able and willing to (1) maintain focused attention during relaxation training, (2) follow instructions regarding tension–release cycles, and (3) engage in regular home practice between treatment sessions. If serious obstacles to any of these three basic requirements exist, it may be wise to work on eliminating those obstacles before beginning a relaxation program.

Compliance, Resistance, and Maintenance

Like most other clinical procedures, APRT requires willingness on the part of the client to comply with the training regimen. In the 29 APRT studies described in Tables 3.1 and 3.2 the average number of training sessions was 9, with training conducted at least twice weekly in 12 studies and once per week in the remaining 17 studies. Home practice was assigned in virtually every study, with the majority of studies encouraging at least one practice session per day. Seventeen of the 29 studies provided participants with audiotapes for home practice. Compliance rates for daily home practice could be determined from data for five studies and ranged from 32% to 82%.

In three studies, home practice tapes were played on tape machines fitted with devices to count the number of "plays" (Hoelscher et al., 1986, 1987; Wisniewski, Genshaft, Mulick, Coury, & Hammer, 1988). Hoelscher et al. (1986) noted that subjects reported an average of 120 minutes of practice per week, whereas the timing device indicated an average of only 100 minutes of practice per week; they also reported that only 32% of subjects actually practiced relaxation daily as prescribed. In a second study, Hoelscher et al. (1987) again found that their subjects overreported practice times (150 minutes vs 126 minutes). Wisniewski et al. (1988) found that their adolescent subjects overreported practice sessions by almost 70%. In a study not reviewed in this chapter because of methodological limitations, Taylor, Agras, Schneider, and Allen (1983) reported that adherence to practice instructions was 39% according to the electronic record and 71% according to self-report. Taken together, these results suggest that compliance does vary and that clients are likely to over-estimate the frequency of their practice. Still, significant improvements in symptom status have been achieved in these studies, despite discrepancies between self-report and actual practice. One research program (Borkovec et al., 1987; Borkovec & Mathews, 1988) has evaluated the relationship between frequency of self-reported practice and treatment outcome. The results are mixed, with one study (Borkovec et al., 1987) finding no effect of reported practice frequency on outcome, and the other study (Borkovec & Mathews, 1988) finding that more frequent practice was associated with greater decreases in symptom severity. In a very recent report concerning the use of APRT for reduction of muscle contraction headache (Blanchard et al., 1991) there was an indication that home practice may lead to greater reductions in headache activity than clinic practice of APRT only. However, these results were marginally significant and based on a small sample size. At this point, it is not clear to what extent practice frequency is linked to symptom improvement, but obviously, less than full compliance with a prescribed practice regimen need not be lethal to treatment effects. It seems important, therefore, to develop individualized criteria for relaxation and to determine the extent to which frequency of practice influences clinical progress in given cases.

Another way to conceptualize compliance is to examine data regarding dropouts from treatment. In the sample of studies summarized in Tables 3.1 and 3.2, dropout rates from the APRT conditions ranged from 0% to 30%, with an average of 9% during the training periods. These results suggest that the role of the therapist may be important in influencing compliance with APRT. However, compliance may also be related to the presenting problems or the client's motivation. Therapist behaviors related to creating and maintaining a positive therapeutic environment; engaging the client's personal expectations, goals, and plans; and employing principles of learning (i.e., reinforcement) are likely to be important factors influencing compliance. Further research is needed, however, to identify more clearly the role that these behaviors may play in promoting compliance with APRT.

As mentioned earlier, the average number of APRT sessions across the 30 studies was 9, with the frequency ranging from 2 to 33. As the present collection of studies illustrates, some clinical problems may require fewer training sessions and some clinical problems may require more training sessions than the average number calculated across representative studies. Long-term follow-up data available for eight studies (average length of follow-up: 11.8 months) were encouraging, with the majority of studies indicating maintenance of treatment gains. Still, additional research is needed on the long-term utility of APRT.

Method

Introducing Relaxation to the Client

Once appropriate assessment has been completed and APRT has been decided upon as a treatment of choice, the method and its specific procedures must be explained to the client in enough detail to promote cooperation and understanding. This presentation should include an explanation of (1) the role that anxiety seems to play in the client's problem and (2) the ways in which APRT may help. The level of discourse and the amount of detail involved in this introductory session should vary from client to client in accordance with individuals' capacities to absorb and integrate the content and concepts involved. At the very least, the clinician should attempt to establish in the client a basic appreciation of how tension is manifested, how it can be reduced, and how that reduction can help alleviate some of the presenting problems. Without such basic understanding, the client's interest in learning and practicing relaxation is not likely to be strong enough for him or her to develop useful skills. Most clients find the idea of APRT intrinsically appealing; however, there will be those who continue to express doubts. If a client remains skeptical but is willing to try APRT seriously, the training itself may relieve the skepticism.

Once the client understands and at least provisionally accepts the conceptualization of his or her problems as partly involving maladaptive levels of tension, the clinician can present a more detailed rationale for the choice of APRT as a part of treatment. This rationale should provide (1) a brief overview of the history of progressive relaxation; (2) a description of APRT as a method whereby one learns a skill, in much the same manner as one learns other skills (such as swimming) that involve muscle control; (3) the stipulation that APRT will require regular practice, so that the client can learn to recognize and control the distinctly different sensations of tension and relaxation; and (4) the clear message that the therapist will not be doing anything to the client—rather, that the client will be developing a capability within himself or herself that can then be used independently.

A sample rationale is reproduced below. It is given merely as an illustration, not as a script. Each therapist should present this material in his or her own natural style.

The procedures I have been discussing in terms of reducing your tension are collectively called "progressive relaxation training." They were first developed in the 1930s by a physiologist named Jacobson, and in recent years we have modified his original technique in order to make it simpler and easier to learn. Basically, progressive relaxation training consists of learning to . . . tense and then [to] relax various groups of muscles all through the body, while at the same time paying very close and careful attention to the feelings associated with both tension and relaxation. That is, in addition to teaching you how to relax, I will also be encouraging you to learn to recognize and pinpoint tension and relaxation as they appear in everyday situations, as well as in our sessions here.

You should understand quite clearly that learning relaxation skills is very much like learning any other kind of skill such as swimming, or golfing, or riding a bicycle; thus, in order for you to get better at relaxing, you will have to practice doing it just as you would have to practice other skills. It is very important that you realize that progressive relaxation training involves learning on your part; there is nothing magical about the procedures. I will not be doing anything to you; I will merely be introducing you to the technique and directing your attention to various aspects of it, such as the presence of certain feelings in the muscles. Thus, without your active cooperation and regular practicing of the things you will learn today, the procedures are of little use.

Now I mentioned earlier that I will be asking you to tense and then to relax various groups of muscles in your body. You may be wondering why, if we want to produce relaxation, we start off by producing tension. The reason is that, first of all, everyone is always at some level of tension during his [or her] waking hours; if people were not tense to some extent, they would simply fall down. The amount of tension actually present in everyday life differs, of course, from individual to individual, and we say that each person has reached some "adaptation level"—the amount of tension under which he or she operates day to day.

The goal of progressive relaxation training is to help you learn to reduce muscle tension in your body far below your adaptation level at any time you wish to do so. In order to accomplish this, I could ask you to focus your attention, for example, on the muscles in your right hand and lower arm and then just to let them relax. Now you might think you can let these muscles drop down below their adaptation level just by "letting them go" or whatever, and to a certain extent, you probably can. However, in progressive relaxation, we want you to learn to produce larger and very much more noticeable reductions in tension, and a way to do this is first to produce a good deal of tension in the muscle group (i.e., to raise the tension well above adaptation level) and then, all at once, to release that tension. We believe the release helps to create a "momentum" which allows the muscles to drop well below adaptation level. The effect is like that which we could produce with a pendulum which is hanging motionless in a vertical position. If we want it to swing far to the right, we could push it quite hard in that direction. It would be much easier, however, to start by pulling the pendulum in the opposite direction and then letting it go. It will swing well past the vertical point and continue in the direction we want it to go.

Thus, tensing muscle groups prior to letting them relax is like giving ourselves a "running start" toward deep relaxation through the momentum created by the tension release. Another important advantage to creating and releasing tension is that it will give you a good chance to focus your attention upon and become clearly aware of what tension really feels like in each of the various groups of muscles we will be dealing with today. In addition, the tensing procedure will make a vivid contrast between tension and relaxation and will give you an excellent opportunity to compare the two directly and to appreciate the difference in feeling associated with each of these states.

Do you have any questions about what I've said so far?[1]

Instead of memorizing this kind of presentation, the therapist may want to use an outline of the main topics to be covered. This is likely to make the material sound less "canned" (see Bernstein & Borkovec, 1973, pp. 61–62, for a sample outline).

[1]Reprinted by permission of Research Press from Bernstein and Borkovec (1973, pp. 19–20).

After any questions about the rationale have been answered, the therapist should begin working with the client to develop optimal tension–release procedures for each of the 16 muscle groups that will be the initial focus of training. These groups and a typical tensing strategy for each are presented below:

Muscle group	*Method of tensing*
1. Dominant hand and forearm	Make a tight fist while allowing upper arm to remain relaxed
2. Dominant upper arm	Press elbow downward against chair without involving lower arm
3. Nondominant hand and forearm	Same as dominant
4. Nondominant upper arm	Same as dominant
5. Forehead	Raise eyebrows as high as possible
6. Upper cheeks and nose	Squint eyes and wrinkle nose
7. Lower face	Clench teeth and pull back corners of the mouth
8. Neck	Counterpose muscles by trying to raise and lower chin simultaneously
9. Chest, shoulders, and upper back	Take a deep breath; hold it and pull shoulder blades together
10. Abdomen	Counterpose muscles by trying to push stomach out and pull it simultaneously
11. Dominant upper leg	Counterpose large muscle on top of leg against two smaller ones underneath (specific strategy will vary considerably)
12. Dominant calf	Point toes toward head
13. Dominant foot	Point toes downward, turn foot in, and curl toes gently
14. Nondominant upper leg	Same as dominant
15. Nondominant calf	Same as dominant
16. Nondominant foot	Same as dominant

In order to facilitate transfer to the actual training situation, it is generally a good idea to have the client assume a reclining position while these tensing strategies are introduced and attempted. It is also advisable to work on the tension–release cycles for each muscle group in the same order as that to be used in subsequent training. When done in this way, the initial "run-through" can provide a reassuring preview of the procedures to come.

Inevitably, some clients will have difficulty achieving tension in the "standard" manner described above. In such a case, the therapist must work with the client to devise alternative methods to achieve significant tension. The client may also find it difficult to tense one muscle group without tensing other groups at the same time. This problem tends to disappear with practice, but the therapist should continue to observe the client and should be ready to provide helpful suggestions and instructions.

Finally, some clients feel self-conscious or silly while tensing certain muscle groups, particularly those involving the face. The therapist can usually put such a client at ease by demonstrating all tensing methods before asking the client to try them.

Description of the Method

Once the relaxation rationale has been presented and discussed, and once a set of muscle-tensing strategies has been agreed upon, a few final instructions should be given. These are presented below in the form a "typical" therapist might employ. Naturally, the specific wording should be adjusted to suit one's own style.

1. I will be instructing you to focus your attention on one muscle group at a time. Please pay attention only to what I am saying and to the sensations you are experiencing in that muscle group, allowing the rest of your body to remain relaxed. I will ask you to tense and relax each of the muscle groups in the same order as we used when we practiced the tensing procedures.

2. When I ask you to tense a group, I will say, for example, "Tense the muscles in your forehead by raising your eyebrows, now." "Now" will be the cue word for you to tense the muscles. Do not tense the muscles until I say "now."

3. When I want you to relax a muscle group, I will say "OK, relax the muscles in your forehead." When I say that, let all the tension go all at once, not gradually.

4. I will ask you to tense and relax each muscle group twice. After the second time, I will ask you to signal if the muscle group is completely relaxed. Please signal by raising the index finger on your right hand [whichever hand is visible to the therapist], but do not signal unless the muscles really feel completely relaxed.

5. During the session, try not to move any more than is necessary to remain comfortable. In order to gain the most benefit from relaxation, it is preferable not to move any muscles that have already been relaxed. This prevents tension from reappearing in those muscles.

6. In order to maintain as much relaxation as possible, I am going to ask you not to talk to me during our session unless it is absolutely necessary. We will mainly use your finger signal as a means of communication, and we will talk about how the session went after we finish today. Questions you may have can be discussed after completion of the relaxation.

7. Our session today will take about 45 minutes, so if you would like to use the restroom before we start, please do so.

8. Now I would like to have you remove or loosen any items (e.g., glasses or tight belts) that may cause discomfort during the session.

9. Do you have any further questions? Is there anything about which you are not clear?

10. OK, get in a comfortable position in your chair—fine. Now please close your eyes and keep them closed during the session. I will dim the lights now to minimize visual stimulation.

At this point, relaxation training can begin. Following the same sequence as the muscle groups presented previously, the therapist should treat each muscle group as follows:

1. Instruct the client to focus attention on the group.

2. Using the predetermined "now" cue, instruct the client to produce tension in that group, repeating the instructions for tensing that group. For example, say, "By making a tight fist, tense the muscles in your right hand and lower arm, now." Allow the client to maintain the tension for 5 to 7 seconds while describing the sensations of tension to the client. Use a shorter tension duration for the feet or other muscles where the client may experience cramping.

3. Using the predetermined "relax" cue, instruct the client to relax the muscle group all at once (not gradually) and to attend to the sensations of relaxation. Allow the client to focus on the relaxation for 30 to 40 seconds while giving him or her some relaxation "patter" to highlight the sensations (see example below).

4. Repeat steps 2 and 3. After the second tension–release cycle, allow the client to maintain the relaxation and to focus on the sensations for 45 to 60 seconds.

5. Before moving on to the next muscle group, ask the client to signal if the current muscle group is completely relaxed. If not, repeat the tension and relaxation steps a third time. If the client still does not signal that the group is relaxed, the procedure may be repeated again. However, if relaxation is not achieved in four or five attempts, alternative means for achieving relaxation may be required. One alternative would be to instruct the client to allow those muscles to relax as much as possible while moving on to other groups, and to return to them at a later point.

6. When the focus is on the chest, shoulders, and upper back, emphasis on breathing should be introduced as part of the procedure. Instruct the client to take a deep breath and hold it while the muscles are tensed and to exhale when instructed to relax. From this point on, breathing cues should be included as a part of the tension–release procedure for all muscle groups. Furthermore, mention of slow, regular breathing can be incorporated into the relaxation "patter."

When these steps are combined, they go something like this:

OK, John, I would like you to focus all of your attention on the muscles of your chest, shoulders, and upper back. And by taking a deep breath and holding it and by pulling your shoulder blades back and together, I'd like you to tense the muscles of the chest, shoulders, and upper back, now. Good, notice the tension and the tightness, notice what the tension feels like, hold it . . . and relax.

Fine, just let all that tension go. Notice the difference between the tension you felt before and the pleasant feelings of relaxation. Just focus all your attention on those feelings of relaxation as they flow into your chest, shoulders, and back. Just focus on your slow and regular breathing and go right on enjoying the relaxation.

[Tension–release cycle is repeated after 30–45 seconds.]

OK, John, I would like you to signal if the muscles in the chest, shoulders, and upper back are as deeply relaxed as those of the neck (i.e., the previous group). OK, fine, just go on relaxing.

When all 16 muscle groups have been relaxed, the therapist should review each group, reminding the client that these muscles have been relaxed and asking him or her to continue to allow them to relax while attending to the accompanying sensations. The client should then be asked to signal if all the groups are indeed completely relaxed. If the client does not signal, the muscle groups should be named, one at a time, and the client should be instructed to signal when the group or groups that are not totally relaxed are mentioned. A tension–release cycle can then be repeated for these groups. Once again, the client should be instructed to signal if any tension remains. Once a signal of total relaxation is given, the client should be allowed simply to enjoy this totally relaxed state for a minute or two before the session is terminated.

To terminate the relaxation session easily and gradually, the therapist can count backwards from 4 to 1. The client can be asked to move his or her feet and legs on the count of 4, to move hands and arms on the count of 3, to move head and neck on the count of 2, and to open the eyes and sit up on the count of 1. At this point, the therapist should ask open-ended questions such as "How do you feel?" or "How was that?" to encourage the client to discuss the feelings of relaxation and any problems that may have been encountered. If the client does not spontaneously report problems, the therapist should ask whether there were any muscle groups the client had difficulty in relaxing and whether the client has any questions about the procedure. The client should be asked whether any particular aspects of the "patter" helped or hindered relaxation.

If the client feels that some muscles were not well relaxed, it may be necessary for the therapist to suggest an alternative means of tensing those muscles and to incorporate the new method at the next session.

The therapist should arrange for the client to practice relaxation skills twice a day for 15 to 20 minutes each time. The therapist may help the client to decide on appropriate times and places for practice, attending to the same issues as those considered in selecting the location for APRT (see below). If the client has difficulty determining a time and place for relaxation practice, it may be necessary to engage in problem solving about these matters with the client, in order to maximize the likelihood that he or she will practice regularly.

Environmental Factors

Environmental factors can have a marked influence on the effectiveness of relaxation training, especially in the early stages. Factors of particular importance include the location at which training and home practice are conducted, the chair or other furniture the client uses, the client's wearing apparel, and the tone of voice used by the therapist.

The therapist should provide a location for training where there will be a minimum of extraneous stimuli. Particular care should be taken to prevent loud noises or the sound of conversation from reaching the treatment room. A sign should be placed on the door to prevent interruptions. Windows and drapes should be closed, and dim lighting should be used. If the client expresses reservations or feels discomfort in this type of environment, the therapist should discuss and resolve these concerns before proceeding.

If the environmental conditions just described cannot be created for some reason, effective APRT is still possible, though it may progress more slowly than usual. It is also true that relaxation skills may be more helpful to some clients if, once learned, they are practiced under somewhat less than optimal conditions. The assumption is that if a client can reach and maintain a state of deep relaxation in the face of some distractions, the relaxation skills will be more robust and useful in dealing with *in vivo* stress or imagined stimuli (as in systematic desensitization). An extreme example of this phenomenon was provided by one of our clients who was very successfully trained in progressive relaxation (and subsequently desensitized to performance anxiety) during sessions accompanied by the continuous and occasionally deafening sounds of construction coming from a building site next door.

As to the client's location during training and practice, a good reclining chair is ideal. It should provide full support for the entire body, so that as the skeletal muscles relax, various limbs do not slip off the chair into uncomfortable positions. For some clients, a small pillow may be needed to provide added lower back support or to prevent head turns. Sometimes a client may be more comfortable with a pillow under the knees. The therapist should encourage the client to experiment with a number of chair positions (and body orientations in each) until the best, most comfortably supportive combination is found.

Prior to the first relaxation session, the client should be advised to wear loose-fitting, comfortable clothing during relaxation training and at-home practice. He or she should remove contact lenses or glasses, and should remove or loosen other articles (such as shoes, belts, or jewelry) that may cause discomfort.

During APRT, the therapist's voice should initially have a normal, conversational tone, volume, and pace. As the session proceeds, it should become smoother, quieter, and more monotonous. During instructions to tense muscles, the voice should have more tension, volume, and speed than during instructions to relax. This discrepancy helps to contrast the sensations of tension and relaxation.

Therapist–Client Relationship

All successful therapeutic endeavors are based, to some degree, upon a good working relationship between client and therapist in which each understands his or her roles and responsibilities. APRT is certainly no exception. Although APRT consists of a specific package of techniques, it should be conducted as part of a broader cooperative learning experience for the client, not as the mere dispensation of a "treatment." Indeed, if the therapist focuses entirely upon the techniques of relaxation, at the expense of integrating the methods into an overall approach to helping the client to deal actively with problems, a "medication mentality" may develop. That is, the client may get the idea that the "relaxation exercises" guided by the therapist will, in some independent and mysterious way, solve the problems that are the focus of concern. This point of view not only may detract from the active practice and utilization of APRT, but may cast the therapist in the role of a remote technician who is simply applying a remedial procedure to a malfunctioning organism. As noted earlier, this problem can be prevented in large measure by placing APRT in its proper perspective during the presentation and discussion of the rationale. When this objective is achieved, and especially when generally good rapport exists between client and therapist, APRT is most likely to contribute to a beneficial outcome.

A word should also be said about the ways in which APRT can aid in the development of the therapeutic relationship. APRT is often useful early in treatment as a means of helping a very tense or confused client to calm down enough to organize his or her thoughts or discuss emotionally volatile material. One or two sessions of APRT can provide a pleasant experience as part of what has been anticipated to be a very trying therapy enterprise, and, in addition, can be very impressive to the client. Helping a very tense, emotionally overaroused person to reach an unfamiliar state of deep relaxation rapidly may leave the client feeling more confident in the therapist's ability and more willing to "open up" regarding matters that might otherwise have remained private much longer.

This rapport-building aspect of APRT stems not only from the pleasant experiences that it engenders, but also from the fact that it provides an opportunity for the therapist actively and clearly to communicate his or her interest in, caring for, and sensitivity to the client. These things can be conveyed in the care with which the therapist presents and explains APRT, answers questions about it, and expresses optimism about the client's ability to learn and use it. During training itself, a warm, caring attitude can be obviously reflected in the numerous requests for assurance that each muscle group is deeply relaxed and in instructions designed to reassure the client that he or she has no need to do anything but relax. Finally, postsession discussion of progress and problems usually centers upon encouragement for the client's efforts, but, perhaps more importantly, may center upon minor points of difficulty that the therapist may have detected but that the client may have thought too trivial to warrant attention. Recognition that the therapist is truly "tuned in" to what is going on can be a very impressive and beneficial experience for the client.

Assessing Progress

In most cases, the client's self-report is the main source of information about the overall success of a program of APRT. Critical positive indicators in such reports include (1) appropriate frequency and regularity of home practice sessions; (2) decreasing time required to reach deep relaxation; (3) changes in general tension; (4) utilization of relaxation to deal with specific stressors; (5) corroborating self-monitoring records, if available; and (6) general references to satisfaction with the procedures.

Such reports carry added weight when accompanied by changing in-session signs such as the following:

1. Decreased total time to achieve relaxation during training sessions.
2. No need to employ more than two tension–release cycles for any muscle group.
3. Increasing depth of relaxation (as indicated by such features as a slack jaw, splayed foot position, slowed relaxation signals, and less vigorous signals).
4. Sleep episodes.
5. Absence of gross motor movement.

6. Apparent total relaxation prior to coverage of all muscle groups.
7. Appearance of drowsiness upon termination of session.

Combining Muscle Groups

If after approximately three formal training sessions (with regular daily practice at home), assessment indicates that the client has become skillful at achieving deep relaxation using 16 muscle groups, a shorter procedure using only 7 muscle groups can be introduced. The 16 muscle groups can be combined into 7 groups as follows:

1. Dominant hand, forearm, and upper arm.
2. Nondominant hand, forearm, and upper arm.
3. All facial muscles.
4. Neck.
5. Chest, shoulders, upper back, and abdomen.
6. Dominant upper leg, calf, and foot.
7. Nondominant upper leg, calf, and foot.

These muscles can be tensed by using combinations of the tensing mechanisms prescribed for the 16 groups, or the therapist can work out some alternate means for achieving optimal tension.

The procedure for relaxation with 7 muscle groups is the same as that for 16 muscle groups. If the client does not achieve satisfactory relaxation after a week or two with this shorter procedure (and regular at-home practice), the therapist should determine which combined groups are not becoming relaxed, and should temporarily divide these into their original components before resuming use of the seven groups. The same type of questioning that follows relaxation with 16 groups should be used after relaxation with 7 groups, in order to encourage the client to express any concerns or questions.

If all goes well, a high level of proficiency in relaxation with 7 muscle groups should be attained after about 2 weeks of practice. However, the therapist should assess the client's skill before moving on to the next abbreviating step—namely, 4 muscle groups. The transition to 4 muscle groups should be treated in the same manner as the transition to 7 muscle groups. The client should be capable of achieving deep relaxation with 7 groups before attempting to use this even shorter procedure. The 7 muscle groups are combined into 4 as follows:

1. Both arms and both hands.
2. Face and neck.
3. Chest, shoulders, back, and abdomen.
4. Both legs and both feet.

Using this 4-group procedure, relaxation should take approximately 10 minutes. As with the 7-group method, questioning should follow each relaxation session.

It is to be expected that the client will require continual, regular practice to achieve deep relaxation using only 4 muscle groups.

Releasing Tension by Recall

When the client is capable of achieving deep relaxation using the 4-group procedure, relaxation through recall can be attempted. In this procedure, each of the 4 muscle groups is focused on individually, as before; however, the tension stage is eliminated. The client is asked to achieve relaxation by merely recalling the sensations associated with the release of tension. Mastery of this step is essential to the ultimate goal of relaxation training, which is to enable the client to control excess tension as it occurs in "real-life" situations. Obviously, the client will not always be able to stop and run through even a short relaxation procedure every time tension occurs. The use of recall, along with other steps yet to be discussed, should ultimately enable the client to maintain minimum levels of tension in anxiety-provoking situations.

The therapist's procedure for teaching relaxation through recall is as follows:

1. Instruct the client to focus on a muscle group (each of the 4 muscle groups is to be dealt with individually) and to attend to any tension that may be present in that group.

2. Instruct the client to recall the sensations associated with the release of tension.

3. Using the cue word as before, instruct the client to relax the muscle group.

4. Allow the client to focus on the relaxation process for 30 to 45 seconds while making statements to help the client attend to the feelings in the muscles.

5. Ask the client to signal if the muscle group is completely relaxed.

6. If the client signals that relaxation has been achieved, proceed to the next muscle group. If the client has not achieved relaxation, repeat the procedure, once again instructing the client to identify the remaining tension in the muscle group and to focus on releasing that tension.

Taken together, these procedures might sound like this:

> OK, Jill, I would like you to focus all of your attention on the muscles of your arms and hands. And I want you to pay close attention to how those muscles feel, and notice any feelings of tightness or tension that might be present in those muscles. OK, now just let those muscles relax, just recalling what it felt like when you let all that tension go. Just let that tension go now and allow the muscles of your arms and hands to become more and more relaxed. [Continue "patter" for 30–45 seconds.]
>
> OK, if the muscles of your arms and hands feel completely relaxed, I'd like you to signal. . . . OK, fine, just go right on relaxing.

If the client experiences a great deal of difficulty achieving relaxation in any group with the recall procedure, it may be necessary to use a tension–release cycle for that group. However, a tensing strategy should be used only for that group and only in the training session. The other groups should be relaxed using recall alone, and the client should try to use recall for all groups when practicing at home. In most cases, relaxation through recall will improve with regular practice.

Termination of the session and questioning is the same for the recall procedures as they are for previous sessions.

Recall with Counting

A "counting" method can be introduced at the end of a recall session, once the recall procedure is a well-established method of achieving relaxation. It should be presented to the client as a simple procedure that will promote even deeper muscle relaxation.

To incorporate counting into the training session, the therapist should instruct the client to continue relaxing and to allow the relaxation to become deeper with each number as the therapist counts from 1 to 10. The counting should be timed to coincide with the client's exhalations. The therapist should provide some "patter" about the sensations of relaxation between counts. For example, after a signal of complete relaxation has been received, the therapist might say:

OK, as you go right on relaxing, I am going to count slowly from 1 to 10. As I count, I would like you to allow all the muscles in your body to become even more deeply and completely relaxed. Just focus on your muscles as they relax more and more on each count. OK, 1 . . . 2. Let your arms and hands relax even more. 3 . . . 4. Focus on the muscles of the neck and face as they relax. 5 . . . 6. Allow the muscles of the chest, shoulders, back, and abdomen to become even more relaxed. 7 . . . 8. Let the muscles in your legs and feet relax more and more. 9 . . . 10. You are relaxing more and more all through your body.

If the client likes this procedure, he or she can be instructed to subvocalize a 1–10 count after relaxation by recall when practicing at home.

Counting Alone

When the client has developed a strong association between counting and relaxation, counting can be used alone to achieve relaxation, both in the consulting room and at home. The counting-alone procedure entails the same basic methods just described, except that the steps for relaxation by recall are eliminated. The therapist merely counts from 1 to 10, timing the counts with the client's exhalations, while presenting brief relaxation "patter" between counts. Once the counting is finished, the client should be asked to signal if any tension remains. If so, the remaining tension should be identified and released through recall (or, in rare cases, through a tension–release cycle).

At this point, the client possesses well-developed skills at relaxation. Practice may be decreased to once a day, but the client should be encouraged to continue practicing regularly to maintain proficiency.

Timetable

The following timetable for progress in an abbreviated relaxation training program illustrates an ideal case (Bernstein & Borkovec, 1973). Many clients will follow this ideal schedule, but it need not be strictly maintained. Indeed, the pace of progress must be adjusted (especially slowed) for clients who are having various kinds of problems in mastering the procedures. There is a corresponding tendency to want to speed things up for clients who are having no trouble, but in the interest of assuring adequate learning (and with the exception of the recall-with-counting procedure), each step should be employed by the therapist in at least two formal training sessions. The therapist should never proceed to a more advanced step until he or she is satisfied that the one being used has been mastered by the client.

Procedure	Session
16 muscle groups, tension–release	1, 2, 3
7 muscle groups, tension–release	4, 5
4 muscle groups, tension–release	6, 7
4 muscle groups, recall	8
4 muscle groups, recall and counting	9
Counting	10

Potential Problems

Many problems may appear in the course of relaxation training. In some cases, the therapist may have to find his or her own unique solutions to them. However, some of the more common problems and some workable solutions are given below.

Muscle Cramps

As mentioned previously, cramping may occur in some muscle groups. If this happens, the client should move the affected muscles to alleviate the cramping, while allowing the rest of the body to remain as relaxed as possible. For areas of the body in which the client experiences frequent cramping, alternative tension means should be employed, along with shorter tension periods (e.g., 3–5 seconds). Once the cramp is relieved, the therapist should provide indirect suggestions to help the client regain the previous level of relaxation.

Movement

Frequent gross motor movement during a session may indicate that the client is not relaxing. The client should be reminded not to move any more than is necessary to remain comfortable, and not to move any parts of the body that have already been relaxed. The therapist may wish to rephrase the relaxation instructions and present them again. Movement may also represent the presence of a serious problem relating to the client's acceptance of the method being used. If so, this issue should be discussed before proceeding.

Laughter

The client may laugh during relaxation, especially in the first session. This, however, should probably not be a cause for stopping the training session. A client's laughter may indicate something about motivation, feelings, or responses that may be helpful to the therapeutic process. Accordingly, it may be useful to explore the meaning of the laughter with the client after the relaxation training session is completed. There is also a possibility that the therapist is eliciting the laughter. Again, discussing the reasons underlying the laughter with the client may clarify the issues and enable further relaxation training sessions to proceed without interruptions from laughter.

Talking

Talking by the client should be ignored unless the client is reporting a serious problem. It may be necessary to repeat the instructions not to talk.

Muscle Twitches

Clients sometimes experience involuntary muscle twitches during relaxation. If such a client seems to be concerned, the therapist should assure the client that such twitches are common, that they indicate deepening relaxation, and that the client should not try to control them.

Anxiety-Producing Thoughts

If the client reports anxiety-producing thoughts during training, the therapist should first try repeating the instructions to focus only on his or her voice and the sensations experienced in the muscles. The therapist can also increase the amount of "patter" during relaxation; this helps distract the client from unpleasant thoughts. Or the therapist and the client together may decide upon some pleasant imagery upon which the client can focus during the session. This imagery can be incorporated in the relaxation "patter," or it can be accomplished by describing to the client the technique of "thought switching," in which the client deliberately changes the focus of his or her thoughts by concentrating on a pleasant image during the release phase of the relaxation training. Another approach may be to assist the client in altering the rate and/or depth of breathing patterns, as described by Fried in Chapter 10 of this volume.

Sexual Arousal

The APRT setting and procedure (a dimly lit room, soft voice, pleasant feelings) can have sexual overtones for some clients. The presence of sexual thoughts and consequent arousal can, in most cases, be dealt with routinely as another form of intrusive thinking that may interfere with the relaxation process. The therapist should recognize and accept the problem, while assuring the client that it is unlikely to remain once the focus of attention is fully upon relaxation in the muscles. Naturally, if the problem persists and more substantive interpersonal issues appear to be involved, a more extended discussion outside the context of APRT may be required.

Sleep

Some clients may fall asleep during relaxation. The therapist can determine whether a client is sleeping by first asking him or her to signal if relaxed, and then, if no signal is made, by asking the client to signal if not relaxed. Obviously, the client, if awake, should signal after one of these requests. To awaken the client, the therapist should gradually increase voice volume, repeating the request for a signal, until the client wakes. The therapist should be careful not to startle the client by making sudden, loud statements.

Coughing and Sneezing

A client's coughing or sneezing may occasionally interrupt relaxation. Infrequent coughing or sneezing will usually not interfere with the procedure, but if the client has a cold or other ailment and coughing or sneezing is frequent, the relaxation should probably be postponed. A smoker's cough can be very disruptive to a relaxation session. Since deep breathing can trigger coughing for heavy smokers, the client can be asked to take only shallow breaths during tension, or, alternatively, to maintain normal breathing during tension and relaxation. Sometimes a change in body position can help reduce the likelihood of coughing.

A Case Example

As noted throughout this chapter, APRT can be used alone or in combination with other treatment methods to deal with a broad range of human problems. For purposes of clarity, we have chosen a case example that illustrates the way in which APRT can work as the primary method of intervention when the presenting problems are rather severe but the time available for treatment is artificially short. Had circumstances allowed, a more elaborate, multidimensional treatment program would probably have been preferable, but these same circumstances created a formidable test of the value of APRT in isolation.

The client in this case was Mr. N, a professional man in his 50s. He had a wife, two children, and a "high-pressure" job, which he felt was in large measure responsible for his psychological and physical problems. At the first session, Mr. N described himself as suffering from "chronic tension." He was well aware of the fact that he was "high-strung," irritable, aggressive, and generally difficult to get along with. He was also in considerable pain most of the time as the result of a severe stomach ulcer, which his physician had attributed to stress. For several years, Mr. N had been taking antacids and other prescribed ulcer medication. He also had a supply of prescription tranquilizers, which he took several times each day to combat his chronically high level of general tension.

Mr. N told the therapist that he was planning to move to the East Coast in less than 2 months in order to start a new and even more demanding job. He sought help at this time because he was afraid that the combined stress of the relocation and the new position might be "too much" for him. There was no question of his reassessing the decision to move, so the therapist was faced with the choice of either rejecting the case or seeking to help the client develop some tension reduction skills—namely, through APRT.

The latter course was chosen, but only on the condition that the client would agree to a consultation between the therapist and Mr. N's physician about discontinuing the tranquilizer medication. This was more than acceptable to the client and, as it turned out, a long-term goal of the physician, since neither was happy with the idea of an open-ended pharmacological approach to the problem of tension. (We should add that the therapist was just as unhappy with a narrow and time-limited approach to psychological treatment, but by this time that issue had been resolved.) The primary purpose in getting the tranquilizing drugs out of the picture was to increase the probability (1) that any relaxation effects observed would be a function of APRT; (2) that the client could learn to experience sensations of relaxation fully without interfering drug effects; and (3) that the skills acquired during APRT would not have to be transferred to a nondrugged state, with possible loss of potency.

Only five training sessions could be scheduled in the time available before the client's departure, so the sequence of events was compressed somewhat. The therapist's goal was merely to teach the client basic relaxation skills and to bring him to a level of competence with them that might serve to combat general tension. Anything more, such as differential or cue-controlled relaxation (see Bernstein & Borkovec, 1973), was clearly unrealistic under the circumstances. Fortunately, the training sessions went very smoothly. The client was, as one might expect, highly motivated and cooperative. He practiced the procedures faithfully between sessions, and at the fifth session was able to achieve deep relaxation through the recall method.

Somewhat to the therapist's surprise, but certainly to his delight, the client reported a number of immediate and significant benefits that he attributed to his newly acquired capability for relaxation. The client claimed to be far less generally tense and irritable than before, and he stated that he did not miss his tranquilizers (to our knowledge, he has never resumed their use). In addition, Mr. N said that he was finding it easier to deal with stressful events at work and at home by using relaxation "breaks" at the office and at the end of each day. The reduction in general and specific tension was also accompanied by reports of greatly reduced gastric discomfort. Some combination of increased physical comfort and decreased tension (and, perhaps, the prospect of a job change) created a noticeable improvement in Mr. N's behavior in relation to his family. Specifically, he began to appear less irritable, more understanding and tolerant, and easier to live with in general. It seems reasonable to suppose that the changes just described, while not brought about directly by APRT alone, were greatly facilitated by it.

Comments and Reflections

After three decades of development, clinical use, and experimental evaluation, APRT remains a major component of social learning approaches to behavior change. It is easy to see why this should be the case. The methods involved are relatively simple, straightforward, and easily adapted for use in isolation or along with more elaborate intervention packages of various kinds. Furthermore, clients usually enjoy learning and practicing the procedures, and seem to make good use of the skills that evolve.

At the same time, the clinicians and researchers who use and investigate APRT have become more and more sophisticated about it. For one thing, there is far less defensiveness about the method. It is now seen not as a semi-magical method that "makes desensitization work," but as one of several related methods through which autonomic overarousal and maladaptive subjective states can be effectively managed. Accordingly, there is now less emphasis on what is "special" about APRT, and more emphasis on how it relates to other relaxation-inducing methods (such as yoga or biofeedback) and what common physiological and cognitive mechanisms might account for all of them (see Smith, 1985; Tarler-Benlolo, 1978). There also appears to be a less rigid adherence to procedural orthodoxy in APRT. Whereas at one time only certain specific relaxation methods were seen as clinically useful, there is a broadening awareness that a single set of procedures, no matter how carefully developed and presented, may not meet the needs (or may "overtreat" the problems) of all clients. Thus, although "live," client-controlled relaxation methods may be desirable in general (e.g., Borkovec & Sides, 1979), there may be clients for whom and circumstances for which less elaborate procedures may be useful as well (see King, 1980; Carlson, Collins, Nitz, Sturgis, & Rogers, 1990). For example, having clients focus their attention during APRT on the physiological sensations of tension and relaxation may be important only for clients reporting certain kinds of problems, and may actually decrease the benefits of training in some cases (e.g., Borkovec & Hennings, 1978).

This provides but one illustration of the way in which clinicians and researchers have turned their attention to individual differences in clients and their problems in the selection of APRT and variations thereof. As another example, it has been suggested that some anxiety or "tension" problems may involve a strong physiological component, that others may incorporate a significant cognitive component, and that still others may include both. Relaxation may be more useful in some cases than in others (e.g., Davidson & Schwartz, 1976, Lehrer, Woolfolk, & Goldman, 1986).

Finally, it should be pointed out that APRT, in whatever client-specific form it may be administered, has enjoyed an expansion of applications—not only in terms of the target problems for which it is used, but in the way it is used. Originally suggested as a relatively passive state that is incompatible with anxiety, relaxation through APRT has also been conceptualized as an active coping skill (e.g., Goldfried & Trier, 1974) that the client can bring to bear in handling stressful situations. As before, it is seen as potentially useful alone (e.g., as in cue-controlled relaxation) or as an adjunct to the development and use of more elaborate cognitive coping skills (King, 1980).

As illustrated by the examples given here, the flexibility and adaptability that are inherent in APRT represent two of its most attractive characteristics. These features, when combined with APRT's convenience, clinical utility, and apparent benefits, suggest that ever-expanding versions and applications of the original Jacobson and Wolpe methods will continue to be an important part of social learning approaches to human problems.

REFERENCES

Adler, C. M., Craske, M. G., & Barlow, D. H. (1987). Relaxation-induced panic (RIP): When resting isn't peaceful. *Integrative Psychiatry, 5,* 94–112.

Agras, W. S., Taylor, C. B., Kraemer, H. C., Southam, M. A., & Schneider, J. A. (1987). Relaxation training for essential hypertension at the worksite: II. The poorly controlled hypertensive. *Psychosomatic Medicine, 49,* 264–273.

Attanasio, V., Andrasik, F., & Blanchard, E. B. (1987). Cognitive therapy and relaxation training in muscle contraction headache: Efficacy and cost-effectiveness. *Headache, 27,* 254–260.

Benson, H. (1975). *The relaxation response.* New York: Morrow.

Bernstein, D. A., & Borkovec, T. D. (1973). *Progressive relaxation training: A manual for the helping professions.* Champaign, IL: Research Press.

Blanchard, E. B., Andrasik, F., Appelbaum, K. A., Evans, D. D., Jurishe, S. E., Teders, S. J., Rodichok, L. D., & Barron, K. D. (1985). The efficacy and cost-effectiveness of minimal-therapist-contact, non-drug treatments of chronic migraine and tension headache. *Headache, 25,* 214–220.

Blanchard, E. B., Andrasik, F., Neff, D. F., Arena, J. G., Ahles, T. A., Jurish, S. E., Pallmeyer, T. P., Saunders, N. L., Teders, S. J., Barron, K. D., & Rodichok, L. D. (1982). Biofeedback and relaxation training with three kinds of headache: Treatment effects and their prediction. *Journal of Consulting and Clinical Psychology, 50,* 562–575.

Blanchard, E. B., Appelbaum, K. A., Guarnieri, P., Neff, D. F., Andrasik, F., & Jaccard, J. (1988). Two studies of the long-term follow-up of minimal therapist contact treatments of vascular and tension headache. *Journal of Consulting and Clinical Psychology, 56,* 427–432.

Blanchard, E. B., Appelbaum, K. A., Radnitz, C. L., Michultka, D., Morrill, B, Kirsch, C., Hillhouse, J., Evans, D. D., Guarnieri, P., Attanasio, V., Andrasik, F., Jaccard, J., & Dentiger, M. P. (1990). Placebo-controlled evaluation of abbreviated progressive muscle relaxation and of relaxation combined with cognitive therapy in the treatment of tension headache. *Journal of Consulting and Clinical Psychology, 58,* 210–215.

Blanchard, E. B., McCoy, G. C., Musso, A., Gerardi, M. A., Pallmeyer, T. P., Gerardi, R. J., Cotch, P. A., Siracusa, K., & Andrasik, F. (1986). A controlled comparison of thermal biofeedback and relaxation training in the treatment of essential hypertension: I. Short-term and long-term outcome. *Behavior Therapy, 17,* 563–579.

Blanchard, E. B., McCoy, G. C., Wittrock, D., Musso, A., Gerardi, R. J., & Pangburn, L. (1988). A controlled comparison of thermal biofeedback and relaxation training in the treatment of essential hypertension: II. Effects on cardiovascular reactivity. *Health Psychology, 7,* 19–33.

Blanchard, E. B., Nicholson, N. L., Taylor, A. E., Steffek, B. D., Radnitz, C. L., & Appelbaum, K. A. (1991). The role of regular home practice in the relaxation treatment of tension headache. *Journal of Consulting and Clinical Psychology, 59,* 467–470.

Borkovec, T. D. (1987). Commentary. *Integrative Psychiatry, 5,* 104–106.

Borkovec, T. D., & Hennings, B. L. (1978). The role of physiological attention-focusing in the relaxation treatment of sleep disturbance, general tension, and specific stress reaction. *Behaviour Research and Therapy, 16,* 7–19.

Borkovec, T. D., & Mathews, A. M. (1988). Treatment of nonphobic anxiety disorders: A comparison of nondirective, cognitive, and coping desensitization therapy. *Journal of Consulting and Clinical Psychology, 56,* 877–884.

Borkovec, T. D., Mathews, A. M., Chambers, A., Ebrahimi, S., Lytle, R., & Nelson, R. (1987). The effects of relaxation training with cognitive or nondirective therapy and the role of relaxation-induced anxiety in the treatment of generalized anxiety. *Journal of Consulting and Clinical Psychology, 55,* 883–888.

Borkovec, T. D., & Sides, J. K. (1979). Critical procedural variables related to the physiological effects of progressive relaxation: A review. *Behaviour Research and Therapy, 17,* 119–125.

Burish, T. G., Carey, M. P., Krozely, M. G., & Greco, F. A. (1987). Conditioned side effects induced by cancer chemotherapy: Prevention through behavioral treatment. *Journal of Consulting and Clinical Psychology, 55,* 42–48.

Burish, T. G., & Lyles, J. N. (1981). Effectiveness of relaxation training in reducing adverse reactions to cancer chemotherapy. *Journal of Behavioral Medicine, 4,* 65–78.

Carey, M. P., & Burish, T. G. (1987). Providing relaxation training to cancer chemotherapy patients: A comparison of three delivery techniques. *Journal of Consulting and Clinical Psychology, 55,* 732–737.

Carlson, C. R., Collins, F. L., Nitz, A. J., Sturgis, E. T., & Rogers, J. L. (1990). Muscle stretching as an alternative relaxation training procedure. *Journal of Behavior Therapy and Experimental Psychiatry, 21,* 29–38.

Carrington, P. (1977). *Freedom in meditation.* Garden City, NY: Doubleday.

Cautela, J. R., & Groden, J. (1978). *Relaxation: A comprehensive manual for adults, children, and children with special needs.* Champaign, IL: Research Press.

Chesney, M. A., Black, G. W., Swan, G. E., & Ward, M. M. (1987). Relaxation training for essential hypertension at the worksite: I. The untreated mild hypertensive. *Psychosomatic Medicine, 49,* 250–263.

Cohen, A. S., Barlow, D. H., & Blanchard, E. B. (1985). Psychophysiology of relaxation-associated panic attacks. *Journal of Abnormal Psychology, 94,* 96–101.

Davidson, R. J., & Schwartz, G. E. (1976). The psychobiology of relaxation and related states: A multiprocess theory. In D. I. Mostofsky (Ed.), *Behavior control and modification of physiological activity* (pp. 399–442). Englewood Cliffs, NJ: Prentice-Hall.

Davison, G. C. (1966). Anxiety under total curarization: Implications for the role of muscular relaxation in the desensitization of neurotic fears. *Journal of Nervous and Mental Disease, 143,* 443–448.

DeGood, D. E., & Williams, E. M. (1982). Parasympathetic rebound following EMG biofeedback training: A case study. *Biofeedback and Self-Regulation, 7,* 461–465.

Edinger, J. D., & Jacobsen, R. (1982). Incidence and significance of relaxation treatment side effects. *Behavior Therapist, 5,* 137–138.

Gellhorn, E. (1958). The influence of curare on hypothalamic excitability and the electroencephalogram. *Electroencephalography and Clinical Neurophysiology, 10,* 697–703.

Gellhorn, E., & Kiely, W. F. (1972). Mystical states of consciousness: Neurophysiological and clinical aspects. *Journal of Nervous and Mental Disease, 154,* 399–405.

Goldfried, M. R., & Trier, C. S. (1974). Effectiveness of relaxation as an active coping skill. *Journal of Abnormal Psychology, 83,* 348–355.

Halonen, J. S., & Passman, R. H. (1985). Relaxation training and expectation in the treatment of postpartum distress. *Journal of Consulting and Clinical Psychology, 53,* 839–845.

Heide, F. J., & Borkovec, T. D. (1983). Relaxation-induced anxiety: Paradoxical anxiety enhancement due to relaxation training. *Journal of Consulting and Clinical Psychology, 51,* 171–182.

Hoelscher, T. J., Lichstein, K. L., Fischer, S., & Hegarty, T. B. (1987). Relaxation treatment of hypertension: Do home relaxation tapes enhance treatment outcome? *Behavior Therapy, 18,* 33–37.

Hoelscher, T. J., Lichstein, K. L., & Rosenthal, T. L. (1986). Home relaxation practice in hypertension treatment: Objective assessment and compliance induction. *Journal of Consulting and Clinical Psychology, 54,* 217–221.

Holmes, D. S., & Roth, D. L. (1988). Effects of aerobic exercise training and relaxation training on cardiovascular activity during psychological stress. *Journal of Psychosomatic Research, 32,* 469–474.

Hyman, R. B., Feldman, H. R., Harris, R. B., Levin, R. F., & Malloy, G. B. (1989). The effects of relaxation training on clinical symptoms: A meta-analysis. *Nursing Research, 38,* 216–220.

Jacobson, E. (1938). *Progressive relaxation* (2nd ed.). Chicago: University of Chicago Press.

Jakes, S. C., Hallam, R. S., Rachman, S., & Hinchcliffe, R. (1986). The effects of reassurance, relaxation training and distraction on chronic tinnitus sufferers. *Behaviour Research and Therapy, 24,* 497–507.

Kiecolt-Glaser, J. K., Glaser, R., Williger, D., Stout, J., Messick, G., Sheppard, S., Ricker, D., Romisher, S., C., Briner, W., Bonnell, G., & Donnerberg, R. (1985). Psychosocial enhancement of immunocompetence in a geriatric population. *Health Psychology, 4,* 25–41.

King, N. J. (1980). Abbreviated progressive relaxation. In M. Hersen, R. M. Eisler, & P. M. Miller (Eds.), *Progress in behavior modification* (pp. 147–182). New York: Academic Press.

Lang, P. J. (1977). Imagery in therapy: An information processing analysis of fear. *Behavior Therapy, 92,* 276–306.

Lang, P. J. (1979). A bio-informational theory of emotion imagery. *Psychophysiology, 16,* 495–512.

Lehrer, P. M. (1982). How to relax and how not to relax: A re-evaluation of the work of Edmund Jacobson—I. *Behaviour Research and Therapy, 20,* 417–428.

Lehrer, P. M., & Woolfolk, R. L. (1984). Are stress reduction techniques interchangeable, or do they have specific effects?: A review of the comparative empirical literature. In R. L. Woolfolk & P. M. Lehrer (Eds.), *Principles and practice of stress management* (1st ed., pp. 404–477). New York: Guilford Press.

Lehrer, P. M., Woolfolk, R. L., & Goldman, N. (1986). Progressive relaxation then and now: Does change always mean progress? In R. J. Davidson, G. E. Schwartz, & D. Shapiro (Eds.), *Consciousness and self-regulation* (Vol. 4, pp. 183–216). New York: Plenum Press.

Ley, R. (1988). Panic attacks during relaxation and relaxation-induced anxiety: A hyperventilation interpretation. *Journal of Behavior Therapy and Experimental Psychiatry, 19,* 253–259.

Long, B. C., & Haney, C. J. (1988). Coping strategies for working women: Aerobic exercise and relaxation interventions. *Behavior Therapy, 19,* 75–83.

Lyles, J. N., Burish, T. G., Krozely, M. G., & Oldham, R. K. (1982). Efficacy of relaxation training and guided imagery in reducing the adverseness of cancer chemotherapy. *Journal of Consulting and Clinical Psychology, 50,* 509–529.

Paul, G. L. (1966). *Insight versus. desensitization in psychotherapy.* Stanford, CA: Stanford University Press.

Paul, G. L., & Bernstein, D. A. (1973). *Anxiety and clinical problems: Treatment by systematic desensitization and related techniques.* New York: General Learning Press.

Reynolds, W. M., & Coats, K. I. (1986). A comparison of cognitive–behavioral therapy and relaxation training for the treatment of depression in adolescents. *Journal of Consulting and Clinical Psychology, 54,* 653–660.

Roth, D. L., & Holmes, D. S. (1987). Influence of aerobic exercise training and relaxation training on physical and psychologic health following stressful life events. *Psychosomatic Medicine, 49,* 355–365.

Sigmon, S. T., & Nelson, R. O. (1988). The effectiveness of activity scheduling and relaxation training in the treatment of spasmodic dysmenorrhea. *Journal of Behavioral Medicine, 11,* 483–495.

Smith, J. C. (1985). *Relaxation dynamics: Nine world approaches to self-relaxation.* Champaign, IL: Research Press.

Southam, M. A., Agras, W. S., Taylor, C. B., & Kraemer, H. C. (1982). Relaxation training: Blood pressure lowering during the working day. *Archives of General Psychiatry, 39,* 715–717.

Tarler-Benlolo, L. (1978). The role of relaxation in biofeedback training: A critical review of the literature. *Psychological Bulletin, 85,* 727–755.

Taylor, C. B., Agras, W. S., Schneider, J. A., & Allen, R. A. (1983). Adherence to instructions to practice relaxation exercises. *Journal of Consulting and Clinical Psychology, 51,* 952–953.

Teders, S. J., Blanchard, E. B., Andrasik, F., Jurish, S. E., Neff, D. F., & Arena, J. G. (1984). Relaxation training for tension headache: Comparative efficacy and cost-effectiveness of a minimal therapist contact versus a therapist-delivered procedure. *Behavior Therapy, 15,* 59–70.

Turner, J. A. (1982). Comparison of group progressive-relaxation training and cognitive-behavioral group therapy for chronic low back pain. *Journal of Consulting and Clinical Psychology, 50,* 757–765.

Wisniewski, J. J., Genshaft, J. L., Mulick, J. A., Coury, D. L., & Hammer, D. (1988). Relaxation therapy and compliance in the treatment of adolescent headache. *Headache, 28,* 612–617.

Wolpe, J. (1958). *Psychotherapy by reciprocal inhibition.* Stanford, CA: Stanford University Press.

4

Yoga-Based Therapy

CHANDRA PATEL

Hypertension in the community is a major challenge to public health today. Hypertension affects as much as a quarter of the adult population in industrialized countries (Office of Health Economics, 1971; Joint National Committee on Detection, Evaluation, and Treatment of High Blood Pressure, 1984). One of the most important complications of hypertension is coronary heart disease, which is the number one killer in most industrialized countries. In this chapter, I describe the contribution that can be expected from a yoga-based stress management therapy in reducing hypertension and the risk of coronary heart disease; the development of the therapy in its present form; the rationale for using it; the types of patients who are most likely to benefit; the essential ingredients for successful outcome; and possible indications and contraindications. The program I have developed for hypertension is described in some detail; its applications to other stress-related conditions are also briefly described.

History of the Method

After having been trained in cardiology and chest medicine, I decided in 1969 to join a general practice in suburban London, as that was the most convenient thing I could do with my family commitments. I had taken many courses in advanced medicine; I knew how to read X-rays or electrocardiograms (EKGs) and could rattle off the normal limits of any biochemical or hematological measures if asked in the middle of the night. I was trained to believe that at the basis of any illness was organic derangement, which could be diagnosed by history, examination, and laboratory investigations. With my extensive knowledge of the pharmacopeia, I thought that general practice would be a walkover. Unfortunately, this turned out to be an illusion. Soon there were many occasions when I realized that it was not appropriate to prescribe tranquilizers, painkillers, or sleeping pills for such symptoms as chronic fatigue, vague aches and pains, or restless nights when extensive investigations had shown no abnormality. Many symptoms appeared to originate from psychological, social, and spiritual malaise, yet patients did not feel that their symptoms warranted their seeing a psychiatrist. Other symptoms seemed actually to be caused by our modern medicine.

I cite just two cases here. One was the case of a young man whose wife had run away with another man for an exciting weekend, but had returned on Monday. He was devastated, and I had no words with which to comfort him. He did not want tranquilizers. He also did not want to divorce his wife, as they had two children under 5 years of age. When I tried to tell him that he would have to try to forget the episode, he asked me "Teach me, Doctor, how to forget!" The second case was that of a middle-aged lady with severe hypertension. At last this was something I knew how to treat! I gave her prescriptions for antihypertensive drugs, one after the other, going to stronger and stronger varieties because her blood pressure was remaining difficult to control. I continued to increase the doses until one day I heard that she had been admitted to a psychiatric hospital with severe depression, probably caused or at least significantly contributed to by the medications she was taking. A few days later, she sent me a messge through her daughter: "Tell the doctor that I did not always take my medications."

Realizing my inadequacy and the fact that I might have been doing harm to my patients, I felt unhappy, and in fact began having some of the same symptoms that my patients were describing! Sometimes I could not sleep until 3:00 A.M., and then I would be tempted to take half a sleeping pill, with the rationalization that I would not otherwise be in a proper state to practice medicine the next day. Within months I knew that this was ridiculous. I was not going to let this happen to me. I started doing yoga breathing and physical exercises twice a day, followed by the deep muscle relaxation and meditation I had learned as a child, and within days I felt quite well. It occurred to me that if this regimen was good for me, it also should be good for my patients.

I could not effectively apply these methods right away, as I was not a qualified yoga teacher, and my office was not really suitable for teaching people physical exercise. Eventually, I bought several books that described and illustrated yoga postures. I started giving these books to suitable patients, only to realize 3–6 months later that they had put the unread books onto a shelf and their symptoms were no better. My patients wanted advice from their doctor, not books. Then, to patients who demanded "Valium or something" to calm their nerves because they had a driving test, a dreaded flight, or an important interview the next day, I began teaching diaphragmatic breathing exercises and deep muscle relaxation in the 10–15 minutes of a consultation session. I immediately felt that most patients were grateful and amazed to know how simple it was to control their own anxiety and how effective these techniques could be.

I also experimented with the same technique with a middle-aged hypertensive lady whose blood pressure had also remained uncontrolled by the strongest antihypertensive drugs I could prescribe. To my surprise, her blood pressure fell from 200/120 to 140/90 mm Hg in only a few days. I continued to see her three times a week for half an hour, and within 3 weeks her blood pressure had reached 120/80 mm Hg. I gradually reduced her medication and eventually stopped it altogether. Every time a pill was withdrawn, her blood pressure would rise to about 140/90, but it quickly fell again to about 120/80. This, I thought, was too good to be true. I next tried these methods with a 42-year-old woman whose hypertension had begun following the toxemia of pregnancy and whose blood pressure was controlled at about 140/90 mm Hg with methyldopa (250 mg, three times a day). The experience with my previous patient was replicated: This patient too was eventually taken off her medication, while her blood pressure was maintained at about 125/80 mm Hg. Several additional patients were then treated with most satisfactory results, although not all of them were able to stop using medication completely. I could not understand why there was so much variability in individual results. Could it be that all patients were not relaxing equally? If only I could measure their level of relaxation, I could determine this.

Soon after this I read, with great excitement, an article by Neal Miller (Miller, 1969) discussing how he and his colleagues had been successful in training rats to increase or decrease heart rate or blood pressure and to perform even more exotic feats (e.g., blushing in one ear but not in the other at the same time!). A blood pressure biofeedback machine had also been developed, and experiments on human control of blood pressure were being published by investigators at Harvard University (Shapiro, Tursky, Gershon, & Stern, 1969; Shapiro, Schwartz, & Tursky, 1972; Benson, Shapiro, Tursky, & Schwartz, 1971). However, their results were tiny compared with the results I was getting. I thought that if I could combine biofeedback with my relaxation procedure, maybe I could achieve even better results, which could deserve the attention of the scientific community. Alas, the cost of a blood pressure biofeedback machine turned out to be beyond my wildest dream of affordability, but I did find a small galvanic skin response (GSR) biofeedback instrument, which was within my means and which I immediately bought.

As I began working in earnest, I found that if patients were left on their own to practice after initial instruction in breathing and relaxation, many would fall fast asleep. I sat beside them and recited relaxation instructions, and also introduced simple meditation procedures involving the repetition of such words as "relaxed," "one," or "harmony" with every exhalation. This mental activity appeared to keep the persons awake and yet profoundly relaxed. My first study with 20 hypertensive patients, treated by this combination of yoga-based physical and mental relaxation and biofeedback, was impressive enough to be promptly published (Patel, 1973). Later I found that after the first few months, patients would not keep up with regular twice-daily practice, and ways had to be found to integrate relaxation into their daily lives and to have them make durable changes in behaviour. Initially, the therapy was conducted on a one-to-one basis and was very much tailored to suit the individuals, but group sessions were later introduced to make treatment more cost-effective, and therapy became more structured. The original results were successfully replicated in randomized controlled trials (Patel, 1975; Patel & North, 1975; Patel, Marmot, & Terry, 1981).

Theoretical Underpinnings

Although the therapy to be described in this chapter can be used for any stress-related condition, my research experience with it has been largely restricted to hypertension and coronary heart disease, and these diseases are used throughout to illustrate the principles. In the use of yoga-based relaxation therapy to reduce hypertension, it is assumed that stress is an important contributory etiological factor; that plausible biological mechanisms exist to explain the pathways through which blood pressure may rise as a result of stress; that a temporal relationship can be demonstrated showing that stress occurs before hypertension and is not merely associated with it; that a dose–response curve exists, with greater stress associated with greater rises in blood pressure; and that stress-reducing techniques can reverse the pathological process and thereby reduce blood pressure. It is further assumed that yoga-based therapy reduces the stress because the stressors are not appraised as threatening; the physiological response to stress is attenuated; or the therapeutic effects counteract mental, emotional, physical, or behavioral effects of stress.

Stress and Hypertension

Unfortunately, no positive proof of an etiological link between stress and hypertension or coronary heart disease exists. The only scientifically accepted fact is that in some 90% of the patients with so-called essential hypertension, no definite cause is known. Despite the lack of acceptable scientific evidence, stress has continued to linger in the minds of the public and a handful of researchers as an important causative factor for both hypertension and coronary heart disease. My hypothesis that yoga-based physical and mental relaxation would be preventive and/or therapeutic was based on these intuitions as well as on some scientific observations.

Clinical and Epidemiological Observations

Many astute physicians in the past observed the association between certain negative emotions or aggressive, hostile behavior and hypertension or coronary heart disease. Even though these observations were largely anecdotal, they are still very pertinent. As early as the 17th century, William Harvey (cited in Inglis, 1965, pp. 179–180) observed the effect of emotions in causing hypertension:

> I was acquainted with another strong man, who having received injury and affront from one more powerful than himself, and upon whom he could not have his revenge, was so overcome with hatred and spite and passion, which he yet communicated to no-one, that at last he fell into a strange distemper, suffering from extreme oppression and pain of the heart and breast and in the course of a few years he died. His friends thought him poisoned by some maleficent influence, or possessed with an evil spirit. . . . In the dead body I found the heart and aorta so much gorged and distended with blood, that the cavities of the ventricles equalled those of a bullock's heart in size. Such is the force of the blood pent up, and such are the effects of its impulse.

From the pathology, it is certain that the patient had sustained high blood pressure leading to angina, and that he probably died of a heart attack.

A number of more recent clinical and epidemiological observations also seem to suggest that stress may be an important contributor. For example, blood pressure tended to rise in casualties after a vast nitrate explosion in Texas City (Ruskin, Beard, & Scaffer, 1948); in a battalion of soldiers in World War II after 2 years of desert fighting (Graham, 1945); in a large number of inhabitants during the siege of Leningrad (Miasnikov, 1962); and in men who were unemployed after a plant shutdown (Kasl & Cobb, 1970). The mean blood pressure or incidence of hypertension rose in people who migrated from primitive areas where they were exposed to unchanging unchallenged traditional roles to areas of "Western," urban civilization (Cruz-Coke, 1960; Cruz-Coke, Etchverry, & Nagel, 1964; Maddocks, 1961, 1967; Scotch & Geiger, 1963); in those living in deprived neighborhoods compared with more affluent neighborhoods (Harburg, Schull, Erfurt, & Shork, 1970); in prisoners forced to live in crowded conditions compared to those living in private cells (D'Atr & Ostfeld, 1975); in air traffic controllers with higher responsibility compared with controllers having less responsibility (Cobb & Rose, 1975); in pregnant women living in parts of Israel facing periodic bombardment (Rofe & Goldberg, 1983); and in London civil servants in lower social classes compared with those in higher social classes (Marmot, Rose, Shipley, & Hamilton, 1978). Henry and Cassel (1969) arranged data from 18 different studies from around the world to show that as societies progressively modernize, the mean blood pressure of their populations begins to rise until the adaptation process is completed, when blood pressure becomes more stable. Similarly, Waldron et al. (1982) pooled data from 84 different societies and showed that blood pressure rises when there is an increased emphasis on market economy and economic competition and a decreased emphasis on extended family systems.

Increased sympathetic activity in essential hypertension is also indicated by the facts that most antihypertensive drugs reduce blood pressure by interfering or blocking the action of the sympathetic nervous system, and that they produce a greater fall in blood pressure in hypertensive than in normotensive subjects (Doyle & Smirk, 1955; Smirk, 1970). Most antihypertensive drugs, such as vasodilators, calcium channel blockers, or diuretics, work by producing effects that are opposite to the physiological effects of sympathetic nervous system or pituitary–adrenocortical axis stimulation. The fact that not everyone exposed to similar stressful environment gets hypertension can be explained by genetic predisposition and the concept of autonomic response stereotypy. According to this concept, people respond to stress with a generalized increase in sympathetic activity, but many individuals consistently show maximal responses in only one or two physiological paremeters (Lacey & Lacey, 1958). In other words, under stress some people manifesting stereotypy show a rise in blood pressure, whereas others may have headaches, indigestion, runny noses, or dizziness.

Evidence from Animal Experiments

It is easier to obtain experimental evidence in animals than in humans. For example, when chronically exposed to stressful environments such as crowding, conflicts, and operant conditioning schedules, mice (Henry, Stephens, & Santisteban, 1975), rats (Friedman & Dahl, 1975), and monkeys (Benson, Herd, Morse, & Kelleher, 1969) developed sustained hypertension. Stress has also been found to augment the effect of other blood-pressure-increasing stimuli, such as excess salt ingestion: The rise in blood pressure resulting from combined exposure to stress and excessive salt was more severe and persistent than the rise that occurred when either stimulus was presented alone (Friedman & Iwai, 1977; Anderson, 1984). It is true that the same exposure to stress does not result in similar rises in blood pressure in all humans or animals. Early environmental experience (Henry, Ely, & Stephens, 1972) and genetic predisposition (Friedman & Iwai, 1976, 1977) play an important role in determining the pathogenic influence of stress in the development of hypertension.

Pathogenesis of Human Hypertension: A Model

A previously suggested model (Patel, 1977) for the pathogenesis of essential hypertension is shown in Figure 4.1. It is generally accepted that the defense alarm reaction or the "fight-or-flight" response is a basic stress response activated by a wide range of stimuli that are evaluated by the cerebral cortex as challenging, demanding, or threatening. An important component of this response is cardiovascular, consisting of a rise in blood pressure, an increase in heart rate and cardiac output, and vasoconstriction. Muscle tension; rapid or irregular breathing pattern; an alert brain showing a fast, low-amplitude desynchronized electroencephalogram (EEG); and an increase in the activity of sweat glands are some of the other changes. As shown in Figure 4.1, the rise in blood pressure occurs as a direct result of stimulation of the cardiac and vascular sympathetic effectors, as well as indirectly through hormonal release. Both the central and peripheral nervous systems and the endocrine system participate in bringing about the final result. Genetic predisposition is suggested by observations that patients with borderline hypertension or normotensive offsprings of hypertensive patients show exaggerated pressor response to stress (Light & Obrist, 1980; Falkner, Onesti, Angelakos, Fernandes, & Langman, 1979). Stress can alter sodium and water excretion more in those susceptible to develop hypertension (Light, Koepke, Obrist, & Willis, 1983). Once initiated, hypertension can be maintained or perpetuated by resetting of the baroreceptors (Kezdi, 1953; Kubicek, Kottke, Laker, & Visscher, 1953; McCubbin, Green, & Page, 1956; Korner, 1971) or structural hypertrophy of the arteriole walls (Folkow, Hallbäck, Lundgren, Sivertsson, & Weiss, 1973), even in the absence of psychological stimuli or stress.

Reduction in Stress Reduces Blood Pressure

The fact that there is an in-built physiological response that counteracts stress or the fight-or-flight response was demonstrated by Hess (1957) in cats. Electrical stimulation of the anterior hypothalamus resulted in skeletal muscle relaxation, a decrease in blood pressure, lower respiratory rate, and pupillary constriction. The fall in blood pressure during sleep probably results from a fall in sympathetic vasoconstrictive tone, since it has been shown that marked reduction occurs in the flow of sympathetic nerve impulses during sleep (Iwamura, Uchino, Ozawa, & Torii, 1969) and that this normal fall in blood pressure during sleep can be prevented or reduced by bilateral thoracolumbar sympathectomy (Zanchetti, Bacelli, Guazzi, & Mancia, 1972). The possibility of inducing this antistress or relaxation response in humans through meditation or similar techniques has been demonstrated (Wallace & Benson, 1972;

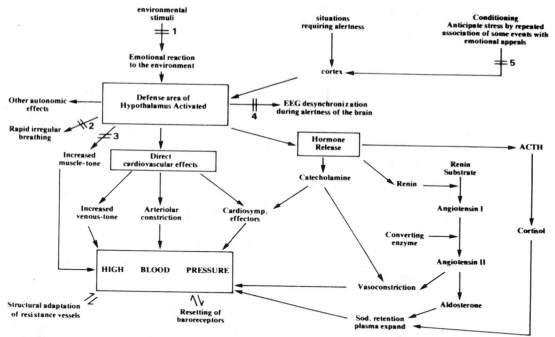

FIGURE 4.1. Suggested pathogenesis of hypertension and behavior modification: 1, educational program; 2, breathing exercise; 3, muscle relaxation; 4, meditation; and 5, deconditioning. Reprinted by permission from Patel (1977, p. 9).

Benson, Beary, & Carol, 1974). The response has been shown to be associated with a decrease in oxygen consumption, respiratory rate, and cardiac output; a marked decrease in arterial blood lactate concentration, which is known to be associated with anxiety; an intensification of slow alpha waves and occasional theta waves in the EEG; and an increase in electrical resistance of the skin, associated with a decrease in sweat gland activity. These findings provide a strong rationale for using a stress management therapy that regulates breathing, reduces muscle tension, synchronizes the EEG pattern, and integrates a stress-reducing philosophy into everyday life. As I demonstrate later, ther is empirical evidence of its efficacy.

Stress and Coronary Heart Disease

In 1768, William Haberden added to his vivid description of angina, "The disease is created by the disturbance of the mind" (Willius & Keys, 1941). John Hunter, a 19th-century surgeon from St George's Hospital in London, is remembered to have said, "My life is at the mercy of any rascal who shall put me in passion." He proved his point by dying abruptly at a boardroom meeting during a heated discussion (Willius & Keys, 1941). An American physician, William Osler (1910), described a coronary-prone man as one who is "keen and ambitious, the indicator of whose engines is set full speed ahead." Kemple (1945) described him as an "aggressive, ambitious individual with an intense emotional drive, unable to delegate authority or responsibility with ease, having no hobbies and concentrating all his thoughts and energy in the narrow groove of his career." Wolf (1958) described him as one who not only meets challenges by putting out extra effort, but who also takes little satisfaction from his accomplishments.

Two cardiologists, Meyer Friedman and Ray Rosenman (1974), have taken this connection from an anecdotal to a more scientific level by describing an overtly stress-prone "Type A" behavior pattern and linking this pattern to premature coronary heart disease. The individual with this behavior pattern is intensely ambitious, hard-driving, and competitive, with a sustained drive for achievement; impatient, with a keen sense of time urgency; constantly preoccupied with occupational deadlines; involved in a chronic struggle to achieve as many things as possible in the shortest possible time; and displaying aggression and hostility if anybody or anything gets in the way. Friedman and Rosenman have shown in an epidemiological study of over 3000 men that those with the Type A behavior pattern were twice as likely to get coronary heart disease as their counterparts with the Type B behavior pattern (Rosenman et al., 1975). It has also been shown that altering Type A behavior by a stress management program in myocardial infarction patients can reduce recurrence rate (Friedman et al., 1984).

Stress can also lead to coronary risk factors. For example, it is recognized that stress can be lead to obesity, alcohol drinking, and cigarette smoking. It may lead to hypertension and Type A behavior as described above, and also to physical inactivity because of time shortage or early fatigue (Nixon, 1976). Overwhelming stress can lead to hyperglycemia (Hinkle & Wolf, 1952) or sudden death as a result of electrical instability (Lown & Verrier, 1976). Stress has been shown to lead to hyperlipidemia in medical students before final examinations (Thomas & Murphy, 1958), in accountants before tax deadlines (Friedman, Rosenman, & Carroll, 1958), in new Air Force Academy cadets (Clark et al., 1975), and in trainees of an underwater demolition team (Rahe, Rubin, Gunderson, & Arthur, 1971). A hypothesis I have suggested earlier (Patel, 1982) linking stress to coronary heart disease is depicted in Figure 4.2.

Yoga Philosophy and Techniques, and How They May Help Reduce Stress

Yoga is a system of Indian philosophy and practice. The word "Yoga" means "union"; it is so called because it teaches the means by which one can learn to be in communion with the Absolute or with universal energy. A human being consists of both material and nonmaterial entities. The material entity is the physical body with all its organs, and the nonmaterial entities are the soul and the mind. Yoga attempts to bring within its perspective all three sides of human life—the body, the mind, and the soul, or, to put it differently, the physical side, the social side (or life in action), and the spiritual side. The physical side also includes the natural elements such as air, water, food, and sunshine, without which humans cannot sustain physical life; a healthy body is necessary to house the inner soul. Unfortunately, the physically robust may lack spiritual awareness, and even those who are both physically fit and spiritually aware may be lacking in their proper relationship with others (Swami Rama, 1972). Yoga philosophy, by presenting us with various values, techniques, and disciplines, teaches us ways of establishing harmony among the various sides of life.

One who follows the path of yoga is called a "yogi" (male) or "yogini" (female).

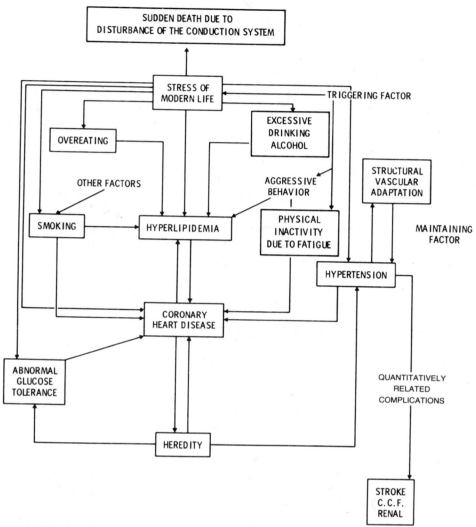

FIGURE 4.2 Relationship between emotional stress and coronary heart disease: a hypothesis. Reprinted by permission from Patel (1982, p. 26).

Yogis have developed "hatha yoga," or the physical path for the development of the body; "gnyana yoga," or the intellectual path; "bhakti yoga," or the devotional path; and "karma yoga," or the path of practical actions for the unfolding of the mind and realization of the soul. The different paths for developing the mind are based on the fact that the mind has three different aspects: knowing, feeling, and willing. In some people intellect predominates, in others emotions, and in still others action. For intellectuals, the yoga of knowledge is prescribed; for emotional people, the devotional yoga of love and faith; and for people of action, the yoga based on daily action. However, this does not mean that intellect, emotion, and action are exclusive of one another. A person who has a pain knows it, feels it, and takes some action to relieve it. Although one quality dominates in each individual, and the individual can thus benefit from adopting the suitable path, it is important to allow cross-currents from other systems to intermingle. "Raja yoga" is designated as the king of yoga because it is here that all systems converge. These systems are briefly described below.

Hatha Yoga, or the Physical Path

The main components of hatha yoga are (1) regulation of the mind and the body through 14 different breathing exercises, of which simple abdominal breathing is only the first exercise (this is described in more detail later in the "Method" section); (2) over 200 balanced physical postures developed to exercise every muscle in the body, in order to prevent skeletomuscular deterioration, to keep the body supple, and to tone up all organs in the body and insure their healthy functioning; and (3) exercises for awakening "kundalini" (a large reservoir of energy thought to be situated at the base of the spinal cord) and making this energy rise upward toward higher power. A detailed description of hatha yoga is beyond the scope of this chapter, but readers are referred to several interesting books (Iyanger, 1968; Liddel, Rabinovitch, & Rabinovitch, 1983; Monro, Nagarathna, & Nagendra, 1990).

Gnyana Yoga, or the Intellectual Path

"Gnyana" means "knowledge." This path of yoga leads to knowledge of one's self. "Who am I?" is the problem the person of knowledge must solve. According to yoga philosophy, ignorance is the cause of pain and misery in life. The lack of discrimination between temporary and permanent, real and unreal, truth and untruth, and self and nonself is at the roots of illness and disease. Intellectual exercise involves learning to discriminate between each of these through the process of self-analysis (Brunton, 1969) on the question of "Who am I?" It is not listing one's vices, virtues, or qualities, but solving the question of who one really is.

The first step involves asking, "Am I my body?" This is the meditation of the first stage. Until one can be sure of the answer, one cannot progress to the next stage; it may take days or even months. Attention must be brought back again and again to this central theme; interest must be captured and held upon it. As Brunton (1969) says, "The light of the mind is vague and diffused in the average man; what we have to do is to concentrate it until it becomes a powerful searchlight; then upon whatever object we throw this powerful beam we shall be able to see it clearly" (pp. 82–83). A discriminatory thought process should demonstrate that people are not their physical bodies, because bodies may be stricken with paralysis or sight, touch, hearing, taste, and smell may be destroyed, but that does not diminish people's perception of themselves as self-conscious beings. They may lose hands or legs or parts of other organs, but the sense of "I" remains as strong as ever. The self is not the body, but it is in the center of consciousness: A person who is in dreamless sleep is not aware of the physical body, yet somehow "I" still exists because the person awakes later and remembers his or her identity. When one has discarded the physical body as the sum total of existence or the "real self," one turns to the next stage of the inquiry into the true nature of the real self.

The second step involves asking, "Am I my mind? Am I what my mind thinks or feels: desire, doubt, hate, anger, like, dislike, passion, lust, hope, greed, fear, sympathy, attachments, hostility, or other thoughts or feelings?" The arguments that apply to the sleeping body also apply to sleeping emotions. Even when these seem dead in dreamless deep sleep, the "I" notion still emerges upon waking. Feelings, desires, and passions take people in many directions, but the sense of self remains unaffected. As in the conscious trance of the medieval Christian monk or a modern Indian yogi, it is possible to withdraw from all experiences of the outer world and from all emotions, but the sense of self-existence is still retained. Thus the self and emotions are two different things. A person's outlook may change with time and ideas are ever in flux, but in the midst of changing mind the sense of real self, the "I," does not change; it remains the same from cradle to grave, and thus neither the mind nor any of the emotional states constitutes the real being.

It is difficult to make these subtle matters comprehensible without indulging in abstract metaphysics, but once the power of discrimination develops, it is possible to dissociate one's self from the body and the mind. The faint recognition of dispassionate pure consciousness, which is capable of viewing the agitations of the body and the mind as an unaffected witness, is the essence of self-knowledge. When the knowledge of self is realized, six spiritual attainments are thought to be achieved (Siddhantalankar & Taraporevala, 1969); this is similar to psychoanalysts' belief that abnormality disappears when the cause of tension and neurosis is brought to the conscious self. Yoga exercises to gain knowledge cannot be claimed to be the only way to spiritual enlightenment. Many saints and wise people of other cultures and religions have attained this state of bliss. The six attainments described in yoga are as follows:

1. The agitation and passion of the mind subside, and the mind finds rest in peace and harmony. This peace and tranquility of the mind are what Jesus Christ may have referred to when He said, "Blessed are the peacemakers, for they shall be called the children of God" and "Peace I leave with you, my peace I give unto you."

2. With knowledge of the spiritual entity separate from the physical body, it becomes possible to control the body—pain and pleasure, heat and cold ("heat" and "cold" here mean different elements of the body, imbalances in which are considered to be at the basis of illness and diseases).

3. There is willing acceptance of one's worldly possessions as well as of the persons one is associated with in life. This does not however, mean that one should become lazy and make no effort to achieve worldly possessions or give up selecting people with whom one associates; it means that one should accept willingly whatever one gets after making the necessary effort.

4. One attains endurance of the hardship of life with a smiling face. This can be compared with the Alcoholics Anonymous prayer: "God grant me the serenity to accept the things I cannot change, courage to change the things I can, and wisdom to know the difference."

5. One develops an abiding faith and confidence in the design of the grand plan of the universe by the Supreme Power. Its acceptance is similar to accepting "Thy will be done."

6. Steadfastness, firmness of purpose, constancy, and resolution comprise a settled condition of the mind.

Bhakti Yoga, or the Devotional Path

The essence of the devotional path is love and sacrifice (Siddhantalankar & Taraporevala, 1969). It is an emotion of the heart. The relationship between the devotee and the object of devotion, between the soul and the personal God, is like a relationship between the lover and the beloved. All the major religions of the world—Hinduism, Islam, Judaism, and Christianity—believe in the existence of a personal God. Every song in the Koran begins with the name of Allah, and everyone is called upon to have faith in Allah: "It is the Allah who bringeth and quickeneth, it is Allah who rewardeth the good and punisheth the wicked." The Ten Commandments from Mount Sinai begin with this one: "I am the Lord thy God . . . Thou shalt have no other gods before me." Christ commanded His disciples to observe the greatest commandment of all: "And thou shalt love the Lord thy God with all thy heart, and with all thy soul, and with all thy mind, and with all thy strength." It is easier to worship a God with physical attributes than without them, and therefore the worship of a personal God is more prevalent in the world than that of an impersonal God. It is only what can be seen that excites the emotions. This is why temples and churches are built and devotees of some religions install images of their God or objects of their devotion. "The devotees of the unmanifest have a harder task, because the unmanifest is very difficult for embodied souls to realize" (Bhagavad-Gita XII-5). The idol installed, however, is not God. According to St. Paul, "Forasmuch then as we are the offspring of God, we ought not to think that the Godhead is like unto gold, or silver, or stone, graven by art and man's device," and according to the Ten Commandments, "Thou shalt not make unto thee any graven image."

The Bhagavad-Gita (XI-19,28) answers the question by metamorphosing the physical form of the beloved into universal form. One can visualize God in the form of the sun or the moon, myriads of twinkling stars, or mighty waves of the ocean; in monumental hills and dales, expanses of forest, or the ripple and roar of rivers; and in millions of men, women, and children who inhabit this earth. According to the Gita, these are His physical forms or glorious manifestations. God in His essential nature is invisible, but He manifests Himself through the magnificence of the universe, the vast expanse of the earth, the unfathomable waves of the deep oceans, the unscaled heights of the mountains, the starry heavens with suns and moons; all are the physical manifestations of the supreme divine power that keeps them animated. Martin Luther said, "Our Lord wrote the promise of the resurrection not in books alone but in every flower that blooms during the springtime." It is with the development of divine vision that one can see God everywhere and in everything.

The devotional path involves concentration on the object of devotion with contancy and faith. "Concentration" means that one is required to enter the core of the object of devotion and love until one feels totally merged into it and feels one with it. One completely loses one's sense of separate identity. This approach has been described in the Bhagavad-Gita (XII-2) as "Mayi Manh Aveshya," the translation of which is similar to the following song: "Penetrating into Me, be absorbed in Me, lodge your mind in Me, make me your dearest delight with devotion undaunted." "Constancy" here means always, day and night, every single moment, abiding in the beloved. The third essential element of devotion is "faith"—not blind faith, but the faith that comes from factual and truthful experience. A devotee surrenders consciousness to the Super-Consciousness; all thoughts, feelings, and actions are surrendered to God. The devotee must accept that human beings are frail and cannot be the sole arbiters of their destiny. "It is the power beyond us that presides over the sprouting of a sapling, chirping of a bird and the throbbing of the human heart. To surrender unto that Will is the only consolation of man and unto that Will have surrendered themselves the saints and sages of the world" (Siddhantalankar & Taraporevala, 1969, p. 309).

Karma Yoga, or the Path of Cause and Effect

The law of "karma" is the spiritual counterpart of the physical law of cause and effect. According to it, human beings are inextricably bound up in the wheel of cause and effect by their past and present actions. The time span covers not only this life but also past and future lives. Persons who are suffering through what they see as no fault of their own are likely to believe that this is injustice. They may rebel against God and ask, "Why was I born poor or ugly while others were born rich or beautiful for no apparent reason? How can it be fair for me to be disabled or in great pain while others seem to be enjoying life to the fullest? "Especially when misfortune befalls a person at birth, it is difficult to assign such emotional distress to the suppressed or repressed desires of Freudian theory. There is no point in accusing God, heaven, fate, or providence for the apparent injustice, for the law of karma can explain everything (Yogi Ramcharaka, 1964). Good and evil acquired through deeds by the soul throughout many incarnations are manifested as enduring characteristics from one incarnation to another, being modified here and there by further karma, but always pressing forward for expression and manifestation at the right time and in the right circumstances. According to this philosophy, there is no injustice. What each one of us is in this life depends upon what we have been and how we have acted in previous lives, and what we do now will decide our future in this life as well as in lives to come. We are not rewarded *for* our good deeds, but we receive our rewards *through and by* characteristics and qualities we acquire. We are our own judges as well as our own executioners.

According to this path, we do not commit sins against the God or Absolute who brought us into being, but rather against ourselves. We cannot possibly harm the Absolute, but we can harm each other and, in the process, write our destiny. As the human soul passes from one life to another, it learns new lessons, gathers new experiences, and learns to recognize the pain that invariably comes from wrong actions and happiness that comes from right actions. Just as a child learns not to touch a burning stove after it has burned its fingers or through the teachings of its parents, the mind learns to recognize how hurtful certain actions are and thus to avoid them. Even why some people fall prey to certain temptations while others do not can be explained by the karma of their past lives: The things that do not tempt the others now have been outlived in some former life, and they have profited by their past experience and teaching. If we do not learn the lesson well, says Yogi Ramcharaka, "we are compelled to sit on the same old school-bench and hear the same old lesson repeated until it is fairly driven into our consciousness" (1964, p. 247).

It is obvious that we can learn from bitter experiences in the present life. If we agonize over these painful experiences and wish that they had not happened, we are forgetting that they are the outcome of our past actions, and that without these painful experiences of the present it is unlikely that we can learn new knowledge or attain wisdom. People often object to this explanation on the ground that they do not remember experiences of their past lives. Karma yoga philosophy insists that these experiences, although not remembered, are not lost to us. They become part of the material of which our minds are composed, and are indelibly imprinted on the fabric of our characters. They exist in the form of our feelings, characteristics, inclinations, likes, dislikes, affinities, and repulsions. We are what we are because of the results of these experiences. Little by little, our characters are molded and shaped by these apparently forgotten pleasures and pains, happiness and sorrows, joys and miseries. The karma that we are acquiring now through our deeds, thoughts, and mental and spiritual relationships will be stored and will spring into action in the future when our bodies and environments are appropriate for its manifestations. We do not even have to wait for future lives, because if there are no opposing karma from our past lives, they may begin to manifest in this life.

According to this philosophy, we should strive to make our actions good, honest, and desirable without expecting fruits thereof. It is the expectations of goals or results that bring sorrow when they are not fulfilled. We must perform our duties and leave the rest to the governance of the universal laws that regulate the scheme of things. Attachment is the cause of every suffering; the only way to get rid of sorrow is through nonattachment. When we work in the form of selfless service to humanity, we can insure our own progress, for our progress depends on the progress of the whole community. Since each action must have a corresponding reaction, it stands to reason that our selfish actions will generate selfish reactions in others. The philosophy of "everyone for himself or herself" will give rise to individualism, groupism, regionalism, or nationalism, and will make people fight against people and nations against nations. Selfish actions thus ends in disintegration. Selfless actions without expectation of rewards as recommended by karma yoga will mirror similar responses in others; bring people closer together; and make divisions between families, communities, regions, and nations heal. "Everyone for others and none for himself or herself" is the quintessence of karma yoga. Not only individuals but races, nations, and the world have their collective karma. If the karma generated in the past is favorable, the races or nations flourish and become rich and influential. If, on the other hand, their collective karma is bad, they suffer and may even disappear from the face of the earth.

It would seem that the acceptance of the law of karma can dissolve anger, hurt, jealousy. mistrust, or resentment, and can lead to acceptance of the present with equanimity. Belief in the law of karma can strengthen our resolve to improve and become wiser. Whatever we have sown in the past must bear fruit, but we are free to sow what we choose in the present. We bring our destiny with us, but we can negate the past and create a new destiny for ourselves by our action. The law of karma teaches us that we should share and care, be compassionate and kind, and reach out to others for the ultimate good of our souls and destinies. The modern theory of advocating social support and discarding goal-directed, angry, hostile Type A behavior is a step in the right direction toward the teachings of karma yoga and bhakti yoga. Altruism, in the end, is for our own good.

Raja Yoga, or the Integrated Path

Raja yoga, the king of yoga, is an integration of all systems of yoga. The exponent of this yoga was Patanjali, who embodied his teachings in 185 aphorisms (see Johnson, 1970) to fight against the afflictions of humankind over 2000 years ago. It is sometimes known as the "eightfold spiritual path." The eight steps are (1) "yama," or the five abstentions; (2) "niyama," or the five observances; (3) "asanas," or over 200 balanced exercise postures; (4) "pranayama," or regulation of the breath or the life force; (5) "pratyahara," or withdrawal of the senses; (6) "dharana," or concentration; (7) "dhyana," or contemplation; and (8) "samathi," or the meditative state. The five abstentions and five observances may be considered the Ten Commandments of yoga and are similar to the Ten Commandments of the Bible. They simply advise people to conduct their everyday lives in a moral and peaceful manner. An individual does not become wise just by listening to a sermon or by reading a good book without making real efforts. If people want their friends and families to be helpful and kind, then they must be helpful and kind to them; if they want their homes to be beautiful and cheerful, then they must bring beautiful things into them. A person who cultivates the habit of being kind, compassionate, loving, and forgiving will be rewarded by similar surroundings. The most important ingredient in the practice of raja yoga is faith. In faith people believe not only with their brains, but also with their bodies and souls.

The five abstentions are abstentions from violence, lying, stealing, sensuality, and greed. As part of nonviolence, yoga also prescribes a strictly vegetarian diet, although dairy products (which do not involve the killing of life) are allowed. Eggs represent potential life and are banned. Abstention from violence does not merely mean no killing; it is equivalent to universal brotherhood. Abstention from lying is considered honesty and truthfulness in everyday behavior. Abstention from stealing is upholding the rights of others. Abstention from sensuality means a life of simplicity. Finally, abstention from greed includes charity to all in words and deeds.

The five observances are purification, contentment, self-discipline, studiousness, and surrender to God or the Higher Self. Purification means purity of the body and the mind. Cleanliness of the body and the environment is necessary in maintaining the health of the body and the mind. It is the meaning behind the saying "Cleanliness is next to godliness." Contentment is willing acceptance of things as they are with regard to oneself as well as others. It does not mean that one should not work for achievement or give up pursuits; all it means is that one should accept what is finally given without blaming others. Self-discipline is defined in the Bhagavad-Gita as restraint of the body, speech, and mind. Its meaning thus includes "See no evil, speak no evil, hear no evil." Studiousness is the study of one's self by whatever means and is generally conveyed by the aphorism "Know thyself." The last observance of surrendering to God is accepting the fact that despite the numerous plans we make for ourselves, the grand plan of the universe is not of our making. Each of us is but a tiny speck in the Maker's plan of this glorious world.

The physical postures involve learning to control, regulate, and become aware of one's physical existence. During the various exercises, breathing, with its inhalation, exhalation, and pause, bears a certain relationship to the sequence of the body movements. One is required to give complete mental attention to each movement, to the exclusion of everything else. Through practice, this awareness is heightened to such an extent that it completely fills the field of consciousness. Similar to hatha yoga in this regard are tai-chi, the dervish dances of the Sufi, and the Alexander technique of sensory awareness. By regularly practicing single-minded concentration on body movements, the practitioner gradually strengthens his or her own personality, and the different bodily functions become more integrated with one another as well as with personality. A great deal of energy that lies dormant in the body is awakened, and the person feels radiant with vitality and energy. Patanjali noted that any posture that is not fatiguing is good for spiritual exercise.

Regulation of breathing is the next stage that enables one to reach the innermost consciousness. The fifth stage, withdrawal of the senses, involves deep muscle relaxation of the body on an empty stomach, bladder, and bowel in a quiet, semidark environment. The reason for observing this rule is to cut down on visceral impulses going to the brain. The next three stages—concentration, contemplation, and the meditative state—together form the practice of meditation. Because breathing regulation, deep relaxation, and meditation are the most important parts of the therapy program my colleagues and I offer, they are described later (see "Method" section) in the manner in which the information about them is imparted to potential clients.

Assessment

Clinical Applications

It would seem that yoga therapy can be useful in many psychosomatic conditions. It has never been tried in the true sense of its teaching in clinical settings, but applications of its various aspects have been made. The majority of the studies have been uncontrolled and have used small samples. Most of the controlled studies are in the area of hypertension and coronary heart disease, and there are promising observations in regard to anxiety states, asthma, and diabetes. Those wishing to review this literature more comprehensively are referred to an extensive bibliography of 1600 references on scientific studies on yoga and meditation (Monro, Ghosh, & Kalish, 1989). A few controlled studies in the areas of hypertension, coronary heart disease, and asthma are described here.

Hypertension and Primary Prevention of Coronary Heart Disease

Although it is not possible to carry out a double-blind trial of behavior therapy, randomized controlled trials have been carefully executed. These have used a variety of relaxation techniques, with or without some form of biofeedback, and often combined with stress mangement techniques. They have been reviewed in detail elsewhere (Johnston, 1987; Patel, 1990). Successful clinical trials require not only experimental vigor, but also clinical flexibility. Resolving such competing demands is not easy in a single trial. However, the sheer number of trials—each with some deficiency, but usually of a different kind—makes it possible to draw broad conclusions. Most experimental groups have shown some reduction in blood pressure, and approximately half of them have shown statistically significant reductions in blood pressure compared with control groups.

Most of the studies that failed to show meaningful reductions in blood pressure with various relaxation techniques, yogic or otherwise, usually omitted some of the essential ingredients of the treatment. In some cases, the procedure was diluted to such an extent that it must fail to achieve an important therapeutic ingredient, namely, a change in day-to-day behavior as well as beliefs and attitudes of the clients (Goldstein, Shapiro, Thananopavarn, & Sambhi, 1982; Crits-Christoph, Luborsky, Kron, & Fishman, 1978). Some investigators made no efforts to generalize therapeutic effects to daily life. Others included inappropriate samples, such as patients who had been on antihypertensive drugs until a few days before the trial and hence failed to show real therapeutic effects, because it is well known that the blood pressure of those who stop medications does not usually rise to its original level immediately but takes several weeks (Luborsky et al., 1982). Some investigators studied patients with rather low initial blood pressure (Surwit, Shapiro, & Good, 1978) or imposed inflexible and demanding schedules, which can interfere with adequate learning (Frankel, Patel, Horwitz, Friedwald, & Gaardner, 1978).

It is important to remember that even where investigators (including my colleagues and I) have claimed to use yoga therapy, they have used only parts of yoga and have also added other components. For example, we apply yoga philosophy in a subtle and indirect manner to enable clients to reduce such negative emotions as anger and hostility, to increase tolerance and forgiveness, and to develop compassion and caring attitudes. We largely omit religious connotations, and point out desirable behaviors without demanding specific drills or record keeping. We predominantly train clients in the techniques of diaphragmatic breathing (pranayama, or Stage 4 of raja yoga), deep muscle relaxation (pratyahara, or Stage 5 of raja yoga), visualization and meditation (dharana, dhyana, and samathi, or Stages 6, 7, and 8 of raja yoga), and integration of these techniques into their daily lives to facilitate balanced attitudes or equanimity. These and the additional educational material we use are summarized in the "Method" section. In our research, we did not prescribe a vegetarian diet or physical exercise to avoid confounding of results, although for ethical reasons we recommended a prudent diet to both the treatment and control groups. In the short term, our program as well as many other relaxation therapies can reduce blood pressure; but unless patients integrate these techniques in daily life and change their stress-prone attitudes and behavior, the long-term maintenance of such reductions is doubtful.

In one study carried out in an industrial setting (Patel, et al., 1981), we randomized 192 high-risk subjects into treatment and control groups. Subjects had been identified through a screening program as having two or more of the following risk factors: blood pressure of 140/90 mm Hg or more and not an antihypertensive medication; plasma cholesterol of 6.3 mmol/liter or more; and currently smoking 10 or more cigarettes per day. Subjects in both groups were given health education leaflets advising them to stop smoking, to reduce animal fat in the diet, and to remain under the supervision of their own doctors. They were also issued a booklet giving general information on blood pressure. In addition, treatment subjects attended light weekly 1-hour group meetings (each group included up to 10 subjects) for training in breathing, relaxation, meditation, and stress management based on yoga (see "Method" section). The training in relaxation was enhanced by the use of GSR biofeedback developed specifically for group use.

The groups were followed up after 8 weeks, 8 months, and 4 years. In a small subsample of 25 subjects in each group, we measured plasma renin activity and plasma aldosterone at the 8-week and 8-month follow-ups. We also assessed dietary changes by using 24-hour dietary recall diaries on 3 consecutive days initially, as well as at the 8-week and 8-month follow-ups. There was a significantly greater drop in blood pressure in the treatment group than in the control group at the 8-month follow-up. In those with an initial blood pressure of 140/90 or more, mean blood pressure fell from 166/101 to 143/89 mm Hg in the treatment group, compared with a fall from 160/98 to 149/97 mm Hg in the control group. We also found a significantly greater reduction in plasma renin activity and plasma aldosterone in the treatment group after 8 weeks, although not after 8 months. Analysis of dietary diaries filled out over a period of 3 consecutive days at entry, after 8 weeks, and after 8 months showed modest changes in the diet (greater in the control group), but no significant differences between the groups with regard to dietary fat, alcohol, or calories consumed. Their mean weight remained unchanged. Thus, the differences between the groups were likely to have resulted from relaxation therapy.

At the 4-year follow-up (Patel et al., 1985) 18% of the treatment group and 20% of the control group were on antihypertensive drugs. Despite the general tendency for blood pressure to rise over 4 years, the differences between the groups were largely maintained. Blindly assessed EKG using the Minnesota code (Rose & Blackburn, 1968) revealed five new events (two probable and three possible myocardial infarction in the control group, compared with one possible myocardial infarction in the treatment group. In addition, there was one fatal myocardial infarction in the control group. Fischer's exact test for this 6:1 difference in the objective data of cardiovascular incidence was statistically significant ($p < .05$).

On the basis of reduction in traditional risk factors, we predicted a 12% reduction in coronary heart disease incidence, using a multiple logistic function. ("Multiple logistic function" is a formula that can be developed from a large prospective epidemiological observational study. By using the magnitude of changes observed in each of the major risk factors in any intervention study, possible reduction in coronary heart disease incidence can be predicted. We used a formula derived from the London Whitehall study; another formula derived from the Framingham study also exists.) The observed reduction in incidence during this 4 years was much greater than that predicted. This could be attributed to chance variation, but it also suggests that relaxation-based psychological therapy may reduce coronary heart disease through pathways other than through the established risk factors.

Transferring Techniques from the Laboratory to Clinical Practice

Nonpharmacological measures are gaining popularity in the reduction of mildly elevated blood pressure. Their efficacy has been reported in a number of clinical trials. However, efficacy in a trial does not automatically guarantee effectiveness in everyday clinical practice. As far as relaxation therapy is concerned, the important questions are these: Can clinicians be successfully trained as relaxation and stress management therapists? Will patients make desirable behavioral changes and maintain them in the longterm?

To see whether we could effectively train general practitioners to implement therapy, we conducted a study of 103 patients (Patel & Marmot, 1988a) who had previously participated in a large trial of drug treatment of mild hypertension (Medical Research Council Working Party, 1985). In Phase 2 (Medical Research Council Working Party, 1986), some 2000 subjects who had completed 6 years of the placebo-controlled antihypertensive drug trial (Medical Research Council Working Party, 1985) were randomly assigned to continue using the drug or placebo or to stop using it. Our subsample of 103 patients was further randomly assigned (according to a factorial design) to receive or not to receive relaxation therapy (relaxation techniques plus stress management). Patients' general practitioners and their nurses were trained over a weekend workshop, and supplied with therapy manuals and handouts for the patients. The training protocol was the same we have used elsewhere (see Table 4.3, below).

The analysis of blood pressure at the 1-year follow-up showed the overall changes in systolic and diastolic blood pressure to be more favorable in the treatment groups (no drug plus relaxation, drug plus relaxation, no placebo plus relaxation, and placebo plus relaxation) than in the control groups (no drug plus no relaxation, drug plus no relaxation, no placebo plus no relaxation and placebo plus no relaxation). An analysis of covariance, controlling for differences in initial blood pressures between the groups, showed the adjusted difference between the groups for systolic blood pressure to be 7.5 mm Hg ($p = .007$) and for diastolic blood pressure to be 2.2 mm Hg (n.s.). The most important observation was that the subgroup that stopped taking antihypertensive drugs but was offered relaxation therapy maintained lower blood pressure, whereas the subgroup that stopped taking drugs but was not offered relaxation showed a significant rise in blood pressure, amounting to 14 mm Hg systolic and 5 mm Hg diastolic; this was comparable to the observation in Phase 2 of the Medical Research Council trial (Medical Research Council Working Party, 1986). The development of new cardiovascular events was assessed by documentation from patients' general practitioners, as well as by blindly coded EKGs. There were five new events in the control group, compared with one in the treatment group. This study was not aimed at studying morbidity, and the number of cardiovascular events was small; nonetheless, when these results are taken in conjunction with our previous report of six events in the control group versus one in the treatment group (Patel et al., 1985), the suggestion that this therapy may reduce coronary risk becomes stronger.

Secondary Prevention of Coronary Heart Disease

Among the investigators using yoga-based techniques including a vegatarian diet, Ornish's group stands out as the most scientific one. In their earlier study (Ornish et al., 1983), they used noninvasive endpoint measures to assess the short-term effects of intervention on coronary heart disease. They reported inprovement in cardiac risk factors and better functional status, including a marked reduction in the frequency and severity of angina as well as the amount of angina medication consumed, improved myocardial perfusion, and improved left ventricular function. However, the subjects in these trials were taken to retreats away from the pressures of everyday life and work, and follow-up periods were short. In their more recent study (Ornish et al., 1990), they randomly assigned 48 middle-aged male and female outpatients with angiographically documented coronary artery disease to experimental and usual-care control groups. The patients in the experimental group were prescribed an extremely low-fat vegetarian diet and moderate aerobic exercise (brisk walking that sustained 50–80% of their maximum heart rate); were given training in stress management, including enhancement of social support among the group members to increase compliance; and were advised to stop smoking. The stress management training included yoga-based stretching exercises, breathing techniques, meditation, relaxation, and visual imagery. The patients were asked to practice these at least 1 hour per day, and were given 1-hour audiocassette tapes to help them practice. The patients in the control group were not asked to make these life style changes, but were free to do so.

In the experimental group, compared with the control group, there was a significantly greater fall in total cholesterol (24.3%) and low-density lipoprotein cholesterol (37.4%), as well as in apolipoprotein B; high-density lipoprotein cholesterol did not change substantially. Patients in the experimental group reported a 91% reduction in the frequency of angina, a 42% reduction in the duration of angina, and a 28% reduction in the severity of angina pain. In contrast, the control group reported a 165% rise in frequency, a 95% rise in duration, and a 39% rise in severity of angina pain. The investigators assessed 195 coronary artery lesions in both groups by quantitative coronary angiography at baseline and after about 1 year. The average percentage diameter of stenosis regressed from 40% to 37.8% in the experimental group, but progressed from 42.7% to 46.1% in the control group ($p = .001$, two-tailed). When lesions only greater than 50% stenosed were analyzed, the average percentage diameter of stenosis regressed from 61.1% to 55.8% in the experimental group, but progressed from 61.7% to 64.4% in the control group ($p = 0.03$, two-tailed). Coronary artery disease, the authors commented, is a progressive disease, and the control group's results demonstrate that the usual advice to change life style and medications is not sufficient to halt progression. On the other hand, the definite evidence of regression over the comparatively short period of 1 year in the experimental group is very encouraging.

Asthma

A number of studies reporting beneficial effects of yoga on asthma have been published (Bhole, 1967; Hoensberger & Wilson, 1973; Erskin & Schonel, 1979; Goyeche, Abdo, & Ikemi, 1982; Murphy, Sahaj, & Silaramaraju, 1983). However, most of these studies have been uncontrolled and have used subjective measures, and follow-up has been short. One controlled study (Nagarathna & Nagendra, 1985), however, recruited 53 pairs of asthmatics (matched for age, sex, and severity) attending hospital outpatient clinics, and randomly allocated each pair to a treatment or a control group. Both groups continued their usual medical treatment. In addition, the treatment group attended 2½-hour sessions daily for 2 weeks, during which they were trained in an integrated set of yoga exercises (including breathing exercises, physical postures, meditation, and devotional practice). After the training, they were asked to continue practising these exercises 65 minutes a day. Long-term follow-up (54 months) showed a significant reduction in the experimental group's number of asthma attacks and amount of medication used; there was also a significant increase in peak flow rate in the treatment group compared with the control group.

Quality of Life and Adverse Effects with Relaxation Therapy

Psychological and social functioning has been assessed in some studies of behavioral therapy of hypertension. The results have shown reductions in anxiety (Bali, 1979; Jorgensen, Housten, & Zurawski, 1981), anxiety and depression (Wadden, 1984), and a variety of psychosomatic symptoms, as well as an increased sense of well-being (Peters, Benson, & Peters, 1977). Four years after the training described in the preceding section, my colleagues and I assessed the following aspects of life: relationships at work, general health, enjoyment of life, personal and family relationships, general level of physical energy, sexual life, concentration at work, mental well-being, and social life (Steptoe, Patel, Marmot, & Hunt, 1987; Patel & Marmot, 1987). For each of these aspects, a greater percentage of subjects in the treatment group than in the control group reported improvements. The differences were statistically significant for the first four aspects of life. Among those who reported continuing to practice relaxation regularly, significant ($p < .01$) improvements occurred in six out of nine aspects: relationships at work, concentration at work, general health, enjoyment of life, personal and family relationships, and mental well-being. However, there was no correlation between improvement in various aspects of life and reduction in blood pressure, nor was such a correlation reported in the other studies cited above. This could mean that such positive effects may represent a different pathway through which relaxation could lead to prevention of coronary heart disease.

Only a very small and nonsignificant number of subjects (more in the control group than in the treatment group) reported deterioration in some of these aspects of life. Therefore, such deterioration could not be ascribed to therapy (Patel & Marmot, 1987). There are, however, some anecdotal reports of clients' reporting hallucinations or having a psychotic episode; in nearly all these cases, the patients had had previous psychiatric illness or disregarded the therapist's advice about practicing only 20–30 minutes once or twice a day. Prolonged practice of meditation has been reported to precipitate psychosis, perhaps as a result of prolonged sensory deprivation (Benson et al., 1974). Occasionally patients do complain of feeling excessively fatigued, but this can nearly always be overcome by changing practice time. Wolpe (1958), on the other hand, reported that some patients became depressed with relaxation. In my experience with hypertensive patients, the technique, if practiced as prescribed, is remarkably safe. None of the side effects has ever resulted in a patient's dropping out of a study, in my experience.

Indications and Contraindications

On the basis of the results my colleagues and I have obtained, I would recommend this therapy for any hypertensive patient—in conjunction with antihypertensive drugs in moderately severe hypertension, but on its own initially in mild hypertension. In the latter case, antihypertensive drugs should be added if blood pressure fails to be controlled satisfactorily. The rationale is as follows.

The benefits of treating severe or moderately severe hypertension by means of antihypertensive drugs have been demonstrated (Hamilton, Thompson, & Wisniewski, 1964; Veterans Administration Cooperative Group, 1967, 1970), but the results of drug trials for mild hypertension are conflicting. The largest placebo-controlled trial of treatment of mild hypertension (diastolic blood pressure 90–109 mm Hg), involving nearly 18,000 patients, showed that the reduction in blood pressure achieved by means of antihypertensive drugs did not reduce coronary heart disease or save lives, whereas the rate of undesirable side effects was quite high (Medical Research Council Working Party, 1981, 1985). However, lowering of mild hypertension is important, because it has been shown that two-thirds of coronary heart disease mortality and three-quarters of stroke mortality occurs in patients with mild hypertension (Rose, 1981). Three-quarters of all hypertensives are in the mild hypertension category (Hypertension Detection and Follow-Up Program Cooperative Group, 1979).

It must, however, be stated that the Hypertension Detection and Follow-Up program Cooperative Group (1979) showed that "stepped-care" treatment of hypertension reduced coronary as well as all-cause mortality significantly, compared with mortality in the "referred-care" group. Those allocated to the referred-care group were referred to their usual source of medical care, while those allocated to the stepped-care group were treated more intensively in specialized centers. This treatment was completely free of charge; appointments were made to suit individual patients, and if an appointment was not kept, the patient was immediately contacted; free transportation was provided if necessary. A doctor was on duty 24 hours a day to deal with any medical problem that might arise. During the 5 years of follow-up mortality from both cardiovascular and noncardiovascular causes was significantly lower in the stepped-care group in Stratum I (diastolic blood pressure 90–104 mm Hg).

The main criticism of the study is that it was not a placebo-controlled study but a comparison of good versus ordinary care. Since the number of noncardiac deaths (from diabetes, gastrointestinal and respiratory diseases, and cancer) also fell in the stepped-care group, it can be argued that the results reflected the quality of care rather than the value of antihypertensive drugs. The fact that the small benefit of reducing mild hypertension by antihypertensive drugs may be outweighed by metabolic and other disadvantages of drugs was also borne out by the Multiple Risk Factor Intervention Trial Research Group (1982): A significantly greater number of deaths occurred in the subgroup of hypterensives receiving antihypertensive drugs in a stepped-care fashion than in the usual-care control group.

Even though a vast number of people may have mildly elevated blood pressure, the rate of complications in this group is low—approximately 1% per year (Hypertension Detection and Follow-Up Program Cooperative Group, 1979). Thus, even if antihypertensive drugs are effective, a large proportion of this population has to be medicated on a lifelong basis to prevent a small number of complications. In view of these facts, a great deal of attention is being paid to nonpharmacological measures; it is not surprising that the Joint National Committee on Detection, Evaluation, and Treatment of High Blood Pressure (1984) from the United States has recommended that in all patients with mild hypertension, nonpharmacological treatment should be tried first and antihypertensive medication should be added only when the initial treatment fails to produce satisfactory control of blood pressure.

Yoga-based therapy is contraindicated in most cases of malignant or secondary hypertension, in view of the critical nature of these conditions. It should also not be tried in depressive or psychotic patients.

Compliance, Resistance, and Maintenance

Long-Term Compliance

Since hypertension is often asymptomatic, motivation to continue with time-consuming relaxation practice tends to be poor, and without compliance long-term benefits cannot be maintained. At our 4-year follow-up we were disappointed with the compliance rate, and frankly surprised. Further analysis (Steptoe et al., 1987) clearly disclosed that the degree of success depended on the degree of compliance, as shown in Table 4.1. At the 4-year follow-up, only 17% of the patients admitted practicing relaxation regularly; these, of course received the greatest benefit. Of the remaining patients, those who had not given up relaxation practice altogether did better than those who had abandoned the practice at least 18 monthe earlier.

All was not lost, however. We probed deeper to look at how often patients were doing their "minirelaxation" (one-breath relaxation) in daily life, which was part of our efforts to generalize the therapeutic effects; we also looked at how often they used intellectual strategies to reappraise or redefine situations as less threatening, and told themselves to calm down or moderate their responses. Fortunately, 80–90% of our patients had practiced both of these strategies "often" or "sometimes," and these patients did retain a considerable reduction in blood pressure compared with those who did not.

On the whole, we concluded that patients who find it easier to fit relaxation into their daily schedule, whose lives are unlikely to be disrupted by relaxation practices, who develop positive attitude to the therapy offered, whose families are generally supportive, and whose quality of life has generally improved are more likely to comply with one or more components of the therapy. Patients with painful or unpleasant symptoms (e.g., tension headaches or migraines) are usually more motivated to comply with prescribed life style changes. Ornish's group (Ornish et al., 1990) found that in patients with angina or proven coronary heart disease, the overall adherence was excellent.

Resistance

Sometimes people feel disappointed because they do not get what they expect from meditation. Others describe all kinds of experiences, such as floating sensation, visions, out-of-body sensations, tingling, or numbness. Beginners, who may never have had such experiences before, may become concerned. Some may feel too energetic while others may feel too lazy after a session. These experiences probably occur as a result of altered sense of consciousness and serve as mere distractions, having no

TABLE 4.1. Degree of Compliance and Change in Blood Pressure from Entry to 4-Year Follow-Up

	% of subjects	Mean change in systolic blood pressure (mm Hg)	Mean change in diastolic blood pressure (mm Hg)
Relaxes regularly	17	−10.9 ± 6.7	−7.0 ± 3.2
Does not relax regularly	83	−6.3 ± 3.0	−1.7 ± 1.9
Last relaxed less than 18 months ago	76	−10.8 ± 3.7	−4.5 ± 2.3
Last relaxed over 18 months ago	24	+2.2 ± 4.4	+4.2 ± 3.0
"Often" or "sometimes" integrates relaxation into daily life	83	−7.6 ± 4.1	−2.3 ± 2.5
"Never" integrates relaxation into daily life	17	−4.6 ± 5.8	+4.4 ± 3.6
"Often" or "sometimes" tells self to calm down	90	−7.9 ± 2.5	−2.9 ± 2.5
"Never" tells self to calm down	10	+6.1 ± 8.7	0.0 ± 3.5

Note. Adapted from Steptoe, Patel, Marmot, & Hunt (1987, pp. 103–104).

other significance. If they are explained as such, the concerns usually disappear. Another factor causing resistance or failure in long-term maintenance in a "quick-fix" society is the demand made upon clients' time to practice this therapy. Similarly, some may feel that yoga and meditation belong to a foreign culture, and that adopting such practices may change their feelings for their own religion or that someone will ridicule them. Proper explanation of the scientific principles underlying yoga-based therapy usually allay these fear or concerns.

Some patients are afraid of taking up meditation because they fear that it will make them neglect their responsibilities and their duties to their families. Meditation is not an escape from social responsibilities or a defense against the problems of life. Neither is it a withdrawal from life, although such withdrawal may occur temporarily when a practitioner seeks solitude purposely for a short period. The experience of most therapists suggests that meditation in fact leads patients to a deeper appreciation of their relationship to their families, friends, communities, nations, and even the world. Meditators play their roles in society just as other people do. They do not have to be politicians or protesters, if that is not their style, but meditation does not prevent them from doing so. Mahatma Gandhi fought social injustice on a grand scale and yet led a spiritual life. Meditation seems to change the way its practitioners tackle problems, not the problems themselves. By keeping their mental state balanced and undisturbed, meditators prevent damage not only to themselves, but also to others.

Maintenance

The biggest problem in maintaining benefit in the long term is motivating patients to comply with recommended practice. In retrospect, we feel that the relative success we had in maintaining benefit in our study in an industrial setting (Patel et al., 1985) must have resulted in large part from the active participation of the physician and a number of nurses from the occupational medical department, who were available on a daily basis for counseling, reassurance, or general reinforcement of the therapy. Unfortunately, not all controlled studies of relaxation therapy have been equally successful, especially in the long term. Three main factors are likely to determine successful outcome: (1) the components of the behavioral treatment package, (2) characteristics of the therapist, and (3) characteristics of the patients to whom the treatment is applied (Patel & Marmot, 1988b).

Therapeutic Program. Many of us talk about relaxation and stress management therapy, but we all mean something different. It varies from providing cursory advice to take things easy or supplying a relaxation tape to offering biofeedback, hypnosis, or cognitive restructuring. In our experience, a more comprehensive program with considerable efforts to generalize the treatment components to everyday life is more likely to be successful. The theoretical assumptions underlying this are as follows: (1) People differ in their needs and in how different components of the treatment package appeal to them; (2) different strategies are required to cope with different situations in daily life; and (3) generalization of behavioral and cognitive techniques is necessary to maintain round-the-clock therapeutic benefit.

Characteristics of the Therapist. A therapist's committment to the therapy, enthusiasm about and belief in the therapy, previous experience, educational background, communication mode, and ability to form rapport with patients are some of the factors that can affect the results. The successful therapist is likely to be the one who is able to develop empathy with patients; who not only listens but also demonstrates interest in and concern for the patients; who makes the patients feel that he or she has time to talk to them; who talks in a language they can understand; who understands patients' medical problems and is able to discuss them intelligently; and, importantly, who is able to help patients remember the advice they have been given.

In an ongoing study, we used five therapists of different backgrounds and experience, but the same intervention protocol and a homogeneous group of patients (all civil servants). We found that the three medically qualified therapists (an internist, a psychiatrist, and a general practitioner) were equally effective, whereas the patients treated by a clinical psychologist and a yoga teacher actually showed a *rise* in both systolic and diastolic blood pressure (Patel & Marmot, 1988b). Even in a study in which all therapists were general practitioners of similar educational background who trained their own long-term patients using the same intervention protocol, there were individual differences in effectiveness as judged by the average reductions in blood pressure the patients achieved (Patel & Marmot, 1988b).

The presence of a therapist does, however, seem to be necessary. Brauer, Horlicks, Nelson, Farquhar, and Agras (1979) reported blood pressure reductions of

11 (systolic) and 6 (diastolic) mm Hg when relaxation was taught by a therapist, compared with 5 and 1 mm Hg, respectively, when patients were supplied with relaxation tapes and were asked to practice at home. At a 6-month follow-up, the therapist-taught patients showed mean reductions in blood pressure of 18 and 10 mm Hg, respectively, compared with increases of 1 and 5 mm Hg, respectively, in the tape-taught patients.

A good therapist is one who can motivate patients to comply with therapy in the long term. This requires the power of tactful persuasion. Patients are also more likely to accept recommendation from a therapist they generally respect. It is not surprising, therefore, that an experienced therapist with a wider educational background is more effective than a younger, inexperienced, or medically naive therapist. It is also important that contact with the therapist and a generally supportive relationship between therapist and patient be maintained over the long term if therapeutic effect is to continue.

Characteristics of the Patients. Successful outcome depends upon patients' initial level of blood pressure, willingness to comply with prescribed practice, attitudes toward therapy, availability of time, support from their families, benefits from the ongoing therapy with respect to other aspects of life, degree of psychological distress, number of life events in the recent past, and personalities. On the whole, the higher the initial blood pressure, the greater the decrease that can be expected from this therapy (Jacob, Kraemer, & Agras, 1977). For long-term efficacy, we have found that belief in the effectiveness of therapy is important. It is not essential that patients believe in the therapy from the outset. Many of our patients, who are not volunteers but recruited through screening programs, do have a healthy skepticism about the benefits until they see their reductions in blood pressure or experience a better quality of life. However, ultimate belief in the treatment is necessary before people can be motivated to comply with its practice. We thought that the best measure of this belief would be patients' willingness to recommend this therapy to other people with a similar condition. At our 4-year follow-up, we found that 75% of men and 91% of women were sufficiently convinced of the treatment's benefits to recommend it to others. Sympathetic support from family members, without reminding patients to do their relaxation practice, also predicted successful outcome.

When patients have been recruited through screening programs, they represent hypertensive patients in the general population, and hence their responses tend to be more satisfactory and predictable. My own experience as well as that of others suggests that such satisfactory outcomes may not be seen when patients are referred from hypertension clinics or by other physicians, because their blood pressure is difficult to control or because they are generally "problem" patients. Patients who are poor compliers with drug therapy (regardless of side effects), those who have difficult home circumstances, those who stand to gain from their sick role, those who are too busy to give this slow-acting therapy an adequate chance to work, and those who are nihilistic are unlikely to benefit from behavioral therapy.

Even when the therapy has been successfully tried and tested before, the patients have been properly recruited and randomized, and previously successful therapists are used, investigators may fail to replicate the results in a randomized controlled trial. As public awareness regarding risk factors and some of the nonpharmacological measures to alter them increases, control group patients feeling deprived of an active therapy are likely to make every effort they can to change their health status for the better. Such changes were thought to play an important part in an inconclusive primary prevention trial of coronary heart disease (Multiple Risk Factor Intervention Trial Research Group, 1982), and may have been partly responsible, along with poor compliance, for the disappearance of the differences between relaxation and control groups at 3-year follow-up in another study (Agras, Taylor, Kraemer, Southam, & Schneider, 1987). Motivating asymptomatic hypertensive patients to comply with time-consuming practice is difficult, although if there is a choice between lifelong medication or modification of behavior, most patients will opt for the latter. Even those patients already on antihypertensive drugs may be willing to try this therapy if there is a possibility that their drug requirements can be reduced substantially or better control of blood pressure can be achieved.

Some researchers have shown that neurotic individuals and those patients with negative self-image seem to do less well (Shkhvatsabaya, 1982; Richter-Heinrich, Knust, Muller, Schmidt, & Sprung 1975) than those with less neuroticism and positive self-image. Eagan, Kogan, Garber, and Jarrett (1983) found that patients with current psychological distress and a higher incidence of stressful life events in the months prior to relaxation therapy also seemed to be more resistant. These investigators did not find that level of compliance or expectation of success predicted outcome during a follow-up of 12 months. On the other hand, Agras, Horne, and Taylor (1982) found the opposite to be true. They told one group to expect immediate lowering of blood pressure and the other group to expect delayed lowering of blood pressure from relaxation, and found that the reductions in systolic blood pressure in the two groups were 17.0 and 2.4 mm Hg, respectively ($p = .001$). Mean diastolic blood pressure did not differ, however. The training in relaxation was carried out over three sessions in a single day, which is not quite the same as long-term relaxation therapy.

Despite some of these observations, the characteristics of patients who are likely to respond well and those who are not likely to benefit much from behavioral therapy need to be investigated further.

Method

The treatment aims as explained to patients in our program are outlined in Table 4.2. First, the nature of stress is explained: what stress is; what external stressors are; what makes a person vulnerable to stressors; and how personality, beliefs, and attitudes can interact with external stressors to create stress. Although stressors can be numerous, most stressful situations can be analyzed in terms of what they create: frustration, conflict, and pressure. The contribution of stress to hypertension is also explained, as well as how to recognize when one is under stress, including its mental, emotional, behavioral, and physiological symtoms and signs. To help reduce stress, various cognitive, behavioral, and physiological coping strategies are discussed throughout the course.

TABLE 4.2.   Treatment Aims

Stressors are the factors that cause stress. They can be external or internally generated, and can cause stress when a person is in a vulnerable state. They can be analyzed in terms of frustration, conflict, and pressure. Stress responses are the body's and the mind's reactions to stressors and can be recognized by mental, emotional, behavioral, or physiological symptoms. The coping strategies can be cognitive (i.e., intellectual), behavioral, or physiological, as shown.

Examples of stressors	Examples of stress responses	Examples of coping strategies
Frustration (a goal's being blocked)	*Mental and emotional signs* (lack of concentration, memory lapses, anxiety, fear, panic, anger, hostility, aggression)	*Cognitive strategies* (developing awareness, detachment, self-esteem, and compassion; learning anger management)
Conflict (uncertainty, making choices)	*Behavioral signs* (smoking, drinking, overeating, Type A behavior, social withdrawal)	*Behavioral strategies* (assertiveness, social support, resilient behavior)
Pressure (time pressure, emotional pressure)	*Physiological signs* (erratic breathing, tense muscles, aches and pains, fatigue, palpitation, sweating, dry mouth, indigestion, allergies, hypertension, depression)	*Physiological strategies* (breathing exercises, relaxation, visualization, meditation, biofeedback)

   To make treatment cost-effective, we carry out therapy for hypertensive patients during eight once-weekly 1½-hour sessions in a group setting. At every session, patients practice breathing and relaxation. Visual imagery is added in the second week, and meditation is added in the third week. Patients are connected to group GSR biofeedback in such a way that they hear their own biofeedback signal on one side of the headphone and simultaneously listen to common breathing, relaxation, and meditation instructions on the other side of the headphone. An outline of our week-by-week treatment protocol is given in Table 4.3.

   In the present chapter, it is not possible to describe in detail everything that is talked about or discussed in group sessions. As examples, however, the ways in which breathing, relaxation, visualization, and meditation are introduced to a group are given below. For a fuller description of the strategies used in our program, readers are referred to my book on stress management (Patel, 1991).

Introduction to the Breathing Exercise: Therapist's Remarks to the Group

Breathing is essential to life. Life cannot exist without breath. Breathing is usually involuntary, being controlled (like all other internal functions) by the autonomic nervous system and generally remaining outside of our awareness. Our brains filter out many of the events that are constantly happening, in order to enable us to focus on more important things at hand. As a result, many people breathe shallowly and haphazardly, going against the natural rhythmic movements without noticing it. However, breathing is unique in that it can also be controlled by an act of will. Since

TABLE 4.3. Summary of Treatment Protocol

Session 1. The treatment plan, the biofeedback concept, and types of breathing in different states are explained; diaphragmatic breathing is demonstrated. A handout explaining some facts about high blood pressure and breathing exercises is distributed, together with relaxation instruction cassettes. The patients are asked to practice relaxation once a day (or, if possible, twice a day). Questions are answered. Relaxation is practiced.

Session 2. The nature of stress, and ways in which it may strain health, are explained. The importance of learning stress management is pointed out. A short film, "Understanding Stresses and Strains," made by Walt Disney Productions, is shown. The human function curve is explained. Creative imagery and its uses are explained. A handout listing biological, behavioral, and emotional signs of stress is distributed. Questions are answered. Relaxation is practiced.

Session 3. How stress responses can be analyzed, and how positive emotions and behaviors can be used to replace harmful or undesirable emotions and behaviors, are explained. The hows and whys of meditation are explained, supported by a handout giving more details on the subject. Questions are answered. Relaxation is practiced.

Session 4. Figures and graphs showing beneficial effects of relaxation and meditation in various studies are shown, to increase patients' belief in the methods used as well as to increase their motivation to comply with practice. Questions are answered. Relaxation is practiced.

Session 5. Ways of integrating relaxation into everyday life are discussed. Each patient is asked to list 10 situations he or she finds stressful and to practice one-breath relaxation either during or before those situations. Management of emotions such as anger, hostility, and aggression is discussed. A handout on how to develop effective communication skills is distributewd. Questions are answered. Relaxation is practiced.

Session 6. The protective effects of social support, as well as cultural and traditional aspects of life, are pointed out. Questions are answered, and general discussion and supportive relationships within the group are encouraged. Relaxation is practiced.

Session 7. The coronary-prone personality, including Type A behavior, is discussed. Those who identify themselves as Type A are encouraged to change their behavior. Possible characteristics of resilient behavior are discussed. Relaxation is practiced.

Session 8. The whole course is summarized. General free discussion is encouraged. The importance of regular practice and integration of the new positive behavior is re-emphasized, without giving the impression that life is going to be regimented with dos and don'ts. The emphasis is on making life more fulfilling and enjoyable. Relaxation is practiced.

---

we breathe between 16,000 and 20,000 times a day, it can be a very powerful tool in gaining some degree of control over autonomic functions.

Breathing According to Yoga and Its Scientific Meaning

Yoga masters spend years learning the intricate aspects of breathing. They believe that besides the body and the mind, there are other levels of existence. The one that links the body and the mind is considered to be the level of functioning, and the one that lies beyond the mind or thoughts is considered to be pure consciousness. The energy required for the level of functioning is called "prana," which literally means "life force." Some 3000 years ago, yogis with highly developed extrasensory perception pronounced that "life is in the breath." By "breath," they meant more than just the gaseous exchange that takes place between inspired air and blood circulating in the lungs. Even now, when someone gets a creative insight into something, we call it an "inspiration." When we hear great and wise people talking, we get "inspired." The more prana or life force one has, the more vital energy and mental alertness and awareness one also has. The person who radiates vitality and energy, and who has a kind of magnetic personality, has a particular abundance of life force. But what is this prana or life force? Here we return to breath, because breath is considered the vehicle for prana. When someone dies and the life force has left him or her, we say that the person has "expired," because life energy has left with the last breath. Thus through the language we use, we convey an intuitive recognition of the relationship between the breath and the vital energy—its necessity for life and its necessity for creativity. We all experience, from time to time, a great deal of vitality and clarity of mind, while at other times we experience a sense of having "no mental energy." The prana, in addition to breathing, includes food, water, and sunshine. In yoga philosophy they are all interconnected.

Yoga philosophy does not pay much attention to uniqueness of the individual. There is a positive longing to unite with the Universe. This may sound very "foreign," but when we realize that our bodies are constantly dissolving and reforming, it may make some sense. The thousands of individual carbon, hydrogen, oxygen, and other atoms that comprise the body are in constant exchange with the world outside. The modern technique of using radioisotopes, which allows us to trace the chemicals that enter and leave the body, demonstrates that 98% of the atoms of the entire body are replaced every year (see Dossey, 1982). Each structure of the body has its own rate of reformation: The lining of the stomach renews itself in 1 week, the skin is entirely replaced in 1 month, the liver is regenerated within 6 weeks. Some tissues are relatively slow to turn over—for example, the supporting tissue of the body, called "collagen." The bone, on the other hand, is especially dynamic. We all know that in the next 5 years we will have completely renewed our hair and our nails, but most people are unaware that in 5 years' time not a single atom of our present bodies will be here, so that in a way it can be said that our bodies will not exist!

There is a constant flow of new parts from the earth and everything we see on the earth, including water, plants, and animals. The vegetation makes the oxygen we breathe, but only in the presence of sunshine, and absorbs the carbon dioxide we throw out as a waste product. We consume animal and vegetable products, and our excrement makes wonderful fertilizer for further vegetation. In fact, this whole process extends beyond the earth and the sun. It is known that certain elements in our bodies, such as phorphorus in our bones, were formed at an earlier stage in the evolution of our galaxy. Like many elements in the earth's crust, these were cycled through a lifetime of several stars before appearing on the earth and finding its way through to our body. The carbon atoms that are part of each of us now will become part of the earth and may become part of someone or something else later. There is an endless exchange of elements between living things and the earth. We do not wait until death to return to where we came from; we are constantly returning to the earth while we are alive (Dossey, 1982). We are part of basic oneness with the universe. Breathing provides a vital link in this equilibrium.

Even with our simple knowledge of human physiology, we know that the oxygen we breathe is very important in the metabolic process. Without it we cannot burn energy, the continuous supply of which is necessary to continue functioning. Without it we cannot utilize the nourishment we take to repair and regenerate our bodies. But it is more than that. The average human breath contains about 10 sextillion atoms, a number that can be written in modern notation as 10^{22}. Since the entire atmosphere of Earth is voluminous enough to contain approximately 10^{22} breaths, we can say that with every inhalation we are, on average, drawing one atom from each of these breaths, and with every exhalation we are, on average, sending one atom to each of these breaths. This exchange is repeated some 16,000–20,000 times a day by each of some $5\frac{1}{2}$ billion people living on this planet. It has been calculated that each breath must contain a quadrillion or 10^{15} atoms breathed by the rest of humankind within the last few weeks, and more than a million atoms breathed personally at some time by each and every person on earth. Thus, without exception, we are all partners in this biodance (Dossey, 1982).

There is no question about the fact that mind effects the body but it also seems certain that everyone affects everyone else, and breathing seems to be the medium for this. That is why we sometimes say, "The atmosphere was congenial," or "The air was rather tense." According to yoga philosophy and the philosophy of many religions, the only way to find peace and harmony for ourselves is to live in peace and harmony with everyone and everything that exists in this universe. We have established through mathematical science that all breathing creatures share the same oxygen molecules, creating a low-frequency chain of chemical contacts among all creatures. What is the significance of this contact at the level of human experience? We know that since ancient times there have been people, the so-called mystics, who claimed to have a direct sense of contact with others, an experience of unity with all human beings at all times. Could they possibly be right? Is it just a question of paying attention?

Breathing and Emotions

The flow of breath creates and sustains the tissues of the body. If some part is poorly supplied with this energy, it will become sick. If breath influences both the body and the mind, not only physical, mental, and emotional states are reflected in the pattern of breath, but through breathing we can also influence our physical, psychological, and spiritual well-being. Breathing patterns reflect states of mind and emotions. For example, an anxious person tends to breathe rapidly and often, using only the upper part of the chest; a depressed person tends to sigh; a person who gets hysterical tends to overbreathe, the condition often known as "hyperventilation"; a child during a temper tantrum holds its breath until it is blue in the face. The anxious person talks at the end of an inhalation in a high-tone voice. The depressed person talks at the end of an exhalation in a low-tone voice. These and other abnormal breathing patterns are discussed elsewhere (Patel, 1991).

Diaphragmatic breathing, in conjunction with physical and mental relaxation, has been found to reduce high blood pressure and anxiety significantly. When we are calm and composed, our breathing is diaphragmatic; since there is a reciprocal relationship between the breathing and the mind, practicing diaphragmatic breathing leads to mental relaxation.

The Respiratory System

The principal muscle involved in abdominal breathing is the diaphragm, a strong dome-shaped sheet of muscle that separates the chest cavity from the abdomen. When a person breathes in, the diaphragm contracts and pushes downwards, causing the abdominal muscles to relax and rise. In this position, the lungs expand, creating a partial vaccum that allows air to be drawn in. When the person breathes out, the diaphram relaxes, and the abdominal muscles contract and expel air containing carbon dioxide. In an infant, the diaphragm is the sole muscle of respiration. Watching a baby breathing conveys a good idea of what diaphragmatic breathing is like. As the diaphragm contracts it pushes the abdominal organs downward and forward, and this rhythmical massage gently compresses the organs and improves their circulation.

It is well to remember that gaseous exchange takes place between air in alveoli and blood in the capillaries. Ideally, there should be a match between the amount of blood flowing through the capillaries and oxygen brought to the alveoli by breathing. However, the physiology of the lungs shows that blood is not evenly distributed throughout the entire lung. Because of gravity, there is more blood in the lower part of the lung than in the upper part when a person is in an upright position. On the other hand, ventilation tends to bring oxygen-bearing air to the upper part of the lung. Thus we have the situation that the physiologists call "ventilation–perfusion mismatch." Learning to breathe diaphragmatically or through the abdomen helps to bring air predominantly into the lower parts of the lungs.

Instructions for the Breathing Exercise

1. Lie on your back with your feet a comfortable distance apart, or sit upright comfortably, but not rigidly.

2. Close your eyes.

3. Place the palm of one hand on your chest and the other on your abdomen. Become aware of the rate and rhythm of your breath. Note which hand is moving with your breathing movements.

4. Inhale and exhale slowly, smoothly, and deeply through the nostrils, without noise, jerks, or pauses.

5. Consciously pull your abdominal muscles in when you exhale, and, if necessary, push the abdominal muscles gently with your hand. When you inhale, be aware of the abdominal wall pushing up.

6. Now place your hands by your side, continue inhaling and exhaling, and concentrate exclusively on the breathing movements. Be aware only of your abdomen rising and falling.

7. Just become aware of the rhythm and rate of your breathing. Normally, we breathe about 12–16 times a minute when we are resting. As the mind becomes calmer, you will notice that breathing becomes slower.

8. Practice for 3–5 minutes a day until you can understand the movement and diaphragmatic breathing becomes your natural pattern of breathing, whether you are sitting, standing, or lying down.

Introduction to Deep Muscle Relaxation: Therapist's Remarks to the Group

Medical research shows that chronic muscle tension contributes to a variety of health problems. Unfortunately, most of this tension remains undetected because the brain pushes the information coming from the body into the subconscious if it is constantly bombarded with that information, particularly if it is also kept busy with pursuing daily jobs that have been given top priority. As an analogy, think about a room with a distinct smell: You become aware of it immediately after you enter it, but the sensation gradually fades if you remain in the room for any length of time. The physiologists call this phenomenon "sensory accommodation." So the first thing you need to learn is to become aware of subtle feelings of tension and relaxation by paying attention.

Relaxation, both mental and physical, means much more than simply sitting down and "taking it easy." It is a skill like driving a car, and it has to be learned until, again like driving a car, it becomes second nature. Like the learning of any new skill, relaxation training requires three things: motivation, understanding, and commitment. You must be motivated to learn. Unless and until you genuinely want to learn yourself, no amount of advice will be sufficient for you to develop the skill. Once you are motivated, you must gain the understanding of what you are trying to achieve, what the principles involved are, and why relaxation is likely to help you. Finally, you must make a commitment to continue using the skill on a regular basis. You must have a strong desire to take control of your health. Learning relaxation is not very difficult; the most difficult aspect is to discipline yourself to comply with it in the long term. If you are prescribed medications to control blood pressure, you know that you have to take them for the rest of your life. It is the same with relaxation, although it is likely that controlling blood pressure may become easier with time, because baroreceptors in your body may be reset at a lower level.

The baroreceptors are pressure-sensing cells situated mainly around blood vessels in your neck, and are important in regulating blood pressure just as a thermostat regulates temperature in a central heating system. If your blood pressure falls sharply during fainting, the baroreceptors will send nerve messages to quicken your heartbeat and constrict your blood vessels, both of which will raise the blood pressure. Conversely, if your blood pressure rises during exercise or anger, the baroreceptors will send different messages; the results will be slowing of the heart rate and vasodilation, both of which will tend to lower the blood pressure. When blood pressure rises repeatedly, the baroreceptors are reset at a higher level; once set at a higher level, they tend to maintain higher blood pressure. Most people with high blood pressure have their baroreceptors set at a higher level. Initially, therefore, you may bring your blood pressure down by relaxation, but your baroreceptors will raise it again. However, if you continue to bring your blood pressure down repeatedly, there is a likelihood that your baroreceptors will be reset at a lower level. When that happens, it becomes easier to maintain lower blood pressure.

Each time one of your muscles contracts, thousands of electrical impulses travel along the nerves to the brain. Scientific evidence suggests that a part of the brain called the hypothalamus, which controls stress responses with their mental, emotional, behavioral, and physical components, becomes highly charged when it is bombarded with a variety of sensory stimulation. When the hypothalamus is sensitized in this way, everyday stressors can easily lead to a stress response. In animal experiments, electrical stimulation of the sensitized hypothalamus causes a sharp rise in blood pressure, as well as behavioral symptoms of stress. On the other hand, if the experiment is repeated when animals are deeply relaxed by injection of muscle relaxant, the rise in blood pressure is greatly attenuated (Hess, 1957). It is possible to cut down drastically on the sensory impulses traveling to the brain simply by lying down, closing your eyes, learning not to be distracted by external noises, and then deeply relaxing the entire body. The result is amazing: Both body and mind return to a state of balance or recuperative rest. Such deep relaxation, in which all senses are withdrawn, is a necessary prerequisite for the next step of meditating.

Relaxation should occur spontaneously after any activity, but, unfortunately, the endless demands of modern life often prevent this. The result is an accumulated state of stress, which can eventually culminate in a stress disorder. You need to learn the art of letting go and allowing your body's restorative ability to take over. If relaxation is to be effective, there are a number of general considerations you must take into account before getting down to practice.

Time

Deep muscle relaxation is most beneficial if it is carried out twice a day, with at least 3–4 hours and preferably 8–10 hours between sessions. Thus, the most suitable times for relaxation would be the morning and evening. If morning is impossible and you do not have time for two periods, then choose the time immediately after work before supper. A recuperative period after work means plenty of energy and maximum enjoyment in the evening with your family. Avoid leaving the practice until late in the evening, because you may tend to fall asleep and then wake up in the middle of the night. It is also not a good idea to practice immediately after a meal, because sudden relaxation of the stomach may occur, which may interfere with digestion and occasionally give you nausea. As a general rule, allow 30 minutes after a snack, 1 hour after a light meal, and 2 hours after a heavy meal. Another reason for practicing on an empty stomach, bladder, and bowel is to cut down on visceral nerve impulses going to the brain. Meditation, which is the next step in the practice, cannot be successful until the stage of sensory withdrawal is complete. Here is an example of how visceral nerve impulses work: If you have had too much coffee or beer before going to bed, your full bladder will wake you up in the middle of the night, because impulses from the bladder will activate the brain. If meditation means complete stilling of the body and the mind, it stands to reason why it is necessary to relax with an empty stomach, bladder, and bowel.

Place

It is essential to have a quiet, warm, comfortable place that affords privacy. There should be no bright lights glaring at you. The fewer the distractions, the better your practice will be. If the phone is likely to ring, it may be a good idea to take it off the hook. The radio and television should be turned off. Make an agreement with your family not to disturb you for half an hour, or let your family join you in the practice. If finding a quiet place at home is impossible, you might consider staying at work after hours. If that too is difficult, go to the public library reading room. This will be quiet, but you will have to make do with sitting in whatever type of chair is available.

Posture

Deep muscle relaxation can be practiced lying on a firm bed or on the floor. Alternatively, it can be practiced sitting in a comfortable armchair with a high back or in a reclining chair to support your back, neck, and head. It should be large enough to support your buttocks and thighs. Make sure you are comfortably dressed in loose-fitting garments. Loosen your tie, belt, and any other constricting clothes. If you are lying flat on your back, make sure that your head, neck, and trunk are in a straight line. Spread your legs slightly so that your feet are approximately 18 inches apart. Allow your feet to flop loosely, with your toes pointing outward and your heels pointing inward. Keep your arms by your sides, a suitable distance away from the trunk, and turn your palms upward and bend your fingers slightly. If you are not used to lying flat, you may find this position somewhat uncomfortable. If so, use a small pillow under your head and a folded towel or cushion behind your knees or under your back. The important thing is to make sure that you are comfortable; otherwise, you will find if difficult to relax deeply.

Instructions for Deep Muscle Relaxation

1. Close your eyes. Very slowly fill your lungs, starting at the diaphragm and working right up to the top of the chest, then very slowly breathe out. After three slow breaths, allow your breathing to become normal and regular. Breathe in and out gently and rhythmically, using your diaphragm. Don't force your breath. Don't try to make it slow deliberately. Just keep your own rhythm. Be completely aware of your breathing pattern. Feel the subtle difference in the temperature of the air you are inhaling and the air you are exhaling. The air you breathe in is cooler, and the air you breathe out is warmer.

2. Now you are consciously going to relax each part of the body in turn. Relaxation means the complete absence of movement, since even the slightest movement means that some of your muscles are contracting. It also excludes holding any part rigid. Concentrate on the part you are relaxing.

3. Now take your mind to your right foot and relax your toes, instep, heel, and the ankle; stay there for a few seconds. Now move your attention slowly up, relaxing your leg, calf, knee, thigh, and the hip. Feel all the muscles, joints, and tissues of your right leg becoming completely relaxed. Relax as deeply as you can. Just keep your awareness on this feeling of deep relaxation in your right leg for a few moments.

4. Now take your mind to your left foot and repeat the process, working up the leg, knee, thigh, and the hip as before. Let all the tension ease away and enjoy the feeling of relaxation for a few seconds.

5. Next concentrate on your right hand. Relax the fingers, thumb, palm, and wrist. Move your attention up to your forearm, elbow, upper arm, and shoulder. Feel every muscle, joint, and tissue in your right arm becoming deeply relaxed. Fix your attention on the sensation of relaxation in your entire right arm for a few moments.

6. Now become aware of your left hand and relax the fingers, thumb, palm, wrist, forearm, elbow, upper arm, and the shoulder. Let all the tension ease away from the left arm.

7. Now concentrate on the base of your spine, vertebra by vertebra, relaxing each vertebra and the muscles on either side of the spine into the floor, Relax your back—first the lower back, then the middle back, and finally the upper back. Release all the tension from your back. Let the relaxation become deeper and deeper. Feel your back merging with the floor.

8. Let the muscles in your neck relax next. Let all the muscles in the front of your neck relax. Let your head rest gently and feel the back of the neck relaxing. Let the relaxation become as deep as possible.

9. Relax your chest. Every time you breathe out, relax a little more. Let your body sink into the floor a little more each time. Let all the nerves, muscles, and organs in your chest relax completely. Now relax the muscles of your stomach. Let all the nerves, muscles, and organs in your stomach relax completely. Just feel them relaxing.

10. Now concentrate on your jaw. Let it relax so that it drops slightly, your lips are just touching each other, and your teeth are apart. Relax your tongue; relax the muscles around your cheekbones. Relax your eyes and muscles around your eyes. Feel them becoming relaxed. Your eyes must become very still. Now relax your forehead; let all the muscles in your forehead become completely relaxed. There is no tension in your facial muscles at all. Now relax your scalp and all the muscles around your head.

11. Your body is now completely relaxed. Keep it relaxed for a few more minutes.

To come out of relaxation, take one deep breath, feeling the energy coming down into your arms and legs. Move your arms and legs slowly. Open your eyes without reacting to the light, and slowly sit up and stretch your body, feeling refreshed and re-energized.

Integrating Relaxation into Everyday Life

Once you have mastered this technique, you should be able to relax appropriately while sitting, standing, or lying down, and within a matter of seconds. The breathing exercise and relaxation techniques are not just rituals to be practiced twice or once a day; they are meant to change our attitudes and the way we cope with our everyday stress. Most of our stress does not come in big packages. Of course, such events as bereavement, getting married, or losing a job after 20 years of service are likely to cause major distress. But we often forget that the little irritations of everyday life—getting caught in traffic jams, being interrupted by numerous telephone calls, being under constant time pressure, not being appreciated for good work, a roof's beginning to leak, a babysitter's not turning up, someone's spilling beer on the sofa, having to put up with an incompetent shop assistant, and so on—accumulate and take a major toll on our health and well-being.

You should practice brief relaxation several times a day, so that stress does not accumulate to the point where it causes distress or stress symptoms. For example, every time you come across a red traffic light when driving a car, release the grip of your steering wheel, take one deep breath, and let your body relax. Another helpful suggestion is to practice a similar brief relaxation before you pick up a phone that is ringing. You will find that by doing this not only do you practice "minirelaxation" several times a day, but also your interaction with the person at the other end of the telephone line is much more calm and friendly. Stick a little colored dot on your wristwatch dial so that every time you look at the watch, which is usually when you are under time pressure, you are reminded to practice your one-breath relaxation. If you are late there is usually nothing you can do about it, and if you compose yourself by doing a brief relaxation rather than expending your energy in worrying about it, you are more likely to achieve your goal. Make a list of 10 situations in your life that are likely to make you tense or upset, and then try to relax briefly before or during those situations; begin with minor situations and then go on to more difficult ones. It will be commendable if you can manage to integrate about 20 such brief relaxation periods into your ordinary day.

Introduction to Creative Visualization: Therapist's Remarks to the Group

"Creative visualization" is an adaptation of a meditative exercise for specific therapeutic purposes. It is a technique of using your imagination to create what you want in life and is based on the principle that mind and body are intimately connected. Changes in the physical state of our bodies create changes in our minds; similarly, every mental image leads to physical changes. We use visual imagery all the time, although most of the time we are not conscious of it.

Whenever we create something, we always create it in the mind or thought first. Without thought there is no action. You do not take a bath before you think about or imagine having a bath. An artist first thinks about what a picture may look like before he or she actually paints it. A dress has to be designed before it can be stitched. When a chef creates a new dish, he or she imagines what the new dish will look and taste like before actually experimenting with it. We create what we imagine. If you think of yourself as beautiful, you usually become beautiful because you take care of yourself and see that you become or remain beautiful. Images supply us with creative energy or enthusiasm. The use and practice of imagery techniques can increase our awareness and understanding of our physical and psychological functioning.

Four Basic Steps of Creative Visualization

For creative visualization to be effective, you need to follow four basic steps (Gawain, 1982):

1. Set a goal that is realistic. To start with, choose goals that are easy to accomplish before setting more difficult or higher goals. Confidence can be built through success only; setting unrealistic goals is a recipe for failure, and repeated failures will shrink your self-esteem and lead you to give up your efforts.

2. Create a clear mental picture. It may not be necessary actually to *see* the image (1 person in every 10 finds it difficult to have a visual image), as long as your thoughts are clear. Think of your goal in the present tense, as if it already exists, and think of yourself within that situation as you desire. This is not cheating yourself, but affirming that situations are first created in the mind.

3. Focus on the picture repeatedly, both in a quiet meditative state as well as casually during the day whenever you happen to think about it. Make it an integral

part of your life. The picture should come to you effortlessly, without striving. Practice before going to sleep or when you wake up in the morning, when your body and mind are more relaxed.

4. Give the picture more positive energy as you focus on it by making positive, encouraging statements—"affirmations," as they are often called—and by picturing yourself as actually achieving your goal. During these affirmations, suspend all doubt or disbelief you may have about achieving your goal.

Dr. Emile Coué, a French chemist and psychotherapist, coined the first positive affirmation used in treatment—the well-known phrase "Day by day in every way, I am getting better and better." Scientists still sometimes laugh at this, but it cured thousands of people with distressing ailments (including rheumatism, asthma, paralysis of the limbs, stammering, ulcers, and even some tumors). Overnight disappearance of multiple warts through faith healing is well known. Unfortunately, we have a tendency to believe that anything that is so simple cannot possibly be good or have any powerful or dramatic effect. José Silva, the founder of the Silva Mind Control Method (Silva & Philip, 1980), suggests that if you spur your imagination with belief, desire, and expectancy and train to visualize your goals so that you can see, feel, hear, taste, and touch them, you will get what you want.

Examples of Creative Visualization Affirmations

Following are some affirmations similar to those suggested by Shakti Gawain, the author of *Creative Visualization* (Gawain, 1982):

- I am beautiful and lovable.
- I am kind and loving, and I have a great deal to share with others.
- I am talented, intelligent, and creative.
- I have a perfect, satisfying, and well-paid job.
- I love my work, and I am richly rewarded, creatively and financially.
- Everything I need is already within me.
- I love and appreciate myself as I am.
- The more love I have for myself, the more love I have to give others.
- This is a rich universe and there's plenty for all of us.
- I am now full of radiant health and energy.
- I am energetic and full of vitality.
- I am good to my body and my body is good to me.
- I love and accept my body completely.
- I am now ready for all my relationships to work.
- My relationship with _____ is growing happier and more fulfilling every day.

You can make up your own affirmations to suit your needs. Provided that they are positive, constructed in the present tense, short, simple, and totally right for you (i.e., not directly contradictory to your present feelings and emotions), they should work for you. For developing the skill of visualization, you will be instructed to visualize relaxing scenery following the breathing exercise and deep muscle relaxation.

Introduction to Meditation: Therapist's Remarks to the Group

Meditation has been a part of most cultures and religions, both Eastern and Western, throughout the ages. The meditation methods described in various branches of yoga are probably the oldest; Christian prayer, Jewish meditation, Japanese Zen, Chinese Tao, Moslem Sufism, and the meditation of Hinduism and Buddhism are some other examples. Only recently, however, have medical men and women realized that it can be used without any religious connotation in the promotion of health (Leshan, 1975; Hewitt, 1978; Yogi Ramacharaka, 1960, 1964). As a result, several hundred papers and books have appeared in the medical literature describing the physiological and psychological effects of meditation, as well as the physical, emotional, and spiritual well-being of its practitioners.

What Is Meditation?

First, meditation practice involves taking a comfortable position—either sitting, lying down, or standing, although sitting is the most usual posture. It then involves being in a quiet environment, regulating the breath, adopting a physically relaxed and mentally passive attitude, and dwelling single-mindedly upon an object. The object of meditation does not have to be physical. It can be an idea, image, or happening; it can be mental repetition of a word or phrase, as in mantra meditation; it can be observing one's own thought, perception, or reaction; or it can be concentrating on some bodily generated rhythm (e.g., breathing). In religious practice, needless to say, the object of concentration is God.

The reason why there are so many possible objects of meditation is that this allows for individual variations. People differ in their intellectual and emotional makeup, and it it important in meditation to feel comfortable with the chosen object. The ultimate idea is to learn the discipline of concentrating on one thing and only one thing at a time, to the exclusion of everything else. The mind does, however, wander off, but it must be brought back as soon as possible to the object of meditation. Giving voluntary concentration to a subject not only enables a person to see and think about that subject with greater clarity, but also brings into consciousness all the different ideas and memories associated with the subject. A practical result is an increased ability to find a solution to any problem.

As a deeper state of concentration is developed, the process becomes more intimate and compelling. The mind that holds an idea becomes held by it. Again, this power of the subconscious can be used to build character. It is known that people who constantly tell themselves that they are failures or are inferior to others eventually come to believe it themselves. In the same way, people who perceive themselves to be in possession of a desired trait over and over again can make the new image a fixed part of their characters.

In the mystical tradition, however, the goal of meditation is to narrow down the focus of attention to a point at which ordinary awareness eventually breaks through to a more intense plane of consciousness. It is a state during which the mind is said to transcend the ordinary plane of awareness and to experience intense joy, happiness, peace, or serenity. It is a state of the greatest silence, an experience of bliss. In other words, meditation is an experience, a state of being.

There are further practical advantages of meditation. We can function more efficiently, feel more complete in ourselves, and realize more of our human potential. We feel closer to ourselves and are better able to relate to others. Our personality structure is strengthened and becomes more integrated. We are able to think and express ourselves with more clarity; we are more effective in our work and clearer in our goals. Other physiological advantages include reductions in oxygen consumption, respiratory rate, and cardiac output (indicating metabolic rest); a marked decrease in blood lactate level (giving an objective measure of reduction in anxiety); increase in electrical resistance of the skin (indicating autonomic rest); and increase in alpha brain waves (indicating mental rest) (Wallace & Benson, 1972).

Meditation in Action

Finally, there is the approach called "active meditation" or "meditation in action." At frequent intervals during the day, if we observe our minds to see what they are doing, it becomes clear that they are busy with wishful thinking, daydreaming, and fantasies of the future. Such useless activity wastes time and energy, and lowers the quality of our work. By learning to concentrate on an everyday task as if that was the most important thing in the world at that moment, and by understanding that each task is but a part of the total harmony with the universe, we become closer to reality.

When a person is completely engrossed in whatever he or she is doing, to the exclusion of everything else in the external world—whether he or she is a painter who is painting, a jogger who is jogging, or a homemaker who is simply washing up—that person is meditating in action. Flower arrangements, archery, aikido, and karate in the Japanese tradition, and rug weaving in the Sufi (Moslem) tradition, are some well-known examples.

Commitment to Meditation

We should not be fooled into believing that the benefits of meditation can be accomplished by just sitting and repeating some word now and again when we have the time. It requires a lifelong commitment. If we just sit and use the simplest form of meditation, such as counting our breaths for 10–15 minutes, we will find out soon enough how hard it is to keep our minds concentrated on it totally and exclusively. The first shock and surprise comes when we realize how undisciplined our minds really are. They constantly refuse to abide by our will, and the more we try to bring ourselves to the task, the more we find ourselves doing all sorts of things: solving old problems, planning tomorrow's work, feeling all kinds of sensations and perceptions. Occasionally we get bored or even sleepy. It is important to realise that serious meditation requires perseverance; it may at times be frustrating, but it is worth all the effort.

Simple Meditation on Breathing

One simple exercise for bringing awareness to a single subject is concentration on breathing. After you have regulated your breathing and relaxed your body as described, either in a sitting or reclining position with the eyes closed, you should fix attention on your breath as it enters and leaves the nostrils. Your entire focus should be on the nostrils, noting the full passage of each inhalation and exhalation from the beginning to the end. You may then feel the breathing at the back of your throat, in the chest and finally at the level of abdomen. You should feel the sensations of the air going in and out. These sensations may change from tickling to itching, to intense pressure, or to countless other feelings. There is no right or wrong way. You should simply be aware of your breathing and keep your attention on it. If you have difficulty in keeping your focus fixed, you might try counting 1 on inhalation and 2 on exhalation. If your mind still wanders off, just bring it back without feeling agitated.

Mantra Meditation

A neutral word, the name of God, a verse from a hymn, or a prayer is called a "mantra" when it is repeated over and over again. It is an effective way of concentrating the mind. In yoga, certain Sanskrit words ending in the letters "m," "h," and "n" qualify as mantras, such as "Ram" or "Shyam," which are names of God. "Aum" or "Om" is considered to be the basic sound, or the basis of everything. According to the ancient scripture, all that is past, present, and future is truly "Om." All that is beyond this conception of time is also "Om." Tibetan Lamas and Buddhists from China, Japan, and Indonesia interpret "Om" similarly. It is also worth noting that Christians and Jews say "Amen" and Muslims "Amin" at the end of their prayers. A mantra can be a short phrase (e.g., "Lord Jesus Christ, have mercy on me"). Healing prayers rely on such repetitive sounds for their fundamental effect. However, it is not necessary to have a mantra with religious connotations. One can just repeat a simple neutral word, such as "relaxed," "one," or "harmony."

The idea is to set up one thought, one wave, and to repeat it over and over again. All you should be consciously thinking of is the mantra. In this way, you become intimate with the sound of the mantra and begin to surrender to or merge into it. Your mind will wander off and distracting thoughts will come, but you should not become frustrated and say, "This is hopeless," or "It won't work with me." You should not be disturbed by doubts, discomforts, boredom, or apparent failures, but should learn to watch them instead.

Meditation on Nature

Nature is the easiest object of contemplation. You can devise meditations in which you draw your surroundings into your being through your senses, until you are led into a quiet and peaceful state. The following suggestions may provide some ideas:

1. Visit a meadow, sit under a tree, and just look at the beautiful green fields.
2. After you have mown the lawn, savor the smell of freshly cut grass.
3. Listen to the music of the ocean or a waterfall. Just forget yourself while you continue to listen. Let the intensity of the sound fill your mind.
4. Keep watching the shadow of a boat while you row. See how it shortens or lengthens, depending on the situation of the sun. See how the shape changes with the waves as it moves up and down.

5. Hold an apple in your hand. Feel its shape and texture; examine its color in detail; smell it. Then close your eyes and just capture all you have seen and felt.

6. Taste the wind. What does it carry? Salt from the sea, perhaps, or the clean essense of pines from far-away mountains?

7. Watch the raindrops falling on the ground. Try to see a rainbow in each drop.

Practical Instructions for Meditation

1. Meditate where the distractions of noise, movement, light, and activity of other people are within tolerance level. You may wish to take the telephone off the hook. Some people are more tolerant than others.

2. Ensure your physical and mental comfort. Make sure that the room is warm. Wear loose clothes. Empty your bladder and bowel. Do not practice for at least 2 hours after a meal. It is most beneficial if you practice twice a day, several hours apart (e.g., in the morning before breakfast and again before supper), for about 15–20 minutes each time.

3. Adopt a poised posture. In the Eastern tradition, the classical lotus, half-lotus, and cross-legged postures are used, but they are not essential. The Japanese tend to use the "thunderbolt" posture, in which you kneel of the floor with knees flexed and buttocks resting on the back of the ankles, heels, and soles. You may simply sit in an upright chair. It is essential to have a straight back without rigidity, a comfortable body, and stillness. Ears should be in line with shoulders, and the tip of the nose should be in line with the navel. Eyes are kept closed. In Zen, the eyes are only partially closed and are directed at a spot on the floor a few feet in front. The body should be relaxed, as described in connection with deep muscle relaxation.

4. Breathe through the nostrils and down into the abdomen. Make sure that your breathing is regular, slow, and rhythmical.

5. Dwell single-mindedly on an object of meditation. This can be a physical object (e.g., a fruit, flower, vase, candle, or mandala), a word or phrase repeated mentally or aloud, or a body rhythm (e.g., breathing). Count your breaths on exhalation from 1 to 10 and start again. Try several methods until you find one that is right for you. Once you choose one, stick to it. Relax your body.

6. Passive awareness is very important. You must develop a passive and relaxed attitude toward distraction. You will find that thoughts and images will flit in and out of your mind. You will find yourself remembering past images or planning your future. Each time you become conscious that your mind has wandered away (and this will happen many times), just bring it back easily and effortlessly to the object of your meditation. Do this as many times as is necessary, always maintaining the relaxed and passive attitude. As you become more experienced, distracting thoughts and images will lessen. Accept that they are inevitable and maintain an attitude of indifference to them. Meditation is ruined if you keep thinking about meditation: "What is to be done next?" "What is the experience like?" "How am I doing?" "This is no good; I must really try to control my mind." Meditation is nondoing. It is passivity combined with perception. It is pure perception that is formless, wordless, and imageless.

7. Practice regularly. With practice it becomes easier to still the mind, but you cannot force results.

Meditation is nearly always at least refreshing, relaxing, and peaceful; for some meditators it occasionally triggers a peak experience, which is blissful and joyous or even ecstatic.

Case Report

In the early 1970s, when I was in the middle of conducting my first study (Patel, 1973), I came across a 39-year-old hypertensive man with a positive family history of hypertension who had been promoted to a position as a manager of a bank a few months earlier, just before he himself was diagnosed as hypertensive. He was a patient of my colleague and business partner, who, after obtaining a blood pressure reading of 165–170/100 mm Hg when the patient's blood pressure 3 years prior had been 130/85 mm Hg, promptly referred him to a specialist in a local hospital. In the outpatient clinic, after waiting for some hours to see the specialist, the patient's blood pressure rose to 230/130! He was duly admitted to the hospital for investigations, which did not show obvious organic reasons for the elevated blood pressure. In fact, the only abnormality detected was moderate left ventricular hypertrophy secondary to hypertension.

The condition was reasonably well controlled on prazosin (a vasodilator) and a diuretic for 5 months, but the patient then developed trigeminal neuralgia. Further medications to control his severe head pains made him rather drowsy. His medications were next changed to methyldopa and diuretics, but he got very depressed on this regimen. His medication was once again changed to clonidine—one 0.1-mg tablet three times a day to start with, and eventually three tablets three times a day, because his blood pressure was becoming more resistant. By now, the patient felt so tired and depressed that he did not think he could continue with his responsible job. He came to our office in order to get medical recommendations to step down from his position on the grounds of his hypertension. Because my colleague was on a vacation, he saw me.

When I asked the patient whether he really wanted to resign from his position, he replied, "Of course not. I do not *want* to resign. In fact it will make my wife unhappy to know that I will not be able to afford the big house we are in now, and that my two sons will have to be transferred from private to public schools. But I just cannot cope with my daily work." As he said this, his eyes were filled with tears. I explained to him that I was getting some good results with relaxation therapy and that he happened to be the next patient eligible to enter the study I was conducting. I asked him whether he would like to enter the study and postpone his decision to resign for 3 months; he agreed. I saw him three times a week for half an hour each. Within a few days, his blood pressure was down to 110/85 mm Hg. We made a joint decision to reduce the clonidine to two tablets three times a day, and after a further month or so to reduce it to one tablet three times a day. Involving him in making the decision motivated him strongly. Each time the medication was reduced, his blood pressure would go up somewhat, but he always managed to bring it down to 110–120/ 85–90 mm Hg. Within months he also felt very much better. Because his blood pressure was so satisfactorily controlled, the specialist discharged him from the hospital outpatient clinic to my care.

Three months later, I asked the patient whether he still wanted to resign from his job. He promptly replied, "No." When I asked him whether he could describe how this therapy had helped him, he was quite clear in his mind that the most helpful aspect was the meditation practice. He said, "Before, I used to come to the office realizing that I had many things to do, so I used to get very apprehensive. Now I take one task and concentrate on that task, and don't even think about the hundreds of other things waiting for my attention. As a result, I am calm and can cope with my daily work and responsibilities without getting unduly anxious." These were his own words, resulting from his own experience. There could not have been a hint of suggestion from me, because in those days I did not know much about the theoretical aspect of meditation, which is described above and which is now part of the standard explanations my colleagues and I give to all patients. Another thing he mentioned was this: "Before, I used to feel victimized by anyone in the hospital who thought that my blood pressure was unsatisfactory or a change in medication was necessary. It was like waiting for punishment to be pronounced! With you I have felt that I do have some say in the matter, that I can truly participate in my progress."

His own general practitioner gradually stopped all medications within the next 2 years, and his blood pressure remained well controlled without any drugs. In 1981, a duty doctor (his own general practitioner was on leave) measured his blood pressure at 130/90 mm Hg and put him on a beta blocker and a diuretic. When he was seen by his own general practitioner 2 months later, his blood pressure was only 110/75 mm Hg, and he stopped most medication except for half a tablet of the beta blocker. He is regularly checked by his doctor and a nurse at work; almost 20 years since his initial training he remains quite fit and healthy, and he is still a manager!

It is important to point out that not everyone responds so well. Also, although this patient felt that meditation was the most beneficial component of treatment, there are others who feel equally convinced that the breathing, or the awareness of stress, or some other component is most beneficial.

Summary and Conclusion

As a practicing physician, I realized that the ability to cope more effectively with life situations was preferable to prescription medication for many illnesses. Drawing upon my earlier training in yoga methods, I gradually developed a behavioral program, and improved upon it over a number of years of clinical and research experience. Encouraging results in the area of hypertension, coronary heart disease, and asthma are described. It is pointed out that yoga philosophy goes beyond its application for health; it is a discipline primarily meant for spiritual awakening to the meaning of life. Various pathways through which this can be attained are described. However, the stress management program I have developed does not delve into the riddle of life The program picks out appropriate aspects of yoga methods and puts them in scientific terminology. Certain basic techniques are described in detail. Other stress management strategies are also used; they are outlined but not described in detail.

On the basis of my results, I would recommend this therapy to all patients with mild hypertension as initial treatment, and would add that drugs should be added only if blood pressure fails to be controlled. For other degrees of hypertension, and for patients with coronary heart disease and other conditions described, these methods may also significantly add to current medical practice (although more research is necessary). For the transient stresses of life, simple relaxation and breathing exercises are commendable. The therapy is admittedly time-consuming, and long-term compliance is a real problem; however, it is remarkably safe and is likely to improve quality of life. Further research work should continue on what seems to be a promising therapeutic program.

REFERENCES

Agras, W. S., Horne, M., & Taylor, C. B. (1982). Expectation and the blood pressure lowering effects of relaxation. *Psychosomatic Medicine, 44,* 389–395.

Agras, W. S., Taylor, C. B., Kraemer, H. C., Southam, M. A., & Schneider, J. A. (1987). Relaxation training for essential hypertension at the worksite: II. The poorly controlled hypertensive. *Psychosomatic Medicine, 49,* 264–273.

Anderson, D. E. (1984). Interactions of stress, salt and blood pressure. *Annual Review of Physiology, 46,* 143–153.

Bali, L. R. (1979). Long term effect of relaxation on blood pressure and anxiety level in essential hypertensive males: A controlled study. *Psychosomatic Medicine, 41,* 637–646.

Benson, H. (1975). *The relaxation response,* New York: Morrow.

Benson, H., Beary, J. F., & Carol, M. P. (1974). The relaxation response. *Psychiatry, 37,* 37–46.

Benson, H., Herd, J. A., Morse, W. H., & Kelleher, R. T. (1969). Behavioral reduction and its reversal. *American Journal of Physiology, 217,* 30–36.

Benson, H., Shapiro, D., Tursky, B., & Schwartz, G. (1971). Decreased systolic blood pressure through operant conditioning techniques in patients with essential hypertension. *Science, 173,* 740–742.

Bhole, M. V. (1967). Treatment of bronchial asthma by yogic methods: A report. *Yoga Mimosa, 9,* 3–41.

Brauer, A., Horlick, L. F., Nelson, B., Farquhar, J. W., & Agras, W. S. (1979). Relaxation therapy for essential hypertension: A Veterans Administration Out-Patients Study. *Journal of Behavior Medicine, 2,* 21–29.

Brunton, P. (1969). *The secret path.* London: Rider.

Clark, D. A., Arnold, E. L., Foulds, J., Foulds, E. L., Brown, D. M., Eastmead, D. R., & Parry, E. H. (1975). Serum urate and cholesterol level in Air Force Academy cadets. *Aviation and Space Environmental Medicine, 46,* 1044.

Cobb, S., & Rose, R. M. (1973). Hypertension, peptic ulcer and diabetes in air traffic controllers. *Journal of the American Medical Association, 224,* 489–492.

Crits-Christoph, P., Luborsky, L., Kron, R., & Fishman, H. (1978). Blood pressure, heart rate and respiratory responses to a single session of relaxation: A partial replication. *Psychosomatic Research, 22,* 493–501.

Cruz-Coke, R. (1960). Environmental influences and arterial blood pressure. *Lancet, ii,* 885–886.

Cruz-Coke, R., Etchverry, R., & Nagel, R. (1964). Influence of migration on blood pressure of Easter Islanders. *Lancet, i,* 697–699.

D'Atr, D. A., & Ostfeld, D. (1975). Crowding: Its effect on elevation of blood pressure in a prison setting. *Preventive Medicine, 4,* 550–566.

Dossey, L. (1982). *Space, time and medicine.* Boulder, CO: Shambala.

Doyle, A. E., & Smirk, F. H. (1955). The neurogenic component in hyptertension. *Circulation, 12,* 543–552.

Eagan, K. J., Kogan, H. N., Garber, A. G., & Jarrett, M. (1983). The impact of psychological distress on the control of hypertension. *Journal of Human Stress, 9*(4), 4–10.

Erskin, J., & Schonel, M. (1979). Relaxation therapy in bronchial asthma. *Journal of Psychosomatic Research, 23,* 131–139.

Falkner, B., Onesti, G., Angelakos, E. T., Fernandes, M. & Langman, C. (1979). Cardiovascular response to mental stress in normal adolescents with hypertensive parents: Haemodynamic and mental stress in adolescents. *Hypertension, 1,* 23–30.

Folkow, B., Hallbäck, M., Lundgren, Y., Sivertsson, R., & Weiss, L. (1973). Importance of adaptive changes in vascular design for establishment of primary hypertension: Studies in men and in spontaneously hypertensive rats. *Circulation Research, 32–33*(Suppl. 1), 2–16.

Frankel, B. L., Patel, D. J., Horwitz, D., Friedwald, M. T., & Gaardner, K. P. (1978). Treatment of hypertension with biofeedback and relaxation techniques. *Psychosomatic Medicine, 40,* 276–293.

Friedman, M., & Rosenman, R. (1974). *Type A behavior and your heart.* New York: Knopf.

Friedman, M., Rosenman, R., & Carroll. V. (1958). Changes in serum cholesterol and blood clotting in men subjected to cyclic variation of occupational stress. *Circulation, 17,* 852–861.

Friedman, M., Thorsen, C. E., Gill, J. J., Powell, L., Ulmer, D., Thompson, L., Price, V. A., Rabin, D. D., Breall, W. S., Dixon, T., Levy, R. A., & Bourg, E. (1984). Alteration of Type A behavior and reduction in cardiac recurrence in post-myocardial infarction patients. *American Heart Journal, 108,* 237–248.

Friedman, R., & Dahl, L. K. (1975). The effects of chronic conflict on blood pressure of rats with genetic susceptibility to experimental hypertension. *Psychosomatic Medicine, 37,* 402–416.

Friedman, R., & Iwai, J. (1976). Genetic predisposition and stress-induced hypertension. *Science, 193,* 161.

Friedman, R., & Iwai, J. (1977). Dietary sodium, psychic stress and genetic predisposition to genetic hypertension, *Proceedings of the Society of Experimental and Biological Medicine, 155,* 449–452.

Gawain, S. (1982). *Creative visualization.* New York: Bantam Books.

Goldstein, I. B., Shapiro, D., Thananopavarn, C., & Sambhi, M. P. (1982). Comparison of drug and behavioral treatment of essential hypertension. *Health Psychology, 1,* 7–26.

Goyache, J. R. M., Abdo, Y., & Ikemi, Y. (1982). The yoga perspective: Part II. Yoga therapy in the treatment of asthma. *Journal of Asthma, 19,* 189–201.

Graham, J. D. P. (1945). High blood pressure after battle. *Lancet, i,* 239–240.

Hamilton, M., Thompson, E. N., & Wisniewski, T. K. M. (1964). The role of blood pressure control in preventing Complications of hypertension. *Lancet, i,* 235–238.

Harburg, E., Schull, W. J., Erfurt, J. C., & Shork, M. A. (1970). A family-set method for estimating hereditary and stress: I. A pilot survey of blood pressure among Negroes in high and low stress areas, Detroit, 1966–1967. *Journal of Chronic Disease, 23,* 69–81.

Henry, J. P., & Cassel, J. C. (1969). Psychosocial factors in essential hypertension: Recent epidemiological and animal experimental studies. *American Journal of Epidemiology, 90,* 171–200.

Henry, J. P., Ely, D. L., & Stephens, P. M. (1972). Changes in catecholamine-controlling enzymes in response to psychosocial activation of the defence and alarm reactions. In *Physiology, emotion and psychosomatic illness* (Ciba Foundation Symposium No. 8). Horsham, England: Ciba.

Henry, J. P., Stephens, P. M., & Santisteban, G. A. (1975). A model of psychosocial hypertension showing reversibility and progression of cardiovascular complications. *Circulation Research, 36,* 156–164.

Hess, W. R. (1957). Hypothalamus and vegetative autonomic function. In J. R. Hughes (Ed.), *Functional organization of the diencephalon.* New York: Grune & stratton.

Hewitt, J. (1978). *Meditation.* London: Teach Yourself Books, Hodder & Stoughton.

Hinkle, L. E., & Wolf, S. (1952). A summary of experimental evidence relating life stress to diabetes mellitus. *Journal of the Mount Sinai Hospital, 19,* 537–570.

Hoensberger, R. W., & Wilson, A. F. (1973). Transcendental meditation in treating asthma. *Respiratory Therapy, 3,* 79–81.

Hypertension Detection and Follow-up Program Cooperative Group. (1979). Five-year findings of the Hypertension Detection and Follow-up Program: I. *Journal of the American Medical Association, 242,* 2562–2570.

Inglis, B. (1965). *A History of medicine.* London: Weidenfeld & Nicholson.

Iwamura, Y., Uchino, Y., Ozawa, S., & Torii, S. (1969). Spontaneous and reflex discharge of a sympathetic nerve during "para-sleep" in decerebrate cat. *Brain Research, 16,* 359–367.

Iyanger, B. K. S. (1968). *Light on yoga.* London: George Allen & Unwin.

Jacob, R. G., Kraemer, H. C., & Agras, W. S. (1977). Relaxation therapy in the treatment of hypertension. *Archives of General Psychiatry, 34,* 1417–1427.

Johnson, C. (1970). *The yoga sutras of Patanjali: An interpretation by Charles Johnson.* London: Stuart & Watkins.

Johnston, D. W. (1987). Behavioral control of high blood pressure. *Current Psychological Research and Review, 6,* 99–114.

Joint National Committee on Detection, Evaluation, and Treatment of High Blood Pressure. (1984). The 1984 report of the Joint National Committee on Detection, Evaluation, and Treatment of High Blood Pressure. *Archives of Internal Medicine, 144,* 1045–1057.

Jorgensen, R. S., Housten, B. K., & Zurawski, R. M. (1981). Anxiety management training in the treatment of essential hypertension. *Behaviour Research and Therapy, 19,* 467–474.

Kasl, S. V. & Cobb, S. (1970). Blood pressure changes in men undergoing job loss: A preliminary report. *Psychosomatic Medicine, 32,* 19–38.

Kemple, C. (1945). Rorschach method and psychosomatic diagnosis. *Psychosomatic Medicine, 7*, 85–89.

Kezdi, P. (1953). Sinoaortic regulatory system: Role in pathogenesis of essential and malignant hypertension. *Archives of Internal Medicine, 91*, 26–34.

Korner, P. I. (1971). Neural cardiovascular control and hypertension. *Journal of the Royal College of Physicians, 5*, 213–221.

Kubicek, W. G., Kottke, F. J., Laker, D. J., & Visscher, M. B. (1953). Adaptation in pressor–receptor reflex: Mechanisms in experimental neurogenic hypertension. *American Journal of Physiology, 175*, 380–382.

Lacey, J. I., & Lacey, B. C. (1958). Verification and extension of the principle of autonomic response-stereotypy. *American Journal of Psychology, 71*, 50–72.

Leshan, L. (1975). *How to meditate.* New York: Bantam Books.

Liddel, L., Rabinovitch, N., & Rabinovitch, G. (1983). *The book of yoga: The complete step-by-step guide.* London: Ebury Press.

Light, K. C., & Orbist, P. A. (1980). Cardiovascular reactivity to behavioral stress in young males with and without marginally elevated causal systolic pressures. *Hypertension, 2*, 802–808.

Light, K. C., Koepke, J. P., Obrist, P. A., & Willis, P. W. (1983). Psychological stress induces sodium and fluid retention in men at high risk of hypertension. *Science, 220*, 429–431.

Lown, B., & Verrier, R. L. (1976). Neural activity and ventricular fibrillation. *New England Journal of Medicine, 294*, 1165–1170.

Luborsky, L., Crits-Christoph, P., Brady, J. P., Kron, R. E., Weiss, T., Cohen, M., & Levy, L. (1982). Behavioral versus pharmacological treatment for essential hypertension: A needed comparison. *Psychosomatic Medicine, 44*, 203–214.

Maddocks, I. (1961). Possible absence of essential hypertension in two complete Pacific Island populations. *Lancet, ii*, 396–397.

Maddocks, I. (1967). Blood pressure in Melanesians. *Medical Journal of Australia, 1*, 1123–1126.

Marmot, M. G., Rose, G., Shipley, M., & Hamilton, P. J. S. (1978). Employment grade and coronary heart disease in British civil servants. *Journal of Epidemiology and Community Health, 32*, 244–249.

McCubbin, J. W., Green, J. H., & Page, I. H. (1956). Baroreceptor function in chronic renal hypertension. *Circulation Research, 4*, 205–210.

Medical Research Council Working Party on Mild to Moderate Hypertension. (1981). Adverse reaction to bendrofluazide and propranolol in the treatment of mild hypertension. *Lancet, ii*, 543–563.

Medical Research Council Working Party. (1985). MRC trial of treatment of mild hypertension: Principal results. *British Medical Journal, 291*, 97–104.

Medical Research Council Working Party on Mild Hypertension. (1986). Course of blood pressure in mild hypertensives: Withdrawal of long-term antihypertensive treatment. *British Medical Journal, 293*, 988–992.

Miasnikov, A. L. (1962). The significance of disturbances of higher nervous activity in the pathogenesis of hypertensive disease. In J. H. Cort (Ed.), *Proceedings of the Prague Sympsoium on the Pathogenses of Essential Hypertension.* Oxford: Pergamon Press.

Miller, N. E. (1969). Learning of visceral and glandular responses. *Science, 163*, 434–445.

Monro, R., Ghosh, A. K., & Kalish, D. (1989). *Yoga research bibliography: Scientific studies on yoga and meditation,* Cambridge, England: Yoga Biomedical Trust.

Monro, R., Nagarathna, R., & Nagendra, H. R. (1990). *Yoga for common ailments.* New York: Simon & Schuster.

Multiple Risk Factor Intervention Trial Research Group. (1982). Multiple Risk Factor Intervention Trial: Risk factor changes and mortality results. *Journal of the American Medical Association, 248*, 1465–1477.

Murphy, K. R. J., Sahaj, B. K., & Silaramaraju, P. (1983). Effects of pranayama (rechaka, puraka, kumbhaka) on bronchial asthma: An open study. *Lung India, 5*, 187–191.

Nagarathna, R., & Nagendra, H. R. (1985). Yoga for bronchial asthma: A controlled study. *Lancet, 291*, 1077–1079.

Nixon, P. (1976). Human function curve with special reference to cardiovascular disorders. *Practitioner, 217*, 765–770.

Office of Health Economics. (1971). *Hypertension: A suitable case for treatment.* London: Author.

Ornish, D. M., Brown, S. E., Scherwitz, L. W., Billings, J. H., Armstrong, W. T., Ports, T. A., McLanahan, S. M., Kirkeeide, R. L., Brand, R. J., & Gould, K. L. (1990). Can lifestyle changes reverse coronary heart disease? *Lancet, 336*, 129–133.

Ornish, D. M., Scherwitz, L. W., Doody, R. S., Kesten, D., McLanahan, S. M., Brown, S. E., De Puey, E., Schuemaker, R., Haynes, C., Lester, J., McAllister, G. K., Hall, R. J., Burdine, J. A., & Gotto, A. M., Jr. (1983). Effects of stress management training and dietary changes in treating ischemic heart disease. *Journal of the American Medical Association, 249*, 54–59.

Osler, W. (1910). The Lumleian Lectures on angina pectoris. *Lancet, i,* 839–844.

Patel, C. (1973). Yoga and biofeedback in the management of hypertension. *Lancet, ii,* 1053–1055.

Patel, C. (1975). Twelve-month follow up of yoga and biofeedback in the management of hypertension. *Lancet, i,* 62–65.

Patel, C. (1977). Biofeedback-aided relaxation and meditation in the management of hypertension. *Biofeedback and Self-Regulation, 2,* 1–41.

Patel, C. (1982). Primary prevention of coronary heart disease. In R. S. Surwit, R. B. Williams, Jr., A. Steptoe, & R. Biersner (Eds.) *Behavioral treatment of disease.* New York: Plenum.

Patel, C. (1990). Psychological and behavioral treatment of hypertension. In D. Byrne & R. Rosenman (Eds.), *Anxiety and the heart.* New York: Hemisphere.

Patel, C. (1991). *The complete guide to stress management.* New York: Plenum.

Patel, C., & Marmot, M. G. (1987). Stress management, blood pressure and quality of life. *Journal of Hypertension, 5*(Suppl. 1), S21–S28.

Patel, C., & Marmot, M. G. (1988a). Can general practitioners use training in relaxation and management of stress to reduce mild hypertension? *British Medical Journal, 296,* 21–24.

Patel, C., & Marmot, M. G. (1988b). Efficacy versus effectiveness of behavioral therapy in reducing hypertension. *Stress Medicine, 4,* 283–289.

Patel, C., Marmot, M. G., & Terry, D. J. (1981). Controlled trial of biofeedback-aided behavioral methods in reducing mild hypertension. *British Medical Journal, 282,* 2005–2008.

Patel, C., Marmot, M. G., Terry, D. J., Carruthers, M., Hunt, B., & Patel, M. (1985). Trial of relaxation in reducing coronary risk: Four year follow-up. *British Medical Journal, 290,* 1103–1106.

Patel, C., & North, W. R. S. (1975). Randomised controlled trial of yoga and biofeedback in the management of hypertension. *Lancet, ii,* 93–95.

Peters, R. K., Benson, H., & Peters, D. (1977). Daily relaxation breaks in the working population: I. Effects on self-reported measures of health, performance, and well-being. *American Journal of Public Health, 67,* 946–953.

Rahe, R. H., Rubin, R. T., Gunderson, E. K. E., & Arthur, R. J. (1971). Psychological correlates of serum cholesterol level in man: A longitudinal study. *Psychosomatic Medicine, 33,* 399–410.

Richter-Heinrich, E., Knust, U., Muller, W., Schmidt, K. H., & Sprung, M. (1975). Psychological investigation in essential hypertensives. Journal of *Psychosomatic Research, 19,* 251–158.

Rofe, Y., & Goldberg, J. (1983). Prolonged exposure to war environment and its effect on the blood pressure of pregnant women. *British Journal of Medical Psychology, 56*(4), 305–311.

Rose, G. A. (1981). A strategy for prevention: Lessons from cardiovascular disease. *British Medical Journal, 282,* 1847–1851.

Rose, G. A., & Blackburn, H. (1968). *Cardiovascular survey methods.* Geneva; World Health Organization.

Rosenman, R. H., Brand, R. J., Jenkin, D., Friedman, M., Straus, R., & Wurm, M. (1975). Coronary heart disease in the Western Collaborative Group Study: Final follow-up experience of $8\frac{1}{2}$ years. *Journal of the American Medical Association, 233,* 872–877.

Ruskin, A., Beard, O. W., & Scaffer, R. L. (1948). Blast hypertension: Elevated arterial pressures in the victims of the Texas City disaster. *American Journal of Medicine, 4,* 228–236.

Scotch, N. A., & Geiger, H. J. (1963). The epidemiology of essential hypertension: A review with special attention to psychologic and sociocultural factors. *Journal of Chronic Diseases, 16,* 1183–1213.

Shapiro, D., Schwartz, G. E., & Tursky, B. (1972). Control of diastolic blood pressure in man by feedback and reinforcement. *Psychophysiology, 9,* 296–304.

Shapiro, D., Tursky, B., Gershon, W., & Stern, M. (1969). Effects of biofeedback reinforcement on the control of human systolic blood pressure. *Science, 163,* 588–589.

Shkhvatsabaya, I. K. (1982). Psychosocial factors and essential hypertension: Pathogenic and medical aspects. In *Hypertension: Biobehavioral and epidemiological aspects. Proceedings of the 1981 joint USA–USSR symposium* (DHHS Publication No. NIH 82-2115). Washington, DC: U.S. Government Printing Office.

Siddhantalankar, S., & Taraporevala, S. J. (1969). *Heritage of Vedic culture.* Bombay: Taraporevala.

Silva, J., & Philip, M. (1980). *The Silva mind control method.* London: Grafton, Books.

Smirk, F. H. (1970). The neurogenically maintained component in hypertension. *Circulation Research, 26–27* (Suppl. 2), II55–II63.

Steptoe, A., Patel, C., Marmot, M. G., & Hunt, B. (1987). Frequency of relaxation practice, blood pressure reduction and the general effects of relaxation following a controlled trial of behavioral modification for reducing coronary risk. *Stress Medicine, 3,* 101–107.

Surwit, R. S., Shapiro, D., & Good, M. I. (1978). Comparison of cardiovascular biofeedback, neuromuscular biofeedback and meditation in the treatment of borderline hypertension. *Journal of Consulting and Clinical Psychology, 46,* 252–263.

Swami Rama. (1972). *Book of Wisdom, Ishopanishad.* Honsdale, PA: Himalayan International Institute.

Thomas, C. B., & Murphy, E. A. (1958). Further studies on cholesterols in the John Hopkins medical students: The effect of stress as examination. *Journal of Chronic Diseases, 8,* 661.

Veterans Administration Cooperative Group on Antihypertensive Agents. (1967). Effects of treatment on morbidity in hypertension: I. Results in patients with diastolic blood pressures averaging 115 through 129 mm Hg. *Journal of the American Medical Association, 202,* 1028–1034.

Veterans Administration Cooperative Group on Antihypertensive Agents. (1970). Effects of treatment on morbidity in hypertension: II. Results in patients with diastolic blood pressure averaging 90 through 114 mm Hg. *Journal of the American Medical Association, 213,* 1143–1152.

Wadden, T. A. (1984). Relaxation therapy for essential hypertension: Specific or non-specific effects. *Journal of Psychosomatic Research, 28,* 53–61.

Waldron, I., Nowotakski, M., Friemer, M., Henry, J. P., Post, N., & Witten, C. (1982). Cross-cultural variation in blood pressure: A quantitative analysis of the relationship of blood pressure to cultural characteristics, salt consumption and body weight. *Social and Scientific Medicine, 16,* 419–430.

Wallace, R. K., & Benson, H. (1972). The physiology of meditation. *Scientific American, 226,* 84–90.

Willius, F. A., & Keys, T. A. (1941). *Cardiac classics.* St. Louis: C. V. Mosby.

Wolf, S. G. (1958). Cardiovascular reactions to symbolic stimuli. *Circulation, 18,* 287–292.

Wolpe, J. (1958). *Psychotherapy by reciprocal inhibition.* Stanford, CA: Stanford University Press.

Yogi Ramacharaka. (1960). *Raja Yoga.* London: Fowler.

Yogi Ramacharaka. (1964). *Gnani Yoga.* London: Fowler.

Zanchetti, A., Bacelli, G., Guazzi, M., & Mancia, G. (1972). The effect of sleep on experimental hypertension. In G. Onesti, K. E. Kim, & J. Moyer (Eds.), *Hypertension mechanisms and management.* New York: Grune & Stratton.

5

Modern Forms of Meditation

PATRICIA CARRINGTON

History of the Method

Modern forms of meditation, simplified and divested of esoteric trappings and religious overtones, possess some outstanding therapeutic properties. This chapter presents ways in which these noncultic techniques can be applied in clinical practice.

Technically, meditation can be classified as "concentrative" or "nonconcentrative" in nature. A concentrative technique limits stimulus input by directing attention to a single unchanging or repetitive stimulus. A nonconcentrative technique expands the meditator's field of attention to include as much of his or her conscious mental activity as possible. In actuality, it is the *experience* of meditation that brings about therapeutic change, rather than the *techniques* used to evoke this experience; nonetheless, for practical purposes, the clinician considering using meditation with clients requires a set of replicable procedures. The modern concentrative forms of meditation presented here are simple to learn. These techniques are typically practiced seated, in a quiet environment, with the object of the meditator's attention being a mentally repeated sound, the breath, or some other appropriate focal point. When the meditator's attention wanders, he or she is directed to bring it back to this attentional object in an easy, unforcing manner.

Although meditation is a basically simple procedure, various forms of it have been used by numerous societies throughout recorded history to alter consciousness in a way that has been perceived as deeply beneficial. Traditionally, its benefits have been defined as spiritual in nature, and meditation has constituted a part of many religious practices. Recently, however, simple forms of meditation have been used for stress management with excellent results. Contributing to the rising interest in the meditative techniques is the fact that these techniques are related to the biofeedback techniques (which also emphasize a delicately attuned awareness of inner processes) and to muscle relaxation and visualization techniques used in behavior therapies.

In addition to providing deep relaxation, however, the meditative disciplines appear to assist the client in an area peripheral to many other therapeutic interventions—the fostering of communication between the client and his or her own self, apart from his or her interpersonal environment. In a world where inner enrichment from any source is scarce, many clients hunger for a more profound sense of self than is implicit in merely "getting along with others." Such people seek an awareness of their identity as *being* (as distinct from identity as *doing*). The inner communion of meditation offers a means of fulfilling this need, thus promising to heal an aspect of the psyche that may be as needful as any other presently identified. The use of meditation along with other forms of therapy may therefore be an inevitable accompaniment of the trend currently seen in the behavioral sciences toward encompassing more and varied aspects of life.

Noncultic Methods

Of all the Westernized forms of meditation, transcendental meditation (TM) has been up until now the most widely known and extensively studied. More accurately described as "transitional" rather than modern, because it retains certain cultic features such as the *puja* (Hindu religious ceremony), TM is taught by an organization that does not permit mental health practitioners to assume an active role in its clinical management (unless they are TM teachers). Despite its popularity with segments of the general public, therefore, the TM method has been relatively little used in clinical settings.

Among the clinically oriented meditation techniques, "clinically standardized meditation" (CSM; Carrington, 1978) and the "respiratory one method" (ROM; Benson, 1975) have been the most widely used to date. These techniques were devised with clinical objectives in mind and are strictly noncultic. The methods differ from each other in several important respects, however. A trainee learning CSM selects a sound from a standard list of sounds (or creates one according to directions) and then repeats this sound mentally, without intentionally linking the sound to the breathing pattern or pacing it in any structured manner. CSM is thus a relatively permissive meditation technique and may be subjectively experienced as almost "effortless." By contrast, when practicing ROM, the trainee repeats the word "one" (or another word or phrase) to himself or herself mentally, while at the same time intentionally linking this word with each exhalation. ROM is thus a relatively disciplined form of meditation with two meditational objects—the chosen word and the breath. Accordingly, ROM requires more mental effort than CSM and may appeal to a different type of person.

Other methods of meditation have also been used in some clinical settings, but these methods are less standardized. Buddhist "mindfulness" meditation is probably the most commonly used of the nonconcentrative methods. It is somewhat more difficult to learn than the modern forms of concentrative meditation, however, and the student's success in learning it thus depends more heavily on the individual expertise and personality of the instructor. Nonstandardized forms of meditation are not discussed here, although their usefulness in the proper hands is not to be negated.

The Physiology of Meditation

All of the simplified meditation techniques—including the transitional form, TM—have in common the fact that they rapidly bring about a deeply restful state that possesses certain well-defined characteristics. Although meditation is not the only intervention that can bring about such a restful state, it is clearly one of the most effective. Research has shown that during meditation, body and mind typically enter a state of profound rest. Oxygen consumption can be lowered during 20 to 30 minutes of meditation to a degree ordinarily reached only after 6 to 7 hours of sleep (Wallace, Benson, & Wilson, 1971), and heart and respiration rates typically decrease during meditation (Allison, 1970; Wallace, 1970). However, the heart rate can also speed up during meditation in response to the introduction of stimuli perceived as stressful (Goleman & Schwartz, 1976)—a finding that has been variously interpreted as suggesting a heightened orientation response during meditation or as being a paradoxical reaction. The latter are occasionally found during meditation and are of considerable theoretical interest, while not altering the general finding that meditation is a deeply restful state. In addition electrical resistance of the skin tends to increase during meditation (Wallace, 1970), suggesting a lowering of anxiety at this time. Similarly, a sharp decline in the concentration of blood lactate may occur (Wallace et al., 1971). Although some studies have failed to show such clear-cut indications of decreased physiological arousal during meditation as these, subjective reports of mediators typically describe marked anxiety reduction during this state, and clinical reports have generally confirmed the anxiety-reducing properties of meditation (Delmonte, 1987a).

During the meditative state also, the electroencephalograph (EEG) shows an alert–drowsy pattern with high alpha and occasional theta wave patterns, as well as an unusual pattern of swift shifts from alpha to slower (more sleep-like) frequencies and then back again (Das & Gastaut, 1957; Wallace et al., 1971). These findings suggest that meditation may be an unusually *fluid* state of consciousness, partaking of qualities of both sleep and wakefulness, and possibly resembling the hypnogogic or "falling asleep" state more than any other state of consciousness. A number of studies have also shown that the physiology of meditation differs from that of ordinary rest with eyes closed and from that of most hypnotic states (Brown, Stewart, & Blodgett, cited in Kanellakos, 1974; Wallace, 1970; Wallace et al., 1971). Other studies, however, have shown that true uninterrupted "rest," as induced in the laboratory, shares many of the same features.

In sum, the research suggests that during meditation deep physiological relaxation, somewhat similar to that occurring in the "deepest" non-rapid-eye-movement (NREM) sleep phase, occurs in a context of wakefulness. Wallace et al. (1971) have thus termed meditation a "wakeful, hypometabolic state," and Gellhorn and Kiely (1972) have called it "a state of trophotropic dominance compatible with full awareness." When practiced regularly, meditation also appears to alter behavior occurring outside of the meditative state itself, with both clinical and research evidence suggesting that a number of beneficial changes may take place in people who meditate. These changes are described later, when clinical indications for meditation are discussed.

Theoretical Underpinnings

Several theories have been proposed concerning the manner in which meditation operates to effect change. Five of the most widely accepted are presented below.

Global Desensitization

There is an interesting similarity between the situation occurring during a meditation session and that occurring during the technique of systematic desensitization used in behavior therapy (Carrington & Ephron, 1975; Goleman, 1971). In the latter process, increasingly greater increments of anxiety (prepared in a graded hierarchy) are systematically "counterconditioned" by being paired with an induced state of deep relaxation. If the treatment is sucessful, presentation of the originally disturbing stimulus ceases to produce anxiety. In meditation, awareness of the meditative "focus" (the mantra,[1] the breathing, a candle flame, or whatever) becomes a signal for turning inward and experiencing a state of deep relaxation. Simultaneously, the meditator maintains a permissive attitude with respect to thoughts, images, or sensations experienced during meditation. Without rejecting or unduly holding onto these thoughts, he or she lets them "flow through the mind" while continuing to direct attention to the focal point of the meditation.

This dual process—free-flowing thoughts occurring simultaneously with a repetitive stimulus that induces a state of calm—sets up a subjective state in which deep relaxation is paired with a rapid, self-initiated review of an exceedingly wide variety of mental contents and areas of tension, both verbal and nonverbal. As thoughts, images, sensations, and amorphous impressions drift through the mind during meditation, the soothing effect of the meditative focus appears to neutralize the disturbing thoughts. No matter how unsettling a meditation session may feel, a frequent response of meditators is that they discover that upon emerging from meditation, the "charge" has been taken off their current concerns or problems. Do the modern forms of meditation "work," then, merely because they are a form of systematic desensitization? Such a reductionist point of view would seem to overlook certain important differences between these approaches. In systematic desensitization, therapist and patient work together to identify specific areas of anxiety, and then proceed to deal with a series of single isolated problems in a sequential, highly organized fashion. During meditation, the areas of anxiety to be "desensitized" are selected by the responding organism (the meditating person) in an entirely automatic manner. At this time, the brain of the meditator might be said to act like a computer programmed to run certain material through "demagnetizing" circuits capable of handling large amounts of data at one time. We might conceptualize subsystems within the brain scanning vast memory stores at lightning speed during the meditative state, with the aim of selecting those contents of the mind that are most likely to be currently tolerated without undue anxiety. For these reasons, meditation would seem to operate with a considerably wider scope than systematic desensitization, although for exactly this reason, it may lack the clinical precision of the latter.

[1]The mantra is a resonant sound used for purposes of meditation. In modern forms of concentrative meditation the mantra is most often repeated silently, by merely thinking it.

Blank-Out

Ornstein (1972) has proposed that mantra meditation (or other forms of concentrative meditation in which stimulus input is intentionally limited) may create a situation similar to that occurring when the eye is prevented from continuously moving over the surface of the visual field, but is instead forced to view a constant fixed image without recourse to scanning. When an image is projected onto a contact lens placed over the retina, the lens can follow the movement of the eye, so that the image becomes stabilized in the center of the visual field. Under such conditions, the image soon becomes invisible; without constantly shifting his or her eyes to different part of the perceived image, the subject apparently cannot register the object mentally. At this point, which Ornstein refers to as "blank-out," prolonged bursts of alpha waves may be recorded in the occipital cortex.

It seems, therefore, that the central nervous system is so constructed that if awareness of any sort is restricted to one unchanging source of stimulation, then consciousness of the external world may be turned off, and the individual may achieve a form of mental blank-out. Since mantra meditation involves continuously recycling the same input over and over, it may result in a blank-out effect, which in turn has the effect of temporarily clearing the mind of all thoughts. The aftereffect of blank-out may be an opening up of awareness, a renewed sensitivity to stimuli. After meditation, some meditators seem to experience an innocence of perception similar to that of the young child who is maximally receptive to all stimuli.

Although Ornstein does not address himself to the therapeutic implications of the blank-out effect, it is evident that at the least such a phenomenon may break up an unproductive mental set, thus giving the meditator the opportunity to restructure his or her thoughts along more productive lines. This could result in a fresh point of view on emotional problems, as well as on other aspects of life. Also, becoming more open to direct sensory experience may in itself be valuable in a world beset by problems deriving from overemphasis on cognitive activity. The enlivened experiencing following meditation (often described by meditators as "seeing colors more clearly" "hearing sounds more sharply," or "sensing the world more vividly") may in fact be a prime reason for the antidepressive effects of meditation.

Effects of Rhythm

In mantra meditation, where a lilting sound is continuously repeated, rhythm is an obvious component. But rhythm also plays a role in all other forms of meditation, as the inner stillness involved allows the meditator to become profoundly aware of his or her own bodily rhythms. In the unaccustomed quiet of the meditative state, one's own breathing may be intimately sensed, the pulse rate may be perceived, and even such subtle sensations as the flow of blood through the veins are sometimes described as emerging into awareness. Some meditative techniques even use bodily rhythms as their object of focus, as when the Zen meditator is instructed to concentrate on his or her own natural, uninfluenced breathing.

This rythmic component of meditation may be a major factor in inducing calm.

Rhythm has universally been used as a natural tranquilizer; virtually all known societies use repeated sounds or rhythmic movements to quiet agitated infants, for example. The world over, parents have rocked children gently, hummed lullabies to them, recited nursery rhymes, repeated affectionate sounds in a lilting fashion, or bounced the children rhythmically on their laps, with an intuitive awareness of the soothing effects of such rhythmic activities on the children's moods. Similarly, in the psychological laboratory, Salk (1973) demonstrated that neonates responded to a recorded normal heartbeat sound (played to them without interruption day and night) by greatly lessening their crying, as compared to a control group of infants who were not exposed to the sounds, and also by gaining more weight than the controls.

If contacting deep biological rhythms in oneself is a prominent component of meditation, then regular meditation might be expected to exert a deeply soothing effect. One might, so to speak, gain considerable stabilization from returning periodically to a source of well-being (in meditation), from which one could draw strength in order to deal more effectively with an outer environment whose rhythms are, more often than not, out of phase with one's own.

Balance between Cerebral Hemispheres

Research suggests that during meditation, a greater equalization in the workload of the two cerebral hemispheres may occur (Banquet, 1973). Verbal, linear, time-linked thinking (processed through the left hemisphere, in the right-handed person) seems to be lessened during meditation as compared to the role it plays in everyday life, while holistic, intuitive, wordless thinking (usually processed through the right hemisphere) comes more to the fore. The therapeutic effects derived from meditation may reflect this relative shift in balance between the two hemispheres.

During the early stages of meditation practice, when the technique is relatively new to the meditator, the left-hemispheric activity of the brain—which predominates during waking life in our modern world, often almost to the exclusion of "right-hemispheric" activity—has been shown to take a lesser role during meditation, with a shift toward right-hemisphere dominance occurring (Davidson, Goleman, & Schwartz, 1976). During the more advanced practices of meditation, however, EEG records of experienced mediators frequently display an unusual balancing of the activity of the two cerebral hemispheres during meditation (Earle, 1981). In terms of the clinical applications of meditation considered here, this distinction is relatively unimportant because the "early" stages of a meditation practice constitute the entire meditative experience for the vast majority of those who take up the modern forms of meditation. An occasional client in psychotherapy does advance beyond these beginning stages, but such a person is likely to be using meditation for exploring altered states of consciousness or for furthering spiritual development rather than for therapeutic purposes. More advanced practices of meditation are, of course, valid in their own right, but a discussion of them is beyond the scope of this chapter.

Since restrictive moral systems are for the most part transmitted verbally, with much role modeling dependent on verbal imitation, ameliorative effects of meditation on self-blame—a clinically relevant benefit of this technique—might be explained by this basic shift away from the verbal left-hemispheric mode during meditation. Minimizing verbal-conceptual experience (yet still remaining awake) may afford the individual temporary relief from self-derogatory thoughts, as well as from excessive demands on the self that have been formulated through internal verbalizations. Having obtained a degree of relief from these verbal injunctions during the meditative state, the meditator may find himself or herself less self-critical when returning to active life. The reduction in the strength of self-criticism may have generalized from the meditative state to the life of action.

Constructivist Therapy

Ornstein (1972) and Delmonte (1987b) have drawn on Kelly's (1955) formulation of personal construct psychology to explain the subjective experiences associated with meditation. Kelly postulates that "reality" as we know it is a result of our personal "constructs"—our ways of organizing mental events to anticipate future events. Through the meditation process, the meditator may reorganize his or her constructs. He or she can either block or constrict them (as in concentrative meditation) or broaden the perceptual field to include fresh elements that change the organization of a construct (as in nonconcentrative meditation). The result is said to be a decrease in cognitive construing, with a subsequent increase in nonverbal construing. The meditator's perception of "reality" thus changes in quality.

There are thus a number of theoretical reasons why meditation may be of benefit in clinical practice. I now turn to the identification of those clinical conditions that have been shown to respond to the technique.

Assessment

Clinical Conditions Responding to Meditation

Based on research and clinical reports, a substantial body of knowledge has accumulated concerning the usefulness of meditation in clinical practice. As in most areas of research, however, not everyone agrees in interpretation of the findings. Holmes (1984), for example, considers meditation to be no more effective in lowering arousal or providing therapeutic benefit than is resting with eyes closed, while other researchers (Benson & Friedman, 1985; Shapiro, 1985; Suler, 1985; West, 1985) cite compelling evidence to support the concept that meditation possesses some special therapeutic properties distinct from those of rest. Since many of the more clinically relevant effects of meditation are not readily identifiable by standard psychometric measures, it is probably only necessary for the clinician to note that the conditions of a meditation experiment tend to create a type of uninterrupted "guilt-free" rest that is atypical of our society. Such rest can occur in the laboratory because the experimenter has carefully set up the conditions for it: Rest has become a "demand characteristic" of the experiment. Laboratory-induced rest may well possess some special therapeutic properties, particularly if, while "resting," the subject experiences what I have called the "meditative mood"[2] (Carrington, 1977). Most people in our fast-paced society find it difficult if not impossible to truly rest during the day, and therefore a practice of meditation may supply a highly structured, especially effective form of enforced rest each day—one that is easier for the average person to observe than are vague therapeutic prescriptions to "take it easy and get more rest."[3] In fact, meditation may be particularly effective in this respect because it is a novel, out-of-the ordinary activity.

Such practical considerations as these constitute the focus of indications and counterindications for meditation in clinical practice. The discussion that follows summarizes the major findings in this area.

Reduction in Tension/Anxiety

In research where the effects of meditation on anxiety have been measured, results have consistently shown anxiety to be sharply reduced in a majority of subjects after they commenced the practice of meditation (Carrington, 1977). There is also some evidence suggesting that the regular practice of meditation may facilitate a reduction in anxiety for subjects with clinically elevated (i.e., high or average) anxiety levels, but that it shows a "floor" effect (i.e., not much change) in those with low anxiety (Delmonte, 1987a). In addition, meditation may be less effective for some patients with long-term severe anxiety neurosis or those who suffer from panic disorder, because such patients can easily be overwhelmed by their symptoms and drop out of the practice. Glueck (1973), however, in a study conducted with a group of psychiatric inpatients, found that dosages of psychotropic drugs could be greatly reduced after these patients had been meditating for several weeks; in a majority of cases, the use of sedatives could also be reduced or eliminated in these patients. Meditation has also successfully been used to lower the anxiety experienced by patients preparing for cardiac surgery (Leserman, Stuart, Mamish, & Benson, 1989) and for ambulatory surgery (Domar, Noe, & Benson, 1987).

The quieting effects of meditation differ, however, from the effects brought about by psychotropic drugs. Whereas the relaxation brought about be drugs may slow the person down and cause grogginess, the relaxation resulting from meditation does not bring with it any loss of alertness. On the contrary, meditation seems, if anything, to sharpen alertness. Groups of meditators have been shown to have faster reaction times (Appelle & Oswald, 1974), to have better refinement of auditory perception (Pirot, 1978), and to perform more rapidly and accurately on perceptual–

---

[2]The meditative mood has been defined as a special drifting sort of consciousness quite similar in its subjective features to hypnogogic (presleep) mentation. It is familiar to most people, since it typically occurs at intervals during waking life when the individual is especially relaxed and quiet. Presence of the meditative mood during a control procedure can thus render comparisons between meditation and "control" conditions misleading.

[3]In the great meditative traditions, meditation is considered to serve a unique function quite different from that of rest. It is important not to confuse the therapeutic goals of modern meditation with the spiritual goals of meditation as traditionally practiced.

motor tasks (Rimol, 1978) than nonmeditating controls. Meditation may therefore be indicated where anxiety is a problem, and can often be used productively in place of tranquilizers or as a supplement to drug treatment.

Improvement in Stress-Related Illnesses

Many stress-related illnesses have proven responsive to meditation. Research has shown meditation to be correlated with improvement in the breathing patterns of patients with bronchial asthma (Honsberger & Wilson, 1973); with decreased blood pressure in both pharmacologically treated and untreated hypertensive patients (Benson, 1977; Patel, 1973, 1975; Hafner, 1982; Friskey, 1984); with reduced premature ventricular contractions in patients with ischemic heart disease (Benson, Alexander, & Feldman, 1975); with reduced symptoms of angina pectoris (Tulpule, 1971; Zamarra, Besseghini, & Wittenberg, 1978); with reduced serum cholesterol levels in hypercholesterolemic patients (Cooper & Aygen, 1979); with reduced sleep-onset insomnia (Miskiman, 1978; Woolfolk, Carr-Kaffashan, McNulty, & Lehrer, 1976); with amelioration of stuttering (McIntyre, Silverman, & Trotter, 1974); with lowered blood sugar levels in diabetic patients (Heriberto, 1988); with amelioration of psoriasis (Gaston, 1988–1989); and with reductions in the symptoms of psychiatric illness (Glueck & Stroebel, 1975). Studies have also shown that meditation may reduce salivary bacteria and thus be useful in treating dental caries (Morse, 1982) and may decrease periodontal inflammation (Klemons, 1978). It may also reduce some coronary-prone behavior patterns (Muskatel, Woolfolk, Carrington, Lehrer, & McCann, 1984) and may be beneficial in lowering central nervous system responsivity to norepinephrine (Benson, 1989). Meditation can thus be a useful intervention in a wide variety of stress-related illnesses.

Increased Productivity

Meditation may bring out increased efficiency by eliminating unnecessary expenditures of energy; a beneficial surge of energy is often noted in persons who have commenced the practice. This can manifest itself variously as a lessened need for daytime naps, increased physical stamina, increased productivity on the job, increased ideational fluency, the dissolution of writer's or artist's "block," or the release of hitherto unsuspected creative potential. Meditation may therefore be useful when it is desirable to increase a client's available energy and/or when a client is experiencing a block to productivity.

Lessening of Self-Blame

A useful by-product of meditation may be increased self-acceptance, often evidenced in clients as a lessening of unproductive self-blame. A spontaneous change in the nature of a meditator's self-statements—from self-castigating to self-accepting—suggests that the noncritical state experienced during the meditation session itself can generalize to daily life. Along with the tendency to be less self-critical, the meditator may show a simultaneous increase in tolerance for the human frailties of others, and there is often concomitant improvement in interpersonal relationships. Meditation may therefore be indicated when a tendency toward self-blame is excessive or when irrational blame of others has become a problem.

Antiaddictive Effects

Several studies (Benson & Wallace, 1971; Shafii, Lavely, & Jaffe, 1974, 1975) have shown that, at least in persons who continue meditating for long periods of time (usually for a year of more), there may be a marked decrease in the use of nonprescription drugs, such as marijuana, amphetamines, barbiturates, and psychedelic substances (e.g., LSD). Many long-term meditators, in fact, appear to have discontinued use of such drugs entirely. Similar antiaddictive trends have been reported in ordinary cigarette smokers and abusers of alcohol as well (Shafii, Lavely, & Jaffe, 1976; Murphy, Pagano, & Marlatt, 1986; Royer-Bounguar, 1989). Meditation may therefore be useful for a patient suffering from an addictive problem, particularly if that problem is in its incipient stage.

Mood Elevation

Both research and clinical evidence suggests that people suffering from mild chronic depression or from reactive depression may experience distinct elevation of mood after commencing meditation (Carrington et al., 1980). People with acute depressive reactions do not generally respond well to meditation, however, and are likely to discontinue practicing it (Carrington & Ephron, 1975). Meditation therefore appears indicated in mild or chronic depressive reactions, but not in acute depressions.

Increase in Available Affect

Those who have commenced meditating frequently report experiencing pleasure, sadness, anger, love, or other emotions more easily than before. Sometimes they experience emotions that have previously been unavailable to them. Release of such emotions may occur during a meditation session or between sessions, and may be associated with the recovery of memories that are highly emotionally charged (Carrington, 1977). Meditation is therefore indicated when affect is flat, when the client tends toward overintellectualization, or when access to memories of an emotional nature is desired for therapeutic purposes.

Increased Sense of Identity

Meditating clients frequently report that they have become more aware of their own opinions since commencing meditation; that they are not as easily influenced by others as they were previously; and that they can arrive at decisions more quickly and easily. They may also be able to sense their own needs better, and thus may become more outspoken and self-assertive and more able to stand up for their own rights effectively. Such effects may not be easily measurable by any existing tests, although it is possible that the trait known as "field independence" may be relevant to some of the effects noted. Two studies (Hines, cited in Carrington, 1977; Pelletier, 1978) have shown changes in the direction of greater field independence (or "inner-directedness") following the commencement of the practice of meditation, whereas other researchers have found no such changes. The clinically important observation that there tends to be an increased sense of identity in mediators may not as yet have been validly tested in an experimental setting.

One result of the increased sense of identity noted by clinicians may be marked improvement in the ability of a meditator to separate from significant others when such separation is called for. Meditation can thus be extremely useful in pathological bereavement reactions, or in cases where an impending separation (threatened death of a loved one, contemplated divorce, upcoming separation from growing children, etc.) presents a problem. Meditation is therefore indicated where separation anxiety is a problem. Since it is particularly useful in bolstering the inner sense of "self" necessary for effective self-assertion, it may also be helpful as an adjunct to assertiveness training.

Lowered Irritability

The meditating person may become markedly less irritable in his or her interpersonal relationships within a relatively short period of time after commencing meditation (Carrington et al., 1980). Meditation thus appears indicated where impulsive outbursts or chronic irritability is a symptom. This recommendation includes cases of organic irritability, since preliminary observations have shown meditation to be useful in increasing overall adjustments in several cases of brain injury (Glueck, 1973).

How to Assess for Use of the Method

A few attempts have been made to identify personality characteristics of the meditation-responsive person. Most of these have led to inconclusive results, with the possible exception of the research on "absorption," a component of hypnotic susceptibility. Absorption refers to the disposition to display episodes of total attention "during which the available representational apparatus seems to be entirely dedicated to experiencing and modeling the attentional object, be it a landscape, a human being, a sound, a remembered incident, or an aspect of one's self" (Tellegen & Atkinson, 1974, p. 274). Meditative skills such as focusing and receptivity may be reflected in items on the Tellegen Absorption Scale. For example, "When I listen to music I can get so caught up in it that I don't notice anything else" may reflect the focusing ability that Smith (1987) considers an essential meditative skill. In the same manner, the statement "I sometimes 'step outside' my usual self and experience an entirely different state of being" may reflect a receptivity to altered states of consciousness useful for meditation. Some evidence (Tjoa, 1975; Davidson & Goleman, 1977; Warrenburg & Pagano, 1982–1983) suggests that the absorption trait may predict a positive response to meditation, although this possibility has not been tested in clinical settings.

The majority of the studies attempting to predict what kind of person responds positively to meditation or stays with the practice over time have used nonclinical populations, and their criteria for "responsiveness to meditation" have generally not been relevant to problems involved in clinical assessment. One of the only measures of clinical improvement that has been experimentally addressed in meditation research in an attempt to identify a correlation with personality factors is improvement in anxiety. Beiman, Johnson, Puente, Majestic, and Graham (1980) noted that the more "internal locus of control" participants reported prior to learning meditation, the greater their reductions in anxiety as measured by the Fear Survey Schedule; and Smith (1978) found that reductions in trait anxiety following meditation training were moderately correlated with two of Cattell's Sixteen Personality Factor Inventory (16-PF) factors: "autia" (preoccupation with inner ideas and emotions) and "schizothymia" (steadiness of purpose, withdrawal, emotional flatness, and "coolness"). However, when my colleagues and I (Carrington et al., 1980) studied employee stress in a large corporation, we found no significant correlations between any of the 16-PF factors (including anxiety) measured at pretest, and subsequent drops in symptomatology as measured by the Symptom Checklist 90—Revised (SCL-90-R; Derogatis, Rickels, & Rock, 1976), a validated self-report inventory.

At this point, therefore, the research is too inconclusive to permit us to predict which clients will respond to meditation by means of standard personality tests. There has, however, been an attempt to identify predictive personality variables correlated with successful meditation practice on a *theoretical* basis. Davidson and Schwartz (1976) have suggested that relaxation techniques have varied effects, depending on the system at which they are most directly aimed. They categorize progressive relaxation as a "somatically oriented technique," because it involves learning to pay closer attention to physiological sensations, particularly muscle tension; they categorize forms of meditation in which a word or sound is internally repeated as "cognitively oriented techniques," since repeating a word (i.e., the mantra) presumably blocks other ongoing cognitive activity. In support of this, Schwartz, Davidson, and Goleman (1978) report questionnaire data showing that meditation produces greater decreases in cognitive symptoms of anxiety than does physical exercise, whereas exercise appears to produce greater decreases in somatic anxiety symptoms.

On the basis of the Davidson–Schwartz hypothesis, some clinicians have felt justified in advising meditation for clients who show symptoms of cognitive anxiety, and in advising physiologically oriented techniques such as progressive relaxation or autogenic training for those who show symptoms of somatic anxiety. Although this criterion has the advantage of offering the therapist clear-cut guidelines, the empirical support of cognitive–somatic specialization remains at best insubstantial (see Lehrer & Woolfolk, Chapter 16, this volume). Given the absence of any solid predictive measures at present, and the fact that even those that show promise (such as the Tellegen Absorption Scale) are not readily available in the clinic, a clinician attempting to assess the suitability of meditation for a particular client will do well to determine whether this client shows one or more of the meditation-responsive symptoms or difficulties. The following is a summary checklist of these primary indicators of meditation:

- Tension and/or anxiety states
- Psychophysiological disorders
- Chronic fatigue states

- Insomnias and hypersomnias
- Abuse of "soft" drugs, alcohol, or tobacco
- Excessive self-blame
- Chronic low-grade depressions or subacute reaction depressions
- Irritability, low frustration tolerance
- Strong submissive trends, poorly developed psychological differentiation, difficulties with self-assertion
- Pathological bereavement reactions, separation anxiety
- Blocks to productivity or creativity
- Inadequate contact with affective life
- A need to shift emphasis from client's reliance on therapist to reliance on self (of particular use when terminating psychotherapy)

If the therapist determines that the client possesses the requisite pathology for use of meditation, he or she should recognize that other modalities may also be used for treating these same symptoms. At this point, therefore, the decision to employ meditation becomes a practical one. The following are some of the factors that may guide this decision:

1. *Self-discipline.* The degree to which the client has a disciplined life style may be an important factor to consider when deciding on meditation as a stress management technique. Meditation requires less self-discipline than do most other methods currently used for stress control. The technique itself can usually be taught in a single session, with the remainder of the instruction consisting of training in practical management of the method. Unlike some other techniques, meditation does not require the memorization and carrying out of any sequential procedures. It does not even require the mental effort involved in visualizing muscle groups and their relaxation, or in constructing "calm scenes" or other images. The modern forms of meditation are simple one-step operations that soon become quite automatic. They are therefore particularly useful for those clients who may not be willing to make a heavy commitment in terms of time or effort, or in situations where relatively rapid results are desired.

2. *Self-reinforcing properties.* For many clients, the peaceful, drifting mental state of meditation is experienced as unusually pleasurable, a "vacation" from all cares. This self-reinforcing property of meditation makes it especially appealing to many clients. Other things being equal, a modern form of meditation is more likely to be continued, once experienced, than are the more focused relaxation procedures. Therefore, when motivation to continue with a program for stress management is minimal, mediation may be an especially useful strategy.

3. *Meditative skills.* Smith (1985, 1986) postulates three meditative skills: "focusing" (the ability to attend to a restricted stimulus for an extended period); "letting be" (the ability to put aside unnecessary goal-directed an analytic activity); and "receptivity" (the willingness to tolerate and accept subjective experiences that may be uncertain, unfamiliar, and paradoxical). He suggests a skills-focused approach to meditation, which can both teach such skills in an organized manner and help select prospective meditators on the basis of whether or not they already possess some components of these skills. This is a promising approach, but one that awaits a test battery to measure "meditation readiness" before it can be applied formally in the

clinic. *Informal* assessment of an individual as to whether or not they may possess meditative skills is a possibility, however.

4. *Contraindication for clients with excessive need to control.* Clients who fear loss of control may equate meditation with hypnosis or forms of mind control, and may thus be wary of learning the technique. If they do learn it, they may experience the meditation as a form of punishment, a surrender, a loss of dominance, or a threat to a need on their part to manipulate others; they may soon discontinue the practice unless therapeutic intervention brings about a sufficient change in attitude. Such overly controlling clients may prefer a more "objective" technique that they can manage through conscious effort (e.g., by tensing and relaxing muscles, dealing with biofeedback hardware, etc.). The response of a client to the clinician's initial suggestion that he or she learn meditation will often be the deciding factor: Those clients who fear loss of control during meditation will usually indicate this and will respond negatively to the suggestion that they learn the technique.

Limitations of the Method

Side Effects of Tension Release

Like all techniques used to effect personality change, meditation has its limitations. One of these is the stress release component of meditation, which must be understood if this technique is to be used effectively. Particularly in the new meditator, physiological and/or psychological symptoms of a temporary nature may appear during or following meditation. These have been described elsewhere (Carrington, 1977, 1978) and appear to be caused by the release of deep-seated nonverbal tensions. Their occurrence can be therapeutically useful, provided that the therapist is trained in handling them properly; however, too rapid a release of tension during or following meditation can cause difficulties and discouragement in a new meditator, and may result in a client's backing off from meditation or even abandoning the practice altogether. For this reason, careful adjustments of meditation time and other key aspects of the technique must be made if this modality is to be used successfully. Such adjustments can usually eliminate problems of tension release in short order; accordingly, adjustment of the meditation to suit each practicer's individual needs is central to such modern forms of meditation as CSM.

Rapid Behavior Change

Another potential problem in the use of meditation stems from the rapidity with which certain alterations in behavior may occur. Some of these changes may be incompatible with the life style or defensive system of the client. Should positive behavioral change occur before the groundwork for it has been laid (i.e., before the client's value system has readjusted through therapy), an impasse can occur, which must then be resolved in one of two ways: (1) The pathological value system must be altered to incorporate the new attitude brought about by the meditation; or (2) the practice of meditation must be abandoned. If the meditator facing such an impasse has recourse to psychotherapy to work through the difficulties involved, this usually allows the individual to continue productively with meditation and make use of it to effect a basic change in life style.

Some of the ways in which meditation-related behavioral changes may threaten a client's pathological life style are as follows:

1. Meditation may foster a form of self-assertion that conflicts with an already established neurotic "solution" of being overly self-effacing. The tendency toward self-effacement must then be modified before meditation can be accepted into the person's life as a permanent and beneficial practice.

2. Meditation tends to bring about feelings of well-being and optimism, which may threaten the playing out of a depressive role that may have served an important function in the client's psychic economy.

3. The deeply pleasurable feelings that can accompany or follow a meditation session can cause anxiety. For example, clients with masturbation guilt may unconsciously equate meditation (an experience where one is alone and gives oneself pleasure) to masturbation, and thus may characterize it as a "forbidden" activity.

4. Meditation can result in an easing of life pace, which may threaten to alter a fast-paced, high-pressured life style that is used neurotically as a defense or in the service of drives for power, achievement, or control. Clients sensing that this may happen may refuse to start meditating in the first place—or, if they start, may quickly discontinue the practice—unless these personality problems are treated.

5. A client may develop negative reactions to the meditation process, or to a meditational object of focus such as a mantra. Some individuals initially view meditation as being almost "magical." When they are inevitably forced to recognize that the technique varies in its effectiveness according to external circumstances, or according to their own mood or state of health, they may then become angry and quit the practice unless the clinician can help them modify their irrational demands.

Fortunately, such complications as these do not occur in all meditating patients. Often meditation assists the course of therapy in such a straightforward fashion that there is little necessity to be overly concerned with the client's reaction to it.

Cautions

1. An occasional person may be hypersensitive to meditation, so that he or she needs much shorter sessions than the average. Such a person may not be able to tolerate the usual 15- to 20-minute sessions prescribed in many forms of meditation, and may require drastic reductions in meditation time before benefiting from the technique. Most problems of this sort can be successfully overcome by adjusting the meditation time to suit the individual's needs.

2. Overmeditation can be dangerous. On the theory that "If one pill makes me feel better, taking the whole bottle should make me feel exceptionally well," some clients may, on their own, decide to meditate 3 or 4 hours (or more) per day instead of the prescribed 15–20 minutes only once or twice a day. Like a tonic or medicine, meditation may cease to have beneficial effects if it is taken in too heavy doses, and may become detrimental instead. Release of emotional material that is difficult to

handle may occur with prolonged meditation; in a person with an adverse psychiatric history, the commencement of meditation training has been known to precipitate psychotic episodes (Glueck & Stroebel, 1975; Carrington, 1977; Lazarus, 1976). Although it is not certain that overmeditation will lead to such serious results in relatively stable people, it is probably unwise for any person to enter into prolonged meditation sessions, except in special settings (such as a retreat) where careful supervision is available.

The fact that meditation may be a tonic and facilitator when taken in short, well-spaced dosages, but may have an antitherapeutic effect when taken in unduly prolonged sessions, is essential to consider when reviewing a psychiatric case history where any form of meditation has previously been practiced by a client. Certain forms of meditation currently promoted by "cults" demand up to 4 hours of daily meditation from their followers—an important factor to note when assessing some of the "brainwashing" effects frequently reported by ex-members of these cults.

3. Meditation may enhance the action of certain drugs in some clients. Requirements for antianxiety and antidepressive drugs, as well as antihypertensive and thyroid-regulating medications, should therefore be monitored in patients who are practicing meditation. Sometimes the continued practice of meditation may permit a desirable low-dosage treatment of such drugs over more prolonged periods, and occasionally may permit the discontinuance of drug therapy altogether.

To avoid such difficulties as these, meditation should therefore be practiced in moderation, with the meditator following instructions in a reliable meditation training program. Full training in the management and adjustment of the technique, not just instruction in how to meditate, is essential in the clinical use of meditation.

The Method

Optimal use of meditation in a clinical setting depends on teaching the client to manage the technique successfully—a consideration that can easily be overlooked. Unless routine problems that arise during the practice of meditation are handled, the likelihood of obtaining satisfactory compliance is poor. If the technique is regulated to meet the needs of the particular client, however, compliance is often excellent.

It is doubtful whether meditation can ever be taught effectively through written instructions, since correct learning of the technique relies on the communication of the "meditative mood"—a subtle atmosphere of tranquility best transferred through nuances of voice and tonal quality. Meditation can be taught successfully by means of tape recordings, however, provided that the latter effectively convey this elusive meditative mood (i.e., that they are not "cold" or "mechanical" in nature) and that the recorded teaching system is sufficiently detailed in terms of the information it conveys, so that the trainee is instructed in handling minor problems that may arise before the technique becomes truly workable.

The CSM method (which incorporates ROM as an alternative form of meditation) teaches meditation through cassette tapes and a programmed instruction text, and comprises a total training program in the management of meditation. Because of these advantages, the following discussion on method is confined to CSM. Some of the points made, however, can be applied to any of the modern meditation methods. The following discussion covers some of the ways in which CSM may be introduced to a client.

Introduction of the Method

Clinicians are in a strategic position to introduce the idea of learning CSM to their clients. This is best done by referring to specific difficulties or symptoms that a client has previously identified. Simply mentioning research that suggests that meditation may be useful for these problems is often all that is needed to motivate the client to learn the technique. To forestall misunderstandings, however, several aspects of the CSM method are useful to mention when the subject of meditation is first introduced.

The clinician will want to indicate that this form of meditation is strictly noncultic in nature. Clients with religious convictions will not want their beliefs violated by competitive belief systems and can be relieved to learn that CSM is a "scientifically developed" form of meditation. In addition, clients who are uncomfortable with seemingly unconventional interventions will also benefit from being reassured about the noncultic nature of the method. The clinician will also want to emphasize that the technique is easily learned, since one of the most prevalent misconceptions about meditation is the notion that it requires intense mental concentration. Most people are reassured by the knowledge that a modern technique such as CSM does not require forced "concentration" at all, but actually proceeds automatically once it has been mastered. The clinician should also routinely check on the client's knowledge about and/or previous experience with meditation in order to clear up any further questions about the method.

The preliminary discussion between therapist and client is typically brief, but certain clients may need to be introduced to meditation in a more planned manner. "Type A" clients, for example, may resist learning meditation (or any other relaxation technique) because the idea of "slowing down" threatens their life style, which is often hectic and high-pressured. When a clinician is recommending CSM to a Type A person, therefore, a useful strategy is to indicate that the time that this person will take out of his or her day for meditation practice is likely to result in increased efficiency. Much research suggests that this is so, and Type A individuals are typically achievement-oriented.

Type A or extremely active people can also be helped to accept meditation by being informed that they can break up their practice into a series of what have been termed "minimeditations" (Carrington, 1978). These are short meditations of 2 or 3 minutes (sometimes only 30 seconds) in duration, which can be scattered throughout the day. Frequent minimeditations may be much more acceptable to an impatient, driven sort of person than longer periods of meditation may be (although these can be used too), and they have the advantage of helping the client reduce transient elevations in stress levels as these occur.

A final strategy useful when recommending meditation to Type A or exceedingly active persons can be to inform them that they can use CSM while simultaneously engaged in some solitary sport that they may already practice and enjoy.

Meditation can be successfully combined with solitary, repetitive physical activities such as jogging, walking, bicycling, or swimming, and this practice may be a salutary one. Benson, Dryer, and Hartley (1978) have shown, for example, that repeating a mantra mentally while exercising on a stationary bicycle can lead to increased cardiovascular efficiency.

The Physical Environment and Equipment

CSM is usually taught by means of several cassette recordings and a programmed instruction workbook, but instruction in the technique can also be carried out in person where indicated.

With the recorded training, the client is introduced to the principles of meditation by an introductory tape played before instruction per se is undertaken. Later (usually on another day), the client listens to the actual instruction recording under quiet conditions in a room arranged to certain specifications. During the instruction session, the trainee repeats his or her mantra out loud in imitation of the instructor, and meditates silently "along with" the instructor. Subsequently, the client fills out a postinstruction questionnaire and completes the instruction session by listening to the other side of the tape, which directs meditation practice for the next 24 hours. On the following day the trainee listens to another tape, which discusses potential problems involved in meditation practice, and plays the final tape of the series 1 week later. This last tape prepares the trainee for a permanent practice of meditation. During the week's training period, the trainee works with the programmed instruction text to master the details of his or her meditation practice and to adjust the technique to suit his or her personal needs. The clinician may also assist in making clinically relevant adjustments of the technique.

Most clients learn CSM in their homes (or hospital or dormitory rooms), making their own arrangements for a suitable instruction environment. Where clients are taught on the premises of the clinician (usually so that the clinician can advise immediately on adjustment of the technique), a quiet, uncluttered room where the client can be alone while learning is made available. This room typically contains a comfortable straight-backed chair and some visually pleasant object such as a plant or vase, upon which the trainee can gaze when entering and exiting from meditation. The arrangements are simple, but must be carefully observed for maximum effect.

Therapist–Client Relationship

Once a clinician has selected meditation as the intervention of choice, he or she must then decide whether to teach CSM by means of the recordings or in person. Factors influencing this decision typically center on special requirements of the client. When the clinician is weighing the factors involved, the following advantages of recorded instruction should be noted:

1. Learning the technique in his or her home or room facilitates the client's generalization of the meditative response to the living situation; this helps to prevent problems that can occur when instruction is given in person in a setting outside the

home. In the latter instance, trainees frequently complain that their subsequent meditation sessions are never "the same as" or "as good as" their initial learning session—a factor that may adversely affect compliance.

2. Learning the technique alone, through his or her own efforts, fosters the client's reliance on self as an initiator of the practice.

3. Replaying the recordings at intervals reinforces the meditation practice. The recordings may also be used to re-establish the meditation routine after the client has temporarily ceased to practice it.

4. The client's family or friends can also learn to meditate from the recordings. Their subsequent involvement in the practice (plus the fact that on occasion they may meditate together with the client) can lend substantial support and improve compliance.

5. Certain clients are embarrassed at the idea of speaking a mantra out loud or sitting with eyes closed in anyone else's presence. Such clients find learning by tape preferable.

There are some situations where tape-recorded instruction is not suitable, however. Clients experiencing severe thought disturbances or other clinical symptoms that make it difficult for them to learn from a recording require personal instruction in the technique. Similarly, non-English-speaking clients, clients who belong to a subculture that uses highly idiomatic speech, clients who are too physically ill to concentrate on a recording, or clients who may have a natural antipathy to learning from recordings will also need to be instructed in person. There is a standardized procedure for teaching CSM by means of personal instruction. People who have successfully used other meditation techniques often make excellent instructors of CSM, since almost all meditation techniques have a number of points in common. Even those trained in some of the more concentrative forms of meditation have been able to teach the nonconcentrative, permissive approach of CSM after first learning the technique themselves and practicing it for several months prior to teaching it. Personal experience with this particular meditative technique is essential, in order for the prospective instructor to understand the basic permissiveness of the technique.

Trainees receiving personal instruction first select a mantra from a list of 16 mantras in the workbook. They are instructed to choose the one that sounds most pleasant and soothing to them, or to make up a mantra according to simple instructions. The mantras used in this method are resonant sounds (often ending in the nasal consonants "m" or "n") that have no meaning in the English language, but that, in pretesting, have been shown to have a calming effect on many people. Such sounds as "Ahnam," "Shi-rim," and "Ra-mah" are among those used. After the trainee has selected a mantra, training is conducted in a peaceful setting removed from any disturbances that may detract from the "meditative mood." The instructor walks quietly, speaks in low tones, and typically conveys by his or her behavior a respect for the occasion of learning meditation.

When teaching meditation, the instructor repeats the trainee's mantra out loud in a rhythmical manner to demonstrate how this is done. The trainee then repeats the mantra in unison with the instructor, and finally alone. He or she is next asked to "whisper it" and then simply to "think it to yourself" silently, with eyes closed. Instructor and trainee then meditate together for a period of 10 minutes, after which the trainee remains seated for a minute or two with eyes closed, allowing the mind to return to "everyday thoughts." The trainee is then asked to open his or her eyes very slowly. At this point the instructor answers any questions the trainee may have about the technique and corrects any misconceptions; he or she then leaves the room so that the trainee can meditate alone for a stated period of time (usually 20 minutes). The experience of meditating on one's own is included in order to "wean" the trainee as soon as possible from dependency on the instructor's presence when meditating.

Immediately following the first meditation session, the trainee completes a postinstruction questionnaire and reviews his or her responses with the instructor. In the postinstruction interview, procedures for a home meditation practice are clarified, and instructions are given for the trainee's meditation program for the next week. The trainee is then apprised of possible side effects of tension release (Carrington, 1978; see "Limitations of the Method," above), and is taught how to handle these should they occur.

Individual follow-up interviews are later held at intervals, or group meetings are scheduled where new meditators can gather to share meditation experiences, meditate in a group, or pick up new pointers on handling any problems that may arise in their practice. These trainees then learn to adjust their techniques to suit their own individual needs and life styles. Whatever the method of instruction (recorded or in person), close clinical supervision of the meditation practice is strongly advised. A careful follow-up program insures much greater participation in a continued program of meditation.

Resistance, Compliance, and Maintenance of Behavior Change

Problems of resistance have been discussed above under "Limitations of the Method." Compliance and maintenance of behavior change are now considered.

Compliance

Researchers have found compliance with the modern forms of meditation to be about 50% among adults in a typical community, with about half of those who learn to meditate discontinuing the practice within 3 years of having learned it, and an even larger number cutting down to once instead of twice a day, or to only occasional use of the practice (Carrington, 1977). Several problems emerge when we try to evaluate the existing compliance figures, however, The trend has been to define "compliance" as "regular daily practice" of the meditation technique in question, a viewpoint undoubtedly influenced by the TM organization's firm conviction that twice-daily practice is necessary in order to obtain benefits from meditation. Some recent findings cast doubt on the necessity of daily meditation for all people, however, and suggest that the degree of compliance that is necessary to produce benefits may be an individual matter.

When my colleagues and I (Carrington et al., 1980) studied the use of two modern meditation techniques (CSM and ROM) in a working population self-selected for symptoms of stress, we found that after $5\frac{1}{2}$ months of practicing meditation, these subjects showed highly significant reductions in symptoms of stress as measured by the SCL-90-R, in comparison with controls. However, when the groups were broken down into (1) "frequent practicers" (subjects who practiced their technique several times a week or more), (2) "occasional practicers" (subjects who practiced it once a week or less), and (3) "stopped practicers" (subjects who no longer practiced their technique), the results were unexpected. Although SCL-90-R improvement scores for stopped practicers and controls did not differ (as might be expected), no differences in degree of symptom improvement were found between frequent and occasional practicers when the scores for these two groups were compared, contrary to our expectation. Nevertheless, when frequent and occasional practicers were collapsed into a single "practicers" group, and stopped practicers and controls into a single "nonpracticers" group, the difference in degree of symptom reduction between these two groups was highly significant. As long as subjects practiced at all, then they were likely to show improvement in symptoms of stress. When they did not practice, they were unlikely to improve more than controls.

The finding in this study—that frequent practice appears unnecessary to produce symptomatic improvement—disagrees with those in several studies using the TM technique. The latter studies have reported positive effects of frequent (as opposed to occasional) practice of meditation on neuroticism (Ross, 1978; Tjoa, 1978; Williams, Francis, & Durham, 1976), trait anxiety (Davies, 1978), autonomic instability (Orme-Johnson, Kiehlbauch, Moore, & Bristol, 1978), intelligence test scores (Tjoa, 1975), and measures of self-actualization (Ross, 1978). However, our findings (Carrington et al., 1980) are in agreement with research that has reported no differences between frequent and occasional practicers with respect to anxiety reduction (Lazar, Farwell, & Farrow, 1978; Ross, 1978; Zuroff & Schwarz, 1978).

It should be noted that there were several differences between our study with the employee group and those studies using the TM technique that did not show effects for frequency of practice. All but one of the TM investigations were conducted with subjects who had signed up to learn TM at training centers. These subjects were not selected for high initial stress levels (although in some cases perceived stress may have played a role in their decision to learn meditation). It is therefore unlikely that they were under the same degree of stress as the employees in the Carrington et al. (1980) study, who had been self-selected for this variable and whose initial SCL-90-R scores fell at the edge of the clinical range. Possibly when stress symptoms approach clinical levels, even a moderate amount of meditation, or the use of meditation when needed, is sufficient to achieve sharp reductions in symptomatology. When the initial stress levels are close to the norm, however, it may be necessary to practice meditation more frequently in order to reduce symptoms to a still lower level.

Another factor differentiating the employee study from the others is that teachers of the TM technique prohibit the use of minimeditations, which they consider harmful to proper meditation practice. In the employee study, however, strong emphasis was laid upon the use of minimeditations in addition to full meditation sessions, and the effectiveness of this teaching was demonstrated by the fact that at the end of $5\frac{1}{2}$ months, 88% of the employees who had learned meditation reported that they were using minimeditations. Minimeditations may therefore have exerted a leveling effect, causing a blurring of expected distinctions between frequent and occasional practicers.

Although frequency of practice could not predict stress reduction in the employee study, this should not be taken to mean that frequent practice of a meditation technique is not valuable. For some subjects in the study, regular daily practice may have been necessary for them to acquire noticeable benefits. Realizing this, such people may have developed the habit of meditating frequently. Other subjects, however, may have found it unnecessary to practice their technique more than a few times a week to obtain noticeable symptom improvement. It is also not presently known whether frequent practice will in time produce beneficial changes in some practicers who do not report benefits from frequent practice during the first 6 months; whether physiological (as opposed to psychological) measures respond to occasional practice as well as they do to frequent practice; or whether effective control of a maladaptive form of behavior (e.g., drug addiction) requires the frequent practice of meditation in order to alter this behavior.

Research findings such as those described above, coupled with clinical reports on the benefits of using meditation on a contingency basis (and/or of using frequent minimeditations), suggest the wisdom of reconsidering our present criteria for compliance. This might serve to lessen some of the current confusion in the field. For example, in the Carrington et al. (1980) study, when "practicing at all" (whether frequent or occasional) was used as the criterion for compliance, 81% of the CSM subjects and 76% of the ROM subjects were still "practicing" their respective techniques at the end of $5\frac{1}{2}$ months. However, when "frequent practice only" was used as the criterion for compliance, 50% of the CSM subjects and 30% of the ROM subjects were "practicing" their techniques by the end of this time. Which figures are the "true" ones?

Spontaneous comments offered by subjects in this study (on a postexperimental questionnaire) may offer some clues. When these comments were examined in relation to frequency of practice, analysis revealed that more occasional practicers than frequent practicers were using their techniques for strategic purposes (i.e., as needed); that more frequent practicers than occasional practicers made strong positive statements about the benefits derived from their technique; and that only occasional practicers qualified their statements about their benefits (e.g., "Under extreme pressure in my department, I don't feel as tensed up, but don't find meditation as beneficial as I had hoped" or "I think there has been some possible effect"). The tentative statements of many of the occasional practicers attest to the "in-between" quality of their evaluative statements, as opposed to the certainty that characterized those of the frequent practicers.

We might summarize the findings to date, then, by saying that the effects of frequency of practice are only partially known. Frequency may not play a major role in symptom reduction per se for certain patients (although it may for others), but it may be positively related to perceived benefits in other areas such as personal growth, and seems clearly related to the degree of enthusiasm subjects experience for their technique. In a practical sense, therefore, it would seem wise to encourage regularity of practice in a client wherever possible, without being unduly alarmed if that client should shift from meditating regularly to using the technique for strategic purposes only, or to relying heavily on minimeditations. The deciding factor should be the degree of benefit that the client is deriving from the practice. If this factor remains satisfactory in the estimation of the clinician, then even if the client meditates only occasionally or uses only minimeditations, his or her decision to employ the technique in this manner should be supported.

Also relevant to compliance is the manner in which meditators stop practicing. In the Carrington et al. (1980) study, the timetable for quitting in the stopped practicers was revealing. The practice of meditation appears to have stabilized markedly within the first 3 months. One-third of the stopped practicers reported that they had abandoned their technique within the first 2 weeks after having learned it; another 27% reported that they abandoned it after between 2 and 6 weeks; and still another 37% reported having abandoned it after between 6 weeks and 3 months. Only one subject had abandoned the technique between 3 and $5\frac{1}{2}$ months (during the final $2\frac{1}{2}$ months of the study). It would seem, therefore, that during the first 3 months of their practice, a more or less permanent stand was taken by these trainees with respect to continuation of their meditation practice. Thereafter, while a trainee might shift from frequent to occasional practice (or back again), he or she was extremely unlikely to stop practicing entirely. This timetable of attrition strongly suggests that once meditation has been successfully adopted and practiced for a period of several months, it may become a permanent coping strategy that can then be called upon by a trainee when he or she has need for it—in short, that the strategic use of meditation is not likely to be abandoned.

It has also been observed that meditators may stop practicing meditation temporarily for a variety of reasons. These "vacations" from meditation appear to be a normal part of the practice for many people and are not evidence of noncompliance. It is important, therefore, that the clinician not label a cessation of meditation practice as "dropping out" until such a fact has been proven correct. The client should be helped instead to understand that such "vacations" can be normal occurrences, and that meditators frequently return to their regular practice later on with renewed enthusiasm. In CSM, reuse by the client of a special renewal-of-practice recording by the client is recommended as a useful means of reinstating the meditation practice after having taken a break from it.

The clinician should also be aware that even if a client eventually abandons his or her technique, this is not necessarily a negative sign. Recent reports from a corporate program using CSM at New York Telephone suggest that after an extended period (e.g., 1 year or more) of successful meditation practice, some people may no longer need to practice meditation on a formal basis, because its benefits have been incorporated into their life style. One telephone company employee reported that he no longer needed to meditate, because he had begun to spend his lunch hour eating by the fountain in the courtyard where he worked, "just watching the water rise and fall." He described this as so peaceful that afterward "I feel better for the rest of the day." He typically spent 20 minutes watching the fountain, but before he learned to meditate (approximately a year earlier), "I would never have thought of such a thing, because then I was always in a hurry, even when I had a lunch break." When asked whether his experience of gazing into the fountain had any features in common with meditation, he replied that although this had not occurred to him before, actually the two processes were "exactly the same, except that I don't think the mantra when I watch the fountain."

Similar reports from other long-term meditators, now being collected at New York Telephone, suggest that formal meditation may be phased out by some clients as a meditative approach to life is phased in. Such people appear to have substituted their own meditation equivalents for formal meditation sessions. This is by no means the case with all meditators, however. A sizable number of people need to continue with the formal practice of meditation indefinitely in order to maintain the beneficial changes brought about by the use of the technique.

Maintenance of Behavioral Change

As noted above, the maintenance of behavioral change is substantial and may be closely linked with compliance in some, but not necessarily in all, instances. However, cases have occasionally been reported where after several years of meditation, meditators have ceased to notice any more benefits accruing from their practice. Since these have all been anecdotal reports, it is unclear whether the people involved were actually no longer benefiting from their meditation practice, or whether benefits were still occurring but were not perceived because the meditators' tension levels had been reduced for so long a time. In clinical practice, an empirical test can be applied in the event of reports of diminished benefits. The client can be asked to stop practicing meditation for a stated period of time; if cessation of meditation brings no change in the clinical condition, or if it results in a beneficial change, then meditation (at least as originally learned and practiced) may have outgrown its usefulness for the client. Substitution of another variant of meditation, if this is desired, is sometimes useful at this point and can result in a revival of beneficial effects in some cases. The reasons for these occasional apparent habituations to the method are unclear, as are the causes of reports of certain meditators' having experienced adverse effects after having practiced their techniques for prolonged periods of time. Although the latter problem can usually be brought under control by proper readjustment of the meditation routine, discontinuance of the practice is in order where it cannot.

Case Example

Training in meditation was recommended for a middle-aged female client because her chronic tension headaches had consistently resisted all forms of intervention, even though her other psychosomatic symptoms (e.g., gastric ulcer and colitis) had abated with therapy. After she commenced meditation, this client's headaches worsened for a period of about a week (temporary symptom acceleration is not unusual following commencement of meditation) and then abruptly disappeared; the patient remained entirely free of headaches for 4 months (for the first time in many years).

During this period, however, she noticed personality changes that disturbed her and that she attributed to meditation. Formerly self-sacrificing and playing the role of a "martyr" to her children, husband, and parents, she now began to find herself increasingly aware of her own rights and impelled to stand up for them, sometimes so forcefully that it alarmed her. Although she was apparently effective in this new self-assertion (her adolescent sons began to treat her more gently, making far fewer scathing comments), other members of her family commented that she was no longer the "sweet person" that she used to be, and the client soon complained that "meditation is making me a hateful person."

At the same time, this client also noticed that she was no longer talking compulsively—a change for which she received favorable comments from others, but which bothered her because she was now able to sense the social uneasiness that had been hidden beneath her compulsive chatter. She related this tendency to remain quieter in social situations directly to meditation, since it was more apt to occur soon after a meditation session. Unable to assimilate the personality changes noted, the client stopped meditating, despite the fact that her tension headaches then returned.

It was necessary at this point in therapy to trace the origins of this client's need to be self-effacing before she could consider reinstating the practice of meditation. In doing so, it was discovered that her competition with an older sister was at the root of much of her difficulty in this respect. This sister had been considered a "saint" by their parents, while the client had always been considered a troublesome, irritating child. During her childhood she had despaired at this state of affairs; however, in her adolescence she developed an intense compulsion to become more "saintly" than her exalted sister, although this often meant total sacrifice of her own wishes or needs to those of others. Even the simple pleasure of a total meditation session seemed to this client to be a self-indulgence out of character for so "self-sacrificing" a person.

After working on these problems in therapy, and after some role playing with respect to positive forms of self-assertion, the client finally agreed to resume daily meditation. It was soon discovered, however, that the meditative process was once again pushing her toward self-assertion at too rapid a rate for her to handle. The therapist then suggested that she reduce her meditation to once weekly. Her meditation session was to take place only at the start of each therapy session, and the therapist was to meditate with the client at these times, giving tacit support to the client's right to independence and self-assertion and serving as a role model in terms of acceptance of a meditation practice in one's life.

These weekly joint meditative sessions proved extremely productive; the client described her sessions with her therapist as being "deeply restful," pleasurable, and constructive. Since her emotional responses to each meditation session could be promptly dealt with in the discussion that followed, guilt over self-indulgence was prevented from occurring. With this approach, the client's headaches again disappeared, and she began to experience personality changes typical of regular daily meditators, such as marked enrichment of a previously impoverished fantasy life. She repeatedly stated, however that this weekly meditation session was all she could "take" of meditation at one time without feeling "pounded" by it. In this moderate dose, the client appeared well able to assimilate the changes in self-concept brought about by meditation, and the client–therapist relationship was used to enhance the effectiveness of the meditation through the joint meditation sessions.

As this case illustrates, the use of other forms of therapy along with meditation can be crucial in certain instances to the success of the technique. In most cases, however, meditation contributes to the patient's therapeutic progress with few if any complications.

Comments and Reflections

A note of caution seems appropriate at this point. Although it is clearly desirable to be clinically oriented in one's approach to meditation training, this need not be defined as making the instruction of the technique impersonal in nature. The clinician should be aware that in zeal for objectivity, he or she could inadvertently "throw the baby out with the bath water." The attitude of quiet respect and the peaceful surroundings that have traditionally accompanied the teaching of meditation may have something important to teach us. They cannot, it seems, be lightly dispensed with without losing something essential to the meditative process. Properly taught, meditation can be a compelling subjective experience. To hand a client a sheet of instructions and tell him or her to "go home and meditate," therefore, is likely to result in a serious decrease in the importance the client will attach to learning the meditation, as well as to deprive him or her of a role model to demonstrate the subtle meditative mood.

Following the old adage "easy come, easy go," clients who are taught meditation in an abbreviated fashion and without attention to the conveying of the delicate mood inherent in this practice are apt to treat meditation casually and may soon discontinue its practice. When field-testing versions of the CSM recorded instructions, I discovered, for example, that clients' compliance increased in direct proportion to the inclusion in later versions of informal, "personal," mood-setting recordings. Similarly, when giving personal instruction in meditation, clinicians are advised to give careful attention to the setting and the mood that accompany the teaching of meditation. The instruction need not reflect any belief system, but it should be pleasant, peaceful, and in some sense rather special in nature. Learning meditation is an important moment in an individual's life. If it is treated as such, the entire practice takes on a new and deeper meaning.

A somewhat related issue is the tendency of some clinicians to view meditation as so "simple" that it can be taught in one session merely by imparting the technique itself, and that the client can then be left to his or her own devices. As Smith (1987) has pointed out, many therapists and researchers tend to use truncated versions or "analogues" of authentic meditation training, on the assumption that these are equivalent to the full training. In fact, the analogues merely supply components of meditation that have been isolated from their context. For proper training in meditation, *context* is extremely important. Although the actual techniques of meditation can often be taught in a single carefully structured session, this does not mean that a successful practice of meditation has been established by doing this. The latter requires that a number of changes be made in the trainee's daily routine, that individual regulation of the technique be provided, and that knowledge of ways to handle problems that may arise in meditation practice be taught. Without full training in the management of meditation, in fact, learning the technique alone can be detrimental, in that it may lead a trainee to believe that he or she is not a likely candidate for meditation (because he or she may have run into some problems with its practice) when in fact this may not be the case at all.

The clinician who recommends meditation to a client must therefore be careful to supply complete training in all the practical aspects of the technique. Only in this manner can he or she insure that the method will have the best opportunity to be successful. Imparted with full respect for both its inherent ease and the problems involved in teaching it, meditation can be a potent tool for personality change—one that greatly enlarges the clinician's repertoire.

REFERENCES

Allison, J. (1970). Respiratory changes during the practice of transcendental meditation. *Lancet, 7651*, 833–834.

Appelle, S., & Oswald, L. E. (1974). Simple reaction time as a function of alertness and prior mental activity. *Perceptual and Motor Skills, 38*, 1263–1268.

Banquet, J. (1973). Spectral analysis of the EEG in meditation. *Electroencephalography and Clinical Neurophysiology, 35*, 143–151.

Beiman, I. H., Johnson, S. A., Puente, A. E., Majestic, H. W., & Graham, L. E. (1980). Client characteristics and success in TM. In D. H. Shapiro & R. N. Walsh (Eds.), *The science of meditation*. Chicago: Aldine.

Benson, H. (1975). *The relaxation response*. New York: Morrow.

Benson, H. (1977). Systemic hypertension and the relaxation response. *New England Journal of Medicine, 296*, 1152–1156.

Benson, H. (1989). The relaxation response and norepinephrine: A new study illuminates mechanisms. *Australian Journal of Clinical Hypnotherapy and Hypnosis, 10*(2), 91–96.

Benson, H., Alexander, S., & Feldman, C. L. (1975). Decreased premature ventricular contractions through use of the relaxation response in patients with stable ischaemic heart disease. *Lancet, ii*, 380.

Benson, H., Dryer, T., & Hartley, H. L. (1978). Decreased CO_2 consumption during exercise with elicitation of the relaxation response. *Journal of Human Stress, 4*, 38–42.

Benson, H., & Friedman, R. (1985). A rebuttal to the conclusions of David S. Holmes's article: "Meditation and somatic arousal reduction." *American Psychologist, 40*(6), 725–728.

Benson, H., & Wallace, R. K. (1971). Decreased drug abuse with transcendental meditation: A study of 1,862 subjects. *Congressional Record*, 92nd Congress, First Session, Serial No. 92-1.

Carrington, P. (1977). *Freedom in meditation*. Garden City, NY: Doubleday/Anchor.

Carrington, P. (1978). *Clinically standardized meditation (CSM) instructor's kit*. Kendall Park, NJ: Pace Educational Systems.

Carrington, P., Collings, G. H., Benson, H., Robinson, H., Wood, L. W., Lehrer, P. M., Woolfolk, R. L., & Cole, J. W. (1980). The use of meditation–relaxation techniques for the management of stress in a working population. *Journal of Occupational Medicine, 22*, 221–231.

Carrington, P., & Ephron, H. S. (1975). Meditation as an adjunct to psychotherapy. In S. Arieti (Ed.), *New dimensions in psychiatry: A world view*. New York: Wiley.

Cooper, M. J., & Aygen, M. M. (1979). A relaxation technique in the management of hypercholesterolemia. *Journal of Human Stress, 5*, 24–27.

Das, N. N., & Gastaut, H. (1957). Variations de l'activité électrique du cerveau, du coeur, et des muscles squelletiques au cours de la méditation et de l'extase yogique. *Electroencephalography and Clinical Neurophysiology, 6*(Suppl.), 211–219.

Davidson, R., & Goleman, D. (1977). The role of attention in meditation and hypnosis: A psychobiological perspective on transformation of consciousness. *International Journal of Clinical and Experimental Hypnosis, 25*, 291–308.

Davidson, R., Goleman, D., & Schwartz, G. (1976). Attentional and affective concomitants of meditation: A cross-sectional study. *Journal of Abnormal Psychology, 85*, 235–238.

Davidson, R., & Schwartz, G. (1976). The psychobiology of relaxation and related states: A multiprocess theory. In D. I. Mostofsky (Ed.), *Behavior control and the modification of physiological activity*. Englewood Cliffs, NJ: Prentice-Hall.

Davies, J. (1978). The Transcendental Meditation Program and progressive relaxation: Comparative effects on trait anxiety and self-actualization. In D. W. Orme-Johnson & J. T. Farrow (Eds.), *Scientific research on the Transcendental Meditation Program: Collected papers* (Vol. 1). Livingston Manor, NY: Maharishi European Research University Press.

Delmonte, M. M. (1987a). Personality and meditation. In M. West (Ed.), *The psychology of meditation*. New York: Oxford University Press.

Delmonte, M. M. (1987b). Constructivist view of meditation. *American Journal of Psychotherapy, 41*(2), 286–298.

Derogatis, L. R., Rickels, K., & Rock, A. F. (1976). The SCL-90 and the MMPI: A step in the validation of a new self-report scale. *British Journal of Psychiatry, 128,* 280–290.

Domar, A. D., Noe, J. M., & Benson, H. (1987). The preoperative use of the relaxation response with ambulatory surgery patients. *Journal of Human Stress, 13*(3), 101–107.

Earle, J. B. (1981). Cerebral laterality and meditation: A review of the literature. *Journal of Transpersonal Psychology, 13,* 155–173.

Friskey, L. M. (1984). *Effects of a combined relaxation and meditation training program on hypertensive patients.* Unpublished doctoral dissertation, University of Arizona.

Gaston, L. (1988–1989). Efficacy of imagery and meditation techniques in treating psoriasis. *Imagination, Cognition and Personality, 8*(1), 25–38.

Gellhorn, E., & Kiely, W. F. (1972). Mystical states of consciousness: Neurophysiological and clinical aspects. *Journal of Nervous and Mental Disease, 154,* 399–405.

Glueck, B. C. (1973, March). *Current research on transcendental meditation.* Paper presented at the Rensselaer Polytechnic Institute, Hartford Graduate Center, Hartford, CT.

Glueck, B. C., & Stroebel, C. F. (1975). Biofeedback and meditation in the treatment of psychiatric illness. *Comprehensive Psychiatry, 16,* 302–321.

Goleman, D. (1971). Meditation as a meta-therapy: Hypothesis toward a proposed fifth state of consciousness. *Journal of Transpersonal Psychology, 3,* 1–25.

Goleman, D. J., & Schwartz, G. E. (1976). Meditation as an intervention in stress reactivity. *Journal of Consulting and Clinical Psychology, 44,* 456–466.

Hafner, R. J. (1982). Psychological treatment of essential hypertension: A controlled comparison of meditation and meditation plus biofeedback. *Biofeedback and Self-Regulation, 7,* 305–316.

Heriberto, C. (1988). *The effects of clinically standardized meditation (CSM) on type II diabetics.* Unpublished doctoral dissertation, Adelphi University, Institute of Advanced Psychological Studies.

Holmes, D. S. (1984). Meditation and somatic arousal reduction: A review of the experimental evidence. *American Psychologist, 39,* 1–10.

Honsberger, R. W., & Wilson, A. F. (1973). Transcendental meditation in treating asthma. *Respiratory Therapy: The Journal of Inhalation Technology, 3,* 79–80.

Kanellakos, D. (Ed.). (1974). *The psychobiology of transcendental meditation.* Menlo Park, CA: W. A. Benjamin.

Kelly, G. A. (1955). *The psychology of personal constructs.* New York: Norton.

Klemons, I. M. (1978). Changes in inflammation in persons practicing the transcendental meditation technique. In D. W. Orme-Johnson & J. T. Farrow (Eds.), *Scientific research on the Transcendental Meditation Program: Collected papers* (Vol. 1). Livingston Manor, NY: Maharishi European Research University Press.

Lazar, Z., Farwell, L., & Farrow, J. T. (1978). The effects of the Transcendental Meditation Program on anxiety, drug abuse, cigarette smoking, and alcohol consumption. In D. W. Orme-Johnson & J. T. Farrow (Eds.), *Scientific research on the Transcendental Meditation Program: Collected papers* (Vol. 1). Livingston Manor, NY: Maharishi European Research University Press.

Lazarus, A. A. (1976). Psychiatric problems precipitated by transcendental meditation. *Psychological Reports, 10,* 39–74.

Leserman, J., Stuart, E. M., Mamish, M. E., & Benson, H. (1989). The efficacy of the relaxation response in preparing for cardiac surgery. *Behavioral Medicine, 15*(3), 111–117.

McIntyre, M. E., Silverman, F. H., & Trotter, W. D. (1974). Transcendental meditation and stuttering: A preliminary report. *Perceptual and Motor Skills, 39,* 294.

Miskiman, D. E. (1978). Long-term effects of the Transcendental Meditation Program in the treatment of insomnia. In D. W. Orme-Johnson & J. T. Farrow (Eds.), *Scientific research on the Transcendental Meditation Program: Collected papers* (Vol. 1). Livingston Manor, NY: Maharishi European Research University Press.

Morse, D. R. (1982). The effect of stress and meditation on salivary protein and bacteria: A review and pilot study. *Journal of Human Stress, 8*(4), 31–39.

Murphy, T. J., Pagano, R. R., & Marlatt, G. A. (1986). Lifestyle modification with heavy alcohol drinkers: Effects of aerobic exercise and meditation. *Addictive Behaviors, 11*(2), 175–186.

Muskatel, N., Woolfolk, R. L., Carrington, P., Lehrer, P. M., & McCann, B. S. (1984). Effect of meditation training on aspects of coronary-prone behavior. *Perceptual and Motor Skills, 58,* 515–518.

Orme-Johnson, D. W., Kiehlbauch, J., Moore, R., & Bristol, J. (1978). Personality and autonomic changes in prisoners practicing the transcendental meditation technique. In D. W. Orme-Johnson & J. T. Farrow (Eds.), *Scientific research on the Transcendental Meditation Program: Collected papers* (Vol. 1). Livingston Manor, NY: Maharishi European Research University Press.

Ornstein, R. (1972). *The psychology of consciousness.* San Francisco: W. H. Freeman.

Patel, C. H. (1973). Yoga and bio-feedback in the management of hypertension. *Lancet, ii,* 1053–1055.

Patel, C. H. (1975). 12 month follow-up of yoga and bio-feedback in the management of hypertension. *Lancet, i,* 62–64.

Pelletier, K. R. (1978). Effects of the Transcendental Meditation Program on perceptual style: Increased field independence. In D. W. Orme-Johnson & J. T. Farrow (Eds.), *Scientific research on the Transcendental Meditation Program: Collected papers* (Vol. 1). Livingston Manor, NY: Maharishi European Research University Press.

Pirot, M. (1978). The effects of the transcendental meditation technique upon auditory discrimination. In D. W. Orme-Johnson & J. T. Farrow (Eds.), *Scientific research on the Transcendental Meditation Program: Collected papers* (Vol. 1). Livingston Manor, NY: Maharishi European Research University Press.

Rimol, A. G. P. (1978). The transcendental meditation technique and its effects on sensory–motor performance. In D. W. Orme-Johnson & J. T. Farrow (Eds.), *Scientific research on the Transcendental Meditation Program: Collected papers* (Vol. 1). Livingston Manor, NY: Maharishi European Research University Press.

Ross, J. (1978). The effects of the Transcendental Meditation Program on anxiety, neuroticism, and psychoticism. In D. W. Orme-Johnson & J. T. Farrow (Eds.), *Scientific research on the Transcendental Meditation Program: Collected papers* (Vol. 1). Livingston Manor, NY: Maharishi European Research University Press.

Royer-Bounguar, P. A. (1989). *The transcendental meditation technique: A new direction for smoking cessation programs.* Unpublished doctoral dissertation, Maharishi International University.

Salk, L. (1973). The role of the heartbeat in the relations between mother and infant. *Scientific American, 228,* 24–29.

Schwartz, G., Davidson, R., & Goleman, D. (1978). Patterning of cognitive and somatic processes in the self-regulation of anxiety: Effects of meditation versus exercise. *Psychosomatic Medicine, 40,* 321–328.

Shafii, M., Lavely, R. A., & Jaffe, R. D. (1974). Meditation and marijuana. *American Journal of Psychiatry, 131,* 60–63.

Shafii, M., Lavely, R. A., & Jaffe, R. D. (1975). Meditation and the prevention of alcohol abuse. *American Journal of Psychiatry, 132,* 942–945.

Shafii, M., Lavely, R. A., & Jaffe, R. D. (1976). Verminderung von zigarettenrauchen also folgc transzendentaler meditation [Decrease of smoking following meditation]. *Maharishi European Research University Journal, 24,* 29.

Shapiro, D. H. (1985). Clinical use of meditation as a self-regulation strategy: Comments on Holmes's conclusion and implications. *American Psychologist, 40*(6), 719–722.

Smith, J. C. (1978). Personality correlates of continuation and outcome in meditation and erect sitting control treatments. *Journal of Consulting and Clinical Psychology, 46,* 272–279.

Smith, J. C. (1985). *Relaxation dynamics: Nine world approaches to self-relaxation.* Champaign, IL: Research Press.

Smith, J. C. (1986). *Meditation: A sensible guide to a timeless discipline.* Champaign, IL: Research Press.

Smith J. C. (1987). Meditation as psychotherapy: A new look at the evidence. In M. A. West (Ed.), *The psychology of meditation.* New York: Oxford University Press.

Suler, J. R. (1985). Meditation and somatic arousal: A comment on Holmes's review. *American Psychologist, 40*(6), 717.

Tellegen, A., & Atkinson, G. (1974). Openness to absorbing and self-altering experiences ("absorption"), a trait related to hypnotic susceptibility. *Journal of Abnormal Psychology, 83,* 268–277.

Tjoa, A. (1975). Increased intelligence and reduced neuroticism through the transcendental meditation program. *Gedrag: Tijdschrift voor Psychologie, 3,* 167–182.

Tjoa, A. (1978). Some evidence that the transcendental meditation program increases intelligence and reduces neuroticism as measured by psychological tests. In D. W. Orme-Johnson & J. T. Farrow (Eds.), *Scientific research on the Transcendental Meditation Program: Collected papers* (Vol. 1). Livingston Manor, NY: Maharishi European Research University Press.

Tulpule, T. (1971). Yogic exercises in the management of ischemic heart disease. *Indian Heart Journal, 23,* 259–264.

Wallace, R. K. (1970). Physiological effects of transcendental meditation. *Science, 167,* 1751–1754.

Wallace, R. K., Benson, H., & Wilson, A. F. (1971). A wakeful hypometabolic state. *American Journal of Physiology, 221,* 795–799.

Warrenburg, S., & Pagano, R. R. (1982–1983). Meditation and hemispheric specialization: Absorbed attention in long-term adherents. *Imagination, Cognition and Personality,* 211–229.

West, M. A. (1985). Meditation and somatic arousal reduction. *American Psychologist, 40*(6), 717–719.

Williams, P., Francis, A., & Durham, R. (1976). Personality and meditation. *Perceptual and Motor Skills, 43,* 787–792.

Woolfolk, R. L., Carr-Kaffashan, K., McNulty, T. F., & Lehrer, P. M. (1976). Meditation training as a treatment for insomnia. *Behavior Therapy, 7,* 359–365.

Zamarra, J. W., Besseghini, I., & Wittenberg, S. (1978). The effects of the Transcendental Meditation Program on the exercise performance of patients with angina pectoris. In D. W. Orme-Johnson & J. T. Farrow (Eds.), *Scientific research on the Transcendental Meditation Program: Collected papers* (Vol. 1). Livingston Manor, NY: Maharishi European Research University Press.

Zuroff, D. C., & Schwarz, J. C. (1978). Effects of transcendental meditation and muscle relaxation on trait anxiety, maladjustment, locus of control, and drug use. *Journal of Consulting and Clinical Psychology, 46,* 264–271.

6

Hypnosuggestive Approaches to Stress Reduction: Data, Theory, and Clinical Applications

THEODORE XENOPHON BARBER

A significant proportion of present-day therapists use hypnosuggestions as one part of their broader approach to treatment. The suggestions are not used alone, but as one component of an eclectic approach that integrates procedures from various other therapies (which may include behavior therapy, cognitive therapy, rational–emotive therapy, and psychoanalytically oriented therapy). The many different types of suggestions that are subsumed under the broader term "hypnosuggestions" derive from the very long and rich historical tradition of suggestive therapeutics and hypnosis, which includes such luminaries as Liebeault, Bernheim, Janet, the early Freud, and Erickson.

The emphasis in hypnosuggestive approaches is on the deliberate use by the therapist of suggestions that are intended to help the client cope with stress and with general or particular life difficulties. Within a mutually trusting and congruent relationship, the hypnosuggestive therapist aims to present useful suggestions that are tailored for each client. The kinds of suggestions that comprise the hypnosuggestive therapist's extensive armamentarium can be illustrated by two examples.

At the conclusion of a session with a smoker, after many suggestions have already been given, the hypnosuggestive therapist (or "hypnotherapist") may be heard to be saying something like the following:

> And as you begin to feel again the strength and energy moving through your body and mind, and as you become aware of the deep sweetness of each day of life, you may begin to experience a determination to live with full health and enjoyment. While looking at a cigarette, you may become aware that you don't want it any more, you don't need it any more. You are free, totally free, free to start a new life.

At the conclusion of a session with a socially isolated, relatively depressed client, the hypnosuggestive therapist may be heard to be saying something like this:

> And when you wake up in the morning you may have a feeling that this is your first day on earth and you are looking at the sky for the first time, and you begin to see the depth of the colors and the beauty of the clouds, the sky, and the sunlight. And as you begin to look around you, as if your eyes are opening for the first time, you may begin to feel as if a fog is lifting and everything is becoming fresh and new and sparkling clean. And you are beginning to see again and feel again and be aware again and come alive again for the first time. And you see yourself touching and smelling and feeling the soft texture of a flower for the first time, and hearing the sounds of the wind and music and human voices for the first time.

A lengthy chapter could be written about the uses and effectiveness of each of the innumerable kinds of suggestions that are used in hypnosuggestive therapeutic approaches. In the present chapter, I have sufficient space to focus on only *one* of these many types of suggestions. However, the type of suggestion I discuss is the one used most often in hypnosuggestive therapy; it is unique, and also has special uses in treating stress-related disorders. This type of suggestion, which aims to produce deep relaxation, calmness, "letting go," and "awayness," is given in a calm and relaxing tone and is worded along the following lines:

> Close your eyes and take a deep breath . . . Breathing slowly and deeply . . . and as you breathe out slowly, you may feel more at ease, calm, relaxed, letting go of tensions, worries, frustrations . . . Breathing slowly and gently and calmly . . . letting go of bothers and concerns . . . more serene, relaxed, at ease, at peace, tranquil . . . Peaceful, quiet, deeper and deeper relaxed. Mind calm and body relaxed . . . Warm and comfortable . . . Deeper and deeper, deeper and deeper relaxed.

These suggestions aim to produce "deep relaxation," which refers not only to physical relaxation, but also concomitantly to a calm mind with a "letting go" of and "awayness" from daily concerns. The suggestions typically succeed in their aim; that is, clients typically show reductions in respiratory rate, skin conductance, electrodermal spontaneous activity, and other psychophysiological indices of arousal, and they typically report that they are relaxed in body and mind (Edmonston, 1981).

These kinds of deep relaxation suggestions are used in the great majority of hypnosuggestive therapeutic sessions, for the following "official" and also unofficial or subtle reasons: (1) They define the situation as "hypnosis." (2) They are "easy" suggestions that most clients can "pass," and they thus provide the clients with the experience of successfully responding to suggestions. (3) They can help reduce critical and analytical thinking. (4) They can change the situation so that imagining and fantasizing are appropriate. Also, during the session, they can produce peace of mind, calmness, "letting go," and "awayness," which are useful in therapy for (5) thinking through solutions to life problems; (6) mentally practicing carrying out particular tasks such as being at ease, calm, and "with it" during an interview or while taking a test; and (7) mentally rehearsing overcoming addictions (such as smoking or alcoholism). Finally, (8) suggestions for deep relaxation can help produce a longer-lasting peace of mind and calmness, which are useful for overcoming stress-related disorders such as migraines, headaches, asthma, insomnia, and hypertension. I now discuss in turn each of these eight uses of deep relaxation suggestions in hypnosuggestive therapy.

Uses of Deep Relaxation Suggestions in Hypnosuggestive Therapy

Using Deep Relaxation Suggestions to Define the Situation as "Hypnosis"

Suggestions for deep relaxation implicitly define the situation to the clients as "hypnosis." Many individuals come to hypnotherapists because their (erroneous) conceptions of hypnosis lead them to believe that hypnosis is a uniquely powerful tool; even when they are given potentially potent therapeutic suggestions, they will not accept that they are in a potent situation if they have not been exposed to a preliminary procedure that they view as a hypnotic induction. Since suggestions for deep relaxation are accepted by virtually all clients as a hypnotic induction, they are at times used by hypnotherapists to define the situation to their clients (and also to themselves) as hypnosis, and to capitalize on their clients' (and also their own) positive excitement and expectancies about hypnosis (Barber, Spanos, & Chaves, 1974; Goldstein, 1981; Stanton, 1979). (Of course, defining the situation as "hypnosis" by utilizing a deep relaxation procedure, or in any other way, can also backfire among clients who have not volunteered for hypnotherapy and/or among those who have negative attitudes and fearful expectations toward what they conceive of as hypnosis.)

Deep Relaxation Suggestions as "Easy" Suggestions That Enhance Response to Later Suggestions

Another implicit or latent function of deep relaxation suggestions derives from a general principle: If individuals are first given easy suggestions that they can experience, they are more likely to expect that they will also experience the later suggestions; consequently, they may be more at ease with and more likely to pass the subsequent suggestions (Barber & DeMoor, 1972; Weitzenhoffer, 1953). Suggestions for deep relaxation are "easy" suggestions that are experienced by a high proportion of subjects (Wilson & Barber, 1978). Consequently, by receiving suggestions for deep relaxation, individuals generally find themselves experiencing what is suggested; they presumably say to themselves such things as "It's easy to experience what the therapist suggests," and thus they have more positive expectancies that they will experience subsequent suggestions.

Using Deep Relaxation Suggestions to Enhance Responsiveness by Reducing Critical, Analytical Thinking

A third goal of the suggestions for deep relaxation is more "official" or explicit: to enhance clients' responsiveness to subsequent suggestions by guiding them to become calm, relaxed, less critical and analytical, and less concerned about time, place, and person. If a client does not have negative attitudes or fears about hypnosis, the suggestions for deep relaxation are usually successful in enhancing the subject's responsiveness (Barber, 1969; Weitzenhoffer & Sjoberg, 1961). However, it should also be noted that heightened response to suggestions can also be elicited by procedures that do not lead to relaxation—for example, by exhortative instructions to use one's mind creatively and to think and imagine the suggested effects (Barber, 1969, 1970; Barber et al., 1974; Barber & Wilson, 1977).

Using Deep Relaxation Suggestions to Change the Situation So That Fantasy Is Appropriate

A fourth goal of suggestions for deep relaxation is to change the situation from a reality-oriented, more or less formal social interaction to one where fantasy, primary processes, and a kind of role playing are appropriate (Fromm, 1979; Sarbin & Coe, 1972). For instance, after administering suggestions for deep relaxation, the hypnotherapist feels more at ease in administering, and the client generally feels more at ease in receiving, such suggestions as "I would now like to speak to your Inner Mind" (Francuch, 1981), or "I now wish to speak to your unconscious mind" (Erickson, 1980), or "It is now 1673" (suggestions for "past-life" regression), or "It is A.D. 2112" (suggestions for age progression). Also, since suggestions for deep relaxation change the situation to one that is more "loose"—more informal and less rigid—the hypnotherapist can now more easily advance (and the subject can more easily accept) suggestions to free-associate more easily, to proffer new or creative ideas, and to interrelate with others present in a more "loose" or informal manner. For instance, when clients in insight-oriented therapy who are expected to free-associate are having an unproductive "dry" period in which "nothing comes to mind," the therapist might consider first giving suggestions for deep relaxation and then suggesting, "Now that you are relaxed . . . calm . . . at peace . . . thoughts will flow more freely . . . you will speak more easily . . . ideas and feelings will come to mind and you will find yourself talking about them in a smooth, free-flowing way" (Wolberg, 1948). Similarly, in group therapy, when the group has reached a relatively unproductive period, the therapist can suggest to the group members and to himself or herself that they all are relaxing deeply; immediately upon completion of a series of relaxation suggestions, the therapist could suggest, "After we open our eyes in a few moments, we will continue to feel at ease, at peace, calm, and relaxed, and we will be able to talk with each other more freely and relate with each other more easily and empathically."

It is important to note that suggestions for deep relaxation can be used for this purpose—that is, to change the situation to one where fantasy and a kind of role playing are appropriate—even when the clients do *not* become especially relaxed. Perhaps more important for this purpose than the actual degree of relaxation is the clients' *belief* that they are now in a different situation wherein they can behave and experience in more "loose," fantasy-related, and play-like ways. This is somewhat analogous to a situation where alcoholic beverages are served (or where individuals believe they have received alcohol in their beverages even when they have not); because of their beliefs about alcohol, they now feel more free to converse, to laugh, and to have fun or be silly, even before there is sufficient time for any alcohol in the beverages to take effect (Marlatt, 1979).

Using Deep Relaxation (a "Calm Mind") for Working on Life Problems

Suggestions for deep relaxation are also at times given in order to foster the solving of life problems. This fifth function is based on the premise that at least some decisions or problems can be approached and solved more easily and satisfactorily when a person is experiencing deep calmness. When the suggestions for deep relaxation appear to have produced a state of calmness, the hypnotherapist may say to the client: "Now that you are calm, at peace, tranquil, relaxed [or in hypnosis], you will be able to see new facets and new approaches to a life problem [or to an issue or decision to be made]. As you now work on the problem by yourself with a calm, relaxed, peaceful mind during the next [10] minutes, you will come up with new ideas, insights, and creative solutions."

   This approach can also be used to help clients stop worrying during their daily lives. For instance, I instruct clients to put aside worries deliberately during the day and to set aside about 15 minutes in the evening, when they first listen to a 7-minute cassette tape I have made for them composed of deep relaxation suggestions. While relaxed, calm, and at ease, they are to take one problem in their lives (e.g., a financial or work problem or a problem in interpersonal relations with children, spouse, parents, coworkers, etc.) and let themselves feel and experience the problem in a new way, with new ideas, insights, and viewpoints on how they can best deal with it. This procedure benefits clients in two ways: It minimizes worrying during the day, and it also provides a calm, productive situation for thinking through a life problem.

Using Deep Relaxation (a "Calm Mind") for Mentally Rehearsing Tasks and Performances

In therapy situations, suggestions for deep relaxation also have a sixth function: While relaxed, the client can mentally rehearse carrying out tasks and performances that can be accomplished most effectively when the person is calm instead of tense or "uptight" (Barber, 1979c). For instance, after receiving suggestions for deep relaxation, a client who is to give a speech in public may be asked to rehearse his or her talk mentally while continuing to experience tranquility. More specifically, the client may be given suggestions for deep relaxation and then told, "Continue to feel calm and at peace as you picture yourself or feel yourself walking to the speaker's stand, as you pause and look at the audience, and as you begin speaking. Now hear yourself calmly and smoothly speaking each word as you practice the talk [while remaining deeply relaxed]." Similarly, student clients may be asked to remain deeply relaxed as they see or feel themselves at their desks preparing to study and as they begin to read and become more and more engrossed in the study material (Barber, 1979a; Donk, Knudson, Washburn, Goldstein, & Vingoe, 1968). While in a state of deep relaxation, student clients may also be guided to a mental rehearsal of taking an examination while remaining calm and at ease and allowing the information and material they have learned to flow easily and smoothly from the unconscious (Stanton, 1977). Athletic or sports performances—running, bowling, tennis, football, baseball, weight lifting—can also be mentally rehearsed immediately after the client has received suggestions for deep relaxation. It appears likely that these kinds of procedures, which have been used by a large number of investigators, are useful to the extent that they reduce performance anxiety; by repeatedly practicing the performance while deeply relaxed, the client may be able to extrapolate the feeling of calmness and to minimize anxiety and worry prior to and during the performance.

Using Deep Relaxation (a "Calm Mind") for Rehearsing Overcoming Addictions

Deep relaxation suggestions have a seventh function in therapy situations: They are used to produce a high level of tranquility, which is useful for mentally rehearsing changing addiction behaviors such as smoking, overeating, or overindulgence in alcohol (Barber, 1979b). After receiving suggestions for deep relaxation, the clients are guided to feel themselves in particular situations where they typically have a desire to smoke, to overeat, or to drink alcoholic beverages, and then are guided to imagine and feel themselves calm, relaxed, and at ease in each situation with no desire to smoke, to overeat, or to drink alcohol. This "hypnotic desensitization" procedure is continued until the client has rehearsed calmly avoiding the addiction behavior in all situations in which it is likely to occur.

Using Deep Relaxation Suggestions for Reducing Stress and Tension

Suggestions for deep relaxation have also been used in therapy situations simply to produce a state of deep relaxation. The deep relaxation that is aimed for—the "trophotropic response" (Hess, 1954) or the "relaxation response" (Benson, Beary, & Carol, 1974)—has been used by hypnotherapists for over a century to reduce stress and tension, especially in individuals with stress-related or psychosomatic ailments such as migraine, headache, asthma, insomnia, or hypertension. During the 1800s, hypnotic treatment for ailments of this type typically consisted simply of suggesting to patients that they would become "deeper and deeper relaxed . . . drowsy, sleepy, going into a relaxed, hypnotic state" (Bernheim, 1886/1957; Liebeault, 1889). In fact, Wetterstrand's (1897) practice of hypnotherapy with stress-related and psychosomatic ailments consisted solely of suggesting over and over to the hospitalized patients continually every few hours for a period of days or even weeks that they would remain deeply relaxed, calm, and at peace. The patients would get up from bed briefly to eat and to relieve bodily needs, but otherwise they remained in bed while receiving continual suggestions to relax deeply. Wetterstrand reported that this prolonged hypnotic deep relaxation had marked effects in relieving a wide variety of illnesses that we would now label hysterical and psychosomatic.

Although modern hypnotherapists do not use Wetterstrand's prolonged relaxation treatment, they commonly suggest deep relaxation to their stressed patients and then suggest that they continue practicing the relaxation procedures by themselves at home. I describe the modern hypnotic relaxation procedures in detail later in this chapter.

A Case Illustrating the Many Uses of Deep Relaxation Suggestions in Therapy Situations

The major contention of this chapter, up to this point, has been that hypnotherapists use deep relaxation suggestions for a variety of implicit and explicit purposes. I now present a case of very brief (one-session) hypnotherapy that concretely illustrates this contention. (After presenting the case illustration, I turn to the second major contention of the chapter—namely, that deep relaxation and "active relaxation" suggestions, as used in modern hypnotherapy, are useful for the treatment of stress-related or psychosomatic disorders such as migraine, headaches, asthma, insomnia, and hypertension.)

This case involved Joe R, a 22-year-old man who had married very recently and found himself impotent with his wife, even though he had functioned satisfactorily in previous sexual situations with other women. A few days after his marriage, after he had attempted and failed at intercourse several times, he came to me for help, because he had heard that I used hypnosis in therapy and he believed that hypnosis could quickly alleviate his problem. After he and I had talked for about 35 minutes, it became clear that the underlying problem was a type of performance anxiety.

Joe and his bride, Mary, were the same age, lived in the same small town, and had had a speaking acquaintance during their high school years. When Mary was 20, she was married for a relatively short time (less than a year) to Zack, who had been the star football player on their hometown high school team. Zack was 6 feet 4 inches tall, weighed about 250 pounds, and was powerfully built. In contrast, my client, Joe, was short and thin. After talking to Joe for about 35 minutes, it became clear that (1) Joe and Mary were excited about each other, loved each other, and were very happy to be married; but that (2) when Joe was in bed with Mary, he was self-conscious—instead of focusing on Mary, on loving, on the erotic, the sexual, and the exciting, he was focusing on his "deficiencies" and thinking to himself that Mary was viewing him as "not built like a man" in comparison with her ex-husband. The task for the remainder of the session was to attempt to guide Joe in such a way that later, when he was in sexual situations with Mary, he would shift his thoughts away from himself and his "deficiencies" and toward Mary, to his feelings of love for her, and to the erotic and sexually exciting.

My quickly formulated therapeutic plan was first to present a series of deep relaxation suggestions to Joe so that (1) he would accept that hypnosis was being used in his treatment (and thus would be confirmed in his expectations and beliefs that hypnosis could cure him); (2) he would experience the relatively easy-to-experience suggestions for relaxation and would thus feel that "hypnosis was working"; (3) he would relax and become more calm and at ease with me and with the therapeutic situation; (4) he would become less "reality-oriented" and thus more ready to accept the instructions that I would give him during the session to imagine, to fantasize, and to rehearse mentally an ideal sexual situation; (5) he would become more receptive to the somewhat unusual therapeutic suggestions that I would give him during and at the end of the session; and (6) he would be able to transfer some of the feelings of calmness that he would experience during the session to actual sexual situations that he would experience with Mary later.

I informed Joe that we would now use hypnosis. However, I also informed him that when hypnosis is used therapeutically—for example, to cure a sexual problem—it differs in a very important way from the hypnosis that is seen on the stage, in movies, or on TV. I stated that hypnosis is helpful in therapy when it helps clients feel deeply calm, relaxed, at ease, and at peace. I also stated that in therapeutic hypnosis clients are conscious; for instance, they hear the therapist's words clearly and may also hear outside noises, but they are not concerned about such extraneous matters because they are so relaxed, calm, and at ease. The aim of this introduction was to obviate the basic misconception that I find in virtually all individuals who come to me for hypnosuggestive therapy—namely, that they will be "put under" and be rendered unconscious and unaware of what is "done to them" or what they are told during the hypnotic session. A second reason why I introduced hypnosis in this way was because the suggestions for deep relaxation that I would give him actually aimed to produce exactly what I said—feelings of deep calmness, relaxation, and peace.

I next suggested to Joe that we both close our eyes and let ourselves feel calm. After a few moments I continued:

> Let's take a deep breath, and as we breathe out slowly, we feel all the tensions leaving . . . Take another deep breath, and as we breathe out slowly we feel calm . . . at ease . . . at peace . . . waves of deep calmness . . . waves of deep peace and relaxation flowing through our body and mind . . . lots of time . . . so much time . . . more and more time . . . feeling so good . . . floating . . . at peace . . . deep waves of calmness and tranquility . . . deeply relaxed . . . deep peace flowing calmly and gently through every muscle, organ, and cell . . . absolutely calm . . . waves of deep relaxation . . . lots of time . . . so much time . . . feeling so good . . . deep peace . . . deeper and deeper relaxation.

After suggesting deep relaxation and calmness for about 7 or 8 minutes, I began to interblend suggestions for feeling good, alive, strong, and healthy:

> Mind calm . . . deeply calm and at peace . . . and feeling so good . . . so healthy . . . and strong . . . with peace of mind . . . waves of calm health and energy . . . mind at peace . . . feeling so good . . . so good to be alive . . . waves of calm strength and health flowing smoothly and peacefully through mind and body.

The intent of these additional suggestions, as soon becomes clear, was to prepare Joe to feel calm and yet healthy, vital, and strong when in a sexual situation with Mary.

Next, we moved into the "fantasy rehearsal" or "mental rehearsal" phase, in which I guided Joe to see himself focusing on sexually exciting, erotic loving with Mary:

> You feel yourself now with Mary . . . you feel so good . . . loving . . . close . . . flowing . . . so close to Mary . . . touching . . . feeling calm . . . so good . . . so calm, relaxed, strong, healthy . . . touching . . . hugging close and warm . . . loving . . . vibrant, healthy . . . so alive . . . enjoying . . . deep calmness . . . close and warm and touching . . . feeling so good.

After guiding Joe in this way for a few minutes, I said to him, "Now you take over." He understood my request perfectly well; slowly, with pauses, he verbalized his ongoing fantasy: "I am moving my fingers slowly around Mary's thigh . . . buttocks . . . hugging . . . kissing . . . entering . . ." He continued with long pauses to describe an exquisite sexual experience, apparently basing his fantasy on his sexual experiences prior to his marriage and his hopes and imaginings of what could take place with Mary.

After several minutes Joe concluded his fantasy; while he was sitting back quietly on the reclining chair with his eyes closed, I gave him "posthypnotic suggestions" in a modern form:

> When you're with Mary you can feel like this . . . calm . . . relaxed . . . at peace . . . feeling so good . . . so alive . . . with lots of time . . . flowing . . . with waves of health and strength and energy . . . able to touch . . . and hug . . . and hold . . . and feel . . . enjoying . . . loving.

The "posthypnotic suggestions" were my way of telling Joe that when he was with Mary, he could let himself feel at ease and calm; feel that there was lots of time; feel good about himself and Mary and about being alive; and, instead of thinking about himself and his performance, focus on what was important in the situation—the loving, the sexual, the exciting, the erotic—and let his body do what it would do naturally.

Joe telephoned the next day and stated that everything was "great" and that the sexual encounter with Mary was quite similar to the one he had imagined in my office. A follow-up telephone call on my part, about a year later, confirmed that their sexual relations continued at a high level. Of course, this was not a difficult case—Joe and Mary loved each other, and Joe had previously experienced satisfactory sexual relations—and he could have been helped relatively quickly by many approaches. The reason for presenting this uncomplicated case here is that it illustrates the first major theme of this chapter—namely, that suggestions for deep relaxation serve many functions in therapy situations.

Let us turn now to the second major theme of this chapter: the usefulness of deep relaxation and "active relaxation" suggestions in the hypnosuggestive treatment of stress-related disorders.

Hypnotherapeutic Treatment of Migraine Combining Deep Relaxation with "Active Relaxation"

A series of studies reviewed by Mitchell and White (1977) and by Adams, Feuerstein, and Fowler (1980) indicates that in individuals with a predisposition to migraine, the migraine headaches are typically precipitated by "negative" thoughts and feelings (negative emotions), such as resentment or anger, associated with life events perceived as stressful (Bakal, 1975; Bihldorf, King, & Parnes, 1971; Henryk-Gutt & Rees, 1973; Mitchell, 1969; Mitchell & Mitchell, 1971; Selby & Lance, 1960). Henryk-Gutt and Rees (1973), for instance, asked migraine patients to observe for a period of 2 months both their emotional state and any other associated events coinciding with the onset of migraine. Although the patients were frequently distracted by the onset of the migraine and had difficulties in carrying out the assignment, they nevertheless were able to associate 54% of the migraines with emotional stress. Other studies, reviewed by Harrison (1975), indicate that unexpressed anger may be the most common emotion related to the onset of migraine. These and other data suggest the hypothesis that reducing negative emotions by using hypnosuggestions for deep relaxation and "active relaxation" (maintaining equanimity during ongoing daily activities) may reduce the severity and frequency of migraine. This hypothesis was supported in studies by Meares (1967, p. 31) and Harding (1967), and in an investigation carried out in London (Anderson, Basker, & Dalton, 1975; Basker, Anderson, & Dalton, 1978).

Anderson, Basker, and Dalton conducted their study with 47 new patients who met strict criteria for migraine (e.g., unilateral recurrent throbbing headaches preceded by a visual or other sensory aura and present for at least 1 year). The patients were randomly assigned to two treatments: Half were to be treated by hypnotic suggestions emphasizing deep relaxation and "active relaxation," and half were to receive the drugs that were typically prescribed for migraine in that medical setting. Four physicians worked on the project, and each treated half his patients with the hypnotic procedures and half with the drug therapy. The patients on drug therapy were seen by the physicians once per month for 12 months and were asked to take 5-mg doses of prochlorperazine (Stemetil) four times daily during the first month and thereafter twice daily. They were also provided with ergotamine to be taken at the first sign of migraine. Patients assigned to the hypnosis treatment were also seen monthly for a year. During the first part of the year, they participated in at least six sessions in which they were exposed to hypnotic procedures, which were comprised of (1) repeated suggestions for deep relaxation, followed by (2) suggestions that the patients would be less tense, anxious, and apprehensive, and more energetic and happier (Hartland, 1965). Next, the patients were instructed and shown how to give themselves daily suggestions of deep relaxation ("self-hypnosis"). They were also instructed to give themselves suggestions for "active relaxation" whenever they first felt the beginning of a migraine, without necessarily closing their eyes and sitting down; at the first indication of a migraine, they were to massage their foreheads lightly and repeat silently to themselves suggestions such as "Becoming more and more calm . . . more and more comfortable . . . I feel the comfort spreading."

As Table 6.1 shows, 43% of the patients treated by the hypnotic relaxation procedures reported no migraine headaches during the last 3 months of the project, as compared to 13% treated by drugs. Also as shown in Table 6.1 the average number of migraines dropped markedly under the hypnotic treatment but not under the drug treatment, and the number of patients suffering very severe, incapacitating attacks of migraine decreased markedly in the hypnotic group but did not drop at all (in fact, went slightly up) in the drug group.

Since individuals receiving the hypnotic therapy apparently received more unique, intense, and close attention from their physicians than did those receiving the drug therapy, they probably had a stronger tendency to overemphasize the success of their treatment. Keeping this reservation in mind, we can interpret the results as follows: Ostensibly useful procedures that can be added to the armamentarium of all therapists who treat migraine include (1) suggestions for deep relaxation given first in the office and then practiced daily at home; (2) positive suggestions for reduced anxiety and apprehension and for heightened well-being; and (3) instructions to use "active relaxation" in daily life, especially when experiencing the first signs of mi-

TABLE 6.1. Hypnosuggestive Therapy versus Drug Therapy of Migraine

Outcome	Hypnosuggestive therapy ($n = 23$)	Drug therapy (prochlorperazine and ergotamine) ($n = 24$)
Median number of migraines each month		
6 months prior to therapy	4.5	3.3
First 6 months of therapy	1.0	2.8
Second 6 months of therapy	0.5	2.9
Number of patients with incapacitating attacks		
6 months prior to therapy	13	10
First 6 months of therapy	4	13
Second 6 months of therapy	5	14
Patients reporting no migraines during last 3 months of therapy	10 (43%)	3 (13%)

Note. The data are from Anderson et al. (1975).

graine. Research would be useful here to determine whether these three components are equally useful in minimizing migraine, or whether one is significantly more useful than the others.

The study described above focused almost exclusively on treating migraines by training patients in deep relaxation and "active relaxation" in a hypnotic context. In another recent study, Andreychuk and Skriver (1975) included in their hypnotic treatment of migraine both suggestions for deep relaxation and direct suggestions for reducing the migraine pain. They reported that the hypnotic treatment reduced the frequency, duration, and intensity of the migraines over the 10-week treatment period, but not more so than two other comparison treatments that also aimed to produce relaxation—namely, an alpha biofeedback treatment, and a skin temperature biofeedback treatment that was combined with autogenic phrases (self-suggestions for calmness and relaxation).

In an earlier study, Basker (1970) taught deep relaxation (which he called "autohypnosis") to 28 migraine patients and also gave them positive suggestions to feel more competent, assertive, happy, and so forth, plus direct suggestions for control of blood flow to the cranium. A follow-up of the patients, which varied for different patients from about 1 year to 3 years, indicated that 16 of the 28 (57%) had experienced complete remission of their migraines.

Migraines have also been reduced in frequency, duration, and intensity by various other procedures that aim to produce a state of deep relaxation. These include thermal biofeedback (Johnson & Turin, 1975; Wickramasekera, 1973); thermal biofeedback together with progressive relaxation and/or together with autogenic phrases for calmness and relaxation (Blanchard, Theobald, Williamson, Silver, & Brown, 1978; Sargent, Green, & Walters, 1972); progressive muscle relaxation (Hay & Madders, 1971; Lutker, 1971); transcendental meditation (Benson, Malvea, & Graham, 1973); and a combination of muscle relaxation and transcendental meditation (Warner & Lance, 1975).

If an individual prone to migraines can learn to maintain calmness and peace of mind (an outlook that is not worried, not irritated, not frustrated, and not bothered), it is highly likely that his or her headaches will be markedly reduced, if not totally alleviated. However, there is no reason to believe that hypnotic training in deep relaxation and active relaxation, or training in other relaxation procedures such as biofeedback and progressive relaxation, is maximally effective in producing a generalized calmness and equanimity. In fact, it appears likely that the equanimity of clients can be maximized by using a variety of therapeutic procedures in addition to training in relaxation.

A pertinent investigation is that done by Mitchell and White (1977). These investigators treated their migraine patients over a period of 48 weeks by training in several relaxation procedures (progressive muscle relaxation, mental relaxation, and self-desensitization), supplemented by instructions to the clients to practice deep relaxation daily and also to practice active relaxation whenever they became aware of negative thoughts, feelings, or emotions. This treatment was associated with a 55% reduction in migraine frequency at a 60-week follow-up (compared to a 4% reduction for control patients who merely self-recorded the frequency of their headaches). However, a more marked 83% reduction in migraine frequency was found in a group of patients who received training in all of the relaxation procedures mentioned above, *plus* training in additional behavioral and cognitive–behavioral procedures such as thought stopping, time out for worry, assertion training, imaginal modeling, *in vivo* desensitization, and rational thinking.

In summary, the data indicate that hypnosuggestive procedures, such as suggestions for deep relaxation to be practiced daily and self-suggestions for active relaxation to be used at the first sign of migraine, are useful in migraine therapy, but that the hypnotherapeutic procedures should be part of a broader armamentarium of useful approaches that are presently available (see Friedman & Taub, 1984, 1985).

Multidimensional Hypnotherapeutic Approach to Tension Headaches

Individuals who often have tension headaches usually have difficulties in coping with life problems and tend to have many negative thoughts and feelings (negative emotions), such as anxiety, worry, anger, loneliness, and depression (Friedman, 1972; Harrison, 1975; Martin, 1978; Ziegler, 1978). Since relaxation training can increase feelings of calmness and reduce negative emotions, it can generally be expected to have an ameliorative effect on tension headaches. This hypothesis has been confirmed in a rather large number of studies, which have shown that procedures that aim to produce relaxation (e.g., training in progressive muscle relaxation, electromyographic [EMG] biofeedback, and hypnotic induction focusing on suggestions for deep relaxation) are generally effective in reducing the frequency and intensity of tension headaches below the levels found with placebos or with a no-treatment control (Chesney & Shelton, 1976; Cox, Freundlich, & Meyer, 1975; Daniels, 1976, 1977; Epstein, Abel, & Webster, 1976; Fichtler & Zimmerman, 1973; Haynes, Griffin, Mooney, & Parise, 1975; Tasto & Hinkle, 1973). Although there are problems in drawing strong conclusions from these studies—for example, the reduction in headaches may have been partly due to the relaxation training's changing the clients' expectancies that they could control their headaches, or to their now interpreting their unchanged headaches as less severe—I can nevertheless agree with Blanchard, Ahles, and Shaw (1979), who carefully reviewed the data, that the "regular practice of some form of relaxation" is a useful approach in the treatment of headaches. (See also Spinhoven, 1988; VanDyck, Zitman, Linssen, & Spinhoven, 1991.)

The important goal, however, is not "muscle relaxation" per se (as some of the earlier work in this area would lead us to believe), but peace of mind; equanimity in the face of situations perceived by others as stressful; and reduction in anxiety; anger, and other negative emotions (Meares, 1967; Philips, 1978; Rachman, 1968). It is, of course, possible for a person to be calm, not worried, at peace, and so on, while simultaneously tensing many muscles—witness, for example, a champion long-distance runner who is continually tensing virtually all muscles while running with equanimity. On the other hand, a person may have virtually all muscles very relaxed and yet may be very frightened, worried, and mentally far from relaxed—witness a person who has been exposed to a muscle-paralyzing drug, such as curare. In fact, if muscle relaxation were especially important, then muscle-relaxing drugs should be especially efficacious in headache therapy; unfortunately, this is not the case (Ostfeld, 1962).

A major aim of a multidimensional approach to the treatment of tension headaches should be to help clients "relax" in a much broader sense—that is, to maintain calmness, peace of mind, and "active relaxation" throughout their daily lives, especially when situations are encountered that tend to arouse negative emotions.

The beginnings of a multidimensional hypnosuggestive approach to the treatment of headaches have been presented by Field (1979), who worked with 17 long-term headache patients, each of whom had previously undergone drug therapy for chronic headaches over many years. The patients were given suggestions for deep relaxation and were encouraged to practice the relaxation at home. Other procedures in the armamentarium of the hypnotherapist (e.g., age regression and scene visualization) were used to uncover attitudes and emotions that underlay the headaches. Suggestions aimed to enhance assertiveness and to heighten self-confidence were also used to help the patients handle life problems more efficiently and with more equanimity. Field reported that after four or five therapy sessions, 5 of the 17 patients (29%) showed total alleviation of their long-standing headaches, and an additional 29% showed marked reduction in the frequency of headaches. Field concluded that in treating tension headaches therapists should utilize a broad armamentarium, including a variety of hypnosuggestive procedures, which aim to enhance personal adjustment by reducing negative attitudes and emotions.

It appears that cost-effective treatments of headaches will be maximized when therapists are able to select, from a large number of potentially useful approaches, those procedures that can help a specific client (Turin, 1981). These approaches may include insight-oriented procedures for uncovering the client's long-standing attitudes and cognitions that underlie present problems; cognitive-behavior therapy procedures, which aim to change the client's self-defeating methods for handling life problems; and hypnosuggestive procedures, which aim to heighten the client's self-esteem and to help him or her maintain calmness and serenity in daily life. To help readers of this chapter incorporate some of the hypnosuggestive procedures into their approaches, I now present my general methods for treating headaches. Since the aim is to highlight the hypnosuggestive procedures, I present these procedures in detail, and I only mention peripherally other procedures I also use that derive from other therapeutic approaches.

The preliminary procedures in my approach to tension headaches include consultation with a physician to exclude brain tumor, subarachnoid hemorrhage, allergies, dietary deficiencies, and other medical causes for headaches; also included is a thorough interview to reconstruct the patient's life history and headache history, with special emphasis on problems pertaining to self-esteem, self-confidence, and interpersonal relations. In the first treatment sessions, I try to attain four goals: to explain to clients how negative thoughts and feelings of resentment, anger, guilt, and self-criticism are related to the onset of headaches; to help them become aware of subtle signs that a headache is beginning; to guide them to look for past and present associations between negative emotions and the beginning of headaches; and to sensitize them to situational cues that trigger negative thoughts and feelings, which in turn can precipitate headaches (Holroyd & Andrasik, 1978; Holroyd, Andrasik, & Westbrook, 1977).

Also early in the treatment, I explain to the clients that headaches can be minimized when they are able to remain calm and avoid negative emotions as they face the day-to-day problems of life. I also explain that they can begin to proceed toward learning to live with equanimity by first practicing deep relaxation and "active relaxation." Since most of my clients come to me for hypnotherapy, I define the deep relaxation procedures as "self-hypnosis"; for those who do not come for hypnosis, I call the same procedures, with equal validity, "deep relaxation."

I then give suggestions for deep relaxation to each client while he or she reclines comfortably on a lounge chair with eyes closed. These suggestions, which are individualized for each client, typically include such phrases as "taking a deep breath and letting all the tensions go . . . relaxed . . . calm . . . deep peace . . . letting go . . . lots of time . . . waves of relaxation, peace, and calmness moving into every cell, every tissue, every muscle . . . deep, deep calmness." While giving the suggestions to the client, I let myself experience the suggested calmness, and I thus present the suggestions slowly and calmly; in fact, peace and calmness are imbedded in the tone, pacing, pauses, and meaning of each word. Also, while giving these suggestions, I simultaneously make a cassette audiotape recording (which usually extends over a period of about 7 to 12 minutes).[1] I give the tape recording to the client and instruct him or her to use it at home. Typically, the client is asked to listen to the tape and to relax deeply every evening immediately before or after supper; also at another specified time earlier in the day; and, if possible, whenever signs of an incipient headache are detected. Further procedural details are also worked out with the client (e.g., how to listen to the tape alone in a quiet room and how to set oneself to relax deeply without falling asleep).

---

[1]With the exception of those cassette tapes that are to be used before the client goes to sleep, the tapes end with statements such as these: "In a few moments you will open your eyes and feel refreshed . . . feeling good . . . alert . . . so alive . . . Opening your eyes while feeling alert, refreshed, very awake."

During the next therapy session, the client's utilization of the cassette tape and the effectiveness of the suggestions are discussed. Toward the end of this session, I often present the client with a revised set of deep relaxation suggestions, which take into account the client's comments regarding the original suggestions. These revised suggestions are also recorded on audiotape, and the client is asked to listen to them at home during the forthcoming week.

Overlapping with the home practice of deep relaxation, I begin to guide the client to use active relaxation. Although clients have been previously instructed to find an isolated place in which to practice deep relaxation whenever they experience the beginnings of a headache, it is also acknowledged that headaches often begin in situations from which people cannot escape. Clients are told that when they become aware of a beginning headache while they are working, interacting with others, or engaging in other activities during the day, they can reinstate a feeling of calmness and peace of mind that can abort the headache by subvocally saying to themselves and feeling the meaning of "cue words," such as "at ease," "relaxed," "lots of time," "take it easy," "peace," "centered," and so on. The instructions for active relaxation are usually worded along the following lines:

> Whenever you feel the slightest sign of what may be the beginning of a headache, or when you begin feeling frustrated, angry, irritated, nervous, or bothered, and it is not possible to leave the situation and to relax deeply, then repeat silently to yourself "cue words" such as "calm" and "centered" and let yourself feel calm and centered as you continue with the task you are performing. By shifting to feelings of calmness, you will remove the conscious or unconscious negative thoughts and feelings that bring on the headache.

Mental rehearsal is then used in the office to practice active relaxation. Clients are asked to close their eyes and to picture or feel themselves in situations that are likely to be followed by a headache or that tend to produce anger, resentment, guilt, feelings of worthlessness, or the like. When clients signal—for instance, by a small finger movement—that they feel themselves in the situation (which can vary from being stuck in a traffic jam to being rejected by a significant person), they are told, "Now feel yourself saying to yourself, 'Calm . . . relaxed . . . flowing with the situation,' and picture and feel yourself calm and relaxed [in the situation]."

The above-described procedures—practice of deep relaxation and of active relaxation—are imbedded in a broader context. One facet of this broader context is the work performed by the client and myself in delineating and analyzing the way the client has approached and is approaching life problems, as well as the ways in which these approaches are determined by his or her specific life experiences. These discussions often involve step-by-step analysis of how the client has handled particular past and is handling particular present problems, plus such procedures as hypnotic age regressions to probe the early background of the problems.

In addition, the broader context includes utilization of suggestions to provide a philosophical context for "flowing with" the problems of life, and also suggestions that aim to raise the client's self-esteem. To teach my clients to "relax" in the most meaningful sense—to be able to meet the major and minor problems of life with equanimity—I have found it necessary to expend much effort in gently guiding them to develop a broader philosophy of life. I next discuss my philosophical hypnosuggestive approach to "flowing with the problems of life," and then I discuss my philosophical hypnosuggestive approach to raising self-esteem.

Philosophical Context for Flowing with Life Problems

To place the active relaxation in the broader context, I discuss with the clients their "philosophy of living," and I gently try to guide them to accept a broader philosophy, which is based on four tenets that I now describe. Whenever appropriate, I also make audiotapes that present the philosophy of living in a way that is acceptable to the client (Barber, 1978). (When I am making the audiotapes in the office, the client is told that I will now employ philosophical hypnosis; he or she is then given suggestions for relaxation, followed by statements that suggest a more useful philosophy of life.)

The major tenets of this philosophical approach for coping with the difficulties of life are as follows:

1. For every human being, life has undesirable aspects. Aging and death are inevitable for me and you and every person we care about. Also, either we or people we love will experience birth defects, paralysis, blindness, deafness, major physical and mental illnesses, severe pain, bodily disfigurement, and many other very undesirable happenings. Every human being will also experience other unwanted events, such as loss of a job or loss of financial security; rejection by parents, lovers, children, or friends; unsavory encounters with others (parents, siblings, spouses, children, friends, coworkers) who are not the way "we want them to be"; and encounters with many undesirable external events (ranging from inclement weather or traffic jams to wars or a world in turmoil). The first and most essential facet of wisdom and ability to live happily is *fully to accept at a very deep level* that life inevitably has problems and that virtually every day we will encounter events and behaviors from others that we do not like at all and that we wish would never occur. When we deeply accept the fact that in living we will sooner or later encounter major undesirable events and also daily unwanted happenings, we meet the problems of life philosophically, with the thought and feeling that "This is a happening that I do not like at all, but it is part of life—one of the many undesirable events that I and every other human being will experience in our lives." This philosophical attitude, which is found in those who have attained wisdom and the ability to live at a high level, is quite different from the implicit philosophy adopted by the great majority of individuals. When encountering their daily quota of unwanted happenings, most people magnify the undesirable aspects by refusing to accept deeply that life has problems, and by repeating to themselves such statements as "It can't be . . . it shouldn't be . . . I can't stand it . . . This can't be happening to me [or my children, spouse, parents, friends, etc.] . . . It isn't fair . . . I'm going to scream . . ." (Ellis, 1962).

2. As stated above, the first principle of wisdom is the deep acceptance that life

has major undesirable events and daily unwanted difficulties. The second principle of wisdom is to accept deeply and calmly the immediate difficulty as one of life's undesirable events that happens to face us now, by stating calmly to ourselves, "I have this undesirable happening now in my life. Can I change it for the better, and, if so, how?"

3. The third principle of wisdom is to realize deeply that we cannot change many things we do not like. We cannot change any event that has already occurred. We cannot change what we have already said or done, or what has happened to us or to people we care about. Also, we can influence only some events that will occur from now on, and then only to a certain degree. We can influence the interpersonal situations and the tasks that we encounter in our lives by thinking and planning ahead, so that we can interrelate with others and perform our tasks and jobs with as much preparation and equanimity as possible. We can influence the happenings in our lives very little if at all for the better by directly trying to change others. Since many difficulties in life are related to the behavior of other people, individuals often try to surmount their problems by attempting to change the behaviors of others. In fact, almost everyone tries to change the attitude and behaviors of significant individuals in their lives by directly or indirectly criticizing them; telling them what they should or should not do; and subtly trying to make them feel guilty, incompetent, inferior, and unlikable. These approaches may change the behaviors of significant others superficially—they may comply to avoid the criticisms or negative reinforcements—but it does not change the attitudes and understandings that underlie their actions, and it is very likely to elicit resentment and hostility (Skinner, 1953).

4. The fourth major principle of wisdom is that we can improve our life situations by (a) thinking ahead calmly so that we can encounter people and situations with preparation and serenity; (b) changing ourselves so that we are more accepting, nonjudgmental, compassionate, and loving toward ourselves and others; (c) emphasizing the positive aspects and the positive potentials of ourselves and others; (d) modeling for others (showing them what they can be by our example); and (e) when others look up to us and wish to learn from us, talking to them and gently guiding them in an accepting and loving way.

These four principles are directly implemented and practiced in the hypnotic situation. Clients choose a specific problem facing them now, such as a financial problem, a health problem, or a problem in interrelating with others (such as a boss, a coworker, a parent, or a spouse). Next, the clients are given suggestions for deep relaxation for about 7 minutes, and then are given suggestions to see themselves handling the problem situation with wisdom and maturity—that is, accepting deeply that life has problems, including this specific problem; calmly deciding whether this is one of the many life difficulties that cannot be changed directly or whether there are steps that can be taken to improve the situation; calmly deciding what steps can be taken; and then calmly rehearsing mentally the actions that will be executed later with equanimity. The client is also given a cassette tape of the instructions to take home and to use at specified times as an aid in relaxing deeply and applying the four principles to immediate life problems.

A Hypnosuggestive Approach for Enhancing "Relaxation" (Equanimity) by Raising Self-Esteem

Virtually all clients who come for therapy have low self-esteem; they feel they are more or less unattractive, unlovable, incompetent, unexciting, unappealing, dull, and so on. This negative self-image is a very serious hindrance in attempting to help the clients relax in the most meaningful sense—facing the day-to-day events of life with equanimity. There appears to be a threshold level of positive self-regard that is necessary to enable clients to utilize active relaxation in everyday life. Some of the hypnosuggestive procedures that I use to help clients raise their levels of self-esteem include the following:

1. First, I look for and emphasize all of the manifest and latent positive characteristics that I can observe about a client. I am always able to find many such attributes, and I sincerely tell the client about them at intervals in our discussion, using statements such as the following:

- You have done so much [or worked so hard or struggled so much] in your life.
- You have been able to overcome so many difficulties [misfortunes, illnesses, rejections, deaths of loved ones].
- You have helped many people in your life.
- You did well in a very difficult situation.
- You really care about people.
- You have much empathy and love for others that you have not been able to express.
- You are a kind person.
- You have so much that you haven't begun to use—so much more love, so much more competence, so much more ability to be at ease, to enjoy life, to live fully.

In addition to interspersing these kinds of statements in our discussions, I also include them as suggestions in the hypnosuggestive procedures; for example, after the client has been given repeated suggestions of deep relaxation, he or she may be given a series of suggestions on various topics, interspersed with suggestions that "Starting now, you can begin to focus more on your strengths and positive aspects . . . you can become more aware of your ability to overcome obstacles . . . your caring and love for people . . . your growing ability to be at ease and to enjoy life," and so on.

2. A second hypnosuggestive approach that aims to enhance self-esteem derives from the fact that clients with low self-regard have typically been criticized by parents or other significant individuals in their early lives, and they have incorporated the criticisms into their self-images. In the therapy sessions, we trace back the destructive criticisms the clients have received from parents, siblings, or other important people ("You're dumb, stupid, ugly, clumsy, rotten, no good," etc.). After we have uncovered some or many of the origins of the low self-esteem, I proceed as follows in a hypnosuggestive session. I first give to the client (and indirectly to myself) suggestions for deep relaxation, and then, when the client and I are both relaxed with eyes closed, I speak to the client from my "inner self"—for instance, somewhat as follows:

We understand now why you have felt you were unattractive, unintelligent, and not likable. It is clear now that your mother had a tremendous amount of resentment and anger and was unable to love you or anyone else because of her own father, who degraded her and made her feel totally unlikable and worthless. It's clear that you were too young to understand why your mother constantly put you down and screamed at you and made you feel there was something wrong with you. You can now see how your negative feelings about yourself were due to negative suggestions you received constantly from your mother, who was negative about everything and everyone because of her own misery. Now you can begin breaking through the negative suggestions you have received, you can begin coming out of the negative hypnosis you have been in for so many years, and you can begin to be your true self that has been held down for so long. You can see more and more clearly that as long as you were negatively hypnotized and believed you were stupid, ugly, and no good, you reacted to events and people around you in a nonconfident, afraid way, which tended to confirm your own beliefs. You can now begin to let go of these negative suggestions and begin to be your true self, realizing more and more each day that you are a good, kind, loving, and lovable person. Each day you can become less and less afraid, more and more at ease, more and more able to enjoy life and to be your true self.

3. As part of the hypnosuggestive approach to raising self-esteem, I make additional cassette tapes for clients (cf. Barber, 1978, 1979a, 1979b). These tapes, which are made when a client and I are in my office, begin with suggestions for deep relaxation, followed by specific suggestions that aim directly or indirectly to enhance self-esteem by guiding the clients to focus on their underlying strengths, virtues, and positive qualities. The clients are asked to listen to the cassette tape at home once a day during the forthcoming week, to let themselves relax deeply, and to let the ideas "go deep in your mind." Although these tapes are individualized for each client, they typically emphasize positive aspects of the client that have been neglected or suppressed and that can be released and expanded. Examples of the kinds of suggestions that are included in the hypnosuggestive tapes are as follows:

You have much caring and concern and love for others that you hold down and keep within you . . . You can begin now to let out these good feelings . . . allowing the kind, caring, good feelings to flow out to others . . . you can begin more and more to be your true self as you release your warmth and empathy toward others.

Starting now, you can be more and more aware of your true self that is being released, and you can stop criticizing yourself. . . . You can stop blaming yourself for what you did that you should not have done or what you did not do that you should have done, and you can forgive yourself as you forgive others . . . you can be kind to yourself as you are to others . . . as loving to yourself as you are to others . . . you can stop criticizing and blaming yourself, and you can be free—free, more and more, to be your true self.

Starting now, you can more and more allow yourself to be the person you can be . . . appreciating again and grateful again to be able to see, to hear, to smell, to touch, to be alive . . . appreciating again as if it's your first day on earth, as if you've never felt the sun before, never heard a bird sing, never smelled a flower before . . . Grateful to be able to touch the rain and a stone, to hear the laughter of children and the sound of the sea, to smell the grass and appreciate tasty food, to see the colors of the earth and the stars . . . Appreciating again the strength and power in your body . . . Feeling the energy and health vibrating and flowing through your being . . . Feeling again the excitement and enthusiasm and the feeling of aliveness that has been suppressed for so long . . . more and more ready to enjoy, to have fun, to play and laugh and sing . . . More and more feeling good to be you and to be alive.

Hypnosuggestive Relaxation Procedures in the Treatment of Asthma

Asthma is characterized by spasms of the bronchial musculature with oversecretion of viscid mucus, resulting in "wheezy" breathing. Although there are many complexities in the etiology of asthma (Alexander, 1981; Weiner, 1977), there is convincing evidence that in at least some asthmatics, attacks are provoked both by allergen inhalation and also by situations that arouse negative emotions (Dekker & Groen, 1956). The relationship between negative emotional reactions and the onset of asthma suggests that hypnosuggestive procedures aiming to produce a feeling of calmness in situations that precipitate asthmatic attacks, or when the individual first becomes aware of the onset of wheezing, should have a beneficial effect on at least some asthmatics. This hypothesis has been tested in a number of studies, of which Collison's (1975, 1978) recent work may serve as the clearest example.

Collison worked with 121 asthmatics who were referred to him by other physicians for hypnosuggestive therapy, either because there were psychological factors associated with their asthma or because it was important to reduce their need for steroid medication. The hypnosuggestive therapy, which apparently extended over a variable period of weeks or months, included suggestions for deep relaxation, suggestions for increased self-confidence, and posthypnotic suggestions for continued relaxation and the ability to remain calm and cope well in life situations. In addition, the patients were taught self-hypnosis, which was comprised of self-suggestions for calmness, ease, and self-confidence. Collison also stated that he used at least two additional hypnosuggestive procedures (discussions of problems under hypnosis, and age regression to uncover early traumatic factors).

The results were as follows: 21% of the patients were relieved of asthma by the hypnosuggestive procedures; they were asymptomatic during a follow-up that extended more than 1 year. An additional 35% of the patients were clearly helped by the treatment—"improved at least 50%"—even though they were not cured. The asthmatic symptoms were not alleviated significantly in the remaining 44% of the patients, but about half of these reported subjective benefits in general well-being from the hypnosuggestive treatment. (Unfortunately, Collison did not take objective measurements of lung function.)

Since it is clear that some asthmatic patients benefit much more than others do from hypnosuggestive procedures, important data in Collison's report pertained to the type of patients who were helped the most. Collison reported that the greatest degree of improvement was found in the younger patients with psychological problems but less severe asthma, who were able to respond well to the suggestions for deep relaxation (hypnosis).

Other therapists utilizing hypnosuggestive procedures (focusing primarily on deep relaxation during the hypnotic session and on the practice of deep relaxation and active relaxation during daily life) have reported that the procedures are generally effective in producing both subjective and objective improvement in a minority of patients, including at times complete remission of asthma (Brown, 1965; Edgell, 1966; Edwards, 1960; Maher-Loughnan, 1970; Maher-Loughnan & Kinsley, 1968; Maher-Loughnan, MacDonald, Mason, & Fry, 1962; McLean, 1965; Meares, 1967, pp. 109–111; Moorefield, 1971; White, 1961). In a representative study by Edwards (1960), six patients who had been admitted to a hospital for treatment of severe asthma were seen for hypnosuggestive therapy. Over a series of sessions, Edwards exposed each patient to a hypnotic induction procedure, comprised primarily of suggestions for deep relaxation, followed without interruption by forceful suggestions that the asthma would gradually disappear. Five of the six patients were followed for more than a year, when they were questioned about their subjective improvement and assessed for objective improvement by measuring respiratory functions. Of the six patients, four had subjectively complete remission of their asthma, and in two of these the remissions were also objectively complete.

As might be expected, other types of relaxation procedures have also been shown to be helpful in treating asthma. For instance, in less severe asthmatics, the same degree of increase in peak expiratory flow measures was found with training in Jacobson's progressive muscle relaxation, with training in progressive relaxation combined with EMG frontalis biofeedback, and also with simple direct instructions to relax (Davis, Saunders, Creer, & Chai, 1973). Scherr, Crawford, Sergent, and Scherr (1975) found that as compared to 22 untrained asthmatic controls, 22 asthmatic children who were trained in relaxation with the aid of EMG frontalis biofeedback showed an increase in peak expiratory flow, a reduction in number of asthmatic attacks, a decrease in number of infirmary visits, and a reduction in steroid use. A significant effect in helping asthmatics has also been shown in other studies that have taught variations of transcendental meditation (Wilson, Honsberger, Chiu, & Novey, 1975) and Jacobson's progressive relaxation (Alexander, 1972; Alexander, Cropp, & Chai, 1979; Alexander, Miklich, & Hershkoff, 1972; Phillip, Wilde, & Day, 1972; Sirota & Mahoney, 1974).

Although various types of relaxation procedures are useful in the treatment of asthma, it is clear that, with rare exceptions, the illness requires a *multidimensional* psychosocial approach to supplement sophisticated medical procedures. In addition to training in deep relaxation and active relaxation, the psychosocial therapy should also focus on enhancement of self-esteem, social skills training, problem-solving procedures, and more general insight training for understanding and dealing with life problems.

I would surmise, however, that hypnosuggestive procedures (and other psychosocial procedures) may help the asthmatic more than they have heretofore if greater emphasis is placed on utilizing either deep relaxation or active relaxation procedures *at the first indication* of respiratory difficulties. When asthmatics begin to experience bronchial spasms, they become anxious, and the "snowballing" effect of the anxiety further constricts the bronchioles (Spiegel & Spiegel, 1978, p. 226). By using either deep relaxation or an active relaxation procedure (e.g., covertly repeating to oneself that one feels "relaxed . . . calm . . . at peace . . .") *at the first signs of respiratory difficulties,* the asthmatic may be able to shift away from the anxious thoughts and feelings—and thus to minimize or abate further constriction of the bronchioles.

Hypnosuggestive Relaxation Procedures in the Treatment of Insomnia

Insomnia is a multifaceted complaint that may include one or a combination of the following components: (1) a long delay in falling asleep, (2) frequent awakenings during the night, (3) early-morning awakening, and (4) feelings of fatigue and dissatisfaction with sleep upon awakening (Price, 1974).

In middle-age and old age, the problem usually lies in frequent awakenings during the night and early-morning awakenings. In younger individuals, the major problem is typically difficulty in falling asleep, which may be related to worry, anxiety, ruminating over problems, and fears of "letting go." Most sleep problems seem to be related to chronic worry and ruminative activity, which may be exacerbated by additional worry regarding inability to sleep or to get sufficient sleep (Hauri, 1975). A series of studies reviewed by Youkilis and Bootzin (1981) indicate that insomniacs tend to be characterized in personality studies as anxious, depressed, neurotic, and introverted. However, although insomnia may have originally derived from anxiety or depression, it may later be maintained by a new set of factors. Also, treatments that successfully reduce or even eliminate insomnia (to be discussed below) may not significantly change the symptoms of anxiety or depression (Nicassio & Bootzin, 1974).

As Youkilis and Bootzin (1981) noted in a useful review of the research, insomnia is a much more complex problem than is at times assumed. For instance, the sleep problem at times lies in a deficiency in "deep" (Stage 4 slow-wave) sleep, rather than an overall shortage in the amount of sleep; some individuals get a sufficient amount of sleep, but are oversensitive to periods of awakening that occur during the night; some individuals are satisfied with 5 or 6 hours of sleep, whereas others are not satisfied with 7 or 8. Another important consideration in understanding the problem arose in a sleep laboratory study with representative insomnia patients who complained that they slept little and required 1 or 2 hours to fall asleep; nearly 50% of these individuals fell asleep relatively rapidly in the laboratory and slept relatively well, according to electroencephalographic (EEG) criteria of sleep (Dement, 1972, pp. 81–83).

Other difficulties in sleeping are due to sleep apnea (a disorder in which the sleeper stops breathing for about 30 seconds and awakens); to nocturnal myoclonus (in which the muscles of the lower leg jerk during sleep and arouse the sleeper); to physical illnesses such as duodenal ulcers, arthritis, and cancer; and to overuse of caffeine, alcohol, and "sleeping pills."

All sleep medications have serious problems. The barbiturates are associated with such problems as deaths from overdose, buildup of tolerance to the drug, hangover effects, and disturbances in an important part of the sleep cycle (rapid-eye-movement [REM] sleep) during both drug administration and withdrawal. The non-barbiturate benzodiazepine hypnotics such as flurazepam (Dalmane) become ineffective after a few weeks of use, can disturb REM sleep, and have disturbing withdrawal effects (Kales & Kales, 1973; Karacan & Williams, 1971). The over-the-counter medications, which rely on some form of antihistamine, often produce drowsiness, but they also produce undesirable side effects and are typically found to be no more effective than a placebo is in improving sleep (Kales, Tan, Swearingen, & Kales, 1971).

Since present-day drugs are generally ineffective and often counterproductive in the treatment of insomnia, researchers have sought new methods that might help the sleep-deprived patient. During recent years, two kinds of useful procedures have been developed—"stimulus control instructions," and a set of procedures that aim to produce deep relaxation and calmness. Let us glance briefly at each in turn.

A new approach to the treatment of insomnia has been labeled as "stimulus control instructions" by its developer (Bootzin, 1972). These instructions aim to strengthen the stimuli or cues for falling asleep and to separate them clearly from the stimulating cues that are associated with other activities. The "stimulus control instructions" that are given to the insomnia patient include the following ideas:

> Lie down to sleep *only* when you are sleepy; with the exception of sexual activity, do not use your bed for anything except sleep (i.e., no reading, watching television, eating, or worrying in bed); if you are unable to sleep in 10 minutes, get up and do other things (work, read, etc.) and return to bed when ready to sleep; set an alarm and get up at the same time each morning; and do not nap during the day.

Several controlled evaluations of these "stimulus control instructions" indicate that they can produce substantial improvement in time for the patient to fall asleep (Bootzin, 1977; Lawrence & Tokarz, 1976; Tokarz & Lawrence, 1974; Zwart & Lisman, 1979). The average improvement in sleep-onset latency in the six studies was 71% (Bootzin & Nicassio, 1978). There is evidence to indicate that these instructions are useful, primarily because they disrupt tossing and turning in bed and the related worries, ruminations, and other bothersome thoughts that prevent the person from sleeping (Zwart & Lisman, 1979).

Since difficulties in falling or staying asleep are commonly associated with anxiety, worry, and ruminating activity, it appears likely that the difficulties would be alleviated if the patient could be helped to relax and attain relative calmness and peace of mind. This hypothesis has been tested in a large number of studies and has been found to be generally valid. A series of studies reviewed by Bootzin and Nicassio (1978) and Borkovec (1979) have shown that a brief form of Jacobson's progressive relaxation (involving the systematic tensing and relaxing of major muscle groups throughout the body) is more effective in alleviating insomnia than are placebo control and no-treatment conditions. Progressive relaxation training has proved helpful for college students with moderate insomnia (e.g., Borkovec, Kaloupek, & Slama, 1975; Haynes, Woodward, Moran, & Alexander, 1974; Steinmark & Borkovec, 1975) and also for chronic insomniacs with severe sleep problems (e.g., Lick & Heffler, 1977; Nicassio & Bootzin, 1974). This improvement has been demonstrated both with daily sleep diaries (e.g., Borkovec et al., 1975; Nicassio & Bootzin, 1974) and with EEG laboratory assessments (e.g., Borkovec, Grayson, O'Brien, & Weerts, 1979; Borkovec & Weerts, 1976; Freedman & Papsdorf, 1976; Haynes, Sides, & Lockwood, 1977). A series of studies have also shown that two additional procedures aiming to produce relaxation and peace of mind—meditation and autogenic training—are as helpful for insomnia patients as is Jacobson's progressive muscular relaxation (e.g., Nicassio & Bootzin, 1974; Woolfolk, Carr-Kaffashan, McNulty, & Lehrer, 1976). Furthermore, three studies found that EMG frontalis biofeedback and progressive muscular relaxation were both more helpful in alleviating insomnia than the control condition was, but that they did not differ significantly from each other (Freedman & Papsdorf, 1976; Haynes et al., 1977; Nicassio, Boylan, & McCabe, 1976).

In brief, four kinds of relaxation-oriented procedures (progressive relaxation, meditation, autogenic training, and EMG biofeedback) are useful for insomnia, but the degree of improvement is usually limited. The average reduction in time needed to fall asleep associated with training in relaxation is less than 50% (Bootzin & Nicassio, 1978). For instance, the severe insomniacs exposed to progressive relaxation training by Nicassio and Bootzin (1974) still required about an hour to fall asleep at the end of the study, even though the time they needed to fall asleep was reduced by 44%.

Since traditional hypnotic induction procedures and self-hypnosis procedures are comprised almost exclusively of suggestions for deep relaxation, we might expect that such procedures would be as effective as other relaxation procedures are in reducing insomnia. This conjecture was confirmed by Borkovec and Fowles (1973), who assigned 37 college students with difficulties in sleeping to one of three treatment groups: progressive muscular relaxation; hypnotic induction comprised of suggestions for deep relaxation; and self-relaxation. The subjects were exposed to their assigned treatment in three sessions a week apart, and also practiced their particular procedure at home twice a day for 10 minutes each time. The treatments were also compared with a no-treatment control group (10 subjects) on a daily questionnaire that assessed sleep latency time, number of awakenings, and restfulness of sleep. In comparison with the no-treatment control, all three treatments resulted in a significant reduction in the number of times the subjects awakened during the night and in how rested they felt in the morning. Progressive muscular relaxation and the hypnotic procedure comprised of repeated suggestions for deep relaxation were equally effective in reducing the amount of time needed to fall asleep.

Graham, Wright, Toman, and Mark (1975) presented data indicating that self-suggestions for deep relaxation may be more effective in reducing sleep latency and amount of time asleep when subjects are told they are being taught "systematic relaxation" rather than "self-hypnosis." Four other studies found that hypnotic procedures comprised primarily of deep relaxation suggestions are useful for insomnia (Barabasz, 1976; Basker, Anderson, & Dalton, 1979; Nuland, 1975; Stanton, 1975). In a controlled study, Stanton (1975) randomly assigned 30 students with insomnia to one of three groups: hypnosis, progressive muscle relaxation, or placebo. All groups were exposed to six therapy sessions. The hypnosis group received suggestions for deep relaxation, suggestions to visualize relaxing scenes, and additional suggestions such as "More relaxed . . . pleasantly tired . . . allowing your whole body to relax . . . feeling of heaviness . . . drowsier." During the study, the subjects recorded their own sleep latencies and nocturnal awakenings. Stanton reported his results in terms of an insomnia index, which was the product of minutes to fall asleep multiplied by the number of awakenings. The hypnosuggestive treatment was the most effective:

The insomnia index was 2.8 for the base level, 2.2 for the placebo treatment, 0.98 for progressive muscle relaxation, and 0.31 for the hypnosuggestive treatment.

Basker et al. (1979) studied the insomnia-reducing effects of nitrazepam (a benzodiazepine), a placebo, and autohypnosis. Eighteen patients aged 16 to 70, with insomnia of 3 months' to 22 years' duration, were randomly allocated to receive a double-blind treatment consisting of either nitrazepam for 2 weeks followed by placebo for 2 weeks, or vice versa (placebo first followed by nitrazepam). During Weeks 5 to 8, the patients continued to receive the same tablets as they had during Weeks 1 to 4; in addition, during Weeks 5 and 6 they were taught autohypnosis (apparently consisting of repeated self-suggestions of relaxation, drowsiness, and sleep). The patients continued using autohypnosis during Weeks 7 and 8, and also in Weeks 9 and 10, by which time all tablets had been withdrawn.

The placebo and nitrazepam did not differ in their effects on the four sleep measures: time needed to go to sleep, hours of sleep, quality of sleep, and after-sleep feelings of tiredness or alertness. The time taken to go to sleep was less while practicing autohypnosis than while receiving either nitrazepam or placebo. Auto-hypnosis was generally effective, regardless of whether or not a tablet was taken as well. The patients slept more hours with autohypnosis; an average of more than 6 hours of sleep per night was attained by 82% of the patients when practicing auto-hypnosis alone, 70% of those receiving nitrazepam alone, and 41% of those receiving the placebo. With regard to the quality of sleep (as restless, normal, etc.), 94% of the patients reported normal sleep when practicing autohypnosis alone, as compared to 40% with nitrazepam and 30% with placebo. With regard to after-sleep feelings of tiredness or alertness, only 12% were tired after autohypnosis, as compared to 40% with nitrazepam and 47% with placebo. Although conclusions from the study should be guarded, because the autohypnosis could not be counterbalanced with the drug treatments and the outcome measures were derived only from the patients' own reports, the study suggests that autohypnosis may have a powerful ameliorative effect on insomnia.

Although hypnotic procedures focusing on deep relaxation are useful in treating insomnia, more effective treatments would probably include suggestions for deep relaxation as only one aspect of a broader-based approach. Nuland (1975) reported enthusiastically on the effectiveness of a broader approach, which includes the following nine dimensions: specifying the precise nature of the sleep problem; helping clients deal with the stresses, tensions, and anxieties that underlie the insomnia; prescribing a drug such as imipramine (Tofranil) for depressed clients; instructing clients to use Bootzin-type "stimulus control instructions" (e.g., not to go to bed until sleepy); instructing clients to maintain relaxing mental activities and to avoid caffeinated beverages, alcohol, and large meals before bedtime; explaining to clients that since calmly resting in bed is about as restorative as sleep per se, they should not worry about whether or not they are asleep at night; exposing clients (in the formal hypnosuggestive sessions) to suggestions of deep relaxation and suggestions that they will sleep soundly when they go to bed; showing clients how to use self-hypnosis (i.e., how to picture themselves in the most pleasant and relaxed surroundings, feeling more and more calm, relaxed, and drowsy); and, finally, showing clients how to practice autogenic training exercises focusing on feelings of heaviness and warmth.

Although Nuland did not present precise figures, he reported that (1) these procedures relieved the sleep problem in the majority of his insomnia patients; (2) the milder cases responded surprisingly quickly; and (3) with very few exceptions, the procedures removed the distress associated with insomnia, and, with the relief of distress, the patients' sleep was improved.

It appears that the procedures listed above, plus additional procedures delineated by other workers, can be utilized in various combinations to construct more effective individualized treatments for patients. For instance, other procedures that promise to be useful, at least for some patients, include (1) all-night sleep recordings to verify the sleep deficiencies and to rule out sleep apnea, nocturnal myoclonus, and narcolepsy; (2) practice in identifying maladaptive thoughts interfering with sleep, and practice in formulating and using more useful thoughts; and (3) identifying factors or events discriminating nights with good sleep from nights with poor sleep (Thoresen, Coates, Kirmil-Gray, & Rosekind, 1981). Additional procedures that I have found effective for some insomnia patients include (1) making individualized cassette tapes for the patients, which slowly and calmly for about 10 minutes present suggestions of relaxation, peacefulness, and drowsiness—suggestions that they are to listen to immediately before or after they go to bed at night; and (2) instructing the more fantasy-prone patients (Wilson & Barber, 1981, 1983) to become immersed in a pleasant fantasy when they have difficulties sleeping (immersion in fantasy while lying quietly in bed at times moves, by a smooth transition, into sleep).

It appears that useful procedures for treating insomnia provide clients with alternatives on which to focus, other than their sleep-preventing concerns, worries, and ruminative thoughts. For instance, progressive relaxation procedures provide the alternative of focusing on the feelings of muscle tension and relaxation (Borkovec, 1979); typical meditation procedures instruct the patient to focus on a mantra such as "Om"; hypnosuggestive procedures provide the alternative of focusing on the ideas and feelings of "relaxed . . . calm . . . at peace"; autogenic training procedures provide the alternative of focusing on feelings of warmth, heaviness, and regular respiration; and "stimulus control instructions" explicitly guide the patient to focus on almost anything except worrisome thoughts. It appears that a parsimonious theory of insomnia reduction can be formulated in terms of providing alternatives for reducing sleep-preventing thoughts.

Hypnosuggestive Relaxation Procedures in the Treatment of Hypertension

After a thorough review of available data, Weiner (1977) concluded that there are many roads to hypertension; it can be brought about by disturbances in any of the large number of systems that regulate blood pressure. Despite the complexities in the predisposition to, initiation of, and sustaining factors in high blood pressure, it appears likely that stress reactivity plays an important role in some phases of the disease in at least some patients. In borderline, labile hypertension, for instance, the increased cardiac output appears to be produced by sympathetic stimulation of the heart (Weiner, 1977, p. 182). In fact, as Harrell (1980) has pointed out, borderline hypertension resembles the blood pressure rise that is an immediate concomitant of stress, in that there is an increase in cardiac activity, a reduction in baroreceptor sensitivity, and a mediation by the sympathetic nervous system in both cases. Also, the sympathetic nervous system may play a role in maintaining elevated blood pressure via its direct influence on blood volume. Most important, the sympathetic nervous system's response to stress may be exaggerated in individuals with a predisposition to hypertension, and the repeated transient, exaggerated elevations in blood pressure may produce structural thickening of the arteries, which may be responsible for permanent hypertension (Folkow, Hallbäck, Lundgren, Sivertsson, & Weiss, 1973; Folkow & Rubinstein, 1966.).[2] These and other considerations (Weiner, 1977) suggest that procedures aiming to reduce "sympathetic arousal" by producing calmness, equanimity, and relaxation may reduce hypertension, provided that it has not yet resulted in structural thickening of the arteries. At least, as Kaplan (1980) has concluded in a medically oriented review, four nondrug interventions should be tried before using drugs to combat hypertension: reduction of salt intake, reduction in weight, increase in exercise, and enhanced relaxation or reduction in reactivity to stress.

Modest reductions in blood pressure have been associated with various types of relaxation treatments (Blanchard & Miller, 1977; Jacob, Kraemer, & Agras, 1977), including mantra meditation (20 minutes twice daily for 6 months) (Benson, Rosner, Marzetta, & Klemchuk, 1974); galvanic skin response (GSR) biofeedback together with mantra meditation (see Patel, Chapter 4, this volume); abbreviated Jacobson's progressive relaxation (Shoemaker & Tasto, 1975); and autogenic training (Luthe, 1972). After reviewing the data in this area, Blanchard and Miller (1977) concluded that when practiced regularly, on virtually a daily basis, these treatments typically result in a modest reduction in blood pressure of 10–15 mm Hg.

A study by Deabler, Fidel, Dillenkoffer, and Elder (1973) suggests that hypnosuggestive procedures should be part of the armamentarium for treatment of hypertension. In this study, six individuals with high blood pressure, who were not receiving medication for their hypertension, served as a control group; they simply returned to the medical setting seven times to have their blood pressure recorded. Fifteen hypertensive individuals were assigned to the experimental (hypnosuggestive) treatment; six of these were not receiving medication for their elevated blood pressure, and the remaining nine were on stabilized antihypertensive medication. These 15 patients participated in eight or nine treatment sessions, comprised of abbreviated Jacobson's progressive muscular relaxation followed by a hypnotic procedure consisting exclusively of suggestions for deep relaxation. The patients were also instructed in self-hypnosis to be used outside the medical setting. During the hypnosuggestive procedure, some of the patients showed a reduction of 40 mm Hg in systolic pressure and 20 mm Hg in diastolic pressure. The overall results were presented separately for the patients who did not receive hypertensive drugs and those who continued their drug treatment during the study. By the end of the study (eight or nine sessions), the

[2]Folkow and Neil (1971) also propose another mechanism: The restriction of renal circulation that is associated with repeated acute elevations in blood pressure gives rise to a release of renin–angiotensin–aldosterone, which is followed by salt and water retension. Salt retention, in turn, gives rise to chronic hypertension.

no-drug group showed, during suggested deep relaxation, an average reduction of 17% in systolic pressure and 19% in diastolic pressure. At the end of the study, the drug group showed, during deep relaxation, a reduction of 16% in average systolic pressure and 14% in average diastolic pressure. (The patients in the control group did not show significant changes in blood pressure.) The authors stated that the vast majority of the patients in the hypnosuggestion group reported improvement in their hypertensive symptoms as a consequence of using muscular relaxation and hypnotic deep relaxation, including reduced time needed to fall asleep at night, deeper sleep, reduction in frequency and intensity of headaches, and decreased anxiety.

Friedman and Taub (1977, 1978) found, at a 6-month follow-up, that seven hypnosuggestive sessions consisting of repeated suggestions for deep relaxation were associated with an average reduction of 12% in diastolic pressure and 11% in systolic pressure. Although these investigators also utilized a biofeedback group and a no-treatment control group and found that the hypnosuggestion group showed larger reductions in blood pressure, no conclusions can be drawn from these data because of failure to assign the patients to the treatments at random (apparently the most responsive subjects were assigned to the hypnosuggestive treatment).

The above-described studies suggest that hypnosuggestive procedures focusing virtually exclusively on suggestions for deep relaxation are associated with a reduction in blood pressure. Another study by Case, Fogel, and Pollack (1980) indicates that hypnosuggestive procedures that do *not* aim to produce deep relaxation should not be expected to reduce hypertension. These investigators found no reduction in blood pressure in 16 mildly hypertensive patients who were instructed to practice 6 to 10 times per day for 4 months a brief exercise consisting of allowing the left arm to levitate as a signal to enter a trance state, and to concentrate on the need to relax and to respect and protect their bodies.

The hypnosuggestive procedures were used in a very restricted sense in the above-mentioned studies. I would conjecture that a more marked effect on hypertension would be observed if we (1) teach clients both deep relaxation and active relaxation; (2) conduct insight-oriented therapy to uncover the historical roots of clients' approach to problems; (3) utilize hypnosuggestive procedures to hep enhance clients' self-regard and to guide them to a deeper philosophy of life; (4) teach clients deep relaxation for calmly thinking through solutions to immediate problems; and (5) expose clients to additional behavioral and cognitive–behavioral procedures, including thought stopping, assertive training, and training in problem solving.

Hypnosuggestions, Relaxation, and Beyond

This chapter develops two themes. The first theme is that suggestions for deep relaxation are used in many ways in therapy situations. Their "official" use is to produce "hypnosis" or "trance," in the sense of an awayness or withdrawal from active daily concerns, with an associated readiness to experience those things that are suggested. Suggestions for deep relaxation are also used more or less "officially" in therapy situations to produce and maintain a state of tranquility while a client mentally rehearses forthcoming tasks and solutions to life problems. "Unofficially," suggestions for deep relaxation are used in therapy situations in order (1) to define the situation as "hypnosis" and thus to capitalize on both the clients' and the therapists' positive expectancies and excitement about hypnosis; (2) to enhance clients' expectancies that they can experience forthcoming suggestions because they have already experienced the relatively easily experienced (relaxation) suggestions; and (3) to change the formal therapeutic situation so that it is more "loose" and more conducive to fantasy, primary processes, and a kind of role playing. An implicit contention behind this delineation of the various "official" and "unofficial" uses of deep relaxation suggestions in therapy situations is to demonstrate that such situations are complex and multidimensional and have many subtle, often unnoticed aspects. The more we understand therapeutic situations, the more we see that the two individuals involved are in relating in complex ways; that the communications from the therapist have many levels of meaning; and that a single set of suggestions can often have many different aims (Field, 1972).

The second theme of this chapter is that hypnosuggestive procedures focusing on deep relaxation and active relaxation are useful in the treatment of stress-related or psychosomatic disorders such as migraine, tension headache, asthma, insomnia, and hypertension. Several subtle themes also are present in this discussion: (1) Many of the studies lacked important controls, and it was not clear to what extent the effectiveness of the relaxation procedure was due to relaxation per se and to what extent it was due to associated variables such as the excitement, positive expectancies, and special efforts that were part of the therapy situation; (2) the hypnosuggestive relaxation procedures were more helpful with some clients than with others; and (3) the usefulness of the procedures appears to depend on many variables, including how, when, and under what conditions they are presented. Also, hypnosuggestive procedures focusing on deep relaxation and active relaxation have not been shown to be generally more effective than other procedures (such as progressive muscular relaxation, autogenic training, meditation, and various kinds of biofeedback) that have similar aims. In fact, it appears that individual differences are very important here; individuals with certain kinds of characteristics may "fit" one type of relaxation procedure and be "misfits" with another. For instance, it may be preferable to use progressive muscular relaxation or EMG biofeedback with individuals who manifest a high degree of muscle tension, show an external locus of control (Ollendick & Murphy, 1977), or have little ability to imagine and to become "absorbed" (Qualls & Sheehan, 1981). Vice versa, it may be more appropriate to use more "cognitive-based" approaches such as hypnosuggestions, autogenic training, and meditation (Davidson & Schwartz, 1976) with individuals who are more philosophical, and also with those who are more imaginative and fantasy-prone (and are thus good hypnotic subjects) (Barrett, 1991; Lynn & Rhue, 1988; Wilson & Barber, 1981, 1983).

Although the goal of "relaxation" can be approached in various ways, therapists should acknowledge more often that the goal is not muscular relaxation per se, but a new level of being that is characterized by peace of mind. Although training in muscle relaxation may be useful at times in the preliminary phase, the end desired is virtually always the equanimity or tranquility that is associated with a marked reduction of negative feelings or emotions, such as anger, resentment, guilt, and fear. By instructing clients to practice deep relaxation, we hope that they can experience what it is like to be without worries and negative feelings. We also hope that the clients will generalize to "real life" the feelings of well-being and tranquility that they attain during deep relaxation. However, instead of assuming that the feeling of serenity will be extrapolated to active living, we try to enhance its extrapolation by asking clients to practice active relaxation; that is, we ask them to practice, while deeply relaxed, mentally rehearsing being in real-life stress situations and coping calmly and successfully.

However, attainment of true relaxation—that is, equanimity or peace of mind—involves far more than the ritualized practice of stereotyped procedures. It involves movement toward a "higher" or, at least, a different state of consciousness, characterized by "detachment" in the sense of accepting that life has unwanted happenings and not demanding that the world be made to please us. The attainment of relaxation in the most important sense has a dimension that has been emphasized by Eastern spiritual approaches—living fully in the present moment instead of in the past or future, and thus excluding worry and negative emotions (White & Fadiman, 1976, pp. 252–253).

Attaining equanimity requires much more than the practice of muscle relaxation or the practice of deep relaxation; it also requires effective therapy to help clients leave behind their self-defeating behaviors by overcoming their feelings of incompetence, unworthiness, guilt, and unlovableness. This requires an individualized, step-by-step, multidimensional approach that utilizes psychoanalytically oriented procedures together with behavioral and cognitive–behavioral procedures to increase self-understanding, enhance self-esteem, and build a new philosophical outlook. This, in turn, requires exceptional therapists who are not only highly skilled and caring individuals, but also models of tranquility and equanimity.

In this chapter I have focused on deep relaxation suggestions, one of the many kinds of suggestions that are part of hypnosuggestive procedures. I discuss a representative sampling of the many other kinds of suggestions that are in the armamentarium of the hypnosuggestive therapist in other publications (Barber, 1979c, 1981a, 1981b, 1982, 1985).

Possible Adverse Effects and Contraindications

If clients believe that they are in a situation where they will be dominated, controlled, or made unconscious—or, more generally, if they have underlying fears or negative expectations regarding "hypnosis" or particular suggestions—hypnosuggestive procedures can fail in their intent and can have undesirable effects such as resistance, hostility, and even "headaches" on the part of the client. To avoid these undesired consequences, I have developed over the years my own uniquely permissive, collaborative, self-directed procedures, which assure the clients' positive attitudes and cooperation. To the maximum extent possible with each client in each particular situation, I now emphasize "modeling by the hypnosuggestive therapist," "mutual hypnosis," and "self-hypnosis." That is, I use myself to demonstrate responsiveness to the suggestions; I ask the client to join with me to mutually experience the suggested effects; and I define both the client's and my own responsiveness to the suggestions in terms of self-control or "self-hypnosis." At the beginning of my interaction with each client, I explain with full confidence and believability that hypnosuggestive procedures do not involve unawareness or dominance–submission, but instead are based on client–therapist collaboration as the therapist acts as a coach or guide in a beneficial process. We discuss the procedures step by step, and I obtain the client's understanding, agreement, and cooperative participation for each procedure. Since I proceed only after the client agrees to each step and since I use collaborative and self-directed procedures, my clients do not show adverse effects or behaviors that would contraindicate the use of hypnosuggestive procedures. To avoid adverse effects, I recommend to therapists that they remove clients' anxieties and misconceptions by using procedures such as those I have described in this chapter.

REFERENCES

Adams, H. E., Feuerstein, M., & Fowler, J. I. (1980). Migraine headache: Review of parameters, etiology, and intervention. *Psychological Bulletin, 87,* 217–237.

Alexander, A. B. (1972). Systematic relaxation and flow rates in asthmatic children: Relationship to emotional precipitants and anxiety. *Journal of Psychosomatic Research, 16,* 405–410.

Alexander, A. B. (1981). Asthma, In S. N. Haynes & I. Gannon (Eds.), *Psychosomatic disorders: A psychophysiological approach to etiology and treatment.* New York: Praeger.

Alexander, A. B., Cropp, G. J. A., & Chai, H. (1979). The effects of relaxation training on pulmonary mechanics in children with asthma. *Journal of Applied Behavioral Analysis, 12,* 27–35.

Alexander, A. B., Miklich, D. R., & Hershkoff, H. (1972). The immediate effects of systematic relaxation training on peak expiratory flow rates in asthmatic children. *Psychosomatic Medicine, 34,* 388–394.

Anderson, J. A. D., Basker, M. A., & Dalton, R. (1975). Migraine and hypnotherapy. *International Journal of Clinical and Experimental Hypnosis, 23,* 48–58.

Andreychuk, T., & Skriver, C. (1975). Hypnosis and biofeedback in the treatment of migraine headache. *International Journal of Clinical and Experimental Hypnosis, 23,* 172–183.

Bakal, D. A., (1975). Headache: A biopsychological perspective. *Psychological Bulletin, 82,* 369–382.

Barabasz, A. F. (1976). Treatment of insomnia in depressed patients by hypnosis and cerebral electrotherapy. *American Journal of Clinical Hypnosis, 19,* 120–122.

Barber, T. X. (1969). *Hypnosis: A scientific approach.* New York: Van Nostrand Reinhold.

Barber, T. X. (1970). *LSD, marihuana, yoga and hypnosis.* Hawthorne, NY: Aldine.

Barber, T. X. (1978). *Positive suggestions for effective living and philosophical hypnosis.* Medfield, MA: Medfield Foundation. (Cassette tape)

Barber, T. X. (1979a). *Hypnotic and self-hypnotic suggestions for study-concentration, relaxation, pain control, and mystical experience.* Medfield, MA: Medfield Foundation. (Cassette tape)

Barber, T. X. (1979b). *Hypnotic suggestions for weight control and smoking cessation.* Medfield, MA: Medfield Foundation. (Cassette tape)

Barber, T. X. (1979c). Training students to use self-suggestions for personal growth: Methods and word-by-word instructions. *Journal of Suggestive–Accelerative Learning and Teaching, 4,* 111–128.

Barber, T. X. (1981a). Innovations and limitations in Erickson's hypnosis. *Contemporary Psychology, 26,* 825–827.

Barber, T. X. (1981b). Medicine, suggestive therapy, and healing. In R. J. Kastenbaum, T. X. Barber, S. C. Wilson, B. I. Ryder, & L. B. Hathaway (Eds.), *Old, sick, and helpless: Where therapy begins.* Cambridge, MA: Ballinger.

Barber, T. X. (1982). Hypnosuggestive procedures in the treatment of clinical pain: Implications for theories of hypnosis and suggestive therapy. In T. Millon, C. J. Green, & R. B. Meagher, Jr. (Eds.), *Handbook of clinical health psychology.* New York: Plenum.

Barber, T. X. (1985). Hypnosuggestive procedures as catalysts for psychotherapies. In S. J. Lynn & J. P. Garske (Eds.), *Contemporary psychotherapies: Models and methods.* Columbus, OH: Charles E. Merrill.

Barber, T. X., & DeMoor, W. (1972). A theory of hypnotic induction procedures. *American Journal of Clinical Hypnosis, 15,* 112–135.

Barber, T. X., Spanos, N. P., & Chaves, J. F. (1974). *Hypnosis, imagination, and human potentialities.* New York: Pergamon Press.

Barber, T. X., & Wilson, S. C. (1977). Hypnosis, suggestions, and altered states of consciousness: Experimental evaluation of the new cognitive–behavioral theory and the traditional trance-state theory of "hypnosis." *Annals of the New York Academy of Sciences, 296,* 34–47.

Barrett, D. (1991). Deep trance subjects: A schema of two distinct subgroups. In R. G. Kunzendorf (Ed.), *Mental imagery.* New York: Plenum.

Basker, M. A., (1970). Hypnosis in migraine. *British Journal of Clinical Hypnosis, 2,* 15–18.

Basker, M. A., Anderson, J. A. D., & Dalton, R. (1978). Migraine and hypnotherapy. In F. H. Frankel & H. S. Zamansky (Eds.), *Hypnosis at its bicentennial: Selected papers.* New York: Plenum.

Basker, M. A., Anderson, J. A. D., & Dalton, R. (1979). Insomnia and hypnotherapy. In G. D. Burrows, D. R. Collison, & L. Dennerstein (Eds.), *Hypnosis 1979.* New York: Elsevier/North-Holland.

Benson, H., Beary, J. F., & Carol, M. P. (1974). The relaxation response. *Psychiatry, 37,* 37–46.

Benson, H., Malvea, B. A., & Graham, J. R. (1973). Physiologic correlates of meditation and their clinical effect in headache: An ongoing investigation. *Headache, 13,* 23–24.

Benson, H., Rosner, B. A., Marzetta, B., & Klemchuk, H. (1974). Decreased blood pressure in pharmacologically treated hypertensive patients who regularly elicited the relaxation response. *Lancet, i,* 289–292.

Bernheim, H. (1957). *Suggestive therapeutics.* Westport, CT: Associated Booksellers. (Original work published 1886)

Bihldorf, J. P., King, S. H., & Parnes, L. R. (1971). Psychological factors in headache. *Headache, 11,* 117–127.

Blanchard, E. B., Ahles, T. A., & Shaw, E. R. (1979). Behavioral treatment of headaches. *Progress in Behavior Modification, 8,* 207–247.

Blanchard, E. B., & Miller, S. T. (1977). Psychological treatment of cardiaovascular disease. *Archives of General Psychiatry, 34,* 1402–1413.

Blanchard, E. B., Theobald, D. E., Williamson, D. A., Silver, B. V., & Brown, D. A. (1978). Temperature biofeedback in the treatment of migraine headaches. *Archives of General Psychiatry, 35.* 581–588.

Bootzin, R. R. (1972). A stimulus control treatment for insomnia. *Proceedings of the American Psychological Association, 4,* 395–396.

Bootzin, R. R. (1977). Effects of self-control procedures for insomnia. In R. B. Stuart (Ed.), *Behavioral self-management: Strategies and outcomes.* New York: Brunner/Mazel.

Bootzin, R., & Nicassio, P. (1978). Behavioral treatments of insomnia. In M. Hersen, R. Eisler, & P. Miller (Eds.), *Progress in behavior modification* (Vol. 4). New York: Academic Press.

Borkovec, T. D. (1979). Pseudo (experiential)-insomnia and idiopathic (objective) insomnia: Theoretical and therapeutic issues. In H. J. Eysenck & S. Rachman (Eds.), *Advances in behavior research and therapy* (Vol. 2). London: Pergamon Press.

Borkovec, T. D., & Fowles, D. C. (1973). Controlled investigation of the effects of progressive and hypnotic relaxation in insomnia. *Journal of Abnormal Psychology, 82,* 153–158.

Borkovec, T. D., Grayson, J. B., O'Brien, G. T., & Weerts, T. C. (1979). Treatment of pseudo-insomnia and idiopathic insomnia via progressive relaxation with and without muscle tension–release: An electroencephalographic evaluation. *Journal of Applied Behavior Analysis, 12,* 37–54.

Borkovec, T. D., Kaloupek, D., & Slama, K. (1975). The facilitative effect of muscle tension in the relaxation treatment of sleep disturbance. *Behavior Therapy, 6,* 301–309.

Borkovec, T. D., & Weerts, T. C. (1976). Effects of progressive relaxation on sleep disturbance: An electroencephalographic evaluation. *Psychosomatic Medicine, 38,* 173–180.

Brown, E. A. (1965). The treatment of asthma by means of hypnosis as viewed by the allergist. *Journal of Asthma Research, 3,* 101–119.

Case, D. B., Fogel, D. H., & Pollack, A. A. (1980). Intrahypnotic and long-term effects of self-hypnosis on blood pressure in mild hypertension. *International Journal of Clinical and Experimental Hypnosis, 28,* 27–38.

Chesney, M. A., & Shelton, J. L. (1976). A comparison of muscle relaxation and electromyographic biofeedback treatments for muscle contraction headache. *Journal of Behavior Therapy and Experimental Psychiatry, 7,* 221–225.

Collison, D. R. (1975). Which asthmatic patients should be treated by hypnotherapy? *Medical Journal of Australia, 1,* 776–781.

Collison, D. R. (1978). Hypnotherapy in asthmatic patients and the importance of trance depth. In F. H. Frankel & H. S. Zamansky (Eds.), *Hypnosis at its bicentennial: Selected papers.* New York: Plenum.

Cox, D. J., Freundlich, A., & Meyer, R. G. (1975). Differential effectiveness of relaxation techniques and placebo with tension headaches. *Journal of Consulting and Clinical Psychology, 43,* 892–898.

Daniels, L. K. (1976). The effects of automated hypnosis and hand warming on migrane: A pilot study. *American Journal of Clinical Hypnosis, 19,* 91–94.

Daniels, L. K. (1977). Treatment of migraine headache by hypnosis and behavior therapy: A case study. *American Journal of Clinical Hypnosis, 19,* 241–244.

Davidson, R. J., & Schwartz, G. E. (1976). The psychobiology of relaxation and related states: A multi-process theory. In D. I. Mostofsky (Ed.), *Behavior control and modification of physiological activity.* Englewood Cliffs, NJ: Prentice-Hall.

Davis, M. H., Saunders, D. R., Creer, T. L., & Chai, H. (1973). Relaxation training facilitated by biofeed-back apparatus as a supplemental treatment in bronchial asthma. *Journal of Psychosomatic Research, 17,* 121–128.

Deabler, H. L., Fidel, E., Dillenkoffer, R. L., & Elder, S. (1973). The use of relaxation and hypnosis in lowering high blood pressure. *American Journal of Clinical Hypnosis, 16,* 75–83.

Dekker, E., & Groen, J. (1956). Reproducible psychogenic attacks of asthma: A laboratory study. *Journal of Psychosomatic Research, 1,* 58–67.

Dement, W. C. (1972). *Some must watch while some must sleep.* San Francisco: W. H. Freeman.

Donk, L. J., Knudson, R. G., Washburn, R. W., Goldstein, A. D., & Vingoe, F. J. (1968). Toward an increase in reading efficiency utilizing specific suggestions: A preliminary approach. *International Journal of Clinical and Experimental Hypnosis, 16,* 101–110.

Edgell, P. G. (1966). Psychiatric approach to the treatment of bronchial asthma. *Modern Treatment, 3,* 900.

Edmonston, W. E., Jr. (1981). *Hypnosis and relaxation: Modern verification of an old equation.* New York: Wiley.

Edwards, G. (1960). Hypnotic treatment of asthma: Real and illusory results. *British Medical Journal, ii,* 492–497.

Ellis, A. (1962). *Reason and emotion in psychotherapy.* New York: Lyle Stuart.

Epstein, L. H., Abel, G. G., & Webster, J. S. (1976). Self-managed relaxation in the treatment of tension headaches. In J. D. Krumboltz & C. E. Thoreson (Eds.), *Counseling methods.* New York: Holt, Rinehart & Winston.

Erickson, M. H. (1980). *The collected papers of Milton H. Erickson on hypnosis* (E. L. Rossi, Ed.) (4 vols.). New York: Irvington.

Fichtler, H., & Zimmerman, R. R. (1973). Changes in reported pain from tension headaches. *Perceptual and Motor Skills, 36,* 712.

Field, P. B. (1972). Humanistic aspects of hypnotic communication. In E. Fromm & R. E. Shor (Eds.), *Hypnosis: Research developments and perspectives.* Chicago: Aldine-Atherton.

Field, P. B. (1979, September 2). *Stress reduction in hypnotherapy of chronic headaches.* Paper presented at the annual meeting of the American Psychological Association, New York.

Folkow, B., Hallbäck, M., Lundgren, Y., Sivertsson, R., & Weiss, L. (1973). Importance of adaptive changes in vascular design for establishment of primary hypertension: Studies in man and in spontaneously hypertensive rats. *Circulation Research, 32–33*(Suppl. 1), 2–16.

Folkow, B., & Neil, E. (1971). *Circulation.* New York: Oxford University Press.

Folkow, B., & Rubinstein, E. H. (1966). Cardiovascular effects of acute and chronic stimulations of the hypothalamic defence area in the rat. *Acta Physiologica Scandinavica, 68,* 48–57.

Francuch, P. D. (1981). *Principles of spiritual hypnosis.* Santa Barbara, CA: Spiritual Advisory Press.

Freedman, R., & Papsdorf, J. D. (1976). Biofeedback and progressive relaxation treatment of sleep onset insomnia. *Biofeedback and Self-Regulation, 1,* 253–271.

Friedman, A. P. (1972). Treatment of headache. *International Journal of Neurology, 9,* 11–22.

Friedman, H., & Taub, H. A. (1977). The use of hypnosis and biofeedback procedures for essential hypertension. *International Journal of Clinical and Experimental Hypnosis, 25,* 335–347.

Friedman, H., & Taub, H. A. (1978). A six-month follow-up of the use of hypnosis and biofeedback procedures in essential hypertension. *American Journal of Clinical Hypnosis, 20,* 184–188.

Friedman, H., & Taub, H. A., (1984). Brief psychological treatment procedures in migraine treatment. *American Journal of Clinical Hypnosis, 26,* 187–200.

Friedman, H., & Taub, H. A. (1985). Extended follow-up study of the effects of brief psychological procedures in migraine therapy. *American Journal of Clinical Hypnosis, 28,* 27–33.

Fromm, E. (1979). The nature of hypnosis and other altered states of consciousness: An ego-psychological theory. In E. Fromm & R. E. Shor (Eds.), *Hypnosis: Developments in research and new perspectives* (2nd ed.). Hawthorne, NY: Aldine.

Goldstein, Y. (1981). The effect of demonstrating to a subject that she is in a hypnotic trance as a variable in hypnotic interventions with obese women. *International Journal of Clinical and Experimental Hypnosis, 29,* 15–23.

Graham, K. R., Wright, G. W., Toman, W. J., & Mark, C. B. (1975). Relaxation and hypnosis in the treatment of insomnia. *American Journal of Clinical Hypnosis, 18,* 39–42.

Harding, C. H. (1967). Hypnosis in the treatment of migraine. In J. Lassner (Ed.), *Hypnosis and psychosomatic medicine.* New York: Springer-Verlag.

Harrell, J. P. (1980). Psychological factors and hypertension: A status report. *Psychological Bulletin, 87,* 482–501.

Harrison, R. H. (1975). Psychological testing in headache: A review. *Headache, 13,* 177–185.

Hartland, J. (1965). The value of "ego-strengthening" procedures prior to direct symptom-removal under hypnosis. *American Journal of Clinical Hypnosis, 8,* 89–93.

Hauri, P. (1975, August). *Psychology of sleep disorders: Their diagnosis and treatment.* Paper presented at the 83rd annual meeting of the American Psychological Association, Chicago.

Hay, K. M., & Madders, J. (1971). Migraine treated by relaxation therapy. *Journal of the Royal College of General Practitioners, 21,* 664–669.

Haynes, S. N., Griffin, P., Mooney, D., & Parise, M. (1975). Electromyographic biofeedback and relaxation instructions in the treatment of muscle contraction headaches. *Behavior Therapy, 6,* 672–678.

Haynes, S. N., Sides, H., & Lockwood, G. (1977). Relaxation instructions and frontalis electromyographic feedback intervention with sleep onset insomnia. *Behavior Therapy, 8,* 644–652.

Haynes, S. N., Woodward, S., Moran, R., & Alexander, D. (1974). Relaxation treatment of insomnia. *Behavior Therapy, 5,* 555–558.

Henryk-Gutt, R., & Rees, W. L. (1973). Psychological aspects of migraine. *Journal of Psychosomatic Research, 17,* 141–153.

Hess, W. R. (1954). *Diencephalon: Autonomic and extrapyramidal functions.* New York: Grune & Stratton.

Holroyd, K. A., & Andrasik, F. (1978). Coping and self-control of chronic tension headache. *Journal of Counseling and Clinical Psychology, 46,* 1036–1045.

Holroyd, K. A., Andrasik, F., & Westbrook, T. (1977). Cognitive control of tension headaches. *Cognitive Therapy and Research, 1,* 121–123.

Jacob, R. G., Kraemer, H. C., & Agras, W. S. (1977). Relaxation therapy in the treatment of hypertension. *Archives of General Psychiatry, 34,* 1417–1427.

Johnson, W. G., & Turin, A. (1975). Biofeedback treatment of migraine headache: A systematic case study. *Behavior Therapy, 6,* 394–397.

Kales, A., & Kales, J. (1973). Recent advances in the diagnosis and treatment of sleep disorders. In G. Usdin (Ed.), *Sleep research and clinical practice.* New York: Brunner/Mazel.

Kales, J., Tan, T. L., Swearingen, C., & Kales, A. (1971). Are over-the-counter sleep medications effective? Allnight EEG studies. *Current Therapeutic Research, 13,* 143–151.

Kaplan, N. M. (1980). The control of hypertension: A therapeutic breakthrough. *American Scientist, 68,* 537–545.

Karacan, M., & Williams, R. L. (1971). Insomnia: Old wine in a new bottle. *Psychiatric Quarterly, 45,* 274–288.

Lawrence, P. S., & Tokarz, T. (1976). *A comparison of relaxation training and stimulus control.* Paper presented at the annual meeting of the Association for Advancement of Behavior Therapy, New York.

Liebeault, A. A. (1889). *Le sommeil provoqué et les états analogues.* Paris.

Lick, J. R., & Heffler, D. (1977). Relaxation training and attention placebo in the treatment of severe insomnia. *Journal of Consulting and Clinical Psychology, 45,* 153–161.

Luthe, W. (1972). Autogenic therapy: Excerpts on applications to cardiovascular disorders and hyper-choleresteremia. In J. Stoyva, T. X. Barber, L. V. DiCara, J. Kamiya, N. E. Miller, & D. Shapiro (Eds.), *Biofeedback and self-control 1971.* Chicago: Aldine–Atherton.

Lutker, E. R. (1971). Treatment of migraine headache by conditioned relaxation: A case study. *Behavior Therapy, 2,* 592–593.

Lynn, S. J., & Rhue, J. W. (1988). Fantasy proneness: Hypnosis, developmental antecedents, and psychopathology. *American Psychologist, 43,* 35–44.

Maher-Loughnan, G. P. (1970). Hypnosis and autohypnosis for the treatment of asthma. *International Journal of Clinical and Experimental Hypnosis, 18,* 1–14.

Maher-Loughnan, G. P., & Kinsley, B. J. (1968). Hypnosis for asthma—controlled trial: A report of the Research Committee of the British Tuberculosis Association. *British Medical Journal, iv,* 71–76.

Maher-Loughnan, G. P., MacDonald, N., Mason, A. A., & Fry, L. (1962). Controlled trial of hypnosis in the symptomatic treatment of asthma. *British Medical Journal, ii,* 371–376.

Marlatt, G. A. (1979). Alcohol use and problem drinking: A cognitive–behavioral approach. In P. C. Kendall & S. D. Hollon (Eds.), *Cognitive–behavioral interventions: Theory, research, and procedures.* New York: Academic Press.

Martin, M. J. (1978). Psychogenic factors in headache. *Medical Clinics of North America, 62,* 559–570.

McLean, A. F. (1965). Hypnosis in "psychosomatic" illness. *British Journal of Medical Psychology, 38,* 211–230.

Meares, A. (1967). *Relief without drugs: The self-management of tension, anxiety and pain.* Garden City, NY: Doubleday.

Mitchell, K. R. (1969). The treatment of migraine: An exploratory application of time-limited behavior therapy. *Technology, 14,* 50–55.

Mitchell, K. R., & Mitchell, D. M. (1971). Migraine: An exploratory treatment application of programmed behaviour therapy techniques. *Journal of Psychosomatic Research, 15,* 137–157.

Mitchell, K. R., & White, R. G. (1977). Behavioral self-management: An application to the problem of migraine headaches. *Behavior Therapy, 8,* 213–221.

Moorefield, C. W. (1971). The use of hypnosis and behavior therapy in asthma. *American Journal of Clinical Hypnosis, 13,* 162–168.

Nicassio, P., & Bootzin, R. (1974). A comparison of progressive relaxation and autogenic training as treatments of insomnia. *Journal of Abnormal Psychology, 83,* 253–260.

Nicassio, P., Boylan, M., & McCabe, T. (1976). *Progressive relaxation, EMG biofeedback, and biofeedback placebo in the treatment of insomnia.* Paper presented at the 16th meeting of the Inter-American Society of Psychology, Miami.

Nuland, W. (1975). The evaluation and treatment of insomnia. In L. Unestahl (Ed.), *Hypnosis in the seventies.* Orebro, Sweden: Veje Forlag.

Ollendick, T. H., & Murphy, M. J. (1977). Differential effectiveness of muscular and cognitive relaxation as a function of locus of control. *Journal of Behavior Therapy and Experimental Psychiatry, 8,* 223–228.

Ostfeld, A. M. (1962). *The common headache syndromes: Biochemistry, pathophysiology, therapy.* Springfield, IL: Charles C Thomas.

Philips, C. (1978). Tension headache: Theoretical problems. *Behaviour Research and Therapy, 16,* 249–261.

Phillip, R. L., Wilde, G. J. S., & Day, J. H. (1972). Suggestion and relaxation in asthmatics. *Journal of Psychosomatic Research, 16,* 193–204.

Price, K. P. (1974). The application of behavior therapy of the treatment of psychosomatic disorders: Retrospect and prospect. *Psychotherapy: Theory, Research, and Practice, 11,* 138–155.

Qualls, P. J., & Sheehan, P. W. (1981). Electromyograph biofeedback as a relaxation technique: A critical appraisal and reassessment. *Psychological Bulletin, 90,* 21–42.

Rachman, S. (1968). The role of muscular relaxation in desensitization therapy. *Behaviour Research and Therapy, 6,* 159–166.

Sarbin, T. R., & Coe, W. C. (1972). *Hypnosis: A social psychological analysis of influence communication.* New York: Holt, Rinehart & Winston.

Sargent, J. D., Green, E. E., & Walters, E. D. (1972). The use of autogenic feedback training in a pilot study of migraine and tension headache. *Headache, 12,* 120–124.

Scherr, M. S., Crawford, P. L., Sergent, C. B., & Scherr, C. A. (1975). Effect of biofeedback techniques on chronic asthma in a summer camp environment. *Annals of Allergy, 35,* 289–295.

Selby, G., & Lance, J. W. (1960). Observations on 500 cases of migraine and allied vascular headache. *Journal of Neurology, Neurosurgery, and Psychiatry, 23,* 23–32.

Shoemaker, J. E., & Tasto, D. L. (1975). The effects of muscle relaxation on blood pressure of essential hypertensives. *Behaviour Research and Therapy, 13,* 29–43.

Sirota, A. D., & Mahoney, M. J. (1974). Relaxing on cue: The self regulation of asthma. *Journal of Behavior Therapy and Experimental Psychiatry, 5,* 65–66.

Skinner, B. F. (1953). *Science and human behavior.* New York: Macmillan.

Spiegel, H., & Spiegel, D. (1978). *Trance and treatment: Clinical uses of hypnosis.* New York: Basic Books.

Spinhoven, P. (1988). Similarities and dissimilarities in hypnotic and nonhypnotic procedures for headache control: A review. *American Journal of Clinical Hypnosis, 30,* 183–194.

Stanton, H. E. (1975). The treatment of insomnia through hypnosis and relaxation. *Terpnos Logos, 3,* 4–8.

Stanton, H. E. (1977). Test anxiety and hypnosis: A different approach to an important problem. *Australian Journal of Education, 21,* 179–186.

Stanton, H. E. (1979). The hypnotherapeutic placebo. In G. D. Burrows, D. R. Collison, & L. Dennerstein (Eds.), *Hypnosis 1979.* New York: Elsevier/North-Holland.

Steinmark, S., & Borkovec, T. (1975). Active and placebo treatment effects on moderate insomnia under counterdemand and positive demand instructions. *Journal of Abnormal Psychology, 83,* 157–163.

Straus, R. A. (1982). *Strategic self-hypnosis.* Englewood Cliffs, NJ: Prentice-Hall.

Tasto, D. L., & Hinkle, J. E. (1973). Muscle relaxation treatment for tension headaches. *Behaviour Research and Therapy, 11,* 347–349.

Thoresen, C. E., Coates, T. J., Kirmil-Gray, K., & Rosekind, M. R. (1981). Behavioral self-management in treating sleep-maintenance insomnia. *Journal of Behavioral Medicine, 4,* 41–52.

Tokarz, T., & Lawrence, P. (1974). *An analysis aof temporal and stimulus factors in the treatment of insomnia.* Paper presented at the 8th annual meeting of the Association for Advancement of Behavior Therapy, Chicago.

Turin, A. C. (1981). *No more headaches! Practical, effective methods for relief.* Boston: Houghton Mifflin.

VanDyck, R., Zitman, F. G., Linssen, A. C. G., & Spinhoven, P. (1991). Autogenic training and future oriented hypnotic imagery in the treatment of tension headache: outcome and process. *International Journal of Clinical and Experimental Hypnosis, 39,* 6–23.

Warner, G., & Lance, J. W. (1975). Relaxation therapy in migraine and chronic tension headache. *Medical Journal of Australia, 4,* 298–301.

Weiner, H. (1977). *Psychobiology and human disease.* New York: Elsevier/North-Holland.

Weitzenhoffer, A. M. (1953). *Hypnotism: An objective study in suggestibility.* New York: Wiley.

Weitzenhoffer, A. M., & Sjoberg, B. M. (1961). Suggestibility with and without "induction of hypnosis." *Journal of Nervous and Mental Disease, 132,* 204–220.

Wetterstrand, O. G. (1897). *Hypnotism and its application to practical medicine.* New York: Putnam.

White, H. (1961). Hypnosis in bronchial asthma. *Journal of Psychosomatic Research, 5,* 272–279.

White, J., & Fadiman, J. (Eds.) (1976). *Relax.* New York: Confucian Press.

Wickramasekera, I. (1973). Temperature feedback for the control of migraine. *Journal of Behavior Therapy and Experimental Psychiatry, 4,* 343–345.

Wilson, A. F., Honsberger, R., Chiu, J. T., & Novey, H. S. (1975). Transcendental meditation and asthma. *Respiration, 32,* 74–80.

Wilson, S. C., & Barber, T. X. (1978). The Creative Imagination Scale as a measure of hypnotic responsiveness. Applications to experimental and clinical hypnosis. *American Journal of Clinical Hypnosis, 20,* 235–249.

Wilson, S. C., & Barber, T. X. (1981). Vivid fantasy and hallucinatory abilities in the life histories of excellent hypnotic subjects ("somnambules"): Preliminary report with female subjects. In E. Klinger (Ed.), *Imagery: Vol. 2. Concepts, results, and applications.* New York: Plenum.

Wilson, S. C., & Barber, T. X. (1983). The fantasy-prone personality: Implications for understanding imagery, hypnosis, and parapsychological phenomena. In A. A. Sheikh (Ed.), *Imagery: Current theory, research, and applications.* New York: Wiley.

Wolberg, L. R. (1948). *Medical hypnosis* (2 vols.). New York: Grune & Stratton.

Woolfolk, R., Carr-Kaffashan, L., McNulty, T., & Lehrer, P. (1976). Meditation training as a treatment for insomnia. *Behavior Therapy, 7,* 359–365.

Youkilis, H. D., & Bootzin, R. R. (1981). A psychophysiological perspective on the etiology and treatment of insomnia. In S. N. Haynes & L. Gannon (Eds.), *Psychosomatic disorders: A psychophysiological approach to etiology and treatment.* New York: Praeger.

Ziegler, D. K. (1978). Tension headache. *Medical Clinics of North America, 62,* 495–505.

Zwart, C. A., & Lisman, S. A. (1979). Analysis of sleep control treatment of sleep-onset insomnia. *Journal of Consulting and Clinical Psychology, 47,* 113–118.

7

The Autogenic Training Method of J. H. Schultz

WOLFGANG LINDEN

The History of Autogenic Training

In a field as young as clinical psychology or the even younger one of stress management, autogenic training (AT) is almost a "grandmother"; it is one of the oldest biobehavioral techniques known and used. Although widely practiced all over Europe, in Russia, and in Japan, AT is much less popular in North America.

The German neurologist Johannes Heinrich Schultz (1884–1970) is credited with the development and promulgation of AT, which he himself described as a self-hypnotic procedure. During his medical training in dermatology and neurology, Schultz became fascinated with heterohypnosis, which, however, had a dubious image to many of his medical supervisors and peers. Initially, Schultz worked with hypnosis only on his own time, outside of his regular clinic duties. The dominant therapeutic approach of the time for mental and psychosomatic problems was psychoanalysis, but Schultz rejected analysis as a promising treatment for psychosomatic disturbances. In a brief biography, Schaefgen (1984) cites Schultz as having said that "it is complete nonsense to shoot with psychoanalytic guns after symptom-sparrows."

The breakthrough of AT came after Schultz opened his own medical practice in neurology and psychiatry in Berlin in 1924, where he could use and promulgate AT without the constraints of medical superiors who did not share his vision. His first formal presentation of his experiences with AT was in 1926, in front of his colleagues in the Medical Society; his first book followed 6 years later (Schultz, 1932). In all he is accredited with over 400 publications, numerous books, and translations of these into six languages. His ground-breaking book on AT had seen 18 editions by 1984.

The development of AT as a novel technique appears to be based on two sources: Schultz's own experiences with clinical hypnosis, and Oskar Vogt's observations in brain research. Schultz himself noted that his hypnotized patients regularly reported two distinct sensations—a strange heaviness, especially in the limbs, and a similarly strange sensation of warmth. He was convinced that hypnosis was not something that the hypnotist actively did to the patient, but something that the patient permitted to happen, and in that sense actually did to himself or herself. In order for the patient to enter this state, there had to be a "switch," a point of change. Provoking this switch—placing the control in the hands of the patient—was what Schultz wanted to achieve. Oskar Vogt's experiences further strengthened Schultz's belief that it was possible to reliably trigger an autogenic state, because Vogt, a brain researcher, had reported to Schultz that his patients could volitionally produce the sensations of heaviness and warmth and could switch into self-hypnotic trance. Herein lay the seed for the autogenic formulas. Over several years, Schultz further developed the idea of formulas in order to reliably achieve deep relaxation and its accompanying sensations in various parts of the body. The publication of his 1932 book on AT was the culmination of his efforts to standardize the procedure.

AT remained essentially unknown on the other side of the Atlantic Ocean until one of Schultz's followers, Wolfgang Luthe, a physician, emigrated to Canada and began clinical work, teaching, and research about AT in English. A benchmark paper appeared in the *American Journal of Psychotherapy* (Luthe, 1963); this was later followed by a six-volume book series that Luthe coauthored with Schultz (Luthe, 1970a, 1970b, 1970c; Luthe & Schultz, 1969a, 1969b; Schultz & Luthe, 1969). These volumes provide a detailed and comprehensive description of all facets of AT, and the truly serious reader may want to invest the time necessary to read these classic works. Schultz and Luthe provide extensive descriptions of supporting experimental research, case studies, and clinical success reports of AT for an enormous range of clinical problems. For the reader with a strong empiricist bent, however, reading the original works will be a challenging and possibly frustrating task, because in the ultimate evaluation of AT's effectiveness no distinction is made by Schultz and Luthe among opinions, single-case reports, and controlled studies (of which there are precious few). For a more selective critical summary, I refer the reader to Pikoff's (1984) review of the literature in English on AT outcome, or to my book *Autogenic Training: A Clinical Guide* (Linden, 1990).

Theoretical Underpinnings

Given the apparent similarities among meditation, hypnosis, biofeedback, muscular relaxation training, and AT (Benson, 1975), it requires a fine-grained analysis to reveal differences in underlying rationale, technique, and—possibly—outcome. Mensen (1975) aptly described AT as the "legitimate daughter" of hypnosis. AT, however, should not simply be equated with hypnosis; nor is it simply another form of relaxation therapy. Among the many descriptors used is "a psychophysiological self-control therapy" (Pikoff, 1984, p. 620) or "a psychophysiologic form of psychotherapy which the patient carries out himself by using passive concentration upon certain combinations of psychophysiologically adapted stimuli" (Luthe, 1963, p. 175). Although these latter two definitions may seem wordy, they emphasize AT's uniqueness as an autonomic self-regulation therapy. The emphasis is on "self-control" and "which the patient carries out"; this also explains why AT manuals do not come with a cassette or record that the patient can (or should) take home. In contrast, progressive muscular relaxation (PMR) as described by Bernstein and Borkovec (1973) combines the written manual with a record to facilitate relaxation practice. In this sense, AT is more nearly similar to Jacobson's (1938) original PMR technique (see McGuigan, Chapter 2, this volume).

The term "autogenic" is derived from the Greek words *autos* and *genos,* and can aptly be translated as "self-exercise" or "self-induction therapy." It is furthermore important to present in detail how in AT a conceptually sensible, physiological rationale and self-hypnotic suggestions are woven into a type of intervention linking "mind" and "body."

The creator of AT, Johannes Heinrich Schultz, was a firm believer in the self-regulatory capacities and ultimately the self-healing powers of the body if it were only left alone to do its work. Homeostatic models (Cannon, 1933) and more recent formulations of biological self-regulation theory (Linden, 1988; Schwartz, 1977) were foreshadowed by Schultz when he conceptualized AT (Schultz, 1932). Although the most typical application of AT is in reducing excessive autonomic arousal (i.e., it serves as a relaxation technique), the AT rationale embraces a bidirectional homeo-static model, suggesting that AT should be equally useful in raising dysfunctionally low levels of an autonomic function (e.g., low blood pressure). The objective of AT is to permit self-regulation in either direction (i.e., deep relaxation or augmentation of a physiological activity) through "passive concentration," also described as "self-hypnosis."

In AT, the patient (or trainee) concentrates on his or her body sensations in a passive manner, without trying to directly or volitionally bring about change. "Passive concentration" may sound paradoxical, in that "concentration" usually suggests effort. What it means in AT is that the trainee is instructed to concentrate on inner sensations rather than environmental stimuli, and this is indeed somewhat effortful. If, however, this concentration does not come easily, the trainee is told to let his or her thoughts wander for a while, or to rearrange the body position for more comfort, rather than to force inner concentration. Not forcing, allowing sensations to happen, and being an observer rather than a manipulator are what "passive" refers to. The AT trainee is warned that trying too hard is counterproductive: It may lead to negative reactions such as muscle spasms, and it stands in the way of acquiring the necessary passive attitude.

The principle of passive concentration clearly differentiates AT from Jacobson's (1936) PMR and biofeedback (Schwartz & Associates, 1987), in which patients actively attempt to acquire control over physiological functions. A feature that AT shares with biofeedback, however, is the assumption that bidirectional change (increase or de-crease of a physiological activity) is possible and, in some instances, desirable as well. Although AT is considered self-hypnotic, the differences between self-hypnosis and heterohypnosis need to be stressed. In heterohypnosis, the hypnotic trance is induced by another individual (i.e., the hypnotist), who will typically make relaxation and trance suggestions, followed by suggestions for behavioral changes such as stopping smoking or feeling release from pain (see Barber, Chapter 6, this volume). The key differences are self- versus other-control, and dependence on versus independence from a therapist. AT is designed to strengthen independence and to give control back to the patient, thus eliminating the need for either physiological feedback devices (as in biofeedback) or a hypnotherapist.

The claimed uniqueness of AT is supported by (1) experimental studies showing that biobehavioral methods have differential effects on a variety of clinical problems (a summary is provided later in this chapter), and (2) basic experimental findings that relaxation and hypnosis can be psychophysiologically distinguished from autogenic states. Diehl, Meyer, Ulrich, and Meinig (1989) investigated regional cerebral blood flow in 12 healthy male volunteers during autogenic training and during hypnosis. Hypnotic states were verified via successfully performed arm levitation and persistent catalepsy of the right arm. These researchers observed that global hemispheric blood perfusion increased significantly, relative to the subjects' own baseline resting values. Perfusion during AT was significantly less than during hypnosis.

Shapiro and Lehrer (1980) contrasted psychophysiological effects in subjects who had learned either PMR or AT in a 5-week training program. All active training reduced anxiety, depression, and reports of physical symptomatology, but only AT triggered self-perceived heaviness and warmth as well as changes in depth of breathing. Unfortunately, published studies suggesting effects specific to AT but not to other methods are rare. These two studies support the potential of distinct physiological and subjective effects for various self-regulation methods, without, however, offering conclusive evidence.

The core ingredients of AT that make it distinct in method are six standard formulas referring to specific body sensations. The formulas are subvocally repeated by the patient; in addition, the patient is encouraged to develop vivid, personally meaningful images to accompany and enhance these formulas. An important feature that also distinguishes AT from PMR (Jacobson, 1938) and meditation (Wallace, 1970) is the inherent claim of specific effects for each formula. Each formula targets a specific bodily function, and the sensations and images suggested by the formulas are derived from patient reports of deep relaxation and trance states rather than being theoretically derived. The formulas suggest sensations that a relaxed trainee is likely to experience anyway, and create positive expectations of distinct somatic experiences; their occurrence then reinforces the effort and lends further credibility to the formulas. The "magic" of hypnosis is thereby tied to a focus on and increasing awareness of real somatic sensations.

The assumption of AT that somatic imagery is reflective of and can trigger underlying physiological activity is also consistent with Lang's (1979) theory of emotional imagery coding and experience-based somatic–visceral responding. In a series of studies (Lang, Kozak, Miller, Levin, & McLean, 1980; Lang, Levin, Miller, & Kozak, 1983), Lang and his collaborators showed experimentally that focusing in imagination on a distinct physiological response (e.g., sweating or heart rate) did indeed provoke the imagined visceral response with reasonable specificity.

The heaviness formula in AT is directed at muscular relaxation and has been found to be associated with reduction in muscle tone, reductions in blood pressure, and increases in skin resistance (Fischel & Mueller, 1962; Ohno, 1965; Schultz, 1973; von Siebenthal, 1952; Wallnoefer, 1972). The warmth formula is directed at vascular dilation, and researchers have observed peripheral vasodilation in hands and face with an accompanying increase in skin temperature, as well as occasional light sweating (Dobeta, Sugana, & Ohno, 1966; Pelliccioni & Liebner, 1980; Polzien, 1953; Schwarz & Langen, 1966). Practice of the heart regulation formula has been associated with reduction in heart rate, reduced cardiac output with simultaneously improved CO_2 utilization, and stabilization of labile electrocardiogram signals (Luthe, 1970a; Polzien, 1953). Subjects practicing the breathing regulation formula displayed reduced breathing rates and volume, and showed shifts from predominantly thoracic to more abdominal breathing patterns (Ikemi et al., 1965; Linden, 1977; Luthe, 1970a; Polzien, 1953). Practice of the "sun rays" formula is supposed to regulate visceral organ activity, and researchers have indeed reported normalization of dysfunctional stomachs and intestines; increased blood flow to the gastric mucous and vasodilation of peripheral blood vessels have also been noted (Ikemi et al., 1965; Sapir & Reverchon, 1965; Lantzsch & Drunkenmoelle, 1975). Finally, the "cool forehead" formula, which is meant to regulate brain activity and forehead blood flow, has been associated with reduced frequencies of beta waves and increased frequencies of alpha and theta waves in the electroencephalogram (Israel & Rohmer, 1958; Jus & Jus, 1968; Katzenstein, Kriegel, & Gaefke, 1974). Dierks, Maurer, and Zacher (1989) also reported increased theta and reduced beta wave activity; alpha wave activity, however, increased slightly with AT practice. Furthermore, Dierks et al. (1989) noted that the reduction in beta wave activity was specific to the right hemisphere, which is commonly presumed to be the site of emotional function. For more details on supporting research, the reader may want to consult the six-volume series by Schultz and Luthe, or Linden (1990).

A phenomenon not described in the literature for other self-regulation techniques is that of "autogenic discharges," which are seen as a sudden and unpredictable form of "unloading" of pent-up thoughts, sensory processes, and muscular activity (Luthe, 1970b). Although AT is presumed to have an overall gentle, slow effect on autonomic self-regulation, the concept of autogenic discharges incorporates the idea that some of the self-regulation may occur through short bursts of central nervous system activity. Luthe (1970b) differentiates (1) reactive discharges (i.e., responses to acute provocation); (2) normally occurring spontaneous discharges (e.g., motor discharges during presleep stages); (3) discharges that originate from the brain and characterize forms of pathology (e.g., epilepsy); and (4) discharges that may occur during sensory deprivation and during the practice of AT.

Luthe (1970b) also reported that some autogenic discharges are experienced as pain memories from previous injuries, illnesses, or operations. Similarly, there have been reports that the quality of the autogenic discharge may be related to the particular formula being practiced at the time. This can take on the form of a discharge sensation experienced in the body part that is currently being concentrated on, and may be functionally related (although typically in the opposite direction) to the target sensation (e.g., heart palpitations during the heart regulation formula).

Unfortunately, the discharge phenomenon is experienced with considerable variation in intensity and can take on many different forms. In consequence, one can debate whether trainees who do not report sudden discharges have them nevertheless but at a subliminal level (Luthe's position; Luthe, 1970b), or whether they do not occur at all. Also, given that the discharges may take on different forms, it cannot be ruled out that the label "autogenic discharge" may simply cover a variety of phenomena with heterogeneous underlying neuro- or psychophysiological origins. One thing, nevertheless, is clear: Autogenic discharges, when noticed by trainees, are usually interpreted as bothersome and unwanted side effects of the procedure. The traditional view in the AT literature, however, is that autogenic discharges are necessary in a "hydraulic" sense and are considered signs of progress, because they suggest a reduction in physiological and psychological inhibition and provide an opportunity for release of excessive pressure in the system. It is important for the AT instructor to interpret discharge experiences for confused trainees and to provide sensible, comforting explanations.

Data collected by Luthe (1970b) on two experimental groups may further serve to explain the phenomenon and illustrate the variety of possible autogenic discharge experiences. The two groups of subjects were all AT trainees who could be classified either as openly sexually active or as sexually deprived because of their particular life situations (i.e., they were members of the clergy or were otherwise prohibited by their religion from being sexually active). The two groups were apparently similar in male–female proportion, age, clinical condition, and level of professional achievement. The experimental prediction was that the sexually deprived individuals would display more sexuality-related autogenic discharges. Luthe's (1970b) observations suggested that the sexually deprived group indeed had more sexuality-related and general discharge symptoms that did the controls. The sexually deprived group reported more itching, tingling, pain, and muscular twitches; they also reported more erections and vaginal spasms, as well as more sexual fantasies. The perceived sites of the most frequent sensory and motor discharges were the thighs, lower abdomen, and genital regions.

Autogenic discharges are similar in some ways to phenomena described in connection with other techniques (e.g., "relaxation-induced anxiety" as described in the PMR literature; see Bernstein & Carlson, Chapter 3, this volume; the "side effects of tension release" described by Carrington, Chapter 5, this volume). The AT literature, however, presents a much more detailed picture of these phenomena than literature on other techniques and gives more specific suggestions for how to manage them when they occur.

Assessment

Studies of therapy effectiveness typically provide statistical demonstrations of between-group means (based on comparisons of treated patients with themselves before training, or with waiting-list or other treatment controls) as "proof" of a positive outcome (Linden & Wen, 1990). Hidden in such mean change comparisons, however, is considerable variability in treatment response: Some patients benefit, whereas others do not change or get even worse (Jacobson, Follette, & Revenstorf, 1984). A particularly striking example of treatment effect variability is provided by Aivazyan, Zaitsev, and Yurenev (1988), who randomly assigned hypertensive patients to either AT or a no-treatment control condition. When mean changes were broken down into "percentage improved" ratings, the following figures emerged: In the treated group, 32% improved, 59% remained unchanged, and 9% deteriorated; in the control group, 59% also remained unchanged, 11% improved, and 30% deteriorated. Clearly, therapy did nothing for the majority of patients, and the between-group difference is effectively attributable to treatment effects consisting of both direct improvement and the prevention of worsening. Thus, valuable health care funds may be better invested if patients who are not going to benefit from treatment can be identified *a priori* and left out of the treatment comparison.

Especially in light of these observations on treatment outcome variability, a clinician treating individual patients cannot be satisfied with knowing that a statistically significant mean change of a treated group occurred; instead, the practitioner needs to attend to each individual's progress. Therefore it is of great importance for practitioners using AT to be aware of what kind of patient can learn and benefit from AT, and to know in advance whether AT is indeed the best method of treatment for a given patient. The question of AT's suitability, given certain patient characteristics, is addressed in this section.

The literature and my own experience indicate clearly that the mechanics of AT can be taught to a wide variety of individuals; nonetheless, some caveats are in order. Adults of all ages and many children have learned AT, but children below school age lack the discipline to master AT. Depending on a child's maturity, intelligence, and imaginative abilities, the youngest age at which AT can be taught effectively is between 6 and 10 years. Retarded individuals, those with acute central nervous system disorders, and those with uncontrolled psychoses are also likely to be unable to process and follow the instructions. Thus, with these relatively few exceptions, AT can be taught effectively to a wide range of populations.

Although there are few individuals unable to learn the mechanical aspects of autogenics, this does not mean that every learner will necessarily show clinical benefit, and the practitioner has to consider the possibility that AT is not the treatment of choice for a given person. Three lines of research contribute valuable information in this respect. The first is research on relaxation-induced anxiety (Heide & Borkovec, 1984). A second pertinent area of research has attempted to predict relaxation training success by considering differences in initial resting levels (Jacobs, Chesney, Williams, Ding, & Shapiro, 1991) and interindividual differences in response to the first training sessions (Vinck, Arickx, & Hongenaert, 1987). And finally, personality factors as predictors of success have been specifically targeted (Badura, 1977).

Heide and Borkovec (1983) offer a number of potential explanations for the paradoxical effect of anxiety increase during relaxation. The first explanation is that during relaxation a shift toward greater parasympathetic dominance occurs, which results in peripheral vasodilation and feelings of warmth and heaviness (the first and second formulas in AT) (Budzynski, Stoyva, & Pfeffer, 1980). The unfamiliarity with parasympathetic activity sensations may be particularly disturbing to chronically tense or anxious individuals. Also, relaxation frequently brings about unfamiliar spontaneous muscular–skeletal events such as myoclonic jerks, spasms, twitches, or restlessness ("autogenic discharges" in AT). Another explanation centers around the notion of fear of loss of control. Chronically anxious individuals may have learned to control their anxieties in the past by never letting go; they typically work in a compulsive, rigid manner and cannot permit themselves to relax (Martin, 1951). Finally, Ley (1985), on the basis of his work with panic disorder, has proposed that relaxation-induced anxiety may be linked to "relative hyperventilation" ("relative" in this context means that the perceived pace of one's own breathing is above what would be metabolically needed in a given situation). The discrepancy between perceived need and actual respiration pace serves as an alarm cue triggering additional anxiety cognitions, which may then create an upward spiral toward even more arousal.

These findings suggest that patient characteristics such as predominant anxiety experience can predict differential relaxation treatment outcome, and deserve consideration in individual treatment plans involving relaxation therapy. Unfortunately, the replicated findings in this research domain involve only meditation, exercise, and PMR, and it is not clear how AT outcome may be affected by individual predispositions such as pretreatment anxiety levels or preferred coping styles.

The second and third lines of research deal with pretreatment or early-treatment differences between individuals. Vinck et al. (1987) attempted to predict blood pressure treatment responses in normotensives who learned either PMR (Jacobson, 1938) or AT. Training was provided weekly for 6 weeks. Relaxation effects were measured as within-session changes during the first treatment session, overall changes in resting values from the first to the last treatment session, and within-session changes during the last treatment session. Although no differential effects for PMR relative to AT were reported, Vinck et al. (1987) did replicate Jacobs, Kraemer, and Agras's (1977) findings that higher initial blood pressure levels also predicted the greatest reduction after relaxation training. A recent review of therapy outcome for hypertension treated via relaxation strategies (Jacobs et al., 1991) clearly confirms the earlier (Jacobs et al., 1977) contention that patients with initially high blood pressure show greater reductions.

Vinck et al. (1987) also found that trainees with the smallest changes within the first training session of either AT or PMR were the ones who showed the greatest reductions during the last training sessions. Attempts to predict blood pressure treatment response via personality indices was unsuccessful. Vinck et al. (1987) may have failed to identify personality factors as predictors of AT success because their subjects were healthy individuals who probably reflected a relatively narrow range of associated personality features. No such range restriction was apparent in the work of Badura (1977), who related Minnesota Multiphasic Personality Inventory (MMPI) profiles to AT outcome in 200 patients who displayed neurotic, functional, and/or psychosomatic symptomatologies. Badura's patients were subdivided into "successes" and "failures" on the basis of their reported ability to achieve formula-specific autogenic sensations. Patients in the "failure" group were characterized by an MMPI profile with relative elevations on the Hypochondriasis, Depression, Hysteria, and Social Introversion subscales. Discriminant function analysis indicated that with these distinct MMPI profiles, 80% of the success–failure incidences in AT could be correctly classified.

A number of conclusions and suggestions appear justified. Patients with elevated baselines on an autonomic index (e.g., blood pressure) profit more from AT (or other relaxation therapies) than those with lower baselines (Jacob et al., 1991); similarly, those patients showing the least initial response to treatment improve relatively more over time. Also, clinical elevations on the MMPI scales noted above predict lack of success with AT. Such individuals may be better served with another form of psychotherapy.

Method

The Training Format

AT can be taught individually or in groups. The advantages for each mode of training are fairly obvious and are the same as for other forms of psychological therapy. Individual training is much more expensive, but training can also be easily adjusted to likely differences in the pace of learning and other individual needs (this is especially true when AT is taught as part of a complex intervention package). The existence of a personal therapeutic relationship may also serve to enhance compliance and credibility. Group training is more cost-effective, but permits less individualized attention and may thus reduce compliance. On the other hand, groups also have the potential to develop cohesion and serve as mutual support systems, which in turn will have a positive impact on compliance. My personal preference is to teach AT in groups of 8–12 participants, as long as the group can be expected to have more or less homogeneous needs and learning paces.

Another important point that cuts across the whole learning process is that of realistic expectations. At the outset of AT, trainees should be alerted to the probability that learning will be slow. The great majority of practitioners feel little if anything during their first practices, and it is perfectly normal for the desired sensations to remain weak for the first week of practice. This is true even for the avid practitioner who is fully compliant with the instruction to practice twice per day.

The Physical Setting

The ideal physical setting is one of comfort, with minimal likelihood of disruption, a room temperature of 20–24°C, a couch or exercise mattress (plus pillows) to stretch out on, and adjustable lighting conditions (a slightly darkened room is best). Training success is facilitated by an environment that permits trainees to concentrate on their inner sensations. Accordingly, any speech while training impedes with the basic principle of "*auto*genics." If the trainer talks during the exercise or plays a record or cassette, the trainee cannot really learn to exercise autogenically (i.e., independently); instead, he or she will go through a light heterohypnosis. Therefore, autogenic training necessitates tranquility. In a tranquil setting, AT, with its focus on six functional systems (muscles, blood vessels, heart, breathing, inner organs, and the head), can be learned best.

In order to go through the training procedure, a very comfortable sitting—or, even better, lying—position is necessary. The entire body position must be comfortable, since body position itself may lead to muscle tension, which will interfere with progress in the exercises. It is most advantageous to exercise in a supine position, so that the neck especially is well supported. The arms should be placed flat beside the body with slightly bent elbows, and the interior of the hands should be placed on the ground. The tips of the feet should fall slightly to the outside.

If lying is not possible (e.g., if a trainee wants to practice in the clinician's office), a chair with a high back and armrests is best, so that the head and arms are supported. The elbows should be bent at nearly a right angle, because this will insure that the stretching and bending muscles in each arm will be in a balanced state. The entire back and the back of the head should be fully supported. Small pillows may facilitate this support. The feet should rest flat on the ground and close to each other, and the knees should fall slightly to the outside, which will help to prevent mechanical tension in the thigh musculature. Most people will tend to close their knees even while sitting, although this position is often associated with unconscious muscular tension.

When it is not possible either to sit comfortably or to lie down, a third position may be used for the exercises: A trainee can sit on a bench or a chair without back support. In this position the head should be allowed to sink into the torso, so that the arms will hang at the sides and the head will be in a perfectly vertical position over the spine. It is important for the trainee not to bend forward; instead, the torso must be in a vertical position, although somewhat reduced in height. In this position, no muscular activity is necessary and no muscular tension is created, because the skeleton is held by the spine and its tendons. Now the arms can be moved loosely and can be supported on the widely spread thighs, so that the underarms (close to the elbow) will be supported by the thighs. The arms are again bent in the above-described manner. The body now hangs without any muscular work in its own bone structure.

These positions need to be assumed carefully before the exercises begin. In one of these positions (preferably lying down), the trainee can now begin with the first exercise. The eyes should be closed to facilitate passive concentration, and the trainee should now try to imagine the sensation in the formula as well as possible, without making any movement or trying to speak or do anything else. The ideas, images, and memories that will necessarily develop in each individual should not be fought off, because this attempt in itself would lead to tension. Ideas and images other than the formula-based sensations should be ignored.

Content and Sequence of Exercises

First Exercise: The Heaviness Experience (Muscular Relaxation)

The first AT exercise involves the musculature, because muscle activity is familiar to people and is most easily influenced by conscious efforts; in addition, experience with hypnosis and relaxation suggestions has shown that notable muscular relaxation can be achieved rapidly. Muscular relaxation is experienced as a heaviness of the extremities. Intentional concentration on outside stimulation is associated with muscular tension (e.g., looking, speaking, and reaching out are based on muscular movement). Attentional anticipation can also justifiably be called "tension," since muscles are already tensed in anticipation of movement. Even profound thinking may be associated with muscular activity, since many individuals crease the forehead while thinking. Each intention, or even vivid imagination, of a motion will result in increased tone of the musculature in the extremities.

It is not advisable to use the entire body as an object of training at once, because in this case the necessary focus would be difficult to achieve. The training should begin with the dominant arm. If this arm has been trained for a reasonable period of time, the experience of heaviness during muscle relaxation will generalize to the other arm, the legs, and other body systems, since all extremities and organs are accessed by the same nervous system. The exercise is executed on the arm until it has generalized to the other three extremities. It is important to achieve a maximal concentration in the one arm first and to permit a generalized overflow of relaxation into the other extremities before good results can be expected.

The steps in the heaviness formula are as follows: (1) "The right (left) arm is very heavy" (this is repeated six times); (2) "I am very quiet" (this is said only once, and then alternates with the first step until six cycles have been completed). In normal individuals a noticeable experience of heaviness will develop soon, particularly in the area of the elbow and lower arm. After the heaviness formula is practiced, the instructions are "taken back." "Taking back" refers to a systematic set of activities designed to bring the trainee gradually from a state of relaxed, low muscle tone back to an alert state. This needs to be performed in a consistent manner to facilitate the reflex nature of the process. It is executed in the following steps: (1) The arm is bent and stretched a few times with an energetic pull; (2) the individual breathes profoundly in and out briefly; (3) the eyes are opened. As brief versions, one can use the following: (1) "Bend arm"; (2) "Breathe deeply"; (3) "Open eyes."

It is important that the trainee pay attention to the timing of the exercise. Training should be repeated in two or three practice sessions per day. In each training session, one can practice the heaviness formula twice for about 1 minute each. If in the beginning the individual steps are extended, because many trainees want to do the exercise particularly well, semiconscious tensions may arise. Trainees will realize that the experience of heaviness, instead of increasing, decreases more and more with excessively long practices.

Within the first week of training, the feeling of heaviness in the trained arm will be more pronounced and will occur more rapidly; also, the same feeling will be experienced in the other extremities, usually at the same time as in the other arm. When the experience of heaviness in both arms is quite pronounced, the formula can now be changed into "Arms are heavy." The taking-back procedure for both arms involves a count from 1 to 4, where each number is associated with a specific instruction: (1) "Make a couple of fists"; (2) "Bend the arms a few times"; (3) "Breathe in deeply"; and (4) "Open the eyes and sit up." Heaviness experience in the legs does not necessitate a particular taking-back procedure, since legs function more autonomically. Normally, within a week, the exercise has proceeded so far that with only a brief moment of inner concentration arms and legs can be perceived as quite heavy. It is then time to approach the second exercise.

Second Exercise: Experience of Warmth (Vascular Dilation)

Muscular exercises are something that the naive individual finds natural, since muscular activity is typically considered to be a voluntary act. It is a more novel idea that blood vessels may constrict or dilate through intentional effort. However, it should be noted that all emotional activity tends to be associated with a change in blood flow (flushing or paleness). Furthermore, there are systematic types of activities (e.g., the sauna) in which individuals systematically train blood vessels; these activities are reasonably familiar to many individuals. The second AT exercise, which aims at the warmth experience, affects the entire peripheral cardiovascular system: It affects blood flow through arteries, capillaries, and veins in the skin, organs, and musculature. The distribution of blood in the vessels is regulated through constriction and dilation, which take place as a response to nervous system innervation; their magnitude and direction are determined by physical activity, general state of arousal, and inhibition.

Once the first exercise with the heaviness experience has been well trained and can be induced rapidly and reliably, training sessions can then be extended by inclusion of the second formula, as follows:

1. "Arms (legs) are very heavy" (this is repeated for a total of six times).
2. "I am very quiet" (this is said once).
3. "The right (left) arm is very warm" (this is repeated six times; the term "quiet" is then repeated once).

A normal individual will notice an inner, streaming, flowing sensation of warmth very rapidly, typically in the area of the elbow and the lower arm. Quite frequently, trainees who master the heaviness sensation will also spontaneously report warmth sensations before they are instructed to imagine them. Specific instructions for "taking back" the experience of warmth are not necessary, since the blood vessels are elastic and governed by a compensatory self-regulation, which will trigger a return to their usual position in an autonomous manner.

The first and second training exercises are executed in the same manner for a period of at least 1 week, until warmth is experienced easily and rapidly in the trained arm first and then in all four extremities. The experience of heaviness and warmth will then also generalize to the entire body. The blood vessel dilation and associated relaxation have a particularly tranquilizing and sleep-inducing effect. Training exercises directed at blood vessel dilation are not necessarily innocuous, since the changed distribution of blood influences the entire organism. The exercise should be instituted only in healthy individuals for whom no vascular risks are known to exist.

When a new exercise step is added in AT (e.g., when the experience of warmth is added to the feeling of heaviness, as above), the subject should always concentrate initially on the already learned exercises and should add a new exercise only for brief periods (typically 1 minute). New exercises are added only for brief periods, in order to keep the overall exercise length brief and to prevent trainees from attempting to achieve "perfect success" (i.e., taking it too seriously). The choice of 1-minute segments is somewhat arbitrary; it is suggested because 1 minute is an even unit of time, and because when all training steps are added together they amount to a reasonable practice length of 10–15 minutes. Once heaviness and warmth are achieved rapidly and reliably, the third exercise can be added.

Third Exercise: Regulation of the Heart

The awareness of heart activity varies considerably among people. How does one feel heart activity? Many individuals are aware of it in times of strain, excitement, and fever, but many others do not feel heart activity without prior training. These trainees need to be sensitized to their own heart activity.

Trainees who do not perceive their heart activity at any particular point in their body can use their pulse for orientation. With further training they will also experience the activity of the heart itself. If this help is not sufficient, a trainee may try to become aware of heart activity by other means. This can be done by lying flat on the back so that the right elbow is fully supported and lies at the same height as the chest. Now the right hand is placed in the heart area; the left arm's position remains unchanged. Now the trainee can go into the usual state of heaviness, warmth, and quietness and can concentrate on the sensations in the chest area just where the hand touches the skin. The pressure of the hand functions as a directional indicator. After a few exercises, the trainee is now likely to recognize heart activity, and with continuing repetition of the entire exercise the experience will become more obvious. The heart formula is "The heart is beating quietly and strongly" (or, in the case of easily arousable individuals, "quietly and regularly"); this formula is repeated six times, and the word "quiet" is added once.

When the heart sensation has been learned (and in a sense "been discovered"), the hand does not need to be placed any longer in the area of the heart, but the exercise can be continued in the usual position. It should be strongly emphasized that the intent of the exercise is not actively to slow down the heartbeat, since this would prevent self-regulation. The emphasis of this exercise is on regular and strong beats, but not on a reduction of the heartbeat frequency.

Fourth Exercise: Regulation of Breathing

Breathing is partially intentional and partially an autonomous activity. In AT the muscular, vascular, and heart relaxation becomes immediately integrated with the rhythm of breathing, much as heaviness and warmth automatically generalize from the trained arm to all the other extremities. In the AT procedure, however, any intentional influence on or modification of breathing is undesired, since an intentional change would be associated through a reflex-type mechanism with tension and voluntary activity. Again, the trainee is to enter all the other exercise levels before the new, fourth formula is added: "It breathes me" is repeated six times, and then the word "quiet" is added.

For many subjects it is very seductive to attempt voluntary changes of breathing, as in a systematic breathing exercise (e.g., in yoga). This intentional modification needs to be prevented in AT, since breathing is supposed to function autonomously and in a self-regulatory system without any active adjustment. In order to prevent intentional change, the passive wording "It breathes me" has been chosen. This statement is intended to make it clear to the trainee that relaxation and the regulation of breathing will come by themselves—that the trainee will be carried by and is to give in to his or her natural breathing rhythm. It typically takes another week to make good progress with this exercise.

Fifth Exercise: Regulation of Visceral Organs ("Sun Rays")

For self-regulation of visceral organs, the trainee focuses on the area of the solar plexus, which is the most important nerve center for the inner organs. The image associated with this nerve center is that of a sun from which warm rays extend into other body areas. The solar plexus is found half-way between the navel and the lower end of the sternum in the upper half of the body. The trainee now concentrates on the solar plexus area: The formula "Sun rays are streaming quiet and warm" is repeated six times, and "quiet" is repeated once. This exercise also takes approximately 1 week for normal individuals to learn. The image that the breath is streaming out of the body when the subject breathes out can also help with this particular exercise.

Sixth Exercise: Regulation of the Head

The well-known relaxing effect of a cool cloth on the forehead forms the basis for the sixth exercise. In order to learn the sixth exercise, the subject will engage in the first five exercises in the same careful and progressive manner as described above, and will then (initially only for a few seconds) proceed with the following formula: "The forehead is cool" (repeated six times). Just as warmth is associated with vasodilation, the experience of freshness on the forehead leads to a localized vasoconstriction and thereby to a reduced supply of blood, which in turn accounts for the cooling effect. Since all blood vessels of the entire organism are interconnected, a localized vasoconstriction may generalize to other blood vessels. This can be demonstrated by placing a finger in a basin filled with cold water; the entire hand (and at times even the opposite hand as well) is likely to feel cool and look pale. During AT the concentrative relaxation will originate from the cortex as a central organ, which also possesses the capability of changing the distribution of blood within the body. The "cool forehead" exercise can be learned in about the same time as the other exercises, although up to a third of trainees never acquire a strong response to this formula (Mensen, 1975).

Since most walls are not entirely airtight, there will always be a slight movement of air in any room. Therefore, the cool forehead may be sensed and described as a cool breeze.

Summary of Exercises

With these six formula-specific exercises, AT has been described in its basic but complete form. The entire exercise sequence can now be summarized as follows:

- "Arms and legs are heavy" six times; "quiet" once.
- "Arms and legs are very warm" six times; "quiet" once.
- "The heart is beating quietly and strongly" six times; "quiet" once.
- "It breathes me" six times; "quiet" once.
- "Sun rays are streaming quiet and warm" six times; "quiet" once.
- "The forehead is cool" six times; "quiet" once.
- Now "taking back": "Make fists" bend arms; breathe deeply; open eyes."

After about 8 weeks of training, most individuals have acquired the complete set of sensations, and the emphasis can be placed on ease in achieving the described sensations reliably and rapidly. Daily training for another 4–6 months will lead to more profound and stronger sensations, and generalization of training to different environments can be targeted. It is important to go through the taking-back procedure after each session (except when the trainee has fallen asleep during AT). Thus the trainee will acquire a readily available mechanism for switching from active tension to deep relaxation and vice versa.

Monitoring Progress and Maximizing Compliance

Compliance and monitoring progress are intricately linked and are therefore discussed jointly in this section. Clearly, a trainee who does not see any progress despite twice-daily practice and weeks of training will quickly lose the motivation to continue. In some ways, this section could also be entitled "Maximizing Motivation," because this is the cornerstone of progress and compliance. Because progress is not immediately obvious, a trainee with high initial motivation is more likely to succeed, and it is extremely important that the therapist radiate confidence and a firmly anchored belief in the effectiveness of AT from the very beginning of training. It is recommended that the therapist give an optimistic but reasonable picture of the success to be expected: "I have trained x number of people or groups, and there is hardly anybody who has not benefited considerably. Even after x number of years I still practice it myself. Within the first 2 weeks you can expect the first training effects, which will only become stronger and easier to trigger as you keep on practicing." It is important to reinforce compliance with daily practice, especially until the training effects themselves become apparent and take over as motivation enhancers. Even motivated patients, however, do not perfectly adhere to relaxation homework assignments (Taylor, Agras, Schneider, & Allen, 1983). Taylor et al. tested compliance with relaxation practice, using a special tape recorder that displayed instructions but also monitored unobtrusively the number of times it was actually used; 71% of patients adhered to the instructions. Hoelscher, Lichstein, and Rosenthal (1986) similarly tested compliance with home practice instructions; they found that self-reported compliance exceeded monitored compliance by 91%, and that only 32% of trainees averaged one practice a day. These results leave no doubt that poor compliance is a major problem and needs to be taken seriously. The implication for clinical researchers, then, is that compliance needs to be monitored carefully and that only those patients who comply should be included in statistical analyses of outcome.

On the basis of empirical findings on compliance and my own past experience with AT, I can recommend a number of concrete steps for monitoring progress and enhancing compliance.

Having Trainees Keep a Diary

Trainees should keep a diary in which they record their daily practices and particular success or failure experiences. Of course, trainees may cheat and record a practice that they actually skipped, but this does not happen often in my experience, and in fact the diary serves as a potent reminder to trainees. It is recommended that trainees rate the intensity of their perceived sensations in order to maximize the principle of the self-fulfilling prophecy. When trainees rate each practice after being told that the sensation will get stronger and stronger, they are likely to expect steady improvement, which will become even more obvious when they see the progressive ratings they have made. The diary is of course very useful for the review of the past week's training experiences, which should be undertaken at the beginning of a given therapy session. For maximum convenience and compliance, as well as to facilitate standardization, I actually supply all trainees with a preprinted diary that has a page for every training week. This prevents uneven record keeping and eliminates the excuse of "I could not find an appropriate booklet for a diary."

Emphasizing Regular Timing of the Home Practice

Lack of compliance is a profound problem plaguing all behavioral prescriptions and treatments that require specific daily routines. Research on medication use (Haynes, Taylor, & Sackett, 1979) has revealed that taking medications at predetermined times of day coupled with other already existing routines is an important vehicle for enhancing compliance. In the same vein, I ask my trainees to think about and commit themselves to such practice times in the first training sessions. I would rather deal with their scheduling difficulties before they start practicing than find out a week later that they did not practice at all because they could not find the time. When I say "predetermined" times, I do not mean "6:47 P.M. every day" but "every time after I finish watching the evening news" or "when I am in bed before falling asleep." AT practice must become a routine that requires no thinking or planning; otherwise, it is much too vulnerable to daily mood fluctuations or outside disturbances.

Emphasizing the Need for Frequent Practice

AT trainees may find the rule of twice-daily practice for 2 months (or more) overly compulsive; when it is combined with other competition for their time, they may be tempted to cut down on practicing. My recommendation is to be understanding if one or two practices a week are skipped; however, trainees should be urged to stick to the rule. Frequent practicing is more likely to occur if trainees clearly understand the reason for this rule. In the first session it should be emphasized that relaxation is a skill that requires practice, just as learning to talk or walk is for a small child, or reacquiring good balance is for somebody with a complicated leg fracture and a cast. One can also compare AT practice with throwing a baseball or playing the backhand in tennis; any and all of these are skills that require practice, practice, practice.

Examining Reasons for Dropout

Although AT is popular, patients drop out for a variety of reasons: They move away; there is too much competition for their time; the training effects are too slow in coming; or a variety of other reasons. Even the most experienced therapist will have to face dropout and noncompletion rates of 20–25% in AT. If the dropout rates are noticeably higher than this, the therapist should question his or her own ability to motivate patients. Lack of trainer enthusiasm, poor communication skills, or poor session planning is sometimes the culprit. I have also seen—although rarely—that some groups never develop cohesion without apparent reason, or that one or more members are considered so obnoxious that other members stay away.

Highlighting Success

Nothing succeeds like success, as the old saying goes. The therapist can use this principle by regularly asking the trainees whether they have tried AT in acute stress situations (e.g., anticipating an exam or facing a confrontation with a superior) and highlighting their success stories. Trainees can be asked regularly whether they have noticed any generalizations of training effects, such as improvement in their ability to fall asleep or to relax after a hard day of work, or reduction in occasional tension headaches. Even if they have not personally experienced such benefits, hearing that somebody else has benefited from AT can serve as an extra motivator.

Also, the trainer should frequently praise the learners not only for apparent positive outcome, but also for coming regularly to the training sessions and keeping up with the home practice.

Knowing Possible Problems and Potential Solutions

Anybody attempting to apply a standardized treatment such as AT will soon find out that clinical reality and full standardization are often incompatible: Trainees lose motivation, have unpredictable and confusing training experiences, have medical or psychological problems that may interfere with learning and/or practicing AT, or have other obligations that may prevent regular practice. Good general clinical skills are required to complement the training manual and still bring training to a fruitful end. Nevertheless, some problems are well known to experienced teachers of AT and are endemic either to specific exercises of AT or to the practice of relaxation at large. Although a full discussion is beyond the scope of this chapter, typical problems that can be anticipated and some suggested solutions are presented in the manual (Linden, 1990).

Clinical Applications and Case Study

This section serves as a bridge between the prescriptive, standardized procedure described above and the recurrent need of practitioners to apply, modify, and adjust this procedure to the realities of the clinical situation. The practical approach taken in this section is of greatest value for the clinician who needs to make therapy plans on a case-by-case basis and who may have to make modifications to "classic" AT or create a multicomponent therapy package. Modifications of the AT formulas to suit specific case needs, a case study, and a possible integration of an AT component into a stress management package are described below to illustrate the clinical applications of AT.

Modifications of Formulas to Suit Specific Clinical Needs

Modifications of the standard formulas are typically of three types: (1) Only a few of the formulas are taught (often the heaviness and warmth formulas only); (2) the standard set is taught, but one specific formula is left out or modified; or (3) the standard formulas are taught and an additional, problem-specific formula is created and appended.

Teaching abbreviated AT would be cost-efficient if comparative effectiveness with the long version had been demonstrated empirically. Unfortunately, no such direct comparisons are available, although some abbreviated applications of AT have been found to produce therapeutic benefit (see Linden, 1992). Given the absence of clear comparative evaluations, I argue that teaching abbreviated AT methods (e.g., the heaviness and warmth formulas only) may be inadvisable if full therapeutic benefit is expected.

The need for elimination or modification of a certain formula from the standard set often results from an unanticipated difficulty. One possibility is that certain formulas trigger negative associations, images, and memories for a particular trainee. Another possibility is that of a rationale–application mismatch: For example, a cardiac patient may (at least initially) be hypersensitive to all cardiac sensations, and elimination of the heart regulation formula may be advisable.

Many other formula-specific patient problems are possible. I noted in one case that a trainee experienced searing heat sensations at the words "very warm" in the warmth formula, and a toning down to "pleasantly warm" was judged more appropriate. The "sun rays" formula may be contraindicated for ulcer patients; a non-heat-related image may be preferable in order to set the desired sensation apart from the burning sensation of ulcer pain. Or the formula may be left out altogether in order not to direct even more attention to a potential pain site. Such decisions require clinical, on-the-spot judgment, and excessive standardization and prescription via a manual may be inappropriate.

A particularly appealing modification for many therapists and their patients is that of a person- or disorder-specific additional formula. Lindemann (1974) has provided a useful catalogue of formulas for specific applications, from which I have selected a subset for demonstration here. There really are no limits for adapting such formulas (also called "intentional formulas") to idiosyncratic preferences in imagery and word choices, or descriptions of desirable target behaviors. Characteristics of effective intentional formulas are brevity, a pleasant rhyme or rhythm, a positive choice of words, high relevance to the trainee, and good match to his or her personality. Guidance for creating formulas with these characteristics can be drawn from Erickson and Rossi (1979).

Some of Lindemann's intentional formulas are as follows:

- "First work, then pleasure" to help against procrastination.
- "I am happy, relaxed, and free of hunger" to accompany a weight reduction program.
- "I sleep deeply, relaxed, and restful" against insomnia.
- "I am calm and relaxed; my cheeks stay cool" against blushing.

- "I am completely relaxed and free; my stomach and bowels are working steadily and smoothly" against gastrointestinal complaints.
- "I am totally quiet and in peace; my joints are moving freely and without discomfort; they feel warm" against arthritis pain.

Case Study

Jane M was referred by her family physician because of elevated blood pressure. This 25-year-old woman had a 10-week-old baby at home, and had developed high blood pressure during the pregnancy. Pregnancy-induced hypertension tends to disappear quickly after birth, but this was not apparent in her case.

The assessment consisted of a 1-hour interview in which Jane and I attempted to identify major sources of distress in her life. Throughout the interview, the patient's blood pressure was sampled at 2-minute intervals, using a fully automated blood pressure monitor with digital displays (Dinamap Model 850, Critikon Corp., Tampa, FL). I routinely use this procedure with all referrals for stress-related problems, because it may help identify emotion triggers that patients themselves may not be aware of (Lynch, 1985). The diagnosis of elevated blood pressure was confirmed, in that the 1-hour average reading was 138/95 mm Hg; these readings also supported her family physician's recommendation that drug treatment was not indicated for blood pressure at this level.

Jane remembered that at the age of 18 she had become aware of the family's positive history for high blood pressure, and she had been preoccupied with her own blood pressure ever since. Although I explained that this was probably not accurate, she claimed an awareness of sudden blood pressure changes and attributed subjective feelings of stress to excessive demands in her job as an administrative assistant. When she became pregnant and developed blood pressure problems, she had quit her job; she did not plan to return in the near future.

Neither Jane's verbal reports nor my attempts to link these reports with accompanying changes in her blood pressure identified specific stress triggers that could have become the targets for a stress management program. Instead, I chose to teach her AT, which appeared to hold credibility as an intervention for her.

Over an 8-week period with a total of seven 1-hour sessions, Jane learned the full AT package with six formulas. Using a daily diary system, she charted her practice times and successes, thus also documenting her compliance with the twice-daily home practice requirement. At the end of the seventh session, she was clearly comfortable with the full six-formula AT procedure. She continued to be puzzled that her subjective evaluations of when her blood pressures were high or low were as inaccurate at the end of training as they had been before. Her average blood pressure during the last session was 128/78 mm Hg, indicating a 10-point drop in systolic blood pressure and a 17-point drop in diastolic blood pressure from the readings in the first session. Although this averaging procedure is probably inferior to 24-hour ambulatory blood pressure monitoring, it is nevertheless better than determinations that are based on two or three readings only. The 1-hour averaging procedure at least captures the adaptation processes typical for repeated measurement (Linden & Frankish, 1988).

At a 3-month follow-up, Jane reported that her blood pressure was still in the normal range (this was verified by her family physician). She continued to practice AT, although less often than during the acute training phase.

Autogenic Training in a Multicomponent Treatment Package

In the clinic patients often present with multiple complaints, and/or the therapist discovers during an individual assessment that a given problem is probably caused or exacerbated by a multiplicity of factors. This in turn calls for a program of therapy with multiple components. Although multicomponent therapy is the norm in everyday clinical work and is associated with better clinical outcome than single-component therapies (Shapiro & Shapiro, 1982), infinite numbers of such treatment combinations are possible; this makes extensive comparative outcome testing for each combination extraordinarily difficult. Clinical judgment, good training, experience, and an awareness of research findings are needed in order to judge the appropriateness of a treatment package for a given patient. The best packages tend to be those with strong individually tailored rationales, and with components that have been shown to be efficacious when tested alone. Because there are so many possible combinations of treatment techniques, only a stress management combination including AT is described here.

A multicomponent package including AT has become the standard stress management approach in my own clinical work. First, the client is provided with a rationale that describes stress as a three-step process, involving (1) environmental stress triggers, (2) behavioral and cognitive responses to the challenge, and (3) the ultimately ensuing physiological stress response. For each of the three elements of the stress process, different intervention techniques are taught: (1) situational analysis for identification of stress triggers, and use of stimulus control procedures to prevent these from triggering stress; (2) modification of the acute response to challenge via cognitive restructuring and assertiveness skill training; and (3) acquisition of a behavioral coping skill for reducing the physiological and subjective arousal via AT. Learning to relax via AT not only has desirable acute effects, but tends to generalize insofar as patients typically learn to perceive themselves as being at the control of their stress responses; this in turn has a positive impact on the way they perceive potential stress triggers and how they respond to them. The reader wanting to learn more about stress management techniques in a manual format is referred to Davis, Eshelman, and McKay's (1988) excellent book on stress reduction.

Reflections on the Clinical Outcome of Autogenic Training

Clinical reports of AT are heavily dominated by case studies and uncontrolled research (Luthe, 1970a; Pikoff, 1984). If taken at face value, these clinical findings suggest that AT possesses treatment potential for almost every psychological and psychosomatic problem ever listed in a medical catalogue. Pikoff (1984) reviewed the available clinical studies published in English and found that the quality of published reseach was very uneven, that controls were frequently lacking, and that AT was often equated with autogenic biofeedback (see Norris & Fahrion, Chapter 8, this volume), which pools AT principles with biofeedback procedures. Also, because most researchers used time-limited training programs and rarely trained subjects in more than the heaviness and warmth formulas, he concluded that AT had never really been tested in this body of literature. Nevertheless, the overall evaluation of AT was quite promising; positive outcomes were reported for AT and insomnia, test anxiety, and migraine.

More recently, I have undertaken a substantive review of AT outcome, covering the literature in both English and German and including a meta-analysis of AT effects (Linden, 1992). I summarize the methodology and key findings of this review here. The literature search included a 20-year retrospective computer search, careful screening of the outcome studies described by Luthe (1970a), and further searches of all secondary sources identified via the first two search strategies. Studies were included only if they met the following criteria: (1) inclusion of an experimental control group or condition; (2) sample size for the smallest cell of 5 or greater; and (3) inclusion of at least one standardized, widely accepted outcome measure for the given target problem. Twenty-nine controlled studies met the inclusion criteria and targeted the following clinical problems: angina pectoris, asthma, childbirth essential hypertension, headaches (including migraines), infertility, insomnia, rehabilitation from myocardial infarction, Raynaud's disease, generalized anxiety, and test anxiety. For purposes of parsimony and standardization, I report AT outcome in terms of effect sizes, defined by Glass, McGaw, and Smith (1981) as

$$ES = \frac{M_e - M_c}{SD_c}$$

M_e and M_c can be defined two ways. They refer to raw means at posttest and pretest, respectively, when change within a group is determined. M_e and M_c can also reflect change scores or means obtained at posttest (but adjusted for pretest differences) for comparisons between treatment groups (e.g., AT vs. attention control groups).

Summed across all target problems, the observed effect size for AT was $d = .495$ for comparisons of pretest versus posttest scores in the same individual. The ES was 0.28 for AT versus no-treatment control groups, and 0.37 for AT compared to placebo or attention control groups, thus suggesting that placebo effects do not account for as much treatment effect as they appear to do in more standard psychotherapy approaches (Shapiro & Shapiro, 1982). These average effect sizes noted for AT are remarkably similar to effect sizes reported for other biobehavioral interventions such as meditation, biofeedback, and PMR, which also ranged from 0.43 to 0.66 (Hyman, Feldman, Harris, Levin, & Malloy, 1989). Comparisons of effect sizes for AT versus other behavioral treatments need to be interpreted with considerable caution, however, because the number of individual effects contributing to average effect size is typically only three to six for a specific target problem. These effect size comparisons suggest the existence of many "ideal" technique–target problem matches. Temperature biofeedback under cold stress conditions (Freedman, Ianni, & Wenig, 1983) clearly turned out to be the treatment of choice for Raynaud's disease.

AT was actually found to worsen the outcome for tension headaches, whereas PMR was associated with significant pain reduction (Janssen & Neutgens, 1986). AT showed some promise for hypertension (averaged *ES* for pre–post comparison = 0.43), birth preparation (*ES* compared to another *active* behavioral treatment = 1.37), and recovery from myocardial infarction (*ES* = 0.62 for pre–post comparison. When effect sizes for AT were averaged and contrasted with effect sizes for other active biobehavioral treatments such as biofeedback or meditation, then a difference of 0.00 emerged, suggesting equivalence of overall effects.

Given the high variability in AT outcomes for different target problems, it is inappropriate to reduce the presentation of results to a single statement that describes AT as a method with medium effect sizes. The considerable variability in outcomes as a function of the specific disorder needs to be emphasized; it suggests that the search for problem–method matches is not in vain.

Meta-analytic reviews by definition reveal nothing about design differences, which could, however, influence treatment outcomes. In this light, it is important to stress that the majority of AT studies have used less than ideal training programs (because of taped instructions, very brief treatments, and/or only a subset of the six-formula set). I suspect that comprehensive training and personal delivery are bound to make AT more effective. The effect sizes reported here may therefore underestimate the maximal effects possible with more appropriate training procedures.

Summary and Conclusions

AT deserves a place in every stress management book, given its long history, its enthusiastic endorsement around the world (although somewhat less prominent in English-speaking countries), and the extensive data base that is now available for critical evaluations of clinical outcome and for basic experimental effects of the AT formulas. However, it is also clear that there are still more remaining questions than available answers. There is tentative evidence that AT may be more useful than other self-regulation methods for certain disorders, whereas for others a different method (e.g., thermal biofeedback) may be better (for a review, see Linden, 1992). Detecting specific effects will remain difficult, however, because the average effect associated with AT is of a medium size when AT's effects are tested in a pre–post manner or compared against those of no-treatment controls. When different target problems are lumped together, the comparison with other active biobehavioral treatments generally reveals that these interventions tend to produce similarly medium-sized effects (probably because of shared nonspecific treatment elements). A more promising approach (at least in the clinical environment) is that of permitting clients to select their own treatment after a range of treatments and their rationales have been presented; clients who then choose AT may respond more strongly because of the *a priori* credibility that self-chosen methods embody.

At this time there is no evidence that full-length training (i.e., suggested to last at least 8 weeks) is superior to brief training with a selected subset of formulas. However, this question has never been subjected to a direct test in a single study that has targeted one clearly delineated clinical problem, and in which trainees have been randomly assigned to either short or full-length training. The conclusion of no evidence for a difference between short and long training is based on comparisons of effect sizes from short versus long treatments across different studies. This also implies likely confounding of effect size with problem severity, in that less severe problems may have received shorter treatment, and quick recovery may have been attributable to lesser problem severity rather than shorter treatment length.

In summary, there is a strong research base supporting AT's rationale and clinical outcome, but it also seems true that clinical enthusiasm continues to be a few steps ahead of the research base.

REFERENCES

Aivazyan, T. A., Zaitsev, V. P., & Yurenev, A. P. (1988) Autogenic training in the treatment and secondary prevention of essential hypertension: Five-year follow-up. *Health Psychology, 7*(Suppl.), 201–208.

Badura, H. O. (1977). Beitrag zur differentialdiagnostischen Validitaet des MMPI zur Prognose der Effizienz des Autogenen Trainings [Contribution to the differential diagnostic validity of the MMPI for predicting the outcome of autogenic training]. *Archiv für Psychiatrie und Nervenkrankheiten, 224,* 389–394.

Benson, H. (1975). *The relaxation response.* New York: Morrow.

Bernstein, D. A., & Borkovec, T. D. (1973). *Progressive relaxation training: A manual for the helping professions.* Champaign, IL: Research Press.

Budzynski, T. H., Stoyva, J. M., & Pfeffer, K. E. (1980). Biofeedback techniques in psychosomatic disorders. In A. Goldstein & E. B. Foa (Eds.), *Handbook of behavioral intentions.* New York: Wiley.

Cannon, W. B. (1933). *The wisdom of the body.* New York: Norton.

Davis, M., Eshelman, E. R., & McKay, M. (1988). *The relaxation and stress reduction workbook* (3rd ed.). Oakland, CA: New Harbinger.

Diehl, B. J. M., Meyer, H. K., Ulrich, P., & Meinig, G. (1989). Mean hemispheric blood perfusion during autogenic training and hypnosis. *Psychiatry Research, 29,* 317–381.

Dierks, T., Maurer, K., & Zacher, A. (1989). Brain mapping of EEG in autogenic training (AT). *Psychiatry Research, 29,* 433–434.

Dobeta, H., Sugano, H., & Ohno, Y. (1966). Circulatory changes during autogenic training. In J. J. Lopez Ibor (Ed.), *IV World Congress of Psychiatry, Madrid* (International Congress Series No. 117.48). Amsterdam: Excerpta Medica.

Erickson, M. H., & Rossi, E. L. (1979). *Hypnotherapy: An exploratory casebook.* New York: Irvington.

Fischel, W., & Mueller, V. P. (1962). Psychogalvanische Hautreaktionen im Autogenen Training und waehrend der Hypnotherapie. *Zeitschrift für Psychologie, 167,* 80–106.

Freedman, R. R., Ianni, P., & Wenig, P. (1983). Behavioral treatment of Raynaud's disease. *Journal of Consulting and Clinical Psychology, 51,* 539–549.

Glass, G. V., McGraw, B., & Smith, M. L. (1981). *Meta-analysis in social research.* Beverly Hills, CA: Sage.

Haynes, R. B., Taylor, D. W., & Sackett, D. L. (1979). *Compliance in health care.* Baltimore: Johns Hopkins University Press.

Heide, F. J., & Borkovec, T. D. (1983). Relaxation-induced anxiety: Paradoxical anxiety enhancement due to relaxation training. *Journal of Consulting and Clinical Psychology, 51,* 171–182.

Heide, F. J., & Borkovec, T. D. (1984). Relaxation-induced anxiety: Mechanisms and their theoretical implications. *Behaviour Research and Therapy, 22,* 1–12.

Hoelscher, T. J., Lichstein, K. L., & Rosenthal, T. L. (1986). Home relaxation practice in hypertension treatment: Objective assessment and compliance induction. *Journal of Consulting and Clinical Psychology, 54,* 217–221.

Hyman, R. B., Feldman, H. R., Harris, R. B., Levin, R. F., & Malloy, G. B. (1989). The effects of relaxation training on clinical symptoms: A meta-analysis. *Nursing Research, 38,* 216–220.

Ikemi, Y., Nakagawa, S., Kimura, M., Dobeta, H., Ono, Y., & Sugita, M. (1965). Blood flow change by autogenic training—including observations in a case of gastric fistula. In W. Luthe (Ed.), *Autogenes Training: Correlationes psychosomaticae* (pp. 64–68). Stuttgart: Thieme.

Israel, L., & Rohmer, F. (1958). Variations électroencéphalographiques au cours de la relaxation autogène et hypnotique. In P. Aboulker, L. Chertok, & M. Sapir (Eds.), *La relaxation: Aspects théoriques et pratiques.* Paris: Expansion Scientifique Française.

Jacob, R. G., Chesney, M. A., Williams, D. M., Ding, Y., & Shapiro, A. S. (1991). Relaxation therapy for hypertension: Design effects and treatment effects. *Annals of Behavioral Medicine, 13*, 5–17.

Jacob, R. G., Kraemer, H. C., & Agras, W. S. (1977). Relaxation therapy in the treatment of hypertension: A review. *Archives of General Psychiatry, 34*, 1417–1427.

Jacobson, E. (1938). *Progressive relaxation* (2nd ed.). Chicago: University of Chicago Press.

Jacobson, N. S., Follette, W. L., & Revenstorf, D. (1984). Psychotherapy outcome research: Methods of reporting variability and evaluating clinical significance. *Behavior Therapy, 15*, 336–352.

Janssen, K., & Neutgens, J. (1986). Autogenic training and progressive relaxation in the treatment of three kinds of headache. *Behaviour Research and Therapy, 24*, 199–208.

Jus, A., & Jus, K. (1968). Das Verhalten des Elektroencephalogramms waehrend des Autogenen Trainings. In D. Langen (Ed.), *Der Weg des Autogenen Trainings* (pp. 359–375). Darmstadt, Germany: Wissenschaftliche Buchgesellschaft.

Katzenstein, A., Kriegel, E., & Gaefke, I. (1974). Erfolgsuntersuchung bei einer komplexen Psychotherapie essentieller Hypertoniker. *Psychiatrie, Neurologie, Medizinische Psychologie, 26*, 732–737.

Lang, P. J. (1979). A bio-informational theory of emotional imagery. *Psychophysiology, 16*, 495–512.

Lang, P. J., Kozak, M. J., Miller, G. A., Levin, D. N., & McLean, A., Jr. (1980). Emotional imagery: Conceptual structure and pattern of somato-visceral response. *Psychophysiology, 17*, 179–192.

Lang, P. J., Levin, D. N., Miller, G. A., & Kozak, M. J. (1983). Fear behavior, fear imagery, and the psychophysiology of emotion: The problem of affective response integration. *Journal of Abnormal Psychology, 92*, 276–300.

Lantzsch, W., & Drunkenmoelle, C. (1975). Studien der Durchblutung in Patienten mit Essentieller Hypertonie [Studies of the circulation in patients with essential hypertension]. *Psychiatria Clinica, 8*, 223–228.

Ley, R. (1985). Blood, breath and fears: A hyperventilation theory of panic attacks and agoraphobia. *Clinical Psychology Review, 5*, 271–285.

Lindemann, H. (1974). *Ueberleben im Stress: Autogenes Training*. München: Bertelsmann.

Linden, M. (1977). Verlaufsstudie des Wechsels der Atmung und des CO_2 Spiegels waehrend des Lernens des Autogenen Trainings. *Psychotherapie und Medizinische Psychologie, 27*, 229–234.

Linden, W. (Ed.). (1988). *Biological barriers in behavioral medicine*. New York: Plenum.

Linden, W. (1990). *Autogenic training: A clinical guide*. New York: Guilford Press.

Linden, W. (1992). *Autogenic training: A narrative and a meta-analytic review of chemical outcome*. Paper presented at the International Conference for Behavioral Medicine, Hamburg, Germany.

Linden, W., & Frankish, C. J. (1988). Expectancy and type of activity: Effects of prestress cardiovascular adaptation. *Biological Psychology, 27*, 227–235.

Linden, W., & Wen, F. (1990). Therapy outcome research, health care policy, and the continuing lack of accumulating knowledge. *Professional Psychology: Research and Practice, 21*, 482–488.

Luthe, W. (1963). Autogenic training: Method, research and application in medicine. *American Journal of Psychotherapy, 17*, 174–195.

Luthe, W. (1970a). *Autogenic therapy: Vol. 4. Research and theory*. New York: Grune & Stratton.

Luthe, W. (1970b). *Autogenic therapy: Vol. 5. Dynamics of autogenic neutralization*. New York: Grune & Stratton.

Luthe, W. (1970c). *Autogenic therapy: Vol. 6. Treatment with autogenic neutralization*. New York: Grune & Stratton.

Luthe, W., & Schultz, J. H. (1969a). *Autogenic therapy: Vol. 2. Medical applications*. New York: Grune & Stratton.

Luthe, W., & Schultz, J. H. (1969b). *Autogenic therapy: Vol. 3. Applications in psychotherapy*. New York: Grune & Stratton.

Lynch, J. J. (1985). *The language of the heart*. New York: Basic Books.

Martin, A. R. (1951). The fear of relaxation and leisure. *American Journal of Psychoanalysis, 11*, 42–50.

Mensen, H. (1975). *ABC des Autogenen Trainings*. München: Goldmann.

Ohno, Y. (1965). Studies on physiological effects of autosuggestion centered around autogenic training. *Fukuoka Acta Medica, 56*, 1102–1119.

Pelliccioni, R., & Liebner, K. H. (1980). Ultraschall-Doppler sonographische Messungen von Blutstroemungsaenderungen waehrend der Grunduebungen im Rahmen des Autogenen Trainings. *Psychiatrie, Neurologie, und Medizinische Psychologie, 32*, 290–297.

Pikoff, H. (1984). A critical review of autogenic training in America. *Clinical Psychology Review, 4*, 619–639.

Polzien, P. (1953). Versuche zur Normalisierung der S-T strecke und T-zacke im EKG von der Psyche her. *Zeitschrift für Kreislauf-Forschung, 42*, 9–10.

Sapir, M., & Reverchon, F. (1965). Modifications objectives—circulatoires et digestives—au cours du Training Autogène. In W. Luthe (Ed.), *Autogenes Training: Correlationes psychosomaticae* (pp. 59–63). Stuttgart: Thieme.

Schaefgen, E. (1984). Lebensweg von J. H. Schultz nach seinem "Lebensbilderbuch eines Nervenarztes." In G. Iversen (Ed.), *Dem Wegbereiter Johann Heinrich Schultz*. Köln, Germany: Deutscher Aerzte Verlag.

Schultz, J. H. (1932). *Das Autogene Training-Konzentrative Selbstentspannung*. Leipzig: Thieme.

Schultz, J. H. (1973). *Das Autogene Training-Konzentrative Selbstentspannung. Versuch einer Klinisch-praktischen Darstellung*. Stuttgart: Thieme.

Schultz, J. H., & Luthe, W. (1969). *Autogenic therapy: Vol. 1. Autogenic methods*. New York: Grune & Stratton.

Schwartz, G. E. (1977). Psychosomatic disorders and biofeedback: A psychological model of dysregulation. In J. D. Maser & M. E. P. Seligman (Eds.), *Psychopathology: Experimental models*. San Francisco: W. H. Freeman.

Schwartz, M. S., & Associates. (1987). *Biofeedback: A practitioner's guide*. New York: Guilford Press.

Schwarz, G., & Langen, D. (1966). Gefaessreaktionen bei Autogenem Training und niedrigen Raumtemperaturen. In J. J. Lopez Ibor (Ed.), *IV World Congress of Psychiatry, Madrid* (International Congress Series No. 117.48). Amsterdam: Excerpta Medica.

Shapiro, S., & Lehrer, P. M. (1980). Psychophysiological effects of autogenic training and progressive relaxation. *Biofeedback and Self-Regulation, 5*, 249–255.

Shapiro, D. A., & Shapiro, D. (1982). Meta- analysis of comparative therapy outcome studies: A replication and refinement. *Psychological Bulletin, 92*, 581–604.

Taylor, C. B., Agras, W. S., Schneider, J. A., & Allen, R. A. (1983). Adherence to instructions to practice relaxation exercises. *Journal of Consulting and Clinical Psychology, 51*, 952–953.

Vinck, J., Arickx, M., & Hongenaert, M. (1987). Predicting interindividual differences in blood pressure response to relaxation training in normotensives. *Journal of Behavioral Medicine, 10*, 395–410.

von Siebenthal, W. (1952). Eine vereinfachte Schwereuebung des Schultz'schen Autogenen Trainings. *Zeitschrift für Psychotherapie und Medizinische Psychologie, 2*, 135–143.

Wallace, R. K. (1970). Physiological effects of transcendental meditation. *Science, 167*, 1751–1754.

Wallnoefer, H. (1972). *Seele ohne Angst-Hypnose, Autogenes Training, Entspannung*. Hamburg: Hoffmann & Campe.

8

Autogenic Biofeedback in Psychophysiological Therapy and Stress Management

PATRICIA A. NORRIS
STEVEN L. FAHRION

History of the Method

The history of autogenic biofeedback training may be somewhat unusual in that the goal, conscious acquisition of physiological self-regulation, was conceived of prior to the development of the specific methodology required to aid acquisition of self-regulatory skills. Elmer Green, a physicist, and his wife, Alyce—the cofounders and developers of autogenic biofeedback treatment methods—decided to pursue their interest in the development of human awareness and volition in order to develop ways of teaching people to become conscious of, and to learn voluntary control of, normally unconscious processes (both physiological and psychological). They began this work by measuring the physiological correlates of autogenic training (Schultz & Luthe, 1969) without feedback, to see, for example, the actual thermal consequences of repeating the phrase "My left hand is warm." While measuring the physiological correlates of autogenic phrases, Green and Green (1975) observed in one subject a strong relationship between relief from a migraine headache and vasodilation in the hands (correlated with a temperature increase in the hands of 10°F in 2 minutes). The discovery led directly to the first integration of autogenic training and simultaneous feedback of the consequent psychophysiological changes.

"Autogenic training," a system of psychosomatic self-regulation that was developed in Germany at about the turn of the century, permits the gradual acquisition of autonomic control (see Linden, Chapter 7, this volume). "Biofeedback training" refers to a collection of techniques useful in accelerating psychosomatic self-regulation. Physiological activity is monitored, and information is presented (fed back) visually and auditorially to show the patient what is happening to bodily functions that are normally unavailable to awareness. Control of a wide variety of physiological parameters has been demonstrated, and seems limited only by the opportunity to monitor the level of function in a physiological system consciously, by the possibility of providing continuous feedback on that level, and by the expectation of success on the part of the patient (Leeb, Fahrion, & French, 1976).

"Autogenic biofeedback training" (Green, Green, Walters, Sargent, & Meyer, 1975) represents an integration of these two self-regulatory techniques; it provides a methodology combining the best features of each. This integrative method has wide-ranging applications in medicine, psychology, and education. Autogenic biofeedback treatment began in 1966 when the wife of one of the Greens' colleagues in their research department, who suffered from migraine headaches, asked if she could learn to eliminate them. Elmer Green explained the limbic–hypothalamic–pituitary rationale described below, gave her an autogenic biofeedback temperature training session, and loaned her one of the just-constructed temperature trainers, cautioning her that the treatment would be experimental. As so often happens in the development of a new treatment modality, the first patient was a great success. Although she had previously experienced an incapacitating headache almost every week, after a month of hand temperature training she had the migraine problem under control, and she eliminated entirely her dependence on headache medication. She remained headache-free during 10 years of follow-up.

The Greens developed a plan to study control of unconscious processes through their physiological correlates in autonomic nervous function. Gardner Murphy, director of research at the Menninger Foundation, was open to and interested in this line of inquiry. With Murphy's encouragement, a proposal was prepared, and a government grant to fund this biofeedback research was obtained from the National Institute of Mental Health in 1967. The study, "Voluntary Control of Internal States" (Green, Ferguson, Green, & Walters, 1970; Green, Green, & Walters, 1970b), concerned the training of college students, with the aid of feedback, simultaneously (1) to reduce the level of muscle firing in the forearm as an indication of striate relaxation (Green, Walters, Green, & Murphy, 1969); (2) to increase hand temperature as an indication of autonomic relaxation (Luthe, 1965); and (3) to increase the density of alpha rhythm in the electroencephalographic (EEG) record as an indication of central nervous system relaxation (Kamiya, 1968). From that project, the first biofeedback research to be funded by the federal government, the Voluntary Controls Program at Menninger, was generated. The term "biofeedback" was actually not coined until the founding meeting of the Biofeedback Research Society 2 years later.

A number of research reports and conceptual papers describing autogenic biofeedback training began to emerge on a variety of topics, including deep relaxation (Green et al., 1969), voluntary control of internal psychological and physiological states (Green, Ferguson, et al., 1970; Green, Green, & Walters, 1970b), self-regulation and healing (Green, Green, & Walters, 1971a), creativity (Green, Green, & Walters, 1971b), migraine headaches (Sargent, Green, & Walters, 1972), and anxiety/tension reduction (Green, Green, & Walters, 1973). By the middle 1970s, other investigators began to use autogenic techniques combined with biofeedback, both clinically and experimentally, but few reports appeared until after 1975.

Theoretical Underpinnings

Scope of Application

In considering theoretical underpinnings for autogenic biofeedback, it is well to examine the scope of application of the technique, in order to assess the range of results for which that theory must account. Whereas a survey of the literature from 1975 to 1982 found papers on autogenic training outnumbering papers on autogenic biofeedback by 15 to 1, during the period from 1983 to 1991 this ratio shrank to 1.7 to 1. The earlier period encompassed a total of 33 papers on autogenic biofeedback training; 118 papers on this topic appeared in the latter period. During the latter period, 194 papers were published on autogenic training. An interesting difference was also seen in the languages and locations of publication for these two sets of papers. Papers on autogenic training were predominantly published in English (59), German (55), Russian (31), Italian (15), French (11), and Spanish (7). Those on autogenic biofeedback were primarily published in English (93) in the United States, with 5 each in German and Russian, and with 4 each in Spanish and Japanese. Autogenic training maintains a strong European influence, whereas autogenic biofeedback is currently more of a U.S. phenomenon.

These papers vary markedly in sophistication of design and conceptualization, in the use of experienced versus untrained therapists, in whether an adequate number of training sessions was used to obtain a clinical result, in the populations from which subjects were drawn, and in the depth of physiological relaxation achieved. Such differences make comparison of results problematic at best. The greatest number of autogenic biofeedback efficacy studies have examined cardiovascular applications (23 papers) and headache (28 papers). Autogenic biofeedback has been used in the *treatment* of alcoholism (Peniston & Kulkosky, 1989; Fahrion, Walters, Coyne, & Allen, 1992), of test anxiety (Sun et al., 1986), of childhood disorders such as incontinence and hyperactivity (Barowsky, 1990), of fibrositis (Rouleau, Denver, Gauthier, & Biedermann, 1985), of collagen vascular disease (Keefe, Surwit, & Pilon, 1981), and of writer's cramp (Akagi, Yoshimura, & Ikemi, 1977); in the *management* of sickle cell crises (Cozzi, Tryon, & Sedlacek, 1987), of pain due to causalgia (Blanchard, 1979), of phantom limb pain (Sherman, Arena, Sherman, & Ernst, 1989; Tsushima, 1982), of dysmenorrhea (Dietvorst & Osborne, 1978), of tinnitus (Kirsch, Blanchard, & Parnes, 1987), of asthma (Meany, McNamera, Burks, Berger, & Sayle, 1988), and of angina pain (Hartman, 1979); and in the *prevention* of psychiatric treatment dropout (Hohne & Bohn, 1988) and of motion sickness (Dobie, May, Fischer, Elder, & Kubitz, 1987; Smirnov, Aizikov, & Kozlovskaia, 1988).

In our experience, these diverse published reports represent only a small indication of the extent to which autogenic biofeedback training is being utilized in clinical treatment. Clinical seminars in the use of these techniques began at the Menninger Foundation in 1971, and several thousand professionals have attended to date. Subsequently, many professionals have incorporated autogenic biofeedback into their clinical practice.

Autogenic biofeedback training has also had an impact on other than clinical areas. It has been used in educational settings with emotionally handicapped children (Walton, 1979); with normal children (Engelhardt, 1976); with incarcerated prisoners (Norris, 1976); in personal growth (Leeb et al., 1976); and in other health, physical exercise, and sports applications (Zaichkowsky & Fuchs, 1988).

Mechanisms

Not all the neuromechanisms involved in voluntary self-regulation of the autonomic nervous system have been delineated, but the limbic–hypothalamic–pituitary axis is clearly an essential part. The classic paper by Papez (1937), "A Proposed Mechanism of Emotion," laid the groundwork for an understanding of biopsychological factors, and additional work has elaborated Papez's position (Brady, 1958). The work of Penfield (1975) and of Heath and Becker (1954) in exploring tumor boundaries, in which brain areas were probed with depth electrodes in conscious patients, has demonstrated that limbic stimulation results in the experience of emotion and sensory perception. MacLean (1955) coined the phrase "visceral brain" for the limbic system, and others have referred to it as the "emotional brain," but the important point is that emotional states are reflected in or correlated with electrophysiological activity in the limbic system. It seems that the limbic system is the major responder to psychological stress, and that chronic psychological problems can manifest themselves in chronic somatic processes through numerous interconnections between the limbic system and autonomic and hormonal control centers in the hypothalamus and pituitary gland.

It may be possible to bring under some degree of voluntary control any physiological process that can be continuously monitored, amplified, and displayed. This is implied by the psychophysiological principle that, as the Greens postulated it, affirms: "Every change in the physiological state is accompanied by an appropriate change in the mental–emotional state, conscious or unconscious; and conversely, every change in the mental–emotional state, conscious or unconscious, is accompanied by an appropriate change in the physiological state" (Green, Green, & Walters, 1970b, p. 3). From a theoretical point of view, when coupled with volition, what is going on inside the skin that makes possible the self-regulation of what are usually "involuntary" physiological processes? A cybernetic model of the underlying neurological and psychological principles is described below (Green & Green, 1977).

Figure 8.1 is a highly simplified representation of processes that occur in the voluntary and involuntary neurological domain, and simultaneously in the conscious and unconscious psychological domain. The upper half of the diagram represents the normal domain of conscious processes—that is, processes of which we normally have awareness when we wish it. The lower half of the diagram represents the normal domain of unconscious processes. The normal neurological locus for conscious processes seems to be the cerebral cortex and the craniospinal apparatus. The normal locus for unconscious processes appears to be the subcortical brain and the autonomic nervous system.

Electrophysiological studies show that every perception of outside-the-skin (OUTS) events (see the upper left box of Figure 8.1) has associated with it (Arrow 1) electrical activity in both conscious and unconscious structures—those involved in emotional and mental responses. The boxes labeled "Emotional and mental re-

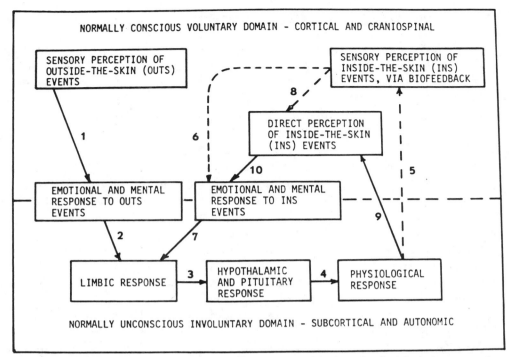

FIGURE 8.1. Simplified operational diagram of "self-regulation" of psychophysiological events and processes. Sensory perception of OUTS events, stressful or otherwise (upper left box), leads to a physiological response along Arrows 1 to 4. If the physiological response is "picked up" and fed back (Arrow 5) to a person who attempts to control the "behavior" of the feedback device, then Arrows 6 and 7 come into being, resulting in a "new" limbic response. This response in turn makes a change in "signals" transmitted along Arrows 3 and 4, modifying the original physiological response. A cybernetic loop is thus completed, and the dynamic equilibrium (homeostasis) of the system can be brought under voluntary control. Biofeedback practice, acting in the opposite way to drugs, increases a person's sensitivity to INS events, and Arrow 8 develops, followed by the development of Arrows 9 and 10. External feedback is eventually unnecessary, because direct perception of INS events becomes adequate for maintaining self-regulation skills. Physiological self-control through classical yoga develops along the route of Arrows 7–3–4–9–10–7, but for control of specific physiological and psychosomatic problems, biofeedback training seems more efficient.

sponse . . ." have been placed on the midline of the diagram, divided by our horizontal center line into conscious and unconscious parts in order to show their two-domain nature. The next box, called "Limbic response," is placed entirely in the "unconscious" section of the diagram, though some neural pathways lead from limbic structures directly to cortical regions, implying that "information" from limbic processes can reach consciousness.

Of major significance to a proper rationale is the fact that the limbic system is connected by many pathways, represented by Arrow 3, to the central "control panel" of the brain, the hypothalamus. Though the hypothalamus weighs only about 4 grams, it regulates a large part of the body's autonomic neural machinery; in addition, it controls the pituitary gland. The pituitary, the so-called "king gland" of the body, is at the top of the hormonal hierarchy, and its action precipitates or triggers changes in other glandular structures. With these concepts in mind, it is easy to see how news from a telephone message could cause a person to faint, or to have a sudden surge of high blood pressure. The perception of OUTS events leads to limbic–hypothalamic–

glandular responses, and, of course, physiological changes are the inevitable consequence.

If a physiological change from the box at the lower right in Figure 8.1 is "picked up" by a sensitive electrical transducer and displayed to the person on a meter (Arrow 5) or made audible by a tone in order to feed back physiological information, then there ensues (Arrow 6) a "new" emotional response, a response to normally unconscious inside-the-skin (INS) information. The new emotional response is associated with a "new" limbic response (Arrow 7). It combines with, or replaces, or modifies, the original limbic response (Arrow 2). This new limbic response in turn develops a "new" pattern of hypothalamic firing and pituitary secretion, and a "new" physiological state ensues. Thus, a biocybernetic control loop is completed as a result of providing the conscious cortex with information about normally unconscious INS processes. Closing the biocybernetic loop bridges the normal gap between conscious and unconscious processes, voluntary and involuntary processes.

In learning voluntary control of normally unconscious processes, we do not become directly aware of the neural pathways and muscle fibers involved, any more than we become aware of what cerebral and subcerebral nerves are involved in hitting a golf ball. But, as in the case of hitting the golf ball, when we get external objective feedback we can learn to modify the internal "setup" so as to bring about changes in the desired direction.

With the advent of biofeedback, certain previously existing distinctions between the voluntary and involuntary nervous system, and between conscious and unconscious processes, are being eroded. Conscious control of the autonomic nervous system (once conceptualized to be unconscious and involuntary) is as possible as conscious control of the muscular system is, and it takes place in much the same way. In picking up a pen the intent is conscious, and visual and proprioceptive feedback are utilized to carry out the activity (consciously or unconsciously). The mechanism whereby the activity is carried out is unconscious; the cortical decision, the visual and motor coordination, and the messages from the visual and motor cortices to spinal ganglia, to motor neurons, and thus to contracting muscles are unconscious; and the result, the pen in hand, is conscious (at least to some extent) and is always available to consciousness.

In the same way, the intent to warm one's fingers is conscious, and visual feedback provided by a temperature trainer is utilized initially to carry out the activity. The mechanism whereby this vasodilation is accomplished (cortex to limbic system to hypothalamus–pituitary, with accompanying neurohormonal changes in the autonomic nervous system) is unconscious; and the result, the change on the meter or the sensation of warmth, is once again conscious or available to consciousness, like the pen in hand. Initially, of course, the result is made conscious through the use of sensitive physiological monitoring and feedback. Through this process certain autonomic nervous system activity, as well as striate, craniospinal activity, can come under conscious, voluntary control.

It is useful to focus attention especially on Arrows 5, 6, 7, 8, 9, and 10 of Figure 8.1. Biofeedback information, along Arrow 5 and then Arrow 6, is often not needed for more than a few weeks. Biofeedback is not addictive, it seems, because voluntary internal control is established instead of dependence on an external agency. In this respect, biofeedback differs considerably from drugs. Dosages of many drugs often need to be increased as time goes by in order to overcome the body's habituation. With biofeedback, however, sensitivity to subtle internal cues is increased rather than decreased. This increased sensitivity, indicated by Arrow 8, is an essential step in closing the internal cybernetic loop, so that the need for feedback devices is only temporary. Eventually the ability to regulate autonomic activity without the aid of machinery can be developed (Green & Green, 1973).

Visualization, Awareness, and Choice

Visualization is an important part of autogenic feedback training. "Making mental contact with the part" (of the body to be regulated) is one of the most interesting concepts in autogenic training. It is clear that consciousness is implicit in learning, and top athletes, musicians, and performers of all kinds have reported that conscious "visualizations" (which may be visual, auditory, and/or kinesthetic) are essential to correct learning and performing. Animal research has clearly demonstrated that perceptual stimuli may result in physiological and behavioral changes. There is, for example, the often-cited case of the stickleback fish that responds to an orange truck parked across the street from its aquarium with the same physiological changes (mating behavior) that would normally be elicited by the orange underbelly of a female fish nearby, because the truck subtends the same angle on the retina (Dobzhansky, 1951).

In humans visualizing events, imagining sources of stimulation can create as great a physiological response as the actual experience of the event can. For many, the image of squeezing lemon juice under the tongue produces increased salivation as effectively as actually doing so does; the physiological effects of sexual fantasies and visual stimulation are well known; advertisers are well aware of the connections between images created and eventual behavior. Whereas animals are regulated almost entirely by the environment, humans are regulated by the environment as perceived by them, and by their own inner fantasies, visualizations, images, and expectancies; humans can thus regulate themselves by choosing appropriate visualizations and expectations of desired goals.

Many authors have focused on the nonspecific elements that all psychotherapies appear to share, including a confiding and emotionally charged relationship, and a treatment rationale that is confidently conveyed and is accepted by both patient and therapist. These are important in the process of autogenic biofeedback training as well. There must be communication of new conceptual and experiential information through percept, example, and the process of self-discovery; a strengthening of the patient's expectation of help; the provision of success experiences; and the facilitation of the arousal of emotions (Frank, 1971). Despite these commonalities, there are also striking contrasts among various therapies, especially when cross-cultural comparisons are made.

Even within the domain of relaxation-based therapies, quite different rationales appear to underlie the different procedures. Lehrer, Atthowe, and Weber (1980) have pointed out that with progressive relaxation, the focus is on achieving very deep levels of muscular relaxation, which may lower physiological activation in general; by contrast, the rationale of autogenic training is to allow the body to re-establish a state of healthy homeostasis through states of deep relaxation and abreactive emotional discharges.

Karasu (1977) has classified the three predominating themes in the development of psychotherapies as "dynamic," "behavioral," and "experiential." This is very similar to the categorization of psychotherapies by Ikemi as "psychoanalytic," "behavioral," and "autogenic self-regulatory" (Ikemi & Aoki, 1976; Ikemi, Nakagawa, Suematsu, & Luthe, 1975). Indeed, Karasu (1977, p. 852) sees autogenic training as experiential psychotherapy, but places biofeedback training as represented by the Greens in the behavioral category. His examples, among others, of the three therapeutic themes include the following: (1) dynamic—classical psychoanalysis (Freud), analytical psychology (Jung), character analysis (Horney), ego analysis (Klein), and biodynamic therapy (Masserman); (2) behavioral—reciprocal inhibition therapy (Wolpe), modeling therapy (Bandura), rational–emotive therapy (Ellis), reality therapy (Glasser), and biofeedback training (the Greens); and (3) experiential—existential analysis (Binswanger), client-centered therapy (Rogers), psychoimagination therapy (Shorr), experiential therapy (Gendlin), and autogenic training (Luthe). An examination of Karasu's (1977, p. 853) description of the thematic dimensions of these psychotherapeutic categories suggests that operant conditioning biofeedback does fit the behavioral paradigm, whereas the Greens' autogenic biofeedback fits the experiential dimension most closely, but combines features of both the behavioral and dynamic dimensions as well.

Behavioral therapies seek, as their primary concern, to reduce anxiety. Behaviorists see pathology as the product of maladaptive learned habits, and they conceive of health as an increased ability to take action or perform—a state enhanced by direct learning, conditioning, systematic desensitization, and shaping. Experiential therapies have as their primary concern a reduction in alienation. The source of pathology is seen as existential despair, fragmentation of self, and lack of congruence with one's experiences, and health is conceived of as actualization of potential, self-growth, authenticity, and spontaneity through immediate experiencing.

An examination of the research literature indicates that biofeedback is used in both behavioral and experiential contexts. Furthermore, it is gradually becoming clear that when biofeedback is applied in a conditioning context, the learning of self-regulatory skills proceeds less effectively than when biofeedback is seen as a method to enhance awareness (Brown, 1978; Green & Green, 1977; Lynch, Thomas, Paskewitz, Malinow, & Long, in press); this perhaps accounts for some of the marked variability in results reported in the biofeedback research literature.

Autogenic biofeedback training as developed by the Greens is an experiential psychotherapy arising in the context of existentialism; it derives from the basic concept that humans have innate regulatory mechanisms that, if given the chance, can restore brain and body processes to optimal homeostatic conditions. Its concept of pathology derives both from experiential concepts of human loss of possibilities and of fragmentation of self, and from the behavioral concept of learned maladaptive habits. Its concept of health emphasizes actualization of potential, self-growth, authenticity, and spontaneity (experiential); symptom removal and anxiety reduction (behavioral); and development of increased ego strength, a more positive self-image, and field independence (dynamic). The treatment model is educational, but takes place in a partnership alliance, an egalitarian existential relationship between therapist and client. This therapy thus emphasizes self-regulation, self-actualization, choice as responsibility, an authentic client–therapist relationship, and awareness. Behavioral techniques such as symptom charting, shaping, and systematic desensitization are used as appropriate, but the therapeutic context is not primarily behavioral, since (1) the locus of control for improvement is seen to reside inside the client, not inside the dispenser of reinforcements; and (2) awareness is considered to be the prime requisite for higher levels of integration.

From this standpoint, it is important to emphasize that the therapeutic goal in autogenic biofeedback training is to maintain and promote desirable levels of functional harmony, rather than simply to reduce anxiety by relaxing deeply. Along with improvements in physiological functioning, a higher-order personality integration often does occur, together with increased empathy, creativity, and productivity.

What stands in the way of these therapeutic improvements is not just chronic, homeostasis-disturbing physiological activation of the autonomic and muscular systems as a result of stress, but also habitual, functionally fragmented patterns of afferent and efferent corticolimbic activity. It is these disturbed psychophysiological patterns ("automatizations," in psychoanalytic terminology) that are corrected ("de-automatized") by the normalizing, self-repair functions and facilitated by autogenic discharge ("abreaction"), thereby overcoming the restricted capacity for self-regulation. This self-neutralizing process seems to be facilitated and stabilized by the patient's insight into the previous antihomeostatic reaction patterns and distorted conditioning; such insight helps to avoid repetition of the same failures (Ikemi et al., 1975).

Luthe (1965) has contrasted the ergotropic nature of active concentration with trophotropic functional change resulting from passive concentration on autogenic formulas. He has also discussed the potential specificity of the physiological effect of visualization through the use of organ-specific formulas. These would seem essential features of the method, as embodied in the psychophysiological principle stated earlier: "Every change in the physiological state is accompanied by an appropriate change in the mental–emotional state, conscious or unconscious; and conversely, every change in the mental–emotional state, conscious or unconscious, is accompanied by an appropriate change in the physiological state" (Green, Green, & Walters, 1970b, p. 3).

Sympathetic Vasodilator System

It is worth noting that other mechanisms may be elicited during hand warming than those associated with the autogenic shift. A series of papers by Freedman and colleagues has recently appeared, purporting to provide evidence that feedback-induced vasodilation is mediated through a non-neural, beta-adrenergic mechanism (see Freedman, 1991). It remains unchallenged that blocking alpha-adrenergic vasoconstrictive responses (e.g., with clonidine) produces comparative vasodilation through a neural mechanism mediated by norepinephrine. Yet these papers have created some degree of confusion among treaters, largely because of a tendency to overgeneralize study results to procedures that have not been examined, including effective autogenic biofeedback.

Specifically, it has *not* been demonstrated that the results of these mechanism studies generalize (1) to hand temperatures above 90°F, including those in the maximally therapeutic range above 95°F; (2) to patients except those with Raynaud's disease; or (3) to methods other than thermal biofeedback alone, such as autogenic biofeedback methods. The last point is notable, since clinicians have long observed that different mechanisms seem to be invoked by using thermal biofeedback alone (which results in increasingly localized response) and by using thermal biofeedback in combination with other relaxation techniques to promote a high thermal criterion (which produces an increasingly generalized, whole-body response). Limits of applicability of results obtained in these mechanism studies have not been explicitly explored in discussions of Freedman's work; more research is necessary to determine to which methodological domains his results apply.

Assessment

Clinical Indications for Autogenic Biofeedback

Autogenic biofeedback therapy, described in detail below, is widely useful in the treatment of stress-related disorders, including such problems as classical and common migraine headache (Sargent et al., 1972; Billings, Thomas, Rapp, Reyes, & Leith, 1984; Blanchard et al., 1985; Boller & Flom, 1979; Chapman, 1986; Daly, Donn, Galliher, & Zimmerman, 1983; Fahrion, 1977; Guarnieri & Blanchard, 1990), tension headache (Budzynski, Stoyva, & Adler, 1970), mixed tension–vascular headache (Fahrion, 1977), idiopathic essential hypertension (Fahrion, 1991; Green, Green, & Norris, 1979; McGrady, Yonker, Tan, Fine, & Woerner, 1981; Sedlacek, 1979), primary idiopathic Raynaud's disease (Taub & Stroebel, 1978; Freedman, 1987), irritable bowel syndrome (Blanchard, Radnitz, Schwarz, Neff, & Gerardi, 1987; Blanchard & Schwarz, 1987; Schwarz, Taylor, Scharff, & Blanchard, 1990), diabetic ulcer (Shulimson, Lawrence, & Iocono, 1986), and cardiac arrhythmias (Brody, Davison, & Brody, 1985).

Autogenic biofeedback therapy is also appropriate as an adjunctive treatment for other disorders where stress may play a part in causing or exacerbating the problem. In neuromuscular rehabilitation with problems of paresis and spasticity following trauma or stroke, for example, autogenic biofeedback training may be used to reduce the impact of the stresses associated with the disability, to improve circulation to damaged areas in the interests of healing, and to restore or improve function in areas affected by paresis. Autogenic biofeedback has also been found useful for self-regulation training in instances of tic, blepharospasm, Bell's palsy, and torticollis. Moreover, autogenic biofeedback therapy may play an important adjunctive role in reducing symptoms and stress while potentiating other medical treatments in such illnesses as cancer, diabetes, and multiple sclerosis.

Psychological dysfunctions ameliorated by autogenic biofeedback therapy include such stress-related disorders as agoraphobia, neurotic depression, impulse disorders (anger, acting out), and other generalized stress syndromes with no underlying organicity—for all of which, in nonpsychiatric medical settings, Valium or other palliatives are often prescribed. Autogenic biofeedback therapy and psychological monitoring also constitute a useful adjunct to desensitization psychotherapy.

We have found that autogenic biofeedback training can be accommodated to any age group; we have treated people from ages 4 through 89 with equally good success. Autogenic biofeedback training can also be accommodated to a wide range of intelligence levels, and has been used with positive results with retarded children (French, Leeb, & Fahrion, 1975).

At another level, assessment proceeds according to psychophysiological considerations, and the initial session as a whole may be seen as an opportunity for both therapist and patient to assess the appropriateness of this treatment approach. Initial physiological levels for a typical patient coming to a therapist's office for the first time provide a sample that represents some degree of the stress response. Then, as the patient goes through the relaxation procedures of the first session, the therapist observes the patient's levels and flexibility of response: To what extent is the patient able to relax at the outset? Thus the initial evaluation and demonstration proceed simultaneously. With this information, the therapist can inform the patient about the observed response, and ask, on the basis of this sample of what the training will involve, whether the patient wishes to proceed. This "self-selection" approach permits the patient to provide truly informed consent for the treatment—an ideal that is all too often missing in practice in most medical treatment.

Limitations and Contraindications

This treatment approach fails, when it does, primarily because of lack of motivation on the part of the patient. Consistent (daily) effort is required to practice psychophysiological control until normal homeostatic functioning is restored. Thus, although we are presently observing 90% of our medicated patients with essential hypertension develop the ability to maintain normal blood pressures while eliminating all antihypertensive medications, those who fail are those who do not learn physiological control (indexed by objective criteria), or those who, having developed such control, do not practice the five to seven times per week required initially to make a significant change in their stress-related problems. Later, patients are able to maintain their gains with only infrequent formal practice, as average before-practice hand and foot temperatures increase through experience of the self-regulatory exercises.

There are no known contraindications to the application of these techniques in themselves. However, patients with psychosomatic and psychophysiological stress disorders—if they are taking medication with major systemic effects, such as antihypertensive drugs, thyroid medication, or insulin—may become overmedicated as they make progress in the acquisition of these self-regulatory skills, with the consequent neurohormonal changes and physiological improvements. Close monitoring of such physiological changes in relation to medications is a necessity to prevent possible overmedication and its consequences, and to be sure that medication levels are reduced when appropriate. This is always done in cooperation with, and at the order of, such patients' managing physicians.

Individuals who have been highly stressed and who become very relaxed physiologically may also find themselves in much better touch with emotion-laden uncon-scious processes. This discharge phenomenon actually represents a part of the therapeutic action of autogenic biofeedback; however, if it should become temporari-ly overwhelming for a patient, the therapist may wish to recommend that the patient engage in several short sessions (5 minutes or less) during the day, rather than in one or two longer sessions, until this process resolves itself. With some more severely disturbed patients, the therapist may find it necessary to conduct all the experiential processes with the patients in the office at first. We have observed that stress manage-ment therapy with seriously disturbed patients often takes much longer, particularly in instances of high levels of psychoactive medications; that it may have definite but only limited beneficial effects; and that in a few instances, improvement may not persist beyond the treatment period.

It is important to recognize in this regard that if a patient is able to maintain a relaxed physiology in the face of this discharge of emotion-laden thoughts and images, a kind of naturalistic desensitization process ensues, and autogenic abreaction and neutralization are facilitated. At any rate, this phenomenon does not represent a contraindication for the experienced therapist so much as a technical problem to be dealt with in the psychotherapeutic process.

The Method

Introducing the Method to the Client

Although there is considerable variability in the procedures used by various prac-titioners in teaching voluntary control of autonomic processes, those described here are fairly typical. At the beginning of psychophysiological therapy, each medically symptomatic patient should have his or her medical records reviewed; if necessary, the patient should have a further medical examination to establish the diagnosis and to assure that any medical treatment that may be required in addition to the psy-chophysiological therapy will be recommended or provided.

That the variability in concepts among the various practitioners using biofeed-back contributes to a rather wide range of procedures and results can be seen from an examination of the literature. With respect to the role of awareness in biofeedback, for example, the paradigms within which biofeedback is used range from "Biofeed-back training has nothing to do with awareness" to ""Biofeedback training is aware-ness training." The latter position is implicit in autogenic training, a procedure that mobilizes intention and volition; it is the position of the founders of autogenic biofeedback therapy, as well as of clinicians who think of biofeedback in terms of self-regulation and voluntary control rather than conditioning.

The philosophy under which autogenic biofeedback is used in treatment has an impact on all aspects of the method, and is the determining factor in such aspects of treatment as the introduction of the method to the client and the nature of the client–therapist relationship. In our practice, we place great emphasis on engendering in the client a clear understanding of the basic mechanisms of stress and anxiety, of self-regulation concepts, of the principles underlying psychosomatic illness and psy-chosomatic health (Green, Green, & Walters, 1970b), and of the rationale for the methods to be employed. To this end, we frequently employ audiovisual aids (graphs, diagrams, films, and videotapes) and assigned readings, as well as a variety of experiential exercises to familiarize patients with their own mind–body coordination.

From the beginning of therapy, we make it clear to patients that the essence of self-regulation of any kind is proper visualization. This is true of all acquired skills, from executing a pole vault or a cartwheel to playing the piano, as well as in the learning of autonomic self-regulation. The neurological rationale described above is provided to patients; every effort is made to "demystify" the topic of mind–body coordination, and to foster a mental set within which physiological self-regulation is easier to learn. We hypothesize that understanding the rationale underlying treatment engages both hemispheres of a client's brain in the therapeutic process: The left cortex, appreciating the rational and practical nature of neurological self-regulation, enhances (or at least does not interfere with) the right cortex in creating appropriate visualizations. Each patient participates in goal setting and in developing the treatment program, and is in every sense a coparticipant in the treatment process.

The Physical Environment and Equipment

Training sessions typically occur in a standard office environment with, at a minimum, a reclining chair for the patient, a nearby table for the equipment, and comfortable seating space for the therapist. The office setting should be pleasant and conducive to relaxation, rather than sterile and emotionally cold. Office temperatures will ideally be well stabilized, and perhaps somewhat warmer than usual (72–74°F); and/or a light blanket should be available to cover the patient during the early phases of training. The office should be quiet and softly lighted, without fluorescent lights to create electrical artifacts that are difficult to filter out. These ideal conditions are facilitative in early training, particularly with patients who are tense, anxious, and in pain. Later in training, it is important for patients to accomplish relaxation in any environment.

Commercially available biofeedback equipment is commonly used; this may vary markedly in complexity, from inexpensive thermometers to multiplexed multichannel microcomputers for data collection and display. Minimal equipment would include simple, stand-alone electronic thermal and electromyographic (EMG) biofeedback units, plus a digital integrator to average data over variable time intervals. In general, the expense of equipment is largely determined by its sensitivity, by the complexity of its data processing, and by the variety of its feedback displays.

No comprehensive literature currently exists to compare the effects of these equipment parameters in training, but clinical observation suggests that individual clients may prefer one or another form of feedback display, and that it is useful to follow these preferences insofar as this is possible. The fact that patients seem to learn self-regulation with many different feedback regimens suggests that these aspects of training are relatively unimportant, as long as the feedback is immediate, continuous, and reasonably pleasant in character.

Some therapeutic advantage may actually accrue from the use of simpler, less expensive equipment, in that it is less likely to suggest to the patient that the equipment itself will "do something to" the patient, rather than simply serving as an electronic mirror. This assures that the mere presence of the equipment will be less likely to induce short-lived, counterproductive placebo effects that may produce initial confusion in the process of learning self-regulatory skills. Simpler equipment is also less subject to "down time," an important consideration for the practicing clinician, since the expense of more complicated units may also inhibit acquisition of backup equipment. Thermal and EMG biofeedback units, together with breathing exercises and other adjunctive strategies, can accomplish symptom alleviation or removal and can increase psychosomatic health in any and all of the patients seen. More specific training can often be facilitated with other feedback modalities, such as EEG, electrodermal response (EDR), electrocardiographic (EKG), sphygmomanometer, and goniometer feedback. These physiological measures may be used both for skills training and for objective measurement of other psychophysiological behaviors being treated.

The Therapist–Client Relationship

Since autogenic biofeedback therapy emphasizes self-regulation, much importance is placed on the client's assuming and/or maintaining responsibility for his or her own stress responses, healing process, and state of wellness. This necessitates several strategies of approach, which differ from those of many other therapies. First, the relationship is not an authoritarian one; rather, it is a healing partnership in which the client participates fully. The patient is not simply a passive receiver of health care, but an active participant in a teamwork approach between therapist and patient. To this end, no information is withheld from any patient. Patients are fully informed of their condition, their physiological parameters and measurements, and the nature of their progress through the treatment process. As part of increasing self-awareness, we encourage patients to know everything possible about themselves and their conditions. If appropriate, X-rays, blood tests, and other medical findings are shared with clients, and these may help form the basis of the visualizations employed.

Effective therapists are generally acute observers. This is an invaluable skill for biofeedback practitioners as well, and is even more invaluable as a skill to pass on to patients. An ability to become an "observer of the self" maximizes choice and is a central part of self-regulation.

Description of the Method

In a typical case, a major portion of the initial appointment is spent in developing rapport with the client, taking a clinical data history from the client's point of view, and introducing the concept of biofeedback training. Particular emphasis is placed on explaining the rationale described above for the way in which biofeedback is applied to the client's specific disorder—that is, what body functions are being measured and how the normalization of these functions can help to alleviate the symptoms. The client may be shown several graphs or other relevant data of successful training outcomes of similar patients, with the intent of inducing a sense of hopefulness and positive expectancy about the treatment process. Patients with psychophysiological disorders have typically undergone a variety of different treatments without successful results, and often feel despondent or skeptical about the prospects of improving their condition.

At the onset of training, the client is monitored for baseline levels of skin temperature and forehead muscle tension at least, and frequently EDR and other parameters are also evaluated. Since the initial training is usually performed with the patient reclining in a chair, the baseline data are also taken in this position in our practice. Each physiological function is monitored and the data recorded, first over a few minutes of baseline and then during the relaxation experience, which together provide an index of the stress level. Some clinicians do initial diagnostic evaluations with stressors administered as well. Although this provides useful information for research and outcome measures, these advantages may be offset by the initial "message" to the client that is implicit in such a procedure.

In addition to the physiological assessment, our diagnostic evaluation includes psychological measures. Each patient completes a Spielberger State–Trait Anxiety Inventory, a Cornell Medical Index, and a Personal Orientation Inventory at the beginning of treatment and again at termination. The test results are generally shared and discussed fully at the end of treatment. Occasionally other psychological measures may also be administered.

In a typical first training session, as soon as the baseline data are taken, the trainee is oriented to the training process with remarks such as the following:

> At this point I'm going to give you some autogenic training phrases, and I want you to say each phrase over and over to yourself. First, your attitude as you do this is quite important. This is the kind of thing where the more you try to relax, the less it will happen. So the best approach is to have the intention to warm and relax, but to remain detached about your actual results. Since everyone can learn voluntary control of these processes, it is only a matter of time until you do, and therefore you can afford to be detached about the results. Second, saying the phrases is good because it keeps them in mind, but it is not enough. The part of the brain that controls these processes, the limbic system, doesn't understand language well, so it is important to translate the content of the phrase into some kind of image. One of the phrases is "My hands are heavy and warm." If you can actually imagine what it would feel like if your hands did feel heavy or if they did feel warm, that helps to bring on the changes that we are looking for. Or use a visual image: Imagine that you are lying out on a beach in the sun, or that you are holding your hands over a campfire. Whatever works for you as a relaxing image or a warmth-inducing image is the thing to use, but the imaging itself is important. Finally, if you simply trust your body to do what you are visualizing it as doing, then you will discover that it will.

The modified autogenic training phrases adapted by Alyce Green, including the "mind-quieting" phrases she developed (see Figure 8.2), are then administered for approximately 20 minutes. Only verbal feedback is typically given during the first autogenic biofeedback experience, because direct instrument feedback may induce performance anxiety at this stage, and because verbal feedback facilitates the focus of attention on internal awareness. The therapist observes the physiological response on the instrument and either provides verbal feedback for improvement in hand temperature between the autogenic phrases (if indicated) or records impressions for

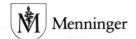 Menninger   Thermal Feedback scoring sheet

Trainee's initials _____   Date _____

Initial temperature _____

Temperature reading   **Phrases**
(at the start of each phrase)

_____   1. I feel quite quiet.

_____   2. I am beginning to feel quite relaxed.

_____   3. My feet feel heavy and relaxed.

_____   4. My ankles, my knees and my hips feel heavy, relaxed and comfortable.

_____   5. My solar plexus, and the whole central portion of my body, feel relaxed and quiet.

_____   6. My hands, my arms and my shoulders feel heavy, relaxed and comfortable.

_____   7. My neck, my jaws and my forehead feel relaxed. They feel comfortable and smooth.

_____   8. My whole body feels quiet, heavy, comfortable and relaxed.

_____   9. Continue alone for a minute.

_____   10. I am quite relaxed.

_____   11. My arms and hands are heavy and warm.

_____   12. I feel quite quiet.

_____   13. My whole body is relaxed and my hands are warm, relaxed and warm.

_____   14. My hands are warm.

_____   15. Warmth is flowing into my hands, they are warm, warm.

_____   16. I can feel the warmth flowing down my arms into my hands.

_____   17. My hands are warm, relaxed and warm.

_____   18. Continue alone for a minute.

_____   19. My whole body feels quiet, comfortable and relaxed.

_____   20. My mind is quiet.

_____   21. I withdraw my thoughts from the surroundings and I feel serene and still.

_____   22. My thoughts are turned inward and I am at ease.

_____   23. Deep within my mind I can visualize and experience myself as relaxed, comfortable and still.

_____   24. I am alert, but in an easy, quiet, inward-turned way.

_____   25. My mind is calm and quiet.

_____   26. I feel an inward quietness.

_____   27. Continue alone for a minute.

_____   28. The relaxation and reverie is now concluded and the whole body is reactivated with a deep breath and the following phrases: "I feel life and energy flowing through my legs, hips, solar plexus, chest, arms and hands, neck and head... The energy makes me feel light and alive." Stretch.

Final temperature _____

05-391 (Rev. 2-88)   The Menninger Clinic

FIGURE 8.2. Autogenic biofeedback training phrases. Reprinted by permission of the Menninger Foundation.

sharing at the conclusion of the experience. The client may be told, "You are beginning to get warmer," and "You're now warming more rapidly," as these events occur. The client is given encouragement and reinforcement. The therapist paces the phrases to correspond to the client's actual physiological changes; it is important for the client to be given sufficient time between phrases to be able to repeat each phrase slowly to himself or herself at least three times.

Toward the end of the first session, auditory or visual feedback may be introduced. Various instruments provide different forms of feedback, but the most widely used is either an analog or digital meter, or a tone that decreases in pitch as the hands warm. Another sensitive and useful form of feedback is a tone that increases in pitch as the rate of warming increases.

In concluding the first training period, the therapist and client discuss the experience and the homework exercises to be practiced daily between office visits. The therapist informs the client that positive results are likely, provided that two criteria are met: (1) The client must perform hand-warming exercises every day until symptoms are overcome, and must be able finally to sustain a hand temperature of at least 95.5°F for 10 minutes or more; and (2) the client must be able to increase hand temperature at a rate of at least 1°F per minute. (These criteria are perhaps somewhat more stringent than those currently used by most biofeedback practitioners, but their achievement has been observed to be essential if the best clinical results are to be obtained and maintained over time.)

In addition to the more formal practice, we also encourage our clients to experiment with the equipment. We may say something like this:

> This equipment is yours to use for the time being, so have fun with it; let the scientist within you come out. If you are watching TV, it is interesting to see what your hand temperature does during the news, during a comedy, or during tender or frightening moments. It may be enlightening to see what happens to your hand temperature if you have a difficult phone call to make . . . do your hands get cold? Can you keep them warm or make them warm? You may want to check this response during any opportunity to explore your own physiological functioning, so let your imagination be your guide.

A thorough description of all the specific training methods is beyond the scope of this chapter. A description of the aims of autogenic biofeedback therapy will suffice to provide a guideline for clinical work and all its ramifications and applications. In autogenic therapy, as developed by Schultz and Luthe, the first four standard exercises are these:

1. Heaviness (associated with neuromuscular quietness).
2. Warmth (associated with autonomic quietness).
3. Cardiac regulation.
4. Respiration.

These exercises are considered mandatory to prepare the client for, and to optimize the effectiveness of, "organ-specific formulas" (Schultz & Luthe, 1969).

In the development of autogenic biofeedback therapy, we have followed a similar paradigm. In order for visualization, intentional formulas, and specific physiological training to be most effective, the client first learns to achieve a quiet body, quiet emotions, and a quiet mind. To that end, the threefold autogenic biofeedback training phrases (see Figure 8.2) were developed by the Greens to help initiate these states; they can be used with any or all of the training modalities, although they are customarily introduced at the outset with thermal training for vascular relaxation and sympathetic deactivation.

Also, to achieve these ends (quiet body, quiet emotions, quiet mind), training proceeds generally in the following order. First, emotional quietness is approached by thermal training, and it is considered to be achieved when criterion levels of hand warming are met. At the second or third session, breathing exercises are introduced, and corrective exercises are given if necessary to switch the patient from thoracic to diaphragmatic breathing. The goals of the breathing exercises are for the patient to do the following:

1. To establish deep diaphragmatic breathing.
2. To extend the breathing cycle until the breathing rate during relaxation is gradually reduced, over a period of weeks, to a maximum of three to four times per minute.
3. To develop awareness of gasping and holding of breath as a means of blocking feelings, and awareness of rapid, shallow breathing at times of anxiety and/or daily life stress.
4. To learn to exhale, let go, and breathe slowly and deeply as an instant destressing technique.

Practice of both thermal training and breathing exercises is continued daily. Some attention must be paid to integrating the practice into the daily life of the client, and homework practice is considered imperative in facilitating a generalization of training skills.

Another technique we have found to be especially useful is one we have dubbed "constant-instance practice." When some mastery of physiological self-regulation is demonstrated (e.g., when a temperature of 95°F or more is reached in the hand a number of times, or a deeply relaxed EMG level is attained), the patient is told to engage in the process of constant-instance practice for 1 week, with the following guidelines:

> Repeat to yourself as often as possible a brief phrase indicating the change you want to occur—for example, "My hands are warm and my muscles relaxed." The primary goal is to become relaxed, so if you forget for a while, don't be concerned; just think, "Good, I remembered now." But bear in mind that the more often you do it, the better—100 times is better than 50. So every time you come to a stop sign, every time you sit down, stand up, use the phone, or start or end any activity, simply think of the phrase and the accompanying sensation briefly, without interference in whatever you are doing, without performance anxiety, without checking to see whether anything is happening. Simply, over and over, generate the feeling and let go.

We have found with the majority of our patients that this practice consolidates the training, is especially facilitative of the transfer of training, and helps to establish the new homeostatic balance.

The patient may practice briefly two or more times a day. Once a day, at the conclusion of a practice session, a short report of the training session is made (see Figure 8.3). This report is an invaluable part of the awareness enhancement, as the patient tunes in to the physical sensations, emotions, and thoughts and fantasies that accompany relaxation. We have observed that psychotherapeutic gains are made by almost every individual learning peripheral temperature regulation. The realization on the part of a patient that he or she can control some internal processes that were thought involuntary is always accompanied by a self-image change and an enhanced sense of self-mastery. Over a period of time, both physical and mental well-being are enhanced, as relaxation and self-regulatory skills are transferred to everyday life.

Third, a quiet body is further enhanced by EMG feedback (commonly introduced in the first or in an early session) and by general relaxation training, until criterion levels of deep relaxation are reached and can be maintained for at least 10 minutes. Often these three steps are sufficient to produce a quiet mind, as well as physical and emotional quietness. If the "quiet mind" condition has not already been met, EEG alpha and theta training may reduce mental stress and aid in the achievement of mental quietness.

This training—the "core" of autogenic biofeedback training and the sine qua non of our stress management training—precedes specific visualizations and training, whether the disorder being treated is agoraphobia, cancer, arthritis, multiple sclerosis, or any disorder in which stress is a complicating or etiological factor.

Maintenance of Treatment Results

Once patients' gains through daily deep relaxation have been achieved and consolidated, in many instances they may begin to taper off the daily practice. This may be achieved by warming only on days on which the hands are cool to begin with, or only every other day. The symptoms are monitored during this process, and symptomatic regression is an indication of need to increase the daily practice once again; otherwise, practice may be reduced and eliminated, except for very stressful periods.

The trainee continues to send the symptom report cards to the therapist for the next few months after treatment is concluded. If it appears from these reports that the trainee is experiencing difficulties, or if he or she does not send in the cards, the therapist telephones the individual to inquire about progress and to recommend whatever modifications in training methodology seem appropriate. As a routine procedure, the therapist telephones each trainee after several months for a follow-up evaluation.

Case Example

The case example we present here has been chosen to illustrate several aspects of the technique and effect of autogenic biofeedback therapy. We discuss a patient treated for a major stress disorder: essential hypertension.

 Menninger   Temperature feedback training questionnaire

Your name _____ Date _____ Time of day _____

Where did you practice? _____ Starting skin temperature _____

Medication or medication changes _____ Highest temperature _____

Were you able to feel the following internal changes?
a. Warmth   Definitely   Moderately   Slightly   Not at all
b. Flushing   Definitely   Moderately   Slightly   Not at all
c. Throbbing/Pulsating Definitely   Moderately   Slightly   Not at all

How did the training session seem?

Were you able to relax?   Yes   No   If not, what seemed to interfere?

Physical sensations that occurred.

Emotional feelings that occurred.

Thoughts, fantasies, and imaginings.

Did your mind wander at all?   Yes   No   If so,   A lot   Moderately   Slightly

Did you have any tendency to fall asleep (or get drowsy)   Yes   No

Did you have any dream-like experiences or mental pictures?   Yes   No
a. If so, did these experiences occur in a particular way?   Visual   Auditory   Spatial   Touch (pressure)   Smell   Taste
b. If so, were you aware of these experiences all of a sudden (very quickly) or in a gradual way?   Sudden   Gradual

Was there anything that you particularly liked or did not like about this training session?

Further experiences you would like to share, or remarks you would like to make (if necessary, use reverse side of this sheet).

The Menninger Clinic

OS-374 (Rev. 7-91)

FIGURE 8.3. Daily report for enhancing psychophysiological self-awareness during home practice. Reprinted by permission of the Menninger Foundation.

Although our treatment program is multifaceted, it is probably not possible or even useful to ascribe relative value to the various components, because of their synergistic nature. Yet in our clinical experience, the autonomic self-regulation gained through autogenic biofeedback procedures is the most synergistically powerful element of the entire package. Autogenic biofeedback training mediates stress reduction; aids visualization; enhances the psychotherapeutic process; and reduces the adversity and probably potentiates the effectiveness of the concurrent medical treatment (medications, diet, and exercise).

Autogenic biofeedback can thus play a significant role in the treatment of patients with essential hypertension (Fahrion, 1991). The major elements of the program are these:

1. Acquisition and daily practice of relaxation skills.
2. Psychotherapy, including exploration of past and present stressors, and self-image.
3. Nutritional counseling.
4. Exercise, including breathing exercises.
5. Goal setting and play: Participating as fully as possible in living, enjoyable activities, and productivity.
6. Visualization and imagery of the specific healing process.

A comprehensive wellness program, but also a straightforward stress management program based on biofeedback-assisted relaxation, can have a significant impact on the lives and well-being of hypertensive patients. It is well to remember that there is often a triple stress associated with hypertension: the stress that may have contributed to developing high blood pressure in the first place; the stress of having a chronic illness such as hypertension; and the stress associated with taking medication and undergoing other aspects of medical treatment of this disease. The capacity to cope with stress through learned self-regulation can reduce blood pressure and the need for hypotensive medication; can ameliorate unpleasant side effects of treatment and potentiate its positive effects; and can enhance a sense of competence, self-esteem, and self-mastery. From a human perspective, self-regulation increases feelings of mastery and well-being, increases coping, and enhances the quality of life.

Ben was a 38-year-old white middle management executive who was referred by his physician to a controlled research study of autogenic biofeedback and psychophysiological therapy for treatment of essential hypertension. He had been diagnosed as hypertensive 10 years prior to entering treatment on the basis of blood pressure readings taken in the physician's office, and he was placed on hypotensive medication (Enduron, 5 mg daily). His records indicated a normal blood chemistry profile and a normal treadmill EKG.

He entered treatment because of health concerns, stating, "I want to learn a technique that will allow me to better control my hypertension. I am frustrated by its controlling me, and disheartened by the need to medicate a response that I should and could control." His attitude, though cautious at first, soon became confident, and his expectations became positive.

Medication Washout and Pretreatment Condition

After signing informed consent forms, the patient was instructed in the use of an aneroid sphygmomanometer with the dual-stethoscope equipment. He was then given a standard sphygmomanometer and asked to take his pressure daily. A stepped medication washout was accomplished over a 2-week period. He was monitored weekly in the office with a random zero sphygmomanometer in order to remove some biases common in blood pressure measurement; the average of his first two weekly unmedicated office blood pressures was 156/107 mm Hg. One month later, his office blood pressures averaged 148/96 mm Hg. He was maintained in an unmedicated condition during cardiac reactivity evaluation.

Cardiac Reactivity Testing: Procedures and Initial Results

Cardiac reactivity testing consisted of a $1\frac{1}{2}$-hour protocol during which the following measurements were taken: systolic and diastolic blood pressure; thoracic impedance (using a BOMED Noninvasive Continuous Cardiac Output Monitor); heart rate (HR); hand and foot temperatures (using a T-68 Temperature Monitor, J & J Electronics); and forehead and forearm muscle tension (using an M-57 EMG Monitor, J & J Electronics). Tasks began with a 20-minute self-relaxation baseline period with the examiner out of the room, followed by a 2-minute tilt-to-supine-position task. The remaining tasks included a 5-minute extemporaneous speech sample (Gottschalk, 1978, 1986), a 3-minute serial 7's subtraction task, a 2-minute hand dynamometer task, a video game, and a 90-second cold-pressor task. Each stressor was followed by a self-relaxation recovery period of 6 minutes. The session concluded with one additional 6-minute postbaseline recovery period with the examiner out of the room. During baseline and all recovery periods, the subject was encouraged to relax as much as possible, but without the aid of physiological feedback.

The reactivity test results are displayed according to the convention developed in 1988 by Dr. Robert Eliot (see Figure 8.4A). Normal hemodynamic functioning is represented by values in the white trapezoid at the lower right of Figure 9.4A, bounded on the top by a mean blood pressure of 107 mm Hg (equivalent to pressures of 140 mm Hg systolic and 90 mm Hg diastolic), and bounded on the left by a total systemic resistance of 1400 (dynes/second/cm^5). These values represent a situation comprising normal blood pressure and a relatively open arterial tree. Although this patient's initial baseline level was in this normal range, his pressures became elevated with all of the stressors except the video game. The direction of the vectors indicates that his stress responses consisted predominantly of elevated beta-adrenergic drive, with the responses to the cold-pressor and speech tasks showing increased alpha-adrenergic drive, with increased systemic resistance and closing down of the arterial tree as well (Eliot, 1988). The video game task produced more beta-adrenergic response, with the vector moving more to the right, than was the case with the other tasks, indicating that the blood pressure increase observed here resulted primarily from an increase in cardiac output rather than in systemic resistance.

Two very different adrenergically mediated hemodynamic stress responses underlie elevated blood pressure to different degrees in different individuals (Eliot,

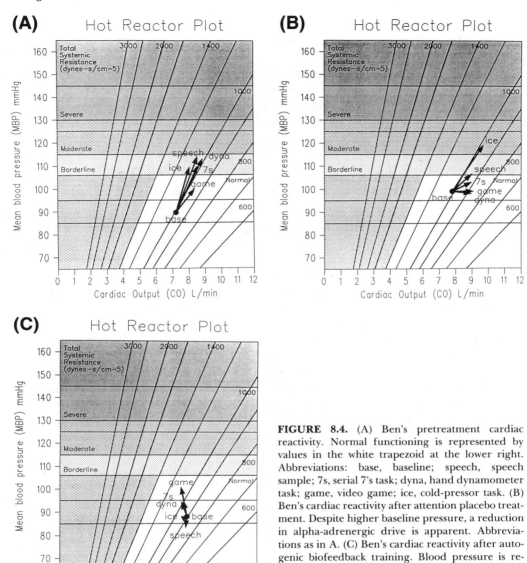

FIGURE 8.4. (A) Ben's pretreatment cardiac reactivity. Normal functioning is represented by values in the white trapezoid at the lower right. Abbreviations: base, baseline; speech, speech sample; 7s, serial 7's task; dyna, hand dynamometer task; game, video game; ice, cold-pressor task. (B) Ben's cardiac reactivity after attention placebo treatment. Despite higher baseline pressure, a reduction in alpha-adrenergic drive is apparent. Abbreviations as in A. (C) Ben's cardiac reactivity after autogenic biofeedback training. Blood pressure is reduced both at baseline and under stress. An overall decrease in both alpha- and beta-adrenergic drive is evident. Abbreviations as in A.

1988; Fahrion, 1991). During stress, the alpha-adrenergic response first moves blood *out* of areas where it is *not* needed for fight or flight: out of the hands and feet, out of the lower abdominal area, and out of the kidney. Second, a beta-adrenergic response moves this available blood *into* the areas where it *is* needed for fight or flight: into the muscles and heart. Beta-adrenergic response includes increased cardiac output (CO) as a result of both increased HR and increased stroke volume (SV). Renin release into the plasma is simultaneously increased as part of this pattern.

Similarly, two basic types of hemodynamic response have been observed. The "hyperkinetic heart syndrome," which is similar to the beta-adrenergic pattern described above (with elevated CO, HR, and SV), is commonly seen in the early stages of essential hypertension. Total systemic resistance (TSR), which usually increases with stress, is usually observed to be normal at this point. How this is possible is explored below.

The second hemodynamic pattern, the "blood loss pattern," is similar to that seen when the body experiences hemorrhage and pulls the blood away from the periphery to maintain pressure and prevent blood loss. This pattern is commonly seen in the later stages of hypertension, when CO, HR, and SV have normalized but TSR has become elevated, increasing blood pressure.

In synthesizing these dynamic patterns, we see that in the first stage of stress, the alpha- and beta-adrenergic patterns occur together. TSR is normal because of increases in the diameter of arteries in muscle tissue (to prepare for fight or flight), providing a significant portion of open arterial tree (in the muscles) through which blood can readily flow, even though it is being squeezed out of other areas. If stress is sustained (i.e., impossible to terminate through physical activity), beta-adrenergic response normalizes, including arterial diameter in the muscles. CO also normalizes, as the body is no longer mobilized for action. Yet alpha-adrenergic response continues, squeezing blood out of the periphery, the kidneys, and the organs of digestion. TSR then becomes elevated, since the arterial tree as a whole is relatively constricted.

One implication of this model is that hypertension is also characterized by two quite different phenomenological stances, which may be observed singly or in combination. On the one hand, those with high systolic hypertension and elevated CO may be seen as evidencing "racehorse" hypertension; they commonly report that they have "too much to do and too little time." On the other hand, those with high diastolic hypertension and high TSR seem to be evidencing "turtle" hypertension; their reports are in concert with a need to have a shell around themselves to avoid emotional suffering, because of perceived vulnerability to others, or fear that they will lose control and express their own emotions in an excessive fashion.

It is important for practitioners to recognize that when medications for hypertension are given, either or both of these psychophysiological stances may be affected, depending upon the action of the medications prescribed. Simplistically, beta blockers reduce "racehorse" hypertension, whereas alpha blockers, calcium channel blockers, and angiotensin-converting enzyme inhibitors tend to reduce "turtle" hypertension.

In terms of this model, at initial testing the patient in this case example was primarily responding with beta-adrenergic increases in CO, the hemodynamic pattern typically seen in early hypertension; yet in response to the cold-pressor stimulus, an alpha-adrenergic vasoconstrictive pattern was also activated. Thus specific hemodynamic response to stress may be seen to be a product of both patient characteristics and stimulus "pull."

"Placebo" Treatment Results

Ben was next randomly assigned to a nondirective "self-exploration" (attention placebo) group conducted by a psychologist for 6 months. He took the self-exploration group very seriously and was an active and open participant in group discussions. Discussions focused on interpersonal stress both at work and in the family, financial stress, and stress related to beliefs and roles. The group members became sensitive to dynamic issues such as shame and guilt that related to present stress in their lives, and Ben developed and expressed greater awareness of how his emotions and his blood pressure interacted. During this time the group leader facilitated interaction between participants, but did not provide suggestions, direction, or presentation of didactic material.

Following this treatment the patient reported, "The group process helped me work through stressful situations and better developed my sense of stress, its source, and how better to deal with it. I have a more sensitive perception of reality and all of its imperfections." Despite these positive comments, at 150/91 mm Hg his average office blood pressure was still hypertensive at the end of the 6-month self-exploration group.

The graph of Ben's cardiac reactivity testing at that point is presented in Figure 8.4B. It reveals that his baseline blood pressure, although still normal, was actually higher than during initial testing. His response to the speech, serial 7's, video game, and dynamometer tasks had normalized, and the direction of the vectors suggested some reduction in alpha-adrenergic response had occurred. His response to the cold-pressor task was somewhat higher than before, but indicated more of a "race-horse" than a "turtle" pattern.

Self-Regulation Results

Next Ben was treated with "self-regulation," a group autogenic biofeedback treatment, for 6 months. At the outset the patient viewed a film on our work with essential hypertension (Hartley, 1981), which presents a rationale, describes the method of treatment, and presents the successful results, including the comments of a number of patients. Ben reported that he had believed there was little more he could do on his own behalf to make a difference in his health; however, seeing and hearing the previously successful patients describe their results awakened him to the possibility that he could be an active participant in the therapeutic processes.

Ben was then introduced to thermal biofeedback and breathing exercises and began daily home practice of these immediately, with the aid of a small electronic digital thermometer. These exercises began to help him with relaxing during the first week of practice, and by the end of the week he was able to achieve a hand temperature of 94.8°F, usually associated with deep autonomic relaxation. He reported practicing both autonomic relaxation and breathing during this time with good results, further reinforcing his sense of ability to control some psychophysiological processes.

After six weekly 1-hour sessions, Ben could usually warm his hands to 96–97°F, and was ready to begin warming his feet. We regularly teach patients with essential hypertension to warm the feet, as this is associated with significant drops in blood pressure in our clinical experience.

Despite his good success with hand warming, Ben had difficulty reliably warming his feet to 93°F until the 24th week of the self-regulation group. To begin with, his feet would often start in the mid-80s (degrees Fahrenheit) and warm only 1–2°F. Ben was a runner, and we have observed with interest that other individuals who run extensively usually have more difficulty than most people in learning to warm their feet. It is worth noting, however, that he succeeded in raising his foot temperature effectively during the coldest part of winter.

Patients with essential hypertension are provided with a home blood pressure monitor and are asked to assume responsibility for taking their pressures every day. During the first week that Ben was taking his pressure daily in the home environment before and after relaxation, his weekly average before relaxing was 136/80 mm Hg, and readings ranged up to 144/94. During the last week of treatment his weekly home pressure before relaxing was 123/78 mm Hg, with his two highest pressures at 126/74 and 118/80.

During the course of treatment, Ben's first sessions with the therapist were spent in thermal training in developing awareness of related physical, emotional, and mental events correlated with autonomic relaxation, as well as awareness of associated imagery and insights. One session was spent in giving the breathing exercises and their rationale. Also during this time, transfer of training of these new autogenic skills was a focus in every session. Ben was found to have fairly high forehead muscle tension levels (3–4 μV), but within three sessions of EMG biofeedback he was able to relax to criterion level (1 μV); he continued to practice with the EMG throughout the training process.

Emphasis on the psychotherapeutic process continued during the sessions and was frequently wide-ranging, covering not only the imagery and insights that arose from the relaxation and visualization themselves, but also past life events, present life stressors, present triumphs and accomplishments, and family concerns. Throughout the self-regulation group, patients were constantly reminded to use their new strategies when under stress. During the entire course of therapy, Ben continually experienced improvements in his blood pressure and in his ability to relax in the face of stressful events. He slept better, had a better appetite, and felt more trim and fit. His coworkers and his family both noticed that he was more relaxed and easygoing, and was better able to cope with daily irritants, deadlines, and other stressors. At the end of treatment he reported, "Generally, I am more in touch with me and my environment, and seem to be more at peace with that relationship. I am more accepting of others and tend not to let them 'push my buttons.'"

The graph of the posttreatment cardiac reactivity evaluation is presented in Figure 8.4C. It demonstrates lowered mean blood pressure both at baseline and under stress compared to the previous testings; in fact, all readings fell within the "normal" range. Baseline TSR was also reduced compared to previous testings, suggesting lowered alpha-adrenergic drive. In contrast, the direction of the vectors suggests a trend of reacting to stressors, particularly the video game, with alpha-adrenergic mechanisms. No increase in beta-adrenergic response in relation to any of the stressors was observed.

Summary

At the present time Ben has eliminated hypotensive medication, and his blood pressures are normotensive with 1 year of follow-up; currently they average 125/75 mm Hg off medication. On the basis of previous clinical experience, it is expected that he will be able to maintain a normotensive stance off medications over the years, with only *ad libitum* practice of formal relaxation skills.

Ben is a person who is participating in life and in gaining health, who feels competent, who has eliminated hypertension and hypotensive medications, and who is enjoying an enhanced quality of life.

Reflections and Comments

Although the initial training in autogenic biofeedback training is oriented toward attaining states of deep relaxation, physiological studies of the passive concentration state of autogenic training have revealed an increased density of 15- to at least 20-cycle-per-second EEG activity, together with concurrent slow-wave activity density (Degossely & Bostem, 1977). Fischer (1978–1979) interprets these data as indicating that the passive concentration state represents not only a state of relaxation, but a state of arousal as well. Focused attention and the increased awareness of formerly unconscious events occurring during relaxed states are both part of the process of effective autogenic biofeedback training. This unusual state, then, appears to share characteristics with both the vigilant rapid-eye-movement dreaming state and the hypoaroused relaxed waking state. Therapeutically, it enables detached introspection concerning the exciting and possibly traumatic material emerging from the unconscious (Fischer, 1978–1979).

Similar observations were made in the Greens' studies of imagery and states of consciousness associated with creativity. Their first studies focused on normal, healthy subjects and used biofeedback methods to explore the relation between specific internal states, or states of consciousness, and specific brain wave patterns. They found theta waves to be associated with a deeply internalized (vigilant) state and with a quieting of the body, emotions, and thoughts, thus allowing usually "unheard or unseen things" to come to consciousness in the form of hypnogogic imagery (Green & Green, 1977).

There has been increasing interest in examining similar psychophysiological correlates of meditation. Fischer (1978–1979) likens the altered state of consciousness that accompanies autogenic training to Theraveda Buddhist meditation. In order to adapt the system for research in states of consciousness, and to shorten the learning time associated with autogenic training, the Greens combined "the conscious self-regulation aspect of yoga and the psychological method of autogenic training with the modern instrumental technique called physiological feedback" (Green, Green, & Walters, 1970a).

Benson, Beary, and Carol (1974), who adapted their methods for achieving the relaxation response from transcendental meditation, note that the physiological states thus achieved resemble those achieved through autogenic training, hypnosis, Zen, yoga, and other meditative techniques. Bostem and Degossely (1978) described, using spectral analysis of EEG data, the progressive spread of a dominant alpha band all over the scalp during autogenic training. These findings are very similar to those of Banquet (1973) in his spectral analysis of EEG during meditation. Fehmi (1978) has also observed a global high-amplitude, high-density alpha state brought about by a spatial-imagery meditative task and enhanced by EEG biofeedback.

Levine (1976) developed a sophisticated method for analyzing EEG correlates of meditation-induced altered states of consciousness, which has not yet been comparatively applied to states associated with other meditative procedures and with autogenic biofeedback training. Using this technique, Orme-Johnson, Clements, Haynes, and Badaoui (1977) found a significant correlation between the subjective experience of meditation and bilateral frontal lobe coherence. Frontal coherence in the alpha band was associated with increases or indices of creativity (ideational fluency on the Torrance Novel Uses Test), whereas frontal coherence in the theta band was associated with increased flexibility of concept formation. Interestingly, global coherence (all frequencies) increased with wakefulness and progressively decreased during sleep stages, with minimum coherence in Stage 4 sleep. On the basis of these studies, we speculate that autogenic biofeedback produces the same global coherence associated with wakefulness, while inducing deep autonomic and muscular relaxation; this may provide a fruitful direction for future research.

Other cerebral changes have also been noted. Mathew et al. (1980) reported cerebral blood flow increases accompanying self-regulated hand warming. (This finding supports the Greens' original hypothesis regarding the mechanism of improvement in migraine headache activity with hand warming.) Since blood flow in the brain is correlated with increased metabolic activity, these results again substantiate the dual nature of the autogenic state—simultaneously concentrated and relaxed, creating ideal conditions for passive volition.

Recent improvements in measurement techniques, together with new paradigms encompassing expanded conceptual frameworks of human psychological functioning, are leading to new understandings of the commonalities underlying different healing and meditative states. The Greens' early observation (Hartley, 1974) that "if there is such a thing as psychosomatic illness, there must be such a thing as psychosomatic health," moves beyond the elimination of disease toward a greater actualization of human potential. Self-regulation for physical and emotional well-being etches a new image of the human being as volitional, well, and strong—self-affirmative and self-responsible.

Summary and Conclusion

Two decades ago, Green, Green, and Walters (1971a) expressed the hope that

> with the resurgence of interest in self-exploration and in self-realization, it will be possible to develop a synthesis of old and new, East and West, pre-science and science, using both yoga and biofeedback training tools for the study of consciousness. . . . Much remains to be researched, and tried in application, but there is little doubt that in the lives of many people a penetration of consciousness into previously unconscious realms (of mind and brain) is making understandable and functional much that was previously obscure and inoperable. (p. 8)

The synthesis of concept and technique continues, while at a practical level, many people have begun to experience the healing and personally integrative consequences of unifying mind and body.

REFERENCES

Akagi, M., Yoshimura, M., & Ikemi, Y. (1977). A clinical study of the treatment of writer's cramp by biofeedback training. *Behavioral Engineering, 4*, 45–50.

Banquet, J. P. (1973). Spectral analysis of the EEG in meditation. *Electroencephalography and Clinical Neurophysiology, 35*, 143–151.

Barowsky, E. (1990). The use of biofeedback in the treatment of disorders of childhood *Annals of the New York Academy of Sciences, 602*, 221–233.

Benson, H., Beary, J. F., & Carol, M. P. (1974). The relaxation response. *Psychiatry, 37*, 37–46.

Billings, R. F., Thomas, M. R., Rapp, M. S., Reyes, E., & Leith, M. (1984). Differential efficacy of biofeedback in headache. *Headache, 24*, 211–215.

Blanchard, E. B. (1979). The use of temperature biofeedback in the treatment of chronic pain due to causalgia. *Biofeedback and Self-Regulation, 4*, 183–188.

Blanchard, E. B., Andrasik, F., Evans, D. D., Ness, D. F., Appelbaum, K. A., & Rodichok, L. D. (1985). Behavioral treatment of 250 chronic headache patients: A clinical replication series. *Behavior Therapy, 16*, 308–327.

Blanchard, E. B., Radnitz, C., Schwarz, S. P., Neff, D. F., & Gerardi, M. A. (1987). Psychological changes associated with self regulatory treatments of irritable bowel syndrome. *Biofeedback and Self-Regulation, 12*, 31–37.

Blanchard, E. B., & Schwarz, S. P. (1987). Adaptation of a multicomponent treatment for irritable bowel syndrome to a small group format. *Biofeedback and Self-Regulation, 12*, 63–69.

Boller, J. D., & Flom, R. P. (1979). Treatment of the common migraine: Systematic application of biofeedback and autogenic training. *American Journal of Clinical Biofeedback, 2*, 63–64.

Bostem, F., & Degossely, M. (1978). Spectral analysis of alpha rhythm during Schultz's autogenic training: A tentative approach to rapid visualization. *Electroencephalography and Clinical Neurophysiology, 34*(Suppl.), 181–190.

Brady, J. (1958). The paleocortex and behavioral motivation. In H. Harlow & C. N. Woolsey (Eds.), *The biological and biochemical bases of behavior*. Madison: University of Wisconsin Press.

Brody, C., Davison, E. T., & Brody, J. (1985). Self regulation of a complex ventricular arrhythmia. *Psychosomatics, 26*, 754–756.

Brown, B. (1978). Critique of biofeedback concepts and methodologies. *American Journal of Clinical Biofeedback, 1*, 10–14.

Budzynski, T. H., Stoyva, J. M., & Adler, C. S. (1970). Feedback-induced muscle relaxation: Application to tension headache. *Journal of Behavior Therapy and Experimental Psychiatry, 1*, 205–211.

Chapman, S. L. (1986). A review and clinical perspective on the use of EMG and thermal biofeedback for chronic headaches. *Pain, 27*, 1–43.

Cozzi, L., Tryon, W. W., & Sedlacek, K. (1987). The effectiveness of biofeedback assisted relaxation in modifying sickle cell crises. *Biofeedback and Self-Regulation, 12*, 51–61.

Daly, E. J., Donn, P. A., Galliher, M. J., & Zimmerman, J. S. (1983). Biofeedback applications of migraine and tension headaches: A double-blinded outcome study. *Biofeedback and Self-Regulation, 8*, 135–152.

Degossely, M., & Bostem, F. (1977). Autogenic training and states of consciousness: A few methodological problems. In W. Luthe & F. Antonelli (Eds.), *Proceedings of the 3rd World Congress, ICPM* (Vol. 4). Rome: Pozzi.

Dietvorst, T. F., & Osborne, D. (1978). Biofeedback-assisted relaxation training for primary dysmenorrhea: A case study. *Biofeedback and Self-Regulation, 3*, 301–305.

Dobie, T. G., May, J. G., Fischer, W. D., Elder, S. T., & Kubitz, K. A. (1987). A comparison of two methods of training resistance to visually induced motion sickness. *Aviation and Space Environmental Medicine, 58*, A34–A41.

Dobzhansky, T. (1951). *Genetics and the origin of species* (3rd ed.). New York: Columbia University Press.

Eliot, R. S. (1988). *Stress and the heart: Mechanisms, measurements and management*. Mount Kisco, NY: Futura.

Engelhardt, L. J. (1976). *The application of biofeedback techniques within a public school setting*. Paper presented at the Seventh Annual Meeting of the Biofeedback Society of America, Colorado Springs, CO.

Fahrion, S. L. (1977). Autogenic biofeedback for migraine. *Mayo Clinic Proceedings, 52*, 776–784.

Fahrion, S. L. (1991). Hypertension and biofeedback. *Primary Care, 18*, 663–682.

Fahrion, S. L., Walters, E. D., Coyne, L., & Allen, T. R. (1992). Alterations in EEG amplitude, personality factors and brain electrical mapping after alpha–theta brainwave training: A controlled case study of an alcoholic in recovery. *Alcoholism: Clinical and Experimental Research, 16*, 547–552.

Femhi, L. (1978). EEG biofeedback, multi-channel synchrony training and attention. In A. A. Sugarman & R. E. Tarter (Eds.), *Expanding dimensions of consciousness.* New York: Springer.

Fischer, R. (1978–1979). Healing as a state of consciousness: Cartography of the passive concentration stage of autogenic training. *Journal of Altered States of Consciousness, 4*, 57–61.

Frank, J. (1971). Therapeutic factors in psychotherapy. *American Journal of Psychotherapy, 25*, 35–361.

Freedman, R. R. (1987). Long term effectiveness of behavioral treatments for Raynaud's disease. *Behavior Therapy, 18*, 387–399.

Freedman, R. R. (1991). Physiological mechanisms of temperature biofeedback. *Biofeedback and Self-Regulation, 16*, 95–115.

French, D., Leeb, C. S., & Fahrion, S. L. (1975). *Biofeedback hand temperature training in the mentally retarded.* Paper presented at the Sixth Annual Meeting of the Biofeedback Society of America, Monterey, CA.

Gottschalk, L. A. (1978). Content analysis of speech in psychiatric research. *Comprehensive Psychiatry, 19*, 387–392.

Gottschalk, L. A. (1986). An objective method of measuring psychological states associated with changes in neural function: Content analysis of verbal behavior. In L. A. Gottschalk (Ed.), *Content analysis of verbal behavior.* New York: Springer-Verlag.

Green, A. M., & Green, E. E. (1975). Biofeedback: Research and therapy. In N. O. Jacobsen (Ed.), *New ways to health.* Stockholm: Natur ock Kultur.

Green, E. E., Ferguson, D. W., Green, A. M., & Walters, E. D. (1970). *Preliminary report on the Voluntary Controls Program: Swami Rama.* Topeka, KS: Voluntary Controls Project, The Menninger Foundation. (Mimeograph)

Green, E. E., & Green, A. M. (1973, Winter). Regulating our mind–body processes. *Fields within Fields . . . within Fields*, pp. 16–24.

Green, E. E., & Green, A. M. (1977). *Beyond biofeedback.* New York: Delacorte Press.

Green, E. E., Green, A. M., & Norris, P. A. (1979). Preliminary observations on a new non-drug method for control of hypertension. *Journal of the South Carolina Medical Association, 75*, 575–586.

Green, E. E., Green, A. M., & Walters, E. D. (1970a). *Psychophysiological training for inner awareness.* Paper presented at the conference of the Association for Humanistic Psychology, Miami.

Green, E. E., Green, A. M., & Walters, E. D. (1970b). Voluntary control of internal states: Psychological and physiological. *Journal of Transpersonal Psychology, 2*, 1–26.

Green, E. E., Green, A. M., & Walters, E. D. (1971a). *Biofeedback for mind–body self-regulation: Healing and creativity.* Paper presented at the symposium, "The Varieties of Healing Experience," De Anza College, Cupertino, CA.

Green, E. E., Green, A. M., & Walters, E. D. (1971b). *Psychophysiological training for creativity.* Paper presented at the meeting of the American Psychological Association, Washington, DC.

Green, E. E., Green, A. M., & Walters, E. D. (1973). Biofeedback training for anxiety tension reduction. *Annals of the New York Academy of Sciences, 233*, 157–161.

Green, E. E., Green, A. M., Walters, E. D., Sargent, J. D., & Meyer, R. G. (1975). Autogenic feedback training. *Psychotherapy and Psychosomatics, 25*, 88–98.

Green, E. E., Walters, E. D., Green, A. M., & Murphy, G. (1969). Feedback technique for deep relaxation. *Psychophysiology, 6*, 371–377.

Guarnieri, P., & Blanchard, E. B. (1990). Evaluation of home based thermal biofeedback treatment of pediatric migraine headache. *Biofeedback and Self-Regulation, 15*, 179–184.

Hartley, E. (1974). *Biofeedback: Yoga of the west.* Cos Cob, CT: Hartley Film Foundation. (Film)

Hartley, E. (1981). *Hypertension: The mind–body connection.* Cos Cob, CT: Hartley Film Foundation. (Film)

Hartman, C. H. (1979). Response of anginal pain to hand warming. *Biofeedback and Self-Regulation, 4*, 355–357.

Heath, R. G., & Becker, H. C. (1954). *Studies in schizophrenia.* Cambridge, MA: Harvard University Press.

Hohne, F., & Bohn, M. (1988). Biofeedback without a technical team—simple and cost effective. *Psychiatrie, Neurologie, und Medizinische Psychologie, Leipzig, 40*, 421–425.

Ikemi, Y., & Aoki, H. (1976). Comprehensive psychosomatic training for internists (at university level). *Dynamische Psychiatrie, 9*, 287–299.

Ikemi, Y., Nakagawa, T., Suematsu, H., & Luthe, W. (1975). The biologic wisdom of self-regulatory mechanism of normalization of autogenic and Oriental approaches to psychotherapy. *Psychotherapy and Psychosomatics, 25*, 99–108.

Kamiya, J. (1968, November). Conscious control of brain waves. *Psychology Today*, pp. 55–60.

Karasu, T. B. (1977). Psychotherapies: An overview. *American Journal of Psychiatry, 134*, 851–863.

Keefe, F. J., Surwit, R. S., & Pilon, R. N. (1981). Collagen vascular disease: Can behavioral therapy help? *Journal of Behavior Therapy and Experimental Psychiatry, 12*, 171–175.

Kirsch, C. A., Blanchard, E. B., & Parnes, S. M. (1987). A multiple baseline evaluation of the treatment of subjective tinnitus with relaxation training and biofeedback. *Biofeedback and Self-Regulation, 12*, 295–312.

Leeb, C., Fahrion, S., & French, D. (1976). Instructional set, deep relaxation and growth enhancement: A pilot study. *Journal of Humanistic Psychology, 16*, 71–78.

Lehrer, P. M., Atthowe, J. M., & Weber, E. S. P. (1980). Effects of progressive relaxation and autogenic training on anxiety and physiological measures, with some data on hypnotizability. In F. J. McGuigan, W. E. Sime, & J. M. Wallace (Eds.), *Stress and tension control*. New York: Plenum Press.

Levine, P. H. (1976). The coherence spectral array (COSPAR) and its application to the study of spatial ordering in the EEG. *Proceedings of the San Diego Biomedical Symposium, 15*, 237–247.

Luthe, W. (1965). *Autogenic training*. New York: Grune & Stratton.

Lynch, J. J., Thomas, S. A., Paskewitz, D. A., Malinow, K. L., & Long, J. M. (in press). Interpersonal aspects of blood pressure control. *Journal of Nervous and Mental Disease*.

MacLean, P. D. (1955). The limbic system ("visceral brain") in relation to central gray and reticulum of brain stem. *Psychosomatic Medicine, 17*, 355–56.

Mathew, R. J., Largen, J. W., Dobbins, K., Meyer, J. S., Sakai, F., & Claghorn, J. L. (1980). Biofeedback control of skin temperature and cerebral blood flow in migraine. *Headache, 20*, 19–28.

McGrady, A. V., Yonker, R., Tan, S. Y., Fine, T. H., & Woerner, M. (1981). The effect of biofeedback-assisted relaxation training on blood pressure and selected biochemical parameters in patients with essential hypertension. *Biofeedback and Self-Regulation, 6*, 343–353.

Meany, J., McNamara, M., Burks, V., Berger, T. W., & Sayle, D. M. (1988). Psychological treatment of an asthmatic patient in crisis. Dreams, biofeedback, and pain behavior modification. *Journal of Asthma, 25*, 141–51.

Norris, P. A. (1976). *Working with prisoners, or, there's nobody else here*. Topeka, KS: Voluntary Controls Program, The Menninger Foundation. (Mimeograph)

Orme-Johnson, D. W., Clements, G., Haynes, C. T., & Badaoui, K. (1977). Higher states of consciousness: EEG coherence, creativity, and experiences of the sidhis. In D. W. Orme-Johnson & J. T. Farrow (Eds.), *Scientific research on the Transcendental Meditation Program: Collected papers* (Vol. 1). Rheinweiler, Germany: Maharishi European Research University Press.

Papez, J. W. (1937). A proposed mechanism of emotion. *Archives of Neurology and Psychiatry, 28*, 725–743.

Penfield, W. (1975). *The mystery of the mind: A critical study of consciousness and the human brain*. Princeton, NJ: Princeton University Press.

Peniston, E. G., & Kulkosky, P. J. (1989). Alpha–theta brainwave training and beta endorphin levels in alcoholics. *Alcoholism: Clinical and Experimental Research, 13*, 271–279.

Rouleau, J. L., Denver, D. R., Gauthier, J. G., & Biedermann, H. (1985). Le biofeedback électromyographique dans le traitement de la fibrosité: Evaluation d'une approche thérapeutique [Electromyographic biofeedback in the treatment of fibrositis: Evaluation of a therapeutic approach]. *Revue de Modification du Comportement, 15*, 7–19.

Sargent, J. D., Green, E. E., & Walters, E. D. (1972). The use of autogenic feedback in a pilot study of migraine and tension headaches. *Headache, 12*, 120–125.

Schultz, J. H., & Luthe, W. (1969). *Autogenic therapy: Vol. 1. Autogenic methods*. New York: Grune & Stratton.

Schwarz, S. P., Taylor, A. E., Scharff, L., & Blanchard, E. B. (1990). Behaviorally treated irritable bowel syndrome patients: A four year follow-up. *Behaviour Research and Therapy, 28*, 331–335.

Sedlacek, K. (1979). Comparison between biofeedback and relaxation response in the treatment of hypertension. *Biofeedback and Self-Regulation, 4*, 259.

Sherman, R. A., Arena, J. G., Sherman, C. J., & Ernst, J. L. (1989). The mystery of phantom pain: Growing evidence for psychophysiological mechanisms. *Biofeedback and Self-Regulation, 14*, 267–280.

Shulimson, A. D., Lawrence, P. F., & Iacono, C. U. (1986). Diabetic ulcers: The effect of thermal biofeedback mediated relaxation training on healing. *Biofeedback and Self-Regulation, 11*, 311–319.

Smirnov, S. A., Aizikov, G. S., & Kozlovskaia, I. B. (1988). Effect of adaptive biofeedback on the severity of vestibulo-autonomic symptoms of experimental motion sickness. *Kosmicheskaya Biologiya i Aviakosmicheskaya Meditsina, 22*, 35–39.

Sun, Z., Zhao, J., Xia, M., Ren, R., Yan, H., Yang, L., Gao, S., & Wang, S. (1986). [Comparative study on the efficiency of EMG and thermal biofeedback training and the combination of biofeedback and autogenic training in reducing test anxiety.] *Acta Psychologica Sinica, 18*, 196–202.

Taub, E., & Stroebel, C. F. (1978). Biofeedback in treatment of vasoconstrictive syndromes. *Biofeedback and Self-Regulation, 3,* 363–373.

Tsushima, W. T. (1982). Treatment of phantom limb pain with EMG and temperature biofeedback: A case study. *American Journal of Clinical Biofeedback, 5,* 150–153.

Walton, W. T. (1979). The use of a relaxation curriculum and biofeedback training in the classroom to reduce inappropriate behaviors of emotionally handicapped children. *Behavioral Disorders, 5,* 10–18.

Zaichkowsky, L. D., & Fuchs, C. Z. (1988). Biofeedback applications in exercise and athletic performance. *Exercise and Sports Sciences Reviews, 16,* 381–421.

9

Biofeedback Methods in the Treatment of Anxiety and Stress Disorders

JOHANN M. STOYVA
THOMAS H. BUDZYNSKI

In this chapter, we explore the use of biofeedback, especially electromyographic (EMG) feedback, as applied to anxiety and stress-related disorders. After offering a brief definition of "biofeedback," we sketch the history and theory of the technique. We then focus on the types of biofeedback most often considered when anxiety reduction and/or stress management is the primary goal.

In general, biofeedback systems operate by detecting changes in the biological environment and, by means of visual and auditory signals, information a patient of these changes. The patient, using this precise and immediate information, engages in a trial-and-error strategy of testing in order to make the signals change in the desired direction. With the biofeedback as a guide, the patient learns in relatively short order how to control the biological response system generating the biofeedback signals. With additional training, the patient learns to calibrate the subtle internal events corresponding to the biological system in question, and can then be gradually weaned away from the biofeedback signal.

The object of such training is to achieve control over biological systems that previously have been operating in a maladaptive fashion and have been beyond conscious control. The term "maladaptive" implies that the system has been operating at a level of functioning that contributes to inefficiency at the very least and to stress-related disease at the worst. Biofeedback training essentially involves three stages (Budzynski, 1973). The first stage is acquiring awareness of the maladaptive response; by means of biofeedback, the client learns that certain thoughts as well as certain bodily events influence the response in question. Next, guided by the biofeedback signal, he or she learns to control the response. Finally, the client learns to transfer the control into everyday life.

It should be noted that biofeedback does more than help individuals bring their physiological activity into a proper range of functioning. For many patients, it also helps to convince them that it is in fact possible to control events that bear on their well-being and on their capacity to cope with stressful circumstances.

History of the Method

In 1966, Kamiya's technique of controlling the alpha electroencephalographic (EEG) rhythm by means of a feedback tone to indicate the presence of the alpha rhythm was already stirring interest on the West Coast. In the same year, Neal Miller captured the attention of a Moscow colloquium with his report that certain autonomic responses could be operantly conditioned in experimental animals.

Later that year, we built an alpha EEG feedback device. It had occurred to us that the pleasant and tranquil characteristics of the "alpha state" as reported by Kamiya (1969) could be used to counter anxiety in the behavior therapy procedure known as "systematic desensitization." We reasoned that with the feedback device we could first teach patients to produce more alpha. Then we could ask them to visualize themselves in anxious or stressful situations. As the percentage of alpha diminished, we could stop the visualization and allow the patients to "recover" the (relaxed) alpha state using the feedback tone. This approach did in fact result in the highly successful desensitization of a patient suffering from a severe death-related phobia (Budzynski & Stoyva, 1973). Desensitization was completed in four sessions. A follow-up 14 years later indicated no return of the anxiety. To our knowledge, this was one of the first applications of electronic biofeedback in a psychotherapy setting.

Subsequent investigation into the possibility of using alpha EEG feedback as an adjunct to systematic desensitization caused us to conclude that surface EMG feedback might be a better way to teach relaxation. We developed our first EMG feedback device for this purpose in 1967. It incorporated the constant-reset level integrator used by Sainsbury and Gibson (1954) in their studies of surface EMG. Our device took the output of the integrator, a series of pulses, and converted it to a digital readout at selected intervals. The device also provided two types of auditory feedback, in addition to a three-level vertical-array visual display.

From the beginning, our goal—first with the alpha EEG and then with surface EMG feedback—was to facilitate the development of relaxation. Much of our initial research with surface EMG feedback was focused on the use of the forehead musculature as a sensor site. Earlier research by Sainsbury and Gibson (1954), Malmo (1975), Goldstein (1972), and Leaf and Gaarder (1971) had indicated that the frontalis or frontal EMG was a useful indicator of anxiety, tension, or arousal.

We next began to work with anxious patients. The first few of these were individuals who had been unable to learn to relax with the brief Wolpe–Jacobson training usually provided by behavior therapists. Others were patients who thought they could relax but were surprised to see that their levels of tension in selected muscles were quite high. We discovered that in the absence of biofeedback, patients would often show an increase of muscular tension throughout a systematic desensitization session, even while reporting that they were still relaxed (Budzynski & Stoyva, 1973). Often this took the form of an inability to return to the relaxed state after the first or second visualization of a scene from the "anxiety hierarchy." Not knowing that they were still tense, the patients would typically report relaxation between visualizations; consequently, the desensitization would proceed even though the patient's level of tension was escalating. With the EMG feedback device, however, we were able to monitor the exact level of muscle tension in selected muscles. Moreover, the patients could use the feedback signal as an aid in returning to relaxation quickly.

We then began work with a series of phobic patients, as well as with patients suffering from chronic, pervasive anxiety. In general, the cases of chronic, pervasive anxiety required approximately twice as many biofeedback relaxation and systematic desensitization sessions as did the cases of circumscribed anxiety (Budzynski & Stoyva, 1975).

Shortly after we had begun our work with anxious patients, we initiated a parallel effort to apply frontal EMG biofeedback to tension headache. Our pilot observations (Budzynski, Stoyva, & Adler, 1970) were later confirmed by a larger controlled study (Budzynski, Stoyva, Adler, & Mullaney, 1973). In this second study, the frontal EMG feedback condition proved superior to both an active placebo condition (self-taught relaxation) and a no-treatment condition in reducing headache frequency and intensity. Considering the fact that tension headache is sometimes referred to as the "common cold" of psychosomatic disease, the development of an effective nondrug treatment for this disorder lent credence to the idea that psychophysiological and behavioral methods could play a growing role in the treatment of stress-related disturbances.

Since the publication of our controlled-outcome study, some scores of additional investigations have reported on the use of psychophysiological and behavioral methods in tension headache. These studies strongly confirm the favorable impact of systematic relaxation procedures on tension headache pain. In their extensive review, Andrasik and Blanchard (1987) note an average reduction of about 50% in frequency and intensity of headaches over this large body of studies. There has, however, been debate on two main points: (1) Some researchers argue that nonbiofeedback relaxation techniques work about as well as the (more targeted) biofeedback methods; and (2) many investigators maintain that cognitive methods of stress reduction are superior to muscle relaxation methods.

In working with anxiety and stress patients, our early rationale for using only EMG feedback was that extensive relaxation of the musculature should theoretically "pull" all of the autonomic responses in the direction of decreased sympathetic and increased parasympathetic activity. It turned out, however, that some individuals could attain low EMG levels but would still report that they felt anxious; in most such instances, they would show either a high electrodermal response (EDR) or a low peripheral temperature or both. Apparently a minority of anxious patients can attain fairly low muscle tonus, and yet remain high in sympathetic activity. Consequently, we began to use the EDR feedback and thermal feedback to augment the impact of EMG feedback. Electronic systems allowed these various forms of feedback to be presented singly or in combinations through patients' headphones. This technique allowed us to carry out a *systematic shaping of low arousal* (Stoyva & Budzynski, 1974). Using such a system, a therapist could monitor all three response systems (some monitored heart rate and EEG as well), and could provide feedback for whichever of the three systems seemed indicated.

Later, we began to combine biofeedback with more traditional therapies for the treatment of anxiety and stress-related disorders (Budzynski, 1973). A systems approach was devised that incorporated training in three basic response systems. This technique involved the use not only of EMG feedback but also of other forms, such as thermal and EDR feedback. The later two, reflecting autonomic activity, contributed to a complete program of training that was sequenced according to certain criteria (Budzynski, Stoyva, & Peffer, 1980).

Biofeedback and Systematic Desensitization

We have already noted that much of our early work with EMG biofeedback focused on relaxing the patient prior to the behavior therapy procedure known as "systematic desensitization" (Wolpe, 1958). Since this procedure involves the counterconditioning of anxiety with relaxation, we felt that EMG biofeedback could be used, first, to aid the patient in achieving the skill of relaxation, and second, to act as a monitor of depth of relaxation during the subsequent desensitization.

A number of researchers have shown that anxious patients typically show elevated levels of muscle tension, particularly during an anxiety episode (Jacobson, 1938; Malmo, 1975). Martin and Grosz (1964), for example, found that when various emotions were hypnotically suggested to a group of psychiatric patients, their arousal indicators changed in the expected direction. When told they were anxious, the patients displayed increases in heart rate and muscle tension over that of the "relaxed" condition. In fact, the researchers noted that the most consistently responsive measure was the level of muscle tension.

Admittedly, not all anxious patients are muscle responders, but even for those who are not, the relaxation of major muscle groups appears to dampen the activity of the sympathetic nervous system (SNS); this produces a shift toward lower arousal, characterized by parasympathetic nervous system (PNS) dominance (Gellhorn, 1964; Germana, 1969; Hess, 1954; Luthe, 1970; Obrist, Webb, Sutterer, & Howard, 1970). Since the state of anxiety, and for that matter the stress response, is characterized by heightened sympathetic tone, it is reasonable to assume that procedures that shift autonomic dominance from the SNS toward the PNS should be effective in moderating stress and anxiety reactions.

A possible neurophysiological basis for the effects of muscle relaxation was advanced by Gellhorn (1964). In commenting on a number of animal studies that dealt with autonomic–somatic relationships, Gellhorn noted that

> a reduction or inhibition of proprioceptive impulses through blocking of the neuromuscular junction reduces sympathetic and increases parasympathetic discharges, and also reduces the state of cortical excitation: synchronous potentials and behavior indicate that sleep has been induced. . . . These experiments are believed to represent a physiological model of the mechanism by which abnormal states of emotional tension are alleviated through various forms of "relaxation therapy." (1964, p. 468)

In his researches, Gellhorn (1967) worked for many years on the issue of ergotropic–trophotropic balance.[1] On the basis of extensive experimental work, in

[1] In the terminology of W. R. Hess (1954), "ergotropic" responding refers to a condition of coordinated activation in the SNS, the cortex, and the skeletal muscle system. Its reciprocal, "trophotropic" responding, refers to a condition of parasympathetic dominance, lowered cortical arousal, and neuromuscular relaxation.

both humans and animals, he concluded that "ergotropic and trophotropic reactions do not occur at the same time. They are reciprocally related, since with the increasing activity of one system the responsiveness of the antagonistic system declines progressively" (Gellhorn, 1967, p. 40). Gellhorn also indicated that systematic muscular relaxation is a useful way to induce a shift from sympathetic to parasympathetic dominance:

> The reduction of skeletal muscle tone in Jacobson's, Schultz's, and Wolpe's relaxation therapy leads to a loss in ergotropic tone of the hypothalamus (Gellhorn, 1958), a diminution of hypothalamic–cortical discharges, and, consequently, to a dominance of the trophotropic system through reciprocal innervation. (Gellhorn & Kiely, 1972, p. 404)

Since it now appeared that we had both a rationale and a technology for muscle relaxation, we turned our efforts toward the desensitization phase. We first monitored EMG levels of patients undergoing systematic desensitization. In the typical behavior therapy situation, patients are given brief training in a modified form of Jacobson's progressive relaxation. They are then instructed to produce this relaxed condition while visualizing scenes from the anxiety hierarchy. The demand characteristics of the typical therapy setting, however, predispose patients to report that they are relaxed after a reasonable period of time, whether this is actually true or not (Budzynski & Stoyva, 1969). Moreover, we found that patients will generally show a rise in tension—especially in frontal EMG levels—just before they are presented with the first hierarchy scene (Budzynski & Stoyva, 1973). Often, too, once aroused by a particular hierarchy visualization, they have difficulty in returning to relaxed levels. In the absence of objective physiological monitoring, however, a patient's arousal level can be difficult to assess.

We found that EMG biofeedback both served to expedite relaxation and provided an accurate monitor of tension level during desensitization. A patient could use it after each visualization in returning to a relaxed baseline condition. And the therapist, watching the biofeedback display, would know when to signal the patient to commence the next visualization.

Pervasive Anxiety Technique

In cases of generalized or pervasive anxiety, it is often difficult for a patient to specify which stimuli actually trigger the anxiety reaction. We found, however, that the frontal (or forehead) EMG could be a sensitive indicator of subtle increases in anxiety in the generally relaxed patient (Budzynski & Stoyva, 1973). Thus, a patient who has first received training in relaxation will simply be told to let his or her thoughts wander while receiving feedback. If the tone suddenly rises in pitch, the patient knows that the thought coincident with, or just preceding, the rise in tone is arousing in nature. He or she next attempts to shift away from the thought—at the same time relaxing and lowering the feedback tone. After this, the patient reintroduces the thought and tries to keep the tone low while doing so. This imagery–relaxation sequence is repeated until the patient can think of the particular thought without a rise in tension. At this point the individual allows the thoughts to begin wandering again, thus repeating the sequence with the next arousing thought (Budzynski & Stoyva, 1975). (For subsequent experimental work confirming the sensitivity of the facial muscles as indicators of emotion, see the review by Carlson & Hatfield, 1992, pp. 213–221.)

Theoretical Underpinnings

When the individual reacts to threat or challenge, multiple integrated physiological reactions are brought into play. Not just one system is active; many are active at the same time. The conception we utilize for our stress management patients postulates a cortical triggering of the defense–alarm reaction. This involves not only physiological and behavioral components, but cognitive ones as well (Stoyva & Carlson, 1993).

Our approach, like that of many therapists engaged in stress management, involves a sequence of interventions and is based on a conceptual framework that divides the individual's response to stress into two alternating parts: a phase of active coping efforts, and a rest phase (Stoyva & Carlson, in press). Patients with stress-related symptoms show many signs of being excessively in the active coping phase. There is evidence of high sympathetic activity and high arousal in one or more systems, as in the anxious patient; there are complaints of tension and of inability to "unwind" or relax when it is appropriate to do so. There are often complaints of disturbed sleep. The patient may be irritable and short-tempered. Type A behavior is often prominent, and catecholamine levels are likely to be elevated (Frankenhaeuser, 1983).

In our review, the individual's endeavors at adaptation may be regarded as consisting of an alternation between active coping efforts and a rest phase. this alternation is reflected at many levels of psychological and physiological organization. In the striated muscle system, there is an alternation between muscular contraction (involved in active coping efforts) and muscular relaxation (as in rest)—an alternation that is integral to the operation of this system. In the autonomic nervous system (ANS), there is an alternation between its two great branches: the SNS, which supports high energy utilization and vigorous physical activity; and the PNS, which acts to promote digestion, sleep, and the rebuilding of energy sources.

Both stress and anxiety are characterized by SNS dominance in the ANS. Perhaps SNS dominance plays a part in the genesis of stress-related disorders? A noted psychophysiologist has presented evidence for such a review. Wenger and colleagues studied the resting autonomic patterns of nearly a thousand young, healthy Army Air Corps cadets during World War II. Wenger then developed a scoring system by which each cadet was given an estimate of autonomic balance called the "$\bar{A}$ score" (Wenger & Cullen, 1972). This score was a composite of the scores obtained on each of seven physiological variables reflecting autonomic functioning. Low $\bar{A}$ scores meant apparent SNS dominance. The cadets' scores formed a normal distribution by means of which Wenger could compare groups with various disorders. He found, for example, that most psychosomatic patients produced low $\bar{A}$ scores, indicating an apparent SNS dominance in the resting stage.

Approximately 15 years after the cadet study, Wenger sent out questionnaires to the former cadets. The questionnaire was designed to reveal which disorders, including mental problems, had arisen among the formerly healthy young men. He found that those individuals who had low $\overline{A}$ scores (apparent SNS dominance) reported the greatest incidence of stress-linked disorders (Wenger & Cullen, 1972). It appears that those individuals who show a resting autonomic pattern characterized by SNS dominance are more susceptible to stress disorders. These findings of Wenger suggest that systematic training in decreasing SNS tone may act as a preventive program.

Even in the neuroendocrine system, there are probably periods of activation and nonactivation—as, for example, in the case of hormone responses to various stressors (Mason, 1972). Moreover, an interlocking series of experiments by Frankenhaeuser (1983) at the University of Stockholm indicate that the human neuroendocrine system is highly reactive to the perceived stress of the individual. In particular, situations demanding a marked degree of active coping efforts generate large increases in catecholamine levels, with adrenalin output being especially responsive. Again, at the experiential level, there are marked differences between periods of active effort and times of tranquility.

We can summarize our argument as follows: Patients with psychosomatic or stress-linked disorders are likely to show signs of high physiological arousal in one or more systems; they are strongly or excessively engaged in the active coping mode. They also show evidence of being deficient in the ability to shift from the coping to the rest mode. It can be hypothesized that this defect in the ability to shift to a rest condition is the principal reason why various relaxation procedures have so often proved useful in the alleviation of stress-related symptoms (Stoyva & Carlson, 1993).

We also find it useful to divide the coping phase and the resting phase further into three main levels of observation: the physiological, the behavioral, and the experiential levels (the last of these is indexed by verbal report). Such a tripartite or three-system model helps the therapist to become attuned to the complex and multidimensional nature of the individual's stress response. The various clinical interventions currently utilized in stress management already reflect the three-system conceptualization of the stress response; it is useful, however, to make the idea explicit. For one thing, it prompts the therapist to note in which system or systems the patient's stress reaction has gone awry. Next, in the treatment phase, interventions can be chosen in accordance with the nature of the maladaptive coping response. For example, if misperceptions and distorted beliefs seem to be the main problems, cognitive interventions may be in order; if physiological arousal appears excessive, relaxation training or biofeedback may be initiated. Lastly, the therapist will need to know whether any change in the maladaptive response has in fact occurred, and whether it has persisted. We believe that a three-system approach to stress management will act to produce a more sophisticated approach to the area, since it encourgaes therapists not to overlook important aspects of the stress response in favor of some single-track strategy, whether this be cognitive restructuring, relaxation training, or something else.

It is also important to note that the various indicators of stress may be discrepant from one another. For example, a Type A individual may indicate verbally that he or she feels "just fine" during stressful situations, yet at the same time may show a powerful physiological reaction. A patient may report the presence of relaxation, but at the same time may show very high EMG levels compared to normal levels. At the very least, such information suggests hypotheses as to what may be involved in patients' stress reactions. It also makes for a more comprehensive treatment approach. In relaxation training, for example, we remain slightly skeptical if we observe just the verbal report of relaxation; we want the physiological indicators of relaxation to be present as well.

In the remainder of this chapter, we describe feedback procedures as they have evolved in our laboratory and clinic since we initiated work in 1966. Most of our stress management procedures fall within the framework of the coping–rest model. Generally, our initial emphasis is on the rest phase; later, the focus shifts more to the reshaping of maladaptive coping efforts.

Biofeedback Compared to Other Relaxation Techniques

In assessments of the use of EMG biofeedback in anxiety disorders, the general conclusion to emerge is that EMG biofeedback enjoys no particular superiority over other relaxation techniques. This conclusion, however, should not be a cause for therapeutic pessimism; the glass should be seen as mainly full rather than mainly empty. And there is indeed reason for optimism. The resounding conclusion to emerge from a large body of work over the past 20 years is that relaxation training of various types brings about a significant reduction in anxiety, and that this reduction is greater than that occurring in various control conditions. (For an extensive review of these matters, see Chapters 16 and 18, this volume.) This favorable outcome is consistent with the many reports over the years that various relaxation techniques bring about a significant reduction, not only in anxiety, but in a range of stress-related symptomatology. It may be noted, too, that this outcome supports the theoretical position that relaxation and stress are opposing conditions of the organism (Gellhorn, 1967; Luthe, 1970; Stoyva & Budzynski, 1974).

Nonetheless, this positive and fortunate outcome does leave us with one considerable puzzle: Are we to conclude that all relaxation techniques generate about the same amount of beneficial effect? Is there nothing special added by some methods as opposed to others? Is a sloppy training just as good as one that is systematic and thorough? Certainly, the progenitors of the major traditions have strongly emphasized that training has to be both correct and thorough (Jacobson, 1938; Schultz & Luthe, 1959). Simply closing one's eyes and assuming a semirecumbent position is no guarantee that good relaxation will automatically occur—a point readily affirmed by those who have worked with patients who are anxious, exasperated, and in doubt as to whether there is any alternative to a lifetime of heavy medication and a state of permanent seminarcotization. (See Chapter 18 for further discussion.) We should also note that in the serious forms of meditation, such as Zen (Kapleau, 1980), the admonition to practice is constantly in evidence, as is the admonition to practice the right thing. This twin emphasis goes back to the original Buddhist teachings.

In the remainder of this section, we take up these issues in greater detail—the central question being whether biofeedback offers any special advantages beyond those offered by more traditional nonbiofeedback therapies. Actually, there is no simple answer to this question, so it is useful to divide the question into several parts:

1. Evidence from controlled comparative studies on the uses of EMG feedback in anxiety disorders.
2. Advantages of EMG feedback in daily clinical practice.
3. Special properties of facial muscle responses.
4. Three techniques that can be added to a general relaxation response.
5. The need for combined interventions.
6. EMG feedback, autogenic exercises, and meditative techniques in combination.

Comparative Studies in Anxiety

Several earlier comparative studies yielded favorable reports regarding the use of EMG feedback in anxiety disorders. Canter, Kondo, and Knott (1975) compared frontal EMG feedback to progressive relaxation with 28 patients who were diagnosed as suffering from anxiety neurosis, and who also complained of muscular tension and insomnia. Both EMG feedback and progressive relaxation training produced significant decreases in frontal EMG activity. However, EMG feedback was found to be generally superior in reducing anxiety symptoms.

Townsend, House, and Addario (1975) contrasted frontal EMG feedback with group psychotherapy as a treatment for chronically anxious patients. In the group receiving EMG feedback, there were significant decreases in EMG levels, mood disturbance, trait anxiety, and (to a lesser extent) state anxiety; these changes were not seen in the group receiving psychotherapy. An interesting related observation was reported by Hiebert and Fitzsimmons (1981). This study showed that frontal EMG feedback alone was at least as effective as the more traditional procedures in reducing anxiety in a nonpatient population (who had initially tested high for anxiety on the IPAT, a 40-item anxiety scale developed by Cattell at the Institute for Personality and Ability Testing in Champaign, Illinois). Moreover, the addition of either systematic desensitization or cognitive monitoring did not magnify the effect produced by EMG feedback.

One of the most intriguing studies reported so far involved a comparison of frontal EMG feedback and Valium in the treatment of chronic, free-floating anxiety (Lavallée, Lamontagne, Pinard, Annable, & Tétreault, 1977). The 40 outpatients were randomly assigned to one of four groups: EMG feedback plus Valium, EMG feedback plus Valium placebo, EMG control (no feedback) plus Valium, and EMG control (no feedback) plus Valium placebo. By the end of the 4-week treatment period, all active treatment groups showed a significant reduction in anxiety. During the follow-up, however, the two Valium groups fared less well than the EMG feedback group. The EMG feedback group continued to show significant anxiety reductions at both the 1- and 3-month follow-ups (though not at the 6-month follow-up). On the other hand, the two Valium groups (in which subjects received either Valium, or Valium plus EMG feedback) failed to show significant reductions in anxiety at either the 3- or

6-month follow-up. The authors conclude that for patients with chronic free-floating anxiety, frontal EMG feedback has a more prolonged treatment effect than does Valium. In other words, frontal EMG feedback produced better results than did the most popular antianxiety drug of the day.

In the interest of full reporting, however, we should add that the most sustained posttreatment reduction in anxiety occurred in the placebo group—which was the condition consisting of EMG control (no feedback) plus Valium placebo. Patients in this group showed significant reductions in anxiety at the 1-, 3-, and 6-month follow-ups, although their anxiety reduction had *not* been significant at the end of the 4-week training period. Lavallée et al. (1977) suggest that a possible reason for the puzzling outcome of the placebo group was that they engaged in more frequent practice of their (self-taught) relaxation response during the follow-up period than did the other groups. Specifically, at the 6-month follow-up, the two Valium groups reported practicing relaxation on only 7 of 30 days per month, the EMG feedback group on 11 of 30, and the placebo group on 14 of 30. The relaxation instructions for the placebo patients had been simply to sit comfortably in a quiet room for 20 minutes a day without falling asleep.

Other comparisons, published mainly in the 1980s, suggest no particular advantage for EMG biofeedback in anxiety disorders, as opposed to other relaxation methods (see Chapter 18, this volume). In fact, a number of investigators report cognitive techniques as being superior to relaxation in the reduction of anxiety. Recently, however, Fahrion and Norris (1990) have written that, to date, the controlled studies of self-regulatory techniques in anxiety have suffered from too narrow a focus. A range of techniques is required. We need to pay attention not just to muscle relaxation, but also to the autonomic components of relaxation, to diaphragmatic breathing, and to the incorporation of the relevant skills into the stressful challenges of everyday living.

As can be seen in later sections of this chapter this view is very close to our own (see "The Need for Combined Interventions," below). Anxiety is a multisystem phenomenon. Accordingly, using a combination of procedures is a logical way to proceed, and in fact reflects current everyday practice. From a scientific standpoint, however, we still face the task of determining what (if anything) is contributed by a given procedure, or by that procedure in combination with another method.

Advantages of Electromyographic Feedback in Daily Practice

In day-to-day clinical practice, EMG feedback offers a number of fairly specific advantages—that is, compared to traditional nonbiofeedback relaxation therapies, such as progressive relaxation or autogenic training.

1. *An objective indicant of relaxation.* The EMG measure gives us an estimate of whether the patient is learning anything. Is muscular relaxation present or not? As Middaugh (1990) has noted, in these days of accountability, we will probably require more than verbal affirmations to buttress our claim that relaxation is in fact occurring. We should note, too, that in the various relaxation therapies, the demand characteristics of the situation are such as to predispose patients to report relaxation even in its

absence (see Budzynski & Stoyva, 1973). The EMG measure, however, provides an objective check on the patient's verbal report of relaxation. The use of physiological monitoring and biofeedback makes the somewhat elusive phenomenon of relaxation more concrete.

2. *An aid to clinical decision making.* When there is a discrepancy between the patient's verbal report of relaxation and the EMG measure, the EMG data help the therapist decide what to do next; in other words, these data aid in clinical decision making. For example, the EMG levels may indicate the need for further relaxation training: A patient may have been doing well at arm and trapezius relaxation, but poorly at relaxing the muscles of the face.

3. *A means of clarifying the idea of "nonstriving."* EMG biofeedback lends itself especially well to demonstrating the idea of "noneffort" or "nonstriving." This idea can be difficult to explain verbally, especially to the extreme Type A individuals likely to present themselves as candidates for stress management; yet the skill it refers to has been recognized as a critical dimension of many kinds of relaxation, biofeedback, and meditation training (Peper, 1976). The use of EMG biofeedback, especially forehead feedback, gets the idea of "noneffort" across quickly and vividly. Patients discover that the "old college try"—the head-on assault—simply drives the tone up! They must learn to do the opposite.

4. *An aid in noting scientific relationships.* The use of biofeedback, and the quantification of physiological parameters that usually accompanies it, increase the possibility of detecting relationships. Such quantification, and the noting of relationships among measures, expedite the task of placing biofeedback and self-regulatory therapies within a scientific explanatory framework. One good example of such a relationship is that when the frontal EMG levels of already relaxed patients decrease even further (usually over a span of 10 to 60 seconds), then patients are drowsy or asleep. (For more examples, see "Some Special Properties of the Facial Muscles," below). In this context, we might call to mind the remark of Eddington (1955) that modern science does not penetrate to the ultimate reality of things. Rather, what is gained is a "knowledge of pointer-readings." The job of the scientist lies "in working out the exact scheme of interconnection of the pointer-readings" (Eddington, 1955, p. 205).

5. *A means of operationalizing the concept of relaxation.* The use of biofeedback and physiological monitoring helps the therapist in analyzing the somewhat amorphous concept of relaxation into identifiable components. As already discussed, we adopt a three-system view of anxiety and stress. We assume that the state of relaxation, like anxiety and stress, consists of behavioral and cognitive as well as physiological components (see "Theoretical Underpinnings," above). This approach helps the therapist become aware of etiological and therapeutic possibilities that might otherwise be easily overlooked. For example, a patient may be progressing well on muscle relaxation but still complain of racing thoughts. Such a situation should prompt the therapist to search for interventions useful in dampening mental activity.

6. *A source of new strategies for dealing with learning difficulties.* Users of non-biofeedback techniques may mainly have to exhort the patient "to keep on trying." Biofeedback methods not only help to pinpoint the source of training problems, but open new possibilities of intervention. For example, they readily allow the systematic

use of shaping procedures. In our relaxation training, for example, we have patients begin with an easy response (such as relaxing the forearm extensor) and then proceed to something more difficult (such as lowering frontal EMG levels). Should frontal EMG prove too difficult, feedback training can temporarily be shifted back to the forearm extensor. Or, if there are problems with the dominant arm, the patient may nonetheless do well with the nondominant arm. For some years, we have referred to this approach as the "shaping of low arousal" (Stoyva & Budzynski, 1974, pp. 381–384).

Admittedly, there are some drawbacks associated with biofeedback. First, patients may develop an excessive reliance on the machines. Second, the machines sometimes break down; what then? And third, biofeedback is comparatively weak in providing cognitive coping strategies for reducing relaxation (Stoyva, 1989). These drawbacks, however, can generally be overcome through the use of autogenic heaviness and warmth exercises, as well as of certain exercises drawn from the meditative disciplines. Some advantages of the autogenic exercises are as follows:

1. The training phrases ("training formulas") help with the cognitive aspects of relaxation, being especially useful in coping with the inevitable interference from "stray thoughts." We tell patients to "just go with the stray thought for a moment, then use the phrase to bring your attention back to your arm."

2. The autogenic exercises foster a type of self-reliance, in that the training phrases can be employed in a great many different situations—even as a brief exercise of 30 to 60 seconds—and do not require the use of a tape recorder or other mechanical device.

3. For some patients, the autogenic exercises help in learning autonomically mediated responses. About 40% of patients, for example, learn to experience hand or arm warmth in response to the peripheral warmth phrase of the second standard exercise. (For details on autogenic training, see Linden, Chapter 7, this volume.)

Some Special Properties of the Facial Muscles

Considerable evidence has accumulated that changes in facial muscle activity are closely associated with changes in bodily systems other than in the skeletal muscle system itself. The existence of a connection between the muscles of facial expression and autonomic activity was recognized, or at least implied, by Charles Darwin. In his judgment, "Most of our emotions are so closely connected with our expression that they hardly exist if the body remains passive" (Darwin, 1872/1965, p. 257). He further wrote that "The free expression by outward signs of an emotion intensifies it" (1872/1965, p. 365).

Darwin's position is consistent with the view of many contemporary researchers on emotion that emotional experience depends, at least to a degree, on feedback from the facial musculature. In a valuable review of contemporary research on the issue of facial expression and autonomic activity, Carlson and Hatfield (1992) conclude that "emotional experience, facial feedback, and ANS activity are tightly linked and seem to influence one another." It appears that "facial feedback shapes both emotional experience and ANS activity" (Carlson & Hatfield, 1992, p. 212).

Increases in Facial Muscle Activity

A number of observations indicate that changes of EMG activity in the facial muscles are reliably associated with physiological changes in ANS and central nervous system (CNS) function. Increased activity in the facial muscles is associated with increased emotionality, with increases in heart rate, and in CNS activation levels. Some relevant observations are the following:

1. Some time ago, Jacobson (1970) and Shagass and Malmo (1954) recognized that the frontalis and other facial muscles were especially likely to be involved in stress and emotional responses. Indeed, a fairly large proportion of Jacobson's progressive relaxation training is devoted to the muscles of the face, eyes, and neck (see McGuigan, 1981). In this context, it is worth reminding ourselves of the famous Penfield–Rasmussen homunculus (Penfield & Rasmussen, 1950). This dwarf-like figure shows that the face and eyes (and hands) enjoy a huge representation in the sensory–motor cortex—about two-thirds of its total area. The torso and legs make up only about a third of the figure.

2. In their series of studies involving the deliberate facial expression of certain emotions, Ekman, Levenson, and Friesen (1983) observed elevations in heart rate for some emotions, but not for others. For example, in anger and fear, there were heart rate increases of 8 beats per minute above resting base levels, whereas in the disgust condition heart rate remained at the base level. On the basis of this and related observations, these investigators concluded that "producing the emotion-prototypic patterns of facial muscle action resulted in autonomic changes of large magnitude" (Ekman et al., 1983, p. 1210).

3. Rubin (1977), in a book titled *Reanimation of the Paralyzed Face,* suggests that the frontalis muscle in particular may possess a dual innervation: Both the alpha motor neurons of skeletal muscle and autonomic fibers are present. In his view, although the frontalis consists mainly of striated muscle, thin layers of nonstriated muscle are also present. According to Mielke's (1973) book on surgery of the facial nerve, these nonstriated layers receive their innervation from the SNS.

4. Eye movements, which result from contractions in the ocular muscles, appear to be related to visual imagery and possibly to the recall of repressed traumatic memories as well. Jacobson (1970, p. 41) stated quite emphatically that eye movements are associated with visual imagery, and that their absence is associated with an absence of such imagery. Subsequent to Jacobson's original research on the "electrophysiology of mental activities" in the early 1930s, it was found that rapid eye movements during sleep are associated with the visual imagery of dreaming (Stoyva & Kamiya, 1968). Recently, Shapiro (1989) has observed that when patients with posttraumatic stress disorder are made to engage deliberately in saccadic eye movements, repressed traumatic memories rise to awareness. Moreover, when patients engage in such saccadic eye movements over several sessions—along with the attendant controlled imagining of the memories—a desensitization to the traumatic event is said to occur.

5. In animal experiments with the trigeminal nerve, part of which is responsible for pain in the facial area, Rosenfeld (1990) has reported that biofeedback training (operant conditioning) of the cortical evoked potentials of this nerve produces a distinct analgesic effect. This analgesic effect, equivalent to that produced by a moderate injection of morphine, is highly specific to the cortical trigeminal area (the

orofacial somatosensory cortex), and is confined to the side of the face represented by the conditioned side of the cortex. Moreover, it does not appear when potentials from the *brainstem* nucleus of the trigeminal are the object of conditioning.

Decreases in Facial Muscle Activity

What about reductions in facial EMG activity? In general, we find that low levels of facial EMG activity are associated with decreased emotional responding, reductions in heart rate, and with drowsiness and sleep.

Before we consider further the special properties of the facial muscles, we should note that the frontal (forehead) electrode placement detects the EMG activity not only of the frontalis, but of most of the other facial muscles as well (Budzynski & Stoyva, 1969). The validity of this statement can be demonstrated to the patient experientially. First, the patient should decrease frontal EMG activity by means of forehead EMB feedback. Then the patient should clench the jaw, or contract the muscles around the mouth or eye, or produce an eye movement, or smile. All of these actions will quickly increase the frequency of the frontalis feedback tone heard by the patient. In other words, the patient learns that the forehead electrode placement is sensitive to the activity of the facial muscles in general.

It has also been noted by Basmajian (1976), the neuroanatomist and electromyographer, that "The integrated EMG from forehead surface electrodes generally reflects the total or global EMG of all sorts of repeated dynamic muscular activities down to about the first rib—along with some postural activity and nervous tension overactivity" (p. 370). As Basmajian also emphasizes, this site reflects activities such as swallowing, breathing, and movements of the tongue, lips, eyelids, and eyeballs. In other words, to reach low levels on the forehead feedback tone, a subject needs to relax the face muscles in general, to breathe quietly, and to refrain from swallowing and eye movements. To put it another way, it is apparent that the forehead electrode placement (Budzynski & Stoyva, 1969) actually detects a wide range of both EMG activity and overt movement. Not surprisingly, low forehead EMG levels are associated with a decrease in arousal.

1. Very low levels of frontal EMG activity are associated with a shift of mental activity toward drowsiness and sleep. Some years ago—in keeping with the motor theory of thinking—Jacobson found that when activity in the facial and laryngeal muscles fell to zero (or close to zero) levels, then the individual was asleep. In Jacobson's own words, "we can cite our clinical and laboratory experience that if the action potential values both from the eye and speech regions are at approximately zero level for a relatively brief period of time, such as about thirty seconds, the individual is asleep" (Jacobson, 1970, p. 41).

Consistent with this report, our own observations have shown that frontal EMG levels below those of relaxed wakefulness are associated with Stage 1 and Stage 2 sleep (Stoyva & Budzynski, 1974, p. 384). As frontal EMG decreases, then EEG theta rhythms (indicative of drowsiness) show a sharp increase. Moreover, when aroused from this very low frontalis EMG condition, subjects usually (90% or more of the time) report that they were drowsy or asleep. Since this observation is highly reliable, it lends itself well to laboratory demonstration purposes.

An important related observation on this topic was reported by Budzynski (1969). His experiment showed that the consequences of frontalis and forearm relaxation are not limited to the specific muscles being trained, but are manifested in CNS changes as well. This experiment drew on the work of Venables and Wing (1962), which showed that the fusion threshold for paired flashes of light may be used to determine cortical activation level. In general, individuals who are anxious or hyperalert are usually able to discriminate smaller differences in the time interval between the pairs of successive light flashes than are individuals with more normal activation levels; that is, the anxious subjects have lower thresholds.

In Budzynski's (1969) experiment, two-flash thresholds were used to assess the CNS effects of profound muscle relaxation. Twelve normal subjects were training to produce muscle relaxation by means of EMG feedback on the frontalis and the forearm. Each of the 12 subjects showed an increased two-flash threshold (their discrimination interval was larger) in the profound-relaxation condition. Similarly, each subject shows decreased heart rate and, generally, decreased respiration rate during relaxation. In sum, when EMG activity diminished, there were also ANS and CNS effects in the direction of lowered arousal.

2. Finley, Niman, Standley, and Ender (1976) provided frontal EMG feedback training to six patients suffering from athetoid cerebral palsy. Although pretraining frontal EMG levels were extremely high (28.9 μV peak-to-peak), these levels were cut approximately in half after 12 training sessions over 6 weeks. Subjects, and their parents as well, reported subtle improvements in various speech and motor functions. These findings are of great interest in regard to what is known about the neurological basis of athetoid cerebral palsy—namely, that a principal feature of this disorder is the continuous discharge of motor neurons even when an individual is at rest. Relaxation training presumably acts to reduce this continuous discharge.

3. An experiment by DeGood and Chisholm (1977) involved a comparison of frontal EMG feedback and parietal alpha EEG feedback. In essence, frontal EMG affected alpha levels, but the converse was not true. Thus, as frontal EMG levels *decreased* (in the EMG feedback condition) alpha levels significantly *increased;* however, in the alpha feedback condition, an increase in alpha did not lead to a significant decrement in frontal EMG. Also, it was observed that when frontal EMG levels decreased, subjects simultaneously showed significant decreases in heart rate and respiration rate, along with increases in alpha levels. Of five measures, only finger pulse volume failed to shift in the expected direction.

4. In a series of studies with asthmatics, Kotses and his associates (Kotses et al., 1991) have shown that feedback-induced relaxation of the facial muscles leads to increases in peak expiratory flow. Relaxation of other muscles, such as those of the arms, does not produce the effect (Glaus & Kotses, 1983). In the controlled clinical trial of Kotses et al. (1991), the feedback patients also reported decreases in anxiety, though not in medication usage or frequency of asthmatic attacks. Kotses et al. (1991) conclude that facial tension and air flow resistance are directly related. They hypothesize that the two are related by a reflexive mechanism having both trigeminal and vagal components. In their model, changes in facial muscle tension induce changes in afferent trigeminal activity, which in turn changes efferent vagal activity, a determinant of bronchomotor tone.

In summary, Darwin was right: The visible expression of emotion is closely connected with the rest of emotion, including its experiential and physiological components. As the face goes, so goes the rest of the person! Moreover, biofeedback technology lends itself especially well to reducing frontal EMG activity—a measure that provides a global index of what the facial muscles are doing. Furthermore, as we (Budzynski & Stoyva, 1969) have shown, frontalis biofeedback appears to be superior to "placebo" relaxation in reducing frontal EMG activity.

Three Techniques That Can Be Added to a General Relaxation Response

Although the notion of a general relaxation response as suggested by Benson (1975) seems plausible, and is a useful working hypothesis, it also seems highly probable that components of the relaxation response can be strengthened by the addition of specific training procedures. For example, teaching patients a (relaxed) abdominal breathing exercise has specific benefits in those anxiety conditions where hyperventilation is a problem. In this context, we should note the theory advanced by Ley (1987). According to Ley, the crucial event in panic attacks is the act of hyperventilation; most if not all of the symptoms accompanying such attacks are attributable to it. The array of symptoms induced by excessively rapid breathing include dyspnea, heart palpitations, chest pain, choking or smothering sensations, dizziness, lightheadedness, paresthesia, and feelings of unreality.

Over the past several years, evidence has mounted that respiratory retraining—usually in the form of learning abdominal (diaphragmatic) breathing—has some definite merits in the modification of stress and anxiety reactions. The rationale for such training is that hyperventilation generates drastic physiological changes, which in turn set the stage for the onset of powerful anxiety. For example, at St. Bartholomew's Hospital in London, Bonn, Readhead, and Timmons (1984) successfully used breathing retraining in treating clinically diagnosed agoraphobics. Twelve agoraphobics entered the treatment program. Of these, seven received two 1-hour breathing retraining sessions followed by seven weekly 2-hour sessions of real-life exposure to the feared situation(s). Breathing retraining consisted of instruction in diaphragmatic respiration (abdominal breathing), which was maintained at a rate of 8–10 breaths per minute. The five patients in the comparison group were simply given nine 2-hour sessions of real-life exposure (i.e., desensitization), but without any breathing retraining. At the end of training, both groups showed a large drop in panic attack frequency (from about four per week to less than one) and in resting breathing rate as well. At the 6-month follow-up, however, the comparison group showed some resurgence in panic attacks, whereas those in the treatment group showed a further decrease (virtually to zero).

Two Dutch investigators used respiratory biofeedback for 25 carefully chosen patients suffering from hyperventilation syndrome (Defares & Grossman, 1988). Auditory feedback informed patients when their breathing tempo exceeded a desired preset rate. In addition, auditory stimuli concerning the correct breathing pattern to follow were simultaneously provided. Patients also practiced at home with the respiratory feedback device for 30 minutes per day over the 8-week training period. Control patients were likewise exposed to respiratory feedback, but no attempt was made to alter their breathing patterns—although they did practice muscle relaxation at home twice per day. Tests conducted 1 month after training showed an interesting pattern of differences between feedback and control patients. Experimental patients were significantly lower on physiological measures—breathing rate and a CO_2 measure. They also had lower scores on state anxiety, trait anxiety, and neurosomatic instability. In the judgment of Defares and Grossman (1988), this shift in trait (long-term) anxiety indicated that a fundamental change in organismic functioning had occurred.

In our Colorado laboratory and clinic, we now include (relaxed) abdominal breathing exercise as a regular part of our basic training sequence. In working with performance anxiety, we find that about 50% of patients report the abdominal breathing exercise as being useful during the feared situation.

Another specific kind of training that can augment the impact of muscle relaxation training is learning the skill of voluntary hand warming. This hand-warming response—whether accomplished by temperature biofeedback from the hands, or through the autogenic peripheral warmth exercise ("My arms and legs are warm," the second standard exercise)—is a function of cutaneous vasodilatation. A decrease in sympathetic outflow from the CNS causes relaxation of the smooth muscle in the wall of the peripheral blood vessels. This relaxation of autonomically mediated smooth muscles may be regarded as a component of relaxation in addition to that provided simply by relaxation of the striated musculature.

The clinical utility of the peripheral warming response has long been noted in the autogenic training literature. For example, Luthe and Schultz (1969, p. 70) observe that a marked reduction of reported stress symptoms frequently occurs as patients attain mastery of the second autogenic standard exercise ("arms and legs warm") and the fifth standard exercise ("solar plexus warm"). Similarly, in one of the most impressive studies to date of self-regulatory methods in essential hypertension, Blanchard and his associates have shown that hand temperature biofeedback confers a definite benefit in addition to that provided by muscle relaxation. Blanchard et al. (1986), rather than using blood pressure reduction as the dependent variable, examined the proportion of patients who were able to cut back from two lines of antihypertensive medication to only one (the diuretic) with two different types of relaxation training. Over an 8-week period, one experimental group received hand temperature biofeedback; the other spent an equal amount of time learning progressive relaxation. The figures for subjects able to discontinue second-stage medications in the biofeedback versus the relaxation condition were 65% and 27%, respectively, at the end of treatment. At the 3-month follow-up, the figures were 47% and 23%, respectively. In other words, more than twice as many temperature feedback patients as muscle relaxation patients were able to discontinue medications.

A third important component of general relaxation—and one that can vary markedly in its degree—is the tempo and amount of mental activity experienced by the patient. Such activity can often occur at quite a frenetic level. The ability to reduce it, and voluntarily to bring about a state of mental quiet, is probably the cardinal skill acquired in an effective training program of relaxation. For example, with patients suffering from sleep-onset insomnia, the inability "to stop racing thoughts" is usally the most prominent single presenting symptom (Hauri & Linde, 1990). We find that "mental quieting" skills, such as those developed in the autogenic heaviness exercise and in the meditation-based exercise of paying quiet and steady attention to respiratory sensations, help the majority of insomniacs to overcome their sleep-onset problem.

Finally, we should note that the foregoing ideas on strengthening the clinical impact of relaxation training by increasing patients' skills in altering some of its major components are very much in agreement with the three-system view of anxiety and stress already discussed in the section on "Theoretical Underpinnings."

The Need for Combined Interventions

In day-to-day practice with stress-related disorders, we often find that the impact of one intervention by itself yields only a marginal treatment effect; however, if we use two or three techniques in combination, a summated effect large enough to be quite clinically significant may occur.

We should also note that in practice, no one relaxation technique works all the time. For example, some patients do not respond well to progressive relaxation; they dislike tensing their muscles. Some patients do not develop the autogenic heaviness or warmth sensations. And some find it difficult to utilize biofeedback successfully. Consequently, it is important to have backup procedures available. A set of such procedures developed in our laboratory and clinic is described in the next section.

In the future, we can expect more work on combinations of techniques—for example, biofeedback plus cognitive interventions plus behavior change techniques such as assertiveness training or anger control. Overall, such combinations are likely to prove more effective than any one technique by itself. Valuable work along these lines has been done by Blanchard and his associates. In one such study (Blanchard et al., 1982), patients with migraine headache or tension headache were first given 10 sessions of nonbiofeedback relaxation training over an 8-week period. This intervention yielded decreased headache levels in 52% of tension headache patients and in 30% of the migraineurs. Treatment failures were then given biofeedback—frontal EMG feedback in the case of the tension headache patients, and hand temperature feedback for the migraineurs. The proportion of treatment successes then increased to 73% for the tension headache group and to 50% for the migraine group. Feedback training, in other words, increased the proportion of treatment successes by roughly 50% in both conditions over that achieved by muscle relaxation alone.

Studies of this type are arduous undertakings, since many comparison conditions need to be examined (see Borkovec, Johnson, & Block, 1984, for a fine discussion of this point). Yet, once we have begun to isolate individual components in a given disorder, it becomes reasonable to ask whether relevant interventions can be combined. Are these interventions additive, or is one simply equivalent in effect to the other? It is also our conviction that in research concerning the various stress reduction techniques, the main question for the future is not so much whether a particular technique enjoys a marginal edge over another, but whether the various techniques "tap into" differing dimensions of the stress reaction. When they do, their effects are likely to be additive.

Electromyographic Feedback, Autogenic Training, and Meditation Combined

A set of training procedures developed in our Colorado laboratory and clinic, and regularly utilized in treating various disorders of hyperarousal (including anxiety reactions), draws explicitly from several independent traditions (Stoyva, 1989). For the laboratory sessions, EMG feedback is used—first from the forearm extensor, then from a forehead placement (for teaching relaxation of the facial musculature). A particular value of the feedback technique is that not only does it provide some quantification of the learning process, but the patient is also taught what is meant by shifting into a "noneffort" or "nonstriving" mode, as discussed earlier. The latter ability is a crucial skill running through various relaxation and meditative techniques.

For home practice exercises, patients learn the autogenic heaviness and warmth exercises, then subsequently two meditative exercises (Stoyva, 1989). About 70% of patients achieve good heaviness sensations, at least in their arms; about 40% report strong warmth sensations, mainly occurring in hands and arms. Physiologically, the autogenic exercises promote a shift from sympathetic to parasympathetic response patterns (Luthe, 1970). In addition, the exercises serve to dampen mental activity—something many patients find especially valuable.

An important additional component we have added in recent years is the regular use of two meditative exercises. These are often helpful for patients who have enjoyed little success with the autogenic exercises. Physically, the first meditative exercise involves a shift to abdominal (diaphragmatic) breathing. Mentally, the patient learns to pay quiet attention to the movement sensations accompanying the rise and fall of the stomach. The second meditative exercise also involves first shifting to abdominal breathing. In addition, the patient is asked to quietly focus attention on the sensation of cool air in the nostrils that accompanies every in-breath: "On every in-breath, swing your attention back to the cool air sensation. This helps to break up the chains of thoughts."

As the reader will note, this set of exercises provides skills relevant to both the physiological and the cognitive (mental quieting) aspects of relaxation. We also make sure to tell patients early in the program that when they become proficient at these two sets of skills and use them frequently, they have at their disposal specific tools for moderating a stress reaction that has spun out of control. Although this assertion may seem a strong statement, it holds true for the great majority of patients.

Assessment

Biofeedback training is used in two general ways in a clinical setting: first, as a way of teaching self-regulation of physiological responses in the prevention of stress-related disorders, and second, as a means of teaching a patient already suffering from a stress disorder to bring the relevant physiological response systems back to within the normal range of functioning.

The efficacy of biofeedback is demonstrated best in those individuals who seem to be unable to relax even when they consciously attempt to do so. Such people are often relatively unaware of the high tension levels that they habitually manifest. Lacking the ability to sense inner tension, these individuals are often unsuccessful with traditional nonbiofeedback relaxation techniques. Biofeedback, however, gives them specific information about tension levels and about whether a particular relaxation strategy is working or not.

Our decision as to whether to use biofeedback training or some other therapeutic intervention depends upon several factors:

1. A major requirement for our biofeedback patients is that they be willing to engage in regular home practice. The aim of such practice is to teach mastery not only of muscular relaxation, but also of the skills of mental quieting. For patients with stress-related disorders, these twin skills are difficult to acquire without regular practice outside the clinic. Typically, we recommend that a patient spend about 5 to 10 minutes a day in home practice during the first week of the program (five to seven episodes a day at about 1 minute each). Then, by the second week, the patient moves to a regimen of two long and two or three short episodes a day at home or at work (i.e., two episodes a day of 8–12 minutes each, and two or three episodes of about 1 minute each). Most patients find this a practical regimen.

2. Does the patient show a maladaptive physiological response pattern? We assess this by using the Psychophysiological Stress Profile (PSP), a procedure that involves physiological monitoring of the patient while he or she (a) relaxes, (b) is asked to subtract serial 7's (a mathematics task), and (c) recovers by relaxing a second time (Budzynski et al., 1980). Further details on the PSP are provided in the following section.

3. Are the symptoms of recent origin, or are they of long standing? Stress disorders of long standing are almost always accompanied by chronically heightened arousal in the skeletal muscle system or ANS, or both. Chronic "bracing" of this sort can usually be eliminated or reduced with biofeedback training. Parenthetically, we should also note that even short-term symptoms may reflect the impact of a recent, severe stress situation superimposed upon a long-term bracing pattern.

4. What are the antecedents of the symptoms? If we can identify the triggering stimuli, we can perhaps modify or eliminate them. Such stimuli can be cognitions, internal sensations, or external events.

5. What are the consequences of the symptoms? Often patients are subtly rewarded for their symptoms. These rewards can take they form of increased attention by others, expressions of sympathy, being taken care of, or monetary settlements for on-the-job injuries or illnesses. A more common situation is that the symptoms facilitate avoidance behavior. Does the patient go home from work, or perhaps not even show up for work, if the symptom appears? Is he or she able to avoid social functions or engaging in sexual activity?

6. Does the symptom appear to be a conversion reaction? If so, biofeedback is probably not the therapy of choice.

7. Does the patient exhibit moderate to severe depression? In this case, a therapy other than biofeedback would be in order.

These various factors must be carefully and tactfully explored in order for a comprehensive and effective program to be designed.

The Psychophysiological Stress Profile

Many biofeedback or behavioral medicine clinics use a type of diagnostic procedure that involves physiological monitoring of relevant responses as the patient is first relaxed, then presented with a mild stressor (usually mental arithmetic), and finally allowed to recover from the stress phase (Budzynski et al., 1980).[2] We have used the PSP for some years to determine the reactivity profile of the patient (i.e., the pattern of responsivity under stress). Maladaptive functioning is suggested by responses that fall outside the normal range. Such aberrant responding is reflected both in the absolute magnitude of the response under stress, and in the slope of the recovery curve.

Under stress, many patients exhibit a profile of heightened EMG levels and cool hands; a smaller number, many of whom are generalized anxiety cases, will show heightened EDR activity as well. It is during the recovery phase that anxious patients are likely to show a maladaptive response. It appears difficult for them to return to baseline relaxation levels after they have been subjected to stress.

The PSP is mainly helpful in defining the most reactive response system in a particular individual. Clients with anxiety problems tend to have high EDRs (over 5 μmhos) and possibly high heart rates (over 100 beats per minute during the stress phase). Migraine clients often tend to have cool hands, as do some patients with hypertension. Frontalis EMG can be very high (>10 μV peak-to-peak) in chronic pain clients and often in headache clients, especially if they are experiencing a headache at the time of determining the PSP.

As already mentioned, the PSP involves a three-phase procedure: rest, stress, and recovery. The measures used are typically EMG (frontalis, trapezius, or wrist-to-wrist), hand temperature, EDR (skin conductance response), and heart rate. The objective of the PSP is to determine the response of the client under the three conditions so that an appropriate program of biofeedback training can be designed. The PSP helps define the physiological "style" of the patient; for example, is the individual a muscle responder or an autonomic responder? Subsequent biofeedback training can be optimized by feeding back from the response system found to be most labile or furthest from the norm. (For comments on EMG bandpass width and on normative data for EMG, EDR, and hand temperature, see the Appendix to this chapter.)

---

[2]In our laboratory, assessment by means of the PSP is undertaken with equipment from Bio-Feedback Systems, Inc., 2736 47th Street, Boulder, CO 80301. The bandpass of the EMG units is 100–1000 Hz.

Disorders Treated in Biofeedback Settings

Certain disorders are frequently treated in most biofeedback clinics. We see patients for tension headache, common and classic migraine, insomnia, Raynaud's disease, irritable bowel, colitis, cardiac rehabilitation (e.g., moderating the Type A behavior pattern), temporomandibular problems, mild essential hypertension, anxiety, certain forms of muscle rehabilitation, and a variety of pain syndromes. Many of the problems we work with can be characterized as disorders of hyperarousal—that is, one or more physiological systems are hyperreactive (see Everly, 1989).

Quantification of Symptoms

It has been our experience that patients progress faster when they are asked to keep a daily record of symptoms. For example, pain symptoms can be rated as to both frequency and intensity. Later, when such data are graphed, certain trends can often be noted; this information is likely to be of value to both patient and therapist.

Limitations and Contraindications

Biofeedback training is not to be regarded as a crisis intervention technique—although in certain types of pain problems dramatic results can sometimes occur rapidly, because of relief of muscle spasms.

When a patient reports constant vascular headaches, and especially when all medications have failed, we would suspect psychogenic head pain. Psychotherapy in such a case would be more appropriate.

Hysterical and conversion reaction symptoms do not usually respond to biofeedback unless parallel psychotherapy is successful in resolving the underlying conflict.

Therapists should employ caution if using biofeedback with insulin-dependent diabetics. Relaxation training may result in a greatly decreased need for insulin; consequently, training should be done under careful medical supervision.

Secondary Gain

Biofeedback training may need to be delayed in the intervention sequence if there is evidence of strong secondary gain. Since biofeedback is a self-regulatory procedure, its success depends upon a patient's desire both to learn and then to apply the new skills in daily life. If secondary gain is operating, then the motivation to learn and apply the self-regulation skills will be weak, and progress will be minimal. Consequently, we attempt to assess for the presence of secondary gain in the initial interview. Once the antecedents and consequences of the symptoms are defined, it is possible to institute change procedures.

For example, one of our patients showed a pattern of avoiding social situations by developing migraine headaches. An analysis of the patient's experience in social situations revealed that she felt deficient in her ability to carry on small talk. She believed that she sounded ignorant when she attempted to converse. It turned out that she neither read very much nor watched the television news. Accordingly, we encouraged her to join a book club, to subscribe to *Time* magazine, and to watch the news on television daily. Soon she became better able to converse with others at social gatherings. At this juncture, she began to make good progress with her biofeedback training, and a dramatic reduction in migraine headaches shortly manifested itself.

If secondary gain is not detected, it may manifest itself in a reluctance on the part of the patient to carry out the home practice exercises; in a seeming inability to acquire relaxation skills; or in the continuing report of symptoms, even though the biofeedback monitoring indicates an ability to achieve good relaxation.

Resistance, Compliance, and Maintenance of Behavior Change

Most of our patients follow their instructions for daily homework and the charting of symptoms. If a patient has difficulty in doing so, we begin to suspect that some resistance to getting well may be present. Perhaps the patient's family is unconsciously attempting to maintain him or her in the "sick" role so that the old family equilibrium is not disturbed. More often, resistance is the result of early learning—as expressed, for example, in such sayings as "The devil finds work for idle hands," or "He who does not work does not eat." Many Type A patients fall into this category. Often a careful probing of the thoughts and feelings generated during home relaxation practice will serve to reveal this resistance to a patient. Once patients become aware of their resistance, they can learn to counter when it occurs with a thought such as "The relaxation allows my body to repair itself," or "I deserve a bit of time for myself."

Compliance can be enhanced both by encouraging positive expectations and by paying careful attention to both charting and home relaxation practice. Patients often need to be reminded that acquisition of biofeedback skills requires frequent practice, just as does a sport such as tennis, jogging, or swimming.

Maintenance of behavior change appears to be enhanced primarily by the development of effective "transfer skills." Most of these involve brief relaxation or cognitive techniques. The patient must first learn to become aware of maladaptive thoughts, behavioral, and physiological responses so that coping skills can then be applied. For this task, certain practices developed in behavior therapy can be very helpful. Bits of colored tape, for instance, can serve as a reminder to check tension levels. Small pieces of tape (to serve as reminders) can be placed on such places as watch faces, steering wheels, briefcases, or refrigerator doors. Another variant of this method is that the patient makes a contract with himself or herself to check tension levels *just prior* to performing some frequently occurring behavior. Picking up a telephone receiver is one example. For one physician of our acquaintance, it was writing a prescription. The rationale for this technique is that when the low-frequency behavior (checking and reducing tension levels) becomes associated with the high-frequency behavior, then the low-frequency behavior begins to occur more often (in accordance with the Premack principle).

The Method

Introducing the Method to Patients

A critical, but often neglected, aspect of biofeedback training is explaining the procedure to patients. If patients lack a clear understanding of how and why biofeedback may be useful for their anxiety disorders, then not much benefit can be expected to accrue. For example, they are unlikely to see the point of engaging in much home practice. As Frank (1961) has pointed out in his discussion of psychological therapies, there must exist a shared assumptive framework between the patient and the therapist. That is, there should be a mutual understanding as to what the problem is and why the proposed course of treatment is likely to be helpful. Briefly, we explain to patients in a conversational way that their anxiety problem is a type of stress reaction—one that has become excessive and maladaptive. The aim of the program is to alter this maladaptive stress reaction.

> Basically, the stress (and anxiety) response is an energization reaction in which a whole cluster of processes are set in motion. Muscles become tense, heart rate and blood pressure increase, and stored glycogen is released into the blood, as are many hormones. The physiological activities associated with rest and digestion diminish. This emergency reaction is one we all possess; it is a basic survival response. What becomes a problem, however, is that some individuals react too strongly. Small or moderate amounts of anxiety help us to meet challenges and to get things done. But the brain often gets a person into trouble; it may, because of the person's life history, begin to interpret all sorts of events and situations as threats. In other words, the interpretive activity of the brain leads to frequent, and sometimes crippling, triggering of the stress (anxiety) reaction. Since the stress reaction is very powerful, and involves many systems, various symptoms may appear in addition to anxiety: elevated blood pressure, migraine and tension headache, duodenal ulcers, skin irritations, sleep disturbances, and irritable bowel syndrome.

At this point, a good justification for biofeedback relaxation training can be developed. The fundamental idea, by now supported by a wealth of evidence (Gellhorn, 1967; Luthe, 1970; Stoyva & Budzynski, 1974), is that the effects of profound relaxation are generally opposite to those produced by psychological stress (and anxiety). With good relaxation, the bodily systems involved in stress-related effort begin to moderate their reactivity, and an individual begins to feel more calm. Patients learn to relax first with feedback, then without it. Other interventions such as systematic desensitization are added later. This last procedure enables patients to think about, and later to confront, situations that previously caused them severe anxiety. As with relaxation training, patients first train in the clinic, then practice their new skills in the real-life anxiety situations troubling them.

The basic principles of biofeedback are explained as follows:

> The main idea of biofeedback is to use instruments to tell you what's happening inside your own body—and to tell you immediately. For example, is your pulse rate going up or down? With biofeedback instruments, we can tell at once. Or what's happening with your muscle tension? In order to find out, we place sensors over the muscle we are interested in. The sensors pick up the tiny electrical signals generated by the muscles. Through your

headphones you'll learn that when you tense the muscle, you hear a high-frequency sound. Then, as soon as you relax, the tone frequency goes down. In other words, the tone tells you instantly whether you're going in the right direction. Is the muscle tensing or relaxing? Let the tone be your guide. We've used this on a lot of people now, and it helps them to relax more effectively.

Some patients know little or nothing about biofeedback. For them, a fairly full explanation is important. In particular, they must know how biofeedback training can be helpful for anxiety. Other individuals may have heard of biofeedback, but may have invested it with magical expectations. Here it is important to clarify what can be expected and to set realistic treatment goals.

As already indicated, we find it useful to convey the idea that the anxiety reaction is part of an excessive stress reaction. This helps place the symptoms in a wider and somewhat reassuring perspective: Moderate amounts of anxiety are adaptive and normal, but large amounts are not. Again, the term "stress," despite its scientific ambiguity, is one readily comprehended by the average individual. On the other hand, if patients hear that their problem is "psychosomatic," they often misinterpret this to mean "They think it's all in my head."

The Physical Environment and Equipment

Biofeedback devices range in size from tiny $\frac{1}{4}$-inch liquid crystal temperature dots to large physiographs and computers connected to input–output peripherals. The majority of biofeedback therapists, however, use stereo-size separate components. Typically, they have in their training rooms one or two EMG units, one thermal unit, and one EDR unit. Also valuable is an electronic "mixer" unit, which greatly simplifies the coordinated presentation of several types of feedback. The "mixer" allows one or more combinations of auditory feedback to be presented simultaneously. "Pink noise" (pleasant "white noise") is also available as a background sound. Another procedure, which can sometimes be useful, is to have tape-recorded instructions presented along with the feedback signals.

The physical environment of most biofeedback clinics varies. Some therapists prefer to use a one-room system, in which the therapist is present in the same room as the patient and the equipment. Other therapists prefer a two-room arrangement, in which the patient sits in a recliner chair in a semidarkened, quiet room, and the trainer and equipment are in the next room. Patient and therapist communicate over an intercom. Having used both systems over the years, we believe that most patients learn faster in the two-room system—particularly those who experience some initial difficulty relaxing in the presence of another person. Since this difficulty often appears in individuals suffering from anxiety or stress-related disorders, we prefer the two-room approach.

In the case of group training in stress management, the smaller, inexpensive temperature sensors are those most often used.[3] Almost any setting can be employed,

[3]Small temperature-sensing devices—which are lightweight, portable, and economical—can be obtained from Bio-Feedback Systems, Inc., 2736 47th Street, Boulder, CO 80301.

although it is useful to insure that each participant can lie down or at least sit comfortably for the relaxation practice.

Therapist–Patient Relationship

Like all psychological therapies, the biofeedback treatment of anxiety requires a relationship of trust and confidence. Such a relationship can be fostered in a number of ways.

1. As mentioned above, the therapist should explain how biofeedback and related procedures can be useful in the treatment of anxiety. This explanation becomes strongly convincing as a patient begins to benefit from his or her relaxation training. One of us (J. M. S.) employs autogenic exercises right from the outset for the home practice phase of relaxation training (Stoyva, 1989). The other author (T. H. B.) starts patients out with the first of the six-phase home training cassette tapes (see Budzynski et al., 1980).

2. The therapist should specify treatment goals. Patients are reassured and given confidence in the therapist when they realize that reliable step-by-step procedures are available for the management and reduction of their anxiety. However, in the case of more-difficult-to-treat disturbances, such as generalized anxiety, agoraphobia, or multiple sources of anxiety, we emphasize that the program will involve a lot of time; that it may require the use of several different procedures; and that the anxiety will probably not vanish completely, although it will be reduced and made more manageable. It is also worth noting that biofeedback per se is not a treatment for a great variety of medical problems, or for relationship problems, marital difficulties, character disorders, or psychoses. Such a disclaimer is especially important in the case of patients harboring magical expectations. Subsequent disappointments are minimized, and the ground is set for a long-term relationship of honesty and mutual respect.

3. The therapist should help the patient cultivate a sense of mastery. This factor is prominent not only in biofeedback and self-regulatory therapies, but probably in all psychological therapies (Strupp, 1970). A feeling of mastery can be promoted by arranging a success experience early in the program. Biofeedback lends itself well to such an endeavor. Generally, we commence biofeedback training with a muscle group that is easy to relax, such as the forearm extensor. However, should relaxation of the right arm prove too difficult, we can shift the feedback site to the other arm. Relaxation can nearly always be accomplished at one or the other of these sites (Budzynski et al., 1980). Even a modest success, especially on a task deemed relevant to one's disorder, acts as a source of encouragement. A sense of mastery, and a sense that one can regain control of oneself and one's life, is set in motion.

4. The therapist should be a sympathetic listener. As in other therapies, the process of listening allows for the expression reassurance and encouragement. Typically, a good time to interact with the patient is right after the feedback portion of the session, a task generally occupying 15 to 20 minutes. At this time, the patient is likely to be communicative and may bring up matters previously undisclosed. We generally begin by asking which relaxation strategies were helpful and which were not (as

indicated by the feedback tone). We then inquire as to how the home practice went this last week, and whether there were any difficulties. This question often leads to a discussion of current life stresses: pressures on the job, difficulties with supervisors or subordinates, problems with children, financial difficulties, self-doubts with regard to performance challenges, difficulties in making an important life transition, and social and marital problems. Clearly, biofeedback and relaxation training can be only of limited help for this array of difficulties, though often they help a patient to feel better rested and give him or her a sense of having more energy to devote to active coping efforts (active problem solutions). This sense of feeling better rested and more energetic is especially likely to occur when the patient is beginning to sleep better.

5. The therapist should ask about home practice. In each session, as noted above, we inquire as to how the home practice exercises have been going. Training difficulties are explored, and suggestions for coping with them may be offered (Stoyva, 1989). These inquiries let patients know of our continuing concern with their problems and emphasize the importance of changing behavior outside the clinic setting.

6. Termination is generally accomplished by spacing the sessions further apart. This allows patients to realize that they can function independently; yet at the same time, there still remains some contact with the therapist should difficulties arise.

Description of the Method

When biofeedback is indicated by virtue of the intake evaluation and the PSP results, we proceed with training. Each patient then has sensors (electrodes) attached for monitoring forearm extensor EMG, frontal EMG, finger temperature, and EDR. These sensors are all easily applied in less than 3 minutes. The patient is told how the sensors function to pick up the small bioelectric signals generated by various types of physiological activity. (For more details on electrode placement and instrumentation, see the Appendix to this chapter. For a valuable discussion of the equipment needs of the psychotherapist, see Peffer, 1989.)

Baseline Measures

Although for research purposes we like to obtain three baseline sessions on each of three separate days, such a protocol is not very practical for everyday clinical work. Instead, the first 4 minutes of each session are used as a no-feedback baseline measure of relaxation ability. The patient sits comfortable in a recliner chair in a softly lighted room, and keeps his or her eyes gently closed. The subsequent feedback portion of the session then occupies about 20 minutes. Following the 20-minute period, there is often 2 or 3 minutes' worth of practice in the absence of biofeedback. As training progresses, the no-feedback levels begin to approximate those obtained during the feedback period itself.

In the frontalis EMG placement, a reference sensor is positioned above the bridge of the nose in parallel with two active sensors, which are placed above the irises of the eyes and approximately $\frac{1}{2}$ inch above the eyebrows.

Biofeedback Training

After the sensors have been attached, the technician leaves the room. Now outside with the equipment, he or she establishes voice contact with the patient, who is reclining in a comfortable chair. This initial voice interchange assures the patient that the trainer is outside and can hear any comments or questions.

The patient is next presented with feedback, usually from the forearm extensor, since this muscle is ordinarily easy to control. As the patient begins to practice increasing and decreasing muscle tension, he or she is told that there are two modes of attending to this task (lowering arousal). One way is called "active striving" and is the way most people have been taught to learn. It involves conscious, active focusing on a task. But this mode does not work in reducing muscle tension or decreasing autonomic tone. The more suitable mode has been labeled "passive volition" or the "nonstriving mode." Oddly enough, the very act of "not trying" allows the patient to succeed at controlling these response systems in the relaxation direction.

After this introductory phase, the patient is asked to practice letting go and to listen to the biofeedback tone for guidance. This stage is one of strategy testing, with the biofeedback tone providing prompt and reliable information as to whether a given strategy is working. It is during this initial session that patients first may realize that a connection exists between thought and physiological responding. They are often amazed that a seemingly benign thought can generate a powerful physiological change.

After the patient becomes successful at lowering arm tension, the gain (or sensitivity) of the feedback loop is increased. This means that the patient will now have to manifest an even lower level of EMG in order to decrease the tone frequency. (These changes of gain are always reported to the patient *before* the change is made, so as not to confuse him or her.)

The sequencing of biofeedback training has been described elsewhere (Budzynski et al., 1980; Stoyva, 1989). When the patient reaches criterion on forearm extensor EMG (1.0 μV peak-to-peak or less), even without feedback, we shift to frontal EMG biofeedback. Not infrequently, however, forearm EMG levels begin to increase after the feedback signal and attention have been shifted to frontal EMG. For this reason, we may leave the patient with some minimal form of biofeedback from the arm (such as a light of varying color) while he or she is at the same time receiving auditory frontal EMG feedback. The two distinct biofeedback modalities make it easier for the patient to maintain the first system in a relaxed state, while simultaneously maintaining passive attention on the second system.

After mastery of the second system, frontal EMG, has been demonstrated by meeting the criterion of 2.5 μV peak-to-peak while simultaneously holding the forearm EMG at a low level, the patient can progress to the third system—namely, hand temperature. In the relaxed condition, with its relatively low SNS tone, the skin of the hands and feet will generally show temperatures of 90°F or greater (our criterion for relaxation in the peripheral skin temperature system). Thermal feedback is useful in helping the patient reach this criterion. Turning to this third system often allows us to discontinue the feedback from the first system (the forearm EMG). Although a patient can learn to control three systems simultaneously, we prefer to use only one or two at any given time during relaxation training. Later, however, during the systematic desensitization phase, the patient may sometimes be monitoring three systems at once.

In the case of EDR activity (skin conductance), criteria are more difficult to establish, since a very low level can indicate a flatness of affect or inhibition of emotion. On the basis of normal patients, however, we have generally found that a level between 0.5 and 2.5 μmhos is associated with good psychological functioning. A high palmar skin conductance (greater than 10 μmhos) is often seen in individuals with generalized anxiety.

Home Practice

Patients are regularly asked about their home practice, which is a vital part of their training. One of us (J. M. S.) uses mainly EMG feedback in the laboratory in order to teach both muscle relaxation and the idea of "nonstriving" or "letting go." The sequence of home exercises involves (1) the autogenic heaviness exercise; (2) the autogenic warmth exercise; (3) an abdominal breathing exercise (drawn from Vipassana meditation); and (4) the mental quieting exercise—paying quiet attention to the cool air sensations in the nose that accompany inhalation (Stoyva, 1989). This sequence offers alternative strategies for seeking the goal of relaxation. Such alternatives are important, since in daily practice, no single technique works for all patients. Consequently, it is extremely valuable to have alternative strategies built into the system.

The other author (T. H. B.) uses a similar sequence of home practice exercises, except that tapes are used. Over the past 15 years, this tape series has been used extensively in both clinical and research settings. For a description of these tapes, see Budzynski et al. (1980). The series may be ordered from Bio-Feedback Systems, 2736 47th St., Boulder, CO 80301.

Systematic Desensitization

If the patient has completed relaxation training and has met our criteria for mastery of the selected responses, but still experiences difficulty in real-life situations, we use the systematic desensitization procedure described earlier. Over the years, since our initial work with EMG feedback, we have added thermal and skin conductance feedback to this procedure. As we present scenes for the fear or stress hierarchy, we monitor all indicators for signs of disruption of the relaxed state. The scene is terminated if one or more of the responses changes significantly in the direction of heightened arousal. Between visualizations, one or more kinds of feedback are used by the patient to return to baseline levels.

As noted earlier, recovery training can be employed after the desensitization phrase as a means of helping the patient resume a calm condition after a surge of anxiety has occurred. Another addition to systematic desensitization is the pervasive anxiety procedure already described. It can be used to identify anxiety sources of which the patient was previously unaware, and can also be used for an unstructured (nonhierarchical) form of desensitization.

Group Training

Up to this point, we have described procedures that are used with one patient at a time. More recent applications, however, include the use of simplified forms of biofeedback in group settings. This type of training is made possible through the use of inexpensive biofeedback devices, such as various types of small liquid crystal temperature sensors or small EDR units. The small temperature sensors allow each participant to monitor hand temperature both inside and outside the clinic setting.

Larger and more expensive pieces of biofeedback equipment can also be used in a group setting. Selected patients can demonstrate the use of the equipment for relaxation or hand warming.

Case Examples

Insomnia and Anxiety

Ms. N, a 33-year-old advertising executive, presented with complaints of insomnia and feelings of "anxiety and tension" at work. Her insomnia, which consisted of difficulties in both falling asleep and staying asleep, had begun during a period of great personal stress 3 years ago and had persisted after the resolution of the stress.

At present, apart from the insomnia, life was going well for Ms. N. She enjoyed good physical health, liked her work, and felt that her relationships with other people were a source of satisfaction. A medical examination confirmed her report of good health, and she was not a user of caffeine, alcohol, or tobacco. Some years previously she had been diagnosed as having a mitral valve prolapse, but neither she nor her medical consultant felt that this problem was a likely factor in her anxiety. For the past 3 years she had regularly taken Halcion for her insomnia, but had become increasingly skeptical as to its usefulness, and worried that she was becoming addicted to it.

Bright and highly energetic, Ms. N characterized herself as an "extreme Type A." She also described herself as feeling "tense and anxious" at work, and as someone "who could not unwind." She had attempted various remedies for her insomnia, none of which had helped for long. She had also tried various hypnotics; these had produced only transient relief, and had caused unpleasant side effects. At the time of treatment onset, she reported feeling extremely exasperated about her sleep problem and despondent as to whether anything could be done about it.

The patient's laboratory training consisted of EMG feedback—first from the forearm extensor in Session 1, then from the frontalis placement in Session 2 and subsequent biofeedback sessions. Her sequence of home practice exercises consisted of the autogenic heaviness exercise, the autogenic warmth exercise, the abdominal breathing exercise, and the mental quieting exercise (as described earlier in this chapter).

Ms. N rapidly learned to develop distinct heaviness sensations in both arms, and later in her legs. At first she was able to develop these sensations only during her practice episodes at work, but not at home—a common pattern for insomniacs (i.e., relaxation for them is most difficult in their regular sleep environment). After about 3 weeks, however, she began to develop the heaviness sensations at home as well, at which point the heaviness exercise sometimes began to help with sleep onset.

A particularly fruitful maneuver for Ms. N was the feedback-induced relaxation of the facial muscles by means of frontal EMG feedback. With the "deep" relaxation of these muscles, she would notice a dissipating of facial tension and the onset of drowsiness sensations. She found, too, that in the laboratory she could be roused from the drowsy condition of low frontal EMG levels (about 1.5 μV peak-to-peak and below), and could then use frontal EMG feedback to return to a drowsy, sleep-onset condition. This interruption sequence could be repeated two or three times in the space of a 30-minute feedback session. The patient also began to report that she was developing some facility at the "cool air" mental quieting exercise.

About 4 weeks into treatment, while Ms. N was on her Christmas break, she independently decided to stop her Halcion usage entirely. She did so because she had recently experienced increasing symptoms of vague anxiety, depression, and stomach upset, for which she felt "there was no good reason." During the withdrawal period, she reported great tension and extremely bad sleep. Throughout this period, however, she persisted in her home practice exercises; about 12 days after she had stopped taking the drug, her sleep began to improve markedly.

Ms. N now reported sleeping about 6 or 7 hours a night instead of her previous 3 or 4, and felt alert and refreshed during the day. Asked what was most useful in overcoming her insomnia, she noted the following: (1) doing the facial relaxation (a maneuver that dampened the "buzz" of mental activity and made her feel sleepy); (2) "knowing that I couldn't go back on the drug" (a realization that solidified her resolve to persist in nondrug approaches to her problem); and (3) the mental quieting exercise (paying quiet attention to respiratory sensations).

She also utilized the exercises to reduce anxiety and tension at work. As a consequence of her relaxation training, she found that she now had developed a sensitivity to cues of rising tension at work—cues she had previously ignored. Several times a day at her office, she now carried out a relaxation episode of 1 or 2 minutes. In particular, she reported the facial relaxation maneuver to be useful in dissipating the feeling of "anxiety and tension."

The treatment course of this patient illustrates several points:

1. Each of several techniques had some usefulness, and could be combined with others to produce a useful effect on insomnia and anxiety.

2. Biofeedback-induced relaxation of the facial muscles appeared to be a specific maneuver helpful in promoting drowsiness and sleep, and also in gaining a sense of control over sleep induction. This same maneuver also proved to be a means of reducing the buildup of situational anxiety at work.

3. Despite the turbulence of Ms. N's Halcion withdrawal period, she persisted in her training, and learned to meet the two major criteria of our program—first, learning physical relaxation; second, learning to become quiet mentally. After she acquired these skills, and after the Halcion rebound had subsided, her insomnia remitted, and she now reported sleeping well on about six out of seven nights.

Trauma-Related Anxiety and Pain

Mrs. R, a 45-year-old wife and mother with post-traumatic stress disorder, reported left-sided facial, chest, and shoulder pain as well as anxiety, panic attacks, and intermittent depression. All her symptoms appeared to be the consequences of an automobile accident 2 years prior to her present admission to the Presbyterian Medical Center.

In the accident, when the family jeep had skidded off a patch of black ice and overturned into a ditch, Mrs. R had suffered six broken ribs, a collapsed lung, a concussion, and internal bleeding. She herself at first remembered very little of the accident. After it occurred, she had been functionally blind for nearly 24 hours, and had also experienced intermittent blackouts during this period. After her ribs had healed, the patient continued to experience crying spells, episodes of depression, and intense anxiety attacks, as well as daily shoulder, chest, and facial pain.

Several sessions were spent in eliciting a detailed chronological account of the accident from Mrs. R. While this was being done, bilateral EMG responses were recorded from face, neck, arm, and shoulder sites. As expected, signals from the left side were generally a good deal more reactive then those from the right as she described various parts of the accident. Heart rate and EDR elevations also occurred during these parts of her account. It became evident that Mrs. R was a victim of traumatic memories, and that through the process of stimulus generalization, her condition had deteriorated to a point where the painful memories could be triggered by a broadening circle of stimuli. Earlier interventions with physical therapy and medications had not yielded satisfactory results.

During her biofeedback treatment, Mrs. R made use of the information feed-back from the several response systems, and learned to reach relaxation criteria in about eight sessions. Then, working in a desensitization paradigm, she learned to keep EMG levels on the left side of her body at about the same level as those on the right while she recounted details of her accident. Finally, she was able to keep EMG activity at low levels on both sides of her body, even while vividly re-experiencing the various parts of the traumatic event.

An additional intervention was for Mrs. R to see herself as remaining reasonably calm and focused after the accident, and to substitute positive for negative thoughts. For example, instead of thinking "I am going to die," she would practice making self-statements such as "I am going to be OK." In order to foster transfer of skills, she practiced the combination of relaxation and positive self-statements several times a day at home, at work, and in her car.

Mrs. R was seen roughly twice a week for a total of 16 sessions until her pain and anxiety symptoms had largely dissipated. The last symptoms to subside were her depressive episodes.

In this case, we may note that monitoring and biofeedback were useful in reducing reactivity in physiological response systems that were contributing to anxiety and pain. Again, we should note that more than one sort of intervention was needed, and that these included biofeedback, systematic desensitization, the uncovering of repressed traumatic memories, and the use of positive self-statements.

Comments and Summary

EMG feedback can be considered a valuable tool for teaching the skills of relaxation. It is especially useful both for assessing that at least some degree of muscular relaxation has occurred (by means of the quantification of EMG activity normally involved), and for teaching the patient what is meant by "noneffort" or "passive volition," a concept often difficult to convey verbally. It can further be used to induce low levels of EMG activity in the facial muscles—a transition generally associated with marked reductions in CNS and ANS arousal.

Biofeedback can also serve as a potent tool in giving the patient a sense of increased control over aberrant physiological reactions. This is an important consideration in the treatment of anxiety and stress-linked disorders, since in these disturbances a sense of defective control over one's own reactions generally looms as a cardinal characteristic of the pathology. Moreover, feedback technology lends itself to the devising of new learning strategies; this is likewise an important matter, especially in working with difficult patients. It should be emphasized and re-emphasized that in daily clinical practice, no single technique works for all patients. Consequently, it is highly desirable to have backup strategies available. Biofeedback technology amplifies the range of alternative strategies.

In the future, given the probability of continuing progress in electronics and in the technology of *in vivo* monitoring, we can also expect further advances in the dynamic assessment of patients' reactivity under active, naturalistic conditions. Increasingly, patients will be taught to moderate physiological reactivity under conditions of active coping in addition to those of the resting mode.

All in all, we can conclude this chapter on an optimistic note. Not only have relaxation and biofeedback methods demonstrated considerable usefulness, but the body of techniques continues to expand from year to year. These developments are particularly encouraging in the light of some prescient comments made a generation ago by René Dubos (1965). In his view, health and prevention measures that have grown out of community action, and that have not required much personal effort, have been comparatively easy to put into practice. One calls to mind examples such as the introduction of clean water supplies, pasteurized milk, vaccination against infectious disease, and safer workplaces. But as Dubos also noted,

> there are many other aspects of the environment that are uncontrollable unless man is willing to make a personal effort and change his ways of life. He may have to curtail his smoking, drinking, or overeating; walk instead of riding; refrain from becoming dependent on drugs; stop polluting his air and streams, even though this means slowing down industrial expansion. Environmental control through collective and anonymous social measures has proved relatively painless, but physicians and hygienists have not yet succeeded in convincing human beings that they should change their ways of life for the sake of health if the change involves a continued personal effort. (Dubos, 1965, p. 366)

The methods described in this book should encourage more people to make the effort.

Appendix: Note on Instrumentation and Physiological Measures

The Electromyographic Signal

EMG activity, it should be noted, is not a direct measure of the force of muscle contraction per se. It is an indirect measure in which surface electrodes are used to detect the electrical activity of motor units. When these units fire, not only do they cause muscle spindles to contract, but part of their electrical energy migrates through the surrounding tissue and can be detected at the skin surface as a fluctuating potential. In other words, what is detected is an electrical aspect of muscle contraction—a dimension that is directly related to the force of the muscular contraction.

The researcher should note that the EMG does not provide an absolute measure, as a thermometer or a ruler does. Its magnitude is critically dependent on such factors as amplifier characteristics, width of filter bandpass, good or poor electrode contact, and the amount of interference from various sources of electrical "noise." It does, however, indicate fluctuations in the electrical aspects of muscle activity, and can therefore be used to assess whether muscle tension is increasing or decreasing.

A good rule for the neophite is to get the feel of the instrument by trying it personally. What are the EMG values when one feels relaxed or tense? What are the *frontal* EMG levels when one feels drowsy? The "drowsy" levels are likely to be among the very lowest that occur for this particular placement.

Electromyographic Bandwidth and Signal Processing

The amplifier of the biofeedback unit provides a window on EMG activity. When we speak of EMG "bandwidth," we are referring to the range of EMG frequencies within which the amplifier is most sensitive. The spectrum of EMG frequencies can vary from 20 to 10,000 Hz (Cram, 1991), although 80% of the signal energy originates in the 30 to 80-Hz band.

The filter bandwidth determines how much electrical energy emerges in the output measure. The wider the bandpass, the larger the signal. In the earlier days of biofeedback, we suggested a bandpass of 95–1000 Hz (Budzynski et al., 1980), although our very first EMG devices featured a bandpass of 20–1000 Hz. The 20-Hz low end permitted the capture of a substantial amount of the EMG energy, but allowed other artifacts (such as the electrocardiogram and 60-Hz noise from electrical power sources) to get through. The 95-Hz low end was a compromise designed to avoid these artifacts and yet to retain as much of the EMG as possible. However, other biofeedback manufacturers later decided to use other filters, such as bandpasses of 100–200 Hz or 100–400 Hz, thus making it difficult to establish normative levels. Cram (1991), however, has recently published normative data from various EMG sites using bandpasses of both 100–200 Hz and 25–1000 Hz.

Normative values on forearm extensor and frontalis EMG, and hand temperature, from approximately 10 years of work, were incorporated into the systems diagrams that appear in Budzynski et al. (1980). These values represented levels that could be expected from relaxed individuals. The levels for forearm extensor and frontalis were 1.0 and 2.5 μV peak-to-peak, respectively, and 90°F for hand temperature.

Emerging from the amplifier of the biofeedback unit, with its particular bandpass, is a fluctuating electrical signal. The voltage of this signal is proportional to the degree of electrical activity in the motor neurons of the muscles under measurement. This signal is often referred to as the "raw EMG." When it is transformed into an auditory signal, this "raw EMG" resembles a rushing sound or radio "static." A less erratic and more pleasing sound can be obtained if the raw EMG is first further processed. This task is accomplished by rectifying and smoothing the signal, which involves evening out the peaks and valleys. The smoothed signal is then used to produce a tone of varying frequency. This smoothed signal can be used for quantifying EMG activity (e.g., as in driving a readout), as well as for providing information feedback.

Skin Preparation and Electrode Placement

Prior to placing EMG electrodes on the skin, its surface must be suitably prepared—a task that nowadays requires only a minute or two. The object of this preparation is to lower skin resistance to the transmission of the EMG signal by removing surface impediments to good conduction, such as oils, salts, makeup, and dead skin cells on the epidermal layer.

In our early work, we used a fine-grained abrasive soap (Brasivol) for this purpose (Budzynski & Stoyva, 1969; Budzynski et al., 1980). Now, however, we simply use "alcohol prep pads," which are quicker and neater than the Brasivol method. The electronic characteristics of EMG devices have improved substantially in recent years, so that the fairly intense scrubbing of the skin, as with the Brasivol method, is no longer necessary.

Skin preparation involves an initial cleaning with slight rubbing of the sensor site with an alcohol pad. Then the alcohol must be allowed to dry thoroughly before the sensor cups are applied. The sensor cups are filled with electrode paste and smoothed off so that no excess paste is present. If there is excess paste, it may form a low-impedance bridge to the other sensor, resulting in an erroneous low reading. Silver/silver chloride sensors are ideal, and they resist polarization and electrode "pop," but stainless steel sensors have also been used.

In the frontalis EMG placement, a reference electrode is positioned above the bridge of the nose in parallel with two active sensors, which are placed above the irises of the eyes and approximately $\frac{1}{2}$ inch above the eyebrows. The exact electrode placement sites for the most commonly used muscles in biofeedback work can be found in Basmajian (1989, pp. 369–382).

Peak-to-Peak Microvolts

The EMG values given in this chapter are of the peak-to-peak type. As Peek (1987, p. 93) points out, EMG machines are alternating-current voltmeters, and "microvolts peak-to-peak" refers to the voltage difference between the positive and the negative peak of an alternating current. A related measure, the "average EMG value," equals the peak-to-peak value divided by 3.14 (it is assumed that the same bandwidths are involved in both measures). In other words, the average level is equal to just less than one-third of the peak-to-peak value.

Another commonly used measure is the "root mean square" (RMS). Unlike peak-to-peak values, which represent voltages, RMS values are a measure of electrical power. There is no simple arithematical operation for converting RMS values to peak-to-peak values. RMS values, however, typically lie within 20% of the average value, which means that RMS values are roughly one-third of peak-to-peak values. This is probably why they are favored by some manufacturers: The smaller values make the machine look more sensitive!

For an excellent and lucidly reasoned exposition of biofeedback electronics and instrumentation, see Peek (1987). Writing for the nonengineer, Peek not only uses "ordinary language," but also makes a point of linking electronic matters to questions of psychological interest.

Skin Temperature

Like EMG activity, skin temperature is an indirect measure. In this case, the phenomenon of interest is peripheral vasoconstriction, which varies with the amount of sympathetic outflow.

Since there is no simple way to measure the diameter of blood vessels directly, we instead use a correlate of peripheral vasoconstriction—namely, skin temperature of the surrounding tissue. As variations occur in the diameter of blood vessels, the temperature of surrounding tissues increases or decreases accordingly. Thus, a thermometer attached to the skin gives us an estimate of vasoconstriction or dilation in the tissue beneath the probe.

Skin Conductance

Skin conductance is an indirect measure of sweat gland activity, the latter being one of the physiological aspects of emotional responding controlled by the ANS. With increasing levels of emotion, more sweat glands become active and more sweat appears on the skin surface, especially on the palms and soles. Crucial to skin conductance measurement is the fact that sweat contains various salts, which render it electrically conductive.

In a skin conductance instrument, a small voltage is applied across two points of skin, usually on the palm or the volar surface of the fingers. The amount of electrical current that the skin allows to pass is expressed in "micromhos." With increasing levels of emotional arousal (and sweating), more current is passed. Although criteria for skin conductance are difficult to establish, we have generally observed that levels between 0.5 and 2.5 μmhos are associated with good psychological functioning. High palmar skin conductance levels (>10 μmhos) are often seen in patients suffering from generalized anxiety disorder.

REFERENCES

Andrasik, F., & Blanchard, E. B. (1987). The biofeedback treatment for headache. In J. P. Hatch, J. G. Fisher, & J. D. Rugh (Eds.), *Biofeedback: Studies in clinical efficacy* (pp. 281–321). New York: Plenum Press.

Basmajian, J. V. (1976). Facts vs. myth in EMG biofeedback. *Biofeedback and Self-Regulation, 1,* 369–371.

Basmajian, J. V. (Ed.). (1989). *Biofeedback: Principles and practice for clinicians* (3rd ed.). Baltimore: Williams & Wilkins.

Benson, H. (1975). *The relaxation response.* New York: Morrow.

Blanchard, E. B., Andrasik, F., Neff, D. F., Teders, S. J., Pallmeyer, T. P., Arena, J. B., Jurish, S. E., Saunders, N. L., Ahles, T. A., & Rodichok, L. D. (1982). Sequential comparison of relaxation training and biofeedback in the treatment of three kinds of chronic headache or, the machines be necessary some of the time. *Behaviour Research and Therapy, 20,* 1–13.

Blanchard, E. B., McCoy, G. C., Musso, A., Gerardi, M. A., Pallmeyer, T. P., Gerardi, R. J., Cotch, P. A., Siracusa, K., & Andrasik, F. (1986). A controlled comparison of thermal biofeedback and relaxation training in the treatment of essential hypertension: I. Short-term and long-term outcome. *Behavior Therapy, 17,* 563–579.

Bonn, J. A., Readhead, C. P., & Timmons, B. H. (1984). Enhanced adaptive behavioral response in agoraphobic patients pretreated with breathing retraining. *Lancet, ii,* 665–669.

Borkovec, T. D., Johnson, M. C., & Block, D. L. (1984). Evaluating experimental designs in relaxation research. In R. L. Woolfolk & P. M. Lehrer (Eds.), *Principles and practice of stress management* (1st ed., pp. 368–403). New York: Guilford Press.

Budzynski, T. H. (1969). *Feedback-induced relaxation and activation level.* Unpublished doctoral dissertation, University of Colorado, Boulder.

Budzynski, T. H. (1973). Biofeedback procedures in the clinic. *Seminars in Psychiatry, 5,* 537–547.

Budzynski, T. H., & Stoyva, J. M. (1969). An instrument for producing deep muscle relaxation by means of analog information feedback. *Journal of Applied Behavior Analysis, 2,* 231–237.

Budzynski, T. H., & Stoyva, J. M. (1973). Biofeedback techniques in behavior therapy. In N. Birbaumer (Ed.), *Reihe Fortschritte der Klinischen Psychologie: Vol. 3. Neuropsychologie der Angst* (pp. 248–270). Munich: Urban & Schwarzenberg.

Budzynski, T. H., & Stoyva, J. M. (1975). EMG-Biofeedback bei unspezifischen und spezifischen Ang stzustanden. In H. Legewie & L. Nusselt (Eds.), *Fortschritte der Klinischen Psychologie*: *Vol. 6. Biofeed-backtherapie*: *Lernmethod in der Psychosomatic, Neurologie und Rehabilitation* (pp. 163–185). Munich: Urban & Schwarzenberg.

Budzynski, T. H., Stoyva, J. M., & Adler, C. S. (1970). Feedback-induced muscle relaxation: Application to tension headache. *Journal of Behavior Therapy and Experimental Psychiatry*, *1*, 205–211.

Budzynski, T. H., Stoyva, J. M., Adler, C. S., & Mullaney, D. J. (1973). EMG biofeedback and tension headache: A controlled outcome study. *Psychosomatic Medicine*, *35*, 484–496.

Budzynski, T. H., Stoyva, J. M., & Peffer, K. E. (1980). Biofeedback techniques in psychosomatic disorders. In A. Goldstein & E. Foa (Eds.), *Handbook of behavioral interventions* (pp. 186–265). New York: Wiley.

Canter, A., Kondo, C. Y., & Knott, J. R. (1975). A comparison of EMG feedback and progressive muscle relaxation training in anxiety neurosis. *British Journal of Psychiatry*, *127*, 470–477.

Carlson, J. G., & Hatfield, E. (1992). *The psychology of emotion*. Fort Worth, TX: Harcourt Brace Jovanovich.

Cram, J. (1991). *Clinical EMG for surface recordings* (Vol. 2). Nevada City, CA: Clinical Resources.

Darwin, C. (1965). *The expression of emotion in man and animals*. Chicago: University of Chicago Press. (Original work published 1872)

Defares, P. B., & Grossman, P. (1988). Hyperventilation, anxiety, and coping with stress. In P. B. Defares (Ed.), *Stress and anxiety* (Vol. 11, pp. 127–140). New York: Hemisphere.

DeGood, D. E., & Chisholm, R. C. (1977). Multiple response comparison of parietal EEG and frontalis EMG biofeedback. *Psychophysiology*, *14*, 258–265.

Dubos, R. (1965). *Man adapting*. New Haven, CT: Yale University Press.

Eddington, A. S. (1955). The domain of physical science. In J. Needham (Ed.), *Science, religion, and reality* (pp. 193–222). New York: Braziller.

Ekman, P., Levenson, R. W., & Friesen, W. V. (1983). Autonomic nervous system activity distinguishes among emotions. *Science*, *221*, 1208–1210.

Everly, G. S. (1989). *A clinical guide to the treatment of the human stress response*. New York: Plenum Press.

Fahrion, S. L., & Norris, P. A. (1990). Self-regulation of anxiety. *Bulletin of the Menninger Clinic*, *54*, 217–231.

Finley, W. W., Niman, C., Standley, J., & Ender, P. (1976). Frontal EMG biofeedback training of athetoid cerebral palsy patients. *Biofeedback and Self-Regulation*, *1*, 169–182.

Frank, J. D. (1961). *Persuasion and healing*. Baltimore: Johns Hopkins University Press.

Frankenhaeuser, M. (1983). The sympathetic–adrenal and pituitary–adrenal responses to challenge. In T. M. Dembroski, T. H. Schmidt, & G. Blumchen (Eds.), *Biobehavioral bases of coronary heart disease* (pp. 91–105). Basel: Karger.

Gellhorn, E. (1958). The influence of curare on hypothalamic excitability and the electroencephalogram. *Electroencephalography and Clinical Neurophysiology*, *10*, 697–703.

Gellhorn, E. (1964). Motion and emotion. *Psychological Review*, *71*, 457–472.

Gellhorn, E. (1967). *Principles of autonomic–somatic integrations*. Minneapolis: University of Minnesota Press.

Gellhorn, E., & Kiely, W. F. (1972). Mystical states of consciousness: Neurophysiological and clinical aspects. *Journal of Nervous and Mental Disease*, *154*, 399–405.

Germana, J. (1969). Central efferent processes and autonomic–behavioral integration. *Psychophysiology*, *6*, 78–90.

Glaus, K. D., & Kotses, H. (1983). Facial muscle tension influences lung airway resistance; limb muscle tension does not. *Biological Psychology*, *17*, 105–120.

Goldstein, I. B. (1972). Electromyography: A measure of skeletal muscle response. In N. S. Greenfield & R. A. Sternbach (Eds.), *Handbook of psychophysiology* (pp. 329–365). New York: Holt, Rinehart & Winston.

Hauri, P., & Linde, S. (1990). *No more sleepless nights*. New York: Wiley.

Hess, W. R. (1954). *Diencephalon: Autonomic and extrapyramidal functions*. New York: Grune & Stratton.

Hiebert, B. A., & Fitzsimmons, G. (1981). A comparison of EMG feedback and alternative anxiety treatment programs. *Biofeedback and Self-Regulation*, *6*, 501–516.

Jacobson, E. (1938). *Progressive relaxation* (2nd ed.). Chicago: University of Chicago Press.

Jacobson, E. (1970). *Modern treatment of tense patients*. Springfield, IL: Charles C Thomas.

Kamiya, J. (1969). Operant control of the EEG alpha rhythm and some of its reported effects on consciousness. In C. T. Tart (Ed.), *Altered states of consciousness* (pp. 507–517). New York: Wiley.

Kapleau, P. (1980). *The three pillars of Zen*. Garden City, NY: Doubleday/Anchor.

Kotses, H., Harver, A., Segreto, J., Glaus, K. D., Creer, T. L., & Young, G. A. (1991). Long-term effects of biofeedback-induced facial relaxation on measures of asthma severity in children. *Biofeedback and Self-Regulation*, *16*, 1–21.

Lavallée, Y. J., Lamontagne, Y., Pinard, G., Annable, L., & Tétreault, L. (1977). Effects of EMG feedback, diazepam and their combination on chronic anxiety. *Journal of Psychosomatic Research*, *21*, 65–71.

Leaf, W. B., & Gaarder, K. R. (1971). A simplified electromyographic feedback apparatus for relaxation training. *Journal of Behavior Therapy and Experimental Psychiatry*, *2*, 39–43.

Ley, R. (1987). Panic disorder: A hyperventilation interpretation. In L. Michelson & L. M. Ascher (Eds.), *Anxiety and stress disorders*: *Cognitive–behavioral assessment and treatment* (pp. 191–212). New York: Guilford Press.

Luthe, W. (1970). *Autogenic therapy*: *Vol. 4. Research and theory*. New York: Grune & Stratton.

Luthe, W., & Schultz, J. H. (1969). *Autogenic therapy*: *Vol. 3. Applications in psychotherapy*. New York: Grune & Stratton.

Malmo, R. B. (1975). *On emotions, needs, and our archaic brain*. New York: Holt, Rinehart & Winston.

Martin, I., & Grosz, H. J. (1964). Hypnotically induced emotions. *Archives of General Psychiatry*, *11*, 203–213.

Mason, J. W. (1972). Organization of psychoendocrine mechanisms. In N. S. Greenfield & R. A. Sternbach (Eds.), *Handbook of psychophysiology* (pp. 3–91). New York: Holt, Rinehart & Winston.

McGuigan, F. J. (1981). *Calm down: A guide to stress and tension control*. Englewood Cliffs, NJ: Prentice-Hall.

Middaugh, S. J. (1990). On clinical efficacy: Why biofeedback does—and does not—work. *Biofeedback and Self-Regulation*, *15*, 191–208.

Mielke, A. (1973). *Surgery of the facial nerve*. Philadelphia: W. B. Saunders.

Obrist, P. A., Webb, R. A., Sutterer, J. R., & Howard, J. L. (1970). The cardiac–somatic relationship: Some reformulations. *Psychophysiology*, *6*, 569–587.

Peek, C. J. (1987). A primer of biofeedback instrumentation. In M. S. Schwartz & Associates, *Biofeedback*: *A practitioner's guide* (pp. 73–127). New York: Guilford Press.

Peffer, K. E. (1989). Equipment needs for psychotherapists. In J. V. Basmajian (Ed.), *Biofeedback*: *Principles and practice for clinicians* (3rd ed., pp. 337–345). Baltimore: Williams & Wilkins.

Penfield, W., & Rasmussen, T. (1950). *The cerebral cortex of man: A clinical study of localization of function*. New York: Macmillan.

Peper, E. (1976). Passive attention: The gateway to consciousness and autonomic control. In E. Peper, S. Ancoli, & M. Quinn (Eds.), *Mind/body integration*: *Readings in Biofeedback* (pp. 119–124). New York: Plenum Press.

Rosenfeld, J. P. (1990). Applied psychophysiology and biofeedback of event-related potentials (brain waves): Historical perspective, review, future directions. *Biofeedback and Self-Regulation*, *15*, 99–119.

Rubin, L. R. (1977). *Reanimation of the paralyzed face*. St. Louis: C. V. Mosby.

Sainsbury, P., & Gibson, J. F. (1954). Symptoms of anxiety and tension and the accompanying physiological changes in the muscular system. *Journal of Neurology, Neurosurgery and Psychiatry*, *17*, 216.

Schultz, J. H., & Luthe, W. (1959). *Autogenic training: A psychophysiologic approach in psychotherapy*. New York: Grune & Stratton.

Shagass, C., & Malmo, R. (1954). Psychodynamic themes and localized muscular tension during psychotherapy. *Psychosomatic Medicine*, *16*, 295–313.

Shapiro, F. (1989). Efficacy of the eye movement desensitization procedure in the treatment of traumatic memories. *Journal of Traumatic Stress*, *2*, 199–223.

Stoyva, J. M. (1989). Autogenic training and biofeedback combined: A reliable method for the induction of general relaxation. In J. V. Basmajian (Ed.), *Biofeedback: Principles and practice for clinicians* (3rd ed., pp. 169–185). Baltimore: Williams & Wilkins.

Stoyva, J. M., & Budzynski, T. H. (1974). Cultivated low arousal—an anti-stress response? In L. V. DiCara (Ed.), *Recent advances in limbic and autonomic nervous systems research* (pp. 369–394). New York: Plenum Press.

Stoyva, J. M., & Carlson, J. G. (1993). A coping/rest model of relaxation and stress management. In L. Goldberger & S. Breznitz (Eds.), *Handbook of stress: Theoretical and clinical aspects* (2nd ed.). New York: Free Press/Macmillan.

Stoyva, J. M., & Kamiya, J. (1968). Electrophysiological studies of dreaming as a prototype of a new strategy in the study of consciousness. *Psychological Review*, *75*, 192–205.

Strupp, H. (1970). Specific versus nonspecific factors in psychology and the problem of control. *Archives of General Psychiatry*, *23*, 393–401.

Townsend, R. E., House, J. F., & Addario, D. (1975). A comparison of biofeedback-mediated relaxation and group therapy in the treatment of chronic anxiety. *American Journal of Psychiatry*, *132*, 598–601.

Venables, P. H., & Wing, J. K. (1962). Level of arousal and the subclassification of schizophrenia. *Archives of General Psychiatry*, *7*, 114–119.

Wenger, M. A., & Cullen, T. D. (1972). Studies of autonomic balance in children and adults. In N. S. Greenfield & R. A. Sternbach (Eds.), *Handbook of psychophysiology* (pp. 535–569). New York: Holt, Rinehart & Winston.

Wolpe, J. (1958). *Psychotherapy by reciprocal inhibition*. Stanford, CA: Stanford University Press.

10

The Role of Respiration in Stress and Stress Control: Toward a Theory of Stress as a Hypoxic Phenomenon

ROBERT FRIED

Current practice in clinical psychophysiology centers largely on the behavioral treatment of symptoms and disorders variously classified as "psychosomatic" or as "stress-related." They either currently impair health or functioning, or pose a determinable risk of doing so in the foreseeable future. A compendium of these symptoms and disorders constitutes an impressive list. It ranges through all known organ systems—for instance, cardiovascular (hypertension, angina, etc.), digestive (gastritis, irritable bowel, etc.), pulmonary (hyperventilation, asthma, etc.), and neurological (migraine, etc.). It also includes psychiatric symptoms (tension, anxiety, etc.), insomnia, libidinal dysfunction, and a host of other problems.

In fact, it is a fairly common though by no means universal practice to assign a "psychosomatic" or "stress" component to virtually all disorders. Assigning one of these labels to persons suffering from a physical disorder sometimes appears to hinge more on the degree to which a clinician is willing to risk offending than on any scientific basis: "Stress" implies success, whereas "psychosomatic" implies emotional problems, and "malingering" (which may also be used in this context) is even more pejorative. Part of this casual labeling may be due to the vague etiology of most diseases, particularly those that are unconnected to a known biological pathogen. But much of it has resulted from incoherence in the definition of stress and its putative role in illness.

We now, however, do have enough clues to the existence of an entity we term "stress" to act as if we knew what it is. And we can point to various models of it, especially the "general adaptation syndrome" of Selye (1974). But a first-hand look at Selye's definition is enlightening: Selye defines stress as "the nonspecific response of the body to any demand made upon it" (1974, p. 27). It is more than "merely nervous tension," and he ultimately goes on to categorize well over 1000 physiological things

For further information about the J & J I-430 Physiological Monitoring System, or the Ohmeda 4700 OxiCap CO_2 monitor, please write the author at 1040 Park Avenue, New York, NY 10028.

that happen in stress and adaptation. Thus his theory is really only a description of what one may reasonably expect in the chronic exposure to stressors, and the body's attempts to adapt and return to "normality." It does nothing to explain its various sources.

What is this nonspecific response? The answer to this question cannot hinge on the conventional meaning of the word "response," which is usually viewed as a unitary composite of elements occurring during some specifiable and limited time epoch; rather, it depends on the meaning of "response" as a more or less set sequence of events evolving over the course of time, and initiated by a more or less fixed event. The initial elements of this sequence appear to be the same for all individuals, but the threshold for the appearance of symptoms, as well as their diversity, may depend upon individual organic tolerances and predispositions.

I agree with Gantt (1970) and other Pavlovians, who have hypothesized that all nonspecific stress reactions begin with an orienting response in which activity, especially breathing, is inhibited; this is followed by an excitatory increased metabolic demand for oxygen. I hypothesize here that the pivotal factor is the ability of the body to sustain intermittent orientation and sympathetic arousal, and to meet increased metabolic demand for oxygen. The evidence strongly suggests that it cannot. Physiologically, we are like quarter horses: We can run fast, but not for very long. If the hypothesis is correct, then "the nonspecific response of the body to any demand made on it" is not so nonspecific after all; it is increased tissue air hunger, and all that this entails.

Hypoxia—The Intervening Variable

Increased metabolic activity requires increased tissue oxygenation, and there are several ways in which the body can accomplish this. First, blood can circulate more frequently, and it can do so under greater pressure to favor diffusion into tissues. Second, the oxygen transport system can adjust to increased oxygen delivery. These two factors are pivotal in increased metabolic demand; their long-term elicitation and compensatory homeostatic adjustments give rise to physiological by-products favoring a compromise that may result in chronic graded hypoxia (Blass & Gibson, 1979; Fried, 1987b, 1990a, in press; Katz, 1982).

"Hypoxia" is decreased oxygen availability. It differs from "anoxia," in which there is no oxygen at all. Anoxia leads to asphyxiation within a matter of a few minutes. Hypoxia may therefore be "graded," meaning that it may occur in varying sublethal degrees. When metabolic demand exceeds oxygen availability, the resulting hypoxia raises the ratio of anaerobic to aerobic metabolism, favoring a concomitant increase in blood lactate levels and leading to lactic acidosis (Cohen & Woods, 1976; Huckabee, 1961; Kreisberg, 1980; Park & Arief, 1980). Lactic acidosis is typically compensated for by increased pulmonary ventilation, causing hyperventilation (Edwards & Clode, 1970; Gamble, 1982; Shapiro, Harrison, & Walton, 1982).

Thus, the recommendation that hyperventilation be viewed as putative evidence of hypoxia—hyperventilation being sometimes characterized as "one extreme of a continuum of more or less normal stress reactions" (van Dixhoorn & Duivenvoorden, 1985, p. 200)—is consistent with the practice of stress reduction by techniques that emphasize breathing (Badawi, Wallace, Orme-Johnson, & Rouzere, 1984; Beary, Benson, & Klemchuck, 1974; Benson, Beary, & Carol, 1974; Fried, 1987a, 1990b, 1990c, in press; Morse, Martin, Furst, & Dubin, 1977; Patel, 1975; Shapiro, 1982; Suess, Barney-Alexander, Smith, Sweeney, & Marion, 1980; van Dixhoorn, 1990; Wallace, 1972). As background for a further discussion of stress as a hypoxic phenomenon, I now provide a simplified explanation of respiration, ventilation, and the oxygen (O_2) and carbon dioxide (CO_2) transport systems, as follows.

The Factors Involved in Breathing

The primary role of breathing is to supply the body with O_2. It has two major features: respiration and ventilation. Respiration oxygenates body cells, and ventilation removes excess CO_2. We usually consider respiration a behavior involving two processes of the lungs: inspiration and expiration. Breathing also involves dynamic and static pulmonary air volumes. Dynamic volumes are those that involve air moving into (inspiratory tidal volume) or out of (expiratory end-tidal volume) the lungs. Static volume is the component that remains more or less as dead space in the lungs.

During inspiration, air fills the lungs; in the alveoli, globe-shaped compartments at the end of pulmonary airways, O_2 diffuses into blood circulation because its pressure is greater than that in blood. Conversely, CO_2 pressure, which is greater in blood, diffuses from blood into the alveoli and is expelled with expiration; this is ventilation. When O_2 diffuses into the blood, most of it passes through the membrane of the red blood cells (RBCs), where it binds to hemoglobin (Hb) to form oxyhemoglobin (OHb). The degree of affinity of Hb for O_2 is a function of the pH of the Hb, which is controlled by buffering the major blood acid, hydrogen ion (H^+). The density of H^+ is related to CO_2 flux in the body.

The CO_2 transport system involves the enzyme carbonic anhydrase and the formation in the blood of volatile carbonic acid and bicarbonate. Both the RBCs and kidneys contain carbonic anhydrase, which helps CO_2 to "hydrolyze" (to combine with water); that is, CO_2 combines with water to form carbonic acid, which can readily break down to H^+, and bicarbonate. Because of carbonic anhydrase, RBCs can more efficiently carry CO_2 as carbonic acid.

Normal pH is about 7.4, slightly basic or alkaline. Decrease of alkalinity favors dissociation of OHb, whereas increased alkalinity, or alkalosis, favors retention of O_2 by OHb. Ordinarily, maintenance of acid–base balance involves the lungs and kidneys. The lungs account for about 85% of this process by expelling CO_2 and carbonic acid; the kidneys can expel "base excess"—bicarbonate. Thus, most of the work of regulating the acid–base balance of the body is controlled on a breath-by-breath basis; the function of Hb, which is extremely intolerant of even very small changes in pH, is thus likewise bound to breath. The O_2 available from each breath is determined by the characteristics of only a few of the breaths preceding it. Cells in the body, reached by the blood, have a lower pH because local metabolism increases CO_2 concentration. Greater acidity favors OHb dissociation, and O_2 diffuses into the cells, whereas CO_2 diffuses back into blood, where its concentration is initially lower. Most of the CO_2 is transported by Hb.

At the turn of this century, Bohr, Hasselbach, and Krogh (1904) described the effect of CO_2 on blood. OHb affinity is a function of CO_2 concentration in blood—that is, the "partial pressure" of CO_2 in arterial blood (PaCO$_2$). In a mixture of gases, the partial pressure, P, is the fractional component contributed by any one of them to the total gas pressure. For instance, barometric pressure is typically 760 mm Hg, or torr, at sea level. O_2 constitutes about 21% of the gases in atmospheric air; consequently, its partial pressure (PO$_2$) is a little over 150 torr—about one-fifth of 760 torr. Normal alveolar concentration of CO_2 in the average person at rest is about 5.00%, or 38 torr (760 × 0.05).

Since PaCO$_2$ affects pH, OHb dissociation is pH-related. Figure 10.1 shows the OHb dissociation curve (ODC) at different values of pH, at normal body temperature (the curve also shifts to the left when body temperature rises, creating, in children, a hypoxic crisis that may lead to febrile seizure). "Dissociation" is decreased O_2–Hb affinity, or the tendency to form deoxyhemoglobin (i.e., desaturated Hb). The curve in the center represents percentage of OHb (saturation) when pH is normal (7.4). At 50% O_2 saturation, PO$_2$ in blood can be expected to be about 27 mm Hg (torr). But if the pH rises (alkalosis) to 7.6, PO$_2$ drops to about 22 torr. When pH drops to 7.2, PO$_2$ will be about 32 torr.

The shift of the ODC to the left is called the "Bohr effect." Under ordinary circumstances, shifts in pH are only momentary, because the homeostatic lung–kidney system will compensate blood pH. But as Kerr, Dalton, and Gliebe (1937) described, in what is generally regarded as the pioneering study of hyperventilation, pH shifts may be profound in some persons and may lead to an astonishing array of symptoms. In the long run, blood pH will be near normal and will not indicate respiratory alkalosis, but excretion of bicarbonate will.

Thus, although a person cannot survive long without O_2, the critical variable in the psychophysiology of stress is not O_2 but CO_2; as will be seen, this occurs for more reasons than the Bohr effect.

Normal Breathing

Taking into account the differences between men and women, the Radford Nomograph (Radford, 1955; see Figure 10.2) estimates breathing at rest in normal in-

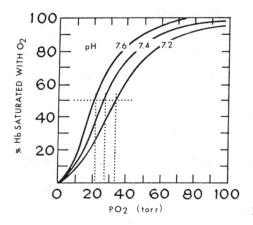

FIGURE 10.1. Blood oxygen dissociation curve.

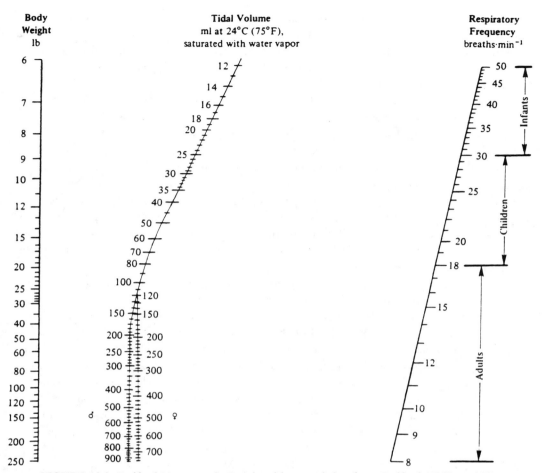

FIGURE 10.2. Radford Nomograph. Reprinted by permission from Radford (1955, p. 451).

dividuals. A nomograph·is an alignment chart for two or more variables so that a straight line cutting all of them intersects related values of each. In this case, a straight line between body weight and breathing rate estimates "tidal volume" (V_t), or the amount of air per breath. V_t multiplied by breathing rate is "minute volume" (V_{min}). Thus, as can be seen in Figure 10.2, a man weighing 150 pounds and breathing 12 times per minute should have a V_t of 500 ml; multiplied by 12, this equals a V_{min} of 6000 ml. In a person with normal metabolism at rest, hyperventilation will obtain with either constant breathing rate and higher V_t, or from constant V_t and increased breathing rate.

Hyperventilation

In an average normal person at rest, alveolar partial pressure of CO_2 (PCO_2) below 38 torr is the commonly accepted criterion for hyperventilation (Comroe, 1974). It is often erroneously defined simply as rapid and shallow breathing. The term "hyperventilation" does not describe behavior, but its outcome—"hypocapnia," or decreased alveolar CO_2. Depending on metabolic CO_2 production, it is possible to breathe rapidly, yet not to be hyperventilating. When hypocapnia reduces arterial blood CO_2 ($PaCO_2$), the condition is called "hypocarbia." The correlation between alveolar PCO_2 and $PaCO_2$, where they equilibrate in the lungs, is about $+.93$ (Collier, Affeldt, & Farr, 1955; Comroe, 1974).

The physiological sequelae of hypocapnia should be of considerable relevance to clinical psychophysiologists concerned with stress reduction. Decreased alveolar PCO_2 (i.e., respiratory alkalosis) requires homeostatic adjustments, many of which result in "stress symptoms." Numerous clinicians employ a "hyperventilation challenge" (Hardonk & Beumer, 1979)—usually having a client breathe fast and deeply for about 2 minutes—to induce hyperventilation-related symptoms. (I recommend against this procedure, because I agree with many physiologists who consider it hazardous.) But when does hyperventilation "cause" symptoms? In my experience, it does so when alveolar PCO_2 drops below 28 torr during a routine "challenge" or early breathing training procedure, or is chronically about 30 torr or less. There are, of course, individual differences in tolerance.

Hypocapnia impairs all organ systems, including muscle, myocardial tissue, and nerves, but especially the blood and arteries. First, it shifts the ODC unfavorably to the left (the Bohr effect); second, it promotes compensatory homeostatic increase in RBC organic phosphate. (RBC organic phosphate increases OHb dissociation by competing with O_2 for binding on Hb, thereby releasing more O_2 into tissues and cells.) In addition, hypocapnia causes profound cerebral and peripheral arterial vasoconstriction, reducing blood flow to body extremities and to the brain (Darrow & Graf, 1945; Kety & Schmidt, 1948; Penfield & Jasper, 1954). This is especially important, since it has been shown unequivocally that unlike arterial blood CO_2 concentration in systemic circulation (also under the influence of sympathetic stimulation and catecholamines), brain arterial blood CO_2 concentration is the only mechanism that affects brain arterial caliber and blood flow (Heistad, Marcus, & Abboud, 1978).

Stress and Breathing

One of the most obvious features of stress is that it affects breathing. Although it is not invariably the case, persons who complain of stress often have breathing-related complaints: "I can't seem to catch my breath—it is unsatisfactory," "I can't seem to get enough air," "I huff and puff." They may also show frequent sighing, swallowing, and chest heaving. Alternatively, they may show no discernible breathing movements at all (Fried, 1987b, 1990a).

Remarkably, most of the symptoms of stress are those that are associated with hyperventilation (i.e., disordered breathing and hypocapnia). The list of hyperventilation symptoms provided by Kerr et al. (1937; see also Table 10.1) closely resembles that for panic disorder, as given in the revised third edition of the *Diagnostic and Statistical Manual of Mental Disorders* (DSM-III-R). Yet, for decades, "hyperventilation" was considered symptomatic of *hysteria* (Lowry, 1967). "Stress" was a term in physics, and "neurocirculatory asthenia," "anxiety neurosis," and "neurasthenia" were used to describe an aggregate of symptoms varying only slightly among reports. The list in

TABLE 10.1. Frequency of Hyperventilation Symptoms and Symptoms Associated with Psychoneurosis and Anxiety Neurosis

No. of patients with symptoms similar to the ones now described as associated with hyperventilation	36
No. of patients without these symptoms	14
No. of patients with the following symptoms:	
Weakness and fatigability	18
Numbness and paresthesia	14
Palpitation and increased cardiac rate	12
Dizziness	10
Nausea and vomiting	4
Muscular contractions:	
Twitching, trembling, convulsive states	14
Tetany (not on basis of hypoparathyroidism)	9
Difficulty in swallowing, talking, breathing (pharyngeal–laryngeal spasm)	8
Precordial pain (intercostal muscle and diaphragmatic spasm)	4
Dyspnea (diaphragmatic spasm)	14
Epigastric pain (diaphragmatic spasm)	2
Constipation (spastic colon)	5

Note. Symptoms were described by 50 patients admitted over a 9-year period to the University of California Hospital whose conditions had been diagnosed as psychoneurosis with anxiety neurosis. The figures given above are compiled from the descriptions of the symptoms and signs that were given, and not from the results of formal experimentation. Reprinted by permission of the *Annals of Internal Medicine* from Kerr, Dalton, & Gliebe (1937, p. 983).

Table 10.2, from Wheeler, White, Reed, and Cohen (1950), illustrates this phenomenon; it bears a remarkable resemblance to hyperventilation, anxiety, and stress symptoms. It should do more than raise an eyebrow to note that symptoms of stress and anxiety, as those terms are used today, are rooted in studies that could not satisfactorily differentiate among effort syndrome, neurasthenia, psychoneurosis, anxiety neurosis, and hyperventilation syndrome. An additional controversy centered on whether these had an organic or psychic basis (Fried, in press).

More recently, Hirsch and Bishop (1981) and Grossman (1983), among many investigators, have also linked stress and hyperventilation. According to Grossman,

> variation in breathing pattern may often modulate cardiovascular function in everyday life. . . . However, under certain conditions, self-regulatory processes may break down because of the dissociation of respiratory and cardiovascular functioning (e.g., hyperventilation). Alteration in ventilatory parameters may then induce such changes as reduced parasympathetic cardiac controls . . . and inadequate myocardial and cerebral oxygenation. (1983, p. 284)

A list of the frequency of common hyperventilation symptoms from a subsequent report by Grossman and DeSwart (1984) is given in Table 10.3. Naturally, the stressful effects of hyperventilation cannot be thought to be restricted to the heart and the brain if they do indeed involve "reduced oxygenation," as some of us contend.

The astonishing overlap of hyperventilation, anxiety, and stress symptoms has also been observed in the Nijmegen Questionnaire (van Doorn, Colla, & Folgering, 1982), tested by van Dixhoorn and Duivenvoorden (1985). And Nixon's patient-specific "think test" provided an excellent demonstration that when asked to recall, or "think back to" unpleasant or stressful events they had experienced, patients hyperventilated (Nixon & Freeman, 1988).

TABLE 10.2. Symptoms of Neurocirculatory Asthenia

Symptoms	Patients	Controls
Palpitation	96.7	8.8
Tires easily	95.0	18.6
Breathlessness	90.0	12.7
Nervousness	87.6	26.5
Chest pain	85.0	9.8
Sighing	79.3	15.7
Dizziness	78.3	15.7
Faintness	70.0	11.8
Apprehension	60.7	2.9
Headache	58.3	25.5
Paresthesias	58.2	7.2
Weakness	50.0	3.0
Trembling	53.5	16.7
Breath unsatisfactory	52.7	3.9
Insomnia	52.7	4.0
Unhappiness	50.0	2.1
Shakiness	46.5	15.7
Fatigued all the time	45.1	5.9
Sweating	44.9	33.0
Fear of death	41.8	2.0
Smothering	39.7	3.9
Syncope	36.7	10.8
Flushes	36.2	—
Yawning	34.6	14.0
Pain radiating to left arm	30.0	2.0
Vascular throbbing	29.0	1.1
Dry mouth	25.1	1.1
Nervous chill	24.4	—
Frequency	18.6	2.1
Nightmares	18.3	9.2
Vomiting and diarrhea	14.0	0.0
Anorexia	12.3	3.0
Panting	7.9	—
Paralysis	0.0	0.0
Blindness	0.0	0.0

Note. Reprinted by permission of the American Medical Association from Wheeler, White, Reed, & Cohen (1950, p. 878). © 1950 American Medical Association.

We may reasonably conclude from such studies and many others, that the variegated symptomatology of the hyperventilation syndrome cannot in many instances be distinguished from that of stress, anxiety, panic, and "psychosomatic" disorders. I do not believe that this ambiguity is adventitious, and it is the thesis of this chapter that the psychophysiology of graded hypoxia (and its attendent chronic lacticacidemia) is the factor common to all of them.

For this reason, I have focused many of my clinical and research efforts over the past 10 years to the development of psychophysiological breathing assessment techniques and protocols, as well as of breathing-based therapeutic strategies aimed at correcting the putative metabolic basis of the common stress-related and (currently labeled) psychophysiological disorders. These efforts have been based in large part on

TABLE 10.3. Frequency of Positive Responses to Complaint Items among Hyperventilation Syndrome (HVS) and Non-HVS Subjects

Item	Percent positive responses		Significance level
	HVS Ss	Non-HVS Ss	
Fits of crying	14.5	6.5	0.01
Unable to breathe deeply enough	44.5	33.5	0.03
Suffocating feeling	54.5	41.0	0.009
Rapid heartbeat	41.5	27.0	0.003
Feeling of unrest, panic	54.5	38.5	0.002
Tingling in feet	20.0	17.0	
Nausea	38.0	31.5	
Confused or dream-like feeling	35.0	27.5	
Feeling of heat	42.0	34.0	
Pounding heart	50.0	27.0	0.0000
Stomach cramps	19.0	18.0	
Toe or leg cramps	10.5	12.5	
Shivering	25.5	16.5	
Irregular heartbeat	18.5	11.5	0.07
Tingling in legs	16.0	11.5	
Feeling anxious	30.0	21.0	0.05
Chest pains around heart region	40.0	37.5	
Stiffness in fingers or arms	18.5	13.0	
Cold hands or feet	20.5	20.5	
Feeling of head warmth	29.0	20.0	0.05
Stiffness about mouth	6.5	4.5	
Stomach feels blown up	21.5	18.0	
Pressure or knot in throat	23.0	13.5	0.02
Tingling in arms	20.5	14.0	
Faster or deeper breathing than normal	42.5	18.5	0.0000
Hands tremble	38.5	25.0	0.005
Dizziness	69.0	50.5	0.0002
Stiffness in legs	7.5	5.0	
Blacking out	45.5	35.5	0.05
Tingling in body	5.0	4.0	
Tenseness	51.5	36.5	0.003
Need for air	27.5	16.0	0.008
Fainting	15.0	15.5	
Tingling in fingers	26.5	17.5	0.04
Tiredness	64.0	55.5	0.10
Headaches	47.0	51.0	
Tingling in face	10.0	4.0	0.03

Note. Reprinted by permission from Grossman & DeSwart (1984, p. 100). ©1984 Pergamon Press, Inc.

the substantial published research pointing to (1) the seemingly crucial effect of respiratory psychophysiology on brain function; (2) the consistent reports of breathing-related symptoms in stress and anxiety; and (3) the reportedly successful treatment of these conditions with strategies centering on breathing. The recent development of affordable means of computerized infrared oximetry and capnography has dramatically opened the door to a systematic examination of the role of blood gases in psychophysiology.

Assessment: The Psychophysiological Respiration Profile

In 1984, I proposed a Psychophysiological Hyperventilation Profile (PHVP) on the basis of the consistently reported relationship among breathing, stress, emotions, and psychophysiological disorders (Fried, Fox, Carlton, & Rubin, 1984). It included breathing rate, mode, and rhythm; alveolar PCO_2; electrocardiographic (ECG) respiratory sinus arrhythmia (RSA); and an electroencephalogram (EEG). It was intended to be the basis for communicating such observations as breaths per minute; chest versus abdominal breathing; breathing pattern over time; and alveolar PCO_2 ($PETCO_2$; i.e., percentage of end-tidal CO_2 [$ETCO_2$]) and, by inference, $PaCO_2$. ECG RSA was added as an index of vagal tone (Fried, 1987b; Grossman, 1983; Hirsch & Bishop, 1981; Porges, McCabe, & Yongue, 1982), and the EEG was added because of the near-linear relationship between fundamental frequency and $PaCO_2$ (Lennox, Gibbs, & Gibbs, 1938).

Since 1984, many technological innovations have made it possible to update the PHVP, and the second-generation Psychophysiological Respiration Profile (PRP) has taken its place. A description of the PRP—its development, testing, and application—follows.

Test Population

The PHVP and $PETCO_2$ biofeedback methods (developed at the ICD—International Center for the Disabled, New York, NY, for behavioral control of seizures; see Fried et al., 1984; Fried, Fox, & Carlton, 1990) were refined and used to treat psychophysiological and stress-related disorders in persons referred to the Stress and Biofeedback Clinic of the Institute for Rational–Emotive Therapy (IRET), New York, NY, where I became director in 1985 (Fried, 1987b, 1990a, in press). These persons were from all walks of life (though predominantly professionals) and ranged in age from 19 to 81 years. About two-thirds were women.

Stress Symptoms

With few exceptions, stress sufferers reported various combinations of the symptoms common to those of the hyperventilation syndrome:

- Tension (a "feeling of tension," muscle ache)
- Irritability, low frustration tolerance
- Anxiety (apprehension, heightened vigilance)
- Dyspnea (inability to catch one's breath, choking sensation, feeling of suffocation, frequent sighing, chest heaving, lump in throat)
- Fatigue, tiredness, burnout
- Insomnia
- Heart palpitations (pounding in chest, seemingly accelerated pulse rate, sensation of heaviness or weight on the chest, diffuse chest pain)

- Depression, restlessness, nervousness
- Dizzy spells, shakiness, trembling
- Coldness of the hands and feet, and occasionally tingling sensations
- Inability to concentrate
- Bloating

In a number of cases, these "stress symptoms" were accompanied by panic attacks, but most commonly physical complaints and symptoms of organic disease were reported, including the following (this is only a partial list):

- Allergies
- Anemia
- Angina
- Arthritis
- Arrhythmias
- Asthma
- Colitis
- Constipation
- Diabetes
- Gastritis
- Headache/migraine
- Heart disease
- Hypertension
- Irritable bowel
- Musculoskeletal trauma and pain
- Raynaud's disease
- Seizures (idiopathic and organic)
- Temporomandibular joint pain, bruxism

The procedures were also applied to persons suffering from psychological disorders, including anxiety, panic, simple phobias, agoraphobia, depression, and obsessive compulsive disorder (OCD). In the case of OCD, the procedures were applied for counterarousal or counterconditioning.

Apparatus

$ETCO_2$ is measured with a small nasal catheter ($\frac{1}{8}$ inch x $\frac{1}{32}$ inch, 6 inches long), inserted about $\frac{1}{4}$ inch into a nostril and held in place by being taped to the upper lip. This nasal catheter segment is attached to a fitting on the tubing conducting to the capnometer. Presterilized latex surgical tubing, packaged in 50-foot rolls, is precut to 6-inch lengths for the nasal segment. *This tubing, in contact with the nose, must be discarded immediately after each use. To protect the client from infection, it must never be reused.*

The capnometer was initially a P. K. Morgan infrared gas analyzer coupled to an Apple II+ computer; it provided average and peak CO_2 per screen epoch, and translated $ETCO_2$ as a trace on a video monitor. This outmoded arrangement supported the PHVP, but it did not permit multiparametric analysis and display, and was discarded as soon as advanced technology became available. However, some of the illustrative tracings provided below were made with it.

The present arrangement employs the same means as the earlier one to conduct end-tidal breath to the capnometer. An Ohmeda 4700 OxiCap is coupled to a computer via a J & J Instruments I-430 Physiological Monitoring System Interface isolation amplifier module (I-801). After a number of such units were examined, the Ohmeda 4700 OxiCap (see Figure 10.3) was chosen for its ease of operation, modest cost, and versatility, which permit its alternative use as a free-standing biofeedback instrument. Alveolar PCO_2 in torr (or $PETCO_2$) pattern trace, arterial blood O_2 saturation (SaO_2), breathing rate, and pulse rate are all displayed on the instrument screen, with programmable data storage and trend analyses.

(A reminder on nomenclature may be in order here. The partial pressure of CO_2 in alveolar air is denoted as PCO_2, in end-tidal breath as $ETCO_2$, and in arterial blood as $PaCO_2$. These values are typically given in torr. PCO_2 and $ETCO_2$ are often interchanged because of the high positive correlation between them. However, when $ETCO_2$ is given in percent, it is percentage of end-tidal CO_2, or $PETCO_2$. Thus, PCO_2 or $ETCO_2$ at 38 torr equals 5.00% $PETCO_2$. $PETCO_2 = 0.05$ means $\frac{1}{2}$% $ETCO_2$.)

The J & J I-430 (see Figure 10.4) will operate with any computer having an RS-232 port. The software was written for IBM-compatible PS/2, PC AT, and XT computers with EGA or VGA monitors. The present computer is an AGI 286-12, with an Everex VGA 400 monitor coupled to an Epson LQ 850 printer. I have given considerable thought to the choice of a physiological monitoring interface system. I chose and recommend the J & J I-430 because I have found it to be versatile and affordable. Furthermore, it is the *only* psychophysiological monitoring system

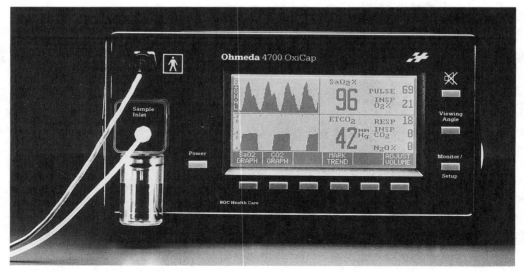

FIGURE 10.3. Ohmeda 4700 OxiCap CO_2 monitor. Upper left quadrant shows pulse waveform; upper right quadrant shows SaO_2 and pulse rate; lower left quadrant shows $ETCO_2$ waveform; and lower right quadrant shows $ETCO_2$ in torr.

FIGURE 10.4. J & J I-430 Physiological Monitoring System. A sample unit is shown with eight preamplifiers. These units can be configued for any desired physiological modalities.

that recognizes, displays, and analyzes blood gas data. In monitoring and biofeedback applications, I invert the PETCO$_2$ trace for convenience, and set screen epoch duration at 30 seconds. Normal PCO$_2$ is 38 torr, or about 5% ETCO$_2$ (or PETCO$_2$ = 5.00).

Arterial Blood Oxihemoglobin Saturation

The delivery of O$_2$ to body tissue depends on its availability in the atmosphere, its inspiration into the lungs, its absorption into blood, its transport by the blood, and its release at the desired site. One of the factors affecting this transport and release is the pH of the Hb molecule to which it is bound.

In most ordinary clinical psychophysiology situations, barring pulmonary obstructive disease, O$_2$ is available in atmospheric air and gets into the alveoli with varying degrees of efficiency. There it is taken up by Hb when it diffuses into blood. Normally, about 95–98% of RBC Hb will be of the OHb, or saturated, type. As noted above, arterial blood O$_2$ saturation is denoted as SaO$_2$.

When PCO$_2$ decreases (hypocapnia), SaO$_2$ elevated above normal indicates a left-shifted ODC, and therefore less O$_2$ delivery to tissue. By contrast, normal PCO$_2$ with elevated SaO$_2$ reflects increased alveolar air pressure and O$_2$ perfusion into the blood—a goal of deep diaphragmatic breathing training. Thus, monitoring SaO$_2$, given PETCO$_2$, provides an indication of O$_2$ delivery to the body and brain tissues.

The Ohmeda 4700 Oxicap oximeter sensor is attached to the index finger of the right hand. The analog output of the oximeter is likewise coupled to an ISA module (I-801) of the J & J I-430 System Interface. The oximeter readout is whole-integer percent SaO$_2$, that is, the percentage of saturated Hb or OHb. But the analog output yields SaO$_2$ to 0.1%. Thus, the computer can display a trace of SaO$_2$, which reflects changing alveolar CO$_2$ concentrations with increased pulmonary blood O$_2$ perfusion, over *each* breathing cycle.

Chest versus Abdominal Breathing Mode and Inspiration–Expiration Breathing Pattern

Strain gauges are held in place by Velcro-fastened cloth bands, one around the chest and another around the abdomen. The pneumograph module (R-301) of the J & J I-430 permits display of trace analogs of the magnitude of the displacement of the chest and abdomen. With biofeedback, a client can also learn a breathing pattern favoring increased V_t by increasing abdominal and decreasing chest excursion during inspiration, and pulling back the abdomen during expiration. This outcome is supported by the observation that if metabolism remains fairly constant, and other factors remain equal, there is a direct relationship between V_{min} and $PETCO_2$: As V_{min} increases, breathing rate decreases, and as breathing rate decreases, $PETCO_2$ normalizes.

The J & J I-430 system does not have a module for volumetric observation. But in most cases, other than in asthma or other pulmonary disease, this is not a problem. The Radford Nomograph (see Figure 10.2) can be used to estimate V_t and V_{min} where necessary. Or forced expiratory volume can be determined with a Spiropet windmill-type spirometer. This measure is taken to estimate the inspiratory limiting effect of chronic dysponetic "bracing" on V_t, common in stress.

Pulse Rate and Respiratory Sinus Arrhythmia

The plethysmograph sensor (PS-400) is attached to the right index finger. The plethysmograph module (P-401) of the J & J I-430 Interface permits observation of beat-to-beat pulse rate variation over time, indicating RSA over the breathing cycle. Vagal tone is an important indication of the status of cardiopulmonary reflexes (Angelone & Coulter, 1964; Davies & Neilson, 1967; Fried, 1987b; 1990a; in press; Melcher, 1976; Porges et al., 1982).

Hand and Head-Apex Temperature

A thermal sensor is taped to the little finger of the nondominant hand. Another is attached to the scalp apex; the hair, where appropriate, is parted, and the thermal probe is placed on the scalp. A cotton wad is placed over the probe and held in place with bobby pins. If the person is bald, the thermistor is taped to the scalp. The rationale for the scalp attachment is derived from reports that increased blood flow in the brain is associated with increased "local" temperature (Gerard, 1937; Jacquy, Piraux, Noel, & Henriet, 1979; Schmidt & Hendrix, 1937; Tachibana, Kuramoto, Inanaga, & Ikemi, 1967). Moreover, cerebral blood flow increases with normocapnia.

It is generally held that warm hands are better than cold hands and that anything below 85.0°F at normal room temperature is not too good. Fortunately, Blanchard, Morill, Wittrock, Scharff, and Jaccard (1989) have recently published norms tables of hand temperatures in several symptom groups as well as in a normal control group. This is most helpful, especially since the symptoms are stress-related (i.e., headache, hypertension, and irritable bowel syndrome).

Blood Pressure

Although blood pressure decreases with deep diaphragmatic breathing and normocapnia (Fried, 1987b), it is seldom monitored as part of the PRP unless hypertension is a primary treatment consideration.

The Profile

A PRP is obtained on the first visit, before training begins. It typically consists of the following parameters:

- Breathing:
    - Rate
    - Mode (chest vs. abdominal)
    - Pattern or rhythm (inspiration–expiration ratio)
    - PETCO$_2$
    - SaO$_2$
- Heart
    - Pulse rate
    - Interbeat interval distribution (RSA)
    - (In rare instances) ECG, lead I
- Circulation:
    - Hand and scalp-apex temperature

A sample profile is shown in Figure 10.5. This 27-year-old professional woman with periodic "stress," anxiety, and mild depression was showing hyperventilation. Her breathing rate was 12 per minute, and PETCO$_2$ = 4.1; SaO$_2$ was slightly elevated at 98.6%; chest excursions (F2) predominated over abdominal ones (F3). Heart rate was normal (68.2 beats per minute), and there was some RSA; pulse rate rose and fell somewhat with the breathing cycle. Head temperature (D1) was normal at 92.1°F, while hand temperature (C1) was somewhat decreased (85°F).

Figure 10.6 shows a modified profile before the first breathing training trial in a 32-year-old woman reporting stress, and Figure 10.7 shows it during breathing/relaxation training. As Figure 10.6 indicates, her pretraining breathing rate was 18 per minute (screen epoch duration was 30 seconds); PETCO$_2$ was 4.3, or 33 torr; SaO$_2$ was 99.8%; pulse rate was 68; hand temperature was 79.5°F; and scalp-apex temperature was 92.8°F (in a room at about 76°F). She was definitely hyperventilating. Her breathing rate was elevated (tachypnea) and CO$_2$ was low (hypocapnia). Judging from her hand temperature, there was profound peripheral vasoconstriction. But her pulse rate was relatively low because she was a runner. At 99.8%, SaO$_2$ was elevated above normal (95–98%) suggesting a left-shifted ODC consistent with hypocapnic alkalosis (see Figure 10.1).

After 10 minutes of deep diaphragmatic breathing training (see Figure 10.7), this woman's breathing rate was down to 6 per minute. But her respiration had not adjusted yet; though breathing was "deeper," there was still chest movement, and loss

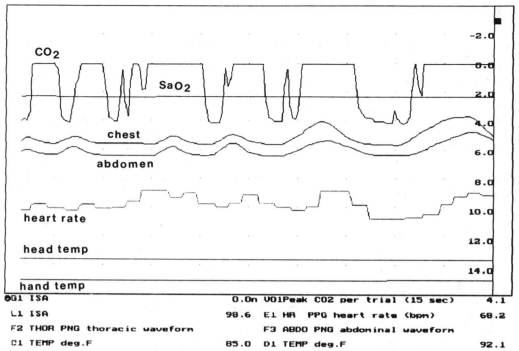

FIGURE 10.5. Sample profile showing PETCO$_2$, SaO$_2$, chest and abdominal excursion, heart rate, and hand and head temperature.

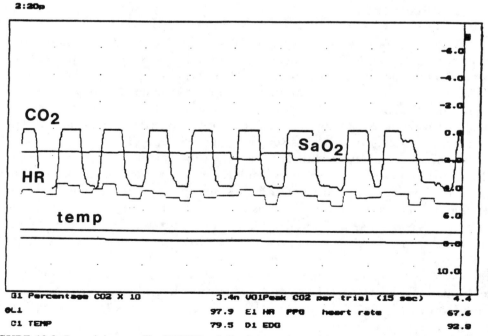

FIGURE 10.6. Pretraining profile (PETCO$_2$, SaO$_2$, heart rate, and hand and head temperature) of a 32-year-old woman reporting stress.

2:30p

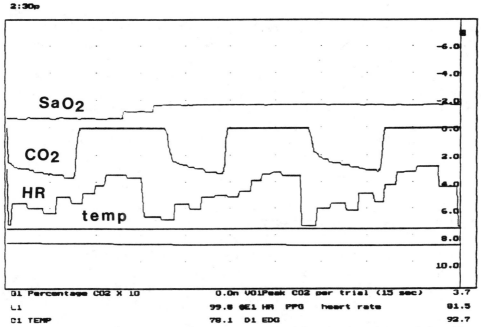

Q1 Percentage CO2 X 10	0.On VO1Peak CO2 per trial (15 sec)	3.7
L1	99.8 @E1 HR PPG heart rate	81.5
C1 TEMP	78.1 D1 EDG	92.7

FIGURE 10.7. Profile of the same woman after 10 minutes of training, showing a decrease in breathing rate from 18 to 6 per minute, with a pronounced increase in SaO_2 and distinct RSA.

of CO_2 continued (PETCO$_2$ was 3.7, or about 28 torr). Hand and scalp-apex temperature dropped somewhat with lower PCO$_2$, and SaO_2 rose about 1% with increased alkalosis. Consequently, training was discontinued until PCO$_2$ stabilized at the higher value. Then it was reinstituted.

Training Procedure

Preliminary Instructions and Tests

The client is seated comfortably in a recliner and is coupled to the physiological monitoring equipment. Each sensor (and the corresponding trace on the video monitor) is explained as it is attached to him or her. The therapist makes physical contact with each sensor to show that it is harmless.

The nasal catheter is then handed to the client who is told:

> Please hold this tubing. I will ask you—not yet—to insert it about $\frac{1}{4}$ inch into a nostril. It doesn't matter which one. The tubing is fresh and sterilized; it will be discarded after use. Please do not push it up your nose, because that will tickle and be uncomfortable . . . just place it at the entrance. I will then tape it to your upper lip so that you will not have to hold it. It collects your breath and sends it to this machine, which translates it to the wave that you see on the screen here. Do you have any questions? If you are uncertain about anything or if anything is uncomfortable, please tell me immediately.

As a first test, the therapist tells the client, "Please close your eyes for a moment. Thank you." I have noted that if breathing slows down, at least slightly, it is more likely that breathing training will occur rapidly. The therapist then continues:

> Please open your eyes and look at the screen. Let's begin with breathing. Please put this book flat on your abdomen, spine up, and please push it out as far as you can. That's good. Now relax. Thank you. Did you feel any pain or discomfort? No? Good.

The purpose of this test is to see whether the client can contract the diaphragm. The degree of outward excursion is observed.

The Rapid Alert Relaxation Exercises

The Rapid Alert Relaxation (RAR^{TM}) exercises combine modified progressive relaxation, deep abdominal breathing, and mental imagery. They were developed over a period of 8 years and have been integrated into the Prudential Insurance Company's Alert Relaxation Training System (ARTSystem^{TM}) (1988). I begin with a description of the abdominal breathing training.

Abdominal/Diaphragmatic Breathing

The therapist introduces breathing training to the client in this manner:

> Now you will be doing an abdominal breathing training exercise that has been very successful in getting people to do more deep, slow abdominal breathing, and to relax. It helps reduce muscle tension, pulse rate, and blood pressure, and helps people to get a general sense of alert well-being, relaxation, and comfort. Here is what happens during diaphragmatic breathing—when you breathe with your abdomen. Your diaphragm, which separates your lungs and heart from your stomach and digestive system, contracts. In so doing, it alters its shape from a dome, vaulted upwards, to a more or less flat sheet. When this occurs, two things happen simultaneously: First, the space created in the chest cavity permits the lungs to expand and fill with air; second, it appears to you that your abdomen is pushed outwards. Then, as you exhale, the diaphragm, no longer directed to contract, relaxes and springs back to its vaulted shape. Because of its elasticity, air is pushed out of your lungs, and your abdomen returns to its original shape.
>
> Since you haven't done anything like this before, I have divided the training procedures over several sessions so that your muscles will have time to adjust and become toned for this task.

It is generally a good idea to do deep abdominal breathing exercises slowly at first, in sets of two to three (or four breaths at most), without straining the diaphragm. The emphasis is on comfort. The therapist continues:

> This is aerobics. You are trying to increase oxygenation of the body by increasing the efficiency of breathing. You do not need to plunge like a "health freak" into pain as a measure of success. If you experience pain and discomfort, you are doing it wrong.

First Session. The therapist instructs the client:

Please sit back, with your back supported by the back of the chair. Unbutton your collar; take off your jacket; loosen your tie, belt, or any other tight-fitting clothing. Place your hands on your knees and pause for a moment.

How do you breathe? Place your left hand on your chest, just over your breastbone, and your right hand over your abdomen (cover your belly button). Look at your hands as you breathe. What is the left hand doing? What is the right hand doing? Are they moving together?

Your left hand, over your chest, should not move. Your right hand, over your abdomen, should be moving *out* as you inhale, and *in* as you exhale. Check and make sure that you are doing this: breathe *in*, belly *out;* breathe *out,* belly *in.* Repeat three times, then stop.

Do you feel dizzy? If not, good. If you feel dizzy, you are overbreathing— hyperventilating. You are putting too much effort into it, too early in the game. Make the motions a little more subtle—not so far out on the inhale and not so far in on the exhale.

If you feel dizzy, stop and rest a little while until it passes. It usually does after a few practice sessions; rarely, it may not stop. *If you don't stop feeling dizzy after a few practice sessions, stop trying!*

If your left hand moves mostly, or if both hands rise and fall at the same time, you are breathing with your chest. Or is your hand movement shallow and slow, or shallow and rapid? Make a note to yourself.

Close your mouth. Breathe in and out only through your nose. Breathing through your mouth tends to promote hyperventilation.

Look at your hands: As you inhale, keep your chest down. Let the hand on your abdomen rise as the air fills your abdomen.

If there is noncompliance, the therapist should try this:

Place this book on your lap (spine up, so that it won't slide off). Now, without coordinat- ing it with your breath at all, push the book out as far as you can with your abdomen. When you inhale, your abdomen should move out about as far as it did when you pushed the book. If it did not move out, don't worry; you may be tense, but that's to be expected. It will improve with practice. On the exhale, slowly—but never so slowly that it creates dis- comfort—pull your abdomen back as far as it will go, but do not let it raise your chest.

Good. Now don't stop. Don't pause; repeat the inhale and exhale procedure once more. Rest for a moment.

After the client has successfully practiced the exercise two or three times, the therapist continues:

You will find after a few days of practicing just 3 to 4 minutes per day—don't do more, now—that your inhale and exhale will be of approximately the same duration. There should be no pause in breathing—not before or after the inhale or exhale—just one smooth motion.

Now, once again: Inhale . . . fill up. And exhale . . . pull all the way back. Repeat this procedure three times, then stop. That's all for today.

Doing more than this much may be counterproductive, and may cause dia- phragmatic cramps or dizziness (though that will pass quickly). There may be a slight tendency to hyperventilate at first; many of my clients do. It will pass, and, with practice, it will disappear.

Second Session. The therapist instructs the client:

Prepare yourself for the exercise in the same way that you did yesterday: Sit back in your chair; place your hands on your knees for a moment, and let yourself relax. Now close your mouth. Place your hands on your chest and abdomen as you did yesterday. Once you get the knack, you can do it without your hands.

Now, looking at your hands, inhale, holding down your chest and letting your abdomen fill up. Then exhale slowly, and pull your abdomen all the way back. Repeat this procedure three more times. That's enough for today.

Did you find it to be any easier? Did your abdomen move further out when you inhaled? Did the hand on your chest remain more or less motionless? Can you pull your abdomen a little further in?

I recommend only very short exercise sessions the first few days. The diaphragm and abdominal muscles need time to tone up.

Third Session. The therapist instructs the client:

Let's see you do the exercise without your hands. Prepare yourself in your chair, as you did yesterday. Try it. Does your chest remain more still as you inhale, and is your abdomen moving outward? If it is, good. If not, go back to using your hands. But if you can, then proceed breathing in and out four times in a row—close your eyes.

If you still need to use your hands, then proceed, eyes closed, and imagine what your hands are doing. Good. That's it for today.

I usually make it a practice to review the pre- and posttraining profile, and to review the frequency and severity of signs and symptoms, after each session.

As soon as the client can sustain deep diaphragmatic breathing for at least 10 to 15 consecutive breaths without trace reversals or hypocapnia, the breathing exercise can be integrated with a modified form of muscle relaxation, imagery, and music. Limitations of space do not permit me to describe the entire procedure here, but I provide enough of it so that readers can reconstruct the rest. For greater detail, readers may wish to consult *The Breath Connection* (Fried, 1990a) or *Breathing and Hyperventilation in Behavioral Medicine, Clinical Psychology, and Psychiatry* (Fried, in press).

Integrating Breathing with Muscle Relaxation and Music

The therapist says to the client:

Are you comfortable? Good. Let's begin. Please put your head back and let yourself relax. Focus on your breathing. When you inhale, I will give you a "relaxation phrase." Please repeat it to yourself as you exhale, and try to focus your attention on the part of the body mentioned.

1. "I am letting the tension out of my forehead."
2. "I am letting the tension in my forehead flow out with my breath."
3. "I am letting the tension out of my face; I am relaxing my jaw."
4. "I am letting the tension in my face and my jaw flow out with my breath."
5. "I am letting the tension out of my neck and my shoulders. I am letting my shoulders down—away from my body."
6. "I am letting the tension in my neck and shoulders flow out with my breath."
7. "I am letting the tension out of my arms and my hands."
8. "I am letting the tension in my arms and hands flow out with my breath."
9. "I am letting the tension out of my thighs and my legs."
10. "I am letting the tension in my thighs and my legs flow out with my breath."

This represents 10 consecutive breaths. If there is any reversal in the PCO_2 trace at any time during the exercise, the therapist should stop the procedure; this indicates diaphragmatic fatigue. Pushing the diaphragm when it is fatigued can cause spasm. Figure 10.8 shows a trace reversal at the beginning of the first inspiration, indicating diaphragmatic fatigue. In later training sessions, when a client is accustomed to sustained deep diaphragmatic breathing, such reversals are seldom observed. But watching the physiological traces on the monitor is the only means of making sure that the clinician is controlling what the client is learning.

Music may also be introduced in the background at any time during the training procedure. I have found it very helpful. It inexplicably promotes slow, deep breath-

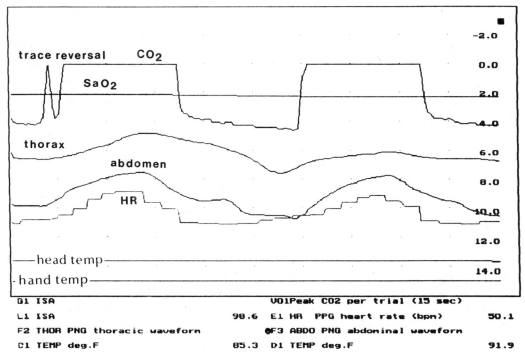

FIGURE 10.8. Profile showing diaphragmatic fatigue in the form of trace reversal. Diaphragm contraction at the start of inspiration cannot be maintained, but is then overridden, and inspiration continues to completion.

ing, and I have described this phenomenon and suggested tentative explanations in several papers (Fried, 1990b, 1990c). I recommend the following:

- Pachelbel's Canon in D Major, played by Daniel Kobialka, *Timeless Motion* (Li-Sem Enterprises; cassette).
- *Oxygene,* Jean-Michel Jarre (Polygram Records; cassette).
- *Infini* (Pan Communications Compact Disc No. 9001).
- *Ocean Sounds—Environments.* (Syntonic Research, Inc., cassette series).

Integrating Breathing with Imagery

It is common to use various forms of imagery to facilitate breathing and relaxation. "Beach imagery" is an example. Here is how I do it:

> Please close your eyes and let yourself relax. (At this point, prerecorded ocean and surf sounds are played on the sound system.) Now imagine that you are at the beach. You are standing on the beach and looking at the ocean: The sky is clear, and the sun bright and warm but not hot.
>
> Can you see the ocean? Can you feel the warmth of the sun on your head? Your shoulders? As you are standing there, imagine that the weight in your body is drifting down to the bottom of your feet, so that you feel very firmly planted on the beach. Now please look at the ocean. Can you see the surf?

I am watching the monitor, and as I see the client inhaling, I say:

> Now, as you begin to inhale, try to feel that you are inhaling ocean air, and feel how cool and refreshing it feels. Watch the surf rolling up on the beach toward your feet. And now, as you exhale, see the surf rolling out to the sea. Let the tension in you body roll out with the surf. (After a few "cued" breaths:) Now, on your own, watch the surf roll in as you inhale and roll out as you exhale.

Additional instructions are given *ad libitum:*

> As you inhale, you feel awake, alert, refreshed. As you exhale, you feel relaxed, warm, comfortable.

Contraindications and Cautions

I do not recommend the RAR^{TM} for persons with psychosis; I have no experience with that population. In some instances, persons with temporal lobe epilepsy may suffer severe depression and may report hallucinations and other psychosis-like sensations and symptoms. Except for those cases, I am in no position to speculate about the benefits or possible harmful effects of these exercises on such patients' condition.

Deep abdominal/diaphragmatic breathing may initially be strenuous for a person who has been holding the diaphragm in partial contraction as part of the physical stress profile. Diaphragmatic cramps are not unheard of. If cramps occur and are anything but mild, or if even mild cramps persist, the exercise should be discontinued immediately. For this reason I give my clients the following instructions:

> If an exercise causes pain of discomfort, stop it immediately. Also, do not do any exercise if you have any physical or medical condition or any injury that would contraindicate its safety. Among such conditions are the following:
>
> 1. Muscle or other tissue or organ malformation or injury—for example, sprained or torn muscles, torticolis, fractures, or recent surgery.
>
> 2. Any condition causing metabolic acidosis, where hyperventilation may be compensatory such as diabetes, kidney disease, heart disease, severe hypoglycemia, etc. If you are in doubt, please bring your condition to my attention.
>
> 3. Low blood pressure or any related condition, such as syncope (fainting). Deep abdominal breathing may cause a significant decrease in blood pressure.
>
> 4. Insulin-dependent diabetes. If you are an insulin-dependent diabetic, you should not do this or any other deep relaxation exercise without the express approval of your physician and his or her close monitoring of your insulin needs.

In the long run, deep relaxation may be beneficial in the management of diabetes, but the sudden reduction in the blood level of the stress hormones has been demonstrated to reduce insulin dependence (Guthrie, Moeller, & Guthrie, 1983; Seeburg & Deboer, 1980). Under certain circumstances, hyperventilation may be the body's protection against diabetic acidosis.

Typical Findings

The application of breathing training procedures with psychophysiological monitoring and some degree of "biofeedback" has been reported in detail elsewhere (Fried et al., 1984; Fried, 1987b, 1990a, in press). Various combinations of elements of the PRP are helpful in assessing pre- and posttreatment breathing and stress status. In general, it can be said that the RAR^{TM} exercises have the effects described below and illustrated in the cases that follow.

1. Breathing rate slows down, and by virtue of the increase in PCO_2, it may be inferred that V_{min} (the total volume of air breathed per minute) either increases or remains constant. It seldom drops. When training has stabilized, breathing rate will be between 3 and 5 per minute—in many cases, below 3 per minute.

2. Breathing mode becomes predominantly abdominal. The rhythm becomes smooth, with equal duration of inspiration and expiration.

3. Alveolar PCO_2 rises after the initial training sessions; SaO_2 normalizes between 95% and 98%, except that it increases (despite PCO_2 increase) during the inspiration phase of breathing with deep diaphragmatic breathing. By inference, this is a result of increased perfusion with increased intrapulmonary air pressure. It does not indicate a left-shifted ODC, because with normal PCO_2, there is no alkalosis.

4. Pulse rate typically drops, except that it rises slightly where there is bradycardia (50 beats per minute or less). Initially, systolic blood pressure may show a slight homeostatic increase if diastolic blood pressure drops. After a few sessions, systolic blood pressure drops also if diastolic pressure remains down.

5. RSA, typically absent before training, may become pronounced—I have seen difference of up to 11 to 12 beats over the breathing cycle.

6. EEG may show elevation of the entire theta range before training. During training, the theta range will drop, as alpha frequency becomes more coherent at a lower frequency in the range and increases in amplitude. These changes are accompanied by reports in some cases of the experience of "thoughtless consciousness," described in the meditation literature as "samadhi" or the altered state of consciousness.

Figure 10.9 shows the EEG power spectrum before and during breathing training in a 42-year-old woman with severe stress, fatigue, depression, and a childhood history of petit mal seizures. She showed pulmonary ventilatory deficiency (i.e., $PETCO_2 = 5.9$). Such ventilatory deficiency is typically accompanied by low alveolar O_2. Before training, the left side showed higher voltage than the right, and both right and left sides showed elevation in theta, with no apparent coherent alpha. During training, right- and left-side voltage equalized; average theta decreased, with coherent alpha on both sides, though more prominently on the right.

In summary, the counterstress breathing-based relaxation strategies described above typically reduce tension and anxiety, as well as the frequency and severity of psychophysiological disorders. Clients report that the strategies makes them feel good, relaxed, and in control, and that they have fewer symptoms as a result. Objective indices of counterarousal include decreased rate and predominantly abdominal mode of breathing, as well as normalization of alveolar CO_2; decreased pulse rate and restoration of RSA; improved circulation (i.e., hand warming); decreased

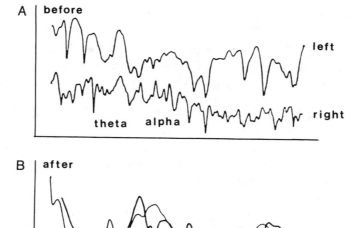

FIGURE 10.9. EEG frequency power spectra of a 42-year-old woman with stress, fatigue, depression, and a childhood history of petit mal seizures. Before breathing training (A), the entire theta range was elevated in both the right and left hemispheres, with the left side showing greater baseline voltage (arousal) than the right. During deep diaphragmatic breathing, theta was normalized, with coherent alpha, in both right and left hemispheres, and with equalization of baseline voltage.

blood pressure; and "normalized" EEG—all of which depend on normocapnia and adequate tissue oxygenation. The following cases illustrate some of these findings and show how the PRP supports the theory of a more or less closed-loop relationship between breathing, on the one hand and stress and psychophysiological disorders on the other.

Case Materials

Case 1

A 29-year-old professional man reported work-related stress, fatigue, anxiety, and mild depression. He reported nothing but mild allergies in his medical history, and nothing of significance in his social and family life. Breathing training showed a paradoxical increase in $PETCO_2$ to 5.9, with SaO_2 slightly below normal at 94.1% (see Figure 10.10A). The choppy exhale looked suspicious, and he confirmed that he had been diagnosed as having asthma (a fact that he had failed to reveal previously) and that he felt his allergies acting up.

Further deep diaphragmatic breathing improved his ventilation: $PETCO_2$ dropped to 5.2, and SaO_2 rose to 95.4%. He also reported feeling better (see Figure 10.10B). This was a case where organic conditions (asthma and allergies) underlay the stress: Through moderate bronchial constriction, pulmonary ventilation decreased and so did blood O_2 level. This was functionally tantamount to anemia. Increased alveolar CO_2 is known to cause diaphragmatic fatigue, further decreasing the ability to breathe and increasing the feeling of tiredness.

Case 2

A 42-year-old woman reported stress and moderate hypertension (146/94 mm Hg). There was nothing of note in her medical history, nor was there a discernible psychological disorder. She was in excellent physical condition, reporting a healthy concern with diet and exercise. At the initial profile (see Figure 10.11A), her breathing rate was found to be elevated (22 per minute); $PETCO_2$ was depressed at 4.10; SaO_2 was normal (97.4%); and pulse rate (52 per minute) was low—typical in a runner. There was no evidence of RSA.

After several rounds of breathing training (3 breaths per round) over a 22-minute period, her breathing rate dropped to a little over 2 per minute; $PETCO_2$ rose to 4.5; SaO_2 rose to 98.5%; pulse rate rose to 63 per minute; and her blood pressure was 153/90 mm Hg (see Figure 10.11B).

It may appear paradoxical, but it happens invariably that with relaxation, systolic blood pressure rises when diastolic blood pressure drops. I never fail to explain to my clients that if both were to drop suddenly, the client might faint (syncope). The initial rise in systolic pressure invariably accompanies a drop in diastolic pressure. This is a compensatory mechanism for blood pressure homeostasis, and a good sign

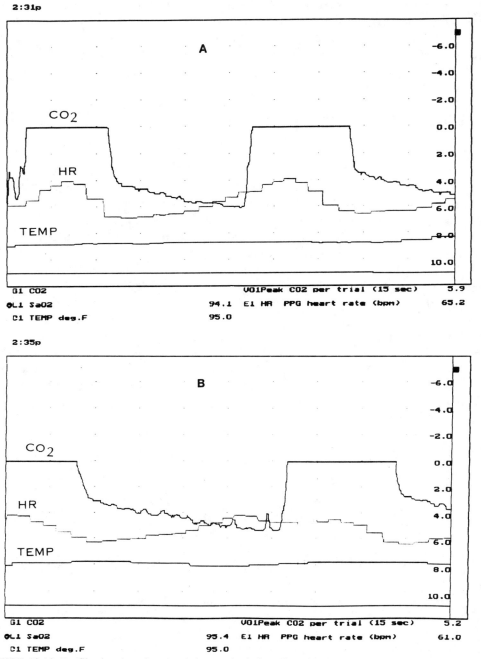

FIGURE 10.10. Profile showing characteristic paradoxical "asthmatic" $PETCO_2$ elevation with slow, deep breathing (A). Continued slow breathing resulted in reduced $PETCO_2$ (B).

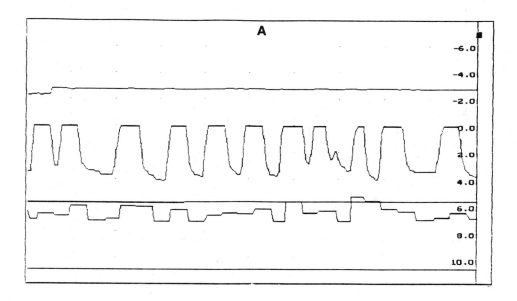

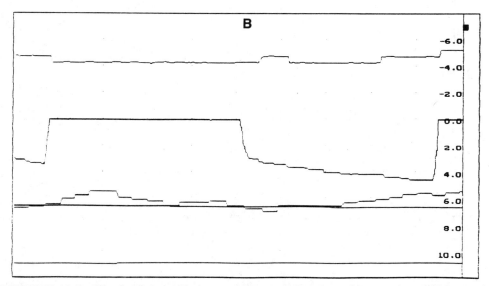

FIGURE 10.11. Profile of a 42-year-old woman with stress and moderate hypertension. Initial pretraining breathing rate was 22 per minute (A). During training (B), breathing rate dropped to 2 per minute, and systolic blood pressure showed a homeostatic increase as diastolic pressure decreased.

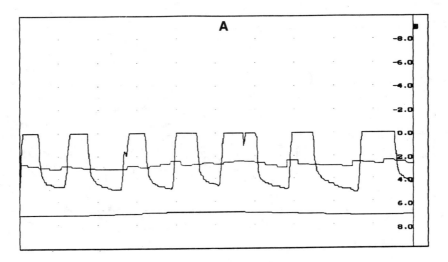

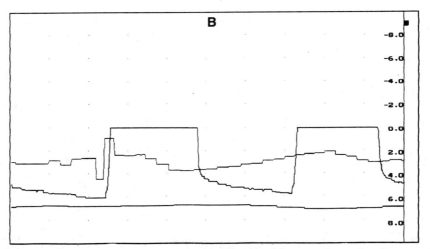

FIGURE 10.12. Pretraining profile (A) in a 37-year-old man with stress, depression, hypertension, and insomnia. Breathing rate was 14 per minute. During breathing training (B), breathing rate dropped to 4 per minute.

that pressure is coming down. Subsequently, systolic pressure drops also if diastolic remains lower.

Case 3

A 37-year-old man reported stress, depression, anxiety, hypertension, and insomnia. His breathing rate (14 per minute) was slightly elevated; his pulse rate (74 per minute) was normal; $PETCO_2$ was normal (4.9); and SaO_2 was low borderline (94.3%) (see Figure 10.12A). Blood pressure was elevated (158/94 mm Hg). No RSA was evident.

His initial profile on the 15th session (Figure 10.12B) showed that breathing rate dropped to 4 per minute; PETCO$_2$ rose slightly to 5.5; SaO$_2$ normalized (95.4%); pulse rate did not change much (71 per minute), but blood pressure dropped considerably (148/80 mm Hg). He now reported that his depression was milder and that he could periodically control his anxiety, but his insomnia was not yet much improved.

ACKNOWLEDGMENT

I wish to thank Dr. Joe Grimaldi of The Calmer Center, Carmel, NY, for his patience and the time he spent in teaching me to operate the J & J I 330 System and unfolding its virtually endless possibilities. I also wish to thank my colleagues at the Institute for Rational–Emotive Therapy (IRET), New York, NY—Drs. Janet Wolfe, Ray DiGiuseppe, Albert Ellis, and Dom DiMatia, and the directors of the IRET—for their encouragement and equipment grant support.

REFERENCES

Angelone, A., & Coulter, N. A. (1964). Respiratory sinus arrhythmia: A frequency dependent phenomenon. *Journal of Applied Physiology, 3,* 479–482.

Badawi, K., Wallace, R. K., Orme-Johnson, D., & Rouzere, A. A. (1984). Electrophysiological characteristics of respiratory suspension periods occuring during the practice of a transcendental meditation program. *Phychosomatic Medicine, 46,* 267–276.

Beary, J. F., Benson, H., & Klemchuck, H. P. (1974). A simple psychophysiologic technique which elicits the hypometabolic changes of the relaxation response. *Psychosomatic Medicine, 36,* 115–120.

Benson, H., Beary, J. F., & Carol, M. P. (1974). The relaxation response. *Psychiatry, 37,* 37–46.

Blanchard, E. B., Morill, B., Wittrock, D. A., Scharff, L., & Jaccard, J. (1989). Hand temperature norms for headache, hypertension, and irritable bowel syndrome. *Biofeedback and Self-Regulation, 14,* 319–331.

Blass, J. P., & Gibson, G. E. (1979). Consequences of mild, graded hypoxia. In S. Fahn, J. N. Davis, & L. P. Rowland (Eds.), *Advances in neurology* (Vol. 26). New York: Raven Press.

Bohr, C., Hasselbach, K. A., & Krogh, A. (1904). Ueber einen in biologischer Beziehung wichtigen Einfluss, den die Kohlensaurespannung des Blutes auf dessen Sauerstoffbindung ubt. *Scandinavian Archives of Physiology, 16,* 402–412.

Cohen, R. D., & Woods, H. F. (1976). *Clinical and biochemical aspects of lactic acidosis.* Oxford: Blackwell.

Collier, C. R., Affeldt, J. E., & Farr, A. F. (1955). Continuous rapid infrared CO$_2$ analysis—Fractional sampling and accuracy in determining alveolar CO$_2$. *Journal of Laboratory and Clinical Medicine, 45,* 526–539.

Comroe, J. H. (1974). *Physiology of respiration* (2nd ed.). Chicago: Year Book Medical.

Darrow, C. W., & Graf, C. C. (1945). Relation of encephalogram to photometrically observed vasomotor changes in the brain. *Journal of Neurophysiology, 8,* 449–461.

Davies, C. T. M., & Neilson, J. M. M. (1967). Sinus arrythmia in man at rest. *Journal of Applied Physiology, 22,* 947–955.

Edwards, R. H. T., & Clode, M. (1970). The effect of hyperventilation on lacticacidemia of muscular exercise. *Clinical Science, 38,* 269–276.

Fried, R. (1987a). Relaxation with biofeedback-assisted guided imagery: The importance of breathing rate as an index of hypoarousal. *Biofeedback and Self-Regulation, 12,* 273–279.

Fried, R. (1987b). *The hyperventilation syndrome.* Baltimore: Johns Hopkins University Press.

Fried, R. (1990a). *The breath connection.* New York: Plenum.

Fried, R. (1990b). Integrating music in breathing training and relaxation: I. Background, rationale, and relevant elements. *Biofeedback and Self-Regulation, 15,* 161–169.

Fried, R. (1990c). Integrating music in breathing training and relaxation: II. Applications. *Biofeedback and Self-Regulation, 15,* 171–177.

Fried, R. (in press). *The psychology and physiology of breathing in behavioral medicine, clinical psychology, and psychiatry.* New York: Plenum.

Fried, R., Fox, M. C., & Carlton, R. M. (1990). Effect of diaphragmatic respiration with end-tidal CO$_2$

biofeedback on respiration, EEG, and seizure frequency in idiopathic epilepsy. *Annals of the New York Academy of Sciences, 602,* 67–96.

Fried, R., Fox, M. C., Carlton, R. M. & Rubin, S. R. (1984). Method and protocols for assessing hyperventilation and its treatment. *Journal of Drug Research and Therapy, 9,* 280–288.

Gamble, J. L. (1982). *Acid–base physiology.* Baltimore: Johns Hopkins University Press.

Gantt, W. H. (1970). *Pavlovian approaches to psychopathology.* Elmsford, NY: Pergamon Press.

Gerard, R. W. (1937). Brain metabolism and circulation. In S. Cobb, A. M. Frantz, W. Penfield, & H. A. Riley (Eds.), *The circulation of the brain and spinal cord.* New York: Hafner.

Grossman, P. (1983). Respiration, stress, and cardiovascular function. *Psychophysiology, 20,* 284–300.

Grossman, P., & DeSwart, J. C. G. (1984). Diagnosis of hyperventilation syndrome on the basis of reported complaints. *Journal of Psychosomatic Research, 28,* 97–104.

Guthrie, D., Moeller, T., & Guthrie, R. (1983). Biofeedback and its application to the stabilization and control of diabetes mellitus. *American Journal of Clinical Biofeedback, 6,* 82–87.

Hardonk, H. J., & Beumer, H. M. (1979). Hyperventilation Syndrome. In P. J. Vinken & G. W. Bruyn (Eds.), *Handbook of clinical neurology* (Vol. 38). Amsterdam: North-Holland.

Heistad, D. D., Marcus, M. L., & Abboud, F. M. (1978). Experimental attempts to unmask the effects of neural stimuli on cerebral blood flow. In M. J. Purves (Ed.), *Cerebral vascular smooth muscle and its control.* Amsterdam: Excerpta Medica.

Hirsch, J. A., & Bishop, B. (1981). Respiratory sinus arrhythmia in humans: How breathing patterns modulate heart rate. *American Journal of Physiology, 241,* 179–180.

Huckabee, W. E. (1961). Abnormal resting blood lactate. *American Journal of Medicine, 30,* 833–840.

Jacquy, J., Piraux, A., Noel, G., & Henriet, M. (1979). A tentative study of regional vasomotor capacitance variations by rheoencephalography. *European Journal of Neurology, 10,* 12–24.

Katz, I. R. (1982). Is there a hypoxic affective syndrome? *Psychosomatics, 23,* 846–853.

Kerr, W. J., Dalton, J. W., & Gliebe, P. A. (1937). Some physical phenomena associated with anxiety states and their relationship to hyperventilation. *Annals of Internal Medicine, 11,* 961–992.

Kety, S. S., & Schmidt, C. F. (1948). The effects of altered arterial tensions of carbon dioxide and oxygen on cerebral blood flow and cerebral oxygen consumption of normal young men. *Journal of Clinical Investigation, 27,* 484–492.

Kreisberg, R. A. (1980). Lactate homeostasis and lactic acidosis. *Annals of Internal Medicine, 92,* 227.

Lennox, W. G., Gibbs, F. A., & Gibbs, E. L. (1938). The relationship in man of cerebral activity to blood flow and blood constitutents. *Journal of Neurology and Psychiatry, 1,* 221–225.

Lowry, T. P. (1967) *Hyperventilation and hysteria.* Springfield IL: Charles C Thomas.

Melcher, A. (1976). Respiratory sinus arrhythmia in man. *Acta Physiologica Scandinavica* (Suppl. 435), 7–31.

Morse, D. R., Martin, J. S., Furst, M. L., & Dubin, L. L. (1977). A physiological and subjective evaluation of meditation, hypnosis and relaxation. *Psychosomatic Medicine, 39,* 304–324.

Nixon, P. G. F., & Freeman, L. J. (1988). The "think test": A further technique to elicit hyperventilation. *Journal of the Royal Society of Medicine, 81,* 277–79.

Park, R., & Arief, A. I. (1980). Lactic acidosis. *Advances in Internal Medicine, 25,* 33.

Patel, C. (1975). 12-month follow-up of yoga and biofeedback in the management of hypertension. *Lancet, i,* 62–64.

Penfield, W., & Jasper, H. (1954). *Epilepsy and the functional anatomy of the brain.* Boston: Little, Brown.

Porges, S. W., McCabe, P. M., & Yongue, B. G. (1982). Respiratory heart-rate interactions: Psychophysiology—Implications for pathophysiology and behavior. In J. T. Cacioppo & R. E. Petty (Eds.), *Perspectives in cardiovascular psychophysiology.* New York: Guilford Press.

Radford, E. P. (1955). Mechanical factors in distribution of pulmonary ventilation. *Journal of Applied Physiology, 7,* 451–460.

Schmidt, K. F., & Hendrix, J. P. (1937). The action of Chemical substances on cerebral blood vessels. In S. Cobb, A. M. Frantz, W. Penfield, & H. A. Riley (Eds.), *The circulation of the brain and spinal cord.* New York: Hafner.

Seeburg, K. N., & Deboer, K. F. (1980). Effects of EMG biofeedback on diabetes. *Biofeedback and Self-Regulation, 5,* 289-293.

Selye, H. (1974). *Stress without distress.* Philadelphia: J. B. Lippincott.

Shapiro, B. A., Harrison, R. A., & Walton, J. R. (1982). *Clinical application of blood gases.* Chicago: Year Book Medical.

Shapiro, D. H. (1982). Overview: Clinical and physiological comparison of meditation with other self-regulation control strategies. *American Journal of Psychiatry, 139,* 267–274.

Suess, W. M., Barney-Alexander, A. B., Smith, D. D., Sweeney, H. W., & Marion, R. J. (1980). The effect of psychological stress on respiration: A preliminary study of anxiety on hyperventilation. *Psychophysiology, 17,* 535–540.

Tachibana, S., Kuramoto, S., Inanaga, K., & Ikemi, Y. (1967). Local cerebrovascular response in man. *Confina Neurologica, 29,* 289–298.

van Dixhoorn, J. (1990). *Relaxation therapy in cardiac rehabilitation.* Rotterdam: Erasmus University Press.

van Dixhoorn, J., & Duivenvoorden, H. J. (1985). Efficacy of Nijmegan Questionnaire in recognition of the hyperventilation syndrome. *Journal of Psychosomatic Research, 29,* 199–206.

van Doorn, P., Folgering, H., & Colla, P. (1982). Control of the end-tidal PCO_2 in the hyperventilation syndrome: Effects of biofeedback and breathing instructions compared. *Bulletin of European Physiopathology and Respiration, 18,* 829–836.

Wallace, R. K. (1972). *The physiological effects of transcendental meditation.* Los Angeles: Students International Meditation Society.

Wheeler, E. O., White, P. D., Reed, E. W., & Cohen, M. E. (1950). Neurocirculatory asthenia (anxiety neurosis, effort syndrome, neurasthenia). *Journal of the American Medical Association, 142,* 878–889.

11

Cognitive Approaches to Stress

AARON T. BECK

Cognitive Model of Stress

Cognitive Structuring

The first principle in the cognitive model of stress reactions is as follows: *The construction of a situation (cognitive set) is an active, continuing process that includes successive appraisals of the external situation and the risks, costs, and gains of a particular response. When the individual's vital interests appear to be at stake, the cognitive process provides a highly selective conceptualization.*

The individual's construction of a particular situation may be likened to taking a snapshot. In taking a photograph, the individual scans the relevant environment and then decides which aspects he or she wants to focus on. The photograph reduces a three-dimensional situation to two dimensions and consequently sacrifices a great deal of information; it also introduces a certain amount of distortion into the system. The specific settings (lens, focus, speed) have an enormous influence on the type of picture that will be obtained. Depending on the type of lens (wide-angle or telephoto), for example, breadth is sacrificed for detail, or vice versa. Certain aspects are also highlighted at the expense of others, and the relative magnitudes and prominence of particular features are distorted. In addition, there may be blurring or loss of detail as a result of inadequate focusing or too rapid exposure; moreover, the use of filters further influences the salience and coloring of particular features. Finally, the lens itself may be distorted, and thus may introduce a distortion into the picture.

Similarly, in conceptualizing a particular event, the cognitive set influences the "picture" obtained by an individual: Whether the mental image or conception is broad, skewed, or narrow, clear or blurred, accurate or distorted depends on the characteristics of the existing cognitive set. These determine which aspects are to be magnified, which minimized, and which excluded. It is probable that a person takes a series of "pictures" before making a final conceptualization. The first "shot" of an event provides data regarding the nature of the situation—for example, whether it is likely to be pleasant, neutral, or noxious. (The discussion that follows is restricted to a consideration only of those reactions that may lead to stress.) This first "shot" provides feedback that either reinforces or modifies the pre-existing cognitive set. An initial impression is formed on the basis of scanty data, and is important in that it indicates the general nature of the situation—specifically, whether it directly affects the individual's vital interests. It should be noted that the first impression (first "shot") is especially important because, unless modified or reversed, it determines (influences) the direction of subsequent steps in conceptualization of and total response to the situation. If the individual judges the situation to be affecting his or her vital interests, he or she shows what I call a "critical response." The critical response, which is of particular importance in the development of stress reactions, may be viewed as including two types of reactions.

One type of critical response is the "emergency response." The response is activated when the individual perceives a threat to his or her survival, domain, individuality, functioning, status, or attachments—that is, attack, depreciation, encroachment, thwarting, abandonment, rejection, or deprivation. Another type of critical response occurs when the individual perceives an event as increasing or facilitating self-enhancement—attainment of personal goals, exhibitionism, or receiving admiration.

An essential feature of the critical response is that it is egocentric. Through a sequence of cognitive processing, the situation is conceptualized in terms of "How does it affect me?" The immediate interests of the individual are central in the conceptualization, and the details are selected and molded (or distorted) to provide a meaningful answer to that question. The kinds of conceptualizations in the critical response tend to be global and to include a limited number of dimensions. The primitive forms of the conceptualization correspond to primitive content—physical danger, predation, social bonding, and so forth. Generally, the critical response tends to be overly inclusive: Some events that in reality are not related to issues of personal identity, survival, or self-enhancement are perceived as though they are relevant.

For our present purpose, let us assume that the individual's first impression of a situation is that it is noxious. This appraisal activates a particular "mode" (assembly of "schemas"), which is used to refine the classification of the stimulus situation. The initial impression of a situation fits into the category of "primary appraisal" (Lazarus, 1966). If the primary appraisal is that the situation is noxious, successive "reappraisals" are made to provide immediate answers to a series of questions:

1. Is the noxious stimulus a threat to the individual or his or her interests?
2. Is the threat concrete and immediate, or abstract, symbolic, and remote? Or,
3. What is the content and magnitude of the threat?
   a. Does it involve possible physical damage to the individual?
   b. Is the threat of a psychosocial nature—for example, disparagement or devaluation?
   c. Does the threat involve violation of some rules that the individual relies on to protect his or her integrity or interest?

At the same time that the nature of the threat is being evaluated, the individual is assessing his or her resources for dealing with it. This assessment, labeled "secondary appraisal" by Lazarus (1966), aims to provide concrete information regarding the individual's coping mechanisms and ability to absorb the impact of any assault. The final picture or construction of the noxious situation is based on an equation that takes into account the amount and the probabilities of damage inherent in the threat as opposed to the individual's capacity to deal with it (the "risk–resources equation"). These assessments are not cool, deliberate computations, but to a large degree are automatic. The equation is based on highly subjective evaluations that are prone to considerable error; two individuals with similar coping capacities might respond in a vastly different manner to the same threatening situation.

If the risk is judged to be high in relation to the coping resources available, the individual is mobilized to reduce the degree of threat through avoidance or escape ("flight reaction"), preparing for defense, or self-inhibition ("freezing"). If the individual judges the threat to be low in relation to available coping mechanisms, he or she is mobilized to eliminate or deflect the threat ("fight reaction").

Another type of critical response, as noted above, occurs when the stimulus situation is perceived as potentially self-enhancing. For example, a person is challenged or invited to compete for a prize. The person then makes rapid evaluations of the desirability of the goal, his or her capacity for reaching it, and the costs to him or her in terms of expenditure of time, energy, and sacrifice of other goals. These factors may be reduced to a cost–benefit ratio analogous to the risk–resources ratio. The final construction of the stimulus situation determines whether the person accepts the challenge or invitation, and consequently whether or not the person becomes mobilized to attain the goal.

The processes involved in the critical response tend to present not only a one-sided but also an exaggerated view of the stimulus situation, because of the exclusionary and categorical nature of the thinking at this primitive level. The processes involved in the critical response are automatic, involuntary, and not within awareness.

The conceptualization presented above is compatible with theories of information processing advanced by other authors. As pointed out by Bowlby (1981), current studies of human perception show that before a person is aware of seeing or hearing a stimulus, the sensory inflow coming through the eyes or ears has already passed through many stages of selection, interpretation, and appraisal. During the course of this process, a large proportion of the original inflow has been excluded. The reason suggested by Bowlby (1981) for this extensive exclusion is that "since the channels responsible for the most advanced processing are of limited capacity, they must be protected from overload to insure that what is most relevant gets through and that the less relevant is excluded." The selection of inflow is under central control. Although this processing is done at extraordinary speeds, and almost all of it is outside awareness, much of the inflow is nonetheless carried to a very advanced state of processing before being excluded.

In the ordinary course of a person's life, the criteria applied to sensory inflow that determine what information is to be accepted and what is to be excluded reflect what appears to be in the person's best interests at any one time. Thus, when a person is hungry, information regarding food is given priority, whereas other information that might ordinarily be useful is excluded.

Yet, should he or she perceive danger, priorities would quickly change so that inflow concerned with issues of danger and safety would take precedence and inflow concerned with food be temporarily excluded. This change in the criteria governing what inflows is to be accepted and what excluded is effected by evaluating systems that are central to the cognitive organizations. (Bowlby, 1981)

Mobilization to Action

The second principle of the cognitive model is this: *The cognitive structuring of a situation is responsible for mobilizing the organism to action. If the mobilization is not adequately discharged, it forms the precursor to a stress reaction.*

Of course, not all stimuli are interpreted as noxious, and not all psychophysiological reactions are "fight" or "flight." Depending on the kind of appraisal, a host of different reactions may be stimulated by a given situation. These reactions may range from a wish to engage in some recreational activity to a desire to undertake a dangerous mission. They have a common theme, however: The individual is mobilized to engage in some kind of action. For a variety of reasons, he or she may not yield to the desire, wish, or drive; nonetheless, the mobilization has a powerful effect. Recent writings have emphasized the emotional response to a stressful stimulus, but have largely neglected the importance of the motivated response.

If a person is activated to perform a particular behavior, the directing force may be labeled a "behavioral inclination." The behavioral inclinations, or action tendencies, constitute one type of motivation. Another class of motivations is concerned with "receiving" rather than "doing" and includes wishes for love, praise, or approval, as well as the appetitive wishes. The intensity of the behavioral inclination is reflected in the degree of arousal. If the behavioral inclination is not translated into action, then the individual remains in a state of arousal for a period of time, even though the instigating stimulus is no longer present.

At the same time that an individual is aroused to action, he or she may experience an affective response. For example, people who believe they are in a dangerous situation generally experience subjective anxiety, as well as a desire to escape; if they judge that other people are mistreating them, they are likely to experience anger, as well as a desire to attack. Similarly, people may experience feelings of excitement as they prepare to engage in a competitive sport. In each case, the behavioral inclination represents the catalyst to action. The affective response occurs independently of the behavior (although these two phenomena are often fused in technical as well as popular concepts). Both the behavioral inclination and the affective response stem from the individual's conceptualizations of the situation, and are related to each other only insofar as they are both related to the cognitive structuring of the situation. It should be noted that a behavioral inclination may be aroused with minimal or no evidence of an emotional response. Persons exposed to a sudden dangerous situation (e.g., an impending automobile collision) may react to avert the danger without experiencing subjective anxiety.

The mobilization of the individual for action is the key to understanding stress reactions. If the arousal is intense and is not dissipated by action, then the individual is likely to experience some degree of stress. The stress is manifested by an interference with the normal functioning of the organism. The term "stress" is applied to the response of the organism and not to the external stimulus. The stimulus that sets up the chain of events leading to this dysfunctional reaction is labeled the "stressor." Depending on the conceptual process, the stressor may be regarded as either trivial or overwhelming by an observer. Similarly, an observer may regard the individual as underreacting or overreacting to the stimulus situation.

Distinction between Behavioral Inclinations and Emotions

The third principle of the cognitive model is as follows: *Overt behavior stems directly from the mobilization of impulses, drives, or wishes (behavioral inclinations). The emotional experience is parallel to the behavioral inclination and is not a determinant of overt action.*

The popular concept of emotions—which is also reflected to some degree in psychoanalytic theory—revolves around the notion that these phenomena are like a fluid or reservoir. When the internal hydraulic system reaches a certain level, it builds up a pressure for overt expression. According to the same metaphor, the suppression of certain emotions such as anger can lead to a wide variety of ills, ranging from headache to hypertension. By the same token, it has been stated that the free and open expression of emotions such as anger or sadness can relieve the psychosomatic disorders.

The question naturally arises: How do we know that people are suppressing or expressing their emotions? Let us take the example of angry people, who may stamp their feet, yell, shout epithets, or physically attack persons whom they regard as adversaries. They may state that they have been unjustly injured and that they are going to "get even" with the other persons. According to the conventional notions, we would label the observed behavior as "anger" or as an "angry reaction." Further reflection, however, forces us to raise questions about this notion. Are we actually seeing in the observed behavior a manifestation of some endopsychic process other than emotion? When we see an individual shake a fist and express condemning words, it seems more logical to infer that we are seeing the direct expression of a *motivation* (behavioral inclination), rather than the expression of an emotion. (As a matter of fact, an individual can play-act this scenario without feeling angry at all.)

If we question individuals who are behaving in this way, they may explain that they are "blowing off steam" or "expressing angry feelings." Similarly, people who have tightened their muscles in an attempt to prevent themselves from engaging in antagonistic behavior are likely to explain this behavior as "bottling up my feelings." (Again, note the use of a fluid metaphor to refer to feelings.) If we ask such persons, "What would you like to do?", they may respond with a description of a series of actions, such as "I would like to punch him in the nose. . . . I would like to humiliate him. . . . I'd like to make him feel the way I feel." If we inquire about such individuals' feelings, they may describe them in terms of "anger swelling up inside me." They believe that if they could release (and thus reduce) the anger, they would feel better. Suppose that such an individual does scold the offender, and that the offender then apologizes. The individual feels better and is no longer angry. This sequence of events thus appears to be consistent with the person's notions regarding the release of anger: He or she felt angry, expressed the anger, is no longer angry, and feels better. Thus, the person "demonstrates" to his or her own satisfaction that the problem lay in "suppressing my anger."

Does this experience really confirm the validity of the conventional notions regarding the expression of emotions? Let us examine the earlier phase of the process, when an individual feels "anger bursting out all over." When we analyze the situation, we might question whether the person is transforming the anger into overt behavior or whether he or she is simply carrying out an *inclination* to act against the adversary. The second formulation—that what we are observing are the *effects of an impulse* to scold, berate, or attack the other person—seems more plausible, because it does not require the notion of some "transmutation" of an emotion into behavior, and fits in general with our idea that goal-directed physical activity is preceded by a wish, drive, or impulse (behavioral inclination). According to this formulation, the behavioral inclination and not the emotional response is involved in the mobilization for action.

Structural Organization

The fourth principle of the cognitive model is this: *Depending on the content of the cognitive constellation, the behavioral inclination may be a desire to flee, attack, approach, or avoid; the corresponding affect would be anxiety, anger, affection, or sadness, respectively. The responses can be regarded as organized into structures, with primacy assigned to the controlling cognitive constellation, which activates and controls the behavioral inclination and the affective response.*

The foregoing discussion lays the foundation for discussing the priority of the conceptual processes in stress reactions. The way in which the cognitive organization processes the information determines the behavioral inclinations and affect. Thus, we can conceive of a chain of events proceeding from the environmental event to the cognitive processing system (the controlling cognitive constellation), to the action-arousing system (the behavioral inclination), to the motoric system, and finally to the observable actions. Concomitantly, the controlling cognitive constellation may activate the affect-arousing system.

The role of the cognitive organization in processing information has been described previously (Beck, 1967, 1976). Briefly, the organization is composed of systems of structural components—namely, "cognitive schemas." When an external event occurs, specific cognitive schemas are activated and are used to classify, interpret, evaluate, and assign a meaning to the event. In normal functioning, the schemas that are activated are relevant to the nature of the event. A series of adjustments occurs so that the appropriate schemas are "fitted" to the external stimulus. The final interpretation of an event represents an interaction between that event and the schemas.

The thematic content of the cognitive schemas determines the nature of the affective response and of the behavioral inclinations. Thus, if the content is relevant to danger, then a wish to flee and the feeling of anxiety are experienced. The theme of personal encroachment stimulates anger and the wish to attack. The perception of receiving desired interpersonal "supplies" (such as love) may stimulate feelings of affection and the desire to approach the other person. Perceived disapproval, on the other hand, produces sadness and often the desire to avoid the other person.

Our view of an individual's interactions with his or her environment must thus include a consideration of certain durable characteristics of the individual's personality. These include not only the relatively stable cognitive schemas, but also other personality structures that are relevant to instigating affect and behavior. (In our schematic representation, these structures are integrated with the cognitive structures to form a triad.) In metaphorical terms, we may visualize the cognitive schemas as energized initially and then energizing the motivational, motoric, and affective schemas. In order to make this formulation complete, we should postulate a feedback loop, with data from the motivational and affective schemas being routed back to the cognitive schemas.

The central role of the cognitive structures is expanded in this formulation to include not only energizing the other structures, but also controlling and modulating them. Whether an impulse will be expressed in overt behavior is dependent on the controlling cognitive constellation. The following example illustrates the sequence: An individual, confronted with a possible assault by another person, structures the situation as noxious and consequently becomes mobilized to attack. The impulse to attack will be transformed into actual behavior, unless the individual decides that counterattack is unwise and that the impulse to do so should be inhibited.

Translating this example into structural terms, I propose that the activation of the cognitive constellation leads directly to the activation of the motor apparatus, which "prepares for action." The feedback to the cognitive schemas triggers a new signal—namely, to control or inhibit action. The result of this interaction is that the organism is mobilized for action, but is prevented by internal controls from carrying it out. It should be noted that the controlling signal does not deactivate the mobilization, which persists. This formulation suggests the need for postulating a system of controls whose functions range from blanket inhibition to sensitive modulation of the impulses. (In a later section, I discuss how modifications in the cognitive constellation can facilitate "demobilization.")

It should be noted that although affect may be stimulated, it has no role in the mobilization for action. Moreover, although the individual may inhibit the inclination to attack, he or she nonetheless experiences anger. Similarly, if the individual carries out the hostile inclinations, he or she also experiences anger. Furthermore, he or she will continue to experience both the inclination and the affect (anger) until there is some modification in the controlling cognitive constellation. This modification, which is discussed later (see "Cognitive Therapy of Stress Reactions," below), results from procedures such as changing the dominant conceptualizations and shifting the cognitive focus.

Cognitive Stress and Thinking Disorders

The fifth principle of the cognitive model is as follows: *The stressors lead to a disruption of the normal activity of the cognitive organization. In addition to erosion of the ability to concentrate, recall, and reason, and to control impulses, there is a relative increase in primitive (primary-process) content.*

Under ordinary conditions, the activation of the cognitive–behavioral–affective configuration does not cause any particular problems. In fact, the configuration can be viewed as the mechanism for producing the wide range of normal emotions and normal behavior. Under certain circumstances, however, the primitive, egocentric cognitive system is activated (Beck, 1967, pp. 281–290). This activation is likely to occur when the individual perceives that vital interests are at stake. Specific idiosyncratic cognitive schemas become hyperactive if the resultant behavioral and affective mobilization is sufficiently intense or prolonged; distress, conceptual distortions, cognitive dysfunctions, and frequently disturbance of physiological functions (such as appetite and sleep) are produced.

Although depression, anxiety, and hostility have at times been included in discussions of stress reactions (e.g., Holroyd, 1979), the cognitive organization per se has rarely been singled out as the "target organ" (Beck, 1967, 1976).

Conceptual Distortions

In stress reactions, deviations in the thinking process play a major role. The stress-prone individual is primed to make extreme, one-sided, absolutistic, and global judgments. Since the appraisals tend to be extreme and one-sided, the behavioral inclinations also tend to be extreme. For example, a hostility-prone employer may be primed to react to a relatively minor error by an employee as though it were criminal negligence, and consequently will be inclined to attack the employee. A person who is susceptible to fear reactions may interpret an unfamiliar noise as the firing of a revolver or an earthquake, and will have an overpowering urge to escape. A depression-prone individual may interpret a humorous comment as a rejection and will want to withdraw.

As I have previously pointed out, conditions such as depression have conventionally been regarded as "affective disorders," pure and simple, and cognitive difficulties have been ignored or glossed over (Beck, 1963). Nonetheless, my colleagues and I observe in those conditions a generalized thinking disorder that we attribute to the dominance of the primitive cognitive system (Beck, Rush, Shaw, & Emery, 1979, pp. 14–15). Disordered individuals tend to personalize events that are not relevant to them and to interpret their experiences in global, categorical, absolutistic terms. These misconstructions of reality are detectable in the various cognitive distortions, such as polarization, selective abstraction, overgeneralization, and arbitrary inference. Some of these characteristics have been described in the psychoanalytic literature under the rubric of "primary-process thinking."

In the primitive mode of thinking, the complexity, variability, and diversity of human experiences are reduced to a few crude categories. In contrast, mature cognition ("secondary-process thinking") integrates stimuli into many dimensions or qualities, is quantitative rather than categorical, and is relativistic rather than absolutistic.

Cognitive Disorganization

The sequential flow of adaptive thinking is disrupted by mental symptoms such as preoccupation, preservation, difficulty in concentration, and forgetfulness, especially in severe stress. A salient feature of these symptoms is the loss of volitional control over the thinking process. Perhaps even more striking is the disruption of such crucial cognitive functions as objectivity and reality testing (see Caplan, 1981).

Impairment of Voluntary Control

It is interesting to note that the characteristics of the primitive cognitive organization are also reflected in the systems relevant to behavioral inclinations, control, and affect. Thus, the content of the impulses tends to be more extreme, and the mechanisms of control also show a dichotomous character. Just as the individual's capacity to "fine-tune" cognitive responses is impaired, so his or her modulation of behavioral inclinations deteriorates into a "choice" between total inhibition and no control at all.

For example, a hostile person may manifest an inclination to respond to an insult with a violent counterattack, as well as reduced control over this impulse. A depressed person has strong regressive desires, such as staying in bed and avoiding constructive action; he or she also has attenuated control over these inclinations. A fearful person has exaggerated impulses to escape from "noxious" stimuli; he or she experiences "overcontrol" (inhibition) of assertiveness and "undercontrol" of the wish to escape.

Another feature of cognitive stress or strain is the relative diminution of what has been described in the psychoanalytic literature as "secondary-process thinking" (Beck et al., 1979, p. 15). Thus, stressed individuals lose, to varying degrees, their capacity to observe their "automatic thoughts" (cognitions) objectively, to subject them to reality testing, and to adjust them to reality. Furthermore, the idiosyncratic cognitions are often so intense that such individuals have difficulty in "turning them off" and shifting their focus to other topics. The processes relevant to reality testing and control have been categorized in the psychoanalytic literature as ego functions.[1]

Erosion of Cognitive Functions

It seems likely that the erosion of secondary-process functions is a combination of the pre-emption of the cognitive organization by the hyperactive idiosyncratic schemas and of "mental fatigue" (depletion of the resources for energizing secondary-process schemas). After long periods of sleep loss or hard mental work, there seems to be not only a weakening of secondary-process thinking, but also a loosening of controls over impulses. These functional impairments are manifested in the phenomena of low stress tolerance.

What situations are likely to lead to the hyperactivity of the idiosyncratic cognitive schemas and impairment of secondary-process functions? Generally, either overwhelming traumatic events (such as an unexpected death in the family or a near-fatal accident) or intermittent or chronic, insidious stressors (such as continuous low-grade danger, repeated thwarting or defeats, or continual rejecting behavior from a spouse) lead to cumulative stimulation of the schemas relevant to loss, danger, or rejection, and a concomitant drain on secondary-process functions. It should be noted that

---

[1]A more complete description of the cognitive organization with specific reference to "primary-process" and "secondary-process" thinking is presented elsewhere (Beck, 1983).

different people have different sensitivities, so that situations that are stressful for one person may be innocuous for another person (see the discussion of the seventh principle, below).

A consequence of the hyperactivity of the idiosyncratic schemas is that they become relatively "autonomous": The conceptualizations and ruminations are far less under the influence of external stimuli than of internal factors. In the normal state, the cognitive organization fluctuates—in an adaptive way—among being predominantly "reactive" (i.e., activated and directed by environmental stimuli), "proactive" (forcing environmental stimuli into a preformed mold), and "detached" (walled off from environmental stimuli). Thus, a person watching a horror film is predominantly reactive; a door-to-door salesman attempting to sell a product and a child building a mud castle are proactive; and a person daydreaming or thinking through the details of a plan is detached. In severe psychopathology, the ability to shift flexibly from one mode to another is greatly reduced. The individual is "stuck" in one of the modes. Thus, a fearful person stamps each environmental event as dangerous and ruminates about catastrophes; a hostile person indiscriminately labels others' behaviors as encroaching on him or her; a manic person perceives his or her reflected glory in environmental events.

Cognitive Constellations and Specific Sensitivities

The sixth principle of the cognitive model is this: *Specific primitive cognitive constellations are "chained" to specific stimuli. This pairing constitutes the specific sensitivity of a given individual and prepares the way for inappropriate or excessive reactions. Since people vary widely in their specific sensitivities, what is a stressor for one person may be a benign situation for another.*

Granted that there are commonalities in the form of the thinking disturbance in the various stress disorders, how do we account for differences in the content? Why does one person tend to react to life experiences with chronic hostility, another with depression, and a third with severe or chronic anxiety? People differ not only in their types of response to stressors, but also in the kinds of stressors to which they overreact. Thus, they are likely to demonstrate individualized hypersensitivities to specific stressors and to experience specific patterns of responses. The differences in the types of susceptibility and response patterns may be attributed to differences in cognitive organization, and in many cases to differences in personality as well.

The preceding section has described how flaws in thinking are associated with stress. However, it has left unanswered the question of why these cognitive dysfunctions are evoked by some situations and not by others. The construct of "specific sensitivity," first described by Saul (1947) as "specific emotional vulnerability," refers to the individual's predilection to overreact to certain highly specific situations (specific stressors). My theoretical formulation postulates that the individual has a number of sensitive areas, and that when a given situation impinges on one of these areas, he or she is likely to respond cognitively in the kind of relatively crude, categorical form characteristic of primary-process cognition. The idiosyncratic cognitive response sets in motion the motivational systems that may lead to stress.

To illustrate the concept of specific sensitivity, let us take a commonplace example. A young man was bitten by a dog as a child. From that time on, he has responded with anxiety to the sight of any dog, to the sound of a dog barking, or even to the picture of a dog. Any stimulus relevant to a dog elicits the thought "It will bite my leg off," and generally an image of the leg being severed at the calf. He then experiences anxiety and a wish to flee. Thus, the young man reacts to an innocuous stimulus as though it were dangerous. The specific stressor in this case is any dog, and the specific cognitive response is automatic, stereotyped, and undifferentiated. Even though he "knows" at one level (the mature cognitive system) that there is no danger, the primitive cognitive system is prepotent for as long as the stimulus is present. Since the reaction disappears after the stimulus is removed, this case can be considered a simple phobia and is not regarded as a stress reaction (unless the exposure to the stressor is prolonged or intense enough to produce a residual dysfunction).

In order to illustrate how a specific sensitivity predisposes an individual to a stress reaction, let us consider the case of a middle-aged man with intense chronic anxiety. The episode of anxiety started shortly after his brother died of a heart attack, when he himself began to have pains in his chest. From that point on, he has been acutely aware of changes in his breathing or heart rate and any perceptible sensations in his chest—all of which make him believe he is having a heart attack and lead to chest pain (because of splinting of the intercostal muscles), anxiety, and a desire to rush to the hospital. He has a similar reaction when he hears of anybody dying of a heart attack. This case qualifies as a stress reaction, because the psychophysiological effects last after exposure to a stimulus and are represented in continued dysfunctional thinking ("I am in danger of dying"), impaired concentration, chronic feelings of discomfort, and increased heart rate.

This anecdote illustrates how a person responds selectively (fear reaction) to an initial stressor (his brother's death) with hypersensitivity to any stimuli suggestive of coronary disease. The hypersensitivity can be understood in terms of the pre-dominance of a cognitive constellation relevant to the danger of "instant death." This constellation remains prepotent, so that most internal stimuli are scanned for signs of an impending heart attack. Moreover, even external stimuli relevant to the concept of heart attack (such as news of a friend's having a coronary episode) are capable of activating or intensifying his fear. In summary, the case can be formulated in terms of three constructs:

1. Specific stressor: Stimuli relevant to heart attack.
2. Specific response: Fear of sudden death.
3. Specific dysfunctions: Preoccupation, chest pain, tachycardia.

A wide variety of sensitivities and response patterns may exist. People with a sensitivity to the same stressor may have notably different response patterns; others may have the same type of response, but to dissimilar stimuli. For example, two students studying together may react strongly when they hear a loud noise, such as the backfiring of a car—one with hostility, the other with fear. The first regards the noise as an encroachment; the other perceives it as a danger (namely, gunfire). Other people may show the same type of response (e.g., fear of bodily damage or death) to quite different stimuli, such as the sight of blood or a barking dog. It is therefore expedient to categorize stress reactions in terms of the cognitive response (fear, hostility, depression) rather than the specific stimulus.

A further word is indicated to explain how a particular cognitive constellation is formed and how it contributes to the specific sensitivity. In the course of development, individuals gradually form a number of concepts (schemas) about themselves and their world. As these concepts are structuralized, they become embedded in a cluster of related memories, meanings, assumptions, expectations, and rules, which the individuals utilize to process incoming data and to mobilize themselves into action. The related schemas (Beck, 1964) may be so broad and pervasive across situations that they may comprise a major dimension of personality type. On the other hand, the schemas may be relatively narrow and applicable only to a highly specific set of stimuli. If a concept (schema) has been formed under stressful conditions, it may assume the characteristic structures of the primitive cognitive system (primary-process thinking): rigid, global, categorical, and absolutistic.

To illustrate a primitive concept, let us take the example of the young man who was bitten by the dog. According to the theory I am proposing, the severity of the trauma was responsible not only for the formation of an extremely negative memory of the dog, but also of an extreme, unidimensional, undifferentiated construction of the category "dog." The primitive concept has a content such as "All dogs are dangerous." When this schema is activated, dogs are appraised according to only one dimension: not whether they are large or small, frisky or passive, shaggy or smooth-coated, but whether they are dangerous or safe. Since the schema is categorical and absolutistic, the specific appraisal excludes the notion "safe." Hence, the cognitive response to the sight of any dog is uniform: "This dog is dangerous." This response occurs even when the dog is objectively harmless, geographically remote, or safely chained. Associated with the concept are a number of assumptions and expectations, such as "If it comes closer, it will bite me" and "I won't be able to ward off the attack." Furthermore, several rules (imperatives), such as "You must get to a safe place," "Get ready to be attacked," and "Freeze!", are derived from the concept. Of course, when the primitive schema is not invoked, the individual is capable of responding realistically to the category "dog" (mature cognitive system).

To return to the sequence, any dog is automatically labeled as "dangerous." Since the young man does not believe that he has the resources to deal with the danger, and believes that the risk is high, he experiences the typical fear reaction described previously:

1. He has the expectation of being attacked.
2. He does not believe that he can safely counterattack or repel the attack.
3. He becomes mobilized to flee.

If flight does not appear possible, he may "freeze" in order to reduce the probability of the attack, and also to prepare his body to sustain the impact of the expected attack. Concomitantly, he will experience anxiety. Freezing may be an anachronistic response stemming from the assumption that a still, silent object will blend into the environment (like an opossum) and thus will not be subject to attack. When freezing occurs in interpersonal encounters, of course, it is highly maladaptive.

It is important to recognize that when a concept or schema is highly structuralized and hypervalent, the power of mature thinking to subject the construction to reality testing, make discriminations, and correct the distortion is greatly diminished. Nonetheless, it is possible in psychotherapy to counterbalance the primitive concept by helping the patient to strengthen and to apply realistic, flexible, multidimensional concepts (secondary-process thinking). As becomes clear later, the task of psychotherapy is much more difficult when the individual has a large assembly of broad primitive concepts organized around a single major theme relevant to a large proportion of his or her experience, such as interpersonal relations.

Stress and Personality

The seventh principle of the cognitive model is as follows: *Differences in personality organization account for some of the wide variations in individual sensitivities to stressors. Thus, the autonomous and sociotropic personality types differ in the kind of stressors to which they are sensitive. The occurrence of a stress reaction is thus contingent to a large degree on specific vulnerabilities related to personality.*

It may not be difficult to understand how a person can react excessively to a highly specific type of stimulus. However, it is puzzling to observe that certain individuals overreact in a relatively uniform way to a wide variety of apparently dissimilar situations. As we get to know such persons better, we find that most of the situations fit into a pattern. Thus, one individual may react with fear and inhibition when making requests, making a phone call, asking for directions, associating with strangers, or traveling alone—in other words, whenever there is any conceivable risk of rejection or isolation. Another person may react with hostility in situations demanding conformity to social norms or institutional requirements. These observations suggest that such people are governed by certain broad expectations and conceptions that they carry with them into every situation. The situations are found to have a common thread—namely, a similar individualized meaning to the person.

In some cases, the individualized meanings seem to pervade every interaction. In structural terms, it appears that a few schemas whose content is relevant to this individualized meaning are activated by the diverse situations. To illustrate this formulation, we can return to the anecdote of the student who becomes hostile when he hears a loud noise while he is studying. In reviewing his reaction to a multitude of varied life situations, we find that he is extremely sensitive to any characteristic of the situation that represents an incursion on his "life space" or an impediment to his goals. He becomes hostile if interrupted while talking, studying, or daydreaming. He is intolerant of being crowded by other people in restaurants, elevators, or conference rooms. He prefers to sit near the exit in theaters or other public places. He reacts strongly against formal rules, orders, and restrictions. He insists on "leaving his options open" and may, for example, break off a love relationship rather than accept a limitation on his freedom of action.

This individual has a host of related concepts that are applied to all interpersonal as well as impersonal relationships. These are organized into a value system whose themes are fulfillment through action, expression of individuality, and preservation of autonomy. (In contrast, the sociotropic person is oriented to receiving, togetherness, and dependency.) Thus, even minimal encroachment on this system elicits such cognitions as "He is interfering with me," "She is pushing me around," "She is trying to trap me," or "I am boxed in." These extreme ideas occur, respectively, in interactions as diverse as someone's expressing an interest in his work, asking him to participate in a group project, asking him personal questions, or expressing love and affection. Whereas these situations might elicit, respectively, gratitude, cooperativeness, friendliness, or affection in other people, they stir up hostility in this individual.

I have previously described this set of characteristics in proposing that "autonomous depressions" tend to occur in people who would be rated high on the personality dimension of individuality and low on sociality. Such individuals may experience depression if blocked from achieving their goals (Beck, 1983). I have applied the label "autonomous personality" to characterize this type of person. Autonomous individuals' conception of other people is slanted toward sensitivity to interference, intrusion, coercion, or restraint. The relevant concept is associated with such assumptions and expectations as these: "In order to reach my objective, I must do it myself," "If other people interrupt me, I won't be able to do what I have to," "I need breathing space in order to survive," and "Since the strong prey on the weak, I must appear strong in every interaction."

Some individuals of this type may show exorbitant reactions even when the noxious situation is impersonal or physical (e.g., crawling through a narrow tunnel). For example, a man who had received many decorations for bravery in World War II experienced a crippling (and demoralizing) anxiety attack when he attempted to crawl through a large cylinder in an amusement park. The possibility of being immobilized in the cylinder threatened his notion of his autonomy, upon which his concept of his identity was based. He could not tell even his best friend about his emotional reaction, because he was afraid of being ridiculed. It is of interest to note that this paratrooper's heroic exploits had centered around escaping from closed-in environments: He had shown extraordinary daring in jumping out of aircraft behind enemy lines and in breaking out of prison camps.

Clinical observations and some preliminary systematic investigation suggest that individuality and sociality are clinically and empirically useful dimensions of personality for purposes of exposition. The two dimensions are described in terms of the type of individual who would score high on one and low on the other. The "autonomous type" is a person whose personality is disproportionally weighted with characteristics of individuality, or who would be rated high on individuality and relatively low on sociality; the "socially dependent type" is one whose personality is excessively weighted toward sociotropism or sociality.

"Individuality" refers to an individual's investment in freedom of action, independence, and mobility. The motif of this cluster is "doing." The sense of well-being for such persons depends on preserving the integrity and autonomy of their domain; on having unrestricted freedom of choice, action, and expression; on directing their own activities; on being free from outside encroachment, restraint, pressure, or interference; and on attaining meaningful goals through action.

"Sociality" or "sociotropism" refers to a person's investment in positive interchange with other people. The motif of this cluster is "receiving." This cluster includes passive, receptive wishes, such as the desire for acceptance, intimacy, understanding, support, guidance, and feedback from other people for purposes of validating beliefs and behavior. Such individuals are dependent on these social inputs not only for the gratification that they bring, but also as a means of motivating and directing their own behavior and helping them to modify ideas and behaviors in order to receive more social approval and avoid social disapproval.

Studies suggest that two types of depression are associated with these two dimensions of personality. Individuals who are high on one of the dimensions have a different set of symptoms and vulnerabilities than do those who score high on the other dimension (Beck, 1983). I have observed that the autonomous type of person is more likely than the socially dependent type to experience acute or chronic hostility, claustrophobia, and "endogenous depression." The sociotropic type of person is more likely to experience "reactive depression," anxiety, and agoraphobia. From the description of the individual types, we can conclude that the autonomous type is more sensitive to restraint, encroachment, and defeat, whereas the sociotropic type is more susceptible to rejection, abandonment, and deprivation.

The difference in the two personality types may be understood in terms of the differing sets of rules, expectancies, and imperatives incorporated in their cognitive organizations. The rules governing the behavior of the autonomous personality include "I must fight for my rights," "I must not let people get in my way," "I should push people away if they crowd me," and "I mustn't let a person get away with crossing me." The application of these rules mobilizes such individuals to fight their way out of situations that symbolize traps to them; to attack people who appear to restrain, coerce, or encroach on them; and to resort to flight if fighting is not possible. If the individuals are overmobilized or are unable to "demobilize" through action, then they are likely to experience stress reactions.

This personality type illustrates how an individual may have a sensitivity to a wide range of stimuli. Such persons may be vulnerable to stress reactions unless they can arrange their social or impersonal environments in such a way as to protect their privacy and independence and to insure the attainment of their goals. Such individuals may compensate for their sensitivities in their customary life situations, but are traumatized when their environment is radically changed—for example, when they are inducted into the Army, get married, are jailed, or are thwarted or demoted in their jobs.

The origin of this particular cognitive organization differs from one person to another, but a typical case might show the following background: An active, action-oriented child strikes out against boundaries set by parents, teachers, and even peer groups. The child forms a concept of parents and other authority figures as obstructionistic and coercive. It seems to the child that the more he or she presses against the boundaries, the more rigid and restraining they become. The child's concern about threats to his or her freedom and autonomy spreads to the entire social and physical environment. If this individual's life situation restricts freedom of mobility, expression, and choice, he or she is susceptible to stress reactions.

A traveling salesman began to experience anxiety attacks after his engagement. For several years after marriage, he was depressed and complained that his wife had trapped him into the marriage and then cemented him in by having several children.

He attributed his lack of advancement in his career to the necessity of restricting his sales territory to the immediate area. The patient had volunteered for active duty during the Korean War. Shortly after his induction, he had begun to experience great hostility toward all of his officers. These reactions had continued until he was discharged for severe chronic headaches. It was clear that his psychological problem stemmed from his extremely low threshold for any type of restriction on his mobility and freedom of action. The headaches arose from muscular tension resulting from his controlled impulse to attack.

The second cluster of personality patterns revolves around the dimension of sociality. When the sociotropic structure is particularly prominent, it is useful to think of the "socially dependent type" as the opposite of the "autonomous type." This type of person is exquisitely sensitive to the possibility of rejection, exclusion, separation, and abandonment. He or she believes that "Life is not meaningful without love," "I can't live unless I have people around who care," and "If a person is unkind to me, there is something wrong with me." Since this type has been described extensively elsewhere (Beck, 1983), I do not elaborate further here.

The typical background of an individual dominated primarily by sociotropic patterns would be as follows: As a child, this individual was driven to receive affection, nurturance, and praise. Although the mother was a "giving" person, older siblings whom the child admired tormented and rejected him or her. The hypersensitivity to rejection that resulted undermined the child's receiving full acceptance into his or her peer group. From adolescence on, the individual has felt like a "loner," and although he or she may have achieved the symbols of success—prestige in a career and a devoted family—the person has continually sought praise and reassurance and is hypersensitive to rejection and separation.

Stress Syndromes

The eighth principle of the cognitive model is this: *Each of the stress syndromes (such as hostility, anxiety, and depression) consists of hyperactive schemas with an idiosyncratic content specific for that syndrome. Each syndrome comprises a specific controlling cognitive constellation and the resultant behavioral inclinations and affect.*

When the schemas have been overstimulated for long enough to produce the symptoms of a well-defined disorder, the term "syndrome" may be applied to designate the triad consisting of the cognitive constellation, behavioral inclination, and affect. A number of different syndromes may be involved in the stress reaction; only three are described at this point.

A characteristic of all the syndromes is that once the cognitive constellation becomes overactive, it tends to select and process stimuli that are congruent with it—a process described by Mahoney (1982) as "feedforward." As a result of extracting only congruent stimuli, the cognitive constellation continues to be hyperactive or becomes more active. Thus, individuals who are fixated on ideas of personal danger are likely to scan their environment for signs of potential harm and to misread innocuous events as dangerous. Consequently, the notion of imminent harm becomes progressively greater. Similarly, the tendency of depressed patients to direct their attention to negative events and to misinterpret or blot out positive events intensifies their negative constructions of their experience. The same vicious cycle may be observed in acute hostile reactions: As hostile individuals misinterpret successive events as challenges or affronts, they are more likely to interpret subsequent neutral occurrences in the same way.

In the "hostility syndrome," individuals are hypersensitive to any events that suggest restraint, interference, assault, or encroachment on their domain (Beck, 1976, pp. 64–75). They may, for example, respond to even gentle suggestions with the idea that they are being controlled, and they are thus stimulated to counterattack. As indicated earlier, any threat to the domain may evoke the hostility "fight" reaction if such individuals place a higher premium on attacking or counterattacking than on the possible risks or costs. The affect associated with hostility reactions may range from mild irritation to intense anger or rage. A key component in the hostility syndrome, therefore, is these individuals' belief that they have the resources to oppose or punish the presumed restrictions, encroachments, or affronts. Unlike individuals with the fear or depressive syndromes, they are not concerned about their inability to negate adverse reactions to their aggressive behavior.

In the "fear syndrome," individuals are hyperreactive to any situation that represents danger to them. Their state of arousal is manifested by a desire to flee to a safe place or to inhibit any behavior that does not ostensibly facilitate reducing the danger. This inhibition, manifested by "freezing," "choking up," or "blocking," is anachronistic and indeed generally increases the danger; it is related to a total focusing on the danger and an automatic blotting out of any other cognitions, including coping strategies. It is seen most frequently in interpersonal situations, such as speaking in public, taking tests, or initiating social contacts. Although some aspects of this automatic inhibition may have had adaptive value in earlier stages of evolution of the species, it is maladaptive in contemporary life. Thus, the disorder is best viewed in terms of an activation of an anachronistic mechanism of defense, rather than as a "neurotic" reaction. Since the emotion associated with this fear syndrome is anxiety, the subsyndromes are generally referred to as "public-speaking anxiety," "test anxiety," or "social anxiety." Although the syndromes are named after the associated affects, they could be labeled more precisely according to the nature of the cognitive constellation—for example, "public-speaking fear," "fear of being tested," or "social fear."

The "depression syndrome" is more complex than the two previously described syndromes and consists of a variety of possible cognitive constellations, behavioral inclinations, and affects. The relationship of the controlling cognitive constellation to the characteristic affects has been described previously (Beck, 1967, 1976). In brief, the prevailing cognitive constellation in depression has a content relevant to sense of loss, thwarting, or defeat and is reflected in negative attitudes toward the self, the future, and external events. The cognitive schemas become prepotent and activate tendencies to withdraw, give up, and become passive. These tendencies may become accentuated because of the "de-energizing" or inhibition of the drives toward goal-directed activity.

Suicidal impulses are directly derived from hopelessness, which is a component of the cognitive constellation. However, since hopelessness and the derivative suicidal wishes occur in conditions other than depression, these particular psychological phenomena should not be considered to be exclusive properties of the depression syndrome.

The "Internal Stressor"

The ninth principle of the cognitive model is as follows: *The principal stressor may be internal, with no apparent referent in the outside world. The assumption that the only road to fulfillment is through total success is intrinsic in achievement-oriented persons prone to stress reactions.*

We can observe that individuals may develop typical stress reactions when there are no external conditions to account for them. In such cases, the origin of the stress may be internal and consist of such phenomena as the demands the individuals place on themselves, their repetitive self-nagging, and their self-reproaches.

A stereotype of one kind of person prone to this form of self-stressing is the "typical" hard-driving businessperson or scientist. Such persons set high goals and drive themselves and others in order to achieve them. Their outward behavior reflects their system of goals and beliefs, which leads to a constant state of tension. Although there may be no objective evidence of pressure from the outside, such patients' occupations present problems for them because of the way they perceive their work. Since they regard each specific task as a major confrontation, they are continually driving, nagging, and pressing themselves. Their self-imposed psychological stress is accompanied by overloading of one or more of their psychophysiological systems.

The excessive momentum behind the work drive may be these persons' chronic concern that they will not reach their goals, or that they or their subordinates will make costly errors. These "worried achievers" react to each new task with strong doubts. They exaggerate the importance or the difficulty of a task (a faulty cognitive appraisal) and underestimate their capacity to deal with it (also a faulty cognitive appraisal). Not only do they magnify the obstacles to completing a task, but they also exaggerate the consequences of failure. They may, for example, visualize a chain of events leading to bankruptcy whenever the outcome of a particular financial venture is uncertain. These individuals are predisposed to excessive tension, because they exaggerate not only the dire consequences of falling short of their goals, but also the probability of these consequences' occurring.

These "irritable achievers" are also in a continuous state of tension because of what they conceive of as unnecessary obstacles in the path toward their goal. They may experience hostility toward their coworkers or subordinates whenever their systems fail to operate at maximum efficiency. Alternatively, they may reproach themselves savagely if they perceive that they have been inefficient or negligent. A system may be so important that the end becomes more important than the means.

Reciprocal Interaction Model of Stress

The 10th principle of the cognitive model is this: *Stressful interactions with other people occur in a mutually reinforcing cycle of maladaptive cognitive reactions. Specific mechanisms, such as the egocentric cognitive mode, framing, and polarization, lead to increased mobilization and consequently to stress.*

In the discussion up to this point, I have regarded the patterning of stress reactions in terms of the responses of single individuals to external stimuli. For purposes of convenience, I have not dealt with the way in which individuals may develop stress reactions in response to complicated interrelationships with other people in their environment.

Stress does not occur in a vacuum. When we look at the interpersonal relations of stressed individuals, we realize that their behavior evokes responses from other people, which are fed back to them and stimulate further responses in them. Ordinarily, interpersonal responses are modulated in such a way as to minimize the amount of friction among people, and also the degree of disturbance within individuals. Thus, people operate as though they have a kind of "thermostat" that regulates their behavior. When these adjustments in behavior do not occur in an adaptive way, the stage is set for stress in individuals and/or in the persons with whom they are interacting (see Lazarus, 1981).

Cognitive–Behavioral Interactions

A more comprehensive reciprocal or interactional model demands the inclusion of cognitive structuring. Thus, an individual structures a particular situation with another person in a specific way. The individual's structuring of the situation will lead to a particular behavior. His or her behavior is interpreted in a specific way by the other person, who then manifests a behavioral response to this interpretation. Thus we get a continuous cycling of cognition → behavior → cognition → behavior.

For example, Bob thinks that it would be nice to do something with Harry and makes a suggestion to Harry. Harry reacts to the overt behavior (the request) with an idiosyncratic interpretation—"He is making an unwarranted demand"—and starts to criticize Bob for his "demandingness." Bob responds to this critical behavior with his own interpretation: "He is treating me unfairly. I would certainly fulfill *his* request. I can't let me get away with this." He then verbally counterattacks.

Harry responds cognitively with the notion "This guy is useless to me; I might as well write him off," and tells Bob, "Look, we just can't get along. Why don't we call the whole thing off?" Bob's cognitions then run something like this: "Harry is being unreasonable. He regards me as a pushover. I can't let him get away with it, or other people will think they can push me around." Bob then becomes overmobilized for further attack. At this point, what he says will be insufficient to restore his mobilization to a baseline level. Consequently, the state of overmobilization persists for a period of time.

This kind of overmobilization is the immediate factor in producing stress. If sustained and repeated over a long enough period, the individual's reactions may move from heightened activity in the neuroendocrine system to specific physiological dysfunctions.

The Egocentric Mode

As pointed out previously, when people consider their vital interests to be at stake, they are likely to shift into the egocentric mode. The egocentric mode organizes present, past, and future situations or events predominantly in terms of how they affect the individuals' own vital interests. Since such individuals are focused on the meanings of the events to them, the meanings of other persons are not part of their phenomenal field. Even when they attempt to view situations from the standpoints of other persons, they will—as long as they are in the egocentric mode—come up with interpretations that are heavily laden with the meanings the events have for them.

In interpersonal relations, clashes are likely to occur when each individual is operating solely within the egocentric mode. Even though an individual may have no desire to hurt (and, indeed, may even want to help), his or her egocentricity places a burden on the other person and ultimately on himself or herself. A clash is inevitable when both individuals view things according to their highly personalized formulations. Each person's constructions of his or her own behavior and of the other person's behavior will inevitably lead to a conflict of interest.

The stressful nature of interactions is well illustrated in the form of the widely recognized frictions that develop in marital relations. The stressful interactions derived from one couple's conflict serve as a model to exemplify the mutually reinforcing nature of stressors. The couple demonstrated completely different cognitive sets in the following situation: The wife asked the husband to stay home with her on a particular night because she felt sick. He refused, because he had already committed ' imself to spending the evening with a business colleague. They then slipped into uch a screaming match that each started to think seriously about getting a divorce.

On exploration, it became apparent that each partner not only was viewing the disagreement in egocentric terms but was "catastrophizing." The wife's thoughts were these: "If he won't do this small favor for me, how can I count on him when I have a major problem? It shows I can't count on him for anything." The husband's interpretation was this: "She is completely unreasonable. She won't give me any freedom. She looks for any excuse to keep me home. If I have to give in, I can't survive."

This anecdote illustrates several characteristics of the egocentric mode. First, neither person was aware of the meaning conveyed by his or her behavior to the spouse. Second, each believed that his or her interpretation of the event was so valid that its reasonableness should be apparent to anybody. The wife, for example, was convinced that her husband's noncompliance with minor requests proved that she would not be able to rely on him for help when she needed it. The husband believed that compliance with the "small request" would place him in a straitjacket. Because the egocentric mode precludes the possibility of integrating crucial interpersonal feedback (in this case, understanding the spouse's perspective), each individual tended to attempt maladaptively to force the spouse to accept his or her frame of reference. The result was that each partner became frozen in his or her own perspective.

It is interesting that the egocentric mode tends to highlight certain dominant personality patterns. In the preceding example, the husband, who had a strong autonomous bent, needed to maintain a certain freedom of action in his relationships. His specific vulnerability was "being tied down." The wife, on the other hand, had a strong sociotropic/dependent pattern, and consequently was especially sensitive to being left alone. Continued abrasion of the sensitive areas could lead to stress in either or both partners.

The therapeutic approach in this case would consist of "decentering" (to use

Piaget's term) each individual's perspective, and facilitating his or her awareness of the mate's perspective. This procedure would require delicate handling by the therapist, because the perspective of one or both partners might be relatively idiosyncratic and might be regarded by the other spouse as either "unreasonable" or "ridiculous."

Framing

When people view other people with whom they are in conflict, they tend to make an appraisal not only of the others' behavior, but of the other persons themselves. Generally, the type of actions that people consider to be most typical of these others, or most salient in terms of their interaction with them, are transformed into images or concepts of the other individuals. For example, somebody who is regarded as acting deviously will emerge in an image as a "sneak" or "cheat." In the preceding example, the husband pictured his wife as a demanding, needy, rigid person; the wife visualized the husband as a self-centered, insensitive, undependable person.

"Framing" consists of focusing on some characteristic one attributes to another person and portraying this individual in such a way that this attribute dominates the picture of that person. The term "frame" is applied to the specific image or concept of an individual with whom one is in conflict. In creating a frame, one not only reduces a highly complex individual to a few (usually negative) character traits, but manufactures additional elements to flesh out the image (which inevitably is a distortion or caricature of the other person). It is possible to have more than one frame of another person: A wife may see her husband at one time as kind and generous, and at other times as selfish and rejecting. The wife in this instance becomes sensitized to certain types of behavior, which she correlates with the negative attributes. When a particular instigating event occurs, the frame that is anchored to that type of stimulus is aroused. For example, whenever the husband places a priority on *his* interests, the wife is likely to visualize him as a bully.

Polarization

As the spouses in the "framing" example discussed their opposing wishes, they became increasingly angry at each other. Moreover, as their discussion progressed, they took more extreme, inflexible, opposing positions. We see two interacting phenomena here: "external polarization" (moving further apart in their expressed opinions) and "internal polarization" (thinking more negatively of each other). Their view of each other became more and more negative until it was finally hardened into a specific frame. The view was expressed also in a vague image, which might be verbalized as follows:

> HUSBAND: She is weak, demanding, incapable of helping herself. She is mush, a weakling.
> WIFE: He is insensitive, ruthless, rejecting, inconsiderate.

The negative constructions by the husband led him to withdraw more. This behavior in turn was processed cognitively by the wife as rejection and abandonment, and led her to become more dependent, clinging, scolding—and ultimately depressed. He structured her depressed behavior as manipulation to induce guilt and force him to comply. Thus, he wanted even more to be free of her. The cognitive processing by each person thus took on the characteristics of a thinking disorder of the neuroses: extreme, unrealistic evaluations of the other person; selective abstraction of data consistent with the "frame" each person had imposed on the other; ablation of favorable data by inattention or forgetting; misinterpretation of the other's behavior; and attribution of unworthy motives to explain the other's behavior.

To describe the phenomena of the interaction, the model must be expanded still further. Cognitive structuring does not lead directly to overt behavior. Interposed between the cognitive process and behavior, there is the motivational component labeled "behavioral inclination." In this case, the behavioral inclination emerged from the cognitive constellation in the form of a wish to scold, demand, complain, withdraw, or punish. The overt behavior (speech) of one spouse was consequently tinged with phrases, inflections, and tones that connoted disapproval and devaluation of the other spouse.

The Unitary Psychophysiological System

The 11th principle of the cognitive model is as follows: *An individual experiences an inclination to respond physically, although the stimulus may be psychosocial or symbolic and although ultimate overt behavior is verbal. The mobilization for "fight or flight" involves the same cognitive–motoric systems, regardless of whether the level of meaning of a threat or challenge is physical or psychosocial.*

An individual may show the same type of response, regardless of whether the noxious stimulus is physical or abstract (psychosocial): The person responds in much the same way to a psychosocial challenge, threat, or injury as he or she does to an actual physical confrontation or attack (see Wolff, 1950). To illustrate, let us examine one of these "real-life dramas." A man was shoved in a ticket line by somebody wanting to move the line along. As he felt the pressure on his back, he became mobilized to counterattack: His voluntary muscles became tense, and he experienced an increase in heart rate and blood pressure as he braced himself to push back the offender. A few weeks later, one of his coworkers was pressing him to speed up his work. The individual experienced *the same type of physical pressure across his back* as when he was shoved in line. Moreover, he felt the same wish and bracing of his muscles to push away his coworker.

The crucial observation is that our protagonist became mobilized to counteract the challenge in the same fashion (voluntary nervous system, autonomic nervous system) when he was psychosocially pressured to do something he did not want to do as when he was subjected to physical pressure from an adversary. Although it may be conceded that there might be some adaptational benefit in preparing to defend oneself against physical encroachments (such as being shoved), there seems little benefit from this total kind of physical mobilization when an adequate response would be a verbal statement employing only the muscles of articulation: "Leave me alone," "Get off my back," "I don't want to do it."

Why do people who are confronted with minor psychosocial challenges respond unnecessarily with a mobilization of the fight-or-flight apparatus when their conscious desire is simply to utter a few words? Certainly, the total mobilization is at best superfluous and at worst self-destructive. It seems that even though humans are generally well trained to respond overtly in an appropriate, "civilized" way to minor challenges, they are nonetheless the victims of an inherited primitive response system. Although they may have a well-functioning system of controls to keep the primitive responses in check, they nonetheless have to contend continually with being mobilized for aggressive action far in excess of the demands of the real situations.

If our protagonist were to be "attacked" verbally—say, by somebody's insulting him—he might experience an urge to strike the offender just as though he had been attacked physically. These examples indicate that there is an equivalence between the abstract, verbal stimulus and the concrete physical stimulus. The initial response to both psychosocial and physical transgressions is identical: Each elicits an impulse to counterattack physically. Whether the transgression is concrete or symbolic in nature, there is a basic physical response.

It is easy to confirm the observation that individuals who have hostile reactions generally experience tightening of their shoulder, arm, back, or leg muscles, even though they may not be aware of the behavioral inclination to use these muscles against an adversary. With introspection, individuals who are retaliating verbally may recognize a concomitant impulse to strike their adversaries. In the disorders characterized by chronic muscular tension, it is important to determine whether individuals are experiencing this kind of behavioral inclination to defend themselves or to counterattack.

The reactions of the fear syndrome are analogous to those of the hostility syndrome. The noxious stimulus may be a threat of psychological injury (e.g., betrayal) or of physical injury (e.g., being stabbed in the back). Such persons may respond both verbally (e.g., by shouting "How can you do this to me?") and physically (by an impulse to protect themselves or to flee). The typical reactions of the voluntary and involuntary (autonomic) nervous systems occur, and such individuals become mobilized for self-protection or flight, regardless of whether the fear is of an abstract (e.g., psychosocial) injury or a concrete (physical) injury.

The similarities in response to either a psychosocial or a physical stimulus suggest the presence of a generalized meaning that encompasses both types of stimulus. In the hostile reaction, the generalized meaning occurs in the form of an idea such as "That person is transgressing against me." In the fear reaction, the meaning assumes a general form such as "I am in danger of having a damaging experience." An encroachment on or danger to the physical integrity of an individual would appear logically to be more serious than a transgression or threat to an individual's psychological status. This notion is exemplified in the old saw "Sticks and stones will break my bones, but words will never hurt me." Despite the common-sense utility of such a saying, the meaning of a verbal assault is so close to that of a physical assault that the same cognitive and motor systems are activated in response to each stimulus.

This formulation suggests that in our "civilized" society, the symbolic meanings of countless social interactions are continuously arousing us to fight, defend, or flee. It seems plausible that since we rarely allow this arousal to be transformed into physical action, our voluntary and autonomic nervous systems are continually overloaded. Beyond a certain point, this overloading leads to a stress reaction.

Cognitive Therapy of Stress Reactions

Relief of Symptoms

To understand the cognitive approach to treatment of stress reactions, let us take a commonplace example and see how this problem would be approached.

Mr. A was a hard-driving businessman who had hypertension, headaches, and a sleep disturbance. Every day he left his house at 7 A.M. in order to avoid the heavy traffic. However, by the time he arrived at his office half an hour later, his face was red, he was perspiring, his pulse was racing, and he had a headache. What happened in the interim?

The following scenario was elicited. Although Mr. A believed that he was simply driving his car to work, it was apparent that he himself *was being driven* by forces that he was only dimly aware of. Practically every second of his trip, he was engaged in sequences of confrontations and challenges with other drivers. The competitive struggle led him to cut in and out of lanes and to attempt to get the jump on the other drivers at stop signals. He believed that the other drivers were similarly trying to beat him, and he was impelled to counterattack if one of them did get an advantage.

Aside from his competitive reactions, Mr. A had his own goal of making the best possible time. He reacted to any loss of momentum as though he were blocked by a major barrier. He mentally or orally attacked a slow driver who impedes forward progress. He regarded it as a personal defeat if he did not beat out a yellow light before it turned red.

It was apparent that Mr. A—far from simply traveling to work—was engaged in a kind of survival course. His maneuvering was not a game, but rather a series of fierce encounters. He was mobilized for aggressive physical action, as manifested by his muscular tension, increased blood pressure, and increased heart rate. Since he had no opportunity to transform the mobilization into action, by the time he reached the office his muscles were taut and he was coiled, prepared to strike. However, there was no opportunity to engage in the kind of physical action that would facilitate "demobilization." Moreover, since his cognitive set revolved around the notion of "attack," he tended to interpret further encounters in terms of this construct, and then to remain in a state of mobilization.

If we take this example as the prototype of a stress reaction, let us consider how the cognitive approach could be applied to alleviate Mr. A's symptoms.

Rationale

The first step in the management of stress reactions is the application of the principles outlined in the first part of this chapter to understanding an individual case. The case needs to be formulated in terms of the theoretical framework, and then the appropriate strategies and techniques can be developed and utilized.

The basic model that provides the rationale for the treatment is that certain idiosyncratic cognitive patterns become hyperactive and lead to overmobilization of the voluntary nervous system and autonomic nervous system. Concurrently, the system of buffers and adaptive functions (objectivity, perspective, reality testing) becomes strained and is progressively less effective in counteracting the dominance of the controlling cognitive constellation. The direct result of the overmobilization may be experienced in terms of the "syndromes" (e.g., anxiety reaction or hostility reaction) or psychosomatic disorders. In the latter disorders, the physical effects are observable in dysfunction of specific systems or organs (musculoskeletal, cardiovascular, gastrointestinal, etc.).

The overall aim of therapy is to reduce the hypervalence of the controlling cognitive constellations and to shore up the adaptive functions. An initial direct approach is to reduce the exposure to situations that serve as stressors (i.e., that serve to increase or maintain the stimulation of controlling cognitive constellations). An example of environmental modification would be for Mr. A to take time away from the job or to stop driving to work. As the overactivity of the cognitive constellation is reduced, there is not only a reduced mobilization of the neuromuscular endocrine system, but also a relative increase in the adaptive functions (particularly objectivity and perspective). As the individual's total involvement in the immediate work-related stimuli is reduced, the person is then able to reflect upon his or her reactions, recognize overreactions, test some of his or her conclusions, and adopt a broader view regarding his or her realistic problems. When this approach is systematized, the specific cognitive techniques are used: identifying automatic thoughts, recognizing and correcting cognitive distortions, and identifying the broad beliefs and assumptions that underlie the hyperactive constellations.

Clarifying and Defining the Problem

It is important to recognize that although we might label Mr. A's symptoms as manifestations of a "stress reaction," environmental stressors—as we generally conceive of them—were not present. If we were to think simply in terms of external factors, we might be hard put to explain why Mr. A experienced his trip as more stressful than the other drivers did. In order for him to achieve an understanding of his problem, he would need to be encouraged to examine the internal factors: his thoughts, impulses, and feelings. It would be especially important for him to grasp the workings of the "internal stressor" (the ninth principle). As noted above, an external situation serves as a stimulus to an internal stressor but is not inherently stress-producing.

Understanding the Meanings

Mr. A needed to become aware, first of all, that his driving had surplus meanings. He was not fully conscious of how he was driven to fight off the other drivers, nor did he see the connection between his combativeness on the road and his symptoms. Preparing himself to observe his attitudes and reactions would enable him to make the crucial observations during his next trip. Once he was prepared to observe, he could delineate the pattern of challenge, confrontation, and competition, as well as his reactions to any difficulty as though it were a major barrier. He would be able to see that he had superimposed a heavy layer of meanings onto the relatively easy task of driving his car to work. This overload of meanings (and their association with primary-process thinking) led to the overmobilization manifested in his stress symptoms: increased heart rate, increased blood pressure, and headache. Moreover, he would be able to see the carryover of these cognitive patterns: Throughout his working day, he reacted to each encounter as though he were engaged in hand-to-hand combat.

Recognizing Egocentrism and Cognitive Distortions

One of the most important characteristics for Mr. A to detect would be his own egocentrism. He viewed all events as though he were the central character in a drama; the behavior of all the other characters had meaning only insofar as he related it to his own "vital interests." He personalized events that are essentially impersonal, and perceived confrontations and challenges when others were conducting their own lives oblivious of him. The egocentric mode could be viewed as responsible for Mr. A's way of interpreting events in terms of factors such as survival, as well as his attaching extreme, negative labels to other drivers.

Once Mr. A understood the problem, he could understand the rationale for various therapeutic maneuvers. To summarize, the steps in formulating the case and understanding the problem would be as follows: First, Mr. A would need to recognize that crucial components of stress were internal (i.e., idiosyncratic meanings were attached to events). Second, he would need to pinpoint the overall idiosyncratic meaning (i.e., that he was prepared for combat). Third, he would need to focus attention on the overmobilization (muscular tension with vegetative sensations). Fourth, he would need to connect the meaning ("combat") with the behavioral inclination ("beat them out") and the affect (anger, etc.). Finally, he would need to recognize how "vital interests" were injected into mundane situations because of the egocentric frame of reference.

Increasing Objectivity

"Objectivity" refers to the capacity of individuals to examine their thinking, motivations, and behavior as though they were disinterested observers. It is essential that patients attain distance from their reactions, so that they can look at their experiences as phenomena instead of being totally absorbed by them. Then they may be able to recognize that their thoughts and conclusions are inferences, not facts—that their beliefs are derived from an internal process and are not pure images of external reality. They may consequently realize that, since their cognitive processes are fallible, they may have been accepting misinterpretations, distortions, and exaggerations as "truth." Furthermore, they can observe that the laws and rules that they apply to themselves and others are not immutable, natural laws (like the laws of gravity and thermodynamics), but are often arbitrary and self-defeating.

With increasing objectivity, patients can recognize that the meanings and significances of events are "man-made" and do not occur independently in nature. Although they do not voluntarily attach irrelevant and self-defeating meanings to events, it is possible to undo the assignment of meaning—to strip away the excess baggage from events.

It is worth emphasizing that simply taking a history and asking the "right" questions can increase a patient's objectivity (and perspective). As a therapist probes for meanings, a patient spontaneously begins to question the validity of his or her conclusions and to see the symptoms in a new light.

Increasing Perspective

"Increasing perspective" refers to individuals' expanding the frames by which they judge events, themselves, and others. The expanded frame of reference facilitates seeing an event in a broader vista. By applying a calibrated measurement, individuals can obtain a more relative concept of magnitude, seriousness, and duration. In contrast, people who have lost perspective think in absolute terms—as though the present instance is of utmost importance and will go on forever.

With increasing perspective, for example, Mr. A could come to see that beating other drivers and getting to work fast was relatively unimportant—not a life-and-death struggle—and could further realize that the encounter with other drivers was time-limited and not a part of a continuous war. The conceptualizations involved in a broader perspective are far more complex and involve many more kinds of shading than those derived from the narrow egocentric frame of reference.

Expanding boundaries means not only processing more information, but also forming conceptualizations that are more heterogeneous and contain contradictory elements. For example, other people might simultaneously feel friendly toward Mr. A and wary of him; they might have a blend of positive and negative characteristics. Moreover, in the course of therapy his beliefs might become more dimensional and less absolutistic. Thus, he would introduce uncertainty into his belief that other drivers were out to get him.

In addition, he could extend his concept of time so that an upsetting incident would not pre-empt his view of the past and the future, but would be just a point on a time continuum. The increasing time perspective would help to reduce the exaggerated significances.

Shifting or Damping Cognitive Set

The crucial element in facilitating demobilization of the neuroendocrine system is changing the cognitive set. Each time Mr. A went out to his car, a specific cognitive set was induced; that is, his view of his world shifted from a relatively peaceful, harmonious outlook during breakfast to an expectation of confrontation and competition. Since this cognitive set was not fixed, it could be changed. All of the techniques listed below would involve his changing from a combative to a noncombative frame of mind.

A cognitive set is the final product of the network of associated attitudes, expectations, memories, and meanings that are activated by a given situation. This set may be induced by specific situations (e.g., Mr. A's trip to work), or it may be relatively stable across all situations, as when a person is depressed. In the earlier portion of this chapter, I have applied the term "controlling cognitive constellation" to designate the basic cognitive structures ("schemas") that are reflected in the cognitive set. Although the structures are out of awareness, the individual has access to the *content* represented in the set. Changing the cognitive set may be achieved by changing the nature of the environmental stimuli, by transferring attention to a different set of stimuli, or by subjecting the content of the set to logical and empirical analysis.

The cognitive set induced by specific stimuli may also be conceptualized as consisting of a composite of primary and secondary appraisals. Thus, therapeutic work may be directed toward modifying the conception of threat or challenge ("primary appraisal") or toward the evaluation of coping resources ("secondary appraisal"). The validity of the primary and secondary appraisals is tested by subjecting them to a series of questions: What is the evidence of a threat? How serious is it? What coping resources are available? The individual can also reduce exaggerated threats through "coping self-statements" (Ellis, 1962; Goldfried, 1977; Meichenbaum, 1977; Novaco, 1975; Turk, Meichenbaum, & Genest, 1983).

Environmental Change

Since the stimuli from Mr. A's driving in traffic led to the arousal of a specific combative pattern, another mode of travel might eliminate this source of stimulation. For example, if Mr. A were to take the train to work, he would be removed from the specific situation that led to the mobilization. A person who is overinvolved in the demands or obligations of business or family might seek a change of scenery by taking a vacation.

Diversion

Mr. A could attempt to shift his attention away from the other drivers, from thinking about competition, and so on. Thus, he might he focus on listening to an audiotape or to the radio, or observe features of his environment to which he had formerly been oblivious. The diversion would vitiate the power of the cognitive set, and would thus reduce the frequency and intensity of Mr. A's hostile inferences regarding confrontations and challenges.

Relaxation

Using a technique such as Edmund Jacobson's progressive relaxation (Jacobson, 1938) might serve several purposes for Mr. A. Training him to relax during his journey might result in a damping down of his physiological arousal, as Jacobson claimed.

Furthermore, relaxation sessions during the day might also lower Mr. A's level of arousal.

Beyond the obvious purposes of relaxation, this procedure would probably help to modify Mr. A's cognitive set. Certainly, focusing on relaxing his muscles might divert Mr. A from his overvigilant attention to the other drivers. In addition, the instruction to "relax" would convey powerful meanings, such as "Things are not as serious as I make them out to be," "I can just sit back and take it easy," and "It's not desirable to keep driving myself." Since the motive force behind Mr. A's tension was the drive to action, the assignment to relax would activate cognitive structures relevant to inaction and passivity.

Cognitive Restructuring and Reality Testing

The techniques of cognitive modification are aimed at improving a patient's way of processing information, and consequently his or her grasp of reality. Take, for example, Mr. A's notion that other drivers were trying to beat him out or to obstruct his progress. A series of questions could be raised: (1) What is the evidence for this conclusion? (2) Is there evidence that contradicts this conclusion? (3) Are there alternative explanations for their presumed hostile behavior?

Such a joint inquiry between therapist and patient has been labeled "collaborative empiricism" elsewhere (Hollon & Beck, 1979). The technique consists of framing a conclusion as a hypothesis, which is then jointly investigated. By assuming an investigative role, the therapist encourages the patient to view his or her ideas as conclusions or inferences to be examined, rather than as beliefs to be defended. The approach has the benefit of increasing the patient's objectivity and reality testing— functions previously ascribed to the "secondary process."

For example, after Mr. A had been asked to look for evidence either consistent with or contradictory to his notion that the other drivers were trying to beat him out (or obstruct him), he reported the following incident: "There was a truck ahead of me. I thought it was deliberately trying to block me, so I gunned my engine to pass it. Then I saw that the driver was busy talking to his buddy and didn't even notice me." Through looking for evidence, he came to realize that, far from engaging in a battle with him, the drivers of other vehicles were not even aware of him. Such an observation not only can correct a misconception, but can also help shake the egocentric perspective—a process I call "decentering." Mr. A's discovery that his attribution of malicious intent was wrong fits into the concept of "disattribution." The cognitive techniques of examining the evidence, looking for alternative explanations, and disattribution have been described in detail in previous writings (Beck, 1963; Beck et al., 1979).

Recognizing and Correcting Dysfunctional Cognitions

Patients with stress reactions show the same kinds of deviations in information processing and logical thinking that have been described previously in regard to depression, anxiety disorders, and hostility reactions (Beck, 1963, 1976). These deviations appear to be manifestations of primary-process patterns of thinking, as well as of relatively reduced secondary-process thinking.

Mr. A gradually became aware of his thoughts and impulses while driving. Each time he was able to identify these cognitions, he increased his objectivity toward them. Some of the categories were these:

1. *Projections (mind reading):* "They think I am a pushover."
2. *Exaggeration:* "I'll never get to work at this rate. . . . This bottleneck is awful."
3. *Imperatives:* "I must get to work as fast as I can," "I can't let him think he can get away with edging me out," "I must show him," "I must not allow myself to be jammed in."
4. *Negative attributions:* "They are deliberately trying to cut me off."
5. *Punitive wishes:* "I will show him how stupid he is by cutting in front of him."

The step after noting and recording a particular cognition is to evaluate it logically. For example, Mr. A was asked to look for evidence that other drivers were deliberately trying to impede his progress. The homework assignment was for him to do this on his next trip by observing other drivers more closely.

Special Cognitive Problems

In addition to the therapeutic techniques listed earlier (examining the evidence, disattribution, decentering, etc.), specific techniques are important to counteract some of the characteristics of primitive or primary-process thinking.

"Premature closure" can be counteracted by asking patients to train themselves to record their immediate conclusions and then to attempt to postpone acting on the conclusions until they have had a chance to review the bases for the conclusion. Some patients develop a real skill in carrying on an internal debate, in lieu of immediately accepting the validity of a conclusion.

Absolutistic or dichotomous thinking can be approached by inducing patients to introduce a scale into their appraisal of situations. For example, a student who had acute diarrhea before exams reported that he had just undergone a "horrible" experience. He and I then had the following interchange:

THERAPIST: On a 100-point scale, how bad was it?
PATIENT: About 100.
THERAPIST: What was the worst experience you ever had?
PATIENT: When my grandfather died.
THERAPIST: If that rated 100, how would you rate yesterday's experience?
PATIENT: Oh, I guess about 60.

The patient then went on to say that it could be "horrible" if he did not do well on a test the next day.

THERAPIST: How horrible could it be?
PATIENT: About 100.

THERAPIST: If your grandfather's death was 100, how bad would this be?
PATIENT: About 40, I guess.

This technique tends to give a patient a greater sense of proportion and a sense that unpleasant events are relative and not absolute. Indeed, the technique reduces the magnitude of the perceived stressor by enabling the patient to view events in terms of degrees of severity, rather than in absolute terms. In actuality, much of the patient's thinking does include perspective, relativism, and dimensionality. The aspects of secondary-process thinking are overridden, however, by the narrow, egocentric, absolutistic categories of primary-process thinking when the individual perceives that his or her vital interests are at stake.

Typical dichotomous thinking is manifested in the patient's framing inferences in terms of "success–failure," "liked–disliked," or "happy–sad." Since the patient has a tendency to set a relatively high standard for an event to be rated in terms of having succeeded, been liked, or felt happy, he or she is particularly vulnerable to the risk of experiencing "failure," "dislikes," or "unhappiness." The student with fear of exams reported the following:

PATIENT: I feel terrible today.
THERAPIST: Why?
PATIENT: I feel like a failure. I really blew the exam.
THERAPIST: What do you think you got?
PATIENT: A really bad score.
THERAPIST: 50, 60, 70?
PATIENT: 80, I guess.
THERAPIST: Does that mean you failed?
PATIENT: No, but I didn't do as well as I wanted.
THERAPIST: What did you want?
PATIENT: At least a 90.
THERAPIST: So anything less than a 90 is a failure?
PATIENT: Sounds silly, but I guess that's right. . . . OK, I didn't blow it, but I wish I had done better.

The "seriousness" attached to anticipated adverse events can be approached in a way illustrated in the following example of the same student before an exam:

PATIENT: I feel like jumping out of my skin. . . . If I fail this exam, I don't know what I'll do.
THERAPIST: What could be a failure?
PATIENT: Anything less than 80.
THERAPIST: Imagine you got a 70. What do you visualize would happen?
PATIENT: I'd flunk out. My parents would be disappointed. My classmates would cut me up.
THERAPIST: Why don't you rate the probabilities?
PATIENT: I guess I would not flunk out. I've got too many A's for that. My parents would be disappointed if I did. The other kids wouldn't cut me up, but their opinion would go down.

This belief interchange was powerful enough to undercut the seriousness of the possible consequences. There was a durable effect, in that the student became less fearful and was less susceptible to diarrhea prior to exams.

Structural Change

The description of Mr. A's driving patterns covers only one aspect of his actual case history. The treatment plan already described is one designed primarily to produce symptom relief. That result, which is no small achievement in itself, is often attained in 5 to 10 interviews. Since this type of relief is dependent on a shift in cognitive set, the improvement may not be durable if there has been no fundamental change in the cognitive organization. I find, however, that many patients need—and often want— more substantial and more lasting change, so that they are less vulnerable to future stress reactions. In addition, the more basic work is important to improve interpersonal relations and overall satisfactions. Structural change consists not only of modifying the habitual cognitive errors (arbitrary inferences, personalization, framing, polarization, etc.), but of modifying the inappropriate system of meaning assignment and the underlying organization of rules, formulas, assumptions, and imperatives.

In conducting a cognitive analysis of a case, it is useful to elicit a broad range of dysfunctional attitudes and behaviors and to specify the circumstances or situations in which they are typically evoked. These data can then be organized or grouped according to the thematic content or some other form of patterning. In treating Mr. A, for example, I was able to list a host of distinctive dysfunctional behaviors and attitudes. (This list, incidentally, is applicable to many individuals who are prone to depression; see Beck, 1983.)

In the following description, I present additional details of Mr. A's life that indicated a need for more work than simply the treatment of his disturbance in driving. After giving more details of his case history, I present an organization of the data in terms of the specific situations (stressors) that elicited dysfunctional responses, and in terms of his specific vulnerabilities. This situational analysis then provides the basis for a structural analysis of his personality.

Case History and Analysis

Mr. A, a 45-year-old businessman, had been referred for psychotherapy for hypertension and chronic tension in all his muscles. The referring therapist, who was highly experienced in the utilization of relaxation techniques and biofeedback, made the referral because these approaches had only been mildly effective in this case.

On interview, the patient was extremely restless and unable to sit still; he asked whether he could move around. He then paced the floor for the first part of the interview. He said that he got little enjoyment out of life, although he was successful in business and (as was confirmed later) had a happy marriage and a good relationship with his children. He complained that he was unable to relax at home, and that he and his wife had to take frequent vacations in order for him to have a period of rest and relaxation. He also reported having a serious case of depression.

In the course of therapy, the case was analyzed in terms of significant factors that appeared to combine to produce his symptoms.

Specific Stressors

The stress situations involved specific "ordinary" business events. These circumstances produced a strong reaction in Mr. A. The kind of events that upset him were (1) the initiation of a new contract, project, or account; and (2) any action by one of the employees that impeded his progress in any way. Taking on a new project added substantially to the feeling of pressure he chronically experienced. Furthermore, he interpreted anything less than optimum efficiency on the part of one of his employees as "negligence," and he would experience hostility toward that employee. Since he considered it unwise to scold his employees, he carried a constant load of hostility. Thus, any performance below his standards (mistakes, delays, etc.) would contribute to the stress he experienced.

Specific Vulnerabilities

It was apparent that Mr. A was hypersensitive to a variety of events that would only minimally disturb other people:

1. If asked to do something, he would feel "put upon." This reaction was a result of his perceiving additional tasks as making his burden unbearable.

2. Any limitation of his freedom of action made him feel "locked in" or "trapped." Thus, unpleasant sensations occurred, whether the limitation was physical or psychological.

3. He was sensitive to any interference in his goal-directed activity. If somebody interrupted him while he was working, he would feel furious at the other person. The same reaction occurred when somebody impeded his progress when he was driving, as described above. He also reacted badly to being in crowds, finding that a door was locked or difficult to open, being told that a rule prohibited a certain course of action, or being asked to finish a project before he was ready.

Rules and Imperatives

1. Mr. A placed a very high value on his standards and goals, and thus was driven to meet his highly valued standards and to achieve his objectives at all costs. He was intolerant of any obstacles, delays, or detours.

2. Just as when driving to work, he was constantly pressing toward a goal and was continually monitoring his progress toward meeting the goals.

3. Since he attached too much significance to his goals, he regarded each activity as a do-or-die matter. He was chronically overmobilized.

4. Simple procedural matters were elevated to the rank of major substantive matters. Thus, he became excessively upset by unexpected problems that could readily be solved.

5. Minor mistakes that either he himself or his other workers committed were labeled as monstrous misdeeds.

6. Problems had to be solved as soon as possible. If there was no immediate solution to a problem, he believed that he was faced with a disaster.

7. The reason he became impatient, restless, and uncomfortable was that his goal seeking was continually activated and he could not deactivate it. Hence, he was impelled to work toward a particular objective even when there was nothing to be done at a given time.

An Analysis of Cognitive Organization

The patterning of rules, expectancies, and imperatives comprises a substantial component of what has been traditionally included in the concept of "personality structure." This patterning determines to a large degree the nature of a person's cognitive responses, motivations, affect, and behavior. The therapy of the "structural" problems can, for purposes of convenience, be divided into certain topical areas; these areas then become the targets for intervention. Three areas were of special importance in Mr. A's structural modification. These were (1) his egocentricity, (2) his system of rules and regulations, and (3) his punitiveness. The first two areas are crucial in most cases regarding personality change.

"Vital Interests" and Egocentricity

Importance of Meanings. Why are the "vital interests" so ubiquitous? Why do individuals react so strongly to events that a disinterested observer would consider trivial? Psychological problems may arise when an event is somehow connected with a central core of meaning that involves fundamental elements—self-enhancement, self-protection, escape, nurturance, and so on. It could be speculated that these elemental meanings take on particular force because they are derived from more primitive concepts and motivations, such as those involved with predatory behavior, protection against attack, and kinship attachments. Regardless of the possible anthropological or developmental roots, our vital interests seem to involve the kind of primitive thinking that one might expect to be precursors to "primitive impulses."

Since each of Mr. A's business activities was connected with a core construct (survival, self-enhancement), then each activity had exaggerated importance for him. Thus, even a trivial matter such as having sharp pencils available to him was invested with the same kind of meaning and degree of seriousness as the availability of capital to carry out one of his ventures. He would become almost as distressed over not finding a sharp pencil or paper on his desk as he would be if he found that part of his bank account had been encumbered by a lien.

On exploration, it was discovered that behind his overreaction to the kind of trivial occurrence such as not having a pencil available was his heavy investment in his "system." Any imperfection in the workings of his organization meant a breakdown in the system. Therefore, his line of reasoning would go something like this: "If I can't count on my staff to have something available that is so tangible and easy to attend to as pens and pencils, how can I count on them for something really important?" In brief, any event that weakened his confidence in the efficient operation of his employees led to a complete loss of confidence in the system. The resulting sense of being let down led to his experiencing anger and a wish to punish the offenders. At a previous time when he was going into a depression, the chain of mental events had led him to believe that he was going bankrupt as a result of the system's breaking down.

Now let us review some of the meanings of "success" to this individual in order to understand why making money was such a vital interest.

1. Financial success, according to Mr. A's system of rules and formulas, was a way of gaining the respect of other people in the same line of business. Thus, making money was a source of gratification because it enhanced his social image. However, it had a far more important meaning than this, in that it afforded him a sense of protection against the disdain of other people and also against destitution. Because of early childhood experiences with the contempt of older siblings, he had a continual expectation of being ridiculed. Thus, whenever there was any question of loss of financial security, he began to experience anxiety and to visualize the contempt of his business associates. During his earlier bout of depression, he had thought that the loss of money would lead to destitution and thus to his death, because he would not be able to afford medical treatment.

2. Mr. A's sense of confidence depended upon the tangible evidence of success. When he did well on a business deal, he would think, "I am successful. I am really bright." If he did not do well, he would think, "I am stupid." Apparently, he had not built up any solid core of self-esteem that would be relatively insensitive to fluctuations in his cash flow.

3. It was very important to Mr. A to be able to provide an adequate standard of living for his family. He took great pride in the material satisfactions that his family had, but always had a nagging sense that he would "lose everything" if his business went under. His dichotomous thinking was evident in his considering his business (and himself) as either a success or a failure. There was nothing in between.

An important part of the therapy consisted of unraveling each of these meanings and then subjecting them to scrutiny. It was possible, first of all, to expose the dichotomous thinking so that Mr. A could start to make evaluations in terms of varying degrees of success (or failure). Then we were able to assess the probabilities of his being considered unworthy by his family and friends if he should indeed show a financial slippage.

Egocentric Mode. Mr. A was able to recognize that he was making his judgments from an egocentric frame of reference. For example, he had decided that people would ridicule him if he failed; he had not, however, considered their reactions from *their* frame of reference. When he was asked to try to determine their frame of reference, he was able to see that he had not even taken into account that they might react differently from the way that he automatically expected. He and I were particularly successful in demonstrating his egocentricity in his expectation that his wife would lose respect for him. When he spoke to her about his financial problems, he was able to see that her frame of reference was completely different from that which he had projected onto her. Specifically, what mattered to her the most were qualities other than his ability to provide the material comforts. He was subsequently able to generalize from this demonstration of his egocentric notions to other situations in which he showed a similar degree of egocentric thinking (e.g., suicidal wishes).

Another point that we were able to explore successfully was that he defined "competence" only in terms of the outcome of his most recent ventures. Even if he had been successful a dozen times in his business ventures, a slight financial loss on the 13th venture would mean that he was incompetent. This example again demonstrated a type of egocentricity, in that he appraised his financial acumen solely in terms of the outcomes of his latest ventures, rather than on the basis of the long-range results of his specific skills. Moreover, he had not taken into account that the outcomes of his ventures were to a large extent determined by such factors as fluctuations in the market, changes in the economy, and information about particular investments that he had not known at the time. He came to recognize that the business cycle was subject to numerous oscillations that he could not predict and over which he had no control. Thus, he came to recognize that a downturn in the economy that affected everybody in his industry was more likely to be the cause of financial problems than a deficiency in his acumen was.

System of Formulas, Rules, and Regulations

Mr. A operated according to a complex set of rules, formulas, injunctions, and prohibitions. Thus, the rules or the system were the instrument for (1) reaching his goals and (2) protecting himself against disgrace, destitution, and death.

As pointed out previously, when a rule was broken, Mr. A was likely to catastrophize. The underlying theme seemed to be this: "If a rule is broken a little bit, then all rules can be broken a lot." When a rule was broken, he would react just as strongly when no damage was done as when there actually was damage. For instance, if he did not receive a message promptly, he would react almost as strongly if no harm resulted as he would if he lost an account because of the delay.

It is also notable that when the pressure built up, the formulas became more rigid. When upset, Mr. A adopted the formula that if he were not very strict with his employees, there could be a serious loss. This concept showed dichotomous thinking. His employees were either "careful" or "negligent." Either he could control them well, or they were completely uncontrolled. His firm either ran smoothly, or it was chaotic. Thus, he needed absolute control to insure his security.

"Personalizing the System." As our discussions continued, it became apparent that Mr. A's system had become an end in itself. He was less fixated on the probable outcomes of deficiencies than on the imperfections themselves. It appeared that the means had become more important than the end. In the course of time, it became apparent that he had identified himself with his system. For example, when he was having some remediable difficulty in the operations of the organization, he experienced feelings of paralysis.

Expectations. Because of Mr. A's overinvestment in the system, he tended to "ride herd" over his employees—an approach that probably engendered a certain amount of resentment and possibly of passive resistance on their part. It is notable that his demands and expectations of himself were just as stringent as those he imposed on his employees. Thus, he would become concerned at any error in judgment that he made. The reason for this was that he saw this as a harbinger of the slide down the road to disaster. A single stone rolling down the hill indicated that an avalanche was about to come. Partly as a result of the presumed disastrous consequences of mistakes, he rarely made mistakes, but he was continually under the impression that he might make a fatal error.

The therapeutic approach to this psychological problem was to ask Mr. A to list his expectations of the key individuals in his organization. Then he was asked to rate their performance periodically. If a person's performance was below his rational expectations, then he could either discuss this with the person or decide whether he was willing to assume the risk of further imperfections in that individual's work. If, on the other hand, the imperfections were what he had anticipated, he could use his observation to counteract his unreasonable expectations.

We found that his discovery of an inefficiency was generally followed by a catastrophic thought ("The whole organization will fall apart"). The therapeutic work of decatastrophizing consisted of making predictions each time he discovered an error and then reviewing the predictions and the outcome several weeks later.

Notions of Causality. Mr. A had primitive notions of causality in reference to business problems. If anything went wrong, then a particular person was to blame. Just as he expected himself to have total knowledge of all the factors necessary to making a decision, he expected the same from his staff. His underlying theme was "I do not expect anything more from them than from myself." It was important in terms of the therapy to demonstrate to him that he indeed expected too much of himself— that he was not the only determinant in the outcome of his ventures. Similarly, the members of his staff would not be the sole causes of the success or failure of any enterprise. In fact, as he explored the situation further, he recognized that many factors other than simply judgment were causes of the fate of the ventures.

Punitiveness

Since Mr. A attributed accountability, responsibility, and causality to both himself and his staff, he was constantly prepared to punish the offending party when something went wrong. Typically, he would conduct an investigation when there was any "foul-up" and would feel a strong urge to come down hard on the offending party. It should be pointed out that he was aware that he could not continually badger his staff, so that a good part of the time he had hostile reactions to the staff, but did not express them. The reasons behind this punitive attitude had to do with the following:

1. Since his vital interests were at stake, it meant that any offense by the staff struck at the heart of these interests. This caused pain and raised a desire to retaliate because of the pain that had been caused him.

2. Part of the punitiveness was intended to "teach them a lesson" so as to prevent a recurrence.

3. A related concept was that he needed to punish members of the staff periodically in order to "tighten the reins."

It is notable that much more hostility was engendered as a result of the rules' being broken than as a result of any real damage that was done. Because of the importance of the rules to Mr. A, he was continually vigilant to make sure that they were followed closely. Thus, he would check his secretary's work to make sure that there were no mistakes in punctuation, and he would monitor the arrival and departure times of the employees to make sure that they were not cheating. Because of this overvigilance, he did indeed perceive a fair number of infractions, and as a result was hostile about these.

Summary

1. The construction of a situation (cognitive set) is an active, continuing process that includes successive appraisals of the external situation and the risks, costs, and gains of a particular response. When the individual's vital interests appear to be at stake, the cognitive structuring of a situation is responsible for mobilizing the organism to action. If the mobilization persists substantially beyond realistic demands, it forms the precursor to a stress reaction.

2. Overt behavior stems directly from the mobilization triggered by activated cognitive structures. Depending on the content of the cognitive constellation, the behavioral mobilization may be directed toward flight, attack, approach, or withdrawal. The concomitant affect would be, respectively, anxiety, anger, affection, or sadness.

3. Specific primitive cognitive constellations are "chained" to specific stimuli. This pairing constitutes the specific sensitivity of a given individual and prepares the way for inappropriate or excessive reactions. Since people vary widely in their specific sensitivities, what is a stressor for one person may be a benign situation for another.

4. The stressors lead to a disruption of the normal activity of the cognitive organization. Deviations in the thinking process occur as a result of the stress. When vital interests are at stake, the primitive, egocentric cognitive system is activated, and the individual is primed to make extreme, one-sided, absolutistic, and global judgments. Furthermore, there is a loss of volitional control over thinking processes; a reduced ability to "turn off" intense, idiosyncratic cognitive schemas; and a reduction in the ability to concentrate, recall, and reason.

5. Differences in personality organization account for some of the wide variations in individual sensitivities to stressors. Thus, the autonomous and sociotropic personality types differ in the type of stressors to which they are sensitive. Consequently, the occurrence of a stress reaction is contingent to a large degree on specific vulnerabilities related to personality.

6. Each of the stress syndromes (such as hostility, anxiety, and depression) consists of hyperactive schemas with an idiosyncratic content specific for that syndrome. Each syndrome comprises a specific controlling cognitive constellation and the resultant behavioral inclinations and affect.

7. The principal stressor may be internal, with no apparent referent in the outside world. The assumption that the only road to fulfillment is through total success is intrinsic in achievement-oriented persons prone to stress reactions.

8. Stressful interactions with other people occur in a mutually reinforcing cycle of maladaptive cognitive reactions. Specific mechanisms, such as the egocentric cognitive mode, framing, and polarization, lead to increased mobilization and consequently to stress.

9. An individual responds physically, although the stimulus may be psychosocial or symbolic and although ultimate overt behavior is verbal. The mobilization for "fight or flight" involves the same cognitive–motoric systems, regardless of whether the level of meaning of a threat or challenge is physical or psychosocial.

10. The cognitive approach to the treatment of stress reactions focuses on reducing the hyperactivity of the controlling schemas and supporting the adaptive functions. The patient is encouraged to examine the internal factors—thoughts, impulses, and feelings—contributing to the stress response. The patient also identifies the meanings he or she has assigned to events that are connected to both behavioral activation and affect. Cognitive techniques, such as identifying automatic thoughts, recognizing and correcting cognitive distortions, and identifying broad beliefs and assumptions that underlie cognition, are used to clarify the problems.

11. Through a process of collaborative empiricism, the cognitive therapist and the patient frame the patient's conclusions as hypotheses, which are investigated and tested by increasing both objectivity and perspective. Logically evaluating dysfunctional cognitions leads to shifts in thinking, with the ultimate goal being structural change. Structural change may come about through the analysis of specific stressors and of vulnerabilities, rules, and imperatives that have governed the person's responses. Structural change, then, extends beyond modifying habitual cognitive errors to the underlying organization of rules, formulas, assumptions, and imperatives that misclassify events as threatening.

REFERENCES

Beck, A. T. (1963). Thinking and depression: 1. Idiosyncratic content and cognitive distortions. *Archives of General Psychiatry, 9*, 324–333.

Beck, A. T. (1964). Thinking and depression: 2. Theory and therapy. *Archives of General Psychiatry, 10*, 561–571.

Beck, A. T. (1967). *Depression: Clinical, experimental, and theoretical.* New York: Hoeber.

Beck, A. T. (1976). *Cognitive therapy and the emotional disorders.* New York: International Universities Press.

Beck, A. T. (1983). Cognitive therapy of depression: New perspectives. In P. Clayton (Ed.), *Depression.* New York: Raven Press.

Beck, A. T., Rush, A. J., Shaw, B. F., & Emery, G. (1979). *Cognitive therapy of depression.* New York: Guilford Press.

Bowlby, J. (1981, April). *Cognitive processes in the genesis of psychopathology.* Invited address to the Biennial Meeting of the Society for Research in Child Development, Boston.

Caplan, G. (1981). Mastery of stress: Psychosocial aspects. *American Journal of Psychiatry, 138*, 413–420.

Ellis, A. (1962). *Reason and emotion in psychotherapy.* New York: Lyle Stuart.

Goldfried, M. R. (1977). The use of relaxation and cognitive relabeling as coping skills. In R. B. Stuart (Ed.), *Behavioral self-management: Strategies and outcomes.* New York: Brunner/Mazel.

Hollon, S. D., & Beck, A. T. (1979). Cognitive therapy of depression. In S. D. Hollon & P. C. Kendall (Eds.), *Cognitive–behavioral interventions: Theory, research, and procedures.* New York: Academic Press.

Holroyd, K. A. (1979). Stress, coping and the treatment of stress. In S. R. McNamara (Ed.), *Behavioral approaches to medicine.* New York: Plenum Press.

Jacobson, E. (1938). *Progressive relaxation* (2nd ed.). Chicago: University of Chicago Press.

Lazarus, R. S. (1966). *Psychological stress and the coping process.* New York: McGraw-Hill.

Lazarus, R. S. (1981). The stress and coping paradigm. In C. Eisdorfer, D. Cohen, A. Kleinman, & P. Maxim (Eds.), *Conceptual models for psychotherapy*. New York: Spectrum.

Mahoney, M. (1982). Psychotherapy and human change processes. In J. H. Harvey & M. P. Parke (Eds.), *Psychotherapy research and behavior change*. Washington, D.C.: American Psychological Association.

Meichenbaum, D. H. (1977). *Cognitive behavior modification: An integrative approach*. New York: Plenum Press.

Novaco, R. (1975). *Anger control: The development and evaluation of an experimental treatment*. Lexington, MA: D.C. Heath.

Saul, L. J. (1947). *Emotional maturity*. Philadelphia: J. B. Lippincott.

Turk, D. C., Meichenbaum, D., & Genest, M. (1983). *Pain and behavioral medicine: A cognitive–behavioral perspective*. New York: Guilford Press.

Wolff, H. G. (1950). Life stress and bodily disease—a formulation. In *Life stress and bodily disease: Proceedings of the Association for Research in Nervous and Mental Disease, December 2 and 3, 1949, New York*. Baltimore: Williams & Wilkins.

12

Stress Inoculaton Training: A 20-Year Update

DONALD MEICHENBAUM

Clinicians who seek to provide help to stressed individuals, on either a treatment or a preventative basis, are confronted with a major challenge. Stressful events come in diverse forms. As Eliot and Eisdorfer (1982) observe, such events may be of the following types:

1. An acute, time-limited variety, including such events as preparing for specific medical procedures (e.g., surgery, dental examinations) or for invasive medical examinations (e.g., biopsies, cardiac catheterization), or having to confront specific evaluations (e.g., a PhD defense).
2. A stressor sequence variety, whereby a specific event (e.g., death of a loved one, divorce, job loss, natural or man-made disaster) may trigger a series of stressful reactions and transitional adjustments (e.g., coping with being raped or otherwise being victimized, becoming unemployed).
3. A chronic intermittent variety, constituting repeated exposures to such stressors as student examinations, competitive performances (e.g., musical or athletic competitions), occasional medical tests or treatments, military combat, or episodic physical disorders (e.g., recurrent headaches).
4. A chronic continual variety, including having to cope with a debilitating or chronic medical or psychiatric illness; prolonged marital or familial discord, often with accompanying physical or sexual abuse; and exposure to persistent occupational dangers and stressors in professions such as policework, nursing, and teaching.

These stressful events may range from those requiring situational adaptational coping efforts to those stressors that challenge, invalidate, and in some instances even shatter an individual's beliefs about himself or herself and the world. Individuals who fail to cope effectively with stressful events may evidence the full array of physiological, emotional, cognitive and behavioral dysfunctions, including post-traumatic stress disorder (PTSD), anxiety, depression, aggressive behavior, addictive behaviors, and the like. Clinicians have employed a full armamentarium of therapeutic and preventative techniques to help individuals cope more effectively with diverse stressors.

One intervention approach that has been employed successfully across the full array of stressed individuals is stress inoculation[1] training (SIT). SIT was first introduced in the early 1970s as a treatment approach to help (1) phobic clients who experienced multiple fears (Meichenbaum & Cameron, 1972); (2) clients who had problems controlling their anger (Novaco, 1975); and (3) individuals who had problems coping with physical pain (Turk, 1977). In 1985, a clinical guidebook on SIT was published (Meichenbaum, 1985); this has now been translated into Spanish, Japanese, German, and Italian. Since its origin, SIT has been applied by investigators in many countries to a wide array of stress-related problems and populations on both a preventative and a treatment basis. In this chapter I "take stock" of the broad application of SIT, itemizing all of the published and unpublished papers that I am aware of (some 200 studies). Following a brief description of SIT, its theoretical underpinnings, and clinical procedures, I provide a brief report on its empirical status and comment on the likely future directions of SIT application and research.

SIT is *not* a panacea. Rather, it is a heuristically useful way to conceptualize both the distress that individuals experience and the factors leading to their behavioral change, as well as a clinically sensitive way to provide help on both a treatment and a preventative basis. SIT does *not* represent a treatment formula that can be routinely applied to distressed individuals; it is a set of general guiding principles and accompanying clinical procedures that must be individually tailored to the unique characteristics of each case. Before a consideration of specific SIT procedures, it is first helpful to turn to Table 12.1, which lists the extensive variety of target populations for whom SIT has been applied. Each of the classes of stressful events that Eliot and Eisdorfer (1982) describe is included in Table 12.1. I have listed each stress-related problem that has been treated by SIT and the accompanying references.

A caveat is warranted in regard to Table 12.1. The list of references covers the full array of clinical and laboratory investigations, including case studies; demonstration projects with limited comparison control groups; and tightly controlled comparative outcome studies that included both appropriate control groups and follow-up assessments, as well as descriptive proposals for future applications of SIT. In addition, laboratory analogue studies are included, especially in the area of experimentally induced pain, where investigators have analyzed the various components of SIT as described in a later section. In some investigations, SIT was included as a component of a broad-based treatment program. The application of SIT ranges from single-case clinical interventions to a preventative application to an entire target population of a country (high school students and their parents in Israel, who received SIT before the students enlisted in the Israeli Defense Forces [IDF]). In Table 12.1, I have also cast a broad net by including illustrative clinical studies that employ closely allied cognitive–behavioral stress reduction interventions, such as Suinn's (1990) anxiety management training or Smith's (1980) stress management training.

In short, we have learned a great deal in the last 20 years about SIT and related stress management interventions. In this chapter, I attempt to convey some of the

---

[1]Parenthetically, it is worth noting that the word "*in*oculation" (not "*inn*oculation") is one of the most frequently misspelled words in the English language. See Brock (1983) for a list of creative misspellings of the word "inoculation."

TABLE 12.1. Applications of SIT and Closely Related Stress Management Procedures

Target problem or population	References
Populations having problems with anger	
Adults with anger control problems	Bistline & Frieden, 1984; Deffenbacher et al., 1987, 1988, 1991; Gaertner et al., 1983; Hazaleus & Deffenbacher, 1986; Moon & Eisler, 1983; Novaco, 1975, 1977a; Stermac, 1986
Adolescents with anger control problems	Feindler & Ecton, 1986; Feindler & Fremouw, 1983; Feindler et al., 1984, 1986; Feindler, 1990; Hains, 1989, in press; Hains & Szyjakowski, 1990; Schlichter & Horan, 1981
Children with anger control problems	Lochman et al., 1981; Lochman & Lampron, 1988; Maag et al., 1988; Saylor et al., 1985; Spirito et al., 1981; Stern & Fodor, 1989
Brain-injured patients with anger control problems	Franzen & Lovell, 1987; Lira et al., 1983
Mentally retarded individuals with anger control problems	Golden & Consorte, 1982
Abusive parents	Denicola & Sandler, 1980; Egan, 1983; Twentyman et al., 1984
Problems with anxiety	
Test anxiety	Deffenbacher & Hahloser, 1981; Holroyd, 1976; Hussain & Lawrence, 1978; Kooken & Hayslip, 1984; Meichenbaum, 1972; Nye, 1979; Suinn & Richardson, 1971
Math anxiety	Avia & Ruiz, 1987
Public-speaking anxiety	Altmaier et al., 1985; Craddock et al., 1978; Fremouw & Zitter, 1978; Fremouw & Harmatz, 1975; Jaremko, 1980; Jaremko et al., 1980; Jones, 1991; Kantor, 1978
Interpersonal and dating anxiety	Glass et al., 1976; Hains, 1992; Jaremko, 1983; Kunzman, 1986
Other performance anxiety (e.g., musical, writing, computer usage)	Avants et al., 1990; Altmaier et al., 1982; Bloom & Haitalouma, 1990; Kendrick, 1979; Salovey & Harr, 1990; Sweeney & Horan, 1982
Vulnerability to criticism	Kirschenbaum et al., 1984
Psychiatric anxiety disorders (panic attacks, generalized anxiety, PTSD)	Fairbank & Brown, 1987; Barlow, 1988; Meichenbaum & Deffenbacher, 1988; Ost, 1985; Foa et al., 1991; Rabin & Nardi, 1991
Problems with circumscribed fears	
Multiple animal phobias	Meichenbaum & Cameron, 1972
Fear of flying	Haug et al., 1987
Prevention of fears in children and adults	Barrios & Shigetomi, 1980
Populations with general stress reactions	
Outpatient psychiatric populations and chronically stressed community residents	Brown, 1980; Holcomb, 1979, 1986; Long, 1984, 1985; Van Hassel et al., 1982; Weston et al., 1987
Women on public assistance	Tableman et al., 1982
Persons in need of general stress education	Dougherty & Deck, 1984; Forman & O'Malley, 1985; Jaremko, 1984; Schulink et al., 1988; Suinn, 1990

(continued)

TABLE 12.1. Continued

Target problem or population	References
Psychiatric populations	
Children with psycho-physiological complaints	Van Broeck, 1985
Self-mutilators	Kaminer & Shahar, 1987
Alcoholics	Marlatt & Gordon, 1985; Milkman et al., 1984; Rohsenow et al., 1985
Stress related to life transitions	
Coping with unemployment	Caplan et al., 1989
Anxiety over transition to high scholl	Jason & Burrows, 1983
Anxiety of adults re-entering university	*Athabasca University Student Services Orientation Guidebook,* 1983
Adjustment to college and medical school	Deck & Dougherty, 1986; Holtzworth-Munroe et al., 1985
Facilitation of IQ in older adults	Hayslip, 1989
Adjustment to joining the military	Israelashvili, 1991
Victimized individuals	
Rape and sexual assault victims	Foa et al., 1991; Frank et al., 1988; Kilpatrick et al., 1982; Oots & Wiegele, 1985; Pearson et al., 1983; Resick et al., 1988; Veronen & Best, 1983; Veronen & Kilpatrick, 1983
Victims of terrorist attacks	Ayalon, 1983
Medical patients—treatment of health-related problems	
Chronic pain patients	Karol et al., 1981; Levendusky & Pankrantz, 1975; Puder, 1988; Rybstein-Blinchik, 1979; Turk et al., 1983; Worthington & Shumate, 1981
Patients with chronic tension headaches	Holroyd & Andrasik, 1978; Holroyd et al., 1977
Cancer patients (adults, or children and their parents)	Jay & Elliot, 1986, 1990; Jay et al., 1987; Moore & Altmaier, 1981; Roffman, 1986; Sobel & Worden, 1981; Turk & Rennert, 1981; Varni et al., 1988; Warner & Swenson, 1991; Weisman et al., 1980
Rheumatoid arthritis patients	Randich, 1982
Burn patients	Wernick, 1983; Wernick et al., 1981
Essential hypertension patients	Amigo et al., 1991; Bloom & Cantrell, 1978; Crowther, 1983; Jorgenson et al., 1981
Patients experiencing dysmenorrhea	Quillen & Denney, 1982
Patients experiencing premenstrual syndrome	Kuczmierczyk, 1989
Multiple sclerosis patients	Foley et al., 1987
Ulcer patients	Berbalk et al., 1984; Brooks & Richardson, 1980
Patients with gag reflex problems	Klepac et al., 1982
AIDS patients	Perry & Markowitz, 1986

(continued)

TABLE 12.1. Continued

Target problem or population	References
Medical patients—preventative interventions	
Patients preparing for general and heart surgery	Blythe & Erdahl, 1986; Erdahl & Blythe, 1984; Langer et al., 1975; Ludwick-Rosenthal & Neufeld, 1988; MacDonald & Kuiper, 1983; Postlethwaite et al., 1986; Wells et al., 1986
Adult patients preparing for cardiac catheterization	Kendall, 1983; Kendall et al., 1979
Type A individuals	Hart, 1984; Jenni & Wollersheim, 1979; Roskies, 1983; Suinn, 1990; Thurman, 1984
Medical outpatients	Cragan & Deffenbacher, 1984
Gynecological and obstetric patients	Cruz, 1991; Deffenbacher & Craun, 1985
Parents preparing for their children's hospitalization	Meng & Zastowny, 1982
Dental patients	
Children and adults preparing for dental examinations	Klepac et al., 1981; Melamed & Siegel, 1975; Moses & Hollandsworth, 1985; Nelson, 1981; Nocella & Kaplan, 1982; Siegel & Peterson, 1980
Athletic competitors	
Athletes participating in such sports as volleyball, scuba diving, gymnastics, basketball, and the like	Allen, 1988; Crocker, 1989; Crocker et al., 1988; Deikis, 1983; Harrison & Feltz, 1981; Kirschenbaum et al., 1984; Long, 1980; Mace & Carroll, 1986; Mace et al., 1986, 1987; Smith, 1980; Smoll & Smith, 1989; Ziegler et al., 1982
Professional groups	
Registered nurses and practical nursing students	West et al., 1984; Wernick, 1984
School psychologists	Forman, 1981, 1983
Teachers and student teachers	Forman, 1982; Cecil & Forman, 1990; Payne & Manning, 1990; Mydgal, 1978; Sharpe & Forman, 1985; Turk et al., 1982
Police officers	Lester et al., 1984; Meichenbaum & Novaco, 1978, 1985; O'Neill, 1982; Novaco, 1977b; Sarason et al., 1979
Probation officers	Novaco, 1980
Military recruit trainees	Novaco et al., 1983
Military parachutists	Dinner & Gal, 1983
Marine Corps drill instructors	Novaco et al., 1983
Staff members working with mentally retarded cients	Keyes & Dean, 1988
Disaster workers	Dunning, 1990
Individuals learning industrial safety prevention	
Operators of automated machinery	Spettel & Liebert, 1986; Starr, 1987
Offshore oil workers	Hytten et al., 1990
Individuals learning cardiopulmonary resuscitation	Starr, 1986

(continued)

TABLE 12.1.   Continued

Target problem or population	References
Laboratory analogues of pain and stress	
Cold-pressor test, muscle ischemia test, electric shock	de Blas & Labrador, 1984; Cassens et al., 1988; Genest, 1979; Girodo & Wood, 1979; Hackett & Horan, 1980; Hackett et al., 1979; Horan et al., 1977; Jaremko, 1979; Klepac et al., 1981; Lustman & Sava, 1983; Miller & Bowers, 1986; Ruiz & Angeles, 1985; Schuler et al., 1982; Spanos et al., 1985–1986; Stone et al., 1977; Turk, 1977; Vallis, 1984; Wald & Fish, 1983; Worthington, 1978; Worthington & Shumate, 1981
Ego-threatening interpersonal encounters	Ulissi, 1978
Stress-engendering films	Ulissi, 1978

major lessons, highlighting the strengths and limitations of SIT. A full-length clinical handbook on SIT is now in preparation.

What Is Stress Inoculation Training?

SIT is a flexible, individually tailored, multifaceted form of cognitive–behavioral therapy. Given the wide array of stressors that individuals experience, SIT provides a set of clinical guidelines for treating stressed individuals, rather than a specific treatment formula. A central concept underlying SIT is that of "inoculation" or "immunization," which has been used both in medicine[2] and in social-psychological research on attitude change (McGuire, 1964). In both areas, the central notion is that bolstering an individual's repertoire of coping responses to milder stressors can serve to defuse maladaptive responses or susceptibility to more severe forms of distress and persuasion, whether in the form of a virus or an attitude change effort. In a similar fashion, SIT is based on the notion that exposing clients[3] to milder forms of stress can serve to defuse responses to major life stressors. As in medical inoculations, a person's resistance is enhanced by exposure to a stimulus strong enough to arouse defenses without being so powerful that it overcomes the individual. Since lack of preparation and surprise contribute to distressing, ineffective coping efforts, SIT bolsters clients'

---

[2]In 1796, Edward Jenner noted that inoculation with cowpox conferred immunity against the more deadly smallpox virus. Since then, the concept of "inoculation" has been employed in a variety of treatment and training arenas (see Meichenbaum, 1985, for a discussion).

[3]Although the term "client" is used in this description, in many SIT studies the participants were not labeled as "clients" or "patients" but rather as "trainees," because an educational rather than a psychotherapeutic framework was employed. Also, SIT has been successfully conducted on a group basis. The reader should consider the potential group application of many of the SIT interventions that will be described.

preparedness and assimilatory processes. In this way, individuals can learn to pace themselves as they learn to master stress gradually.

In order to enhance an individual's coping repertoire and to empower him or her to use already existing coping skills, an overlapping three-phase intervention approach is employed. In the initial conceptualization phase, a collaborative relationship is established between the client(s) and the trainer. A Socratic exchange is used to help the client better understand the nature of stress and its effects on his or her emotions and behavior. A variety of clinical techniques, including interviewing, psychological testing, and client self-monitoring, are used to help the client make sense of the stress he or she is experiencing. One objective of this phase is to help clients appreciate that how they appraise both events and their ability to cope with these events plays an important role in the stress they experience. Individuals are taught that they do *not* react to events directly, but do so only through their interpretation of events; moreover, they are shown that alternative interpretations and explanations are available. In addition, after empathically listening, the SIT trainer/therapist helps individuals/clients to do the following:

1. To appreciate that the stress they experience is *not* abnormal and not a sign that they are "going crazy" or "losing their minds"; rather, their distressing symptoms reflect a normal reaction to a difficult situation.

2. To reframe their stressful symptoms as aspects of a normal, spontaneous reconstructive or rehabilitative process or as adaptive reactions, and not as signs of weakness or failure. For example, intrusive images and nightmares are reframed as both conscious or deliberate and unconscious or automatic efforts to work through stressful events or as ways to search for meaning; emotional numbing, denial, and avoidance are characterized as ways individuals who have experienced traumatizing events "dose" or "pace" themselves, dealing with only so much stress at a given time. As Epstein (1990) metaphorically characterizes the denial process, "the mind is taking a time out from overstimulation."

3. To understand the nature and course of their disorder, and to appreciate that there are *not* prescribed emotional stages that stressed individuals go through, nor is there a correct way to cope; moreover, to appreciate that some individuals may experience distress many years after stressful events occur (Wortman & Silver, 1987).

4. To discover and appreciate the transactional nature of stress, and how they themselves unwittingly, unknowingly, and often inadvertently exacerbate and help maintain the very stress reactions they experience.

5. To facilitate their discovery of a sense of meaning, or, to use Figley's (1989) term, to collaboratively formulate a "healing theory" or explanation of what happened and why.

6. To develop gradual mastery of stress by providing a more manageable reconceptualization of it, which acts as the basis for coping more effectively. Frank (1987) has noted that such a reconceptualization acts as "articles of faith" and provides the "basis of hope." The reconceptualization conveys to clients that their stress consists of different components and that they go through different phases. The plausibility and acceptability, rather than the scientific validity, of the specific reconceptualization

model that is offered are most important. The specific model offered is individually tailored to a specific client's or client group's problems.[4]

7. To draw a distinction between "changeable" and "unchangeable" aspects of stressful situations, and to "fit" either problem-focused or emotion-focused coping efforts to the perceived demands of the situation, as Folkman et al. (1991) have described.

8. To break down or disaggregate global stressors into specific short-term, intermediate, and long-term coping goals.

Thus, in a collaborative fashion, a more helpful reconceptualization of the client's presenting problem or stressful experience is formulated. This process involves the client's conceptualizing his or her negative emotional arousal problems and coping efforts in terms that are addressable, rather than conceiving of them as overwhelming, uncontrollable, and unpredictable. As a result of such a reconceptualization, feelings of hopefulness, empowerment, and a sense of "learned resourcefulness" are nurtured in the client, as compared to feelings of despair, unpredictability, uncontrollability, and "learned helpfulness."

The second phase of SIT, which follows naturally from the conceptualization phase, focuses upon coping skills acquisition and rehearsal. In some instances, clients may already possess adequate coping skills, and such clients are encouraged to use their own preferred coping strategies in a skill consolidation and rehearsal phase. In this latter instance, the second phase of SIT focuses on removing any inhibiting factors that may interfere with adequate coping, such as maladaptive beliefs, feelings of low self-efficacy, and the like. The coping skills are taught and practiced primarily in the clinic or training setting and then gradually rehearsed *in vivo*. In order to consolidate these skills, individuals may even be asked to help others with similar problems.

The final phase of application and follow-through includes opportunities for the client to apply the variety of coping skills on a graduated basis across increasing levels of stressors (the "inoculation" concept). Such techniques as imagery and behavioral rehearsal, modeling, role playing, and graded *in vivo* exposure are employed. A central feature of this application phase is the use of relapse prevention procedures (Marlatt & Gordon, 1985). The trainer explores with the client the variety of high-risk stressful situations that he or she is likely to encounter, and then the client rehearses in a collaborative fashion with the trainer (and with other clients in a group setting, or with a spouse if SIT is conducted on a couples basis) the various coping techniques that might be employed. The client is taught how to view lapses, should they occur, as learning occasions rather than as occasions to "catastrophize" and relapse. The follow-through feature is designed to extend the SIT training into the future. In many SIT

---

[4]Different conceptualizations are collaboratively developed by the therapist/trainer and the clients. For example, with patients who experience chronic pain, Melzack and Wall's (1965) gate control model of pain has been used; with clients who have anger problems, Schachter's (1966) model of emotions has been employed; with panic patients, Clark and Salkovskis's (1989) model of anxiety has been employed; with phobic patients, Lang's (1968) tripartite model of fear has been offered. In each instance, the model is presented in lay terms, using the client's stress reactions as the basis for the reconceptualization. (See Meichenbaum, 1985, for examples.)

programs, follow-up or booster sessions of some type have been built into the training regimen.

In short, SIT helps clients acquire sufficient knowledge, self-understanding, and coping skills to facilitate better ways of handling expected stressful encounters. SIT combines elements of Socratic and didactic teaching, client self-monitoring, cognitive restructuring, problem solving, self-instructional and relaxation training, behavioral and imagined rehearsal, and environmental change. With regard to the notion of environmental change, SIT recognizes that stress is transactional in nature. The stress that a client experiences is often endemic, institutional, and unavoidable. As a result, SIT interventions often need to go beyond the client to involve significant others. For example, in preparing patients for stressful medical examinations, the trainer can focus on teaching coping skills to distressed patients, but the trainer can also attempt to work with the hospital staff in order to reduce the nature and level of institutional stress (see Kendall, 1983). In competitive sports, a trainer can help athletes develop their coping skills in order to better handle the stress of competition, but as Smith (1980) observes, a trainer can also attempt to influence coaches' and parents' behaviors, thus reducing a major source of competitive stress. Similarly, in work with victims of rape, terrorist attacks, and the like, "secondary victimization" of clients from community agents (doctors, police, judges, teachers, peers) can often prove additionally distressing (Ayalon, 1983; Veronen & Kilpatrick, 1983). It would be short-sighted to delimit interventions to just the target victimized group and not to attempt to influence the stress-engendering behaviors and attitudes of community members. SIT has adopted the dual-track strategy of working directly both with the stressed population and with significant others and community agents who inadvertently and unwittingly may exacerbate stress.

Finally, SIT recognizes that some stressful situations do not lend themselves to direct-action problem-solving coping efforts, since solutions are not always readily available (e.g., in the case of incurable illness, irreversible loss, etc.). In such instances, an emotionally palliative set of coping responses—such as perspective taking, attention diversion, adaptive affective expression, and humor—should be nurtured, as described by Lazarus and Folkman (1984). There are no "correct" ways to cope. What works with one client in one situation, or with the same client at different times, may not be applicable with other clients or at other times. Thus, the objective of SIT is to teach each client a flexible coping repertoire and to nurture the client's sense of confidence that he or she can cope resourcefully with the changing variety of daily stressors and life events.

How Is Stress Inoculation Training Conducted?

One of the strengths of SIT is its flexibility. SIT has been carried out with individuals, couples, small groups, and large groups. The length of the intervention has varied, being as short as 20 minutes for preparing patients for surgery (Langer, Janis, & Wolfer, 1975) to forty 1-hour weekly and biweekly sessions administered to psychiatric patients or to individuals with chronic medical problems (Turk, Meichenbaum, & Genest, 1983). In most instances in the clinical domain, SIT consists of some 8 to

15 sessions, plus booster and follow-up sessions conducted over a 3- to 12-month period.

Obviously, the manner in which the three phases of SIT (conceptualization; skills acquisition and rehearsal; application and follow-through) are conducted varies, depending upon both the nature of the population and the length of the training. The content of the conceptualization phase, the specific skills trained, and the nature of the application phase are all specifically geared to the targeted population. There is, however, sufficient congruence across SIT applications that a flow chart of the SIT treatment procedures can be outlined as shown in Table 12.2. More detailed clinical presentations of SIT are offered in Meichenbaum (1976, 1977, 1985), Meichenbaum and Cameron (1982), Meichenbaum and Deffenbacher (1988), Meichenbaum and Jaremko (1983), Turk et al. (1983), and Wertkin (1985).

Theoretical Underpinnings

Before I provide some illustrative examples of how SIT has been employed, a brief consideration of the theoretical underpinnings of this cognitive–behavioral approach is instructive. SIT adopts a transactional view of stress as espoused by Lazarus and Folkman (1984); this model proposes that stress occurs whenever the perceived demands of a situation tax or exceed the perceived resources of the system (individual, group, community) to meet those demands, especially when the system's well-being is perceived as being at stake. This relational, process-oriented view of stress emphasizes the important roles of cognitive–affective appraisal and coping activities. As Lazarus and Folkman (1984) highlight, stress is neither a characteristic of the environment alone nor a characteristic of the person alone. Instead, stress is defined as a particular type of relationship between the person and the environment, in which the individual perceives the adaptive demands as taxing or exceeding available coping resources.

The affinity between the transactional model of stress and the SIT approach is evident from the fact that SIT is designed to facilitate adaptive appraisals (conceptualization phase), to enhance the repertoire of coping responses (skill acquisition and rehearsal phase), and to nurture the client's confidence in and utilization of his or her coping capabilities (application and follow-through phase). Thus, the SIT approach recognizes both personal and environmental determinants of stress, and it attempts to provide training in a variety of coping skills designed to help a client deal more effectively with the varied sources of stress. In some instances, helping clients alter their cognitive appraisals may be indicated, while at other times considerable therapeutic benefit may be derived from restructuring stressful situations and training clients to do this for themselves. As noted, what constitutes effective coping is likely to vary from situation to situation, and thus nurturing a flexible coping repertoire is necessary.

Another related literature that has influenced the development of SIT highlights the impact of stressors on cognitive–affective processes. A number of investigators (Epstein, 1990; Horowitz, 1986; Janoff-Bulman, 1985; McCann & Perlman, 1990; Roth & Newman, 1991; Silver & Wortman, 1980) have reported that traumatic stressful events can "destabilize," "invalidate," and "shatter" an individual's

TABLE 12.2.   A Flow Chart of SIT

Phase 1: Conceptualization

• In a collaborative fashion, identify the determinants of the presenting clinical problem or the individual's stress concerns by means of (1) interviews with the client and significant others; (2) the client's use of an imagery-based reconstruction and assessment of a prototypic stressful incident; (3) psychological and situational assessments; and (4) behavioral observations. (As Folkman et al., 1991, suggest, have the client address "who, what, where, and when" questions; "Who is involved?" "What kind of situations cause stress?" "Where is this kind of situation likely to occur?" "When did it occur last?" Also see interview in Meichenbaum & Turk, 1987, p. 89.)

• Permit the client to tell his or her "story" (solicit narrative accounts of stress and coping, and collaboratively identify the client's coping strengths and resources). Help the client to transform his or her description from global terms into behaviorally specific terms.

• Have the client disaggregate global stressors into specific stressful situations. Then help the client break stressful situations and reactions into specific behaviorally prescriptive problems. Have the client consider his or her present coping efforts and evaluate which are maladaptive and which are adaptive.

• Have the client appreciate the differences between changeable and unchangeable aspects of stressful situations.

• Have the client establish short-term, intermediate, and long-term behaviorally specifiable goals.

• Have the client engage in self-monitoring of the commonalities of stressful situations stress-engendering appraisals, internal dialogue, feelings, and behaviors. Help the client appreciate the trans-actional nature of his or her stress, and the ways in which he or she inadvertently, unknowingly, and unwittingly contributes to stress reactions. Train the client to analyze problems independently (e.g., to conduct situational analyses and to seek disconfirmatory data—"check things out").

• Ascertain the degree to which coping difficulties arise from coping skills deficits or are the results of "performance failures" (namely, maladaptive beliefs, feelings of low self-efficacy, negative ideation, secondary gains).

• Collaboratively formulate with the client and significant others a reconceptualization of the client's distress. Socratically educate the client and significant others about the nature and impact of stress, and the resilience and courage individuals manifest in the face of stressful life events. Using the client's own "data," offer a reconceptualization that stress is composed of different components (physiological, cognitive, affective, and behavioral) and that stress reactions go through different "phases" (viz., preparing for the stressor, confronting the stressful situation, handling feelings of being overwhelmed, and reflecting on how the coping efforts proceeded—sometimes well and sometimes not as effectively as one had hoped). The specific reconceptualization offered will vary with the target population; the plausibility of the reconceptualization is more important than its scientific validity. In the course of this process, facilitate the discovery of a sense of meaning, nurture the client's hope, and highlight the client's strengths and feelings of resourcefulness.

• Debunk myths concerning stress and coping, such as these: (1) People go through uniform emotional stages of reaction in response to stress; (2) there is a "right" way to cope; (3) people should not expect to experience stressful reactions well after stressful life events occur.

Phase 2: Skills acquisition and rehearsal

A. Skills training (tailor to the specific population and to the length of training)

• Ascertain the client's preferred mode of coping. Explore with the client how these coping efforts can be employed in the present situation. Examine what intrapersonal or intrapersonal factors are blocking such coping efforts.

• Train problem-focused instrumental coping skills that are directed at the modification, avoidance, and minimization of the impact of stressors (e.g., anxiety management, cognitive restructuring, self-instructional training, communication, assertion, problem solving, anger control, applied cue-controlled relaxation training, parenting, study skills, using social supports). Select each skill according to the needs of the specific client or group of clients. Help the client to break complex stressful problems into more manageable subproblems that can be solved one at a time.

(continued)

TABLE 12.2.   Continued

- Help the client engage in problem-solving activities by identifying possibilities for change, considering and ranking alternative solutions, and practicing coping behavioral activities in the clinic and *in vivo*.
- Train emotionally focused palliative coping skills, especially when the client has to deal with unchangeable and uncontrollable stressors (e.g., perspective taking; selective attention diversion procedures, as in the case of chronic pain patients; adaptive modes of affective expression such as humor, relaxation, and reframing the situation).
- Train clients how to use social supports effectively (i.e., how to choose, obtain, and maintain support). As Folkman et al. (1991) observe, help clients appreciate what kind of support is needed (informational, emotional, tangible), from whom to seek such support, and how to maintain support resources.
- Aim to help the client develop an extensive repertoire of coping responses in order to facilitate flexible responding. Nurture gradual mastery.

B. Skills rehearsal

- Promote the smooth integration and execution of coping responses by means of behavioral and imagery rehearsal.
- Use coping modeling (either live or videotape models). Engage in collaborative discussion, rehearsal, and feedback of coping skills.
- Use self-instructional training to help the client develop internal mediators to self-regulate coping responses.
- Solicit the client's verbal commitment to employ specific coping efforts.
- Discuss possible barriers and obstacles to using coping behaviors.

Phase 3: Application and follow-through
A. Encouraging application of coping skills
- Prepare the client for application by using coping imagery, together with techniques in which early stress cues act as signals to cope.
- Expose the client to more stressful scenes, including using prolonged imagery exposure to stressful and arousing scenes.
- Expose the client in the session to graded stressors via imagery, behavioral rehearsal, and role playing.
- Use graded exposure and other response induction aids to foster *in vivo* responding.
- Employ relapse prevention procedures: Identify high-risk situations, anticipate possible stressful reactions, and rehearse coping responses.
- Use counterattitudinal procedures to increase the likelihood of treatment adherence (i.e., ask and challenge the client to indicate where, how, and why he or she will use coping efforts).
- Bolster self-efficacy by reviewing both the client's successful and unsuccessful coping efforts. Insure that the client makes self-attributions for success or mastery experiences (provide attribution retraining).

B. Maintenance and generalization

- Gradually phase out treatment and include booster and follow-up sessions.
- Involve significant others in training (e.g., parents, spouse, coaches, hospital staff, police, administrators), as well as peer and self-help groups.
- Have the client coach someone with a similar problem (i.e., put client in a "helper" role).
- Help the client to restructure environmental stressors and develop appropriate escape routes. Insure that the client does not view escape or avoidance, if so desired, as a sign of failure, bur rather as a sign of taking personal control.
- Help the client to develop coping strategies for recovering from failure and setbacks, so that lapses do not become relapses.

fundamental beliefs and implicit assumptions about himself or herself and the world. The basic tacit rules that guide a person's life—such as the beliefs that the world is benign and benevolent; events are predictable, controllable, and just; life is meaningful; and the self is worthy—can be challenged and nullified by stressful events (Janoff-Bulman, 1990). As Epstein (1990) observes, "threatening events invalidate at a deep experimental level the most fundamental beliefs in a personal theory of reality. . . . Recovery is contingent upon building a new assumptive world that can assimilate the victimization experience in an adaptive manner" (p. 80). SIT helps clients find a way of explaining, conceptualizing, reframing, minimizing, and coping with stress. In short, SIT helps clients to experientially rescript their lives, or to create a new narrative about their ability to cope. Through carefully arranged proactive learning trials both in the clinic and *in vivo*, clients can collect "data" that they can take as evidence to "unfreeze" their beliefs about themselves and the world. In this fashion, clients can formulate new schemas and develop more differentiated assumptions, and thus inoculate themselves to future stressors. Let us now consider how SIT has been implemented on both a treatment and a preventative basis.

Applications to Medical Problems on a Preventative Basis

Since SIT is a generic approach, it has been applied to a wide variety of medical problems (see Ludwick-Rosenthal & Neufeld, 1988; Turk et al., 1983). SIT has been used to help patients reduce their stress levels in dealing with such medical challenges as preparing for surgery and invasive medical examinations and dental treatments. A description of several illustrative studies conveys the potential of the SIT approach in helping patients to cope more effectively. For instance, Langer and her colleagues (1975) provided 20 minutes of coping skills training to patients prior to their surgery. The conceptualization phase of SIT in this context highlighted the extent to which stress can be elevated or reduced as a result of selective attention and cognition. Collaboratively, the trainer was able to help patients direct their attention to more favorable aspects of the surgical situation and to develop more adaptive coping responses. The group receiving the coping skills intervention, relative to information and assessment control groups, evidenced significantly less preoperative anxiety and fewer postoperative requests for pain relievers and sedatives; there was also a trend for the SIT coping group to remain in the hospital for a shorter period of time.

Another short-term (45-minute) innovative application of SIT was offered by Kendall and his colleagues (1979) with patients undergoing cardiac catheterization. The SIT patients received individual training in the identification of those hospitalization procedures that aroused anxiety and in the application of their own idiosyncratic coping strategies that could be used to reduce anxiety about the catheterization. The trainer highlighted that the experience of stress in such situations is normal. In fact, the trainer even self-disclosed some stressful incidents and accompanying coping efforts that he or she had experienced (i.e., the trainer acted as a coping model). Finally, the trainer had the patients rehearse specific coping responses that could be employed in response to anxiety-producing cues. Relative to an attention placebo group and to a current-hospital-conditions control goup, the SIT group evidenced

significantly less tension and anxiety and better adjustment, as judged by both physicians and medical technicians. The use of the patients' own preferred coping strategies, the trainer's modeling coping, and the patients' rehearsal of coping procedures
were particularly helpful.

Although a number of other SIT intervention studies for medical and dental
procedures are noted in Table 12.1 (e.g., pain, headache, burns, arthritis, ulcers,
multiple sclerosis, etc.), the two studies that are highlighted here involved the treatment of hypertension and cancer. A recent study in Spain by Amigo, Buceta, Becona,
and Bueno (1991) demonstrated the effectiveness of 6 weeks of SIT in significantly
reducing both systolic and diastolic blood pressure, relative to an attention placebo
condition. This relative improvement was also evident at a 6-month follow-up.

The potential application of SIT for the treatment of cancer patients and their
family members was highlighted by Turk and Rennert (1981). Their suggestions were
picked up by a number of investigators such as Jay and Elliott (1986, 1990), who
developed an innovative videotape application of SIT for parents of pediatric leukemia patients (aged 3 to 12) who were undergoing bone marrow aspirations or lumbar
punctures. Approximately 1 hour prior to each child's medical procedure, SIT was
offered to the parents in the form of an 11-minute film of a model who employed
coping self-statements, relaxation efforts, and coping imagery rehearsal. Relative to
parents receiving a child-focused intervention, the SIT-treated parents evidenced less
anxiety and better coping skills.

Turk and Rennert (1981), Warner and Swensen (1991), and other authors listed
in Table 12.1 also describe the successful application of SIT directly to cancer
patients. But not all applications of SIT to medical populations have yielded positive
results. An examination of the failures can also prove instructive. For example, within
the cancer arena, Roffman (1986) used SIT to treat cancer patients in order to help
them cope with the nausea and vomiting that often accompany chemotherapy. Some
50% of cancer patients who undergo chemotherapy experience distressing side
effects; moreover, 30–40% do not find antiemetic medication effective. This difficulty
contributes to the high rate of treatment nonadherence (see Meichenbaum & Turk,
1987). Roffman taught cancer patients coping skills (self-instruction, imagery, and
relaxation) in order to minimize the side effects (disorientation, anxiety) accompanying the use of the antiemetic THC, a synthetic cannabinoid. No differences were
found between the SIT and the placebo information group. Roffman questioned
whether a $1\frac{1}{2}$-hour SIT intervention was adequate to achieve the desired effects; a
more extensive training approach distributed over time and over trials would be likely
to prove more effective. A similar problem arose in a study by Postlethwaite, Stirling,
and Peck (1986), who provided SIT for patients undergoing coronary artery graft
surgery. Relative to attention control and no-treatment control groups, the SIT group
evidenced minimal change. The two 90-minute SIT trials were not sufficient to
control for the severe pain and life-threatening complications of the coronary surgery. Tan and Poser (1982) reported similar limited effectiveness of SIT for treating
the pain accompanying a knee arthrogram. In explaining these negative results, Turk
et al. (1983) have proposed that for such intense medical problems SIT intervention
should include multiple trials of rehearsal, both imaginal and behavioral. In general,
the length of treatment should be individually tailored rather than arbitrarily es-

tablished beforehand. The length of training should also be performance-based rather than time-based.

With the phenomenal growth of behavioral medicine, we can expect continued application of SIT interventions. There is a need to provide medical patients not only with procedural and sensory information, but also with information about possible coping efforts. They should also be given the opportunity to rehearse their coping skills, receive feedback, correct their strategies accordingly, and make personal attributions about the changes they were able to bring about. The nature of the training must be tailored, however, to the age of the patient population (e.g., see Melamed & Siegel, 1975) and to the patient's coping style. As Andrews (1970), Shipley, Butt, and Horwitz (1979), and others have reported, patients classified as "avoiders" may evidence increased stress in response to explicit, directive coping intervention efforts.

Finally, an innovative way to present SIT in medical settings was offered by Wernick, Jaremko, and Taylor (1981). They taught nurses working on a burn unit to employ SIT with their patients as they debrided their patients' burned wounds. The notion of "giving SIT away" or training other professional groups to use SIT *in vivo* is most promising. For example, I am presently consulting on research in which nurses are being taught how to do short-term SIT with outpatients who suffer from chronic medical conditions, such as arthritis, multiple sclerosis, and pain problems.

Applications to the Treatment of Psychiatric Patients

In working with psychiatric populations, the SIT trainer recognizes that individuals' counterproductive coping solutions originate earlier in life and often continue to operate in the present. A number of investigators have employed SIT for the general class of both inpatient and outpatient psychiatric clients, the latter of whom have to make a readjustment to nonhospital life. In addition, they have employed SIT in the treatment of specific target client groups (e.g., patients who have panic attacks or phobias, who suffer from PTSD, who experience problems controlling their anger, etc.).

I begin this examination with the general clinical psychiatric population. In most studies, SIT has been combined with other multifaceted psychoeducational and pharmacological interventions. For example, Holcomb (1986) examined the relative efficacy of eight 1-hour SIT sessions with and without medication in the treatment of 26 psychiatric inpatients. In terms of anxiety, depression, and overall subjective distress, Holcomb reported that SIT was superior to pharmacological interventions; impressively, this relative improvement was evident at a 3-year follow-up, as indicated by fewer patient readmissions for psychiatric problems.

Weston, Gordon, Bush, Holder, and Lieberman (1987) embedded SIT into a social skills board game training program in order to help discharged psychiatric hospital patients. In the course of the game, patients discussed and practiced various coping skills for high-risk situations. Other studies cited in Table 12.1 under "General stress reactions," especially those by Long (1984, 1985), indicate the general prophylactic potential of SIT.

Another major clinical challenge are those individuals who experience PTSD as a result of victimization (e.g., rape, abuse, other crime, terrorist attacks, etc.) or of exposure to an intense stressor (e.g., military combat). Following the "inoculation" metaphor, the SIT approach helps PTSD clients to assimilate less distressing aspects of trauma before they deal with more distressing aspects. This is nicely illustrated in an innovative cognitive–behavioral psychoeducational intervention conducted in Israel by Rabin and Nardi (1991). Under the heading "Ko'ach" (meaning "strength"), they provided training for 41 PTSD casualties of the Lebanon war and their wives. Since war can have a "toxic" effect on relationships, as evident in the finding that 38% of marriages of Vietnam veterans broke up within 6 months after their return from war (cited by Rabin & Nardi, 1991), the inclusion of spouses was viewed as critical. The SIT concept of gradualism was implemented by exposing the soldiers to a 4-week military training camp conducted by experienced mental health officers. The participants were systematically and gradually exposed to stress-inducing military stimuli that they tended to avoid (e.g., noise of firearms). They were also taught such coping skills as relaxation, self-talk, goal analysis, and problem solving concerning their civilian and work roles. Within a psychoeducational framework, their wives were given information about PTSD symptomatology, interpersonal skills training, and cognitive skills training, each of which was designed to nurture hope. A major treatment focus both in individual sessions and in couples group sessions was on identifying and nurturing the participants' particular strengths, thus fostering their sense of personal efficacy. Two additional innovative features of the Rabin and Nardi intervention are worth highlighting: (1) the use of trained wives in reaching out to more resistant wives, helping them to overcome their hesitancy and fear of participating in the program; and (2) the development of self-help couples groups after the Ko'ach program was completed, in order to conduct the follow-through aspects of SIT. Although the initial results of this comprehensive, multifaceted cognitive–behavioral intervention are encouraging, more careful evaluative study is required.

A more explicit evaluation of SIT with PTSD clients—in this case, rape victims—was conducted by Foa, Rothbaum, Biggs, and Murdock (1991). Instead of gradually exposing distressed clients to trauma-related cues in a desensitizing fashion, Foa et al. employed prolonged exposure or emotional flooding. The prolonged-exposure form of inoculation involves having the client repeatedly imagine scenes of the traumatic event over several sessions. Despite high levels of distress, anxiety, and anger, the client is required to "stay" with her self-generated images of the traumatic scenes until the accompanying anxiety and distress subside. As Epstein (1990) observes, the therapist encourages the client to vividly imagine the traumatic scenes, thus facilitating an intense re-experiencing of what is most feared. Clients may even be given audiotapes of their affectively charged imagery reconstructions to listen to as "homework," in order to further "defuse" or "uncouple" the accompanying anxiety and distress. Such imagery exposure is accompanied by the trainer's encouraging and arranging for the client's re-exposure on a gradual basis to the previous stressful setting, such as revisiting the scene of a traumatic event with the aid of others. Foa et al. found that such a prolonged-exposure intervention (without accompanying relaxation and coping imagery training), which encouraged the rape victims to confront fear-engendering stimuli both imaginally and behaviorally, was most successful in reducing intrusive thoughts, arousal symptoms, and avoidance behaviors.

The prolonged-exposure procedure employed by Foa et al. (1991) is similar to the induced intense affect exposure that Smith and his colleagues (Smith & Nye, 1989; Smith & Rohsenow, 1987) use in their stress management procedures and that Suinn (1990) uses in his anxiety management training. Although those who adopt a conditioning framework explain the diminished emotional reactions that follow from prolonged exposure in terms of "extinction" and "habituation," a cognitive–behavioral perspective hypothesizes that prolonged imaginal and behavioral exposure and intense affective imagery rehearsal provide clients with "data" indicating that they are indeed able to cope with distressing events. Such repeated exposure provides clients with opportunities to practice their coping skills, or, in SIT terms, to "inoculate" themselves against future stressful encounters. These training opportunities help clients to develop an adaptive personal narrative about their ability to cope, reinstituting a sense of personal control and predictability. With repeated experiential trials, they learn that fear and anxiety need not be overwhelming, and in time their fear is no longer appropriate. As Epstein (1990) posits, the distressed individuals develop a more differentiated and integrated conceptual system that they can accept life with all its imperfections; thus they each build a new assumptive world, assimilating their victimization in an adaptive manner. (See Janoff-Bulman, 1985, 1990, for discussions of how recovery is contingent upon a client's building a new assumptive world.)

Since distressed clients (especially those suffering from PTSD) are viewed as entering treatment with an internal dialogue characterized by feelings of helplessness, victimization, and demoralization, as well as a belief system that has been seriously challenged if not invalidated, SIT employs diverse experientially affective learning trials in order to nurture more adaptive and resourceful personal narratives. The more emotionally convincing the training opportunities, the more likely it is that a client's narrative, as well as his or her accompanying affect, will change.

A colleague and I (Meichenbaum & Fitzpatrick, in press) have analyzed a variety of stress management procedures, as well as individual and group coping rituals, from a constructive narrative perspective. For example, we describe how such diverse procedures as (1) religious ceremonies; (2) sweat lodge healing rituals, as employed with Vietnam veterans; (3) detached cathartic reporting of traumatic events (e.g., describing an incest episode as if one were a reporter telling a story); (4) ceremonial testimonials by torture victims; and (5) SIT, each attempt to help distressed clients "rescript" their internal dialogues and reconstruct their narrative belief systems. Such reconstructive efforts are not limited to adult victims, as illustrated by the innovative work of Ayalon (1983), who used play and fantasy to help children master the distress that followed being victims of terrorist attacks. Both imaginal and behavioral exercises, as well as gradual re-exposure to the stressful setting, were used to "inoculate" the victimized children to the stress they had experienced.

The value of an SIT format is further underscored in the important clinical work with panic patients. For example, Barlow (1988) has successfully extended the SIT model to panic disorder patients. During an initial conceptualization phase, the patients are offered an explanation (a conceptual model based on their own symptoms) about the interactive role that their hypervigilance about bodily cues, their catastrophic misinterpretations of physiological arousal, and their hyperventilation play in eliciting and exacerbating anxiety reactions. Such a reconceptualization of panic attacks readily leads to the use of (1) practice relaxation skills in order to control physical tenseness and hyperventilation; (2) cognitive coping skills in order to control catastrophic misinterpretations; and (3) cognitive restructuring procedures in order to alter appraisals, attributions, expectations, and avoidance behaviors. Following the SIT format, Barlow and other cognitive–behavioral therapists provide anxiety disorder patients with imaginal and behavioral rehearsal (e.g., behavioral coping trials to deal with self-induced hyperventilation; coping imagery rehearsal to anxiety-producing scenes). Finally, patients are challenged and encouraged to behaviorally rehearse, in a graduated fashion, their coping efforts *in vivo* (e.g., confronting what were formerly panic-inducing situations). Relapse prevention and self-attribution treatment components are also included in the SIT of panic patients. Barlow (1988), Clark and Salkovskis (1989), and Rapee (1987) have each documented the clinical efficacy of this cognitive–behavioral SIT approach, relative to pharmacological and other psychological interventions. The application of SIT for anxiety disorder patients is a clear success story, as documented by Michelson and Marchione (1991).

Another clinical area where SIT has been effectively employed is in work with clients who have problems controlling their anger. Many diverse aggressive populations have been treated with SIT, including children, adolescents, adults, and abusive couples, some of whom have limiting physical conditions (such as mental retardation or head injuries) that contribute to their impulsive and explosive behavior. Space does not permit a comprehensive review of these studies, and the interested reader should examine the multiple references by Deffenbacher, Feindler, and Novaco cited in Table 12.1. A critical treatment feature of many of these SIT interventions is to help angry and aggressive clients to view interpersonal provocations as "problems to be solved," rather than as personal threats. Moreover, there is a need to teach them a variety of coping skills, including cognitive skills (e.g., self-instructional procedures), behavioral skills (e.g., time-out procedures), and self-regulation of affective arousal (e.g., relaxation). We (Meichenbaum & Novaco, 1978) have described how SIT can be employed on a preventative basis with police officers who have problems with anger control, while Novaco, Cook, and Sarason (1983) implemented a SIT program with Marine drill instructors. Given the widespread nature of anger-related problems and the often accompanying attitudinal concerns about exerting power (e.g., in the case of spouse abuse), a cognitive–behavioral SIT approach seems quite promising, as described in a case study later in this chapter.

Applications to the Treatment of Performance Anxiety

From its origin, SIT has continually been employed with individuals who experience debilitating anxiety in evaluative situations. As noted in Table 12.1, this may take the form of test, speech, math, computer, dating, and writing anxiety, as well as anxiety associated with athletic competition. Major literature reviews already exist in many of these anxiety areas (e.g., Hembree, 1988, has offered a meta-analysis of 562 studies in the area of test anxiety). In many instances, SIT has been combined with skills training programs, such as in the treatment of speech anxiety (public-speaking training; Jones,

1991), writing skills practice for anxious writers (Salovey & Harr, 1990), and study skills training for those who have examination anxiety (Hembree, 1988). There are no consistent findings across these varied populations in terms of the incremental benefits that accrue from combining an explicit skills training component and other SIT features. In some studies the combination of skills training and SIT has been found to facilitate performance, while in other studies there have been no synergistic effects from the combination. The marked diversity of populations, varied lengths of treatments, and different levels of initial anxiety preclude adequate comparisons across studies.

Another arena that has combined various features of SIT is that of athletic competition. For instance, Smoll and Smith (1988) advocate that interventions need to go beyond the stress management of athletes and should influence the nature of both the coaches' and parents' communications with the athletes. In fact, Smith (1980) has provided guidelines based on observational studies of coaches' "dos and don'ts" of coaching.

The promise of employing SIT with athletes is highlighted in a series of studies by Mace and his colleagues. For example, Mace, Eastman, and Carroll (1987) offered a case study of an Olympic gymnast who developed difficulties in performing in a competitive pommel horse event. The gymnast's tenseness, worry, and doubts interfered with his ability to engage in mental preparation and gymnastic performance. Twelve sessions of SIT, consisting of relaxation, visualization, and positive coping self-statements, were used successfully to improve his athletic skills; consequently, he won a regional championship. In this clinical case, as well as in other cognitive–behavioral treatment studies of athletes (squash players, Mace & Carroll, 1986; gymnasts, Mace, Eastman, & Carroll, 1986; basketball players, Harrison & Feltz, 1981), SIT was expanded to include both visualization and actual practice in the gym (inoculation trials), videotape feedback, and the constructive involvement of the coach in arranging for athletic practice under competitive rules. The long-term (6-month follow-up) potential usefulness of such stress management interventions was reported by Crocker and his colleagues (Crocker, 1989; Crocker, Alderman, & Smith, 1988). They proposed the need for intermittent follow-up sessions to maintain the acquired coping skills.

Smith (1980) has highlighted the value of labeling such stress management procedures as a form of "mental toughness training" for athletes and their coaches. They are told that the training is designed to help athletes "control the emotional responses that might interfere with performance and also is designed to help athletes focus their attention on the tasks at hand" (p. 157). Such a rationale is more likely to be accepted than that of "reducing stress," as if stress is something to be avoided, when indeed many athletes believe that they need to experience stress in order to "peak." Under the aegis of "mental toughness training," Smith has developed a cognitive–behavioral group training program that is offered in six twice-weekly, 1-hour sessions. The initial educational/conceptualization phase orients the participants to the nature of stress and emotion, the role mental processes play, and various ways to develop an "integrated coping response." The skills acquisition phase focuses upon cue-controlled relaxation, imagining stressful situations, and cognitive rehearsal of "anti-stress" coping self-statements. The goal of training is *not* to eliminate emotional arousal, but rather to give athletes greater control over their emotional responses. The athletes are given an opportunity to rehearse their coping skills under conditions of trainer-induced high arousal and strong affect, which are stimulated by the trainer's offering highly charged imagery scenes. In this inoculating fashion, the athletes are taught to focus their attention on intense feelings and then to practice turning them off in order to reduce and prevent high arousal levels from getting out of hand. The trainer also attends to the excessively high performance standards and distorted fear of the consequences of possible failure that distressed athletes, their coaches, and their parents may hold. In addition, the trainer, in collaboration with a coach and an athlete, can set up *in vivo* practice trials and can implement a training program to improve relevant sport skills. In short, SIT with athletes is packaged as an educational program in self-control, and not as a form of psychotherapy.

Applications to Problems with Adjustment to Life Transitions

Among the most widespread forms of stress that individuals have to cope with are transitional demands that set off a series of adjustments. Entry, re-entry, displacement, unemployment, and the like have all been occasions for the application of SIT, as noted in Table 12.1. An illustrative instance is the demonstration project by Deck and Dougherty (1986), who successfully included SIT as part of their student services study skills program in order to improve student retention rates. SIT was offered for six class meetings lasting 50 minutes each. The students kept coping logs, role-played, and then implemented the practiced skills. The initial results from this demonstration project are encouraging, but a more adequate comparison group study is required.

On a much grander scale, another demonstration project was conducted in Israel by Israelashvili (1991). He used SIT with Israeli senior high school students who must serve in the IDF. In order to help these youths develop realistic expectations, flexible coping repertoires, and self-confidence, and to heighten their preparedness to deal with the stress of unfamiliarity, humiliation, home separation, and adaptation to new demands, SIT training was provided in postprimary schools throughout the country. The training was conducted on an interdisciplinary basis, involving members of the IDF, representatives of the Ministry of Education, and school personnel. Following the SIT clinical guideline of employing a coping model, an additional SIT trainer was a recent graduate of each school who had enlisted and who could relate coping experiences Another critical feature of SIT is the involvement of significant others, and Israelashvili thoughtfully involved the youths' parents in separate SIT group meetings. The parents were instructed and guided on how to become positive and helpful sources of coping for their children during this transition period.

The initial conceptualization phase of SIT focused on educating the military candidates about the nature of the IDF, providing needed information about possible stressors and flexible coping efforts, and helping candidates in deciding which military branch they wished to serve in. The acquisition and rehearsal phase focused on coping and adaptation techniques. Some sessions in the rehearsal phase were conducted separately by sex in order to tailor the training individually. The final phase of application and follow-through provided the participants with a week-long opportunity to try out their respective coping techniques on army bases and then to reflect in group sessions on their personal reactions to the tryout. The application phase also provided an opportunity to identify those recruits who required additional individualized SIT.

Whereas the SIT provided a heuristically valuable model for interventions in both the Deck and Dougherty (1986) and Israelashvili (1991) projects, systematic comparative outcome data are only now being collected. More empirical encouragement for SIT was offered in a randomized field experiment by Caplan, Vinokur, Price, and van Ryn (1989), who addressed the challenging problem of the effects of unemployment. As part of a comprehensive program, eight 3-hour group sessions were conducted with the unemployed over a 2-week period. Inoculation about possible setbacks was incorporated as a critical feature of the comprehensive treatment package (which also included job-seeking skills, problem-solving skills, decision-making training, and ways of further developing social skills). Caplan et al. highlighted the critical need for the trainer to establish trust and foster collaboration by means of self-disclosure. This comprehensive cognitive–behavioral package contributed to higher rates of re-employment, higher motivation, and greater job satisfaction in the treatment group, relative to a matched attention control group. This important study warrants replication and extension.

Applications for Highly Stressed Occupational Groups

Whereas SIT initially emerged as a stress reduction procedure for psychiatric clients, innovative researchers quickly highlighted its potential for highly stressed occupational groups as noted in Table 12.1. Since many of these SIT occupational preventative studies have been summarized in Meichenbaum (1985), the more recent innovative SIT work by Hytten and his colleagues warrants special mention here. Working with Norwegian disaster prevention investigators, Hytten, Jensen, and Skauli (1990) examined the relative effectiveness of short-term (1-hour) SIT for offshore oil workers who must learn how to use smoke-diving equipment and how to escape quickly from an oil platform in free-fall lifeboats. The SIT was designed to nurture realistic expectations and to help the workers control their thoughts and emotions and perform efficiently. Interestingly, SIT resulted in improvement in the smoke-diving situation, but not in the free-fall situation, where more uncertainty was evident. More extensive performance-based training, perhaps using coping modeling films and multiple practice trials, might prove helpful. The SIT procedures that Starr (1986) successfully employed to enhance recall and performance of cardiopulmonary resuscitation by nonmedical personnel could be readily employed by Hytten and his group.

Finally, another common feature of several of the SIT studies with highly stressed occupational groups was that they employed trainers who came from the same occupational group as the targeted treatment group. For instance, in the study by Novaco et al. (1983), Marine drill instructors were taught how to cope by other drill instructors; Sarason, Johnson, Berberich, and Siegel (1979) used police officers to train other police officers. Another innovative way to use SIT was offered by Novaco

(1980), who trained probation officers to conduct SIT with their adolescent parolees. According to this diffusion paradigm, the psychologist acts as a trainer and consultant to others who conduct SIT directly.

Lessons Learned from Component Analysis of Stress Inoculation Training

An examination of Table 12.2, which describes the multifaceted features of SIT, indicates its complexity. What are the "active" ingredients of SIT? Are the various phases of SIT equally important in facilitating change? The number of studies that have dismantled and compared various components of SIT is still limited. Moreover, most of these studies have been laboratory analogue studies of subjects exposed to experimentally induced pain. For example, component-analytic studies by Horan, Hackett, Buchanan, Stone, and Demchik-Stone (1977) and Vallis (1984) indicated that the skills acquisition phase of SIT plays a critical role in contributing to treatment effectiveness. When this phase was dropped, the efficacy of SIT was significantly lowered. There was also evidence that with laboratory-induced pain, the improvement was mediated by the subjects' use of relaxation and by an accompanying decrease in their use of negative thinking (catastrophizing ideation). Kendall (in press) has argued that the reduction of negative ideation, or what he describes as "the power of non-negative thinking," is both a by-product and mediator of behavioral change. In fact, he reports that it is not the absence of negative thinking, but a 2:1 ratio of positive to negative thinking, that characterizes adaptive coping.

In other laboratory studies, Cassens, Stallings, and Ahles (1988) reported on the important role of verbal feedback as a component of SIT, while Smith and Nye (1989) reported that the failure to provide subjects with rehearsal opportunities resulted in less effective outcomes. We (Meichenbaum & Turk, 1987) have highlighted the important role of the initial conceptualization phase as a critical component in fostering client treatment adherence. Such client noncompliance issues take on specific importance when we learn that adherence to daily practice of relaxation procedures (a skill taught in SIT) is only about 40%, and moreover that the overall attrition rate from all forms of psychotherapy is approximately 70% by the third session (Phillips, 1986).

SIT was conceived and developed as an integrative, clinically sensitive treatment package, and it is likely that each of the three specific treatment phases contributes important elements to the change process. Although component analysis can prove informative, the primary research emphasis should be on assessing the clinical usefulness of SIT on both a short-term and a long-term basis, relative to appropriate control treatments. The field needs more documented evidence that SIT in indeed effective before we begin to take it apart. In particular, there is a need to determine whether SIT is contraindicated in any specific population. At this point there is no evidence to suggest that any specific client group should not be treated with SIT. Instead, the clinical caveat to follow is that the style and manner with which SIT is implemented needs to be individually tailored. Moreover, in some instances SIT needs to be supplemented by other forms of intervention ranging from psychotropic medication to community involvement.

Case Study

The following case study illustrates how SIT has been applied successfully. Novaco (1977a) used SIT to treat Tom, a 38-year-old credit manager for a national firm, who had been hospitalized for tension, depression, and feelings of worthlessness and inadequacy; he was even considering suicide. He had been under considerable job pressure, and he had developed headaches and chest pains. He was married and had six children, one of whom had been diagnosed as hyperactive.

Clinical interviews revealed that Tom had a great deal of anger and hostility toward his colleagues and supervisors. He kept his feelings "bottled up" and often reacted in an overcontrolled fashion. He would actively suppress his anger, but periodically explode in "verbal fireworks." At home he was intolerant and easily provoked. The children's fights frequently elicited anger, which Tom readily expressed both verbally and physically; as he stated, he was "reacting out of proportion." He felt overwhelmed and helpless.

During hospitalization, SIT was conducted three times a week for $3\frac{1}{2}$ weeks. Follow-up sessions were conducted twice weekly for 2 months. The initial phase of treatment focused on making Tom aware of his personal anger pattern and of the multiple functions of anger (e.g., what caused his anger and how anger could be self-regulated). The psychotherapeutic discussions focused on such topics as (1) recognizing the first signs of tension and arousal; (2) identifying persons and situations that triggered stress and anger; (3) discriminating between justified and unnecessary anger; and (4) appreciating how sometimes he inadvertently exacerbated his stress (i.e., "lit his own fuse"). These discussions took place in a collaborative fashion.

The second phase of SIT was devoted to bolstering, learning, and rehearsing coping skills. Tom was taught how to view stressful situations as problems to be solved, instead of as personal threats and provocations. Tom was encouraged to identify the results (goals) that he wanted and to realize that anger and aggression were only one of several ways to achieve such goals. SIT helped Tom to deautomatize his response in stressful situations, as well as to enumerate and consider the best possible means of achieving his desired outcome. Tom also received training in how to use relaxation and self-regulatory cognitions, how to take perspective and maintain a sense of humor, and how to communicate his feelings more effectively without stridency.

During the final phase of SIT, Tom underwent graded doses of anger stimuli by means of imagery and behavioral rehearsal and role playing. For instance, Tom was asked to imagine a series of scenes ranging from those least likely to provoke anger to those that had driven him into fury and frustration in the past. While imagining these scenes, Tom mentally rehearsed the various anger control coping skills he had already developed. Coping imagery scenes were used in which Tom would envision himself beginning to "lose his cool"; he would then imagine himself "noticing," "catching," "interrupting," and "choosing" alternative ways of handling his distress. Tom was learning that he had choices, and that he was not a victim of stressful situations or of his own distressing feelings. Later, these imaginal scenes were actually played out, with Tom and the therapist taking opposing roles. Finally, Tom was encouraged to use his anger control coping skills in real life (*in vivo*), initially in relatively safe situations and then, with practice, in more demanding and stressful social situations.

The therapist carefully anticipated and subsumed any possible setbacks or lapses that Tom might encounter by including relapse prevention procedures. The therapist also insured that Tom made personal attributions for the changes he was able to bring about.

SIT proved successful in helping Tom to deal with his anger and to reduce his accompanying depression. For example, Tom found it much easier to control his irritation with his children, even though there were many highly provocative incidents. At work, too, he was much more able to express his feelings in a constructive manner.

SIT has been applied successfully to many similar clinical problems (see Meichenbaum, 1985). Let us now consider some possible future directions of SIT practice and research.

Future Directions

One major new direction for SIT will be the continued application of the procedure to diverse clinical and nonclinical populations. In fact, a number of authors have already written thoughtful and creative descriptions of how SIT might be applied to their particular arenas. Divorcing spouses and their children (Turner, 1985), victims of terrorist and hostage attacks (Oots & Wiegele, 1985), children who come from high-risk families (Pellegrini, 1990), and operators of automated machinery (Spettell & Liebert, 1986) are but a few of the populations suggested as possible candidates for SIT. Another good example of the potential applicability of SIT was highlighted by Walton (1990), who has analyzed the stressors that individuals from business and governmental agencies experience when they have to cope with overseas placement and adapt to differences in culture, climate, and the many other dimensions of living and working abroad. SIT could be used to reduce the 20–50% of international business relocations that end with premature return.

Another innovative extension of SIT has been in the form of bibliotherapy, which provides clients with a conceptualization, describes coping strategies, and provides application exercises (see Register, Beckham, May, & Gustafson, 1991, for test-anxious students; *Athabasca University Student Services Orientation Guidebook*, 1983, for mature returning college students). A cautionary note is required, however, given the high rate of noncompliance with bibliotherapeutic forms of intervention (Meichenbaum & Turk, 1987). A more personalized interactive format of SIT is now being explored in our laboratory: computer-based SIT for distressed populations. With the advent of voice-operated computers and accompanying video disks that can include coping modeling films, a new generation of individualized SIT instructional packages is possible. Such SIT modules could be used in clinic settings and hospitals, military settings, business organizations, and the like, on both a treatment and a preventative basis.

In formulating these new SIT programs, it is important for us to keep in mind a number of clinical guidelines:

1. Stress management must not merely focus on altering the individual's or group's response to stressors; it must also focus on changing the environment in order to reduce the stress load.

2. SIT must *not* be applied in a uniform fashion or in a strict therapeutic sequence, regardless of the presenting problem or the individual's particular coping style.

3. SIT must be sensitive to the nature of the stressor and whether it poses emotion-focused or problem-focused demands, and the trainer and client must intervene accordingly.

4. The literature on client resistance, noncompliance, and treatment nonadherence indicates that a collaborative therapeutic or training alliance is a critical component in SIT (see, Meichenbaum & Turk, 1987, for a discussion of what is needed to achieve adherence and nurture generalization).

5. The packaging of the stress management intervention is critical. In some instances, characterizing the SIT as a form of teaching "mental toughness" or "toughening up" is more appropriate than describing it as a set of stress management procedures (see Holtzworth-Munroe, Munroe, & Smith, 1985). As noted, much forethought should be given as to who should offer SIT. The message to be conveyed is that SIT is *not* designed to eliminate stress; rather, it encourages clients to learn flexible adaptive responses to be used in stressful situations.

The next 20 years are likely to see even more clinical application and research activity on SIT. I hope that this chapter has "inoculated" the reader to possible pitfalls and highlighted the potential of cognitive–behavioral interventions.

REFERENCES

Allen, T. W. (1988). The cognitive bases of peak performances: A classroom intervention with student athletes. *Journal of Counseling and Development, 67,* 202–204.

Altmaier, E. M., Leary, M. R., Halpern, S., & Sellers, J. E. (1985). Effects of stress inoculation and participant modeling on confidence and anxiety. *Journal of Social and Clinical Psychology, 34,* 500–505.

Altmaier, E. M., Ross, S., Leary, M. R., & Thornbrough, M. (1982). Matching stress inoculation's treatment components to client's anxiety mode. *Journal of Counseling Psychology, 29,* 331–334.

Amigo, I., Buceta, J. M., Becona, E., & Bueno, A. M. (1991). Cognitive behavioral treatment for essential hypertension: A controlled study. *Stress Medicine, 7,* 103–108.

Andrews, J. (1970). Recovery from surgery with and without preparatory instructions for three coping styles. *Journal of Personality and Social Psychology, 15,* 223–226.

Athabasca University Student Services Orientation Guidebook. (1983). Athabasca, Alberta: Athabasca, University.

Avants, S. K., Margolin, A., & Salovey, P. (1990). Stress management techniques: Anxiety reduction, appeal and individual differences. *Imagination, Cognition and Personality, 10,* 3–24.

Avia, M. D., & Ruiz, M. A. (1987). Systematic desensitization, stress inoculation, and nonspecific therapy on the treatment of mathematics anxiety. *Estudios de Psicologia, 31,* 41–52.

Ayalon, O. (1983). Coping with terrorism: The Israeli case. In D. Meichenbaum & M. Jaremko (Eds.), *Stress prevention and management: A cognitive behavioral approach.* New York: Plenum Press.

Barlow, D. (1988). *Anxiety and its disorders: The nature and treatment of anxiety and panic.* New York: Guilford Press.

Barrios, B., & Shigetomi, C. (1980). Coping skills training: Potential for prevention of fears and anxieties. *Behavior Therapy, 11,* 431–439.

Berbalk, H., Kollenbaum, V., E. & Volkel, H. (1984). Biochemical effects of stress inoculation: An important and neglected method of therapeutic control demonstrated on a group of ulcer patients. *Zeitschrift für Klinische Psychologie, 13,* 276–287.

Bistline, J. L., & Frieden, F. P. (1984). Anger control: A case study of a stress inoculation treatment for a chronic aggressive patient. *Cognitive Therapy and Research, 8,* 551–556.

Bloom, A., & Haitalouma, J. E. (1990). Anxiety management training as a strategy for enhancing computer user performance. *Computers and Human Behavior, 6,* 337–349.

Bloom, L., & Cantrell, D. (1978). Anxiety management training for essential hypertension in pregnancy. *Behavior Therapy, 9,* 377–382.

Blythe, B. J., & Erdahl, J. C. (1986). Using stress inoculation to prepare a patient for open heart surgery. *Health and Social Work, 11*, 265–274.

Brock, T. D. (1983). Why copy editors exist: The misspelling of the word inoculation. *American Society for Microbiology, 49*, 501.

Brooks, G., & Richardson, F. (1980). Emotional skills training: A treatment program for duodenal ulcer. *Behavior Therapy, 11*, 198–207.

Brown, S. (1980). Coping skills training: An evaluation of a psychoeducational program in a community mental health setting. *Journal of Counseling Psychology, 27*, 340–345.

Caplan, R. D., Vinokur, A. D., Price, R. H., & van Ryn, M. (1989). Job seeking, reemployment, and mental health: A randomized field experiment in coping with job loss. *Journal of Applied Psychology, 74*, 10–20.

Cassens, H. L., Stalling, R. B., & Ahles, T. A. (1988). The influence of positive feedback and stress inoculation training in the response to cold pressor pain. *Journal of Social Behavior and Personality, 3*, 117–126.

Cecil, M. A., & Forman, S. G. (1990). Effects of stress inoculation training and coworker support groups on teacher stress. *Journal of School Psychology, 28*, 105–118.

Clark, D. M., & Salkovskis, P. M. (1989). *Panic disorder treatment manual*. Oxford: Pergamon Press.

Craddock, C., Cotler, S., & Jason, L. (1978). Primary prevention: Immunization of children for speech anxiety. *Cognitive Therapy and Research, 2*, 389–396.

Cragan, M., & Deffenbacher, J. (1984). Anxiety management training and relaxation as self-control in the treatment of generalized anxiety in medical outpatients. *Journal of Counseling Psychology, 31*, 123–131.

Crocker, P. R. (1989). A follow-up of cognitive–affective stress management training. *Journal of Sport and Exercise Psychology, 11*, 236–242.

Crocker, P. R., Alderman, R. B., & Smith, F. M. (1988). Cognitive–affective stress management training with high performance youth volleyball players: Effects on affect, cognition and performance. *Journal of Sport and Exercise Psychology, 10*, 448–460.

Crowther, J. H. (1983). Stress management training and relaxation imagery in the treatment of essential hypertension. *Journal of Behavioral Medicine, 6*, 169–187.

Cruz, R. A. (1991). *Immunización al stress en pacientes pre-operatorios [Stress inoculation in preoperative patients]*. Unpublished manuscript, Universidad Autonoma de Nuevo Leon, Nuevo Leon, Mexico.

de Blas, M. R. & Labrador, F. J. (1984). The efficacy of the techniques of relaxation, RPg biofeedback and stress inoculation for changing preceptions of experimentally induced pain. *Analisis y Modificación de Conducta, 10*, 513–532.

Deck, M. D., & Dougherty, A. M. (1986). *SITting on stress: A retention emphasis through study skills*. Cullowhee, NC: Student Services, Western Carolina University.

Deffenbacher, J., & Craun, A. (1985). Anxiety management training with stressed student gynecology patients: A collaborative approach. *Journal of College Student Personnel, 26*, 513–518.

Deffenbacher, J., & Hahloser, R. (1981). Cognitive and relaxation coping skills in stress-inoculation. *Cognitive Therapy and Research, 5*, 211–215.

Deffenbacher, J., McNamara, K., Stark, R., & Sabadell, P. (1991). A combination of cognitive relaxation, and behavioral coping skills in the reduction of anger. *Journal of College Student Development, 26*, 114–212.

Deffenbacher, J., Story, D., Brandon, A., Hogg, J., & Hazaleus, S. (1988). Cognitive and cognitive–relaxation treatment of anger. *Cognitive Therapy and Research, 12*, 167–184.

Deffenbacher, J., Story, D., Stark, R., Hogg, J., & Brandon, A. (1987). Cognitive–relaxation and social skills intervention in the treatment of general anger. *Journal of Counseling Psychology, 34*, 171–176.

Deikis, J. G. (1983). *Stress inoculation training: Effects on anxiety, self-efficacy, and performance in divers*. Unpublished doctoral dissertation, Temple University.

Denicola, J., & Sandler, J. (1980). Training abuse parents in child management and self-control skills. *Behavior Therapy, 11*, 263–270.

Dinner, R., & Gal, R. (1983). *Stress-inoculation training and Israeli defense airborne soldiers*. Unpublished manuscript, Department of Behavioral Sciences, Israeli Defense Forces, Tel Aviv, Israel.

Dougherty, A., & Deck, M. D. (1984). Helping teachers to help children cope with stress. *Journal of Humanistic Education and Development, 23*, 36–44.

Dunning, C. (1990). Mental health sequelae in disaster workers: Prevention and intervention. *International Journal of Mental Health, 19*, 91–103.

Egan, K. (1983). Stress management and child management with abusive parents. *Journal of Clinical Child Psychology, 12*, 292–299.

Eliot, G. R., & Eisdorfer, C. (1982). *Stress and human health*. New York: Springer-Verlag.

Epstein, S. (1990). The self-concept, the traumatic neurosis, and the structure of personality. In D. J. Ozer, J. M. Healy, & A. J. Stewart (Eds.), *Perspective on personality: Self and emotion*. Greenwich, CT: JAI Press.

Erdahl, J., & Blythe, B. (1984). *Single-case evaluation of stress inoculation training to prepare a cardiac patient for open-heart surgery*. Paper presented at the National Association of Social Work Health Conference, Washington, DC.

Fairbank, J. A., & Brown, T. A. (1987). Current behavioral approaches to the treatment of posttraumatic stress disorder. *The Behavior Therapist, 10*, 57–64.

Feindler, E. L. (1990). A review of adolescent behavior therapy. In E. L. Feindler & G. R. Kalfus (Eds.), *Adolescent behavior therapy*. New York: Springer.

Feindler, E. L., & Ecton, R. B. (1986). *Adolescent anger control: Cognitive–behavioral techniques*. Elmsford, NY: Pergamon Press.

Feindler, E. L., Ecton, E. B., Kingsley, D., & Dubey, D. (1986). Group anger control training for institutionalized psychiatric male adolescents. *Behavior Therapy, 17*, 109–123.

Feindler, E. L., & Fremouw, W. (1983). Stress inoculation training for adolescent anger problems. In D. Meichenbaum & M. Jaremko (Eds.), *Stress prevention and management: A cognitive behavioral approach*. New York: Plenum Press.

Feindler, E. L., Marriott, S., & Iwata, M. (1984). Group anger control training for junior high school dropouts. *Cognitive Therapy and Research, 8*, 299–311.

Figley, C. R. (1989). *Helping traumatized families*. San Francisco: Jossey-Bass.

Foa, E. B., Rothbaum, B. O., Riggs, D. S., & Murdock, T. B. (1991). *Treatment of PTSD in rape victims: A comparison between cognitive–behavioral procedures and counseling*. Unpublished manuscript, Medical College of Pennsylvania.

Foley, F. W., Bedell, J. R., & LaRocca, N. G. (1987). Efficacy of stress inoculation training in coping with multiple sclerosis. *Journal of Consulting and Clinical Psychology, 55*, 919–922.

Folkman, S., Chesney, M., McKusik, L., Ironson, G., Johnson, D. S., & Coates, T. J. (1991). Translating coping theory into an intervention. In J. Eckenrode (Ed.), *The social context of coping*. New York: Plenum Press.

Forman, S. G. (1981). Stress management training: Evaluation of effects on school psychological services. *Journal of School Psychology, 19*, 233–241.

Forman, S. G. (1982). Stress management for teachers: A cognitive–behavioral program. *Journal of School Psychology, 20*, 180–187.

Forman, S. G. (1983). Occupational stress management: Cognitive–behavioral approaches. *Children and Youth Services Review, 5*, 277–287.

Forman, S. G., & O'Malley, P. L. (1985). A school-based approach to stress management education of students. *Special Services in the Schools, 1*, 61–71.

Frank, E., Anderson, B., Stewart, B. D., Dancu, C., Hughes, C., & West, D. (1988). Efficacy of cognitive behavior therapy and desensitization in the treatment of rape trauma. *Behavior Therapy, 19*, 403–420.

Frank, J. D. (1987). Psychotherapy, rhetoric, and hermeneutics: Implications for practice and research. *Psychotherapy, 24*, 293–302.

Franzen, M. D., & Lovell, M. R. (1987). Behavioral treatments of aggressive sequelae of brain injury. *Psychiatric Annals, 17*, 389–396.

Fremouw, W., & Harmatz, M. (1975). A helper model for behavioral treatment of speech anxiety. *Journal of Consulting and Clinical Psychology, 43*, 652–660.

Fremouw, W., & Zitter, R. (1978). A comparison of skills training and cognitive restructuring-relaxation for the treatment of speech anxiety. *Behavior Therapy, 9*, 248–259.

Gaertner, G., Craighead, L., & Horan, J. (1983). *A component analysis of stress inoculation applied to institutionalized public offenders with anger and aggression management deficiencies*. Unpublished manuscript, Pennsylvania State University.

Genest, M. (1979). *A cognitive–behavioral bibliotherapy to ameliorate pain*. Unpublished master's thesis, University of Waterloo, Waterloo, Ontario.

Girodo, M., & Wood, D. (1979). Talking yourself out of pain: The importance of believing you can. *Cognitive Therapy and Research, 3*, 23–33.

Glass, C., Gottman, J., & Shmurak, S. (1976). Response acquisition and cognitive self-statement modification approaches to dating skill training. *Journal of Counseling Psychology, 23*, 520–526.

Golden, W. L., & Consorte, J. (1982). Training mildly retarded individuals to control their anger through the use of cognitive behavior therapy techniques. *Journal of Contemporary Psychotherapy, 13*, 182–187.

Hackett, G., & Horan, J. (1980). Stress inoculation for pain: What's really going on? *Journal of Counseling Psychology, 27*, 107–116.

Hackett, G., Horan, J., Buchanan, J., & Zumoff, P. (1979). Improving exposure component and generalization potential of stress inoculation for pain. *Perceptual and Motor Skills, 48,* 1132–1134.

Hains, A. A. (1989). An anger-control intervention with aggressive delinquent youths. *Behavioral Residential Training, 4,* 213–230.

Hains, A. A. (1992). A stress inoculation training program for adolescents in a high school setting: A multiple baseline approach. *Journal of Adolescence, 15,* 163–175.

Hains, A. A. (in press). A comparison of cognitive–behavioral stress management with adolescent males. *Journal of Counseling and Development.*

Hains, A. A., & Szyjakowski, M. (1990). A cognitive stress-reduction intervention program for adolescents. *Journal of Consulting and Clinical Psychology, 37,* 79–84.

Harrison, R. P., & Feltz, D. (1981). Stress inoculation for athletes: Description and case example. *Motor Skills: Theory into Practice, 5,* 53–61.

Hart, K. (1984). Stress management training for Type A individuals. *Journal of Behavior Therapy and Experimental Psychiatry, 15,* 133–140.

Haug, T., Brenne, L, Johnsen, B. H., & Bernstein, D. (1987). A three-systems analysis of fear of flying: A comparison of a consonant and non-consonant treatment method. *Behaviour Research and Therapy, 25,* 187–194.

Hayslip, B. (1989). Alternative mechanisms for improvements in fluid ability performance among older adults. *Psychology and Aging, 4,* 122–124.

Hazaleus, S., & Deffenbacher, J. (1986). Relaxation and cognitive treatments of anger. *Journal of Consulting and Clinical Psychology, 54,* 222–226.

Hembree, R. (1988). Correlates, causes, effects and treatment of test anxiety. *Review of Educational Research, 58,* 47–77.

Holcomb, W. R. (1979). *Coping with severe stress: A clinical application of stress inoculation therapy.* Unpublished doctoral dissertation, University of Missouri, Columbia.

Holcomb, W. R. (1986). Stress inoculation therapy with anxiety and stress disorders of acute psychiatric patients. *Journal of Clinical Psychology, 42,* 864–872.

Holroyd, K. A. (1976). Cognition and desensitization in the group treatment of test anxiety. *Journal of Consulting and Clinical Psychology, 44,* 99–101.

Holroyd, K. A., & Andrasik, F. (1978). Coping and the self-control of chronic tension headache. *Journal of Consulting and Clinical Psychology, 46,* 1036–1045.

Holroyd, K. A., Andrasik, F., & Westbrook, T. (1977). Cognitive control of tension headache. *Cognitive Therapy and Research, 1,* 121–133.

Holtzworth-Munroe, A., Munroe, M., & Smith, R. E. (1985). Effects of stress management training program on first- and second-year medical students. *Journal of Medical Education, 60,* 417–419.

Horan, J., Hackett, G., Buchanan, J., Stone, C., & Demchik-Stone, D. (1977). Coping with pain: A component analysis of stress inoculation. *Cognitive Therapy and Research, 1,* 211–221.

Horowitz, M. (1986). *Stress response syndromes.* New York: Basic Books.

Hussain, R., & Lawrence, P. (1978). The reduction of test, state and trait anxiety by test-specific and generalized stress inoculation training. *Cognitive Therapy and Research, 2,* 25–37.

Hytten, K., Jensen, A., & Skauli, G. (1990). Stress inoculation training for smoke divers and free fall lifeboat passengers. *Aviation, Space, and Environmental Medicine, 61,* 983–988.

Israelashvili, M. (1991). *A model for preparation of adolescents for recruitment into military service in Israel.* Unpublished manuscript, Tel Aviv University, Tel Aviv, Israel.

Janoff-Bulman, R. (1985). The aftermath of victimization: Rebuilding shattered assumptions. In C. R. Figley (Ed.), *Trauma and its wake.* New York: Brunner/Mazel.

Janoff-Bulman, R. (1990). Understanding people in terms of their assumptive worlds. In D. J. Ozer, J. M. Healy, & A. J. Stewart (Eds.), *Perspectives on personality: Self and emotion.* Greenwich, CT: JAI Press.

Jaremko, M. E. (1979). A component analysis of stress inoculation: Review and prospectus. *Cognitive Therapy and Research, 3,* 35–48.

Jaremko, M. E. (1980). The use of stress inoculation training in the reduction of public speaking anxiety. *Journal of Clinical Psychology, 36,* 735–738.

Jaremko, M. E. (1983). Stress inoculation training for social anxiety, with emphasis on dating anxiety. In D. Meichenbaum & M. Jaremko (Eds.), *Stress prevention and management: A cognitive behavioral approach.* New York: Plenum Press.

Jaremko, M. E. (1984). Stress inoculation training: A generic approach for the prevention of stress-related disorders. *Personnel and Guidance Journal, 62,* 544–550.

Jaremko, M. E., Hadfield, R., & Walker, W. (1980). Contribution of an educational phase to stress inoculation of speech anxiety. *Perceptual and Motor Skills, 50,* 495–501.

Jason, L., & Burrows, B. (1983). Transition training for high school seniors. *Cognitive Therapy and Research, 7,* 79–92.

Jay, S. M., & Elliott, C. H. (1986). *Coping with childhood leukemia and its treatment: A parent's perspective.* Urbana, IL: Carla Medical Communication. (Videotape)

Jay, S. M., & Elliott, C. H. (1990). A stress inoculation program for parents whose children are undergoing painful medical procedures. *Journal of Consulting and Clinical Psychology, 58,* 799–804.

Jay, S. M., Elliott, C. H., Katz, E., & Siegel, S. E. (1987). Cognitive–behavioral and pharmacological interventions for children's distress during painful medical procedures. *Journal of Consulting and Clinical Psychology, 55,* 860–865.

Jenni, M., & Wollersheim, J. (1979). Cognitive therapy, stress management, and the Type A behavior pattern. *Cognitive Therapy and Research, 3,* 61–73.

Jones, M. C. (1991). *The effects of stress inoculation training and skills training on the treatment of speech anxiety.* Unpublished masters' thesis, Laurentian University, Sudbury, Ontario.

Jorgensen, R., Houston, B., & Zurawski, R. (1981). Anxiety management training in the treatment of essential hypertension. *Behaviour Research and Therapy, 19,* 467–474.

Kaminer, Y., & Shahar, A. (1987). The stress inoculation training management of self-mutilating behavior: A case study. *Journal of Behavior Therapy and Experimental Psychiatry, 18,* 289–292.

Kantor, L. (1978). *Stress inoculation as a means of teaching anxiety management skills.* Unpublished doctoral dissertation, Bowling Green State University.

Karol, K., Doerfler, L., Parker, J., & Armentraut, D. (1981). A therapist manual for the cognitive–behavioral treatment of chronic pain. *JSAS Catalogue of Selected Documents in Psychology, 11,* 15–61. (Ms. No. 2205).

Kendall, P. C. (1983). Stressful medical procedures: Cognitive–behavioral strategies for stress management and prevention. In D. Meichenbaum & M. Jaremko (Eds.), *Stress prevention and management: A cognitive behavioral approach.* New York: Plenum Press.

Kendall, P. C. (in press). Healthy thinking. *Behavior Therapy.*

Kendall, P. C., Williams, L., Pechacek, F. F., Graham, L. E., Shisslak, C., & Herzoff, N. (1979). Cognitive–behavioral and patient education intervention in cardiac catheterization procedures: The Palo Alto Medical Psychology Project. *Journal of Consulting and Clinical Psychology, 47,* 49–58.

Kendrick, M. (1979). *Reduction of musical performance anxiety by attentional training and behavioral rehearsal: An exploration of cognitive medicational processes.* Unpublished doctoral dissertation, University of British Columbia.

Keyes, J. B., & Dean, S. F. (1988). Stress inoculation training for direct contact staff working with mentally retarded persons. *Behavioral Residential Treatment, 3,* 315–323.

Kilpatrick, D. G., Veronen, L. J., & Resnick, P. A. (1982). Psychological sequelae to rape: Assessment in treatment strategies. In D. M. Doleys & R. L. Meredith (Eds.), *Behavioral medicine: Assessment in treatment strategies.* New York: Plenum Press.

Kirschenbaum, D. S., Wittrock, D. A., Smith, R. A., & Monson, W. (1984). Criticism inoculation training: Concept in search of strategy. *Journal of Sport Psychology, 6,* 77–93.

Klepac, R. K., Hague, G., & Dowling, J. (1982). Treatment of overactive gag reflex: Two cases. *Journal of Behavior Therapy and Experimental Psychiatry, 13,* 141–144.

Klepac, R. K., Hague, G., Dowling, J., & McDonald, M. (1981). Direct and generalized effects of three components of stress inoculation for increased pain tolerance. *Behavior Therapy, 12,* 417–424.

Kooken, R. A., & Hayslip, B. (1984). The use of stresss inoculation in the treatment of test anxiety in older students. *Educational Gerontology, 10,* 39–58.

Kuczmierczyk, A. R. (1989). Multicomponent behavioral treatment of premenstrual syndrome: A case report. *Journal of Behavior Therapy and Experimental Psychiatry, 20,* 235–240.

Kunzman, G. G. (1986). Cognitive behavioral counseling with isolated university students. *International Journal for the Advancement of Counseling, 9,* 231–236.

Lang, P. (1968). Fear reduction and fear behavior. In J. Shlien (Ed.), *Research in psychotherapy.* Washington, DC: American Psychological Association.

Langer, T., Janis, I., & Wolfer, J. (1975). Reduction of psychological stress in surgical patients. *Journal of Experimental Social Psychology, 11,* 155–165.

Lazarus, R. S., & Folkman, S. (1984). *Stress, appraisal and coping.* New York: Springer-Verlag.

Lester, D., Leitner, C., & Posner, I. (1984). The effects of a stress management training programme on police officers. *International Review of Applied Psychology, 33,* 25–31.

Levendusky, P., & Pankratz, L. (1975). Self-control techniques as an alternative to pain medication. *Journal of Abnormal Psychology, 85,* 165–168.

Lira, F. T., Carne, W., & Masri, A. M. (1983). Treatment of anger and impulsivity in a brain damaged patient: A case study applying stress inoculation. *Clinical Neuropsychology, 5,* 159–160.

Lochman, J. E., & Lampron, L. B. (1988). Cognitive behavioral interventions for aggressive boys: 7 month follow-up effects. *Journal of Child and Adolescent Psychotherapy, 2,* 21–25.

Lochman, J. E., Nelson, W. M., & Sims, J. P. (1981). A cognitive behavioral program for use with aggressive children. *Journal of Clinical Child Psychology, 10,* 146–148.

Long, B. C. (1980). Stress management for the athlete: A cognitive behavioral model. In C. Nadeau, W. Halliwell, K. Newell, & G. Roberts (Eds.), *Psychology of motor behavior and sport—1979.* Champaign, IL: Human Kinetics.

Long, B. C. (1984). Aerobic conditioning and stress inoculation: A comparison of stress-management interventions. *Cognitive Therapy and Research, 8,* 517–542.

Long, B. C. (1985). Stress management interventions: A 15-month follow-up of aerobic conditioning and stress inoculation training. *Cognitive Therapy and Research, 9,* 471–478.

Ludwick-Rosenthal, R., & Neufeld, R.W. (1988). Stress management during noxious medical procedures: An evaluative review of outcome studies. *Psychological Bulletin, 104,* 326–342.

Lustman, P. J., & Sava, C. J. (1983). Comparative efficacy of biofeedback and stress inoculation for stress reduction. *Journal of Clinical Psychology, 39,* 191–197.

Maag, J. W., Parks, B. T., & Rutherford, R. B. (1988). Generalization and behavior covariation of aggression in children receiving stress inoculation therapy. *Child and Family Behavior Therapy, 10,* 29–47.

MacDonald, M., & Kuiper, N. (1983). Cognitive–behavioral preparations for surgery. *Clinical Psychology Review, 3,* 27–39.

Mace, R. D., & Carroll, D. (1986). Stress inoculation training to control anxiety in sport: Two case studies in squash. *British Journal of Sports Medicine, 20,* 115–117.

Mace, R. D., Eastman, C., & Carroll, D. (1986). Stress inoculation training: A case study in gymnastics. *British Journal of Sports Medicine, 20,* 139–141.

Mace, R. D., Eastman, C., & Carroll, D. (1987). The effects of stress inoculation training on gymnastics performance on the pommelled horse: A case study. *Behavioural Psychotherapy, 15,* 272–279.

Marlatt, G. A., & Gordon, J. R. (Eds.). (1985). *Relapse prevention: Maintenance strategies in the treatment of addictive behaviors.* New York: Guilford Press.

McCann, I. L., & Pearlman, L. A. (1990). *Psychological trauma and the adult survivor.* New York: Brunner/Mazel.

McGuire, W. (1964). Inducing resistance to persuasion: Some contemporary approaches. In L. Berkowitz (Ed.), *Advances in social psychology* (Vol. 1). New York: Academic Press.

Meichenbaum, D. (1972). Cognitive modification of test anxious college students. *Journal of Consulting and Clinical Psychology, 39,* 370–380.

Meichenbaum, D. (1976). A self-instructional approach to stress management: A proposal for stress inoculation training. In C. Spielberger & I. Sarason (Eds.), *Stress and anxiety in modern life.* New York: Winston.

Meichenbaum, D. (1977). *Cognitive behavior modification: An integrative approach.* New York: Plenum Press.

Meichenbaum, D. (1985). *Stress inoculation training.* Elmsford, NY: Pergamon Press.

Meichenbaum, D., & Cameron, R. (1972). *Stress inoculation training: A skills training approach to anxiety management.* Unpublished manuscript, University of Waterloo, Waterloo, Ontario.

Meichenbaum, D., & Cameron, R. (1982). The nature of effective coping and the treatment of stress-related problems: A cognitive–behavioral perspective. In L. Goldberger & S. Breznitz (Eds.), *Handbook of stress.* New York: Free Press.

Meichenbaum, D., & Deffenbacher, J. L. (1988). Stress inoculation training. *Counseling Psychologist, 16,* 69–90.

Meichenbaum, D., & Fitzpatrick, D. (in press). A narrative constructivist perspective of stress and coping: Stress inoculation applications. In L. Goldberger & S. Breznitz (Eds.), *Handbook of stress* (2nd ed.). New York: Free Press.

Meichenbaum, D., & Jaremko, M. (Eds.). (1983). *Stress prevention and management: A cognitive behavioral approach.* New York: Plenum Press.

Meichenbaum, D., & Novaco, R. (1978). Stress inoculation: A preventative approach. In C. Spielberger & I. Sarason (Eds.), *Stress and anxiety* (Vol. 5). Washington, DC: Hemisphere.

Meichenbaum, D., & Novaco, R. (1985). Stress inoculation: A preventative approach. *Issues in Mental Health Nursing, 7,* 419–425.

Meichenbaum, D., & Turk, D. C. (1976). The cognitive behavioral management of anxiety, anger and pain. In P. Davidson (Ed.), *The behavioral management of anxiety, depression and pain.* New York: Brunner/Mazel.

Meichenbaum, D., & Turk, D. C. (1987). *Facilitating treatment adherence: A practitioner's guidebook.* New York: Plenum Press.

Melamed, B., & Siegel, L. (1975). Reduction of anxiety in children facing hospitalization and surgery by use of filmed modeling. *Journal of Consulting and Clinical Psychology, 43,* 511–521.

Melzak, R., & Wall, P. (1965). Pain mechanisms: A new theory. *Science, 50,* 971–979.

Meng, A., & Zastowny, T. (1982). Preparation for hospitalization for parents and children. *Maternal–Child Nursing Journal, 11,* 87–94.

Michelson, L. K., & Marchione, K. (1991). Behavioral, cognitive and pharmacological treatments of panic disorder with agoraphobia: Critique and synthesis. *Journal of Consulting and Clinical Psychology, 59,* 100–114.

Milkman, H., Werner, S. E., & Sunderworth, S. (1984). Addiction relapse. *Advances in Alcohol and Substance Abuse, 3,* 119–134.

Miller, M. E., & Bowers, K. S. (1986). Hypnotic analgesia and stress inoculation in the reduction of pain. *Journal of Abnormal Psychology, 95,* 6–14.

Moon, J. R., & Eisler, K. M. (1983). Anger control: An experimental comparison of three behavioral treatments. *Behavior Therapy, 14,* 493–505.

Moore, K., & Altmaier, E. (1981). Stress inoculation training with cancer patients. *Cancer Nursing, 10,* 389–393.

Moses, A. N., & Hollandsworth, J. G. (1985). Relative effectiveness of education alone versus stress inoculation training in the treatment of dental phobia. *Behavior Therapy, 16,* 531–537.

Mydgal, W. (1978). The acquisition of stress management skills by student teachers: An outcome of stress inoculation and anxiety management. *Dissertation Abstracts International, 39*(5), 2839A–2840A.

Nelson, W. M. (1981). A cognitive–behavioral treatment of disproportionate dental anxiety and pain: A case study. *Journal of Clinical Child Psychology, 10,* 79–82.

Nocella, J., & Kaplan, R. M. (1982). Training children to cope with dental treatment. *Journal of Pediatric Psychology, 7,* 125–128.

Novaco, R. (1975). *Anger control: The development and evaluation of an experimental treatment.* Lexington, MA: D. C. Heath.

Novaco, R. (1977a). Stress inoculation: A cognitive therapy for anger and its application to a case of depression. *Journal of Consulting and Clinical Psychology, 45,* 600–608.

Novaco, R. (1977b). A stress inoculation approach to anger management in the training of law enforcement officers. *American Journal of Community Psychology, 5,* 327–346.

Novaco, R. (1980). Training of probation officers for anger problems. *Journal of Counseling Psychology, 27,* 385–390.

Novaco, R., Cook, T., & Sarason, I. (1983). Military recruit training: An arena for stress-coping skills. In D. Meichenbaum & M. Jaremko (Eds.), *Stress prevention and management: A cognitive behavioral approach.* New York: Plenum Press.

Nye, S. (1979). *Self-instructional stress management training: A comparison of the effects of induced affect and covert modeling in a cognitive restructuring treatment program for test anxiety.* Unpublished doctoral dissertation, University of Washington.

O'Neill, M. W., Hanewicz, W. B., & Fransway, L. M. (1982). Stress inoculation training and job performance. *Journal of Police Science and Administration, 10,* 388–397.

Oots, K. L., & Wiegele, T. C. (1985). Terrorist and victim: Psychiatric and physiological approaches from a social science perspective. *Terrorism, 8,* 1–32.

Ost, L. G. (1985). Coping techniques in the treatment of anxiety disorders: Two controlled case studies. *Behavioural Psychotherapy, 13,* 154–161.

Payne, B. D., & Manning, B. H. (1990). The effect of cognitive self-instructions on preservice teacher's anxiety about teaching. *Contemporary Educational Psychology, 15,* 261–267.

Pearson, M. A., Poquette, B. M., & Wasden, R. E. (1983). Stress inoculation and the treatment of post-rape trauma. A case report. *The Behavior Therapist, 6,* 58–59.

Pellegrini, D. S. (1990). Psychosocial risk and protective factors in childhood. *Journal of Developmental and Behavioral Pediatrics, 11,* 201–209.

Perry, S. W., & Markowitz, J. (1986). Psychiatric interventions for AIDS-spectrum disorders. *Hospital and Community Psychiatry, 37,* 1001–1005.

Phillips, E. L. (1986). *Are theories of psychotherapy possible?* Paper presented at the Fifth National Conference on Cognitive-Behavior Therapy, Clearwater Beach, FL.

Postlethwaite, R., Stirling, G., & Peck, C. L. (1986). Stress inoculation for acute pain: A clinical trial. *Journal of Behavioral Medicine, 9*, 219–227.

Puder, R. S. (1988). Age analysis of cognitive behavioral group therapy for chronic pain outpatients. *Psychology and Aging, 3*, 204–207.

Quillen, M., & Denney, D. (1982). Self-control of dysmenorrhea symptoms through pain management training. *Journal of Behavior Therapy and Experimental Psychiatry, 11*, 229–232.

Rabin, C., & Nardi, C. (1991). Treating post traumatic stress disorder couples: A psychoeducational program. *Community Mental Health Journal, 27*, 209–224.

Randich, S. (1982). *Evaluation of stress inoculation training as a pain management program for rheumatoid arthritis.* Unpublished doctoral dissertation, Washington University, St. Louis.

Rapee, R. (1987). The psychological treatment of panic attacks: Theoretical conceptualization and review of evidence. *Clinical Psychology Review, 7*, 427–438.

Register, A. C., Beckham, J. C., May, J. G., & Gustafson, D. J. (1991). Stress inoculation bibliotherapy in the treatment of test anxiety. *Journal of Counseling Psychology, 38*, 115–119.

Resick, P. A., Jordan, C. G., Girelli, S. A., Hutler, C. K., & Marhoefer-Dvorak, S. (1988). A comparative outcome study of behavioral group therapy for sexual assault victims. *Behavior Therapy, 19*, 385–401.

Roffman, R. A. (1986). Stress inoculation training in the control of THC toxicities. *International Journal of the Addictions, 21*, 883–896.

Rohsenow, D. J., Smith, R. E., & Johnson, S. (1985). Stress management training as a prevention program for heavy social drinkers: Cognitive, affect, drinking, and individual differences. *Addictive Behaviors, 10*, 45–54.

Roskies, E. (1983). Stress management for Type A individuals. In D. Meichenbaum & M. Jaremko (Eds.), *Stress prevention and management: A cognitive behavioral approach.* New York: Plenum Press.

Roth, S., & Newman, E. (1991). The process of coping with sexual trauma. *Journal of Traumatic Stress, 4*, 279–297.

Ruiz, F., & Angeles, M. (1985). The efficacy of the different components of stress inoculation applied to experimentally induced pain. *Boletin de Psicologia Spain, 6*, 107–119.

Rybstein-Blinchik, E. (1979). Effects of different cognitive strategies on chronic pain experience. *Journal of Behavioral Medicine, 2*, 93–105.

Salovey, P., & Haar, M. D. (1990). The efficacy of cognitive behavior therapy and writing process training for alleviating writing anxiety. *Cognitive Therapy and Research, 14*, 515–526.

Sarason, I., Johnson, J., Berberich, J., & Siegel, J. (1979). Helping police officers to cope with stress: A cognitive–behavioral approach. *American Journal of Community Psychology, 7*, 593–603.

Saylor, C. F., Benson, B., & Einhaus, L. (1985). Evaluation of an anger management program for aggressive boys in inpatient treatment. *Journal of Child and Adolescent Psychotherapy, 2*, 545.

Schachter, S. (1966). The interaction of cognitive and physiological determinants of emotion. In C. Spielberger (Ed.), *Anxiety and behavior.* New York: Academic Press.

Schlichter, K., & Horan, J. (1981). Effects of stress inoculation on the anger and aggression management skills in institutionalized juvenile delinquents. *Cognitive Therapy and Research, 4*, 359–365.

Schuler, K., Gilner, F., Austrin, H., & Davenport, D. G. (1982). Contribution of the education phase of stress inoculation training. *Psychological Reports, 51*, 611–617.

Schulink, E. J., Gerards, F. M., & Bouler, L. M. (1988). The effect of stress education: A review of the literature. *Pedagogische Studien, 65*, 425–436.

Sharpe, J. J., & Forman, S. G. (1985). A comparison of two approaches to anxiety management for teachers. *Behavior Therapy, 16*, 370–383.

Shipley, R. H., Butt, J. H., & Horwitz, E. A. (1979). Preparation to reexperience a stressful medical examination effect of repetitious videotape exposure and coping style. *Journal of Consulting and Clinical Psychology, 47* 485–492.

Siegel, L., & Peterson, L. (1980). Stress reduction in young dental patients through coping skills and sensory information. *Journal of Consulting and Clinical Psychology, 48*, 785–787.

Silver, R. L., & Wortman, C. B. (1980). Coping with undesirable life events. In J. Garber & M. Seligman (Eds.), *Human helplessness.* New York: Academic Press.

Smith, R. E. (1980). A cognitive–affective approach to stress management training for athletes. In C. H. Nadeau, W. R. Halliwell, K. M. Newell, & G. C. Roberts (Eds.), *Psychology of motor behavior and sport—1979.* Champaign, IL: Human Kinetics.

Smith, R. E., & Nye, S. L. (1989). Comparison of induced affect and cover rehearsal in the acquisition of stress management coping skills. *Journal of Counseling Psychology, 36*, 17–23.

Smith, R. E., Rohsenow, D. J. (1987). *Cognitive–affective stress management training: A treatment and resource manual.* San Rafael, CA: Select Press.

Smoll, F. L., & Smith, R. E. (1988). Reducing stress in youth sport: Theory and application. In F. L. Smoll, R. A. Magell, & M. J. Ash (Eds.), *Children in sport.* Champaign, IL: Human Kinetics.

Sobel, H, & Worden, J. (1981). *Helping cancer patients cope: A problem-solving intervention for health care professionals.* New York: BMA/Guilford Press. (Audiocassette)

Spanos, N. P., Ollerhead, V. G., & Gwynn, M. I. (1985–1986). The effects of three instructional treatments on pain magnitude and pain tolerance. *Imagination, Cognition and Personality, 5,* 321–337.

Spettell, C. M., & Liebert, R. M. (1986). Training for safety in automated person–machine systems. *American Psychologist, 41,* 545–550.

Spirito, A., Finch, A. J., Smith, T. L., & Cooley, W. H. (1981). Stress inoculation for anger and anxiety control: A case study with an emotionally disturbed boy. *Journal of Clinical Child Psychology, 10,* 67–70.

Starr, L. M. (1986). *Stress inoculation training applied to cardiopulmonary resuscitation.* Unpublished manuscript, Villanova University.

Starr, L. M. (1987). Training for safety in automated person–machine systems. *American Psychologist, 42,* 1029.

Stermac, L. E. (1986). Anger control treatment for forensic patients. *Journal of Interpersonal Violence, 1,* 446–457.

Stern, J. B., & Fodor, I. G. (1989). Anger control in children: A review of social skills and cognitive behavioral approaches to dealing with aggressive children. *Child and Family Behavior Therapy, 11,* 1–20.

Stone, C. I., Demchik-Stone, D. A., & Horan, J. J. (1977). Coping with pain: A component analysis of Lamaze and cognitive–behavioral procedures. *Journal of Psychosomatic Research, 21,* 429–438.

Suinn, R. M. (1990). *Anxiety management training.* New York: Plenum.

Suinn, R. M. & Richardson, F. (1971). Anxiety management training: A non-specific behavior therapy program for anxiety control. *Behavior Therapy, 2,* 498–510.

Sweeney, G., & Horan, J. (1982). Separate and combined effects of uncontrolled relaxation and cognitive restructuring in the treatment of musical performance anxiety. *Journal of Counseling Psychology, 29,* 486–497.

Tableman, B., Marciniak, D., Johnson, D., & Rodgers, R. (1982). Stress management training for women on public assistance. *American Journal of Community Psychology, 10,* 357–367.

Tan, S. Y., & Poser, E. G. (1982). Acute pain in a clinical setting: Effects of cognitive–behavioural skills training. *Behaviour Research and Therapy, 20,* 535–545.

Thurman, C. (1984). Cognitive–behavioral interventions with Type A faculty. *Personnel and Guidance Journal, 2,* 358–362.

Turk, D. C. (1977). *A coping skills approach for the control of experimentally produced pain.* Unpublished doctoral dissertation, University of Waterloo, Waterloo, Ontario.

Turk, D. C., Meeks, S., & Turk, L. (1982). Factors contributing to teacher stress: Implications for research prevention and remediation. *Behavioral Counseling Quarterly, 2,* 3–25.

Turk, D. C., Meichenbaum, D., & Genest, M. (1983). *Pain and behavioral medicine: A cognitive–behavioral perspective.* New York: Guilford Press.

Turk, D. C., & Rennert, D. (1981). Pain and the terminally ill cancer patient: A cognitive social learning perspective. In H. J. Sobell (Ed.), *Behavior therapy in terminal care.* Cambridge, MA: Ballinger.

Turner, N. W. (1985). Divorce: Dynamics of decision therapy. *Journal of Psychotherapy and the Family, 1,* 27–38.

Twentyman, C., Rohrbeck, C., & Amish, P. (1984). A cognitive–behavioral model of child abuse. In S. Saunders (Ed.), *Violent individuals and families: A practitioner's handbook.* Springfield, IL: Charles C Thomas.

Ulissi, S. (1978). *The efficacy of stress inoculation training and induced anxiety.* Unpublished doctoral dissertation, University of Mississippi.

Vallis, M. (1984). A complete component analysis of stress inoculation in pain tolerance. *Cognitive Therapy and Research, 8,* 313–329.

Van Broeck, N. (1985). Cognitive and behavior modification in the treatment of psychophysical complaints by children. *Gedragstherapie, 18,* 127–141.

Van Hassel, J., Bloom, L. J., & Gonzales, A. C. (1982). Anxiety management training with schizophrenic outpatients. *Journal of Clinical Psychology, 38,* 280–285.

Varni, J., Jay, S., Masek, B., & Thompson, K. (1988). Cognitive–behavioral assessment and management of pediatric pain. In A. Holzman & D. Turk (Eds.), *Pain management: A handbook of psychological treatment approaches.* Elmsford, NY: Pergamon Press.

Veronen, L. J., & Best, C. L. (1983). Assessment and treatment of rape induced fear and anxiety. *Clinical Psychologist, 36,* 99–101.

Veronen, L. J., & Kilpatrick, D. (1983). Stress management for rape victims. In D. Meichenbaum & M. Jaremko (Eds.), *Stress prevention and management: A cognitive behavioral approach*. New York: Plenum Press.

Wald, M., & Fish, J. M. (1983). Visual–nonvisual cognitive style and response to behavior therapies. *Journal of Mental Imagery, 7*, 101–118.

Walton, S. J. (1990). Stress management training for overseas effectiveness. *International Journal of Intercultural Relations, 14*, 507–527.

Warner, J. E., & Swensen, C. (1991). *Effectiveness of stress inoculation training for cancer pain patients*. Unpublished manuscript, Purdue University.

Weisman, A., Worden, J., & Sobel, H. (1980). *Psychological screening and intervention with cancer patients*. Unpublished manuscript, Harvard Medical School.

Wells, J. K., Howard, G. S., Nowlin, W. F., & Vargas, M. J. (1986). Presurgical anxiety and postsurgical pain and adjustment: Effects of a stress inoculation procedure. *Journal of Consulting and Clinical Psychology, 54*, 831–835.

Wernick, R. L. (1983). Stress inoculation in the management of clinical pain: Applications to burn pain. In D. Meichenbaum & M. Jaremko (Eds.), *Stress prevention and management: A cognitive behavioral approach*. New York: Plenum Press.

Wernick, R. L., Jaremko, M., & Taylor, P. (1981). Pain management in severely burned adults: A test of stress inoculation. *Journal of Bahavioral Medicine, 4*, 103–109.

Wertkin, R. A. (1985). Stress inoculation training: Principles and appalications. *Social Casework, 12*, 611–616.

West, D., Horan, J., & Games, P. (1984). Component analysis of occupational stress inoculation applied to registered nurses in an acute care hospital setting. *Journal of Counseling Psychology, 31*, 209–218.

Weston, R. E., Gordon, A., Bush, C. A., Holder, M. P., & Lieberman, H. J. (1987). *The community skills training game: The development of a game approach to skill training*. Unpublished manuscript, South Beach Psychiatric Center, Staten Island, NY.

Worthington, E. (1978). The effects of imagery content, choice of imagery and self-verbalization on the self-control of pain. *Cognitive Therapy and Research, 2*, 225–239.

Worthington, E., & Shumate, M. (1981). Imagery and verbal counseling methods in stress inoculation training for pain control. *Journal of Counseling Psychology, 28*, 1–6.

Wortman, C. B., & Silver, R. C. (1987). Coping with irrevocable loss. In G. R. Vandenbox & B. K. Bryant (Eds.), *Cataclysms, crises, and catastrophes: Psychology in action*. Washington, DC: American Psychological Association.

Ziegler, S. G., Klinzery, J., & Williamson, K. (1982). The effects of two stress management training programs on cardiorespiratory efficiency. *Journal of Sport Psychology, 4*, 280–283.

13

Music Therapy and Stress Management

CHERYL DILEO MARANTO

History of the Method

Music is ubiquitous in the vast majority of cultures. It is integral to daily life; it is pervasive in all areas of human functioning. Aside from its aesthetic and entertainment values, there are repeated and consistent descriptions of its use for nonaesthetic or nonentertainment goals. Out of the interest in examining its uses to promote human health and well-being has grown the discipline of music therapy. Its use to facilitate relaxation has been one of its most important therapeutic aspects (Scartelli, 1989).

The use of music to treat health problems is firmly rooted in history. The close association between music and medicine can be traced to ancient cultures, where music was closely allied with medical practice (Boxberger, 1962). The oldest account of medical practices, the Kahum Papyrus, details the use of incantations for healing purposes (Light, Love, Benson, & Morch, 1954, cited in Standley, 1986).

Although the uses of music to treat various psychological and physiological problems extend throughout antiquity, the Middle Ages, and the Renaissance, its modern history began at the end of the 19th century. This period marked the advent of empirical studies on physiological and psychological responses to music. These studies pointed to the effects of music on neurosis (Corning, 1899); insomnia and fevers (Davison, 1899); and blood pressure, circulation, cardiac contraction, and respiration (Dogiel, 1880, cited in Eagle, 1972). Davison (1899) further postulated that it was important to match the music to the psychological state of the patient (Pratt & Jones, 1987). Other early researchers concluded that physiological functions responded reflexively to music (Hyde, 1924), and that the subject's appreciation for the music was the important determinant of physiological response (Vincent & Thompson, 1929). These ideas, among others, have established a foundation for using music to affect health.

Music therapy as a formalized discipline began during and immediately following World War II, when its effects on convalescing and "shell-shocked" patients were noted. To advance scientific knowledge in this discipline and to provide standards and support for its practitioners, the National Association for Music Therapy, was formed in 1950, and the American Association for Music Therapy was founded in 1971.

Because of the breadth of music therapy's applications, various areas of clinical intervention have been emphasized during the past 40 years. To judge by the literature, applications of music therapy in psychiatry were emphasized during the 1950s and 1960s, and its applications with the developmentally disabled and handicapped were emphasized during the 1970s. Since the 1980s, there has been a growing focus on its medical/physiological applications. This emphasis has undoubtedly coincided with changes in the health care profession, as well as with technological advances that have permitted more accessible and valid measures of physiological responses.

Theoretical Foundations

Defining Music Therapy

Because music therapy is such a broad area, with many possible applications, a working definition must be adopted that provides a foundation for its therapeutic potential in stress management. Thus, "music therapy is a systematic process of intervention wherein the music therapist helps the client to achieve health, using medical experiences and the relationships that develop through them as dynamic forces of change" (Bruscia, 1989, p. 47). Necessary components of music therapy based on this definition include the following: a client with a defined health need, a trained music therapist, a goal-oriented music process, music materials, and an evaluation of therapeutic effectiveness.

Music Therapy Classification

Whereas the presence of these components differentiates music therapy from other uses of music (e.g., self-help methods), further amplification and classification of how music therapy can be used, particularly in stress management, are in order. Conceptually, music therapy may be used in treating stress in one of five categories, based on the relative importance of the music versus the therapeutic relationship and on the role of music therapy in stress management treatment (Maranto, 1991, 1992a):

1. Music in stress management
2. Music as stress management
3. Music therapy and stress management
4. Music therapy in stress management
5. Music therapy as stress management

This classification system may also in the future serve as the basis of research hypotheses about the effectiveness of music therapy in stress management; however, to date no systematic research has made comparisons to determine whether the use of music is more or less effective among these categories. It is speculated at this point that the choice of a category for clinical intervention will depend upon the individual needs of the client.

When music is the primary method of treatment, it is used directly to reduce anxiety and tension; the therapeutic relationship is of lesser significance, although it is still a vital component. When the therapeutic relationship is the primary method of treatment, music is of lesser significance, although it too remains a necessary component of treatment (Maranto, 1991, 1992a). Music and the therapeutic relationship can serve in either primary or supportive roles with regard to stress management treatment. Music therapy can be used as the primary mode of intervention to effect health changes in the individual; alternatively, music therapy can be equal or subordinate to other methods of stress management intervention, such as autogenic training, meditation, or medication.

1. *Music in stress management.* In this category, music is more important than the therapeutic relationship in effecting change. In addition, music therapy is used to support another treatment modality. An example in this category is music to support progressive relaxation.

2. *Music as stress management.* In this category, music is of greater significance than the therapeutic relationship, and the music is used as the primary or sole method of therapeutic intervention. An example in this category is "entrainment" of physiological responses via listening to music or actively performing music (e.g., singing, "toning," "improvisation") to reduce stress. (See the Appendix to this chapter for definitions.)

3. *Music therapy and stress management.* In this category, the music and the therapeutic relationship are of equal significance in treatment, and music therapy is in equal partnership with other methods of treatment. An example in this category is music-facilitated imagery for stress management.

4. *Music therapy in stress management.* In this category, the therapeutic relationship is more important than the music, and music therapy is subordinate to or supportive of stress management treatment. An example in this category is the use of music in counseling to facilitate life changes regarding stress.

5. *Music therapy as stress management.* In this category, the therapeutic relationship again is more important than the music, and music therapy assumes a primary role in treatment. An example in this category is music psychotherapy to overcome long-term problems associated with stress.

Physiological Responses to Music

It appears that music elicits physiological responses; these can be used to support a rationale for the use of music in stress management. However, it is not always possible to predict the direction of physiological responses to music, because of the complexity of the musical stimuli and the complexity of individual differences in responses to music. More data than those reported in individual studies are often needed to understand the findings of these studies.

An important caveat in interpreting some of the literature on physiological responses to music is the lack of standardization of musical stimuli; different studies use different genres of music to measure physiological responses. Also, various researchers have used ambiguous categories of "stimulative" and "sedative" music.

Therefore, as Taylor (1973) points out, it is virtually impossible to generalize beyond one piece of music. In addition, as stated above, responses to music are complex and multidimensional, occurring on several levels simultaneously (i.e., physiological, psychological, cognitive, etc.). Thus, information on physiological responses cannot be adequately interpreted without simultaneous data from these other domains. Moreover, much of the research on physiological responses to music is dated and has not necessarily been replicated; generalizations should not be made until more consistent, systematic research is undertaken. It is also possible that differences in research findings can be attributed to inconsistencies in the power of various statistical and experimental designs employed and to the size of samples. Finally, it should be noted that these studies are primarily laboratory studies examining the effect of music on physiology, and not necessarily in the presence of anxiety; clinical studies involving the use of music to treat stress and other clinical problems are considered in a subsequent section of this chapter.

Hodges (1980) has provided a review of the research on physiological responses to music; this review, with additions of later research as appropriate, is presented in Table 13.1. Some of the results of the studies reviewed provided contradictory findings, perhaps because of the reasons stated above. However, the important factors to understand as one reviews there findings, regardless of the various inconsistencies, are these: the breadth of physiological parameters that may be affected by music; the significance and potential significance of these findings for future research; the complexity of music stimuli; the various affective and cognitive factors that may influence physiological responses to music; and the complexity of measurement of responses to music.

A number of reasons may account for these contradictory findings in the area of physiological responses to music:

1. As Dainow (1977) suggests, inappropriate statistical analysis, inadequate control measures, nonstandardized measurement techniques, differing instructions to subjects, subjects' expectancies, volume of the musical stimuli, influence of subjects' attention to the music, faulty equipment, and substandard baselines may have greatly influenced research findings and their subsequent generalizability.

2. The misconception that responses among subjects to music are similar and predictable is often operating (Thaut, 1989b).

3. Psychophysiological processes are unique to each individual and involve attentional and processing differences (Lacey, 1956).

4. Cognitive interpretations of music events influence autonomic reactivity (Schacter, 1957, 1964).

5. There are response patterns unique to each individual resulting from differences in autonomic reactivity; these differences are attributable to factors such as age, health, life style, fitness, and situational variables (Thaut, 1989b).

6. Individuals may exhibit unique emotional reactions as a result of individual interpretations of various situations.

7. Individual attitudes, preferences, and nonmusical associations influence physiological responses (Harrer & Harrer, 1977).

In summary, Thaut (1989a) concludes that physiological responses to music are the product of each individual's unique, idiosyncratic physiological makeup, which is

TABLE 13.1. Summary of Research Findings on Physiological Responses to Music

---

Music and heart rate

1. Stimulative music increases heart rate; sedative music decreases heart rate (Coleman, 1920; Darner, 1966; DeJong, van Mourik, & Schellekens, 1973; Hincke, 1970; Hyde, 1927; Landreth & Landreth, 1974; Lovell & Morgan, 1942).

2. Any type of music increases heart rate (Binet & Courtier, 1895; Ellis & Brighouse, 1952; Shatin, 1957; Wascho, 1948; Weld, 1912).

3. Both sedative music and stimulative music cause changes in heart rate; however, the directions of these effects are not predictable (Bierbaum, 1958/1989; Lisco, 1980/1989; M. Sears, 1954).

4. Music does not affect heart rate (Barger, 1979; Coutts, 1965; Hyde & Scalapino, 1918; Johnson & Trawick, 1938; Misbach, 1932; Ruiz, 1979/1989; Trenes, 1937; Zimny & Weidenfeller, 1963).

5. Listening to music or toning reduces heart rate (Rider, Mickey, Weldin, & Hawkinson, 1991).

Elements of music and heart rate

1. There is no influence of various frequencies on heart rate (Clarke, 1981/1989).

2. Fast-tempo melodies and slow-tempo rhythms affect heart rates of premature infants (Spaulding, 1977/1989).

3. Heart rate acceleration is correlated with loudness, tempo, and musical complexity; heart rate deceleration is correlated with resolutions of musical conflict, decreasing loudness, and slowing tempo (Edwards, Eagle, Pennebaker, & Tunks, 1991).

4. Heart rate decelerates to rock music (Wilson & Aiken, 1977).

5. Tachycardia is associated with driving rhythms, and increasing dynamics; bradycardia is associated with changes in rhythm, texture, and dynamics (Landreth & Landreth, 1974).

Skin temperature

1. Arousing, negative music terminates skin temperature increases and facilitates skin temperature decreases. Calming, positive music has the opposite effect; affective ratings of music are related to skin temperature responses (McFarland, 1985).

2. Listening to music, singing, or toning does not affect skin temperature (Rider et al., 1991).

3. Sedative music significantly increases finger temperature (Kibler & Rider, 1983).

Skin conductance level (SCL)

1. SCL habituates to music; interrupted SCL habituation and SCL increases are correlated with tempo, loudness, and musical complexity. Decreases in SCL are correlated with resolutions of musical conflict (Edwards et al., 1991).

Galvanic skin response (GSR)

1. Stimulative and sedative music have different, unpredictable effects on GSR (Michel, 1952; Shrift, 1955; Taylor, 1973; Weidenfeller & Zimny, 1962; Zimny & Weidenfeller, 1963).

2. There is a relationship between liking–disliking of the music and GSR responses (DeJong et al., 1973; Dreher, 1948; Peretti & Swenson, 1974; Wechsler, 1925). (Ries, 1969, found no such relationship.)

3. Elements of music affect GSR ratings (DeJong et al., 1973; Henkin, 1957; Misbach, 1932; Wilson & Aiken, 1977).

Blood pressure

1. Blood pressure is affected by music listening, but the type of music that effects these changes is unknown (Binet & Courtier, 1895; Dogiel, 1880, cited in Eagle, 1972; Foster & Gamble, 1906; Hyde, 1927; Hyde & Scalapino, 1918; Wascho, 1948; Weld, 1912).

2. Music does not influence blood pressure (Trenes, 1937).

3. Music is effective in reducing blood pressure in essential hypertensives (Hoffman 1974/1989).

Respiration

1. Stimulative music increases respiration and sedative music decreases it (Ellis & Brighouse, 1952; Foster & Gamble, 1906; Johnson, 1964; Kneutgen, 1974; Lovell & Morgan, 1942; Miles & Tilly, 1935; Weld, 1912; Wilson & Aiken, 1977).

2. Any music increases respiration (Binet & Courtier, 1895; Dogiel, 1880, cited in Eagle, 1972).

(continued)

TABLE 13.1. Continued

3. Music that is enjoyed increases respiration (DeJong et al., 1973; Plutchic, 1959; Poole, Goetyinger, & Rousey, 1966; Ries, 1969; Weld, 1912).

4. Sedative music decreases minute ventilation, minute oxygen usage, and metabolic rate; stimulative music increases these measures slightly (Metera & Metera, 1975).

5. Music does not significantly influence airway resistance (Metera, Metera, & Warwas, 1975).

6. Slow-tempo rhythms and fast-tempo melodies influence respiration in premature infants (Spaulding, 1977/1989).

7. Music rhythms facilitate respiratory entrainment, particularly among musicians (Haas, Distenfeld, & Axen, 1986).

Digestion/gastric motility
1. Disliking of the music causes a cessation of gastric motility; sedative music produces stronger stomach contractions (Wilson, 1957/1989; M. Sears, 1954).

2. Music decreases stomach acid production (Demling, Tszchoppe, & Classen, 1970).

3. Music has no influence on pancreatic output (Unkefer, 1952).

Muscle responses
1. Stimulative music increases muscular activity (W. W. Sears, 1952, 1958, 1960; Brickman, 1950; Holdsworth, 1974; Patterson, 1959; Stevens, 1971).

2. There is no significant difference in muscular activity between stimulative and sedative music (Lord, 1968).

3. Listening to music reduces electromyographic (EMG) activity (Rider et al., Hawkinson, 1991).

4. Music has no effect on EMG activity (Miller & Bornstein, 1977).

5. Specific emotions cause distinct muscle activity in the fingertips (Clynes, 1978).

Pupillary responses
1. Stimulative music causes dilation of the pupils (Slaughter, 1954).

Brain waves
1. Listening to music produces more alpha brain waves in musicians than in nonmusicians (Wagner, 1975a, 1975b; Wagner & Menzel, 1977; McElwain, 1974).

2. Children produce more alpha waves during silence than during aural conditions (Furman, 1978; Inglis, 1972).

3. There is no difference in alpha wave production between sedative and stimulative music conditions (Borling, 1981).

4. Popular music produces more electroencephalographic (EEG) changes than classical music, particularly in middle-aged subjects. Popular music causes a decrease in blood flow to the brain in young adults; classical music promotes brain blood flow enhancement in middle-aged subjects (Mitkov, Moldovanska, & Roglev, 1981).

5. Musicians show greater EEG activation for complex musical stimuli; nonmusicians demonstrate greater EEG activation for simpler musical stimuli (Paley, 1991).

6. Attentiveness to music, familiarity with the music, and emotional reactions correlate moderately to substantially with EEG measures (Walker, 1977).

Thrill responses
1. Music produces thrill responses (Goldstein, 1980).

Immune responses
1. Music significantly increases secretory immunoglobulin A (IgA) (Tsao, Gordon, Maranto, Lerman, & Murasko, 1991; Rider et al., 1990, 1991; Rider, 1988).

2. Entrainment music significantly increases leukocyte circulation (Rider & Achterburg, 1989), and live entrainment music and imagery significantly increases secretory IgA (Rider & Weldin, 1990).

Note. Adapted by permission of the author from Hodges (1980, Appendix A, pp. 393–395).

further influenced by the individualized psychological experience of the music. Finally, because music occurs on a moment-to-moment basis, pre–post measurements (used in much of the literature) may not adequately reflect the effects of music on anxiety. Therefore, continuous measurements of responses to music may provide more information on the nature of this relationship.

Cognitive Aspects of Music Listening

The research on hemispheric processing of musical stimuli is vast; however, several studies point to the fact that music is generally processed in the right hemisphere (Cook, 1973; Kimura, 1964; McCarthy, 1969; Roederer, 1975). Therefore, according to Scartelli (1982), music may be used in relaxation to decrease left-hemisphere activity and increase right-hemisphere functioning.

Psychological Responses to Music

Most of the relatively limited literature dealing with affective responses to music has been concerned with the power of music to influence an individual's mood. According to Abeles (1980), much of the research has focused on a number of questions: the length of time an affective response lasts, the relationship between affective responses and personality traits, and the influence of short-term affective states on mood responses. Affective/mood responses to music are highly individualistic, complex and difficult to define. In addition, a variety of dependent measures and experimental approaches have been employed in the literature, making results difficult to summarize. In spite of this, the results can be summarized as follows:

1. Musical training appears to influence mood intensity and mood responses elicited by music (Brenneis, 1970; Sopchak, 1955).

2. There are contradictory findings regarding the influence of gender on mood responses to music (Sopchak, 1955; Hart & Cogan, 1976; Fisher & Greenberg, 1972; Greenberg & Fisher, 1966).

3. Research suggests that the existing mood of the listener affects subsequent reactions to music (Eagle, 1971; Wheeler, 1985). Wheeler's results suggest that preference for the music may interact with mood in terms of music's potential to alter moods. Questions concerning the stability of the mood response to music have yet to be answered (Abeles, 1980).

4. There have been specific attempts to alter mood deliberately via music. The "iso-" principle (see the Appendix to this chapter) has been employed in two studies (Shatin, 1970; Orton, 1953). According to this principle, music is matched to the existing emotional state of the individual. Subsequently, changes in the affective qualities of the music are expected to yield similar changes in the mood of the individual.

5. Other attempts to alter mood via music have shown support for this phenomenon. Pignatiello, Camp, and Rasar (1986) significantly altered subjects' moods to correspond with a 20-minute music tape progressing from neutral to either elating or

depressing. Geary (1989) indicated that music and imagination instruction could induce either positive or negative moods in subjects. Similar results with mood induction through music were reported by Straseske (1988).

6. Psychiatric patients responded appropriately to the moods suggested by words and music; these patients responded more often and consistently than did nonpatient controls (Burns, 1958).

7. The delivery of the music may have an effect on mood. Magill (1980) found significant positive mood changes in cancer patients exposed to live music.

Music and Imagery

McKinney (1990) studied the influence of music on spontaneous imagery. Music had no effect on aspects of imagery, including the number of senses involved, types of imagery, vividness, activity within the imagery, or the amount of time the subjects generated imagery. However, music significantly affected the intensity of the emotions experienced while listening. On the other hand, Summer (1983) found a significant influence of music on subjects' self-rated level of involvement in the imagery, and Quittner (1980) found that music was more effective than progressive relaxation or silence in increasing imagery vividness.

Theoretical Concepts Supporting the Use of Music Therapy

There are a number of theoretical concepts, some derived from research findings, that support the use of music therapy as a unique treatment modality in stress management and provide a rationale for its use:

1. Music elicits physiological responses; however, the direction of these responses is difficult to predict in a consistent manner.

2. Music elicits psychological (mood/affective) responses.

3. Music may evoke imagery and associations.

4. Music elicits cognitive responses.

5. Music has the potential for physiological and/or psychological entrainment (see the Appendix).

6. Physiological, psychological, and cognitive responses to music are unique for each individual.

7. Music can elicit psychological, cognitive, and physiological responses simultaneously; these responses may be interrelated.

8. An individual's history with, understanding of, and liking for the music are significant factors in psychological and/or physiological responses elicited; furthermore, a number of other individual variables may influence responses to music.

9. Elements of music, as well as the music gestalt, affect psychological and physiological responses.

10. Music may have an enhancing or diminishing effect on other methods of treatment.

11. Psychological and physiological responses to music may be inconsistent and/or contradictory.

12. A number of music experiences in addition to listening may contribute to stress management.

13. Vibrational aspects of music may be powerful factors in stress management.

14. Physiological, psychological, and/or cognitive responses to music may vary with music training.

15. Music, because it is predominantly a right-hemisphere function, may be used to "block left-hemispheric activity and/or enhance right-hemispheric process" (Scartelli, 1982, p. 212).

16. Music can be a reinforcing stimulus for desired behaviors; music listening or participation is a pleasurable experience (Saperston, 1989).

17. Music can serve as a structural prompt by providing cues for physiological aspects of relaxation and serving as a focus for attenion, thereby redirecting attention from distractions or anxiety-provoking thinking (Saperston, 1989).

18. Music can serve as an eliciting stimulus for perceived states of relaxation and positive affective response (Saperston, 1989).

19. Music may serve as a "conditioned stimulus for both sympathetic and parasympathetic autonomic activity" (Rider & Weldin, 1990, p. 211).

Assessment

Applications of Music in Stress Management

A number of uses of music in stress management have been described in the literature. Studies have dealt with the influence of music on anxiety, as well as with the uses of music to manage stress in a number of anxiety-provoking clinical situations, ranging from test taking to medical procedures. It should be noted that the scientific rigor employed in these studies has varied; also, few of these studies have used long-term follow-up measures. Thus, the reader should exert caution in interpreting these results.

Music and Anxiety

The results of studies using music to treat anxiety are inconsistent. This may be partly or totally attributable to the lack of standardized methodologies in approaching the topic, as well as to the lack of a universal definition of "relaxing music." In addition to the selection of music for these studies, methodological differences (the length of treatment, number of treatments, etc.) may also contribute differences in findings.

Some studies point to the effectiveness of music as a way to decrease physiological tension and/or anxiety scores (Ballard, 1981; Candler, 1978; Kibler & Rider, 1983; Kooyman, 1988; Landreth & Landreth, 1974; Peretti, 1975; Peretti & Swenson, 1974; Stoudenmire, 1975; Thaut, 1989b; Webster, 1973). Beneficial effects of music and imagery combined have also been noted (Russell, 1987). Several studies have identified an interaction of music's effectiveness with gender (i.e., females tend to benefit more from the sedative aspects of music than males) and with music training (i.e., musicians seem to benefit more than nonmusicians) (Peretti, 1975; Peretti & Swenson, 1984; Peretti & Zweifel, 1983). In addition, music was found to significantly enhance recovery from a stressful situation (Little, 1986). On the other hand, several studies have found that music has no effect on anxiety—specifically, in institutionalized adolescent females (Kampfer, 1989), in female college students (Howard, 1985), and in subjects receiving only four treatment sessions (Sime & DeGood, 1975).

The type of music used for relaxation may influence the potential for anxiety reduction. Some types of music may increase tension, such as atonal music, some "new-age" music (Logan & Roberts, 1984), and "happy" music (Biller, Olsen, & Breen, 1974; Smith & Morris, 1976). Conversely, types of music that may decrease anxiety include "sad" music (Biller et al., 1974; Smith & Morris, 1976), "popular" music (Ballard, 1980), and "preferred" music (David & Thaut, 1989; Stratton & Zalanowski, 1984; Smith & Morris, 1977; Peretti & Zweifel, 1983). Furthermore, both contemplative and classical music significantly increased susceptibility to hypnotic induction and depth of trance state (Morris, 1985).

Several studies have also noted differences between physiological, self-report, and/or behavioral measures of anxiety. Jellison (1975) found that subjects with experimentally induced anxiety had decreases in anxiety test scores in response to background music; however, physiological measures of systolic blood pressure, pulse rate, finger pulse volume, and GSR did not decrease accordingly. Davis and Thaut (1989) found significant decreases in state anxiety to preferred music, but simultaneous increases in physiological measures. Similarly, Hanser, Martin, and Bradstreet (1982) found lack of concordance between substantial verbal reports of relaxation to music and physiological measures. Katkin (1975, cited in Hanser, 1985) stated that individuals who differed on trait anxiety measures demonstrated "differential autonomic responsiveness to a stress situation" (p. 154). Hanser (1985) believes that this finding may explain the lack of consistency between these measures, as attention to the music may produce autonomic activity similar to that which occurs during stress. Thus, attention to a music stimulus, although psychologically interpreted as an orienting response, may manifest itself physiologically as an increase in autonomic activity.

It is possible that other variables may contribute to these findings. For example, music may have more effect in situations where stress is greater (e.g., during medical procedures). Thus, there may be differential effects of music as a relaxation technique in studies where stress is minimal versus studies where stress is intense (such as those clinical settings described in subsequent sections). Perhaps the effects of music are less striking when the goal of therapy is to teach relaxation skills, which must then be generalized to other situations.

These findings can also be explained in terms of Lang's "three-system" model (Lang, 1971, cited in Craske & Craig, 1984). The three systems—behavioral, physiological, and verbal—can be highly interactive and can also be independent to some extent. These systems may differ in their sensitivity to stress factors (Agras & Jacob, 1981) and across individuals (Lang, 1977). In addition, physiological indices may be the least sensitive to stress events (Agras & Jacob, 1981). This model can explain the results of several studies cited above (Jellison, 1975; Hanser et al., 1982; David & Thaut, 1989), wherein anxiety test scores and verbal reports showed decreases in anxiety, but physiological measures did not.

There are five hypotheses (discussed in Craske & Craig, 1984) that describe concordance among the three systems (Hodgson & Rachman, 1974): Concordance is most often correlated with severely stressful stimuli, found in low-demand situations, correlated with specific therapeutic interventions, found during follow-up measures, and correlated with specific physiological measures (i.e., heart rate vs. SCL). Some of these hypotheses have been supported empirically. Further research is needed to apply this model to stress reduction strategies employing music.

Finally, it is possible that cognitive effects to music may be more reliable and predictable than physiological effects, and these effects need to be compared systematically. In these investigations, the influence of expectancy effects would need to be carefully examined.

Music in Biofeedback Procedures

Several studies support the use of music in biofeedback procedures; studies comparing music and biofeedback treatments are considered in a subsequent section.

Greater decreases in muscle tension were observed when sedative music was paired with EMG-assisted biofeedback relaxation training (Scartelli, 1982, 1984; music, relaxation, and biofeedback were effective in decreasing frontalis muscle tension (Martin, 1987); and contingent music and biofeedback reduced frontalis EMG levels of two moderately/severely mentally retarded, aggressive subjects, although these levels did not reach clinical significance (Putnam, 1984). Similarly, contingent music was effective in reducing EMG levels in a patient with tension headache; however, the effects did not generalize after biofeedback was terminated (Epstein, Hersen, & Hemphill, 1974). Finally, it has been suggested that sequenced (as opposed to simultaneous) presentations of music and EMG biofeedback training may more dramatically assist relaxation (Scartelli & Borling, 1986).

Music and Test Anxiety

The results of studies examining the sedative effects of music on anxiety in test situations are inconsistent; the effects of various types of music have been contrasted in some of these studies.

Anxiety levels appear to rise in the absence of music, while these are held constant with music (Hardie, 1990). In addition, music may have more effect on highly anxious subjects (Stanton, 1973). In comparisons of various types of music, it is suggested that stimulative music increases worry and emotionality (Smith & Morris, 1976) more than sedative music decreases them (Smith & Morris, 1977; Rohner & Miller, 1980). Various types of music may significantly reduce physiological symptoms of anxiety and significantly increase exam scores in college students (Blanchard, 1979) and in learning disabled students (Kleckley, 1989).

Smith and Morris (1977) conclude that in test situations "effects of music are to be understood in terms of cognitive processes such as worry, expectancy, and concentration rather than primarily on the basis of the arousal or reduction of physiological–affective responses to musical stimuli" (p. 1052).

Music and Performance Anxiety

Performance anxiety or "stage fright" is a pervasive problem in performing musicians and music students (Habboushe & Maranto, 1991). Although the idea may seem paradoxical, music may be influential in reducing anxiety associated with music performance (Maranto, 1989a, 1989b, 1992b). Music therapy techniques (improvisation, performance, awareness techniques, and verbal processing) significantly reduced anxiety scores, significantly increased confidence scores, and significantly decreased narcissism scores in musicians (Montello, 1989). Also, a preliminary study using music, desensitization, and biofeedback has suggested favorable results (Maranto & Murphy, 1991).

Music and Stress Associated with Medical Procedures

The effect of music in reducing stress and anxiety associated with various medical procedures has been studied. The success of music varies to some extent with the procedure examined. Positive results of anxiety reduction have been reported with gynecological patients undergoing punch biopsy (David, 1991); with children undergoing bone marrow transplants and lumbar punctures (Schur, 1986); with patients receiving debridement for burns (Barker, 1991); and for patients undergoing bronchoscopy procedures (Metzler & Berman, 1991). However, no significant effects of music on anxiety were found for patients undergoing dialysis (Schuster, 1985) or femoral arteriograms (Mandle, 1988).

Music in the General Hospital and Intensive Care Unit

Music activities appear to improve mood and comfort of adult patients in general hospitals (Goloff, 1981) and to reduce trait anxiety significantly in chronically ill patients (Levine-Gross & Swartz, 1981). Furthermore, music listening improves mood for patients and other visitors in medical reception rooms (Roter, 1957).

Background music in an intensive care unit was responsible for a drop in myocardial infarction and a mortality rate of 8–12% below the national average (St. Joseph's Hospital, 1972); for decreased heart rates, lessened anxiety and depression, and greater tolerance for pain and suffering (Bonny, 1983); and for significantly improved moods in patients (Davis-Rollans & Cunningham, 1987).

Music in Pregnancy, Labor, and Delivery

Several studies have reported successful applications of music to reduce anxiety during pregnancy (Winslow, 1986; Lindquist, 1985). Pregnant adolescents receiving music during the third trimester experienced significantly less state anxiety than controls (Liebman, 1989). Music therapy also appears to facilitate relaxation during labor and delivery (Burt & Korn, 1964; Clark, McCorkle, & Williams, 1981; DiFranco, 1988; Hanser, Larson, & O'Connell, 1983; Winokur, 1984). In addition, music is reported to decrease pain responses during labor (Hanser et al., 1983; McDowell, 1966; Burt & Korn, 1964; Codding, 1982; Winokur, 1984; Livingston, 1979) and to elicit positive psychological responses (McDowell, 1966; Livingston, 1979).

Music and Pediatrics

Music appears to have a favorable influence on a variety of behaviors related to stress among neonates and pediatric patients:

1. Music significantly reduced stress behaviors, initial weight loss, and hospital stay, and significantly increased average weight, volume of formula intake, and caloric intake, among premature and low-birth-weight neonates (Caine, 1989).

2. Instrumental and vocal music were found to be effective in reducing crying behaviors of newborns (Lininger, 1987) and with a patient with Stevens–Johnson syndrome (Schieffelin, 1988).

3. Music plus interaction with the therapist effectively reduced stress in hospitalized infants and toddlers (Marley, 1984).

4. Music therapy was more effective than play therapy in eliciting verbalizations about hospitalization in pediatric patients (Froelich, 1984).

5. Taped music produced significant reductions in respiration rates for infants in respiratory distress (Ammon, 1968).

6. Music simulating intrauterine sounds significantly improved oxygen saturation levels and behavioral states (arousal levels) in premature infants (Collins & Kuch, 1989).

Music in Surgery

The vast majority of studies report that music has significant positive effects, as shown by a variety of dependent measures, as a treatment for anxiety prior to surgery. Thus, effects of "anxiolytic" music, defined as music designed to minimize psychophysiological aspects of anxiety (Spintge, 1991), are fairly consistent. Also, substantial effects of music on other psychophysiological parameters (e.g., pain) are found in these studies. These results can be summarized as follows:

1. Music listening produces significant reductions in stress hormone levels during surgery (Halpaap, 1988; Halpaap, Spintge, Droh, Kummert, & Kugel, 1987; Kamin, Kamin, Spintge, & Droh, 1983; Oyama, 1983; Oyama, Sato, Kugo, Spintge, & Droh, 1983; Spintge & Droh, 1988; Tanioka et al., 1983).

2. Music used with nitrous oxide anesthesia reduces struggling, delirium, and vomiting, and enables rapid emergence from anesthesia (Cherry & Pallin, 1948).

3. Music and suggestion produce favorable effects on pain, sleep, anxiety, and amounts of analgesics in patients undergoing open heart surgery (Crago, 1980).

4. Music appears to reduce anxiety in preoperative pediatric patients up to and during the administration of anesthesia (Chetta, 1981), and also in adolescent and adult surgical patients (Tanioka et al., 1983; Sanderson, 1986; Stein, 1991; Steinke, 1991; Moss, 1988).

5. Music administered postoperatively reduces pulse rates (Locsin, 1981) and stabilizes blood pressure (Sanderson, 1986); music administered preoperatively significantly reduces blood pressure, pulse rate, mean arterial pressure, double product index, and anxiety (Updike & Charles, 1987).

6. Music listening reduces postoperative pain (Locsin, 1981, 1988; Crago, 1980; Sanderson, 1986; Shapiro & Cohen, 1983); the need for pain medication (Locsin, 1981; Siegel, 1983; Sanderson, 1986); and the need for sedatives during regional anesthesia, but not the feelings of anxiety during this procedure (Walther-Larsen, Diemar, & Valentin, 1988).

7. Music reduces the amount of anesthesia needed for surgery (Spintge, 1983).

8. Research involving 8000 patients receiving music during surgery showed

significantly better outcomes in psychological, behavioral, and physiological parameters for these patients than for those not receiving music (Spintge & Droh, 1988).

Music in Dentistry

A number of studies examining the effects of music in dental procedures have utilized music in "audio-analgesia" (see the Appendix). Specifically, music is combined with white noise, and the patient has direct control over the amounts of music and/or white noise needed to reduce anxiety and control pain. Significantly favorable self-report data as a result of hearing taped music were reported by Jacobsen (1957) and Gardner and Licklider (1959). Treatment results for 5000 patients revealed that for 90%, audio-analgesia was the only pain control required (including during tooth extractions) (Gardner, Licklider, & Weisz, 1960).

Music listening causes significant reductions in heart rate, blood pressure, and stress hormones (Oyama, Hatano, et al., 1983); favorable reductions in autonomic sensations and anxiety (Corah, Gale, Pace, & Seyrek, 1981); significant decreases in the uses of other analgesics (Monsey, 1960); improvement in patients' feelings of helplessness (Gfeller, Logan, & Walker, 1988); and increases in pain threshold and tolerance (Morosko & Simmons, 1966) during dental procedures.

There are a number of possible explanations for the successful applications of music in dentistry, medicine, and pain relief: (1) Auditory stimuli may directly suppress pain neurologically (i.e., parts of the auditory and pain systems come together in the reticular formation in the lower thalamus, and the interactions between the two systems may be largely inhibitory); (2) auditory stimuli may mask the sound of medical or dental instrumentation (e.g., the dental drill); (3) focus on the music may serve as a distraction; (4) controlling the volume of the music may allow the patient to exercise control over the situation; and (5) additional benefits may be achieved through the use of suggestion (Standley, 1986).

Music in Oncology and Terminal Illness

Results of studies using music to reduce stress in various aspects of the care of oncology and terminally ill patients have shown encouraging results. The use of music to reduce anxiety in terminally ill patients approached significance (Curtis, 1986). Bailey (1983) found that cancer patients receiving live (versus taped) music reported significantly less anxiety, more vigor, more changes in physical discomfort, and more positive changes in mood. In addition, cancer patients increased their self-disclosure verbalizations through music therapy activities (Sedei, 1980).

Patients showed highly favorable responses to the use of background music during radiotherapy (Mowatt, 1967). Similarly, music and guided visual imagery produced favorable improvement in nausea, vomiting, and anxiety associated with chemotherapy (Frank, 1985), and music listening was significantly effective in increasing relaxation in chemotherapy patients (Cotanch & Strum, 1987).

Music in Vibroacoustic Therapy

"Vibroacoustic therapy is the therapeutic use of VibroAcoustic equipment and software that emit low frequency sound signals mixed with special audio cassettes" (Skille,

1989, p. 62). It is a process wherein low-frequency tones generated via vibrations are applied directly to the body. Anecdotal and clinical reports have indicated that this type of therapy reduces sympathetic activation, improves circulation, and enhances relaxation and well-being (Skille, 1987a, 1987b, 1989). In vibroacoustic therapy, the following operational principles are implemented: Low pitches facilitate relaxation, and high pitches cause stress; rhythmic music increases energy, while nonrhythmic music decreases energy; loud music activates the body, whereas soft music serves as a pacifier (Skille, 1989).

An empirical study using vibroacoustic therapy (Somatron) has revealed positive results on self-report measures (Madsen, Standley, & Gregory, 1991). Further pilot studies using the RestRider (see the Appendix) have revealed increases in self-reported relaxation (Page, 1991; Hiller, 1991; Kremling, 1991), improved identification of specific resonance areas in the body (Hiller, 1991), some effect on back pain (Brooks, 1991), and preference for vibroacoustic treatment over free-field music (Kremling, 1991).

Music and Immune Response

Several studies have examined the positive influences of music on immune responses. College students showed significant increases in secretory IgA after listening to music for a 20-minute period (Tsao et al., 1991). Significant effects on IgA for groups receiving imagery alone and music listening alone over a control group were found by Rider et al. (1990) and Rider (1988). Rider et al. (1991), comparing various active and passive musical experiences, found significant advantages for listening and control conditions over singing. The toning condition was not significantly different from other treatments.

In addition, entrainment music significantly increased leukocyte circulation (Rider & Achterburg, 1989), and entrainment music and imagery significantly increased secretory IgA (Rider & Weldin, 1990).

Comparison Studies

The findings of studies combining or contrasting music with other relaxation strategies generally fall into one of five categories: Music enhances the efficacy of other treatment(s); (2) music does not enhance treatment efficacy; (3) music is not as effective as other methods of intervention; (4) music is as effective as other methods of intervention; or (5) music is more effective than other methods of intervention.

Music Enhances the Efficacy of Other Treatments

Results of studies in the first category are as follows:

1. Music appears to enhance progressive relaxation, and this combination may be more effective than either of these treatments alone (Kibler & Rider, 1983).

2. Music, imagery, and autogenic relaxation procedures in psychiatric and normal subjects produced significant increases in skin temperature and perceived

relaxation. On the average, subjects experienced three different modes of imagery during a session (Peach, 1984).

3. A program combining music, guided imagery, and progressive relaxation significantly decreased circadian amplitude and entrained corticosteroid and temperature rhythms (Rider, Floyd, & Kirkpatrick, 1985).

4. Music and imagery were significantly more effective than music alone, and also more effective than cognitive treatment, in the reduction of state and trait anxiety scores in highly anxious college students (Russell, 1987).

5. Music alone and music with suggestions of positive experiences were compared for their influence on the subjective and objective indices of stress and recovery of patients undergoing open heart surgery. It was found that the music–suggestion treatment was more effective than music alone in facilitating relaxation (Crago, 1980).

Music Does Not Enhance Treatment Efficacy

Results of studies in the second category are as follows:

1. Music did not appear to have an enhancing effect on anxiety reduction (EMG measures and self-report) when paired with muscle relaxation, intermediate relaxation, mental relaxation, or self-relaxation. It should be noted that the treatment time for this study was only a 30-minute period (Miller & Bornstein, 1977).

2. Neither relaxation suggestion training nor music significantly lowered anxiety scores of older persons (Dicker, 1989).

Music Is Not as Effective as Other Modes of Treatment

EMG biofeedback, progressive relaxation, and music were compared as treatments for tension reduction of inpatient alcoholics. At the end of seven sessions, subjects receiving biofeedback or progressive relaxation were significantly more relaxed than the music group, according to EMG measurements (Sisson, 1981).

Music Is as Effective as Other Modes of Treatment

Results of studies in the fourth category are as follows:

1. Both an imagery scene and this scene paired with music produced significant reductions in heart rate from baseline in college students (Friedman, 1979).

2. Music, progressive relaxation, and music plus progressive relaxation each significantly increased finger temperature in college students. Although the difference was not significant, scores of subjects in the group receiving music plus progressive relaxation were higher than scores in the other groups (Kibler & Rider, 1983).

3. Music was as effective as taped relaxation instruction in reducing frontalis muscle tension in preschool children (Reese, 1987).

4. There were no significant treatment effects among autogenic training, progressive relaxation, and music (as a control condition) (Van Fleet, 1986).

5. Both music and progressive relaxation were significantly effective in reducing state anxiety; neither decreased trait anxiety (Stoudenmire, 1975).

Music Is More Effective Than Other Modes of Treatment

Results of studies in the fifth category are as follows:

1. Type A subjects receiving music or progressive relaxation produced significantly lower EMG levels than subjects receiving a visual relaxation technique (Jenkins, 1986).

2. Music and imagery were significantly more effective than cognitive treatment in the reduction of state and trait anxiety scores in highly anxious college students (Russell, 1987).

3. EMG levels of subjects receiving music only and music plus autogenic training were significantly lower than those of controls. Music plus autogenic training resulted in the lowest levels among all the methods tested (biofeedback only, autogenic training only, and control) (Reynolds, 1984).

4. High school students receiving modified anxiety training with and without music significantly lowered their anxiety scores; students receiving music also significantly improved their academic achievement (Vaughn, 1989).

5. Yulis et al. (1975) recommend that music be used in place of other, more complicated relaxation training methods, because it is equally effective and less time-consuming.

From the comparison studies presented above, the following may be concluded (with caution):

1. The effectiveness of music as an enhancement for other relaxation interventions may depend on the relaxation method(s) used. Techniques involving progressive relaxation, autogenic methods, imagery, and suggestion appear to be enhanced by music.

2. Music may have limited effectiveness in enhancing relaxation treatments of very short duration.

3. The effectiveness of music in comparison to other treatments may vary with the clinical population under investigation.

4. Music may be as effective or as ineffective as other modes of relaxation training, depending upon the clinical population.

5. Highly anxious subjects may benefit more from music than relatively nonanxious groups.

6. Music may provide beneficial effects in addition to relaxation in some populations.

Adverse Effects

Perhaps one of the main advantages of using music in stress reduction is its relative lack of negative side effects, particularly when it is used by a trained music therapist. In the vast majority of the literature, the only negative effect of music reported (if, indeed, it can be considered a negative response) was the lack of the desired response. However, it is emphasized that adverse reactions can happen more frequently when these techniques are used by individuals without appropriate training in music therapy—that is, when music is used casually as a supplement to other techniques. Music can be a very powerful tool in therapy, because of its ability to access physiological, psychological, and cognitive reactions simultaneously; thus, it cannot be used in a cavalier manner. Moreover, because music can access feelings and responses directly and immediately, caution should be exercised in its use without consultation from trained professionals.

In the present section, I list possible adverse reactions as determined in clinical work, and suggest remedial measures in the event that these adverse responses occur.

Displeasure with the Music

Arbitrary selection of music by an untrained clinician can elicit responses that are counterproductive to treatment. This may be considered the most common reason for any adverse reactions. It cannot be assumed that one particular piece or genre of music is universally effective with patients; rather, music can only be selected for therapeutic use following an individualized assessment process with direct input from the client.

If inappropriate music is selected for use, a variety of psychological and physiological reactions are possible, including irritation, anger, frustration, and increases in psychological and physiological measures of tension. The severity of these reactions can be minimized and remediated by a careful observation of the patient's physiological and behavioral reactions while listening to the music. If adverse effects are noted, a change in music is warranted immediately. Also, a discussion with the client of these reactions should take place; the clinician should obtain more feedback from the client on the nature of these reactions, so that these can be avoided in the future. Throughout this process, it is important that the integrity of the therapeutic relationship be preserved and that the patient–therapist trust inherent in this relationship be maintained. This can only be accomplished by an open relationship with the client, in which the client's feedback on the music and methodology is acknowledged and respected.

Cathartic Reactions

Even when a careful assessment of the client has been completed, it is possible that very strong feelings, associations, memories, and imagery may be elicited by the music. It is even possible that music that has been used successfully for stress reduction at one time may cause these reactions at another time. The reason for this is that relaxed states minimize the client's defenses and allow psychological issues to emerge. Specific techniques in music therapy, such as guided imagery and music (see the Appendix), are in fact effective by virtue of this phenomenon. A relaxed state makes a client more vulnerable to imagery and feelings; this vulnerability is intensified when imagery-evoking music is used. It may be impossible for the inexperienced or untrained therapist to know how evocative a particular piece of music may be for a given individual. Reactions that may occur include intense affect, vivid memories, and physiological reactions. When the goal of treatment is the resolution of psychotherapeutic issues in the client, the uncovering of these reactions may be an important component of the process and may facilitate therapy. However, if stress reduction is the goal of therapy, these reactions may be considered counterproductive in the short term. Furthermore, they must be handled with therapeutic skill and cannot be dismissed by an ethical therapist.

Once these reactions occur, they usually will not be averted by simply changing the music. However, it is likely that they can be minimized by gently stopping the music and guiding the person back to an alert state. If these reactions are considered part of the goals of therapy, they may be continued if the therapist is competent in dealing with these issues. Again, it must be emphasized that these reactions can be minimized by careful selection of the music by a trained music therapist. In addition, therapeutic skill is necessary to deal with these reactions when they occur, to give the client the needed support, and to refer the client to appropriate resources, if necessary, for further work on issues that have come to the surface.

It is important to note at this point that music selected for psychotherapeutic work and music selected for stress reduction may be vastly different in nature and quality.

Combining Techniques

Music is often used in combination with other methods, such as hypnosis, biofeedback, meditation, and visualization. Although typically not considered an "adverse reaction," positive results of interventions with music can be minimized or reduced when combined with methods involving verbal or cognitive elements. In some of the research, music has not always enhanced these techniques. It can be speculated that combining methods may create a sensory overload for the client and actually produce tension. An example of combining techniques is the use of verbal directions for progressive or autogenic relaxation accompanied by music. The client must cognitively switch back and forth between the music and the directions; in a number of clients this can cause stress reactions. Another example is the use of music with biofeedback, where an auditory click is used to provide feedback to the client on his or her physiological state and the music plays simultaneously with the auditory feedback; in this situation, the auditory clicks and the music can demand cognitive shifts from the client and potentially counteract relaxation.

In combining music with another technique, several factors must be addressed:

1. Can music enhance the technique, or can music alone be used to facilitate the desired response?

2. If music is used in combination with the technique, what is the perceptual role of the music; that is, is it designed to be in the foreground or background?

3. Is the music appropriate for the technique; for example, if verbal instructions are used, does music match these instructions in content or does it divert the person from the instructions?

4. Would it be more appropriate to sequence the music following the technique or to provide music simultaneously?

Contraindications

Although there are no substantive contraindications provided in the literature on music therapy and stress management, there are some conditions that, if present, might logically preclude the use of music (see Table 13.2).

TABLE 13.2. Contraindications for Music Therapy in Stress Management

Condition	Clinical modification
Musicogenic epilepsy	Avoid using music known to elicit seizures; avoid using music therapy
Neurological impairments	Avoid using music that lacks structure or is overly stimulating
Psychosis	Avoid using music and relaxation techniques that elicit detachment from reality
Borderline personality disorders	Same as above
Dementia	Same as above

Compliance, Resistance, and Maintenance

There are no known compliance or dropout rates for music therapy treatment of stress and anxiety published in the literature. Several factors may account for this phenomenon:

1. The use of music in treating stress and anxiety is relatively new. Authors of the published research appear to be examining effects of music on various aspects of anxiety with different client groups as a first step. Once these findings become more conclusive, more information about specific methodological issues will be forthcoming, perhaps as a second step in the research process.

2. It may also be possible that because music as a treatment is not a foreign or alien modality to clients in stress treatment and because few other treatments allow pleasurable affective responses, compliance for music treatment may be very high and dropout rates minimal.

Similarly, few if any studies report specific details about the regularity with which treatment must be offered in both the short and the long term. One may speculate in a rather optimistic manner that music as a treatment for stress works relatively quickly; indeed, this suggestion is confirmed in the data on immune responses elicited by music (Tsao et al., 1991) and in conclusions by various authors (Yulis et al., 1975).

Another possible explanation for this is that music therapy is not just one technique; there are *many* techniques in music therapy that may facilitate relaxation. Both active and passive methods are described in the literature. Specific techniques include music biofeedback; music and imagery; music psychotherapy; music improvisation; entrainment music; group music sessions; instrumental playing; contingent music; music and suggestion; guided imagery and music; music and progressive relaxation; music desensitization; music and autogenic training; music and hypnosis; music and play therapy; live music; taped music; various styles and genres of music; and so on (Maranto & Scartelli, 1992). Specific details of short- and long-term treatment methodology certainly vary with each technique as well as with each individual. It is unrealistic to expect such details when so many techniques are available to the clinician at such an early stage in the development of the discipline. Furthermore, as stated previously, because of the individual differences in response to music noted in many of the research articles, an approach to using music therapy must be highly individualized. Indeed, although music therapy is rapidly becoming a "science," it is still an "art."

Several of the techniques listed above are described in the following sections.

The Method

The "music-based individualized relaxation training" (MBIRT) method (Saperston, 1989)[1] is the primary method described in this section. MBIRT is selected because it is geared to individuals for whom relaxation training is particularly difficult (e.g., the developmentally disabled and/or behaviorally disturbed). This method incorporates a number of other techniques: biofeedback, entrainment, progressive relaxation, contingent music, "iso-music," and imagery. Also, it uses music in a number of different ways to elicit relaxation responses. It provides an excellent example of the use of music therapy in stress reduction, and can be easily adapted to a number of clinical populations with simple modifications in the sophistication of instructions and procedures.

Content and Sequence of Instruction

MBIRT is a behavioral approach incorporating elements of music in training strategies to shape or elicit behaviors prerequisite to relaxation. Its goals are "to move the client from respondent procedures to operant procedures so that relaxation skills can be performed independently" (Saperston, 1989, p. 26). MBIRT is sequenced according to four levels:

Level I: The development of enabling behaviors. During this level, overt prerequisites to relaxation are shaped (e.g., lying still, eyes closed); incompatible behaviors are reduced or extinguished. Also, therapist–client rapport is established, and both contingent music or respondent "iso-music" may be utilized. Criterion for this level is lying still for 15 minutes with eyes closed (Saperston, 1989).

Level II: The development of therapist-directed relaxation responses. During this level, clients initially learn to perform progressive relaxation and breath control with instructions given through songs or chants sung by the therapist and client. Participation in the songs or chants by clients may directly reduce or regulate respiration. The sequence of a session may be as follows: (1) listening to preferred music; (2) using songs with relaxation messages and cues for relaxation (i.e., breathing and muscles); (3) using chants of decreasing tempi to focus attention and decrease breathing rate; (4) using improvised or prerecorded entrainment music at progressively slower tempi; (5) using guided imagery or biofeedback training; and (6) returning the client to an alert state. During this level also, client music preferences may be modified to facilitate the relaxation response. Criterion for this level consists of lying still and performing muscle relaxation and breath control aided by musical prompts (songs, chants, rhythms), with minimal prompting from the therapist (Saperston, 1989).

[1]Cited by permission of the National Association for Music Therapy.

Level III: The development of independent relaxation responses. During this level, musical prompts are replaced with verbal instruction with musical background, using fading procedures; respondent techniques give way to operant techniques. Biofeedback training is of longer duration. Criterion for this level is the achievement of both relaxation skills in response to verbal instruction and an increasingly relaxed physiological state in response to the relaxation procedures (Saperston, 1989).

Level IV: The development of transfer and generalization skills. During this level, the client learns to identify when he or she can self-implement the relaxation techniques, and to transfer these skills to different times and settings (Saperston, 1989).

Physical Environment and Equipment

Equipment and settings vary, depending on the music therapy relaxation method used. For the most part, however, the following are needed:

1. A small, comfortable room with minimal visual and auditory distractions. This is essential, since auditory distractions in particular will interfere with the music procedures. Lighting in the room should be controllable via shades and lamps. The furnishings of the room should be conducive to relaxation.

2. A comfortable bed, cot, mat, or reclining chair for the client; several of these should be available to accommodate different clients' preferences and physical conditions.

3. An appropriate audio system with a clear, nondistorted delivery system and high-quality headphones. The system should include capabilities for both audiocassettes and compact discs.

4. A wide selection of pretested tapes and discs from various musical genres (classical, jazz, New Age, popular, country–western, etc.), which can be selected according to clients' preferences. It is important that the therapist be familiar enough with these tapes and discs to make selections on the basis of their sedative and entrainment qualities, their potential for eliciting or not eliciting imagery, and the preferences of different clients.

5. Appropriate equipment for physiological monitoring, including biofeedback equipment. Software designed to permit music or vibrational feedback instead of auditory or visual feedback is optimal.

6. Musical instruments (piano, rhythm instruments, etc.) to be used for live music, improvisation, and entrainment.

7. Vibroacoustic equipment, such as the RestRider.

Therapist–Client Relationship

As the definition of music therapy and the classification model presented earlier in this chapter indicate, a supportive therapist–client relationship is an essential requisite of music therapy intervention. The client–therapist relationship in music therapy, particularly in its application in medicine, may differ from other clinical relationships for several reasons:

1. In music therapy, the personality of the therapist and the relationship developed with the client may both effect change, along with the music (Maranto, 1991, 1992a). Thus, it is the intent of the music therapist to establish a warm, supportive environment in which therapy can take place; the music therapist is concerned with the whole individual, including all biophysical data and not only the presenting problem.

2. The music therapist, because of the medium used, is able to focus on "healthy" or creative parts of the individual rather than on aspects of sickness.

3. Clients associate music therapy with pleasure and relaxation rather than discomfort and stress.

4. Because music is pervasive in everyday life, it may be less threatening to clients than other forms of therapy.

5. The use of music as a therapy may be less stigmatizing to the client than other methods of intervention.

As stated previously, the presence of a trained therapist differentiates music therapy from other uses of music. Curricula for the training of music therapists have been in existence for almost 40 years. These studies, accomplished either at the graduate or the undergraduate level, provide students with training in music, music therapy, behavioral sciences, social sciences, and physiology. Students learn how to use music therapy techniques with a wide variety of clinical conditions. Following an extended full-time internship of 900–1040 hours, students are eligible for registration and/or certification by a professional organization (i.e., the National Association for Music Therapy or the American Association for Music Therapy), and may sit for the national board certification examination in music therapy. Graduate work in music therapy is strongly encouraged if individuals are to use more in-depth methods of music therapy, including applications in medicine. Approximately 70 universities now offer undergraduate training and certification coursework, 17 offer master's degrees, and 7 offer doctoral studies in related areas with an emphasis in music therapy (Maranto & Bruscia, 1987, 1988, 1989).

Methods for Enhancing Compliance

One aspect of music therapy, as noted above in the description of MBIRT, is its ability to be transferred into the client's own environment. Music may be portable via a Walkman or similar devices, and thus may be used in a variety of nonclinical settings (e.g., in the car, at home, at work, or wherever there is a perceived need). Again, there is no stigma attached to listening to music.

Typically, following music therapy sessions and the learning of skills, therein, clients are given detailed instructions on how to transfer skills to their own situations and use them most efficiently for their own needs. Because music is a pleasurable experience, resistance is not generally an issue.

Change is maintained through the music therapist's continued monitoring of the client and the evaluation of self-report data. Ways of incorporating music in the day-to-day environment that are compatible with the client's own routine and life style are explored and implemented. Indeed, the inclusion of music as a stress management device can be virtually effortless when it is done creatively and in conjunction with the client's own preferences. Clients can use music in a cue-controlled manner or in a preventative way to prevent situations from becoming stressful. The accessible aspects of music allow clients to feel "in control" of their treatment and perhaps more motivated to continue its use in stress reduction.

Case Materials

Two case examples are provided in this section to demonstrate several music therapy techniques, as well as applications with various clinical populations that may benefit from music therapy.

Music-Based Individualized Relaxation Training

In a case described by Saperston (1989),[2] Ronald was classified as severely disturbed with hyperactivity, anxious behaviors, aggression, tantrums, stereotyped behaviors, and inappropriate talking to himself. His chronological age was 32 and his IQ was 64. Medications were used on an average of twice weekly to control outbursts. The following describes his treatment over a 38-month period.

Ronald had great difficulty lying still and keeping his eyes closed, in addition to other inappropriate behaviors while listening to music. He liked music and singing, however, so the use of MBIRT was implemented. He attended four 30-minute sessions per week. Level I procedures included using concept songs for relaxation and using improvised music contingently to control behaviors incompatible with treatment. In the fourth month of treatment, Ronald could already, without instruction, transfer these new relaxation skills to a different anxiety-provoking situation.

After 1 year of treatment, Ronald achieved the criterion for Level II, no longer exhibited incompatible behaviors, and needed no medication for behavior control. EMG instrumentation was acquired and introduced during the 14th month of treatment (Level III). His EMG levels were lowest during live music, which consisted of music improvised according to EMG levels. Melodic music elicited higher EMG levels, perhaps because of an orienting response; atonal music elicited lower levels. Also, shorter natural pauses in the music elicited lower EMG levels than longer pauses. During sessions, Ronald's singing of the relaxation concept song initially and rapidly increased EMG levels. However, once the song was completed, his attention was more focused and lower EMG levels resulted.

Ronald then learned to perform relaxation skills with verbal instruction only. For the first month, his EMG levels were higher than in Level II, but by the fifth month he could relax as well with the verbal instructions as with the music cues. He began to transfer skills actively during the sixth month of Level III.

During the last months of sessions, Ronald demonstrated progressively lower EMG levels (an average of 2–3 μV). Other behavioral areas appeared to benefit from the training: No medications were used during the 38-month period, his social behaviors improved, and he also entered a voacational training program for the first time.

[2]Cited by permission of the National Association for Music Therapy.

Music and Imagery with the Terminally Ill

Joe was a 75-year-old man with inoperable cancer of the lung and diaphragm. He lived at home with his wife; prior to his diagnosis, he had enjoyed a very active life style that included dancing several times a week and part-time employment. He was referred to the therapist by his surgeon because of his interest in music to improve the quality of his life and to reduce his anxiety concerning his illness. Joe was a very quiet, gentle person, who was unable to share his feelings about his illness with his family for fear of creating a burden for them.

Joe was seen in his home for sessions that lasted for 2 hours each. Sessions were held every 2–3 weeks; he received no other interventions besides medical ones. Joe was very interested in assuming an active role with regard to his illness and read the latest books and articles on the topic of mind–body relationships. Still, he was worried about the progression of the disease, not being able to continue his former level of activity, and becoming a burden to the family that he continued to care for. An assessment by the therapist indicated that "big band" music was his favorite, yet he liked many styles of music and was willing to experiment with new types.

During the first session, a version of progressive relaxation that involved tensing and releasing various muscle groups was used; an imagery focus of going to a favorite comfortable place was given; and sedative "New Age" music was used. The music played for 15 minutes, after which Joe was guided back to an alert state and there was a discussion of feelings and imagery that occurred during the music. Because biofeed-back equipment was unavailable throughout therapy, the achievement of relaxation was noted from observation of physiological signs such as respiration rate, muscle tension, and movement; also, information was gleaned from the patient's self-report. After the music and imagery of the first session, the patient reported that it was the most relaxed he had been in months. His imagery had been very comforting to him, and he couldn't believe that he could feel that peaceful again. Tears of gratitude came to his eyes as the session was concluded.

At subsequent sessions, similar techniques were used. However, different imagery focuses were chosen to reflect Joe's needs for different sessions, as determined via initial discussions; music was chosen in a similar manner. For example, at one session Joe reported having difficulty breathing because of his tumor and the humid weather. The imagery focus chosen was that of being on a beach; music was chosen that could entrain slow, relaxed breathing. Guided imagery was used throughout the music selection—imagery of "breathing in" the music and letting it open his airways, as well as imagery of letting the music enter the body through the breath, having it travel to different parts of the body, and letting any tension found be removed from the body via exhalation. The results of this session were extraordinary. The effects of the music and imagery procedures lasted several days. During the course of treatment, relaxation inductions were also varied, but consistently less and less time was needed until relaxation was achieved. The procedures never failed to elicit a deep state of relaxation in the patient.

Following the music sessions, the therapist spent considerable time processing the images with Joe, along with the feelings that emerged. It seemed that the music was able to relax him sufficiently to allow him to address his fears and concerns about the illness, as well as to release emotions that had been pent up for many years. The music-facilitated relaxation also permitted the patient to attempt a review of difficult situations in his life and to come to resolutions on various issues. Joe commented on several occasions that because of music therapy, he was able to gain control again over his life.

Tapes were provided by the therapist, and Joe used them daily, particularly when he felt tension mounting. However, he reported that this was not as effective as having sessions with the therapist.

Although the cancer ultimately took Joe's life, he remained fairly active until his demise, and his family reported that music therapy was the only thing that appeared to help him deal with his illness. He knew that music therapy was a safe place to "let go" of tension and to face and resolve his fears concerning his illness.

Comments and Reflections

Music therapy is and will undoubtedly continue to be an important therapeutic modality to treat stress associated with a variety of conditions. I believe that the value of this therapeutic modality lies in its ability to address the *whole* person concurrently and simultaneously—that is on physical affective, cognitive, and social levels. Music appears to be a noninvasive technique with few if any side effects, with relative ease of administration, with no stigma attached, and with increasing therapeutic promise as seen in the literature.

There are still a number of questions and issues in using music therapy that remain unanswered. Future research will undoubtedly provide needed information regarding the relationship of music to various health processes. This research will allow therapists to predict responses to music more accurately and to apply music in more systematic ways. However, it is not likely that this research will lead to "music for the masses." Music therapy will continue to be a process designed and modified on the basis of each individual's needs, as well as the individual's own unique pattern of responding and history with the music.

It is predicted that the need for music as a primary or supportive therapy in stress reduction will continue to grow as individuals seek treatment that complements their need to manage their own health in a humanistic health care delivery system.

Summary and Conclusions

Music is a method of treatment that humankind has relied on for many centuries. Although music is a complex stimulus, and responses to music are equally complex, research has supported its effectiveness as a treatment modality with many clinical problems. Because music is a personal and unique experience to each individual, research methodology has yet to reveal an operational paradigm for its many applications. In spite of this, clinical uses of music are fairly widespread and successful. Recent research, particularly that concerning the immune system's responsiveness to music and the entrainment possibilities of music, will certainly open many new frontiers to music therapy practitioners. Among the reasons for the existence of music in virtually every culture, its ability to elicit and maintain human health and well-being stands out.

Appendix: Glossary

Anxiolytic music: Music that is designed to elicit a relaxed state (i.e., to eliminate the psychophysiological aspects of anxiety).

Audio-analgesia: The suppression of sound directly through listening to music, white noise, or the combination thereof.

Contingent music: Music (generally preferred by the client) that is used to consequate behavior.

Entrainment: A process in physics describing the influence that one vibrating body has on another body vibrating at a similar frequency: The two bodies will eventually vibrate at the same frequency. In music and medicine, this term refers to the use of music matched to the physiological state of the patient; changes in the music will subsequently affect the patient's physiology in the desired direction.

Guided imagery and music: A technique that involves listening to specially designed music tapes while in a very relaxed state. Spontaneous imagery and feelings elicited by the music are reported as they occur to a guide, who focuses and deepens the imagery experience.

Improvisation: Spontaneous music making on instruments or with the voice.

Iso-music: Music that is matched to a particular psychological state of the patient. Changes in the music are expected to effect changes in the patient's psychological state.

RestRider: A vibroacoustic bed designed to aid in stress reduction through the use of a special music delivery system and vibrations generated by low frequencies present in the music.

Toning: A process wherein vowel sounds are sustained by the voice on various pitches.

REFERENCES

Abeles, H. F. (1980). Responses to music. In D. A. Hodges (Ed.), *Handbook of music psychology* (pp. 105–140). Lawrence, KS: National Association for Music Therapy.

Agras, W. S., & Jacob R. (1981). Phobia: Nature and measurement. In M. Mavissakalin & D. H. Barlow (Eds.), *Phobia: Psychological and pharmacological treatment* (pp. 35–62). New York: Guilford Press.

Ammon, M. K. (1968). The effects of music on children in respiratory distress. *American Nurses Association Clinical Sessions*, 127–134.

Bailey, L. M. (1983). The effects of live music versus taped-recorded music on hospitalized cancer patients. *Music Therapy, 3*, 17–28.

Ballard, B. (1981). Effects of background music on anxiety during the initial counseling interview. *Dissertation Abstracts International, 41*, 3002A.

Barger, D. A. (1979). The effects of music and verbal suggestion on heart rate and self-reports. *Journal of Music Therapy, 16*, 158–171.

Barker, L. W. (1991). The use of music and relaxation techniques to reduce pain of burn patients during daily debridement. In C. D. Maranto (Ed.), *Applications of music in medicine* (pp. 123–140). Washington, DC: National Association for Music Therapy.

Bierbaum, M. A. (1989). Variations in heart action under the influence of musical stimuli. In C. Maranto & K. Bruscia (Eds.), *Master's theses in music therapy: Index and abstracts* (p. 7). Philadelphia: Esther Boyer College of Music, Temple University. (Original unpublished work 1958)

Biller, J. E., Olson, P. J., & Breen, T. (1974). The effect of "happy" versus "sad" music and participation on anxiety. *Journal of Music Therapy, 11,* 68–73.

Binet, A., & Courtier, J. (1985). Recherches graphiques sur la musique. *Année Psychologique, 2,* 201–222.

Blanchard, B. E. (1979). The effect of music on pulse rate, blood pressure and final exam scores of university students. *Journal of School Health, 49,* 470–471.

Bonny, H. L. (1983). Music listening for intensive coronary care units: A pilot project. *Music Therapy, 3,* 4–16.

Borling, J. E. (1981). The effects of sedative music on alpha rhythms and focused attention in high-creative and low-creative subjects. *Journal of Music Therapy, 18,* 101–108.

Boxberger, R. (1962). Historical bases for the use of music in therapy. In E. H. Schneider (Ed.), *Music therapy 1961: Eleventh book of proceedings of the National Association for Music Therapy* (pp. 125–166). Lawrence, KS: National Association for Music Therapy.

Brennes, N. C. (1971). Mood differential responses in music as reported by secondary music and nonmusic students from different socio-economic groups. *Dissertation Abstracts International, 31,* 5837A.

Brickman, H. R. (1950). Psychiatric implications of functional music for education. *Music Educators Journal, 36,* 29–30.

Brooks, D. (1991). *The effects of musical vibrational frequencies on the reduction of lower back pain.* Unpublished research, Temple University.

Bruscia, K. E. (1989). *Defining music therapy.* Spring City, PA: Spring House Books.

Burns, R. F. (1958). *A study of the influence of familiar hymns on moods and associations: Potential application in music therapy.* Unpublished master's thesis, Florida State University.

Burt, R. K., & Korn, G. W. (1964). Audioanalgesia in obstetrics: "White sound" analgesia during labor. *American Journal of Obstetrics and Gynecology, 88,* 361–366.

Caine, J. (1989). *The effect of music on the selected stress behaviors, weight, caloric and formula intake, and length of hospital stay of premature and low birth weight neonates on a newborn intensive care unit.* Unpublished master's thesis, Florida State University.

Candler, W. L. (1978). A comparison of externally-controlling pausing and self-controlled pausing procedures in relaxation training of anxiety neurotics. *Dissertation Abstracts International, 39*(1), 1591B.

Cherry, H., & Pallin, I. (1948). Music as a supplement in nitrous oxide anesthesia. *Anesthesiology, 9,* 391–399.

Chetta, H. D. (1981). The effect of music and desensitization on preoperative anxiety in children. *Journal of Music Therapy, 18,* 74–87.

Clark, M. E., McCorkle, R. R., & Williams, S. (1981). Music therapy-assisted labor and delivery. *Journal of Music Therapy, 18,* 88–100.

Clarke, G. L., (1989). The influence of frequencies equated for subjective loudness on heart rate. In C. D. Maranto & K. Bruscia (Eds.), *Master's theses in music therapy: Index and abstracts* (p. 18). Philadelphia: Esther Boyer College of Music, Temple University. (Original work published 1981)

Clynes, M. (1978). *Sentics: The touch of emotions.* Garden City, NY: Doubleday/Anchor.

Codding, P. A. (1982). *An exploration of the uses of music in the birthing process.* Unpublished master's thesis, Florida State University.

Coleman, W. M. (1920). On the correlation of heart rate, breathing, bodily movement and sensory stimuli. *Journal of Physiology, 54,* 213–217.

Collins, S., & Kuch, K. (1989). *Music therapy in the neonatal intensive care unit.* Unpublished manuscript.

Cook, R. B. (1973). Left–right differences in the perception of dichotically presented music stimuli. *Journal of Music Therapy, 10,* 59–63.

Corah, N. L., Gale, E. N., Pace, L. F., & Seyrek, S. K. (1981). Relaxation and musical programming as means of reducing psychological stress during dental procedures, *Journal of the American Dental Association, 103,* 232–234.

Corning, T. L. (1899). The uses of musical vibrations before and during sleep. *Medical Record, 55,* 79–86.

Cotanch, P., & Strum, R. (1987). Progressive muscle relaxation as antiemetic therapy for cancer patients. *Oncology Nursing Forum, 14,* 33–37.

Coutts, C. A. (1965). Effects of music on pulse rates and work output of short duration. *Research Quarterly, 36,* 17–21.

Crago, B. R. (1980). Reducing the stress of hospitalization for open heart surgery. *Dissertation Abstracts International, 41* (7), 2752B.

Craske, M. G., & Craig, K. D. (1984). Musical performance anxiety: The three systems model and self-efficacy theory. *Behaviour Research and Therapy, 22,* 267–280.

Curtis, S. L. (1986). The effect of music on pain relief and relaxation of the terminally ill. *Journal of Music Therapy, 23,* 10–24.

Dainow, E. (1977). Physical effects and motor responses to music. *Journal of Research in Music Education, 25,* 211–221.

Darner, C. L. (1966). Sound pulses and the heart. *Journal of the Acoustical Society of America. 39,* 414–416.

Davis, C. A. (1991). *The effects of music and relaxation techniques on pain and anxiety of women undergoing in-office gynecological procedures.* Unpublished master's thesis, Florida State University.

Davis, W. B., & Thaut, M. H. (1989). The influence of preferred relaxing music on measures of state unxiety, relaxation, and physiological responses. *Journal of Music Therapy, 26,* 168–187.

Davison, J. T. H. (1899, October). Music in medicine. *Lancet,* pp. 1159, 1160, 1162.

Davis-Rollans, C., & Cunningham, S. G. (1987). Physiologic responses of coronary care patients to selected music. *Heart and Lung, 16,* 370–378.

DeJong, M. A., van Mourik, K. R., & Schellekens, H. M. (1973). A physiological approach to aesthetic preference—music. *Psychotherapy and Psychosomatics, 22,* 46–51.

Demling, L., Tzschoppe, M., & Classen, M. (1970). The effect of various types of music on the secretory function of the stomach. *American Journal of Digestive Diseases, 15,* 15–20.

Dicker, M. T. (1989). Didactic and practice relaxation and suggestion training for older persons. *Dissertation Abstracts International, 50*(5), 1250A.

DiFranco, J. (1988). Relaxation: Music. In F. H. Nichols & S. S. Humenick (Eds.), *Childbirth education: Practice, research and theory* (pp. 201–215). Philadelphia: W. B. Saunders.

Dreher, R. E. (1948). The relationship between verbal reports and galvanic skin response. *American Psychologist, 3,* 275–276. (Abstract)

Eagle, C. T., Jr. (1971). Effects of existing mood and order of presentation of vocal and instrumental music on rated mood responses to that music. *Dissertation Abstracts International, 32,* 2118A.

Eagle, C. T., Jr. (1972). *A review of human physiological systems and their response to musical stimuli.* Paper presented at the Southeastern Conference of the National Association for Music Therapy, Tallahassee, FL.

Edwards, M. C., Eagle, C. T., Pennebaker, J. W., & Tunks, T. W. (1991). Relationships among elements of music and physiological responses of listeners. In C. D. Maranto (Ed.), *Applications of music in medicine* (pp. 41–57). Washington, DC: National Association for Music Therapy.

Ellis, D. S., & Brighouse, G. (1952). Effects of music on respiration and heartrate. *American Journal of Psychology, 65,* 39–47.

Epstein, L. H., Hersen, M., & Hemphill, D. P. (1974). Music feedback in the treatment of tension headache: An experimental case study. *Journal of Behavior Therapy and Experimental Psychiatry, 5,* 59–63.

Fisher, S., & Greenberg, R. P. (1972). Selective effects upon women of exciting and calm music. *Perceptual and Motor Skills, 34,* 987–990.

Foster, J. C., & Gamble, E. A. (1906). The effect of music on thoracic breathing. *American Journal of Psychology, 17,* 406–141.

Frank, J. M. (1985). The effects of music therapy and guided visual imagery on chemotherapy induced nausea and vomiting. *Oncology Nursing Forum, 12*(5), 47–52.

Friedman, H. G. (1979). *The effect of heart rate of music paired with an imagery relaxation scene.* Unpublished master's thesis, Florida State University.

Froelich, M. A. (1984). A comparison of the effect of music therapy and medical play therapy on the verbalization behavior of pediatric patients. *Journal of Music Therapy, 21,* 2–15.

Furman, C. E. (1978). The effect of musical stimuli on the brainwave production of children. *Journal of Music Therapy,* 108–117.

Gardner, W. J., & Licklider, J. C. (1959). Auditory analgesia in dental operations. *Journal of the American Dental Association, 59,* 1144–1150.

Gardner, W. J., Licklider, J. C., & Weisz, A. Z. (1960). Suppression of pain by sound. *Science, 132,* 32–33.

Geary, C. M. (1989). Mood induction procedures: A review and direct comparison of Velten and music plus imagination instruction methods. *Dissertation Abstracts International, 51*(3), 1495B.

Gfeller, K., Logan, H., & Walker, J. (1988). *The effect of auditory distraction and suggestion on tolerance for dental restorations in adolescents and young adults.* Unpublished manuscript, University of Iowa.

Goldstein, A. (1980). Thrills in response to music and other stimuli. *Physiological Psychology, 8*(1), 126–129.

Goloff, M. S. (1981). The responses of hospitalized medical patients to music therapy. *Music Therapy, 1,* 51–56.

Greenberg, R. P., & Fisher, S. (1966). Some differential effects of music on projective and psychological tests. *Psychological Reports, 28,* 817–820.

Haas, F., Distenfeld, S., & Axen, K. (1986). Effects of perceived musical rhythm on respiratory pattern. *Journal of Applied Physiology, 61*(3), 1185–1191.

Habboushe, F., & Maranto, C. D. (1991). Medical and psychological problems of musicians: An overview. In

C. D. Maranto (Ed.), *Applications of music in medicine* (pp. 201–221). Washington, DC: National Association for Music Therapy.

Halpaap, B. B. (1988). *Musiz als anxiolytikum in der geburtshilfe [Music as an anxiolytic agent in obstetrics].* Unpublished doctoral dissertation, FU, Berlin.

Halpaap, B., Spintge, R., Droh, R., Kummert, W., & Kugel, W. (1987). Angstloesende muzik in der geburtshilfe [Anxiolytic music in obstetrics]. In R. Spintge & R. Droh (Eds.), *Muzik in der medizin [Music in medicine]* (pp. 232–242). Berlin: Springer-Verlag.

Hanser, S. B. (1985). Music therapy and stress reduction research. *Journal of Music Therapy, 22*, 194–206.

Hanser, S. B., Larson, S. C., & O'Connell, A. S. (1983). The effect of music on relaxation of expectant mothers during labor. *Journal of Music Therapy, 22*, 50–58.

Hanser, S. B., Martin, P., & Bradstreet, K. (1982, November). *The effect of music on relaxation of dental patients.* Paper presented at the annual conference of the National Association for Music Therapy, Baltimore.

Hardie, M. H. (1990). The effect of music on mathematics anxiety and achievement, *Dissertation Abstracts International, 51*(6), 1943A.

Harrer, G., & Harrer, H. (1977). Music, emotion and autonomic function. In M. Critchley & R. A. Henson (Eds.), *Music and the brain.* London: Heinemann Medical Books.

Hart, J. H., & Cogan, R. (1976). Sex and emotional responses to classical music. *Perceptual and Motor Skills, 36*, 170–176.

Henkin, P. (1957). The prediction of behavior response patterns to music. *Journal of Psychology, 44*, 111–127.

Hiller, J. M. (1991). *An investigation of perceived body resonance to low frequency tones on the RestRider.* Unpublished research, Temple University.

Hincke, M. D. (1970). *The effect of rhythmic sound on heart rate.* Unpublished honors thesis, Acadia University, Wolfville, Nova Scotia, Canada.

Hodges, D. A. (Ed.). (1980). *Handbook of music psychology.* Lawrence, KS: National Association for Music Therapy.

Hodgson, R., & Rachman, S. (1974). Desynchrony in measures of fear. *Behaviour Research and Therapy, 12*, 319–326.

Hoffman, J. (1989). Management of essential hypertension through relaxation with sound. In C. D. Maranto & K. Bruscia (Eds.), *Master's theses in music therapy: Index and abstracts* (p. 53). Philadephia: Esther Boyer College of Music, Temple University. (Original unpublished work 1974)

Holdsworth, E. (1974). *Neuromuscular activity and covert musical psychomotor behavior: An electromyographic study.* Unpublished doctoral dissertation, University of Kansas.

Howard, N. H. (1985). Effects of sedative music and applied relaxation training on anxiety levels of female college students. *Dissertation Abstracts International, 47*(2), 459A.

Hyde, I. M. (1927). Effects of music upon electrocardiograms and blood pressure. *Journal of Experimental Psychology, 7*, 213–224.

Hyde, I., & Scalapino, W. (1918). Influence of music upon electrocardiogram and blood pressure. *American Journal of Psychology, 46*, 35–38.

Inglis, T. J. (1972). *The effects of unfamiliar music on electroencephalograms of secondary school music students and non-music students.* Unpublished doctoral dissertation, University of Minnesota.

Jacobson, H. L. (1957). The effect of sedative music on the tensions, anxiety and pain experienced by mental patients during dental procedures. In E. T. Gaston (Ed.), *Music therapy 1956* (pp. 231–234). Lawrence, KS: National Association for Music Therapy.

Jellison, J. A. (1975). The effect of music on autonomic stress response and verbal reports. In C. K. Madsen & C. H. Madsen (Eds.), *Research in music behavior: Modifying music behavior in the classroom.* New York: Teachers College Press.

Jenkins, D. L. (1986). The effects of verbal and nonverbal relaxation techniques on psychophysiological levels of arousal with demographic correlates. *Dissertation Abstracts International, 47*(8), 3526B.

Johnson, D. M., & Trawick, M. (1938). Influence of rhythmic sensory stimuli upon the heart rate. *Journal of Psychology, 6*, 303–310.

Johnson, J. M. (1964). *Changes in heart rate and respiration of young and old subjects produced by sedative and stimulative musical selections.* Unpublished master's thesis, University of Kansas.

Kamin, A., Kamin, H., Spintge, R., & Droh, R. (1983). Endocrine effect of anxiolytic music and psychological counseling before surgery. In R. Droh & R. Spintge (Eds.) *Angst, schmerz, muzik in der anesthesie* (pp. 163–166). Grenzach: Editiones Roche.

Kampfer, K. M. (1989). *The effect of music therapy on depression and anxiety in institutionalized adolescent females.* Unpublished master's thesis, University of Nevada.

Katkin, E. S. (1975). Electrodermal lability: A psychophysiological analysis of individual differences in response to stress. In I. G. Sarason & C. D. Spielberger (Eds.), *Stress and anxiety.* New York: Wiley.

Kibler, V. E., & Rider, M. S. (1983). Effects of progressive muscle relaxation and music on stress as measured by finger temperature response. *Journal of Clinical Psychology, 39,* 213–215.

Kimura, D. (1964). Left–right differences in the perception of melodies. *Quarterly Journal of Experimental Psychology, 16,* 335.

Kleckley, D. M. (1989). The effects of stress and music on test performance for the learning-disabled and students in remedial classes. *Dissertation Abstracts International, 50* (6), 1507A.

Kneutgen, J. (1974). Eine musikform und ihre biologische funktion: Uber die wirkungsweise der weigenlieder. *Psychological Abstracts, 45,* 6016.

Kooyman, R. J. (1988). An investigation of the effect of music upon the academic, affective, and attendance profiles of selected fourth grade students. *Dissertation Abstracts International, 49* (11), 3265A.

Kremling, K. (1991). *A comparison of the effects of music on relaxation as presented by the RestRider or tape recorder.* Unpublished research, Temple University.

Lacey, J. I. (1956). The evaluation of autonomic responses: Toward a general solution. *Annals of the New York Academy of Sciences, 67,* 123–164.

Landreth, J. E., & Landreth, H. F. (1974). Effects of music on physiological response. *Journal of Research in Music Education, 22,* 4–12.

Lang, P. (1971). Physiological and subjective measures of anxiety during flooding. *Behaviour Research and Therapy, 20,* 81–88.

Lang, P. (1977). Physiological assessment of anxiety and fear. In J. Cone & R. Hawkins (Eds.) *Behavioral assessment: New directions in clinical psychology.* New York: Brunner/Mazel.

Levine-Gross, J., & Swartz, R. (1981). The effects of music therapy on anxiety in the chronically ill. *Music Therapy, 1,* 43–52.

Liebman, S. S. (1989). The effects of music and relaxation on third trimester anxiety in adolescent pregnancy. *Dissertation Abstracts International, 51*(3), 779A.

Light, G. A., Love, D. M., Benson, D., & Morch, E. T. (1954). Music in surgery. *Current Researches in Anesthesia and Analgesia, 33,* 258–264.

Lininger, L. (1987). *The effects of instrumental and vocal lullabies on the crying behavior of newborn infants.* Unpublished master's thesis, Southern Methodist University.

Lindquist, R. (1985). *The role of GIM in the birthing process.* Unpublished fellow's paper, Institute for Consciousness and Music, Port Townsend, WA.

Lisco, J. D. (1989). The effect of stimulative and sedative music on heart rate and verbal reports. In C. D. Maranto & K. Bruscia (Eds.), *Master's theses in music therapy: Index and abstracts.* Philadelphia: Esther Boyer College of Music, Temple University. (Original work published 1980)

Little, P. A. (1986). Effects of a stressful movie and music on physiological and affect arousal as a function of sensation seeking trait. *Dissertation Abstracts International, 47*(9), 3962B.

Livingston, J. C. (1979). Music for the childbearing family. *JOGN Nursing, 8*(6), 363–367.

Locsin, R. (1981). The effect of music on the pain of selected post-operative patients. *Journal of Advanced Nursing, 6,* 19–25.

Locsin, R. (1988). *Effects of preferred music and guided imagery music on the pain of selected post-operative patients.* Unpublished doctoral dissertation, College of Nursing, University of the Philippines.

Logan, T. G., & Roberts, A. R. (1984). The effects of different types of relaxation music on stress levels. *Journal of Music Therapy, 21,* 177–183.

Lord, W. (1968). *The effect of music on muscle activity during exercise as measured by heart rate.* Unpublished manuscript, University of Kansas.

Lovell, G., & Morgan, J. (1942). Physiological and motor responses to a regularly recurring sound: A study in monotony. *Journal of Experimental Psychology, 30,* 435–451.

Madsen, C. K., Standley, J. M., & Gregory, D. (1991). The effect of a vibrotactile device, Somatron, on physiological responses: Musicians versus nonmusicians. *Journal of Music Therapy, 28,* 14–22.

Magill, L. A. (1980). *The effects of live versus tape-recorded music on hospitalized cancer patients.* Unpublished master's thesis, New York University.

Mandle, C. L. (1988). The use of the relaxation response with patients during femoral arteriograms. *Dissertation Abstracts International, 49*(12), 5563B.

Maranto, C. D. (1989a). *Performance anxiety: A meta-analysis of experimental research and clinical implications.* Paper presented at the Seventh Annual Symposium on Medical Problems of Musicians and Dancers, Snowmass, CO.

Maranto, C. D. (1989b). *The use of music therapy in the treatment of performance anxiety in musicians.* Paper presented at the IV International MusicMedicine Symposium, Rancho Mirage, CA.

Maranto, C. D. (1991). A classification model for music and medicine. In C. D. Maranto (Ed.) *Applications of music in medicine* (pp. 1–6). Washington, DC: National Association for Music Therapy.

Maranto, C. D. (1992a). A comprehensive definition of music therapy with an integrative model for music medicine. In R. Spintge & R. Droh (Eds.), *MusicMedicine* (pp. 19–29). St. Louis: MMB Music.

Maranto, C. D. (1992b). The use of music therapy in the treatment of performance anxiety in musicians. In R. Spintge & R. Droh (Eds.), *MusicMedicine* (pp. 273–283). St. Louis: MMB Music.

Maranto, C. D., & Bruscia, K. E. (Eds.). (1987). *Perspectives on music therapy education and training.* Philadelphia: Esther Boyer College of Music, Temple University.

Maranto, C. D., & Bruscia, K. E. (1988). *Methods of teaching and training the music therapist.* Philadelphia: Esther Boyer College of Music, Temple University.

Maranto, C. D., & Bruscia, K. E. (Eds.). (1989). *Master's theses in music therapy: Index and abstracts.* Philadelphia: Esther Boyer College of Music, Temple University.

Maranto, C. D., & Murphy, K. (1991). *The influence of music desensitization and biofeedback on performance, anxiety in musicians.* Unpublished manuscript, Temple University.

Maranto, C. D., & Scartelli, J. (1992). Music in the treatment of immune-related disorders. In R. Spintge & R. Droh (Eds.), *MusicMedicine* (pp. 142–154). St. Louis: MMB Music.

Marley, L. S. (1984). The use of music with hospitalized infants and toddlers: A descriptive study. *Journal of Music Therapy, 21,* 126–132.

Martin, M. (1987). *The influence of combining preferred music with progressive relaxation and biofeedback techniques on frontalis muscle.* Unpublished master's thesis, Southern Methodist University.

McCarthy, J. F. (1969). Accuracy of recognition for verbal and tonal stimuli presented to the left and right ears. *Bulletin of the Council for Research in Music Education, 16,* 18.

McDowell, C. R. (1964). Obstetrical applications of audioanalgesia. *Hospital Topics, 44,* 102–104.

McElwain, J. M. (1974). *Effect of music stimuli and music chosen by subjects on the production of alpha brainwave rhythms.* Unpublished master's thesis, Florida State University.

McFarland, R. A. (1985). Relationship of skin temperature changes to the emotions accompanying music. *Biofeedback and Self-Regulation, 10*(3), 255–267.

McKinney, C. H. (1990). The effect of music on imagery. *Journal of Music Therapy, 27,* 34–46.

Metera, A., & Metera, A. (1975). Influence of music on the minute oxygen consumption and basal metabolic rate. *Anaesthiology, Resuscitation, and Intensive Therapy, 3,* 259–264.

Metera, A., Metera, A., & Warwas, I. (1975). Effect of music on airway resistance in patients. *Anaesthiology, Resuscitation, and Intensive Therapy, 3,* 265–269.

Metzler, R., & Berman, T. (1991). The effects of sedative music on the anxiety of bronchoscopy patients. In C. D. Maranto (Ed.), *Applications of music in medicine* (pp. 163–178). Washington, DC: National Association for Music Therapy.

Michel, D. E. (1952). *Effects of stimulative and sedative music on respiration and psychogalvanic reflex as observed in seventh grade students.* Unpublished manuscript, University of Kansas.

Miles, J. R., & Tilly, C. R. (1935). Some psychological reactions to music. *Guy's Hospital Gazette, 39,* 319–322.

Miller, R. K., & Bornstein, P. H. (1977). Thirty-minute relaxation: A comparison of some methods. *Journal of Behavior Therapy and Experimental Psychiatry, 8,* 291–294.

Misbach, L. E. (1932). Effect of pitch on tone-stimuli upon body resistance and cardiovascular phenomena. *Journal of Experimental Psychology, 15,* 167–183.

Mitkov, V., Moldovanska, P., & Roglev, M. (1981). The effect of music on brain electrical activity and hemodynamics and on some vegetative parameters. *Folia Medica, 23,* 41–46.

Monsey, H. L. (1960). Preliminary report of the clinical efficacy of audio-analgesia. *Journal of the California State Dental Association, 36,* 432–437.

Montello, L. (1989). Utilizing music therapy as a mode of treatment for the performance stress of professional musicians. *Dissertation Abstracts International, 50*(10), 3175A.

Morris, R. E. (1985). The effect of music on hypnotic induction. *Dissertation Abstracts International, 47*(3), 1280B.

Morosko, T. E., & Simmons, F. F. (1966) The effect of audioanalgesia on pain threshold and pain tolerance. *Journal of Dental Research, 45,* 1608–1617.

Moss, V. A. (1988). Music and the surgical patient. *AORN Journal, 43*(1), 64–69.

Mowatt, K. S. (1967). Background music during radiotherapy. *Medical Journal of Australia, 1,* 165–171.

Orton, M. R. (1953). *Application of the iso-moodic principle in the use of music with psychotic and "normal" subjects.* Unpublished master's thesis, University of Kansas.

Oyama, T. (1983). *Endocrinology and the anaesthetist.* Amsterdam: Elsevier.

Oyama, T., Hatano, K., Sato, Y., Kudo, M., Spintge, R., & Droh, R. (1983). Endocrine effects of anxiolytic music in dental patients. In R. Droh & R. Spintge (Eds.), *Angst, schmerz, muzik in der anesthesie* (pp. 143–146). Grenzach: Editiones Roche.

Oyama, T., Sato, Y., Kudo, T., Spintge, R., & Droh, R. (1983). Effect of anxiolytic music on endocrine function in surgical patients. In R. Droh & R. Spintge (Eds.) *Angst, schmerz, muzik in der anesthesie* (pp. 147–152). Grenzach: Editiones Roche.

Page, F. (1991). *Self vs. therapist-selected music for reducing stress in musicians.* Unpublished research, Temple University.

Paley, B. E. (1991). The effects of rhythm, tempo, syncopation, and tonality on EEG asymmetry and subjective responses in musicians and nonmusicians. *Dissertation Abstracts International, 15*(12), 3981B.

Patterson, C. H. (1959). *An experimental study of the effect of soothing background music on observed behavior indicating tension of third grade pupils.* Unpublished doctoral dissertation, University of Virginia.

Peach, S. C. (1984). Some implications for the clinical use of music facilitated imagery. *Journal of Music Therapy, 21,* 27–34.

Peretti, P. O. (1975). Changes in galvanic skin response as affected by musical selection, sex, and academic discipline. *Journal of Psychology, 89,* 183–187.

Peretti, P. O., & Swenson, K. (1974). Effects of music on anxiety as determined by physio.ogical skin response. *Journal of Research in Music Education, 25,* 211–221.

Peretti, P. O., & Zweifel, J. (1983). Affect of musical preference on anxiety as determined by physiological skin responses. *Acta Psychiatrica Belgica, 83,* 437–442.

Pignatiello, M. F., Camp, C. J., & Rasar, L. (1986). Musical mood induction: An alternative to the Velten technique. *Journal of Abnormal Psychology, 95,* 295–297.

Plutchic, R. (1959). The effects of high intensity intermittent sound on performance, feeling and physiology. *Psychological Bulletin, 56,* 113–151.

Poole, R., Goetyinger, C. P., & Rousey, C. L. (1966). A study of the effects of auditory stimulation on respiration. *Acta Otolaryngologica, 61,* 141–152.

Pratt, R. R., & Jones, R. W. (1987). Music and medicine: A partnership in history. In R. Spintge & R. Droh (Eds.), *Music in medicine* (pp. 377–388). Berlin: Springer-Verlag.

Putnam, R. F. (1984). The utilization of EMG biofeedback to teach relaxation skills with moderately and severely mentally retarded subjects. *Dissertation Abstracts International, 46*(8), 2267A.

Quittner, A. L. (1980). *The facilitative effects of music on visual imagery: A multiple measures approach.* Unpublished master's thesis, Florida State University.

Reese, J. T. (1987). Effects of a selected stress reduction exercise on ability to relax in preschool children. *Dissertation Abstracts International, 48*(8), 2027A.

Reynolds, S. B. (1984). Biofeedback, relaxation training and music: Homeostasis for coping with stress. *Biofeedback and Self-Regulation, 9*(2), 169–179.

Rider, M. S. (1988). Effect of cell-specific, music-mediated mental imagery on secretory immunoglobulin A (IgA). *Dissertation Abstracts International, 49*(10), 4598B.

Rider, M. S., & Achterburg, J. (1989). The effect of music-mediated imagery on neutrophils and lymphocytes. *Biofeedback and Self-Regulation, 14*(3), 247–257.

Rider, M. S., Achterburg, J., Lawlis, G. F., Goven, A., Toledo, R., & Butler, J. R. (1990). Effect of biological imagery on antibody production and health. *Biofeedback and Self-Regulation, 15,* 317–333.

Rider, M. S., Floyd, J. W., & Kirkpatrick, J. (1985). The effect of music, imagery and relaxation on adrenal corticosteroids and the re-entrainment of circadian rhythms. *Journal of Music Therapy, 22,* 46–58.

Rider, M. S., Mickey, C., Weldin, C., & Hawkinson, R. (1991). The effects of toning, listening and singing on psychophysiological responses. In C. D. Maranto (Ed.), *Applications of music in medicine.* Washington, DC: National Association for Music Therapy.

Rider, M. S., & Weldin, C. (1990). Imagery, improvisation and immunity. *The Arts in Psychotherapy, 17,* 211–216.

Ries, H. A. (1969). GSR and breathing amplitude related to emotional reactions to music. *Psychonomic Science, 14,* 62–64.

Roederer, J. (1975). *Introduction to the physics and psychophysics of music* (2nd ed.). New York: Springer-Verlag.

Rohner, S. J., & Miller, R. (1980). Degrees of familiar and affective music and their effects on anxiety states. *Journal of Music Therapy, 17,* 2–15.

Roter, M. (1957). *The use of music in medical reception rooms.* Unpublished master's thesis, University of Kansas.

Ruiz, O. (1989). Effect of music on heart rate. In C. D. Maranto & K. Bruscia (Eds.), *Master's theses in music therapy: Index and abstracts* (p. 102). Philadelphia: Esther Boyer College of Music, Temple University. (Original work published 1979)

Russell, L. A. (1987). Comparisons of cognitive, music and imagery techniques on anxiety reduction. *Dissertation Abstracts International, 48*(8), 1990A.

Sanderson, B. (1986). *The effect of music on reducing preoperative anxiety and postoperative anxiety and pain in the recovery room.* Unpublished master's thesis, Florida State University.

Saperston, B. M. (1989). Music-based individualized relaxation training (MBIRT): A stress-reduction approach for the behaviorally disturbed mentally retarded. *Music Therapy Perspectives, 6,* 26–33.

Scartelli, J. P. (1982). The effect of sedative music on electromyographic feedback assisted relaxation training of spastic cerebral palsied adults. *Journal of Music Therapy, 19,* 210–218.

Scartelli, J. P. (1984). The effect of EMG biofeedback and sedative music, EMG biofeedback only, and sedative music only on frontalis muscle relaxation. *Journal of Music Therapy, 21,* 67–78.

Scartelli, J. P. (1989). *Music and self-management methods: A physiological model.* St. Louis: MMB Music.

Scartelli, J. P., & Borling, J. E. (1986). The effects of sequenced versus simultaneous EMG biofeedback and sedative music on frontalis relaxation training. *Journal of Music Therapy, 23,* 157–165.

Schachter, S. (1957). Pain, fear, and anger in hypertensive and nonhypertensives. *Psychosomatic Medicine, 19,* 17–29.

Schachter, S. (1964). The interaction of cognitive and physiologic determinants of emotional states. *Advances in Experimental Social Psychology, 1,* 49–80.

Schieffelin, C. (1988, April). *A case study: Stevens–Johnson syndrome.* Paper presented at the annual conference of the Southeastern Association for Music Therapy, Tallahassee, FL.

Schur, J. M. (1986). Alleviating behavioral distress with music or Lamaze pant–blow breathing in children undergoing bone marrow aspirations and lumbar punctures. *Dissertation Abstracts International, 48*(3), 889B.

Schuster, B. L. (1985). The effect of music listening on blood pressure fluctuations in adult hemodialysis patients. *Journal of Music Therapy, 22,* 146–153.

Sears, M. (1954). *Study of the vascular changes in the capillaries as effected by music.* Unpublished master's thesis, University of Kansas.

Sears, W. W. (1952). Postural responses to recorded music. In E. G. Gilliland (Ed.), *Music therapy, 1951* (pp. 197–198). Chicago: Allen Press.

Sears, W. W. (1957). The effect of music on muscle tonus. In E. T. Gaston (Ed.), *Music therapy, 1957* (pp. 199–205). Lawrence, KS: Allen Press.

Sears, W. W. (1960). *A study of some effects of music upon muscle tension as evidence by electromyographic recordings.* Unpublished doctoral dissertation, University of Kansas.

Sedei, C. A. (1980). The effectiveness of music therapy on specific statements verbalized by cancer patients. Unpublished master's thesis, Colorado State University.

Shapiro, A. G., & Cohen, H. (1983). Auxiliary pain relief during suction curettage. In R. Droh & R. Spintge (Eds.) *Angst, schmerz, muzik in der anesthesie* (pp. 89–93). Basel: Editiones Roches.

Shatin, L. (1957). The influence of rhythmic drumbeat stimuli upon the pulse rate and general activity of long term schizophrenics. *Journal of Mental Science, 103,* 172–188.

Shatin, L. (1970). Alteration of mood via music: A study of the vectoring effect. *Journal of Psychology, 75,* 81–86.

Shrift, D. C. (1955). Galvanic skin responses to two types of music. *Bulletin of the National Association for Music Therapy, 10,* 5–6.

Siegel, S. L. (1983). *The use of music as a treatment in pain perception with post-surgical patients in a pediatric hospital.* Unpublished master's thesis, University of Miami.

Sime, W. E., & DeGood, D. E. (1977). Effect of EMG biofeedback and progressive muscle relaxation training on awareness of frontalis muscle tension. *Psychophysiology, 14,* 522–530.

Sisson, R. W. (1981). The effect of three relaxation procedures on tension reduction and subsequent drinking of inpatient alcoholics. *Dissertation Abstracts International, 42*(5), 2085B.

Skille, O. (1987a). The music bath: Possible uses as an axiolytic. In R. Spintge & R. Droh (Eds.), *Music in medicine* (pp. 253–256). Berlin: Springer-Verlag.

Skille, O. (1987b). Low frequency sound massage—the music bath: A follow-up report. In R. Spintge & R. Droh (Eds.), *Music in medicine* (pp. 257–260). Berlin: Springer-Verlag.

Skille, O. (1989). Vibroacoustic therapy. *Music Therapy, 8*(1), 61–77.

Slaughter, F. (1954). *The effect of stimulative and sedative types of music on normal and abnormal subjects as indicated by auxiliary reflexes.* Unpublished master's thesis, University of Kansas.

Smith, C. A., & Morris, L. W. (1976). Effects of stimulative and sedative music on cognitive and emotional components of anxiety. *Psychological Reports, 38,* 1187–1193.

Smith, C. A., & Morris, L. W. (1977). Differential effects of sedative and stimulative music on anxiety, concentration, and performance. *Psychological Reports, 41,* 1047–1053.

Sopchak, A. L. (1955). Individual differences in responses to music. *Psychological Monographs, 69*(11), 1–20.

Spaulding, S. (1989). The effects of vocal music and drumbeat rhythms varied by pitch, tempo, and volume on respiratory and cardiac responses of premature infants. In C. D. Maranto & K. Bruscia (Eds.), *Master's theses in music therapy: Index and abstracts* (p. 112). Philadelphia: Esther Boyer College of Music, Temple University. (Original work published 1977)

Spintge, R. (1983). Psychophysiological surgery preparation with and without anxiolytic music. In R. Droh & R. Spintge (Eds.), *Angst, schmerz, muzik in der anesthesie* (pp. 77–88). Grenzach: Editiones Roche.

Spintge, R. (1991). The neurophysiology of emotion and its therapeutic applications in music therapy and music medicine. In C. D. Maranto (Ed.), *Applications of music in medicine* (pp. 59–72). Washington, DC: National Association for Music Therapy.

Spintge, R., & Droh, R. (1988). Ergonomic approach to treatment of patients' perioperative stress. *Canadian Journal of Anesthesia, 35*, S104–S106.

Standley, J. M. (1986). Music research in medical/dental treatment: Meta-analysis and clinical implications. *Journal of Music Therapy, 23*(2), 50–55.

Stanton, H. E. (1973). The effects of music on test anxiety. *Australian Psychology, 8*, 220–228.

Stein, A. M. (1991). Music to reduce anxiety during cesarean births. In C. D. Maranto (Ed.), *Applications of music in medicine* (pp. 179–190). Washington, DC: National Association for Music Therapy, Inc.

Steinke, W. (1991). The use of music, relaxation and imagery in the management of postsurgical pain for scoliosis. In C. Maranto (Ed.), *Applications of music in medicine* (pp. 141–162). Washington, DC: National Association for Music Therapy.

Stevens, E. A. (1971). Some effects of tempo changes on stereotyped rocking movements of low-level mentally retarded subjects. *American Journal of Mental Deficiency, 76*, 76–81.

St. Joseph's Hospital. (1972). In this intensive care unit, the downbeat helps the heartbeats. *Modern Hospital, 118*, 91.

Straseske, C. A. (1988). Musically induced moods: Effects on judgments of self-efficacy. *Dissertation Abstracts International, 50*(1), 355B.

Stratton, V. N., & Zalanowski, A. H. (1984). The relationship between music, degree of liking, and self-reported relaxation. *Journal of Music Therapy, 21*, 184–192.

Stoudenmire, J. (1975). A comparison of muscle relaxation training and music in the reduction of state and trait anxiety. *Journal of Clinical Psychology, 31*, 490–492.

Summer, L. (1983). *The use of music as a catalyst for involvement in imagery.* Unpublished master's thesis, Hahnemann University.

Tanioka, F., Takazawa, T., Kamata, S., Kudo, M., Matsuki, A., & Oyama, T. (1983). Hormonal effects of anxiolytic music in patients during surgical operations under epidural anesthesia. In R. Droh & R. Spintge (Eds.), *Angst, schmerz, muzik in der anesthesie* (pp. 285–290). Grenzach: Editiones Roche.

Taylor, D. (1973). Subjective responses to precategorized stimulative and sedative music. *Journal of Music Therapy, 10*, 86–94.

Thaut, M. H. (1989a). Physiological responses to musical stimuli. In R. Unkefer (Ed.), *Music therapy in the treatment of adults with mental disorders.* New York: Schirmer Books.

Thaut, M. H. (1989b). The influence of music therapy interventions on self-rated changes in relaxation, affect and thought in psychiatric prisoner–patients. *Journal of Music Therapy, 26*, 155–166.

Trenes, N. E. (1937). Study of the effects of music on cancer patients. *Hospital Social Service, 16*, 131.

Tsao, C. C., Gordon, T. F., Maranto, C. D., Lerman, C., & Murasko, D. (1991). The effects of music and directed biological imagery on immune response (S-IgA). In C. D. Maranto (Ed.), *Applications of music in medicine* (pp. 85–121). Washington, DC: National Association for Music Therapy.

Unkefer, R. F. (1952). The effect of music in insulin-coma therapy. In E. G. Gilliland (Ed.), *Music therapy, 1951.* Chicago: Allen Press.

Updike, P. A., & Charles, D. M. (1987). Music Rx: Physiological and emotional responses to taped music programs of preoperative patients awaiting plastic surgery. *Annals of Plastic Surgery, 19*, 29–33.

Van Fleet, J. N. (1986). The effect of autogenic training phrases and progressive relaxation phrases on cognitive and somatic anxiety. *Dissertation Abstracts International, 47*(8), 3506B.

Vaughn, S. J. (1989). A comparison of modified anxiety management with music versus modified anxiety management training without music on academic achievement, self-esteem and state anxiety of high school students. *Dissertation Abstracts International, 50*(7), 1950A.

Vincent, S., & Thompson, J. H. (1929). The effects of music upon the human blood pressure. *Lancet, i*, 534–537.

Wagner, M. J. (1975a). Effect of music and biofeedback on alpha brain wave rhythms and attentiveness. *Journal of Research in Music Education, 23*, 3–13.

Wagner, M. J. (1975b). The effect of music stimuli and biofeedback on the production of alpha brainwave rhythms and verbal reports of musicians and nonmusicians. Reviewed by S. Hedden. *Council for Research in Music Education, 41,* 1–10.

Wagner, M. J., & Manzel, M. B. (1977). The effect of music listening and attentiveness training on the EEG's of musicians and nonmusicians. *Journal of Music Therapy, 14,* 151–164.

Walker, J. L. (1977). Subjective reactions to music and brainwave rhythms. *Physiological Psychology, 5*(4), 483–489.

Walther-Larsen, S., Diemar, V., & Valentin, N. (1988). Music during regional anesthesia: A reduced need of sedatives. *Regional Anesthesia, 13,* 69–71.

Wascho, A. (1948). The effects of music on pulse rate, blood pressure, and mental imagery. In D. Soibelman (Ed.), *Therapeutic and industrial uses of music.* New York: Columbia University Press.

Webster, C. (1973). Relaxation, music and cardiology: The physiological and psychological consequences of their interrelation. *Australian Occupational Therapy Journal, 20,* 9–20.

Wechsler, D. (1925). The measurement of emotional reactions. Researches on the psychogalvanic reflex. *Archives of Psychology, 76,* 1–181.

Weidenfeller, E. W., & Zimny, G. H. (1962). Effects of music upon GSR of depressives and schizophrenics. *Journal of Abnormal Social Psychology, 64,* 307–312.

Weld, H. P. (1912). An experimental study of musical enjoyment. *American Journal of Psychology, 2,* 245–308.

Wheeler, B. L. (1985). Relationship of personal characteristics to mood and enjoyment after hearing live and recorded music and to musical taste. *Psychology of Music, 13,* 81–92.

Wilson, C. V., & Aiken, L. S. (1977). The effect of intensity levels upon physiological and subjective affective response to music. *Journal of Music Therapy, 13,* 60–76.

Wilson, V. M. (1989). Variations in gastric motility due to musical stimuli. In C. D. Maranto & K. Bruscia (Eds.), *Master's theses in music therapy: Index and abstracts* (p. 128). Philadelphia: Esther Boyer College of Music, Temple University. (Original work published 1957)

Winokur, M. A. (1984). *The use of music as an audio-analgesia during childbirth.* Unpublished master's thesis, Florida State University.

Winslow, G. A. (1986). Music therapy in the treatment of anxiety in hospitalized high-risk mothers. *Music Therapy Perspectives, 3,* 29–33.

Yulis, S., Brahm, G., Charnes, G., Jacard, L. M., Picota, E., & Rutman, F. (1975). The extinction of phobic behaviour as a function of attention shifts. *Behaviour Research and Therapy, 13*(2–3), 173–176.

Zimny, G. H., & Weidenfeller, E. W. (1963). Effects of music upon GSR and heart rate. *American Journal of Psychology, 76,* 311–314.

14

The Use of Aerobic Exercise as a Method of Stress Management

ROGER B. FILLINGIM
JAMES A. BLUMENTHAL

Exercise has become an increasingly popular leisure-time activity in recent years, perhaps largely because of its potential health benefits, such as improved weight control and reduced risk of cardiovascular disease. In addition, there has been considerable interest in the potential psychological benefits of physical activity. Anecdotally, many individuals report "feeling better" following physical activity, and many health care professionals recommend exercise as a stress management technique. However, anecdotal data alone do not justify promoting exercise as a method of psychological health enhancement.

In considering the value of exercise, a basic understanding of the physiology of exercise may be useful. There are two fundamental kinds of exercise, which are defined on the basis of how the energy sources used to perform muscle contractions are derived. Energy is released when either adenosine triphosphate (ATP) or creatine phosphate (CP) is broken down within the cell. The available stores of ATP are limited, and the effects of ATP are transient; consequently, ATP must be constantly resynthesized within working skeletal muscles in order for the muscles to perform continuously. To sustain exercise, ATP is synthesized aerobically, primarily from carbohydrates and fats (i.e., via the Krebs cycle). When sufficient oxygen is available, oxygen is combined with hydrogen ions to form water and carbon dioxide, and thus a higher yield of ATP. In contrast, when not enough oxygen is available, hydrogen accumulates and blocks the aerobic cycle, so that the cells must rely on anaerobic metabolism for energy. "Aerobic exercise" refers to the repetitive movement of large muscle groups in which the energy is derived from aerobic metabolism. Activities such as walking, biking, swimming, and jogging are considered aerobic exercises. "Anaerobic exercise" utilizes anaerobic metabolism for energy, and includes activities such as weight lifting. The cardiovascular adjustments to aerobic exercise, referred to as the "training effect," result from participation in aerobic activities over an extended period of time. Indeed, most studies have focused on the effects of chronic exercise (i.e., exercise performed for 8 to 12 weeks). The effects of acute exercise (i.e., a single "bout" or exercise session) have also been studied, but to a lesser extent.

With regard to the psychological effects of exercise, many investigators have reported that both acute exercise and chronic exercise lead to mood improvements, such as decreased anxiety and depression and increased feelings of vigor (e.g., Blumenthal, Williams, Needels, & Wallace, 1982; Boutcher & Landers, 1989; Emery & Blumenthal, 1988; Moses, Steptoe, Matthews, & Edwards, 1989; Roth & Holmes, 1987; Steptoe, Edwards, Moses, & Matthews, 1989). A related line of research has examined the effects of exercise on individuals' responses to stress (Crews & Landers, 1987; Fillingim & Blumenthal, 1992). In this chapter we review the effects of exercise on mood, and examine the relationship of both chronic and acute physical exercise to subjective and psychophysiological stress responses. A number of theoretical and methodological issues that are relevant for research in this area are discussed first. Then research concerning the potentially stress-reducing effects of aerobic fitness and acute and chronic exercise on anxiety, depression, and stress responses is reviewed. Next, guidelines for establishing and maintaining an aerobic exercise regimen are presented, along with a case report illustrating these principles. Lastly, a summary of this area with an emphasis on directions for future research is presented.

Theoretical Issues

Theoretical formulation in this area of research remains in the preliminary stages. The primary rationale for examining the effects of exercise and stress responses stemmed from the fact that improved physical fitness (i.e., exercise) reduces autonomically mediated cardiovascular responses to physical stress; therefore, it was hypothesized that responses to psychosocial stress might likewise be reduced (Shulhan, Scher, & Furedy, 1986). Consistent with this hypothesis are findings that exercise training reduces plasma norepinephrine concentrations (Duncan, Farr, Upton, Hagan, & Oglesby, 1985; Meredith et al., 1990). Relatedly, decreased adrenergic responses to stressful laboratory tasks following one session or "bout" of exercise (Peronnet, Massicotte, Paquee, Brisson, & de Champlain, 1989) and down-regulation of beta-adrenergic receptors following a single exercise session (Friedman, Ordway, & Williams, 1987) have been reported. Thus, there is indirect support of the hypothesis that exercise reduces responses to stress by altering autonomic sensitivity; however, more direct evidence for reduced sympathetic activity underlying the effects of exercise on stress responses is lacking.

Methodological Issues

Because research in this area spans several disciplines (e.g., exercise physiology, psychophysiology, and psychological stress research), it is particularly important to attend to methodological issues when considering this body of work. The experimental design used is an important factor, and two basic experimental designs, cross-sectional and longitudinal, have been used. Correlational designs typically assess aerobic fitness and stress responses concurrently, and examine the relationship of the two. A cross-sectional study typically identifies groups of fit and unfit subjects and compares the stress responses of the two groups. Correlational designs are easier to conduct but do not permit causal inferences, whereas longitudinal designs are more time-consuming but often do permit causal conclusions. Another important design issue is choice of control conditions. It is important that a control condition be matched fairly closely to the experimental condition (i.e., exercise) on nonspecific variables, such as subject expectations, presence of social support, demand characteristics, and experimenter contact.

Accurate assessment of aerobic fitness is also an important methodological issue, because fitness is used as an independent variable in correlational designs, and assessment of aerobic capacity is critical for evaluating the effect of exercise training in longitudinal studies. Many methods are available, including questionnaires, as well as submaximal and maximal exercise testing. Ideally, a multistage maximal exercise test on a treadmill or cycle ergometer, with direct measurements of oxygen consumption ($\dot{V}O_2$), is performed to provide the most accurate measure of aerobic fitness. This must be done under adequate medical supervision, and the American College of Sports Medicine (ACSM) guidelines for exercise testing should be followed (ACSM, 1986). After assessment of aerobic fitness, the exercise training is an important part of research in this area. Exercise programs can vary along a number of dimensions, including the type, intensity, duration, and frequency of the exercise regimen, all of which can affect the subsequent stress responses. Aerobic exercise programs are the most widely used in this field, and guidelines for establishing such programs are briefly discussed later.

Compliance is another important factor in exercise research. Aerobic exercise training requires a significant commitment of time, and dropout rates are typically high (Dishman, 1982). Such strategies as goal setting and use of distraction or dissociation during exercise may improve compliance (Martin & Dubbert, 1987). These authors also suggest that the exercise program (1) be convenient, (2) use group exercise formats, (3) use a participant/supervisor, (4) emphasize individual responsibility for exercise, (5) reinforce the exercise habit, (6) use generalization training, and (7) use continued feedback and testing.

The potential adverse effects of exercise, including orthopedic injury, major cardiac events, and other risks for individuals with pre-existing medical conditions such as diabetes or asthma, must be considered when conducting exercise research (Haskell, 1984). Although exercise is widely believed to be beneficial, it should also be emphasized that the value of exercise is not universally accepted. In an editorial in a publication of the ACSM, John Holloszy (1983) noted:

> If it were necessary to obtain approval from the Food and Drug Administration for the use of strenuous exercise in health maintenance and if approval were based on the same criteria used by the FDA for a new drug, i.e. proof of efficacy and extensive evidence that it does not cause cancer or other harmful effects, it seems unlikely that approval for the use of exercise could be granted on the basis of currently available information. (p. 2)

Although the risks of exercise cannot be entirely eliminated, they can be controlled through proper medical screening of high-risk patients, adequate supervision, and appropriate guidelines for exercise training.

Research in this area has also focused on modification of stress responses. The selection of stressors is another important methodological issue that can affect results. The stressor must elicit a robust subjective and/or psychophysiological response pattern that is measurable and modifiable. The most common stressors in this area of research have been mental arithmetic (e.g., Blumenthal, Emery, et al., 1988; Blumenthal et al., 1990), various cognitive tasks such as the Stroop test (e.g., Holmes & Roth, 1987; Hull, Young, & Ziegler, 1984; Sinyor, Golden, Steinert, & Seraganian, 1986), public speaking (Blumenthal et al., 1991), and the cold-pressor test (Blumenthal et al., 1991). Optimally, a battery of behavioral stressors, perhaps varying along important dimensions such as intensity or active–passive coping, may be useful to evaluate the generality of changes in stress reactivity and to help identify the most effective and valid laboratory stressors (e.g., Hull et al., 1984; Light, Obrist, James, & Strogatz, 1987; Peronnet et al., 1989; Roskies et al., 1986).

Another important methodological issue concerns the dependent measure used to assess mood and/or stress response. The choice of dependent measures should be based on both practical and conceptual considerations. When one is measuring the physiological stress response, the nature of the stressor is important, since different stressful tasks elicit different physiological response patterns (Allen, Obrist, Sherwood, & Crowell, 1987; Sherwood, Allen, Obrist, & Langer, 1986). Because of their ease of measurement, heart rate and blood pressure are the most commonly employed dependent variables. In some studies, these measures have been found to be sensitive to fitness-related differences in stress reactivity; however, they offer relatively little information regarding the mechanisms underlying such differences. Thus, if a study aims to clarify mechanisms for decreased stress responses, more specific measures (such as circulating catecholamines and other factors) may need to be considered (see De Geus, Van Doornen, De Visser, & Orlebeke, 1990; Van Doornen & De Geus, 1989). In addition, assessing subjective and behavioral responses to stress is often overlooked, but can provide information not reflected in physiological indices. Subjective mood should be assessed by means of psychometrically sound instruments that are sensitive to short-term changes in emotional response.

Cross-Sectional Studies of Physical Fitness and Stress Responses

Several studies have examined differences in stress responses among subjects who differ in physical fitness. Holmes and Roth (1985) assessed the aerobic fitness of 72 females by means of a submaximal cycle ergometer test, and compared the heart rate and subjective arousal responses to a memory test of the 10 least and 10 most fit subjects. It was found that the most fit subjects showed a smaller increase in heart rate during the memory task than the least fit subjects, but that fitness had no effect on subjective response. Other studies have reported similar results. One study found that diastolic blood pressure responses to a cognitive task were smaller for fit subjects over 40 years of age than for their same-age unfit counterparts (Hull et al., 1984). These authors also reported less subjective anger and depression in fit subjects following an unpleasant film. Light et al. (1987) categorized subjects on the basis of self-reported exercise habits and found that cardiovascular reactivity (pre-ejection period, heart rate, and systolic blood pressure) to a reaction time task was greater in subjects reporting lower levels of exercise. Relatedly, Van Doornen and de Geus (1989) reported that highly fit subjects (as determined by a maximal exercise test) showed smaller increases in heart rate, diastolic blood pressure, and total peripheral resistance than low-fitness subjects during a reaction time task.

It has also been found that aerobically fit borderline hypertensives tend to show smaller increases in systolic and diastolic blood pressure than their unfit counterparts (Perkins, Dubbert, Martin, Faulstich, & Harris, 1986). In another study (Shulhan et al., 1986), low-fitness subjects showed greater T-wave amplitude attenuation than highly fit subjects during mental arithmetic, but no differences in heart rate response emerged. Sothmann, Horn, Hart, and Gustafson (1987) reported decreased plasma norepinephrine in fit subjects following stress, but no differences in self-reported mood. A recent study found decreased diastolic blood pressure reactivity to stress in highly fit subjects, and the authors attributed some of the decreased reactivity to differences in anger between the two groups (Czajkowski et al., 1990). These cross-sectional findings suggest that aerobic fitness reduces psychophysiological responses to stress. However, only one study assessed fitness with a maximal exercise test (Van Doornen & De Geus, 1989), and the physiological measures used varied quite widely; therefore, it is difficult to compare findings across studies. In addition, no causal conclusion is warranted on the basis of these cross-sectional studies.

Other cross-sectional research has only partially supported these results. For example, some investigators have reported that while aerobic fitness was not related to decreased psychophysiological reactivity during stress, highly fit subjects showed more rapid physiological recovery from stress than did low-fitness subjects (Cox, Evans, & Jamieson, 1979; Holmes & Cappo, 1987; Sinyor, Schwartz, Peronnet, Brisson, & Seraganian, 1983). In addition, Sinyor et al. (1983) reported lower state anxiety in physically fit subjects following mental stress. Furthermore, Plante and Karpowitz (1987) reported that although subjects who reported more exercise showed less cardiovascular reactivity (i.e., lower heart rate and pulse volume) than low-exercise subjects, there were no differences during stress or recovery when baseline differences were controlled. One study actually reported that aerobic fitness was associated with greater blood pressure reactivity during a competitive game; however, these subjects were Type A college athletes as opposed to regular college students, and their high level of competitiveness rather than their fitness level may have affected the results (Lake, Suarez, Schneiderman, & Tocci, 1985).

Longitudinal Studies of Physical Fitness and Cardiovascular Reactivity

Although much of the early research in this area was correlational, more recent studies have employed longitudinal designs with random assignment of subjects to exercise training programs, in order to manipulate levels of aerobic fitness. Table 14.1 summarizes the major methodological aspects and the results of these studies.

TABLE 14.1. Summary of Longitudinal Studies of Aerobic Exercise and Cardiovascular Reactivity

Study	Subjects	Control condition	Exercise training	Fitness test	Stressor(s)[b]	Significant effects[a]
Blumenthal, Emery, et al. (1988)	36 Type A men (age 44.4)	Strength training	3 times/week, 12 weeks	Maximal treadmill	MAT[b]	RCV: HR, SBP, RPP LL: SBP, DBP, HR, RPP SP: HR, RPP
Blumenthal et al. (1990)	37 Type A men (age 42)	Strength training	3 times/week, 12 weeks	Maximal treadmill	MAT	LL: HR, DBP, RPP SP: SBP, DBP, HR, RPP
Blumenthal et al. (1991)	46 women (age 50)	Strength training	3 times/week	Maximal treadmill	Speech, cold-pressor task	NS
De Geus et al. (1990)	26 men (ages 18–28)	Waiting list	4 times/week	Maximal cycle ergo.	Memory, tone avoidance	NS
Holmes & McGilley (1987)[c]	67 women (ages 17–20)	Psychology class	2 times/week, 13 weeks	Submax. walk/run	Digits backward	SP: HR (Low-fitness subjects only)
Holmes & Roth (1987)	49 students (ages unknown)	Relaxation, no treatment	3 times/week, 11 weeks	Submax. treadmill	Digits backward	LL: HR
Roskies et al. (1986)	107 Type A men (age 37)	Stress management, strength training	3 times/week, 10 weeks	Unknown	MAT, Raven's matrices	NS: HR, SBP, DBP
Sherwood et al. (1989)	27 Type A men[d] (age 41.4)	Strength training	3 times/week, 12 weeks	Maximal treadmill	Competitive reaction time task	SP: DPB (border-line hypertensives)
Sinyor et al. (1986)	38 men (age 23)	Strength training, no treatment	3–4 times/week, 10 weeks	Submax. treadmill	"EKG quiz," Stroop task	NS: HR

[a]Significant effects: SP, stress period, indicates decreased reactivity in exercise group; RCV, recovery period, indicates more rapid return to baseline following stress in exercise group; LL, lower levels, indicates only lower absolute physiological activity during stress in exercise group; NS, nonsignificant. Other abbreviations: HR, heart rate; SBP, systolic blood pressure; DBP, diastolic blood pressure; RPP, rate–pressure product (an indirect measure of myocardial oxygen consumption).

[b]MAT, mental arithmetic test.

[c]Holmes & McGilley (1987) used nonrandom assignment to groups.

[d]Sherwood, Light, & Blumenthal (1989) classified subjects as normotensive or borderline hypertensive. Based on some of the same subjects as Blumenthal et al. (1988).

Three well-controlled studies have demonstrated that aerobic exercise affects stress responses. In an initial study, Blumenthal, Emery, et al. (1988) compared 12 weeks of aerobic training to nonaerobic strength training in a sample of 36 healthy Type A men. Subjects' cardiovascular reactivity to a mental arithmetic test (MAT) was assessed before and after the exercise training period. Results indicated that the aerobic group showed more rapid recovery of heart rate, systolic and diastolic blood pressure, and myocardial oxygen consumption following the MAT; there was also an attenuation of heart rate, systolic blood pressure, and myocardial oxygen consumption reactivity to the task. Using a similar experimental design in which cardiovascular and neuroendocrine responses were assessed in a new sample of 37 healthy Type A men, Blumenthal et al. (1990) reported that, compared to strength-trained subjects, aerobically trained Type A men showed reduced heart rate, diastolic blood pressure, and myocardial oxygen consumption. Epinephrine levels during recovery also tended to be lower for the aerobic group. There was no clear-cut reduction in reactivity to the MAT as a function of exercise condition, however, and Blumenthal et al. concluded that aerobic exercise training did not reduce cardiovascular and neuroendocrine *reactivity*, but that aerobic training reduced absolute *levels* of blood pressure and heart rate. In a third study based upon a subgroup of subjects from the initial cohort, Sherwood, Light, and Blumenthal (1989) showed that diastolic blood pressure responses during a competitive reaction time task were attenuated in a subgroup of Type A borderline hypertensive subjects who were aerobically conditioned.

Other studies have reported more equivocal results. For example, Holmes and McGilley (1987) found that, compared to a no-treatment control group, aerobic training decreased heart rate reactivity during a memory task for subjects who initially had low aerobic fitness, but not for subjects who were highly fit, even though fitness increased significantly in both groups. However, subjects were not randomly assigned to treatment groups. Holmes and Roth (1987) found lower absolute heart rates during a memory task in subjects who were aerobically trained versus strength-trained; however, the groups did not differ when reactivity (i.e., changes in heart rate from baseline to stress) was compared.

In addition, other studies failed to find any fitness effects. Sinyor et al. (1986) compared aerobic exercise to strength training and found no group differences in heart rate or subjective response to a series of mental tasks. Similarly, Roskies et al. (1986) compared the effects of stress management, strength training, and aerobic training in a group of healthy Type A men. The results of their 10-week program indicated that cognitive–behavioral stress management reduced behavioral reactivity, but there were no differential treatment effects on physiological reactivity to a series of mental stressors. Blumenthal et al. (1991) compared the effects of aerobic exercise training with nonaerobic strength training in a group of 46 healthy pre- and post-menopausal women. Although the results were complex, in general the data indicated that the reductions in cardiovascular or neuroendocrine responses to a public speaking task and to a cold-pressor procedure were not consistently greater for the participants in the aerobic exercise group than for the strength training group. Another recent study combined cross-sectional and longitudinal methodology and found that lower cardiovascular stress responses were related to higher initial fitness levels, but a 7-week aerobic exercise program did not reduce psychophysiological responses to stress (De Geus et al., 1990).

Although the above-described studies examined psychophysiological responses to laboratory stress, several studies by Roth and colleagues have examined whether fitness may moderate the adverse health effects of negative life events. In a correlational study, highly stressed college students who were also highly fit reported less depression than low-fitness, high-stress students (Roth & Holmes, 1985). In a related experimental study, high-stress college students who participated in an exercise program showed greater decreases in depression than those who participated in relaxation training or received no treatment (Roth & Holmes, 1987). In another study, although fitness was related to better health, fitness did not promote health by moderating the negative effects of stress (Roth, Wiebe, Fillingim, & Shay, 1989). These studies provide equivocal support for the hypothesis that fitness reduces the adverse health effects of stress.

In the research as a whole, there is some, but not universal, support for the efficacy of aerobic exercise in reducing stress reactivity. Cross-sectional studies generally support the notion that subjects who are more highly aerobically fit show smaller psychophysiological responses to laboratory stressors than do less fit subjects. Findings from the longitudinal research are inconsistent. In addition, there is some evidence that fitness modulates the adverse health effects of negative life events.

Effects of Acute Aerobic Exercise on Stress Responses

It has been suggested that many of the psychosocial benefits of chronic exercise may be attributable to the cumulative benefits of individual bouts of exercise (Haskell, 1987). Research in both humans (Raglin & Morgan, 1987) and nonhumans (Overton, Joyner, & Tipton, 1988) suggests that acute exercise reduces resting blood pressure. In this regard, a few studies have examined the effects of single sessions of aerobic exercise on subsequent cardiovascular reactivity to stress.

Several studies found that subjective and psychophysiological responses to mental tasks were not altered by single bouts of exercise (McGowan, Robertson, & Epstein, 1985; Russell, Epstein, & Erickson, 1983). However, these studies were plagued by methodological problems. For example, Russell et al. (1983) allowed only a 5-minute postexercise recovery period before assessing reactivity, and subjects' residual exercise-induced arousal probably obscured any potential reactivity changes. Also, McGowan and colleagues (1985) presented the same stressor to subjects multiple times, thus providing an opportunity for habituation; the stressor apparently was innocuous, as subjects showed very little heart rate reactivity (i.e., <5 beats per minute [bpm]), regardless of treatment condition.

In a recent well-designed study, Roth (1989) found no effect of 20 minutes of cycle ergometry on heart rate or blood pressure reactivity to a memory task. Conversely, Fillingim, Roth, and Cook (1992) reported smaller peripheral pulse volume responses to aversive emotional imagery following cycle ergometry relative to quiet rest, but no differences in subjective or facial electromyographic responses to the imagery. In addition, Peronnet and coworkers (1989) found decreased adrenergic responses to physical and mental tasks following 2 hours of cycle ergometry. The discrepancies in these studies of physiological reactivity could result from differences in the timing of postexercise tasks, since the last two experiments assessed stress reactivity while subjects remained cardiovascularly aroused from exercise; on the other hand, Roth allowed a substantial recovery period. Moreover, different psychophysiological indices were used in these studies. Roth measured heart rate and blood pressure, whereas Fillingim et al. and Peronnet et al. found differences in peripheral pulse volume and epinephrine, respectively. In fact, Peronnet et al. also assessed heart rate and blood pressure responses to the stressor, but no exercise-induced changes emerged. Thus, certain physiological variables may be more sensitive as indices of stress reactivity than others.

Effects of Exercise on Mood

In addition to its effects on physiological responses to stress, exercise has also been shown to affect subjective mood states. Initial findings were generally based on uncontrolled observations with nonrandom designs. More recent studies, however, have stronger experimental designs and greater methodological rigor; results suggest that both acute and chronic exercise may improve various mood states, particularly anxiety and depression. Several of these studies are discussed below, but for more complete reviews the interested reader is referred elsewhere (Folkins & Sime, 1981; Hughes, 1984; Plante & Rodin, 1990; Simons, Epstein, McGowan, Kupfer, & Robertson, 1985).

Several investigators have reported that single bouts of physical exercise produce anxiolytic effects. Bahrke and Morgan (1978) reported decreases in anxiety for subjects in an exercise group and those in a meditation group; however, the control subjects showed comparable anxiety reductions. In another study, psychological tension was significantly reduced by moderate and intense exercise but not by mild exercise (Farrell, Gustafson, Morgan, & Pert, 1987). On the other hand, Steptoe and Cox (1988) found increases in tension and fatigue following high-intensity exercise and positive mood changes after low-intensity exercise. In another report, swimmers showed decreases in anger, tension, depression, and confusion and an increase in vigor following exercise, whereas controls showed no changes (Berger & Owen, 1983). Boutcher and Landers (1988) found a decrease in anxiety following running in subjects who were regular runners but not in nonrunners. Conversely, Roth (1989) found decreases in anxiety and tension following stationary cycling in both active and inactive subjects.

Other studies have examined the effects of prolonged exercise training on mood. Blumenthal et al. (1982) found improvements on several measures of mood in subjects who participated in a 10-week exercise program compared to a no-treatment control group. In a random crossover design, no mood effects were reported following a 12-week exercise program (Hughes, Casal, & Leon, 1986). Lobitz, Brammell, Stoll, and Nicoli (1983) found that a 7-week exercise program produced decreases in state anxiety, while anxiety management training produced decreases on both state and trait measures. Goldwater and Collins (1985) reported significant improvements in anxiety and well-being in subjects who participated in a 6-week exercise group compared to a placebo control group. Roth and Holmes (1987) found that an exercise program produced greater reductions in depression than did relaxation training or no treatment; the antidepressant effect emerged only 5 weeks into the 11-week program. Moses et al. (1989) reported improvements in tension/anxiety and confusion immediately after a 12-week moderate exercise program, and improvements in perceived coping ability at a 3-month follow-up, but no improvements after high-intensity exercise or a placebo control condition. In a similar study of anxious adults, a 12-week program of moderate exercise was found to reduce anxiety/tension and depression significantly (Steptoe et al., 1989). Finally, King, Taylor, Haskell, and DeBusk (1989) found that a 6-month home-based aerobic conditioning program was related to improvements in perceived physical fitness and satisfaction with physical shape and weight, but did not produce significant mood changes.

The above-described studies have examined the mood effects of exercise in nonclinical subjects; however, some trials have been conducted with patient populations. Greist et al. (1979) reported decreased depression scores in individuals with mild depression, but they provided no statistical comparison of the efficacy of exercise versus psychotherapy. Doyne, Chambless, and Beutler (1983) used a multiple-baseline design to examine the effects of exercise versus placebo in four depressed women. The results indicated decreased depression following exercise but not the placebo condition. In another study, these investigators found that both aerobic and anaerobic (weight training) exercise led to decreased depression in a group of 40 women with clinical depression (Doyne et al., 1987). Fremont and Craighead (1984) found that aerobic exercise and cognitive therapy were equally effective at reducing depression in mild to moderately depressed men and women. Martinsen (1984) found greater reductions in depression for patients who participated in exercise training in addition to psychotherapy and occupational therapy, compared to patients who only had the latter two treatments but no exercise. In a more recent study, both aerobic and nonaerobic exercise treatments were found to improve anxiety in patients with diagnosed anxiety disorders, but the two treatments had no differential effects (Martinsen, Hoffart, & Solberg, 1989).

In general, these studies indicate that acute and chronic exercise both enhance mood in normal and clinical populations, but the intensity of exercise and the exercise status of the subjects may influence the results. Moreover, the aerobic benefits of exercise appear not to be entirely responsible for these effects; mood changes have occurred with nonaerobic exercise, and the mood changes following aerobic exercise often occur before any aerobic adaptation would be expected.

A variety of explanations for the mood-enhancing effects of exercise have been proposed, but none has been systematically investigated. Two major physiological explanations have been proposed: the monoamine hypothesis and the endorphin hypothesis (see Morgan, 1985). The former derives from the notion that depression is characterized by depletion of monoamine neurotransmitters such as norepinephrine and serotonin (Schildkraut, 1965; Schildkraut & Kety, 1967; Weiss, 1982), and that exercise increases circulating levels of metabolites of these transmitters in rats (Barchas & Freedman, 1963), depressed patients (Ebert, Post, & Goodwin, 1972; Post, Kotin, Goodwin, & Gordon, 1973), and nondepressed persons (Galbo, Christensen, & Holst, 1977). In addition, antidepressant medications enhance central nervous system (CNS) levels of these amines (Glowinski & Axelrod, 1964; Glowinski & Baldessarini, 1966). Therefore, exercise may exert antidepressant effects by increasing CNS monoamine activity (Ransford, 1982). This theory has intuitive appeal; however, direct empirical support is lacking, and it does not seem to account for the putative anxiolytic effects of exercise.

The endorphin hypothesis proposes that exercise releases endogenous opioid peptides, which produce a euphoric feeling. This hypothesis has also not been strongly supported. Many studies have failed to demonstrate an increase in endorphinergic activity with exercise (Farrell et al., 1987; Grossman et al., 1984; Grossman & Sutton, 1985). From a physiological perspective, changes in monoamines (Ransford, 1982) or endorphins resulting from exercise have been suggested as the mechanism for improved mood, but empirical support is lacking.

Two major psychological hypotheses of the affective benefits of exercise are the distraction hypothesis and the self-attitude hypothesis. The distraction hypothesis (Morgan, 1980, 1985) posits that exercise produces positive mood effects by providing distraction or time out from stressful stimuli. Evidence cited as supporting this theory is largely comprised of negative findings (e.g., Bahrke & Morgan, 1978; Raglin & Morgan, 1987). These are studies in which exercise was followed by decrements in anxiety, but exercise did not differ from other experimental conditions (e.g., quiet rest) in reducing reported anxiety. Such factors as statistical regression and natural reductions in anxiety upon completion of a threatening task (i.e., the experiment) can readily explain these data. At present, there is no compelling evidence to support this hypothesis.

The self-attitude hypothesis holds that the positive mood effects of exercise are results of enhanced self-esteem and self-efficacy; it has been applied more often to prolonged exercise training than to the acute effects of exercise. Training has been found to improve self-attitudes in some physically and mentally handicapped groups (see Ben-Shlomo & Short, 1983, for a review). However, in many of the studies exercise was part of an overall treatment program, which makes it difficult to determine the unique effects of exercise on self-attitudes. These authors also reported that healthy individuals do not consistently show improved self-attitudes following exercise training. In his review, Sonstroem (1984) reported that exercise has generally been found to improve self-esteem, but methodological problems preclude strong conclusions. Therefore, the self-attitude hypothesis is tenable but not well supported.

The Exercise Prescription

As mentioned earlier, most of the research discussed above has involved aerobic exercise. This form of activity involves the rhythmic, repetitive movement of large muscle groups (e.g., the arms or legs). The main criterion for aerobic exercise is that it be continuous and of sufficient intensity to elevate the heart rate to a particular level. Measurement of the amount of physical exertion associated with exercise and other forms of activity can be quantified by measuring metabolic activity. A common standard of measurement is the metabolic unit, or MET. One MET is equivalent to the resting oxygen uptake relative to the total body mass, which is generally considered 3.5 ml of oxygen per kilogram of body weight per minute. Thus, a MET level of 5 would indicate five times the energy expenditure during resting conditions.

When the individual exercises aerobically above the resting metabolic level for a period of time, a series of cardiovascular and neuroendocrine adaptations occurs; this has been termed the cardiovascular "training effect." The term refers to the ability to perform more work at a lower submaximal heart rate and to exercise for longer duration. The training effect is achieved by exercising at or above a prescribed training range for an average of 8–12 weeks.

In order to establish an exercise training range, exercise testing is typically employed. Guidelines for equipment and staffing of exercise laboratories are described in detail in the American College of Sports Medicine's publication *Guidelines for Exercise Testing and Prescription* (1986).

There are two basic exercise testing protocols that are employed in most exercise testing settings. The Bruce protocol varies both treadmill speed and grade. These changes occur in 3-minute stages, in which Stage 1 is set at a low speed and moderate grade (1.7 mph and 10% grade), equivalent to 5 METs, and speed and grade are systematically increased: Stage 2 is set at 2.5 mph and 12% grade (7 METs); Stage 3 is set at 3.4 mph and 14% grade (10 METs); and Stage 4 is set at 4.2 mph and 16% grade (13.5 METs). The Bruce protocol is a good protocol for healthy individuals, and typical testing usually lasts 10 minutes. However, the disadvantages include that it is not appropriate for low-functioning individuals, because the starting workload is relatively high (5 METs); the relatively severe grade can be difficult for even healthy but deconditioned persons; and the large grade requires most individuals to hold on to the treadmill railings, which may spuriously affect the results. Moreover, if the subject does not complete the 3-minute, stage it is difficult to assign a precise MET level.

The other commonly employed protocol is the Balke protocol. With this protocol, the treadmill speed is usually kept constant (typically 3 or 3.3 mph) and the grade changes every minute. For example, Stage 1 is set at 3 mph and 0% grade (3 METs); Stage 2 is set at 3 mph and 2% grade (4 METs); and Stage 3 is set at 3 mph and 3% grade (4.5 METs). This protocol is particularly good for low-functioning individuals, because the grade increases are small and the speed can be preselected on the basis of the subject's fitness level. The disadvantages of the Balke protocol are that the increases are too gradual for each workload and the actual protocol can last for more than 15 minutes. Typically, the lengthy protocol results in muscular fatigue, and the speed of 3 mph may be too slow for many individuals.

A protocol recently developed in collaboration with researchers at Duke University Medical Center and the Bowman Gray School of Medicine combines the principles of the Bruce and Balke protocols such that both speed and grade are changed systematically (Blumenthal, Rejeski, et al., 1988); however, our new protocol consists of a series of 1-minute stages, with each stage increasing by 1 MET or less. Stage 1 is set at 2 mph and 0% grade (2.5 METs); Stage 2 is set at 2.5 mph and 0% grade (3.0 METs); Stage 3 is set at 2.5 mph and 2% grade (3.5 METs); Stage 4 is set at 3.0 mph and 2.5% grade (4.3 METs); Stage 5 is set at 3.0 mph and 5% grade (5 METs). Each subsequent change involves a 1-MET increase, and speed is increased to 3.3 mph at 9 minutes. The advantages of this protocol are as follows: The initial three workloads are good for low-level individuals, and this initial period also provides good warmup for more fit individuals. Since grade and speed change, the average adult finishes the test in 10 minutes (10 METs). Finally, this protocol is more vigorous than the Balke protocol but not as rigorous as the Bruce protocol; therefore, it can be used for individuals with a broad range of functional capacities. The major disadvantage of this protocol is that it may discriminate against individuals who are highly fit.

It is also important that regardless of the specific protocol employed, the personnel conducting the treadmill test should be well trained in the collection of subjective data (e.g., ratings of perceived exertion and symptoms such as chest pain) and objective data (heart rate, blood pressure, and $\dot{V}O_2$) from the patient. It also is essential that the subject and testing personnel communicate, so that the test can be terminated appropriately. Exercise stress testing requires continuous electrocardiographic (EKG) monitoring to record heart rate, cardiac rhythm, and changes in the ST segments. The capability to determine blood pressure quickly and accurately is also a necessity.

The exercise prescription is typically based upon a percentage of the maximum percentage of heart rate achieved during the exercise stress testing. The best-known method for establishing a cardiovascular training range is the so-called Karvonan formula: maximum heart rate − resting heart rate × 0.75 + resting heart rate ± 6. In order for a clinician to write an exercise prescription, the type, intensity, duration, and frequency of activity need to be defined. As noted earlier, aerobic exercise typically involves regular rhythmic movements of large muscle groups, such as in jogging, swimming, and bicycling. The emphasis is typically not on isometric exercises, such as weight lifting, which increase muscle strength but may also produce rapid increases in myocardial oxygen demand and blood pressure.

A Clinical Case Example

Mr. Radford was a 53-year-old man who developed chest pain upon physical exertion. He underwent a cardiac catheterization, which revealed the presence of significant blockage in two of his coronary arteries. He was enrolled in the Duke Center for Living program for exercise training and underwent an initial treadmill test with our standard exercise testing protocol. His resting blood pressure was 124/96 mm Hg, and his resting heart rate was 79 bpm. He then exercised for 11 minutes and achieved a maximal heart rate of 163 bpm. His maximum blood pressure was 166/90 mm Hg, which was achieved at peak exercise. His rating of perceived exertion at maximal exercise was 18 (out of a possible 20). He also reported chest pain, which he rated 1 out of a possible 10 at 9 minutes and 3 out of 10 at peak exercise. The test was stopped because of general fatigue, and the EKG revealed 2 mm ST segment depression at a heart rate of 155 bpm. His maximum $\dot{V}O_2$ was recorded as 30.5 ml/kg/minute. He was assigned a 12-beat training range, equivalent to 75% of his maximal heart rate reserve. The heart rate where the EKG was positive was used to determine the maximum heart rate (155). Thus, his training rate was established at 155 − 79 × 0.75 + 79 = 136 bpm, and his training range was set at 130–142.

Mr. Radford completed a psychometric test battery to provide information about his subjective mood state; the battery included the Cook Medley Hostility Scale, the State–Trait Anxiety Inventory, the Karasak Job Stress Inventory, and the Beck Depression Inventory. He also underwent an interview designed to reveal manifestations of the Type A behavior pattern. Mr. Radford was a typical Type A: overly ambitious, competitive, and aggressive. He complained a great deal about his work situation, where he was employed as a manager for a large company. He reported having considerable job strain; both he himself and his employer placed high demands upon him, and he had relatively little control over the decision-making process.

His initial exercise routine was set as follows: bicycle ergometry 1.0 kilopond (kp) for 10 minutes; arm ergometry 1.0 kp for 5 minutes; stretching and light calisthenics for 10 minutes; and 35 minutes of continuous walking on an outdoor track. Mr. Radford completed 41 sessions during the 16-week training period. He exercised three times per week at the same time each day. He progressed from walking 7–8 laps on a 400-meter outside track in 35 minutes to jogging a total of 150 meters and completing 10 laps. He was unable to advance past jogging more than 150 meters because of chest pain. He maintained his heart rate in the prescribed training range 70% of the time. Mr. Radford also completed a daily exercise log (see Figure 14.1), in which he recorded his heart rate at random intervals and his overall level of perceived exertion for each exercise session. He was re-evaluated after 4 months of exercise training.

EXERCISE LOG

Name_____   Training Range 130 - 142 bpm

Group 6:15AM, 7:45AM, 8:45AM, (5:15PM)

				Leg Ergometer			Arm Ergometer							
Date	Wt.	BP	HRrest	Wkld	Time	HRs	Wkld	Time	HRs	Floor exer.	Track HRs	# of laps	RPE	Comments
1/23/90	206	112/86	78	1.0kp	10:00	102 114	1.0kp	5:00	114	✓	121 136	8	12	Good 1st day! ☺
1/25/90	206	120/90	84	1.0kp	10:00	114 120	1.0kp	5:00	114	✓	120 126	8	13	
1/29/90	206	/	84	1.25kp	10:00	120 126	1.0kp	5:00	114	✓	120 126	8	14	Keep up the good work!
1/30/90	205	138/96	78	1.25kp	10:00	96 108	1.0kp	5:00	102	✓	120 138	8	13	
2/1/90	205	128/96	96	1.25kp	10:00	120 120	1.0kp	5:00	108	✓	120 178	8	13	Any problems? No
2/6/90	206	116/88	96	1.25kp	10:00	120 120	1.0kp	5:00	114	✓	118 130	8	14	
2/8/90	205	114/86	96	1.25kp	10:00	126 144	1.0kp	5:00	126	✓	120 138	7	13	What was leg wkld set at? Snored it up myself!
2/12/90	206	/	96	1.5kp	10:00	114 126	1.25kp	5:00	120	✓	126 138	7	14	Try to speed up walking!
2/13/90	206	122/84	90	1.5kp	10:00	120 126	1.25kp	5:00	120	✓	126 132	8	14	Please report any pain/problems!
2/15/90	206	106/78	96	1.5kp	10:00	120 120	1.25kp	5:00	114	✓	120 138	8	13	- a little angina at max HR
2/19/90	206	/	96	1.5kp	10:00	126 120	1.25kp	5:00	114	✓	126 140	8	14	Please see me before today's session.
2/20/90	206	104/74	90	1.5kp	10:00	102 108	1.25kp	5:00	108	✓	121 138	6	11	Not feeling well! Good last month!

FIGURE 14.1. Sample exercise log, including date, weight (Wt.), resting blood pressure (BP), and resting heart rate (HRrest) at the time the patient checked in with the exercise leader. The warmup period included leg and arm ergometry in which the workload (Wkld), time, and heart rates (HRs) were recorded, along with attendance during the light calisthenics (Floor exer.). Walking and jogging were performed on an outdoor track. The exercise heart rates (measured at random intervals during the exercise sessions) on the track (Track HRs), number of laps completed (# of laps), ratings of perceived exertion (RPE), and the leader's comments are also recorded.

Upon retesting, Mr. Radford exercised for 12 minutes on the treadmill, following the same protocol that he had completed initially. His maximal heart rate was 165 bpm, and his maximal blood pressure was 162/84 mm Hg. He rated his perceived exertion at peak exercise at 18 out of 20. He again reported chest pain, which he rated 1 out of 10 at 7 minutes and 5 out of 10 at maximal exercise. The test was stopped because of general fatigue and chest pain. The EKG was interpreted as positive at 142 bpm. His maximum $\dot{V}O_2$ was 36.4 ml/kg/minute, a 10% increase from his pretraining treadmill test. His improvement was typical for the average cardiac patient. He was able to exercise longer and achieved greater work capacity. In addition, his "anginal threshold" was increased, so that he could perform more work without experiencing symptoms. It should be noted that healthy subjects, and certain individuals with coronary disease, can achieve even greater improvements in exercise capacity with 3–4 months of regular (three to four times per week for 20–45 minutes) exercise. Moreover, Mr. Radford indicated that he felt more relaxed, less depressed and angry, and more "in control." He also appeared to display less exaggerated Type A responses; his volume and speed of speech were reduced, and he displayed less "potential for hostility" during the Type A interview at retesting.

Summary and Conclusions

There is growing evidence to suggest that physical exercise may reduce psychophysiological stress responses. Cross-sectional studies have shown that fit individuals generally show reduced physiological responses to psychological stress, compared to their unfit counterparts (Crews & Landers, 1987, De Geus et al., 1990; Holmes & Roth, 1985; Hull et al., 1984; Light et al., 1987; Perkins et al., 1986; Shulhan et al., 1986; Van Doornen & De Geus, 1989); however, results have not been entirely consistent (Cox et al., 1979; Holmes & Cappo, 1987; Plante & Karpowitz, 1987; Sinyor et al., 1983). Longitudinal investigations in which exercise training has increased fitness levels have also shown that exercise may attenuate stress responses (Blumenthal, Emery, et al., 1988; Blumenthal et al., 1990; Sherwood et al., 1989). Once again, however, results have not always been consistent (Blumenthal et al., 1991; De Geus et al., 1990; Holmes & Roth, 1987; Roskies et al., 1986; Sinyor et al., 1986). The results of studies that included measures of subjective response to stress in high- versus low-fitness subjects have been mixed, with some studies reporting less subjective arousal following stress in fit subjects (Hull et al., 1984; Sinyor et al., 1983) and others reporting no fitness-related differences in subjective responses (Holmes & Roth, 1985; Sinyor et al., 1983; Sothmann et al., 1987). There are a few studies suggesting that fitness may moderate the adverse effects of stressful life events (e.g. Roth & Holmes, 1985, 1987). Differences in subject characteristics, experimental design, and exercise training regimens appear to be responsible for some of the variable results. In addition, research into the emotional effects of exercise indicates that acute and chronic exercise both tend to enhance mood by reducing depression and anxiety and increasing feelings of vigor.

Future research in the area should address several important issues. It will be important to investigate individual-difference factors that may be critical for understanding the relationship of fitness to stress responses. For example, such factors as Type A behavior, initial fitness level, medical status (e.g., hypertension), age, and gender may all be relevant.

Second, it will be important to identify mechanisms by which exercise may attenuate stress responses and enhance mood. Modification of stress responses has been attributed to several processes, including reduced sympathetic activity, increased vagal tone, and reduced adrenoreceptor sensitivity; however, direct evidence in support of these hypotheses is lacking. Moreover, the mechanisms whereby exercise improves mood are unclear. Systematic investigations in this area are clearly needed.

Finally, the clinical utility of exercise in stress management should be addressed more directly. Do the stress-modulating effects of exercise discussed above translate to clinically meaningful physical or psychological health benefits? For example, there is some evidence to suggest that exercise reduces blood pressure in hypertensives (see Siegel & Blumenthal, 1991, for a review; see also Martin, Dubbert, & Cushman, 1990; Meredith et al., 1990).This effect may be attributable in part to altered autonomic response to stress, and this possibility should be investigated further. Relatedly, clinical trials of exercise in the treatment of various "stress-related" disorders (e.g., anxiety, depression, hypertension, peptic ulcer disease) are needed. Also, additional comparisons of exercise with other established stress management techniques (e.g., relaxation, meditation, cognitive–behavioral therapy) would be informative. Specifically, it would be helpful to identify certain patient populations (e.g., hypertensives or peptic ulcer disease patients) or subpopulations (e.g., Type A hypertensives) for whom exercise is a particularly effective stress management strategy. This will help distinguish those individuals for whom the benefits of exercise outweigh any potential risks.

ACKNOWLEDGMENT

The writing of this chapter was supported in part by Grant Nos. HL43028 and HL30675 from the National Institutes of Health.

REFERENCES

Allen, M. T., Obrist, P. A., Sherwood, A., & Crowell, M. D. (1987). Evaluation of myocardial and peripheral vascular responses during reaction time, mental arithmetic, and cold pressor tasks. *Psychophysiology, 24,* 648–656.

American College of Sports Medicine (ACSM). (1986). *Guidelines for exercise testing and prescription* (4th ed.). Philadelphia: Lea & Febiger.

Bahrke, M. S., & Morgan, W. P. (1978). Anxiety reduction following exercise and meditation. *Cognitive Therapy and Research, 2,* 323–333.

Barchas, J. D., & Freedman, D. X. (1963). Brain amines response to physical stress. *Biochemical Pharmacology, 12,* 1232–1235.

Ben-Shlomo, L. S., & Short, M. A. (1983). The effects of physical exercise on self-attitudes. *Occupational Therapy in Mental Health, 3,* 11–28.

Berger, B. G., & Owen, D. R. (1983). Mood alteration with swimming: Swimmers really do "feel better." *Psychosomatic Medicine, 45,* 425–433.

Blumenthal, J. A., Emery, C. F., Walsh, M. A., Cox, D. R., Kuhn, C. M., Williams, R. B., & Williams, R. S. (1988). Exercise training in healthy Type A middle-aged men: Effects on behavioral and cardiovascular responses. *Psychosomatic Medicine, 50,* 418–433.

Blumenthal, J. A., Fredrikson, M., Kuhn, C. M., Ulmer, R. A., Walsh-Riddle, M., & Appelbaum, M. (1990). Aerobic exercise reduces levels of cardiovascular and sympathoadrenal responses to mental stress in subjects without prior evidence of myocardial ischemia. *American Journal of Cardiology, 65,* 93–98.

Blumenthal, J. A., Fredrikson, M., Matthews, K. A., German, D., Steege, J., Walsh-Riddle, M. A., Kuhn, C., Rifai, N., & Rodin, J. (1991). Stress reactivity and exercise training in pre and postmenopausal women. *Health Psychology, 10,* 384–391.

Blumenthal, J. A., Rejeski, J., Walsh-Riddle, M. A., Emery, C. F., Miller, H., Roark, S., Ribisl, P. M., Morris, P. B., Brubaker, P., & Williams, R. S. (1988). Comparison of high- and low-intensity exercise training early after acute myocardial infarction. *American Journal of Cardiology, 61,* 26–30.

Blumenthal, J. A., Williams, R. S., Needels, T. L., & Wallace, A. G. (1982). Psychological changes accompany aerobic exercise in healthy middle-aged adults. *Psychosomatic Medicine, 44,* 29–36.

Boutcher, S. H., & Landers, D. M. (1988). The effects of vigorous exercise on anxiety, heart rate, and alpha activity of runners and nonrunners. *Psychophysiology, 25,* 696–702.

Cox, J. P., Evans, J. F., & Jamieson, J. L. (1979). Aerobic power and tonic heart rate responses to psychological stressors. *Personality and Social Psychology Bulletin, 5,* 160–163.

Crews, D. J., & Landers, D. M. (1987). A meta-analytic review of aerobic fitness and reactivity to psychosocial stressors. *Medicine and Science in Sports and Exercise, 19*(Suppl.), S114–S120.

Czajkowski, S. M., Hindelang, R. D., Dembroski, T. M., Mayerson, S. E., Parks, E. B., & Holland, J. C. (1990). Aerobic fitness, psychological characteristics, and cardiovascular reactivity to stress. *Health Psychology, 9,* 676–692.

De Geus, E. J. C., Van Doornen, L. J. P., De Visser, D. C., & Orlebeke, J. F. (1990). Existing and training induced differences in aerobic fitness: Their relationship to psychological response patterns during different types of stress. *Psychophysiology, 27,* 457–478.

Dishman, R. K. (1982). Compliance/adherence in health related exercise. *Health Psychology, 1,* 237–267.

Doyne, E. J., Chambless, D. L., & Beutler, L. E. (1983). Aerobic exercise as a treatment for depression. *Behavior Therapy, 14,* 434–440.

Doyne, E. J., Ossip-Klein, D. J., Bowman, E. D., Osborn, K. M., McDougal-Wilson, I. B., & Neimeyer, R. A. (1987). Running versus weight lifting in the treatment of depression. *Journal of Consulting and Clinical Psychology, 55,* 748–754.

Duncan, J. J., Farr, J. E., Upton, S. J., Hagan, R. D., & Oglesby, M. E. (1985). The effects of aerobic exercise on catecholamines and blood pressure in patients with mild hypertension. *Journal of the American Medical Association, 204,* 2609–2613.

Ebert, M. H., Post, R. M., & Goodwin, F. K. (1972). Effect of physical activity on urinary MHPG excretion in depressed patients. *Lancet, ii,* 766.

Emery, C. F., & Blumenthal, J. A. (1988). The effects of exercise training on psychological functioning in healthy Type A men. *Psychology and Health, 2,* 367–379.

Farrell, P. A., Gustafson, A. B., Morgan, W. P., & Pert, C. B. (1987). Enkephalins, catecholamines, and psychological mood alterations: Effects of prolonged exercise. *Medicine and Science in Sports and Exercise, 19,* 347–353.

Fillingim, R. B., & Blumenthal, J. A. (1992). Does aerobic exercise reduce stress responses? In J. R. Turner, A. Sherwood, & K. C. Light (Eds.), *Individual differences in cardiovascular response to stress* (pp. 203–214). New York: Plenum Press.

Fillingim, R. B., Roth, D. L., & Cook, E. W., III. (1992). The effects of aerobic exercise on cardiovascular, facial EMG, and subjective responses to emotional imagery. *Psychosomatic Medicine, 54,* 109–120.

Folkins, C. H., & Sime, W. E. (1981). Physical fitness training and mental health. *American Psychologist, 36,* 373–389.

Fremont, J., & Craighead, L. W. (1984). *Aerobic exercise and cognitive therapy for mild/moderate depression.* Paper presented at the meeting of the Association for Advancement of Behavior Therapy, Philadelphia.

Friedman, D. B., Ordway, G. A., & Williams, R. S. (1987). Exercise-induced functional desensitization of canine cardiac beta-adrenergic receptors. *Journal of Applied Physiology, 62,* 1721–1723.

Galbo, H., Christensen, N. J., & Holst, J. J. (1977). Catecholamines and pancreatic hormones during autonomic blockade in exercising man. *Acta Physiologica Scandinavica, 101,* 428–437.

Glowinski, J., & Axelrod, J. (1964). Inhibition of uptake of tritiated-noradrenaline in the intact rat brain by imipramine and structurally related compounds. *Nature, 204,* 1318–1319.

Glowinski, J., & Baldessarini, R. J. (1966). Metabolism of norepinephrine in the central nervous system. *Pharmacological Review, 18,* 1201–1238.

Goldwater, B. C., & Collins, M. L. (1985). Psychological effects of cardiovascular conditioning: A controlled experiment. *Psychosomatic Medicine, 47,* 174–181.

Greist, J. H., Klein, M. H., Eischens, R. R., Faris, J., Gurman, A. S., & Morgan, W. P. (1979). Running as treatment for depression. *Comprehensive Psychiatry, 20,* 41–53.

Grossman, A., Bouloux, P., Price, P., Drury, P. L., Lam, K. S. L., Turner, T., Thomas, J., Besser, G. M., & Sutton, A. J. (1984). The role of opioid peptides in the hormonal responses to acute exercise in man. *Clinical Science, 67,* 483–491.

Grossman, A., & Sutton, J. R. (1985). Endorphins: What are they? How are they measured? What is their role in exercise? *Medicine and Science in Sports and Exercise, 17,* 74–81.

Haskell, W. L. (1984). Overview: Health benefits of exercise. In J. D. Matarazzo, J. D. Weiss, J. A. Herd, & N. E. Miller (Eds.), *Behavioral health: A handbook of health enhancement and disease prevention* (pp. 409–423). New York: Wiley-Interscience.

Haskell, W. L. (1987). Developing an activity plan for improving health. In W. P. Morgan & S. E. Goldston (Eds.), *Exercise and mental health* (pp. 37–55). Washington, DC: Hemisphere.

Holloszy, J. O. (1983). Exercise, health, and aging: A need for more information. *Medicine and Science in Sports and Exercise, 15,* 1–5.

Holmes, D. S., & Cappo, B. M. (1987). Prophylactic effect of aerobic fitness on cardiovascular arousal among individuals with a family history of hypertension. *Journal of Psychosomatic Research, 31,* 601–605.

Holmes, D. S., & McGilley, B. M. (1987). Influence of a brief aerobic training program on heart rate and subjective response to a psychologic stressor. *Psychosomatic Medicine, 49,* 366–374.

Holmes, D. S., & Roth, D. L. (1985). Association of aerobic fitness with pulse rate and subjective responses to psychological stress. *Psychophysiology, 22,* 525–529.

Holmes, D. S., & Roth, D. L. (1987). Effects of aerobic exercise training and relaxation training on cardiovascular activity during psychological stress. *Journal of Psychosomatic Research, 32,* 469–474.

Hughes, J. R. (1984). Psychological effects of habitual aerobic exercise: A critical review. *Preventive Medicine, 13,* 66–78.

Hughes, J. R., Casal, D. C., & Leon, A. S. (1986). Psychological effects of exercise: A randomized cross-over trial. *Journal of Psychosomatic Research, 30,* 355–360.

Hull, E. M., Young, S. H., & Ziegler, M. G. (1984). Aerobic fitness affects cardiovascular and catecholamine responses to stressors. *Psychophysiology, 21,* 353–360.

King, A. C., Taylor, C. B., Haskell, W. L., & DeBusk, R. F. (1989). Influence of regular aerobic exercise on psychological health: A randomized controlled trial of healthy middle-aged adults. *Health Psychology, 8,* 305–324.

Lake, B. W., Suarez, E. C., Schneiderman, N., & Tocci, N. (1985). The Type A behavior pattern, physical fitness, and psychophysiological reactivity. *Health Psychology, 4,* 169–187.

Light, K. C., Obrist, P. A., James, S. A., & Strogatz, D. S. (1987). Cardiovascular responses to stress: II. Relationships to aerobic exercise patterns. *Psychophysiology, 24,* 79–86.

Lobitz, W. C., Brammell, H. L., Stoll, S., & Nicoli, A. (1983). Physical exercise and anxiety management training for cardiac stress management in a nonpatient population. *Journal of Cardiac Rehabilitation, 3,* 683–688.

Martin, J. E., & Dubbert, P. M. (1987). Exercise promotion. In J. A. Blumenthal & D. C. McKee (Eds.), *Applications in behavioral medicine and health psychology: A clinician's sourcebook* (pp. 361–398). Sarasota, FL: Professional Resource Exchange.

Martin, J. E., Dubbert, P. M., & Cushman, W. C. (1990). Controlled trial of aerobic exercise in hypertension. *Circulation, 81,* 1560–1567.

Martinsen, E. W. (1984). Interaction of exercise and medication in the psychiatric patient. In *Coping with mental stress: The potential and limits of exercise intervention* (NIMH Workshop). Washington, DC: National Institute of Mental Health.

Martinsen, E. H., Hoffart, A., & Solberg, O. Y. (1989). Aerobic and non-aerobic forms of exercise in the treatment of anxiety disorders. *Stress Medicine, 5,* 115–120.

McGowan, C. R., Robertson, R. J., & Epstein, L. H. (1985). The effect of bicycle ergometer exercise at varying intensities on the heart rate, EMG and mood state responses to a mental arithmetic stressor. *Research Quarterly for Exercise and Sport, 56,* 131–137.

Meredith, I. T., Jennings, G. L., Esler, M. D., Dewar, E.M., Bruce, A. M., Fazio, V. A., & Korner, P. I. (1990). Time-course of the antihypertensive and autonomic effects of regular endurance exercise in human subjects. *Journal of Hypertension, 8,* 859–866.

Morgan, W. P. (1980). Alterations in anxiety following acute physical activity. In S. I. Fuenning, K. D. Rose, & F. Strider (Eds.), *Proceedings of the First Research Seminar on Physical Fitness and Mental Health* (pp. 40–48). Lincoln: University of Nebraska Press.

Morgan, W. P. (1985). Affective beneficence of vigorous physical activity. *Medicine and Science in Sports and Exercise, 17,* 94–100.

Moses, J., Steptoe, A., Matthews, A., & Edwards, S. (1989). The effects of exercise training on mental well-being in the normal population: A controlled trial. *Journal of Psychosomatic Research, 33,* 47–61.

Overton, J. M., Joyner, M. J., & Tipton, C. M. (1988). Reductions in blood pressure after acute exercise by hypertensive rats. *Journal of Applied Physiology, 64,* 748–752.

Perkins, K. A., Dubbert, P. M., Martin, J. M., Faulstich, M. E., & Harris, J. K. (1986). Cardiovascular reactivity to psychological stress in aerobically trained versus untrained mild hypertensives and normotensives. *Health Psychology, 5,* 407–421.

Peronnet, F., Massicotte, D., Paquee, J. E., Brisson, G., & de Champlain, J. (1989). Blood pressure and catecholamine responses to various challenges during exercise-recovery in man. *European Journal of Applied Physiology, 58,* 551–555.

Plante, T. G., & Karpowitz, D. (1987). The influence of aerobic exercise on physiologic stress responsivity. *Psychophysiology, 24,* 670–677.

Plante, T. G., & Rodin, J. (1990). Physical fitness and enhanced psychological health. *Current Psychology: Research and Reviews, 9,* 3–24.

Post, R. M., Kotin, J., Goodwin, F. K., & Gordon, E. K. (1973). Psychomotor activity and cerebrospinal fluid amine metabolites in affective illness. *American Journal of Psychiatry, 130,* 67–72.

Raglin, J. S., & Morgan, W. P. (1987). Influence of exercise and quiet rest on state anxiety and blood pressure. *Medicine and Science in Sports and Exercise, 19,* 456–463.

Ransford, C. P. (1982). A role for amines in the antidepressant effect of exercise: A review. *Medicine and Science in Sports and Exercise, 14,* 1–10.

Roskies, E., Seraganian, P., Oseasohn, R., Hanley, J. A., Collu, R., Martin, N., & Smilga, C. (1986). The Montreal Type A Intervention Project: Major findings. *Health Psychology, 5,* 45–69.

Roth, D. L. (1989). Acute emotional and psychophysiological effects on aerobic exercise. *Psychophysiology, 26,* 593–602.

Roth, D. L., & Holmes, D. S. (1985). Influence of physical fitness in determining the impact of stressful life events on physical and psychologic health. *Psychosomatic Medicine, 47,* 164–173.

Roth, D. L., & Holmes, D. S. (1987). Influence of aerobic exercise training and relaxation training on physical and psychologic health following stressful life events. *Psychosomatic Medicine, 49,* 355–365.

Roth, D. L., Wiebe, D. J., Fillingim, R. B., & Shay, K. (1989). Life events, fitness, hardiness, and health: A simultaneous analysis of proposed stress resistance effects. *Journal of Personality and Social Psychology, 57,* 136–142.

Russell, P. O., Epstein, L. H., & Erickson, K. T. (1983). Effects of acute exercise and cigarette smoking on autonomic and neuromuscular responses to a cognitive stressor. *Psychological Reports, 53,* 199–206.

Schildkraut, J. J. (1965). The catecholamine hypothesis of affective disorders: A review of supporting evidence. *American Journal of Psychiatry, 122,* 509–522.

Schildkraut, J. J., & Kety, S. S. (1967). Biogenic amines and emotion. *Science, 58,* 117–128.

Sherwood, A., Allen, M. T., Obrist, P. A., & Langer, A. W. (1986). Evaluation of beta-adrenergic influences on cardiovascular and metabolic adjustments to physical and psychological stress. *Psychophysiology, 23,* 89–104.

Sherwood, A., Light, K. C., & Blumenthal, J. A. (1989). Effects of aerobic exercise on hemodynamic responses during psychosocial stress in normotensive and borderline hypertensive Type A men: A preliminary report. *Psychosomatic Medicine, 51,* 123–136.

Shulhan, D., Scher, H., & Furedy, J. J. (1986). Phasic cardiac reactivity to psychological stress as a function of aerobic fitness level. *Psychophysiology, 23,* 562–566.

Siegel, W. C., & Blumenthal, J. A. (1991). The role of exercise in the prevention and treatment of hypertension. *Annals of Behavioral Medicine, 13,* 23–30.

Simons, A. D., Epstein, L. H., McGowan, C. R., Kupfer, D. J., & Robertson, R. J. (1985). Exercise as a treatment for depression: An update. *Clinical Psychology, 5,* 553–568.

Sinyor, D. S., Golden, M., Steinert, Y., & Seraganian, P. (1986). Experimental manipulation of aerobic fitness and the response to psychosocial stress: Heart rate and self-report measures. *Psychosomatic Medicine, 48,* 324–337.

Sinyor, D. S., Schwartz, S. G., Peronnet, F., Brisson, G., & Seraganian, P. (1983). Aerobic fitness level and reactivity to psychosocial stress: Physiological, biochemical, and subjective measures. *Psychosomatic Medicine, 45,* 205–217.

Sonstroem, S. (1984). Exercise and self-esteem. *Exercise and Sports Sciences Reviews, 12,* 123–155.

Sothmann, M. S., Horn, T. S., Hart, B. A., & Gustafson, A. B. (1987). Comparison of discrete cardiovascular fitness groups on plasma catecholamine and selected behavioral responses to psychological stress. *Psychophysiology, 24,* 47–54.

Steptoe, A., & Cox, S. (1988). Acute effects of aerobic exercise on mood. *Health Psychology, 7,* 329–340.

Steptoe, A., Edwards, S., Moses, J., & Matthews, A. (1989). The effects of exercise training on mood and perceived coping ability in anxious adults from the general population. *Journal of Psychosomatic Research, 33,* 537–547.

Stoney, C. M., Davis, M. C., & Matthews, K. (1987). Sex differences in physiological responses to stress and in coronary heart disease: A causal link? *Psychophysiology, 24,* 127–131.

Van Doornen, L. J. P., & De Geus, E. J. C. (1989). Aerobic fitness and the cardiovascular response to stress. *Psychophysiology, 26,* 17–28.

Weiss, J. M. (1982). *A model for neurochemical study of depression.* Paper presented at the annual convention of the American Psychological Association, Washington, DC.

15

Pharmacological Approach to the Management of Stress and Anxiety Disorders

LASZLO A. PAPP
JACK M. GORMAN

Stress is part of human existence. Interestingly, the severity of a given stress does not usually predict the kind and degree of the subsequent stress reaction. Such reactions range from benign, transitional anxiety to severe, debilitating anxiety disorders. Although the pharmacological approach has been traditionally reserved for the management of anxiety disorders, the recent availability of efficacious and safe medications makes this approach a compelling alternative in the treatment of many stress reactions. At the same time, it should be emphasized as a principle that an equally efficacious nonpharmacological treatment is almost always preferable to medications.

In this chapter we outline the principles of the pharmacological management of anxiety. Three major classes of medications are discussed in detail: benzodiazepines (BZDs), cyclic antidepressants, and noncyclic antidepressants. In addition to these most frequently used antianxiety medications, a number of pharmacological agents are mentioned under the category of "other antianxiety medications." Throughout, we focus on the anxiety disorders delineated by the revised third edition of the *Diagnostic and Statistical Manual of Mental Disorders* (DSM-III-R; American Psychiatric Association, 1987). Whenever the data clearly support the benefit of medications, other (non-DSM) diagnostic categories are also discussed.

Medications and Anxiety

"Normal" anxiety serves many useful purposes. Anxiety insures that we prepare for a job interview, seek the doctor's advice when feeling sick, and pay our taxes on time. In these situations, anxiety motivates us to take necessary actions and prevent potential dangers; once the problem is resolved, the anxiety lifts. Eliminating this type of "normal" anxiety by the use of prescription medications, alcohol, or other licit and illicit drugs is counterproductive and can be quite dangerous.

In some instances, however, anxiety can become excessive. A critical comment from one's superior may be blown out of proportion. Undue rumination about being fired from the job may then spread to social and family functioning and may cause temporary disruption in sleep. However, after a few weeks and some reassurance, normal functioning is usually restored. This type of "excessive" anxiety serves no useful purpose and stays beyond the time of stress. Although treatment is usually recommended, medications are rarely required.

Unlike "normal" and "excessive" anxiety, "anxiety disorders," except for post-traumatic stress disorder (PTSD), do not directly result from real-life stresses. Untreated, they can become lifelong disabilities that seriously interfere with everyday functioning. Anxiety disorders have been found to be the most common psychiatric illnesses in the United States. The 6-month prevalence rate for anxiety disorders has been estimated to be 5% (Myers et al., 1984). Although adequate psychiatric evaluation and treatment are clearly indicated, they are rarely received by these patients. Some will decline help because of the stigma attached to psychiatric treatment; some will be disappointed by their physicians' approach and their lack of empathy; and others will resort to self-medication with alcohol or some other drugs.

However, anxiety disorders are highly treatable, and many of the treatments involve the judicious use of medications. The strategy of "pharmacological dissection" (Klein, 1964) of the formerly homogeneous category of "anxiety neurosis" into distinct and meaningful diagnostic groups has contributed to an unprecedented growth in the field of anxiety research. In return, the establishment of separate anxiety disorder categories has given renewed impetus to the development of anxiety-disorder-specific medications. The cross-fertilization between anxiety research and psychopharmacology has led to sophisticated understanding and consequently to significantly improved treatment of anxiety disorders.

The enormous pharmacological advances have generated both overenthusiasm about and unjustified skepticism toward the use of psychotropic medications in general. Psychiatric treatment has become polarized. The artificial dichotomy and the subsequent hostility between so-called "biological" and "psychological" approaches has damaged the image of the profession and confused patients. Fortunately, an increasing number of clinicians and researchers recognize that this division is unjustified. Rather than insisting on "purity," these "pragmatists" advocate an eclectic approach. This chapter provides guidelines for the use of medication by the "pragmatic practitioner."

Historical Background

The oldest antistress drug is alcohol; to date, it remains the most frequently used nonspecific tranquilizer. The introduction of paraldehyde in 1882 and bromides in the early 20th century, followed shortly by the first use of barbiturates in 1903, heralded the beginning of modern anxiolysis. Although at present the use of these drugs should be severely limited by the availability of safer and more effective anxiolytics, paraldehyde and some of the barbiturates retain certain specialized utilities.

Intramuscular or oral paraldehyde is an old-fashioned treatment for alcohol withdrawal. Phenobarbital is still used in the emergency treatment of seizures, as well as in cases of congenital hyperbilirubinemia. It is also used to decrease oxygen utilization during anesthesia, and to reduce cerebral edema following head trauma. Barbiturates may exert their sedative effects by decreasing presynaptic neurotransmitter release, by enhancing the postsynaptic effects of the inhibitory neurotransmitter gamma-aminobutyric acid (GABA), or by blocking calcium entry into neurons. Barbiturates are respiratory depressants and are contraindicated in patients with respiratory insufficiency. Abrupt discontinuation of the drug may result in severe, potentially life-threatening withdrawal reactions. Barbiturates are clearly addicting and lethal in overdose.

In the 1930s, in response to the deficiencies of barbiturates, a whole series of "nonbarbiturate, non-BZD" hypnotics was developed. Unfortunately, these drugs turned out to be just as problematic as the barbiturates, and most of them have retained only historic significance. Glutethimide (Doriden) overdose, for instance, can result in convulsions and fluctuating coma, since the drug is episodically released from tissue stores. Methaqualone (Quaalude) and methyprylone (Noludar) are both highly addicting and can be fatal in overdose. Meprobamate (Miltown) and tybamate (Benvil, Solacen) are modestly effective anxiolytics but possess a very low therapeutic index (low therapeutic–toxic ratio). The synthesis in 1957 of the first BZD, chlordiazepoxide (Librium), introduced a new era in the safe pharmacological management of anxiety.

Benzodiazepines

Currently, BZDs are the most popular choices in the pharmacological management of anxiety. Other therapeutic indications for BZDs include insomnia, seizures, muscle spasms, and the induction of anesthesia. All BZDs possess similar anxiolytic, sedative, and anticonvulsant properties; pharmacokinetic differences explain their various indications. Because of their safety, efficacy, and high therapeutic index, BZDs have almost entirely replaced barbiturates and most "nonbarbiturate, non-BZD" sedatives. From the time of their availability in the mid-1960s, BZD use in the United States increased steadily until 1985. Since then the number of BZD prescriptions filled annually in retail pharmacies has leveled off at approximately 61 million. The most commonly prescribed BZD was chlordiazepoxide in 1965, surpassed by diazepam by 1970 and alprazolam by 1987 (Nelson, 1987). According to a 1981 survey, approximately 1 out of every 10 American adults had taken BZDs during the previous year; nevertheless, only one-third of those found to be in need of pharmacological treatment for an anxiety disorder received any medication. Contrary to public perception, scientific data conclusively show that BZDs are safe, that they are not overused, and that tolerance to their therapeutic effects is extremely rare (American Psychiatric Association Task Force, 1990). A case can be made that, given the high prevalence of severe anxiety disorders, BZDs are actually underprescribed.

Pharmacology of Benzodiazepines

BZDs bind to the BZD–GABA receptor complex and enhance the postsynaptic inhibitory effects of GABA. This is mediated by opening of a postsynaptic chloride channel (Tallman, Paul, Skolnick, & Gallagher, 1980; Pritchett et al., 1989). Because of their high lipid solubility, all BZDs readily cross the blood–brain barrier. The so-called "long-acting" BZDs (such as chlordiazepoxide or diazepam) produce active metabolites that require the hepatic mixed-oxidase system for degradation. The elimination half-life (time needed for the concentration to fall by 50%) of these BZDs tends to be over 24 hours, sometimes several days. By contrast, "short-acting" BZDs (such as lorazepam or oxazepam) have no active metabolites, do not require the mixed-oxidase system, and therefore have half-lives that are shorter than 24 hours. The active metabolites of alprazolam and triazolam do not lengthen their half-lives. The BZDs currently available in the United States are listed in Table 15.1.

Principles of Benzodiazepine Use

A number of factors should be taken into account when BZDs are being considered for use with anxious patients:

1. All BZDs are equally sedating. Tolerance to the sedative–hypnotic effect of benzodiazepines usually develops within a few weeks of continued use. Tolerance to their anxiolytic effects, however, is extremely rare. Evidence consistently shows that once a therapeutic dose of a BZD is reached, it is rarely necessary to raise the dose again in order to maintain the same level of therapeutic benefit (Rickels, Schweizer, Csanalosi, Case, & Chung, 1988). In fact, panic disorder patients have been shown to reduce their BZD dose over time (Sheehan, 1987). Because of their increased sensitiv-

TABLE 15.1 Benzodiazepines

Generic name	Trade name	Usual daily dose (mg)
Long-acting		
Chlordiazepoxide	Librium	15–100
Clonazepam	Klonopin	0.5–6
Clorazepate	Tranxene	7.5–60
Diazepam	Valium	2–60
Flurazepam	Dalmane	15–30
Halazepam	Paxipam	80–160
Prazepam	Centrax	20–60
Quazepam	Doral	7.5–15
Short-acting		
Alprazolam	Xanax	0.5–6
Estazolam	Prosom	1–2
Lorazepam	Ativan	1–6
Oxazepam	Serax	30–120
Temazepam	Restoril	15–30
Triazolam	Halcion	0.125–25

ity to sedation, older patients should take significantly lower doses of BZDs. Other occasionally observed side effects necessitating dose reduction include ataxia, incoordination, dysarthria, diplegia, vertigo, impaired memory, and dizziness. Hence, it is critical that patients on BZDs be regularly monitored by a physician.

2. Some patients, frequently those with histories of organic brain disease or significant character pathology, become disinhibited on BZDs. These patients should be placed on a significantly reduced BZD dose and followed carefully.

3. BZD abuse by patients with prior histories of alcohol or other substance abuse is common (Ciraulo, Sands, & Shader, 1988). Only as a last resort should BZDs be prescribed for these patients.

4. Like most drugs, if BZDs are taken for a long period of time, they may produce physiological dependence as evidenced by discontinuance syndrome when stopped abruptly (Roy-Byrne, Dager, Cowley, Vitaliano, & Dunner, 1989). The symptoms of this discontinuance syndrome commonly include insomnia, anxiety, agitation, muscle twitching, tremor, headache, and nausea. They may represent a transient and more intense return of the original anxiety symptoms (rebound), the return of the pattern of the original anxiety (recurrence or relapse), and/or the development of new symptoms that were not part of the original anxiety (withdrawal or abstinence). The most severe but fortunately the least frequent discontinuance symptoms are withdrawal seizures. The severity of the discontinuance syndrome is proportional to the dose, the length of administration, and the rate of taper of the medication. Therefore, as a rule, BZDs should be used at the lowest efficacious dose and the shortest time needed for improvement. Upon tapering, the dose should be reduced by less than 10% every 3 days.

5. Some studies suggest that benzodiazepines can induce or exacerbate depression, although this hypothesis is controversial. If depression develops during the course of BZD treatment, lowering the dose or discontinuing the drug may be indicated. Alprazolam has been found to have antidepressant effects (Rickels & Schweizer, 1987).

6. Although reported fetal abnormalities associated with BZD use have not been confirmed by animal studies, the consensus is that BZDs should be avoided during the entire pregnancy.

Benzodiazepine Treatment Recommendations

The presence of anxiety does not necessarily indicate the use of anxiolytics. As noted earlier, mild anxiety may actually improve performance. Even moderate anxiety that interferes with performance may still be best managed with psychotherapy. If it is determined that drug treatment is necessary for an acute anxiety episode, rapid relief is usually achieved by a single oral dose of diazepam. Because of its high lipid solubility, diazepam works within 15 minutes—more rapidly than any other benzodiazepine. On the other hand, if the intramuscular route is preferred, lorazepam is a better choice.

For short-term use (less than 1 week), short-half-life BZDs have the advantage of lacking "hangover effect" and causing less sedation than long-half-life BZDs. Their rapid, simple metabolism is preferred in the elderly and in patients with impaired liver function. For longer-term use, long- and short-half-life BZDs are equally useful. Studies provide mixed indications as to whether the discontinuance syndrome is any less troublesome with long-acting than with short-acting BZDs.

The length of BZD treatment is highly individual. Some patients continue their medications at stable doses for several years without any evidence of loss in efficacy. Long-term anxiolytic treatment should probably continue for at least 2 weeks beyond complete symptom remission. At that point the dose should be reduced, and, if possible, the medication should be discontinued. If the original symptoms return, the medication should be reinstituted; at a later date, tapering should be attempted again. Rebound with withdrawal symptoms should not be confused with the return of the original symptoms. They are best managed by slower tapering.

Recommendations for the use of BZDs in the treatment of specific anxiety disorders are given later in the chapter.

Antidepressants

The success of imipramine in controlling panic attacks in patients with panic disorder provided the first evidence that antidepressants may alleviate anxiety independently of their antidepressant effects (Klein & Fink, 1962). This historic observation in the late 1950s also heralded the beginning of attempts to differentiate among the anxiety disorders on the basis of their response to medications.

The currently available antidepressants are listed in Table 15.2. They include cyclic antidepressants, monoamine oxidase inhibitors (MAOIs), and "novel" antidepressants.

Cyclic Antidepressants

Following the seminal studies with imipramine, a series of cyclic antidepressants was tested in patients with panic disorder and other anxiety disorders. Most controlled studies found these drugs to be superior to placebo in most anxiety disorders (Liebowitz et al., 1988). The advantages of cyclic antidepressants over BZDs (once-a-day administration, fewer and less troublesome withdrawal symptoms, less sedation, less depression, less dependence), in spite of some disadvantages (later onset of action, anticholinergic side effects, initial agitation), make them a good treatment alternative in certain patients with anxiety disorders.

Most side effects of the cyclic antidepressants, though they can be quite bothersome, are benign and do not represent clinically significant limitations. Orthostatic hypotension is only problematic in the elderly, who are more susceptible to falls and subsequent injuries. In most cases the inconvenience of positional drops in blood pressure can be minimized by avoiding sudden postural changes, increasing salt intake, or using constrictive support hose. For patients with severe orthostatic hypotension, nortriptyline can still be successfully utilized.

Most cyclic antidepressants prolong the PR and QRS intervals on the electrocar-

TABLE 15.2 Antidepressants

Generic name	Trade name	Usual daily dose (mg)
Cyclic antidepressants		
Amitriptyline	Elavil, Endep	150–300
Amoxapine	Asendin	300–600
Clomipramine	Anafranil	50–250
Desipramine	Norpramin, Pertofrane	150–300
Doxepin	Sinequan, Adapin	150–300
Imipramine	Tofranil, Janimine	75–300
Maprotiline	Ludiomil	75–225
Nortriptyline	Aventyl, Pamelor	50–150
Protriptyline	Vivactil	20–60
Trimipramine	Surmontil	100–300
Monoamine oxidase inhibitors		
Isocarboxazid	Marplan	20–50
Pargyline	Eutonyl	75–150
Phenelzine	Nardil	45–90
Selegiline/deprenyl	Eldepryl	30–60
Tranylcypromine	Parnate	30–60
"Novel" antidepressants		
Bupropion	Wellbutrin	300–450
Fluoxetine	Prozac	5–80
Trazodone	Desyrel	200–400

diogram (EKG), but in an otherwise healthy patient, these EKG changes are not clinically significant. Anticholinergic side effects are the most frequent causes of premature termination or intolerance of cyclic antidepressants. Significant weight gain, urinary hesitancy or block, severe constipation, sexual dysfunction, and cognitive impairment may be managed by lowering the dose, or by adding bethanecol, stool softeners, or (in the case of anorgasmia) the antihistamine cyproheptadine. Most cyclic antidepressants cause photosensitivity.

If medications with anticholinergic side effects are contraindicated (i.e., because of prostatic hypertrophy or closed-angle glaucoma), the least anticholinergic cyclic antidepressant, desipramine, or an antidepressant with no anticholinergic side effects (e.g., fluoxetine) should be used. The only cyclic antidepressant found beneficial in the treatment of patients with obsessive compulsive disorder (OCD) is clomipramine.

Monoamine Oxidase Inhibitors

Close to the time of the identification of imipramine as an antipanic drug in the United States, investigators in England showed that "hysterical" patients with phobic symptoms responded favorably to MAOIs. Patients in this diagnostic category share a number of features with agoraphobic panic patients. Subsequent comparative trials in phobic patients have shown that the MAOI phenelzine is marginally more effective than imipramine, and that both drugs are significantly more effective than placebo

(Sheehan, Bach, Ballenger, & Jacobsen, 1980). The reluctance to prescribe MAOIs stems from the fact that unless patients adhere to a special tyramine-free diet, MAOIs can induce hypertensive crisis. Following in the footsteps of their British colleagues, American psychiatrists increasingly acknowledge the unique benefits of MAOIs, and realize that the diet is easy to follow and that hypertensive reactions are exceedingly rare (Tollefson, 1983).

Orthostatic hypotension is a more common and a more serious side effect of MAOI than of cyclic antidepressant treatment; its management includes the techniques recommended for the cyclic antidepressants. Severe postural hypotension usually responds well to the addition of fludrocortisone (0.1 mg two to three times a day) for 2 weeks. Weight gain, sexual dysfunction, peripheral edema, and hypomania, in addition to weak anticholinergic symptoms, may require adjusting the dose or switching to a different class of antidepressant. Agitation and insomnia are more likely with tranylcypromine.

Fluoxetine

Of the numerous "novel antidepressants," fluoxetine (Prozac) is among the select few that has proven to be a real advance over the traditional antidepressants. Fluoxetine was introduced in the U.S. market in 1988, and by 1990 it was the best-selling antidepressant in the country. The drug is a serotonin reuptake blocker with only minimal effect on noradrenergic and dopaminergic neurotransmission. Its advantages over the more traditional antidepressants are numerous.

Fluoxetine has substantially fewer side effects than most other antidepressants (no anticholinergic effects, minimal cardiovascular side effects); moreover, it is not lethal in overdose, and it is easy to administer. The disadvantages of fluoxetine include its high price, its delayed onset of action, and the fact that most patients with panic attacks cannot tolerate the only available 20-mg capsule. A number of patients also complain of delayed orgasm while on fluoxetine. Because of the agitation and insomnia frequently reported by patients, fluoxetine is usually taken in the morning. The elimination half-life of several days allows for once-a-day administration. Patients with OCD may require substantially higher doses than other anxiety disorder patients.

Although optimism seems justified, the relatively short U.S. career of fluoxetine should caution us against overenthusiasm. Contrary to some reports of increased suicidal ideation associated with fluoxetine treatment, a recent comparison of suicidality among patients taking fluoxetine or other antidepressants found no significant differences (Fava & Rosenbaum, 1991).

Pharmacology of the Antidepressants

The efficacy of antidepressants is probably related to their ability to alter neurotransmission in the synapse. They can block the reuptake of neurotransmitters back into the presynaptic nerve ending, antagonize certain receptors, or inhibit certain neurotansmitter-degrading enzymes. Most antidepressants directly affect the central regulation of respiration, suggesting that correcting respiratory abnormalities in anxiety may be an important aspect of their utility. The exact mechanism of their action is the subject of intensive research (Snyder & Peroutka, 1984).

Most antidepressants have long elimination half-lives and a number of active metabolites. Therefore, most of them can be taken once a day. Other than in the monitoring of compliance, antidepressant blood levels have limited use in clinical practice. The exception is nortriptyline: A blood level of nortriptyline between 50 and 150 ng has been found to be associated with good results and should be maintained. In the case of other antidepressants, however, blood levels fluctuate widely and do not predict or correspond with clinical status (American Psychiatric Association Task Force, 1985).

Antidepressant Treatment Recommendations

Antidepressants are not recommended for the treatment of episodic anxiety or excessive anxiety; they should be reserved for managing anxiety disorders. In the absence of conclusive evidence for differential efficacy, the choice of an antidepressant will usually be determined by its side effect profile. The exception to this rule is the preference to use primarily serotonergic drugs (fluoxetine, clomipramine) in patients with OCD.

In order to minimize initial agitation, the starting dose of the antidepressant may have to be a small fraction of the usual antidepressant dose. For the same reason, strongly serotonergic drugs such as fluoxetine may have to be abandoned in favor of more noradrenergic antidepressants. The dose of antidepressant needed for symptom control varies widely from individual to individual. The general rule here is to raise the dose either until symptoms remit completely or until bothersome side effects prevent further increase. The length of antidepressant treatment for various anxiety disorders varies greatly; specific recommendations are given later in the chapter. In general, although exceptions do exist, most anxiety disorders run a chronic fluctuating course. The pharmacological approach should match this course, with periodic attempts to taper and discontinue the drug following a prolonged symptom-free period, but willingness to restart the effective drug upon relapse (Klein, Gittelman, Quitkin, & Rifkin, 1980).

Other Antianxiety Medications

Neuroleptics

As a general rule, neuroleptics or antipsychotics (also incorrectly referred to as "major tranquilizers") should not be used in the treatment of anxiety or anxiety disorders because of the possibility of inducing tardive dyskinesia. Tardive dyskinesia, characterized by involuntary muscle movements, is a frequently irreversible side effect of neuroleptics following long-term use. As possible exceptions to this rule, neuroleptics may be necesssary to treat agitation in the elderly and to manage anxiety in patients with organic brain disease. These patients may become delirious on usual doses of antianxiety medications such as BZDs, but may benefit greatly from low doses of neuroleptics. Short-term treatment with neuroleptics reduces the risk in these patients of developing tardive dyskinesia.

In select situations, neuroleptics may be indicated as "last-resort" antianxiety agents. For example, in managing patients with borderline personality disorder, patients with histories of drug dependence, or patients for whom all other alternatives have failed, periodic short-term use of neuroleptics may be justified (Klein et al., 1980). Extrapyramidal side effects must be monitored during any length of neuroleptic treatment.

Beta-Adrenergic Receptor Antagonists (Beta Blockers)

Beta blockers are probably the most frequently used medications in the treatment of hypertension, angina, and migraine headache. Their mechanism of action is to reduce adrenergic stimulation by antagonizing beta-adrenergic receptors located in the cardiovascular system (Frishman, 1981).

Autonomic symptoms (e.g., rapid heartbeat, tremor, tingling, perspiration, blushing, and chest constriction) are frequent concomitants of anxiety. These symptoms may be induced by increased adrenalin secretion during anxiety. Anxious patients may have a tendency to misinterpret these symptoms as dangerous, and are also often hyperaware of normal adrenergic functioning. For instance, innocuous palpitations may be perceived as evidence of an impending heart attack; catastrophic thinking, in turn, may augment the original symptom. Beta-adrenergic receptor antagonist drugs may derive their benefit from blocking these symptoms. A number of beta blockers have been found effective in the treatment of both generalized anxiety and situationally provoked anxiety, such as social phobia and performance anxiety (Kathol et al., 1980; Gorman, Liebowitz, Fyer, Campeas, & Klein, 1985).

It is somewhat controversial at present whether these drugs exert their beneficial effects only through the reduction of peripheral autonomic symptoms or through central mechanisms as well (Gottschalk, Stone, & Gleser, 1974; Gorman et al., 1983). In support of peripheral action are treatment studies that divide anxious patients into predominantly psychic versus somatic groups. Somatic anxiety seems to respond both to BZDs and to beta blockers more than to placebo, but only BZDs and not beta blockers seem superior to placebo in treating psychic anxiety. Also, practolol and atenolol, two selective peripheral beta blockers, seem to be effective antianxiety agents. Since neither of these beta blockers enters the brain to any significant degree, this finding is consistent with peripheral efficacy for beta blockers.

Beta blockers are contraindicated in patients with a history of asthma or serious allergies that produce wheezing. Relative contraindications include hypotension, bradycardia, congestive heart failure, and diabetes mellitus.

All beta blockers are rapidly absorbed from the gastrointestinal tract. Depending on their lipid solubility, they may cross the blood–brain barrier. For instance, the highly lipid-soluble propranolol may exert considerable central effects, such as sedation. The weakly lipid-soluble atenolol does not cross the blood–brain barrier and has many fewer central effects. Some of the beta blockers are local anesthetics, and some are intrinsically sympathomimetic (i.e., they also stimulate some beta-adrenergic receptors).

Selective beta blockers (atenolol, metoprolol) only antagonize $beta_1$-adrenergic receptors, located primarily on the myocardium. Nonselective beta blockers (propranolol, pindolol) antagonize both $beta_1$- and $beta_2$-adrenergic receptors. Since $beta_2$-adrenergic receptors are located on the vascular and bronchial smooth muscles, nonselective beta blockers can cause airway constriction. In general, beta blockers are safe and relatively easy to administer. The side effects of beta blockers are relatively mild and may include nightmares, depression, tingling sensations in the hands and feet, and occasionally fatigue and sedation. Beta blockers are not habit-forming. Although there are no withdrawal symptoms, tapering is recommended upon discontinuation in order to avoid rebound blood pressure changes.

Buspirone

Buspirone (BuSpar), a novel antianxiety agent, is pharmacologically unrelated to BZDs or any other marketed anxiolytics. The increasing popularity of buspirone is related to the fact that it causes less sedation and has lower potential for abuse and dependence than any other anxiolytics.

Buspirone enhances dopaminergic neurotransmission and antagonizes serotonergic ($5-HT_{1A}$) and GABA neurotransmission. It has no cross-tolerance with BZDs and seems less effective in patients previously exposed to BZDs than in BZD-naive populations. In contrast to the rapid onset of action of BZDs, response to buspirone may take as long as 4 weeks. Multiple dosing is necessary because of its short half-life.

Even though the experience with buspirone is limited to a few years, there appears to be little tolerance to its therapeutic effects over time. Buspirone produces relatively few side effects and no known irreversible somatic effects with long-term administration. Unlike discontinuation of BZDs, discontinuation of buspirone does not induce withdrawal syndrome. A major disadvantage of buspirone is the 4-week lag in clinical efficacy, compared to the rapid onset of improvment with BZD treatment (Rickels et al., 1988).

Disorder-Specific Treatment Recommendations

Generalized Anxiety Disorder

According to DSM-III-R, generalized anxiety disorder (GAD) patients suffer from "unrealistic or excessive anxiety and worry" for at least 6 months. They experience motor tension, autonomic hyperactivity, and hypervigilance. The usual course of GAD includes periods of quiescence and exacerbation. Depression is a common complication.

BZDs are the traditional pharmacological choice in the treatment of GAD. These medications have been clearly established as efficacious in relieving the symptoms of GAD. A few studies have suggested that tricyclic antidepressants (e.g., imipramine and amitriptyline) and buspirone may also be used in treating GAD (Rickels & Schweizer, 1987). Since the purity of GAD diagnoses in most of these studies is questionable, the prescription of tricyclic drugs and buspirone for GAD remains an interesting possibility requiring further study.

If the patient is willing and able to wait for several weeks for relief, buspirone can be tried first. If there is no response or immediate relief is needed, a short- or long-half-life BZD should be started. If long-term treatment (over 2 weeks) is likely, a switch to a long-acting BZD may be necessary. The dose of any medication should be kept as low as possible, and drug discontinuation should be attempted every 6 months. Emergence of depression should prompt vigorous antidepressant treatment. Concomitant psychotherapy (simple stress management, problem-solving assistance, cognitive or psychodynamic treatments) may shorten the length of time the patient needs to be on medication.

Panic Disorder with or without Agoraphobia

The hallmark of panic disorder is the panic attack. These sudden, unexpected, episodic bursts of anxiety are characterized by autonomic symptoms (e.g. sweating, hyperventilation, palpitation, light-headedness) and fear of impending doom. They last from 5 to 30 minutes. Frequent complications include anticipatory anxiety, which is the almost constant fear of panic attacks; agoraphobia or phobic avoidance of situations associated with panic attacks; and secondary demoralization, which occasionally leads to severe depression.

Medication treatment is targeted at the panic attacks. Once the attacks are blocked, the anticipatory anxiety, agoraphobia, and depression usually remit as well. Antidepressants and BZDs are the medications most often used to treat panic attacks. The traditional antipanic drug is the tricyclic antidepressant imipramine. In addition to most cyclic antidepressants, the MAOIs including phenelzine and tranylcypromine; alprazolam, clonazepam, and other BZDs; and fluoxetine have been shown to posses antipanic properties.

A careful psychiatric and medical differential diagnosis should be followed by a physical exam, an EKG, and blood work, including thyroid function tests. The patient is then started on medication, if this is indicated. The target symptom is the panic attack and not the associated features.

If speedy recovery is the main goal, BZDs are the best choice. BZDs may be sedating initially, but are easier to tolerate later than the anticholinergic antidepressants. Withdrawal from BZDs is more problematic than withdrawal from antidepressants. Patients who can tolerate the initial agitation and insomnia and can wait for symptom relief, but are sensitive to the anticholinergic side effects and concerned about withdrawal, should be placed on fluoxetine. If these first-line drugs fail following an adequate trial (at least 4 weeks on a therapeutic dose), one of the MAOIs may be substituted. The rules about transition to an MAOI and the dietary restrictions should be strictly observed.

Medications should be continued for 6 to 9 panic-free months and than gradually discontinued. Once a patient is panic-free, exposure to fearful situations should be attempted. Panic disorder is a cyclical illness, with sometimes many months or years of complete remission; a treatment approach that helped once is likely to be successful again. Proper medication treatment is successful in about 80% of panic patients.

Although its antipanic efficacy has not been established to the same degree as that of pharmacotherapy, focused, time-limited cognitive–behavioral treatment is a promising alternative in situations when medications are contraindicated (e.g., pregnancy) or when patients are reluctant to take medications. Even if formal antipanic psychotherapy is not employed, such techniques as breathing retraining, relaxation exercises, and exposure may prolong remission in the drug-free state.

Social Phobia

Patients with social phobia experience significant anxiety and autonomic discharge in one or more social situations. Their fear of embarrassing or humiliating themselves in these situations usually leads to significant avoidance. Limited social phobia involves one situation (e.g., public speaking); patients with generalized social phobia are anxious in and tend to avoid many different social situations. Social phobia appears to be a chronic condition, beginning in late adolescence and often resulting in lifelong disability. Substance abuse and secondary depression are frequent complications. Nevertheless, research on social phobia was largely neglected by American psychiatry until the publication of DSM-III in 1980.

Over the past few years, however, a number of promising medication trials have been carried out. As a result, the efficacy of phenelzine has been clearly established in the treatment of social phobia (Liebowitz et al., 1990). A few uncontrolled studies (Hartley, Ungapen, & Davie, 1983; Gorman et al., 1985), as well as anecdotal evidence, support the efficacy of beta blockers. Our own promising personal experience with fluoxetine in treating social phobia remains to be confirmed by double-blind studies. Finally, there is no convincing support for the use of BZDs, buspirone, or tricyclic drugs for this condition.

In the absence of sufficient published long-term treatment studies of patients with social phobia, the following recommendations must currently be regarded as tentative. Because of their relative safety, rapid onset of action, and ease of administration, an initial trial with beta blockers is warranted. If they work, the beneficial effects of beta blockers are obvious after the first week of treatment. Approximately 50% of social phobics will benefit substantially from beta blockers. A higher success rate can be expected in limited than in generalized social phobia.

If after 2 weeks there is no response to beta blockers, the social-phobic patient should be switched to phenelzine; if this is successful, the patient should be maintained on the same dose for approximately 6 symptom-free months. Then an attempt should be made to taper the patient off phenelzine over 2 weeks. By that time, some patients will have developed sufficient self-confidence to function well without medication. Certain psychotherapies may prolong remission, although this is currently the subject of investigation. If symptoms recur, the effective medication can be reinstituted.

For the relief of simple performance anxiety (possibly a mild version of limited social phobia), the medications most frequently recommended are beta blockers. In cases of predictable and relatively infrequent performance anxiety, propranolol may be taken approximately 1 hour before the stressful event. The medication will control such symptoms as trembling, sweating, blushing, or palpitation for about 3 to 6 hours.

If the anxiety is more generalized and less predictable, a longer-acting drug (e.g., atenolol taken at night) will usually provide symptom control for the subsequent 24-hour period.

Obsessive Compulsive Disorder

Patients with OCD experience repetitive, usually senseless thoughts or impulses, occasionally accompanied by repetitive and also senseless behaviors (e.g., washing, counting, or checking). OCD is a disabling disorder with poor prognosis. Spontaneous remissions are rare, and without appropriate treatment most OCD patients will remain symptomatic and impaired. Because of its distinct features, some investigators do not even consider OCD an anxiety disorder.

The treatment of OCD is difficult. Although some behavioral treatments seem beneficial, most patients will resort to taking medications in addition to psychotherapy. The most promising medications available in the United States are the prominently serotonergic antidepressants clomipramine and fluoxetine.

Clomipramine, a cyclic antidepressant with powerful serotonergic-reuptake-blocking properties, has been found to be effective in relieving the symptoms of OCD (Pato, Zohar-Kadouch, Zohar, & Murphy, 1988). Although it has only been available in the United States since 1990, the drug has been tested extensively around the world. With the exception of a slightly higher risk of seizure, the side effects are identical to those described for cyclic antidepressants. Clomipramine will substantially reduce the duration and/or the amount of obsessions and compulsions, and alleviate the anxiety experienced, in about 50% of OCD patients.

The only pharmacological alternative to clomipramine is fluoxetine (Turner, Jacob, & Beidel, 1985). Although it is not as well established in the treatment of OCD as clomipramine, some clinicians consider fluoxetine the first-line drug for OCD because of its fewer side effects. Refractory cases may benefit from combining these drugs with lithium or fenfluramine, or from a trial with intravenous clomipramine. If effective, medications will often have to be taken permanently; drug discontinuation can result in rapid relapse. Behavioral psychotherapy is usually recommended to supplement the medication treatment of OCD.

Post-Traumatic Stress Disorder

PTSD is diagnosed when the patient persistently re-experiences a traumatic event that is outside of the range of usual human experience. Since features of the illness include flashbacks to the trauma, "psychic numbness," and affective symptoms in addition to anxiety, it is still being debated whether PTSD belongs in the anxiety disorder category.

Placebo-controlled medication trials in patients with PTSD are few and usually involve small numbers of patients. Therefore, treatment recommendations are mostly based on anecdotal evidence. In general, pharmacological treatment should focus on the presenting symptoms. Anxiety should be managed with BZDs, whereas depression requires antidepressant treatment.

There is some evidence that beta blockers (Yudofsky, Williams, & Gorman, 1981) and the alpha$_2$-adrenergic agonist clonidine (Bond, 1986) may control explosive behavior, hyperalertness, intrusive thoughts, and nightmares. If these results are replicated, they would point toward noradrenergic dysfunction as a possible etiology in PTSD. Unless overt psychosis is present, neuroleptics are not recommended in PTSD. Psychotherapy (or, at the very least, counseling) is probably needed to supplement pharmacotherapy, although this has not been studied in a controlled design.

Conclusion

The availability of specific and effective antianxiety medications has significantly increased the number of anxiety disorder patients who can be helped by psychiatric treatment. However, most anxiety disorders, like many medical conditions, are often well controlled but not cured. This phenomenon should not be considered a failure of treatment; rather, it is a function of the chronic nature of the illness. Chronic conditions require long-term management.

Since the currently recommended antianxiety medications are safe and are not known to produce permanent side effects even after long-term use, medication treatment is a viable alternative to a less effective nonpharmacological treatment. An unbiased, open approach to treating these chronic conditions is strongly recommended. From a pharmacological point of view, the principle of the lowest effective dose for the shortest possible period of time should always be followed. Periodic drug discontinuation should be attempted. If the patient cannot be maintained symptom-free without medication, however, drugs should be continued for as long as necessary. Psychotherapeutic approaches should be used to supplement medication effects and to reduce symptoms and impairment.

REFERENCES

American Psychiatric Association. (1987). *Diagnostic and statistical manual of mental disorders* (3rd ed., rev.). Washington, DC: Author.

American Psychiatric Association Task Force. (1985). Tricyclic antidepressants: Blood level measurements and clinical outcome. *American Journal of Psychiatry, 142,* 155–165.

American Psychiatric Association Task Force. (1990). *Benzodiazepine dependence, toxicity, and abuse.* Washington, DC: American Psychiatric Association Press.

Bond, W. S. (1986). Psychiatric indications for clonidine: The neuropharmacologic and clinical basis. *Journal of Clinical Psychopharmacology, 6,* 81–90.

Ciraulo, D. A., Sands, B. F., & Shader, R. I. (1988). Critical review of liability for benzodiazepine abuse among alcoholics. *American Journal of Psychiatry, 145,* 1501–1506.

Fava, M., & Rosenbaum, (1991). Suicidality and fluoxetine: Is there a relationship? *Journal of Clinical Psychiatry, 52*(3), 108–111.

Frishman, W. H. (1981). Beta-adrenoceptor antagonists: New drugs and new indications. *New England Journal of Medicine, 305,* 500.

Hartley, L. R., Ungapen, S., & Davie, T. (1983). The effect of beta adrenergic blocking drugs on speaker's performance and memory. *British Journal of Psychiatry, 142,* 512.

Gorman, J. M., Levy, G. F., Liebowitz, M. R., McGrath, P., Appleby, I. L., Dillon, D. J., Davies, S. O., & Klein, D. F. (1983). Effect of acute beta-adrenergic blockade on lactate-induced panic. *Archives of General Psychiatry, 40,* 1079.

Gorman, J. M., Liebowitz, M. R., Fyer, A. J., Campeas, R., & Klein, D. F. (1985). Treatment of social phobia with atenolol. *Journal of Clinical Psychopharmacology, 5,* 298.

Gottschalk, L. A., Stone, W. N., & Gleser, C. G. (1974). Peripheral versus central mechanisms accounting for antianxiety effects of propranolol. *Psychosomatic Medicine, 36,* 47.

Kathol, R. G., Noyes, R., Jr., Slymen, D. J., (1980). Propranolol in chronic anxiety disorders: A controlled study. *Archives of General Psychiatry, 37,* 1361.

Klein, D. F. (1964). Delineation of two drug-responsive anxiety syndromes. *Psychopharmacology Bulletin, 5,* 397.

Klein, D. F., & Fink, M. (1962). Psychiatric reaction patterns to imipramine. *American Journal of Psychiatry, 119,* 432–438.

Klein, D. F., Gittelman, R., Quitkin, F. M., & Rifkin, A. (1980). *Diagnosis and treatment of psychiatric disorders: Adults and children* (2nd ed.). Baltimore: Williams & Wilkins.

Liebowitz, M. R., Fyer, A. J., Gorman, J. M., Campeas, R. B., Sandberg, D. P., Hollander, E., Papp, L. A., & Klein, D. F. (1988). Tricyclic therapy of the DSM-III anxiety disorders: A review with implications for further research. *Journal of Psychiatric Research, 22* (Suppl. 1), 7–31.

Liebowitz, M. R., Schneier, F., Campeas, R., Gorman, J., Flyer, A., Hollander, E., Hatterer, J., & Papp, L. (1990). Phenelzine and atenolol in social phobia. *Psychopharmacology Bulletin 26*(1), 123–125.

Myers, J. K., Weissman, M. M., Tischkler, G. L., Holzer, C. E. III, Leaf, P. J., Orvaschel, H., Anthony, J. C., Boyd, J. H., Burke, J. D., Kramer, M., & Stroltzman, R. (1984). Six-month prevalence of psychiatric disorders in three communities: 1980–1982. *Archives of General Psychiatry, 41,* 959–967.

Nelson, R. C. (1987). *Estimates of benzodiazepine use, doses, and duration of use; data on seizures and other reported withdrawal.* Washington DC: U.S. Food and Drug Administration.

Pato, M. T., Zohar-Kadouch, R., Zohar, J., & Murphy, D. L. (1988). Return of symptoms after discontinuation of clomipramine in patients with obsessive–compulsive disorder. *American Journal of Psychiatry, 145*(12), 1531–1525.

Pritchett, D. B., Sontheimer, H., Shivers, B., et al. (1989). Importance of a novel $GABA_A$ receptor subunit for benzodiazepine pharmacology. *Nature, 338,* 582–590.

Rickels, K., & Schweizer, E. (1987). Current pharmacotherapy of anxiety and panic. In H. Y. Meltzer (Ed.), *Psychopharmacology: The third generation of progress.* New York: Raven Press.

Rickels, K., Schweizer, E., Csanalosi, I., Case, W. G., & Chung, H. (1988). Long-term treatment of anxiety and risk of withdrawal. *Archives of General Psychiatry, 45*(5), 444–450.

Roy-Byrne, P. P., Dager, S. R., Cowley, D. S., Vitaliano, P., & Dunner, D. L. (1989). Relapse and rebound following discontinuation of benzodiazapine treatment of panic attacks: Alprazolam versus diazepam. *American Journal of Psychiatry, 146,* 860–864.

Sheehan, D. (1987). Benzodiazepines in panic disorder and agoraphobia. *Journal of Affective Disorders, 13,* 169–181.

Sheehan, D., Bach, M. B., Ballenger, J., & Jacobsen, G. (1980). Treatment of endogenous anxiety with phobic, hysterical, and hypochondriacal symptoms. *Archives of General Psychiatry, 37,* 51–59.

Snyder, S. H., & Peroutka, S. J. (1984). Antidepressants and neurotransmitter receptors. In R. M. Post & J. C. Ballenger (Eds.), *Neurobiology of mood disorders.* Baltimore: Williams & Wilkins.

Tallman, J. F., Paul, S. M., Skolnick, P., & Gallagher, D. W. (1980). Receptors for the age of anxiety: Pharmacology of the benzodiazepines. *Science, 207,* 274–281.

Tollefson, G. D. (1983). Monoamine oxidase inhibitors: A review. *Journal of Clinical Psychiatry, 44,* 280.

Turner, S. M., Jacob, R. G., & Beidel, D. C. (1985). Fluoxetine treatment of obsessive–compulsive disorder. *Journal of Clinical Psychopharmacology, 5,* 201–212.

Yudofsky, S., Williams, D., & Gorman, J. (1981). Propranolol in the treatment of rage and violent behavior in patients with chronic brain syndromes. *American Journal of Psychiatry, 138,* 218–220.

INTEGRATION

16

Specific Effects of Stress Management Techniques

PAUL M. LEHRER
ROBERT L. WOOLFOLK

This chapter reviews the empirical literature on selected comparisons among treatments described in this book. We focus on the theme of differential effects of the various techniques, and examine various other factors that may bear on the choosing of one technique over another.

Many additional studies have been reported since the first edition of this book (Woolfolk & Lehrer, 1984). There is much new information about mechanisms of action, predictors of success with specific techniques, and clinical effectiveness. However, the conclusions regarding the specificity of action of the various techniques are remarkably similar to those presented in 1984: There is considerable evidence for symptom–treatment specificity, but this is superimposed on a general "relaxation response." As we discuss in Chapters 18 and 19, the added effects of treatment–symptom specificity are clinically important for some disorders.

Models for Differential Selection of Techniques

The "Specific Effects" Model

The specific-effects hypothesis was formulated by Davidson and Schwartz (1976), who cited frequent findings of desynchronies among behavioral, cognitive, and somatic measures of anxiety. The specific-effects hypothesis suggests that a treatment oriented to one of these modalities will particularly benefit symptoms of that modality: cognitive treatments for cognitive symptoms, behavioral treatments for behavioral symptoms, and somatic treatments for somatic symptoms.

Davidson and Schwartz classified Jacobson's progressive relaxation (PR) technique (see McGuigan, Chapter 2, this volume) as a somatically oriented technique, because it focuses almost exclusively on muscular control. Some of the modified Jacobsonian procedures (see Bernstein & Carlson, Chapter 3, this volume) might also be thought of as having a primarily somatic emphasis, but they contain additional cognitive components, particularly suggestion. Similarly, biofeedback has a primarily somatic focus. Cognitive therapy is obviously a cognitive technique. Autogenic training (AT) has both cognitive and somatic aspects. It involves saying a formula (a cognitive activity), but it also involves paying attention to somatic processes, and has a greater emphasis than muscle relaxation techniques on autonomic effects. Davidson and Schwartz (1976) first classified mantra meditation as a somatic technique. Later, however, they reclassified it as a cognitive technique, because saying a verbal mantra might be expected to block verbal anxiety-related thoughts very directly (Schwartz, Davidson, & Goleman, 1978).

The "Relaxation Response" Model

The antithesis of the specific-effects hypothesis has been put forward by Benson (1975, 1983). Benson has argued that all the relaxation techniques produce a single "relaxation response," characterized by diminished sympathetic arousal and perhaps mediated by decreased norepinephrine receptor activity. He has stated that all relaxation methods involve verbal repetition and a passive attitude toward external stimuli (Benson, 1983). He concludes that their results are similar.

Compromise Position

A possible compromise position grew out of the research of Schwartz et al. (1978), who concluded that the specific effects of various relaxation techniques may be superimposed upon a general "relaxation response."

Smith's Hierarchical Model

A new model for categorizing relaxation therapies has been proposed by Smith (1986, 1988). In his view, relaxation training involves a set of specific behaviors and cognitions, which by their nature prescribe a preferred order for the teaching of relaxation skills. These include mental focusing, passivity, a redirection of attention, and receptivity to unusual and sometimes discrepant experiences (such as relaxation-induced anxiety). Effective relaxation training also involves making changes in basic beliefs and values, as well as committing oneself to have relaxation become more a salient and treasured component of daily life. Smith hypothesizes that physical relaxation techniques, such as PR and some hatha yoga exercises, are the easiest to learn. He notes that these tend to be used as an introduction to more complex methods before instruction in the latter is offered. The physical relaxation techniques are relatively concrete and require little change in basic cognitive structures for effectiveness. Next in difficulty are techniques with less structure and direction from the therapist. These involve concentration on a single stimulus, such as a word or a physical sensation. The most difficult level involves a state of complete passivity, without a specific attentional focus.

Although it would be useful to fit various techniques into specific levels of this model, the task is not easy, because most of the techniques involve multiple levels. PR, for example, is described by Smith as a concrete method. Its proponents, however, view it as more complex, involving several levels of Smith's hierarchy. Consistent with Smith's categorization, PR (Jacobson, 1938) begins by training areas of the body whose movements are easy to see as well as feel (i.e., the limbs). However, toward the end of treatment PR provides training to the eye and speech areas, which can be self-monitored only by proprioception, and which are brought into action during the process of thinking. This is a more abstract level in Smith's scheme. Also, to the Jacobsonian, true relaxation is a *completely* passive condition, including mental as well as physical passivity. Tension–release activity and even directed mental concentration on specific muscles are used only in the didactic phase of training. They are not used to produce relaxation in daily life, because they themselves produce increases in muscle tension—in the eyes as well as in the target area.

Nevertheless, Smith's model is of heuristic value, and it raises important questions about the complexity of factors involved in effective relaxation training. However-er, the model is still too new to have been adequately evaluated experimentally, so it is examined here only in passing.

Subject Populations

Choice of subject population is a problem in many of the studies we reviewed. Using college students as the subject population may have contributed to the small between-groups differences found in some studies. Lehrer (1978) found that subjects who are not psychiatric patients tend to show a "floor effect" in psychophysiological studies of relaxation. With little or no relaxation training, they can relax very deeply, and differences among techniques may thus be expected to appear as very small or nonexistent when tested in nonclinical populations. Thus the effects of various treat-ments and differences among them may be stronger than many of the studies discussed here seem to show.

Procedural Variables in Progressive Relaxation: Jacobson's Method versus "Modified Jacobsonian Procedures"

In Chapter 2, McGuigan describes Jacobson's original technique of PR. In Chapter 3, Bernstein and Carlson describe the modified PR techniques that are currently in vogue. Elsewhere (Lehrer, Woolfolk, & Goldman, 1986), we have discussed differ-ences between the two approaches in more detail. They can be summarized briefly as follows:

1. The Jacobson technique is focused on changing levels of muscle tension per se, whereas the revised techniques emphasize *perception* of physical and emotional tension, or cognitive activity associated with doing relaxation instruction.

2. The Jacobson technique eschews such training aids as taped instructions,

hypnotic suggestion, biofeedback, and an especially relaxing ambience for relaxation training. The latter elements are thought to produce dependence on these external aids; in so doing, they are thought to reduce both the motivation and specific training required to learn the skill of PR. The revised techniques use these aids to enhance compliance and perception of relaxation effects. Although Jacobsonian practitioners may use electromyographic biofeedback (EMG BFK) equipment to assess the effectiveness of their training, they tend not to use it as a training device.

3. The revised methods use gross tension–release instructions, whereas the Jacobsonian practitioners tend to use the "method of diminishing tensions" to produce more sensitive perception of very low levels of muscle tension. Proponents of the gross tension–release method hypothesize that it induces muscle relaxation because tension automatically decreases below baseline level after a period of deliberate muscle clenching. This hypothesis has been challenged experimentally (Lehrer, Batey, Woolfolk, Remde, & Garlick, 1988); we found *elevated* muscle tension in the period immediately after release of a voluntary muscle contraction. It is possible that slowed relaxation after maximal contraction may result from ischemia associated with muscle fatigue (Styf, 1990). Maximal contractions can slow relaxation by at least two parallel chemical processes (Cady, Elshove, Jones, & Moll, 1989). In a more recent study, Lucic, Steffen, Harrigan, and Stuebing (1991) found the lowest EMG levels after detailed instructions to relax various muscle groups without tensing them first. Prior tension–release training had been given, however. This finding appears to conflict with that obtained in an earlier study by Borkovec and Hennings (1978). In this study greater tension-reducing effects occurred for tension–release instructions than for suggestions to relax the muscles. Presumably, the prior tension–release instructions in the study by Lucic et al. (1991) provided more effective training, even though they were delivered by tape recording (see "Live versus Taped Training," below).

4. In the Jacobson technique, training sessions are devoted to teaching muscular relaxation skills and developing competence with them over time. A state of emotional or cognitive relaxation may not be experienced *during* training sessions, particularly toward the beginning. The revised techniques do emphasize creating a sense of relaxation during the sessions.

5. Both techniques contain methods for generalization of relaxation skills. The Jacobson technique does this through "differential relaxation" training. As described by McGuigan (Chapter 2), the trainee deliberately practices relaxation in daily life, particularly in situations that might elicit emotional or physical tension. Jacobson emphasized the development of voluntary conscious control of muscle tension in all situations. In the revised methods, on the other hand, there tends to be a greater emphasis on "conditioned relaxation." This involves cognitive creation of associational bridges among various words and cues that are repeated in a state of deep relaxation. These cues are used as "relaxation stimuli" during times of stress, and are described as producing an almost "automatic" relaxation response. Jacobson doubted the usefulness of this perceived response unless it was accompanied by a genuine reduction in neuromuscular tension.

Because of the many differences between these Jacobson's PR technique and the modified PR methods, we believe that the two are sufficiently distinct to be considered as two separate approaches. There has been little empirical investigation of differences between the two. So far, we have found only two studies (Snow, 1977/1978; Turner, 1978) that have compared Jacobson's technique with some modified ones. These studies showed some marginal advantages for Jacobson's original technique on measures of anxiety and heart rate. Both, however, were flawed by their use of "normal" college students as their subject population. In these subjects, as noted earlier, a "floor effect" may have obscured some real differences between the two PR approaches. Several *components* of differences between the approaches have been studied, however.

Live versus Taped Training

Elsewhere, we have reviewed the voluminous literature on live versus taped relaxation training (Lehrer, 1982; Lehrer & Woolfolk, 1984), and concluded that only live relaxation training provides subjects with skills that enable them to lower the level of physiological arousal outside the training session. Both techniques work equally well *within* training sessions, however (see the more recent study by Stefanek & Hodes, 1986). This is consistent with the acceptability of taped relaxation training in some revised PR methods that emphasize feelings of relaxation during a training session. Taped relaxation training is not always effective even here, however, particularly when the outcome criterion is a physiological response. We have found no data evaluating the effects of relaxation tapes for use during home practice, as an *adjunct* to live training.

Why is live training more psychophysiologically effective? Paul and Trimble (1970) hypothesize that immediate feedback to the subject and response-contingent training are the critical ingredients. The "response-contingent training" component involves advancing the pace of training when a skill is being learned rapidly and giving additional instruction when some difficulties occur. The reasons for the advantages of live training become self-evident when one thinks about the training of other analogous muscular skills. Could anyone doubt that live training in (say) learning to play tennis, to dance, or to play the piano would be more effective than taped training?

The advantage of live training in producing physiological effects is not attributable simply to repetition of instructions when subjects have difficulty feeling tension in a particular muscle group (Godsey, 1979/1980; Quayle, 1979/1980). Both of these studies examined subject-contingent versus program-contingent repetition of instruction. In the subject-contingent condition, instructions were repeated when a subject was having difficulty locating a sensation of tension or difficulty relaxing a particular muscle. In the program-contingent condition, instructions were presented at a predetermined pace, independent of the progress of individual subjects. Quayle (1979/1980) found that subject-contingent instruction produced greater decreases in EMG levels and skin temperature than program-contingent instructions, but that program-contingent instructions were more effective in reducing self-report measures of anxiety. Similarly, Godsey (1979/1980) found no significant differences between subject-contingent and program-contingent instruction on heart rate or skin conductance. (In both studies, live training produced greater decreases than taped training in the physiological measures mentioned above.)

It is also possible that the advantages for relaxation training may be explained by interpersonal factors in the relationship between client and therapist. Taub (1977; Taub & School, 1978) found that even the relatively mechanical procedure of raising hand temperature through biofeedback could not be learned from an instructor with an aloof, matter-of-fact style. It was, however, readily learned when the instructor was interpersonally warm. Contrary to these findings, Blanchard et al. (1983) found no relationship between subjects' perceptions of therapists' warmth, competence, or helpfulness and reduction in headache activity with various relaxation–biofeedback strategies. Therapist warmth may therefore not be a critical factor in all circumstances.

Another ingredient in the differential success of live PR training might be the amount of feedback that the live instructor can give to the learner during training. When the subject is unable to feel tension, the instructor may intervene in several ways. The instructor may simply point out the remaining tension, or may illustrate it kinesthetically by passively flexing a muscle or by putting resistance against an attempted limb movement. Relaxation instruction involves teaching the trainee to be his or her own biofeedback machine. All possible methods of effective communication (demonstration, reinforcement, etc.) may be used.

One recent study using "enhanced" tape-recorded PR training did produce significant generalizable effects on EMG, heart rate, and subjective measures of anxiety and stress (Hoshmand, Helmes, Kazarian, & Tekatch, 1985). Enhanced training included cue control training, "application" training (i.e., differential relaxation, as described by McGuigan in Chapter 2 of this volume), and reminders to practice relaxation and to use it in stressful situations. It is possible that the enhancing conditions were critical for the success of the technique.

Use of Electromyographic Biofeedback

Elsewhere, we have reviewed the comparative literature on EMG BFK and PR (Lehrer, 1982; Lehrer, Woolfolk, & Goldman, 1986). Studies of EMG BFK combined with taped relaxation instructions suggest that EMG BFK may help to potentiate the effectiveness of taped relaxation training. However, these findings are only strong when the primary outcome measure is EMG from the muscle under the biofeedback electrodes. More recent data suggest that taped PR training provides marginally greater cognitive effects (defined as including self-reports of somatic activity) than EMG BFK. Funch and Gale (1984) found taped PR training to be more effective than EMG BFK in producing decreases in self-reported bruxing activity among sufferers from temporomandibular joint pain. Burish and Hendrix (1980) found that EMG BFK was more effective than simple suggestions to relax in reducing frontal EMG activity toward the end of a 30-minute session. This was not noted toward the beginning of the session. The two methods produced equivalent EMG reductions following threat of electric shock. The combination of EMG BFK and relaxation suggestions did not differ from those of EMG BFK alone.

Comparisons between live PR training and EMG BFK have produced mixed results. In the our review in the first edition of this book (Lehrer & Woolfolk, 1984), we concluded that live EMG BFK appears to add little to the effectiveness of live PR instruction. This conclusion was consistent with Jacobson's view that EMG BFK is not useful as either an adjunct to or a substitute for PR. More recent data, however, show that although PR may produce greater cognitive effects than EMG BFK, the latter appears to have greater effects in reducing surface EMG levels. Scandrett, Bean, Breeden, and Powell (1986) found that modified PR instructions produced greater reductions in self-reported anxiety than did EMG BFK, although the reverse was the case for reductions in EMG levels. These instructions included considerable cognitive and suggestive components, which perhaps accounted for the cognitive emphasis in their effects. Subjects in this study were anxious psychiatric patients. Denkowski and Denkowski (1984) found that PR and EMG BFK both resulted in improved academic achievement and decreased disruptive classroom behavior among hyperactive children. PR, however, produced a greater shift toward internal locus of control. Although the authors suggest that this reflected subjects' relative boredom with EMG BFK, the greater cognitive emphasis of PR may have played a role in this finding. The fact that PR was taught in a group while EMG BFK was administered individually may also have enlisted peer pressure on the side of more acceptable school behavior in this study. Other comparisons between EMG BFK and live relaxation instruction have generally shown that the latter has greater effects on a variety of self-report measures (see reviews by Lehrer, 1982; Lehrer, Woolfolk, & Goldman, 1986).

Similarly, LeBoeuf and Lodge (1980) found larger effects for EMG BFK than for PR in frontalis EMG during a training session. However, the advantage of EMG BFK did not generalize to heart rate or to anxiety levels. An opposite finding was reported by Rawson, Bhatnagar, and Schneider (1985). They did a within-subject comparison and devoted one session to each treatment; they found smaller decreases in heart rate with PR than with either EMG BFK or self-relaxation. It is possible, however, that the tension–release instructions in this single session may have produced transient physiological arousal, thus producing this anomalous result. A classic study by Alexander (1975), however, casts doubt on whether EMG BFK to a single muscle site is at all an effective method for teaching general relaxation. He found no generalization from frontalis EMG BFK to EMG levels in the limbs, and no differences between the EMG BFK condition and a control condition in subjective level of relaxation.

Also, some disorders may respond differentially to EMG BFK. In Chapter 19, in our discussion of relaxation therapy for asthma, we note studies showing that facial EMG BFK may be a critical element in the success of this technique.

Relaxation versus Meditation

Because he believes that all relaxation techniques have approximately the same effects, Benson (1975) argues that the best technique is the one that is simplest to teach and to learn. His own early technique involved simply saying the word "one" with each exhalation; in the present volume this is called "respiratory one meditation"

(ROM). Benson has asserted that the effects of ROM are at least equivalent to those of more complex techniques (see Greenwood & Benson, 1977). Furthermore, because of the ease of administering it, Benson argues that ROM is preferable to other techniques. More recently, Benson and Proctor (1985) have suggested that prayer or other individualized verbal devices can be substituted for the word "one."

Schwartz et al. (1978), in contrast to Benson, have described some evidence that transcendental meditation (TM) produces specific cognitive effects. They compared people who meditated regularly with people who exercised regularly. The meditators had fewer cognitive symptoms of stress than the exercisers, whereas the exercisers had fewer self-reported somatic symptoms of stress than the meditators. This finding was inconclusive, however: Because subjects had not been randomly assigned to the two groups, individual differences between groups may have accounted for the findings. Norton and Johnson (1983) provided other data showing cognitive–somatic specificity for meditation and relaxation. Studying snake phobics in a snake approach situation, they compared PR with agni yoga (comprising primarily imaginal meditative exercises). They found that subjects scoring high on cognitive anxiety approached the snake more closely after agni yoga than after PR, whereas subjects high on somatic anxiety approached more closely after PR. Additional evidence comes from data on hypertension (reviewed in Chapter 19), suggesting that meditation may have a weaker effect than PR in reducing blood pressure.

Some evidence has accumulated that PR does indeed produce greater reductions in somatic tension than mantra meditation does. Warrenberg, Pagano, Woods, and Hlastala (1980) found that resting heart rates were lower among long-term practitioners of PR than among long-term practitioners of TM. This is not surprising, since PR is specifically directed at the skeletal muscles, and heart rate is directly affected by muscle tension. This result is consistent with Davidson and Schwartz's (1976) hypothesis. English and Baker (1983) found greater decreases in systolic blood pressure with PR than with Benson's ROM technique, although the effects on reaction time and diastolic blood pressure were similar. Both treatments produced greater blood pressure decreases than control conditions did in a healthy population.

In contrast, Carlson, Bacaseta, and Simanton (1988) found that tape-recorded instructions in "devotional meditation" (listening to scriptural passages and thinking about their meaning) produced lower levels of anxiety and lower EMG levels than did either tape-recorded PR or a waiting-list control. The poor showing of PR here, however, may be attributable to the use of taped instructions. A study of long-term practitioners of PR and TM by Curtis and Wessberg (1980) failed to find any differences between the groups on heart rate, skin conductance, or respiration rate. Warrenburg et al. (1980), however, noted that the levels of arousal in Curtis and Wessberg's subjects were unusually high, perhaps suggesting a problem in the experimental method.

Eppley, Abrams, and Shear (1989) conducted a meta-analysis of the effects of various relaxation techniques on trait anxiety. Their results were consistent with the specific-effects theory: They found a greater effect size for TM than for other relaxation techniques in reduction of trait anxiety. On the other hand, Shapiro (1982) has concluded that meditation does not produce specific physiological patterns differing from those produced by other relaxation techniques.

There is some evidence that mantra meditation may, under some circumstances, produce a desynchrony between cortical and somatic indices of arousal. The most consistent physiological effects of meditation appear to be effects on electroencephalographic (EEG) rhythms. Reviews conclude that meditative ecstasy is often accompanied by increases in beta rhythms and suppression of alpha activity, whereas alpha activity is enhanced in states of relaxation that may occur during meditation (see reviews by Delmonte, 1984a; West, 1980; Woolfolk, 1975). One study (Lehrer, Schoicket, Carrington, & Woolfolk, 1980) found more EEG alpha activity but higher heart rate and muscle tension in a testing session after training in mantra meditation than after either PR or a control condition. Thus, meditation appeared to produce cortical relaxation with simultaneous somatic arousal. However, these results were not replicated in a subsequent study (Lehrer, Woolfolk, Rooney, McCann, & Carrington, 1983). Delmonte (1984a) observed in his literature review that "meditators more readily demonstrate alpha [and theta] levels than controls, even when not meditating" (p. 219). We have hypothesized that frontal EEG alpha may be a physiological marker for diminished cognitive activity (Lehrer, Schoicket, et al., 1980); this would make our own results consistent with the Davidson and Schwartz (1976) hypothesis.

PR does not appear to have consistent effects on EEG activity. Lehrer (1978) found that PR produced increases in occipital alpha activity among anxiety neurotics, but borderline-significant *decreases* among normal subjects. Lindholm and Lowry (1978) found that prior training in PR did not facilitate learning in an EEG alpha biofeedback experiment. Lehrer (1978) found no effects for PR training on the sensory–motor rhythm (approximately 13 Hz, recorded from near the motor cortex). However, Carter, Johnson, and Borkovec (1986) found that PR produced diminution in cortical activation, less asymmetric left-hemispheric dominance, and diminished worry activity.

Although the effects of meditation on tonic muscle tension and heart rate may be quite variable, the effects on cardiac reactivity are more consistent. In two studies, we found greater cardiac decelerations in meditation than in PR in response to noxious stimuli (Lehrer, Schoicket, et al., 1980; Lehrer et al., 1983). The relation between this result and the EEG findings is unclear. Perhaps both reflect cognitive relaxation. The augmented cardiac decelerations to noxious stimuli in our studies may reflect a tendency to react to changes in the environment with curiosity, acceptance, and interest, rather than with anxiety; thus, they may be interpreted as "orienting" rather than as "defensive" reflexes (see Graham & Clifton, 1966; Sokolov, 1963). Similar results were reported by Goleman and Schwartz (1976), who found greater autonomic responsivity to stressful scenes in a movie among meditators than among nonmeditators, but faster autonomic recovery among meditators. It is possible that such a response set over a long period may diminish tonic cardiovascular activity, and thus may be helpful in overcoming psychosomatic disease.

A recent paper by Kokoszka (1990) focuses on the philosophical underpinnings of relaxation and meditation therapies, and concludes that they differ in important respects. Meditation is a means toward achieving personal growth and finding a system of values and philosophy of life, whereas most relaxation techniques are designed as treatments for particular disorders. These functions may overlap, however, because re-evaluating one's philosophy of life is often a necessary component of learning to master stress (see Patel, Chapter 4, and Beck, Chapter 11, this volume).

Meditation versus Biofeedback

The hypothesis presented by Davidson and Schwartz (1976) predicts that biofeedback for various somatic functions should produce more somatic effects and meditation should produce more cognitive effects. A study by Cuthbert, Kristeller, Simons, Hodes, and Lang (1981) provides some support and some contrary evidence for this hypothesis. Self-report measures of anxiety (i.e., cognitive measures) were reduced more by Benson's meditation technique (ROM) than by heart rate biofeedback. However, contrary to the specific effects theory, ROM also was more effective than heart rate biofeedback in reducing skin conductance and heart rate. The effects of EMG BFK were similar to those of heart rate biofeedback. It is possible that this contrary finding can be attributed to the brief training (three sessions) provided in biofeedback. ROM, a very simple technique, can be mastered more quickly than biofeedback, and specific effects may only be observable after more lengthy training.

Strong findings consistent with this interpretation were reported by Sedlacek, Cohen, and Boxhill (1979). Twenty sessions of combined training in thermal biofeedback (TBFK) and EMG BFK were compared with the same number of training sessions in ROM. The effects for EMG BFK in lowering blood pressure were dramatically greater than those for meditation. Here, however, the large number of sessions devoted to ROM may have hurt the technique. People can easily learn ROM in only one or two sessions; it is difficult to imagine how people could be kept interested and involved during 20 sessions of training. At the very least, subjects may have wondered why so much training was needed, and this may have undermined the credibility of the procedure. Hafner (1982) studied patients with essential hypertension and found greater blood pressure reductions among subjects given one session of mantra meditation plus skin resistance biofeedback or EMG BFK than among those just given meditation. Two other studies (Fee & Girdano, 1978; Zaichkowsky & Kamen, 1978) found no differences between EMG BFK and ROM in reducing frontalis EMG.

Although these studies are supportive of the specific-effects hypothesis, further research is needed to find how stable the results are. A study with discrepant results was reported by Pollard and Ashton (1982), who found a greater decrease in heart rate with meditation than with heart rate biofeedback.

Autogenic Training and Thermal Biofeedback

Comparison with Muscle Relaxation Methods

The six standard exercises in AT emphasize sensations involving the autonomic nervous system (e.g., warm hands, slow heart rate, a cool forehead, a warm solar plexus). According to the specific-effects hypothesis, the technique should have greater effects on autonomic activity than PR and/or EMG BFK should have. The latter two techniques should have greater effects on the musculoskeletal system. Similarly, TBFK might be expected to have greater effects than muscle relaxation techniques on measures of blood flow and on disorders associated with blood flow.

With a few exceptions, AT and TBFK have been found to have greater effects than PR or EMG BFK on autonomic measures and disorders associated with autonomic dysfunction. Gamble and Elder (1983) found greater forehead cooling with forehead TBFK training than with EMG BFK or PR training. Lehrer, Atthowe, and Weber (1980) found greater decreases in heart rate during AT than during PR in subjects who initially scored high on the IPAT Anxiety Inventory (Krug, Scheier, & Cattell, 1976). Both groups showed decreases in anxiety and in various other self-report measures of psychological distress. Fray (1975) found AT to be superior to EMG BFK in maintaining blood pressure reductions at follow-up. Three papers from Blanchard's laboratory (Blanchard et al., 1984, 1986; McCoy et al., 1988) reported greater reductions in mean arterial blood pressure and plasma norepinephrine after TBFK than after PR. However, another paper from this laboratory reported greater decreases in heart rate reactivity to laboratory stressors after PR than after TBFK in the same population (Blanchard, McCoy, et al., 1988). An additional study found greater reductions in blood pressure with TBFK or breathing–relaxation training (comprising a combination of PR and concentrating on the words "in" and "out" during breathing) than with AT (Aivazyan, Zaitsev, Salenko, Yurenev, & Patrusheva, 1988). In this study, it is possible that breathing training may have augmented the autonomic effects of muscle relaxation alone, rendering it equivalent to TBFK. Similarly, as described in Chapter 19, in the section on headaches, migraine headaches appear to be more effectively treated by AT and/or TBFK than by PR and/or EMG BFK.

Conversely, there is evidence that PR and EMG BFK have greater effects on muscular tension and symptoms associated with it than AT and TFBK do. A study by Staples, Coursey, and Smith (1975) found lower frontalis EMG levels during the last of 10 sessions of taped training in PR and in EMG BFK than in the corresponding session of taped AT. In the section on headaches in Chapter 19, we review data showing that PR and EMG BFK have stronger effects than AT and TBFK in the treatment of muscle contraction headaches. In a mixed clinical population, Schneider, Rawson, and Bhatnagar (1987) found that EMG BFK produced bigger decreases in EMG than AT and self-relaxation. Gamble and Elder (1983) found that EMG BFK produced greater decreases in muscle tension than forehead TFBK among sufferers from migraine headaches. Banner and Meadows (1983) found no cognitive or physiological differences among AT, EMG BFK, and the combination of the two. However, this study was done on normal subjects recruited from advertisements for volunteers; moreover, no differences were found between any of the relaxation techniques and a placebo condition, perhaps suggesting the existence of a floor effect on this healthy population.

There is some evidence that the effectiveness with which a technique is taught and learned may be as important as the specific technique used. In a study comparing PR and TBFK as treatments for hypertension, Wittrock, Blanchard, and McCoy

(1988) found a significant association between improvement in blood pressure and appropriate measures of having learned the two techniques effectively (self-reported depth of relaxation for the PR group, and increase in finger temperature for the TBFK group).

Autogenic Training and Hypnosis

Comparisons between AT and hypnosis are reviewed in the "Hypnosis versus Other Methods" section below. There is, however, a definitional problem in these comparisons, because some argue that AT *is* a form of self-hypnosis. Krenz (1986) notes that AT "looks, sounds, and feels like hypnosis," and that the German Society for Hypnosis and Autogenic Training defines AT as a method of self-hypnosis. On the other hand, he notes that Wolfgang Luthe, whose writings introduced AT to the English-speaking world, defined the two methods as distinctly separate therapies. It has been claimed that J. H. Schultz, the originator of the technique, replaced hypnosis with AT in his own practice because he found hypnosis to be unreliable, but this has been disputed. No direct comparisons have been made between AT and formal hypnosis.

Cognitive Effects of Autogenic Training, Thermal Biofeedback, and Progressive Relaxation

As mentioned above, Davidson and Schwartz (1976) hypothesized that AT should have more cognitive effects than such purely somatically oriented techniques as biofeedback or PR, because it contains a mixture of cognitive and somatic elements. There is evidence that the specific suggestions regarding warmth, heaviness, and so forth in AT may have the specific effect of producing these sensations, compared with PR (Lehrer, Atthowe, & Weber, 1980; Shapiro & Lehrer, 1980). There is also evidence that AT may produce more vivid images and emotions than PR (Borgeat, Stravynski, & Chaloult, 1983). Some equivocal data, which nevertheless favor the specific-effects theory, were obtained in a recent Chinese study. Sun et al. (1986) found that the combination of AT and EMG BFK was more effective in reducing self-reported test anxiety (i.e., a cognitive measure) than EMG BFK alone, but that the combination of AT and TBFK appeared to have no greater effect than TBFK alone. Both biofeedback methods alone produced greater decreases in anxiety than those produced in a waiting-list condition. Only the group receiving EMG BFK and AT showed greater decreases in anxiety than a false-feedback condition. The incremental effectiveness of adding AT to EMG BFK is consistent with the specific-effects theory. The greater effects of EMG BFK than of TBFK remain unexplained.

   Not all results have supported the notion of specific cognitive effects for AT. Negative results were obtained by Staples et al. (1975), who found no cognitive differences between the two techniques. Similarly, in a study of anxious pregnant women, Yang, Xin, Chen, and Hu (1987) found no greater anxiety reduction when AT was added to EMG BFK. The opposite relationship was found by Detrick (1977/

1978), who observed greater decreases in self-reported anxiety (a cognitive measure) for the combination of PR and EMG BFK than for that of AT and TBFK. Hartman (1982) studied a group of subjects with anxiety-based disorders, who had been classified as having either high or low vividness of imagery. Subjects with high imagery showed greater reductions in cognitive and somatic anxiety after PR than after AT, whereas no differential effects were found for the two techniques among low-imagery subjects.

Differences between Autogenic Training and Thermal Biofeedback

It has long been assumed that the effects of AT on peripheral temperature are quite similar to those of TBFK (see Surwit, 1982). There is, in fact, considerable evidence for a large overlap in effects. For example, Surwit, Pilon, and Fenton (1978) found no differences between TBFK and the combination of TBFK and AT on physiological or self-report measures of symptoms associated with Raynaud's disease. Kluger, Jamner, and Tursky (1985) examined changes in hand temperature among normal college students, and found no differences among TBFK, finger pulse volume biofeedback, and tape-recorded "autogenic-like" instructions emphasizing warmth and heaviness. Blanchard, Khramelashvili, et al. (1988) found similar effects for the two techniques in treatment of mild hypertension.

However, Freedman (1991) has noted some discrepancies between effects of finger-warming procedures and those of various relaxation therapies, and has proposed a physiological mechanism that may explain them. He reported evidence that TBFK produces greater rises in finger temperature than AT, EMG BFK, or simple instructions to increase finger temperature (Freedman & Ianni, 1983; Freedman, 1989). Similar results were obtained from repeated assessment of two individuals by Kelso and Bryson-Brockmann (1985). Freedman and his colleagues also found that TBFK produces greater symptom reduction and tolerance to cold stressors among patients with Raynaud's disease (Freedman, Ianni, & Wenig, 1983), as well as more durable effects (Freedman, 1987). These findings are consistent with data described by Sargent, Solbach, Coyne, Spohn, and Sergerson (1986). These investigators also found borderline-significant findings of greater symptom reduction with TBFK than with AT or EMG BFK for treatment of migraine headaches. As described above, Aivazyan et al. (1988) found greater blood pressure reductions with TBFK than with AT.

Freedman hypothesizes that the effects of TBFK may not all be in the direction of producing a global relaxation response, and that this may explain some specific effects of the technique. Relaxation tends to reduce both alpha and beta sympathetic activity. Although it has long been known that alpha sympathetic activity produces peripheral vasoconstriction, Freedman et al. (1988) have produced some data showing that beta sympathetic arousal may produce peripheral *vasodilation*. Thus relaxation therapy may *inhibit* one mechanism for hand warming. TBFK, in contrast, may enhance the beta sympathetic component in finger warming.

The addition of biofeedback to AT may have two combined effects: It may increase the motivational power of AT, and it may increase the effectiveness of AT in treating certain problems. Sakai and Takeichi (1985) treated 39 individuals with psychosomatic or affective disorders, and noted that combinations of AT and other relaxation or biofeedback techniques were more effective than was AT alone. Hohne and Bohn (1988) noted that the addition of TBFK to AT decreased the dropout rate among psychiatric patients.

Autogenic Training versus Meditation

Mantra meditation and AT both contain cognitive components, inasmuch as both involve saying something to oneself. AT also involves suggestions related to the autonomic nervous system. The specific-effects hypothesis would therefore predict a greater autonomic effect for AT, and equivalent cognitive effects for the two techniques.

Consistent with the specific-effects theory were the results of a study on hypertensives, reported by Cohen and Sedlacek (1983). In this study, Benson's ROM procedure was compared with a combined procedure that included PR, AT, relaxing imagery, EMG BFK, and TBFK. The combined procedure produced both greater decreases in diastolic blood pressure and increases in field independence than did either ROM or a waiting-list control. The effective components in the combined method were not evaluated separately. It is, however, interesting that its components included two techniques with a strong autonomic component (AT and TBFK). It also included a treatment specifically entailing imagery—hence, perhaps, the particularly strong effects on outcome measures involving an autonomic variable (blood pressure) and visualization (field independence).

Other studies have yielded results that are less clear. Gallois and colleagues (Gallois, 1984; Gallois, Forzy, & Dhont, 1984) found that regular practitioners of TM showed lower baseline levels of prolactin and cortisol than did individuals who regularly practiced AT. Meditators also manifested significantly greater decreases in these hormones and more frequent periods of suspended respiration during meditation. Both groups showed decreased urinary catecholamines and increased simple reaction time. By contrast, catecholamines increased and reaction time decreased in a control group during testing. The major problem in this research was lack of random assignment to treatments, and the various biasing factors may have contributed to subjects' selection of one treatment over another. Also, demand characteristics of the testing situation may have been very different for subjects in the three groups.

Zeier (1985) used a "within-subject" design, in which all subjects were experienced in AT and were given one session of training in a meditation technique. He used a "respiratory meditation" procedure, involving saying a mantra upon every exhalation—a technique similar to Benson's ROM technique. Subjects listened to slow baroque music during this procedure. Zeier found a greater decrease in skin conductance, respiration rate, and a combined index of physiological arousal with the meditation technique. An obvious problem in this study was failure to control for the possibility that adding *any* new technique may predispose subjects to take it more seriously during testing. It nevertheless suggests that this type of meditation shows promise of enhancing autogenic instructions.

In summary, there is no conclusive evidence for systematic differential effects between AT and meditation. It is surprising that AT has not yielded greater autonomic effects than meditation, given its greater autonomic focus. Perhaps the emphasis on breathing in many meditation techniques augments the somatic focus of the latter. Cognitively, the two procedures are similar, with each involving repetition of simple verbal material.

Listening to Music versus Other Stress Management Techniques

There is evidence that listening to music may potentiate the effects of other relaxation techniques, at least during a training session. Music is highly suitable as a component in a multimodal treatment, because it can be presented while other techniques are being practiced. Using repeated observations on 35 normal subjects in a Latin square design, Chaloult, Borgeat, and Elie (1988) compared relaxing music with autogenic suggestions and the combination of the two. They found greater psychological effects for the combination than for either technique separately. The autogenic instructions were given at several degrees of loudness compared with the music, ranging from "subliminal" suggestion to a condition in which the suggestions were louder than the music; generally, greater effects were obtained with louder suggestions. No physiological differences among conditions were obtained. Reynolds (1984) compared four relaxation techniques in a population of healthy undergraduates during stressful imagery. All subjects received EMG BFK training. Significant decreases in EMG activity were found among subjects who also listened to music and among subjects receiving both music and AT, but not in groups receiving AT or EMG BFK without music.

Scartelli (1984) found that "sedative music" enhanced the effects of EMG BFK in reducing facial EMG among a group of music students. In a second study, Scartelli and Borling (1986) found the enhancing effects of music to be greater when it either preceded or followed EMG BFK, rather than co-occurring with it. Kimmel, Palomba, and Stegagno (1986) found a more prolonged decrease in heart rate after visual heart rate biofeedback when subjects were listening to music during training than when they were not. An earlier study from the same laboratory, however, had found no differences among music, listening to a pure tone, and silence in heart rate or in transfer of heart rate training during or after heart rate biofeedback training (Kimmel, Palomba, & Stegagno, 1984). Delle-Chiaie, Guerani, and Biondi (1981) reported a significantly greater decrease in self-reported anxiety among a group of anxious subjects given EMG BFK with relaxing music, compared with simple tones, as a feedback signal. Guyer and Guyer (1984) compared relaxing music with taped PR and a waiting-list control among healthy adolescents. They found no differences among groups in several measures of emotions and moods. Similar results were obtained on adults by Miller and Bornstein (1977). Stoudenmire (1975) found equivalent decreases in state anxiety while subjects listened to a single session of relaxing music or a tape of PR instructions. No decreases in trait anxiety occurred.

Several studies have compared the effects of music with suggestion. The results are variable, but indicate that the effects of the two interventions may be comparable.

Edelman (1970) found greater decreases in systolic blood pressure while subjects listened to "semiclassical music" than while receiving relaxation suggestions. There were no differences between the music condition and taped PR. Fowler and Lander (1987) found that music was more effective than hypnotic suggestion in treating injection pain in 200 young children. Combining the two techniques did not produce more beneficial effects than music alone. Opposite findings, however, were reported by Stanton (1984), who found significant reductions in anxiety among 60 anxious adults who received either hypnotic suggestions or music. Sessions with each technique were held once weekly for 3 weeks, and were compared with a no-treatment control. The suggestion group showed greater anxiety reduction than the music group. Tsao, Gordon, Maranto, Lerman, and Murasko (1991) found significant increases in salivary immunoglobulin A (a measure of immune function) in three treatment conditions than in a waiting-list control condition among college students. The conditions were listening to music that was judged to be relaxing and imagery-inducing; imagining the body producing immune cells (a suggestion-like procedure); and a combination of the two procedures. No differences were found among the three active treatment conditions.

Kibler and Rider (1983) found no differences among PR, relaxing music, and the combination of the two in increasing finger temperature. Treatment effects in this study may have been attenuated, however, by the fact that the subjects were asymptomatic students in a college music class. Schilling and Poppen (1983) found that music was not as effective as either EMG BFK or PR in reducing EMG activity. Similar findings were obtained by Page and Schaub (1978) for the combination of PR and EMG BFK among subjects with chronic tension and anxiety.

The relaxing effects of music appear to depend on the kind of music used. Rider (1985) used an "entrainment" condition, which involves having the subject listen initially to music appropriate to his or her level of arousal, and only gradually shifting to relaxing music. He found that this procedure was more effective in reducing EMG activity and pain ratings among patients with spinal cord injuries than listening to relaxing music alone or a no-music condition. Stratton and Zalanowski (1984) reported, not surprisingly, that the type of music most preferred by subjects tended to have the most relaxing effects, as measured by self-report. Comparisons between music and more physiological techniques tend to show fewer somatic effects for music. This has been shown in comparisons with EMG BFK on frontalis EMG (Page & Schaub, 1978).

In summary, the research literature shows that music sometimes has relaxing effects as powerful as those of suggestion and various relaxation techniques, and may potentiate the effects of other relaxation techniques when used properly. However, despite the well-known adage that "music soothes the savage breast," music is relatively rarely used by stress management therapists. Studies comparing music with PR and biofeedback tend to show that music produces fewer physiological effects. An apparent drawback is that music cannot be transported to sites where "real-life" stress management is needed; this difficulty, however, can now easily be overcome by using a miniature portable tape recorder. The knotty problems involved in choice of musical selections, discussed earlier in this volume by Maranto (Chapter 13), render conclusions about the relative and potential effects of music difficult to draw at this time.

Respiratory Strategies versus Other Methods

Research thus far suggests that methods involving alterations in respiratory patterns may be effective for alleviating the effects of stressors, particularly symptoms related to hyperventilation. (See the section in Chapter 18 on anxiety and panic.) Zeier (1984) found that a "breathing–biofeedback" technique, presented along with suggestions similar to those used in AT and with relaxing music, produced lower levels of physiological arousal than the music and suggestions alone. This study used within-subject comparisons and a healthy population. The breathing–biofeedback technique involved concentrating on exhalation and receiving respiratory biofeedback. Using a multiple-baseline design with agoraphobics, Franklin (1989) compared cognitive therapy, PR, and respiratory retraining for treating agoraphobia. The results were consistent with the specific-effects theory: Cognitive therapy produced the greatest decrease in cognitive distress, muscle relaxation the greatest decrease in anxiety, and respiratory retraining the greatest decrease in the physiological accompaniments of panic. Longo (1984) studied blood pressure reductions in normotensive students, and compared taped PR training, guided imagery, and a method involving slow, deep breathing. He found that the deep breathing technique had the greatest effect on systolic blood pressure, and that guided imagery had a smaller effect than the other techniques on diastolic blood pressure.

Relaxation versus Cognitive Therapies

The hypothesis of specific effects should be even more applicable to the distinction between cognitive therapies and relaxation therapies than to that among different forms of relaxation therapy. Cognitive therapies do not necessarily teach people to reduce physiological arousal directly, and most relaxation therapies teach little about cognitive control, although Lazarus (1977) has argued the opposite. He suggests that even biofeedback, the least cognitive of relaxation therapies, is mediated by cognition. He also theorizes that the critical effect of biofeedback is cognitive. That is, it occupies clients' attention with somatic processes, and thereby blocks stressful thoughts or events; or, alternatively, the self-knowledge gained about stress responses and the events that produce them leads people to rethink the meaning of these events, and to change their behavior accordingly. A similar argument has been made by Holroyd (1979).

Studies reviewed in Chapters 18 and 19 suggest that cognitive therapy produces greater changes than relaxation therapy in disorders that are assessed by cognitive measures (e.g., anxiety, pain), whereas problems assessed primarily by somatic measures tend to show a greater response to somatically oriented interventions. Cognitive therapy also may have an advantage in modifying stress-related overt behavior.

There is even evidence that cognitively oriented therapies have greater effects than relaxation therapies on self-report measures of *somatic* symptoms. The process of self-observation and self-report obviously requires kinds of mental activity similar to those needed for other cognitive tasks (i.e., all require verbal and analytic skills—those that are commonly associated with dominant-hemisphere brain function). Self-report of stress symptoms involves interpretation of the environment as stress-producing, as well as interpretation of somatic perceptions as indicating pain or stress. Thus, when we review data in Chapter 19 on treatment of pain conditions, we find evidence that cognitive therapy adds significantly to the effects of relaxation or biofeedback therapy, and may even be superior to the latter.

Applied Training in Relaxation: Combining Somatic and Cognitive Training

For all the treatments described in this book, generalization from treatment sessions to everyday life is critically important. Since generalization often does not occur automatically, several techniques include specific methods for achieving it. Thus, as described by McGuigan (Chapter 2, this volume), Jacobson's version of PR includes specific training in "differential relaxation." This comprises training in procedures for relaxing the muscles not needed for specific tasks while engaging in various activities. Similarly, practitioners of AT are also trained to produce various physiological changes during everyday activities. These components have not been systematically evaluated. However, many approaches to stress management specifically combine relaxation methods with various cognitive and behavioral methods, with the explicit rationale of rendering the various techniques more effective in managing "real-life" stress. One such method is Meichenbaum's "stress inoculation training" (see Chapter 12, this volume).

Another therapy package that combines relaxation and cognitive therapies is called "anxiety management training" (Deffenbacher & Suinn, 1982; Suinn, 1975, 1990; Suinn & Richardson, 1971). This approach combines live training in PR with deep breathing and imagining a relaxing scene. In addition, clients are trained to imagine anxiety-provoking scenes and to use their relaxation skills to reduce the anxiety elicited by the scenes. Clients are also trained to recognize "early warning signs" of stress, to use their relaxation skills when these occur, and to relax *while* they are imagining the anxiety scenes without avoiding them. One study (Shoemaker, 1976/1977) found anxiety management training to be more effective than PR training alone in reducing self-reported general anxiety among anxiety neurotics.

Several studies have compared relaxation therapy with various other combinations of cognitive and behavioral interventions aimed at helping people to apply their relaxation skills in daily life. Goldfried and Trier (1974) found that specific training in applying PR skills to public-speaking anxiety potentiated the effects of PR. Chang-Liang and Denney (1976) found their technique of applied relaxation training (PR training combined with instructions on how to use it in daily life) to be more effective than Wolpe's (1958) technique of systematic desensitization in reducing trait anxiety and test anxiety. However, PR training alone and a no-treatment control condition did not differ from either of the other two training conditions. Mitchell and Mitchell (1971) compared the combination of relaxation, desensitization, and assertiveness training to each component individually. They found the combination to be more effective for treatment of migraine headaches than any of the individual treatments. Another study, however, found no differences between relaxation therapy and applied relaxation training (Comer, 1977/1978).

Results of studies comparing PR with systematic desensitization suggest that desensitization is altogether a more powerful technique, probably because it combines good training in PR with an additional technique. Several studies have found this to be true on self-report measures or behavioral assessments of phobic behavior (Aponte & Aponte, 1971; Cooke, 1968; Freeling & Shemberg, 1970; Johnson & Sechrest, 1968). One study also found desensitization to have greater effects on a physiological measure than PR: Moore (1965) found greater decreases in respiratory resistance for desensitization than for PR among asthmatics. In a study of treatment for test anxiety, Kroner, Frieg, and Niewendiek (1982) compared the following conditions: AT alone, AT combined with systematic desensitization, the preceding two along with training in using them in everyday life, and a waiting-list control. They found greater anxiety reduction among subjects receiving the combined treatments than among those receiving only AT.

A possibly less effective method of training people to generalize relaxation skills has been called "cue-controlled relaxation." This procedure involves training a person to think of a word such as "relax" or "calm" while in the relaxed state. By association, the word acquires the characteristics of a cue that *elicits* relaxation. In reviewing the empirical outcome literature on cue-controlled relaxation, Grimm (1980) found that the method does not appear to have advantages over PR alone. Indeed, some studies have found superior results for PR (see Holstead, 1978; Franklin, 1986). It is difficult to explain why, in this instance, one part of a training package might be more effective than the whole package. Perhaps in these studies, the relaxation training has been greatly truncated because of the need to fit cue-controlled training into the therapy program within allowable time limits. The number of training sessions given to people in studies of cue-controlled relaxation has typically not been greater than the number given to people trained in PR alone. The relaxation training thus probably was not as intensive or effective as in studies of PR alone. It is also, of course, possible that the procedure of pairing relaxation with a "cue" word is simply not an effective intervention. It should be mentioned, however, that two studies using cue-controlled relaxation have yielded significant results. Studies by Sweeney and Horan (1982) and by Lent (1979), reviewed in the section in Chapter 18 on anxiety disorders, found significant advantages for cue-controlled relaxation. Because of methodological confounds, however, they do not definitively prove its effectiveness. Lent combined the procedure with a desensitization routine, which may have accounted for the positive results; and Sweeney and Horan did not include a placebo relaxation condition.

In summary, despite the weak effects found in studies of cue-controlled relaxation, most combinations of relaxation and cognitive training are more effective than is either therapy alone. Specific training in how to apply relaxation skills in daily life is an advisable addition to relaxation therapy. Also, relaxation therapy may be a useful accompaniment to cognitive approaches in treatment of stress-related problems.

Behavioral Interventions versus Relaxation Therapies

Behavioral measures often do not correlate well with cognitive and somatic measures. For example, Lang (1971) reviewed evidence that in snake phobics, the correlations are very small among three variables: autonomic response to a snake, performance on a behavioral approach test, and self-ratings of anxiety. Lehrer and Leiblum (1981) found only moderate correlations among behavioral, somatic, and self-report measures of nonassertiveness and assertion anxiety; each kind of measure may be valid, however. In the latter study, nonassertive female clients at a community mental health center differed from normal women on all three types of measures. At low levels of anxiety, Craske and Craig (1984) found desynchrony among behavioral, cognitive, and physiological indices of performance anxiety among musicians; at high levels, however, these symptoms converged. Elsewhere, we (Lehrer & Woolfolk, 1982) have presented data showing that self-reported social avoidance is less closely related to self-reported cognitive and somatic symptoms of anxiety than the latter two are to each other.

The kind of symptom that is most important to treat should depend upon which is most debilitating. When a person avoids important tasks or relationships, or functions inadequately in them, the specific-effects theory would call for a behaviorally oriented intervention, aimed at overcoming these behavioral deficits. Marks (1981, 1987) concludes that exposure to feared situations is by far the most effective component in treatment of phobias and obsessive–compulsive symptoms, both of which are usually assessed by changes in overt behavior. He argues that relaxation therapy contributes little more than a placebo effect in treatment of obsessive–compulsive conditions, whereas directly preventing such individuals from engaging in obsessions and/or compulsions can produce dramatic reductions in symptoms; he also contends that relaxation therapies are less effective than exposure therapy in treatment of phobic disorders, and do not effectively enhance exposure therapy. Marks does not review any of the studies using breathing techniques, however. Breathing techniques have been found particularly helpful for the treatment of panic-related conditions.

Exposure therapy has a particularly powerful effect on reducing avoidance behavior. Consistent with Marks's contentions, several studies have examined cognitive and cognitive–behavioral strategies involving exposure and rationales that can be used to enhance motivation for exposure. Most investigators have found these procedures to be more effective than relaxation therapy for reducing phobic avoidance and self-report of phobic anxiety (e.g., Michelson, Marchione, Marchione, Testa, & Mavissakalian, 1988). However, researchers at the same laboratory (Michelson, Mavissakalian, & Marchione, 1985, 1988) had previously found no differences between the two techniques, other than a higher dropout rate for subjects given exposure treatment. An additional study (Michelson, Mavissakalian, Marchione, Dancu, & Greenwald, 1986) found that subjects given relaxation training actually engaged in *more* exposure behavior than did subjects given graduated exposure therapy. Presumably, relaxation was effective in increasing the courage necessary to engage in exposure. Biran and Wilson (1981) found greater effects for a form of exposure therapy than for rational–emotive therapy in an approach test among individuals afraid of heights or elevators. Some cognitive effects, however, were greater for rational–emotive therapy.

The specific effects theory would predict greater reductions in physiological arousal with PR than with exposure therapy. Michelson et al. (1990) found that both methods produced deeper decreases in heart rate than did paradoxical intention, although the decreases were statistically significant only for PR.

Social skills training appears to have the greatest effects on measures of social competence, particularly among individuals with deficits in this area. The large literature on assertion training and social skills training has been reviewed extensively elsewhere (Alberti, 1977; Twentyman & Zimering, 1978). Generally, these behavioral techniques reduce anxiety as well as improve behavioral functioning. Öst, Jerremalm, and Johansson (1981) classified a group of 40 psychiatric outpatients according to whether they were primarily physiological reactors or behavioral reactors in a test situation involving social interaction under conditions of stress. They compared applied relaxation training with social skills training. Subjects who were treated according to their primary symptoms showed greater decreases than others did on a combined measure of change in anxiety and stress. Heart rate during the posttest exposure to the social stressor decreased in physiological reactors, but not in behavioral reactors. There was a nonsignificant tendency for heart rate to decrease more after applied relaxation training among the physiological reactors and more after social skills training among the behavioral reactors. Similarly, self-reported social activity increased among behavioral reactors during and after social skills training. This did not happen for applied relaxation training or among physiological responders. Self-ratings of anxiety during the test situation decreased more after applied relaxation training than after social skills training.

A more dramatic finding of specific effects was obtained in a study of the treatment of asthma in children (Hock, Bramble, & Kennard, 1977). Relaxation therapy improved airway resistance and asthmatic symptoms, whereas assertion therapy actually made the symptoms worse.

Thus there is substantial evidence for specific behavioral effects for behavioral treatments, when compared with treatments that are clearly somatic or cognitive—although some generalization across modalities does occur. People whose problems have greater behavioral components appear to show a preferential response to behaviorally oriented treatments.

Hypnosis versus Other Methods

As discussed by Barber (Chapter 6, this volume), the hypnotic state is difficult to define, and the procedures for inducing it are varied. Also, the literature comparing hypnosis with other techniques is difficult to interpret. These studies have compared only the immediate effects *during* the hypnotic situation, and therefore have tended to give very cursory training in *all* the techniques that were used. In addition, only very few of the studies used random assignment, a sufficiently large *n*, and adequate controls for expectancy or therapist contact.

One can perhaps consider all the techniques included in this book to be forms of hypnosis or to involve some form of suggestion. Several investigators have commented that people practicing relaxation techniques slip in and out of hypnotic states (Mather & Degun, 1975), particularly highly hypnotizable subjects (Humphreys, 1983). Edmondston (1981) notes the common use of relaxation for hypnotic induction, and argues that the processes involved in relaxation and hypnosis are identical. He does not, however, consider the wide use of nonrelaxation inductions, or the varying effects found for hypnotic and nonhypnotic *procedures*. Humphreys (1983) reviewed the literature on relaxation and hypnosis and concluded that the effects of relaxation and hypnosis are generally equivalent, despite the occasional differences found in specific studies. However, he lumped subjective and physiological changes together in this overview; moreover, in our opinion, he may have disregarded some important differences that do exist.

In our view, hypnosis must at the very least include a cognitive component, since it involves the specific redirection and concentration of attention, and the following of specific suggestions. According to the specific-effects theory, it therefore should have specific cognitive effects. From an operational perspective, the sine qua non of the hypnotic experience is the subject's understanding that he or she is being hypnotized; this is a cognition. In reviewing the empirical studies comparing hypnosis with other methods, we have considered all self-report measures (including self-assessment of anxiety and pain) to be cognitive. We have done this even when the reports were about somatic activity or overt behavior. We are thus classifying the acts of self-observation, self-conceptualization, and self-report as essentially cognitive processes, primarily because they all involve verbal behavior.

There is considerable evidence that more physiologically based interventions tend to produce stronger physiological effects than do hypnotic suggestions, when such suggestions are unaccompanied by specific training in control of physiological activity. The earliest of the comparative studies were done in Gordon Paul's laboratory, and confirmed the physiological predictions of the specific-effects theory. This research found that live training in PR had more powerful effects than hypnotic suggestions to relax in reducing levels of physiological arousal and in diminishing physiological reactivity to stressful imagery. Both methods were superior to an elaborate placebo procedure (Paul, 1969a, 1969b). When the procedures were delivered via tape recording, however (Paul & Trimble, 1970), the conditions did not differ. Similarly, Borkovec and Hennings (1978) found greater physiological effects associated with PR than with suggestions to relax the various muscles (without specific training in tension–release methods). Also, Crosson (1980) found greater skin temperature effects during TBFK than during hypnosis; and Fernandez-Abscal and Miguel-Tobal (1979) found greater decreases in respiration rate with PR or AT than with hypnotic relaxation or a no-treatment control. The effects of hypnosis did not differ from those of the control condition on this measure.

More ambiguous findings emanate from studies yielding no differences between hypnosis and relaxation methods. It is impossible to deduce whether these findings truly do signify "no differences," or whether they reflect too small a sample size or other methodological difficulties that may have obscured results. Deabler, Fidel, Dillenkoffer, and Elder (1973) found significant but equivalent reductions in blood pressure for PR and hypnosis. Borkovec and Fowles (1973) measured frontalis EMG, respiration rate, heart rate, and skin conductance. They found no differences on these measures between three sessions of PR and three sessions of hypnotic relaxation.

One would think that cognitive measures (e.g., pain ratings) should be particularly sensitive to hypnotic effects when used as outcome criteria. This has not been the case, however. Spanos, Ollerhead, and Gwynn (1985–1986) compared subjects' responses to the cold-pressor test after exposure to one of three experimental conditions (hypnotic analgesia, instructions to "do whatever you can to reduce pain," and stress inoculation training) or a no-instruction control. They found decreases in self-reported pain magnitude and pain tolerance for the three instructional groups, with no differences among them. In a similar study, Tripp and Marks (1986) administered a cold-pressor test to 56 subjects under one of four conditions: analgesia suggestions alone, analgesia suggestions with hypnosis, analgesia with relaxation instructions, and no treatment. Analgesia instructions with hypnosis were superior to analgesia instructions alone, but did not differ from analgesia instructions with relaxation in reducing self-reported pain. Interestingly, both the hypnosis and *relaxation* groups reported themselves as having been more deeply hypnotized than the control group, with no differences between these two groups. Apparently some suggestion components were present in the PR technique used in this study, and this may have obscured some of the differences between the two techniques. Nilsson (1990) reported equal effects from hypnosis and one session of taped PR in increasing the vividness of visual imagery; both methods were superior to a control condition involving listening to a tape on study habits. Rickard, Crist, and Barker (1985) found greater effects for taped PR than for suggestions to relax on self-report of relaxation. The "suggestion" procedure in this study, however, did not involve a formal hypnotic induction.

Hypnosis may facilitate developing control of physiological variables, perhaps through helping subjects to focus more intently on learning the self-control task. Barabasz and McGeorge (1978) found significantly greater increases in skin temperature for relaxation instructions plus hypnotic hand-warming suggestions than for continuous TBFK, a false-feedback control, or relaxation instructions alone. Charlesworth and Doughtie (1982) found greater reductions in EMG activity when subjects were told that they were under hypnosis than when subjects were given the identical instructions but were told, as in PR, that they were being taught a relaxation skill. They reported that the hypnosis suggestions appeared to produce a more passive state than the "learned relaxation" instructions. Diehl, Meyer, Ulrich, and Meinig (1989) found greater global hemispheric blood perfusion for both cerebral hemispheres with a hypnotic induction than with AT. They studied a group of 12 male subjects who had all previously been given AT. Blood perfusion was higher than the normative average in both conditions and even at rest, particularly among subjects who responded to catalepsy suggestions.

Combining hypnosis with biofeedback, however, does not appear to enhance the somatic effects of hypnosis. Friedman and Taub (1977) reported greater diastolic blood pressure reductions during seven sessions of hypnosis than during a no-treatment control condition, or than during a combination of hypnosis and biofeedback. Significant decreases in blood pressure occurred only in the hypnosis group and in a group receiving biofeedback without hypnosis. If the results of this study are replicated in subsequent research, we may be forced to conclude that, in combination, the two techniques weaken rather than potentiate each other.[1] The unrelenting truth

---

[1]The results of this study are not conclusive. The biofeedback-only group was not found to differ significantly from any of the other groups, including the control groups. This raises questions about the manner in which the biofeedback treatment was administered. Also, subjects were not randomly assigned to groups, and the groups differed at pretest on the major dependent variable. Subjects in the hypnosis groups were screened for high hypnotizability, while the other groups were not; and subjects in the biofeedback-only group had higher initial blood pressures than subjects in the other groups.

of the biofeedback machine may undermine the more flexible "suggested truth" that must be believed if one is to enter a hypnotic trance; and the hypnotic set may detract from learning the biofeedback task. The latter effect, in fact, was implicitly assumed by Jacobson (1938, 1970) when he deliberately avoided using suggestion as an aid to learning muscle relaxation. These arguments are similar to those advanced by Qualls and Sheehan (1979) and by Sigman and Phillips (1985) that biofeedback and hypnosis involve antithetical processes. We have previously presented a similar argument (Lehrer, Woolfolk, & Goldman, 1986). The data on hypnotizability presented in Chapter 17 are also consistent with this position.

Cognitive therapy and hypnosis appear to have equivalent effects on various cognitively based outcome measures of pain (Edelson & Fitzpatrick, 1989; Wall & Womack, 1989). These studies are reviewed in the section on pain conditions in Chapter 19.

Delmonte (1984b) has noted that hypnosis and meditation procedures show a large amount of overlap. They share many characteristics: a shift to more "primary-process" thinking; heightened suggestibility; a greater response in individuals high in hypnotic susceptibility and absorption; right-hemispheric cortical dominance; the appearance of hypnagogic phenomena; rhythmical and monotonous verbal material; increased EEG alpha and theta activity; and generally lower physiological arousal. He has also noted, however, that similarities between the effects of the two techniques may be more apparent among novices than among experienced practitioners. In addition, he has outlined several similarities between hypnotic and meditational *procedures:* "(1) focused and selective attention; (2) reduced exteroceptive and pro-prioceptive sensory input; (3) passive volition; (4) a receptive attitude; (5) a relaxed posture; (6) closed eyes; and (7) monotonous, rhythmic vocal (or subvocal) repetition" (p. 30). He concludes that differences between meditation and hypnosis are blurred, particularly for individuals inexperienced with these techniques.

A few more recent studies suggest that the incremental effectiveness of hypnosis may depend on the particular task that accompanies the hypnotic procedure. In a study of pain reduction during oral surgery, Katcher, Segal, and Beck (1984) found that hypnosis augmented the procedure of "contemplating" a poster, but not that of contemplating an aquarium. The latter procedure alone was just as effective as the hypnotic procedures. Zika (1987) found greater increases in time competence, inner-directedness, existentiality, and self-regard with hypnosis than with TM, a Western meditation technique, a placebo control, or a no-treatment control. TM produced the greatest improvements in spontaneity and capacity for intimate contact, but these changes were not significantly different from those obtained in the control groups. The results for the Western meditation technique approximated those for the placebo condition. Soskis, Orne, Orne, and Dinges (1989) found no differences between meditation and a self-hypnotic procedure in a study of stress management.

Finally, if the effects of all relaxation techniques result from procedures and processes that are indistinguishable from hypnosis, then presumably the effects of all should be related to hypnotic susceptibility. The data reviewed in the next three chapters show that this is only partially true. Although success in most methods is related to various measures of hypnotic susceptibility, no such relationship is found for biofeedback; moreover, the relationship is greater with formal hypnosis than with any of the other methods.

These results all lead us to conclude that although hypnosis bears some similarities to other stress management techniques, it specifically emphasizes focusing attention, having particular thoughts or feelings (e.g., anesthesia, age regression, amnesia, etc.), and engaging in particular actions. Its effects are dependent on the nature of the suggestions that are given. Hypnosis may amplify various within-session relaxation effects, particularly in the absence of extensive prior relaxation training; it may do this by helping the individual to focus on the relaxation task more single-mindedly. However, unless accompanied by specific training in physiological control, hypnotic suggestion produces weaker physiological effects than do various somatically oriented techniques. Also, the activities and processes involved in hypnosis may conflict sufficiently with those in biofeedback to render these two techniques mutually incompatible.

Exercise versus Other Methods

Exercise, particularly aerobic exercise, has been touted by many people as an effective stress reduction method (see Fillingim & Blumenthal, Chapter 14, this volume). Several studies and literature reviews have concluded that exercise may be significantly helpful in the treatment of depression (see the section on depression in Chapter 18). Keller and Seraganian (1984) found a greater decrease in stress-induced electrodermal reactivity after a 10-week program of aerobic exercise than after a program in meditation or a music appreciation course.

Other comparative studies found no such advantages for exercise, however. Berger, Friedmann, and Eaton (1988) found a greater reduction in self-reported stress symptoms among undergraduates put on a regimen of either jogging or Benson's ROM technique than among subjects given group support or assigned to a no-treatment condition. No differences were found between Benson's technique and exercise. Steptoe and Kearsley (1990) attempted an expanded replication of Schwartz et al.'s (1978) findings of greater somatic relaxation for exercise and greater cognitive relaxation for meditation. They studied 340 meditators, competitive athletes, recreational exercisers, and sedentary controls, and found no differences among groups on any of three scales designed to differentiate cognitive from somatic anxiety. Murphy, Pagano, and Marlatt (1986) found that meditation and exercise had equivalent (and significant) effects in reducing alcohol consumption among a group of alcoholics. Bruning and Frew (1987) found no differences among meditation, exercise, and management skills training in reducing basal levels of physiological arousal in a work setting. No additive effects were found for combinations of these techniques. Long and Haney (1988) found no differences between exercise and PR in a 14-month follow-up on a group of 39 stressed working women. Both procedures produced lasting improvements on a variety of measures of stress and coping.

Several studies have yielded weaker effects for exercise than for other stress management methods. Roskies et al. (1986) found greater reductions in behavioral measures of Type A responding during an interpersonal stressor with a cognitive–behavioral intervention than with aerobic exercise. However, they found only trivial changes for either group in physiological reactivity to the stress. Hughes, Casal, and Leon (1986) found no effects of an exercise program on mood, compared to a control condition, among a group of sedentary males without known psychopathology. The authors voiced doubts about the usefulness of exercise in treatment programs for various pathological emotional states; however, the use of a population chosen for *absence* of psychopathology may have minimized the chances for finding any beneficial effect. The results from another study of normal subjects, however, are not so equivocal. Caprara et al. (1986) used the Buss "aggression machine" paradigm to examine whether exercise reduces aggressiveness. Subjects who were administered a bicycle ergometer exercise task subsequently delivered *higher* electric shocks than subjects who simply waited for the 10 minutes that the experimental subjects spent pedaling.

In summary, the literature comparing exercise with other relaxation techniques is small. With some exceptions, however, it suggests that exercise may have effects similar to but smaller than those of some other relaxation techniques described in this book. There is some evidence that it has specific effects in relieving depression, and that it has greater somatic than cognitive effects. There also is evidence that in some circumstances, it may disinhibit aggressive behavior.

Relaxation-Induced Anxiety

Meditation may produce more negative side effects than PR (Carrington et al., 1980; Heide & Borkovec, 1983; Lehrer et al., 1983; Norton, Rhodes, Hauch, & Kaprowy, 1985). Specifically, more people report sensations of transient anxiety during practice of meditation than during practice of PR. This is consistent with the heightened physiological arousal and physiological reactivity that are sometimes found in meditation. Heide and Borkovec (1983) call it "relaxation-induced anxiety," despite the fact that they report more frequent occurrences of it in meditation than in PR. Carrington (1977) interprets it as an "unstressing" phenomenon, reflecting a state of high emotional tension prior to meditation. Such anxiety reactions may be less common in PR because of its more direct effects in lowering somatic tension. If the problem of relaxation-induced anxiety becomes troublesome in the training of particular individuals, the research literature thus suggests that PR may be easier for the person to tolerate.

The causes of relaxation-induced anxiety are not entirely clear. One contributor may be an increased somatic awareness that occurs during deep relaxation, coupled with an anxiety-producing interpretation of the meaning of the remaining perceptions of somatic arousal. It is known that anxious individuals are more sensitive to these perceptions and are more likely to interpret them as anxiety. Thus, in patients with panic disorder, the heightened physiological arousal produced by an injection of lactate can produce a full-fledged panic attack. In other people, it produces only the *somatic* sensation of being anxious without the "mental fear" (see review by Ackerman & Sachar, 1974). A person's interpretation of the meaning of the somatic sensations and of the threat content in the situation appears to be critical to the development of fear in this situation. Patients who do not experience the fear tend to credit the reassuring presence of the doctor for their calmness.

More recent theories have also emphasized the influence of cognitive interpretations of physiological changes experienced during anxiety (Clark, 1986). On the other hand, Ley (1988) interprets relaxation-induced anxiety as a product of panic patients' tendency to overbreathe, and to fail to react to their bodies' low level of metabolic activity during deep relaxation. In this sense relaxation-induced anxiety stems completely from the experience of hyperventilation, which is a frequent occurrence in this population.

Similar phenomena are given particular prominence in the AT literature (see Linden, Chapter 7, this volume), where they are labeled "autogenic discharges" (see Schultz & Luthe, 1969). These are emotional or physical experiences that are usually unpleasant; they may consist of pain, anxiety, palpitations, muscle twitches, and the like. Crying is also often experienced. Although these events must be treated carefully during therapy, they are not necessarily countertherapeutic. Indeed, according to Schultz and Luthe, autogenic discharges may occur as by-products in the process of achieving homeostasis. Sometimes, however, they may make the technique too unpleasant to practice, and influence an individual to give up the technique; alternatively, they may produce effects that are medically dangerous (e.g., increases in blood pressure among hypertensives). Thus subjects must be carefully monitored to be sure that they do not experience intolerable autogenic discharges. Also, the duration of autogenic exercises is purposely kept very short in order to diminish the intensity of autogenic discharges.

There is some evidence that autogenic discharges may occur more frequently with AT than with PR, just as relaxation-induced anxiety occurs more often in meditation than in PR. Lehrer, Atthowe, and Weber (1980) found that subjects in an AT group reported having experienced sensations of palpitations when they were first introduced to the autogenic formula "My heartbeat is calm and regular." No analogous phenomena occurred during PR. This was a transient experience and was not associated with a negative outcome of AT. Indeed, subjects in the AT group achieved lower heart rates than subjects in other groups during a posttraining stress test.

Braith, McCullough, and Bush (1988) examined personality correlates of relaxation-induced anxiety. They found a positive relationship with internal locus of control, fear of losing control, and fear of becoming anxious. The latter two factors, however, may *result* from the frequent experience of panic, as well as contribute to maintaining both panic disorder and relaxation-induced anxiety.

Although relaxation-induced anxiety may be seen as a problem in relaxation therapy, and may even contribute to the high dropout rate in relaxation therapies, Smith (1988) reminds us that the symptoms of relaxation-induced anxiety can be therapeutic: If subjects can learn to relax through the experience, they learn to develop the attitude of "receptivity," which is an important benefit of this kind of training. The meditation and AT literatures deal with this problem specifically, and conclude that these experiences are to be expected, worked with systematically, and ultimately accepted as bearable and nonthreatening. This attitude is similar to that now widely recommended for the treatment of panic disorder (Michelson et al., 1990). Several treatment regimens for this problem prescribe deliberate exposure to the experience of panic—even drug-induced panic, if necessary. Thus the clients learn to tolerate the experience, much as meditators and practitioners of AT learn to tolerate "unstressing" experiences or autogenic discharges. However, data from a study of combined relaxation and cognitive therapy in the treatment of generalized anxiety disorder show that the experience of relaxation-induced anxiety predicts poor prognosis in treatment (Borkovec et al., 1987).

Drug Therapy versus and Combined with Other Stress Reduction Therapies

Despite the safety of most medications used to treat stress-related conditions, a nonpharmacological alternative is always preferable if it is equally effective, if it is of reasonably equivalent cost, and if it generates equivalent compliance. No medication is *completely* without risks or side effects, and it is therefore prudent not to use this approach if psychological strategies are of equal potency and availability. We propose that practitioners examine the following list of considerations before turning to drug treatment of stress-related disorders. Indeed, Tyrer (1978) has cautioned that it is *unethical* to treat patients with medication for problems that are social in nature. In general, however, one or more of the following questions should be clearly answerable in the affirmative before drug treatment is undertaken.

1. Is medication treatment more effective than the best available psychological treatment in reducing symptoms, both immediately and in the long run? If drug therapy produces more immediate results, as it often may, does the need for fast effects outweigh any expected long-term adverse consequences (including physical or psychological dependence, state-dependent learning, habituation of drug effects, etc.)?

2. Is the drug treatment so much less expensive than psychological methods over the entire course of treatment that many individuals would prefer it, despite the additional possible risks?

3. Does drug treatment potentiate psychological treatment, which might be much less effective without medication (e.g., does it enable phobic individuals to engage in a course of exposure therapy, which they otherwise would refuse to do)?

4. Is improvement maintained after the drug is withdrawn? Alternatively, is long-term (perhaps lifelong) drug therapy an acceptable solution?

5. Would patient compliance with a drug regimen be higher than with a regimen of psychological treatment?

As is shown below, the empirical literature does not provide a clear answer to any of these questions. The art of therapy, then, is to arrive at the best method for treating each individual, with this literature serving more as a rough guide than as a precise blueprint.

The largest group of studies comparing drug and behavioral treatments is found in the literature on anxiety. It is reviewed in detail in the section on treatment of anxiety disorders in Chapter 18. This research suggests that drug treatments and behavioral treatments (relaxation, biofeedback, cognitive therapy, exposure, etc.) tend to have approximately equivalent short-term effects. However, drug therapy is not effective in treating phobic avoidance unless some attempt at exposure to the phobic object is also made. Combinations of imipramine and exposure therapy are effective, and there is some evidence that the medication may increase willingness to engage in exposure. Benzodiazepine treatments, on the other hand, tend to foster medication dependency and appear to render people less willing to use relaxation strategies to control anxiety. Long-term outcome studies suggest better effects for behavioral strategies than for drug treatments.

As outlined in Chapter 18 in the section on stress management training for children, both relaxation therapies and methylphenidate tend to produce improvements in various manifestations of childhood hyperactivity and attention deficit disorder. Differences between the pharmacological and nonpharmacological therapies have been noted, but they appear to be equivocal. It is unclear whether combining drug therapy with relaxation therapies increases effectiveness.

The poor long-term outcome results of drug therapy for stress-related disorders can be attributed to several factors. These include psychological and physical dependence upon drugs, and a negative effect on the development of effective psychological coping skills. Wooley, Blackwell, and Winget (1978) review evidence that medical treatment, if used alone, actually worsens some psychosomatic disorders. Schneider (1988) investigated reasons for the reported dependence of many insomniacs on low doses of benzodiazepines. He found that these medications tend to diminish hypnotic activity and duration of delta and rapid-eye-movement sleep. Despite the apparent *decrease* in actual deep sleep, patients with low-dose benzodiazepine dependence think that they sleep more and better than before. After the dependence is broken, their insomnia does not increase, but their awareness of it does. This relationship may explain the difficulty that many insomniacs experience in withdrawing from these medications.

There is evidence that relaxation–biofeedback interventions may be particularly helpful when withdrawal from some medications is indicated. Blanchard, McCoy, et al. (1988) found that TBFK and PR were both helpful in decreasing blood pressure and heart rate reactivity to various laboratory stressors after withdrawal from sympatholytic antihypertensive medications. PR had a stronger effect than TBFK. Blanchard, McCaffrey, Musso, Gerardi, and McCoy (1987) found that psychological effects of withdrawal from second-stage antihypertensive medication were ameliorated by relaxation or TBFK. This was especially true when these treatments were administered before the termination of drug therapy. The side effects of antihypertensive medications can be particularly troublesome, and relaxation techniques show promise of decreasing the dosage needed for many cases of hypertension. However, Oakley and Shapiro (1989) report that methodological problems in the research literature "preclude definite conclusions."

Studies of various relaxation, biofeedback, and cognitive therapies have shown that these techniques allow diminished use of medications for such diverse problems as asthma (Lehrer, Hochron, McCann, Swartzman, & Reba, 1986), hypertension (Blanchard et al., 1986; Lasser et al, 1987), back pain and other chronic pain (Biedermann, Monga, Shanks, & McGhie, 1986; Kabat-Zinn, Lipworth, & Burney, 1985), and attention deficit disorder (Whalen, Henker, & Hinshaw, 1985).

Much research remains to be done in the area of pharmacological treatments for stress. Findings from one medication may not be relevant for others, and few medications have been put to the tests listed above. The empirical literature on the interaction between drug therapy and psychological treatment is paltry, despite the often-proclaimed rationale that pharmacological treatment facilitates psychotherapy. Whitehead and Blackwell (1979) suggest that differences in professional backgrounds and interests between investigators with a background in psychopharmacology and those interested in behavior therapy may explain why so few collaborative studies have compared the interactive effects of the two treatments. The National Institute of Mental Health is now encouraging such collaborative research, but the results of it, for the most part, are still forthcoming.

Conclusions

Specificity of Treatment Effects

Unquestionably, the various therapeutic approaches described above have highly specific effects, as well as more generally stress-reducing effects. The somatic–cognitive–behavioral distinction is useful as a predictor. Therapies directed to one of these modalities appear to have their greatest and most consistent effects on that particular modality.

Thus, AT appears to have specific effects on the particular autonomic functions included in the autogenic exercises, even if AT and PR both produce general decreases in physiological arousal. Similarly, PR appears to have specific effects on the musculoskeletal system, and biofeedback seems to have specific effects on the various particular response systems addressed in the training.

Techniques with a greater preponderance of cognitive elements tend to have more cognitive and fewer somatic effects. In comparisons between meditation and either PR or biofeedback, the latter techniques have more powerful somatic effects. Meditation may have stronger cognitive effects. Cognitive therapy has specific effects on various self-report measures of stress. Comparisons between cognitive therapy and various relaxation therapies have revealed clear examples of somatic–cognitive specificity.

Training to relax generally produces greater somatic effects than do *suggestions* to relax, hypnotic or otherwise. Depending on the types of instructions given, however, hypnosis is not an exclusively cognitive technique. Often hypnotic suggestions are directed specifically at somatic processes, and in some reports, hypnosis has greater somatic effects than biofeedback. Several studies have found no differences between hypnosis and various somatically oriented self-control techniques.

To be sure, some generalization does take place from one modality to another. In most of the studies we reviewed, all the treatments produced significant decreases on a broad array of measures. Still tenable is Schwartz et al.'s (1978) early hypothesis that specific effects are superimposed upon a more global relaxation response.

The specific-effects hypothesis thus remains viable, although some studies found no differences among the effects of various contrasting stress reduction techniques. In most of these studies, the methods themselves contain elements of more than one treatment modality. Thus, for example, mantra meditation may contain somatic components, and hypnosis may include behavioral or somatic suggestions as well as a manipulation to alter attention and cognition. Also, many of the studies are poorly controlled, and particular treatments have often been compared in only very few studies.

Jacobsonian versus "Revised Jacobsonian" Progressive Relaxation

Although little scientific work has been done in differentiating Jacobson's PR from various revised PR techniques, the two approaches nevertheless are distinguishable from each other in theoretically important respects. Jacobson's technique has a more exclusively somatic emphasis, so we would expect it to have more specific somatic effects. The revised techniques may have greater cognitive and behavioral effects. However, although one unreplicated finding has shown a small *general* advantage for Jacobson's technique, no evidence for specific effects has yet been obtained. The data relevant to this question are few, so definite conclusions cannot be drawn. No studies of this problem have been done on clinical populations. Also, only a handful of the studies reported in this book have used Jacobson's original technique. The modified techniques are so widely accepted as equivalent to Jacobson's that they are routinely described as "Jacobsonian relaxation." The evidence reviewed here does indicate that the modified techniques have some therapeutic effects, especially when they are administered live and in an individualized fashion. Although some of the components that differentiate the two approaches have been well studied (e.g., taped vs. live training, length of training, use of EMG BFK, cue-controlled training), others have received less attention (e.g., the use of "tension–release cycles" for producing relaxation; training in all muscle groups vs. only a few during a single training session; presentation of the technique as entirely a set of muscular skills).

The Use of Suggestion

Related to the issue of distinctions between Jacobson's technique and the modified techniques is the issue of suggestion. Although differences between PR and pure suggestion have been studied, there is little information about how relaxation training and suggestion may complement each other. All the techniques, including Jacobson's, necessarily include some elements of suggestion. Merely paying money and spending time in learning to relax produce a suggestive effect. Future research must determine the specific forms of suggestion that are most powerful (or harmful) in particular circumstances.

Music and Exercise

There have been fewer studies published thus far on music and exercise than on other techniques described in this book. We have included these techniques, however, because of the rapidly growing interest in these areas, as well as the existence of an empirical literature with at least suggestive results.

Combinations of Techniques

Various techniques described in this book often work synergistically, and several methods involve a variety of modalities (e.g., stress inoculation training, yoga). In clinical use, few of these methods are ever used in isolation from others. Nevertheless, it should be remember that these methods are not *always* mutually compatible. A striking example of this is the combination of hypnosis and biofeedback, which appears to have a weaker effect than does either component individually. Perhaps this is because hypnosis depends upon a person's *perceiving* a particular somatic effect, even if the corresponding actual physiological event is not occurring; by contrast, biofeedback teaches somatic control, regardless of how the client perceives it. The mechanisms by which various techniques facilitate or detract from each other require further investigation.

Hierarchical Model for Stress Management Strategies, and the Issue of "Receptivity"

Evidence that might validate Smith's (1986, 1988) hierarchical model of stress management training remains sketchy. There has been little research into the order in which stress management techniques are most effectively introduced. It also should be noted that Smith's model suggests a manner for dealing with relaxation-induced anxiety—that is, using it as a way to increase the client's "receptivity" to various body experiences. A clear-cut use of a specific method designed to promote such receptivity is encompassed in exposure treatments for various anxiety-related disorders, as described in Chapter 18. Thus, for example, in treatment of panic disorder, people are trained to tolerate some of the uncomfortable body experiences associated with panic. Most relaxation techniques include systematic strategies for managing some of the uncomfortable sensations that may accompany relaxation itself, or the abrupt transition between the states of hyperarousal relaxation. Further research is necessary to delineate the most effective methods for addressing these experiences.

ACKNOWLEDGMENT

Work on this chapter was supported in part by Grant No. HL44097 from the Heart, Lung and Blood Institute of the National Institutes of Health.

REFERENCES

Ackerman, S. H., & Sachar, E. J. (1974). The lactate theory of anxiety: A review and reevaluation. *Psychosomatic Medicine, 36,* 69–81.
Aivazyan, T. A., Zaitsev, V. P., Salenko, B. B., Yurenev, A. P., & Patrusheva, I. F. (1988). Efficacy of relaxation techniques in hypertensive patients: Fifth joint USA–USSR symposium on arterial hypertension. *Health Psychology, 7*(Suppl.), 193–200.
Alberti, R. E. (1977). *Assertiveness: Innovations, applications, issues.* San Luis Obispo, CA: Impact.
Alexander, A. B. (1975). An experimental test of assumptions relating to the use of electromyographic biofeedback as a general relaxation training technique. *Psychophysiology, 12,* 656–662.
Aponte, J. F., & Aponte, C. E. (1971). Group programmed desensitization without the simultaneous presentation of aversive scenes with relaxation training. *Behaviour Research and Therapy, 9,* 337–346.

Banner, C. N., & Meadows, W. M. (1983). Examination of the effectiveness of various treatment techniques for reducing tension. *British Journal of Clinical Psychology, 22,* 183–193.

Barabasz, A. F., & McGeorge, C. M. (1978). Biofeedback, mediated biofeedback and hypnosis in peripheral vasodilation training. *American Journal of Clinical Hypnosis, 21,* 28–37.

Benson, H. (1975). *The relaxation response.* New York: Morrow.

Benson, H. (1983). The relaxation response and norepinephrine: A new study illuminates mechanisms. *Integrative Psychiatry, 1,* 15–18.

Benson, H., & Proctor, W. (1985). *Beyond the relaxation response.* New York: Berkley.

Berger, B. G., Friedmann, E., & Eaton, M. (1988). Comparison of jogging, the relaxation response, and group interaction for stress reduction. *Journal of Sport and Exercise Psychology, 10,* 431–447.

Biedermann, H. J., Monga, T. N., Shanks, G. L., & McGhie, A. (1986). EMG biofeedback in the treatment of back pain patients: Treatment protocol. *Clinical Biofeedback and Health: An International Journal, 9,* 139–145.

Biran, M., & Wilson, G. T. (1981). Treatment of phobic disorders using cognitive and exposure methods: A self-efficacy analysis. *Journal of Consulting and Clinical Psychology, 49,* 886–899.

Blanchard, E. B., Andrasik, F., Neff, D. F., Saunders, N. L., Arena, J. G., Pallmeyer, T. P., Teders, S. J., Jurish, S. E., & Rodichok, L. D. (1983). Four process studies in the behavioural treatment of chronic headache. *Behaviour Research and Therapy, 21,* 209–220.

Blanchard, E. B., Khramelashvili, V. V., McCoy, G. C., Aivazyan, T. A., McCaffrey, R. J., Salenko, B. B., Musso, A., Wittrock, D. A., Berger, M., Gerardi, M. A., & Pangburn, L. (1988). The USA–USSR collaborative cross-cultural comparison of autogenic training and thermal biofeedback in the treatment of mild-hypertension. *Health Psychology, 7* (Suppl.), 175–192.

Blanchard, E. B., McCaffrey, R. J., Musso, A., Gerardi, M. A., & McCoy, G. L. (1987). A controlled comparison of thermal biofeedback and relaxation training in the treatment of essential hypertension: III. Psychological changes accompanying treatment. *Biofeedback and Self-Regulation, 12,* 227–240.

Blanchard, E. B., McCoy, G. C., Andrasik, F., Acerra, M., Pallmeyer, T. P., Gerardi, R., Halpern, M., & Musso, A. (1984). Preliminary results from a controlled evaluation of thermal biofeedback as a treatment for essential hypertension. *Biofeedback and Self-Regulation, 9,* 471–495.

Blanchard, E. B., McCoy, G. C., Musso, A., Gerardi, M. A., Pallmeyer, T. P., Gerardi, R., Cotch, P. A., Siracusa, K., & Andrasik, F. (1986). A controlled comparison of thermal biofeedback and relaxation training in the treatment of essential hypertension: I. Short term and long term outcome. *Behavior Therapy, 17,* 563–579.

Blanchard, E. B., McCoy, G. C., Wittrock, D., Musso, A., Gerardi, R. J., & Pagburn, L. (1988). A controlled comparison of thermal biofeedback and relaxation training in the treatment of essential hypertension: II. Effects on cardiovascular reactivity. *Health Psychology, 7,* 19–33.

Borgeat, F., Stravynski, A., & Chaloult, L. (1983). The influence of two different sets of information and suggestions on the subjective effects of relaxation. *Journal of Human Stress, 9,* 40–45.

Borkovec, T. D., & Fowles, D. C. (1973). Controlled investigation of the effects of progressive relaxation and hypnotic relaxation on insomnia. *Journal of Abnormal Psychology, 82,* 153–158.

Borkovec, T. D., & Hennings, B. L. (1978). The role of physiological attention-focusing in the relaxation treatment of sleep disturbance, general tension, and specific stress reaction. *Behaviour Research and Therapy, 16,* 7–19.

Borkovec, T. D., Mathews, A. M., Chambers, A., Ebrahimi, S., Lytle, R., & Nelson, R. (1987). The effects of relaxation training with cognitive or nondirective therapy and the role of relaxation-induced anxiety in the treatment of generalized anxiety. *Journal of Consulting and Clinical Psychology, 55,* 883–888.

Braith, J. A., McCullough, J. P., & Bush, J. P. (1988). Relaxation induced anxiety in a subclinical sample of chronically anxious subjects. *Journal of Behavior Therapy and Experimental Psychiatry, 19,* 193–198.

Bruning, N. S., & Frew, D. R. (1987). Effects of exercise, relaxation, and management skills training on physiological stress indicators: A field experiment. *Journal of Applied Psychology, 72,* 515–521.

Burish, T. G., & Hendrix, E. M. (1980). Importance of relaxation instructions in the EMG biofeedback training package. *Journal of Psychosomatic Research, 24,* 137–145.

Cady, E. B., Elshove, H., Jones, D. A., & Moll, A. (1989). The metabolic causes of slow relaxation in fatigued human skeletal muscle. *Journal of Physiology* (London), *418,* 327–37

Caprara, G. V., Renzi, P., D'Augello, D., D'Imperio, G., Rielli, I., & Travaglia, G. (1986). Interpolating physical exercise between instigation to aggress and aggression: The role of irritability and emotional susceptibility. *Aggressive Behavior, 12,* 83–91.

Carlson, C. R., Bacaseta, P. E., & Simanton, D. A. (1988). A controlled evaluation of devotional meditation and progressive relaxation. *Journal of Psychology and Theology, 16,* 362–368.

Carrington, P. (1977). *Freedom in meditation.* Garden City, NY: Doubleday/Anchor

Carrington, P., Collings, G. H., Jr., Benson, H., Robinson, H., Wood, L. W., Lehrer, P. M., Woolfolk, R. L.,

& Cole, J. W. (1980). The use of meditation–relaxation techniques for the management of stress in a working population. *Journal of Occupational Medicine, 22,* 221–231.

Carter, W. R., Johnson, M. C., & Borkovec, T. D. (1986). Worry: An electrocortical analysis. *Advances in Behaviour Research and Therapy, 8,* 193–204.

Chaloult, L., Borgeat, F., & Elie, R. (1988). Utilisation de suggestions préconscientes et conscientes combinées à des musiques comme technique de relaxation [Use of preconscious and conscious suggestions combined with music as a relaxation technique]. *Canadian Journal of Psychiatry, 33,* 734–740.

Chang-Liang, R., & Denney, D. R. (1976). Applied relaxation as training in self control. *Journal of Counseling Psychology, 23,* 183–189.

Charlesworth, E. A., & Doughtie, E. B. (1982). Modification of baseline by differential task presentation as either hypnosis or "learned" relaxation. *Perceptual and Motor Skills, 55,* 1131–1137.

Clark, D. M. (1986). A cognitive approach to panic. *Behaviour Research and Therapy, 24,* 461–470.

Cohen, J., & Sedlacek, K. (1983). Attention and autonomic self-regulation. *Psychosomatic Medicine, 45,* 243–257.

Comer, J. F. (1978). Meditation and progressive relaxation in the treatment of test anxiety (Doctoral dissertation, University of Kansas, 1977). *Dissertation Abstracts International, 38,* 6142B. (University Microfilms No. 78-09,340)

Cooke, G. (1968). Evaluation of the efficacy of the components of reciprocal inhibition psychotherapy. *Journal of Abnormal Psychology, 73,* 464–467.

Craske, M. G., & Craig, K. D. (1984). Musical performance anxiety: The three-systems model and self-efficacy theory. *Behaviour Research and Therapy, 22,* 267–280.

Crosson, B. (1980). Control of skin temperature through biofeedback and suggestion with hypnotized college women. *International Journal of Clinical and Experimental Hypnosis, 28,* 75–87.

Curtis, W. D., & Wessberg, H. W. (1980). A comparison of heart rate, respiration, and galvanic skin response among meditators, relaxers, and controls. *Journal of Altered States of Consciousness, 2,* 319–324.

Cuthbert, B., Kristeller, J., Simons, R., Hodes, R., & Lang, P. J. (1981). Strategies of arousal and control: Motivation, meditation, and biofeedback. *Journal of Experimental Psychology: General, 110,* 518–546.

Davidson, R. J., & Schwartz, G. E. (1976). Psychobiology of relaxation and related states. In D. Mostofsky (Ed.), *Behavior modification and control of physiological activity.* Engelwood Cliffs, NJ: Prentice-Hall.

Deabler, H. L., Fidel, E., Dillenkoffer, R. L., & Elder, S. T. (1973). The use of relaxation and hypnosis in lowering high blood pressure. *American Journal of Clinical Hypnosis, 16,* 75–83.

Deffenbacher, J. L., & Suinn, R. M. (1982). The chronically anxious patient. In D. M. Doleys, R. L. Meredith, & A. R. Ciminero (Eds.), *Behavioral medicine: Assessment and treatment strategies.* New York: Plenum Press.

Delle-Chiaie, R., Guerani, G., & Biondi, M. (1981). EMG BFB con segnale di rinforzo musicale nella terapia dell'ansia cronica [EMG-BFB with musical reinforcement in the treatment of anxiety neurosis]. *Rivista di Psichiatria, 16,* 455–472.

Delmonte, M. M. (1984a). Electrocortical activity and related phenomena associated with meditation practice: A literature review. *International Journal of Neuroscience, 24,* 217–231.

Delmonte, M. M. (1984b). Meditation: Similarities with hypnoidal states and hypnosis. *International Journal of Psychosomatics, 31,* 24–34.

Denkowski, K. M., & Denkowski, G. C. (1984). Is group progressive relaxation training as effective with hyperactive children as individual EMG biofeedback treatment? *Biofeedback and Self-Regulation, 9,* 353–364.

Detrick, P. F. (1978). Demonstration and comparison of the efficacy of EMG biofeedback assisted relaxation versus autogenic feedback training for the treatment of tension headaches (Doctoral dissertation, University of Southern Mississippi, 1977). *Dissertation Abstracts International, 38,* 5009B. (University Microfilms No. 78-02,902)

Diehl, B. J. M., Meyer, H. K., Ulrich, P., & Meinig, G. (1989). Mean hemispheric blood perfusion during autogenic training and hypnosis. *Psychiatry Research, 29,* 317–318.

Edelman, R. I. (1970). Effects of progressive relaxation on autonomic processes. *Journal of Clinical Psychology, 26,* 421–425.

Edelson, J., & Fitzpatrick, J. L. (1989). A comparison of cognitive behavioral and hypnotic treatments of chronic pain. *Journal of Clinical Psychology, 45,* 316–323.

Edmonston, W. E. (1981). *Hypnosis and relaxation: Modern verification of an old equation.* New York: Wiley.

English, E. H., & Baker, T. B. (1983). Relaxation training and cardiovascular response to experimental stressors. *Health Psychology, 2,* 239–259.

Eppley, K. R., Abrams, A. I., & Shear, J. (1989). Differential effects of relaxation techniques on trait anxiety: A meta analysis. *Journal of Clinical Psychology, 45,* 957–974.

Fee, R. A., & Girdano, D. A. (1978). The relative effectiveness of three techniques to induce the trophotropic response. *Biofeedback and Self-Regulation, 3,* 145–157.

Fernandez-Abscal, E. G., & Miguel-Tobal, J. J. (1979). Breathing styles in different relaxation methods. *Informes del Departmento de Psicologia General, University of Madrid, 2,* 127–141.

Fowler, K. S., & Lander, J. R. (1987). Management of injection pain in children. *Pain, 30,* 169–175.

Franklin, J. A. (1986). Isometric relaxation. *Australian Psychologist, 21,* 413–425.

Franklin, J. A. (1989). 6 year follow up of the effectiveness of respiratory retraining, in situ isometric relaxation, and cognitive modification in the treatment of agoraphobia. *Behavior Modification, 13,* 139–167.

Fray, J. M. (1975). Implications of electromyographic feedback for essential hypertensive patients (Doctoral dissertation, Texas Technological University). *Dissertation Abstracts International, 36,* 3036B. (University Microfilms No. 75–26, 839)

Freedman, R. R. (1987). Long-term effectiveness of behavioral treatments for Raynaud's disease. *Behavior Therapy, 18,* 387–399.

Freedman, R. R. (1989). Quantitative measurements of finger blood flow during behavioral treatments of Raynaud's disease. *Psychophysiology, 26,* 437–441.

Freedman, R. R. (1991). Physiological mechanisms of temperature biofeedback. *Biofeedback and Self-Regulation, 16,* 95–116.

Freedman, R. R., & Ianni, P. (1983). Self-control of digital temperature: Physiological factors and transfer effects. *Psychophysiology, 20,* 682–679.

Freedman, R., Ianni, P., & Wenig, P. (1983). Behavioral treatment of Raynaud's disease. *Journal of Consulting and Clinical Psychology, 51,* 539–549.

Freedman, R. R., Sabharwal, S.C., Ianni, P., Desai, N., Wenig, P., & Mayes, M. (1988). Nonneural beta-adrenergic vasodilating mechanism in temperature biofeedback. *Psychosomatic Medicine, 50,* 394–401.

Freeling, N. W., & Shemberg, K. M. (1970). The alleviation of test anxiety by systematic desensitization. *Behaviour Research and Therapy, 8,* 293–299.

Friedman, H., & Taub, H. A. (1977). The use of hypnosis and biofeedback procedures for essential hypertension. *International Journal of Clinical and Experimental Hypnosis, 27,* 335–347.

Funch, D. P., & Gale, E. N. (1984). Biofeedback and relaxation therapy for chronic temporomandibular joint pain: Predicting successful outcomes. *Journal of Consulting and Clinical Psychology, 52,* 928–935.

Gallois, P. (1984). Modifications neurophysiologiques et respiratoires lors de la pratique des techniques de relaxation [Neurophysiological and respiratory changes induced by relaxation]. *Encephale, 10,* 139–144.

Gallois, P., Forzy, G., & Dhont, J. L. (1984). Changements hormonaux durant la relaxation [Hormonal changes induced by relaxation]. *Encephale, 10,* 79–82.

Gamble, E. H., & Elder, S. T. (1983). Multimodal biofeedback in the treatment of migraine. *Biofeedback and Self-Regulation, 8,* 383–392.

Godsey, R. L. (1980). Efficacy of response contingent and program contingent progression in live and taped progressive relaxation training (Doctoral dissertation, Texas A&M University, 1979). *Dissertation Abstracts International, 40,* 3928B. (University Microfilms No. 80-03,135)

Goldfried, M. R., & Trier, C. S. (1974). Effectiveness of relaxation as an active coping skill. *Journal of Abnormal Psychology, 83,* 348–355.

Goleman, D. J., & Schwartz, G. E. (1976). Meditation as an intervention in stress reactivity. *Journal of Consulting and Clinical Psychology, 44,* 456–466.

Graham, F. K., & Clifton, R. K. (1966). Heart rate change as a component of the orienting response. *Psychological Bulletin, 65,* 305–320.

Greenwood, M. M., & Benson, H. (1977). The efficacy of progressive relaxation in systematic desensitization and a proposal for an alternative competitive response. *Behaviour Research and Therapy, 15,* 337–343.

Grimm, L. G. (1980). The evidence for cue-controlled relaxation. *Behavior Therapy, 11,* 283–293.

Guyer, N. P., & Guyer, C. G. (1984) Implementing relaxation training in counseling emotionally healthy adolescents: A comparison of three modes. *American Mental Health Counselors Association Journal, 6,* 79–87.

Hafner, R. J. (1982). Psychological treatment of essential hypertension: A controlled comparison of meditation and meditation plus biofeedback. *Biofeedback and Self-Regulation, 7,* 305–316.

Hartman, L. M. (1982). Anxiety, imagery, and self regulation. *Journal of Psychiatric Treatment and Evaluation, 4,* 333–336.

Heide, F. J., & Borkovec, T. D. (1983). Relaxation-induced anxiety: Paradoxical anxiety enhancement due to relaxation training. *Journal of Consulting and Clinical Psychology, 51,* 171–182.

Hock, R. A., Bramble, J., & Kennard, D. W. (1977). A comparison between relaxation and assertive training with asthmatic male children. *Biological Psychiatry, 12,* 593–596.

Hohne, F., & Bohn, M. (1988). Biofeedback ohne Technikerteam einfach und kostengunstig [Biofeedback without a team of technicians—simple and cost effective]. *Psychiatrie, Neurologie und Medizinische Psychologie, 40,* 421–425.

Holroyd, K. A. (1979). Stress, coping, and the treatment of stress-related illness. In J. R. McNamara, (Ed.), *Behavioral approaches to medicine: Application and analysis.* New York, Plenum Press.

Holstead, B. N. (1978). Cue-controlled relaxation: An investigation of psychophysiological reactions to a stressor film (Doctoral dissertation, University of Mississippi). *Dissertation Abstracts International, 39,* 2987B. (University Microfilms No. 78-05,763)

Hoshmand, L. T., Helmes, E., Kazarian, S. S., & Tekatch, G. (1985) Evaluation of two relaxation training programs under medication and no-medication conditions. *Journal of Clinical Psychology, 41,* 22–29.

Hughes, J. R., Casal, D. C., & Leon, A. S. (1986). Psychological effects of exercise: A randomized crossover trial. *Journal of Psychosomatic Research, 30,* 355–360.

Humphreys, A. (1983). Neutral hypnosis, progressive muscular relaxation and the relaxation response: A review. *British Journal of Experimental and Clinical Hypnosis, 2,* 19–27.

Jacobson, E. (1938). *Progressive relaxation* (2nd ed.). Chicago: University of Chicago Press.

Jacobson, E. (1970). *Modern treatment of tense patients.* Springfield, IL: Charles C Thomas.

Johnson, S. M., & Sechrest, L. (1968). Comparison of desensitization and progressive relaxation in treating anxiety. *Journal of Consulting and Clinical Psychology, 32,* 280–286.

Kabat-Zinn, J., Lipworth, L., & Burney, R. (1985). The clinical use of mindfulness meditation for the self regulation of chronic pain. *Journal of Behavioral Medicine, 8,* 163–190.

Katcher, A., Segal, H., & Beck, A. (1984). Comparison of contemplation and hypnosis for the reduction of anxiety and discomfort during dental surgery. *American Journal of Clinical Hypnosis, 27,* 14–21.

Keller, S., & Seraganian, P. (1984). Physical fitness level and autonomic reactivity to psychosocial stress. *Journal of Psychosomatic Research, 28,* 279–287.

Kelso, H. G., & Bryson-Brockmann, W. A. (1985). Peripheral temperature control using biofeedback and autogenic training: A comparison study. *Clinical Biofeedback and Health: An International Journal, 8,* 37–44.

Kibler, V. E., & Rider, M. S. (1983). Effects of progressive muscle relaxation and music on stress as measured by finger temperature response. *Journal of Clinical Psychology, 39,* 213–215.

Kimmel, H. D., Palomba, D., & Stegagno, L. (1984). Biofeedback for HR reduction in different contexts. *Scandinavian Journal of Behaviour Therapy, 13,* 153–161.

Kimmel, H. D., Palomba, D., & Stegagno, L. (1986). Enhanced retention of biofeedback-assisted HR slowing due to training context. *Scandinavian Journal of Behaviour Therapy, 15,* 65–70.

Kluger, M. A., Jamner, L. D., & Tursky, B. (1985). Comparison of the effectiveness of biofeedback and relaxation training on hand warming. *Psychophysiology, 22,* 162–166.

Kokoszka, A. (1990). Axiological aspects of comparing psychotherapy and meditation. *International Journal of Psychosomatics, 37,* 78–81.

Krenz, E. W. (1986). Hypnosis versus autogenic training: A comparison. *American Journal of Clinical Hypnosis, 28,* 209–213.

Kroner, B., Frieg, H., & Niewendiek, U. (1982). Einsatz verschiedener Programme des Autogenen Trainings bei Prüfungsangst [Application of different procedures of autogenic training for test anxiety]. *Zeitschrift für Klinische Psychologie und Psychotherapie, 30,* 254–266.

Krug, S. E., Scheier, I. H., & Cattell, R. B. (1976). *Handbook for the IPAT Anxiety Scale.* Champaign, IL: Institute of Personality and Ability Testing.

Lang, P. J. (1971). The application of psychophysiological methods to the study of psychotherapy and behavior change. In A. E. Bergin & S. L. Garfield (Eds.), *Handbook of psychotherapy and behavior change: An empirical analysis.* New York: Wiley.

Lasser, N., Batey, D. M., Hymowitz, N., Lasser, V., Kanders, B. S., & Lehrer, P. M. (1987). The hypertension intervention trial. In T. Strasser & D. Ganten (Eds.), *Mild hypertension: From drug trials to practice.* New York: Raven Press.

Lazarus, R. S. (1977). A cognitive analysis of biofeedback control. In G. E. Schwartz & J. Beatty (Eds.), *Biofeedback: Theory and Research.* New York: Academic Press.

LeBoeuf, A., & Lodge, J. (1980). A comparison of frontalis EMG feedback training and progressive relaxation in the treatment of chronic anxiety. *British Journal of Psychiatry, 137,* 279–284.

Lehrer, P. M. (1978). Psychophysiological effects of progressive relaxation in anxiety neurotic patients and of progressive relaxation and alpha feedback in nonpatients. *Journal of Consulting and Clinical Psychology, 46,* 389–404.

Lehrer, P. M. (1982). How to relax and how not to relax: A re-evaluation of the work of Edmund Jacobson. *Behaviour Research and Therapy, 20,* 417–428.

Lehrer, P. M., Atthowe, J. M., & Weber, E. S. P. (1980). Effects of progressive relaxation and autogenic training on anxiety and physiological measures, with some data on hypnotizability. In F. J. McGuigan, W. Sime, & J. M. Wallace (Eds.), *Stress and tension control.* New York: Plenum.

Lehrer, P. M., Batey, D., Woolfolk, R. L., Remde, A., & Garlick, T. (1988). The effect of repeated tense–release sequences on EMG and self-report of muscle tension: An evaluation of Jacobsonian and post-Jacobsonian assumptions about progressive relaxation. *Psychophysiology, 25,* 562–569.

Lehrer, P. M., Hochron, S. M., McCann, B. S., Swartzman, L., & Reba, P. (1986). Relaxation decreases large-airway but not small-airway asthma. *Journal of Psychosomatic Research, 30,* 13–25.

Lehrer, P. M., & Leiblum, S. L. (1981). Physiological, behavioral, and cognitive measures of assertiveness and assertion anxiety. *Behavioral Counseling Quarterly, 1,* 261–274.

Lehrer, P. M., Schoicket, S., Carrington, P. & Woolfolk, R. L. (1980). Psychophysiological and cognitive responses to stressful stimuli in subjects practicing progressive relaxation and clinically standardized meditation. *Behaviour Research and Therapy, 18,* 293–303.

Lehrer, P. M., & Woolfolk, R. L. (1982). Self-report assessment of anxiety: Somatic, cognitive, and behavioral modalities. *Behavioral Assessment, 4,* 167–177.

Lehrer, P. M., & Woolfolk, R. L. (1984). Are stress reduction techniques interchangeable, or do they have specific effects?: A review of the comparative empirical literature. In R. L. Woolfolk & P. M. Lehrer (Eds.), *Principles and practice of stress management* (1st ed.). New York: Guilford Press.

Lehrer, P. M., Woolfolk, R. L., & Goldman, N. (1986). Progressive relaxation then and now: Does change always mean progress? In R. Davidson, G. E. Schwartz, & D. Shapiro (Eds.), *Consciousness and self-regulation* (Vol. 4). New York: Plenum Press.

Lehrer, P. M., Woolfolk, R. L., Rooney, A., McCann, B. S., & Carrington, P. C. (1983). Progressive relaxation and meditation: A study of psychophysiological and therapeutic differences between two techniques. *Behaviour Research and Therapy, 21,* 651–662.

Lent, R. W. (1979). A comparison between cue-controlled desensitization, cognitive restructuring, and a credible placebo in alleviating public speaking anxiety (Doctoral dissertation, Ohio State University). *Dissertation Abstracts International, 40,* 1899B. (University Microfilms No. 79-22,513)

Ley, R. (1988). Panic attacks during relaxation and relaxation-induced anxiety: A hyperventilation interpretation. *Journal of Behavior Therapy and Experimental Psychiatry, 19,* 253–259.

Lindholm, E., & Lowry, S. (1978). Alpha production in humans under conditions of false feedback. *Bulletin of the Psychonomic Society, 11,* 106–108.

Long, B. C., & Haney, C. J. (1988). Long term follow up of stressed working women: A comparison of aerobic exercise and progressive relaxation. *Journal of Sport and Exercise Psychology, 10,* 461–470.

Longo, D. J. (1984, May 23–26). *A psychophysiological comparison of three relaxation techniques and some implications in treating cardiovascular syndromes.* Paper presented at the annual meeting of the Society for Behavioral Medicine, Philadelphia.

Lucic, K. S., Steffen, J. C., Harrigan, J. A., & Stuebing, R. C. (1991). Progressive relaxation training: Muscle contraction before relaxation? *Behavior Therapy, 22,* 249–256.

Marks, I. M. (1981). *Cure and care of neuroses: Theory and practice of behavioral psychotherapy.* New York: Wiley.

Marks, I. M. (1987). *Fears, phobias and rituals: Panic, anxiety, and their disorders.* New York: Oxford University Press.

Mather, M. D., & Degun, G. S. (1975). A comparative study of hypnosis and relaxation. *British Journal of Medical Psychology, 48,* 55–63.

McCoy, G. C., Blanchard, E. B., Wittrock, D. A., Morrison, S., Pagburn, L., Siracusa, K., & Pallmeyer, T. (1988). Biochemical changes associated with thermal biofeedback treatment of hypertension. *Biofeedback and Self-Regulation, 13,* 139–150.

Michelson, L., Marchione, K., Marchione, N., Testa, S., & Mavissakalian, M. (1988). Cognitive correlates and outcome of cognitive, behavioral and physiological treatments of agoraphobia. *Psychological Reports, 63,* 999–1004.

Michelson, L., Mavissakalian, M., & Marchione, K. (1985). Cognitive and behavioral treatments of agoraphobia: Clinical, behavioral, and psychophysiological outcomes. *Journal of Consulting and Clinical Psychology, 53,* 913–925.

Michelson, L., Mavissakalian, M., & Marchione, K. (1988). Cognitive, behavioral and psychophysiological treatments of agoraphobia; A comparative outcome investigation. *Behavior Therapy, 19,* 97–120.

Michelson, L., Mavissakalian, M., Marchione, K., Dancu, C., & Greenwald, M. (1986). The role of self-directed in vivo exposure in cognitive, behavioral, and psychophysiological treatments of agoraphobia. *Behavior Therapy, 17,* 91–108.

Michelson, L., Mavissakalian, M., Marchione, K., Ulrich, R. F., Marchione, N., & Testa, S. (1990). Psychophysiological outcome of cognitive, behavioural and psychophysiologically-based treatments of agoraphobia. *Behaviour Research and Therapy, 28,* 127–139.

Miller, R. K., & Bornstein, P. H. (1977). Thirty-minute relaxation: A comparison of some methods. *Journal of Behavior Therapy and Experimental Psychiatry, 8,* 291–294.

Mitchell, K. R., & Mitchell, D. M. (1971). Migraine: An exploratory treatment application of programmed behavior therapy techniques. *Journal of Psychosomatic Research, 15,* 137–157.

Moore, N. (1965). Behavior therapy with bronchial asthma: A controlled study. *Journal of Psychosomatic Research, 9,* 257–274.

Murphy, T. J., Pagano, R. R., & Marlatt, G. A. (1986). Lifestyle modification with heavy alcohol drinkers: Effects of aerobic exercise and meditation. *Addictive Behaviors, 11,* 175–186.

Nilsson, K. M. (1990). The effect of subject expectations of "hypnosis" upon vividness of visual imagery. *International Journal of Clinical and Experimental Hypnosis, 38,* 17–24.

Norton, G. R., & Johnson, W. E. (1983). A comparison of two relaxation procedures for reducing cognitive and somatic anxiety. *Journal of Behavior Therapy and Experimental Psychiatry, 14,* 209–214.

Norton, G. R., Rhodes, L., Hauch, J., & Kaprowy, E. A. (1985). Characteristics of subjects experiencing relaxation and relaxation-induced anxiety. *Journal of Behavior Therapy and Experimental Psychiatry, 16,* 211–216.

Oakley, M. E., & Shapiro, D. (1989). Methodological issues in the evaluation of drug–behavioral interactions in the treatment of hypertension. *Psychosomatic Medicine, 51,* 269–276.

Öst, L. G., Jerremalm, A., & Johansson, J. (1981). Individual response patterns and the effects of different behavioural methods in the treatment of social phobias. *Behaviour Research and Therapy,* 1–16.

Page, R. D., & Schaub, L. H. (1978). EMG biofeedback applicability for differing personality types. *Journal of Clinical Psychology, 34,* 1014–1020.

Paul, G. L. (1969a). Physiological effects of relaxation training and hypnotic suggestion. *Journal of Abnormal Psychology, 74,* 425–437.

Paul, G. L. (1969b). Inhibition of physiological response to stressful imagery by relaxation training and hypnotically suggested relaxation. *Behaviour Research and Therapy, 7,* 249–256.

Paul, G. L., & Trimble, R. W. (1970). Recorded vs. "live" relaxation training and hypnotic suggestion: Comparative effectiveness for reducing physiological arousal and inhibiting stress response. *Behavior Therapy, 1,* 285–302.

Pollard, G., & Ashton, R. (1982). Heart rate decrease: A comparison of feedback modalities and biofeedback with other procedures. *Biological Psychology, 14,* 245–257.

Qualls, P. J., & Sheehan, P. W. (1979). Capacity for absorption and relaxation during electromyograph biofeedback and no-feedback conditions. *Journal of Abnormal Psychology, 88,* 652–688.

Quayle, C. M. (1980). The relative effectiveness of audio-taped and live therapist presented relaxation in terms of physiological parameters (Doctoral dissertation, Utah State University, 1979). *Dissertation Abstracts International, 40,* 3960B. (University Microfilms No. 80-05,114)

Rawson, J. R., Bhatnagar, N. S., & Schneider, H. G. (1985). Initial relaxation response: Personality and treatment factors. *Psychological Reports, 57,* 827–830.

Reynolds, S. B. (1984). Biofeedback, relaxation training, and music: Homeostasis for coping. *Biofeedback and Self-Regulation, 9,* 169–179.

Rickard, H. C., Crist, D. A., & Barker, H. (1985). The effects of suggestibility on relaxation. *Journal of Clinical Psychology, 41,* 466–468.

Rider, M. S. (1985). Entrainment mechanisms are involved in pain reduction, muscle relaxation, and music-mediated imagery. *Journal of Music Therapy, 22,* 183–192.

Roskies, E., Seraganian, P., Oseasohn, R., Hanley, J. A., Collu, R., Martin, N., & Smilga, C. (1986). The Montreal Type A Intervention Project: Major findings. *Health Psychology, 5,* 45–69.

Sakai, M., & Takeichi, M. (1985). [Clinical application and problems of autogenic training in psychiatric clinical work: II.] *Kyushu Neuro-Psychiatry, 31,* 282–287.

Sargent, J., Solbach, P., Coyne, L., Spohn, H., & Sergerson, J. (1986). Results of a controlled, experimental, outcome study of nondrug treatments for the control of migraine headaches. *Journal of Behavioral Medicine, 9,* 291–323.

Scandrett, S. L., Bean, J. L., Breeden, S., & Powell, S. (1986). A comparative study of biofeedback and progressive relaxation in anxious patients. *Issues in Mental Health Nursing, 8,* 255–271.

Scartelli, J. P. (1984). The effect of EMG biofeedback and sedative music, EMG biofeedback only, and sedative music only on frontalis muscle relaxation ability. *Journal of Music Therapy, 21,* 67–78.

Scartelli, J. P., & Borling, J. E. (1986). The effects of sequenced versus simultaneous EMG biofeedback and sedative music on frontalis relaxation training. *Journal of Music Therapy, 23,* 157–165.

Schilling, D. J., & Poppen, R. (1983). Behavioral relaxation training and assessment. *Journal of Behavior Therapy and Experimental Psychiatry, 14,* 99–107.

Schneider, H. D. (1988). Why low dose benzodiazepine dependent insomniacs can't escape their sleeping pills. *Acta Psychiatrica Scandinavica, 78,* 706–711.

Schneider, H. G., Rawson, J. C., & Bhatnagar, N. S. (1987). Initial relaxation response: Contrasts between clinical patients and normal volunteers. *Perceptual and Motor Skills, 64,* 147–153.

Schultz, J. H., & Luthe, W. (1969). *Autogenic therapy: Vol. 1. Autogenic methods.* New York: Grune & Stratton.

Schwartz, G. E., Davidson, R. J., & Goleman, D. T. (1978). Patterning of cognitive and somatic processes in the self-regulation of anxiety: Effects of meditation versus exercise. *Psychosomatic Medicine, 40,* 321–328.

Sedlacek, K., Cohen, J., & Boxhill, C. (1979). *Comparison between biofeedback and relaxation response in the treatment of hypertension.* Paper presented at the annual meeting of the Biofeedback Society of America, San Diego.

Shapiro, D. H. (1982). Overview: Clinical and physiological comparison of meditation with other self-control strategies. *American Journal of Psychiatry, 139,* 267–274.

Shapiro, S., & Lehrer, P. M. (1980). Psychophysiological effects of autogenic training and progressive relaxation. *Biofeedback and Self-Regulation, 5,* 249–255.

Shoemaker, J. (1977). Treatments for anxiety neurosis (Doctoral dissertation, Colorado State University, 1976). *Dissertation Abstracts International, 37,* 5377B. (University Microfilms No. 77-68,13)

Sigman, A., & Phillips, K. (1985). Biofeedback and hypnosis: A review of recent literature. *British Journal of Experimental and Clinical Hypnosis, 3,* 13–24.

Smith, J. C. (1986). Meditation, biofeedback, and the relaxation controversy: A cognitive–behavioral perspective. *American Psychologist, 41,* 1007–1009.

Smith, J. C. (1988). Steps toward a cognitive–behavioral model of relaxation. *Biofeedback and Self-Regulation, 13,* 307–329.

Snow, W. G. (1978). The physiological and subjective effects of several brief relaxation training procedures (Doctoral dissertation, York University, Canada, 1977). *Dissertation Abstracts International, 40,* 3458B.

Sokolov, E. N. (1963). *Perception and the conditioned reflex.* New York: Macmillan.

Soskis, D. A., Orne, E. C., Orne, M. T., & Dinges, D. F. (1989). Self hypnosis and meditation for stress management. *International Journal of Clinical and Experimental Hypnosis, 37,* 285–289.

Spanos, N. P., Ollerhead, V. G., & Gwynn, M. I. (1985–1986). The effects of three instructional treatments on pain magnitude and pain tolerance: Implications for theories of hypnotic analgesia. *Imagination, Cognition and Personality, 5,* 321–337.

Staples, R., Coursey, R., & Smith, B. (1975, February). *A comparison of EMG biofeedback, autogenic, and progressive training as relaxation techniques.* Paper presented at the annual meeting of the Biofeedback Research Society, Monterey, CA.

Stanton, H. E. (1984). A comparison of the effects of an hypnotic procedure and music on anxiety level. *Australian Journal of Clinical and Experimental Hypnosis, 12,* 127–132.

Stoudenmire, J. (1975). A comparison of muscle relaxation training and music in the reduction of state and trait anxiety. *Journal of Clinical Psychology, 31,* 490–492.

Stefanek, M. E., & Hodes, R. L. (1986). Expectancy effects on relaxation instructions: Physiological and self-report indices. *Biofeedback and Self-Regulation, 11,* 21–29.

Steptoe, A., & Kearsley, N. (1990). Cognitive and somatic anxiety. *Behaviour Research and Therapy, 28,* 75–81.

Stratton, V. N., & Zalanowski, A. H. (1984). The relationship between music, degree of liking, and self reported relaxation. *Journal of Music Therapy, 21,* 184–192.

Styf, J. (1990). The influence of external compression on muscle blood flow during exercise. *American Journal of Sports Medicine, 18,* 92–95.

Suinn, R. M. (1975). Anxiety management training for general anxiety. In R. Suinn & R. Weigel (Eds.), *The innovative therapies: Creative and critical contributions.* New York: Harper & Row.

Suinn, R. M. (1990). *Anxiety management training: A behavior therapy.* New York: Plenum Press.

Suinn, R. M., & Richardson, F. C. (1971). Anxiety management training: A nonspecific behavior therapy program for anxiety control. *Behavior Therapy, 2,* 498–510.

Sun, Z., Zhao, J., Xia, M., Ren, R., Yan, H., Yang, L., Gao, S., & Wang, S. (1986). [Comparative study on the efficiency of EMG and thermal biofeedback training and the combination of biofeedback and autogenic training in reducing test anxiety.] *Acta Psychologica Sinica, 18,* 196–202.

Surwit, R. S. (1982). Biofeedback and the behavioral treatment of Raynaud's disease. In L. White & B. Tursky (Eds.), *Clinical biofeedback: Efficacy and mechanisms.* New York: Guilford Press.

Surwit, R. S., Pilon, R. N., & Fenton, C. H. (1978). Behavioral treatment of Raynaud's disease. *Journal of Behavioral Medicine, 1,* 323–335.

Sweeney, G. A., & Horan, J. J. (1982). Separate and combined effects of cue controlled relaxation and cognitive restructuring in the treatment of musical performance anxiety. *Journal of Counseling Psychology, 29,* 486–497.

Taub, E. (1977). Self-regulation of human tissue temperature. In G. E. Schwartz & J. Beatty (Eds.), *Biofeedback: Theory and research*. New York: Academic Press.

Taub, E., & School, P. J. (1978). Some methodological considerations in thermal biofeedback training. *Behavior Research Methods and Instrumentation, 10*, 617–622.

Tripp, E. G., & Marks, D. (1986). Hypnosis, relaxation and analgesia suggestions for the reduction of reported pain in high- and low-suggestible subjects. *Australian Journal of Clinical and Experimental Hypnosis, 14*, 99–113.

Tsao, C. C., Gordon, T. F., Maranto, C. D., Lerman, C., & Murasko, D. (1991). The effects of music and directed biological imagery on immune response (S-IgA). In C. D. Maranto (Ed.), *Applications of music in medicine*. Washington, DC: National Association for Music Therapy.

Turner, P. E. (1978). A psychophysiological assessment of selected relaxation strategies (Doctoral dissertation, University of Mississippi). *Dissertation Abstracts International, 39*, 3010B. (University Microfilms No. 78-24,063)

Twentyman, C. T., & Zimering, R. T. (1978). Behavioral training of social skills: A critical review. In M. Hersen, R. M. Eisler, & P. M. Miller (Eds.), *Progress in behavior modification* (Vol. 7). New York: Academic Press.

Tyrer, P. (1978). Drug treatment of psychiatric patients in general practice. *British Medical Journal, ii*, 1008–1010.

Wall, V. J., & Womack, W. (1989). Hypnotic versus active cognitive strategies for alleviation of procedural distress in pediatric oncology patients. *American Journal of Clinical Hypnosis, 31*, 181–191.

Warrenburg, S., Pagano, R. R., Woods, M., & Hlastala, M. A. (1980). Comparison of somatic relaxation and EEG activity in classical progressive relaxation and transcendental meditation. *Journal of Behavioral Medicine, 3*, 73–93.

West, M. A. (1980). Meditation and the EEG. *Psychological Medicine, 10*, 369–375.

Whalen, C. K., Henker, B., & Hinshaw, S. P. (1985). Cognitive behavioral therapies for hyperactive children: Premises, problems, and prospects. *Journal of Abnormal Child Psychology, 13*, 391–410.

Whitehead, W. E., & Blackwell, B. (1979). Interactions between drugs and behavior therapy. In R. McNamara (Ed.), *Behavioral approaches to medicine*. New York: Plenum Press.

Wittrock, D. A., Blanchard, E. B., & McCoy, G. C. (1988). Three studies on the relation of process to outcome in the treatment of essential hypertension with relaxation and thermal biofeedback. *Behaviour Research and Therapy, 26*, 53–66.

Wolpe, J. (1958). *Psychotherapy by reciprocal inhibition*. Stanford, CA: Stanford University Press.

Wooley, S., Blackwell, B., & Winget, C. (1978). A learning model of chronic illness behavior: Theory, treatment and research. *Psychosomatic Medicine, 40*, 379–401.

Woolfolk, R. L. (1975). Psychophysiological correlates of meditation. *Archives of General Psychiatry, 32*, 1326–1333.

Woolfolk, R. L., & Lehrer, P. M. (Eds.). (1984). *Principles and practice of stress management* (1st ed.). New York: Guilford Press.

Yang, L., Xin, Y., Chen, H., & Hu, Z. (1987). [The effects of EMG biofeedback and autogenic training in relieving the anxiety of pregnant women.] *Acta Psychologica Sinica, 19*, 420–426.

Zaichkowsky, L., & Kamen, R. (1978). Biofeedback and meditation: Effects on muscle tension and locus of control. *Perceptual and Motor Skills, 46*, 955–958.

Zeier, H. (1984). Arousal reduction with biofeedback-supported respiratory meditation. *Biofeedback and Self-Regulation, 9*, 497–508.

Zeier, H. (1985). Entspannung durch biofeedbackunterstutze Atemmeditation und autogenes Training [Relaxation through feedback-supported respiratory meditation and autogenic training]. *Zeitschrift für Experimentelle und Angewandte Psychologie, 32*, 682–695.

Zika, B. (1987). The effects of hypnosis and meditation on a measure of self-actualization. *Australian Journal of Clinical and Experimental Hypnosis, 15*, 21–28.

17

Research on Clinical Issues in Stress Management

PAUL M. LEHRER
ROBERT L. WOOLFOLK

Stress management is an active, directive, educational, instigative form of therapy. A client describes his or her difficulties, and client and therapist work collaboratively to understand the presenting complaints and what they signify in the context of a unique human life. The therapist then brings technical expertise to bear upon those problems of living that have been shown to respond to techniques of stress management. The expertise of the therapist in deciding upon techniques and teaching them is, however, only a part of the clinical story. At one time, the clinical context of stress management was the subject of little systematic research. But in the last decade a substantial body of data on such factors as individual differences in response to treatment and the variables that predict adherence to treatment has emerged. In this chapter, we review the empirical research on clinical issues in stress management.

Adherence

Stress management is initiated and taught in the consulting room, but is practiced primarily in the natural environment. Virtually all forms of stress management assume the model of skills training. Practice between therapy sessions is considered the sine qua non of developing the ability to manage stress. Once mastered, coping skills are thought to require continual use. Stress management techniques do not make stress vanish, nor do they confer permanent immunity to stressors; they are tools that aid individuals in work that is perennial.

It is typically assumed that more frequent use of stress reduction methods results in more rapid learning and in more powerful therapeutic effects. In view of the great emphasis placed upon extramural practice of stress reduction methods, it is often discouraging for beginning practitioners to confront the less-than-perfect adherence to treatment regimens that is common. The problem of imperfect adherence is not, of course, unique to stress management. It is common to all forms of instigative behavior therapy, medical treatment, and health education—indeed, probably to all spheres of human practice where the dictates of reason and inclination are not in harmony.

Research on adherence has revealed a varied pattern of results. In an early study, Otis (1974) observed that only half of a group of individuals who began transcendental meditation (TM) training were still meditating a year later. Smith (1976) found a 59% attrition rate after 3.5 months of training in TM. Shafii, Lavely, and Jaffe (1974) observed that 46% of meditators had either stopped or decreased practicing after 3 months. Soskis, Orne, Orne, and Dinges (1989) reported that with meditation and self-hypnotic techniques, the dropout rate at 6 months neared 60%. As reasons for dropping out, subjects reported difficulty finding time, as well as some adverse experiences with their techniques. Approximately 50% of subjects reported having used their techniques at least 10 times during the 6-month period. In a literature review on the effects of meditation, Delmonte (1988) reported a dropout rate of 54% over 2 years. Zuroff and Schwartz (1980) reported that 2 years after initial training, fewer than 20% of college student subjects who had volunteered for training continued to practice either progressive relaxation (PR) or meditation at least once per week. Lutz, Silbret, and Olshan (1983) reported a 42% overall compliance rate with a multifaceted program for pain that included relaxation and self-hypnosis. Sallis et al. (1987) found that approximately 50% of participants in a worksite stress management program practiced relaxation at least once per week at a 3-month follow-up assessment.

Adsett, Bellissimo, Mitchell, Wilczynski, and Haynes (1989) found the rate of compliance with relaxation training to be comparable to that of adherence to a medication regimen. In a study of chronic pain patients, Kabat-Zinn, Lipworth, and Burney (1985) found a 30% dropout rate from their technique of mindfulness meditation, but this measure was taken at a variable time after treatment, ranging from only 2.5 to 15 months. The lower dropout rate may have been attributable to the shorter average follow-up period in this study or perhaps to higher motivation among pain patients.

Validity Issues in the Assessment of Adherence

Recent research has called into question the validity of subjects' reports of how frequently they practice stress reduction techniques. Lichstein and Hoelscher (1986) have developed an unobtrusive, objective measure of time spent in relaxation practice, which they call a "relaxation assessment device" (RAD). The RAD is a portable audiotape player with a relaxation tape sealed in the tape compartment and a cumulative stopwatch that is activated when and only when the "play" button is pressed. Another assessment technique asks subjects to report the approximate location of a cue tone located somewhere on the relaxation tape (Collins, Martin, & Hillenberg, 1982). Jacob, Beidel, and Shapiro (1984) evaluated adherence by asking subjects to identify one of four possible code words that were placed on each day's relaxation tape.

A problem in these procedures is the necessity of using taped relaxation procedures. Although Jacobson once personally told the first author that he disapproved of this procedure, and the effects of taped training alone appear to be dubious, there are few data to back up Jacobson's distaste for the use of tape recordings as *adjuncts* to live training. Jacobson felt that this would produce reliance on the presence of the tape and would prevent the learning of a generalizable skill.

The use of tape-recorder-dependent techniques may be justified for research purposes, especially in light of evidence that subjects tend to give exaggerated reports of practice time. Wisniewski, Genshaft, Mulick, Coury, and Hammer (1988) found that a group of 10 adolescent headache patients overreported their home practice of relaxation therapy by an average of 70%. Hoelscher, Lichstein, and Rosenthal (1984) found that subjects selected for high generalized anxiety overreported practice time by 126%. In a study of hypertensives, these same authors (Hoelscher, Lichstein, & Rosenthal, 1986) found that self-reports exceeded objectively monitored practice by 91%.

Even objective methods of monitoring practice do not guarantee the validity of assessment of time spent relaxing. Automatic clocking of tape recorder time is not the same as actually observing practice itself. This procedure can be invalid in a different way from subjective reporting. For example, Wisniewski et al. (1988) found that unauthorized use of the tape recorder by family members sometimes occurred; this resulted in inflated "objective" estimates of time spent in relaxation practice.

Effects of Regularity of Practice

Implicit in most approaches to clinical stress management is the assumption that regular practice of relaxation, biofeedback, or meditation techniques is, to some degree at least, related to learning them and to their effectiveness. Sherman (1982) noted decreases in anxiety among anxious patients who reported using tape-recorded PR instructions given to them, but no improvement among those who reported not using the tapes. Blanchard et al. (1983) found a relationship between regularity of relaxation practice at home and reduction in headache activity among individuals with various kinds of chronic headaches. Murphy, Pagano, and Marlatt (1986) reported a significant decrease in drinking among heavy alcohol drinkers who were classified as showing high compliance with requirements for meditation practice (based on a median split), but no change in drinking among those who practiced less. The median number of practice sessions was 5.3 per week. They also studied the effects of an exercise regimen, and found no differences between high and low compliers with this procedure. However, the median number of exercise sessions was lower than for meditation (3.5 per week), and this may have been responsible for the lack of differences between high and low compliers with this treatment.

Libo and Arnold (1983) followed pain patients 3–5 years after treatment and found that continued relaxation practice was significantly related to the maintenance of therapeutic gains. They also discovered that occasional or "as-needed" practice of relaxation methods was sufficient to maintain long-term gains among clients treated for various stress-related disorders. Lutz et al. (1983) found a positive relationship between frequency of relaxation or self-hypnosis practice and long-term improvement in both life style and pain among patients in a multidisciplinary pain program. In a study of 8th- through 12th-grade students with public-speaking anxiety, Hiebert, Boelle, and Jaknavorian (1989) found significantly better results for PR than for the control condition among 11th- and 12th-graders, but not among younger students. They attributed the greater success in this age group to greater treatment compliance (i.e., more home practice) in the older group.

Wittrock, Blanchard, and McCoy (1988) found a relationship between practice time and decreases in blood pressure with both PR and thermal biofeedback (TBFK). Hoelscher et al. (1986) found a relationship between relaxation practice time and decreases in systolic but not diastolic blood pressure. This pattern was present for both self-reported and automatically monitored assessment of practice time. Hoelscher et al. (1984) observed that anxiety reduction was significantly correlated with objectively assessed practice time, but not with self-reported practice. Peters, Benson, and Porter (1977) found few changes in self-reported indices of stress among employees at a manufacturing firm who practiced fewer than three times per week; two practice periods per day did not appear to be necessary to produce positive results. Somatic symptoms tended to improve with less practice time than behavioral symptoms and general sense of well-being.

Carrington et al. (1980), however, found that regular practice was not necessary for maintenance of decreases in Symptom Checklist 90—Revised (SCL-90-R) scores among stressed employees of a major corporation. Treatment gains were maintained equally well among subjects who used their techniques only occasionally or when under stress and among subjects who continued to practice daily. Symptoms rebounded to original levels among subjects who had stopped practicing their techniques entirely. Similar findings were obtained by Hughes, Brown, Lawlis, and Fulton (1983) among people with acne vulgaris who were treated with biofeedback-assisted relaxation and cognitive imagery. Flanders and McNamara (1987b) found that minimal home practice was necessary for anxiety reduction, but that the amount of practice (among subjects who practiced at all) did not correlate with reductions in anxiety. Hafner (1982) found no relationship between home practice time and decreases in blood pressure in either meditation or biofeedback-assisted relaxation training; Wisniewski et al. (1988) found no relationship between practice time and effectiveness of PR in treating headaches among children. Jacob et al. (1984) failed to ascertain any relationship between relaxation practice and reduction of hypertension.

A problem in the above-mentioned studies is that some subjects may not have practiced regularly, or may have stopped practicing altogether, because the relaxation techniques were initially ineffective; thus, the causal relationship between compliance and therapeutic effects is not clear. A more rigorous approach to understanding the effects of home practice would be to compare a group of subjects deliberately instructed to practice at home with another group told not to practice. DeBerry (1982) found that among individuals selected for anxiety, sadness, irritability, or the like, follow-up assessment of state anxiety tended to rebound after a meditation–relaxation therapy among subjects who were specifically instructed not to continue practicing at home, whereas the values continued to decrease among those instructed to continue practicing. Similarly, Hillenberg and Collins (1983) compared home-practice with no home practice in the treatment of anxious mental health clinic patients, and found a greater decrease in symptoms of anxiety and tension among subjects told to practice at home. No differences in physiological activity or self-reported tension were found during a laboratory session, however. Blanchard, Nicholson, Radnitz, Steffek, and Appelbaum (1991) studied the effect of home practice on the effects of TBFK among headache patients. One group was provided with a home practice trainer and instructed to practice regularly; no mention of practice was made to a second group. Blanchard et al. concluded that home practice produced no advantages, either in reduction of headaches or in acquisition of a hand-warming skill.

It should be noted that some differences between relaxation techniques in regard to subjects' willingness to practice them may exist. PR may be somewhat more motivating than autogenic training (AT). Several studies, including two of ours (Carrington et al., 1980; Lehrer, Woolfolk, Rooney, McCann, & Carrington, 1983), found that subjects reported enjoying meditation more than PR and practicing it somewhat more. The differences between groups on these measures were not large, but they were significant and consistent across studies. Zuroff and Schwarz (1978) also reported that college student subjects (at least at their university in the late 1970s) had higher expectancies for meditation than for PR. Lehrer, Atthowe, and Weber (1980) found that subjects given PR reported having engaged in more home practice than subjects given AT. Data reported by Bird, Wilson, and Blanchard (1985), however, showed that subjects at a stress management clinic did not report any preferences between these two techniques. Sallis et al. (1987) found that participants in a worksite stress management program practiced deep breathing more than abbreviated PR, and abbreviated PR more than relaxing imagery. Compliance with a longer PR procedure (involving 16 muscle groups) was lowest of all. Glueck and Stroebel (1975) reported the results of a small pilot study showing that psychiatric inpatients tended to have greater motivational difficulties following AT instructions than TM instructions.

In summary, it appears that *some* home practice of relaxation techniques is necessary to produce clinical success, although lengthy and regular practice does *not* appear necessary. Also, techniques vary in the extent to which people are willing to practice them. Meditation appears to produce a particularly high rate of compliance and AT a relatively low rate, although there is considerable individual variability in response to treatment, as we describe later in the chapter.

Factors Influencing Adherence

In understanding adherence to stress management treatment programs, a useful analogy is that to compliance with medical regimens. Leventhal and his colleagues (Leventhal, Meyers, & Nerenz, 1980; Meyers, Leventhal, & Gutmann, 1985) have formulated what they call a "common-sense model of illness," which predicts for various diseases the seeking of medical care and adherence to treatment. This model includes interacting elements of symptom levels, perception of vulnerability, and anxiety. The greatest compliance and care seeking would be expected among individuals who experience anxiety and high symptom levels and who interpret their symptoms as indicating the presence of disease. This model is similar to Becker's (1976, 1979) health belief model, which bases predictions of adherence on the patient's perception of vulnerability to and seriousness of the problem, as well as the costs and effectiveness of the treatment.

A number of factors appear to influence the extent to which clients will practice and utilize stress management techniques. In a review of literature addressing compliance with meditation practice, Delmonte (1981b) found that higher expectations of success were associated with more regular practice. Hoelscher et al. (1986) also found a positive relationship between home practice of relaxation and expectations of benefit. Self-efficacy was positively correlated with compliance with PR practice in two studies (Hoelscher et al., 1984, 1986). Hart (1982) found dropout rates from treatment to be greater for individuals reporting less severe symptoms (i.e., fewer headaches) and higher levels of depression. Warrenburg and Pagano (1982–1983) found the capacity for absorbed attention to predict adherence to meditation. Delmonte (1988) reported that regularity of practice was negatively related to neuroticism and introversion; this suggests that the greatest positive effects for stress management therapies may be obtained by individuals needing these techniques the least. In a study of mental health clinic patients attending an anxiety management course, however, compliance with home practice of taped PR instructions was *positively* associated with subjects' self-report of the severity of their problem (Bennett & Millard, 1985). It is not possible to know whether the disparity in results in these two reports can be attributed to differences in relaxation methods, in subject populations, in measures of problem severity, or in all of these. Flanders and McNamara (1987a) found that achievement orientation and self-motivation were most predictive of amount of home practice time, although significant negative correlations also occurred with measures of anger and anxiety.

Some interventions have been found to enhance adherence to practice of stress management outside of therapy sessions. Cox, Tisdelle, and Culbert (1988) found that supplying trainees with written behavioral prescriptions for home practice led to better adherence than did a condition in which trainees received only oral instructions. Hypertensive subjects who practiced relaxation with their spouses showed significantly better compliance with treatment instructions than individuals who practiced alone (Wadden, 1983). Taylor, Agras, Schneider, and Allen (1983) reported a significant therapist effect on practice rates, indicating that individual therapists may engender different rates of adherence.

Ley (1982) has emphasized the importance of the patient's understanding of the physician's recommendations in predicting satisfaction with and adherence to medical treatment. However, supplying subjects with a rationale for home practice has not been found to increase compliance over control conditions involving no rationale (Bennett & Millard, 1985; Riley, Berry, & Kennedy, 1986). Bennett and Millard (1985), however, did find that providing additional information about PR did reduce dropout rates and enhance satisfaction with training. Adding contingency contracting to group training in relaxation actually *reduced* adherence to practice instructions (Hoelscher et al., 1986). Monetary deposits did not increase relaxation practice or program adherence in a population with generalized anxiety (Lewis, Biglan, & Steinbock, 1978).

Individual-Difference Factors in Effects of Stress Management Techniques

Expectancy

Expectancy for success is an important ingredient in the success of any psychological treatment. Thus Beiman (1976) found that when negative expectancies were deliberately given, the within-session effects of a single session of PR were negligible. Woolfolk and Rooney (1981) found expectations to have little influence on the psychological and physiological effects of a single meditation session. Brown (1977) found that positive expectancy was important in treating hyperkinesis with relaxation therapy. Borkovec and his colleagues describe an ingenious "counterdemand" procedure, whereby subjects expect poor success for a limited time (e.g., the first four sessions). This manipulation does not appear to interfere with willingness to practice, and it successfully differentiates the effects of training from those of a belief that the method works. Generally, active treatments are found to produce positive effects during the counterdemand periods, although further improvement is usually obtained after that period is over (Borkovec & Hennings, 1978; Borkovec & Weerts, 1976; Carr-Kaffashan & Woolfolk, 1979). Agras, Horne, and Taylor (1982) used a similar procedure in a study of relaxation therapy for hypertension, and found a difference of 14 mm Hg in immediate decreases in systolic blood pressure between subjects who were told to expect immediate decreases and subjects who were not. There were no differences between conditions in diastolic blood pressure or, surprisingly, in perceived relaxation.

Expectancies do not appear to account for whatever differences there are between various techniques. Although some of the studies comparing meditation and relaxation show slightly higher expectancies produced by the meditation, the effects of most of the techniques have been to raise expectancies by an equivalent amount.

Locus of Control

The effect of expectancy may interact with internal locus of control in making training more effective with internally oriented clients. If a person does not believe that a treatment method will work, or if the person does not believe that various symptoms of stress can be overcome by his or her own effort, then the person probably will not practice the relaxation method consistently, and its effects will thus be weakened. Subjects who believe that they can exercise personal control over events occurring in their bodies might therefore be expected to practice any relaxation technique more than subjects who believe that events in their bodies are controlled by external forces. Lewis, Biglan, and Steinbock (1978) found that subjects high in internal control also had high expectancies for success and practiced their relaxation instructions more at home. Consequently, they showed greater reduction in trait anxiety than others. Long and Haney (1986) found an interaction between expectancy and internal locus of control in predicting the willingness of sedentary women to undertake an exercise program. A discrepant study was reported by Kaplan, Atkins, and Reinsch (1984), who found no relationship between locus of control and adherence to exercise prescriptions among patients with chronic obstructive pulmonary disease; however, they found a positive relationship between exercise participation and expectancy for efficacy.

Locus of control also appears to be independently associated with willingness to engage in various self-management strategies. Carlson and Petti (1989) found that internal locus of control was positively related to metabolic demand in exercise programs undertaken by college students. Dinning and Crampton (1989) found locus of control to be positively associated with engaging in preventive health behaviors among college students, and Rauckhorst (1987) found a similar relationship among elderly widows. McCready and Long (1985) found a weak relationship between locus of control and increase in aerobic exercise among a group of sedentary women participating in an aerobic fitness program. Hjelle (1974) found higher levels of internal control among a group of experienced meditators than among a group of novices. However, since pretraining measures were not taken, it is not possible to know whether internality caused subjects to remain with the meditation program or whether meditation produced greater internality. Two studies found no relationship between novice meditators and nonmeditators in locus of control (Dick, 1973/1973–1974; Stek & Bass, 1973).

Perhaps because of increased adherence, some studies of relaxation techniques revealed larger effects among subjects high in internal locus of control. Spoth (1983) found greater anxiety reduction among internal than among external subjects undergoing cue controlled relaxation. Denkowski, Denkowski, and Omizo (1984) found a relationship between locus of control and the effects of electromyographic biofeedback (EMG BFK) on control of hyperactivity. Hudzinski and Levenson (1985) found a relationship between internal locus of control and improvement of headaches after a biofeedback program.

Having an internal locus of control does not necessarily make self-regulation techniques more powerful within a given training session, however. No relationship was found between locus of control and autonomic changes during a single session of alpha biofeedback control among college students (Knox, 1982), or between locus of control and learning of blood pressure control in one session of biofeedback among normotensive college students (Mullins & Sharpley, 1988).

Even over time, not all studies found significant relationships between locus of control and stress management therapies. Delmonte (1988) found no relationship between locus of control and regularity of meditation practice. Lacroix, Clarke, Bock, and Doxey (1986) found no relationship between locus of control and improvement in chronic pain symptoms after relaxation or biofeedback therapies.

Two studies found greater effects among external than among internal subjects. Prager-Decker (1978/1979) found that individuals high on external locus of control learned to reduce EMG activity more quickly during EMG BFK sessions than subjects high on internal locus of control. These findings may be explainable by the fact that subjects were not asked to practice the technique at home between sessions, so individuals' belief in their own ability to control the symptoms had no chance to affect their practice behavior. Also, all biofeedback instruction was given from an external source (i.e., the biofeedback machine), and this treatment may thus have been particularly appealing to externally oriented subjects. No such differences between internal and external locus of control were found for PR in this study. More difficult to explain are the findings of Hendricksen (1977/1978) that meditation, PR, and a placebo all produced greater decreases in state anxiety among inpatient alcoholic subjects with external (vs. internal) locus of drinking control. The fact that this measure did not show differences between placebo and treatment conditions perhaps indicates that external subjects were merely being more sensitive to demand characteristics of the situation (i.e., they may have thought that the experimenters were most interested in producing changes in their anxiety levels). Changes on a measure that did show differences between treatment and control conditions (the Confusion–Bewilderment scale on the Profile of Mood States) were not related to internality–externality. Also, external–internal locus of drinking control may be quite different from other forms of externality–internality. External subjects may perhaps have felt able to control their anxiety levels but not their drinking, so this study does not necessarily contradict previous findings of greater relaxation effects on anxiety among those with internal than among those with external locus of control. In addition, external subjects had manifested higher pretest (and posttest) anxiety than had internal subjects, thus raising the possibility of a floor effect in the latter group, and raising further questions about the interpretability of these results.

As Prager-Decker's (1978/1979) study suggests, locus of control may have a different predictive relationship to success in various treatments, depending on the extent to which the treatments rely on external agents (e.g., biofeedback machines) or internal processes. These methods generally do not allow subjects to practice between sessions, where internal locus of control may provide an advantage. Cognitive interventions may not depend on practice for success, but may rely heavily on the individuals' willingness to exert cognitive control over their behavior and thoughts, thus giving the edge to individuals high on internal locus of control. In a single-session study, Ollendick and Murphy (1977) found that PR produced greater reductions in heart rate and state anxiety among those with external than among those with internal locus of control, whereas cognitive relaxation training (focusing on pleasant thoughts and feelings) had greater effects for those with internal locus of control. Abramowitz, Bell, Folkins, Wolfe, and DuRand (1984) found a relatively positive relationship between internal control and success in decreasing headaches with psychotherapy, but the opposite relationship with biofeedback. Two studies found a positive relationship between externality and ability to produce voluntary decreases in heart rate (Ray & Lamb, 1974; Gatchel, 1975), although other studies found no such relationship (Fenz, Pye, & Favaro, 1984; Lang, 1975; Lang, Troyer, Twentyman, & Gatchel, 1975; Levenson & Ditto, 1981; Bell & Schwartz, 1975). Chellsen (1984) found that providing instructions on how to control heart rate voluntarily allowed internal subjects to achieve greater control of heart rate acceleration through biofeedback than external subjects or subjects given biofeedback without instructions. Other studies also showed a differential ability for internal subjects to increase their heart rates (Schneider, Sobol, Herrmann, & Cousins, 1978; Blankstein & Egner, 1977). Russell, Dale, and Anderson (1982) found that deliberately providing positive expectancies tended to disrupt learning of relaxation by EMG BFK among external subjects.

There is evidence that internal locus of control may be a positive predictor of success in programs with multimodal stress management programs, which include biofeedback, relaxation training, and cognitive interventions. These programs tend to involve multiple sessions and require participants to practice and use their methods in various stressful situations. Hudzinski and Levenson (1985) found this to be the case among headache patients. On the other hand, cancer patients receiving relaxation and/or biofeedback therapy to help them manage side effects of chemotherapy tended to show lower posttreatment levels of physiological arousal and self-reported negative affect if they manifested an external locus of control (Burish et al., 1984). It is possible that this population does in fact have less control over their physical discomfort than the more usual recipients of such treatment (viz., people with psychophysiological disorders), and thus that an external orientation is more adaptive for them. There is also some evidence that relaxation or biofeedback training can produce a shift to greater internality (e.g., Denkowski, Denkowski, & Omizo, 1983; Denkowski & Denkowski, 1984; Porter & Omizo, 1984; Rivera & Omizo, 1980; Roome & Romney, 1985; Rohsenow, Smith, & Johnson, 1985; Stanton, 1982).

In summary, success with most stress management methods appears to be associated with internal locus of control. This relationship may reflect a greater willingness on the part of internally oriented subjects to practice and apply their techniques at home, perhaps stemming from their assumption that they can in fact exercise control over their stress levels. An interesting exception to this may be in the case of biofeedback, which involves an external agent (i.e., the biofeedback machine). The success of biofeedback may be less reliant on internal motivation for home practice, unless machines are available for home use. Biofeedback tends to be favored by externally oriented individuals.

Depression

It is well-known clinical lore among stress management practitioners that persons who are depressed are often not helped by stress management techniques (see Glueck & Stroebel, 1975). There is some evidence for this. In a study of individuals with primarily psychophysiological disorders, Ford, Stroebel, Strong, and Szarek (1982) found a negative correlation between depression and improvement at a 2-year follow-up. Their treatment package comprised PR, AT, EMG BFK, TBFK, and Stroebel's "quieting response" training (which includes some elements of relaxation, suggestion, and cognitive refocusing). Delmonte (1984, 1988) has reported that subjects with lower levels of maladjustment tend to enjoy and practice meditation more than others. As outlined in the section in Chapter 18 on depression, however, there is some evidence that relaxation and other stress management techniques may be helpful adjuncts in the treatment of depression, so the presence of this problem is not a definite contraindication for their use.

Psychophysiological Reactivity

Some complex relationships have been found between levels of physiological arousal or reactivity and responses to various stress reduction treatments. A number of investigators have found a positive association between initial resting heart rate and subsequent response to various behavioral treatments for anxiety (Craske, Sanderson, & Barlow, 1987; Jansson, Jerremalm, & Öst, 1986; Lang, Levin, Miller, & Kozak, 1983; Vermilyea, Boice, & Barlow, 1984; Watson & Marks, 1971). For hypertension, however, responsiveness to relaxation therapy appears to be associated with relatively lower levels of urine epinephrine and less cardiovascular reactivity to laboratory challenges (Larkin, Knowlton, & D'Alessandri, 1990).

Hypnotic Susceptibility

Although response to various relaxation techniques does tend to be related to hypnotic susceptibility, specifically hypnotic techniques tend to show a somewhat higher relationship. This probably results from the greater similarity of hypnotic procedures to those used in tests of hypnotic susceptibility, and indicates that hypnosis is not identical to the other techniques.

Miller and Cross (1985) found that the Harvard Group Scale of Hypnotic Susceptibility predicted decreases in frontalis EMG activity achieved through hypnosis but not EMG BFK, and that low-hypnotizable subjects showed greater EMG reductions with EMG BFK than with hypnosis. Spanos, Ollerhead, and Gwynn (1985–1986) found an association between hypnotic susceptibility and reduction in cold-pressor pain among normal subjects with hypnosis, but not with stress inoculation training; however, both techniques tended to lower pain reactivity compared to control conditions. In a literature review, Delmonte (1985) concluded that hypnotizability is a predictive factor for anxiety reduction with meditation. Pekala and his colleagues (Pekala & Forbes, 1988, 1990; Pekala, Forbes, & Contrisciani, 1988–1989) found consistent differences between high- and low-hypnotizable subjects in response to PR and hypnosis. Among low hypnotizable subjects, PR, compared with hypnosis, produced a greater number of hypnoidal events, more absorption, a greater sense of control, more alterations in experience and state of awareness, and a greater diminution in volitional control. The authors conclude that PR is a more powerful technique than hypnosis for low-hypnotizable subjects. They also note that highly hypnotizable subjects tended to show greater responses than low-hypnotizable subjects on most of the measures listed above, in both conditions.

Qualls and Sheehan (1979) found *smaller* decreases in frontalis EMG after EMG BFK than in a no-feedback condition among subjects scoring high on absorption, but the opposite relationship among low-absorption subjects. Absorption is generally considered to be a key component in hypnotic susceptibility. This "interference" effect of EMG BFK for high-absorption subjects was verified in a second study (Qualls & Sheehan, 1981b). The addition of imaginal strategies overcame the "interference" effect of biofeedback in high-absorption subjects (Qualls & Sheehan, 1981a). It was concluded that subjects high in absorption require concurrent use of imaginal strategies along with the more "objective" and somatic approach of biofeedback for effective learning of somatic control.

The cognitive emphasis in hypnosis is reflected in a greater association between hypnotic susceptibility and changes in cognitive measures than changes in somatic ones. Rickard, Crist, and Barker (1985) found a significant relationship between suggestibility and relaxation scores for cognitive and mood dimensions of relaxation, but not physiological dimensions. The relationship was approximately equal for taped PR and suggestions to relax the various muscles. Subjects for this study were normal college students. This study used a version of relaxation instruction that included some hypnotic-like suggestions, so it is possible that the equivalence of the two techniques could be attributed to this factor.

Despite these findings, however, some investigators have nevertheless continued to hold the position that hypnotic susceptibility is correlated to an equal degree with response to all relaxation techniques. Stam, McGrath, and Brooke (1984) found an equivalent relationship between hypnotic susceptibility and temporomandibular joint pain reduction for a technique involving relaxation therapy and one involving hypnosis. Tripp and Marks (1986) found a positive or equivalent relationship between hypnotizability and response to analgesic instructions in both hypnosis and relaxation conditions. In a literature review, Spinhoven (1988) found greater headache improvement among highly hypnotizable subjects than others with a range of psychological techniques, both hypnotic and nonhypnotic. He speculates that an important element in treatment may be the extent to which the context of it activates a person's hypnotic ability, and that this may be more important than other aspects of the techniques used.

Not all studies have found a relationship between hypnotic susceptibility and effects of nonhypnotic stress management therapies. Lehrer et al. (1980) found no relationship between scores of hypnotic susceptibility and response either to PR or AT. Smith, Womack, and Pertik (1987) found no relationship among children between hypnotic susceptibility and learning to control finger temperature by biofeedback. In a review of the literature to that date, Sigman and Phillips (1985) concluded that hypnotic susceptibility may not be predictive of the power of biofeedback training to help people self-regulate, although it may predict a more general responsiveness to instructions. Radtke, Spanos, Armstrong, Dillman, and Buisvenue (1983) found no relationship between hypnotic susceptibility and changes in EMG after EMG BFK or PR training

The relationship between hypnotic susceptibility and relaxation or meditation practice may be bidirectional. There is some evidence that relaxation therapy may increase hypnotic susceptibility (e.g., Delmonte, 1981a; Kaplan & Barabasz, 1988; Wickramasekera, 1973). Radtke et al. (1983), however, found no changes in hypnotic susceptibility after PR or EMG BFK.

In summary, although improvement with some stress management methods may, debatedly, be related to the trait of hypnotic susceptibility, it is not related to improvement with biofeedback and is most highly related to improvement with formal hypnosis. These findings may be related to the definition and measures of hypnostic susceptibility, which tend to emphasize aspects of hypnosis related to attentional and cognitive aspects of the hypnotic experience. These measures tend to include tasks that are most similar to those employed in techniques described as formal "hypnosis." Hilgard (1965) reviews data indicating separate factors for cognitive and physiological dimensions of hypnotic susceptibility. The physiological component tends to be much easier, and does not as easily differentiate highly hypnotizable subjects from others. Biofeedback, the most strictly "physiological" of all self-regulation techniques, also includes direct information about the individual's actual physiological state, which at times can be at variance with the person's own *perceived* physiological state. This conflict may in fact undermine a hypnotic trance, since the hypnotic procedure may involve instructing subjects to feel sensations that are incompatible with actual physiological events. Information that is discrepant with such sensations (which may be the case when the biofeedback machine indicates physiological activity that is not perceived by the subject) may undermine a hypnotic trance. Thus the lack of correlation between hypnotic susceptibility and biofeedback may reflect major differences in the ways that these techniques work, whereas the close association between hypnotic susceptibility and response to formal hypnosis may be related to the close similarity of the tasks used in each.

Conclusions

It is perhaps obvious that motivational effects of the various techniques are important. If people stop practicing a technique, it will have little therapeutic effect. Our own work has suggested that subjects enjoy meditating more than practicing PR, and that they enjoy PR more than AT. However, these are only group differences; techniques do differ in their appeal to particular individuals. Similarly, the tendency to experience negative effects in one or another treatment may motivate some people to drop out. Given the serious dropout problem, the motivational effects of various techniques on particular individuals may be among their most important differential characteristics. Some people prefer to meditate, others to relax their muscles, others to talk about their thoughts and feelings, and still others to use machines. A sensitive therapist will take these factors into account in designing a treatment. On the average, meditation is one of the most motivational techniques, whereas AT and biofeedback are the least motivational.

Data on internal–external locus of control appear to show that internally oriented individuals master relaxation techniques more easily than do externally oriented people. Externally oriented people tend to do better with biofeedback. The advantage for internality is most apparent when subjects must practice their techniques between sessions, but all effective techniques require this in the clinical situation. Hypnotic susceptibility is sometimes a predictor of response to various interventions, particularly if they are labeled as "hypnosis." It is not related to improvement with biofeedback.

Dropout from treatment and noncompliance with it are major problems for all the methods described in this book. Although a substantial amount of long-term practice is not necessary for clinical effectiveness, some continued use of stress management techniques is necessary for well-being in the long term. Important factors influencing compliance include positive expectancy of success, absorption capability, psychological health, and achievement motivation. Additional factors include the therapist's supplying of written instructions.

REFERENCES

Abramowitz, S. I., Bell, N. W., Folkins, C. H., Wolfe, D., & DuRand, C. (1984). Internal external control and headache response to biofeedback and psychotherapy. *Psychotherapy and Psychosomatics 41*, 57–63.
Adsett, C. A., Bellissimo, A., Mitchell, A., Wilczynski, N., & Haynes, R. B. (1989). Behavioral and

physiological effects of a beta blocker and relaxation therapy on mild hypertensives. *Psychosomatic Medicine, 51,* 523–536.

Agras, W. S., Horne, M., & Taylor, C. B. (1982). Expectation and the blood-pressure-lowering effects of relaxation. *Psychosomatic Medicine 44,* 389–395.

Becker, M. H. (1976). Sociobehavioral determinants of compliance. In D. L. Hackett & R. B. Haynes (Eds.), *Compliance with therapeutic regimens.* Baltimore: Johns Hopkins University Press.

Becker, M. H. (1979). Understanding patient compliance. In S. J. Cohen (Ed.), *New directions in patient compliance.* Lexington, MA: Lexington Books.

Beiman, I. (1976). The effects of instructional set on physiological response to stressful imagery. *Behaviour Research and Therapy 14,* 175–179.

Bennett, G., & Millard, M. (1985). Compliance with relaxation training: The effect of providing information. *Behavioural Psychotherapy, 13,* 110–119.

Bell, I. R., & Schwartz, G. E. (1975). Voluntary control and reactivity of human heart rate. *Psychophysiology, 12,* 339–448.

Bird, E. I., Wilson, V. E., & Blanchard, E. B. (1985). Characteristics of stress clinical attendees. *Biofeedback and Self-Regulation, 10,* 343–348.

Blanchard, E. B., Andrasik, F., Neff, D. F., Saunders, N. L., Arena, J. G., Pallmeyer, T. P., Teders, S. J., Jurish, S. E., & Rodichok, L. D. (1983). Four process studies in the behavioural treatment of chronic headache. *Behaviour Research and Therapy, 21,* 209–220.

Blanchard, E. B., Nicholson, N. L., Radnitz, C. L., Steffek, B. D., & Appelbaum, K. A. (1991). The role of home practice in thermal biofeedback. *Journal of Consulting and Clinical Psychology, 59,* 507–512.

Blankstein, K. R., & Egner, K. (1977). Relationship of the locus of control construct to the self-control of heart rate. *Journal of General Psychology, 97,* 291–306.

Borkovec, T. D., & Hennings, B. L. (1978). The role of physiological attention-focusing in the relaxation treatment of sleep disturbance, general tension, and specific stress reaction. *Behaviour Research and Therapy, 16,* 7–19.

Borkovec, T. D., & Weerts, T. C. (1976). Effects of progressive relaxation on sleep disturbance: An electroencephalographic evaluation. *Psychosomatic Medicine, 38,* 173–180.

Brown, R. H. (1977). An evaluation of the effectiveness of relaxation training as a treatment modality for the hyperkinetic child (Doctoral dissertation, Texas Technological University). *Dissertation Abstracts International, 38,* 2847B. (University Microfilms no. 77-25,502)

Burish, T. G., Carey, M. P., Wallston, K. A., Stein, M. J., Jamison, R. N., & Lyles, J. N. (1984). Health locus of control and chronic disease: An external orientation may be advantageous. *Journal of Social and Clinical Psychology, 2,* 326–332.

Carr-Kaffashan, L., & Woolfolk, R. L. (1979). Active and placebo effects in the treatment of moderate and severe insomnia. *Journal of Consulting and Clinical Psychology, 47,* 603–605.

Carlson, B. R., & Petti, K. (1989). Health locus of control and participation in physical activity. *American Journal of Health Promotion, 3,* 32–37.

Carrington, P., Collings, G. H., Jr., Benson, H., Robinson, H., Wood, L. W., Lehrer, P. M., Woolfolk, R. L., & Cole, J. W. (1980). The use of meditation–relaxation techniques for the management of stress in a working population. *Journal of Occupational Medicine, 22,* 221–231.

Chellsen, J. A. (1984). Effects of locus of control and strategy instructions on acquisition of cardiac control. *Perceptual and Motor Skills, 58,* 426.

Collins, F. L., Martin, J. E., & Hillenberg, J. B. (1982). Assessment of compliance with relaxation instructions: A pilot validation study. *Behavioral Assessment, 4,* 219–223.

Cox, D. J., Tisdelle, D. A., & Culbert, J. P. (1988). Increasing adherence to behavioral homework assignments. *Journal of Behavioral Medicine, 11,* 519–522.

Craske, M. G., Sanderson, W. C., & Barlow, D. H. (1987). How do desynchronous response systems relate to the treatment of agoraphobia?: A follow-up evaluation. *Behaviour Research and Therapy, 25,* 117–122.

DeBerry, S. (1982). The effects of meditation relaxation on anxiety and depression in a geriatric population. *Psychotherapy: Theory, Research and Practice, 19,* 512–521.

Delmonte, M. M. (1981a). Suggestibility and meditation. *Psychological Reports, 48,* 727–737.

Delmonte, M. M. (1981b). Expectation and meditation. *Psychological Reports, 49,* 699–709.

Delmonte, M. M. (1984). Meditation: Similarities with hypnoidal states and hypnosis. *International Journal of Psychosomatics, 31,* 24–34.

Delmonte, M. M. (1985). Meditation and anxiety reduction: A literature review. *Clinical Psychology Review, 5,* 91–102.

Delmonte, M. M. (1988). Personality correlates of meditation practice frequency and dropout in an outpatient population. *Journal of Behavioral Medicine, 11,* 593–597.

Denkowski, K. M., & Denkowski, G. C. (1984). Is group progressive relaxation training as effective with hyperactive children as individual EMG biofeedback treatment? *Biofeedback and Self-Regulation, 9,* 353–364.

Denkowski, K. M., Denkowski, G. C., & Omizo, M. M. (1983). The effects of EMG-assisted relaxation training on the academic performance, locus of control, and self-esteem of hyperactive boys. *Biofeedback and Self-Regulation, 8,* 363–375.

Denkowski, K. M., Denkowski, G. C., & Omizo, M. M. (1984). Predictors of success in the EMG biofeedback training of hyperactive male children. *Biofeedback and Self Regulation, 9,* 253–264.

Dick, L. D. (1973–1974). A study of meditation in the service of counseling (Doctoral dissertation, University of Oklahoma, 1973). *Dissertation Abstracts International, 34,* 4037B.

Dinning, W. D., & Crampton, J. (1989). The Krantz Health Opinion Survey: Correlations with preventive health behaviors and intentions. *Psychological Reports, 64,* 59–64.

Fenz, W. D., Pye, D., & Favaro, P. (1984). Individual differences in voluntary heart rate control. *Archiv für Psychologie, 136,* 125–146.

Flanders, P., & McNamara, R. (1987a). Predicting compliance with home relaxation training. *Psychological Reports, 60,* 313–314.

Flanders, P., & McNamara, R. (1987b). Relaxation training and home practice in the treatment of anxiety. *Psychological Reports, 61,* 819–822.

Ford, M. R., Stroebel, C. F., Strong, P., & Szarek, B. L. (1982). Quieting response training: Treatment of psychophysiological disorders in psychiatric inpatients. *Biofeedback and Self-Regulation, 7,* 331–339.

Gatchel, R. J. (1975). Locus of control and voluntary heart-rate change. *Journal of Personality Assessment, 39,* 634–638.

Gatchel, R. J. (1982). EMG biofeedback in anxiety reduction. In L. White, & B. Tursky (Eds.), *Clinical biofeedback: Efficacy and mechanisms.* New York: Guilford Press.

Glueck, B., & Stroebel, C. (1975). Biofeedback and meditation in the treatment of psychiatric illness. *Comprehensive Psychiatry, 16,* 303–321.

Hafner, R. J. (1982). Psychological treatment of essential hypertension: A controlled comparison of meditation and meditation plus biofeedback. *Biofeedback and Self Regulation, 7,* 305–316.

Hart, J. D. (1982). Failure to complete treatment for headache: A multiple regression analysis. *Journal of Consulting and Clinical Psychology, 50,* 781–782.

Hendricksen, N. E. (1978). The effects of progressive relaxation and meditation on mood stability and state anxiety in alcoholic inpatients (Doctoral dissertation, University of Missouri, 1977). *Dissertation Abstracts International, 39,* 981B. (University Microfilms No. 78-14,120)

Hiebert, B., Boelle, K., & Jaknavorian, A. (1989). School-based relaxation: Attempting primary prevention. *Canadian Journal of Counselling, 23,* 273–287.

Hilgard, E. R. (1965). *Hypnotic susceptibility.* New York: Harcourt, Brace & World.

Hillenberg, J. B., & Collins, F. L., Jr. (1983). The importance of home practice for progressive relaxation training. *Behaviour Research and Therapy, 21,* 633–642.

Hjelle, L. (1974). Transcendental meditation and psychological health. *Perceptual and Motor Skills, 39,* 623–628.

Hoelscher, T. J., Lichstein, K. L., & Rosenthal, T. L. (1984). Objective versus subjective assessment of relaxation compliance among anxious individuals. *Behaviour Research and Therapy, 22,* 187–193.

Hoelscher, T. J., Lichstein, K. L., & Rosenthal, T. L. (1986). Home relaxation practice in hypertension treatment: Objective assessment and compliance induction. *Journal of Consulting and Clinical Psychology, 54,* 217–221.

Hudzinski, L. G., & Levenson, H. (1985). Biofeedback behavioral treatment of headache with locus of control pain analysis: A 20 month retrospective study. *Headache, 25,* 380–386.

Hughes, H., Brown, B. W., Lawlis, G. F., & Fulton, J. E. (1983). Treatment of acne vulgaris by biofeedback relaxation and cognitive imagery. *Journal of Psychosomatic Research, 27,* 185–191.

Jacob, R. G., Beidel, D., C., & Shapiro, A. P. (1984). The relaxation word of the day: A simple technique to measure adherence to relaxation. *Behavioral Assessment, 6,* 159–165.

Jansson, L., Jerremalm, A., & Öst, L. G. (1986). Follow-up of agoraphobic patients treated with exposure *in vivo* or applied relaxation. *British Journal of Psychiatry, 149,* 486–490.

Kabat-Zinn, J., Lipworth, L., & Burney, R. (1985). The clinical use of mindfulness meditation for the self regulation of chronic pain. *Journal of Behavioral Medicine, 8,* 163–190.

Kaplan, G. M., & Barabasz, A. F. (1988). Enhancing hypnotizability: Differential effects of flotation restricted environmental stimulation technique and progressive muscle relaxation. *Australian Journal of Clinical and Experimental Hypnosis, 16,* 39–51.

Kaplan, R. M., Atkins, C. J., & Reinsch, S. (1984). Specific efficacy expectations mediate exercise compliance in patients with COPD. *Health Psychology, 3,* 223–242.

Knox, S. S. (1982). Alpha enhancement, autonomic activation, and extraversion. *Biofeedback and Self-Regulation, 7*, 421–433.

Lacroix, J. M., Clarke, M. A., Bock, J. C., & Doxey, N. C. (1986). Predictors of biofeedback and relaxation success in multiple pain patients: Negative findings. *International Journal of Rehabilitation Research, 9*, 376–378.

Lang, P. J. (1975). Acquisition of heart-rate control: Method, theory, and clinical implications. In D. C. Fowles (Ed.), *Clinical applications of psychophysiology.* New York: Columbia University Press.

Lang, P. J., Levin, D. N., Miller, G. A., & Kozak, M. J. (1983). Fear behavior, fear imagery and the psychophysiology of emotion: The problem of affective response integration. *Journal of Abnormal Psychology, 92*, 276–306.

Lang, P. J., Troyer, W. G., Twentyman, C. T., & Gatchel, R. J. (1975). Differential effects of heart rate modification training on college students, older males, and patients with ischemic heart disease. *Psychosomatic Medicine, 37*, 429–446.

Larkin, K. T., Knowlton, G. E., & D'Alessandri, R. (1990). Predicting treatment outcome to progressive relaxation training in essential hypertensive patients. *Journal of Behavioral Medicine, 13*, 605–618.

Lehrer, P. M., Atthowe, J. M., & Weber, E. S. P. (1980). Effects of progressive relaxation and autogenic training on anxiety and physiological measures, with some data on hypnotizability. In F. J. McGuigan, W. Sime, & J. M. Wallace, (Eds.), *Stress and tension control.* New York: Plenum Press.

Lehrer, P. M., Woolfolk, R. L., Rooney, A., McCann, B. S., & Carrington, P. C. (1983). Progressive relaxation and meditation: A study of psychophysiological and therapeutic differences between two techniques. *Behaviour Research and Therapy, 21*, 651–662.

Levenson, R. W., & Ditto, W. B. (1981). Individual differences in ability to control heart rate: Personality, strategy, physiological, and other variables. *Psychophysiology, 18*, 91–100.

Leventhal, H., Meyers, D., & Nerenz, D. (1980). The commonsense representation of illness danger. In S. Rachman (Ed.), *Contributions to medical psychology.* Oxford: Pergamon Press.

Lewis, C. E., Biglan, A., & Steinbock, E. (1978). Self-administered relaxation training and money deposits in the treatment of recurrent anxiety. *Journal of Consulting and Clinical Psychology, 46*, 1274–1283.

Ley, P. (1982). Satisfaction, compliance, and communication. *British Journal of Clinical Psychology, 21*, 241–254.

Libo, L. M., & Arnold, G. E. (1983). Relaxation practice after biofeedback therapy: A long-term follow-up study of utilization and effectiveness. *Biofeedback and Self Regulation, 8*, 217–227.

Lichstein, K. L., & Hoelscher, T. J. (1986). A device for unobtrusive surveillance of home relaxation practice. *Behavior Modification, 10*, 219–233.

Long, B. C., & Haney, C. J. (1986). Enhancing physical activity in sedentary women: Information, locus of control, and attitudes. *Journal of Sport Psychology, 8*, 8–24.

Lutz, R. W., Silbret, M., & Olshan, N. (1983). Treatment outcome and compliance with therapeutic regimens: Long-term follow-up of a multidisciplinary pain program. *Pain, 17*, 301–308.

McCready, M. L., & Long, B. C. (1985). Locus of control, attitudes toward physical activity, and exercise adherence. *Journal of Sport Psychology, 7*, 346–359.

Meyers, D., Leventhal, H., & Gutmann, M. (1985). Common-sense models of illness: The example of hypertension. *Health Psychology, 4*, 115–135.

Miller, L. S., & Cross, H. J. (1985). Hypnotic susceptibility, hypnosis, and EMG biofeedback in the reduction of frontalis muscle tension. *International Journal of Clinical and Experimental Hypnosis, 33*, 258–272.

Mullins, R. M., & Sharpley, C. F. (1988). Vividness of imagery and locus of control as predictors of normotensives' ability to learn downward control of blood pressure. *Behaviour Change, 5*, 66–73.

Murphy, T. J., Pagano, R. R., & Marlatt, G. A. (1986). Lifestyle modification with heavy alcohol drinkers: Effects of aerobic exercise and meditation. *Addictive Behaviors, 11*, 175–186.

Ollendick, T. H., & Murphy, M. J. (1977). Differential effectiveness of muscular and cognitive relaxation as a function of locus of control. *Journal of Behavior Therapy and Experimental Psychiatry, 8*, 223–228.

Otis, L. S. (1974, April). The facts on transcendental meditation: III. If well-integrated but anxious, try TM. *Psychology Today*, pp. 45–46.

Pekala, R. J., & Forbes, E. J. (1988). Hypnoidal effects associated with several stress management techniques. *Australian Journal of Clinical and Experimental Hypnosis, 16*, 121–132.

Pekala, R. J., & Forbes, E. J. (1990). Subjective effects of several stress management strategies: With reference to attention. *Behavioral Medicine, 16*, 39–43.

Pekala, R. J., Forbes, E. J., & Contrisciani, P. A. (1988–1989). Assessing the phenomenological effects of several stress management strategies. *Imagination, Cognition, and Personality, 8*, 265–281.

Peters, R. K., Benson, H., & Porter, D. (1977). Daily relaxation response breaks in a working population: I. Effects on self-reported measures of health, performance, and well-being. *American Journal of Public Health, 67*, 946–953.

Porter, S. S., & Omizo, M. M. (1984). The effects of group relaxation training/large muscle exercise, and parental involvement on attention to task, impulsivity, and locus of control among hyperactive boys. *Exceptional Child, 31,* 54–64.

Prager-Decker, I. J. (1979). The relative efficacy of progressive muscle relaxation, EMG biofeedback and music for reducing stress arousal of internally vs. externally controlled individuals (Doctoral dissertation, University of Maryland, 1978). *Dissertation Abstracts International 39,* 3177B. (University Microfilms No. 79-00,924)

Qualls, P. J., & Sheehan, P. W. (1979). Capacity for absorption and relaxation during electromyograph biofeedback and no-feedback conditions. *Journal of Abnormal Psychology, 88,* 652–688.

Qualls, P. J., & Sheehan, P. W. (1981a). Imagery encouragement, absorption capacity, and relaxation during electromyogram biofeedback. *Journal of Personality and Social Psychology, 41,* 370–379.

Qualls, P. J., & Sheehan, P. W. (1981b). Role of the feedback signal in electromyograph biofeedback: The relevance of attention. *Journal of Experimental Psychology: General, 110,* 204–216.

Radtke, H. L., Spanos, N. P., Armstrong, C. A., Dillman, N., & Buisvenue, M. E. (1983). Effects of electromyographic feedback and progressive relaxation training on hypnotic susceptibility: Disconfirming results. *International Journal of Clinical and Experimental Hypnosis, 31,* 98–106.

Rauckhorst, L. M. (1987). Health habits of elderly widows. *Journal of Gerontological Nursing, 13,* 19–22.

Ray, W. J., & Lamb, S. B. (1974). Locus of control and the voluntary control of heart rate. *Psychosomatic Medicine, 36,* 180–182.

Rickard, H. C., Crist, D. A., & Barker, H. (1985). The effects of suggestibility on relaxation. *Journal of Clinical Psychology, 41,* 466–468.

Riley, W. T., Berry, S. L., & Kennedy, W. A. (1986). Rationale exposure and compliance to relaxation training. *Psychological Reports, 58,* 499–502.

Rivera, E., & Omizo, M. M. (1980). The effects of relaxation training and biofeedback on attention to task and impulsivity among male hyperactive children. *Exceptional Child, 27,* 41–51.

Rohsenow, D. J., Smith, R. E., & Johnson, S. (1985). Stress management training as a prevention program for heavy social drinkers: Cognitions, affect, drinking, and individual differences. *Addictive Behaviors, 10,* 45–54.

Roome, J. R., & Romney, D. M. (1985). Reducing anxiety in gifted children by inducing relaxation. *Roeper Review, 7,* 177–179.

Russell, C. M., Dale, A., & Anderson, D. E. (1982). Locus of control and expectancy in electromyographic biofeedback. *Journal of Psychosomatic Research, 26,* 527–532.

Sallis, J. F., Trevorrow, T. R., Johnson, C. C., Hovell, M. F., Johnson, C. C., Hovell, M. F., & Kaplan, R. M. (1987). Worksite stress management: A comparison of programs. *Psychology and Health 1,* 237–255.

Schneider, R. D., Sobol, M. P., Herrmann, T. F., & Cousins, L. J. (1978). A re-examination of the relationship between locus of control and voluntary heart rate change. *Journal of General Psychology, 99,* 49–60.

Shafi, M., Lavely, R., & Jaffee, R. (1974). Meditation and marijuana. *American Journal of Psychiatry, 131,* 60–63.

Sherman, R. A. (1982). Home use of tape recorded relaxation exercises as initial treatment for stress related disorders. *Military Medicine, 147,* 1062–1066.

Sigman, A., & Phillips, K. (1985). Biofeedback and hypnosis: A review of recent literature. *British Journal of Experimental and Clinical Hypnosis, 3,* 13–24.

Smith, J. C. (1976). Psychotherapeutic effects of transcendental meditation with controls for expectation of relief and daily sitting. *Journal of Consulting and Clinical Psychology, 44,* 630–637.

Smith, M. S., Womack, W. M., & Pertik, M. (1987). Temperature biofeedback and hypnotic ability in children and adolescents. *International Journal of Adolescent Medicine and Health, 3,* 91–99.

Soskis, D. A., Orne, E. C., Orne, M. T., & Dinges, D. F. (1989). Self hypnosis and meditation for stress management. *International Journal of Clinical and Experimental Hypnosis, 37,* 285–289.

Spanos, N. P., Ollerhead, V. G., & Gwynn, M. I. (1985–1986). The effects of three instructional treatments on pain magnitude and pain tolerance: Implications for theories of hypnotic analgesia. *Imagination, Cognition, and Personality, 5,* 321–337.

Spinhoven, P. (1988). Similarities and dissimilarities in hypnotic and nonhypnotic procedures for headache control: A review. *American Journal of Clinical Hypnosis, 30,* 183–194.

Spoth, R. (1983). Differential stress reduction: Preliminary application to an alcohol abusing population. *International Journal of the Addictions, 18,* 835–849.

Stam, H. J., McGrath, P. A., & Brooke, R. I. (1984). The effects of a cognitive-behavioral treatment program on temporo-mandibular pain and dysfunction syndrome. *Psychosomatic Medicine, 46,* 534–545.

Stanton, H. E. (1982). Increasing teachers' internality through the RSI technique. *Australian Psychologist, 17,* 277–284.

Stek, R., & Bass, B. (1973). Personal adjustment and perceived locus of control among students interested in meditation. *Psychological Reports, 32,* 1019–1022.

Taylor, C. B., Agras, W. S., Schneider, J. A., & Allen, R. A. (1983). Adherence to instructions to practice relaxation exercises. *Journal of Consulting and Clinical Psychology, 51,* 952–953.

Tripp, E. G., & Marks, D. (1986). Hypnosis, relaxation and analgesia suggestions for the reduction of reported pain in high- and low-suggestible subjects. *Australian Journal of Clinical and Experimental Hypnosis, 14,* 99–113.

Vermilyea, J. A., Boice, R., & Barlow, D. H. (1984). Rachman and Hodgson (1974) a decade later: How do desynchronous response systems relate to the treatment of agoraphobia? *Behaviour Research and Therapy, 22,* 615–621.

Wadden, T. A. (1983). Predicting treatment response to relaxation therapy for essential hypertension. *Journal of Nervous and Mental Disease, 171,* 683–689.

Warrenburg, S., & Pagano, R. (1982–1983). Meditation and hemispheric specialization: I. Absorbed attention in long-term adherence. *Imagination, Cognition and Personality, 2,* 211–229.

Watson, J. P., & Marks, I. M. (1971). Relevant and irrelevant fear in flooding: A cross-over study of phobic patients. *Behavior Therapy, 2,* 275–295.

Wickramasekera, I. (1973). Effects of electromyographic feedback on hypnotic susceptibility: More preliminary data. *Journal of Abnormal Psychology, 82,* 74–77.

Wisniewski, J. J., Genshaft, J. L., Mulick, J. A., Coury, D. L., & Hammer, D. (1988). Relaxation therapy and compliance in the treatment of adolescent headache. *Headache, 28,* 612–617.

Wittrock, D. A., Blanchard, E. B., & McCoy, G. C. (1988). Three studies on the relation of process to outcome in the treatment of essential hypertension with relaxation and thermal biofeedback. *Behaviour Research and Therapy, 26,* 53–66.

Woolfolk, R. L., & Rooney, A. J. (1981). The effect of explicit expectations on initial initial meditation experiences. *Biofeedback and Self-Regulation, 6,* 483–492.

Zuroff, D. C., & Schwarz, J. C. (1978). Effects of transcendental meditation and muscle relaxation on trait anxiety, maladjustment, locus of control and drug use. *Journal of Consulting and Clinical Psychology, 46,* 264–271.

Zuroff, D. C., & Schwartz, J. C. (1980). Transcendental meditation versus muscle relaxation: A two-year follow-up of a controlled experiment. *American Journal of Psychiatry, 137,* 1229–1231.

18

Differential Effects of Stress Management Therapies on Emotional and Behavioral Disorders

PAUL M. LEHRER
RICHARD CARR
DEEPA SARGUNARAJ
ROBERT L. WOOLFOLK

This chapter reviews the literature on comparisons among stress reduction techniques as applied to emotional and behavioral disorders. In it we include only those disorders for which such comparisons have been made experimentally, and/or for which a particularly large body of literature confirms the effectiveness of stress reduction methods.

Anxiety and Panic Disorders

Nonpharmacological Approaches

This section describes comparative outcome studies that include two or more non-pharmacological approaches. A separate section below reviews comparisons of drug versus nondrug approaches.

Anxiety is primarily assessed by self-report, which necessarily involves cognitive processes. The specific-effects theory would predict that cognitively oriented therapies have greater effects than other modalities in modifying these aspects of anxiety. Somatic manifestations of anxiety (e.g., autonomic lability), on the other hand, might be expected to respond more readily to somatically oriented therapies, and behavioral manifestations (e.g., avoidance of situations and/or behaviors associated with the occurrence of panic symptoms) to behaviorally oriented ones. With a few notable exceptions, these predictions have been verified. This is true even when anxiety is measured as a "process" variable in the treatment of other problems. For example, in a study of blood pressure reduction, Lustman and Sowa (1983) found that electromyographic biofeedback (EMG BFK) produced greater decreases in blood pressure than stress inoculation training, whereas the latter produced greater decreases in self-reported anxiety.

The efficacy and long-term benefits of a variety of relaxation techniques for clinically diagnosable anxiety conditions have been well established over the years (e.g., Borkovec & Sides, 1979; Bernstein & Borkovec, 1973; Öst, 1989). More recent comparative outcome studies of anxiety disorders have used more complex therapy protocols. Besides targeting physiological arousal, these have incorporated a variety of techniques specifically aimed at decreasing avoidance behavior, panic attacks, and anxiety-arousing cognitions. We begin with a review of anxiety disorders with a predominant avoidance component (phobias), followed by disorders in which avoidance is a less essential characteristic (e.g., panic and generalized anxiety). The section then reviews the treatment of social phobia, which often presents as a mix of social/evaluative (i.e., cognitive) anxiety and phobic avoidance. Finally, it contains a section on test anxiety, which also includes both cognitive (self-perception) and behavioral (test performance) components.

Phobic Avoidance

Michelson and Mavissakalian (1983, 1985) concluded that self-directed exposure is the most critical ingredient in treating panic disorder with moderate to severe agoraphobia. Post-traumatic stress disorder (Keane, Fairbank, Caddell, & Zimering, 1989), and blood/injury phobia (Öst, 1987) have also been successfully treated with exposure, without training in any relaxation technique.

One study of panic disorder with severe avoidance compared progressive relaxation (PR), therapist-led graduated exposure, and paradoxical intention (Michelson, Mavissakalian, & Marchione, 1985). All groups received instructions for extensive self-directed exposure, besides training in their respective coping technique. Graduated exposure led to higher end-state functioning on cognitive and behavioral measures of phobic anxiety and avoidance. PR was as potent as graduated exposure but progressed at a slower rate. PR and graduated exposure were also equally effective in modifying psychophysiological variables. Paradoxical intention was the least effective.

Although agoraphobia is predominantly characterized by avoidance, several comparative studies have examined the benefits of adding cognitive techniques to behavioral exposure interventions. Michelson, Marchione, and Greenwald (1989) compared cognitive therapy (CT) to PR in a sample of patients with panic disorder and severe agoraphobic avoidance. All subjects received programmed practice (self-exposure instructions) and therapist-aided prolonged exposure. A third group received only further homework discussion, beyond programmed practice and therapist exposure. CT plus self- and therapist exposure produced the best overall effects, as assessed by multiple, tripartite measures. Eighty-six percent of CT subjects, 73% of PR subjects, and 65% of subjects receiving only programmed practice and graduated exposure fell into the category of high end-state functioning. Michelson and Marchione (1991) concluded in their review that CT and prolonged, therapist-led exposure, along with programmed practice, is the most effective treatment for severe agoraphobia.

Panic Symptoms

Panic disorder with little or no avoidance has received much research attention in recent years. One major line of this work has focused on the role of breathing abnormalities, specifically hyperventilation (Ley, 1988, 1989). In this theory the physiological symptoms of panic are attributed to hyperventilatory hypocapnia (decreased end-tidal carbon dioxide). Gorman et al. (1990) have proposed that panic symptoms are produced by hypersensitivity to carbon dioxide, rather than to hyperventilation per se. Clark (1989) and Beck (1988) offer a cognitive explanation for panic symptoms. According to this model, panic attacks result from the catastrophic interpretation of a wide range of innocuous bodily sensations, especially those related to hyperventilation (e.g., dizziness, numbness and tingling, choking, etc.).

Recent comparative-treatment studies of panic disorder with mild or no avoidance and generalized anxiety disorder (i.e., disorders with a prominent cognitive component) have emphasized the relative and combined effects of cognitive techniques. Barlow, Craske, Cerny, and Klosko (1989) compared PR to exposure plus CT and to a combination of the three. All three groups improved more than waiting-list subjects on a variety of measures. PR, in contrast to the combined components CT and exposure, did not lead to a significantly higher percentage of subjects who were panic-free at posttreament, compared to waiting-list subjects. However, PR subjects showed greater decreases on measures of general anxiety. (PR subjects had a higher dropout rate as well.) Barlow's package of cognitive–behavioral techniques combines cognitive restructuring and rebreathing/relaxation skills and generally achieves success with 80% of panic subjects or better (i.e., panic-free at posttreatment). Beck (1988) has reported the complete elimination of panic attacks in 16 patients receiving CT, and has found significantly better results with this approach than with supportive therapy.

Other studies of panic disorder have investigated treatments that target panic directly through breathing retraining (Clark, 1986; Clark, Salkovskis, & Chalkley, 1985). These treatments show outcomes similar to those of CT and cognitive–behavioral treatment, with success rates of 80–100% panic-free at posttreatment. Several of these studies include small sample sizes. However, the elimination of panic attacks via cognitive or breathing techniques in at least 80–90% of subjects is highly consistent across studies (Barlow, 1988). The problem arises in separating the breathing from the cognitive components. Use of any breathing technique suggests to the client, at least implicitly, that body sensations associated with panic are easily reversible and are not signs of serious organic disease. Similarly, cognitive techniques often incorporate deliberate hyperventilation as a "behavioral test" of a patient's catastrophic interpretations. Thus, patients receiving either CT or breathing retraining alone are also learning the association between breathing and the experience of (and therefore control over) unpleasant somatic sensations.

Generalized Anxiety Symptoms

Lindsay, Gansu, McLaughlin, Hood, and Espie (1987) randomly assigned patients diagnosed with generalized anxiety disorder to one of three therapies. Two were multicomponent nondrug treatments: anxiety management training, and cognitive–

behavioral therapy (which included a take-home relaxation tape). The third was benzodiazepine pharmacotherapy. A waiting-list control group was also included. Subjects receiving cognitive–behavioral therapy and anxiety management training had clearly superior outcomes at posttreatment and follow-up, compared to waiting-list and benzodiazepine-treated subjects. Borkovec et al. (1987) compared CT with nondirective therapy for the treatment of generalized anxiety disorder, but included PR in both conditions. CT produced greater decreases in self-report measures of anxiety than nondirective therapy. This suggested that CT is incrementally effective over PR. This conclusion is not definitive, however, because it is conceivable (although improbable) that the group differences might be explained by possible deleterious effects of nondirective therapy.

Butler, Cullington, Hibbert, Klimes, and Gelder (1987), treating a group of people with generalized anxiety disorder, compared an anxiety management package to a waiting-list control. The package included cognitive, relaxation, and exposure techniques. They found significant reductions on the State–Trait Anxiety Inventory and a 59% reduction on the Hamilton Anxiety Scale. At a 6-month follow-up, there was an improvement to 69% reduction on the Hamilton scale. Further studies are needed comparing the effect of single versus combined stress management techniques for generalized anxiety. In their review of cognitive–behavioral treatments of generalized anxiety disorder, Deffenbacher and Suinn (1987) recommended teaching relaxation as a self-control procedure. They concluded specifically that anxiety management training is the strongest package. A similar technique, applied relaxation, as developed by Öst and colleagues, has been compared favorably with several of the commonly used individual anxiety management techniques for treating various phobic disorders (e.g., dental and social phobias, claustrophobia) and panic disorder (Öst, 1987). However, further research is necessary to isolate the effective components in these therapy programs. For example, the effects of PR by itself have not yet been compared with those of a multicomponent package for treating generalized anxiety disorder.

Social Phobia

In a comparative study of social phobia, subjects categorized as "physiological" reactors responded more to applied relaxation, whereas "behavioral" reactors responded better to social skills training (Öst, Jerremalm, & Johansson, 1981). It has been suggested that "behavioral" reactors may be more appropriately labeled "socially dysfunctional" or even "avoidant," and would not be classified as social phobics according to the revised third edition of the *Diagnostic and Statistical Manual of Mental Disorders* (DSM-III-R) (Heimberg, Dodge, & Becker, 1987). Furthermore, Heimberg et al. (1987) note that methodological flaws and diagnostic confusion limit the interpretation of studies of social skills training. They also suggest that exposure, which is an inseparable component of social skills training, may be the critical ingredient of that treatment. Another comparative treatment study of social phobia examined the effects of PR, exposure, supportive therapy, and a control condition (Alstrom, Nordlund, Persson, Harding, & Ljungqvist, 1984). Unlike previous studies of anxiety management training or applied relaxation, this study found that PR was inferior to exposure. However, subjects receiving PR had not been trained to apply it in daily life. This underscores the importance of exposure and of teaching relaxation as a coping skill technique in the treatment of social phobia. Both are direct or indirect elements of anxiety management training and applied relaxation (Heimberg, 1989). It is even an important component in Jacobson's approach to PR (see McGuigan's discussion of "differential relaxation" in Chapter 2 of this volume).

Mattick and Peters (1988) reported a significant advantage for adding cognitive restructuring to exposure in the treatment of social phobia. Gross and Fremouw (1982) found no differences between PR and CT in modifying physiological or cognitive aspects of speech anxiety. However, they found a weaker effect for PR among subjects who showed a smaller physiological response component. The investigators interpret this finding as suggesting that in such individuals, speech anxiety is primarily cognitive, and therefore not as amenable to a specifically physiological treatment. Studies with more equivocal findings include one by Lent (1979), who found rational–emotive therapy to be inferior to cue-controlled desensitization (a combination of cue-controlled relaxation and desensitization) in reducing self-reported public-speaking anxiety. The cue-controlled desensitization condition may have produced greater effects because the procedure includes major cognitive as well as somatic components. Kantor (1979/1980) found stress inoculation training, systematic desensitization, and speaking skills training to be equally effective in reducing public-speaking anxiety. Sweeney and Horan (1982) compared cue-controlled relaxation with cognitive restructuring in treatment of music performance anxiety. The two methods produced equal decreases in pulse rate and in state anxiety during a performance. Cue-controlled relaxation also reduced trait anxiety and improved musical performance, while cognitive restructuring reduced behavioral manifestations of anxiety, compared with a control condition involving musical analysis training and a waiting-list control.

Heimberg's (1989) review of social phobia concluded that either exposure, relaxation as self-control (e.g., applied relaxation), or CT is an effective treatment for social phobia. However, further evaluation of these procedures is warranted. In future research, Heimberg recommends improved research designs, larger and better-defined samples, longer follow-up, and comparisons of combined treatments.

Test Anxiety

Various methods of relaxation instruction appear to be equally effective in the treatment of test anxiety and signficantly better than no-treatment controls. Differences between relaxation procedures and placebo conditions are present, but small. Where significant differences do occur, the superiority of EMG BFK over taped relaxation instruction manifests itself (see the discussion of taped PR instruction in Chapter 16 of this volume). Cognitive methods appear to be more effective than relaxation methods, and the addition of cognitive methods to relaxation procedures may produce greater therapeutic improvements than the addition of relaxation to cognitive methods. (In these generalizations, we are considering systematic desensitization to be a cognitive technique that also includes a relaxation component. Systematic desensitization does not seem to be as powerful as CT, but it has been found to be somewhat superior to PR.) Differences among active treatments are more pronounced on self-report measures of test anxiety than on test performance, but sometimes also occur on the latter. The studies are summarized in Table 18.1. A negative finding was reported by Deffenbacher and Hahnloser (1981). They found no differences between relaxation therapy and CT in the treatment of test anxiety. Both methods were superior to a control, and the combination of the two methods was superior to either one individually, particularly at follow-up.

There is conflicting evidence about the usefulness of hypnosis in treatment of test anxiety. Four studies found positive effects for hypnotic interventions (Boutin & Tosi, 1983; Johnson & Johnson, 1984; Palan & Chandwani, 1989; Stanton, 1984). Two other studies using hypnosis found no therapeutic effect for this approach (Farnhill, 1985; Spies, 1979). The effectiveness of hypnosis probably depends upon the specific hypnotic suggestions that are used.

Cavallaro, Donna, and Meyers (1986) reported results showing that an intervention combining relaxation and cognitive restructuring had a greater impact on test anxiety for those subjects with good (vs. poor) study habits. These results suggest that stress management treatments may be less relevant for students whose test anxiety reflects a genuine inability to master the course material.

Pharmacological versus Nonpharmacological Treatments

Elsewhere in this volume, Papp and Gorman (Chapter 15) review the effects of medication on anxiety-related disorders, and conclude that a wide array of agents is pharmacologically effective in reducing symptoms. This section devotes itself only to comparisons between drug therapy and various nonpharmacological treatments, and to evaluations of drug–nondrug treatment interactions.

In a comprehensive literature review of drug therapies and behavior therapy for phobias, panic disorder, and obsessive compulsive disorder, Marks (1987) concluded (1) that "antidepressants are compatible with exposure therapy and sometimes enhance it" (p. 539); (2) that behavioral exposure to anxiety-producing circumstances is a necessary concomitant for drug therapies to be effective with phobia, panic, or obsessive compulsive disorder; and (3) that antidepressant drugs are particularly effective when various anxiety-related problems are accompanied by depressed mood. This last conclusion has been contested by Zitrin, Klein, and Woerner (1980), who found a negative correlation between depression and outcome in agoraphobia with imipramine. Marks (1987) has reported that the compliance rate for pharmacotherapy is approximately equivalent to that for exposure therapy, and that the costs of the two approaches are similar, particularly when self-guided exposure methods are used. Marks does not believe that relaxation therapies are effective components in the treatment of phobias and obsessive compulsive disorder.

It should be noted, however, that the pharmacological effects of various medications (particularly antidepressants) may not produce decreased levels of *somatic* activation. Michelson and Mavissakalian (1985) found that exposure treatment tended to produce lower levels of autonomic arousal among agoraphobics, whereas imipramine produced the opposite result. Similar findings were reported by Roth, Telch, Taylor, and Agras (1988). The clinical importance of this finding is questionable, however, because antidepressant medications may produce increased desynchrony between

TABLE 18.1. Summary of Findings on Test Anxiety

Authors	Effects on test anxiety	Effects on test performance
Studies finding differences among techniques		
Johnson & Sechrest (1968)	PR > SD > NT (but individual comparisons were n.s.).	SD > PR = NT on final exam scores.
Freeling & Shemberg (1970)	SD > PR = visual imagery.	SD = PR = visual imagery on an anagrams test.
Chang-Liang & Denney (1976)	1. Applied relaxation training > NT. 2. PR and SD did not differ from either group.	Applied relaxation training > PR = SD = NT on Wonderlink Personnel Test.
Pesta & Zwettler (1977)	Cognitive methods > PR = combined.	
Counts, Hollandsworth, & Alcorn (1978)	CCR + EMG BFK = placebo > NT.	CCR + EMG BFK > CCR = placebo = NT.
Baither & Godsey (1979)	Rational–emotive therapy > NT. PR differed from neither.	
Reed & Saslow (1980)	1. EMG BFK > taped PR, NT on debilitating anxiety. 2. EMG BFK = PR > NT on STAI State Anxiety during test.	
Boutin & Tosi (1983)	Cognitive–hypnosis > hypnosis > placebo = NT on STAI, Test Anxiety Scales.	
Stanto (1984)	Clenched-fist technique in hypnotic state > clenched-fist technique only on pre- to posttreatment academic performance.	
Dendato & Diener (1986)	Cognitive methods = study skills + cognitive methods > PR = NT.	Cognitive methods + study skills > PR = cognitive methods = NT.
Cavallaro, Donna, & Meyers (1986)	Cognitive restructuring + PR > PR + study skills.	
Studies finding that techniques are equivalent, but more powerful than control conditions		
Snyder & Deffenbacher (1977)	Relaxation as self-control = SD > placebo (SD produced the greatest *increases* in facilitative anxiety).	
Comer (1977/1978)	On self-report measure, no differences among groups.	MED = applied MED = PR = applied PR > NT (on performance measure only).
Rothman (1979)	PR + SD = EMG BFK + SD > NT.	PR + SD = EMG BFK + SD = NT on academic performance.
Spies (1979)	SD + hypnosis = SD + relaxation + EMG BFK > waiting list on Suinn Test Anxiety Behavior Scale.	

(*continued*)

TABLE 18.1. Continued

Authors	Effects on test anxiety	Effects on test performance
Studies finding differences among techniques		
Thompson, Griebstein, & Kuhlenschmidt (1980)	Treatment group[a] > NT on STAI State Anxiety.	
Wise & Haynes (1983)	Rational restructuring = attentional training > NT.	Both treatments > NT on analogue test.
Hurwitz, Kahane, & Mathieson (1986)	EMG BFK = PR > NT.	EMG BFK = PR = NT on academic performance.
Other studies		
Bernthal (1977)	PR = EMG BFK = TBFK. All groups were given visualization and coping imagery.	
Finger & Galassi (1977)	Suggestions to relax = suggestions to pay attention to test materials.	Suggestions to relax = suggestions to pay attention to test materials on Wonderlink Personnel Test and Digit Symbols Test.
Dawson & McMurray (1978)	Random-item SD without relaxation = SD.	
Khan (1978)	EMG BFK = EMG BFK + relationship therapy.	EMG BFK = EMG BFK + relationship therapy on the WISC-R.
Schuchman (1977/1978)	EMG BFK + SD = PMR + SD = nondirective counseling.	
Maxwell (1979)	PR + deep breathing + cognitive restructuring alone = placebo.	PR + deep breathing = cognitive restructuring = cognitive restructuring alone = placebo on diagnostic reading test.
Deffenbacher & Michaels (1980)	PR = SD.	
Kindlon (1983)	MED = placebo. Both improved from pre- to posttreatment. Not moderated by Scholastic Aptitude Test score, frequency of practice, repression, or expectancy of relief.	
Johnson & Johnson (1984)	Hypnosis = placebo on simple = recall task. Hypnosis > placebo on reading comprehension test.	
Palan & Chandwani (1989)	Self-hypnosis > placebo on academic performance.	Self-hypnosis = placebo.

Note. PR, progressive relaxation; EMG BFK, electromyographic biofeedback; TBFK, thermal biofeedback; SD, systematic desensitization; NT, no treatment; CCR, cue-controlled relaxation; MED, meditation; STAI, State–Trait Anxiety Inventory; WISC-R, Wechsler Intelligence Scale for Children–Revised; n.s., nonsignificant.
[a]Live administration of two multifaceted stress management programs, crossed with forearm EMG BFK or taped supplemental instruction in these methods.

autonomic and emotional effects. Hoehn-Saric, McLeod, and Zimmerli (1988) found that imipramine tended to produce improvement primarily in cognitive symptoms of anxiety, whereas alprazolam produced changes primarily in somatic symptoms. Mavissakalian and Michelson (1986) found equivalent improvements with exposure therapy, flooding, and imipramine for agoraphobia. Several studies have found that drugs facilitate therapist-assisted exposure therapy (Mavissakalian & Michelson, 1986; Sheehan, Ballenger, & Jacobsen, 1980; Telch, Tearnan, & Taylor, 1983; Zitrin et al., 1980).

Our own review suggests that drug therapies, particularly those involving benzo-diazepines, are prone to higher relapse rates than behavior therapies for anxiety-related conditions. Lavallée, Lamontagne, Pinard, Annable, and Tétreault (1977) conducted a two-way factorial experiment of chronically anxious psychiatric patients. The factorial dimensions were EMG BFK-assisted relaxation therapy versus a self-relaxation control, and diazepam (5 mg three times a day) versus a placebo. Treatment was conducted over an 8-week period. Although EMG levels were reduced during treatment in both drug and EMG BFK/relaxation therapies, there were no differences between groups in self-ratings or psychiatric ratings of anxiety during that time. All groups showed decreases in anxiety. The authors interpret the good showing of the placebo–self-relaxation group as demonstrating the power of regular rest in decreasing anxiety symptoms. During the course of a 6-month follow-up, however, subjects who had received diazepam showed increases in anxiety, whereas the anxiety levels in the placebo groups remained low. During this time the authors also found that diazepam-treated subjects were taking more drugs and doing less relaxation practice than subjects who had been given the placebo. Thus, it appeared that diazepam reduced the motivation to try to cope with anxiety through relaxation, and thereby led to a resurgence of symptoms. Similar results were reported by Hoshmand, Helmes, Kazarian, and Tekatch (1985). In a study of psychiatric inpatients, they found greater relaxation effects among subjects not given benzodiazepine treatment than among those given it. At a 6-week follow-up, individuals treated without drugs showed better generalization of relaxation effects and a tendency to take fewer drugs.

These studies both suggest that "state-dependent learning" may occur with benzodiazepines, such that people learn to be less anxious. However, in the study by Lavallée et al. (1977) there was a large dropout rate at the 6-month follow-up assessment, so the results of this study are not conclusive. In the study by Hoshmand et al. (1985), subjects were not randomly assigned to treatment, so selection factors may have played a role.

Nevertheless, these results raise a question about the use of benzodiazepines for the treatment of anxiety. With these medications, drug treatment may interfere with nonpharmacological treatment. Also, the relapse rate is very high for psy-chopharmacological treatments, particularly after the drug is withdrawn. Marks (1987) cited a study by Sheehan (1984) reporting that a relapse rate as high as 84% occurred after 1 year of antidepressant and benzodiazepine therapy. This rate is considerably higher than that generally reported for exposure therapies. Abrupt withdrawal from benzodiazepines is widely known to produce rebound anxiety (Fontaine, Chouinard, & Annable, 1984). It is possible that at least some subjects in the studies by Lavallée et al. (1977) and by Hoshmand et al. (1985) did not withdraw from these drugs gradually enough; this would explain the rebound effects. Catalan, Gath, Edmonds, and Ennis (1984) found no differences at a 7-month follow-up on measures of health and emotionality between anxiolytic medication and brief counseling administered by general practitioners. It is probable that the counseling effects were attenuated by the physicians' lack of specialized training in counseling. Nevertheless, these results argue strongly against the routine use of tranquilizing medication for minor problems with anxiety.

However, benzodiazepines may still be useful as adjuncts to some behavioral methods. Whitehead and Blackwell (1979) reviewed studies showing that minor tranquilizers and short-acting barbiturates can, under some circumstances, facilitate desensitization or flooding therapy, but they reported that findings of "no effects" have also occurred. None of these studies assessed long-term effects of drug-aided versus non-drug-aided desensitization. Hafner and Marks (1976) found that diazepam did not enhance exposure therapy. Similarly, Mitchell and Mitchell (1971) found that a combined behavioral treatment (consisting of relaxation, desensitization, and assertive training) was more effective among people who had not previously received drug therapy than among those who had. Presumably most of the drugs taken were benzodiazepines. In this study, however, subjects were not selected randomly for the two groups. It is thus possible that subjects who had been taking medication and who later presented themselves for relaxation therapy may have been untreatable by any intervention. We found no studies specifically evaluating the effect of benzodiazepines or any other drugs on increasing the willingness of subjects to undergo exposure therapy.

Ganguli and Detre (1982) report having found several studies that show no effects for beta-adrenergic blocking drugs (e.g., propranolol) in facilitating exposure in agoraphobic patients, although they criticize these studies on methodological grounds. Among these studies, however, was one by Hafner and Milton (1977), which found that propranolol *impeded* progress with exposure therapy.

Studies of monoamine oxidase inhibitors suggest that they are not helpful as adjuncts or substitutes for behavior therapy in treatment of phobias (see the review by Whitehead & Blackwell, 1979). A study by Solyom et al. (1973) compared an array of behavioral interventions with phenelzine and with brief psychotherapy. The phenelzine group also received the psychotherapy. Although the effects of behavior therapy and of phenelzine were equivalent at the end of the treatment period, the relapse rate was greater in the drug group. Tyrer and Steinberg (1975) compared phenelzine with a package of behavioral techniques for treating agoraphobia, and found no differences in treatment effectiveness between the two. The subjects who received the drug, however, showed a greater tendency to relapse after drug therapy was discontinued.

Conclusions

In summary, more recent comparative studies of anxiety disorders have investigated multicomponent treatment packages with a focus on the major response mode: behavioral avoidance, catastrophic cognitions, physiological arousal, or hyperventilation. Phobic disorders are clearly best treated by prolonged exposure. For phobias, exposure is central to treatment, and training in a relaxation coping strategy may be unnecessary (although such a technique may facilitate exposure). Severe agoraphobia is best treated with a combination of exposure and cognitive therapy. Cognitive strategies seem to be a useful addition to exposure for the treatment of social phobia; however, treatment research for this disorder lags behind that for most other anxiety disorders (Liebowitz, Gorman, Fyer, & Klein, 1985).

Although benzodiazepines may be useful as adjuncts to some behavioral methods, some "state-dependent learning" may occur. Also, some medications may at times inhibit the effects of nonpharmacological treatments or show poorer long-term effects than behavioral approaches. Furthermore, the relapse rate is very high for several psychopharmacological treatments, particularly after the drug is withdrawn. Monoamine oxidase inhibitors do not appear to be useful as adjuncts to behavioral approaches. Comparisons between antidepressant therapy and behavior therapies, and possible synergistic or antagonistic effects of combinations of these, remain to be determined conclusively; however, these drugs show the most promising results. Relaxation therapies and CT both appear to be effective components in treatments for test anxiety and may function additively. They have more consistently positive effects on anxiety than on test performance, although test performance is also sometimes positively affected. Patients with generalized anxiety disorder or panic disorder accompanied by little or no avoidance respond well to relaxation-based packages (e.g., anxiety management training, applied relaxation). Breathing retraining is an important strategy in the treatment of panic disorder, as is CT (Clark, 1986; Clark et al., 1985).

Anger and Aggressive Behavior

Although not often treated with relaxation techniques per se as a primary method, hostility has received much attention from stress management therapists. It has been identified as the component of the Type A personality pattern having the greatest association with coronary heart disease (Lohr & Hamberger, 1990; Wielgosz et al., 1988).

Several studies done by our reseach group showed decreases in self-rated (Symptom Checklist 90—Revised [SCL-90-R]) symptoms of hostility produced by various relaxation techniques, including PR, meditation, and autogenic training (AT) (Carrington et al., 1980; Lehrer, Woolfolk, Rooney, McCann, & Carrington, 1983). Although differences were found between active treatment groups and no-treatment control groups, no differences were found among the active treatments. Another study, however, found that mantra meditation reduced self-rated hostility more than PR, at a marginally significant level (Woolfolk, Lehrer, McCann, & Rooney, 1982). No group maintained a significant decrease on this measure at a 6-month follow-up. Woolfolk (1984) reported the successful treatment of a case of chronic hostility by methods of meditation. Muskatel, Woolfolk, Carrington, Lehrer, and McCann (1984) found that practicing a mantra meditation technique decreased self-reported hostility during a forced-waiting task, compared with a waiting-list control condition.

In another laboratory, Hafner (1982) found decreases in hostility among female hypertensives after both meditation and biofeedback-aided relaxation. Male hypertensives did not score as highly as females on hostility, and did not show a treatment-related decrease. Negative results were obtained by Shapiro and Lehrer (1980), using five sessions of live individual training in PR or AT. Neither treatment produced significant changes in self-rated hostility, compared with a no-treatment control group. It should be noted that none of the above-cited studies specifically selected subjects for having problems with hostility. Therefore, no conclusions about clinical usefulness can be drawn from them without further verification on clinical populations.

The combination of CT and relaxation therapies may be particularly effective in treating excessive anger (Green & Murray, 1975; Meichenbaum & Novaco, 1985; Novaco, 1975). A similar combination of methods has been found effective for treating aggressive behavior in children (see the review by Kendall & Braswell, 1986). Cognitive stress management and relaxation therapy appear to be approximately equally effective, although perhaps not as much as a combination of the two approaches. Bott (1979) compared PR (including training in deep breathing and situational use of relaxation) with group training in alternative coping strategies for retarded individuals. A combined-treatment group was also included. All groups showed improvements in staff ratings of aggressiveness, but the most significant improvement was noted in the combined group. In several post hoc measures, the coping strategies group and the combined group showed greater decreases than the relaxation group. Similarly, Schlichter (1977/1978) found that stress inoculation training was more effective than any one of the elements that comprise it (i.e., PR and behavior rehearsal). Stress inoculation training was also more effective than a no-treatment condition in reducing verbal anger in a role-playing situation. However, no differences were found between the treatment elements and the complete package, either in verbal aggressiveness reported from imaginary scenes or in self-reported anger. Greater reduction in anger occurred in the treatment groups than in the no-treatment control.

Deffenbacher, Demm, and Brandon (1986) combined relaxation therapy and coping skills training, and found significant anger reductions and better coping among undergraduates scoring high on a paper-and-pencil test for anger. Deffenbacher, McNamara, Stark, and Sabadell (1990) evaluated a program combining relaxation, cognitive, and behavioral coping skills for anger control among students scoring high on an anger scale. Compared with a control condition, the treatment produced greater decreases in the frequency and intensity of anger and in anger-related physiological arousal. In another study from the same laboratory, Deffenbacher (1988; Deffenbacher, Story, Stark, Hogg, & Brandon, 1987) found significant and equivalent decreases in self-reported anger in a similar population, after cognitive relaxation and social skills treatments, at a 1-year follow-up. Feindler, Ecton, Kingsley, and Dubey (1986) found that a cognitive–behavioral intervention, presented in groups, produced significant decreases in aggressive behavior among aggressive institutionalized adolescent males. These effects were detectable beyond the ongoing effects of an operant program that included contingencies for aggressive behavior.

Achmon, Granek, Golomb, and Hart (1989) describe results consistent with the specific-effects theory from a comparison between heart rate biofeedback and CT:

> (1) a significant decrease of blood pressure for both treatments as compared with control, (2) a significant decrease of blood pressure with heart rate biofeedback as compared with cognitive therapy, and (3) a better control in anger achieved with cognitive therapy and a lesser control in heart rate as compared with biofeedback. (p. 152)

However, Sallis, Trevorrow, Johnson, Hovell, and Kaplan (1987) found no differences among relaxation therapy, a multicomponent stress management therapy, and an education/social support group in hostility reduction in a worksite program. Deffenbacher and his colleagues (Deffenbacher et al., 1986; Hazaleus & Deffenbacher, 1986) compared relaxation therapy with CT and a control condition in the treatment of anger among angry undergraduates. They found equivalent decreases in various paper-and-pencil measures of anger in the two treatment groups. Both treatments were superior to the control condition. In measures of "constructive coping" with imaginal provocations, however, only subjects in the CT condition showed superiority over those in the control condition. Deffenbacher, Story, Brandon, Hogg, and Hazaleus (1988) found significantly greater hostility reduction with CT than with a control condition among healthy undergraduates. A cognitive relaxation technique did not differ initially from either condition. After 15 months, however, both active treatment groups showed equal reductions, which were significantly greater than those among the control group. Lochman, Burch, Curry, and Lampron (1984) compared four treatment conditions in a group of aggressive boys: goal setting, a cognitive–behavioral anger coping treatment, a combination of the two, and a no–treatment control. At a 1-month follow-up, only the groups receiving the cognitive–behavioral treatment showed a significant decrease in aggressive behavior, both at home and at school.

There is some mixed evidence that specific social skills training for dealing with anger-provoking situations may be more effective than cognitive approaches in improving assertion skills in these situations. Moon and Eisler (1983) found that a problem-solving program and a social skills training program both improved assertiveness and socially skilled behavior and reduced anger-provoking cognitions, whereas stress inoculation training only reduced anger-provoking cognitions. At a 1-year follow-up, Thurman (1985) found that subjects who received cognitive behavior modification reported lower levels of hostility than subjects in the minimal-treatment group. Subjects given this procedure plus assertion therapy did not. During the period immediately following treatment, both methods had produced greater decreases in hostility than the minimal-treatment group.

In a literature review on behavioral interventions for aggressive behavior in children, Sallis (1983) found that programs focusing on changing environmental contingencies (e.g., operant conditioning programs) were most effective in reducing the amount of aggressive behavior in that particular environmental context. Programs oriented to altering "person variables" (e.g., social skills training programs) were most effective in enhancing generalization and maintenance of behavior change. Consistent with this, a literature review by Wilson (1984) reported that there is still insufficient evidence for the effectiveness of behavioral self-control procedures for managing aggressive behavior, and that external procedures produce better results. Our own review also suggests that CT may be particularly effective in reducing self-reported (i.e., cognitively interpreted) hostility. These findings are all consistent with the specific-effects theory.

Depression

Although much attention has been given to the use of CT for treatment of depression (see Beck, Rush, Shaw, & Emery, 1979), relatively little has been devoted to the use of relaxation therapies. Most studies reporting the effects of relaxation techniques on depression have examined depressive symptoms in patients undergoing treatment for other problems. Two studies demonstrated improvement in depressive symptoms following relaxation training for headaches (Grazzi, Frediani, Zappacosta, & Boiardi, 1988; Sorbi, Tellegen, & du Long, 1989). Improvement in self-rated depression following PR has also been reported in cardiac patients undergoing rehabilitation (Bohachick, 1984). Significant reductions in depression have occurred following EMG BFK for chronic low back pain (Bush, Ditto, & Feuerstein, 1985), and following meditation among Vietnam veterans with adjustment problems (Brooks & Scarno, 1985). Carrington et al. (1980), using taped training, found significantly greater decreases on the SCL-90-R Depression scale after meditation instruction than after a no-treatment control among a group of volunteer participants in an employee work-site stress management program. Changes in depression after PR did not differ significantly from those in either of the other two conditions.

Lehrer et al. (1983), on the other hand, using live training, found greater decreases on the SCL-90-R Depression scale among anxious normal subjects given PR than among those given meditation, although both active treatment groups showed greater decreases than a no-treatment control group. Similarly, Gilbert, Parker, and Clairborn (1978), in a single taped training session with hospitalized alcoholics, found greater increases in self-reported vigor and decreases in self-reported depression with PR than with Benson's meditation technique (denoted "respiratory one meditation" [ROM] in this book, because it involves saying the word "one" in synchrony with respiration) or with a self-relaxation control. Woolfolk et al. (1982), on the other hand, using a procedure almost identical to that used by Lehrer et al. (1983), found no differences among relaxation, meditation, and the no-treatment control group on the SCL-90-R Depression scale. Shapiro and Lehrer (1980) found significantly greater decreases on the SCL-90-R Depression scale among normal volunteers after training in PR or AT than in a no-treatment control. No differences were found between the two active treatments.

Several studies have investigated the effects of stress management therapies on depression. Wheeler (1976/1977) studied psychiatric inpatients scoring high on the Beck Depression Inventory, who also were anxious and scored high on external locus of control. The subjects were divided among a PR group, a group receiving an attention placebo, and a group that received only standard hospital care. Compared to the two control groups, the PR group showed the greatest decreases in self-rated depression and anxiety. Reynolds and Coats (1986) randomly assigned 30 moderately depressed high school students to either cognitive–behavioral therapy, relaxation training, or a waiting-list control condition. Both active treatments led to significant reductions in depressive symptoms (subjects went from moderately depressed to nondepressed) and improvements in self-esteem and academic self-confidence, compared with the control condition, at both posttest and 5-week follow-up. Similarly, Kahn, Kehle, Jenson, and Clark (1990) investigated the efficacy of short-term cognitive–behavioral therapy, relaxation training, and self-modeling interventions for the treatment of depression among 68 depressed sixth-, seventh-, and eighth-graders. Subjects were assigned to one of the three active treatments or a waiting-list control. Self-report and interview measures of depression and self-esteem were used to assess treatment effects. All treatment conditions, compared with the waiting-list control, evidenced a significant decrease in depression and an increase in self-esteem. Parent report data and data from treated controls provided further support for the effectiveness of the interventions.

In a study examining the incremental effectiveness of nonpharmacological behavioral treatments over drug therapy (Bowers, 1990), 30 adult inpatients received one of three treatments: medication (nortriptyline) alone (MA), relaxation therapy plus medication (RT + M), or cognitive therapy plus medication (CT + M). RT + M and CT + M groups participated in 12 therapy sessions. Symptoms of depression and related cognitive variables were assessed at Sessions 1, 6, and 12 and at discharge; the measures used included the Beck Depression Inventory and the Dysfunctional Attitude Scale. All groups improved over the course of the study. CT + M and RT + M subjects reported significantly fewer depressive symptoms and negative cognitions at discharge than MA subjects. The number of subjects judged depressed at discharge was lower in the CT + M group than in the MA and RT + M groups. A different study found nonsignificant effects for PR in the treatment of clinical depression. McLean and Hakstian (1979) found PR to be less effective than cognitive–behavioral therapy, and no more (or less) effective than psychotherapy or tricyclic antidepressant therapy. This study did not use a control group, so it is not possible to tell whether the latter treatments were equally effective or equally ineffective.

A newer therapy, known as "interpersonal therapy," has recently been introduced for the treatment of depression. It is a short-term therapy that (as its name denotes) is derived from psychodynamically oriented interpersonal therapies, and emphasizes the client's feelings about and relationships with other important people. Its effects in treating depression have been found to be comparable to those of CT. There is some evidence that this method may have particular advantages in treating depressed people who do not have concurrent personality disorders, whereas CT may be more powerful for individuals with such concurrent disorders (Shea et al., 1990).

Exercise has also been shown to improve depressed mood; its effects may be stronger than those of relaxation therapy, and equal to those of CT. In one study, subjects with low self-esteem and elevated muscular tension were randomly assigned to physical fitness training, relaxation training, or a combination (de Piano, de Piano, Carter, & Wanlass, 1984). The findings showed that physical fitness training resulted in significantly more improvement in physical fitness, muscular tension reduction, and alleviation of depression (Minnesota Multiphasic Personality Inventory [MMPI]

Depression scale) than did either relaxation training or the combination of the two. Fremont and Craighead (1987) found no differences among CT, aerobic exercise, and a combination of the two in the treatment of dysphoric mood. Martinsen (1987) has reviewed nine studies of exercise intervention for clinically depressed subjects (whose diagnoses were nonbipolar depressions of mild to moderate severity). Results showed that aerobic exercise was more effective than placebo or no treatment and was as effective as other treatment methods (e.g., meditation–relaxation, group therapy). Aerobic exercise was the most commonly used form of exercise, but the importance of the aerobic element to outcome is still not clear.

In summary, it appears that many stress management techniques described in this book are helpful treatment components in a comprehensive approach to management of depression. Although CT and exercise appear to have the strongest effects, relaxation therapies also have a statistically significant effect in reducing depression. Among relaxation therapies, some studies found meditation to have greater effects than PR, whereas others found the opposite. Reasons for these discrepancies are not clear; they may result from subtle methodological differences between studies. The clinician should be cautioned that high levels of depression often render these techniques less powerful (see the discussion in Chapter 17 on personality characteristics that predict success with stress management techniques). A possible reason for this is the difficulty in motivating depressed people to practice and use various stress management techniques. Also, caution is always necessary when treating this population because of the possibility of suicidal behavior. None of these techniques has been proven to be an effective treatment for depression by itself. The relative effectiveness of these techniques and the optimal combination of them also remain to be determined.

Substance Abuse

The use of stress management strategies to treat abuse of alcohol and other drugs presupposes that these conditions are, at least in part, either caused or maintained by stress and tension. Conger (1956) proposed a heuristic theory in which he postulated that alcohol intake results in tension relief, which reinforces the drinking response. However, Nathan and Goldman (1979), in an extensive review, have argued that tension reduction is inadequate as an explanation for most cases of alcoholism. Sher (1986) maintains that at a sufficient dosage, alcohol consumption does lead to a decreased stress response, and this reinforces the consumption; however, Sher contends that the high-risk groups are at either extreme (i.e., those for whom alcohol is reinforcing at lower doses and those who must dring large quantities to reduce stress). Mann, Chassin, and Sher (1987) report that *expectancy* of such an effect may also be one of several psychological mechanisms by which drinking may be reinforced. For those who drink to avoid experiencing stress or in response to stress ("self-medicators"), relaxation training could perhaps serve as a substitute for alcohol.

There certainly is research evidence to validate the existence of anxious alcoholics. Kushner, Sher, and Beitman (1990) reported high comorbidity rates of alcohol and anxiety problems from epidemiological surveys and family studies. However, the relationship between alcohol problems and anxiety is variable among the anxiety disorders. In agoraphobia and social phobia, alcohol problems appear more likely to follow from attempts at self-medication of anxiety symptoms. Panic disorder and generalized anxiety disorder, on the other hand, may be more likely to follow from pathological alcohol consumption. Cox, Norton, Swinson, and Endler (1990) reported that 10–40% of alcoholics have a panic-related anxiety disorder and that 10–20% of anxiety disorder patients abuse alcohol or other drugs. They found that most alcoholics believe that self-medication is efficacious even though they are susceptible to higher rates of depression. Hesselbrock, Meyer, and Keener (1985) found high rates of depression, phobias, obsessive compulsive disorder, and panic disorder among a group of 321 hospitalized alcoholics.

A number of studies used various relaxation and self-management techniques with alcoholics, and found significant decreases in various measures of anxiety and tension. Page and Schaub (1978) compared taped PR plus frontalis EMG BFK with music as a control. Within the experimental group, clients with MMPI profiles associated with chronic tension and anxiety reduced their muscle tension levels significantly; clients with other kinds of profiles and the control group did not. However, mood state improved with time for all subjects. A series of studies (Gilbert et al., 1978; Parker & Gilbert, 1978; Parker, Gilbert, & Thoreson, 1978) compared PR, meditation, and a "quiet rest" control. Diastolic blood pressure dropped significantly after the 3-week training in both the PR and the meditation groups; the active treatment groups did not differ from each other. The rest controls showed increases in diastolic and systolic blood pressures from the beginning to the end of the study. All groups manifested a significant uniform decrease in state anxiety over time. Roszell and Chaney (1982) used AT with 23 opiate-dependent and polydrug-dependent individuals. The 11 patients who completed nine training sessions rated their symptoms as 52% inproved on the average. Tarbox (1983) compared frontalis auditory EMG BFK, false auditory EMG BFK, and relaxation instruction among alcoholic volunteers and nondrinking controls. Tarbox hypothesized that alcoholics are less able to reduce tension by nonalcoholic means than most people. The results showed that alcoholics functioned at a higher baseline level of muscle tension, but that they could learn to reduce this tension.

There is some evidence that relaxation and stress management methods may lead to less alcohol and drug abuse, at least among some abusers. Feely (1978) found a better relapse rate after narcotics detoxification for the combination of taped PR and biofeedback than for biofeedback alone, despite the lack of differences between groups in the initial response to treatment. Khatami and Rush (1982) compared contingent EMG BFK with noncontingent pretaped "pseudobiofeedback" conditions among narcotic addicts in an outpatient methadone clinic. The two groups did not differ significantly, but both groups improved on ratings of anxiety, depression, and psychiatric symptoms. They also reported decreases in anxiety and cravings for narcotics. The lack of differential improvement could be attributable either to biofeedback-related placebo effects or to the concurrent use of methadone. Olson, Ganley, Devine, and Dorsey (1981) compared a "behavioral package" of covert sensitization and PR to transactional analysis and to a "milieu therapy" control treatment with chronic alcholics. The behavioral package produced lower drinking and higher abstinence rates than transactional analysis up to 18 months after treatment, but not afterwards (as long as 4 years). It did not, however, differ from the control "milieu therapy" at any point. Since all the subjects received the milieu therapy in addition to other treatments, the milieu treatment could well account for the initial positive changes shown by the behavioral treatment group.

Aron and Aron (1980) reviewed research showing that the transcendental meditation program has a positive effect on various addictive behaviors. Wong, Brochin, and Gendron (1981) taught a group with chemical dependence to meditate as part of a continuing rehabilitation program. This group was compared with a noninstructed control group at the termination of training and 6 months later. At termination the meditators reported improved ability to relax, heightened level of self-awareness, and tendency to increase the ability to concentrate; these differences were no longer in evidence after 6 months, however. Subjects who reported continuing at least minimal meditative practices showed improvements in social adjustment, work performance, and use of drugs and alcohol, compared with nonpracticers. These differences were even manifest when subjects who had continued meditating were compared with others in the study who had stopped meditating but had remained involved in Alcoholics Anonymous. Klajner, Hartman, and Sobell (1984) criticized this study for the lack of randomization, absence of a placebo control group, high dropout rate during follow-up, a brief (3-week) training period, and the use of global retrospective self-reports as a measure of alcohol use.

Stress reduction methods appear to be most effective among alcoholics or drug abusers who are particularly anxious, and/or who use the substances specifically to manage stress or anxiety. Rosenberg (1978/1979) found greater reduction in state anxiety at posttreatment in a biofeedback-assisted group than in an alcohol education control group. At the 2-month follow-up, experimental subjects who initially reported high anxiety related to drinking indicated that they were abstinent significantly more often than control subjects who did not report such an association. Furthermore, subjects who practiced relaxing 7 to 21 times per week during the follow-up period reported abstinence significantly more often than those with infrequent practice.

The fact that many alcoholics and drug abusers are *not* helped by relaxation therapies suggests alternative models for examining the effects of various therapies on alcoholism and chronic drug abuse. Marlatt and Gordon (1985) have advanced a coping model, which postulates that a deficit in coping skills increases the probability that an alcoholic will drink when experiencing a negative mood state. This implies that stress management is but one of many coping skills that may be useful in treatment. There is, in fact, considerable evidence that improvement in various kinds of coping skills (often at best only peripherally related to formal stress management therapy) may have stronger results than therapies that are more narrowly directed at treating stress. Monti, Abrams, and Binkoff (1990) compared communication skills training, communication skills training with family participation, and cognitive–behavioral mood management training with inpatient alcoholic subjects. Both the skills training groups drank significantly less alcohol per drinking day during the 6-month follow-up than those in the mood management group. Those receiving communication skills training improved most in an alcohol-specific high-risk role-playing situation and in ability to relax after the role playiong. Skills training has an advantage over mood management training because it helps the individual to deal with interpersonal high-risk situations as well as with the cognitive or affective reaction to these situations. Hedberg and Campbell (1974) offered subjects a choice of either abstinence or controlled drinking as treatment goals. Subjects were assigned to one of four groups: systematic desensitization plus PR, covert sensitization, electric shock conditioning, or behavioral family counseling. At a 6-month follow-up, 74% of subjects receiving behavioral family counseling had achieved their treatment goals, as had 67% of subjects receiving systematic desensitization. Goal attainment was significantly lower for the other groups.

In summary, it appears likely that stress management methods may be helpful in the treatment of at least some alcoholics and other drug abusers. This may be particularly true among individuals who are particularly anxious and who abuse various substances to reduce their symptoms. Relatively broad-spectrum coping skills training may have advantages over particular relaxation or biofeedback techniques, although the latter still may be of great use to some people with these conditions.

Schizophrenia

Relaxation and biofeedback methods are generally thought to be contraindicated in schizophrenia (Fuller, 1977; Gardner & Montgomery, 1977), primarily because schizophrenics are thought to lack the cognitive clarity or motivation to learn self-regulation of physiological responses. Glueck and Stroebel (1975) observed that the limited attention span of schizophrenics resulted in ineffectiveness of biofeedback and AT, although transcendental meditation could be used effectively by some. Adler and Morrisey-Adler (1983) discussed the possibility of increased hallucinations with biofeedback training.

The conclusion that schizophrenics cannot benefit from stress management therapies may be too pessimistic, however. Weiner (1979) found that chronic schizophrenics could be taught to alter EMG levels as required, using an operant conditioning paradigm. Schneider and Pope (1980) provided nine chronic schizophrenics with five sessions of both auditory and visual electroencephalographic (EEG) feedback. The feedback signal continuously reflected discrepancies between the patients' EEG power spectral profile and the spectral profile associated with neuroleptic-induced clinical improvement. Their posttraining EEGs were similar to those of normal subjects. The authors did not report any behavioral concomitants to the altered EEGs. Nigel and Jackson (1979) compared the effects of six sessions of PR and EMG BFK on 10 medicated schizophrenics and a group of normal controls. The clinical group had significantly lower levels of muscle tension after treatment and lower ratings for pathological symptomatology. In comparison to another clinical sample receiving standard psychiatric treatment, the treatment group had a reduced length of hospital stay. The authors conclude that severely impaired schizophrenics can learn to reduce muscle tension without an increase in psychotic symptomatology, and that EMG BFK training can interact positively with major tranquilizers to enhance relaxation.

A controlled study was reported by van Hessel, Bloom, and Gonzalez (1982), who evaluated 6 weeks of anxiety management training and applied relaxation training with 27 medicated schizophrenic outpatients. They reported a significant decrease in general anxiety in both treatment groups, compared to a waiting-list control group. Also, significant positive changes were reported by the outpatient therapists on unrelated nontargeted behaviors (e.g., reported and observed anxiety, and the abilities to work effectively in therapy, to manage anger appropriately, and to achieve personal goals). Pharr and Coursey (1989) compared frontalis and forearm EMG BFK with PR in 30 chronically hospitalized psychiatric patients, and included an attention placebo control group. After six sessions, subjects receiving EMG BFK had significantly lower muscle tension than those in the PR group. Both treatment groups showed greater EMG reductions than the control group. There was no increase in psychopathology and an increase in social competence in the EMG BFK group. Acosta and Yamamoto (1978) taught six chronically tense schizophrenics to relax with 10 sessions of EMG BFK. There was a significant decrease in muscle tension levels from pre- to posttreatment, showing that these individuals were able to learn the relaxation task.

There is some evidence that schizophrenics whose symptomatology includes high manifest anxiety may benefit particularly from relaxation therapies. Hawkins, Doell, Lindseth, Jeffers, and Skaggs (1980) identified a subgroup of "anxious" schizophrenics characterized by high state and trait anxiety, low emotional withdrawal, and conceptual disorganization, who showed a substantial decrease in anxiety following treatment with thermal biofeedback and relaxation.

Hypnotherapy, despite its complications, has been used successfully with schizophrenics, although some incidences of "posthypnotic trauma" have been reported; these are reportedly akin to post-traumatic stress disorder (Haberman, 1987). Scagnelli (1976) described the use of hypnotherapy with eight schizophrenic and borderline individuals. The techniques included anxiety reduction, ego building, insight therapy, use of hypnotic dreams, and imagery shifts. The participants were able to reduce medication, achieved partial or full-time status as students or job holders, and achieved varying levels of reintegration of personality. No controlled studies of this intervention have been reported, however.

In summary, research on stress management with schizophrenics suggests that relaxation techniques may be useful as adjuncts to treatment of certain schizophrenics, particularly those with high manifest anxiety. Contrary to the widely held assumption that schizophrenics are incapable of practicing and learning these skills, acquisition of relaxation skills has been verified in a number of schizophrenics. However, very few systematic studies have been done with this population, and most of these have been completely uncontrolled. The available data suggest that further investigation of stress management methods is warranted with this population.

Stress Management Therapies with Children

Children can learn relaxation techniques at least as well as adults, and they seem to be better able than adults to master some methods. For example, it is widely known that preadolescent children usually have the highest scores on tests of hypnotizability (Hilgard, 1965). Although many children can be treated with the standard relaxation techniques described in this book, modifications in the techniques have been devised to cater to children's particular needs, abilities, and motivational levels (see Koeppen, 1974).

Setterlind (1983) described a study involving the routine teaching of relaxation skills to 294 children from the sixth grade through the second year of high school in Sweden. Instruction took place in physical education classes, via tape recording; the procedure was designed specifically for children, using modifications of PR training and Benson's ROM technique. Setterlind concluded that the children readily learned relaxation skills in such a setting, and that the psychological effects were strong, although the physiological effects were weaker. Approximately 25% of subjects responded by experiencing deep relaxation, 50% medium, and 25% light. As reflected in self-report of relaxation experiences and improvement in various behaviors and symptoms, the results were strongest among older students and those manifesting high anxiety. One-third of the subjects considered relaxation training to have been "of great value," while only 8% considered it to have been worthless. In addition, subjects receiving relaxation training showed lower respiration rates before, during, and after exercise than a control group; however, heart rate effects were minimal, and there were no differences between groups in catecholamine blood levels.

Zaichkowsky and Zaichkowsky (1984) found that 18 sessions of live training in muscle relaxation and stress management reliably reduced heart rate and respiration rate among 9- and 10-year-old children in a school-based program. A study on younger children (ages 6 to 9), using biofeedback-assisted relaxation instructions, found similar but somewhat smaller effects (Zaichkowsky, Zaichkowsky, & Yeager, 1986). In a study of 8th- through 12th-graders with public-speaking anxiety, Hiebert, Kirby, and Jaknovorian (1989) found significantly better results for PR than for the control condition among 11th- and 12th-graders but not among younger students. They attributed the greater success in this age group to greater treatment compliance (i.e., more home practice) in the older group.

A pediatric disorder that has been widely treated with stress reduction techniques is childhood hyperactivity. A review by Cobb and Evans (1981) concludes that hyperactive children can learn to lower EMG levels via EMG BFK and PR training. Subjects given relaxation training showed greater decreases than those given a placebo in impulsivity scores on the Matching Familiar Figures test. Various beneficial effects among hyperactive children have been found in response to both EMG BFK and PR, including diminished impulsivity and distructive behavior, and improved academic performance and self-concept (Bhatara, Arnold, Lorance, & Gupta, 1979; Braud, 1978; Brown, 1977; Dunn & Howell, 1982; Hampstead, 1979; Omizo & Williams, 1982; Omizo, 1980a, 1980b). Brown (1977) found that the addition of instructions that "encourage participation and outline expected positive outcomes" (p. 2847B) are necessary for effective use of relaxation therapy with hyperactive children. Klein and Deffenbacher (1977) found no differences between relaxation training and an exercise program in a measure of reflectivity–impulsivity or on the Continuous Performance Task (a task involving alertness and simple categorizing). Both treatments improved reflectivity, but neither affected subjects' scores on the Continuous Performance Task. This study had no control group, however. There is some evidence that improvements in hyperactivity may stem from the greater sense of self-control that accompanies demonstrated control over one's body (Denkowski, Denkowski, & Omizo, 1983; Denkowski & Denkowski, 1984; Varni, 1976; Carlson, 1977). Some nonsignificant findings for effects of EMG BFK and PR on hyperactivity-related variables should also be noted (Denkowski & Denkowski, 1984; Vacc & Greenleaf, 1980; Wright, 1978).

In a study of anger control among hyperactive boys, Hinshaw, Henker, and Whalen (1984) found that methylphenidate produced decreases in intensity of anger behavior, whereas a cognitive–behavioral intervention produced greater changes in self-control. No advantage was found for a combination of methylphenidate and the cognitive–behavioral treatment. Brown, Wynne, and Medenis (1985) found equal effects for CT and methylphenidate in improving attention in hyperactive boys, but found the drug to be superior in controlling behavior. Combined use of CT and the drug provided no advantage. Braud (1978) found greater improvement in behavioral ratings among nonmedicated than among medicated hyperactive children after relaxation or EMG BFK therapy, although there were no differences between the two groups in EMG scores. Braud interpreted these findings as suggesting that "medication inhibited the learning or utilization of self-control procedures" (p. 85). Potashkin and Beckles (1990) compared EMG BFK with methylphenidate for treatment of hyperactivity. They found that EMG BFK produced better results on one of the three ratings of hyperactivity, as well as on EMG amplitude reduction. However, an attention placebo condition did not differ from the EMG BFK condition on any of the behavioral ratings, thus suggesting that positive adult support may have been the critical therapeutic ingredient.

Relaxation therapies have also been used for the treatment of anxiety-related academic difficulties. Padawer (1977) found that relaxation was more effective than classroom activities in improving attention, memory, and concentration among poor readers in an inner-city school. Khan (1978) found that EMG BFK alone and the combination of EMG BFK and relationship therapy both produced decreases in state anxiety (although not trait anxiety), and produced increases in Wechsler Intelligence Scale for Children–Revised (WISC-R) scores, among elementary school children who had been diagnosed as having problems with high anxiety levels. Palmari (1980) found that the combination of cue-controlled relaxation and CT was more effective than either CT alone or standard educational treatment in improving scores on the Peabody Individual Achievement Test and teachers' ratings of aggressiveness and attentiveness. Robertin (1979/1980) found that PR training and a procedure emphasizing right-hemisphere learning both improved scores on mathematics tests among special education students. Right-hemisphere learning, on the other hand, was superior to PR in improving vocabulary scores and in decreasing state anxiety during the testing situation. On the other hand, Paull (1980) found 4 weeks of daily stress management training followed by 7 weeks of weekly training to have no effect on a rote learning task or on a test of social maturity.

Thus, although not all studies find significant effects for relaxation in improving behaviors associated with learning, most of the studies show that it can make a contribution in some populations. This is probably because poor learning ability is often accompanied by feelings of anxiety in the learning situation, which further inhibits intellectual functioning. Relaxation cannot be considered a substitute for good remedial teaching, but it may serve as a useful adjunct. Amerikaner and

Summerlin (1982) compared relaxation training with social skills training for a group of learning-disabled first- and second-grade children, and found greater improvements in social self-concept with social skills training. Relaxation training, on the other hand, led to greater improvements in teachers' ratings of "acting-out" behaviors and distractibility. There is also evidence that relaxation therapy may be a helpful adjunct in improving handwriting (Carter & Synods, 1974; Jackson & Hughes, 1978; Jackson, Jolly, & Hamilton, 1980), in improving the recall of didactic material (Barnes, 1976), and in ameliorating various psychosomatic disorders (see the review by Richter, 1984). Meador and Ollendick (1984) reviewed the large literature on cognitive–behavioral therapies for various childhood stress-related disorders. They found equivocal results for hyperactivity and impulsivity, but despite the methodological problems in the literature, they concluded that these methods have positive effects on academic and classroom interaction behaviors. There is also consistent evidence for long-term generalization of effects.

Conclusions

It probably surprises few people that stress management methods are effective treatments for a variety of what are commonly considered to be "emotional" disorders. These include most of the problems discussed in this chapter. In one way or another, these involve dysfunctions of the body's response to stress. The dysfunctions often are not limited to a specific response or a specific organ system; they appear in many forms, and each may include a variety of behavioral, cognitive, and physiological manifestations. (By contrast, the next chapter focuses on applications to behavioral medicine, where by definition a disorder tends to be localized in a particular organ system, and where physiological dysfunctions are often, but not always, paramount.) Consequently, a variety of therapeutic modalities tend to be useful in treating these problems.

Considerable evidence does exist supporting the "specific-effects" theory. Physiological manifestations of panic disorder tend to be best treated by breathing retraining, whereas cognitive interventions appear to be critical for generalized anxiety disorder and the fearfulness component in panic. Behavioral approach strategies appear to be critical for success in treating avoidance components in anxiety disorders. However, most of the disorders described in this chapter repond well to several treatment modalities, and most may be best treated by a combination of techniques. This parallels the frequent observation that the various components in anxiety may work in vicious synchrony with each other. People with a tendency to label their internal and/or external environment as threatening may display heightened physiological reactivity to places, people, and/or bodily sensations. Frequent or prolonged experience of heightened physiological reactivity may foster a predisposition to worry and to avoid physiologically arousing situations. Fearsome or uncomfortable experiences may elicit a variety of cognitive and physiological responses.

Similar conclusions may be drawn about other disorders described in this chapter. Depression, schizophrenia, substance abuse, test anxiety, and hyperactivity, are all complex patterns with a multitude of cognitive, physiological, and behavioral aspects. No single therapeutic approach holds "the" solution to any.

This last point bears particular re-emphasis now that various groups with proprietary interests (drug companies, proponents of a particular psychotherapy, or biofeedback equipment manufacturers) are becoming increasingly strident in their claims for particular interventions. Cognitive and behavioral components appear to be critical for success in therapy programs for most of these disorders, although in some cases (particularly major depression and schizophrenia), medication must often play a prominent role in treatment. However, the positive effects of nonmedical stress management strategies for these particular disorders, including relaxation therapies, are stronger than expected. Some medications (e.g., benzodiazepines in the treatment of chronic anxiety) may actually be deleterious in the long run. Although biofeedback techniques have been shown to be helpful in the treatment of several psychological and behavioral disorders, they have not yet been shown to have a stronger effect than various relaxation techniques or an incremental effect over these methods.

The exact mix of therapeutic modalities that is ideal for each person cannot, at this time, be prescribed by formula.

REFERENCES

Achmon, J., Granek, M., Golomb, M., & Hart, J. (1989). Behavioral treatment of essential hypertension: A comparison between cognitive therapy and biofeedback of heart rate. *Psychosomatic Medicine, 51,* 152–164.

Acosta, F. X., & Yamamoto, J. (1978). Application of electromyographic biofeedback to the relaxation training of schizophrenic, neurotic and tension headache patients. *Journal of Consulting and Clinical Psychology, 46,* 383–384.

Adler, C. S., & Morrisey-Adler, S. (1983). Strategies in general psychiatry. In J. Basmajian (Ed.), *Biofeedback: Principles and practice for clinicans.* Baltimore: Williams & Wilkins.

Alstrom, J. E., Nordlund, C. L., Persson, G., Harding, M., & Ljungqvist, C. (1984). Effects of four treatment methods on social phobic patients not suitable for insight-oriented psychotherapy. *Acta Psychiatrica Scandinavica, 70,* 97–110.

Amerikaner, M., & Summerlin, M. L. (1982). Group counseling with learning disabled children: Effects of social skills and relaxation training on self-concept and classroom behavior. *Journal of Learning Disabilities, 15,* 340–343.

Aron, A., & Aron, E. (1980). The transcendental meditation program's effect on addictive behaviour. *Addictive Behaviours, 5,* 3–12.

Baither, R. C., & Godsey, R. (1979). Rational emotive education and relaxation training in large group treatment of test anxiety. *Psychological Reports, 45,* 326.

Barlow, D. H. (1988). *Anxiety and its disorders: The nature and treatment of anxiety and panic.* New York: Guilford Press.

Barlow, D. H., Craske, M., Cerny, J., & Klosko, J. (1989). Behavioral treatment of panic disorder. *Behavior Therapy, 20,* 261–282.

Barnes, L. L. (1976). The effects of relaxation and music on stabilizing recall of didactic material (Doctoral dissertation, U.S. International University). *Dissertation Abstracts International, 37,* 1397B–1398B.

Beck, A. T. (1988). Cognitive approaches to panic disorder: Theory and therapy. In S. Rachman & J. D. Maser (Eds.), *Panic: Psychological perspectives.* Hillsdale, NJ: Erlbaum.

Beck, A. T., Rush, A. J., Shaw, B. F., & Emery, G. (1979). *Cognitive therapy of depression.* New York: Guilford Press.

Bernstein, D. A., & Borkovec, T. D. (1973). *Progressive relaxation training.* Champaign, IL: Research Press.

Bernthal, J. R. (1977). EMG biofeedback, thermal biofeedback, and progressive relaxation in the treatment of examination anxiety of adult education students (Doctoral dissertation, University of Michigan). *Dissertation Abstracts International, 38,* 1292A–1293A. (University Microfilms No. 77–17, 952)

Bhatara, V., Arnold, L. E., Lorance, T., & Gupta, D. (1979). Muscle relaxation therapy in hyperkinesis: Is it effective? *Journal of Learning Disabilities, 12,* 182–186.

Bohachick, P. (1984). Progressive relaxation training in cardiac rehabilitation: Effect on psychologic variables. *Nursing Research, 33,* 283–287.

Borkovec, T. D., Mathews, A. M., Chambers, A., Ebrahimi, S., Lytle, R., & Nelson, R. (1987). The effects of relaxation training with cognitive or nondirective therapy and the role of relaxation-induced anxiety in the treatment of generalized anxiety. *Journal of Consulting and Clinical Psychology, 55,* 883–888.

Borkovec, T. D., & Sides, K. (1979). Critical procedural variables related to the physiological effects of progressive relaxation: A review. *Behaviour Research and Therapy, 17,* 119–126.

Bott, R. A. (1979). A study of complex learning: Theory and methodologies. *Dissertation Abstracts International, 40*(1), 471B.

Boutin, G. E., & Tosi, D. J. (1983). Modification of irrational ideas and test anxiety through rational stage directed hypnotherapy (RSDH). *Journal of Clinical Psychology, 39,* 382–391.

Bowers, W. A. (1990). Treatment of depressed in-patients: Cognitive therapy plus medication, relaxation plus medication, and medication alone. *British Journal of Psychiatry, 156,* 73–78.

Braud, L. W. (1978). The effects of frontalis EMG biofeedback and progressive relaxation upon hyperactivity and its behavioral concomitants. *Biofeedback and Self-Regulation, 3,* 69–89.

Brooks, J. S., & Scarno, T. (1985). Transcendental meditation in the treatment of post-Vietnam adjustment. *Journal of Counseling and Development, 64,* 212–215.

Brown, R. H. (1977). An evaluation of the effectiveness of relaxation training as a treatment modality for the hyperkinetic child (Doctoral dissertation, Texas Technological University). *Dissertation Abstracts International, 38,* 2847B. (Univerity Microfilms No. 77–25, 502)

Brown, R. T., Wynne, M. E., & Medenis, R. (1985). Methylphenidate and cognitive therapy: A comparison of treatment approaches with hyperactive boys. *Journal of Abnormal Child Psychology, 13,* 69–87.

Bush, C., Ditto, B., & Feuerstein, M. (1985). A controlled evaluation of paraspinal EMG biofeedback in the treatment of chronic low back pain. *Health Psychology, 4,* 307–321.

Butler, G., Cullington, A., Hibbert, G., Klimes, I., & Gelder, M. (1987). Anxiety management for persistent generalized anxiety, *British Journal of Psychiatry, 151,* 535–542.

Carlson, J. G. (1977). Locus of control and frontal electromyographic response training. *Biofeedback and Self-Regulation, 2,* 259–271.

Carter, J. L., & Synods, D. (1974). Effects of relaxation training upon handwriting quality. *Journal of Learning Disabilities, 7,* 53–55.

Carrington, P., Collings, G. H., Jr., Benson, H., Robinson, H., Wood, L. W., Lehrer, P. M., Woolfolk, R. L., & Cole, J. W. (1980). The use of meditation–relaxation techniques for the management of stress in a working population. *Journal of Occupational Medicine, 22,* 221–231.

Catalan, J., Gath, D., Edmonds, G., & Ennis, J. (1984). The effects of non-prescribing of anxiolytics in general practice: I. Controlled evaluation of psychiatric and social outcome. *British Journal of Psychiatry, 144,* 593–602.

Cavallaro, D. M., Donna, M., & Meyers, J. (1986). Effects of study habits on cognitive restructuring and study skills training in the treatment of test anxiety with adolescent females. *Techniques, 2,* 145–155.

Chang-Liang, R., & Denney, D. R. (1976). Applied relaxation as training in self control. *Journal of Counseling Psychology, 23,* 183–189.

Clark, D. M. (1986). A cognitive approach to panic. *Behaviour Research and Therapy, 24,* 461–470.

Clark, D. M. (1989). Anxiety states: Panic and generalized anxiety. In K. Hawton, P. M. Salkovskis, J. Kirk, & D. M. Clark (Eds.), *Cognitive behaviour therapy for psychiatric problems: A practical guide.* New York: Oxford University Press.

Clark, D. M., Salkovskis, P. M., & Chalkley, A. J. (1985). Respiratory control as a treatment for panic attacks. *Journal of Behavior Therapy and Experimental Psychiatry, 16,* 23–30.

Cobb, D. E., & Evans, J. R. (1981). The use of biofeedback techniques with school-aged children exhibiting behavioral and/or learning problems. *Journal of Abnormal Child Psychology, 9,* 251–256.

Comer, J. F. (1978). Meditation and progressive relaxation in the treatment of test anxiety (Doctoral dissertation, University of Kansas, 1977). *Dissertation Abstracts International, 38,* 6142B. (University Microfilms No. 78–09, 340).

Conger, J. J. (1956). Alcoholism: Theory, problem and challenge. II. Reinforcement theory and the dynamics of alcoholism. *Quarterly Journal of Studies on Alcohol, 17,* 296–305.

Counts, D. K., Hollandsworth, T. D., & Alcorn, J. D. (1978). Use of electromyographic biofeedback and cue controlled relaxation in the treatment of test anxiety. *Journal of Consulting and Clinical Psychology, 46,* 990–996.

Cox, B. J., Norton, G. R., Swinson, R. P., & Endler, N. S. (1990). Substance abuse and panic-related anxiety: A critical review. *Behaviour Research and Therapy, 28,* 385–393.

Dawson, R. W., & McMurray, W. E. (1978). Desensitization without hierarchical presentation and concomitant relaxation. *Australian Journal of Psychology, 30,* 119–132.

Deffenbacher, J. L. (1988). Cognitive–relaxation and social skills treatments of anger: A year later. *Journal of Counseling Psychology, 35,* 234–236.

Deffenbacher, J. L., Demm, P. M., & Brandon, A. D. (1986). High general anger: Correlates and treatment. *Behaviour Research and Therapy, 24,* 481–489.

Deffenbacher, J. L., & Hahnloser, R. M. (1981). Cognitive and relaxation coping skills in stress inoculation. *Cognitive Therapy and Research, 5,* 211–215.

Deffenbacher, J. L., McNamara, K., Stark, R. S., & Sabadell, P. M. (1990). A combination of cognitive, relaxation, and behavioral coping skills in the reduction of general anger. *Journal of College Student Development, 31,* 351–358.

Deffenbacher, J. L., & Michaels, A. C. (1980). Two self-control procedures in the reduction of targeted and nontargeted anxieties: A year later. *Journal of Counseling Psychology, 27,* 9–15.

Deffenbacher, J. L., Story, D. A., Brandon, A. D., Hogg, J. A., & Hazaleus, S. L. (1988). Cognitive and cognitive relaxation treatments of anger. *Cognitive Therapy and Research, 12,* 167–184.

Deffenbacher, J. L., Story, D. A., Stark, R. S., Hogg, J. A., & Brandon A. D. (1987). Cognitive-relaxation and social skills interventions in the treatment of general anger. *Journal of Counseling Psychology, 34,* 171–176.

Deffenbacher, J. L., & Suinn, R. (1987). Generalized anxiety syndrome. In L. Michelson & L. M. Ascher (Eds.), *Anxiety and stress disorders: Cognitive–behavioral assessment and treatment.* New York: Guilford Press.

Dendato, K. M., & Diener, D. (1986). Effectiveness of cognitive/relaxation therapy and study-skills training in reducing self-reported anxiety and improving the academic performance of test-anxious students. *Journal of Counseling Psychology, 33,* 131–135.

Denkowski, K. M., & Denkowski, G. C. (1984). Is group progressive relaxation training as effective with hyperactive children as individual EMG biofeedback treatment? *Biofeedback and Self-Regulation, 9,* 353–364.

Denkowski, K. M., & Denkowski, G. C., & Omizo, M. M. (1983). The effects of EMG-assisted relaxation training on the academic performance, locus of control, and self-esteem of hyperactive boys. *Biofeedback and Self-Regulation, 8,* 363–375.

de Piano, F. A., de Piano, L. C., Carter, W., & Wanlass, R. L. (1984). Physical fitness training: Adjunctive treatment for the depressed, low self-esteem, muscular tense patient. *Psychotherapy in Private Practice, 2,* 75–83.

Dunn, F. M., & Howell, R. J. (1982). Relaxation training and its relationship to hyperactivity in boys. *Journal of Clinical Psychology, 38,* 92–100.

Farnhill, D. (1985). A comparison of hypnosis and computer-assisted biofeedback in computer-anxiety reduction. *Australian Journal of Clinical and Experimental Hypnosis, 13,* 31–35.

Feely, T. M. (1978). The effects of electromyographic biofeedback training and EMG biofeedback with progressive relaxation training on narcotics addicts during medical detoxification (Doctoral dissertation, St. Louis University). *Dissertation Abstracts International, 39,* 1474B–1475B.

Feindler, E. L., Ecton, R. B., Kingsley, D., & Dubey, D. R. (1986). Group anger control training for institutionalized psychiatric male adolescents. *Behavior Therapy, 17,* 109–123.

Finger, R., & Galassi, J. P. (1977). Effects of modifying cognitive versus emotional responses in the treatment of test anxiety. *Journal of Consulting and Clinical Psychology, 45,* 280–287.

Fontaine, R., Chouinard, G., & Annable, L. (1984). Rebound anxiety in anxious patients after abrupt withdrawal of benzodiazepine treatment. *American Journal of Psychiatry, 141,* 848–852.

Freeling, N. W., & Shemberg, K. M. (1970). The alleviation of test anxiety by systematic desensitization. *Behaviour Research and Therapy, 8,* 293–299.

Fremont, J., & Craighead, L. W. (1987). Aerobic exercise and cognitive therapy in the treatment of dysphoric moods. *Cognitive Therapy and Research, 11,* 241–251.

Fuller, G. D. (1977). *Biofeedback: Methods and procedures in clinical practice.* San Francisco: Biofeedback Press.

Ganguli, R., & Detre, T. (1982). Psychopharmacology and behavior therapy. In L. Michelson, M. Hersen, & S. M. Turner (Eds.), *Future perspectives in behavior therapy.* New York: Plenum Press.

Gardner, K. R., & Montgomery, P. S. (1977). *Clinical biofeedback: A procedural manual.* Baltimore: Williams & Wilkins.

Gilbert, G. S., Parker, J. C., & Clairborn, C. D. (1978). Differential mood changes in alcoholics as a function of anxiety management strategies. *Journal of Clinical Psychology, 34,* 229–232.

Glueck, B., & Stroebel, C. (1975). Biofeedback and meditation in the treatment of psychiatric illness. *Comprehensive Psychiatry, 16,* 303–321.

Gorman, J. M., Papp, L. A., Martinez, J., Goetz, R. R., Hollander, E., Liebowitz, M. R., & Jordan, F. (1990). High-dose carbon dioxide challenge test in anxiety disorder patients. *Biological Psychiatry, 28,* 743–757.

Grazzi, L., Frediani, F., Zappacosta, B., & Boiardi, A. (1988). Psychological assessment in tension headache before and after biofeedback treatment. *Headache, 28,* 337–338.

Green, R. A., & Murray, E. J. (1975). Expression of feeling and cognitive reinterpretation in the reduction of hostile aggression. *Journal of Consulting and Clinical Psychology, 43,* 375–383.

Gross, R. T., & Fremouw, W. J. (1982). Cognitive restructuring and progressive relaxation for treatment of empirical subtypes of speech-anxious subjects. *Cognitive Therapy and Research, 6,* 429–436.

Haberman, M. A. (1987). Complications following hypnosis in a psychotic patient with sexual dysfunction treated by a lay hypnotist. *American Journal of Clinical Hypnosis, 29,* 166–170.

Hafner, R. J. (1982). Psychological treatment of essential hypertension: A controlled comparison of meditation and meditation plus biofeedback. *Biofeedback and Self-Regulation, 7,* 305–316.

Hafner, R. J., & Milton, F. (1977). The influence of propranolol on the exposure in vivo of agoraphobics. *Psychological Medicine, 7,* 419–426.

Hafner, R., & Marks, I. M. (1976). Exposure in vivo of agoraphobics: Contributions of diazepam, group exposure, and anxiety evocation. *Psychological Medicine, 6,* 71–88.

Hampstead, W. J. (1979). The effects of EMG-assisted relaxation training with hyperkinetic children. *Biofeedback and Self-Regulation, 4,* 113–125.

Hawkins, R. C., Doell, S. R., Lindseth, P., Jeffers, V., & Skaggs, S. (1980). Anxiety reduction in hospitalized schizophrenics through thermal biofeedback and relaxation training. *Perceptual and Motor Skills, 51,* 475–482.

Hazaleus, S. L., & Deffenbacher, J. L. (1986). Relaxation and cognitive treatments of anger. *Journal of Consulting and Clinical Psychology, 54,* 222–226.

Hedberg, A., & Campbell, L. (1974). A comparison of four behavioral treatments of alcoholism. *Journal of Behavior Therapy and Experimental Psychiatry, 5,* 251–256.

Heimberg, R. G. (1989). Cognitive and behavioral treatments for social phobia: A Critical analysis. *Clinical Psychology Review, 9,* 107–128.

Heimberg, R. G., Dodge, C. S., & Becker, R. E. (1987). Social phobia. In L. Michelson & M. Ascher (Eds.), *Anxiety and stress disorders: Cognitive–behavioral assessment and treatment.* New York: Guilford Press.

Hesselbrock, M. N., Meyer, R. E., & Keener, J. J. (1985). Psychopathology in hospitalized alcoholics. *Archives of General Psychiatry, 42,* 1050–1055.

Hiebert, B., Kirby, B., & Jaknovorian, A. (1989). School-based relaxation: Attempting primary prevention. *Canadian Journal of Counselling, 23,* 273–287.

Hilgard, E. R. (1965). *Hypnotic susceptibility.* New York: Harcourt, Brace & World.

Hinshaw, S. P., Henker, B., & Whalen, C. K. (1984). Self control in hyperactive boys in anger inducing situations: Effects of cognitive behavioral training and of methylphenidate. *Journal of Abnormal Child Psychology, 12,* 55–77.

Hoehn-Saric, R., McLeod, D. R., & Zimmerli, W. D. (1988). Differential effects of alprazolam and imipramine in generalized anxiety disorder: Somatic versus psychic symptoms. *Journal of Clinical Psychiatry, 49,* 293–301.

Hoshmand, L. T., Helmes, E., Kazarian, S. S., & Tekatch, G. (1985). Evaluation of two relaxation training programs under medication and no-medication conditions. *Journal of Clinical Psychology, 41,* 22–29.

Hurwitz, L. R., Kahane, J., & Mathieson, C. (1986). The effect of EMG biofeedback and progressive muscle relaxation on the reduction of test anxiety. *Educational and Psychological Research, 6,* 291–298.

Jackson, K. A., & Hughes, H. (1978). Effects of relaxation training on cursive handwriting of fourth grade students. *Perceptual and Motor Skills, 47,* 707–712.

Jackson, K. A., Jolly, V., & Hamilton, B. (1980). Comparison of remedial treatments for cursive handwriting of fourth-grade students. *Perceptual and Motor Skills, 51,* 1215–1221.

Johnson, R. L., & Johnson, H. C. (1984). Effects of anxiety-reducing hypnotic training on learning and reading-comprehension tasks. *Journal of the National Medical Association, 76,* 233–235.

Johnson, S. M., & Sechrest, L. (1968). Comparison of desensitization and progressive relaxation in treating anxiety. *Journal of Consulting and Clinical Psychology, 32,* 280–286.

Kahn, J. S., Kehle, T. J., Jenson, W. R., & Clark, E. (1990). Comparison of cognitive–behavioral, relaxation, and self-modeling interventions for depression among middle-school students. *School Psychology Review, 19,* 196–211.

Kantor, L. E. (1980). Stress inoculation as a means of teaching anxiety management skills: An evaluation of stimulus generalization (Doctoral dissertation, Bowling Green State University, 1979). *Dissertation Abstracts International, 40,* 3401B. (University Microfilms No. 80-00,043)

Keane, T. M., Fairbank, J. A., Caddell, J. M., & Zimering, R. T. (1989). Implosive (flooding) therapy reduces symptoms of PTSD in Vietnam combat veterans. *Behavior Therapy, 20,* 245–260.

Kendall, P. C., & Braswell, L. (1986). Medical applications of cognitive behavioral interventions with children. *Journal of Developmental and Behavioral Pediatrics, 7,* 257–264.

Khatami, M., & Rush, A. J. (1982). A one year follow-up of the multimodal treatment for chronic pain. *Pain, 14,* 45–52.

Khan, M. A. (1978). The effects of EMG biofeedback assisted relaxation training upon problem-solving abilities of anxious children (Doctoral dissertation, Western Michigan University). *Dissertation Abstracts International, 39,* 2476B. (University Microfilms No. 78-21,838)

Kindlon, D. J. (1983). Comparison of use of meditation and rest in treatment of test anxiety. *Psychological Reports, 53,* 931–938.

Klajner, F., Hartman, L. M., & Sobell, M. B. (1984). Treatment of substance abuse by relaxation training: A review of its rationale, efficacy and mechanisms. *Addictive Behaviours, 9,* 41–55.

Klein, S. A., & Deffenbacher, J. L. (1977). Relaxation and exercise for hyperactive impulsive children. *Perceptual and Motor Skills, 45,* 1159–1169.

Koeppen, A. S. (1974). Relaxation training for children. *Elementary School Guidance and Counseling, 9,* 14–21.

Kushner, M., Sher, K., & Beitman, B. (1990). The relation between alcohol problems and the anxiety disorders. *American Journal of Psychiatry, 147,* 685–695.

Lavallée, Y. J., Lamontagne, G., Pinard, G., Annable, L., & Tétreault, L. (1977). Effects of EMG biofeedback, diazepam and their combination on chronic anxiety. *Journal of Psychosomatic Research, 21,* 65–71.

Lehrer, P. M., Woolfolk, R. L., Rooney, A., McCann, B. S., & Carrington, P. C. (1983). Progressive relaxation and meditation: A study of psychophysiological and therapeutic differences between two techniques. *Behaviour Research and Therapy, 21,* 651–662.

Lent, R. W. (1979). A comparison between cue-controlled desensitization, cognitive restructuring, and a credible placebo in alleviating public speaking anxiety (Doctoral dissertation, Ohio State University). *Dissertation Abstracts International, 40,* 1899B. (University Microfilms No. 79-22,513)

Ley, R. (1988). Panic attacks during relaxation and relaxation-induced anxiety: A hyperventilation interpretation. *Journal of Behavior Therapy and Experimental Psychiatry, 19,* 253–259.

Ley, R. (1989). Dyspneic-fear and catastrophic cognitions in hyperventilatory panic attacks. *Behaviour Research and Therapy, 27,* 549–554.

Liebowitz, M. R., Gorman, J. M., Fyer, A. J., & Klein, D. F. (1985). Social phobia: Review of a neglected anxiety disorder. *Archives of General Psychiatry, 42,* 729–736.

Lindsay, W. R., Gansu, C. V., McLaughlin, E., Hood, E. M., & Espie, C. A. (1987). A controlled trial of treatments for generalized anxiety. *British Journal of Clinical Psychology, 26,* 3–15.

Lochman, J. E., Burch, P. R., Curry, J. F., & Lampron, L. B. (1984). Treatment and generalization effects of cognitive behavioral and goal setting interventions with aggressive boys. *Journal of Consulting and Clinical Psychology, 52,* 915–916.

Lohr, J. M., & Hamberger, L. K. (1990). Cognitive behavioral modification of coronary prone behaviors: Proposal for a treatment model and review of the evidence. *Journal of Rational Emotive and Cognitive Behavior Therapy, 8,* 103–126.

Lustman, P. J., & Sowa, C. J. (1983). Comparative efficacy of biofeedback and stress inoculation for stress reduction. *Journal of Clinical Psychology, 39,* 191–197.

Mann, L. M., Chassin, L., & Sher, K. J. (1987). Alcohol expectancies and the risk for alcoholism. *Journal of Consulting and Clinical Psychology, 55,* 411–417.

Marks, I. M. (1987). *Fears, phobias, and rituals: Panic, anxiety, and their disorders.* New York: Oxford University Press.

Marlatt, G. A., & Gordon, J. R. (Eds.). (1985). *Relapse prevention: Maintenance strategies in the treatment of addictive behaviors.* New York: Guilford Press.

Martinsen, E. W. (1987). The role of aerobic exercise in the treatment of depression. *Stress Medicine, 3,* 93–100.

Mattick, R. P., & Peters, L. (1988). Treatment of severe social phobia: Effects of guided exposure with and without cognitive restructuring. *Journal of Consulting and Clinical Psychology, 56,* 251–260.

Mavissakalian, M., & Michelson, L. (1986). Agoraphobia: Relative and combined effectiveness of therapist-assisted *in vivo* exposure and imipramine. *Journal of Clinical Psychiatry, 47,* 117–122.

Maxwell, M. S. (1979). Experimental evaluation of theoretically differentiated treatments of test anxiety (Doctoral dissertation, University of Texas at Austin). *Dissertation Abstracts International, 40,* 1363A. (University Microfilms No. 79-20,167)

McLean, P. D., & Hakstian, A. R. (1979). Clinical depression: Comparative efficacy of outpatient treatments. *Journal of Consulting and Clinical Psychology, 47,* 818–836.

Meador, A. E., & Ollendick, T. H. (1984). Cognitive behavior therapy with children: An evaluation of its efficacy and clinical utility. *Child and Family Behavior Therapy, 6,* 25–45.

Meichenbaum, D., & Novaco, R. (1985). Stress inoculation: A preventative approach. *Issues in Mental Health Nursing, 7,* 419–435.

Michelson, L., & Marchione, K. (1991). Behavioral, cognitive, and pharmacological treatments of panic disorder with agoraphobia: Critique and synthesis. *Journal of Consulting and Clinical Psychology, 59,* 100–114.

Michelson, L., Marchione, K., & Greenwald, M. (1989, November). *Cognitive–behavioral treatments of agora-*

phobia. Paper presented at the annual meeting of the Association for Advancement of Behavior Therapy, Washington, DC.

Michelson, L., & Mavissakalian, M. (1983). Temporal stability of self-report measures in agoraphobia research. *Behaviour Research and Therapy, 21,* 695–698.

Michelson, L., & Mavissakalian, M. (1985). Psychophysiological outcome of behavioral and pharmacologic treatments of agoraphobia. *Journal of Consulting and Clinical Psychology, 53,* 229–236.

Michelson, L., & Mavissakalian, M., & Marchione, K. (1985). Cognitive and behavioral treatments of agoraphobia: Clinical, behavioral, and psychophysiological outcomes. *Journal of Consulting and Clinical Psychology, 53,* 913–925.

Mitchell, K. R., & Mitchell, D. M. (1971). Migraine: An exploratory treatment application of programmed behavior therapy techniques. *Journal of Psychosomatic Research, 15,* 137–157.

Monti, P., Abrams, D., & Binkoff, J. (1990). Communication skills training, communication skills training with family and cognitive behavioral mood management training for alcoholics. *Journal of Studies on Alcohol, 51,* 263–270.

Moon, J. R., & Eisler, R. M. (1983). Anger control: An experimental comparison of three behavioral treatments. *Behavior Therapy, 14,* 493–505.

Muskatel, N., Woolfolk, R. C., Carrington, P., Lehrer, P. M., & McCann, B. S. (1984). Effect of meditation training on aspects of coronary prone behavior. *Perceptual and Motor Skills, 58,* 515–518.

Nathan, P. E., & Goldman, M. S. (1979). Problem drinking and alcoholism. In O. F. Pomerleau & J. P. Brady (Eds.), *Behavior therapy: Theory and practice.* Baltimore: Williams & Wilkins.

Nigel, A. J., & Jackson, B. (1979). Electromyograph biofeedback as an adjunct to standard psychiatric treatment. *Journal of Clinical Psychiatry, 40,* 433–436.

Novaco, R. W. (1975). *Anger control: The development and evaluation of an experimental treatment.* Lexington, MA: D.C. Heath.

Olson, R. P., Ganley, R., Devine, V. T., & Dorsey, G. C., Jr. (19810. Long-term effects of behavioral versus insight-oriented therapy with inpatient alcoholics. *Journal of Consulting and Clinical Psychology, 49,* 866–877.

Omizo, M. M. (1980a). The effects of biofeedback-induced relaxation training on hyperactive adolescent boys. *Journal of Psychology, 105,* 131–138.

Omizo, M. M. (1980b). The effects of relaxation training and biofeedback on dimensions of self-control among hyperactive male children. *Educational Research Quarterly, 5,* 22–30.

Omizo, M. M., & Williams, R. E. (1982). Biofeedback-induced relaxation training as an alternative for the elementary school learning-disabled child. *Biofeedback and Self-Regulation, 7,* 139–148.

Öst, L. G. (1987). Applied relaxation: Description of a coping technique and review of controlled studies. *Behaviour Research and Therapy, 25,* 397–409.

Öst, L. G. (1989). A maintenance program for behavioral treatment of anxiety disorders. *Behaviour Research and Therapy, 27,* 397–409.

Öst, L. G., Jerremalm, A., & Johansson, J. (1981). Individual response patterns and the effects of different behavioral methods in the treatment of social phobias. *Behaviour Research and Therapy,* 1–16.

Padawer, D. D. (1977). Reading performance of relaxation trained children. *Dissertation Abstracts International, 38,* 1306A.

Page, R. D., & Schaub, L. H. (1978). EMG biofeedback applicability for differing personality types. *Journal of Clinical Psychology, 34,* 1014–1020.

Palan, B. M., & Chandwani, S. (1989). Coping with examination stress through hypnosis: An experimental study. *American Journal of Clinical Hypnosis, 31,* 173–180.

Palmari, J. J. (1980). Relaxation and cognitive coping statements as supplemental remedial interventions for learning problems in children (Doctoral dissertation, Hofstra University). *Dissertation Abstracts International, 40,* 5796B. (University Microfilms No. 80-12,855)

Parker, J. C., & Gilbert, G. (1978). Anxiety management in alcoholics: A study of generalised effects of relaxation techniques. *Addictive Behaviours, 3,* 123–127.

Parker, J. C., Gilbert, G. S., & Thoreson, R. W. (1978). Reduction of autonomic arousal in alcoholics: A comparison of relaxation and meditation techniques. *Journal of Consulting and Clinical Psychology, 46,* 879–886.

Paull, R. C. (1980). The effect of relaxation training on a rote learning task and the psychosocial maturity of inner city black seventh graders: A program in holistic education (Doctoral dissertation, University of Southern California). *Dissertation Abstracts International, 41,* 602A.

Pesta, K., & Zwettler, S. (1977). Influence of cognitive desensitization in test anxiety in school children: A therapeutic comparison. *Zeitschrift für Klinische Psychologie, 6,* 130–143.

Pharr, O. M., & Coursey, R. D. (1989). The use and utility of EMG biofeedback with chronic schizophrenic patients. *Biofeedback and Self-Regulation, 14,* 229–245.

Potashkin, B. D., & Beckles, N. (1990). Relative efficacy of Ritalin and biofeedback treatments on the management of hyperactivity. *Biofeedback and Self-Regulation, 15,* 305–313.

Reed, M., & Saslow, C. (1980). The effects of relaxation instructions and EMG biofeedback on test anxiety, general anxiety, and locus of control. *Journal of Clinical Psychology, 36,* 683–690.

Reynolds, W. M., & Coats, K. I. (1986). A comparison of cognitive–behavioral therapy and relaxation training for the treatment of depression in adolescents. *Journal of Consulting and Clinical Psychology, 54,* 653–660.

Richter, N. C. (1984). The efficacy of relaxation training with children. *Journal of Abnormal Child Psychology, 12,* 319–344.

Robertin, H. (1980). Anxiety reduction and academic progress (Doctoral dissertation, Union Graduate School, Ohio, 1979). *Dissertation Abstracts International, 40,* 4500A. (University Microfilms No. 80-02,948)

Rosenberg, S. D. (1979). Relaxation training and a differential assessment of alcholism (Doctoral dissertation, California School for Professional Psychology, San Diego, 1978). *Dissertation Abstracts International, 39,* 1498B.

Roszell, D. K., & Chaney, E. F. (1982). Autogenic training in a drug abuse program. *International Journal of the Addictions, 17,* 1337–1349.

Roth, W. T., Telch, M. J., Taylor, C. B., & Agras, W. S. (1988). Autonomic changes after treatment of agoraphobia with panic attacks. *Psychiatry Research, 24,* 95–107.

Rothman, H. S. (1979). Electromyographic biofeedback training vs. progressive muscle relaxation training in the treatment of test anxiety (Doctoral dissertation, Washington State Uniersity). *Dissertation Abstracts International, 40,* 463B. (University Microfilms No. 79-15,148)

Sallis, J. F. (1983). Aggressive behaviors of children: A review of behavioral interventions and future directions. *Education and Treatment of Children, 6,* 175–191.

Sallis, J. F., Trevorrow, T. R., Johnson, C. C., Hovell, M. F., & Kaplan, R. M. (1987). Worksite stress management: A comparison of programs. *Psychology and Health, 1,* 237–255.

Scagnelli, J. (1976). Hypnotherapy with schizophrenic and borderline patients: Summary of therapy with eight patients. American *Journal of Clinical Hypnosis, 19,* 33–38.

Schlichter, K. J. (1987). An application of stress inoculation training in the development of anger-management skills in institutionalized juvenile delinquents (Doctoral dissertation, Pennslyvania State University, 1977). *Dissertation Abstracts International, 38,* 6172B. (University Microflims No. 78-08,420)

Schneider, S. J., & Pope, A. T. (1980). Neuroleptic-like electroencephalographic changes in schizophrenics through biofeedback. *Biofeedback and Self-Regulation, 7,* 479–490.

Schuchman, M. C. (1978). A comparison of three techniques for reducing scholastic aptitude test anxiety (Doctoral dissertation, Hofstra University, 1977). *Dissertation Abstracts International, 38,* 2010A. (University Microfilms No. 77-20,673)

Setterlind, S. (1983). *Avslappningsträning i skolan: Forskningsöversikt och empiriska studier [Teaching relaxation in school: A survey of research and empirical studies].* Göteborg, Sweden: Acta Universitatis Gothoburgensis.

Shapiro, S., & Lehrer, P. M. (1980). Psychophysiological effects of autogenic training and progressive relaxation. *Biofeedback and Self-Regulation, 5,* 249–255.

Shea, M. T., Pilkonis, P. A., Beckham, E., Collins, J. F., Elkin, I., Sotsky, S. M., & Docherty, J. P. (1990). Personality disorders and treatment outcome in the NIMH Treatment of Depression Collaborative Research Program. *American Journal of Psychiatry, 147,* 711–718.

Sheehan, D. V., Ballenger, J., & Jacobsen, G. (1980). Treatment of endogenous anxiety with phobic, hysterical, and hypochondriacal symptoms. *Archives of General Psychiatry, 37,* 51–59.

Sher, K. J. (1986). Stress response dampening. In H. T. Blane & K. E. Leonard (Eds.), *Psychological theories of drinking and alcoholism.* New York: Guilford Press.

Snyder, A. L., & Deffenbacher, J. L. (1977). Comparison of relaxation as self-control and systematic desensitization in the treatment of test anxiety. *Journal of Consulting and Clinical Psychology, 45,* 1202–1203.

Solyom, L., Heseltine, G. F. D., McClure, D. J., Solyom, C., Ledwidge, B., & Steinberg, G. (1973). Behaviour therapy versus drug therapy in the treatment of phobic neurosis. *Canadian Psychiatric Association Journal, 18,* 25–32.

Sorbi, M., Tellegen, B., & du Long, A. (1989). Long-term effects of training in relaxation and stress-coping in patients with migraine: A 3-year follow-up. *Headache, 29,* 111–121.

Spies, G. (1979). Desensitization of test anxiety: Hypnosis compared with biofeedback. *American Journal of Clinical Hypnosis, 22,* 108–111.

Stanton, H. E. (1984). A comparison of the effects of an hypnotic procedure and music on anxiety level. *Australian Journal of Clinical and Experimental Hypnosis, 12,* 127–132.

Sweeney, G. A., Horan, J. J. (1982). Separate and combined effects of cue controlled relaxation and cognitive restructuring in the treatment of musical performance anxiety. *Journal of Counseling Psychology, 29,* 486–497.

Tarbox, A. R. (1983). Alcoholism, biofeedback and internal scanning. *Journal of Studies on Alcohol, 44,* 246–261.

Telch, M. J., Tearnan, B. H., & Taylor, C. B. (1983). Antidepressant medication in the treatment of agoraphobia: A critical review. *Behaviour Research and Therapy, 21,* 505–517.

Thompson, J. G., Griebstein, M. G., & Kuhlenschmidt, S. L. (1980). Effects of EMG biofeedback and relaxation training in the prevention of academic underachievement. *Journal of Counseling Psychology, 27,* 97–106.

Thurman, C. W. (1985). Effectiveness of cognitive behavioral treatments in reducing Type A behavior among university faculty: One year later. *Journal of Counseling Psychology, 32,* 445–448.

Tyrer, P. J., & Steinberg, D. (1975). Symptomatic treatment for agoraphobias and social phobias: A follow-up study. *British Journal of Psychiatry, 127,* 163–168.

Vacc, N. A., & Greenleaf, S. M. (1980). Relaxation training and covert positive reinforcement with elementary school children. *Elementary School Guidance and Counseling, 14,* 232–235.

van Hessel, J. H., Bloom, L. J., & Gonzalez, A. M. (1982). Anxiety management with schizophrenic outpatients. *Journal of Clinical Psychology, 38,* 280–285.

Varni, J. W. (1976). *A cognitive-behavior self-regulation approach to the treatment of the hyperactive child.* Unpublished doctoral dissertation, University of California, Los Angeles.

Weiner, H. (1979). On altering muscle tensions with chronic schizophrenics. *Psychological Reports, 44,* 527–534.

Wheeler, M. C. (1977). Relaxation training as a prescriptive therapy for anxious and external depressives (Doctoral dissertation, Syracuse University, 1976). *Dissertation Abstracts International, 37,* 5849B. (University Microfilms No. 77-99,13)

Whitehead, W. E., & Blackwell, B. (1979). Interaction between drugs and behavior therapy. In R. McNamara (Ed.), *Behavioral approaches to medicine.* New York: Plenum Press.

Wielgosz, A. T., Wielgosz, M., Biro, E., Nicholls, E., MacWilliam, L., & Haney, T. (1988). Risk factors for myocardial infarction: The importance of relaxation. *British Journal of Medical Psychology, 61,* 209–217.

Wilson, R. (1984). A review of self control treatments for aggressive behavior. *Behavioral Disorders, 9,* 131–140.

Wise, E. H., & Haynes, S. N. (1983). Cognitive treatment of test anxiety: Rational restructuring versus attentional training. *Cognitive Therapy and Research, 7,* 69–77.

Wong, M. R., Brochin, N. E., & Gendron, K. L. (1981). Effects of meditation on anxiety and chemical dependency. *Journal of Drug Education, 11,* 91–105.

Woolfolk, R. L. (1984). Self-control meditation applied to a case of chronic anger. In D. S. Shapiro (Ed.), *Meditation: Classic and contemporary perspectives.* Hawthorne, NY: Aldine.

Woolfolk, R. L., Lehrer, P. M., McCann, B. S., & Rooney, A. J. (1982). Effects of progressive relaxation and meditation on cognitive and somatic manifestations of daily stress. *Behaviour Research and Therapy, 20,* 461–468.

Wright, J. (1978). An investigation of the effectiveness of a relaxation training model on discipline referrals. *Dissertation Abstracts International, 39(4),* 2162A.

Zaichkowsky, L. B., & Zaichkowsky, L. D. (1984). The effects of a school-based relaxation training program on fourth grade children. *Journal of Clinical Child Psychology, 13,* 81–85.

Zaichkowsky, L. B., Zaichkowsky, L. D., & Yeager, J. (1986). Biofeedback assisted relaxation training in the elementary classroom. *Elementary School Guidance and Counseling, 20,* 261–267.

Zitrin, C. M., Klein, D. F., & Woerner, M. G. (1980). Treatment of agoraphobia with group exposure in vivo and imipramine. *Archives of General Psychiatry, 37,* 63–72.

19

Differential Effects of Stress Management Therapies in Behavioral Medicine

PAUL M. LEHRER
RICHARD CARR
DEEPA SARGUNARAJ
ROBERT L. WOOLFOLK

In this chapter we review applications of stress management methods in treatment of various somatic disorders. As in the preceding chapter on applications to emotional and behavioral disorders, we include only disorders for which a body of controlled research provides evidence of effectiveness. For some disorders, stress management approaches now appear to be comprehensive treatments in themselves, and sometimes should be chosen in preference to various medical treatments, which pose more risks and sometimes show poorer long-term benefit. For other problems reviewed in this chapter, stress management methods are useful as adjuncts to medical treatment.

Cardiovascular Disorders

Hypertension

In controlling mild essential hypertension, behavioral treatments such as relaxation and anxiety management training appear to have an advantage over no-treatment, delayed-treatment, and waiting-list control procedures (e.g., Agras, Southam, & Taylor, 1983; Basler, Brinkmeier, Buser, Haehn, & Molders-Kober, 1982; Crowther, 1983; Jorgenson, Houstin, & Zurawski, 1981; Seer & Raeburn, 1980; Southam, Agras, Taylor, & Kraemer, 1982). However, when relaxation therapies are compared with daily home blood pressure monitoring, the results are less consistent. Some studies reveal an advantage for relaxation training (Goldstein, Shapiro, Thananopavarn, & Sambhi, 1982; Glasgow, Gaarder, & Engel, 1982), whereas others do not (Chesney, Black, Swan, & Ward, 1987; Jacob, Fortmann, Kraemer, Farquahar, & Agras, 1985). Nevertheless, Agras, Taylor, Kraemer, Southam, and Schneider (1987) found that 69% of those in a relaxation training group maintained adequate control of blood pressure at a 1-year follow-up, while only 41% in a blood pressure monitoring group also did so. The differences between groups did not persist at a 30-month follow-up.

Relaxation-based interventions have been shown in one study to have a prophylactic effect against heart disease. In a sample of industrial employees at high risk for coronary heart disease, Patel, Marmot, and Terry (1981) evaluated the efficacy of a behavioral treatment program (galvanic skin response biofeedback, progressive relaxation [PR], meditation, and stress education) against a control procedure (standard medical treatment only). Both groups received health education literature. After 8 weeks of training and again after 8 months, the behavioral treatment group showed a significantly greater reduction in systolic and diastolic blood pressure than the control group. Plasma renin activity and plasma aldosterone concentration both showed a greater decrease in the treatment group as well. The most interesting results were obtained 4 years later: The differences in blood pressure remained; more subjects in the control group reported having had angina and treatment for hypertension; and the incidence of ischemic heart disease, fatal myocardial infarction, and electrocardiographic evidence of ischemia was significantly greater in the control group (Patel et al., 1985).

Behavioral treatments, when used alone, are not as effective as antihypertensive medications in reducing blood pressure. Luborsky, Aucona, Masoni, Scolari, and Longoni (1980) compared standard pharmacological treatment with autogenic training (AT) and their combination. They found that drug treatment produced significantly greater decreases in both systolic and diastolic blood pressure than did AT alone. In a later study, Luborsky et al. (1982) used metronome-conditioned relaxation, biofeedback, and a physical exercise control procedure. They found that the advantage for drug treatment persisted throughout a 6-week period. Similar results were reported by Jacob et al. (1986), who compared PR, AT, a beta blocker, and a diuretic. Blood pressure decreased more in response to the two drugs than in response to the self-regulation techniques. Goldstein et al. (1982) compared the effects of drug treatment versus relaxation versus blood pressure feedback versus self-monitoring over a 2-month period. Both drug treatment and biofeedback resulted in decreased diastolic blood pressure, with the former resulting in greater changes in systolic blood pressure.

A meta-analytic comparison of nonpharmacological treatments with standard drug regimens showed that the latter produced greater decreases in blood pressure (Andrews, MacMahon, Austin, & Byrne, 1982). The treatment of essential hypertension by weight reduction, yoga, and PR each appeared to produce smaller but appreciable changes in blood pressure. Furthermore, the effects of meditation, exercise training, blood pressure feedback, and salt restriction tended to be inferior to those of other nonpharmacological regimens and were not significantly different from those of placebo treatment.

There is evidence that stress management techniques can decrease the doses of antihypertensive medications that may be needed (Blanchard et al., 1986; Glasgow, Engel, & D'Lugoff, 1989; Hatch et al., 1985; Lasser et al., 1987). In these studies, the behavioral treatment conditions were associated with significantly less medication consumption (without compensatory increases in blood pressure), compared to various control conditions. In view of the pronounced side effects of most anti-hypertensive medication and the low level of patient compliance when it is prescribed, behavioral procedures appear to hold considerable promise in the treatment of this problem. It should be noted, however, that the overall cost of combined medication and behavioral treatment has been found to be higher than that of medical treatment alone (Glasgow et al., 1989).

There is some inconsistent evidence that combinations of pharmacological and behavioral therapies have greater effects than either treatment individually (Agras & Jacob, 1979). Richter-Heinrich et al. (1981) observed that a combination of psychological/behavioral treatments resulted in a significantly greater decrease in blood pressure than a regimen of beta blockers over a 3-month period. The combination included relaxation training, systolic blood pressure biofeedback, blood pressure monitoring, physical exercise, and a psychoeducational program. The positive effects persisted over 1 year. Goldstein, Shapiro, and Thananopavarn (1984) found that drug treatment combined with relaxation and/or electromyographic biofeedback (EMG BFK) was superior to either pharmacological or nonpharmacological therapy alone.

Early reviews of the literature on behavioral treatment of hypertension reported no difference between blood pressure biofeedback and PR instruction, or among various forms of relaxation treatment (see Agras & Jacob, 1979; Frumkin, Nathan, Prout, & Cohen, 1978; Goldstein, 1982; Seer, 1979; Tarler-Benlolo, 1978). Nevertheless, there is evidence that various relaxation techniques do have differential effects on blood pressure. Techniques with a more direct autonomic focus tend to have greater antihypertensive effects than strictly muscularly oriented ones. At a follow-up session, Fray (1975) found that AT had a greater antihypertensive effect than EMG BFK. Longo (1984) found that deep breathing had a greater effect than guided imagery and PR. It is known that slow deep breathing has direct effects on the cardiovascular system (Kaufman & Schneiderman, 1986). However, two studies (McCoy, Blanchard, et al., 1988; Aivazyan, Zaitsev, Salenko, Yurenev, & Patrusheva, 1988) found thermal biofeedback (TBFK) to have even greater effects than breathing retraining combined with PR. Presumably TBFK produces more direct autonomic effects than breathing retraining, since it focuses on a particular autonomic response.

Three studies found TBFK to have greater effects than AT (Aivazyan et al., 1988; Blanchard, Khramelashvili, et al., 1988; Blanchard et al., 1986). These results can be compared with Freedman's (1991) data (described in Chapter 16), which suggest that TBFK may enlist two physiological mechanisms for peripheral vasodilation (decreased alpha and increased beta sympathetic activity), whereas AT produces general decreases in both varieties of sympathetic activity. The greater peripheral vasodilation produced by TBFK may be responsible for its greater antihypertensive effects. Similarly, Goldstein et al. (1982) found a definite advantage for the highly specific technique of blood pressure biofeedback over relaxation or self-monitoring.

Glasgow et al. (1982) controlled for differences in medication and compared a blood pressure monitoring condition, a systolic blood pressure feedback condition, and a PR plus meditation procedure. Biofeedback had an additive effect when combined with relaxation and a greater effect than either technique used alone. Slightly greater long-term effects were obtained for biofeedback than for relaxation alone. A follow-up of the same sample (Engel, Glasgow, & Gaarder, 1983) found that subjects receiving behavioral treatment could achieve and sustain decreases in blood pressure for at least 18 months. People who discontinued diuretic therapy tended to maintain reductions in blood pressure for at least 9 months. The authors advocate a stepped-care approach to the treatment of borderline hypertension: self-monitoring followed by systolic blood pressure feedback and then relaxation training. If on further follow-up blood pressure is then still uncontrolled, they recommend that drugs be introduced. One anomalous study produced findings opposite to this pattern: Blanchard, McCoy, et al. (1988) found greater antihypertensive effects for PR than for TBFK. One study found that TBFK, self-relaxation, and AT resulted in similar changes in blood pressure (Blanchard, Khramelashvili, et al., 1988).

Additional support for the notion that behavioral treatments with a specific autonomic focus are particularly helpful in controlling blood pressure comes from studies showing that mantra meditation (which we classify as having a predominantly cognitive focus) tends to have weaker antihypertensive effects than other relaxation or biofeedback techniques. Hafner (1982) found meditation to have weaker effects than biofeedback of skin resistance or EMG. Cohen and Sedlacek (1983) found meditation to have weaker effects than a combination of PR, AT, relaxing imagery, and both TBFK and EMG BFK. English and Baker (1983) found meditation to have weaker antihypertensive effects than PR; Sedlacek, Cohen, and Boxhill (1979) found meditation to have weaker effects than EMG BFK. An anomalous earlier study by Parker, Gilbert, and Thoreson (1978) found greater effects for meditation than for PR, although in a population of nonhypertensive alcoholics.

In a recent meta-analysis of studies funded by the National Institutes of Health, however, Kaufmann et al. (1988) found no significant effects of self-regulation on systolic blood pressure, compared with various control conditions, and no differences among the various approaches. (Unfortunately, however, in this analysis, TBFK and EMG BFK were combined into the same category.) Small (an average of 2 mm Hg) but significant effects with these techniques were obtained for diastolic blood pressure among nonmedicated patients. Effects were larger for subjects with initially higher levels of blood pressure. The investigators reported some evidence for more powerful effects among subjects who were given techniques that they themselves selected than among subjects who were offered no choice.

In a further recent review of relaxation therapy for hypertension, Jacob, Chesney, Williams, Ding, and Shapiro (1991) found a highly significant effect for relaxation therapies. In their review of studies, they did not include any that used biofeedback without concurrent relaxation therapy, but they did include some studies that were less rigorous than covered in Kaufmann et al.'s (1988) review, and noted that the demands of rigorous experimental design sometimes require compromises in doing therapy in the most clinically effective way. Jacob et al. (1991) found the best results for studies using multicomponent stress management strategies, followed by those using EMG BFK, and then those using TBFK. The poorest results were obtained from studies using relaxation methods alone. These conclusions differ from those we have drawn. However, in Jacob et al.'s review AT was lumped together with PR as a "relaxation therapy," whereas we consider it to be a technique with a greater autonomic focus than PR. Inconsistencies may also result from the wide variations in methodology among studies. This factor may have affected Jacob et al.'s results more than ours, because that review contrasted treatments used in different studies, whereas our review has focused on differences between treatments in comparative studies. Nevertheless, our review also draws conclusions from studies with diverse hypertensive populations, outcome criteria, baseline procedures. Thus, results should be interpreted with caution.

Several individual-difference factors may predict response to self-management therapies for hypertension. One is severity of hypertension, as described just above. Also, McGrady and Higgins (1989) found particularly striking results among hypertensives characterized by "autonomic overactivity . . . [and] chronic response to stress, such as high anxiety scores and high normal cortisol levels" (p. 277). However, Jacob et al. (1991) note that response to relaxation therapy is not diminished by pretreatment with beta blockers, thus indicating that a high level of adrenergic activity is not in itself a predictive factor, and perhaps that the mechanism for relaxation therapy effects is other than through reduction in sympathetic arousal. Jacob et al. also show that across studies, initial levels of anxiety and hostility are not consistent predictors of response to relaxation therapy. They conclude that the best predictors may be expectancy and motivation for behavioral treatment, but indicate that further research is necessary to confirm this.

Suggestion has also been used in the treatment of hypertension, and has produced significant therapeutic effects. Minsky (1978) found that suggestions to direct imagery toward expanding the arteries produced greater reductions in diastolic blood pressure among hypertensives than did general relaxation imagery (e.g., lying in a hammock). Similarly, Redmond, Gaylor, McDonald, and Shapiro (1974) found that suggestions to "make your heart beat slower and less forcefully, and your vessels less resistant to the flow of blood" (p. 287) had effects equivalent to those of three sessions of live instruction in PR. Agras, Horne, and Taylor (1982) found large differences in systolic blood pressure changes in a group told to expect immediate blood pressure decreases, compared to a group told to expect delayed decreases. They concluded that "cognitive processes can interfere with or promote the blood-pressure-lowering effect of muscle relaxation" (p. 394). However, these studies only examined the brief effects of suggestion over a few sessions, so the implications of these results for clinical treatment of hypertension are not clear.

In Chapter 16 we have argued that processes involved in hypnotic suggestion necessarily involve cognition, so that hypnosis might best be classified as a relatively more "cognitively" oriented technique than relaxation training or biofeedback. When cognitive approaches are compared with various relaxation and biofeedback therapies, the former appear to have weaker effects on blood pressure. Lustman and Sowa (1983) found greater antihypertensive effects for EMG BFK than for stress inoculation training. Longo (1984) found greater decreases in diastolic blood pressure after breathing retraining or PR than after training in guided imagery, and greater decreases in systolic blood pressure after deep breathing than after guided imagery. Achmon, Granek, Golomb, and Hart (1989) found greater decreases in blood pressure following heart rate biofeedback training (for slowing heart rate) than following cognitive therapy (CT) for control of anger. However, a study combining CT and relaxation therapy produced results consistent with those produced by studies of suggestion. Chesney et al. (1987) found that the addition of CT to a relaxation therapy program resulted in larger decreases in blood pressure than did relaxation therapy alone.

Combinations of some individually effective nonpharmacological treatments do not appear to be more effective than single techniques. For example, in a sample of medicated hypertensives, Hafner (1982) evaluated the efficacy of meditation alone and of meditation plus biofeedback against a no-treatment control. Biofeedback-assisted relaxation enhanced the effects of meditation by producing an earlier decrease in diastolic blood pressure and heart rate, but the differences between the groups were not significant. Lasser et al. (1987) found that the effects of stress management training (primarily PR) for mildly hypertensive subjects on no medication were equivalent to those produced by controlling diet. Combining dietary and stress management did not produce an additive effective in keeping subjects from requiring antihypertensive medication. All active nonpharmacological treatments had greater effects than a control condition, in which no nonpharmacological treatments were given. Adding specific autonomically focused training, however, may augment the effects of other relaxation techniques (see Glasgow et al., 1982, as discussed above). Additional research is necessary to verify this conclusion.

In their review of the literature on behavioral treatment of hypertension, Wadden and Luborsky (1984) concluded that behavioral treatments are generally superior to no treatment and to attention placebo procedures, and that drug treatments produce greater benefits than behavioral approaches. McCaffrey and Blanchard (1985) observed in their review that a lack of significant differences among techniques in some studies may be attributable to various differences in methodologies. These include differing definitions of mild hypertension and variations in the degree to which initial differences in blood pressure are controlled. The Joint National Committee on Detection, Evaluation, and Treatment of High Blood Pressure (1988) concluded that relaxation therapies require further evaluation before they can be considered to be definitive treatment for hypertensive patients; however, the committee did recommend that they be used for treatment of mild hypertension, and as an adjunct to medication for treatment of more severe hypertension.

In summary, despite some studies' finding no differences between relaxation methods and blood pressure monitoring, the balance of the evidence indicates that some forms of stress management training should play a role in the treatment of hypertension. However, antihypertensive medications generally produce larger antihypertensive effects than stress management techniques. Where blood pressure is significantly elevated, it should not be considered safe to maintain hypertensive patients on behavioral treatment alone, unless blood pressure levels are well controlled by these methods. Nevertheless, stress management therapies can, under some circumstances, reduce the amount of antihypertensive medication required to maintain safe levels of blood pressure; indeed, they can sometimes eliminate the need for it altogether. More strongly physiologically oriented techniques may have stronger effects than those with a more cognitive focus, and techniques with a specific autonomic focus tend to have stronger effects than muscularly oriented ones. Although the addition of CT or suggestion to a relaxation regimen may augment the effects of the latter, cognitive interventions appear to have weaker effects on blood pressure control than relaxation or biofeedback training. Meditation appears to have smaller effects than other relaxation techniques, perhaps because of its more cognitive focus. Although there is some inconsistent indication that self-monitoring of blood pressure may be just as powerful as a complete behavioral package, methodological problems may obscure some of the behavioral treatment effects in the studies that support this conclusion.

Oakley and Shapiro (1989) offer the following suggestions in the design of drug versus nondrug comparisons: (1) Pretreatment assessments should be performed while the subjects are drug-free or taking very small doses of drugs, so that everyone begins treatment at a natural and comparable level of blood pressure; (2) changes in medication during treatment should be made according to systematic criteria; (3) a minimum of a 1-year follow-up should be required following any drug withdrawal; and (4) in studies of drug–behavioral treatment interactions, one or two classes of drugs with defined dose levels should be used. McCoy, Fein, et al. (1988) have recommended that future research use 24-hour blood pressure and end-organ changes as outcome criteria. Blanchard (1990) recommends that a model be constructed relating expectations, task performance, home practice, and biochemical variables to the effects of TBFK. Also, a more careful evaluation of cognitively oriented therapies is necessary, as are identification of treatment response predictors and assessment of dropout rates (see Jacob, Wing, & Shapiro, 1987).

Raynaud's Disease

In Raynaud's disease, blood flow to the periphery of the body is severely restricted because of spasms in the peripheral blood vessels. It is a disease with potentially very deleterious consequences, including the possibility of gangrene and the loss of fingers and toes. Medical treatment for this condition often involves major surgery (e.g., sympathectomy) or medication to dilate the blood vessels. These often have severe side effects. Behavioral approaches are not invasive and have few adverse side effects, and thus present an attractive alternative. Most behavioral research has focused on biofeedback and relaxation strategies, although two studies using classical conditioning have also been reported.

The classical conditioning studies involved repeated associations of hand immersions in hot water with exposure of the whole body to cold. At the end of 6 weeks, a group given classical conditioning did not differ from those trained with EMG BFK and digital TBFK. At a 1-year follow-up, however, only the classical conditioning group retained the ability to increase skin temperature (Jobe, Sampson, Roberts, & Beetham, 1982; Jobe, Sampson, Roberts, & Kelly, 1986). The clinical effects were positive, but the technique requires replication and further evaluation.

Early reviews of self-control techniques such as PR, AT, and TBFK (Blanchard, 1979; Pinkerton, Hughes, & Wenrich, 1982; Sappington, Fiorito, & Brehony, 1979; Surwit, 1982) suggested that relaxation and finger TBFK training were approximately equally effective for treating Raynaud's disease. Different conclusions were reached in a more recent study by Kelson and Bryson-Brockmann (1985), however. They compared the efficacy of TBFK and AT in increasing finger temperature in subjects complaining of chronically cold hands. Only TBFK training produced consistent increases in finger temperature. In a recent review, Rose and Carlson (1987) conclude that several methods of biofeedback and relaxation training are superior to no treatment. They report that a combination of TBFK and the cold stress technique seems superior to TBFK or AT alone, but caution that differences among methods are not consistent.

Studies by Freedman and his coworkers have conclusively shown an advantage for TFBK. The potency of the intervention increased when cold stress was used in training (Freedman, Lynn, Ianni, & Hale, 1981; Freedman, Ianni, & Wenig, 1983, 1985). The superiority over EMG BFK, AT, and cognitive stress procedures suggests that the effects of TBFK can be attributed to a specific physiological mechanism, which is partially independent of a general reduction in sympathetic arousal (Freedman, 1985). This issue has been discussed in more detail in Chapter 16 in the section comparing TBFK with AT.

In conclusion, it appears that various stress management techniques are beneficial in the treatment of Raynaud's disease. TBFK has the greatest effects, and treatment is potentiated by training during cold stress. Classical conditioning procedures may be useful adjuncts to relaxation or biofeedback techniques, but require further evaluation. Differential and additive effects of pharmacological and nonpharmacological treatments have not yet been evaluated.

Pain

Headache

The literature comparing PR and biofeedback for treatment of tension and vascular headaches has been reviewed extensively (Andrasik & Blanchard, 1987; Blanchard, Andrasik, Ahles, Teders, & O'Keefe, 1980; Blanchard & Andrasik, 1987; Holroyd & Penzien, 1986). A review by Blanchard, Ahles, and Shaw (1979) concluded that relaxation or biofeedback training helps between 40% and 80% of randomly assigned tension headache sufferers. In a meta-analysis of client variables in the behavioral treatment of tension headache, Holroyd and Penzien (1986) found that response to treatment was related to age (individuals under the age of 35 did better), sex (women did better), and source of referral (individuals referred to the study by their physicians did more poorly than individuals who volunteered in response to advertisements). It was not related to type of treatment (EMG BFK, PR, or the combination of the two); as we will show later, however, comparative studies show a different picture here. Neither was it related to therapist contact time, or to whether the treatment protocol specifically focused on transfer of training to outside the therapy situation. The largest proportion of outcome variance was explained by age (30%). Response to the active treatments was significantly greater than response to pseudotreatment controls. Studies reporting follow-up data showed significantly greater improvement at follow-up than immediately after treatment.

Earlier reviews of this literature had concluded that EMG BFK and PR both have substantial therapeutic benefits, and that their effects are approximately equivalent (Beaty & Haynes, 1979; Blanchard, Andrasik, & Silver, 1980; Silver & Blanchard, 1978). An implication that had been drawn from these conclusions—namely, that relaxation therapies are preferable to biofeedback because they do not require expensive equipment—may no longer be valid. The price of clinically useful biofeedback equipment is now less than that of several individual therapy sessions, and a month's rental of more elaborate equipment can cost as little as one session. Under these conditions, it may be even more economical to have the client do much of the biofeedback training at home than it is to have a highly trained professional administer relaxation therapy.

More recent research suggests that biofeedback treatment may be incrementally helpful to some headache sufferers. Blanchard et al. (1982) administered biofeedback therapy to headache patients who were initially unimproved after relaxation therapy. Significant improvement occurred in headache activity, with the greatest amount occurring among individuals with combined migraine and tension headaches. Tension headache sufferers in this study received frontalis EMG BFK, and migraine headache sufferers and sufferers from both kinds of headaches received TBFK. Another study from the same laboratory, using the same research design with migraine headache sufferers, found very similar results (Blanchard et al., 1982). Thus biofeedback may have a critically important treatment role for some individuals, even when relaxation therapy also is used.

For migraine headaches, autonomically focused techniques (e.g., TBFK, AT) are often used in preference to muscularly focused ones (e.g., PR, EMG BFK). The rationale for this lies in the presumed mechanism of action. The prodromal phase of a classical migraine headache is characterized by vasoconstriction, followed by severe vasodilation, the latter of which causes migraine pain. Peripheral vasodilation (via TBFK) is believed to reduce migraine headaches by blocking the preheadache cephalic vasoconstriction, either through direct biofeedback-induced effects on the vasculature, or indirectly, via a reduction in general autonomic arousal (Lisspers & Öst, 1990). Lacroix et al. (1983) found greater reductions in migraine symptoms with TBFK than with PR or EMG BFK. This study also found an association between decreases in migraine symptoms and improved thermal control. Daly, Donn, Galliher, and Zimmerman (1983) compared relaxation training with TBFK for the treatment of migraine and tension headache. They found a greater decrease in hours per month of headache activity with TBFK. In the latter study, however, the poorer showing of PR, particularly among the subjects with tension headaches, may have resulted from the use of taped instructions.

Despite the advantages of autonomically over muscularly oriented techniques for treating vascular headaches, a narrow autonomic focus may be a liability in treatment of migraine headache. A partial-crossover-design study by Huber and Huber (1979) reported that the combination of rational–emotive therapy (a kind of CT) and AT provided relief to migraine sufferers who previously had been unsuccessfully treated by medication and relaxation therapy alone. Blanchard and Andrasik (1982) reported that TBFK alone (in contrast to TBFK plus AT) was not statistically superior to a placebo (34.6% improvement vs. 27.6%, according to an index incorporating measures of frequency, intensity, and duration of headaches). They concluded that relaxation plays a crucial role in the treatment of migraine headache. The advantages of AT in this study probably did not emanate from the specific cognitive components in AT. This is suggested in the results of a recent well-controlled study of the incremental effects of CT over a combination of TBFK and PR. This study included four contrasting groups: TBFK plus PR; TBFK plus PR combined with CT; a credible attention placebo control; and headache monitoring (Blanchard, Appelbaum, Radnitz, Morrill, et al., 1990). The subjects were a sample of 116 vascular headache patients. No differences emerged between the two active treatment groups; that is, CT added nothing to TBFK alone.

An apparent contradiction to this theory was described in several studies, where training in hand cooling (vasoconstriction) showed outcome results equivalent to training in the more traditional hand-warming strategy (Gauthier, Bois, Allaire, & Drolet, 1981; Kewman & Roberts, 1980; Largen, Mathew, Dobbins, & Claghorn, 1981; for a review see Beatty, 1982). Gauthier et al. (1981) suggested that stabilization, not directional control, may be the key to successful treatment of vascular headache. It is also possible that learning to cool the hands taught subjects the general skill of peripheral vascular control, which they then were able to use *bidirectionally* to control their headaches.

The rationale for using muscularly focused treatments for tension headaches is that excessive muscle tension, particularly in the facial area, is believed to cause tension headaches. Thus, reducing muscle tension via frontalis EMG BFK or PR should reduce headache activity. There is evidence that muscularly oriented therapies produce more impressive reductions in tension headache activity than autonomically oriented ones do. A study by Staples, Coursey, and Smith (1975) found lower frontalis EMG levels during the last of 10 sessions of training in PR and in EMG BFK than in AT. There were no EMG differences between groups at follow-up, however, and no differences in anxiety between groups at any time. All groups showed anxiety reductions. Detrick (1977/1978) compared a combination of AT and TBFK with a combination of EMG BFK and PR, and found the latter to be more effective in reducing self-reported tension headache activity and frontalis EMG levels. Janssen and Neutgens (1986) found PR to be more effective than AT for muscle contraction headaches, and found no differences between these treatments for migraine headaches.

Blanchard et al. (1982) reported that 52% of a sample of tension headache sufferers were clinically improved (50% reduction in headache index) following training in relaxation alone; 37% were clinically improved in another study (Teders et al., 1984). Blanchard, Andrasik, Ahles, et al.'s (1980) meta-analysis showed approximately a 60% reduction in tension headache activity for PR, frontal EMG BFK, and their combination (PR plus EMG BFK), all of which were superior to psychological and medication placebos. Blanchard et al. (1985) found greater improvement with PR among tension headache sufferers than among subjects with a vascular component in their headaches, but a greater effect for adding a TBFK procedure among the latter subjects.

Biofeedback alone appears to be less effective than a combination of biofeedback and a relevant relaxation technique. Blanchard and Andrasik (1982) reported that TBFK alone (in contrast to TBFK plus AT) is not statistically superior to a placebo in treatment of migraine headaches. They concluded that relaxation plays a crucial role in the treatment of this problem. In another study PR fared better than

EMG BFK only at a 4-year follow-up (Blanchard, Andrasik, Guarnieri, Neff, & Rodichok, 1987).

Cognitive factors appear to be particularly important in the treatment and, perhaps, etiology of tension headache. Andrasik and Holroyd (1980) found that reductions in frontalis EMG did not correlate with headache improvement after PR and EMG biofeedback training. *Perception* of an increased sense of control did correlate, however. In a later attempt to replicate those results, they found that experimentally manipulating subjects to believe that they were successful at the biofeedback task (i.e., that they successfully increased frontalis muscle tension or successfully decreased muscle tension) was more important than obtaining actual relaxation of the frontalis (Holroyd et al., 1984). The investigators speculated that perceived control over the muscles may lead to increases in perceived self-competence, and to the belief that tension headaches can be controlled. This may in turn lead to a greater sense of relaxation and diminished physiological activity, including lower muscle tension in the head and neck.

Consistent with this, CT appears to be a particularly potent method for treating tension headaches. Holroyd and Andrasik (1982) found greater effects for CT than for biofeedback therapy in treatment of tension headaches. These results persisted through a 2-year follow-up. Similar results were reported by Murphy, Lehrer, and Jurish (1990). These results persisted, and were even exaggerated, at a 3-year follow-up. A comparison of home-based treatments for tension headaches found stronger effects for a combination of CT and relaxation–biofeedback therapy than for the relaxation–biofeedback therapy alone (Tobin, Holroyd, Baker, Reynolds, & Holm, 1988). An intriguing study on two subjects by Kremsdorf, Kochanowicz, and Costell (1981) found that CT reduced self-reported headache activity but not EMG levels, while EMG BFK reduced EMG levels but not self-reported headache activity. Blanchard, Appelbaum, Radnitz, Michultka, et al. (1990) found no significant differences in reduction of tension headache activity between PR and a combination of PR and CT. However, they did note a nonsignificant tendency toward greater improvement in the latter group. Using a 50% reduction in headache index as a criterion for clinical improvement, they found improvement rates of 31.6% for PR (a lower percentage than in previous studies), 62.5% for CT plus PR, 43.8% for placebo controls, and 20% for headache monitoring only.

The effects of CT on *migraine* headache are less clear. No systematic differences have been found between relaxation–biofeedback therapy and CT for migraine headache. Knapp (1982) found no differences in maintenance of migraine headache treatment gains at a 1-year follow-up between a cognitive–behavioral stress coping treatment and biofeedback for temporal artery vasoconstriction. Sorbi and colleagues (Sorbi & Tellegen, 1986; Sorbi, Tellegen, & du Long, 1989) found equivalent effects on migraine headaches for a cognitive–behavioral approach to stress coping training and AT at 6-month and 3-year follow-ups.

Hypnosis does not appear to offer advantages over other therapies described in this book for treatment of headache. Andreychuk and Skriver (1975) found that alpha biofeedback, hypnotic induction, and hand TBFK produced equivalent decreases on a self-reported headache index among migraine headache sufferers. Schlutter, Golden, and Blume (1980) studied response to experimentally induced pain among sufferers from tension headaches. They found no differences among hypnotic suggestion, EMG BFK, and a combination of biofeedback and PR. The measures included self-rated pain and tolerance for pain. Spinhoven (1988) concluded from a literature review that there are no differences in effectiveness between hypnotic and nonhypnotic headache control procedures.

Finally, a group of "chronic, daily, high-intensity headache sufferers," who appear to be refractory to the treatments described here, has been identified. These individuals are more anxious and hysterical, and complain of more physical symptoms, than other headache patients (Blanchard, Appelbaum, Radnitz, Jaccard, & Dentinger, 1989). These patients may represent a homogeneous and diagnosable subset that may respond to more long-term treatment and more training in cognitive stress coping methods.

In summary, although issues regarding their mechanisms of action remain unresolved, CT, relaxation, and biofeedback all appear to have a role in the treatment of headaches. Patients with tension headache show about a 60% reduction after either PR or frontalis EMG BFK. The results of PR seem to persist longer than those of frontalis EMG BFK only, although some nonresponders to PR eventually respond successfully to EMG BFK, suggesting that the two treatments operate through different pathways (Blanchard, 1987). CT is consistently found to be more effective than muscle relaxation methods for treating tension headaches. Thus chronic tension headaches may partially result from hypersensitivity or hyperreactivity to stress and/or unpleasant body sensations. These reactions may produce diminished pain tolerance and perhaps increased muscle contractions, which, in a vicious spiral, may augment pain sensations. Consistent with this, Lehrer and Murphy (1991) reported diminished pain tolerance and augmented somatic and cognitive reactivity to laboratory stressors among tension headache sufferers; and Murphy (1986/1987) reported less effective use of stress coping strategies among this population. Chronic vascular headache (migraine, migraine–tension combined) is somewhat less amenable to behavioral treatment, and is probably best treated by TBFK with abbreviated AT (approximately 51% improvement). Training in PR can also help, although it is less effective, apparently because of its lack of specific autonomic focus. The combination of AT and TBFK appears to be more powerful than either element alone, although the reasons for this must be studied in greater detail. The role, if any, of cognitive components in treatment of migraine headache has yet to be determined.

Comparisons between drug and behavioral treatments have tended to show slightly better effects for behavioral treatments, but research on these comparisons has just begun. One recent study (Holroyd, Nash, Pingel, Cordingley, & Jerome, 1991) compared cognitive–behavioral therapy with amitriptyline among a population of sufferers from tension headaches. Both treatments were clinically effective, with stronger results for cognitive–behavioral therapy. Holroyd et al. (1991) also found greater effects for a combination of relaxation and CT than for amitriptyline in treatment of tension headaches. Holroyd et al. (1989) compared relaxation plus TBFK with a course of ergotamine tartrate for treating migraine headaches. At a 3-year follow-up assessment, they found better maintenance of therapeutic effects with the behavioral treatment. However, in a meta-analysis of the literature on propranolol and relaxation–TBFK approaches to treating migraine headaches,

Holroyd and Penzien (1990) reported equivalent effects for the two approaches (55% reduction in headache activity for each).

Other Pain Conditions

In a study of patients with lower back pain, Kravitz (1977/1978) found equivalent improvements with PR and with a combination of PR and EMG BFK. Resting paralumbar EMG among the patients did not differ from corresponding levels among normal subjects, although patients' EMG levels were higher during various isometric contractions not directly connected with movement of the back. Paralumbar EMG levels during isometric exercises were reduced more in those receiving EMG BFK plus PR than in those receiving simple PR. However, interpretation of this finding is clouded somewhat, because control subjects also reduced EMG levels more than PR subjects. No differences between treatment groups were found under rest conditions. In a similar study by Jerome (1978/1979), PR was found to be effective in reducing lower back pain and paraspinal muscle tension. This study also found advantages for combining PR with electrocautery and facet injections. Barlow (1977) reported several cases of low back pain successfully treated by the Alexander technique. This method involves training in less stressful use of the body while physically active.

Several studies provide data consistent with the notion that pain has an important cognitive component, which is specifically amenable to cognitively oriented treatments. Turner (1982) found slightly stronger effects for CT than for relaxation therapy in the treatment of back pain. Similarly, in a study of patients with severe burns, Achterberg, Kenner, and Lawlis (1988) found that adding a guided imagery procedure to taped PR and breathing instructions produced greater decreases in pain ratings. In a study of dental phobia, hypnotic relaxation and suggestions of pain reduction were more effective than PR in reducing self-reported pain caused by an injection (McAmmond, Davidson, & Kovitz, 1971). Hypnosis was also more effective in convincing subjects that the treatment was effective, and in inducing subjects to visit a dentist within 5 months after treatment. The results were not unequivocal, however. In a test of pain tolerance, hypnosis was superior to PR only for subjects with initially "medium" levels of skin conductance. There were no between-group differences for subjects who initially had low skin conductance levels, and PR was the more effective treatment among subjects with initially high skin conductance levels. Thus, reduction of somatic arousal may be a particularly important intervention among pain patients with initially high skin conductance levels (see studies by Sternbach, 1968, and Mersky & Spear, 1967, showing relationships between pain and anxiety, which is often accompanied by elevated physiological arousal). Among persons with lower arousal, however, pain perception may be more closely related to cognitive factors than to physiological arousal. Some doubt may be cast on the interpretability of this study by the fact that hypnotic subjects were given live inductions, whereas PR instructions were delivered via tape recording.

Hypnosis does not appear to produce incremental effects when combined with other stress management methods. Stam, McGrath, and Brooke (1984) assigned individuals suffering from temporomandibulor joint pain to three conditions: hypnosis and cognitive coping skills, relaxation and cognitive coping skills, and a no-treatment control. The signs and symptoms of temporomandibular dysfunction decreased more in the two treatment groups than in the control group, with no differences between the active treatments. However, actual differences between relaxation and hypnosis may have been obscured by the presence of CT in both groups. In a population of adult patients with chronic pain, Edelson and Fitzpatrick (1989) similarly reported no differences between hypnosis and a cognitive coping procedure that was identical to the hypnotic one, but without induction of a formal hypnotic trance. They found equivalent improvement in both groups in pain intensity, compared with a group receiving an attention placebo. Wall and Womack (1989) compared hypnosis with a cognitively based coping strategy for management of pain among children undergoing painful bone marrow aspiration or lumbar puncture procedures. Both procedures produced decreases in reports of pain, but no changes in anxiety; no differences were found between these treatments. Pain reduction was not related to degree of hypnotizability. It is notable that literature reviews have consistently reported hypnosis to be one of the standard effective behavioral treatment modalities for pain (Bush, 1987; Carey & Burish, 1988; Estlander & Laaksonen, 1984; Jay, Elliott, & Varni, 1986; O'Brien & Weisbrot, 1983; Place, 1984; Whipple, 1987).

Gastrointestinal Disorders

Peptic Ulcer

Peptic ulcer is a potentially life-threatening condition that occurs when the walls of the stomach or duodenum are eroded by hydrochloric acid and pepsin. These lesions are associated with acid secretions and with abdominal pain during periods of gastric motility. There may be perforations in the stomach lining and at times extensive blood loss. Stress management training is promising as an adjunctive intervention for this condition.

An early study (Chappel, Stafano, Rogerson, & Pike, 1936) applied 6 weeks of didactic training that included education about etiology, relaxation training, and training in use of positive self-statements. Subjects receiving this interventions showed greater reduction in ulcer symptoms than did a group receiving only dietary and drug treatment. The treatment gains persisted at a 1-year follow-up. An uncontrolled study by Beaty (1976) suggests that relaxation training, when taught as a stress management technique, can reduce or elminate the symptoms of peptic ulcer. At a 30-month follow-up, Brooks and Richardson (1980) found fewer recurrences of ulcerative symptoms among subjects receiving assertiveness training and relaxation, compared with untreated controls.

In a review of this literature, Whitehead and Basmajian (1982) concluded that there is a need for a large extended trial comparing relaxation training to medical management with antacids and cimetidine. They recommended that X-rays and endoscopy be used as outcome measures. To our knowledge, this has not yet been done.

Irritable Bowel Syndrome

Irritable bowel syndrome (IBS) is characterized by abdominal pain and/or altered bowel habits persisting longer than 3 months, in the absence of demonstrable disease. It may also include other symptoms, such as nausea, headaches, insomnia, fatigue, anxiety and depression. Treatment of IBS through psychological interventions has had encouraging results.

Hislop (1980) found that brief psychotherapy aimed at increasing insight and self-reliance resulted in symptom remission for 50% of a sample of unmedicated IBS sufferers. A follow-up assessment a year later revealed an improvement in anxiety, fatigue, insomnia, mood, diarrhea, and nausea. Abdominal pain tended to be less responsive. Svedlund (1983) added psychotherapy to a standard medical regimen (i.e., bulk-forming agents, anticholinergic drugs, antacids, and mild tranquilizers), and found significant decreases in reports of abdominal pain, depression, anxiety, and bowel dysfunction.

A specific focus on relaxation and gastrointestinal motility appears to be more effective than more general psychotherapy. Whorwell, Prior, and Faragher (1984) found that hypnotherapy aimed at general relaxation and control of intestinal motility was more effective than supportive psychotherapy centering on exploration of common problems and stressful life events. After 3 months of hypnotherapy, clients reported a significant decrease in bowel dysfunction, abdominal pain, and distension, as compared to the psychotherapy group.

Several studies combining relaxation and CT have also found positive results. Lynch and Zamble (1987) found significant decreases in symptoms following a combination of relaxation, assertiveness training, and cognitive restructuring. Neff and Blanchard (1987) reported successful treatment of IBS clients with PR, TBFK, educational information, and cognitive stress coping strategies. Use of this program in a small-group format also resulted in a significant decrease in abdominal pain and diarrhea (Blanchard & Schwarz, 1987). The clients classified as "successes" reported improvement in depression, state anxiety, and psychosomatic symptoms; the "failures" did not deteriorate on any of the measures (Blanchard, Radnitz, Schwarz, Neff, & Gerardi, 1987). The treatment gains persisted at a 2-year follow-up (Blanchard & Schwarz, 1988). Definitive conclusions require more evidence from controlled studies using objective outcome measures (Langeluddecke, 1985). Stern, Koch, Stewart, and Vasey (1987) suggested that the electrograstrogram may be useful as an index of gastric motor activity.

Other Disorders

Asthma

In many studies, relaxation-based treatments have been shown to produce statistically significant improvement in asthma. However, the magnitude and consistency of these effects have generally fallen short of *clinical* significance, according to criteria for effectiveness generally accepted for drug studies (King, 1980; Richter & Dahme,

1982). A more recent study (Lehrer, Hochron, McCann, Swartzman, & Reba, 1986) did produce a clinically significant improvement on the methacholine challenge test, reflecting a decrease in asthmatic reactivity of the airways (a definitional characteristic of asthma). This study utilized frontalis and trapezius EMG BFK along with PR, and also demonstrated greater relaxation effects in individuals with primary asthmatic obstruction in the upper airways. In the latter population, parasympathetic activation is thought to produce bronchoconstriction. Neither of these latter findings was replicated in a subsequent study, however, which used PR alone and prestabilized subjects on asthma medication before behavioral intervention (Lehrer et al., 1991). Possible reasons for the discrepancies in results may be (1) the use of biofeedback in the former study but not the latter; and (2) the possibility that relaxation may not have an incremental effect over an optimal medical regime.

Although several of the studies of relaxation therapy showing significant effects on asthma used EMG BFK to the facial and/or respiratory areas as a component of training (Davis, Saunders, Creer, & Chai, 1973; Lehrer et al., 1986; Scherr & Crawford, 1978; Scherr, Crawford, Sergent, & Scherr, 1975), only one study has directly compared relaxation training alone and relaxation combined with facial EMG BFK (Davis et al., 1973). As pointed out in the comprehensive review by Kotses and Glaus (1981), although the biofeedback procedure produced a greater improvement in pulmonary function than relaxation therapy alone, this difference could not be ascribed to differential effects on facial muscle tension, because the two groups did not differ on this measure. However, the work of Kotses and his coworkers (Harver & Kotses, 1984; Glaus & Kotses, 1983; Kotses et al., 1991; Kotses & Miller, 1987) does suggest that facial muscle EMG BFK produces specific effects on decreasing parasympathetically mediated bronchoconstriction. EMG BFK to the limbs produces no such effect (Glaus & Kotses, 1983; Harver & Kotses, 1984). Kotses and his colleagues ascribe these changes to a direct link between facial muscle tension and vagus nerve activity, through a hypothesized vagal–trigeminal reflex. A clinical trial on 29 asthmatic children compared the long-term (8-month) effects of training to decrease facial muscle tension with training to hold it at the same level (Kotses et al., 1991). Subjects in the group trained to decrease muscle tension produced higher rates of air flow (FEV$_1$/FVC) in both short-term and long-term assessments. These subjects also showed greater improvements in their attitudes toward asthma and in anxiety.

Peper and his colleagues (Peper, Smith, & Waddell, 1987; Tibbetts & Peper, 1989) focused on the muscles involved in respiration. They used trapezius EMG BFK to help asthmatics decrease the use of muscles of the upper trunk in respiration. Hyperventilation is a common occurrence in asthma and may be produced by thoracic breathing (Ley, 1985a, 1985b). It may be responsible for some of the increases in asthmatic symptoms associated with anxiety and panic (Brooks et al., 1989; Clark, 1982; Kinsman, Luparello, Banion, & Sheldon, 1973; Kinsman, Dahlem, Spector, & Staudenmayer, 1977).

Peper theorizes that less effortless breathing is produced by simultaneous relaxation in the trapezius and lower torso areas. He and his coworkers demonstrated that maneuvers involving increased muscle tension in the diaphragmatic area actually can induce wheezing in asthmatic individuals (Peper et al., 1987). Consistent with Peper's theory is a case described by Hibbert and Pilsbury (1988), in which asthma was triggered by episodes of stress-induced hyperventilation. Asthmatic exacerbations were eliminated by training in controlled breathing, directed at avoidance of hyperventilation. Peper's procedure also includes biofeedback for increased inspiratory force, using an incentive inspirometer. Although he has reported clinically significant improvement in a number of individuals using the procedure, a controlled evaluation is still lacking.

Cancer

Various relaxation strategies have been used to treat the side effects of cancer therapy, such as nausea, emesis, and anorexia; however, the literature in this area is still small and tentative. We nevertheless include it here because of the important potential for applications of stress management therapies with this dreaded disease.

Dixon (1984) evaluated the relative effects of relaxation and nutritional supplementation in 55 cancer patients (mean age 59.6 years) assessed as nutritionally at risk. Subjects were randomly assigned to one of four conditions: (1) nutritional supplementation; (2) relaxation training; (3) both nutritional supplementation and relaxation training; or (4) neither nutritional supplementation nor relaxation training. Gain was greatest for the relaxation group; the most severe loss occurred in the control group. The findings suggest that the cachexia of cancer may be slowed or reversed through relaxation training. Morrow (1986) evaluated the effects of various interventions on anticipatory nausea to chemotherapy drugs. Ninety-two ambulatory patients (ages 19–76) were assigned to one of four conditions: systematic desensitization (SD), relaxation only, Rogerian counseling, and a no-treatment control. Subjects received standard clinic treatment for symptom control. Compared with the other three groups, subjects given SD reported a significant decrease in the severity and duration of anticipatory nausea from baseline to follow-up. Both SD and relaxation produced a significant decrease in the duration and severity of posttreatment nausea, compared with that of controls. Results were independent of subjects' ratings of their expectation for success, the credibility of the procedure, or the credibility of the experimenter. The authors conclude that anticipatory side effects are conditioned, and that both relaxation and the use of a stimulus hierarchy are necessary components of SD treatment for anticipatory nausea resulting from chemotherapy.

There is some evidence that administration of stress management therapies by competent professionals is necessary for their success in this application. Carey and Burish (1987) evaluated the effectiveness of three strategies for delivering relaxation training to cancer chemotherapy patients who were experiencing treatment-related side effects. Forty-five patients were randomly assigned to one of four treatment conditions: (1) PR and guided relaxation imagery provided by a professional therapist; (2) PR and guided imagery provided by a trained volunteer (i.e., paraprofessional) therapist; (3) PR and guided imagery provided by professionally prepared audiotapes; or (4) standard treatment (i.e., antiemetic only) control. Patients were assessed on self-report, physiological, and nurse observation measures during five sequential chemotherapy sessions. The results showed that professionally administered PR and guided imagery reduced emotional distress and physiological arousal and increased food intake in cancer patients undergoing chemotherapy, compared with both audiotaped and paraprofessionally administered training. The latter two strategies did not reduce symptoms more than the standard treatment.

In a study of relaxation therapy for insomnia secondary to cancer, 30 subjects were randomly assigned to either routine care or PR (Cannici, Malcolm, & Peek, 1983). PR training was administered in individual sessions on 3 consecutive days. Twenty-six of the subjects were available for follow-up 3 months later. Mean sleep onset latency was reduced from 124 to 29 minutes in the 15 patients receiving PR. Those receiving routine care had means of 116 and 104 minutes, in comparison; the mean differences in sleep latency were maintained at follow-up.

There are few studies comparing the effects of various nonpharmacological strategies for managing the side effects of cancer therapy, or comparing these treatments with various pharmacological alternatives. This is an important area for future investigation.

Insomnia

The study of nonmedical treatments for insomnia has become more sophisticated in the last decade. One reason for this has been the publication of a diagnostic system (Association of Sleep Disorders Centers, 1979) that underscores the importance of assessing beyond the subjective complaint of a sleep problem. Borkovec (1979) drew the distinction between "idiopathic insomnia" (i.e., insomnia that is evidenced in all-night electroencephalographic [EEG] recordings) and "pseudoinsomnia" (i.e., insomnia that is revealed only in self-report measures). He described data showing that PR is an effective treatment for the former, but not for the latter, when compared with appropriate placebo conditions.

Research on behavioral treatment of insomnia using self-report measures has suggested that insomnia is helped approximately equally by various behavioral methods. Woolfolk, Carr-Kaffashan, McNulty, and Lehrer (1976) found equivalent improvements in self-reports of predormital insomnia for meditation and PR; Nicassio and Bootzin (1974) found equivalent effects for PR and AT; Turner and Ascher (1979) found equivalent effects for PR training, paradoxical intention, and stimulus control procedures; and Haynes, Sides, and Lockwood (1977) found equivalent effects for taped PR and EMG BFK. All the methods were superior to control treatments. Gershman and Clouser (1974) found taped PR training and SD to be equally effective in improving self-reported ability to fall asleep. Both were more effective than a no-treatment control condition on this measure; however, only PR improved subjects' self-reported ability to go back to sleep after having been awakened. This possibly resulted from the greater amount of time devoted to relaxation training in the PR condition than in the SD condition, of which relaxation is only one component.

Borkovec and Fowles (1973) found no differences among hypnotic relaxation, PR, and a self-relaxation control in sleep improvement. It is possible, however, that the self-relaxation condition included important components of active treatment: regular relaxation during the day and focus on internal bodily states. All three treatments were more effective than a no-treatment control. When, in another study, an adequate control for expectancy and demand characteristics was used, PR and SD were found to be more effective than a pseudodesensitization placebo (Steinmark & Borkovec, 1974). Using similar procedures in other studies, Borkovec, Kaloupek, and Slama (1975) and Borkovec and Hennings (1978) found PR to be more effective than suggestions to relax (i.e., without training). In a literature review, Knapp, Downs, and Alperson (1976) concluded, "Almost any variant of relaxation training produces statistically significant reductions in latency to sleep onset and a reduction in number of awakenings" (p. 623). Graham, Wright, Toman, and Mark (1975) found decreases in self-reported symptoms of insomnia among subjects told that they were receiving relaxation instructions, but not among subjects told that they were being hypnotized. Actually, all subjects were given a procedure similar to AT. Differences between groups were not found to be significant. The authors note that hypnosis subjects had lower expectation of success. When EEG rather than self-report was used as the criterion for improvement in sleep onset, PR was clearly superior to no treatment and to a placebo (Borkovec & Weerts, 1976).

Recent research has also begun to investigate the interaction between treatment and type of sleep problem (Lacks, Bertelson, Sugarman, & Kunkel, 1983; Hauri, Percy, Hellekson, Hartmann, & Russ, 1982), and between treatment type and severity of insomnia (Lacks, Bertelson, Gans, & Kunkel, 1983), as described below. Closer scrutiny has been given to the effects of nonspecific factors (demand characteristics) versus specific factors (Carr-Kaffashan & Woolfolk, 1979).

Centrality of Cognitive Factors

There is evidence that cognitive rather than physiological arousal is critical to the cause and/or maintenance of insomnia. The content of cognitive arousal may include a variety of personal and/or interpersonal problems, which, when interfering with sleep, are typically compounded (if not superseded) by worry about the sleep problem itself; a vicious cycle is thereby produced. Thus Mitchell and White (1977) found that the combination of mental relaxation and taped PR instruction reduced self-reported latency to sleep more than PR alone. In the group that was given mental relaxation after PR training, decreases in latency to sleep were noted both after PR training *and* after mental relaxation training. Similarly, only subjects receiving training in the combination of treatments showed increases in ratings of sleep satisfaction after training. At a 1-month follow-up, however, both groups had improved. Consistent with the specific-effects theory, PR alone (i.e., the control condition) appeared to reduce ratings of presleep tension, but not of intrusive cognitions. The addition of mental relaxation reduced presleep tension still further, and also reduced intrusive cognitions. Woolfolk and McNulty (1983) found some evidence that sleep onset insomnia is largely mediated by presleep cognitive intrusions. They also found that cognitive components of an insomnia treatment had a greater impact on measures of sleep disturbance than did somatic aspects of the procedure.

One way of studying the strength of cognitive factors on sleep is through experimental manipulations of patients' beliefs about their ability to sleep. Nicassio, Boylan, and McCabe (1982) compared PR with frontalis EMG BFK. They found significant reductions in self-reported sleep onset latency compared to a no-treatment control, but no between-group differences when the two treatments were compared individually with a bogus biofeedback placebo condition. They conclude that the effectiveness of relaxation therapies lies in the patients' "expectancies related to the ability to relax" (Nicassio et al., 1982, p. 159). They point out that although previous research has shown placebo interventions (e.g., self-relaxation) to be ineffective with severely insomniac patients, a placebo *pill* given with the suggestion that it produces relaxation can lead to significant improvement (Bootzin, Herman, & Nicassio, 1976). Thus, they attribute the mechanism of action to patients' immediate and strong beliefs that they are relaxing, whether or not they actually are. In fact, in the study by Nicassio et al. (1982), despite an average 40-minute decrease in sleep onset latency, the bogus biofeedback group displayed no EMG reduction across sessions. This strongly suggests that decreasing cognitive arousal (in this case, worry about the sleep problem itself) is more important than muscle relaxation in improving sleep.

Similarly, the various relaxation strategies appear to contain active common ingredients for successfully treating insomnia, and their relative differences are over-shadowed by the strong effects of positive demand instructions (Carr-Kaffashan & Woolfolk, 1979). The success of bogus biofeedback and placebo pills compared to these treatments also suggests that these therapies may contain rather weak specific effects, although the implied nonspecific effects (i.e., treatment demands, beliefs, or expectancies about sleep) may affect sleep through a viable treatment target— cognitive activity.

Other evidence suggests that cognitive arousal is more important than physi-ological arousal to the cause and/or maintenance of insomnia. In Lichstein and Rosenthal's (1980) survey of 296 insomniacs, 90% rated cognitive arousal as a factor in their sleep difficulties, while only 5% implicated physiological arousal. Of those implicating both physiological and cognitive arousal, the majority rated the latter as most important. Experimentally inducing cognitive arousal (without physiological arousal) has been shown to delay the onset of sleep in good sleepers (Gross & Borkovec, 1982). Nicassio, Mendlowitz, Fussell, and Petas (1985) found correlations with sleep difficulties to be stronger for self-reported cognitive arousal than for self-reported somatic arousal. Moreover, the only process variable that has been shown to correlate with sleep improvement is presleep cognitive intrusions (Woolfolk & McNulty, 1983). The major reviews (Borkovec, 1982; Lichstein & Fischer, 1985; Lacks, 1987) over the past 10 years all suggest that successful treatment of insomnia must on some level affect the arousing, sleep-preventing cognitions and worries.

Consistent with the centrality of cognitive arousal in chronic insomnia is the finding that improvement after behavioral treatment is uncorrelated with decreases in somatic arousal. Coursey, Frankel, Gaarder, and Mott (1980) compared EMG BFK and AT with a nonrelaxation technique, electrosleep, in a group of 22 patients with chronic sleep onset insomnia. Whereas none of the electrosleep subjects improved on all-night EEG measures or self-report, about one-half of the relaxation (EMG BFK or AT) subjects improved significantly, with maintenance at a 1-month follow-up. However, neither the level of frontalis EMG, nor the relationships of both posttreat-ment EEG and self-reported sleep latency to EMG level, differentiated the successful from the unsuccessful subjects. One variable that did differentiate these groups was the level of external stress (e.g., marital or business problems, worries about physical health). This finding suggests that although high levels of muscular tension did not affect sleep, cognitive arousal (i.e., "worries" about various daily hassles) may have. Coursey et al. (1980) conclude that EMG BFK and AT do not by themselves represent an optimal treatment program for insomnia, and should be combined with therapy that targets a patient's stressful patterns of living.

Electroencephalographic Biofeedback

If EEG changes are critical in evaluating success of insomnia treatments, it would be reasonable to assume that EEG biofeedback would be a particularly effective treatment. There is evidence that effectiveness of various forms of EEG biofeedback is related to characteristics of specific cases of insomnia. Hauri et al. (1982) found both theta and sensorimotor rhythm feedback to be equally effective according to self-report. However, according to electrocortical measures, only insomniacs characterized as relaxed at bedtime benefited from sensorimotor rhythm feedback. Anxious insomniacs benefited only from theta feedback. According to electrocortical indices, inappropriate treatment (e.g., theta feedback administered to relaxed insomniacs) led to significant deterioration. Hauri et al. attributed subjective reports of improvement that are not correlated with EMG improvement or not supported by sleep EEG measures (as reviewed above) to a "rekindling of hope" in the patients. They also point out the importance of electrocortical sleep laboratory outcome measures.

Stimulus Control

Stimulus control has also been successfully used in treating insomnia. This procedure usually involves instructing clients to get out of bed when they have difficulty sleeping, so that negative emotions associated with insomnia become dissociated from the bed situation. Although stimulus control is not covered in this volume, it is an important behaviorally focused technique for treating this disorder. Stimulus control treatments have consistently produced significant reductions in sleep onset latencies, compared to placebo and no-treatment controls. More importantly, when compared to the relaxation therapies reviewed here, as well as to paradoxical intention (a treatment aimed specifically at performance anxiety), stimulus control consistently produces best results (Lacks, 1987; Borkovec, 1982; Lichstein & Fischer, 1985).

Lacks, Bertelson, Gans, and Kunkel (1983) found a 50% reduction in sleep onset latency for stimulus control, compared to a range of 18–23% for PR, paradoxical intention, and a credible placebo. In addition, they reported the percentages of improved subjects as 93% for stimulus control and 57–68% for the other groups. This study included subjects classified as mildly, moderately, and severely insomniac, with the most severely insomniac subjects showing the most gains across all treatment groups. The authors specifically recommended against paradoxical intention, especially for mildly and moderately insomniac patients, as this group reported increases in sleep onset latency throughout treatment. Turner and Ascher (1982), in failing to replicate their previous results (Turner & Ascher, 1979), also found a negative outcome with paradoxical intention.

Espie, Lindsay, Brooks, Hood, and Turvey (1989) included measures of sleep quality and sleep pattern in addition to onset latency in their study comparing PR, paradoxical intention, and stimulus control. Although stimulus control was the only intervention to significantly reduce sleep onset latency compared to a control condition (60% reduction), PR led to significant improvement in sleep quality and daytime measures of general well-being. They also found that paradoxical intention initially increased sleep onset latency in one-third of subjects. Lacks and his colleagues demonstrated the comparative superiority of stimulus control procedures with a group of sleep maintenance insomniacs as well (Lacks, Bertelson, Sugarman, & Kunkel, 1983). The major drawbacks of the stimulus control studies reviewed here are the lack of sleep lab EEG measures and the small sample sizes (7 to 10 subjects per group). Borkovec (1982) has proposed that stimulus control procedures may exert their therapeutic effects through their disruption of sleep-incompatible cognitions, worries, or performance anxiety.

Drug Therapy

It should be kept in mind that chemotherapy for insomnia is used far more commonly than treatment by any of the behavioral modalities described above. In summarizing this research, Lacks (1987) concluded that although sleep medications provide some initial improvement, the added sleep time is only about 20 to 40 minutes. Over time, hypnotics can disrupt sleep architecture (i.e., the pattern and timing of the various sleep stages), reduce rapid-eye-movement sleep, and exacerbate symptoms of insomnia. Furthermore, sleep medications tend to lose their effects over time, and tolerance to many hypnotic medications tends to develop within a few weeks. This results in the need for increased dosages, the possibility of addiction, and even the chance of accidental death from an overdose (Kripke, Ancoli-Israel, Mason, & Messin, 1983). The magnitude of the side effects of medical treatment for insomnia indicates that a nonpharmacological treatment approach would be preferable, if it were found to be at least equally effective. No reports could be found of comparisons between behavioral and pharmacological treatment strategies, however.

Conclusion

According to the reviews, reductions in self-reported sleep onset latency are between 58% and 70% for stimulus control and approximately 45% for PR. However, when EEG-defined sleep onset latency is used as the outcome criterion, PR has been associated with reductions of 59–71% (Borkovec, 1982; Lichstein & Fischer, 1985). Comparative studies show that stimulus control should generally be the treatment of choice, although Espie et al. (1989) suggest that PR may be preferable when the patient's goal is improvement in quality rather than quantity of sleep. Because of side effects and poor long-term benefits, we believe that medication should be avoided as a treatment for chronic insomnia. Paradoxical intention is not recommended, at least by Lacks, Bertelson, Gans, and Kunkel (1983). Finally, the wealth of evidence pointing to cognitive arousal as a key etiological factor is matched only by the dearth of comparative studies evaluating cognitive control techniques such as meditation (Lacks, 1987). This clearly points to an important area for future research.

Dysmenorrhea

Empirical research on stress reduction treatments for dysmenorrhea has shown positive results for a variety of procedures. Comparative studies have found few significant differences among nonpharmacological techniques, including SD with PR, PR alone, EMG BFK, TBFK, cognitive restructuring, time scheduling, and nondirective therapy (Balick, Elfner, May, & Moore, 1982; Bennink, Hulst, & Benthem, 1982; Duson, 1976/1977; Rosenthal, 1978; Sigmon & Nelson, 1988).

Stress management procedures appear to be more effective with spasmodic than with congestive dysmenorrhea. The former is assumed to stem from muscle cramping, while the cause of the latter is presumed to involve fluid retention. Chesney and Tasto (1975) found a relaxation–SD procedure to be effective in treating spasmodic but not congestive dysmenorrhea, compared to pseudotherapy and a waiting-list control. Treatment gains were maintained at a 2-month follow-up. Amodei, Nelson, Jarrett, and Sigmon (1987) also found that relaxation training was beneficial for spasmodic but not for congestive dysmenorrhea. In a subsequent experiment, sufferers from congestive dysmenorrhea were given a coping skills package and, in addition, either relaxation or no relaxation. Neither group showed significant improvement. Quillen and Denney (1982) reported no differences between spasmodic and congestive dysmenorrhea in response to anxiety management training. Women with both types reported improvement in symptoms, compared with a no-treatment control group.

Two comparative studies found vaginal temperature biofeedback to be particularly effective with dysmenorrhea. Heczey (1977/1978) found vaginal temperature biofeedback to be more effective than AT, and found both treatments to be more effective than a no-treatment control. Improvement in the treatment conditions ranged from 64% in group-administered AT to 92% in biofeedback. Heczey (1980) found that a combination of AT and vaginal temperature feedback was significantly superior to AT alone and to a no-treatment control. Follow-up data showed that subjects who continued to practice relaxation daily maintained improvement.

Two literature reviews have appeared covering nonpharmacological treatment for dysmenorrhea. Denney and Gerrard (1981) found significant reductions in menstrual symptoms in seven of the nine studies using SD. They note that SD is an effective treatment and advise research on whether this technique operates directly on the pain or only indirectly by reducing tension that might exacerbate it. They also suggest research to identify the active components of the various treatment packages, and they recommend additional studies using adequate controls for nonspecific factors, such as expectancy and attention. Lewis, Wasserman, Denney, and Gerrard (1983) suggest using physiological measures such as intrauterine pressure data (see Smith & Powell, 1980), in addition to self-report measures of outcome. These reviews mention several needs and problems in the literature on nonpharmacological treatment of dysmenorrhea. Some women have symptoms of both spasmodic and congestive dysmenorrhea; there is a need for studies on women who show this mix of symptoms. Furthermore, careful screening and selection of research subjects are necessary. Eliminating subjects who use intrauterine devices or hormonal medication is essential, because of the effects of these on dysmenorrhea and the consequent bias introduced into descriptive and treatment research. Also, researchers have tended to rely on subject populations who are already receiving various kinds of therapy, or on college students. Both these groups are nonrepresentative of women in general.

In summary, the literature suggests that PR may be more effective with spasmodic than with congestive dysmenorrhea, and that stress management techniques in general have a positive effect on dysmenorrhea. They are viable alternatives to pharmacological treatment, which often has debilitating side effects. Treatments such as oral contraceptives, prostaglandin-inhibiting drugs, analgesics, antispasmodic drugs, and ketocaine compresses are known to cause one or more side effects: skin irritation, central nervous system symptoms (drowsiness, headache, depression), visceral and urinary problems, hypertension, gastrointestinal symptoms, and increased agitation. However, before behavioral techniques can be definitively recommended as a treatment of choice for dysmenorrhea, more careful research with better controls and diagnostic procedures is necessary.

Other Conditions

A study of childbirth preparation comparing biofeedback training with Lamaze training found the former to produce greater decreases in the emotional lability of the infant, as well as shortened labor time (Schwartz, 1980). Andrews, Warner, and Stewart (1986) found equivalent improvement in several signs of hyperfunctional dysphonia (high laryngeal muscle tension, lack of control of vocal fold vibration, abnormal voice quality) with laryngeal EMG BFK and PR, when these techniques were imbedded in a graded voice training program. This study lacked a control group, but showed that relaxation and biofeedback techniques warrant further investigation for treating this problem.

Conclusions

The following conclusions can be drawn from the literature reviewed in this chapter:

1. *Stress management therapies as effective treatments or adjuncts for a wide variety of somatic disorders.* Although stress management therapies may only be useful where emotional stress is involved in the etiology or maintenance of a particular disorder, this covers a very large variety of ailments. In some cases, a link with the fight or flight reflex is very obvious (disorders characterized by elevated alertness, reactivity, and sympathetic arousal, such as anxiety, insomnia, hypertension, etc.). Also included, however, may be disorders characterized by parasympathetically mediated symptoms, such as ulcers, fainting, and nausea. These may result from a "parasympathetic rebound" phenomenon, as part of the process by which the body reconstitutes itself after mobilization for stress. These homeostatic processes have been understood for a long time (Cannon, 1939, Gellhorn, 1957). The particular symptoms experienced by an individual can depend on a variety of biological, psychological, and environmental factors. Schwartz (1981) has described the interaction of these elements in terms of "systems theory."

In this chapter we have reviewed data on selected disorders for which stress management therapies have received substantial evaluation as a treatment. In this explosively growing field, it is certain that many more diseases will be added to this list in the future.

2. *Specificity of treatment effects.* There is evidence for greater reductions in muscular problems (e.g., tension headaches) following muscular interventions (EMG BFK or PR) as opposed to autonomic interventions (e.g., AT or TBFK). Disorders that primarily involve cognitive processes (e.g., insomnia and disorders describe in Chapter 18, such as test anxiety, anxiety, phobias, depression, and anger) tend to respond particularly well to CT, and in some instances to respond better to CT than to relaxation therapies. CT may also be particularly effective with tension headaches, thus suggesting that cognitions, as well as muscle tension, may play a critical role in the development of this problem. Vascular headaches and hypertension, on the other hand, do not respond as well to CT, and tend to respond differentially to autonomically focused self-management therapies (TBFK, blood pressure biofeedback, and breathing retraining).

In comparisons between biofeedback and relaxation therapies, the specific training provided by biofeedback may be of particular value to some headache sufferers, as well as to asthmatics and others whose problem involves a specific physiological locus. The addition of relaxation therapy may be of incremental value in some cases. Physiological mechanisms that may explain some specific biofeedback effects have been discovered in recent years. Most dramatic among these are the beta sympathetic components in peripheral vasodilation, which may explain specific effects of TBFK on a variety of cardiovascular disorders; and a vagal–trigeminal reflex, which may explain specific effects of frontalis EMG BFK on asthma.

3. *Use of medication.* For most of the conditions described in this chapter, medication is a quick and inexpensive way to produce dramatic improvement. For some conditions (e.g., hypertension and asthma), nonpharmacological methods might best be considered important *adjuncts* to medical treatment; they may reduce reliance on medications to some extent. Nonpharmacological alternatives are clearly preferable for treating most other stress-related problems. Drug therapies all have some side effects, and tend to produce psychological if not physical dependence; long-term results tend to favor effective nonpharmacological treatments, when such are available.

4. *Real versus imagined physiological change.* Is the predominant goal of treatment to produce the *belief* or *feeling* of being relaxed, or to produce physiologically measurable changes? This question is central to the rationales of several relaxation techniques. The answer depends on the particular condition for which these techniques are used. When the severity of the disorder is defined by a person's self-report (e.g., anxiety, depression, pain), interventions producing the *belief* of relaxation may be as effective as those that produce real changes. Indeed, for these disorders, cognitive interventions may be the most effective of all. Insomnia may also fall into this category, even when EEG is used as an outcome measure. Disorders that are defined in terms of physiological response (e.g., hypertension, asthma) are probably better treated by techniques that produce real physiological change. Migraine headaches may be among this group, even though it is primarily assessed by self-report. This may be so because the severity of the pain is sufficient to outweigh fluctuations in cognitive interpretation of the physiological events involved.

5. *Combinations of techniques.* For some psychosomatic problems, combinations of

techniques appear to produce better cumulative effects than one technique alone. This is not the case, however, when using a combination of techniques means administering one or all of the component techniques only superficially. Although some disorders unquestionably respond best to somatically focused treatments, it remains possible that therapeutic results emanate from the sense of self-efficacy produced by these techniques, rather than from the somatic control per se. Similarly, some medications may render subsequent behavioral treatments ineffective, perhaps because of physical or psychological drug dependency. At times, the therapist must decide whether symptom change (such as in headaches) or physiological change (such as in hypertension) is more important to achieve.

6. *The need for individualized treatment.* In most cases, the research literature provides a guide, not a prescription. Although the results of scientific investigations of stress management therapies give us appreciably more guidance than a decade ago, use of these therapies cannot be reduced to a series of formulas. Despite the large volume of research on these methods, the needs of a suffering human being are infinitely more complex than any series of parametric studies can describe. Although we think it necessary that therapists familiarize themselves with the research literature and use it as a guide, the practice of healing is still an art. This has been true for centuries, and it probably will be so forever. Let us hope that the tools of science will render this art ever more powerful in years to come.

ACKNOWLEDGMENT

Work on this chapter was supported in part by Grant No. HL44097 from the Heart, Lung and Blood Institute, National Institutes of Health.

REFERENCES

Achmon, J., Granek, M., Golomb, M., & Hart, J. (1989). Behavioral treatment of essential hypertension: A comparison between cognitive therapy and biofeedback of heart rate. *Psychosomatic Medicine, 51,* 152–164.

Achterberg, J., Kenner, C., & Lawlis, G. F. (1988). Severe burn injury: A comparison of relaxation, imagery, and biofeedback for pain management. *Journal of Mental Imagery, 12,* 71–87.

Aivazyan, T. A., Zaitsev, V. P., Salenko, B. B., Yurenev, A. P., & Patrusheva, I. F. (1988). Efficacy of relaxation techniques in hypertensive patients: Fifth joint USA–USSR symposium on arterial hypertension. *Health Psychology, 7*(Suppl.), 193–200.

Agras, W. S., Horne, M., & Taylor, C. B. (1982). Expectation and the blood-pressure-lowering effects of relaxation. *Psychosomatic Medicine, 44,* 389–395.

Agras, W. S., & Jacob, R. (1979). Hypertension. In O. F. Pomerleau & J. P. Brady (Eds.), *Behavioral medicine: Theory and practice.* Baltimore: Williams & Wilkins.

Agras, W. S., Southam, M. A., & Taylor, C. B. (1983). Long-term persistence of relaxation-induced blood pressure lowering during the working day. *Journal of Consulting and Clinical Psychology, 51,* 792–794.

Agras, W. S., Taylor, C. B., Kraemer, H. C., Southam, M. A., & Schneider, J. A. (1987). Relaxation training for essential hypertension at the worksite: II. The poorly controlled hypertensive. *Psychosomatic Medicine, 49,* 264–273.

Amodei, N., Nelson, R. O., Jarrett, R. B., & Sigmon, S. (1987). Psychological treatments of dysmenorrhea: Differential effectiveness for spasmodics and congestives. *Journal of Behavior Therapy and Experimental Psychiatry, 18,* 95–103.

Andrasik, F., & Blanchard, E. B. (1987). Task force report on the biofeedback treatment of tension headache. In J. P. Hatch, J. D. Rugh, & J. G. Fisher (Eds.), *Biofeedback: Studies in clinical efficacy.* New York: Plenum Press.

Andrasik, F., & Holroyd, K. A. (1980). A test of specific and non-specific effects in the biofeedback treatment of tension headache. *Journal of Consulting and Clinical Psychology, 48*, 575–586.

Andrews, G., MacMahon, S. W., Austin, A. & Byrne, D. G. (1982). Hypertension: Comparison of drug and non-drug treatments. *British Medical Journal, 284*, 1523–1526.

Andrews, S., Warner, J., & Stewart, R. (1986). EMG biofeedback and relaxation in the treatment of hyperfunctional dysphonia. *British Journal of Disorders of Communication, 21*, 353–369.

Andreychuk, T., & Skriver, C. (1975). Hypnosis and biofeedback in the treatment of migraine headache. *International Journal of Clinical Hypnosis, 23*, 172–183.

Association of Sleep Disorders Centers. (1979). Diagnostic classification of sleep and arousal disorders (1st ed.), prepared by the Sleep Disorders Classification Committee, H. P. Roffwarg, Chairman. *Sleep, 2*, 1–37.

Balick, L., Elfner, L., May, J., & Moore, J. D. (1982). Biofeedback treatment of dysmenorrhea. *Biofeedback and Self-Regulation, 7*, 499–520.

Barlow, W. (1977). *The Alexander technique*. New York: Knopf.

Basler, H. D., Brinkmeier, U., Buser, K., Haehn, K. D., & Molders-Kober, R. (1982). Psychological group treatment of essential hypertension in general practice. *British Journal of Clinical Psychology, 21*, 295–302.

Beatty, J. (1982). Biofeedback in the treatment of migraine: Simple relaxation or specific effects? In L. White & B. Tursky (Eds.), *Clinical biofeedback: Efficacy and mechanisms*. New York: Guilford Press.

Beaty, E. T. (1976). Feedback assisted relaxation training as a treatment for peptic ulcers. *Biofeedback and Self-Regulation, 1*, 323–324.

Beaty, E. T., & Haynes, S. N. (1979). Behavioral intervention with muscle-contraction headache: A review. *Psychosomatic Medicine, 41*, 165–179.

Bennink, C. D., Hulst, L. L., & Benthem, J. A. (1982). The effect of EMG biofeedback and relaxation training on primary dysmenorrhea. *Journal of Behavioral Medicine, 5*, 329–341.

Blanchard, E. B. (1979). Biofeedback: A selective review of clinical applications in behavioral medicine. In R. McNemara (Ed.), *Behavioral approaches to medicine: Application and analysis*. New York: Plenum Press.

Blanchard, E. B. (1987). Long-term effects of behavioral treatment of chronic headache. *Behavior Therapy, 18*, 375–385.

Blanchard, E. B. (1990). Biofeedback treatments of essential hypertension. *Biofeedback and Self-Regulation, 15*, 209–228.

Blanchard, E. B., Ahles, T. A., & Shaw, E. R. (1979). Behavioral treatment of headaches. In M. Hersen, R. M. Eisler, & P. M. Miller (Eds.), *Progress in behavior modification* (Vol. 8). New York: Academic Press.

Blanchard, E. B., & Andrasik, F. (1982). Psychological assessment and treatment of headache: Recent developments and emerging issues. *Journal of Consulting and Clinical Psychology, 50*, 859–879.

Blanchard, E. B., & Andrasik, F. (1987). Biofeedback treatment of vascular headache. In J. P. Hatch, J. D. Rugh, & J. G. Fisher (Eds.), *Biofeedback: Studies in clinical efficacy*. New York: Plenum Press.

Blanchard, E. B., Andrasik, F., Ahles, T. A., Teders, S. J., & O'Keefe, D. M. (1980). Migraine and tension headache: A meta-analytic review. *Behavior Therapy, 11*, 613–631.

Blanchard, E. B., Andrasik, F., Evans, D. D., Neff, D. F., Appelbaum, K. A., & Rodichok, L. D. (1985). Behavioral treatment of 250 chronic headache patients: A clinical replication series. *Behavior Therapy, 16*, 308–327.

Blanchard, E. B., Andrasik, F., Guarnieri, P., Neff, D. F., & Rodichok, D. F. (1987). Two-, three-, and four-year follow-up on the self-regulatory treatment of chronic headache. *Journal of Consulting and Clinical Psychology, 55*, 257–259.

Blanchard, E. B., Andrasik, F., Neff, D. F., Arena, J. G., Ahles, T. A., Jurish, S. E., Pallmeyer, T. P., Saunders, N. L., Teders, S. J., Barron, K. D., & Rodichok, L. D. (1982). Biofeedback and relaxation training with three kinds of headache: Treatment effects and their prediction. *Journal of Consulting and Clinical Psychology, 50*, 562–575.

Blanchard, E. B., Andrasik, F., & Silver, B. V. (1980). Biofeedback and relaxation in the treatment of tension headaches: A reply to Belar. *Journal of Behavioral Medicine, 3*, 227–232.

Blanchard, E. B., Appelbaum, K. A., Radnitz, C. L., Jaccard, J., & Dentinger, M. P. (1989). The refractory headache patient: I. Chronic, daily, high intensity headache. *Behaviour Research and Therapy, 27*, 403–410.

Blanchard, E. B., Appelbaum, R. A., Radnitz, C. L., Michultka, D., Morrill, B., Kirsch, C., Hillhouse, J., Evans, D. D., Guarnieri, P., Attanasio, V., Andrasik, F., Jaccard, J., & Dentineer, M. P. (1990). Placebo-controlled evaluation of abbreviated progressive muscle relaxation and of relaxation combined with cognitive therapy in the treatment of tension headache. *Journal of Consulting and Clinical Psychology, 58*, 210–215.

Blanchard, E. B., Appelbaum, K. A., Radnitz, C. L., Morrill, B., Michultka, D., Kirsch, C., Guarnieri, P.,

Hillhouse, J., Evans, D. D., Jaccard, J., & Barron, K. D. (1990). A controlled evaluation of thermal biofeedback combined with cognitive therapy in the treatment of vascular headache. *Journal of Consulting and Clinical Psychology, 58,* 216–224.

Blanchard, E. B., Khramelashvili, V. V., McCoy, G. C., Aivazyan, T. A., McCaffrey, R. J., Salenko, B. B., Musso, A., Wittrock, D. A., Berger, M., Gerardi, M. A., & Pangburn, L. (1988). The USA–USSR collaborative cross-cultural comparison of autogenic training and thermal biofeedback in the treatment of mild-hypertension. *Health Psychology, 7*(Suppl.), 175–192.

Blanchard, E. B., McCoy, G. C., Musso, A., Maryrose, A. G., Pallmeyer, T. P., Gerardi, R. J., Cotch, P. A., Siracusa, K., & Andrasik, F. (1986). A controlled comparison of thermal biofeedback and relaxation training in the treatment of essential hypertension: I. Short-term and long-term outcome. *Behaviour Therapy, 17,* 563–579.

Blanchard, E. B., McCoy, G. C., Wittrock, D., Musso, A., Gerardi, R. J., & Pagburn, L. (1988). A controlled comparison of thermal biofeedback and relaxation training in the treatment of essential hypertension: II. Effects on cardiovascular reactivity. *Health Psychology, 7,* 19–33.

Blanchard, E. B., Radnitz, C., Schwarz, S. P., Neff, D. F., & Gerardi, M. A. (1987). Psychological changes associated with self-regulatory treatments of irritable bowel syndrome. *Biofeedback and Self-Regulation, 12,* 31–38.

Blanchard, E. B., & Schwarz, S. P. (1987). Adaptation of a multicomponent treatment for irritable bowel syndrome to a small-group format. *Biofeedback and Self-Regulation, 12,* 63–69.

Blanchard, E. B., & Schwarz, S. P. (1988). Two-year follow-up of behavioral treatment of irritable bowel syndrome. *Behaviour Therapy, 19,* 67–73.

Bootzin, R., Herman, C. P., & Nicassio, P. (1976). The power of suggestion: Another examination of misattribution and insomnia. *Journal of Personality and Social Psychology, 34,* 673–679.

Borkovec, T. D. (1979). Pseudo- (experimental) insomnia and idiopathic (objective) insomnia: Theoretical and therapeutic issues. *Advances in Behaviour Research and Therapy, 2,* 27–55.

Borkovec, T. D. (1982). Insomnia. *Journal of Consulting and Clinical Psychology, 50,* 880–895.

Borkovec, T. D., & Fowles, D. C. (1973). Controlled investigation of the effects of progressive relaxation and hypnotic relaxation on insomnia. *Journal of Abnormal Psychology, 82,* 153–158.

Borkovec, T. D., & Hennings, B. L. (1978). The role of physiological attention-focusing in the relaxation treatment of sleep disturbance, general tension, and specific stress reaction. *Behaviour Research and Therapy, 16,* 7–19.

Borkovec, T. D., Kaloupek, D. G., & Slama, K. M. (1975). The facilitative effect of muscle tension-release in the relaxation treatment of sleep disturbance. *Behavior Therapy, 6,* 301–309.

Borkovec, T. D., & Weerts, T. C. (1976). Effects of progressive relaxation on sleep disturbance: An electroencephalographic evaluation. *Psychosomatic Medicine, 38,* 173–180.

Brooks, C. M., Richards, J. M., Bailey, W. C., Martin, B., Windsor, R. A., & Soong, S. S. (1989). Subjective symptomatology of asthma in an outpatient population. *Psychosomatic Medicine, 51,* 102–108.

Brooks, G. R., & Richardson, F. C. (1980). Emotional skills training: A treatment program for duodenal ulcer. *Behaviour Therapy, 11,* 198–207.

Bush, J. P. (1987). Pain in children: A review of the literature from a developmental perspective. *Psychology and Health, 1,* 215–236.

Cannici, J., Malcolm, R., & Peek, L. A. (1983). Treatment of insomnia in cancer patients using muscle relaxation training. *Journal of Behavior Therapy and Experimental Psychiatry, 14,* 251–256.

Cannon, W. B. (1939). *The wisdom of the body.* New York: Norton.

Carey, M. P., & Burish, T. G. (1987). Providing relaxation training to cancer chemotherapy patients: A comparison of three delivery techniques. *Journal of Consulting and Clinical Psychology, 55,* 732–737.

Carey, M. P., & Burish, T. G. (1988). Etiology and treatment of the psychological side effects associated with cancer chemotherapy: A critical review and discussion. *Psychological Bulletin, 104,* 307–325.

Carr-Kaffashan, L., & Woolfolk, R. L. (1979). Active and placebo effects in the treatment of moderate and severe insomnia. *Journal of Consulting and Clinical Psychology, 47,* 603–605.

Chappel, M. N., Stafano, J. J., Rogerson, J. S., & Pike, F. H. (1936). The value of group psychological procedures in the treatment of peptic ulcer. *American Journal of Digestive Diseases, 3,* 813–817.

Chesney, M. A., Black, G. W., Swan, G. E., & Ward, M. M. (1987). Relaxation training for essential hypertension at the worksite: I. The untreated mild hypertensive. *Psychosomatic Medicine, 49,* 250–263.

Chesney, M. A., & Tasto, D. (1975). The effectiveness of behavior modification and spasmodic and congestive dysmenorrhea. *Behaviour Research and Therapy, 13,* 240–253.

Clark, P. S. (1982). Emotional exacerbations in asthma caused by overbreathing. *Journal of Asthma, 19,* 249–251.

Cohen, J., & Sedlacek, K. (1983). Attention and autonomic self-regulation. *Psychosomatic Medicine, 45,* 243–257.

Coursey, R. D., Frankel, B. L., Gaarder, K. R., & Mott, D. E. (1980). A comparison of relaxation techniques with electrosleep for chronic, sleep-onset insomnia: A sleep-EEG study. *Biofeedback and Self-Regulation, 5*, 57–73.

Crowther, J. H. (1983). Stress management training and relaxation imagery in the treatment of essential hypertension. *Journal of Behavioral Medicine, 6*, 169–187.

Daly, E. J., Donn, P. A., Galliher, M. J., & Zimmerman, J. S. (1983). Biofeedback applications of migraine and tension headaches: A double-blinded outcome study. *Biofeedback and Self-Regulation, 8*, 135–152.

Davis, M. H., Saunders, D. R., Creer, T. L., & Chai, H. (1973). Relaxation training facilitated by biofeedback apparatus as a supplemental treatment in bronchial asthma. *Journal of Psychosomatic Research, 17*, 121–128.

Denney, D. R., & Gerrard, M. (1981). Behavioral treatments of primary dysmenorrhea: A review. *Behaviour Research and Therapy, 19*, 303–312.

Detrick, P. F. (1978). Demonstration and comparison of the efficacy of EMG biofeedback assisted relaxation versus autogenic feedback training for the treatment of tension headaches (Doctoral dissertation, University of Southern Mississippi, 1977). *Dissertation Abstracts International, 38*, 5009B. (University Microfilms No. 78-02,902)

Dixon, J. (1984). Effect of nursing interventions on nutritional and performance status in cancer patients. *Nursing Research, 33*, 330–335.

Duson, B. M. (1977). Effectiveness of relaxation–desensitization and cognitive restructuring in teaching the self-management of menstrual symptoms to college women (Doctoral dissertation, University of Texas at Austin, 1976). *Dissertation Abstracts International, 37*, 6322B. (University Microfilms No. 77-11,508)

Edelson, J., & Fitzpatrick, J. L. (1989). A comparison of cognitive behavioral and hypnotic treatments of chronic pain. *Journal of Clinical Psychology, 45*, 316–323.

Engel, B. T., Glasgow, M. S., & Gaarder, K. R. (1983). Behavioral treatment of high blood pressure: III. Follow-up results and treatment recommendations. *Psychosomatic Medicine, 45*, 23–29.

English, E. H., & Baker, T. B. (1983). Relaxation training and cardiovascular response to experimental stressors. *Health Psychology, 2*, 239–259.

Estlander, A. M., & Laaksonen, R. (1984). Psychological assessment of chronic pain patients. *Scandinavian Journal of Behaviour Therapy, 13*, 25–37.

Espie, C. A., Lindsay, W. R., Brooks, D. N., Hood, E. M., & Turvey, T. (1989). A controlled comparative investigation of psychological treatments for chronic sleep-onset insomnia. *Behaviour Research and Therapy, 27*, 79–88.

Fray, J. M. (1975). Implications of electromyographic feedback for essential hypertensive patients (Doctoral dissertation, Texas Technological University). *Dissertation Abstracts International, 36*, 3036B. (University Microfilms No. 75-26, 839)

Freedman, R. R. (1985). Behavioral treatment of Raynaud's disease and phenomenon. *Advances in Microcirculation, 12*, 138–156.

Freedman, R. R. (1991). Physiological mechanisms of temperature biofeedback. *Biofeedback and Self-Regulation, 16*, 95–116.

Freedman, R. R., Ianni, P., & Wenig, P. (1983). Behavioral treatment of Raynaud's disease. *Journal of Consulting and Clinical Psychology, 51*, 539–549.

Freedman, R. R., Ianni, P., & Wenig, P. (1985). Behavioral treatment of Raynaud's disease: Long-term follow-up. *Journal of Consulting and Clinical Psychology, 53*, 136.

Freedman, R. R., Lynn, S. J., Ianni, P., & Hale, P. A. (1981). Biofeedback treatment of Raynaud's disease and phenomenon. *Biofeedback and Self-Regulation, 6*, 355–365.

Frumkin, K., Nathan, R. J., Prout, M. F., & Cohen, M. C. (1978). Nonpharmacologic control of essential hypertension in man: A critical review of the experimental literature. *Psychosomatic Medicine, 40*, 294–320.

Gauthier, J., Bois, R., Allaire, D., & Drolet, M. (1981). Evaluation of skin temperature biofeedback training at two different sites for migraine. *Journal of Behavioral Medicine, 4*, 407–419.

Gellhorn, E. (1957). *Autonomic imbalance and the hypothalamus.* Minneapolis: University of Minnesota Press.

Gershman, L., & Clouser, R. A. (1974). Treating insomnia with relaxation and desensitization in a group setting by an automated approach. *Journal of Behavior Therapy and Experimental Psychiatry, 5*, 31–35.

Glasgow, M. S., Engel, B. T., & D'Lugoff, B. C. (1989). A controlled study of a standardized behavioral stepped treatment for hypertension. *Psychosomatic Medicine, 51*, 10–26.

Glasgow, M. S., Gaarder, K. R., & Engel, R. D. (1982). Behavioral treatment of high blood pressure: II. Acute and sustained effects of relaxation and systolic blood pressure biofeedback. *Psychosomatic Medicine, 44*, 155–170.

Glaus, K. D., & Kotses, H. (1983). Facial muscle tension influences lung airway resistance; limb muscle tension does not. *Biological Psychology, 17,* 105–120.

Goldstein, I. B. (1982). Biofeedback in the treatment of hypertension. In L. White & B. Tursky (Eds.), *Clinical biofeedback: Efficacy and mechanisms.* New York: Guilford Press.

Goldstein, I. B., Shapiro, D., & Thananopavarn, C. (1984). Home relaxation techniques for essential hypertension. *Psychosomatic Medicine, 46,* 399–414.

Goldstein, I. B., Shapiro, D., Thananopavarn, C., & Sambhi, M. P. (1982). Comparison of drug and behavioral treatments of essential hypertension. *Health Psychology, 1,* 7–26.

Graham, K., Wright, G., Toman, W., & Mark, C. (1975). Relaxation and hypnosis in the treatment of insomnia. *American Journal of Clinical Hypnosis, 18,* 39–42.

Gross, R. T., & Borkovec, T. D. (1982). Effects of a cognitive intrusion manipulation on the sleep-onset latency of good sleepers. *Behavior Therapy, 13,* 112–116.

Hafner, R. J. (1982). Psychological treatment of essential hypertension: A controlled comparison of meditation and meditation plus biofeedback. *Biofeedback and Self-Regulation, 7,* 305–316.

Harver, A., & Kotses, H. (1984). Pulmonary changes induced by frontal EMG training. *Biological Psychology, 18,* 3–10.

Hatch, J. P., Klatt, K. D., Supik, J. S., Rios, N., Fisher, J. G., Bauer, R. L., & Shimotsu, G. W. (1985). Combined behavioral and pharmacological treatment of essential hypertension. *Biofeedback and Self-Regulation, 10,* 119–138.

Hauri, P. J., Percy, L., Hellekson, C., Hartmann, E., & Russ, D. (1982). The treatment of psychophysiologic insomnia with biofeedback: A replication study. *Biofeedback and Self-Regulation, 7,* 223–235.

Haynes, S. N., Sides, H., & Lockwood, G. (1977). Relaxation instruction and frontalis electromyographic feedback intervention with sleep-onset insomnia. *Behavior Therapy, 8,* 644–652.

Heczey, M. D. (1988). Effects of biofeedback and autogenic training on menstrual experiences: Relationships among anxiety, locus of control and dysmenorrhea (Doctoral dissertation, The City University of New York, 1977). *Dissertation Abstracts International, 38,* 5571B. (University Microfilms No. 78-05,763)

Heczey, M. O. (1980). Effects of biofeedback and autogenic training on dysmenorrhea. In A. J. Dan, E. A. Graham, & C. P. Beecher (Eds.), *The menstrual cycle: A synthesis of interdisciplinary research* (Vol. 1). New York: Springer.

Hibbert, G., & Pilsbury, D. (1988). Demonstration and treatment of hyperventilation causing asthma. *British Journal of Psychiatry, 153,* 687–689.

Hislop, I. G. (1980). Effect of very brief psychotherapy on the irritable bowel syndrome. *Medical Journal of Australia, 2,* 620–623.

Holroyd, K. A., & Andrasik, F. (1982). Do the effects of cognitive therapy endure? A two year follow-up of tension headache sufferers treated with cognitive therapy or biofeedback. *Cognitive Therapy and Research, 6,* 325–334.

Holroyd, K. A., Holm, J. E., Penzien, D. B., Cordingley, G. E., Hursey, K. G., Martin, N. J., & Theofanous, A. G. (1989). Long-term maintenance of improvements achieved with (abortive) pharmacological and nonpharmacological treatments for migraine: Preliminary findings. *Biofeedback and Self-Regulation, 14,* 301–308.

Holroyd, K. A., Nash, J. M., Pingel, J. D., Cordingly, G. E., & Jerome, A. (1991). A comparison of pharmacological (amitriptyline HCl) and nonpharmacological (cognitive–behavioral) therapies for chronic tension headaches. *Journal of Consulting and Clinical Psychology, 59,* 387–393.

Holroyd, K. A., & Penzien, D. B. (1986). Client variables and the behavioral treatment of recurrent tension headache: A meta-analytic review. *Journal of Behavioral Medicine, 9,* 515–536.

Holroyd, K. A., & Penzien, D. B. (1990). Pharmacological versus non-pharmacological prophylaxis of recurrent migraine headache: A meta-analytic review of clinical trials. *Pain, 42,* 1–13.

Holroyd, K. A., Penzien, D. B., Hursey, K. G., Tobin, D. L., Rogers, L., Holm, J. E., Marcille, P. J., Hall, J. R., & Chila, A. G. (1984). Change mechanisms in EMG biofeedback training: Cognitive changes underlying improvements in tension headache. *Journal of Consulting and Clinical Psychology, 52,* 1039–1053.

Huber, H. P., & Huber, D. (1979). Autogenic training and rational–emotive therapy for long-term migraine patients: An explorative study of a therapy. *Behavior Analysis and Modification, 3,* 169–177.

Humphreys, A. (1988). Etiology and treatment of the psychological side effects associated with cancer chemotherapy: A critical review and discussion. *Psychological Bulletin, 104,* 307–325.

Jacob, R. G., Chesney, M. A., Williams, D. M., Ding, Y., & Shapiro, A. (1991). Relaxation therapy for hypertension: Design effects and treatment effects. *Annals of Behavioral Medicine, 13,* 5–17.

Jacob, R. G., Fortmann, S. P., Kraemer, H. C., Farquahar, J. W., & Agras, W. S. (1985). Combining behavioral treatments to reduce blood pressure: A controlled outcome study. *Behaviour Modification, 9,* 32–54.

Jacob, R. G., Shapiro, A. P., Reeves, R. A., Johnson, A. M., McDonald, R. H., & Coburn, C. (1986). Relaxation therapy for hypertension: Comparison of effects for concomitant placebo, diuretic and beta-blocker. *Archives of Internal Medicine, 146,* 2335–2340.

Jacob, R. G., Wing, R., & Shapiro, A. P. (1987). The behavioral treatment of hypertension: Long-term effects. *Behavior Therapy, 18*(4), 325–352.

Janssen, K., & Neutgens, J. (1986). Autogenic training and progressive relaxation in the treatment of three kinds of headache. *Behaviour Research and Therapy, 24,* 199–208.

Jay, S. M., Elliott, C., & Varni, J. W. (1986). Acute and chronic pain in adults and children with cancer. *Journal of Consulting and Clinical Psychology, 54,* 601–607.

Jay, S. M., Elliott, C., & Varni, J. W. (1988). Similarities and dissimilarities in hypnotic and nonhypnotic procedures for headache control: A review. *American Journal of Clinical Hypnosis, 30,* 183–194.

Jerome, J. A. (1979). Decreasing musculoskeletal tension via biofeedback and relaxation training procedures for the treatment of chronic low back pain (Doctoral dissertation, Michigan State University, 1978). *Dissertation Abstracts International, 40,* 969B. (University Microfilms No. 79-17,721)

Jobe, J. B., Sampson, J. B., Roberts, D. E., & Beetham, W. P. (1982). Induced vasodilation as treatment for Raynaud's disease. *Annals of Internal Medicine, 97,* 706–709.

Jobe, J. B., Sampson, J. B., Roberts, D. E., & Kelly, J. A. (1986). Comparison of behavioral treatments for Raynaud's disease. *Journal of Behavioral Medicine, 9,* 89–96.

Joint National Committee on Detection, Evaluation, and Treatment of High Blood Pressure. (1988). The 1988 report of the Joint National Committee on Detection, Evaluation, and Treatment of High Blood Pressure. *Archives of Internal Medicine, 148,* 1023–1038.

Jorgenson, R. S., Houston, B. K., & Zurawski, R. M. (1981). Anxiety management training in the treatment of essential hypertension. *Behaviour Research and Therapy, 19,* 467–474.

Kaufman, M. P., & Schneiderman, N. (1986). Physiological bases of respiratory psychophysiology. In G. H. Coles, E. Donchin, & S. W. Porges (Eds.), *Psychophysiology: Systems, processes, and applications.* New York: Guilford Press.

Kaufmann, P. G., Jacob, R. G., Ewart, C. K., Chesney, M. A., Muenz, L. R., Doub, N., Mercer, W., & HIPP Investigators. (1988). Hypertension Intervention Pooling Project. *Health Psychology, 7*(Suppl.), 209–224.

Kelson, H. G., & Bryson-Brockmann, W. A. (1985). Peripheral temperature control using biofeedback and autogenic training: A comparison study. *Clinical Biofeedback and Health, 8,* 37–44.

Kewman, D., & Roberts, A. H. (1980). Skin temperature biofeedback and migraine headache: A double-blind study. *Biofeedback and Self-Regulation, 5,* 327–345.

King, N. J. (1980). The behavioral management of asthma and asthma-related problems in children: A critical review of the literature. *Journal of Behavioral Medicine, 3,* 169–189.

Kinsman, R. A., Dahlem, N., Spector, S., & Staudenmayer, H. (1977). Observations on subjective symptomatology, coping, behavior, and medical decisions in asthma. *Psychosomatic Medicine, 39,* 102–119.

Kinsman, R. A., Luparello, T., Banion, R., & Sheldon, S. (1973). Multidimensional analysis of the subjective symptomatology of asthma. *Psychosomatic Medicine, 35,* 250–267.

Knapp, T. J., Downs, D. L., & Alperson, J. R. (1976). Behavior therapy for insomnia: A review. *Behavior Therapy, 7,* 614–625.

Knapp, T. W., (1982). Treating migraine by training in temporal artery vasoconstriction and/or cognitive behavioral coping: A one-year follow-up. *Journal of Psychosomatic Research, 26,* 551–557.

Kotses, H., & Glaus, K. D. (1981). Applications of biofeedback to the treatment of asthma: A critical review. *Biofeedback and Self-Regulation, 6,* 573–593.

Kotses, H., Harver, A., Segreto, J., Glaus, K. D., Creer, T. L., & Young, G. A. (1991). Long-term effects of biofeedback-induced facial relaxation on measures of asthma severity in children. *Biofeedback and Self-Regulation, 16,* 1–22.

Kotses, H., & Miller, D. J. (1987). The effects of changes in facial muscle tension on respiratory resistance. *Biological Psychology, 25,* 211–219.

Kravitz, E. A. (1978). EMG biofeedback and differential relaxation training to promote pain relief in chronic low back pain patients (Doctoral dissertation, Wayne State University, 1977). *Dissertation Abstracts International, 39,* 1485B–1486B. (University Microfilms No. 78-16,047)

Kremsdorf, R. B., Kochanowicz, N. A., & Costell, S. (1981). Cognitive skills training versus EMG biofeedback in the treatment of tension headaches. *Biofeedback and Self-Regulation, 6,* 93–102.

Kripke, D. F., Ancoli-Israel, S., Mason, W., & Messin, S. (1983). Sleep-related mortality and morbidity in the aged. In M. H. Chase & E. D. Weitzman (Eds.), *Sleep disorders: Basic and clinical research.* Jamaica, NY: SP Medical & Scientific Books.

Lacks, P. (1987). *Behavioral treatment for persistent insomnia*. Elmsford, NY: Pergamon Press.

Lacks, P., Bertelson, A. D., Gans, L., & Kunkel, J. (1983). The effectiveness of three behavioral treatments for different degrees of sleep onset insomnia. *Behavior Therapy, 14*, 593–605.

Lacks, P., Bertelson, A. D., Sugarman, J., & Kunkel, J. (1983). The treatment of sleep-maintenance insomnia with stimulus-control techniques. *Behaviour Research and Therapy, 21*, 291–295.

Lacroix, J. M., Clarke, M. A., Bock, J. C., Doxey, N., Wood, A., & Lavis, S. (1983). Biofeedback and relaxation in the treatment of migraine headaches: Comparative effectiveness and physiological correlates. *Journal of Neurology, Neurosurgery and Psychiatry, 46*, 525–532.

Langeluddecke, P. M. (1985). Psychological aspects of irritable bowel syndrome. *Australian and New Zealand Journal of Psychiatry, 19*, 218–226.

Largen, J. W., Mathew, R. J., Dobbins, K., & Claghorn, J. L. (1981). Specific and non-specific effects of skin temperature control and migraine management. *Headache, 21*, 36–44.

Lasser, N., Batey, D. M., Hymowitz, N., Lasser, V., Kanders, B. S., & Lehrer, P. M. (1987). The hypertension intervention trial. In T. Strasser & D. Ganten (Eds.), *Mild hypertension: From drug trials to practice*. New York: Raven Press.

Lehrer, P. M., Hochron, S. M., Mayne, T., Morales, D., Isenberg, S., Carlson, V., Lasoski, A. M., Gilchrist, J., & Rausch, L. (1991, March). *Relaxation therapy for primarily upper-airway asthma: An unsuccessful replication attempt*. Paper presented at the annual meeting of the Association for Applied Psychophysiology and Biofeedback, Dallas.

Lehrer, P. M., Hochron, S. M., McCann, B. S., Swartzman, L., & Reba, P. (1986). Relaxation decreases large-airway but not small-airway asthma. *Journal of Psychosomatic Research, 30*, 13–25.

Lehrer, P. M., & Murphy, A. I. (1991). Stress reactivity and perception of pain among tension headache sufferers. *Behaviour Research and Therapy, 29*, 61–69.

Lewis, R. J., Wasserman, E., Denney, N. W., & Gerrard, M. (1983). The etiology and treatment of primary dysmenorrhea: A review. *Clinical Psychology Review, 3*, 371–389.

Ley, R. (1985a). Agoraphobia, the panic attack, and the hyperventilation syndrome. *Behaviour Research and Therapy, 23*, 79–81.

Ley, R. (1985b). Blood, breath, and fears: A hyperventilation theory of panic attacks and agoraphobia. *Clinical Psychology Review, 5*, 271–285.

Lichstein, K. L., & Fischer, S. M. (1985). Insomnia. In M. Hersen & A. S. Bellack (Eds.), *Handbook of clinical behavior therapy with adults*. New York: Plenum Press.

Lichstein, K. L., & Rosenthal, T. (1980). Insomniacs' perceptions of cognitive versus somatic determinants of sleep disturbance. *Journal of Abnormal Psychology, 89*, 105–107.

Lisspers, J., & Öst, L. G. (1990). BVP-biofeedback in the treatment of migraine: The effects of constriction and dilation during different phases of the migraine attack. *Behavior Modification, 14*, 200–221.

Longo, D. J. (1984, May). *A psychophysiological comparison of three relaxation techniques and some implications in treating cardiovascular syndromes*. Paper presented at the annual meeting of the Society for Behavioral Medicine, Philadelphia.

Luborsky, L., Aucona, L., Masoni, A., Scolari, G., & Longoni, A. (1980). Behavioral versus pharmacological treatments for essential hypertension: A pilot study. *International Journal of Psychiatry in Medicine, 10*, 33–40.

Luborsky, L., Crits-Christoph, P., Brady, J. P., Kron, R. E., Weiss, T., Cohen, M., & Levy, L. (1982). Behavioral versus pharmacological treatments for essential hypertension: A needed comparison. *Psychosomatic Medicine, 44*, 203–213.

Lustman, P. J., & Sowa, C. J. (1983). Comparative efficacy of biofeedback and stress inoculation for stress reduction. *Journal of Clinical Psychology, 39*, 191–197.

Lynch, P. M., & Zamble, E. (1987). Stress management training for irritable bowel syndrome: A preliminary investigation. *Clinical Biofeedback and Health, 10*, 123–134.

McAmmond, D., Davidson, P., & Kovitz, D. (1971). A comparison of the effects of hypnosis and relaxation training on stress reduction in a dental situation. *American Journal of Clinical Hypnosis, 13*, 233–242.

McCaffrey, R. J., & Blanchard, E. B. (1985). Stress management approaches to the treatment of essential hypertension. *Annals of Behavioral Medicine, 7*(1), 5–12.

McCoy, G. C., Blanchard, E. B., Wittrock, D. A., Morrison, S., Pagburn, L., Siracusa, K., & Pallmeyer, T. (1988). Biochemical changes associated with thermal biofeedback treatment of hypertension. *Biofeedback and Self-Regulation, 13*, 139–150.

McCoy, G. C., Fein, S., Blanchard, E. B., Wittrock, D. A., McCaffrey, R. J., & Pangburn, L. (1988). End-organ changes associated with the self-regulatory treatment of mild essential hypertension? *Biofeedback and Self-Regulation, 13*(1), 39–46.

McGrady, A., & Higgins, J. T., Jr. (1989). Prediction of response to biofeedback-assisted relaxation in hypertensives: Development of a Hypertensive Predictor Profile (HYPP). *Psychosomatic Medicine, 51,* 277–284.

Mersky, H., & Spear, F. G. (1967). *Pain: Psychological and psychiatric aspects.* London: Balliere, Tindall, & Cassell.

Minsky, P. J. (1978). High blood pressure and interpersonal "disengagement": A study of maladaptive coping styles and ameliorative treatments. *Dissertation Abstracts International, 38,* 5580B.

Mitchell, K. R., & White, R. G. (1977). Self management of severe predormital insomnia. *Journal of Behavior Therapy and Experimental Psychiatry, 8,* 57–63.

Morrow, G. R. (1986). Effect of the cognitive hierarchy in the systematic desensitization treatment of anticipatory nausea in cancer patients: A component comparison with relaxation only, counseling, and no treatment. *Cognitive Therapy and Research, 10,* 421–446.

Murphy, A. I. (1987). Stress and coping: An investigation of muscle-contraction headache sufferers (Doctoral dissertation, Rutgers University, 1986). *Dissertation Abstracts International, 47,* 4659B.

Murphy, A. I., Lehrer, P. M., & Jurish, S. (1990). Cognitive coping skills training and relaxation training as treatments for tension headaches. *Behavior Therapy, 21,* 89–98.

Neff, D. F., & Blanchard, E. B. (1987). A multi-component treatment for irritable bowel syndrome. *Behavior Therapy, 18,* 70–83.

Nicassio, P. M., & Bootzin, R. (1974). A comparison of progressive relaxation and autogenic training as treatment for insomnia. *Journal of Abnormal Psychology, 83,* 235–260.

Nicassio, P. M., Boylan, M. B., & McCabe, T. G. (1982). Progressive relaxation, EMG biofeedback and biofeedback placebo in the treatment of sleep-onset insomnia. *British Journal of Medical Psychology, 55,* 159–166.

Nicassio, P. M., Mendlowitz, D. R., Fussell, J. J., & Petas, L. (1985). The phenomenology of the pre-sleep state: The development of the Pre-Sleep Arousal Scale. *Behaviour Research and Therapy, 23,* 263–271.

Oakley, M. E., & Shapiro, D. (1989). Methodological issues in the evaluation of drug–behavioral interactions in the treatment of hypertension. *Psychosomatic Medicine, 51,* 269–276.

O'Brien, C. P., & Weisbrot, M. M. (1983). Learned aversions to chemotherapy treatment. *National Institute on Drug Abuse Research Monograph Series, 45,* 36–45.

Parker, J. C., Gilbert, G. S., & Thoreson, R. W. (1978). Reduction of autonomic arousal in alcoholics: A comparison of relaxation and meditation techniques. *Journal of Consulting and Clinical Psychology, 46,* 879–886.

Patel, C., Marmot, M. G., & Terry, D. J. (1981). Controlled trial of biofeedback-aided behavioral methods in reducing mild hypertension. *British Medical Journal, 282,* 2005–2008.

Patel, C., Marmot, M. G., Terry, D. J., Carruthers, M., Hunt, B., & Patel, M. (1985). Trial of relaxation in reducing coronary risk: Four year follow-up. *British Medical Journal, 290,* 1103–1106.

Peper, E., Smith, K., & Waddell, D. (1987). Voluntary wheezing versus diaphragmatic breathing with inhalation (Voldyne) biofeedback: A clinical intervention in the treatment of asthma. *Clinical Biofeedback and Health: An International Journal, 10,* 83–88.

Pinkerton, S., Hughes, H., & Wenrich, W. W. (1982). *Behavioral medicine: Clinical applications.* New York: Wiley.

Place, M. (1984). Hypnosis and the child. *Journal of Child Psychology and Psychiatry and Allied Disciplines, 25,* 339–347.

Quillen, M. A., & Denney, D. R. (1982). Self-control of dysmenorrheic symptoms through pain management training. *Journal of Behavior Therapy and Experimental Psychiatry, 13,* 123–130.

Redmond, D. P., Gaylor, M. S., McDonald, R. H., & Shapiro, A. P. (1974). Blood pressure and heart rate response to verbal instructions and relaxation in hypertension. *Psychosomatic Medicine, 36,* 285–297.

Richter, R., & Dahme, B. (1982). Bronchial asthma in adults: There is little evidence for the effectiveness of behavioral therapy and relaxation. *Journal of Psychosomatic Research, 26,* 533–540.

Richter-Heinrich, E., Homuth, V., Heinrich, B., Schmidt, K. H., Wiedemann, R., & Gohkle, H. R. (1981). Long-term application of behavioral treatments in essential hypertensives. *Physiology and Behaviour, 26,* 915–920.

Rose, G. D., & Carlson, J. G. (1987). The behavioral treatment of Raynaud's disease: A review. *Biofeedback and Self-Regulation, 12,* 257–272.

Rosenthal, R. L. (1978). Differential treatment of spasmodic and congestive dysmenorrhea (Doctoral dissertation, Washington University). *Dissertation Abstracts International, 39,* 1498B. (University Microfilms No. 78-16,421)

Sappington, J. T., Fiorito, E. M., & Brehony, K. A. (1979). Biofeedback as therapy in Raynaud's disease. *Biofeedback and Self-Regulation, 4,* 155–169.

Scherr, M. S., & Crawford, P. L. (1978). Three-year evaluation of biofeedback techniques in the treatment of children with chronic asthma in a summer camp environment. *Annals of Allergy, 38,* 288–292.

Scherr, M. S., Crawford, P. L., Sergent, C. B., & Scherr, C. A. (1975). Effect of bio-feedback techniques on chronic asthma in a summer camp environment. *Annals of Allergy, 35,* 289–295.

Schlutter, L., Golden, C., & Blume, H. (1980). A comparison of treatments for prefrontal muscle contraction headache. *British Journal of Medical Psychology, 53,* 47–52.

Schwartz, G. E. (1981). A systems analysis of psychobiology and behavior therapy: Implications for behavioral medicine. *Psychotherapy and Psychosomatics, 36,* 159–184.

Schwartz, R. A. (1980). Biofeedback relaxation training in obstetrics: Its effect on the perinatal and neonatal states (Doctoral dissertation, California School of Professional Psychology, San Diego). *Dissertation Abstracts International, 40,* 3967B. (University Microfilms No. 80-04,364)

Sedlacek, K., Cohen, J., & Boxhill, C. (1979). *Comparison between biofeedback and relaxation response in the treatment of hypertension.* Paper presented at the annual meeting of the Biofeedback Society of America, San Diego.

Seer, P. (1979). Psychological control of essential hypertension: Review of the literature and methodological critique. *Psychological Bulletin, 86,* 1015–1043.

Seer, P., & Raeburn, J. U. (1980). Meditation training and essential hypertension: A methodological study. *Journal of Behavioral Medicine, 3,* 59–71.

Sigmon, S. T., & Nelson, R. O. (1988). The effectiveness of activity scheduling and relaxation training in the treatment of spasmodic dysmenorrhea. *Journal of Behavioral Medicine, 11,* 483–495.

Silver, B. V., & Blanchard, E. B. (1978). Biofeedback and relaxation training in the treatment of psychophysiological disorders: Or, are the machines really necessary? *Journal of Behavioral Medicine, 1,* 217–239.

Smith, R. P., & Powell, J. R. (1980). The objective evaluation of dysmenorrhea therapy. *American Journal of Obstetrics and Gynecology, 137,* 314–319.

Sorbi, M., & Tellegen, B. (1986). Differential effects of training in relaxation and stress-coping in patients with migraine. *Headache, 26,* 473–481.

Sorbi, M., Tellegen, B., & du Long, A. (1989). Long-term effects of training in relaxation and stress-coping in patients with migraine: A 3-year follow-up. *Headache, 29,* 111–121.

Southam, M. A., Agras, W. S., Taylor, C. B., & Kraemer, H. C. (1982). Relaxation training: Blood pressure lowering during the working day. *Archives of General Psychiatry, 39,* 715–717.

Spinhoven, P. (1988). Similarities and dissimilarities in hypnotic and nonhypnotic procedures for headache control: A review. *American Journal of Clinical Hypnosis, 30,* 183–194.

Stam, H. J., McGrath, P. A., & Brooke, R. I. (1984). The effects of a cognitive–behavioral treatment program on temporo-mandibular pain and dysfunction syndrome. *Psychosomatic Medicine, 46,* 534–545.

Staples, R., Coursey, R., & Smith, B. (1975, February). *A comparison of EMG biofeedback, autogenic, and progressive training as relaxation techniques.* Paper presented at the annual meeting of the Biofeedback Research Society, Monterey, CA.

Steinmark, S., & Borkovec, T. D. (1974). Active and placebo treatment effects on moderate insomnia under counterdemand and positive demand instructions. *Journal of Abnormal Psychology, 83,* 157–163.

Stern, R. M., Koch, K. L., Stewart, W. R., & Vasey, M. W. (1987). Electrogastrography: Current issues in validation and methodology. *Psychophysiology, 24,* 55–64.

Sternbach, R. A. (1968). *Pain: A psychophysiological analysis.* New York: Academic Press.

Surwit, R. S. (1982). Biofeedback and the behavioral treatment of Raynaud's disease. In L. White, & B. Tursky (Eds.) *Clinical biofeedback: Efficacy and mechanisms.* New York: Guilford Press.

Svedlund, J. (1983). Psychotherapy in irritable bowel syndrome: A controlled outcome study. *Acta Psychiatrica Scandinavica, 67*(Suppl. 306), 4–86.

Tarler-Benlolo, L. (1978). The role of relaxation in biofeedback training: A critical review of the literature. *Psychological Bulletin, 85,* 727–755.

Teders, S. J., Blanchard, E. B., Andrasik, F., Jurish, S. E., Neff, D. F., & Arena, J. G. (1984). Relaxation training for tension headache: Comparative efficacy and cost-effectiveness of a minimal therapist contact versus a therapist-delivered procedure. *Behavior Therapy, 15,* 59–70.

Tibbetts, V., & Peper, E. (1989). Follow up study on EMG/incentive inspirometer training to reduce asthmatic symptoms. *Biofeedback and Self-Regulation, 14,* 172.

Tobin, D. L., Holroyd, K. A., Baker, A., Reynolds, R. V. C., & Holm, H. (1988). Development and clinical trial of a minimal contact, cognitive–behavioral treatment of tension headache. *Cognitive Therapy and Research, 12,* 325–339.

Turner, J. A. (1982). Comparison of group progressive relaxation training and cognitive–behavioral group therapy for low back pain. *Journal of Consulting and Clinical Psychology, 50,* 757–765.

Turner, P. E. (1978). A psychophysiological assessment of selected relaxation strategies (Doctoral dissertation, University of Mississippi). *Dissertation Abstracts International, 39*, 3010B. (University Microfilms No. 78-24,063)

Turner, R. M., & Ascher, L. M. (1979). Controlled comparison of progressive relaxation, stimulus control, and paradoxical intention therapies for insomnia. *Journal of Consulting and Clinical Psychology, 47*, 500–508.

Turner, R. M., & Ascher, L. M. (1982). Therapist factors in the treatment of insomnia. *Behaviour Research and Therapy, 20*, 33–40.

Wadden, T. A., & Luborsky, L. (1984). The behavioral treatment of essential hypertension: An update and comparison with pharmacological treatment. *Clinical Psychology Review, 4*, 403–429.

Wall, V. J., & Womack, W. (1989). Hypnotic versus active cognitive strategies for alleviation of procedural distress in pediatric oncology patients. *American Journal of Clinical Hypnosis, 31*, 181–191.

Whipple, B. (1987). Methods of pain control: Review of research and literature. *Image: Journal of Nursing Scholarship, 19*, 142–146.

Whitehead, W. E., & Basmajian, L. S. (1982). Behavioral medicine approaches to the gastrointestinal disorders. *Journal of Consulting and Clinical Psychology, 50*, 972–983.

Whorwell, P. J., Prior, A., & Faragher, E. B. (1984). Controlled trial of hypnotherapy in the treatment of severe refractory irritable bowel syndrome. *Lancet, ii*, 1232–1234.

Woolfolk, R. L., Carr-Kaffashan, L., McNulty, T. F., & Lehrer, P. M. (1976). Meditation training as a treatment for insomnia. *Behavior Therapy, 7*, 359–365.

Woolfolk, R. L., & McNulty, T. F. (1983). Relaxation treatment for insomnia: A component analysis. *Journal of Consulting and Clinical Psychology, 47*, 113–118.

Index